ABOUT THE COVER IMAGE

Iznik Dish with Flower Sprays. Regarded by collectors throughout the world as one of the most valuable forms of the art of ceramics, Iznik pottery takes its name from the town in western Anatolia (modern Turkey) where most of it was made. Iznik already was an established center for the production of simple earthenware pottery when in the last quarter of the 15th century craftsmen in the town began to manufacture high-quality ceramics painted with cobalt blue under a colorless transparent lead glaze that combined traditional Ottoman arabesque patterns with Chinese elements. The change was almost certainly a result of the active intervention and patronage by the recently established Ottoman court in Istanbul, which greatly admired Chinese blue-and-white porcelain. During the 16th century Iznik decoration gradually changed in style, becoming looser and more flowing and featuring, as this dish from 1530–1550 shows, floral as well as geometric designs. Iznik ceramic wares, referred to as "chini" in Ottoman documents, were intended for the domestic market of the Ottoman Empire but were soon exported to eager buyers in Europe, where the coveted wares would give rise to local imitations.

Cultures of the West

A History

Second Edition

Cultures of the West

A History

Second Edition

Clifford R. Backman

Boston University

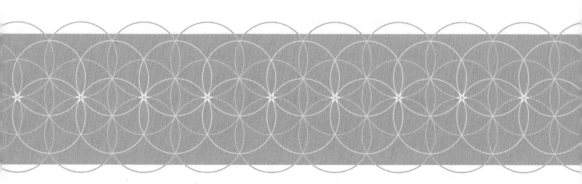

New York   Oxford

OXFORD UNIVERSITY PRESS

Oxford University Press is a department of the University of Oxford.
It furthers the University's objective of excellence in research,
scholarship, and education by publishing worldwide.

Oxford New York
Auckland   Cape Town   Dar es Salaam   Hong Kong   Karachi
Kuala Lumpur   Madrid   Melbourne   Mexico City   Nairobi
New Delhi   Shanghai   Taipei   Toronto

With offices in
Argentina   Austria   Brazil   Chile   Czech Republic   France   Greece
Guatemala   Hungary   Italy   Japan   Poland   Portugal   Singapore
South Korea   Switzerland   Thailand   Turkey   Ukraine   Vietnam

For titles covered by Section 112 of the US Higher Education
Opportunity Act, please visit www.oup.com/us/he for the
latest information about pricing and alternate formats.

Published by Oxford University Press
198 Madison Avenue, New York, New York 10016
http://www.oup.com

Oxford is a registered trademark of Oxford University Press

Library of Congress Cataloging-in-Publication Data
Backman, Clifford R., author.
   The cultures of the west : a history / Clifford R. Backman. — Second edition.
      pages cm
   "Combined volume" includes both volumes 1 and 2.
   ISBN 978-0-19-024045-5   Paperback
   ISBN 978-0-19-061728-8   Loose Leaf
  1. Civilization, Western. 2. Religion and civilization. 3. Science and civilization.
4. Philosophy and civilization. I. Title.
   CB245.B324 2015
   909'.09821--dc23   2015021290

Printing number: 9 8 7 6 5 4 3 2

Printed in the United States of America
on acid-free paper

This book is for
Graham Charles Backman
Puero praeclaro, Scourge of Nations

and for my mother
Mary Lou Betker
with my best love

and in memory of my brother
Neil Howard Backman, U.S.N. (ret.)
(1956–2011)
who found his happiness just in time

BRIEF CONTENTS

CONTENTS

1. Water and Soil, Stone and Metal: The First Civilizations 3

The interaction of the Indo-European groups and the primarily Semitic-speaking peoples of the Fertile Crescent opened the way for the development of the Greater West—a civilization that bridged Europe and western Asia.

2. Law Givers, Emperors, and Gods: The Ancient Near East. 37

3. The People of the Covenant. 71

The romanticization of David and Solomon introduced an entirely new element into Greater Western culture, or at least one for which no earlier evidence survives—namely, the popular belief in a past paradise, a lost era of former glory, when humanity had attained a perfection of happiness.

The Greeks, especially the Athenians, came to regard the mid-5th century bce with a determined awe, recalling it as a lost halcyon era that outshone anything that came before it or since. Through the centuries, much of Western culture has continued the love affair and has extolled "the glory that was Greece" as a pinnacle of human achievement.

The story fascinates, thrills, comforts, angers, and embarrasses at every turn, often all at once. It has touched everything from Western political ideas to sexual mores. Christianity began as an obscure reformist sect within Palestinian Judaism, at one time numbering no more than fifty or so believers. It went on, after three centuries of persecution by the Roman Empire, to become the world's most dominant faith.

The Western world had never seen a military juggernaut like this: in 622 Muhammad and his small group of followers had been forced from their home in Mecca, yet within a hundred years those followers had conquered an empire that stretched from Spain to India, an area twice the size of that conquered by Alexander the Great.

Latin Europe's history had been shaped by two opposed waves of development. The dual economic and cultural engine of the Mediterranean region spread its influence northward, bringing elements of cosmopolitan urban life, intellectual innovation, and cultural vibrancy into the European heartlands. Political leadership, however, came from the north, as the monarchies of England and France and the Holy Roman Empire pushed their boundaries southward, drawn by Mediterranean commerce and the gravitational pull of the papal court. The cross-fertilization of north and south benefited each and fostered Europe's ability to reform and revitalize itself.

13. Worlds Old and New................... 449

14. The Wars of All against All............... 493

The three elements most characteristically associated with the Renaissance— classicism, humanism, and modern statecraft— represent no essential break with medieval life at all. They may in fact be thought of as the culmination of medieval strivings.

Though often referred to as the "wars of religion," the wars that wracked the Greater West in the sixteenth and seventeenth centuries enmeshed religious antagonisms with economic, social, and political conflict. A more accurate term might come from English philosopher Thomas Hobbes (1588–1679): "the war of all against all."

The philosophes may have been the most influential group of talented amateurs in European history, not only because of their influence on their own age but because of the way they and their assumptions about human nature still affect us today.

18. Industrialization and Its Discontents 663

19. The Birth of Modern Politics 703

20. Nationalism and Identity 745

The choices made at the Congress of Vienna emerged in the dramatically changed context of England's rapid and unchallenged industrialization. Investment in industrial technologies was necessary – but was that the responsibility of the state or of individuals? Were the social troubles caused by industrialization the responsibility of the state too? If so, why? Who, ultimately, is responsible for the poor?

The question arises: Why were the dominant European states—the states with the most developed economies, highest literacy rates, most established democratic systems, and most elaborate and sophisticated networks of communication—so resistant to extend suffrage to women?

A new generation, raised to believe in the unique injustice of their suffering, came of age determined to rescue their honor as well as their livelihoods. And they were willing to take desperate action.

The aspiration to unite was cultural, moral, even spiritual. At stake were shared values and beliefs, a commitment to human rights, civic-mindedness, reason, and personal freedom. Politics and the economy played their roles, but what mattered most was the idea of Europe as a civilization, not just a commercial entity.

More was involved in these debates than reconciling figures in a ledger. The Greater West entered the 21st century engaged in full-throttle disputes over the purpose and limits of government and the responsibilities of individuals in society.

Maps

Preface

Iwrote this book with a simple goal in mind: to produce the kind of survey text I wished I had read in college. As a latecomer to history, I wondered why I so enjoyed studying a subject whose textbooks I found dry and lifeless. People, after all, are enormously interesting; and history is the story of people. So why were so many of the books I was assigned to read tedious?

Part of the problem lay in method. Teaching and writing history is difficult, in large part because of the sheer scope of the enterprise. Most history survey books stress their factual comprehensiveness and strict objectivity of tone. The trouble with this approach is that it too often works only for those few who are already true believers in history's importance and leaves most students yawning in their wake. I chose a different option—to teach and write history by emphasizing ideas and trends and the values behind them; to engage in the debates of each age rather than to narrate who won them. Students who are eagerly engaged in a subject, and who understand its significance, can then appreciate and remember the details. Moreover, twenty-five years of experience has taught me that they will do so.

This book adopts a thematic approach, but a theme seldom utilized in contemporary histories. While paying due attention to other aspects of Western development, it focuses on what might be called the *history of values*—that is, on the assumptions that lie behind political and economic developments, behind intellectual and artistic ventures, and behind social trends and countertrends. Consider, for example, the achievements of the Scientific Revolution. The advances made in fields like astronomy, chemistry, and medicine did not occur simply because individuals smart enough to figure out new truths happened to come along. William Harvey's discovery of the circulatory system was possible only because the culture in which he lived had begun, albeit hesitantly, to allow the dissection of human corpses for scientific research. For many centuries, even millennia, before Harvey's time, cultural and religious taboos had forbidden the desecration of bodies. But the era of the Scientific Revolution was also the era of political absolutism in Europe, a time when prevailing sentiment held that the king should hold all power and authority. Any enemy of the king—for example, anyone convicted of a felony—therefore deserved the ultimate penalty of execution and dissection. No king worship, no discovery of the circulation of the blood. At least not at that time.

A history that emphasizes the development of values runs the risk of distorting the record to some extent, because obviously not every person living at a given time held those values. Medieval Christians did not uniformly hate Jews and Muslims, believe the world was about to end, support the Inquisition, and blindly follow the dictates of the pope. Not every learned man and woman in the 18th century was "enlightened" or even wanted to be. The young generation of the 1960s was not composed solely of war protesters, feminist reformers, and rock-music lovers. With this important caveat in mind, however, it remains possible to offer general observations about the ideas and values that predominated in any era. This book privileges those ideas and sensibilities and views the events of each era in relation to them.

And it does so with a certain amount of opinion. To discuss value judgments without ever judging some of those values seems cowardly and is probably impossible anyway. Most large-scale histories mask their subjectivity simply by deciding which topics to discuss and which ones to pass over; I prefer to argue my positions explicitly, in the belief that to have a point of view is not the same thing as to be unfair. Education is as much about teaching students to evaluate arguments as it is about passing on knowledge to them, and students cannot learn to evaluate arguments if they are not presented with any.

In a second departure from tradition (which in this case is really just habit), this book interprets Western history on a broad geographic and cultural scale. All full-scale histories of Western civilization begin in the ancient Near East, but after making a quick nod to the origins of Islam in the 7th century, most of them focus almost exclusively on western Europe. The Muslim world thereafter enters the discussion only when it impinges on European actions. This book overtly rejects that view and insists on including the region of the Middle East in the general narrative, as a permanently constitutive element of the Greater West. For all its current global appeal, Islam is essentially a Western religion, after all, one that has its spiritual roots in the Jewish and Christian traditions and the bulk of whose intellectual foundations are in the classical Greco-Roman canon. To treat the Muslim world as an occasional sideshow on the long march to western European and American world leadership is, I believe, to falsify the record and to get the history wrong. The "European world" and the "Middle Eastern world" have been in a continuous relationship for millennia, buying and selling goods, sharing technologies, studying each other's political ideas, influencing each other's religious beliefs, learning from each other's medicine, facing the same challenges from scientific advances and changing economies. We cannot explain who we are if we limit ourselves to the traditional scope of Western history; we need a Greater Western perspective, one that includes and incorporates the whole of the monotheistic world.

Because religious belief has traditionally shaped so much of Greater Western culture—whether for good or ill is every reader's responsibility to determine—I have placed it at the center of my narrative. Even for the most unshakeable of modern agnostics and atheists, the values upheld by the three great monotheisms have had, and continue to have, a profound effect on the development of our social mores, intellectual pursuits, and artistic endeavors as well as on our politics and international relations.

In another break with convention, the book incorporates an abundance of primary sources into the narrative. I have always disliked the boxed and highlighted source snippets that pockmark so many of today's textbooks. It seems to me that any passage worth quoting is worth working into the text itself—and I have happily done so. But a word about them is necessary. For the first three chapters I have needed considerable help. I am ignorant of the ancient Middle Eastern languages and have relied on the current version of a respected and well-loved anthology.[1] When discussing the sacred texts of Judaism, Christianity, and Islam, I have used their own authorized translations. Simple courtesy, it seems to me, calls for quoting a Jewish translation of the Bible when discussing Judaism; a Catholic, Orthodox, or Protestant Bible whenever discussing those main branches of Christianity; and the English version of the Qur'an prepared by the royal publishing house in Saudi Arabia when discussing Islam.[2] Last, some of the political records I cite (for example, the Cairo Declaration of Human Rights) are quoted from their official English versions. But apart from these special cases—all duly noted—every translation in this book, from chapter 4 onward, is my own.

CHANGES TO THE SECOND EDITION

Since the publication of the first edition of *Cultures of the West*, I have received, thankfully, a great number of notes and e-mails from teachers and students who appreciated the book, as well as dozens of formal critiques commissioned by the press. A textbook, unlike most scholarly works, affords historians the rare chance to revise the original work and to make it better. This second edition gave me the opportunity to realize my vision of the book, and I am pleased and grateful to point to the following main changes, all intended to make *Cultures of the West* a text that will engage students and teachers alike:

---

[1] Nels M. Bailkey and Richard Lim, *Readings in Ancient History: Thought and Experience from Gilgamesh to St. Augustine*, 7th ed. (Wadsworth, 2011).

[2] *Tanakh: The Holy Scriptures*, by the Jewish Publication Society; *New American Bible*, published by the U.S. Conference of Catholic Bishops; *New Revised Standard Version*, published by Oxford University Press; and *The Orthodox Study Bible*. For the Qur'an I have used *The Holy Qur'an: English Translations of the Meanings, with Commentary*, published by the King Fahd Holy Qur'an Printing Complex (A.H 1410).

- *Consistent reinforcement of the history of values*—as evidenced most easily by new chapter introductions and conclusions, but I highlighted the book's central theme throughout the narrative.
- *A more comprehensive treatment of Western Europe to ground students' exploration of the Greater West*—as evidenced, for example, by fuller coverage of the Middle Ages, the French Revolution, and the world wars. To keep the length of the book manageable for readers, I compensated for these additions by streamlining or excising outright subjects and passages that instructors found too advanced for the survey course.
- *A new chapter in Volume 1 and two fewer chapters in Volume 2* for a more course-friendly periodization. The new chapter (9), *The Expansive Realm of Islam, 30–900*, parallels the chapters on early Judaism (3) and Christianity (7) for a full treatment of the monotheistic cultures that gave rise to the Greater West. Basically a reworking of materials previously scattered among different chapters, I am especially proud of this newcomer to the Western civilization textbook literature. To reduce the number of chapters in Volume 2, I combined directly related first-edition chapters 20 and 23 into the new chapter 22, *The Challenge of Secularism*, and the final two first-edition chapters into chapter 29, *Global Warmings: Since 1989*.
- *Consistent treatment of women and gender in the central narrative.* The warm reception to a chapter devoted to the modern woman encouraged me to keep a carefully revised version of this chapter (21) in the new edition, but elsewhere I worked hard to integrate women's history and gender issues into the main story of events.
- *New marginal headings that identify key events and developments* to supplement the book's well-received single-heading structure of the narrative.
- *Expanded map program.* The second edition includes twenty-four new maps. All of the maps have been corrected and redesigned for improved clarity.
- *New Prologue: Before History,* for readers of Volume 1 and the combined edition. Because the first edition neglected the Paleolithic and Neolithic eras, I was especially happy to add this illustrated discussion.

- *Updated scholarship.* The research that goes into revision of a single-authored textbook is as rewarding as it is time consuming. I am pleased to include many new titles in the chapter bibliographies that inform the narrative.

ACKNOWLEDGMENTS

Working with Oxford University Press has been a delight. Charles Cavaliere has served as point man, guiding me through the entire project with grace and kindness. His cheery enthusiasm kept me going through many a difficult hour. If the prose in this book has any merit, please direct your compliments to John Haber and Elizabeth Welch, the talented editors who guided me through, respectively, the first and second editions. Beth did more than edit; she reenvisioned and gave new life to the book (and its author) by her enthusiasm, rigor, and good humor. Christi Sheehan, Debbie Needleman, Theresa Stockton, Lisa Grzan, Eden Kram-Gingold, Kateri Woody, Meg Botteon, and Michele Laseau shepherded me through the production and marketing phases and deserve all the credit for the wonderful physical design of the book and its handsome map and art programs.

I am also deeply grateful to the many talented historians and teachers who offered critical readings of the first edition. My sincere thanks to the following instructors, whose comments often challenged me to rethink or justify my interpretations and provided a check on accuracy down to the smallest detail:

Robert Brennan, Cape Fear Community College
Lee L. Brice, Western Illinois University
Keith Chu, Bergen Community College
Jason Coy, College of Charleston
Marc Eagle, Western Kentucky University
Christine Eubank, Bergen Community College
Jennifer L. Foray, Purdue University
Edith Foster, Case Western Reserve University
Matthew Gerber, University of Colorado at Boulder
David M. Head, John Tyler Community College
Brian Hilly, Suffolk County Community College
Christopher Howell, Red Rocks Community College
Andrew Keitt, University of Alabama at Birmingham
Christina Bosco Langert, Suffolk County Community College
Ryan Messenger, Monroe Community College
Alexander Mikaberidze, Louisiana State University–Shreveport
Kathryn Ordway, Colorado Community College Online

Jennifer Popiel, Saint Louis University
Matthew Ruane, Florida Institute of Technology
Nicholas L. Rummell, Trident Technical College
Robert Rusnak, Trident Technical College
Sarah Shurts, Bergen Community College

I thank as well the good folks at Trident Tech Community College in Charleston, South Carolina, who hosted a workshop in June 2014 that provided a forum for me to sound out the revision plan. Professors Donald West, Barbara Tucker, Robert Rusnak, Nicholas Rummell, and several other History TTCC faculty members were kind enough to spend a morning with me sharing their experiences using *Cultures of the West* and offering suggestions for how it could be improved. I hope they are pleased with the result. I especially want to thank Katherine Jenkins of Trident Tech Community College, who prepared many of the excellent supplementary materials for the second edition and saved me from several embarrassing errors.

My former student at Boston University, Christine Axen (PhD, 2015), has been a support from the start. She has taught with me, and occasionally for me, through the past three years, and I appreciate the time she took away from her own dissertation research to assist me on this project—pulling books from the library, running down citations, suggesting ideas. When Oxford asked me to prepare a companion volume of primary texts for this book, Christine proved to be such an immense help that she deserves to share the title page with me. The sourcebook too is appearing in a second edition.

To my wife, Nelina, and our sons, Scott and Graham, this book has been an uninvited houseguest at times, pulling me away from too many family hours. They have put up with it, and with me, with patience and generosity that I shall always be thankful for. Their love defines them and sustains me.

SUPPORT MATERIALS FOR *CULTURES OF THE WEST*

Cultures of the West comes with an extensive package of support materials for both instructors and students.

- **Dashboard** Dashboard delivers quality content, tools and assessments to track student progress in an intuitive, web-based learning environment. Assessments are designed to accompany *Cultures of the west*, and automatically graded so instructors can easily check students' progress as they complete their assignments. The color-coded gradebook illustrates at a glance where students are succeeding and where they can improve so busy instructors can adapt lectures to student needs. Dashboard features a streamlined interface that connects instructors and students with the functions they perform most, and simplifies the learning experience by putting student progress first. All Dashboard content is engineered to work on mobile devices, including the iOS platform. Our goal is to create a platform that is simple, informative, and mobile. Please contact your local Oxford University Press representative for a demonstration of Dashboard.

- **Oxford First Source** (www.oup.com/us/firstsource) Oxford First Source is an online database, with custom print capability, of primary source documents in World History. The continuously updated collection consists of approximately 300 documents for European and World History, both textual and visual, selected and organized to complement any World History survey text. These documents cover a broad range of political, social, and cultural topics. The documents are indexed by date, title, subject, and region and are fully searchable. Each is accompanied by a headnote and study questions. Six-month access to Oxford First Source is $10.00 when bundled with *Cultures of the West*, or can be purchased standalone for $19.95. Please contact your local Oxford University Press representative for details.

- *Sources for Cultures of the West, Volume 1: To 1750* and *Sources for Cultures of the West, Volume 2: Since 1350*. Edited by Clifford R. Backman and Christine Axen, it includes approximately 175 primary sources, organized to match the chapter organization of *Cultures of the West*. Forty-one of the sources are new to the second edition. Each source is accompanied by a headnote and reading questions. The sourcebooks are significantly discounted when bundled with the text.

  - **Companion Website (http://www.oup.com/us/ backman/**): For students, the open-access site includes quizzes, flashcards, documents, interactive maps, and links to YouTube videos. Access to the student site is unrestricted.

  - **Ancillary Resource Center** (ARC): Includes PowerPoint slides and JPEG and PDF files for all the maps and photos in the text; an additional four hundred map files, in PowerPoint format, from *The Oxford Atlas of World History*; and approximately 250 additional PowerPoint-based slides organized by theme and topic. The ARC also includes an Instructor's Resource Manual, which includes, for each chapter, a detailed chapter outline, suggested lecture topics, learning objectives, suggested Web resources, and digital media files. It also includes, for each chapter, approximately thirty multiple-choice, short-answer, true-or-false, and fill-in-the-blank questions as well as numerous essay questions. The test questions are available in a computerized test bank that can be customized by the instructor.

- *Mapping the Cultures of the West, Volume 1: To 1750*: Includes approximately forty full-color maps, each accompanied by a brief headnote. Free when bundled with the text.

- *Mapping the Cultures of the West, Volume 2: Since 1350*: Includes approximately forty full-color maps, each accompanied by a brief headnote. Free when bundled with the text.

- *Now Playing: Studying Western Civilization through Film* (available in both student and instructor editions) is a concise print supplement that provides synopses, recommended scenes, and discussion questions for thirty of the most commonly assigned films in Western Civilization classes. Qualified adopters can receive a Netflix subscription with their adoption. *Now Playing* can be bundled with *Cultures of the West* at no additional cost.

- **E-book for** *Cultures of the West* **(both volumes):** An e-book is available for purchase at **http://www.course smart.com.**

BUNDLING OPTIONS

Cultures of the West can be bundled at a significant discount with any of the titles in the popular Very Short Introductions or Oxford World's Classics series, as well as other titles from the Higher Education division world history catalog (**http://www.oup.com/us/catalog/he/**). Please contact your OUP representative for details.

About the Author

Clifford Backman has been a member of the History Department at Boston University since 1989. In addition to the two-semester Western Civilization course, he teaches several courses on medieval Europe, the Mediterranean, the Crusades, piracy, and the history of sexual morality. He also teaches in the university's Core Curriculum, a four-semester sequence in the humanities and the social sciences. He is currently at work on a book that traces the development of toleration and interpersonal forgiveness in medieval Christianity, Judaism, and Islam.

Note on Dates

I follow a few basic conventions. Instead of the old BC ("before Christ") and AD (*anno Domini,* "in the year of the Lord") designations for centuries, I use the new norms of BCE ("before the common era") and CE ("common era"). Dates are given, whenever possible, for every figure mentioned in the book. Political leaders are identified by the years they were in power. All other personal dates, unless otherwise noted, are birth and death dates.

Prologue: Before History

Strictly speaking, history is a textual discipline: When human beings developed writing, they started to create written records, the foundation of history (from the Greek word *historia*, meaning "inquiry"). Study of the human world before the advent of writing is the domain of archeology and anthropology. All three disciplines share the same aim—to understand how human life, in all its variety, has developed over time—but they use different tools and methods. Apart from a handful of early markings found in southeastern Europe, dating to the 6th century BCE, which may or may not be examples of writing (scholars have been debating them since they were discovered), the first definite use of writing appeared around the year 3200 BCE in the ancient Near East.

Although it was a long time ago, 3200 BCE should be considered the end, even the culmination, of a story that began much, much earlier.

Archeology and anthropology tell us that human beings (the species *Homo sapiens sapiens*) appeared in eastern Africa approximately 200,000 years ago.[3] Other humanlike (hominid) species still existed in far greater numbers across Africa, Europe, and Asia—species like *Homo neanderthalensis* and *Homo erectus*—but *Homo sapiens sapiens* had several advantages over their distant relatives, the most important being the large forebrain that rests above, rather than behind, the eyes. Increased brain capacity contributed to the use of stone tools and the development of fire, and the raised forehead that accompanied it made possible more subtle communicative abilities. The appearance of human beings marks the beginning of the Paleolithic (or "Old Stone") Age, which lasted until approximately 10,000 BCE.

Two broad hypotheses dominate research into the Paleolithic Age. First, the long-standard "Out of Africa" hypothesis maintains that soon after their appearance in today's country of Ethiopia, humans branched out across Africa. Crossing Egypt's Sinai Peninsula sometime around 125,000 BCE, they settled in the Near East before fanning out in all directions (see Map P.1). Those who ventured westward crossed Anatolia (modern Turkey) and moved on into Europe by 40,000 BCE. Those who migrated eastward reached India as early as 60,000 BCE and advanced as far as southeast Asia and Australia by 50,000 BCE. At still

---

[3] Why *sapiens sapiens*? Because it turns out that we humans are a subspecies rather than a species proper. Also known to specialists as AMH, or Anatomically Modern Humans, we are an offshoot of the *Homo sapiens* species. Fossils of another offshoot, *Homo sapiens idaltu*, now extinct, were discovered by archeologists in Ethiopia in 1997.

another turn of direction, groups of humans moved northward through China, crossed the Siberian–Alaskan ice bridge around 15,000 BCE, and between three and five thousand years later migrated southward into the Americas. By 10,000 BCE, in other words, humans had expanded throughout the entire world. Around that same time, human beings began to practice agriculture—the stage of development at which the Paleolithic Age ends and the Neolithic ("New Stone") Age begins.

The Out of Africa thesis makes geographical and chronological sense, insofar as it places humans at sites and times around the globe that correspond with the fossil record—and this is why it has dominated the thinking about human development and the Paleolithic Age for the past two centuries. But in the past few decades, a second hypothesis has emerged that utilizes previously unknown evidence. The discovery of DNA and genetic coding has made it possible to analyze the Paleolithic remains in greater detail and has revealed a problem with the Out of Africa model—namely, that there should be vastly greater genetic diversity

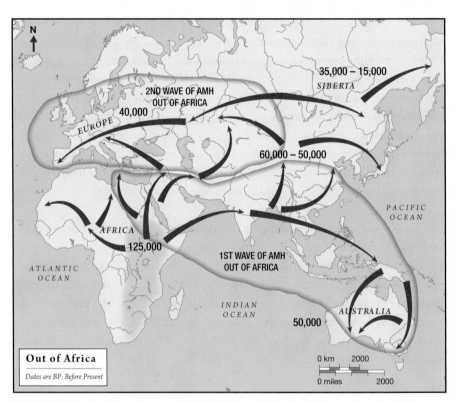

MAP P.1   The map shows the general chronology and migration patterns of anatomically modern humans (AMH) out of Africa. The migrations occurred in two waves: the first directed primarily to the east, and a second, later wave that moved into Europe.

among human beings than there is, given the age of our species. At some point, therefore, something must have happened to decrease dramatically the gene pool. Some researchers have argued that the entire human population must have been reduced to as few as five thousand people to account for the smallness of the genetic variation observable. What could such an event have been? Around 70,000 BCE there was a catastrophic explosion of the supervolcano at Lake Toba, in Indonesia, which scientists reckon (by analyzing ash deposits) was the most violent event on earth in the past 25 million years. So enormous was the blast that it spewed enough ash and sulfur dioxide into the air to alter dramatically the earth's climate, dropping global average temperatures as much as 5°C (41°F) for a decade and triggering a mini ice age that lasted for a thousand years. This "Toba Event" happened early enough in the process of human expansion (when human beings coming out of Africa had made it only as far as Anatolia and India) to nearly eradicate the entire species, thus accounting for the diminished gene pool of the survivors.

The Toba Event hypothesis thus fine-tunes, rather than contradicts, the Out of Africa hypothesis. Researchers still debate the details, but the modified model of human migration in the Paleolithic Age has won broad acceptance. It also helps to explain the abrupt disappearance of the other hominids. Only *Homo sapiens sapiens* had the ability to recover from the biological apocalypse and adapt to the new environment. Peoples' ability to use tools for hunting, building shelter, producing fire, constructing watercraft, and self-defense enabled them to survive when other species could not. For tens of thousands of years they survived as hunter–gatherers, people literally traveling through the earth in search of food.

In the Neolithic Age (10,000–3000 BCE) people everywhere gradually learned agriculture, and populations consequently began to concentrate in areas where the soil and climate were amenable to producing food. The earliest sites of farming discovered by archeologists appear in the region known as the Fertile Crescent, the broad arc of land that stretches from Mesopotamia, in today's southern Iraq, skirts the highlands of northern Syria, and passes along the eastern Mediterranean into Egypt. The domestication of cattle, goats, pigs, and sheep followed soon after; fossils reflecting the domestication of goats date as early as 8900 BCE, and pig domestication dates to roughly 7000 BCE. Most people lived in rural communities made up of various clans, with some of these villages holding several hundred people. The men plowed the fields and harvested, spending the months in between hunting and gathering. Women and children tended to growing crops and the farm animals. Most homes were simple constructions of stone or clay brick—because the region is not rich in timber, most of the wood available was used for cooking.

Archeologists in 1958 discovered a site of unusual size and development in southern Anatolia at a place called Catalhüyük, which was settled around 7500 BCE, where Neolithic peoples lived for two thousand years. As its height, Catalhüyük had as many as six thousand inhabitants, possibly even more, living

A "Mother Goddess"?   This figurine from Catalhüyük is generally thought to depict a corpulent and fertile Mother Goddess in the process of giving birth while seated on her throne. Because no contemporary texts exist to explain the significance of the figurine's obesity and pronounced sexual characteristics, however, we can only speculate about the complex meanings that prehistoric peoples extracted from them.

in a nest of connected mud houses that the people entered through holes in their roofs. (Since no footpaths existed between the buildings, the contiguous rooftops served as an open-air market square.) The interior walls of each house were covered in plaster. No buildings have been identified as anything other than homes and storage units. There were no temples, no ruler's court. This fact suggests that social stratification had not yet developed, nor had any organized political life. Some individual rooms have been identified as shrines, but little is known of the people's religion. People appear to have buried their dead in pits beneath their homes, and surviving artifacts suggest they may have practiced a form of ancestor worship. Hundreds of figurines survive, as do examples of their textiles, tools, and pottery.

Although writing was unknown to them, the inhabitants of Catalhüyük showed considerable artistic skill. Murals covered many walls, and surviving figurines are beautifully made. Obviously people were seeking ways to express themselves through art well before the development of "civilization," the subject of chapter 1. Three concerns seem to have been predominant: death, reproduction, and survival. Numerous mural paintings at Catalhüyük depict vultures pecking at human corpses (the people seem to have left their dead exposed until nothing remained but the bones, which they buried beneath their homes), whereas others portray large-breasted women, who may or may not have served as fertility symbols, either copulating with, or giving birth to, bulls—presumably images of virility. Hunting scenes featuring large wild cattle are another common motif.

The people who settled in Europe lived in more difficult circumstances because the dense woodlands and heavy soil were difficult to work with stone tools. Hunting and gathering remained the mode of existence, and agriculture hence did not begin until at least a thousand years after it appeared in the Fertile Crescent. The first sites of settled agriculture did not appear until sometime around 2500 BCE, in the Balkans. The earliest Europeans are known above all for the giant stone structures they erected. Called megaliths, these structures were raised all across western Europe, from Scandinavia to the Mediterranean. The best-known of these is Stonehenge, on the Salisbury plain in southern England. Initially a ring of pits dug into the ground, it developed around 2300 BCE into a circle of tall standing stones. The stones were quarried far away, in Wales. No one knows precisely what the purpose or function of Stonehenge was, but its mere existence is evidence of a high degree of social organization, skilled labor, and engineering proficiency.

It is a long story, from the emergence of *Homo sapiens sapiens* in Ethiopia to the start of civilization in the Fertile Crescent. Humankind showed its

Stonehenge   Possibly Britain's greatest national icon, Stonehenge symbolizes mystery, power, and endurance. Its original purpose is unclear, but some scholars speculate that it was a temple made for the worship of ancient earth deities.

remarkable adaptability to circumstances, and life progressed from a mere struggle for daily survival to a continuous search for more than that—a search for meaning. The murals and figurines of Catalhüyük and the mysterious grandeur of Stonehenge, whatever their precise interpretation, bear witness to the human desire to make sense out of life's struggle and to find value and purpose in it.

Cultures of the West

A History

Second Edition

CHAPTER 1

Water and Soil, Stone and Metal: The First Civilizations

10,000–2100 BCE

The origins of Western civilization lie in southern Iraq. The region was called Sumer five thousand years ago, and it was the first site of the features that historians associate with civilization: consistent use of agriculture, the domestication of animals that made farming possible, the construction of cities, and the invention of writing. At first glance it seems an unlikely place for civilization to begin. The soil is sandy, summertime temperatures regularly surpass 110°F (43°C), and the dull flatland receives a scant 8 inches of annual rainfall. (By comparison, most of the Mediterranean basin receives nearly four times as much.) There is no stone to quarry, no metal ores to mine, and little timber with which to build. Bordered by the relatively low-lying Zagros Mountains of Iran to the east, Sumer nevertheless lay exposed to raiding groups from the Iranian steppe.

But it was in Sumer that Greater Western civilization began. Many nomadic groups had passed through the region as early as 7000 BCE, following their herds, pursuing prey, or fleeing from rivals. The appearance of the Sumerians around four thousand years

THE ANCIENT NEAR EAST

The Invention of Writing
Unassuming clay objects such as this one from Sumer, in the south of modern Iraq, reveal human beings' earliest ability to record information for the future. Dating to 3300–3100 BCE, this tablet is impressed with cuneiform signs that represent a grain (barley) inventory.

later, however, marks the start of **civilization**. *Civilization*, of course, is an expansive term; it is also value laden. After all, its alternative—to be *uncivilized*—implies barbarism. But historians use it in a nonjudgmental sense to designate a society that has advanced beyond a basic search for sustenance. Agriculture, specialization of labor, and trade, under the right conditions, produce surpluses that release people from the daily struggle for survival and allow them to pursue other endeavors like investigating the physical world and the heavens (the seed of science); creating images, objects, and sounds for pleasure (the origin of art); and wondering where human life came from and what, if anything, it is for (the root of religion and philosophy). These are the elements that make up civilization, and in the case of Sumer they appeared around 3000 BCE. Under different circumstances, they appeared more or less contemporaneously in Egypt's Nile River valley.

Civilization, because it involves the desire for something beyond mere survival, entails the search for values—the ideas, assumptions, and hopes on which human beings rely to give their lives meaning. As the examples of ancient Sumer and Egypt show, the earliest values that emerged in what became the Greater West ranged widely, from a resigned acceptance of life's inherent purposelessness to a conviction in the perfect and eternal order of the world.

CHAPTER TIMELINE

9000 BCE	8500 BCE	7000 BCE	5500 BCE	4500 BCE

■ ca. 9000 BCE **Evidence of grain storage, Jericho**

■ ca. 7000 BCE **Earliest evidence of farming, Sumer**

■ ca. 5500 BCE **Appearance of cities in Eridu and Ur, Sumer**

THE TIGRIS, THE EUPHRATES, AND THE LAND BETWEEN THE RIVERS

Sumer lay in the narrowing plain between the lower reaches of the Tigris and Euphrates rivers. Indeed, the region is also known as Mesopotamia ("between the rivers"), which derives from the ancient Greek name for the area (see Map 1.1). The Sumerians had access to the Persian Gulf, whose headlands reached about 100 miles farther inland in ancient times than they do today. Yet they never developed a maritime tradition and remained resolutely bound to the soil. Sandy though that soil was, it was made fertile by the flooding of the two great rivers, as the winter rains of Syria and the spring thaws of the snows of the Taurus Mountains to the far north brought layer upon layer of silt to fertilize the land. Twisting slowly eastward through narrow gorges until they reached the high plains of Syria and Kurdistan, the rivers then plunged dramatically southward, picking up speed as they approached the site of today's city of Baghdad in Iraq. The Tigris River, with its deep bed, flooded less widely but with a strong current. The Euphrates, on the other hand, was broad and shallow, overran its banks easily, and scattered highland silt over a wide expanse. The faster-flowing Tigris usually reached its high-water mark in April, whereas the Euphrates generally reached full flood about a month later. By managing this water via an elaborate network of levees, reservoirs, and irrigation canals, the Sumerians were able to produce abundant

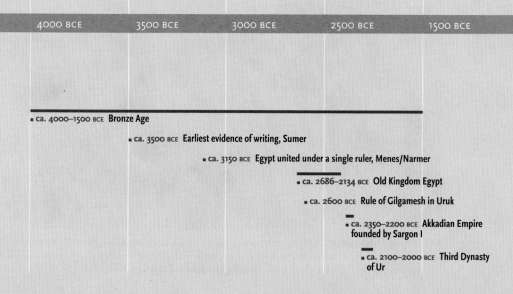

4000 BCE   3500 BCE   3000 BCE   2500 BCE   1500 BCE

- ca. 4000–1500 BCE **Bronze Age**
- ca. 3500 BCE **Earliest evidence of writing, Sumer**
- ca. 3150 BCE **Egypt united under a single ruler, Menes/Narmer**
- ca. 2686–2134 BCE **Old Kingdom Egypt**
- ca. 2600 BCE **Rule of Gilgamesh in Uruk**
- ca. 2350–2200 BCE **Akkadian Empire founded by Sargon I**
- ca. 2100–2000 BCE **Third Dynasty of Ur**

yields of summer grains for themselves and prairie grasses for their herds. Crop yields may have reached ratios as high as 30:1—that is, 30 bushels of grain harvested for every bushel of seeds planted.

Spread of Agriculture   Archeological evidence suggests that the Ubaids—the first identifiable group to settle in the region—began farming in Sumer perhaps as early as 7000 BCE. Remnants of irrigation tunnels, built of stone, date to at least 5900 BCE and possibly earlier. Archeologists have discovered even older settlements involving agriculture in other sites throughout the Middle East. At Jericho in Palestine, for example, evidence of grain storage—although not necessarily of grain production—reaches back to 9000 BCE. Agriculture also developed in northern Mesopotamia only two hundred years later, then on the south-central Anatolian plateau around 7500 BCE, and finally in southern Russia and along the banks of the Black Sea about 7000 BCE, after the geological shifting of continental plates opened the Dardanelles and let the saltwater of the Mediterranean pour in, to create the Black Sea out of what used to be a freshwater lake. But only Sumer gives evidence of continuous settlement, systematic agriculture, developed urban life, and the use of writing. From its location in the **Fertile Crescent**—the belt of rich farmland that extends from Mesopotamia in the east through Syria in the north and down to Egypt in the west—the techniques of agriculture spread eastward into India, westward

At Home in Çatalhöyük   This reconstruction shows a typical village home, ca. 6000 BCE, at Çatalhöyük, in modern central Turkey. The entrance to the house was through the roof. The opening in the floor led to the underground graves of the family's dead.

to the coastal plains of the eastern Mediterranean, and even as far as western Europe (see Map 1.1).

Early agriculture depended on collective labor, and lots of it: until native animals such as oxen were domesticated, the brutal work of cutting open the soil, planting seeds, weeding, pruning vines, cutting stalks, and grinding grains had to be done by hand. Skeletal remains of early agriculturalists—chiefly women— display agonizingly curved spines. Men, on the other hand, hunted, gathered, and ruled. Villages began to appear, some of them rather large; for safety, the people at most sites constructed stone or earthen walls to protect them from attack. The early settlement at Jericho had a population of roughly two thousand people by 7000 BCE and a fortification wall that may have reached 30 feet in height. In west-central Anatolia, at about the time Jericho was completing its wall, cattle breeders settled at Çatalhöyük, where their population swelled to between eight and ten thousand. They built a village of closely placed mud-brick houses without streets in between; roofs served as walkways, and residents entered their homes through holes in their roofs.

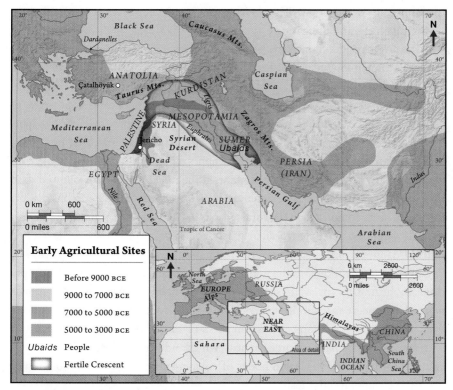

MAP 1.1   Early Agricultural Sites   The earliest agricultural societies appeared in northern Syria and Palestine, where archeological evidence survives from before 9000 BCE. These areas benefited from the higher rainfall of the Mediterranean basin.

Start of the Bronze Age

Primitive metal tools appeared around 7000 BCE as well, when small bits of raw copper were hammered into shape with stones. By 5000 BCE early settlers had learned how to smelt copper ore into the pure metal, which they then either cast into molds or, by 4000 BCE, mixed with tin to produce bronze. Bronze was significantly stronger than its component parts, and its use in weaponry and farm implements spread throughout the Near East quickly—inaugurating the **Bronze Age** (ca. 4000–1500 BCE).

EARLY MESOPOTAMIA: KINGS AND PRIESTS

Rich in potential for grain producing but lacking the stone and metal needed to bring it about, the Sumerians had to develop trade relations. These reached to the ore-rich but grain-poor settlements along the upper Tigris River and westward into Palestine and lower Anatolia. Sumerian grain traveled well in the arid atmosphere of the Near East, and the masses of heavy stone and metal they needed to produce it were easily transported down the strong current of the Tigris. But maintaining these important commercial ties over such long distances compelled the Sumerians to develop writing. With it they could keep records of orders, shipments, revenues, and obligations.

The origins of the Sumerians are unknown since their language is unrelated to any other known tongue, whether ancient or later. It is likely that they entered the Tigris–Euphrates plain, as did most of their subsequent invaders, from the Zagros Mountains in Iran. Sumerians were not the only inhabitants of Mesopotamia, of course, but they were the dominant group until their conquest by the Akkadians around 2500 BCE. Their founding myths identify Eridu and Ur as their first cities; archeological evidence confirms that these appeared as early as 5500 BCE and contained as many as fifty thousand inhabitants at their peak. They were followed soon by settlements at Uruk, Lagash, Nippur, and Kish; Sumerian cities were considerably larger and more complex than the rural villages in Palestine, Syria, and Anatolia.[1]

Although most people worked the land, economic specialization developed quickly. Stonemasons, merchants, rivermen, weavers, dyers, civil and hydraulic engineers, metalworkers, potters, and scribes—all emerged as distinct occupations. In the first centuries, these cities were governed by clan elders, who perhaps worked in concert as a primitive form of municipal council. They could not, however, defend the Sumerians against invaders or satisfy the whims of the deities who controlled the natural forces of heat, wind, and water. These constant needs resulted in the rise of new twin nodes of power—militarily backed monarchies and divinely appointed priesthoods.

---

[1]   Settlements were also heavily fortified. Uruk had a full 6 miles of battlements surrounding it.

Kingship and priesthood commonly emerged together in Western societies, sometimes in contest with each other and sometimes elided into a single office. Military action was most efficiently directed by a single commander to whom everyone owed obedience—the king, whose formal title was **lugal**. Protection against the gods, especially the unpredictable deities that the Sumerians believed in, required the priests. This large and permanent caste was charged with anticipating the gods' desires, interpreting their actions, and above all placating their wrath through prayer and sacrifice. Given their joint responsibility for protecting the people from harm, kings and priests have traditionally worked together: kings stand as bulwarks and standard-bearers of the priests' institutionalized religion, whereas priests serve to consecrate kings and bless their actions. In the ancient Near East, and well into Europe's own history, the worst crises frequently occurred when the secular and religious powers were at cross-purposes.

Secular and Religious Power

The Sumerians' own king list, written around 2100 BCE but reflecting a much older oral tradition, fancifully boasted that an unbroken string of monarchs had governed Sumer for well over 200,000 years. This tradition reached back even before the worst crisis of all: a mythical Great Flood sent by capricious gods that covered the entire earth and all but annihilated mankind. Much like the biblical tale of Noah and the ark, for which it served as a model, the Great Flood never happened but retained its psychological power because of the people's genuine fear of actual flooding. The Tigris and Euphrates occasionally swelled to unusual size and covered farms, fields, and flocks.[2] This legend, told in the great Mesopotamian poem the *Epic of Gilgamesh* (discussed in chapter 2), served to remind the people of the unpredictability of the gods while creating a reference point for the start of their own history.

Sumer consisted of a sprawl of independent city-states, each governed by a lugal, a priestly caste, or an uneasy combination of the two (see Map 1.2). The earliest king we can identify with any certainty was En-Mebaragesi, who ruled over Kish, near the site of the later city of Babylon, around 2600 BCE. His most significant achievement was the construction of the temple in Nippur, dedicated to the great sky god Enlil. En-Mebaragesi ruled during the so-called Early Dynastic Period, which lasted from about 2900 to 2350 BCE. By far the most famous of the Early Dynasts was **Gilgamesh**, who ruled Uruk around 2600 BCE. Tradition credits him with building the battlements surrounding that city and claims that after his death the grateful people of Uruk gave him a magnificent burial: they diverted the Euphrates River, buried his body in the exposed riverbed, and then released the waters once again into their original channel so their ruler would lie

The Early Dynasts

---

[2]   It seems likely that the legend of the Great Flood, if it had any basis in historical fact at all, originated with the creation of the Black Sea, described above.

MAP 1.2   The Ancient Near East   Agriculture formed the foundation of civilization, but other necessary components were cities, literacy, and organized religion. Shown here are the major temple sites in Sumer.

forever beneath the great river.[3] But Gilgamesh is best known as a literary figure, the hero of the later Babylonian epic that bears his name.

The Akkadian Conquest   A Semitic-speaking people called the Akkadians overwhelmed the Sumerian city-states around 2350 BCE, thus establishing what historians call the Akkadian Period, which lasted until about 2100. They had lived for several centuries along the upper Tigris, trading with the Sumerians and the peoples of Syria. Although they were foreigners, the Akkadians respected Sumerian culture and adopted its language, institutions, and religion. The most successful of the Akkadian kings was the first, **Sargon I**, who conquered everything from lower Sumer to northern Syria, all the way to the Mediterranean. This fierce conqueror boasted constantly of his cruelty as a matter of policy, making him perhaps the first ruler who found that simply maintaining a reputation for savagery can hold a large population in check as effectively as actual savagery can.

---

[3]   In 2003 a team of German archeologists discovered what they believe to be the ancient city of Uruk. The excavation is still underway; Gilgamesh's grave has yet to be located.

THE IDEA OF EMPIRE

Sargon placed family members in control of the territories he conquered, thereby governing a knitted-together **empire** (see Map 1.3). This was a surprisingly new idea. The Sumerians had fought plenty of wars over the centuries, but their custom had always been to defeat a neighbor and then to withdraw and receive annual tribute from the conquered. The notion of actually governing the lands they conquered seems never to have occurred to them. Sargon, however, saw that a hitherto unimagined level of wealth and power could result not only from controlling grain-rich Sumer but also from commanding the trade routes of upper Mesopotamia. Through this region Sumerian grain traveled northward, while textiles, metalwork, and animal products of the northern portions of the Fertile Crescent moved south. His empire far exceeded any earlier kingdom in its magnificence, but its real significance lay in the model of strategic authority that it established. By recognizing the Fertile Crescent's connective role—that is, its status as a commercial center or meeting point for the central Asian and eastern Mediterranean economies—he highlighted what was to become perhaps the dominant trait of

MAP 1.3   The Akkadian Empire, ca. 2350–2200 BCE   The Akkadian ruler Sargon was the first political figure to envision a state that united the territories of the Fertile Crescent under a single government.

Middle Eastern history, its strategic significance as the connection point between East and West.

The Sumerians had commonly referred to their rulers as shepherds of the people. The Akkadians, however, would have none of that. The *Babylonian Chronicle of Early Kings* declares, "Sargon, King of Agade, came to power during the reign of Ishtar and had neither rival nor equal. His splendor spread over the land and crossed over the sea to the east. And in the eleventh year he conquered to the west as far as it went." An inscription from the reign of one of Sargon's successors—his grandson Naram-Sin—describes him as "the Strong, the Ruler of Akkad" and claims his own share of his grandfather's glory:

> Even when the four corners of the earth were united in opposition to him, [Naram-Sin] emerged victorious . . . and took captive all the kings who had united against him. Because he had saved Akkad in time of crisis, all the people of the city begged of the gods—of Ishtar, in Eanna; of Enlil, in Nippur; of Dagan, in Tuttel; of Ninhursaga, in Kesh; of Enki, in Eridu; of Sin, in Ur; of Shamash, in Sippur; and of Nergal, in Kutha— that Naram-Sin might be worshipped as a god in Akkad. Accordingly, they built a temple for him in the center of the city.

The Akkadians thus appear to have introduced the cult of king worship.

Sargon's empire collapsed roughly one hundred years after his death, and control of the region passed to a series of native kings known collectively as the Third Dynasty of Ur (ca. 2100–2000 BCE). This was the last period of Sumerian history, since new waves of invaders who poured over Mesopotamia (sometimes en route to Palestine) ultimately displaced the Ur dynasts after 2000 BCE: the Semitic-speaking Amorites from southern Iran (2000–1600 BCE); the Hittites, an Indo-European group from central Anatolia (1600–1400 BCE); the Mitanni, also Indo-Europeans (1500–1300 BCE); and the Assyrians, a Semitic-speaking group from the northernmost reaches of the Tigris River (1500–600 BCE). There were others, too. But these groups generally disdained Sumerian culture and did their best to suppress or supplant it. Their interests lay more in the northern and western reaches of the Fertile Crescent, from Syria and Anatolia down through Palestine and approaching Egypt. As Sumer declined, the priestly caste went into elegiac mode, writing and preserving hymns to their gods and laments for the lost glories of the early city-states.

There is some evidence that economic decline contributed to the invaders' disdain for the Sumerian way of life. Centuries of flooding and irrigation had left high quotients of mineral salts in the farm fields. Since these salts rose to the surface as the water was absorbed into the land, the quality of the soil deteriorated, reducing productivity. Local farmers attempted to stop the decline by introducing new grains, but it seems clear that the gradual corrosion of the alluvial plain, which worsened the farther south one went toward the confluence of the two great rivers, brought an end to Sumerian life. It was no coincidence that the Amorites, the group to succeed the Akkadians, built a new capital for themselves considerably farther to the north, a city that remained the dominant Mesopotamian city for many centuries thereafter: Babylon.

MESOPOTAMIAN LIFE: FARMS AND CITIES, LETTERS AND NUMBERS

So much for the political framework. But what do we know about how people in early Mesopotamia lived, what they valued and believed, and how they understood the world?

Since agriculture is what brought them there in the first place, it is fitting to start with their working of the land. Farming occupied probably 90 percent of the *Farmers* population, who used wooden plows, bronze-tipped seed drills, and stone-bladed hoes. Mesopotamia comprised roughly 8,000 square miles of land fed by a network of major stone canal ways and an elaborate sprawl of subsidiary smaller channels, which divided the land into relatively regularly spaced and equally sized plots. Whereas the largest estates belonged to the kings and temple priests, most farmland was held privately. Whole clans, rather than individuals, owned each plot of land, and they worked out for themselves the distribution of tasks and profits. In most cases the consent of the whole clan was needed before any parcel of land could be sold. Yet it remains unclear how that consent was achieved—whether by all the adults equally, solely by the men, under the leadership of the clan elders, or by some other means. Clans who wanted to relinquish their land-ownership, perhaps to migrate northward into Syria or into Palestine, resorted to adopting would-be buyers into their clan to facilitate the sale of their property. Inheritance practices were **patrilinear**, through male heirs, although in the absence of one, women could own property and give evidence in courts.

A barter economy predominated, with farmers giving grain portions to the various craftsmen—carpenters, smiths, potters, and weavers—who produced the tools they needed to work the land. Payments in kind were likewise made to the priests in the local temples. Commoners also owed a certain amount of labor to their communities, usually for the all-important tasks of maintaining the irrigation canals and urban fortifications. All adult men fought to defend the city-state from attack and were responsible for supplying their own weapons and equipment. Law allowed for divorce and remarriage, although women were not considered equal partners of their husbands.

City Life   The cities that dominated Sumer were built of sunbaked brick and surrounded by deep moats and fortified battlements. The major streets within each city ran from the gates to the market squares and then to the temples and the royal palace. These streets could accommodate two-way traffic of chariots and ass-drawn wagons and carts; branching off these were tangles of narrow byways and alleys where the bulk of the people lived in cramped, low-roofed huts. Open space came at a premium; the wealthy displayed their status and good fortune by building interior courtyards in their palaces. Larger towns like Ur, Uruk, Lagash, Kish, and Nippur held populations as large as forty or fifty thousand, but five to ten thousand was more common. Rank and filthy, these towns had no sewers; human waste was simply dumped into the unpaved streets, where it was foraged (and added to) by crowds of swine, goats, oxen, and dogs. Clean water to drink was a luxury, which accounts for the Sumerians' early invention of beer—the alcohol in it forestalled the proliferation of pathogens. A Sumerian drinking song of the mid-2nd millennium BCE bears witness to the importance of beer:

> Fellow, I will teach you truly who your god is:
> Cast down unhappiness in triumph, forget the silence of death!
> Let one day of happiness make up for 36,000 years of the silence of death!
> Let the Beer Goddess rejoice over you as if you were her own child!
> That is the destiny of humankind.

The practice of slavery appeared early in Sumer; it was a decidedly urban phenomenon. Two principle sources of slaves existed: debt bondage and the taking of captives in war. People who owed money to landlords or merchants seldom sold themselves into slavery; instead, they sold their family members. The practice may have begun as the offering of a child as collateral for a loan or as a ransom against a promise to repay a debt. Failure to pay resulted in the child's permanent loss of freedom. War captives and their descendants, however, probably represented the larger portion of the slave population. The frequent warring between the city-states, and between the Sumerians and their invaders, resulted in a steady supply of new slaves—which was a necessity in ancient times, since the harshness of slave life meant that slave populations were seldom self-sustaining. Their mortality rates almost always exceeded their birth rates. Given the vulnerability of this population, therefore, the Sumerians kept their slaves from the backbreaking work of tilling the land and maintaining the irrigation canals. Too, the Sumerians generally avoided using slave labor in the fields because the opportunities for escape were too great. Instead, slaves remained in the cities, working as domestic servants, laborers in workshops, and concubines.

Ziggurat at Ur   Built in honor of the moon god Nanna/Sin, the patron deity of the city of Ur, this great temple was constructed in the reign of Ur-Nammu, ca. 2000 BCE.

Temples dotted the cityscape. Sumerians believed in and sacrificed to hosts of deities, but each city observed the formal recognition of a particular patron god, for whom they erected vast terraced, pyramid-like mounds called **ziggurats**, atop which stood lavishly decorated temples that served as the earthly home of the god or goddess. Sumerian religion maintained that the gods had invented humans to serve them and perform the labor that they would otherwise have to do for themselves; hence temple worship involved prayer, the singing of hymns, and the offering to deities of an array of gifts. Priests received a percentage of every farmer's produce and of every manufacturer's wares. In return, they presided over the temples' rites and sought to keep the gods appeased. Human life was subject to the whims of the gods. The Sumerians believed that their deities commanded the forces of nature, and although the deities were generally benevolent (hence Sumerian prosperity), they could nevertheless act capriciously and were easily roused to anger.

Priests often worked alongside the king to govern the city-state, creating a de facto theocracy. To aid in that work, and to keep a careful tally of payments made or yet owed to the deities, the priestly caste invented writing—Mesopotamia's greatest single contribution to the world. The earliest surviving documents (records of payments received from temple worshippers, primarily) come from Uruk and Kish around 3500 BCE. Sumerian scribes wrote by pressing figures into mud or clay tablets that were then either sun dried or baked until hardened. They started with pictograms, or drawn representations of objects. These gave way to a script that is called **cuneiform**—a sophisticated system of ideograms, which

Invention of Writing

Cuneiform Writing This clay receipt from about 2300 BCE tallies the number of sheep and goats in a particular herd. Perhaps part of a bill of sale, it may also be a record for taxation purposes.

represent concepts, and phonograms, or marks indicating syllabic phonetic values.[4] The latter are similar to the shortcuts used by today's text messagers. Sumerian writing used nearly two thousand symbols, which meant that literacy remained a tightly held monopoly of professional scribes, who consequently enjoyed positions of great significance in society. Without them, kings and priests could not compile records, issue decrees, or establish legal or liturgical canons.

Once the script had become established, Sumerian scribes set to work recording economic transactions, astronomical charts, religious poems and prayers, medical regimens, legal decrees, arithmetical calculations—all manner of things. Among the most interesting writings are early word lists. These lists were not dictionaries, but rather groups of related nouns—four-legged animals, birds of various sizes, types of flowers and other plants, species of fish, and varieties of precious stones and metals. Such lists probably originated as study guides for learning the cuneiform script. Yet they also represent human beings' first documented efforts to make sense of the world by classifying its components and seeking order among its bewildering variety.

The first author in the Greater Western tradition whose name is known was **En-Heduanna** (2285–2250 BCE), the daughter of Sargon. En-Heduanna served as the high priestess of the Akkadian moon goddess Nanna and left behind a sizable collection of religious poetry. Among her best-known works is a hymn in honor of the love goddess Inanna, who, as the protectress of the city of Uruk, often doubled as a war goddess. En-Heduanna extols Inanna as much for her ferocity on the battlefield as for her beauty and power at inspiring love:

> Great queen of queens, issue of a holy womb for righteous divine powers,
> More holy even than your own mother, wise and sage,
> Lady of all the foreign lands, life-force of the teeming people—
> I will recite your holy song!
> True goddess fit for divine powers, your splendid utterances are
>   magnificent.
> Deep-hearted, good woman with a radiant heart,
> I will enumerate your divine powers!
> . . .

---

[4]   Cuneiform literally means "wedge shape" in Latin, after the indentation made into the clay by a reed stylus.

Be it known that you are lofty as the heavens!
Be it known that you are broad as the earth!
Be it known that you destroy the rebel lands!
Be it known that you roar at the foreign lands!
Be it known that you crush heads!
Be it known that you devour corpses like a dog!

. . .

You have become the greatest!
My lady, beloved by [the sky god] An, I shall tell
Of all your rages. I have heaped up coals in the censer,
And prepared the purification rites. The shrine awaits you.
Might your heart not be appeased towards me?

A second set of markings depicted numbers. Sumerian mathematics used place-value numerals, with both base-ten and base-sixty notations. (The latter *Mathematics* survives in our division of time into sixty-minute hours and sixty-second minutes.) By 2300 BCE they had either invented or imported the abacus, a manual computing device. They used arithmetic to keep financial accounts and to study the constellations and the movement of the planets in the night sky. Since their survival depended on knowing when to expect the spring floods, the Sumerians paid close attention to measuring time. They followed a solar calendar but divided it into twelve lunar months, which necessitated the insertion of a thirteenth month every third year. The flooding of the rivers eroded the Sumerians' mud-brick buildings and boundary markers, so they quickly became adept at basic geometry to re-create their washed-away property lines.

Oral custom and written law structured Sumerian life, and as early as 2300 BCE at least one ruler, Ur-Ukagina of Lagash, had brought these laws *Written* into a single, published code that articulated the pursuit of justice, not the *Law* preservation of inherited right, as the aim of government. Economic specialization in the cities had created a degree of social stratification that ancient custom could neither address nor restrain, leaving thousands vulnerable to exploitation in every city. Written law emerged from this as an effort to reform society by restricting the rights of the powerful. Ur-Ukagina's law code survives only in fragments and in references found in later texts. The portions that survive limit the rights of the priestly caste and wealthy landowners to evict tenants and seize their property, exempt widows and orphans from paying taxes, and oblige the government to meet the funeral expenses of the poor. One inscription reads, "[Ur-Ukagina] freed the people of Lagash from usury, burdensome controls, hunger, theft, murder, and seizure of their property. He established freedom. Widows and orphans were no longer at the mercy of powerful individuals."[5] This effort to relieve oppression did not last long, however: the Akkadians conquered Sumer shortly after Ur-Ukagina's reign. Subsequent rulers, however, continued to produce reformist codes, the most famous of all being that instituted around 1700 BCE by the Babylonian ruler Hammurabi (discussed in chapter 2).

RELIGION AND MYTH: THE GREAT ABOVE AND GREAT BELOW

Sumerian religion, as reconstructed from myths and ritual prayers written in Babylonian times, consisted of a complex web of relations. It encompassed at least three strata of existence: Heaven, the Great Above, and the Great Below.

Major Gods and Goddesses

The Sumerians regarded the day and night sky as the high overarching bowl of Heaven, a fixed semisphere where dwelt Anu (meaning "sky" literally but representing the divine force itself) and a group of spirits known as the Igigi. The Great Above consisted of the space from the dome of the sky down to the surface of the earth; this was the dwelling of the Annunaki—the assemblage of gods and goddesses to whom the people of Sumer sacrificed and offered prayers and whose aid they invoked. Enlil, the god of the air, reigned supreme here. Other chief gods were Utu, the sun god (called Shamash by the Akkadians); Nanna Suen, the moon god (Sin to the Akkadians); Nin-Khursaga, the earth goddess (Akkadian Ishtar); and Enki, the god of waters (later identified with the Babylonian god Ea), but the names of at least fifty other Annunaki survive. Humanity was the creation of Enki, who had made human beings specifically to provide food and comfort for the gods. People, in other words, were the servants of the gods in the most literal sense. Interestingly, the Annunaki—all forces of nature—did not create the world but were in fact created by it.

The world itself came about through the movement of two primordial forces—the male and female principles (Abzu and Tiamat, respectively)—which resulted in the creation of the physical world and then of the gods themselves. But the Annunaki feared the creation of even more gods, who presumably might have supplanted them, and so Enlil killed their mother, Tiamat, and Enki slew Abzu. The murdered parents thus descended into the Great Below, the world beneath the surface of the earth. Also beneath the earth was Kur (Ersetu to the Akkadians), which was the Land of No Return, the place to which all humans went after death. The Sumerians believed there existed two separate entrances to the world of the dead, one in the caves of the Zagros Mountains and another in a secret staircase hidden in the city of Uruk. After dying, all Sumerians entered Kur by one

---

[5] This inscription contains the first known use of the word for "freedom" in any Western language: *ama-gi.*

of these portals, whereupon they received judgment from a council of six hundred gods. It is hard to say what the purpose of such judgment was, however, since all the dead—kings and commoners alike—were consigned to spending eternity wandering naked and exposed through an endless expanse of darkness, dust, and heat.

Each city-state possessed its own unique patron deities, and it was the joint responsibility of the lugal and his corps of priests to lead their societies in ritual worship. Sumerian gods numbered more than three thousand, but most of them remained unknown outside their local cult centers. Only the major deities like Enlil, Enki, and Nin-Khursaga enjoyed wide recognition, through the stories that made up Sumerian mythology. Anthropomorphic in form and all too humanlike in behavior, the gods nonetheless stood well beyond human understanding. A crude barter characterized human–divine relations: the Sumerians courted favor from the gods by offering them prayers and appeasing them with gifts, and the gods blessed the people (when it suited them) by sending favorable conditions for the growing of abundant food. *Local Deities*

The gods were capricious, however, and could lash out in anger by sending a burning drought, a devastating flood, a plague of crop-eating insects, or a wave of foreign invaders. Sumerian priests guarded against such divine fickleness by reading omens in the organs of animals sacrificed in the temple, by interpreting dreams, or by seeing coded messages in the flight patterns of birds. Religious life in Sumer thus consisted largely of maintaining favorable but distant relations with the gods and goddesses. Heavenly interaction with humans spelled doom as often as it brought delight.

The Standard of Ur   Excavated in the 1920s, the "Standard of Ur" of about 2500 BCE is actually a wooden box, about 8-1/2 × 20 inches, with an inlaid mosaic of lapis lazuli, limestone, and shells. This panel portrays farmers, carters, scribes, merchants, and priests en route to offer their sacrifices to the deities.

In earliest times Sumerian myths lacked a strong moral element: the gods exhibited the same self-interest that humans did and pursued their pleasures and whims accordingly. By the start of the 2nd millennium BCE, however, as urban culture developed and social stratification increased, myths appeared that bore witness to a heightened interest in justice and a sense of rational moral order. A hymn to the goddess Nanshe of Lagash, for example, lauds her as the deity who "sees the oppression of man over man, who is the guardian of orphans, . . . the caregiver of widows, who seeks justice for the poor, . . . who comforts the homeless and shelters the weak."

The best known of the moralized Sumerian hymns is called the Shamash Hymn after the Babylonian name for the sun god Utu. The hymn offers praise for the god's relentless protection of the weak and troubled:

> You care for all the peoples of the lands,
> And everything that Enlil/Ea . . . has created is entrusted to you.
> All that draws breath you shepherd without exception. . . .
> The whole of mankind bows to you,
> Shamash, the universe longs for your light. . . .
> You stand by the traveler whose road is difficult,
> To the seafarer in dread of the waves you give [comfort]. . . .
> You save from the storm the merchant carrying his capital;
> The [boatman] who sinks in the ocean you equip with wings;
> You point out settling places to refugees and fugitives, and
> To the captive you point out [escape] routes known only to you.

The hymn goes on to praise Utu/Shamash for punishing corrupt judges and dishonest merchants, for granting long life to those who work for justice, and for rewarding the honest and kindly. The lugals, too, came to be valued for the extent to which they provided justice, since their temple duties of leading sacrifices and observing the chief festivals of the religious year gained in significance.

A contrary tradition in Sumerian myth laments the unpredictability of the gods' affections and care to protect the righteous. "The Poem of the Righteous Sufferer" expresses the agonies of an unnamed Sumerian who, despite his strict ritual observance, has nevertheless suffered the loss of his wealth and social position:

> Who knows the will of the gods in heaven?
> Who understands the plans of the underworld gods?
> Where have mortals learnt the way of a god?
> He who was alive yesterday is dead today.
> For a minute he was dejected, suddenly he is exuberant.
> One moment people are singing in exaltation,

Another they groan like professional mourners.
Their condition changes like the opening and shutting of the legs,
When starving they become like corpses,
When replete they vie with the gods.
In prosperity they speak of scaling heaven,
Under adversity they complain of going down to hell.
I am appalled at these things; I do not understand their significance.

A later Babylonian writer reworked this poem into a song of praise for the god Marduk. This patron deity of Babylon comes to the sufferer's aid and restores him to happiness, ending with a paean to traditional teaching and ritual.[6] In the original tale, however, the dominant tone is despair. The narrator seeks not an end to human suffering but merely an explanation for it. Why do the wicked prosper? Why are the lives of the righteous filled with want, fear, violence, and confusion? Why will the gods not spare humans from the pain of life?

To judge from their literary remains, the people of Mesopotamia thought long and deeply about these matters. The precarious nature of life almost demanded it. *Search for* After all, the land they inhabited had many natural blessings but was vulnerable to *Meaning* invasion by raiders seeking to snatch away the very blessings the Sumerians worked so hard to procure. Moreover, the rivers that gave such abundant life to the region also destroyed it by unpredictable and uncontrollable flash flooding. The more the Sumerians prospered, the more likely they were to be attacked. These were ironies of a most soul-searching kind. If the gods could alternately bless and batter humans so capriciously, is it vain to regard the world as being in any way ethically ordered? And if life lacks moral sense, is it worth the agony of living it? Can we have trust in heaven? Attitudes shifted with time and fortune, but the Sumerians recognized that life is serious business. Among their many important contributions to Western culture was the invention of the conscious search for meaning in life. And that may be their most fundamental contribution of all.

ANCIENT EGYPT, GIFT OF THE NILE

Southwest of the Fertile Crescent, along the banks of the Nile River in Africa, lay the second cradle of Western civilization. The Nile originates in two sub-Saharan tributaries—one in northern Ethiopia, fed by Lake Tana, and the other stretching all the way south to Lake Victoria in Uganda. They meet near today's Sudanese capital city of Khartoum. From there the Nile flows northward, dropping through

---

[6]   The Babylonian tale may have provided a model for the Hebrew author of the biblical Book of Job, in which the unmerited sufferings of an upright man are also discussed in detail.

a series of dramatic cataracts, or waterfalls, before reaching the gentle sloping plane of Egypt itself.

For 600 miles it meanders slowly northward, cutting a green swath of fertile land on either side of the riverbed, until about 100 miles shy of the Mediterranean it branches out in a delta with no fewer than seven major openings to the sea, spread over nearly 250 miles of coastline. This delta region forms "Lower Egypt," and the 600-mile-long river valley directly south of it comprises "Upper Egypt" (see Map 1.4). Ancient Egypt thus consisted of two extremely long strips of land on either side of the Nile, between 4 and 12 miles across, and a vast triangular delta. The waters of the Nile swelled annually, beginning in August. At their peak in September, they reached nearly 20 feet above their low ebb in April and May, bringing more than 100 million tons of rich sediment to replenish the banks. Spring planting thus began when the greatest amount of land was exposed, and the harvest was brought in just before the next replenishing flood began. People lived in small communities along the river's edge as early as 5000 BCE but did not begin to farm the land until approximately 3500 BCE. Until then, they tended their flocks, living off the plants and trees that grew naturally along the shores.

Egyptian ships moved constantly on the great river, bringing foodstuffs, building materials, and laborers to wherever they were needed. Given the Nile's gentle flow, most boats were open and flat bottomed, which made it easy to load and unload cargo. Rowers propelled the boats downstream—that is, from south to north—because the prevailing winds blew southward; boats heading upriver therefore were sail driven. The "Hymn to the Nile," one of ancient Egypt's key religious texts, bears witness to the importance of the river to daily life:

> [The Nile] shines when he issues forth from the darkness
> To cause his flocks to prosper.
> It is his force that gives existence to all things;
> Nothing remains hidden from him.
> Let men clothe themselves to fill his gardens.
> He watches over his works,
> Producing the inundation during the night. . . .
> A festal song is raised for thee on the harp,
> With the accompaniment of the hand.
> The young men and children acclaim thee
> And prepare their long exercises.
> Thou art the august ornament of the earth,
> Letting thy bark advance before men,
> Lifting up the heart of women in labor,
> And loving the multitude of the flocks.

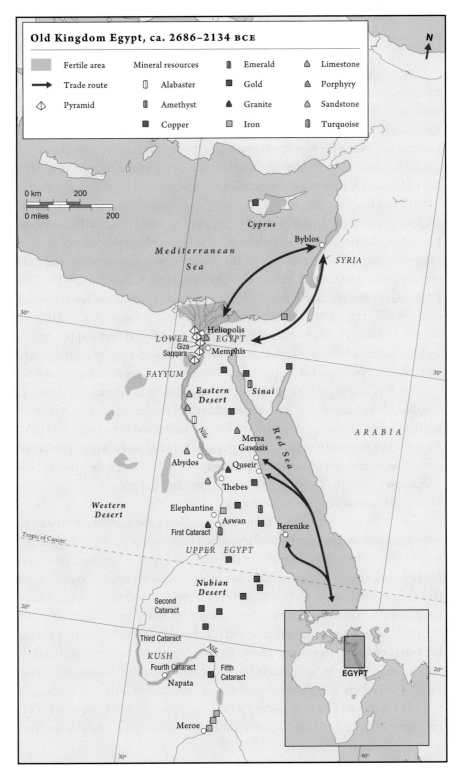

Old Kingdom Egypt, ca. 2686–2134 BCE

N

Fertile area	Mineral resources	Emerald	Limestone
Trade route	Alabaster	Gold	Porphyry
Pyramid	Amethyst	Granite	Sandstone
	Copper	Iron	Turquoise

0 km   200
0 miles   200

Cyprus

Mediterranean Sea

Byblos

SYRIA

30°

Heliopolis
LOWER EGYPT
Giza
Saqqara Memphis

FAYYUM

30°

Eastern Desert   *Sinai*

ARABIA

Mersa Gawasis

Abydos   Quseir

Red Sea

Thebes

Western Desert

Elephantine
Aswan   Berenike
First Cataract

Tropic of Cancer

UPPER EGYPT

Nubian Desert

20°

Second Cataract

Third Cataract

Nile

KUSH
Fourth Cataract   Fifth Cataract
Napata

EGYPT   20°

Meroe

30°   40°

MAP 1.4 Old Kingdom Egypt, ca. 2686–2134 BCE The banks of the Nile grew more fertile the farther downstream (that is, to the north) one traveled, as shown here. But most of Egypt's mineral wealth lay along the upper reaches of the river (to the south).

Away from the cultivated shores of the Nile, the rest of Egypt was all but uninhabitable, with nothing but arid desert to the east, west, and south. The relatively small land bridge of the Sinai Peninsula, the only point of contact between the African and Asian continents, narrowed to a span of 40 miles as it approached Egypt proper. Controlling the movement of peoples through so small an area posed little trouble for ancient Egypt, blessed not only with a concentrated abundance of fertile soil and an easy means of communication and transport, but also with a protective surrounding that kept invaders out for nearly fifteen hundred years. The marshy delta's port cities comprised Egypt's only exposure to other peoples, and hence the fortification of the harbors represented the only significant military expense of its rulers. Moreover, and unlike Sumer, Egypt had abundant resources in stone and metal ores and hence could engage in impressive building projects, most notably the Great Pyramids of Giza, the monumental royal tombs counted among the Seven Wonders of the World. Timber was the only vital natural resource unavailable, but this was procured relatively easily via trade through the delta cities and then shipped upriver. By such natural advantages Egypt unified early, developed a strong central government, and enjoyed more lasting peace and prosperity than any other early culture.

The first languages used in the region belonged to the Hamitic and Semitic families. These suggest that the earliest settlers arrived around 5000 BCE from the northern coast of Africa to the west and from Palestine and Syria to the northeast. By 4000 BCE the construction of rafts made of papyrus reeds, which grew abundantly in the marshlands, enabled the groups stretched along the river to be in continuous contact. Technologies of tool making, copper mining, irrigation, swamp drainage, and stone carving spread accordingly.

Unification of Egypt   Given the quantity of arable land along the river, the earliest Egyptians did not congregate in cities but instead spread out more or less evenly in hundreds of small villages; hence the first organized states emerged as regional groupings, called *nomes*, along segments of the river. These nomes eventually coalesced into larger units, until finally, around 3150 BCE, the entire kingdom was unified under a single ruler. Tradition credits a man named **Menes** with the feat; after him Egyptian kings wore a crown that joined the characteristics of crowns of the earlier rulers of Lower Egypt and Upper Egypt.[7] Many scholars have replaced the semilegendary Menes with **Narmer**, whose position as first ruler of a united Egypt is corroborated by an engraved palette that illustrates the combined kingship. The division of Egypt's history into thirty dynasties was the invention of a native historian of the Hellenistic era named Manetho, after Alexander the Great

---

[7]   The word *pharaoh*, which means "palace" or "great house," did not come into general use until the period of the New Kingdom, discussed in chapter 2. Since the Egyptians believed their ruler to be a god, to speak his name aloud was blasphemy.

(discussed in chapter 5) had conquered the kingdom in 332 BCE. Manetho divided Egyptian history into the periods of the Old, Middle, and New Kingdoms, with so-called Intermediate Periods separating them. The thirty dynasties were then parceled out between the kingdoms and periods. Scholars have since tinkered with the details but have kept Manetho's general scheme (see Table 1.1).

TABLE 1.1 Ancient Egypt

Archaic Period: ca. 3150–2686 BCE (Dynasties 1–2)

Old Kingdom: ca. 2686–2134 BCE (Dynasties 3–6)

First Intermediate Period: ca. 2134–2035 BCE (Dynasties 7–10)

Middle Kingdom: ca. 2035–1640 BCE (Dynasties 11–12)

Second Intermediate Period: ca. 1640–1570 BCE (Dynasties 13–17)

New Kingdom: ca. 1570–1070 BCE (Dynasties 18–20)

Third Intermediate Period: ca. 1070–664 BCE (Dynasties 21–26)

Late Period: ca. 664–332 BCE (Dynasties 27–30)

Narmer Palette   This plaque commemorates King Narmer (a.k.a. Menes—Old Kingdom rulers had as many as five names each), the king who united Lower and Upper Egypt. The front image (left) portrays Narmer as he prepares to smash the skull of a rival with a mace. To the right the god Horus, in the shape of a falcon, brings him captives. Narmer wears a kilt, with the tail of a bull (symbol of strength) attached to his backside. The reverse side of the plaque (right) shows another bull, at the bottom, breaking through the fortifications of a city and trampling a victim, while above, servants attend to two great beasts whose long necks are entwined, a scene that presumably represents the union of the Lower and Upper Kingdoms. On top, a ruler with his servants carries banners and the spoils of war.

An identifiable Egyptian civilization thus took shape at roughly the same time that organized Sumerian society began—around the start of the 3rd millennium BCE. This corresponds with the appearance of writing in both societies. The Egyptians—who had established trade relations with the Sumerians by that early time—may have acquired the idea of writing from Mesopotamia. Unlike the Sumerian cuneiform, however, the Egyptians developed a system of **hieroglyphs** (literally, "sacred carving"), based on a combination of pictograms and phonetic signs. The Egyptians wrote on a kind of paper made of woven strips of papyrus reed that was much easier to use than the Sumerians' clay tablets and that made it possible for Egyptian scribes to devise two cursive scripts (known as demotic and hieratic scripts) that made record keeping considerably easier. As a result, the written records of Egypt vastly exceed those of Mesopotamia in both number and variety, and the arid condition of the local environment enabled them to survive the long centuries more or less intact. For the first four dynasties, in fact, more of their writings survive than the buildings they lived in because the latter were made of baked mud-brick, which

Egyptian Hieroglyphs   In this paint-on-plaster portrait dating from around 2550 BCE, Nefertiabet, the daughter of the pharaoh Cheops (or Khufu), is shown wearing a leopard skin. Surrounding the table at which she sits are a variety of tribute-gifts: linens, loaves of bread, and offerings of beer or wine.

erodes rapidly even in Egypt's dry climate. They reserved expensive stone for the palaces and tombs of the wealthy and for the temples presided over by the influential priestly caste.

LIFE AND RULE IN OLD KINGDOM EGYPT

As in Mesopotamia, most Egyptians worked the land. Slavery existed but was not as widespread as in Mesopotamia. Egypt's relative insulation from outsiders de- *Social* prived it of the main source of slaves: prisoners of war. Besides, the king had an *Strata and* unquestioned right to force his subjects to join labor crews for public-works proj- *Daily Life* ects. Society was strictly stratified, with social distinctions expressed by dress codes. Slightly above the farmers in social status were the simple artisans: brewers, weavers, stonemasons, bricklayers. Higher were the makers of luxury items for the elites: goldsmiths, jewelry makers, perfumers. A smaller corps of professionals stood above these: physicians, scribes, architects, priests, and civic officials. In theory, all Egyptians were equal under the law regardless of class or sex, and even the lowliest farmer could hope to petition for redress of a legal complaint—but that was theory, not reality.

Monogamous marriage was the norm for Egyptians, although law did not require it, and men of all classes frequently took additional wives or concubines. Women, however, were subject to harsh legal punishment and social ostracism for engaging in sex outside of marriage to a single husband. Both sexes, however, could own property, enter contracts, and settle disputes in court.

The basic Egyptian diet consisted of varieties of grain—whether as bread, gruel, or beer—supplemented with a few vegetables (leeks, garlic, squash, and lettuce, especially), along with figs, dates, and fish. Meat was a rare treat for commoners, as was wine. Two other food practices date back to the Old Kingdom: the keeping of bee colonies, for honey and wax, and the netting of wild geese as they followed their own food trail along the river's edges.[8] June to September was the flooding season, October to February saw the growing of the grain fields, and March to May was the harvest. Given the often extreme heat, most Egyptians wore little clothing. Children, in fact, generally went naked until they entered puberty, and it was common for men to shave and oil their entire body. Most people's homes, too, were designed to offset the heat: simple mud-brick, often painted white, remained relatively cool throughout the day, and all cooking was done in small open-air patios. They covered their homes' packed-earth floors with reed mats. The Egyptians followed a solar calendar but never felt compelled to develop the technological tools or scientific expertise of

---

[8]   The Egyptians learned early the trick of fattening the geese by feeding them large quantities of raw bread dough.

the Sumerians. Remarkably, the monumental architectural marvels for which the Old Kingdom is known were created without the wheel.

Agricultural abundance was the hallmark of Old Kingdom life. Papyrus texts, wall paintings, and tomb inscriptions describe masses of men and women at work in every aspect of food production—little other industry receives much attention—and preserve hundreds of popular songs that the farmers reportedly sang as they toiled. The composers of the songs clearly either came from or consciously extolled the upper classes.

> A good day—it is cool.
> The cattle are pulling
> And the sky does according to our desire.
> Let us work for the noble!

Another song was apparently a favorite of the grain-threshers:

> Thresh ye for yourselves, O cattle!
> Straw to eat, and barley for your masters.
> Let not your hearts be weary, for it is cool.

A last song expressed the joy of the slaves who carried their masters on palanquins, seats held aloft on poles:

> Go down into the palanquin—it is sound and it is well!
> The carrying poles are on the shoulders of the carriers.
> O palanquin of Ipi, be as heavy as you wish.
> It is pleasanter full than when empty!

Ideology of Kingship

Ruler worship dominated Old Egyptian life—or at least it was the dominant characteristic of the regimes that produced the evidentiary record. The king presented himself as a living god, the source of justice and stability, the munificent owner of the whole of Egypt and its people, and the embodiment of the people's hopes and love. Officials who wanted to remain in the king's good graces took great care to reinforce the royal self-image:

> To the great King, my Lord, the Sun-God from Heaven, thus I, Prince Zatatna of Acre, Your servant, the most humble servant of the Great King—indeed, the very dirt beneath Your feet, the ground upon which You tread—sends greeting. Seven times, O Great King, seven times, O Sun-God from Heaven, I fall, prostrate and helpless, at Your feet.

So began a typical piece of provincial administration. The glorification given to the king in the 3rd and 2nd millennia BCE, much of it on a colossal scale, would have brought an envious tear to the eye of many a 20th-century dictator. The **Great Pyramids** at Giza, massive royal tombs built by moving huge stones from a quarry and dragging and lifting them into place, tell only part of the tale. Statues of the kings adorned every temple; inscriptions praising their magnificence appeared in every city; hymns in their honor rang out in every religious service.

From their palace at the capital city of Memphis, strategically and symbolically located at the meeting point of Lower and Upper Egypt, the kings controlled every aspect of public life through cults of personality backed up by armies of bureaucratic and military officials. Each nome was administered by a nomarch appointed by

The Pyramids of Giza This striking photograph shows the proximity of the vast structures to the present city of Cairo. There is still no general agreement on how the pyramids were constructed. Most archeologists follow the idea that long ramps were constructed, up which the quarried stones were transported.

the king, and they all reported to a central official called a vizier. The nomarchs oversaw all public-works projects, coordinated food distribution, heard appeals, and dispensed justice. Assisting all these was an army of scribes who kept census records, tallied tax revenues, noted expenditures, and issued the government's decrees. Members of the royal family held many of these posts.

Few states in Western history have experienced such completely centralized rule. As evidence, despite its invention and wide use of writing, Egypt never created a law code. Since the king, a living god, walked the earth, whatever he said at any moment was, in effect, the law. When the king, who was identified as the sun god Horus, died, he became an even greater deity by being absorbed into Osiris, an amalgam of all kings merged into one, the ruler of the underworld, where his supreme authority never ended. Royal officials received estates from the king in return for their service, rather than salaries. The kings likewise endowed mortuary cults and temples to promote the worship of themselves after their deaths on earth.

It was an efficient way to govern, to be sure, and under benevolent rulers and judicious officials ancient Egypt enjoyed a material standard of living that vastly exceeded that of any contemporary society until the end of the Old Kingdom. By then, the pharaohs had transferred so much of their land that they began to have trouble meeting their enormous administrative costs, prompting the nomarchs to challenge royal power for the first time and thereby inaugurating the First

Intermediate Period. In the early centuries, however, safe from foreign aggression because of the surrounding deserts, easily unified by the quiet-flowing Nile, and fed by the abundance of grain and fruit sprouting along its banks, Egypt had only not to disturb nature's rhythms to reap its rewards.

Commitment to Ma'at   Accordingly, the supreme virtue of Egyptian culture was **ma'at**—a recognition of the world's ordering and a commitment to preserve it. Scholars commonly translate ma'at as "justice," which is too generous. Ma'at, in practice, was an acceptance of the world as it is, a reluctance to change anything for fear that the result might be worse than the (often beneficent) reality.

Prominent among the remains of Old Kingdom literature are "Instructions," or self-help guides written by fathers for their heirs, texts that repeatedly emphasize the message not to disturb ma'at. For example, the Instructions written for his son by Ptah-hotep, a royal official during the Fifth Dynasty, begin with the pronouncement that "a great thing is ma'at, enduring and surviving; it has not been upset since the time of Osiris. He who departs from its laws is punished." What actions maintain ma'at? Above all, never to question any established social custom or institution. Married life, for example, is valuable for the stability it brings. "If you are prosperous you should establish a household and love your wife as is fitting. Fill her belly and clothe her back. . . . Make her heart glad as long as you live. She is a profitable field for her lord." Loyal service to one's patron or employer is essential as well. "If you are a worthy man sitting in the council of your lord, confine your attention to excellence. Silence is more valuable than chatter. Speak only when you can resolve difficulties. . . . Bend your back to him who is over you, your superior in the administration; then your house will endure by reason of its prosperity, and your reward will come in due season. Wretched is he who opposes his superior, for one lives only so long as he is gracious."

Above all, Ptah-hotep writes, one must know the limits established by tradition and do nothing to challenge them. Ma'at must be preserved from generation to generation:

> If the son of a man accepts what his father says, no plan of his will fail. . . . Failure follows him who does not listen. A son who hears is a follower of Horus; there is good for him who listens. When he reaches old age and attains honor, he tells the like to his children, renewing the teaching of his father. Every man teaches as he has acted. He speaks to his children so that they may speak to their children.

The cultural contrasts between ancient Egypt and Mesopotamia are striking. The separate city-states of Mesopotamia were in perennial conflict—challenging, experimenting, wondering, often failing, but always adapting to new circumstances and searching for meaning in the apparent jumble of it all. Unified nearly from the start, ancient Egypt created a wealthy, profoundly religious, and strongly centralized society that revolved around the king—and a worldview intended to preserve this social order. Thus it embodied a conservative principle that may be ancient Egypt's most significant legacy to Western culture.

THE KINGDOM OF THE DEAD

Although king worship was a key part of religious life, ancient Egyptian religion was a mix of local myths and traditions that defies easy description. Each nome revered a specific local deity, most of them animal shaped, and a statue of whom stood in the local temple and whose cults formed the center of village religious life. The temple statue was believed to be the god or goddess, not merely to represent him or her; individual homes often would have small statuettes to the deity in a corner, to whom the people offered small gifts of grain, oil, or wine at mealtimes.

A company of major deities ruled over the local gods and probably served to create a sense of shared culture among the peoples of Lower and Upper Egypt. One of these major gods, named Ptah, was credited with creating the world, but beyond this he played little role in Egyptian mythology. The most important deities by far were the incestuous brother and sister Osiris and Isis, whose love for each other set the whole cosmology in motion. Osiris became the first god-king of the earth that Ptah had created, but his brother Seth, jealous of Osiris's kingship and possibly of his relations with Isis, killed Osiris, chopped him up, and scattered bits of his body all along the length of the Nile. Distraught, Isis searched out every piece and with the help of Anubis, the god of mummification, reassembled Osiris's body, bringing it miraculously back to life just long enough for Isis to enjoy one last sexual union with her brother, who promptly died again after completing the deed. But the job was done: Isis became pregnant and in time gave birth to the god Horus—who eventually grew to manhood, avenged his father by killing Seth, and took over the rulership of the world. Every king was thus believed to be a new incarnation of Horus, the god himself walking the earth. And on his death every king transformed into Osiris, who ruled over the realm of the dead for eternity.

Gods and Kings

The Isis–Osiris myth remained central to Egyptian culture for thousands of years, until it was supplanted by Christianity in the early centuries CE—which was itself largely succeeded by Islam in the 7th and 8th centuries CE. Rather than a tale of resurrection, of life defeating death—Osiris, after all, was revived only briefly—his tale expresses the notion of life's renewal, a cycle of generation, death, and regeneration that paralleled the rhythm of flood, planting, and harvest along the great Nile's banks. Temples and statues to Isis and Osiris were erected all

A Tomb with a View   Archeologists have unearthed several hundred ancient Egyptian aristocratic tombs called *mastabas* ("houses for eternity"). These were raised structures, 20 to 30 feet tall, made of mud-brick, with inward-slanting walls. This detail of an inscription on one mastaba (belonging to the head butcher for the royal court) shows part of an invocation to the god Osiris.

throughout the kingdom and reminded people everywhere of the universality of the king's authority. In the afterworld Osiris judged the souls of the dead kings before admitting them to his realm—a realm that was remarkably similar to life along the Nile: not a better life but simply *more* life, which the Egyptians seem to have regarded as blessing enough. Common people in the Old Kingdom received vastly simpler burials, the arable land on the bank being too precious to use for commoners' graves. Buried well away from the great pyramid valleys and far from the Nile itself, they were assumed to move easily into the afterworld—where they continued to farm, mine, and manufacture, in service to the redeemed kings forever.

Admission to the afterworld was not automatic for a king, yet neither was it tied closely to ethical behavior in his lifetime. Ancient Egyptian religion held that the soul of the deceased wandered through a dim wasteland, beset by various demon-spirits, in search of the House of Judgment where Osiris, along with forty-two other judges, would decide whether the dead soul could enter. One could in theory remain lost in the wasteland for eternity, but the ancient Egyptians created a canon of texts intended to lead the king to paradise. These incantations, magic spells, proclamations, and hymns were inscribed on the walls of the royal tombs—hence their collective name of Pyramid Texts. They guided the dead through the wasteland and provided sets of prayers and incantations to deploy against the demons. Moreover, they supplied the answers needed to satisfy the questions posed by Osiris and the other judges. With such scripted clues, the king's eternal reward was assured. After passing the examination, the dead ruler then made a final solemn declaration:

> I have not done evil to mankind.
> I have not oppressed the members of my family. . . .
> I have not brought forward my name for exaltation to honors.
> I have not ill-treated servants.
> I have not belittled a god.
> I have not defrauded the oppressed of their property.
> I have not done that which is an abomination to the gods. . . .
> I have made no man to suffer hunger.
> I have made no one to weep.
> I have done no murder.
> I have not given an order for murder to be done for me.
> I have not inflicted pain. . . .
> I have not committed fornication. . . .
> I have not encroached on the fields of others. . . .
> I have not cut into a canal of running water. . . .
> I have not obstructed a god in his procession
> *I am pure! I am pure! I am pure! I am pure!*

After the declaration the god Anubis weighed the dead king's heart on a scale, and if the purified heart weighed no more than a feather, the soul was admitted to the eternal presence of Osiris.

Note that the departed king's confession before Osiris lacks a positive spirit of morality: virtue consists of not performing evil rather than actively doing good. Just as ma'at did not equal justice, neither did the spiritual purity that entitled one to enter paradise imply anything more than correct behavior. In the earliest centuries only members of the royal family could receive the supreme reward, but the privilege of salvation was extended to the nobles in the Middle Kingdom period and to all Egyptians eventually—although only in the New Kingdom many centuries later. This is not to say that the ancient Egyptians were immoral or amoral. Rather, as with their contemporaries in Mesopotamia, their sense of moral values was distinct from the tenets and practices of their religion.

◆

Although it lacked the emotional complexity of Sumerian religion, Egyptian religion possessed an attractively hopeful belief in the unstoppable resilience of life.

Death, although not exactly a thing to be yearned for, did not need to be feared. It represented only a rite of passage—back to the shores of the Nile, where time would run as endlessly as the great river itself. The tumultuous history of ancient Egypt after the end of the Old Kingdom would test that faith.

WHO, WHAT, WHERE

Bronze Age	Fertile Crescent	ma'at
civilization	Gilgamesh	Menes/Narmer
cuneiform	Great Pyramids	patrilinear
empire	hieroglyphs	Sargon I
En-Heduanna	lugal	ziggurats

SUGGESTED READINGS

Primary Sources

Instructions of Ptah-hotep

Laws of Ur-Ukagina

Poem of the Righteous Sufferer

Shamash Hymn

Anthologies

Bailkey, Nels, and Richard Lim, eds. *Readings in Ancient History: Thought and Experience from Gilgamesh to St. Augustine* (2011, orig. 1987).

Bryce, Trevor. *Letters of the Great Kings of the Ancient Near East: The Royal Correspondence of the Late Bronze Age* (2014, orig. 2003).

Coogan, Michael D. *A Reader of Ancient Near Eastern Texts: Sources for the Study of the Old Testament* (2013).

Foster, John L., trans. *Ancient Egyptian Literature: An Anthology* (2001).

Glassner, Jean-Jacques. *Mesopotamian Chronicles* (2004).

Lichtheim, Miriam. *Ancient Egyptian Literature: A Book of Readings*, 3 vols. (2006, orig. 1973).

Vanstiphout, Herman, and Jerrold S. Cooper. *Epics of Sumerian Kings: The Matter of Aratta* (2004).

Studies

Anthony, David W. *The Horse, the Wheel, and Language: How Bronze-Age Riders from the Eurasian Steppes Shaped the Modern World* (2010, orig. 2007).

Aruz, Joan. *Art of the First Cities: The Third Millennium BC from the Mediterranean to the Indus* (2003).

Assmann, Jan. *The Mind of Egypt: History and Meaning in the Time of the Pharaohs* (2003).

Assmann, Jan. *The Search for God in Ancient Egypt* (2001).

Bottéro, Jean. *Everyday Life in Ancient Mesopotamia* (2001).

Bottéro, Jean. *Religion in Ancient Mesopotamia* (2001).

Brewer, Douglas J., and Emily Teeter. *Egypt and the Egyptians* (2007).

Charvát, Petr. *Mesopotamia before History* (2008).

Crawford, Harriet. *Sumer and the Sumerians* (2004).

Foster, Benjamin R., and Karen Polinger Foster. *Civilizations of Ancient Iraq* (2011).

Germonde, Philippe. *An Egyptian Bestiary: Animals in Life and Religion in the Land of the Pharaohs* (2001).

Glassner, Jean-Jacques. *The Invention of Cuneiform: Writing in Sumer* (2007).

Harris, David R. *Origins of Agriculture in West Central Asia: An Environmental–Archaeological Study* (2010).

Hodder, Ian. *The Leopard's Tale: Revealing the Mysteries of Çatalhöyük* (2011).

Kemp, Barry J. *Ancient Egypt: Anatomy of a Civilization* (2005, orig. 1992).

Leick, Gwendolyn. *Mesopotamia: The Invention of the City* (2003).

Leick, Gwendolyn. *Sex and Eroticism in Mesopotamian Literature* (2003, orig. 1994).

Liverani, Mario. *Uruk: The First City* (2006).

Maynes, Mary Jo, and Ann Waltner. *The Family: A World History* (2012).

O'Brien, Cormac. *The Fall of Empires: From Glory to Ruin, an Epic Account of History's Ancient Civilizations* (2009).

Robins, Gay. *The Art of Ancient Egypt* (2008, orig. 1997).

Romer, John. *A History of Ancient Egypt: From the First Farmers to the Great Pyramid* (2013).

Silverman, David P., ed. *Ancient Egypt* (2003).

Wilkinson, Toby. *The Rise and Fall of Ancient Egypt: The History of a Civilization from 3000 BC to Cleopatra* (2013).

For additional resources, including maps, primary sources, visuals, web links, and quizzes, please go to **www.oup.com/us/backman**.

Law Givers, Emperors, and Gods: The Ancient Near East

2100–486 BCE

THE MIDDLE EAST AND
THE EASTERN MEDITERRANEAN

The second millennium BCE can hardly be topped for drama. Droughts, famines, civil wars, foreign invasions, deadly new weapons, and powerful empires—all these characterized the age and marked its major turning points. Four empires dominated the era: Egypt's Middle and New Kingdoms, the Babylonian (and later Persian) Empire in southern Mesopotamia, the Assyrian Empire of northern Mesopotamia, and the Hittite Empire in Anatolia (modern Turkey). Between them lay a sprawl of smaller states along the eastern Mediterranean coastline and skirting the southern edges of the Anatolian mountains. Once established, this patchwork of big and small states lived in relative harmony, in a dense web of commercial, cultural, and diplomatic connections that inspired some remarkable advances in each society.

Hatshepsut as Pharaoh This sculpture of the New Kingdom Egyptian ruler Hatshepsut (r. 1479–1458 BCE) depicts her as a male, with ceremonial beard. A prolific builder, Hatshepsut oversaw hundreds of construction projects, but her greatest achievement may have been the reestablishment and expansion of Egyptian trading networks.

Around 1200 BCE, however, newcomers appeared—groups of outsiders who operated separately but were loosely related by their dialects of a language family known as Indo-European. Little is known about these mysterious bands, but their waves of invasion set off a chain reaction of political collapse and economic ruin that wiped out nearly every state in the Near East. It left the peoples adrift and unsure, vulnerable to new regimes and exposed to new ideas about values such as human fate, man's relationship with the divine, the purpose of government, and the essence of morality. By 1000 BCE, or thereabouts, Western history had taken on a radical realignment that would have been unthinkable only two hundred years earlier. This realignment led to the birth of Western culture's first two great religions, Judaism and Zoroastrianism.

Moreover, the interaction of the Indo-European groups and the primarily Semitic-speaking peoples of the Fertile Crescent opened the way for the development of the Greater West—a civilization that bridged Europe and western Asia. This Greater West was composed not of a single hybrid culture but rather of the sense of a shared destiny in a large matrix of individual cultures. Europe and the Middle East have remained connected ever since by bonds of trade, intellectual cross-fertilization, cultural overlap, and religious rivalry.

OLD BABYLON

The city of Babylon was founded around 1950 BCE by the Semitic-speaking Amorites, who seized control of Sumer soon after the turn of the second millennium. Its location at the nexus of several trade routes through the Mesopotamian plain made it a strategic base for extending power out of Sumer itself and northward toward Syria, from which the Amorites themselves had come. The most famous of the early Babylonian rulers was **Hammurabi** (r. 1792–1750 BCE). A large archive of his diplomatic records survive, which document his crafty rise

CHAPTER TIMELINE

2250 BCE	2000 BCE	1750 BCE	1500 BCE	1250 BCE

- ca. 2035–1640 BCE Middle Kingdom Egypt
- ca. 2000 BCE Beginning of Indo-European migrations
- ca. 1950 BCE Amorites seize control of Sumer
- 1792–1750 BCE Reign of Hammurabi of Babylon
- ca. 1640–1570 BCE Hyksos ascendancy in Egypt
- ca. 1570–1070 BCE New Kingdom Egypt
- ca. 1478–1458 BCE Reign of Egyptian queen Hatshepsut
- ca. 1200 BCE Appearance of invaders known as the Sea Peoples

to power. At the start of his reign Babylon was simply one among many Amorite *Law Code of* kingdoms and was by no means the largest or strongest. Unable or unwilling *Hammurabi* to challenge his neighbors on the battlefield, Hammurabi instead managed to convince all of them of the existence of numerous conspiracies against their crowns. He passed endless false rumors, usually of his own making and reiterated in person by his many ambassadors. Believing the lies, the other Amorite kings continually attacked one another for nearly twenty years and exhausted themselves in the process. Hammurabi then went on the offensive and in less than a decade conquered them all. He emerged as the sole ruler of virtually the entire Tigris–Euphrates region; thus was built the great Babylonian Empire (see Map 2.1).

Shortly thereafter, he issued a set of laws known as the Code of Hammurabi, texts of which presumably were distributed throughout the empire. He also had the entire Code engraved upon an 8-foot column of basalt as a permanent record of his greatness as a ruler. As propaganda, the Code could hardly have been

Propaganda Device   Hammurabi set up several tall stone pillars (steles) throughout his kingdom to proclaim his laws. The top portion shown here depicts the king receiving symbols of justice from the seated god Marduk.

1100 BCE	750 BCE	500 BCE	250 BCE	0

- ca. 1100 BCE **Iron weapons proliferate throughout ancient Near East**
- 669–627 BCE **Reign of Assyrian ruler Ashurbanipal**
- 559–530 BCE **Reign of Persian emperor Cyrus the Great**
- 521–486 BCE **Reign of Persian emperor Darius**

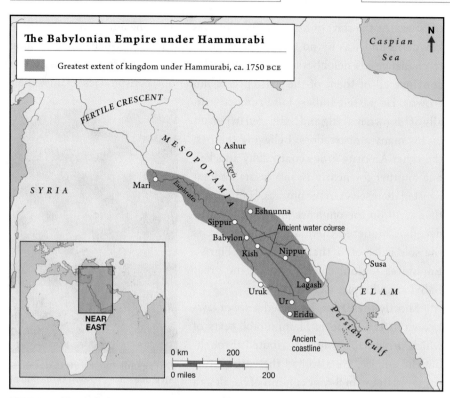

MAP 2.1 The Babylonian Empire under Hammurabi Hammurabi's conquests rivaled those of Sargon the Great in their extent (see Map 1.3). Best known for the law code he implemented, Hammurabi should be remembered also for his introduction of religious imperialism, as he made worship of the Babylonian deity Marduk mandatory for all his subjects.

more successful, since scholars have credited Hammurabi as the first great law giver in Western history ever since. In fact, however, the Code is only a partial law code: although it addresses issues like property rights, water rights, marriage, violent crime, and wage regulations, it neglects to mention many equally vital aspects of Babylonian life, such as the commercial marketplace that formed the lifeblood of the economy. More significantly, the Code is never mentioned in the actual judicial records that survive from Hammurabi's reign or from those of later Babylonian kings. Its statutes may simply represent new laws added to an already-existing body of legislation.

The prologue and epilogue together make up half of the Code's text and proclaim the king's magnificence in glowing terms:

> When the lofty Anu, king of the Anunnaki gods, and Enlil, lord of heaven and earth, he who determines the destiny of the land, committed the rule of all mankind to Marduk, the chief son of Ea; when they made

him great among the Igigi gods; when they pronounced the lofty name of Babylon; when they made it famous among the quarters of the world and in its midst established an everlasting kingdom whose foundations were firm as heaven and earth—at that time, Anu and Enlil appointed me, Hammurabi, the exalted prince, the worshiper of the gods, to cause justice to prevail in the land, to destroy the wicked and evil, to prevent the strong from oppressing the weak, to go forth like the sun over the black-headed people, to enlighten the land and to further the welfare of the people. . . .

These are the just laws which Hammurabi, the wise king, established and by which he gave the land stable support and good government. Hammurabi, the perfect king, am I. . . . The great gods called me, and I am the guardian shepherd whose scepter is just and whose beneficent shadow is spread over my city. In my bosom I carried the people of the land of Sumer and Addad; under my protection they prospered; I governed them in peace; in my wisdom I sheltered them. . . . The king who is pre-eminent among kings am I. My words are precious, my wisdom is unrivaled. By the command of Shamash, the great judge of heaven and earth, I make justice to shine forth on the land. By the order of Marduk, my lord, no one may scorn my statutes, and my name shall be remembered with favor in Esagila forever. . . . In the days that are yet to come, for all future time, may the king who is in the land observe the words of justice which I have written upon my monument! . . . My words are weighty; my deeds are unrivalled; only to the fool are they vain; to the wise they are worthy of every praise.

The actual statutes of the Code seem an afterthought in comparison.

Nonetheless, the Code tells us much about how Babylonian society differed from the Sumerian one it supplanted. As we saw in chapter 1, the Sumerian chief military executive (or lugal), assisted by scribes and priests, had supervised a battery of local officials—with a complex web of traders, craftsmen, and farmers. The Babylonians replaced this norm with a top-heavy and decidedly heavy-handed **plutocracy**, a governing class composed of the wealthy. Hammurabi's conquests resulted in the monopolization of wealth by his royal court and armed supporters. Vast estates and commercial concerns controlled by the Babylonian elites took the place of the more diverse economy of the Sumerians. Most of Babylonia's inhabitants remained legally free but were nevertheless land tenants or commercial dependents of the nobles who dominated the palaces and temples. The Babylonians also expanded the use of slave labor on their estates and began to buy and sell slaves on the international market.

Babylonian Society and Culture

Social stratification increased as well, and the penalties for offenses against one's superiors were severe. Women of all classes, except for slaves, had the right to divorce abusive husbands and to receive financial support from husbands who divorced them without good cause. Capital punishment was meted out unhesitatingly for any number of crimes—murder, assault, rape, theft, and adultery (applicable to women only) were the most common—but the means varied according to sex: men were killed by the blade, women by drowning.

Hammurabi also introduced a form of religious imperialism that both paralleled and legitimated his political oppression. The worship of Marduk, the patron god of the city of Babylon, became required throughout the empire; Hammurabi's subjects could continue to worship their old gods only if they accepted Marduk as the supreme Babylonian deity. Interpreting his military conquests as the worldly enactment of Marduk's spiritual victory over all other gods and goddesses, Hammurabi stands at the beginning of a long Greater Western tradition of justifying warfare as a religious duty. If the Divine Authority demands that His followers engage in warfare to fulfill His own cosmic aims, then what else can pious followers do? Such warfare is not only morally justifiable, because it is divinely sanctioned, but also in fact an act of religious devotion itself.

It is striking how frequently religious warfare, such as Hammurabi's conquests, occurs throughout Greater Western history. We shall see it again and again in later chapters: the *milhemet mitzvah* ("war of religious obligation") that inspired the Hebrews to seize their Promised Land from the Canaanites, Philistines, and Amalikites; the *jihad*-stoked conquests and the Crusades of medieval Muslims and Christians; the Wars of Religion of early modern Europe; the efforts to tame the "Godless heathen" of the New World or "to bring Christianity to the savages" of Africa in the 18th and 19th centuries; and the battles waged against "infidels" by extremist sects in 21st-century Islam. Western culture is not unique in this regard, of course, and wars without an explicitly religious motive have been equally numerous, but religiously based conflict is a notably recurring element in Greater Western history. Hammurabi is our first religious zealot, and the society he created, although it lasted only two centuries after his death, left a bitter legacy of lies, greed, and brutality. Few people mourned the passing of the Old Babylonian Empire.

It did produce a literary masterpiece, however. An anonymous Babylonian scribe gathered a number of folktales about the legendary Sumerian king Gilgamesh—ruler of Uruk some eight hundred years before the Babylonian conquest—and wove them together into an epic of remarkable sophistication. The ***Epic of Gilgamesh*** relates the adventures of a powerful but egotistical king whose arrogance leads him to offend the gods. Unexpectedly, the gods' subsequent plot to kill him fails when Gilgamesh tames the savage half-man half-beast Enkidu, whom they had sent to destroy him, and the two become friends and pursue a series of heroic adventures. When the gods strike again by slaying his beloved new friend, Gilgamesh is filled with panic at the inevitability of death. He

Epic of Gilgamesh

spends the rest of the story on a doomed quest for enlightenment and the secret to eternal life.

The poem notably credits women for their civilizing influence on men. Enkidu, for example, is tamed by an encounter with a temple priestess:

> The lass beheld him, the savage man,
> The barbarous fellow from the depths of the steppe. . . .
> [She] freed her breasts, bared her bosom,
> and he possessed her ripeness.
> She was not bashful as she welcomed his ardor.

They spend six days and seven nights in nonstop passion; then Enkidu undergoes a transformation that estranges him from the other animals of the steppe:

> After he had had his fill of her charms,
> He set his face toward his wild beasts.
> On seeing him, the gazelles ran off,
> The wild beasts of the steppe drew away from [him]. . . .
> His [legs] became motionless. . . . Things were not as they were before.
> Now he had wisdom, broader understanding.
> Returning he sat at the feet of the [priestess]. . . . She says to him,
> "Thou art wise now, Enkidu; thou art become like a god."

Gilgamesh himself, seeking to drown his sorrows after Enkidu's death, receives some sensible advice from a kindly barmaid who is actually the grain goddess Sippur in human form:

> Gilgamesh, . . . the life thou pursueth, thou shalt not find.
> When the gods created mankind,
> Death for mankind they set aside,
> Life in their own hands retaining.
> Thou, Gilgamesh, let full be thy belly,
> Make thou merry by day and by night.
> Of each day make thou a feast of rejoicing,
> Day and night dance thou and play!
> Let thy garments be sparkling fresh,
> Thy head be washed; bathe thou in water.
> Pay heed to the little one that holds on to thy hand,
> Let thy spouse delight in thy bosom!
> For this is the task of mankind!

Gilgamesh, however, obsessively continues his quest and learns of a magic plant growing on the floor of the sea. Whoever pulls the plant from its root and eats it will in fact gain eternal life. Eventually Gilgamesh locates the plant by tying heavy stones to his feet and walking the ocean floor. When he arrives back on shore and is about to eat the plant, however, a giant serpent emerges from the sea, snatches the plant from his hand, and pulls it back to the depths. Gilgamesh is left alone and hopeless on the shore, doomed to the death he could not avoid.

The poem depicts old Sumerian culture but was written down, in the full version in which it survives, in Babylonian times and in the Babylonian dialect. Little seems added to the original Sumerian folktales. The Babylonian compiler merely changed the names of several of the characters and of the gods into Babylonian ones. Thus the figure who tells Gilgamesh about the Plant of Life is named Ziusudra in the Sumerian fragments that survive but is called Utnapishtim, a Babylonian name, in the full compiled version. Was the compiler merely trying to make the text more appealing to a Babylonian audience?

A more subversive aim is possible too: perhaps the compiler hoped the epic could inspire the Babylonians to strive after something more than the wealth and power they hoarded so single-mindedly. Gilgamesh at the beginning of the poem is arrogant, self-centered, and boastful. He sounds more than a bit like Hammurabi in the bombastic claims of the Code. At the end he is broken, fearful, and sad beyond expression, but he has grown into spiritual maturity. He has become deserving of pity and even forgiveness.

MIDDLE KINGDOM EGYPT

The erosion of royal authority, beginning in the Fifth Dynasty of the Old Kingdom, brought about the First Intermediate Period in Egypt (ca. 2134–2035 BCE). In this relatively brief but turbulent period, the local nomarchs usurped royal power, plundered farmers' property, and engaged in widespread lawlessness. Mentuhotep II, the first king of the Eleventh Dynasty, however, was able to subdue the nomarchs and restore central authority from Thebes. It was the start of several periods of empire, including the reigns of the most active and powerful kings and the origins of a new religious tradition, monotheism.

Restoration of Royal Control   Mentuhotep II's reign ushered in the Middle Kingdom (ca. 2035–1640 BCE). Thebes lay in Upper Egypt, roughly 300 miles south of the traditional capital at Memphis (see Map 2.2). Moving the capital there allowed for closer oversight of the nomarchs. It also provided a base for launching new military expeditions southward, up the great river, into Nubia, to secure control of the strategic cataracts (high waterfalls) and to acquire the vast stone quarries and gold deposits found there.

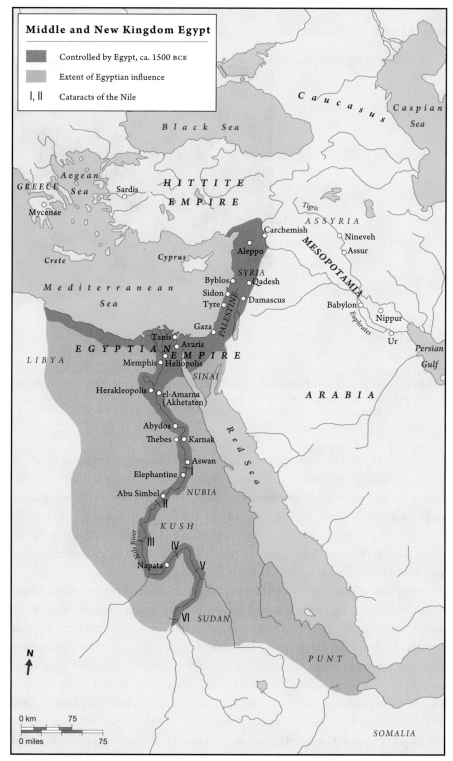

Middle and New Kingdom Egypt

- Controlled by Egypt, ca. 1500 BCE
- Extent of Egyptian influence
- I, II Cataracts of the Nile

Caucasus

Caspian Sea

Black Sea

GREECE

Aegean Sea

Sardis

HITTITE

EMPIRE

Mycenae

Tigris

ASSYRIA

Carchemish

Nineveh

Crete

Cyprus

Aleppo

Assur

MESOPOTAMIA

Mediterranean Sea

SYRIA

Byblos Qadesh

Sidon Damascus

Tyre

Babylon

Nippur

Euphrates

Gaza

PALESTINE

Ur

Persian Gulf

Tanis Avaris

EGYPTIAN EMPIRE

Memphis Heliopolis

LIBYA

SINAI

ARABIA

Herakleopolis el-Amarna (Akhetaten)

Abydos

Red Sea

Thebes Karnak

Aswan I

Elephantine

NUBIA

Abu Simbel II

KUSH

Nile River III

IV

Napata V

VI *SUDAN*

N

PUNT

0 km   75

0 miles   75

SOMALIA

MAP 2.2 Middle and New Kingdom Egypt Waves of invasion drove home to the Egyptians that they could no longer rely on geographical barriers to preserve them from attack, and hence they went on the offensive. As shown here, by 1500 BCE they had extended their control as far north as the southern reaches of the Hittite Empire in Anatolia.

Voyage to the Next World   This wonderfully preserved wooden coffin held the remains of a Middle Kingdom priest named Nekhtankh. The hieroglyphs invoke the gods Osiris, Isis, Nephthys, and others to provide Nekhtankh with all the food and comforts he will need in the afterlife. The vivid eyes represent the priest's soul looking expectantly to the voyage into the next world.

With restored fortunes, the kings of the Middle Kingdom were able to renew public building programs—such as land reclamation in the delta and the extension of irrigation networks and reservoirs along the river. They could even pursue military expansion beyond Egypt's natural borders, into Sinai and along the Syrian coast. These projects required more laborers than the local population could provide, however, which may have led the kings to recruit groups of foreigners (*hyksos* in Egyptian) to work in the mines and fields.

Developments in Egyptian Culture and Society

Egyptian religion continued to be a myriad of local cults rather than a single organized faith. The cults remained *henotheistic*: although they recognized the existence of other deities, each locale proclaimed allegiance to a particular god or goddess as its special protector. In the case of the king's court, new prominence was won by Amon-Ra, patron deity of the city of Thebes. The most significant development in religion, however, was the extension of salvation (that is, entry to the House of Judgment) to the nomarchs, other nobles, and wealthy commoners. The heavenly reward was no longer a monopoly of the kings. The cause of this development is unknown, but the means of it is clear: the contents of the Pyramid Texts (formerly confined to the walls of royal tombs, as we saw in chapter 1) began to circulate among the well-to-do. They were also inscribed into papyrus books, or coffin texts, placed alongside the bodies in their tombs.

By the end of this period, the various coffin texts had been consolidated into the ***Book of the Dead***, an anthology of incantations, magical spells, boilerplate praise poems, and cribbed solutions to the riddles put to souls by Osiris at the entrance to the House of Judgment. This book, when placed in a casket, theoretically opened the gates of paradise, such as it was, to anyone who died with it in his or her possession. Ma'at, acceptance of the world's right ordering, remained the dominant focus and the supreme virtue. To the extent that Osiris and his council truly judged anyone's ethical behavior in life, they did so according to the dead soul's record of sustaining ma'at, which in most cases meant not performing injustice.

The Middle Kingdom did produce an exceptionally large body of writing—mythological stories, folktales, handbooks of practical advice, medical regimens, travelogues, love poetry, personal letters, and professional treatises (on being a successful merchant, civil administrator, estate manager, or whatever). The mix suggests that the intellectual tenor of the age was above all else pragmatic and industrious. The popular father-to-son advice handbooks—the "Instructions"—urge the recipient to work hard at his trade, to obey his superiors, and to cultivate a modest demeanor; they praise charitable acts and denounce corruption and exploitation of the poor. Should one fall short of the moral standard, the *Book of the Dead* was there to help.

The Instructions left behind by several Middle Kingdom kings have an altogether different tenor, one that reflects the less elevated general position these rulers held in comparison to their godlike Old Kingdom predecessors. In Amenemhet I's (r. 1991–1962 BCE) Instruction to his son, for example, he urges, "Hold yourself apart from those subordinate to you . . . and be on guard even when you

Ushabti Funerary figures who accompanied the new dead on their journey were called *ushabtis*. They were the servants of the dead, charged with providing food and water, performing physical labor, and in some cases providing sexual amusement. The hieroglyphs found most frequently on ushabtis quote a passage from the sixth chapter of the *Book of the Dead*: "Hail, ushabti! If [the deceased] be decreed to do any work in the afterlife, let every task that stands in his way be removed—whether plowing fields, tending the water channels, or carrying sand."

are asleep." Trust no one, neither family nor friend, and be especially watchful of the treacherous nomarchs, he warns. The advice, in this case, was sound: Amenemhet left his Instruction unfinished, and a later scribe completed it with a wry note that the great king had been assassinated by one of the officials in the royal court before he could finish the memo.

Middle Egypt's most renowned arts were architecture and sculpture—practical arts both, since most of the works produced served the purpose of promoting or extending the might of the king. Painting and sculpture followed stylistic and iconographic norms that dated to the Old Kingdom, with simple lines, flat surfaces, and a modest palette of colors. Funerary figurines made of clay or wood were exceedingly common. Although simple in design, these figures (called *ushabti*, or "those who respond") represented the servants who continued to work for souls in the afterlife. Science and technology mattered little, since Egypt's technological needs were amply met by the might of the river and the availability of the virtual slave labor of the masses. Mathematical knowledge was not widespread. Government officials probably understood and used all four computational operations—addition, subtraction, multiplication, and division. They employed fractions and discovered how to estimate the area of a circle by measuring the diameter, subtracting one-ninth of its value, and squaring the result. Egypt also did not develop wheeled vehicles until the New Kingdom and relied on oxen and donkeys (for plowing and carting, respectively) long after the Babylonians had already domesticated horses for farming and for pulling wheeled chariots.

The Hyksos Ascendancy   The modest stability of the Middle Kingdom collapsed quickly when the Semitic-speaking foreigners admitted to the realm suddenly rose in revolt and took control of most of the delta region around 1700 BCE. The precise identity of this group is still debated, and Egyptian sources refer to them only as the Hyksos ("foreigners"), but it seems likely that they were the Amorites from Palestine or a group closely related to them. Armed with recurve bows, long lances, and swords made of bronze, the Hyksos quickly seized control of the Nile Delta and forced the rulers in far-southern Thebes to recognize their overlordship. The Hyksos style of warfare unnerved the Egyptians, who used neither cavalry nor archers (since trees to make bows were relatively rare) and had traditionally relied on swarms of infantrymen armed with spears and stone-headed clubs.

For seventy years, from 1640 to 1570 BCE (the Second Intermediate Period), the Hyksos dominated Egypt; thus this period is also known as the **Hyksos ascendancy**. The Hyksos forged extensive commercial and diplomatic links with Palestine, Syria, and the islands of the Aegean Sea. During this time the Nubians to the far south broke away from the rulers in Thebes and established an independent kingdom called Kush. The Theban rulers thus found themselves trapped between foreigners at each end of the Nile, but they capitalized on the direness of the situation by inspiring their soldiers to pursue the noble cause of national liberation— which they promptly did, after quickly studying the new techniques of war. With their modernized army, they drove the Hyksos from Egypt around 1570 BCE and pursued them all the way to Palestine, a campaign that inaugurated Egypt's golden age—that of the New Kingdom (ca. 1570–1070 BCE).

THE NEW KINGDOM EMPIRE

The years of rule by the Hyksos proved to the Egyptians that the defense provided by their surrounding deserts no longer sufficed. Realizing that Egypt's relative isolation was at an end, the kings of the New Kingdom—now called **pharaohs**— decided to seize the initiative by extending their might to other lands. They subdued the Nubians to the south, which guaranteed Egypt's access to the gold mines of the region—a necessity now that gold had been established as the international standard for commerce throughout the Near East. From this vantage point they opened new trade routes down the western shores of the Red Sea and as far away as present day-Sudan and Somalia (see Map 2.2).

Militarily, the reinvigorated army—now led on the battlefield by the chariot-mounted pharaoh himself—conquered all of Palestine and advanced into Syria *Egyptian* as far north as the city of Aleppo. The most aggressive of the New Kingdom pha- *Expansion* raohs was Thutmose I (r. 1504–1492 BCE), who led his army into Syria until he reached the banks of the upper Euphrates, where he erected a victory plaque and proclaimed himself the greatest of Egypt's rulers. He had "surpassed the achievements of all the kings who lived before me. . . . The gods have delighted in my reign, and their temples have been filled with celebration. . . . I have pushed the boundaries of Egypt as far as the sun shines, . . . and I have made her triumphant over every land." His victories consisted more of looting raids than true conquests; nevertheless, his reign marked Egypt's transition into a fully militarized society in which army officers replaced civil officials as the backbone of the administration. Booty and tribute poured into the royal coffers, as did Nubian gold, and the increased wealth allowed him to construct scores of luxurious palaces for the high military caste and a network of new temples to gods both old and new. The god of military victory, named Amen, predictably rose in religious

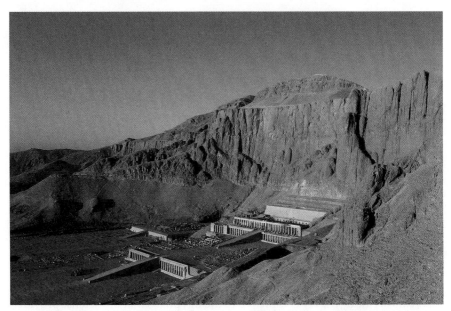

Valley of the Kings   Though grander than most, the temple complex of Queen Hatshepsut is characteristic of the New Kingdom period. Instead of remote pyramids, notable Egyptians constructed elaborate malls with administrative offices, altar rooms, libraries, treasuries, and living quarters.

prominence during this period. His main temple at Karnak, just across the river from Thebes, received a series of massive additions and embellishments until it became a vast complex of halls, temples, administrative buildings, and storehouses, making it by far the largest religious compound in the ancient world.

The reign of Queen **Hatshepsut** (r. ca. 1478–1458 BCE) was notable for its prosperity and peace, evident from the spectacular mortuary temple she had constructed at Deir el-Bahri, near Thebes—a series of terraced gardens and broad colonnades carved into the high cliffs of the river valley. All the pharaohs of the New Kingdom after Thutmose I chose to be buried in this Valley of the Kings, their answer to the Great Pyramids at Giza. The burial sites were separate from the mortuary temples themselves. They hoped that this manner of entombment—in deep caves whose entrances were then concealed—would foil grave robbers.

The royal family practiced traditional brother–sister marriage, the idea *Pharaonic* behind it being that only the daughter of a pharaoh was sufficiently exalted to be *Rule* the queen of another pharaoh. These marriages were usually but not always asexual. Every pharaoh, however, had dozens if not hundreds of wives in his harem, by whom he produced his heirs. Hatshepsut was the daughter of Thutmose I, the queen of Thutmose II (r. 1492–1478 BCE), and the bane of her stepson Thutmose III (r. 1458–1425 BCE). Egyptian law allowed for a woman to rule in her own right, although the occurrence was rare enough that royal monuments sometimes portrayed Hatshepsut with a fake beard. During her rule Hatshepsut extended her realm's commercial contacts as far as the lower reaches of the Red Sea and used much of the improved revenue to undertake ambitious building programs. According to some sources, she also led a military expedition or two.

Although Thutmose III officially began his reign upon his father's death in 1478 BCE, he was a child and lived for twenty tense years under the firm control of his stepmother. Once he took power for himself, he ordered his stonemasons to deface Hatshepsut's images and erase her name from all monuments. He dedicated his reign to extending Egypt's might even farther into Palestine and Syria, personally leading as many as sixteen campaigns. He left a network of client kings to do the actual work of governing the empire, taking their sons with him back to Thebes to be indoctrinated in Egyptian law and custom. In this way, when these children grew to maturity, they could govern their lands in a reliably Egyptian context. Diplomatic marriages between the daughters of the client kings and the Egyptian royal sons were also common. No Egyptian princess was ever wedded to a foreign king, however. Instead, princesses were either dedicated as temple priestesses or given a ceremonial marriage to a male family member.

In 1887 a treasure-trove of cuneiform tablets was discovered at Amarna, in Upper Egypt, that provide an intriguing view of Egyptian governance in the 14th century BCE. Known now as the Amarna Letters, the archive consists of 382 clay tablets, written in Akkadian (the language of international diplomacy at the time), containing letters between the pharaohs from Amenhotep III (r. 1388–1351) to Tutankhamen (r. 1332–1323) and their regional administrators. Several letters mention a group of people called the Apiru or Habiru—which some historians believe to be the first external reference to the Hebrews. In this example, the Egyptian governor of Jerusalem asks for additional military assistance against some rebels:

> They seized Rubutu. The land of the king deserted to the Apiru. And now, besides this, a town belonging to Jerusalem, Bit-Ninurta by name, a city of the king, has gone over to the side of the men of Qiltu. May the lord king give heed to Abdi-Heba [the governor writing this letter], your servant. And send archers to restore the land of the king to the king. If there are no archers, the land of the king will desert to the Apiru.

The goal of bringing the broader Near East under Egyptian influence had less to do with extending values and culture than with simply bringing more people, whether slave or free, into the service of the pharaoh. If Egypt could no longer retain its splendid isolation, then the rest of the world should at least recognize the need to sustain the ma'at that only acceptance of pharaonic rule could effect. Driving the point home were the huge reliefs of Egyptian armies and their

Family Hour at the Pharaoh's   This bas relief from about 1350 BCE portrays Akhenaten and Nefertiti along with three of their six daughters. Akhenaten is best remembered for his effort to replace traditional Egyptian religion with a new cult devoted to a single god called Aten. In this scene, the royal family offers prayers to this sun deity. The image continues a little-understood artistic tradition that portrays Akhenaten in androgynous fashion. Note that his body is curvier than that of his queen, a famous beauty.

victorious generals that bedecked palace and temple walls everywhere they went. Additions to the temple complexes at Karnak and Luxor further attest to the grandeur of imperial Egypt at its height.

The reigns of Amenhotep III (r. 1390–1352 BCE) and his son Amenhotep IV (r. 1352–1338 BCE) mark both the pinnacle of the New Kingdom and the start of its decline. The priests who presided over the temples now controlled roughly a quarter of the empire's land. Concerned about their growing power—especially that of the priests at Karnak, home of the sun god Amon-Ra—Amenhotep IV instituted a radical change: renaming himself **Akhenaten**, he elevated a minor solar deity called Aten to supreme status among the gods. The pharaoh's new name meant, literally, "the one devoted to Aten." Egyptian mythology in fact maintained separate cults for different phases and aspects of the sun. The god of the sunrise was different from the god of the sun at noontime, for example, and the god of sunset was yet another distinct entity. Amon-Ra was thought of principally as the heat energy of the sun.[1] Akhenaten closed the temples to Amon-Ra, violently suppressed their cults,

Akhenaten's Religious Reforms

and, with his queen Nefertiti, promoted Aten as the sole true and universal deity. He even had Amon-Ra's name chiseled out of royal inscriptions. He hoped to forestall popular protest by emphasizing that it was the royal family's obligation to worship Aten, whereas the obligation of the Egyptian people was to continue worshipping the pharaoh as always. He abandoned the palace at Thebes and erected a new capital some 300 miles to the north at a place called Akhetaten ("the horizon of the Aten"), now known as el-Amarna (see Map 2.2).

The belief in a single, supreme deity—or **monotheism**—was a novelty, and it did not go over easily with the people. They still craved the consolation of their all but certain eternal blessedness in the old faith. Akhenaten and Nefertiti, however, although undoubtedly motivated in part by a desire to break the power of the

---

[1]   The new god Aten was originally the physical sphere comprising the sun. Under Akhenaten's imposed monotheism, however, Aten incorporated all the many aspects of the sun.

priests, were genuine enthusiasts for the new religion. Tradition credits the pharaoh with composing the heartfelt Hymn to Aten:

> Thou appearest beautifully on the horizon of heaven,
> Thou living Aten, the beginning of life!
> When thou art arisen on the eastern horizon,
> Thou hast filled every land with thy beauty.

Central to the hymn is Aten's provision for the human world. All good things are connected with the life-giving sun.

Akhenaten's plans went awry, however, because he underestimated both the *Reign of* popularity of Amon-Ra and the priests' determination to hold onto their lofty po- *Ramses* sition. Akhenaten gradually became something of a religious recluse, isolated in *the Great* his palace and ignoring the needs of the empire. His successors on the throne— Tutankhamen, Ay, and Horemheb—quickly suppressed the new cult and restored the old faith. Eventually, a new pharaoh arose from the ranks of the military and restored the empire's fortunes. **Ramses II** (r. 1279–1212 BCE), Egypt's only ruler known as "the Great," built temples, palaces, and statues on a colossal scale. Perhaps one-half of all the Egyptian monuments that survive today belong to Ramses II's reign. Nevertheless, the reign of Ramses II was a last gasp of glory before Egypt once again fell to outsiders. Peoples from far away swept through the Aegean Sea and over Egypt, and rampaged through the rest of the Near East around 1200 BCE.

THE INDO-EUROPEAN ARRIVAL

The newcomers were a motley crew, related to one another by language: each group spoke one of a family of languages known today as **Indo-European**. In 1786 an English philologist named Sir William Jones, then serving as a judge in colonial India, delivered a paper to the Asiatic Society in which he observed that ancient Sanskrit (the tongue from which the major languages spoken in northern India are derived) shared an exceptional number of word roots and grammatical forms with Greek, Latin, and the Gothic and Celtic languages; from this he argued that ancient Indian and European languages must therefore be related. This common ancestor eventually came to be called Proto-Indo-European and is now believed to have originated somewhere north of the Black Sea. The idea of a single source for the family of languages from Ireland to India had been put forth in a more general way a hundred years earlier by a Dutch philologist. But Jones (who spoke thirteen languages fluently and could read another fifteen) produced enough data to make the theory rightly his own.

MOVEMENT OF INDO-EUROPEAN PEOPLES

▪ Indo-European homeland, ca. 2000 BCE
→ Spread of Indo-Europeans, 2nd millennium BCE

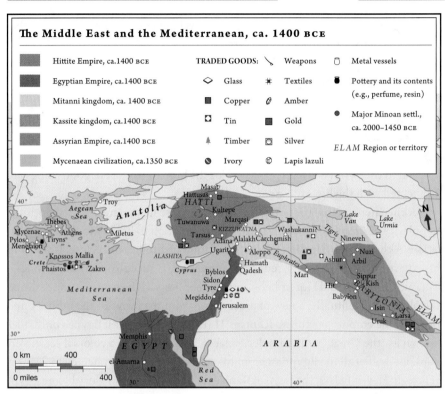

MAP 2.3 **The Middle East and the Mediterranean, ca. 1400 BCE** By 1400 BCE the political composition of the Western world consisted of a half-dozen well-defined states—Mycenaean Greece, the
Hittite Empire, and New Kingdom Egypt along the Mediterranean coast and the Mitanni kingdom,
the Kassite kingdom, and the Assyrian Empire dividing the Mesopotamian lands.

The Indo-European peoples, a collection of nomadic shepherding populations, began to radiate from their homeland near the Black Sea as early as
2000 BCE. Several groups moved into western Europe, the forerunners of the
Goths and the Celts. One strain migrated into the Aegean Sea, where they established the base for what was to become the Greek-speaking world. Many other
groups—most notably the Hittites and the Mitanni—settled throughout Anatolia and the Iranian plain.

The Hittites

The Hittites initially settled in north-central Anatolia in a sprawl of small
states, but by 1700 BCE they had united into a single kingdom (see Map 2.3).
From the time they appeared on the scene, archeology reveals an aggressive warrior society. Although they raided Mesopotamia regularly (even sacking Babylon
in 1595 BCE), the Hittites focused their military efforts on the Egyptian-held portions of Syria and Palestine. They advanced slowly. Although superior in arms,
the Hittites could not put as many soldiers on the field as the Egyptian army
could. The turning point came in 1286–1285 BCE, when Egypt, under Ramses II,
and the Hittites, under their king Hattusilis III, declared a truce after an

inconclusive battle at the Syrian city of Qadesh and established the first written peace treaty in Western history:

> Behold: Hattusilis, the great chief [of the Hittites], has made a treaty with [Ramses], the great ruler of Egypt, beginning this day, to establish good peace and brotherhood between us forever. . . . And the children of the children of the great ruler of the Hittites shall live in brotherhood and peace with the children of the children of Ramses, . . . and hostilities between them shall cease forever.

The peace did not last long. The Hittites, it turned out, had a gift for conquest but little for government, and their unified kingdom faced continual challenges from regional warlords who preferred their own local despotism to the national brand. When yet another wave of Indo-European invaders swept through the area, the Hittite Empire collapsed.

Before it fell, however, the Hittite Empire acquired literacy. The Hittites adopted a version of Mesopotamian cuneiform script and left behind a large archive of government records, including the peace treaty quoted above. Two features stand out in these documents. First, government actions were prefaced by a summary of the events that had led up to them; thus the Hittites contributed to the development of historical writing as a way not only to preserve but also to shape the memory of past events. Second, by presenting the historical context for their actions, the Hittites showed a unique willingness to recognize the failures and mistakes of their rulers. Such a willingness was unthinkable in Egypt or Babylon. In fact, the Hittites likely pioneered the use of critical history as a means of undercutting monarchical pretensions and ambitions.

Another new Indo-European arrival was the mysterious group labeled by the Egyptians as the Sea Peoples, who ran over much of the Aegean and the eastern Mediterranean between 1300 and 1200 BCE. Little is known of them, but they were probably a loose confederation of tribes, clans, and warrior-pirate crews. They moved first into Greece before branching farther south and east; by 1200 BCE they controlled most of the Nile Delta, a move that effectively ended Egyptian rule in Palestine, since the pharaohs no longer had direct access to the sea. *The "Sea Peoples"*

The Sea Peoples fought on land as an infantry, wielding bronze double-edged swords and spears. They also brought to the battlefield an innovation: bronze plate armor, which protected their soldiers far more reliably than any earlier type of protective covering. The Hittites and the Egyptians who slowly learned from them had relied on lightly clad archers who rode lightweight chariots; their greater speed and agility could wreak havoc on most ancient infantries, armed as they mostly were with clubs and spears. But the bronze armor of the Sea Peoples gave them enough protection against archers that they could hold their formations and defeat the Egyptian and Hittite forces.

No one knows precisely who the Sea Peoples were, although theories abound. Were they the Philistines described in the Hebrew Bible? A rival tribe of the Mycenaean Greeks? Or the Trojans, the Hebrews, the Siculi (the indigenous people of Sicily)? Egyptian records occasionally identify specific subgroups among the Sea Peoples, which suggests that they used the name as a catchall for a whole swarm of different ethnic groups.[2] Whoever they were, and wherever they came from, the invaders left behind a trail of annihilation so great that virtually no records survive to describe the wreckage until they reached Egypt. In Greece alone, 90 percent of the population was obliterated.

In Egypt, our first written and pictorial evidence of the Sea Peoples comes from an inscription set up by Ramses III (r. 1186–1155 BCE) to commemorate a rare (for him) victory around 1176 BCE over the intruders. The carved relief shows attackers of many varieties, wearing distinctive clothing and headdresses and carrying an assortment of weapons. The text of the inscription clearly was intended to revive flagging hopes. One portion depicts Ramses in his war chariot, leading his brave troops to battle. Its caption reads in part,

> The king, rich in strength as he rides forth, filling the hearts of the [Sea Peoples] with fear and awe; sole lord, whose hand is capable, conscious of his strength, like a valiant lion lying in wait for wild cattle, freely going forward, his heart confident, smashing thousands into heaps in the space of a moment. His power in the fray is like a fire, making all who assail him to collapse in ashes.

The inscription goes on to depict Ramses in the midst of the battle, scattering an army of terrified Sea Peoples:

> Behold him, as when Set rages, overthrowing the enemy, . . . trampling down the plains and hill-countries; the enemy lies prostrate, beaten from head to tail before his horse. His heat burns up their bodies like a flame. Hacked to pieces are their bodies, throughout eternity.[3]

The destruction caused by the Sea Peoples was vast. In southern and southeastern Europe, they annihilated whole cities. Few ancient Near Eastern cities

---

[2]   Among the specific peoples named by the Egyptians were the "Habiru," whom some believe to have been the Hebrews. This seems unlikely, however. The Habiru spoke an Indo-European, not a Semitic, tongue, and several centuries separate the Habiru and the Hebrews—if, indeed, the Hebrews ever were present in Egypt (see chapter 3).

[3]   Set (also spelled Seth) was the wrathful war god of the desert.

The Sea Peoples Defeated   This wall engraving from the mortuary temple of Ramses III at Medinet Habu in the western district of Thebes shows the pharaoh, at right, leading an ambush of the Sea Peoples. Ramses had blocked the channels of the Nile Delta, which prevented the Sea Peoples' advance, and then unleashed an archery assault on the ships as they struggled to turn course and escape to the sea.

disappeared altogether, but the invaders smashed old trade routes and splintered the diplomatic connections that had kept the region relatively stable from 1500 to 1200 BCE. The three major states of the era—New Kingdom Egypt, Hittite Anatolia, and Babylonian Mesopotamia—had generally managed to keep the wider region peaceful and had kept commerce moving. Even the smaller states that provided a sort of buffer zone among the major empires had thrived for those three centuries. But the advance of the Indo-Europeans sent shockwaves of displacement and despair through all three empires

The disappearance of the Sea Peoples is as much a mystery as is their origin. Despite Ramses III's fanciful inscriptions, no evidence exists of an annihilating defeat of them or of their continued horrific progress. Hence it is likely that they were absorbed into the indigenous populations. This assumption helps to explain the unusual degree of cultural innovation, economic realignment, political recon-figuration, and religious change that occurred in their wake. And an important part of that change was the perfecting of an old technology: the refining of iron.

THE AGE OF IRON BEGINS

Iron ore was plentiful in the ancient Near East, and people had been mining it for a long time. Objects made of iron have been dated to as early as 5000 BCE. By 1200 BCE, metalworkers had begun to perfect their methods. By repeating the

Iron Weapons   Armies in the ancient Near East fought primarily with spears, arrows, and knives, rather than swords. Swords did not become common until the arrival of the Indo-European peoples.

process of heating, quenching, and hammering, they could produce iron objects of ever-greater strength. With new weapons and new trading goods, power shifted again and again. The changes culminated in a new model of statecraft under the Persians and a new religion of fire, Zoroastrianism.

Iron ore was not an obvious choice, however. It is brittle and will produce a usable metal only after it is melted and its impurities burned away. The process, although simple to describe, is difficult to master. Iron melts at a much higher temperature than copper (the main constituent element in bronze) and must remain in its melted state for a considerably longer time to fashion into objects. The constant temperature needed is difficult to achieve with primitive wood fires. Moreover, iron is a weaker metal than bronze and is more susceptible to deterioration by moisture. Even in the dry climate of the Near East, iron can easily oxidize (that is, rust). A clash between an iron sword and a bronze sword would invariably end with the iron sword shattered.

Given these disadvantages, what was gained by producing iron weapons and tools? Simply put, mass production. Iron ore is abundant throughout the region, and, consequently, once the production process was perfected, people of all walks

of life could afford iron implements.[4] By 1100 BCE iron weapons began to proliferate; by 800 BCE most common homes were well supplied with iron pots, tools, and
utensils. The problem with bronze was that its two constituent parts—copper and
tin—are both considerably rarer than iron ore and are seldom found in the same
region. To maintain a constant supply of bronze, the Near East had to maintain
steady commercial relations; any disruption in the long-distance movement of
these metals, and the available supply of bronze disappeared. This is precisely what
happened with the incursions of the Indo-Europeans and the mass waves of refugees they set in motion. Trade networks that had proliferated during the centuries
from 1600 to 1200 BCE simply disintegrated. The abrupt decline in the availability
of copper and tin gave the advantage to the iron-brandishing newcomers.

With the Hittite Empire destroyed, Babylon set reeling, and Egypt sent into yet
another Intermediate Period (the Third, ca. 1070–664 BCE), the political map of the
ancient Near East changed dramatically. New peoples and states arose, some of
them of old provenance, others of newcomers. The region resembled a busy intersection whose traffic lights have gone out at rush hour. Groups like the Phoenicians, the
Philistines, the Kassites, the Amorites, the Mitanni, and the Hurrians—to name
only some of the best known—appeared on the scene in a bewildering tangle.

The Phoenicians were particularly successful, since they took to the sea from
their home base (roughly today's Lebanon) to establish a network of trading *The*
colonies that stretched across the major Mediterranean islands (Cyprus, Sicily, *Phoenicians*
Sardinia, the Balearics) and along the northern coast of Africa. Their name,
which the ancient Greeks translated from a West Semitic dialect as "the purple
people," refers to their expertise in dyeing. (The waters off the shore of Phoenicia
had large populations of murex snails, from whose shells a distinctive reddish-
purple dye was made.) Later writers like the Greek historian Herodotus reported
that Phoenician sailors claimed to have circumnavigated Africa, although this is
doubtful. The Phoenicians' most important contribution to Western culture was
the dissemination of their alphabet, which simplified the task of writing. Among
the first alphabets in Western history, it provided the model for the alphabet later
adopted by the Greeks and hence led directly to the development of the alphabet
used in the Western world today. The most famous of Phoenician cities was
Carthage, founded sometime in the 9th century BCE in present-day Tunisia,
which later challenged Rome for mastery of the entire Mediterranean.

The Philistines, by contrast, settled in the territory just south of the Phoenician
homeland. They are best known as the villains of the Hebrew scriptures (discussed in *The*
chapter 3). Possibly an offshoot of the Peleset (one of the groups singled out by the *Philistines*
Egyptians as being among the Sea Peoples), the Philistines in fact were an urban,

---

[4]   Iron is actually the sixth most abundant element in the universe. It makes up roughly 5 percent of the
earth's crust.

commercial people who practiced little agriculture—just enough to put them at odds with pastoralist groups like their Hebrew neighbors.[5] Little is known of their language, but archeological remains link them with ancient Greek culture. The Philistines introduced to the Levant grape and olive vines, which are indigenous to the Greek archipelago, for example. Their architectural styles—as exemplified by the great citadels at Ashdod, Ashkelon, and Gaza—likewise resemble the fortified palaces of the Mycenaeans. The Philistines lived in the cities but controlled the agricultural hinterland and the regional trade routes. Most important, the Philistines occupied the region of Palestine that provided much of the copper and tin needed to produce bronze. Their control of such strategic sites and their access to superior weaponry, while making it impossible for their foes to forge similar weapons of their own, is what made the Philistines so substantial a foe to the advancing Hebrews.

The Assyrians

The Assyrians, who lived along the upper reaches of the Tigris, created one of the most feared of the new kingdoms. Caught between strangers to the west and unsure of the Hittites and Babylonians to their north and south, respectively, Assyrian culture turned militant and relied overtly on the use of violence and terror to maintain order. Their political fortunes rose and fell, depending on the relative ruthlessness of subsequent rulers, but from the mid-12th century BCE Assyria earned a well-deserved reputation for savagery that lasted for at least six centuries. From their imposing capital at Nineveh, the Assyrians maintained a large standing army of more than 100,000 soldiers divided into specialized units (infantry, cavalry, archers, engineers, and so on) that, uniquely among ancient armies, trained to work in concert (see Map 2.4).

The Assyrians were the first army to use iron weapons extensively and may also have pioneered another technological advance: the addition of carbon and nickel to refined iron to produce steel. Steel blades were significantly stronger than both iron and bronze blades and resisted decomposition. Producing it was expensive, however, which meant that many centuries would pass before steel production became widespread. The Assyrians knew the value of broadcasting their fearsome strength at arms, however. The victory monuments they erected depicted brutal scenes of slaughter, decapitation, rape, and torture, often in chilling detail. Their goal was to frighten people into submission, and it usually worked. When warnings failed, the army did its dirty work with gusto—going so far on occasion as to annihilate entire populations. This was the fate of the "ten lost tribes of Israel," who fell to the Assyrians in 722 BCE. Assyrian law dictated corporal punishments for hosts of crimes, resulting in thousands of publicly performed mutilations a year. On the other hand, at least one Assyrian ruler (Ashurbanipal, r. 669–627 BCE) built the first known library in Western

---

[5]   Traditionally, societies based on permanent settlement do not get along well with nomadic groups. Think of the conflicts between the cattle ranchers and farmers of the American West in the 19th century.

MAP 2.4   The Assyrian Empire, ca. 720–650 BCE   At its height, the Assyrian Empire united the whole of the ancient Near East. Renowned for their military might, the Assyrians were also the first Greater Western people to engage in the large-scale resettlement of populations. The practice aimed to weaken subject peoples' attachment to their homelands (thereby hopefully increasing their sense of identity as members of the Assyrian realm in general) and to maximize agricultural and manufacturing output by bringing manpower to areas with insufficient supplies of labor.

history. Archeologists have recovered thirty thousand clay tablets from its ruins in Nineveh. Most of this treasure store consisted of foreign literary works preserved in Assyrian cuneiform. For example, many modern editions of the *Epic of Gilgamesh* are based on Assyrian redactions unearthed at Nineveh.

Assyria's cruelty earned it the furious hatred of its neighbors. In 612 BCE an alliance led by the Medes, an Indo-European people, and the Chaldeans, the Semitic-speaking residents of southern Babylonia—known also as neo-Babylonians—stormed into Nineveh and reduced it to ashes and dust. Within another decade all vestiges of Assyrian might were destroyed. The new victors did not introduce an era of good feeling, however. The Medes were happy to return to Iran, knowing that the Assyrians were gone once and for all. That left the neo-Babylonians in control of all of Mesopotamia and much of the Levant, where they adopted Assyrian methods and ruled by brute force. One of the neo-Babylonian kings, Nebuchadnezzar II (r. 605–562 BCE), led his army into

The Neo-Babylonians

Ashurbanipal's Library at Nineveh   This cuneiform fragment contains a passage from the *Epic of Gilgamesh*. The remnants of Ashurbanipal's library are now housed in the British Museum.

Jerusalem, destroyed the Hebrew Temple, and carried tens of thousands of Hebrews into slavery back east, in Babylon.

PERSIA AND THE RELIGION OF FIRE

Still another group arose in the middle of the 6th century BCE, a people who toppled the neo-Babylonians and brought some stability to this near-hopeless situation that had continued, off and on, since 1200 BCE. These were the Persians, an Indo-European people whose origins are unknown. Led by an energetic and charismatic ruler named **Cyrus the Great** (r. 559–530 BCE), they lived near the midpoint of the eastern shore of the Persian Gulf. Suddenly and unexpectedly, the Persians united their various tribes, freed themselves from the overlordship of the Medes, and defeated their next neighbor, the Lydians. They then invaded Mesopotamia so quickly that Babylon surrendered without a fight.

Persia's Multicultural Empire   Cyrus was the undisputed master of the east, the largest empire the Western world had yet seen. He freed the Hebrews and allowed them to return to Jerusalem, where they quickly established a semiautonomous vassal state. Such largess was

The Persian Empire at Its Height, ca. 500 BCE

—— Royal road   ········ Boundaries of the satrapies

MAP 2.5   The Persian Empire at Its Height, ca. 500 BCE   Cyrus the Great (r. 559–530 BCE) founded the Persian Empire, which his successors expanded to be even larger than the Assyrian Empire that it replaced. The Persians were notably tolerant of local customs, religions, and social norms. What they provided was a single legal and administrative system that aimed above all to increase trade.

typical of Persian rule, but it resulted from strategic, not altruistic, thinking. The Persian Empire was simply too large for a central government to administer effectively. It was a land empire that, in contrast to Egypt, did not have a grand reliable waterway running through its center to allow easy unification. Cyrus thus portioned out his empire with care and forethought. Why govern a group like the Hebrews, when they could do so themselves? So long as they recognized Persian overlordship, caused no trouble, and sent payments of tax and tribute on time, Cyrus was wisely content to let them go their own way. The Hebrews were not the only people treated in this manner.

Cyrus's son and heir, Cambyses (r. 530–522 BCE), conquered Egypt itself and advanced far into Anatolia, uniting the entire Near East for the first time. The great Persian Empire ultimately stretched from the Aegean coast in the west to the Indus River in the east, from the upper Nile in the south to the middle reaches of the Black, Caspian, and Aral seas in the north. It covered well over 2,000 miles on an east–west axis and more than 1,000 miles from north to south. The ancient world had seen nothing like it (see Map 2.5). The Persians instituted a single currency and a standardized system of weights and measures, but otherwise allowed their subject peoples to govern themselves according to their own traditions. After centuries of Babylonian, Egyptian, Hittite, and Assyrian brutality and control, the light-handed imperial approach of the Persians was a welcome relief—which explains the relative absence of rebellion against the new rulers. The conquered could consider, and perhaps even admire, Persian culture, science, and religion.

The death of Cambyses triggered a dynastic crisis, since he died young and without an heir. Eventually a cousin named Darius carried the day. His reign lasted from 521 to 486 BCE, during which time he reformed the administration and undertook an extensive campaign to improve the empire's infrastructure. His projects included an unprecedented 1,600-mile roadway from Sardis (near the Aegean coast, in Asia Minor) to Susa (near the Persian Gulf, in modern-day Iran) that became the main artery for moving goods, capital, services, information, and soldiers through the heart of the empire (see Map 2.5). Darius also cut a canal that connected the Nile to the Red Sea, to facilitate trade with Egypt, and brought systematic irrigation to the Iranian plateau for the first time, which dramatically increased the agricultural production of the land. Last, he built a vast new capital in Persepolis, 200 miles east of Babylon. The move calmed people's concerns about having an emperor breathing down their necks and brought the eastern half of his empire, which extended to India, within his gaze.

With a calm and peaceful interior at last, with a single currency, and with physical barriers to efficient interaction removed, the economy of the Near East roared

Bringing Tribute to the Emperor   This relief from the Apadana (a high-columned open-air royal hall) in Persepolis shows the various peoples of the Persian Empire bringing tribute to the ruler, Darius I (r. 550–486 BCE). In the upper level, Babylonians bring amphorae filled with wine and oil, linens, and a hump-backed bull; in the lower level, Phoenicians bring gifts of bracelets, bowls, and a two-horse chariot.

to new life. The material standard of life improved for most people, and for most of those it improved dramatically. The Persians had created not just a new state but also a new model of statecraft: imperialism via accommodation and tolerance.

The stunning political and social success of the Persians paved the way for a revolution in religious life because they brought with them a new religion that spread rapidly throughout the Near East and remained the dominant faith of that part of the world until the rise of Islam in the 7th century CE.

The Persians originally had a polytheistic religion not unlike the ancient Sumerian faith, with deities of various types representing natural ele- *Zoroastrianism* ments and forces. In what may have been a self-conscious effort at reform, a man named Zoroaster began to preach the supremacy of a single god and the requirement of an ethical basis of life as the proper way of worshipping him. It was the beginning of **Zoroastrianism**, the first transnational Western religion.

We know little of Zoroaster (the Greek version of his Persian name, Zarathustra); he lived sometime around 1300 BCE and claimed to have received a vision of this "Wise Lord," Ahura Mazda. Ahura Mazda, he preached, was the one true and eternal God, altogether wise, just, and good; significantly, however, Ahura Mazda was not all-powerful—because he had an adversary named Angra Mainyu, later known as Ahriman. "Truly there are two primal spirits, twins renowned to be in conflict. In thought, word, and act they are two: the Good and the Bad," as one of Zoroaster's holy texts attests. It was to defeat Ahriman, Zoroaster taught, that Ahura Mazda created the world and all living things, to provide a battleground for the cosmic struggle between the forces of good and evil.

Zoroaster composed a sequence of hymns to Ahura Mazda. These seventeen poems—known as the Gathas—were passed on orally for many centuries until the Persians acquired writing. By the time the Gathas were written down in the 3rd century CE, a great number of other holy texts had been produced by Zoroastrian priests. These were combined with the original Gathas, and the result was the **Avesta**—the holy book of the Zoroastrians.[6]

The creation myth of this new faith maintained that Ahura Mazda disseminated his spirit to form seven principal elements: Sky, Water, Earth, Plants, Cattle, Man, and Fire. Ahriman brought death into the world, but Ahura Mazda so ordained that the first five elements would be self-regenerating, always bringing more life and therefore more good into the world. Man alone bears the responsibility of choice. The ethical quality of our lives determines not only our own fates but also the fate of the world.

---

[6] The Avesta consisted of twenty-one books, but only fragments remain, since the Muslim conquerors of the Middle Ages searched out every copy they could and destroyed them.

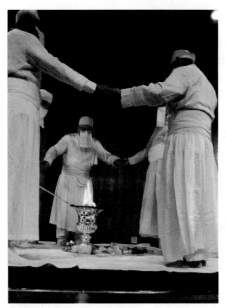

Keeping the Flame Alive   A ring of Zoroastrian priests celebrate their New Year festival with a ritual dance around the sacred flame. Once the most widespread religion in the ancient world, Zoroastrianism today has only about 200,000 followers worldwide. Low birth rates and high rates of conversion to more mainstream religions are contributing to their rapid decline.

Zoroaster wanted to emphasize the unity of mankind, the fact that all peoples regardless of ethnicity are linked by moral necessity and that all lives have value. In his teachings, our lives have a vast purpose—not merely, as in the Sumerian and Egyptian religions, an obligation to serve—that ennobles us and gives meaning to our suffering. God's final element, Fire, exists to inspire and assist us. It represents God's righteousness and truth, his purifying strength, and our hope. Living righteously meant regular prayer (five times daily), always in the presence of fire; performing various temple rituals; and following a high ethical standard of honesty, charity, cleanliness, and respect for nature. In this way, Zoroastrians had every hope of personal salvation, which meant joyous reunion with Ahura Mazda in paradise and the satisfaction of playing a role in God's ultimate victory over Evil. The Gathas enjoined believers to love all peoples, to aid the poor, to practice generous hospitality. They showed respect for nature by not eating animals before the animals had attained maturity and could reproduce. Persian temples drew freely on Sumerian, Akkadian, Babylonian, Assyrian, and Egyptian architectural styles to emphasize that Ahura Mazda was the god of all peoples.

Zoroastrian priests were called **magi**. Their primary responsibility was to tend the sacred fires in the temples, where various rituals central to Zoroastrian life were conducted: marriage, initiation rites, burial rites. Special study was required to become a magus, mostly involving study of the fast-multiplying Avesta texts and memorization of liturgical prayers, but the magi, although highly respected, were not regarded as possessing supernatural powers. Priests and laity remained distinct, but they interacted socially and even intermarried. Priests wore white garments that represented purity; initiated laity were identified primarily by wearing a lengthy cord called a kusti. Zoroastrianism recognized differences between the sexes. It had special temple rites, for example, to help women conceive and to purify them after childbirth. But it allowed all men and women, boys and girls, equal access to the temples and performed the same initiation rites for them all. Away from the temple, female believers could lead the family in prayers and even perform certain rituals.

Zoroastrian belief spread rapidly. The state did not forbid other religions or attempt to suppress them, which may have been the key to Zoroastrianism's success. For many subjects of the empire, Ahura Mazda became a kind of benevolent overlord, whereas their traditional deities were left as immortal spirits in service to the great God. But the ethical element of the faith needs emphasizing. Before Zoroaster, early religions posited no connection between religion and morality. The Sumerian gods, for example, cared only how people treated them, not how they treated each other. The Egyptians were required to obey the divine pharaoh and never upset the order of ma'at—but the only moral expectation placed on them by their religion was not to do harm. Zoroastrian faith gave people the deep satisfaction of feeling that their actions mattered: the way they treated each other helped to create a better world. It appealed to the millions who wanted meaning in life. It assured them that they were good, that their deeds and strivings had purpose, and that a higher ethical standard made life more tolerable for everyone.

◆

The 2nd millennium BCE, for all its political drama and military conflict, marks an important stage in the development of Greater Western values: the rise of pluralistic empires. Whether under the leadership of the New Kingdom Egyptians, the Hittites, the Assyrians, or the Persians, previously independent and ethnically based states were united under a strong central authority. The degree to which subject peoples assimilated and the sources of the most influential traditions varied enormously, but the emergence of pluralistic empires marked the recognition that, despite its cultural diversity, the Greater West was—or at least could be—a single civilization.

WHO, WHAT, WHERE

Akhenaten	Hammurabi	monotheism
Avesta	Hatshepsut	pharaohs
Book of the Dead	Hyksos ascendancy	plutocracy
Cyrus the Great	Indo-European	Ramses II
Epic of Gilgamesh	magi	Zoroastrianism

SUGGESTED READINGS

Primary Sources

Avesta

Book of the Dead

Epic of Gilgamesh

Source Anthologies

Black, Jeremy, trans. *The Literature of Ancient Sumer* (2004).

Chavalas, Mark W., ed. *The Ancient Near East: Historical Sources in Translation* (2006).

Hoffner, Harry A., Jr., trans. *Letters from the Hittite Kingdom* (2009).

Luckenbill, Daniel David, ed. *Annals of Sennacherib* (2005).

Moran, William L., ed. and trans. *The Amarna Letters* (2000).

Simpson, William Kelley. *The Literature of Ancient Egypt: An Anthology of Stories, Instructions, Stelae, Autobiographies, and Poetry* (2003).

Studies

Akkermans, Peter M. M. G., and Glenn Martin Schwartz. *The Archaeology of Syria: From Complex Hunter-Gatherers to Early Urban Societies, ca. 16,000–300 BC* (2004).

Aubet, Maria Eugenia. *The Phoenicians and the West: Politics, Colonies, and Trade* (2001).

Boardman, John. *Persia and the West: An Archaeological Investigation of the Genesis of Achaemenid Persian Art* (2000).

Briant, Pierre. *From Cyrus to Alexander: A History of the Persian Empire* (2006).

Brosius, Maria, ed. *Ancient Archives and Archival Traditions: Concepts of Record-Keeping in the Ancient World* (2003).

Brosius, Maria, ed. *The Persians: An Introduction* (2006).

Bryce, Trevor. *The Kingdom of the Hittites* (2005).

Bryce, Trevor. *Life and Society in the Hittite World* (2004).

Curtis, John E., and Nigel Tallis. *Forgotten Empire: The World of Ancient Persia* (2005).

Day, John V. *Indo-European Origins: The Anthropological Evidence* (2001).

Fleming, Daniel E. *Democracy's Ancient Ancestors: Mari and Early Collective Governance* (2004).

Galil, Gershon. *The Lower Stratum Families in the Neo-Assyrian Period* (2007).

Grajetzki, Wolfram. *The Middle Kingdom of Ancient Egypt: History, Archaeology, and Society* (2006).

Holloway, Steven W. *Aššur Is King! Aššur Is King!: Religion in the Exercise of Power in the Neo-Assyrian Empire* (2002).

Joannès, Francis. *The Age of Empires: Mesopotamia in the First Millennium BC* (2005).

Killebrew, Ann E., and Gunnar Lehmann. *The Philistines and Other Sea Peoples in Text and Archeology* (2013).

Leick, Gwendolyn. *The Babylonians: An Introduction* (2002).

Meskell, Lynn. *Private Life in New Kingdom Egypt* (2004).

Morris, Ian, and Walter Scheidel, eds. *The Dynamics of Ancient Empires: State Power from Assyria to Byzantium* (2009).

Oates, Joan, and David Oates. *Nimrud: An Assyrian Imperial City Revealed* (2001).

O'Brien, Cormac. *The Fall of Empires: From Glory to Ruin—An Epic Account of History's Ancient Civilizations* (2009).

Oren, Eliezer D. *The Sea Peoples and Their World: A Reassessment* (2000).

Ray, John. *Reflections of Osiris: Lives from Ancient Egypt* (2001).

Roehrig, Catharine H., ed. *Hatshepsut: From Queen to Pharaoh* (2005).

Silverman, David P., Josef W. Wegner, and Jennifer Houser Wegner. *Akhenaten and Tutankhamun: Revolution and Restoration* (2006).

Tyldesley, Joyce A. *Ramesses: Egypt's Greatest Pharaoh* (2001).

Van de Mieroop, Marc. *A History of Ancient Egypt* (2010).

Van de Mieroop, Marc. *A History of the Ancient Near East, ca. 3000–323 BC* (2007).

Van de Mieroop, Marc. *King Hammurabi of Babylon: A Biography* (2005).

Wiesehöfer, Josef. *Ancient Persia from 550 BC to 650 AD* (2001).

Yasur-Landau, Assaf. *The Philistines and Aegean Migration at the End of the Late Bronze Age* (2010).

For additional resources, including maps, primary sources, visuals, web links, and quizzes, please go to **www.oup.com/us/backman.**

א אֱלֹהִים אֵת הַשָּׁמַיִם וְאֵת הָאָרֶץ׃ וְהָאָרֶץ הָיְתָה תֹהוּ וָבֹהוּ
שֶׁךְ עַל־פְּנֵי תְהוֹם וְרוּחַ אֱלֹהִים מְרַחֶפֶת עַל־פְּנֵי הַמָּיִם׃ וַיֹּאמֶר
לֹהִים יְהִי אוֹר וַיְהִי־אוֹר׃ וַיַּרְא אֱלֹהִים אֶת־הָאוֹר כִּי־טוֹב וַיַּבְדֵּל
לֹהִים בֵּין הָאוֹר וּבֵין הַחֹשֶׁךְ׃ וַיִּקְרָא אֱלֹהִים ׀ לָאוֹר יוֹם וְלַחֹשֶׁ
רָא לַיְלָה וַיְהִי־עֶרֶב וַיְהִי־בֹקֶר יוֹם אֶחָד׃ פ וַיֹּאמֶר אֱלֹהִים
הִי רָקִיעַ בְּתוֹךְ הַמָּיִם וִיהִי מַבְדִּיל בֵּין מַיִם לָמָיִם׃ וַיַּעַשׂ אֱלֹהִים
ת־הָרָקִיעַ וַיַּבְדֵּל בֵּין הַמַּיִם אֲשֶׁר מִתַּחַת לָרָקִיעַ וּבֵין הַמַּיִם אֲשֶׁ
עַל לָרָקִיעַ וַיְהִי־כֵן׃ וַיִּקְרָא אֱלֹהִים לָרָקִיעַ שָׁמָיִם וַיְהִי־עֶרֶב וַיְהִי־
קֶר יוֹם שֵׁנִי׃ פ וַיֹּאמֶר אֱלֹהִים יִקָּווּ הַמַּיִם מִתַּחַת הַשָּׁמַיִם אֶל
קוֹם אֶחָד וְתֵרָאֶה הַיַּבָּשָׁה וַיְהִי־כֵן׃ וַיִּקְרָא אֱלֹהִים ׀ לַיַּבָּשָׁה אֶר
מִקְוֵה הַמַּיִם קָרָא יַמִּים וַיַּרְא אֱלֹהִים כִּי־טוֹב׃ וַיֹּאמֶר אֱלֹהִי

The People of the Covenant

1200–350 BCE

Sometime between 1800 and 1700 BCE, according to the Biblical story, a tired old man in the city of Ur, near the confluence of the Tigris and Euphrates rivers, began to hear a voice in his head. His name was Abram, and according to the legends passed on about him he was then seventy-five years old, poor, and childless. The voice came from heaven, and it told Abram to take his family—which consisted of his wife Sarai, his nephew Lot, and their servants—and to leave Ur and go where God would lead him. "The LORD said to Abram, 'Go forth from your native land and from your father's house to the land that I will show you. I will make you a great nation, and I will bless you; I will make your name great, and you shall be a blessing. I will bless those who bless you and curse him that curses you; and all the families of the earth shall bless themselves by you'" (Genesis 12.1–3).

It is a tale filled with complex meanings. Part of the collection of books now called the Hebrew Bible (or, to use the Christian term, the Old Testament), it is also a tale of the origins of two peoples—the Jews and the Arabs—and three world religions—Judaism, Christianity, and Islam. Before entering the debate over the tale's factual accuracy, let us follow the narrative a bit further.

In the Beginning This page of the opening of the book of Genesis—here showing its Hebrew name *Bereshit* ("in the beginning") in enlarged letters— comes from a multivolume edition of the Bible planned for publication in Germany in the 1930s. This first volume appeared just before Hitler's rise to power in 1933; the rest of the project was never completed. By long-standing Jewish tradition the text of the scriptures is never adorned with representational imagery, in order to maintain attention on the holy word. Decorative elements consist almost entirely of the beautiful presentation of the script itself.

Being pious, Abram and his family obeyed the call without hesitation. Their trek followed the course of the Fertile Crescent. God led them northward through the Mesopotamian plain, westward across Syria, then southward into the land of the Canaanites in Palestine. At Shechem, which was roughly in the center of Canaan, the Lord appeared to Abram and promised to give all the surrounding land to his offspring. That promise is only the beginning of the tale's complex relationship to history.

Abram built the Lord an altar as a way of giving thanks, but he may have wondered whether the gift was such a blessing. The land was then suffering from a horrific famine, which forced Abram and his family to continue traveling southward in search of food, past the Negev desert, then westward across Sinai and into Egypt. This was a dangerous move, because Abram's wife was an exceptionally beautiful woman, and he believed the Egyptians to be so lecherous that someone might kill him to capture her. Pleading his self-concern, he persuaded Sarai to pose as his (presumably unmarried) sister. Pharaoh's agents saw her beauty and sent her to the royal palace as a new addition to his harem. "And because of her, it went well with Abram; he acquired sheep, oxen, asses, male and female slaves, she-asses, and camels" (Genesis 12.16). But the Lord sent a plague upon the pharaoh because of the wrong done to Sarai, and so the pharaoh sent her and Abram packing. They returned to Palestine, where the Lord repeated his promise of dominion over the land and descendants as numberless as the stars in the night sky.

CHAPTER TIMELINE

1300 BCE	1200 BCE	1100 BCE	1000 BCE	900 BCE

- ca. 1200 BCE **Hebrews move into Palestine**

- ca. 1005–965 BCE **Creation of a unified monarchy under King David**

- ca. 965–928 BCE **Reign of King Solomon; construction of First Temple at Jerusalem**

Yet a decade passed without either promise fulfilled. When Abram was eighty-six, Sarai sent her own servant, an Egyptian maiden named Hagar, into his bed so that he might produce a child by her. Hagar became pregnant, and Sarai, embarrassed at the ease with which Hagar had achieved what she herself had never been able to accomplish, beat her harshly. Hagar eventually gave birth to a son to whom Abram gave the name Ishmael. Another dozen years passed. The Lord appeared to Abram again and repeated his promises yet again, but this time he told Abram to change his name to Abraham (meaning "father of a multitude"), whereas Sarai was henceforth to be called Sarah ("noble-woman"). The new names signaled a sort of spiritual promotion in their relationship with God. Moreover, God ordered Abraham to circumcise himself and Ishmael and to promise to circumcise all their male offspring henceforth on the eighth day after their birth. Abraham did indeed cut off his own foreskin, and some short time later, remarkably, the ninety-nine-year-old Abraham and the ninety-year-old Sarah did conceive a child—a son. They named him Isaac and duly circumcised him on the eighth day. Sarah was joyful to have a child at last but could not help resenting the continued presence of Ishmael and his mother, Hagar, so she ordered them to leave the household. The story takes a bittersweet turn when the Lord, speaking to Hagar for the first time, assures her that he has a plan for Ishmael as well: "I will make a great nation of him" (Genesis 21.18).

950 BCE	800 BCE	700 BCE	600 BCE	500 BCE

- ca. 950 BCE **Composition of first biblical texts**
- ca. 937 BCE **Kingdom splits into Israel (north) and Judah (south)**
- ca. 721 BCE **Assyrians conquer Israel**
- ca. 587 BCE **Neo-Babylonians conquer Judah and destroy Temple**
- 586–539 BCE **Babylonian Captivity**
- ca. 538 BCE **Persian emperor Cyrus the Great allows exiles to return to Judah**
- ca. 515 BCE **Second Temple is dedicated**

Whether or not it accords with historical truth, the story reflects a tradition that this one man, Abram/Abraham, was the patriarch of two great peoples. Through Sarai/Sarah he fathered the nation of the Hebrews, out of which developed the religion of Judaism, and with his Egyptian concubine Hagar he produced the line that resulted in the nation of the Arabs and their faith of Islam.

The tale bristles with difficulties: Why was Abram/Abraham chosen? Why was his family led to the land promised to them at a time of famine, when they could not live there? How could Abram/Abraham justify handing his beloved wife over to the pharaoh's lust? After their release from Egypt, why did God repeat his promise to Abram/Abraham's family, only to let another ten years go by before fulfilling it? After Hagar produced Ishmael, why did he let another twelve years pass before allowing Isaac to be born? And why he did make Hagar endure twelve years of Sarai/Sarah's bullying before extending any consoling promise to her?

But even this is only the beginning of the complexities that frustrate the effort to know the origins of the Hebrews. Political and religious ideologies play an important role in this problem, of course, but even more fundamental is the vexing question of the Bible itself and its usefulness as a historical source. The debate is as old as the Bible itself.

THE BIBLE AND HISTORY

To begin, the Bible is not a book but a library. The Hebrew Bible consists of twenty-four books written over a period of nearly one thousand years. According to Jewish tradition, the entire set of books was finally established, ordered, and canonized around 450 BCE by a group remembered as the "Men of the Great Assembly." Most scholars, however, would regard that as too early a date and prefer something around 250 or 200 BCE—and they place the composition of the first biblical texts around 950 BCE.

Approaching the Hebrew Bible

Many Christians will be surprised by a first look at the Hebrew Bible, since it organizes the books in a way unfamiliar to Christian tradition. The Hebrew Bible is commonly known as the **Tanakh**—an acronym based on the letters *T* (for *Torah*, meaning "Instructions"), *N* (for *Nevi'im*, or "Prophets"), and *K* (for *Ketuvim*, or "Writings")—and it groups its books accordingly. Moreover, there are two distinct versions of the Hebrew Bible: the Masoretic text compiled in Hebrew in the 2nd century CE and the Greek text, the Septuagint, compiled around 200 BCE for the Greek-speaking Jews of the Hellenistic era (discussed in chapter 5). Jewish tradition, supported by textual evidence, regards the Masoretic text as a definitive re-creation of the lost version put together by the Men of the Great Assembly. It thus has priority over the Greek version, which is actually five hundred years older. The Septuagint text varies from the Masoretic in some significant ways,

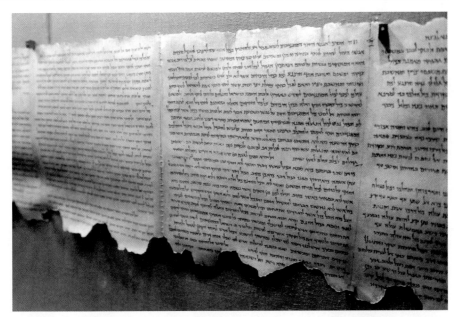

The Dead Sea Scrolls   The scrolls are a collection of 972 ancient texts found in caves near the west bank of the Dead Sea beginning in the late 1940s. They consist largely of Hebrew biblical texts like the ones shown here (roughly 40 percent of the total), with a somewhat smaller number of apocryphal biblical writings. The rest of the collection consists of legal and devotional texts. Most of the scrolls are on parchment and are written in Hebrew, Aramaic, Greek, and Nabataean.

most especially in its acceptance of certain additional books that do not appear in the Hebrew tradition.[1] The variations in the canon are important: the Hebrew scriptures did not emerge fully formed at a single moment in history but rather evolved over centuries.

The problems are obvious. For one, the Bible ascribes impossibly long lives to the early leaders of the Hebrews. Abraham, we are assured, died in his 175th year, and his son Isaac died at the age of 180. We are told that Isaac's son Jacob died when he was very old, although a precise age is never given, but Jacob's son Joseph reportedly lived to be 110. A second problem is that the scriptures coopt stories from other ancient Near Eastern cultures as if they had occurred uniquely to the Hebrews. The biblical legend of Noah and the ark clearly echoes the Sumerian tale of the Great Flood, to pick the most obvious example. Even the single most important episode in defining the Hebrews as a people presents a problem. Here, Moses is chosen by God to lead the Hebrews out of Egyptian bondage, receives the **Torah** (laws for righteous living, collected in the first five books of the Hebrew Bible) on Mount Sinai in the desert northeast of Egypt, and—in return for

---

[1]   The Roman Catholic and the Orthodox churches regard the Septuagint version as normative. Protestant churches usually print the Septuagint's extra books (which they call the *Apocrypha*) as a type of appendix.

agreeing to worship God exclusively and to live by his laws—guides the Hebrews to a promised land of safety and prosperity. The escape from Egypt establishes the Hebrews' special **covenant**, or contract, with God, and yet there is virtually no archeological or documentary evidence for it outside of the Bible itself.

These difficulties hardly negate the Bible's value as a historical source. Rather, we must read the texts on their own terms. They portray not human history in the usual sense but the development of a relationship—the growth of a people's understanding of their connection to a transcendent deity (see Table 3.1).

Whatever the Hebrew Bible lacks in historical accuracy, it makes up for with a searing depiction of a difficult, demanding, and inscrutable God. He places extraordinary obligations on a small, persecuted minority from whom he expects the highest degree of ethical behavior. And their failures to live up to that standard are narrated again and again. The Hebrews are depicted as the Chosen People—but that status confers more obligations than rewards. They are chosen, but not in the sense of favored. Rather, they are held responsible for maintaining a standard of moral behavior and pursuing justice on earth. How else can one interpret the travails of Abraham? Along with the repeated promises and the constant requirement of waiting for fulfillment, he must undergo tension and division within his own household. God tests Abraham far more frequently than he rewards him, and those tests are severe.

Debate over Authorship

The origins of the Bible remain subject to debate even after three thousand years of intense study. The first texts to be composed, scholars agree, were the five books of the Torah, which began to appear, in various forms, around 950 BCE and perhaps a bit later than that. What makes dating the texts so challenging is that several authors and editors had a hand in the process. Most biblical scholars hold

---

TABLE 3.1   **The Central Tenets of Judaism**

Although Judaism does not have an official statement on doctrine, most Jews accept the statement of "The Thirteen Essential Beliefs" as summarized by the great medieval scholar R. Moses ben Maimon (d. 1204):

1. God will reward the good and punish the wicked.
2. The messiah will come.
3. The dead will be resurrected.
4. God exists.
5. God is one and unique.
6. God is incorporeal.
7. God is eternal.
8. Prayer is to be directed to God alone.
9. The words of the prophets are true.
10. The prophecies of Moses are true, and Moses was the greatest of the prophets.
11. The written Torah and the oral Torah were both given to Moses.
12. There will be no other Torah.
13. God knows the thoughts and deeds of all people.

to the so-called **Documentary Hypothesis**, which posits that the texts as they survive result from the intertwining of several writers' work, writers known by the initials J, E, D, and P. These indicate, respectively, the Yahwist author (ca. 950 BCE), the Elohist author (ca. 750 BCE), the Deuteronomist author (ca. 650 BCE), and the Priestly author (ca. 550 BCE). Some scholars add a still later figure known as R, for the Redactor.

The Yahwist (J) is believed to have been the first, and his writings can be identified by his use of the term **YHWH** to stand for God. J is presumed to have written most of the biblical book of Genesis and certainly those parts of it that relate the stories of Abraham and his descendants.[2] J's God is always YHWH in Hebrew (which English-language Bibles represent by the all-capitals word LORD), and as we have seen, YHWH frequently intervenes directly in his human characters' lives.

The Elohist (E), by contrast, uses a different word—Elohim, meaning simply "god" or "deity"—and never depicts any direct human encounters with him. In Genesis, the long final section telling the tale of Joseph and his brothers comes from E. (Joseph is the first human being in the Bible who never sees or hears God personally, yet still believes.) E's handiwork is the patchiest, with few long passages apart from the Joseph story, which suggests that it reflects an oral as opposed to a written tradition, something interwoven here and there throughout the J narrative. Around 750 BCE, the argument goes, as the Assyrian armies drew nearer to the Hebrew lands, E set to work, trying to preserve the tales handed down among those who settled in the northern part of Palestine as a counterbalance to J's heavy emphasis on the Hebrews in southern Palestine. This desire to preserve the traditions of the northern Hebrews may explain why E so frequently tells stories of sibling rivalry, such as that between Jacob and Esau (Isaac's sons) and between Joseph and his brothers.

The Deuteronomist (D) is the most controversial of the purported authors. Some scholars consider him the author of the book of Deuteronomy but of little else, whereas others regard him as the most critical figure in biblical transmission. D insists on the absolute centrality of allegiance to Torah and worship in the Jerusalem Temple, but also relentlessly describes the crisis of the Assyrian conquest and the approach of the neo-Babylonians as the result of the Hebrews' failure of morals and observance.

Finally, the Priestly author (P), or more likely authors, set to work after the fall of Jerusalem to the neo-Babylonians around 587 BCE and inserted a vast body of

---

[2] The Hebrew letter *yod* can be transliterated as either the English J or Y. The name of God is not to be spoken—hence the use of the abbreviation YHWH. Christians, not being subject to the traditional restriction, expand the abbreviation as Yahweh or Jehovah.

priestly ordinances from the time of the First Temple into the traditional material of the Torah. P's handiwork is woven throughout the first books of the Bible but is especially evident in the book of Leviticus and in the first ten chapters of Numbers. P is also responsible for the first chapter of Genesis (J's version of creation had begun with chapter 2), a priestly version of Abraham's covenant with God.

Not all biblical scholars adhere to the Documentary Hypothesis. Some prefer other explanations for the Bible's abrupt shifts, numerous repetitions, and frequent contradictions. Everyone agrees, however, that the Bible is a patchwork of many writers' contributions—as well as the product of considerable revision, expansion, editing, and rearrangement. It is above all a testament to the Hebrews' perseverance, their determination to make sense of their experience, and their faith in God. As we shall see, much of that experience consisted of repeated persecution and oppression.

THE LAND OF CANAAN

Whatever their legendary origins, the Hebrews moved into Palestine sometime around 1200 BCE. This is a long time after their biblical arrival under Abraham in 1800 BCE. The Bible tells of four hundred years of enslavement in Egypt, followed by a heroic march of liberation and the conquest of Canaan (Palestine), also referred to as the Promised Land.

In the Bible the march of liberation was led by Moses, to whom was given the first elements of the Torah. As mentioned before, however, no nonbiblical evidence exists for a large Hebrew presence in Egypt at any time during the New Kingdom. Nor is there evidence for a dramatic Hebrew rebellion and subsequent release from bondage. It seems unlikely that events of such magnitude would leave no trace in the hundreds of thousands of Egyptian records that survive from the New Kingdom era. Yet it seems equally unlikely that a people would invent a legend of their own humiliating enslavement if it had no basis in fact. All that can be said with certainty is that when the Hebrews moved into Palestine, they brought with them an unshakeable conviction: God, they believed, had vouchsafed the land to them. In return, they felt a special obligation to live according to an exacting ethical and ritual code, to care for the poor and downtrodden, and to serve the cause of justice.

Tribal Organization

They were not necessarily a single people and may instead have been a loose assemblage of speakers of related dialect groups. Ancient sources describe the Hebrews' division into twelve tribes. Figures known as **judges** held a combination of religious and political authority over each tribe, together with military leadership in times of war. The Hebrews communicated with the other groups who had already settled the land—the Amalekites, Amorites, Aramaeans, Philistines, and Phoenicians—but the Hebrews were overwhelmingly a pastoral people. Their movement over the land with their herds put them at odds with the other groups, who were chiefly farmers and town dwellers. Although they remained seminomadic, the Hebrew tribes had carved out certain zones for themselves by 1000 BCE. Those in the hilly south called themselves the people of **Judah**, whereas the northern-based tribes took the name of **Israel** (see Map 3.1).

Religious life centered on the family, with daily prayers and rituals to observe the emerging body of Torah. The judges and a caste of priests led communal services that frequently involved some form of animal sacrifice (the "burnt offerings" referred to in the Bible). The Hebrews did not proselytize to non-Hebrews and focused instead on broadening the acceptance of YHWH among their own people. For a long time even after the YHWH cult was established, the Hebrews practiced a henotheistic religion—that is, a religion that recognizes the existence of other gods but insists on the supremacy of its one individual god.

The Hebrews preserved the political autonomy of each tribe for as long as they could, but when the Philistines conquered the southern coastal plain of the *Philistine* Levant, they were forced to mount a united defense against annihilation. They *Conquest*

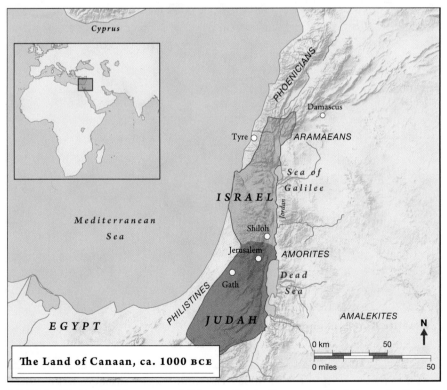

MAP 3.1   The Land of Canaan, ca. 1000 BCE   Originally organized by tribes under the leadership of religious judges, the Hebrews may have contended with one another as bitterly as they did with the peoples they displaced. The Hebrew Bible's book of Judges tells much of this story.

entered the alliance thinking it would be temporary, and internal bickering made concerted action difficult. In 1050 BCE, or thereabouts, the Philistines demolished the main Hebrew sanctuary at Shiloh and carted off the **Ark of the Covenant**—the chest that held the stone tablets of the Torah as received by Moses—as a war trophy. After that military catastrophe, the bulk of the people called out for the creation of a Hebrew monarchy. Only a clear central command under a charismatic figure with military skill, they argued, could hold the confederation together and destroy the Philistines.

DREAMS OF A GOLDEN AGE

Their choice fell ultimately upon David, a low-born but ambitious soldier. **David** (r. ca. 1005–965 BCE) united the kingdoms of Judah and Israel and pushed the borders of the newly unified Israelite kingdom to their greatest expanse, from the Gulf of Aqaba in the south to 50 miles north of the Sea of Galilee (see Map 3.2).

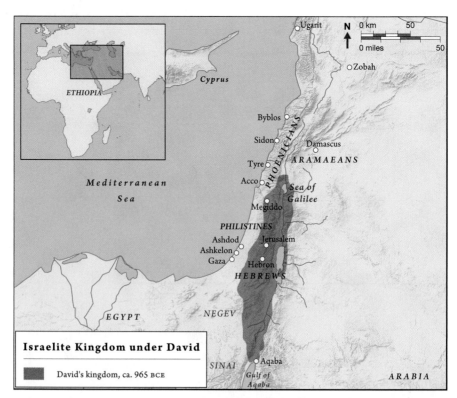

MAP 3.2   Israelite Kingdom under David   The unified kingdom established by King David had its capital at Jerusalem. The choice of city was strategic: Jerusalem had no special significance for any of the Hebrew tribes, so there was no worry about any particular tribe holding pre-eminence over the others.

Politically, the Israelites under David were among the most powerful peoples in the Near East. The choice of Jerusalem for the new capital of his kingdom showed David's shrewdness because its central location made it well placed to watch over both the northern and the southern tribes. Even more important, the city, which had been founded centuries earlier by the Canaanites, had no prior religious significance for the Hebrews and hence was unlikely to fuel tribal competition for privilege. David brought the Ark of the Covenant into the city and began to construct a magnificent palace for himself (which he financed with a combination of heavy taxation, forced loans, and slave labor). Of the 150 prayer-songs that make up the Bible's book of Psalms, tradition ascribes most of them to David's own pen, although modern scholars generally believe that if he did in fact compose any of them, these were most likely Psalms 1 through 41. *Unification under David*

David's son **Solomon** (r. ca. 965–928 BCE) succeeded him and threw his considerable energy into enlarging his father's palace complex. He also began construction of a temple to house the Ark of the Covenant. The Bible devotes three entire chapters to describing the Temple (1 Kings 6–8). Everything about it deserved mention, starting with its size—30 feet wide, 90 feet long, three stories tall. It had latticed windows, inlaid wood paneling, carved cherubim, chains that secured double doors leading into the inner sanctuary where the Ark was placed, and statuary embossed with gold leaf. This was, the Bible assures us, a house fit for the Lord. Solomon also expanded the royal palace until it formed a vast complex with the Temple. *Reign of Solomon*

Moreover, he built the Israelites' first commercial fleet, which sailed out of the Gulf of Aqaba at the kingdom's far southern tip on the Red Sea (see Map 3.2). It put Israel in direct contact with Upper Egypt, Ethiopia, and the coastal peoples of the Arabian peninsula. The Israelites sold the copper that they—or their slaves, actually—mined from the rich veins found in the southern Negev desert. This trade was highly lucrative and helped to finance the palace and Temple projects. Records survive that indicate commercial ties as far as southern India—the source of the incense and spices used in Temple rites and of the sandalwood used to decorate the sacred space.

Solomon, like his father, survives in Hebrew tradition as a wise and great ruler who championed the causes of justice and piety.[3] Solomon wrote psalms, too, and is credited with writing the book of Proverbs and the Song of Songs. Both men, however, could be selfish and despotic and were nowhere near as popular in their lifetimes as in later centuries. Their sexual appetites were tireless: David pursued married women as well as servant girls, and Solomon, we are told, had

---

[3]   "King Solomon excelled all the kings on earth in wealth and in wisdom. All the world came to pay homage to Solomon and to listen to the wisdom with which God had endowed him" (1 Kings 10.23–24).

The Temple in Jerusalem   No one knows exactly what the Temple built by King Solomon looked like, despite the detailed description of it given in the Bible. This representation comes from the Nuremberg Chronicle by Hartmann Schedel, which appeared in 1493.

seven hundred wives and three hundred concubines, including "the daughter of Pharaoh, women of the Moabites, Ammonites, Edomites, Zidonians, and Hittites" (1 Kings 11.1). Solomon's consorts were of an exceptionally large number, but his bed-hopping was not regarded as intrinsically wrong. Polygamy was common among the early Israelites, especially among the elites. Both men had cruel streaks, too. In the story of the beautiful Bathsheba, David intentionally ordered her husband into a ferocious battle so that he could then claim his widow for himself. After a victory over the people of Zobah, David took more than twenty thousand Canaanite soldiers captive as slaves and had all their horses hamstrung.

Most likely, the overwhelmingly flattering nature of the Bible's portrayal of these men resulted from the role they played in strengthening the cult of YHWH. All their conquests, their building projects, their artistic endeavors, their efforts to provide justice for the people—everything was done in service to the God whose great Temple they had raised in Jerusalem. Compared to this, what did some sexual peccadilloes matter? The Bible's compilers gladly held up the David–Solomon era as the golden age of ancient Israel, and the tales of these two kings entered Jewish folklore.

The romanticization of David and Solomon introduced an entirely new element into Greater Western culture, or at least one for which no earlier evidence survives—namely, the popular belief in a past paradise, a lost era of former glory, when humanity had attained a perfection of happiness. This is more than mere nostalgia, and it has been a hallmark of Greater Western life ever since. Throughout the centuries societies have attempted to evoke or re-create a golden age—a past from which we have declined and to which we hope to return. Our reformations therefore tend to be *re*formations, efforts to restore past glories rather than to create new ones. It might be the Jews' struggle to reestablish themselves in the Promised Land. It might be American mythmaking about the Founding Fathers or the old West. It might be modern Muslims' longing for the fabled tolerance and high culture of the classical Islamic world. In each case, Greater Western culture has sought to return to a perfection we have lost.

The northern tribes refused to accept Solomon's son Rehoboam as their king and broke away to form a separate realm. Hence from 937 to 721 BCE there were *Conquest* two Hebrew kingdoms—the kingdom of Israel in the north and the kingdom of *of Israel* Judah in the south, still centered on Jerusalem (see again Map 3.1). Judah, al- *and Judah* though smaller, had the advantage of its relatively isolated position in the hills. As a state and, more importantly, as a people, Israel disappeared with its fall to the Assyrians around 721 BCE. These brutal conquerors annihilated tens of thousands and sent the rest off into slavery throughout the Assyrian Empire, where they eventually vanished—the famed ten lost tribes of Israel.

The people of Judah held out until they themselves were overwhelmed by the neo-Babylonians, or Chaldeans, under their ruler Nebuchadnezzar, around 587 BCE. Thus began the **Diaspora** ("exile" or "scattering"). The neo-Babylonians destroyed the Temple at Jerusalem and drove the Judaeans eastward into the **Babylonian Captivity** (ca. 586–539 BCE). Exile and enslavement forced the people to redefine, or at least to reinterpret, their religious identity. Did their defeat by the Chaldeans mean that the Hebrews had lost their status of YHWH's Chosen People? If not, how were they to understand their enslavement—as a punishment for their failings or as a challenge to be overcome? More specifically, how could they observe their laws now that they lived in exile from the Holy Land and the Temple? With the Temple in ruins, was the authority of the priests rendered null and void? And what of the demands of Torah? For example, the Torah instructed that no Hebrew should eat a meal under the roof of a non-Hebrew (to ensure adherence to biblical dietary restrictions)—but as slaves in Babylon they had no option but to live and eat under their masters' roofs. Was the Law therefore temporarily suspended?

Ten Lost Tribes of Israel   The Assyrians invaded the northern Hebrew kingdom of Israel around 732 BCE and completed its conquest of the land by about 721 BCE. Campaigns against towns along the former border with the kingdom of Judah continued for another quarter century. This relief depicts Israelite captives loading provisions onto a cart, in preparation for their long trek into enslavement in the east. An Assyrian soldier stands guard in the center. One entire room in the Assyrian palace at Nineveh was devoted to depicting this particular campaign of the ruler Sennacherib (r. 705–681 BCE) against the Israelite city of Lachish. This relief forms just one small component of the larger pictorial narrative.

Questions like these demanded a new reckoning of the identity, values, and traditions of YHWH's people. The question immediately facing them was: Who had the right to decide, and on what basis? The problem touched every aspect of their culture, from the Torah itself, to the status of traditional priestly leadership, to the mundane details of daily life—and it raised particularly important questions about the status and role of women in Hebrew life.

WOMEN AND THE LAW

Fixing the status of women in ancient Jewish society is no easy task, but not, as with other Near Eastern peoples, because of a dearth of evidence. The Bible devotes hundreds of pages to describing, praising, criticizing, legislating, berating, lamenting, and thanking the women of the Hebrew world. The image that emerges is complex and sometimes self-contradictory, and yet it is clear that the

Hebrews gave their women more social autonomy, legal rights, education, and respect than any other ancient group, with the possible exception of the Persian Zoroastrians—whose treatment of women remains far less understood because of the paucity of sources. (As noted in chapter 2, most of the archives and libraries of the Zoroastrians were destroyed, often intentionally, during the Islamic conquests of the 7th and 8th centuries CE.)

The biblical passages depicting the pre-Mosaic era invariably describe women as having been created to help, if not to serve, men. From Sarai/Sarah on, Hebrew women appear overwhelmingly in the roles of dutiful daughters, obedient wives, and loving mothers. Enough exceptions to the pattern exist, however, to suggest that many women did carve out different paths for themselves. Moses's

Women's Expansion of Proscribed Roles

own sister, the prophetess Miriam, helped to guide the Hebrews across the Red Sea and led their celebration of thanksgiving once they had reached the other side. Another prophetess, Deborah, actually governed one of the twelve tribes, according to the book of Judges. And a married woman named Huldah was so respected for her knowledge of Hebrew law that King Josiah of Judah (r. 641–609 BCE) entrusted her with validating a newly discovered Torah-scroll fragment found in Jerusalem. Two other women, whether historical or not, were deemed significant enough to deserve entire biblical books devoted to their stories: Esther, a young Jewish girl who becomes queen of Persia and uses her position to forestall a plot to annihilate the Jews within the empire, and Ruth, the main character (and a convert to Judaism) in a charming story about long-suffering love, faithful friendship, and fulfillment.[4]

Story of Ruth   The tale of Ruth, the widowed daughter-in-law of the widowed Naomi, is among the best-loved of biblical stories. Ruth's tender loyalty to Naomi is rewarded, ultimately, when Naomi arranges a new marriage for her. This painting by Julius Huebner (1806–1882) was long believed to have been destroyed in World War II but was rediscovered and restored in 2005.

---

4   To this day, Jews in Iran are referred to colloquially as *Esther's children*.

Rules for Women

The Torah established the framework for women's roles in Jewish society. As usual, the discrepancies between male and female prerogatives are first to draw one's attention. The Law strictly demands virginity of girls before marriage but lays no comparable burden on boys; women cannot give testimony in civil or criminal cases; a husband can divorce his wife for cause, but not vice versa unless the husband agrees to the split. On the other hand, tradition gave girls the right to a basic education (usually enough to allow them to read the scriptures and guide their own children's early religious education), guaranteed their entitlement to inherit property, allowed them limited economic autonomy, and accorded protection to widows. The bans on women entering the Temple or performing other liturgical rites during menstruation or immediately after giving birth, times when they are labeled "impure" or "unclean" (Hebrew *tumeh*), may seem misogynistic but appear less so when one considers the more numerous conditions that rendered a man *tumeh*—such as touching the carcasses of proscribed animals, experiencing nocturnal emissions, developing a rash or sore on his skin, or even just acquiring a bald patch in his beard. To be *tumeh* did not denote sinfulness or a loss of self-worth; it meant only that one was not ceremonially fit for certain religious rites and needed to undergo a ritual purification or cleansing. Nevertheless, women of all ages were generally regarded as individuals needing higher degrees of protection and guidance.

The fifth commandment given to Moses on Mount Sinai enjoined all Hebrews to honor their mothers and fathers equally, and a later rabbinical judgment declared—rhetorically, not legally—"Death to him who strikes or curses his own mother." But the tenth commandment forbade men from coveting their neighbors' wives, houses, work animals, "or any other thing belonging to your neighbor," a command that would seem to regard wives as possessions rather than people. Within marriage, the Law required husbands to honor, support, and work on behalf of their wives at least to an extent that matched the value of the property a woman brought into the marriage by her dowry. Wives who brought no domestic servants into their marriage were expected to perform six specific household tasks for their husbands: grinding grain, cooking, cleaning, spinning and weaving, bed preparation, and child nursing. A Jewish wife was entitled to relinquish one of these essential labors for every servant provided by her dowry. Wives were exempt from performing fieldwork. The Law expected women as well as men to make annual visits to the Temple in Jerusalem, especially for their most important holy days, and provided special bathing spaces for women to prepare themselves for entering the House of the Lord. Mothers led the prayers that preceded the main daily meal, and in pre-Temple times they participated in performing ritual sacrifices.

One of the biblical books, the Song of Songs (also known as the Song of Solomon), consists of a poetic dialogue between a bride and bridegroom that celebrates married love in all its emotional and physical intimacy. Centuries of religious commentary have interpreted the text as an allegory of the covenant between God and his people, but a simpler reading sees in it a hymn to the joy that married union brings in equal measure to man and wife. The bride speaks first:

> Oh, give me the kisses of your mouth,
> For your love is more delightful than wine.
> Your ointments yield a sweet fragrance,
> Your name is like finest oil—
> Therefore do maidens love you.
> Draw me after you, let us run!
> The king has brought me to his chambers.
> Let us delight and rejoice in your love,
> Savoring it more than wine. (Song of Songs 1.2–4)

To which the bridegroom sings in reply:

> You have captured my heart,
> My own, my bride,
> You have captured my heart
> With one glance of your eyes,
> With one coil of your necklace.
> How sweet is your love,
> My own, my bride!
> How much more delightful your love than wine,
> Your ointments more fragrant
> Than any spice!
> Sweetness drops
> From your lips, O bride;
> Honey and milk
> Are under your tongue;
> And the scent of your robes
> Is like the scent of Lebanon. (4.9–11)

Sexual delight is an intrinsic element of married love, and the Law recognizes a wife's right to full enjoyment of it. But pleasure is not the only reason for marriage. God's first instruction to Adam and Eve—the first man and woman, according to the book of Genesis—was to reproduce: "Be fertile and increase, fill the earth and master it." Every Jewish man was expected to marry as early as possible, which most priests and rabbis interpreted to mean the onset of puberty. The Torah not only declines to praise celibacy, it never even mentions it.[5] A girl could not be forced into marriage before puberty and retained a limited right to refuse a marriage partner proposed by her father after she had reached it. The Law does not demand marriage of all females as it does of males, but rabbinical tradition advises women not to remain single, lest they come under suspicion by their neighbors as sexual adventuresses.

Women in ancient Israel and Judah, on the whole, were better off than most of their contemporaries. They could own and inherit property, received at least a basic education, enjoyed legal rights in marriage, participated actively in the religious life of the community, and received the respect of their peers and the veneration of their families. So long, that is, as they obeyed the Law.

PROPHETS AND PROPHECY

In Jewish tradition, the splitting of the Israelite kingdom and the subsequent disappearance of successor states prompted the arrival of the age of the great prophets, messengers of God. Samuel, last of the Judges, was the first of the great prophets. After him came Elijah and Elisha (both mid- to late 9th century BCE), Amos and Hosea (mid-8th century BCE), Isaiah and Micah (late 8th century BCE), Jeremiah (late 7th to early 6th centuries BCE), and Ezekiel (early 6th century BCE). The minor prophets—so called for the length, not the significance, of their prophetic books—came too. Allowing for differences among them as individuals, the **prophets** as a group shared a calling to warn the Hebrews of the approaching Assyrian and Babylonian dangers and to interpret those dangers as signs of YHWH's growing displeasure. By failing to uphold standards of justice, decency, and observance of the Torah, they cautioned, the people had placed themselves in both mortal and spiritual peril. As Jeremiah put it in his Temple sermon,

> Thus said the LORD of Hosts, the God of Israel: "Mend your ways and your actions, and I will let you dwell in this place. Don't put your trust in illusions and say, 'The Temple of the LORD, the Temple of the LORD, the Temple of the LORD are the [buildings].' No, if you really mend your ways and your actions; if you execute justice between one man and another; if you do not oppress the stranger, the orphan, and the

---

[5]   The prophet Jeremiah is the only Jewish figure in the Hebrew Bible known to have been celibate (see Jeremiah 16.2).

widow; if you do not shed the blood of the innocent in this place; if you do not follow other gods, to your own hurt—then only will I let you dwell in this place, in this land that I gave to your fathers for all time." (Jeremiah 7.3–7)

In casting the blame for their misfortunes on themselves, the Hebrews introduced the essential notions of self-criticism and moral responsibility into Western culture. It hardly seems possible to imagine a Sumerian interpreting a calamity like the Hittite invasion as anything other than divine whim or to picture an Egyptian interpreting the Hyksos catastrophe as the consequence of a moral failing on Egypt's part. Earlier societies had senses of morality, but those morals usually existed alongside their religions. The Jews, however, conflated faith and morals to a degree that they could not be separated or distinguished. She'ol was the biblical underworld, and yet the Hebrews did not believe in separate places of reward and punishment in the afterlife. A good life of devotion to YHWH, ethical behavior, and commitment to justice was desirable for its own sake, not as a means to a heavenly end. Ethic and action were necessary components of each other, intrinsic and inextricable.

The Value of Moral Responsibility

This was a revolutionary development in Western life, but one that hardly made the Jews any happier a people. Joy and agony are both present on every page of the Bible, and indeed the scriptures are often at their greatest expressive power when crying out in pain. Among the psalms attributed to David, one that has entered Jewish liturgy as a daily prayer for supplication is the following:

> O LORD, do not punish me in anger,
>> do not chastise me in fury.
>> Have mercy on me, O LORD, for I languish;
>> heal me, O LORD, for my bones shake with terror.
>> My whole being is stricken with terror,
>> while You, LORD—O, how long!
> O LORD, turn! Rescue me!
>> Deliver me as befits Your faithfulness.
>> For there is no praise of You among the dead;
>>> in Sheol, who can acclaim You?
>> I am weary with groaning;
>>> every night I drench my bed.
>> I melt my couch in tears.
>> My eyes are wasted by vexation,
>>> worn out because of all my foes.
>> Away from me, all you evildoers,

> for the LORD heeds the sound of my weeping.
> The LORD heeds my plea,
>   the LORD accepts my prayer.
> All my enemies will be frustrated and stricken with terror;
>   they will turn back in an instant, frustrated. (Psalm 6)

Few ancient texts expressed comparable sentiments. Only the Sumerian "Song of the Righteous Sufferer" (excerpted in chapter 1) comes close to such power.

THE STRUGGLE FOR JEWISH IDENTITY

The loss of Jerusalem, the Temple, and the land of their fathers as well as captivity in Babylon represented crises of the highest order. Had YHWH abandoned the Hebrews, revoking the promises he had made to Abraham and Moses? These concerns had inspired the prophets to call the Hebrews to stricter observance of Torah, to stamp out immoral behavior, and to turn their hearts and minds to YHWH. But how was stricter observance of Torah possible when the Hebrews no longer lived in their own society?

For nearly five hundred years Hebrew religious life had been centered on the home and the Temple. To live an observant life, although ethically challenging, was logistically simple in a homogeneous Hebrew society: the distances involved were, after all, not so great. The daily disciplines of prayer, charity, fair dealing, and hospitality were practiced in the home. The ritual demands of communal worship could be observed by intermittent journeys to the Temple in Jerusalem. The high priests controlled Temple life, performed the rituals, resolved disputes, and represented the community of the Chosen. The king administered the realm, defended the people, and worked to keep the economy afloat.

Now the Hebrews were shorn of centuries of tradition—exiled from their Temple, the ritual prayers, ceremonies, and sacrifices that provided spiritual sustenance and communal identity. They were in captivity and in the minority, facing day-to-day situations that had never occurred in their own kingdom. In these times, established law no longer clearly applied. Might a Hebrew slave indentured to a Persian obey his boss's commands on the Sabbath? Should he risk death by refusing to work? Under what conditions might a Hebrew enter a business partnership with a nonbeliever? Such problems had been addressed to some extent in the past, but usually in the abstract. These questions, and others like them, were now urgent.

Origins of Rabbinical Judaism   Compounding the difficulties, the priestly caste had been largely eradicated or marginalized. To whom, then, could the Hebrews turn for answers? During the nearly fifty years of their Babylonian Captivity, they turned increasingly to their rabbis. The status of **rabbi** had a long lineage going back centuries. Originally an honorific term, the word meant something like "master," in the sense of a person of skill: a man who learned a craft from an expert might call that expert his rabbi, just as a person might honor a special tutor. By the 6th century BCE, however, a rabbi was specifically a teacher of Hebrew Law. Shorn of their Temple lives, the Hebrews in exile turned to the rabbis, who became their de facto leaders. Rabbis continued to teach Torah but also increasingly became religious judges. Their role was to extrapolate from the principles of Torah, so as to redefine an authentic Hebrew life in radically changed circumstances. The incremental growth of a body of rabbinical law—analogous to the tort law of modern societies—came to heavily influence Hebrew life and identity, even to the point where legal scholars started to refer to rabbinical judgments as the expression of an oral Torah that supplemented the written Law. In response, groups of exiled priests began to revise the codified Torah, inserting laws and rituals associated with the P author and re-emphasizing the centrality of priestly worship in Hebrew life.

In 538 BCE the Persian emperor Cyrus the Great released the Hebrews and allowed them to return to Judah. His decision triggered a predictable conflict. Should *Return* the new generations of Hebrews—now known as Jews from the name of their *to Judah* homeland—who had never known Temple worship or the authority of the priests relinquish rabbinical teaching and leadership? Was rabbinical Judaism merely a temporary measure in an emergency, or was it a new and authentic way of being a Jew? Moreover, who would decide—the priests? The rabbis? The people themselves?

Ezra and Nehemiah, the two most prominent prophets of the mid-5th century BCE and ardent champions of Temple worship, leapt into the debate and railed against Jews who had married outside the faith and those who undeservingly claimed the traditional self-identification of "children of Israel" and "children of Abraham." Ezra condemned all mixed marriages and declared them formally dissolved. (The Jews who accepted Ezra's judgments simply dismissed their wives and renounced any children they might have produced.) In Jewish tradition Ezra is a figure of immense stature, a second Moses in his authority, for his dual role of rebuilding the Temple and purifying the community, thus giving his people a religious rebirth.

The prophets Haggai and Zechariah, who appeared next, likewise urged the rebuilding of the Temple and the reestablishment of priestly authority. Did the construction of a Second Temple on the ruins of the First mean the restoration of the old order, or could rabbinical tradition somehow embrace and even subsume the traditions of the past? This debate motivated much of the compiling, editing, and rewriting of the Bible described earlier in this chapter. The territory of Judah would continue under Persia's political control for another two hundred years, but the social and cultural situation remained in flux.

Factions of Jews debated not only the proper ways of worshipping YHWH and adhering to his laws but also even the fundamental issue of who exactly was a Jew. The neo-Babylonians had not forcibly relocated every single Jew to the east. They had carted off primarily the elite members of Hebrew society, along with professionals and artisans, in an effort to decapitate Jewish society and render it more pliant. The numbers involved were small. The population of Judah before the Exile had been perhaps as low as thirty thousand, one-quarter of whom were sent into captivity. Certainly that was enough to end Judean life as it had existed. The economy of the fifty-year Persian era declined to mere subsistence level; effective government ended and was replaced by Persian overseers whose chief interest was the collection of tribute. The biblical book of Lamentations vividly depicts the despair felt by the people who interpreted Judah's fall as a sign of God's rejection of them:

> The Lord has laid waste without pity
> All the habitations of Jacob;
> He has razed in His anger
> Fair Judah's strongholds.
> He has brought low in dishonor
> The kingdom and its leaders.
> In blazing anger He has cut down
> All the might of Israel;
> He has withdrawn His right hand
> In the presence of the foe;
> He has ravaged Jacob like flaming fire,
> Consuming on all sides. (Lamentations 2.2–3)

Adding to the biblical portrayal of misery, many Hebrews decided to abandon the YHWH cult altogether and assimilated into the culture and religion of their captors. Jeremiah, who was among the Hebrews deported to Egypt, prophesied YHWH's further wrath upon the apostates who gave themselves over to foreign gods:

> And now, thus said the LORD, the God of hosts, the God of Israel: "Why are you doing such great harm to yourselves, so that every man and woman, child and infant of yours shall be cut off from the midst of Judah, and no remnant shall be left of you? For you vex me by your deeds, making offerings to other gods in the land of Egypt where you have come to sojourn, so that you shall be cut off and become a curse and a mockery among all the nations of earth. . . . I am going to set my face against you for punishment, to cut off all of Judah. I will take the remnant of Judah

who turned their faces toward the land of Egypt, to go and sojourn there, and they shall be utterly consumed in the land of Egypt. They shall fall by the sword, they shall be consumed by famine; great and small alike shall die by the sword and by famine, and they shall become an execration and a desolation, a curse and a mockery. I will punish those who live in the land of Egypt as I punished Jerusalem, with the sword, with famine, and with pestilence. Of the remnant of Judah who came to sojourn here in the land of Egypt, no survivor or fugitive shall be left to return to the land of Judah. Though they all long to return and dwell there, none shall return except [a few] survivors." (Jeremiah 44.7–8, 11–14)

Few of the Jews who had remained behind in Judah welcomed the idea of reinstalling the old hierarchy, so relations between the population and the returnees remained tense. The elites, widely suspected of collusion with the Persian over-lords, made matters worse by referring to themselves as the "children of the Exile" while dismissing the rest of the population as the "people of the land." Intention-ally or not, the Temple faction, with Ezra and Nehemiah its leaders, implied that they alone were the true bearers of Jewish tradition. Economic factors played a role in this conflict too. Many of the returnees had put up their old properties as collateral for loans: they needed cash to recapitalize their business concerns. When some of those concerns failed, their property was often seized.

With so much at stake, it hardly comes as a surprise that a great amount of recording, revising, expanding, editing, and reinterpreting of the scriptures took place in this era. The Jews of the 6th and 5th centuries BCE were in a crucible of intense political and economic heat that compounded and aggravated the painful struggle to define Jewish identity. YHWH was proving to be a harsh taskmaster, and his people were learning that to be chosen was not necessarily to win.

SECOND TEMPLE JUDAISM

Inspired by their prophets, the Jews rebuilt their Temple in about twenty years; the new building was dedicated around 515 BCE. Tested by exile and enslave-ment, and purified by their prophets, the Jews were determined to reestablish their authority over the Holy Land that had been promised them by YHWH and to maintain themselves as a people set apart. An inscription from the new Temple (a fragment now on display in the Istanbul Archeological Museum) reads, "Let no foreigner pass beyond the balustrade that surrounds the sanctuary and its court-yard. Any [foreigner] who is caught doing so shall have only himself to blame for [his] death that will surely follow." Conflicts over Jewish identity persisted for centuries, however. The traces of these conflicts are evident in the numerous

The "Wailing Wall"   The Western Wall in Jerusalem is the holiest of Jewish sites, sacred because it is a remnant of the retaining wall that once enclosed and supported the Second Temple. European observers named it the "Wailing Wall" because for centuries Jews have gathered here to lament the loss of their Temple.

efforts to expand, rewrite, and edit the canon of holy books that had sustained the people through the centuries.

The Jews entered the fourth century BCE engaged in intense debate about their communal identity. The two principal factions—the "children of the Exile" and the "people of the land"— soon divided into a multiplicity of sects, distinguished by doctrinal divisions, tribal and political loyalties, class distinctions, and linguistic identities. Opposing notions of political overlordship played a role, too. The Hellenistic kingdoms of Ptolemaic Egypt and Seleucid Asia (discussed in chapter 5) both claimed jurisdiction over Judea until 198 BCE, forcing the multiple Jewish factions to perform a careful balancing act between the two foreign powers.[6] Judea held no interest for either power, so long as the Jews paid the taxes levied upon them. Yet the rival imperial claims on the land led to the development of large Jewish communities within both Egypt and Anatolia.

In Alexandria alone, as many as fifty thousand Jews resided. These Jews retained their religious identity but became so assimilated into Hellenistic culture that by around 260 BCE they needed to have the Bible translated into Greek, since they no longer understood Hebrew sufficiently. According to a text known as the *Letter of Aristeas*, a group of seventy-two biblical scholars gathered in Alexandria and carried out the task, thus producing the version of scripture called the Septuagint (that being the Latin word for "seventy"). The *Letter of Aristeas* further reports, delightfully, that the seventy-two translators miraculously spoke as

---

6   The parade of similar-sounding (and imprecise) place-names can be confusing. The *Holy Land* or the *Land of Israel* consists of the territory believed by the ancient Hebrews to have been given them by YHWH. The specific borders of this territory, however, are unclear since the various biblical passages that describe them are inconsistent. The term *Kingdom of Israel* denotes both the kingdom established under King David and passed on to his son King Solomon, and the smaller northern splinter kingdom that resulted from the splitting of the Davidic–Solomonic realm into two states. The southern state that resulted from the split is the *Kingdom of Judah*, and *Judah* (minus the *Kingdom of* portion) is likewise the name given to the restored realm after the Hebrews' return from Babylonian enslavement. *Judea*, by contrast, is the name used by the Greeks for the kingdom of Judah after it had been made into a province of Alexander the Great's empire. When the Roman Empire supplanted the Greeks, they retained the name *Judea* for the now-Roman province. In the ancient world the word *Palestine* was a geographical term only; it denoted an area, but not a specific state or institutional province.

Inscription from the Ruins of the Second Temple   Written in Greek, the inscription
(preserved here in a plastic cast) stood outside the outermost wall of the Temple grounds.
It states that only Jews may enter the Temple precinct itself. Non-Jews found within the walls
potentially faced the penalty of death.

one throughout the entire project, agreeing on each and every word of the
translation. Aristeas was a Greek-speaking Jewish historian who lived roughly
one hundred years after the Septuagint was completed.

Jewish Hellenization involved more than adoption of the Greek language.
A partial religious **syncretism**, or union of doctrines, occurred as well, as Judaism *Influence of*
made contact with and adopted certain characteristics of the dominant Zoroastrian *Zoroastrianism*
faith. This is most apparent in the development of an apocalyptic tradition (with
its tenets regarding the approach of a messiah) within mainstream Judaism and
among some lesser strands such as the Gnostic sects. YHWH's justice shall come
upon earth, scatter and destroy His enemies, and reward faithful Israel:

> Behold the LORD Himself
> Comes from afar
> In blazing wrath,
> With a heavy burden—
> His lips full of fury,
> His tongue like devouring fire,
> And His breath like a raging torrent
> Reaching halfway up the neck—
> To set a misguiding yoke upon nations

> And make a misleading bridle upon the jaws of peoples,
> For you, there shall be singing
> As on a night when a festival is hallowed;
> There shall be rejoicing as when they march
> With flute, with timbrels, and with lyres
> To the Rock of Israel on the Mount of the LORD.
> For the LORD will make His majestic voice heard
> And display the sweep of His arm
> In raging wrath,
> In a devouring blaze of fire,
> In tempest, and rainstorm, and hailstones. (Isaiah 30.27–30)

Some of the intense moralism of Zoroastrianism can be detected in a passage like this, showing the two faiths as complementary. Persian generosity had allowed the Jews to return to the homeland, and Persian money had even financed the start of the construction of the new Temple. If the Persians' faith had injected a note of moral earnestness in Judaism, the Jews' faith had inspired a concern for justice for all peoples in Zoroastrianism. After such cross-fertilization, and having endured so many travails, the Jews of the Second Temple era had learned an important lesson: to expect more trouble.

◆

Judaism's genius for reinvention helped it to survive tumultuous changes in its social and political fortunes. Whatever their earliest origins, the Hebrews had entered Palestine with a developing understanding of their uniqueness. Rare monotheists in an overwhelmingly polytheistic world, they sustained a faith in their responsibility to God and in their exclusive rights to a particular homeland. Its dissolution and loss were only the first of many catastrophes that prompted them to reengage with their tradition, to reinterpret their past and present lives, and to chart new paths for their future.

WHO, WHAT, WHERE

Ark of the Covenant	Documentary Hypothesis	rabbi
Babylonian Captivity	Israel	Solomon
covenant	Judah	syncretism
David	judges	Tanakh
Diaspora	prophets	Torah
		YHWH

SUGGESTED READINGS

Primary Sources

Berlin, Adele, and Marc Zvi Brettler, eds. *The Jewish Study Bible: Jewish Publication Society Tanakh Translation* (2004).

Friedman, Richard Elliott. *The Bible with Sources Revealed: A New View into the Five Books of Moses* (2005).

Anthologies

Arnold, Bill T., and Bryan E. Beyer, eds. *Readings from the Ancient Near East: Primary Sources for Old Testament Study* (2002).

Hallo, William W., ed. *The Context of Scripture* (2002).

Studies

Bartor, Assnat. *Reading Law as Narrative: A Study in the Casuistic Laws of the Pentateuch* (2010).

Esler, Philip F. *Ancient Israel: The Old Testament in Its Social Context* (2006).

Finkelstein, Israel, and Neil Asher Silberman. *The Bible Unearthed: Archaeology's New Vision of Ancient Israel and the Origin of Its Sacred Texts* (2002).

Finkelstein, Israel, and Neil Asher Silberman. *David and Solomon: In Search of the Bible's Sacred Kings and the Roots of the Western Tradition* (2007).

Flusser, David. *Judaism of the Second Temple Period.* Vol. 1, *Qumran and Apocalypticism* (2007).

Flusser, David. *Judaism of the Second Temple Period.* Vol. 2, *The Jewish Sages and Their Literature* (2009).

Golden, Jonathan M. *Ancient Canaan and Israel: An Introduction* (2004).

Halpern, Baruch. *The First Historians: The Hebrew Bible and History* (2003).

Hays, J. Daniel, and Tremper Longman. *The Message of the Prophets: A Survey of the Prophetic and Apocalyptic Books of the Old Testament* (2010).

Hendel, Ronald. *Remembering Abraham: Culture, Memory, and History in the Hebrew Bible* (2005).

King, Philip J., and Lawrence E. Stager. *Life in Biblical Israel* (2002).

Liverani, Mario. *Israel's History and the History of Israel* (2007).

Pardes, Ilana. *The Biography of Ancient Israel: National Narratives in the Bible* (2002).

Person, Raymond F., Jr. *The Deuteronomic History and the Book of Chronicles: Scribal Works in an Oral World* (2010).

Schiffman, Lawrence H. *Qumran and Jerusalem: Studies in the Dead Sea Scrolls and the History of Judaism* (2010).

Schiffman, Lawrence H. *Understanding Second Temple and Rabbinic Judaism* (2003).

Smith, Mark S. *The Memoirs of God: History, Memory, and the Experience of the Divine in Ancient Israel* (2004).

Stavrakopoulou, Francesca, and John Barton. *Religious Diversity in Ancient Israel and Judah* (2010).

Van der Toorn, Karel. *Scribal Culture and the Making of the Hebrew Bible* (2009).

Vaughn, Andrew G., and Ann E. Killebrew. *Jerusalem in Bible and Archeology: The First Temple Period* (2003).

Weinfeld, Moshe. *Normative and Sectarian Judaism in the Second Temple Period* (2010).

Weinfeld, Moshe. *The Place of the Law in the Religion of Ancient Israel* (2004).

For additional resources, including maps, primary sources, visuals, web links, and quizzes, please go to **www.oup.com/us/backman.**

CHAPTER 4

Greeks and Persians

2000–479 BCE

Origin myths are rarely pretty. According to the ancient Greeks, the cosmos began with primordial Chaos, out of which emerged the elemental forces of Gaia (Earth), Eros (Love), Tartarus (Abyss), and Erebus (Darkness). Earth brought forth

GREECE AND PERSIA

Uranus (Sky)—which is when the trouble began. Uranus took his own mother, Gaia, as his wife, and they produced the twelve Titans.

One of these giants, Kronos, castrated his father, overthrew his mother, and took up lordship of the heavens, subjecting his Titanic brothers and sisters to his rule, except for his sister Rhea (Fertility), whom he took as his queen. Fearing that one of his children might do to him what he had done to his own father, Kronos took each child that Rhea produced and ate it. Rhea, we are told, disliked this, so she hid the next child who came along—Zeus, the god of Thunder—and gave Kronos a stone wrapped in a blanket to eat instead. When Zeus grew to manhood, he drugged his father with a potion that made him vomit all

Koure Starting in the Archaic Age, Greek sculptors popularized the use of figures called *kouros* ("youth") and *koure* ("maiden"). The purpose of the statues is still debated, though the frequent discovery of them in temples dedicated to Apollo suggest worship of the Greek sun god. Male kouroi are usually nude, beardless, and standing erect in a posture reminiscent of Egyptian statuary. This statue of a *koure* dates from about 550 BCE and was used to mark the grave of the woman who modeled for it. The artist's inscription at the base gives her name, Phrasikleia. It reads: "The grave marker of Phrasikleia. I shall be called a maiden *[koure]* forever, since the gods allotted me this identity instead of a marriage. Aristion of Paros carved me."

the children he had eaten. Zeus then rallied his revived siblings to join him in killing Kronos and seizing control of heaven.

All this is just the beginning of the story. Greek mythology consists of hundreds of tales regarding the great Olympian deities (Zeus and his siblings, who lived on the mythical Mount Olympus), demigods, and heroes, whose adventures display astonishing creative power and vitality. Themes of incest, patricide, and rebellion occur with unnerving frequency. Like some of their Near Eastern peers, Greek gods and goddesses can be petulant, vain, and full of self-importance, but they also embody virtues of honor, justice, and love. They do not always act admirably, but they do not act without reason. If anything, the myths portray life as an intricate web of passionate feeling and reaction. Each myth leads into and influences the next. A spurned wife here emerges as a wrathful lover there. A proud king in one story becomes the humbled fallen in another. Greek mythology presents a universe of emotion, ambition, and a search for justice—but it also portrays, often with horrifying effect, the unexpected consequences of every action. Life began with Chaos, as the Greeks saw it, and it usually ends in tragedy.

THE FIRST GREEKS

Ancestors of the Greeks had moved into the mainland region of Greece by perhaps 8000 BCE, but the first culture definitely identified as Greek (because of its Indo-European language) arose only around 1600 BCE. We know these people as

CHAPTER TIMELINE

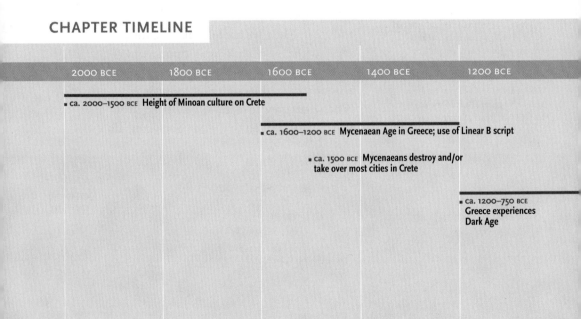

2000 BCE	1800 BCE	1600 BCE	1400 BCE	1200 BCE

ca. 2000–1500 BCE **Height of Minoan culture on Crete**

ca. 1600–1200 BCE **Mycenaean Age in Greece; use of Linear B script**

ca. 1500 BCE **Mycenaeans destroy and/or take over most cities in Crete**

ca. 1200–750 BCE **Greece experiences Dark Age**

the Mycenaeans, a name derived from the hilltop site of Mycenae. Although the Mycenaean settlers may have been of diverse origins, they quickly developed a sense of cultural unity and began to refer to themselves by another name—as a single people, the Hellenes (Greeks). They inhabited a larger territory than the Greek mainland itself. In ancient times, the term for Greece meant the rough circle of land consisting of the Greek peninsula to the west, the coasts of Macedonia and Thrace to the north, coastal Anatolia to the east, and the island of Crete to the south, plus the scores of smaller islands throughout the Aegean Sea (see Map 4.1). The climate is magnificent, with year-round sun and modest rainfall, but the land itself is harsh. Greece proper has a wild, jagged coastline with few harbors broad and deep enough for mooring large vessels. Inland the countryside is mountainous and irregular: less than 20 percent of the land is arable. The land was covered with forests in the Neolithic Age, but by the time the Mycenaeans arrived most of the trees had long since disappeared. Complicating matters, mineral ores were scarce, rivers even scarcer, and the waters of the Aegean Sea not particularly well stocked with fish.

What made the Aegean rim so attractive was the sea: sailing through the calm waters was easy at any time of the year. Distances were short, and the sheer abundance of islands meant that one never risked getting lost. (Ancient mariners navigated more by landmarks than by the stars.) Hundreds of coastal communities could thus be in constant contact with one another. The Hellenes may have settled in a vast sprawl of isolated sites, but by devoting themselves to trade they

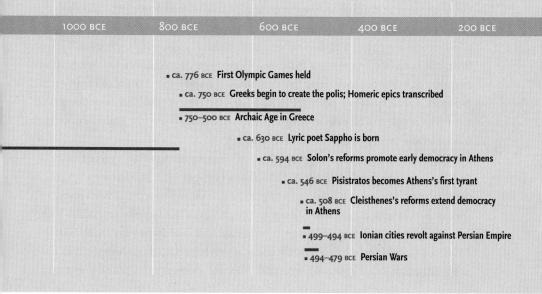

1000 BCE	800 BCE	600 BCE	400 BCE	200 BCE

- ca. 776 BCE **First Olympic Games held**
- ca. 750 BCE **Greeks begin to create the polis; Homeric epics transcribed**
- 750–500 BCE **Archaic Age in Greece**
- ca. 630 BCE **Lyric poet Sappho is born**
- ca. 594 BCE **Solon's reforms promote early democracy in Athens**
- ca. 546 BCE **Pisistratos becomes Athens's first tyrant**
- ca. 508 BCE **Cleisthenes's reforms extend democracy in Athens**
- 499–494 BCE **Ionian cities revolt against Persian Empire**
- 494–479 BCE **Persian Wars**

MAP 4.1   Minoan and Mycenean Greece, ca. 1500 BCE   With a dearth of natural resources to support manufacturing, and with only one-tenth of its land suitable for agriculture, Greece became a distributive economy. Its position in the eastern Mediterranean (especially with its links to Crete) gave it an advantage in transporting goods throughout the eastern sea basin.

could prosper. Although they were generally able to feed and clothe themselves, the ancient Greeks never developed much of a manufacturing base; they shipped goods from one site to another rather than producing goods of their own. Transport, not industry, made their fortunes. Their high degree of contact with other cultures meant more than an active economy; it also exposed them to ideas, technologies, value systems, political institutions, artistic styles, and religious practices. The result was an exhilarating cultural adaptivity—a willingness to criticize old ideas and to experiment with new ones.

Minoan Culture

The first signs of Aegean prosperity and creative energy emerged in Crete. In 1899 a British archeologist, Sir Arthur Evans (1851–1941), unearthed a magnificent palace complex at Knossos—with three stories and nearly thirteen hundred rooms. Evans mistakenly identified it as the palace of the Greeks' legendary king Minos and gave the name Minoan to a culture that had its heyday from 2000 to 1500 BCE (see Map 4.1). Subsequent excavations have found numerous other palaces, although none quite so splendid. Vibrant decoration—murals, statuary,

Palace at Knossos The palace complex on Crete was brightly colored, with scenes of real and imaginary creatures, people, flowers, rocks, and geometric patterns. Shown here is a school of dolphins (common to the Mediterranean) decorating a wall of what scholars surmise to be the queen's private room.

frescos, tiling, pottery, textiles, and metalwork—characterized them all, which suggests that Minoan wealth was widely spread. Moreover, none of the palaces had fortifications of any kind, which likely means that naval defenses were sufficient to keep marauders away. Homes of town dwellers have been found, too—more modest, but still more attractive and comfortable than common urban homes in Middle Kingdom Egypt or Hittite Anatolia. Minoan ships carried tons of Egyptian wheat, Greek olive oil and wine, Palestinian metalwork, Anatolian textiles, and Babylonian spices.

Like the other great commercial cultures of ancient times, the Minoans invented a system of writing to keep records of their activities. Two distinct scripts have survived, which are known as **Linear A** (in use by 1800 BCE) and **Linear B** (which appeared about three hundred years later, after the island was overrun by the Mycenaean Greeks). Linear A remains a mystery, although most scholars agree that the language it records is not Indo-European. Linear B, however, records an early form of Greek. Apparently the trader culture on Crete predated the arrival of the Mycenaeans, and the success of that earlier culture may have been what attracted them into the Aegean in the first place. Numerous legends, after all, describe the ancient Greeks' enduring fascination with Minoan life and magnificence. The stories about the Greek hero Theseus are among the best known. Theseus, a prince from the city of Athens, traveled to Crete to pay tribute to King

The Phaistos Disk This disk was found in 1908 by archeologists working at the Minoan palace of Phaistos on the island of Crete. Nearly six inches in diameter, it has a spiral of various symbols stamped into the clay on each side. All efforts to decipher the code have failed, leading some historians to suggest that the disk is a hoax. Others argue that it is a calendar, an astronomical chart, or even a game board.

Minos, who sent the hero into his famed Labyrinth, built to hold the monstrous Minotaur (a freakish beast created when Minos's lecherous wife mated with a bull). Theseus, keen to prove his heroism, finds the Minotaur, slays it, and retraces his path out of the maze and into the arms of Minos's daughter. Legend also has it that the god Zeus, seeking to evade his cannibalistic father, went to Crete and hid inside another labyrinth until he was ready to rebel against Kronos.

Minoan Crete taught the Mycenaeans seafaring, commerce, writing, and the rudiments of government. In short, the Minoans deeply influenced ancient Greek culture. By 1400 BCE, however, disaster struck Crete. Whether it was an invasion or a natural calamity like an earthquake, the island was devastated, and the Minoans' vibrant culture and economy—now in the hands of the Hellenes—began to fade.

The Mycenaean Age

The Hellenes living on the Greek mainland then began to dominate the Aegean. The years from roughly 1600 to 1200 BCE are known as the Mycenaean Age, after the city of Mycenae, which according to tradition was ruled by the legendary king Agamemnon. Like their mythical king, the Mycenaeans were haughty and militaristic.[1] What kept them from becoming a powerful empire was their internal division. The Greek mainland consists of hundreds of highland valleys and plains separated by irregular mountains and deep gorges; by controlling a handful of mountain passes, a tribal leader could effectively seal off an entire plateau area and create an autonomous, if isolated, miniature kingdom for himself. Once in control, these leaders governed through a tightly centralized royal court made up of military officers and bureaucrats, who lived and worked in enormous citadel-palaces constructed from large stone blocks. Common peasants, nominally free but little better off because of it, and slave teams worked the land and tended the herds.

---

[1] Archeological records are fairly abundant for parts of Mycenaean history. A wealthy (and somewhat shady) businessman and amateur archeologist from Germany named Heinrich Schliemann (1822–1890) dedicated three decades to the search for the palace of King Agamemnon and the ancient city of Troy. His methods were not exactly state-of-the-art (he liked to use dynamite), but he did unearth the cities of Mycenae in Greece and Troy in Anatolia. He built himself a mansion in Athens, where he kept much of his stolen booty; the building is today a museum. So great was his passion for the Mycenaeans that he named his son and daughter (by his second wife) Agamemnon and Andromache, and he "baptized" them by placing a copy of Homer's *Iliad* on each child's head while reciting from memory one hundred lines from the text. Agamemnon Schliemann (1878–1954) in adulthood became the Greek ambassador to the United States.

Peasant women wove fabric, minded children, and prepared food. Handfuls of artisans engaged in leatherwork, winemaking, and metalsmithing.

Virtually all of the surviving Linear B tablets consist of supply lists for the kings' armies. They detail grain rations, wine allowances, clothing, and armor allotments. Larger kingdoms engaged in mass manufacture. The palace at Pylos, for example, maintained more than four hundred bronzesmiths on site. Since this number of smiths would produce vastly more armor and weapons than their king needed, it seems clear that Mycenaean Pylos specialized as an arms manufacturer.

The intense competition for raw materials, markets, and control of trade routes kept the Mycenaeans in more or less constant conflict with one another—which, in turn, validated their militarism. A king kept his position of dominance by acquiring the things his people needed, which he did by trade when possible but by force when necessary. Royal tombs, shaped like inverted beehives, dotted the landscape, and they and the royal palaces were veritable display-houses of weaponry and armor, all surrounded by wall drawings of war scenes and the slaughtering of captives.

Little is known of Mycenaean religion. Various texts mention the names of several gods—most notably Zeus, Poseidon (the god of the sea), and Demeter (the goddess of grain). Since the Mycenaeans built no temples, which might have left some record of their activities, however, we know nothing about communal religious life, or indeed whether any existed at all. Homes had individual shrines within them, either for the worship of ancestors or for petitioning the few gods whose names have survived. Yet no prayers or inscriptions survive to describe the content of their faith. The beehive tombs and their militaristic contents tell us more about Mycenaean life than any afterlife they might have believed in.

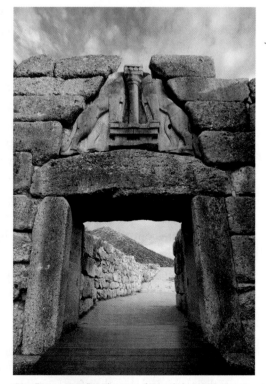

The "Lion Gate" This gate formed the main entrance to the citadel at Mycenae and is the only surviving piece of monumental architecture from the Mycenaean age. The lionesses carved at the top symbolize the power of the Mycenaean kings and may also represent the goddess Hera. The gate was constructed in the 13th century BCE.

THE SEARCH FOR MYTHIC ANCESTORS IN ARCHAIC AGE GREECE

The later Greeks insisted on claiming the Mycenaeans as their ancestors, ascribing to them the epic adventures of their mythical heroes. When the poet or poets known as **Homer** composed the *Iliad* and the *Odyssey*, sometime around 750 BCE, he chose a subject set in Mycenaean times—the events of the Trojan War. In reality, the war, named for Troy, an important trading city in northwestern Asia Minor, was one of many struggles by the newcomer Greeks to seize part of the Aegean rim, but in Homer's reimagining, the tale becomes one of Greek honor and military destiny. Paris, son of King Priam of Troy, has been appointed the judge of a beauty contest among three goddesses. Each goddess bribes Paris, who ultimately selects the goddess (Aphrodite) who offers him the most beautiful mortal woman on earth. That woman is Helen, wife of King Menelaus of Sparta (also brother of Agamemnon), who is promptly delivered to Troy as Paris's prize. The war then begins when all the Mycenaean kings join forces to avenge the injury done to Menelaus's honor. Homer assuredly based his epic on ancient oral traditions, but the *Iliad* can hardly be taken to represent Mycenaean culture accurately. If anything, it describes aspects of the era known as Greece's "Dark Age" (ca. 1200–750 BCE), which separated Homer's world from Agamemnon's. But telling tales of Mycenaean heroes, powerful rulers, and their origins in a murky distant era of violently contending gods gave the Greeks a sense of rootedness. It tied them to their new Aegean home and helped them to make sense out of the chaos of their lives.

The Aegean Dark Age

The Mycenaean age ended abruptly with the invasion, around 1200 BCE, of one or more of the unidentified Indo-European groups who caused so much damage in Egypt and the Levant, as we saw in chapter 2. The newcomers spoke a dialect of early Greek and may well have been present already in the Aegean rim for some time. The Mycenaeans had thrown up a considerable number of new fortifications (and reinforced existing ones) around 1250 BCE, which suggests they saw trouble coming. But the invaders, by themselves, could hardly have brought about the decline of the Mycenaeans and the start of Greece's Dark Age, because the calamity that hit the ancient Mediterranean and Near East proved so monumental that it must have resulted from other factors as well—whether plague, famine, civil strife, emigration, or a combination of them all.

A single, astonishing fact drives the point home: between 1200 and 800 BCE Greece lost 90 percent of its population. The agrarian peasants in Greece were the least well-off farmers of the ancient Mediterranean and Near East, given the harshness of their land, and were therefore least able to survive the catastrophe. The town dwellers of the Aegean cities were in a better position, but once the demographic hemorrhage interrupted the trade cycle, there was little they could do to compensate. Hence everyone presumably fled or was cut down by war, famine, or disease before they could flee. By the time the Dark Age ended, around 750 BCE, the Greeks had not only declined dramatically in numbers but also shifted tenancy. A majority of those who survived had moved from the inland plateaus to the coastal towns, where they attempted to take up new trades. The days of isolated rural kingdoms were over.

And that is precisely what Homer mourns in the *Iliad* and *Odyssey*. These epic poems, like all great art, work on many levels; on the political level, they are con- *Homer* servative, romanticized nostalgia, another instance of lament for a lost, idealized *and the* past. The *Iliad*'s heroes are all kings, and the conflicts dramatized by the poem *Heroic* center on the issue of the honor due to them. In an early scene in the *Iliad*, as the *Tradition* Greeks take the field to prepare for yet another battle, Priam leads Helen to the ramparts that surround Troy so that she can identify the Greek leaders for him:

> "Come, Helen," said Priam, "and tell me who is that great and powerful
> man over there? Others are taller than he, but never have I seen a warrior
> more finely formed, more noble in bearing; surely he is a king."
> Beautiful Helen replied, . . . "That is Agamemnon, the son of Atreus,
>   the lord
> of the Argos plain, a noble ruler and dread warrior." . . .
> Then old Priam looked out again, and this time he beheld Odysseus,
>   and asked,
> "And who is that one? He is a head shorter than Atreus's son, but has
> broader shoulders and a more powerful chest. He has laid his armor and
> weapons on the ground, and strides commandingly up and down
>   the ranks
> like a burly ram keeping a flock of silver-fleeced sheep in line."
> And Helen, the heavenly beauty, answered him, "That is Odysseus,
>   the son
> of Laertes, the skillful mastermind, Ithaca-born (that raw, stony island!),
> who knows every trick and stratagem of war." (*Iliad* 3.150–220)

Thus Homer lauds the heroic age of landed kings.

The *Odyssey* treats the same theme. With the end of the Trojan War, wily Odysseus, the king of Ithaca, spends ten years struggling to get home to his devoted wife, Penelope, and his loving son, Telemachus.[2] In the meantime, his royal palace has been taken over by Penelope's suitors—young upstarts from the town who try to persuade the queen that Odysseus is dead and to choose one of them as a new husband. Hence we have the noble king's adventure, in which he proves his

---

[2]   Odysseus battles giant beasts, survives shipwrecks, is seduced by a goddess, visits the underworld, taunts the sea god Poseidon, encounters witches, and outwits one foe after another.

The Trojan Horse   This is one of the earliest representations (ca. 670 BCE) of the stratagem that supposedly ended the Trojan War. Greek soldiers hid inside the wooden sculpture that was offered as a parting gift to the victorious Trojans and emerged from it at night and opened the city gates to the entire Greek army. The story does not appear in the *Iliad* but is mentioned in the *Odyssey*. In this image, taken from an amphora (a large storage vessel for wine, oil, or water) found at Mykonos, the Greeks are shown as though peering through windows.

superiority to every challenge, and a society, Ithaca, paralyzed with self-doubt. The suitors represent the "new" society of Homer's own time—brash, pushy, and self-interested. The Ithacans ask, "When, oh when, will our king come back? Oh, if only our king were here, we would then see justice and right order restored!"

Rise of the Polis

The Dark Age obviously had its share of calamities. Still, once the demographic collapse had occurred and the migration of the survivors to the coasts had taken place, Greece was not a place of unrelenting misery. The decreased population meant that the amount of food needed to maintain it also declined, to the point where the mainland was able to feed itself unaided by imports from the Near East. Since the foodstuffs produced in Greece—grain, oil, wine, and meat—were difficult to preserve in the bright heat, the rulers of Homer's time tended to distribute surpluses among the people, thus ensuring at least an absence of famine. The upland villages and coastal towns were small enough to be self-governing, which inspired a sense of independence among the people. Identifying themselves as the sustainers of their own communal lives, they gradually coined a new word—**polis** (plural poleis)—for their communities. The polis, or Greek city-state, referred to the physical town and its agrarian hinterland, the people who resided in them, and the group identity they shared. To belong to a polis meant more than to reside in a particular locale. It meant being a constituent element of something larger than oneself, participating in a web of mutual obligations, responsibilities, and rights.

COLONISTS, HOPLITES, AND THE PATH TOWARD CITIZENSHIP

As the Homeric era gave way to the Archaic period (ca. 750–500 BCE), the poleis of Greece began to extend their reach by following the example of the Phoenicians and establishing networks of colonies. These networks extended around the Aegean rim, then into the Black Sea, and ultimately westward into the Mediterranean. With the expanded reach of the poleis came other changes as well—including a society built for war.

The colonies were not military expansions, however. The Greeks generally searched out uninhabited harbors, established small coastal settlements around them, and then opened trade relations with inland populations. Inheritance practices lay behind this growth. Greek custom dictated that a man's estate be divided by his legitimate heirs—an easy enough matter when it came to cash, flocks and herds, and portable property. But what about a man's farmland? A farm might be large enough to survive subdivision among a man's sons, but what happened to those subdivisions when the next generation came along? At a certain point (and usually an early one), the portions of land received by individual heirs could not support a family. This forced many heirs to sell their land, usually to a sibling but in theory to anyone with available funds. With the money, they would then relocate to a colony and set up anew.

Greek Colonization

The colonists, in other words, were neither military adventurers nor impoverished exiles but landholders—specifically, landholders who had cashed out their equity and were looking for new investments. Groups of these entrepreneurs would set out together from a polis in search of new settlement. Personal connections and a sense of shared identity also caused them to establish commercial ties with the polis from which they had come. In this way, the Greek colonies established were not just dependencies of the home city-state, to be exploited for domestic gain. Rather, they took on the character of smaller reproductions of the home city. They were independent and self-governing, yet united in identity with the original polis.

Between 750 and 500 BCE, the Greeks established hundreds of colonies around the Mediterranean and Near East (see Map 4.2). A handful of colonies appeared along the North African coast as well.[3] This explosive growth coincided

---

[3] There were two types of colonies: *apoidikiai* and *empora*; the first were self-governing, and the second were governed from the mainland as trading outposts.

MAP 4.2   Greek and Phoenician Colonies, ca. 500 BCE   Between them, the Greeks and Phoenicians established colonies around the perimeters of both the Mediterranean and the Black seas.

almost exactly with the collapse of Israel under the Assyrians (ca. 722 BCE) and the conquest of Judah by the neo-Babylonians (ca. 587 BCE). And for a reason: the turmoil in the Holy Land interrupted the commercial activity of the Phoenicians, who had previously been the main actors on the sea-lanes. The Greeks thus had few competitors for control of the sea-lanes, and certainly none with the geographical advantages they had. Because of the opportunities abroad, most Greek cities maintained fairly stable population levels in the Archaic period, and many colonies outstripped their home cities in size.

The colonists actively sought out contact with their neighboring or host populations, but were careful not to assimilate. Ethnic pride forbade that—because the Greeks, like many ancient cultures, regarded themselves as superior to other peoples, whom they called "barbarians," peoples whose speech, to Greek ears, sounded like nonsense ("bar-bar-bar"). Moreover, the ease and speed of contact with the mainland kept the colonists' cultural identity as Greeks strong. **Panhellenic** ("all-Greek") religious festivals and competitions like the Olympic Games (the first of which took place in 776 BCE) helped to keep the scattered Greek colonists in close contact with one another.[4] But because the overseas

---

4   Several mythical tales give different stories behind the start of the Games. Most likely, they began as annual foot-races of girls to determine who would become that year's priestess of the goddess Hera at a sacred site outside the town of Olympia. The idea of regular competitions among male athletes soon won out. The Panhellenic Games consisted of four separate tournaments (held in sequence, one per year)— the Olympic, Isthmian, Nemean, and Pythian Games. The Olympic Games were held in the highest regard. By 720 BCE, if not earlier, the tradition had developed of staging all athletic contests in the nude. The Games continued until 394 CE, when the Roman emperor Theodosius I, a Christian, banned all pagan religious festivals.

Greeks encouraged contact with their non-Greek neighbors, a steady exposure to new ideas, technologies, and practices helped promote innovation. It is no accident that many of ancient Greece's greatest thinkers and artists came from the colonies rather than the mainland.

One did not have to be a prominent merchant, civic official, or intellectual to serve one's polis. During the Archaic Age, the effective defense of a polis increasingly required a standing militia. Accordingly, every male between the ages of eighteen and sixty served in the polis's military force. The use of trained infantry did not originate with the Greeks, but with the Assyrians—although there is no clear evidence that the Greeks learned the technique from them. Earlier military strategy, if it can be called that, consisted of mass swarmings of foot soldiers under the leadership of chariot-riding kings or generals. Once the battle lines were drawn up, the fighting quickly devolved into a free-for-all. The Greeks, however, perfected fighting in trained units. What they came up with was the notion of groups of foot soldiers holding tight formation as a block, eight horizontal lines of ten to twenty men each, who stood shoulder to shoulder and moved as a single unit. Called a **phalanx**, such a unit rushed at the enemy and smashed through them, like a kind of foot-powered armored tank. Each of these soldiers, known as **hoplites**, wore a breastplate and helmet, had a short sword at his belt, and carried a round shield and a thrusting spear. By combining their weight and momentum, they made up a powerful force.[5]

The Hoplite Army

It required long hours of training to develop an effective phalanx because each soldier had to overcome the instinct to fend for himself by thrusting his spear or stabbing his sword at everything that moved. Instead, the hoplites had to hold formation and fight as a single unit. This had two important consequences. First, since all men fought in their polis's army, all had to attain a degree of physical conditioning—and hence the Greek emphasis on exercise. Athletic competitions (such as the Olympics), public training facilities, sporting events, and the like all played important roles in Archaic Age culture, a fact we can see in the artwork of the time. Greek painting, sculpture, and poetry emphasize the beauty of a fit male physique more so than any other ancient culture. To be fit and strong, the Greeks believed, was more than to be beautiful: it was freedom itself. Second, the hoplite army underscored and confirmed the interdependence of the polis. It was the body politic, the community that literally stood together as one or perished. A phalanx was living proof that people are stronger together than apart.

And this led to trouble. The more the Greek cities relied on the new armies, the more important the commoners who made up their ranks became. These

---

[5]   The name for these soldiers, *hoplites*, derives from the shields they carried.

Hoplites (left)   This Greek vase painting from around 650 BCE is the earliest known depiction of hoplites fighting in phalanx formation. The phalanx's discipline and group-mindedness are evident here in the uniformly faceless soldiers, the perfect alignment of their marching feet, and the parallel lines formed by their spears.

Athletes (right)   Scenes of wrestling, boxing, and racing were common decorations on Greek vases in the Archaic Age. As shown here, athletic contests were performed in the nude, the better to appreciate the beauty of the human form.

Challenges to the Social Order   soldiers paid for their own equipment and took battlefield instructions from one another through a combination of verbal and manual signals. The aristocrats who made up the charioted officer class declined in importance accordingly, which had important repercussions for political life. A city that depends on its common men for survival cannot long deny them political power. This is why the Archaic Age was filled with social strife—and why Homer's great epics are politically significant. Under pressure from hoplites, colonists, merchants, and workers, the stratified society ruled by noble kings and aristocratic heroes was giving way to a nascent egalitarian order.

A CULT OF MASCULINITY

Archaic Greece developed a cult of masculinity that distinguished it from other ancient cultures. Their's was a society built for war, in which every able-bodied man eighteen to sixty was expected to serve in the hoplite army. Girls received little or no education and were raised with the idea that their sole function in life was to marry, produce children, and care for their household. At marriage a young woman became the legal dependent of her husband, having the same (and no more) rights as the children she would produce. Apart from going to the market or the public well, visiting family members, and attending funerals and a handful of religious ceremonies, women seldom appeared alone in public. Doing so would bring shame on the household and give the father or husband leave to punish her severely. Most homes in fact were physically divided into male and female zones, often with the female rooms enclosed behind a locked door to which the husband kept the key.

Citizenship in a polis, like ownership of property, was hereditary and a right so precious as to inspire an obsession with legitimate birth. Maintaining a *Roles for* woman's seclusion was the best way, men determined, to ensure her chastity *Women* before marriage and fidelity within it. Female virginity was an absolute requirement for marriage, except for cases of a man wedding a widow. Before the ceremony, young brides typically offered special prayers and presented gifts at a temple to the virgin goddess Artemis; these gifts often consisted of the toys enjoyed by the bride in her girlhood. As a sexually experienced wife, she would no longer have need of them.

Marriages were arranged, and a woman's guardian would often engage her to another man's son while she was still a child. The wedding usually took place when the girl was in her early teens and the groom ten to fifteen years older. In most poleis monogamy was the rule, as was a nuclear family (parents and children living together without other relatives in the same house). Although male citizens were free to have sexual relations with slaves, prostitutes, or willing males, female citizens had no such freedom. Sex between a wife and anyone other than her husband carried harsh penalties for both parties. Street prostitutes worked in most cities, but for wealthier patrons a caste of women known as courtesans emerged as a semirespectable profession. Called *hetairai* in Greek ("companions," literally), these women were professional hostesses, usually foreigners, who offered meals and music in addition to sex. They received customers in their own residences, for the most part, but higher-priced hetairai also offered a kind of catering service, attending aristocratic symposia (drinking parties) and entertaining guests with music, dancing, and witty banter, in addition to the expected sexual couplings.

Homosexual contact was accepted, and even approved of, by society so long as *Attitudes* certain norms were followed. Generally it was a unique privilege of the aristocracy, *toward* who did not regard wives as intellectual partners. Older men took noble youths, usu- *Homo-* ally aged twelve to fifteen, under their protection, to guide them in the ways of soci- *sexuality* ety, government, and elite culture. Sexual relations were understood to be a part of this tutoring. In Sparta same-sex activity also existed, although, given Sparta's proud tradition of egalitarianism among its people, the relationships usually involved individuals of equal age. The city-state of Thebes, in the 4th century BCE, famously possessed an elite military unit composed solely of 150 pairs of lovers—the so-called

Sacred Band, which won every battle it engaged in until defeat finally came in 338 BCE at the hands of Philip of Macedonia (discussed in the next chapter).

CIVILIZED PURSUITS: LYRIC POETRY

Archaic Age aristocrats were deeply invested in the heroic ideal enshrined in the Homeric epics. But they also strove to express their unique culture in newer poetic forms like lyric and elegy—the first sung to accompaniment on a lyre, the second to the music of a flute. The range of Greek lyric is impressive, from songs in praise of war, of love, of justice, and of sensual delights to bawdy invectives against real or imagined enemies. An early poet named Tyrtaeus lived in Sparta in the 7th century BCE and composed patriotic songs:

> March forward, sons of men of Sparta,
> the land of brave men!
> With your shields in your left hands
> and your spears in your right,
> march bravely forward with no fear for your lives!
> For the fear of death is unbecoming to a Spartan.

Bacchylides, from the Aegean island of Ceos, in the 5th century BCE sang in praise of peace:

> Great gifts, Peace brings to mortals:
> Wealth; the bursting forth of sweet-sounding music;
> in bright flames atop carved altars
> choice pieces of cattle and woolly sheep roasting
> in honor of the gods; and beautiful youths keen
> for sports, and the arts, and revelry.

The two greatest lyric poets were Pindar (ca. 522–443 BCE) and Sappho (ca. 620–570 BCE). Pindar, who lived and worked in Thebes, made his name by composing odes for special occasions. Among his most popular verses were a series of odes in honor of victors in athletic contests like the Olympic Games. His poetry is notoriously difficult to translate since he delights in sophisticated meters and rhetorical flourishes.

Sappho

Sappho, however, invites translation. Her poetry depends less on technical tricks, more on acute observation and emotional directness. According to tradition she wrote some nine volumes of poetry, although only one poem survives in its entirety, a hymn to Aphrodite. Many of the surviving fragments express homoerotic love, and Sappho's homeland of the island of Lesbos has given its name to lesbianism. Here she describes her feelings at a dinner party with her beloved at the table:

> That man seems to me equal to the gods,
> the one who sits opposite you
> and listens so closely
> to your sweet voice
> and your beguiling laughter—
> oh, how the heart in my chest is stirred!
> For whenever I look at you, even for a moment,
> to speak is beyond me—not one single word;
> my tongue freezes in silence;
> a lick of flame runs beneath my skin;
> my eyes can see nothing;
> my ears hear only a din;
> a cold sweat covers me;
> my body trembles—and I sigh
> and turn greener than grass
> and think I might die.

The only surviving complete poem from Sappho, it leaves one wishing for more—the case, indeed, for most of Greek imaginative literature. As a culture that cherished physical beauty, intellectual engagement, and civic vitality, ancient Greece has never ceased to fascinate. One special element of that fascination was the Greeks' adaptive capacity—their ability and willingness to try different means to a particular end—as we see in the varieties of political and social organization they employed.

SPARTA: THE MILITARIZATION OF THE CITIZENRY

Evidence attests to roughly nine hundred poleis in the Archaic period, and about most of them we know very little. To appreciate the variety of forms political life could take in Archaic Greece, we will examine three particularly well-documented poleis. Sparta, Miletus, and Athens were the most powerful city-states of the age. And each was powerful in a different way.

Sparta boasted the most impressive military. Governed since the 7th century BCE by a council of elders known as the *gerousia* (literally, "group of old men"), it *The Helots* was a brutally efficient city—a large community in which an exceptionally sizable slave population (as much as three-quarters of the city's inhabitants) performed the labor of producing food, building homes, tending animals, weaving cloth, and doing basic craftwork. The slaves' labor freed the Spartan citizens to pursue the solitary goal of preparing for war. They did so neither to repel foreign invasion nor to seek overseas conquests of their own but simply to keep their economic foundation—the enormous state-owned slave population—in check. A revolt by these state-owned slaves, called **helots**, in the mid-7th century BCE had nearly toppled the Spartans and persuaded them to stay on their guard.

Education and Training

The militarization of the citizenry in the mid-7th century was nearly absolute and began at childbirth. City officials examined every infant born to judge whether he or she was healthy enough to keep; those who failed to pass muster were abandoned in the nearby mountains. Military training began at age seven for boys, with group exercise, marching drills, and athletic competitions, especially wrestling and javelin hurling. Girls, also starting at age seven, received group exercise and athletic training. The sexes separated at age twelve, with girls taught elementary reading and writing and domestic economy, whereas boys were handed over to live in military barracks and instructed in fighting with weapons.

A Spartan Youth   This handle from a water jug (ca. 540 BCE) depicts a young Spartan boy—identifiable by the long braids of his hair—holding the tails of two young lions.

Diets were sharply restricted—not to combat obesity, but to inspire the boys to become effective thieves. Food thieves were punished harshly for the crime of getting caught. The food they stole was from their own farms. When training began at age seven, each boy was awarded a farm by the state. This farm was run for him by helots. A hungry Spartan lad was expected to sneak from his barracks, dash to his own farm, steal his own food, and make it back without being caught or observed at either end. The idea was to acquire real-life experience of enduring the pains of hunger, of learning to move about without being seen, and of becoming self-reliant.

Boys were taught basic literacy, but the bulk of their training was military. At age twenty they began active service in the hoplite army. If they served ten straight years, they were granted full Spartan citizenship, which involved the right to speak in the assembly and to hold leadership positions in the polis. If a Spartan married while in his twenties, he still lived in his barracks—and had to sneak out at night to visit his wife. He was then punished, if he was caught, for the crime of being caught.

The superhuman rigor of Spartan training is easily overstated, and it is significant that the only detailed contemporary description of Spartan life comes from Xenophon (427–354 BCE), an Athenian who witnessed the humiliating defeat of his city by the Spartans in the Peloponnesian War (431–404 BCE), as we will see in chapter 5. He dramatizes Spartan life in his book *Hellenica* ("Greek History"), in which he narrates the failure of Athenian democracy and his own disillusionment with his city. A later work, *The Constitution of the Lacedaemonians*, written in 388 BCE, provides the colorful detail. And the better-known *Life of Lycurgus* by Plutarch (ca. 50–120 CE) draws heavily on Xenophon's treatise but adds considerable amounts of gossip and hearsay.[6] Plutarch relates a popular story in which a young Spartan, having gone off in search of food, caught a fox. On the way back to his barracks, some older Spartans came upon him in the dark. Rather than face the humiliation of being caught, the young man hid the live fox under his cloak and never gave a hint of it to the elders, even as the fox bit and clawed its way into his entrails.

Xenophon blames Athens's defeat on its lack of order and discipline, the very traits he proclaims of his adopted Sparta. All Spartan men, he insists, had the right to beat any Spartan youth for misbehavior, and the father of that youth, after learning of the beating, would beat the child again to show his solidarity with his peers. To discourage materialism and greed, he reports, Sparta forbade the use of gold and silver and instituted a new coinage made of iron—which was so valueless that it would require a wagonload of cash to make even a modest purchase. A Spartan man who was too old to satisfy his wife's sexual longings and produce children, he says, was required by law to appoint a young stud to be his wife's lover—which the elder Spartan always did with equanimity, knowing that he was doing what was best for the polis. Xenophon's description of the relentless rigor of Spartan life can hardly be believed, but it began a tradition that the Spartans were keen to propagate. It was also a tradition that the Athenians wished to elaborate, since it lessened the embarrassment of their defeat in the Peloponnesian War. Who could blame them for falling to such superhumans?

Despite such exaggerations, Sparta was a notably disciplined and austere place. Spartan life aimed at a central goal—keeping its citizens strong and resolute enough to keep the helots in place. The deadening effect on the society of this narrowness of vision might well have been the undoing of Sparta, had it not been

---

6   When the war ended, Xenophon went into voluntary exile and ultimately ended up in Sparta, where he lived for twenty years before finally returning to Athens in 366 BCE.

for a slow-gathering threat—a Persian invasion of Greece. Military dangers jus-tify military precautions and give their founders an aura of foresight. The enor-mity of the Persian danger enhanced the perceived wisdom of Sparta's military reformers and added to their reputation for superhuman fortitude.

MILETUS: THE BIRTHPLACE OF PHILOSOPHY

Miletus offered a sharp contrast to Sparta. Located on the western coast of Asia Minor, it was a commercial and cultural hub, involved equally in mainland Greek and Anatolian affairs. Miletus (modern Milet) originated in the Mycenaean period, declined during the Dark Age, and then reemerged as one of the Archaic Age's most vibrant cities. It had as many as a hundred colonies, most of these in the Black Sea region, like Sinope and Trapezus, its two most important colonies and the Turkish cities of Sinop and Trabzon today (see Map 4.2).[7]

A Cosmopolitan Crossroads   Located on a small but strategic peninsula, Miletus was one of the principal way stations for Greek goods entering Asia Minor. There was also a fair-sized harbor, although accumulating sediment from the Maeander River has since filled it, and it now lies roughly 3 miles from the sea. It was also close to the inland city of Sardis, the western terminus of the Royal Highway built by the Persians as the main thoroughfare running through the heart of their empire. This made it a natural distribution point for Persian goods throughout the eastern Mediterranean. In constant contact with the Greek, Hittite, Phoeni-cian, and Egyptian worlds in addition to the Lydian and Persian ones, Miletus was among the most cosmopolitan of cities in the 7th and 6th centuries BCE. It acquired a reputation for producing both high-quality ceramics and remark-able intellectuals—like the philosophers Thales (ca. 624–546 BCE), Anaximander (ca. 610–546 BCE), and Anaximenes (ca. 585–528 BCE) and the early historian Hecataeus (ca. 550–476 BCE).

Governed by a merchant council, the people of Miletus saw greater potential for growth in the Mediterranean than in the land trade with Persia, and so they organized the other coastal cities of Anatolia into an alliance called the **Ionian League**, a confederation of poleis pledged to support one another. This was the first such organization in the Greek world.

The First Philosophers   Miletus's greatest claim to fame, however, is as the birthplace of philosophy ("love of wisdom"). The first three true philosophers in Western history—Thales, Anaximander, and Anaximenes—all appeared there. The city's es-sence as a cultural crossroads no doubt contributed much to this development,

---

7   Miletus's colonies focused on shipping slaves, timber, and wheat from the region of southern Russia. All were in short supply in the Aegean.

although evidence of a heightened appreciation for **rationalism** is present in Greek culture going back to Mycenaean times. What Thales and his followers began was the effort to systematize the observations one draws from everyday experience. Cause and effect surround us at all times, of course, and to notice that fact does not take genius. We observe the world's workings every day: seeds buried in soil grow into plants; wood placed in fire is itself inflamed, whereas metal or stone is not; wine, when drunk, produces lightheadedness; the shadow produced by a stick placed vertically in the ground lengthens, shortens, and changes direction as the sun moves through the sky. To explain the relation of cause and effect, when discussing details of the natural word, is the realm of science. Thales and his followers, however, tried to ascertain whether all of nature follows a rational order. Is nature in fact a system? Is there a set of universal truths that hold together the material world—and if so, how can we learn them? Does human life exist within an eternal code of truths larger than anything our cultural traditions or religions teach us? This is the realm of philosophy.

Thales, the first philosopher, never wrote a word. Philosophy, he believed, is best explored in conversation. The answer to every question, after all, raises another question (at least if the answer is interesting). A written text, however, is finite and fixed and therefore cannot possibly be completely right. Anaximander, his student, disagreed on that point and wrote reams, although only a few fragments survive. Consciously or not, they and Anaximenes all began with an assumption that provides the foundation of all of modern physics—the conservation of matter. Everything came from somewhere, and since the complexity and variety of the world is obviously increasing as we move forward in time, then everything must be traceable to a single point, a single element, if we move backward through time.

What was this universal source? For Thales it was water, the primordial substance from which everything derives. Anaximander posited the existence of a single infinite ether, a malleable goo that took different forms when subjected to opposing forces of heat and cold, wetness and dryness. Anaximenes went even further and added the complicating factor of air, which affects the shape-shifting of the ether by its relative density or lightness. What is interesting about these speculations is the way they hint at a theory of evolution. If the entire physical cosmos has a common beginning, and if the world we observe is still constantly changing, then surely we ourselves came to be through a process of change in the past.[8]

Nothing quite like this had ever been attempted before. The mutability of the physical world has always been known. The Sumerians complained about it

---

[8] Anaximenes even asserted that humans must have been at one time fish.

incessantly, and the Egyptians saw it as a deviation from the stability offered by obedience to the pharaoh. The Hebrews initially regarded it as the fulfillment of YHWH's design, then later feared that he had turned his back on them and his plan. The Ionian Greeks, however, were the first to approach the mutability of the physical world as a rational problem and to test their interpretations of it with logical arguments. This was to be one of the ancient world's greatest legacies for Greater Western culture—a sense of order, a search for meaning, and a tradition of submitting one's ideas to critical inspection.

The Ionian thinkers even submitted religion to critical analysis. The boldest figure of all was Xenophanes of Colophon (ca. 570–480 BCE), who noted that deities in every culture tend to have the physical characteristics of the culture: thus Ethiopian gods and goddesses have black skin and curly hair, whereas Greek artists portray their divinities with olive skin and dark wavy hair, and the barbarians of Thrace (a region well to the north of Greece) worship deities with fair skin, reddish hair, and blue eyes. His conclusion? Humans make gods in their own image—not, as the Hebrew Bible says, the other way around. If cattle could speak, Xenophanes quips, they would pray to gods who looked like cattle. His main concern was to turn people away from the Olympian-deity cults, which he regarded as poetic nonsense, and to examine life through critical reason. Although it is impossible to know the truth with absolute certainty, the point, Xenophanes insists, is to make the effort.

Radical speculation like this declined in Ionia after the Persians conquered Lydia in 494 BCE and acquired control of Miletus, as we will see. The philosophers either fled or joined the resistance. The mode of critical thinking begun in Miletus spread quickly to the Greek mainland, however, where it took root especially in the city of Athens.

ATHENS: HOME TO DEMOCRACY

Athens is older than Jerusalem, older than Nineveh, older than Sparta or Miletus. Perhaps only Jericho, of all the cities of the Greater Western world, has a longer history of continuous human settlement. As early as 3000 BCE, Neolithic tribesmen built a fort atop the rocky hill known as the Acropolis ("high-point of the city"), and people have lived there ever since. Geography favors it: the hilltop provides a natural defensive position from which to control the nearby plains, which provide farmland and pasturage. The Eridanus River flowed through the center of the town (it has long since dried up), and the port of Piraeus lies only 6 miles away. Athens thus had ready access to natural resources and communication links but was also sufficiently isolated to enjoy natural protection. Already a leading city in Mycenaean times, Athens was able to hold out against the so-called

Sea Peoples, although it then went into the same sharp decline as the other cities of the Dark Age.

As the clouds cleared by 700 BCE, Athens stood ready to take advantage once again of its uniquely strong position, and under the leadership of the landholding aristocracy the city slowly seized control of the entire region of Attica.[9] By the mid-600s BCE, however, so many new people had been added to the roster of Athenians that they began to challenge the authority of the nobles and wealthy merchants who ran the polis as an oligarchy. The clash between the privileges of the few and the demands of the many is what would ultimately lead to the invention of Athenian democracy.

An early effort at social revolution occurred at Athens in 632 BCE, when a popular athlete named Cylon tried unsuccessfully to rouse the masses against the aristocrats. Forty years later, in 594 BCE, the city council gave extraordinary authority to a fellow aristocrat named Solon, who instituted widespread reforms to free the city from class strife. Specifically, **Solon** made all adult (male) citizens members of the Athenian Assembly—which was the group that elected the city's governing officials; he also lowered the social and financial qualifications an individual had to have before being elected to office. On the economic front, Solon permitted foreign tradesmen who settled in Athens to become citizens, so long as they brought their families with them. This maneuver helped to bring skilled craftsmen into the city and increase foreign trade. His most celebrated reform, however, was the cancellation of all agrarian debts and the manumission of all poor farmers who had fallen into debt-slavery.

Solon's Reforms

Solon's efforts ultimately failed, however, which resulted in a more populist figure named Pisistratos seizing power around 560 BCE. Pisistratos (d. 527 BCE) was Athens's first **tyrant**. The word *tyrant* carries a pejorative meaning in English, but in ancient Greek a tyrant (*tyrannos*) was simply a person who wielded power temporarily to bring about dramatic reform in a politically deadlocked state. Tyranny was thus a kind of administrative receivership. In terms of social class, the tyrants were aristocrats but were usually allied with the masses. Tyrannies seldom lasted longer than a decade or two, by which time the reasons for the tyranny had either been achieved or were deemed hopeless. In either case the tyrant lost the popular support of the hoplites, which put an end to his power.

Greek Tyranny

Tyrants were installed to reform the state and were judged good or ill according to that standard alone. The methods they employed were of less significance. Pisistratos went so far as to wound himself with a spear so that he could ride his chariot into the Athenian marketplace, blood dripping from his injury, and claim to

---

9   Athens grew by bringing smaller neighboring towns into its jurisdiction—what classical historians call *synoikismos* ("gathering together in a single home"). "Urban sprawl" works just fine.

Cleisthenes This modern bust of the founder of Athenian democracy stands in the Ohio Statehouse. Photograph © 2015 Museum of Fine Arts, Boston

have survived an assassination attempt from his rivals. All this was to whip the crowd of his supporters into a frenzy and quiet his rivals. Pisistratos ruled Athens three times, from 561 to perhaps 557 BCE, again from 556 to 555 BCE, and finally again from 546 to 527 BCE. Each time, Pisistratos saw to it that municipal offices were parceled out more equitably among the social classes, lowered taxes, and increased the number of judges to break up a backlog of criminal and civil cases. (Pisistratos also deserves credit for ordering the permanent archiving of the texts of Homer's *Iliad* and *Odyssey*.) He was succeeded in power by his two sons, Hippias and Hipparchus, who followed their father's policies, but when rivals murdered Hipparchus in 514 BCE, Hippias grew increasingly bitter, suspicious, and vindictive. He was thrown out of office in 510 BCE and eventually replaced by **Cleisthenes**, whom tradition regales as "the father of Athenian democracy."

The system as established under Cleisthenes remained more or less in place until Alexander the Great conquered Athens in 338 BCE, and it provides the model for our understanding of Athenian **democracy**.

Cleisthenes's Reforms

Cleisthenes's most important reform involved changing the political organization from a reliance on clans and clients to a new structure organized around urban precincts called *demes* (the origin of the English word *democracy*). Representatives in council thus represented whole neighborhoods rather than individual families and alliances.

The main body of the government was the citizens' Assembly (*ekklesia* in Greek), which met to consider new legislation, adjudicate trials, and set policies. As many as five to six thousand men comprised the assembly at any one time, which was obviously too cumbersome a group for any effective governance; hence most day-to-day government was performed by a smaller group called the council (*boule*). Chosen by lots and serving for only one day, the members of the council selected the leading magistrates; these were not elections in the modern sense, but an actual lottery. Elections were reserved for the positions of *strategoi*—the military commanders in charge of the citizen army. Magistracies and command positions were for one-year terms, and whereas popular strategoi could serve an unlimited number of consecutive terms, all magistrates were removed from office after a single term.

Full participatory citizenship was restricted to somewhere between 5 and 10 percent of the population: slaves, women, the working poor, and most lesser craftsmen and artisans were denied the right to vote in the assembly and to hold municipal office. The numbers come from the Athenian historian Thucydides (ca. 455–399 BCE), who reckoned the number of citizens at forty thousand. He put the number of slaves in Athens as high as 400,000 and the number of noncitizen residents at seventy thousand. Called *metics*, these resident aliens had no democratic rights and had to pay for the privilege of residing in the city.

Still, no other ancient society placed power in the hands of so many of its people. Further, the real accomplishment of the constitution lay not in the size of the electorate, but in its strict definition and supervision of the powers of civic officials. In other ancient societies, officeholders served a king or regarded their own will as the constitution. In Athens, officeholders served the city and its constitution. In the context of its time, Athens's experiment with government by (some of) the people was a rare and beautiful thing.

THE PERSIAN WARS

By the 490s BCE Sparta, not Athens, was the strongest polis in Greece, however. Most other cities of the time would have named it as their leader, if asked. As tensions rose with the advancing Persian Empire, more and more poleis turned to the Spartans for guidance. Not only was their army the strongest in Greece, but also Sparta—alone among Greek cities—did not have overseas colonies. This assured people that Sparta's leadership in a Panhellenic military force would play no favorites. Few people trusted the Athenians to be so selfless.

The Persian Wars (494–479 BCE) did not have to happen. Persia had been eager enough to conquer all of the Near East, but the empire initially showed no signs of determination, or even desire, to add Greece to its dominion. Doing so, after all, would require the Persians to develop maritime skills that they neither had nor needed. The Greeks controlled the sea-lanes throughout the eastern Mediterranean and the Black Sea. Since the Persians controlled everything else, the Greeks had no one else with whom to trade. Conquering the people would have been a waste of resources.

Revolt by the Ionian Greeks, aided by sympathetic rebels from the island of Naxos, changed all of that. The trouble started in Miletus, which had been gov- *Ionian* erned by a brief series of Persian-affiliated tyrants. The Ionian Greek colonies *Revolt* tired of sending their taxes and tribute eastward and waited only for a leader to organize them into a full-scale rebellion. The rebels' chance came when the tyrant of Miletus, Aristagoras, turned on the Persians. Apparently convinced that he had lost the emperor Darius's favor, Aristagoras roused the Milesians and the rest of Ionia to revolt against Persian rule. He gambled that the Greek mainland would come to the Ionians' assistance and that the Persians, lacking a navy, would let the Ionian colonies go. He was right and wrong in equal measure. The coastal colonies did unite in seceding from Persia, and the mainland Greeks did come to their aid. But Persia refused to let the challenge to their authority go unanswered.

Athens Takes Command

When Sparta—ever concerned over the threat to national security that the helots presented—balked at sending its troops to Miletus, the Athenians, sensing an opportunity, leaped in. In 499 BCE they led a force that sacked the Persians' provincial capital at Sardis (modern Sart). But then the Athenians declared victory and went home, leaving the Ionian cities to face the Persian emperor's wrath alone. Darius decided to teach the Athenians a lesson, and in 490 BCE he sent an army of twenty thousand to thirty thousand elite troops across the Aegean with orders to land on the mainland and to march on Athens and destroy it. The armies met on the plain at Marathon, where the Athenian phalanxes routed the Persian forces. The Greek historian Herodotus records that 6,400 Persians were killed, whereas the Athenians lost only 192. Darius, humiliated, withdrew.[10] Athens rejoiced in its victory and its new standing as the champion of all of Greece (see Map 4.3).

One of the city's leading politicians, Themistocles (ca. 524–459 BCE), advised the polis that the Persians would undoubtedly come back and that the Athenians should therefore prepare. They did so by investing in a fleet of two hundred new warships called **triremes**, thereby turning Athens into a major naval power. Invented by the Phoenicians in the 8th century BCE and introduced in Greece, according to Thucydides, in the 5th century, triremes were oared warships, with three tiers of rowers. Constructed of pine or fir, they were relatively light ships that, with a well-trained crew, could attain high speed. With a bronze-tipped hardwood prow, they were extremely effective at ramming into the hulls of opposing ships.[11]

---

[10] The Athenians took the field in a long horizontal line, hoping to appear more numerous than they were, but with their middle ranks intentionally shallow, only a few ranks deep, and their forces bulked up on either flank. When the Persians charged, the Athenian line quickly broke in the center, as planned, and the strong flanks then wheeled inward in a pincer movement and trapped the Persians between them. Herodotus's casualty numbers cannot be believed but have entered tradition. The battle later lent its name to the "Marathon" foot-race—supposedly a messenger ran the 26 miles from Marathon to Athens, bringing the news of the great Athenian victory. Herodotus mentions no such messenger but does relates the story of Pheidippides running from Athens to Sparta to ask for help. In the lead-up to the battle he ran all the way to Sparta—a distance of 150 miles—to request reinforcements, only to race back again with the news that the Spartans' arrival was going to be delayed and that the Athenians were on their own. A later writer, Lucian of Samosata (125–180 CE), was the first to describe the supposed Marathon-to-Athens run, with the melodramatic conclusion of Pheidippides crying out, "Victory is ours!" before collapsing in death.

[11] Another favorite tactic was to build up speed, approach alongside an enemy ship, withdraw the oars, and let the momentum of the trireme shear away the oars of the foe, leaving him helplessly adrift.

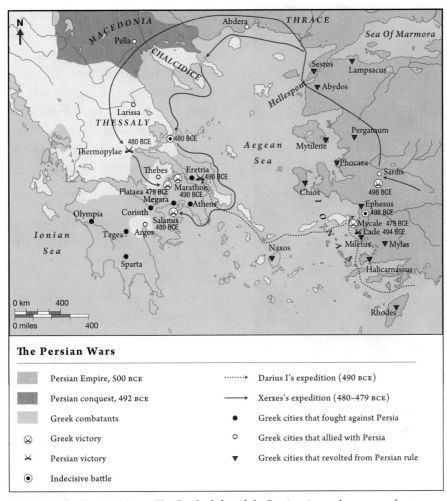

MAP 4.3 The Persian Wars The Greeks defeated the Persians in nearly every confrontation. Shown here are the most important battle sites: Marathon, Thermopylae, Salamis, and Plataea.

The empire did strike back, in 480 BCE. Darius's son Xerxes (r. 486–465 BCE) was then in charge, and he assembled the largest army in ancient history for a land assault. Herodotus reckoned it at 1.7 million soldiers, but most historians estimate the real figure was about one-tenth of that. The Persians marched north from Sardis, crossed the Hellespont, moved westward across Thrace and Macedonia, and prepared to invade Greece from the north. The Persian threat finally persuaded most of the rebel Greeks to unite in defense. Sparta fought a heroic frontline action at the battle of Thermopylae (480 BCE), while the Athenians harried the Persians, supply ships. Spartan bravery at Thermopylae has long been remembered, deservedly, as one of the greatest military feats of Western

The Battle of Salamis   This is a modern rendering of the decisive naval battle that culminated in the defeat of Xerxes's army. Note the ramming prow (complete with smiley face) on the Athenian trireme.

history. With only three hundred soldiers they held off the Persians for three days before succumbing, which gave the rest of the Greek armies time to muster.[12] Subsequent Greek victories at Salamis (480 BCE)—a naval battle—and at Plataea (479 BCE) finally forced Xerxes to give up and return to Persia. Greece was poised to enter its golden age.

Greece's recovery from its Dark Age produced a new set of personal and civic values, and a new form of political and social organization: the polis, a city-state based on citizenship and shared governance. The degree of power sharing varied widely in the Greek poleis. Some, like Sparta and Miletus, were oligarchies. Over time, Athens developed the most extensive democracy, in which political power was extended to all male citizens.

WHO, WHAT, WHERE

Cleisthenes	Linear A	Sappho
democracy	Linear B	Solon
helots	Panhellenic	triremes
Homer	phalanx	tyrant
hoplites	polis	
Ionian League	rationalism	

---

12   Thermopylae ("Hot Springs," literally—so named because of sulfurous hot springs nearby) is a coastal floodplain and the only place where an ancient army could pass from Thessaly into Greece. The plain is considerably wider now than in ancient times, because of sedimentary deposition; in fact, a modern highway now passes through the site.

SUGGESTED READINGS

Primary Sources

Herodotus. *The Persian Wars.*

Hesiod. *Theogony.*

Hesiod. *Works and Days.*

Homer. *The Iliad.*

Homer. *The Odyssey.*

Thucydides. *The Peloponnesian War.*

Xenophon. *Hellenica.*

Xenophon. *Constitution of the Lacedaemonians.*

Anthologies

Buckley, Terry. *Aspects of Greek History, 750–323 BC: A Source-Based Approach* (2010).

Lefkowitz, Mary R., and Maureen B. Fant, comps. *Women's Life in Greece and Rome: A Source Book in Translation* (2005).

Nagle, D. Brendan, and Stanley M. Burstein. *Readings in Greek History: Sources and Interpretations* (2006).

Rice, David G., and John E. Stambaugh. *Sources for the Study of Greek Religion* (2000).

Studies

Bagnall, Nigel. *The Peloponnesian War: Athens, Sparta, and the Struggle for Greece* (2006).

Brunschwig, Jacques, and Geoffrey E. R. Lloyd, eds. *Greek Thought: A Guide to Classical Knowledge* (2000).

Camp, John M. *The Archaeology of Athens* (2002).

Cartledge, Paul A. *The Spartans: An Epic History* (2003).

Cawkwell, George. *The Greek Wars: The Failure of Persia* (2005).

Davidson, James. *The Greeks and Greek Love: A Bold New Exploration of the Ancient World* (2009).

De Souza, Philip. *The Greek and Persian Wars, 499–386 BC* (2003).

Dickinson, Oliver. *The Aegean from Bronze Age to Iron Age: Continuity and Change between the Twelfth and Eighth Centuries BC* (2007).

Ducat, Jean. *Spartan Education: Youth and Society in the Classical Period* (2006).

Gere, Cathy. *Knossos and the Prophets of Modernism* (2009).

Graham, Daniel W. *Explaining the Cosmos: The Ionian Tradition of Scientific Philosophy* (2006).

Hall, Jonathan M. *A History of the Archaic Greek World, ca. 1200–479 BCE* (2006).

Hughes, Bettany. *Helen of Troy: The Story Behind the Most Beautiful Woman in the World* (2007).

Langdon, Susan. *Art and Identity in Dark Age Greece, 1100–700 BCE* (2010).

Morris, Ian, and Barry B. Powell. *The Greeks: History, Culture, and Society* (2009).

Osborne, Robin. *Athens and Athenian Democracy* (2014).

Osborne, Robin. *Greece in the Making, 1200–479 BC* (2009).

Pedley, John. *Sanctuaries and the Sacred in the Ancient Greek World* (2005).

Pomeroy, Sarah B. *Spartan Women* (2002).

Pomeroy, Sarah B., Stanley M. Burstein, Walter Donlan, Jennifer Tolbert Roberts, and David Tandy. *Ancient Greece: A Political, Social, and Cultural History Third Edition* (2012).

Schofield, Louise. *The Mycenaeans* (2007).

Snodgrass, Anthony M. *The Dark Age of Greece: An Archaeological Survey of the Eleventh to Eighth Centuries BC* (2000).

Thomas, Rosalind. *Herodotus in Context: Ethnography, Science, and the Art of Persuasion* (2002).

Waterfield, Robin. *The First Philosophers: The Presocratics and the Sophists* (2009).

For additional resources, including maps, primary sources, visuals, web links, and quizzes, please go to **www.oup.com/us/backman.**

CHAPTER 5

Classical Greece and the Hellenistic World

479–30 BCE

The Classical and Hellenistic ages witnessed all the best and worst of ancient Greek life. The first, the Classical Age, dates from the successful defense of Greece against Persia to the conquest of Persia by the Greeks under Alexander the Great (479–323 BCE). The Hellenistic Age that followed ran from Alexander's death to the conquest of the East by the Romans (323–30 BCE). A sense of euphoria swept through the Greek people after their victory over Xerxes, and the Athenians felt more euphoric than any. Their bravery at Marathon and their de-

THE CLASSICAL AND HELLENISTIC AGES

cision to build a fleet of triremes had led directly to the Persians' defeat. Now, with the exception of Sparta and a few outliers, every polis in Greece recognized Athens's new position of leadership.

Its leadership involved more than military achievements. Mid-5th-century BCE Greece, especially Athens, witnessed a remarkable vitality in civic life, economic prosperity, artistic expression, and literary and scientific achievement. Yet it seems

The Discus Thrower Carved around 450 BCE, the original *Diskobolos* ("discus thrower") of Myron is lost, but this classical Greek masterpiece is known through numerous Roman copies, such as this marble sculpture. The discus throw was one of the events in the ancient pentathlon: discus, javelin, long jump, sprint, and wrestling. All five events took place in one day.

only right that one of its greatest achievements was tragedy, because its Golden Age ended with the disastrous war between Athens and Sparta known as the Peloponnesian War (431–404 BCE), which lasted twenty-seven years and consumed much of the Greek peninsula. As it happened, of the period's greatest philosophers—Socrates, Plato, and Aristotle—the last taught the military heir to the disaster, Alexander the Great. Alexander's conquests had far-reaching consequences. By defeating Persia, he brought the entire Near East and the eastern Mediterranean under a single command for the first time, an achievement that confirmed and highlighted the ties that held together the Greater West as a single, although pluralistic, civilization. The intentional cross-fertilization of Greek and Persian cultures that followed, atop the traditional values of the indigenous Semitic-speaking societies across the region, catalyzed the development of a cosmopolitan culture that defined the Hellenistic Age and laid the foundations for the development of Christianity and eventually of Islam.

ATHENS'S GOLDEN AGE

Despite their victory in 479 BCE, none of the Greeks believed they had seen the end of the Persian threat. Athens argued successfully for the creation of a military alliance among all the poleis, one dedicated to maintaining a strong defense and,

CHAPTER TIMELINE

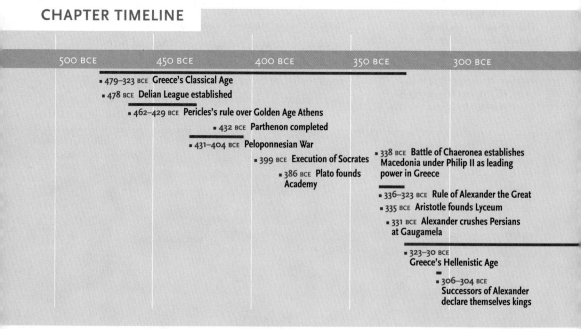

500 BCE	450 BCE	400 BCE	350 BCE	300 BCE

- 479–323 BCE **Greece's Classical Age**
- 478 BCE **Delian League established**
- 462–429 BCE **Pericles's rule over Golden Age Athens**
- 432 BCE **Parthenon completed**
- 431–404 BCE **Peloponnesian War**
- 399 BCE **Execution of Socrates**
- 386 BCE **Plato founds Academy**
- 338 BCE **Battle of Chaeronea establishes Macedonia under Philip II as leading power in Greece**
- 336–323 BCE **Rule of Alexander the Great**
- 335 BCE **Aristotle founds Lyceum**
- 331 BCE **Alexander crushes Persians at Gaugamela**
- 323–30 BCE **Greece's Hellenistic Age**
- 306–304 BCE **Successors of Alexander declare themselves kings**

if possible, even pressing the offensive into Persian territory. The alliance was called the **Delian League**, named for the Aegean island of Delos where the group's treasury was kept. By 470 BCE, in other words, Greece was victorious, independent, organized, self-confident, and quickly amassing wealth. The Greeks could be forgiven if they felt a bit of pride. They could be forgiven, too, if they did not foresee that the next great conquests, following their downfall, were to come from peoples they knew as little more than barbarians. They could have noticed even earlier the return of the Jews, freed by the Persians, to Judea.

Golden ages seldom last long, and the Greek one was no different. They also are seldom as golden as people believe them to have been. The Greeks, especially the Athenians, came to regard the mid-5th century BCE with a determined awe, recalling it as a lost halcyon era that outshone anything that came before it or since. Through the centuries, much of Western culture has continued the love affair and has extolled "the glory that was Greece" as a pinnacle of human achievement. A more sober viewer can admire the brilliance of the time without overlooking its less praiseworthy elements.

Most of the great achievements of the age were connected in some fashion to Athens. That city, in the heady atmosphere of patriotic victory over Persia and its newfound prosperity, had ample material and spiritual resources to devote to education, urban development, artistic expression, and religious ritual. Moreover, Athenian ties to the Ionian cities grew closer with the creation of the Delian

250 BCE	200 BCE	150 BCE	100 BCE	50 BCE

■ 167–142 BCE **Maccabean Revolt**

■ 30 BCE
Rome completes conquest of Hellenistic East

League, which brought an injection of the vigorous intellectualism of the Near East into Athenian life. The stimulus was significant.

Periclean Athens

The greatest of the Athenian leaders, **Pericles** (495–429 BCE), lavished money on building temples, theaters, schools, and public meeting houses. He held the office of *strategos* ("general") from 462 to 429 BCE. This was an elected office with a one-year term, but the Athenian constitution placed no limit on the number of terms a strategos could serve; Pericles won reelection thirty-two times. Although he himself had a high aristocratic lineage, he had an ardent populist streak, as a result of which he broadened the scope of Athenian democracy to include all free-born (male) citizens. Poor Athenian free men, if they could afford the time away from their work, could attend the assembly and vote on legislation. Pericles made it easier for them to participate in civic life by offering to reimburse their lost day wages if they wished to attend the municipal council meeting.

Athens's gain was the rest of Greece's loss—because no other city had anything like the cultural flowering of Periclean Athens, many of the best architects, sculptors, playwrights, scholars, scientists, and poets across Greece rushed to partake of Pericles's patronage. But even with all its advantages, Golden Age Athens was possible only because Athens controlled the treasury of the whole Delian League and appropriated its funds.

The Parthenon The chief temple of ancient Athens, dedicated to the city's patron goddess Athena, the Parthenon was built when the city was at the height of its power. The temple also doubled as the Athenian treasury.

THE POLIS: RITUAL AND RESTRAINT

Although prosperous, Greek life in the Classical Era was surprisingly modest. Most homes were comfortable but simple; no palaces were built, not even by those few who did achieve great wealth. Personal luxuries were spurned. Instead, prosperous Greeks spent their money on commercial investment, public building projects, and supporting arts and education. Temples, public halls, amphitheaters, baths, and athletic fields all benefited from private largess.

Public Religion

Each polis administered its major religious celebrations, which naturally differed from one another depending on the particular deities associated with each city. In Athens itself, the two most significant festivals were the Panathenaia, a celebration held every May in honor of the goddess Athena, and the Great Dionysia, a festival honoring Dionysius. Religion was ritualistic, and it neither asserted a creed nor promoted an ethical code.[1] People presented offerings, performed their prayers, consulted their oracles (priests or priestesses through whom the gods spoke directly to people), and honored the gods in song. No uniformity of opinion existed regarding the afterlife, although the great majority of Greeks believed in Hades, a shadowy afterworld to which all who received funeral rites went, regardless of the morality or immorality of their earthly lives. Those who did not receive a proper funeral were thought to wander the world as ghosts.

The Panathenaia?   This scene was long thought to depict the preparations for the opening ceremony of the Panathenaia, the high point of which was the solemn procession of Athena's sacred robes to the Acropolis. Recent scholarship suggests a different interpretation, however, arguing that the scene illustrates the preparations for the sacrificial slaying of Chthonia, the daughter of an Archaic Age king named Erechtheus. An oracle demanded the sacrifice as the price for Athens's victory in a war against Eleusis.

---

[1]   The ancient Greek language had no word corresponding to the English word "belief" or "beliefs" in its religious sense.

Daily Life

The Greeks disdained the luxurious diets of the Persians, which they considered a sign of the Persians' supposed decadence, and most ate simple meals. In his *History of the Persian Wars*, Herodotus is bemused by Persian eating and drinking habits:

> The day they value most of all is a birthday; on one of those they think it right to set up a greater banquet than usual—for wealthier Persians will arrange to have an ox, horse, camel, or ass roasted whole and set out before them (the less well-to-do use smaller beasts). They eat only a little of their main course but an abundance of desserts; moreover, they never use salt. This is why the Persians say that we Greeks are still hungry when we finish eating, for there is nothing worth having after we finish our main course—but if some delicacies were given us, we would eat our fill. The Persians are very devoted to wine (but they never vomit or piss in front of one another). Such are their customs. They will get drunk even when discussing the most important matters. The following day the host of the house they are in will ask them—now that they are sober—to reconsider their decisions of the night before. If they are still so inclined, the matter is settled; if not, not. If it happens that they deliberate an issue when sober, they reconsider it later when they are drunk. (1.133)

For the Greeks, grains, olive oil, and wine formed the basis of all meals. Breakfast commonly consisted of barley bread dipped in wine. Lunch was usually a form of soup or stew (made chiefly of lentils, onions, and beans, since fresh vegetables were hard to come by in the cities), accompanied by cheese and honey. Dinner was eaten at nightfall and was the largest meal of the day. For most people this was the only meal at which meat was served. Pork was the cheapest meat, and each city had its own favorite preparation.[2] Fish was relatively rare inland; the coastal cities and the Aegean islanders had little success transporting it inland without spoiling. Men and women always ate separately; in a small house with limited dining area the men ate first, then the women, then the male servants, and finally the female servants. Most Greek houses did not have stone ovens; instead, women cooked by heaping red-hot coals on a flat stone and setting an inverted clay bowl over the pile. Once the stone was hot, they scraped away the coals, placed the food on the heated stone, covered it with the hot bowl, and surrounded the bowl with the coals again. Holding little regard for such artful food preparation, however, the Greeks tended to devalue the role that women played in it. Food was fuel, not pleasure.

---

[2]   The Spartans' signature dish was *melas zomos*, a dark, thick stew made of pork, vinegar, and pigs' blood. In Aristophanes's play *Peace* (1.374), a small piglet is said to cost three days' wages for a civil servant.

Drinking, however, was another matter. The Greeks developed the first vintage wines, and among the many civic officials in local government was the person responsible for affixing the municipal seal to wines for export. By reputation, the best wines came from three Aegean islands: Chios, Lesbos, and Thasos; the wine produced in Achaea, the mainland district surrounding Athens, was among the worst. Claudius Aelianus (d. 235 CE), a Roman historian who wrote in Greek, records that Achaean wine was reputed to induce miscarriages in pregnant women.

Wine was drunk throughout the day, always cut (diluted) with water. Drinking uncut wine was considered barbarous, as was the drinking of wine by women, except in Sparta, where moderate wine drinking was thought to increase a woman's fertility. Drinking to excess was also looked down upon, except at symposia, the all-male drinking parties where testing one's limits was the whole point—to drink as much as possible without getting drunk, as a sign of one's manliness.

Divine Wine A 5th-century BCE drinking cup depicting the goddess Athena pouring wine for the famous hero Herakles.

Plato's dialogue *The Symposium* is the most famous depiction of one of these parties, although it is not characteristic. Few people can drink that much and still engage in such intelligent discussion. Still, some Greeks, like the philosopher Socrates, earned renown for their ability to imbibe.[3]

THE EXCLUDED: WOMEN, CHILDREN, AND SLAVES

Pericles's democratic reforms extended only to poor free men: Athenian women, children, and slaves remained without political rights, and women remained largely out of public view. Every polis had its own standards. Corinth, for instance, was renowned for the number, beauty, and prominence of its temple priestesses (hetairai) dedicated to the goddess Aphrodite. (According to the Roman poet Horace, they were also famously expensive to hire.) Women in the polis of Ephesus, on the Anatolian coast, enjoyed considerable liberality of social movement and economic rights; under the protection of the goddess Artemis, the polis produced several female artists of high repute. Women in Delphi, Megara, and Sparta were able to own land independently. Athens, it turns out, was unique (or nearly so) in the low value it placed on women. But certain customs were widely recognized. Every home had a specially designated "woman's zone" (*gynaeceum*), in which women passed the time with their children and servants. A woman never entered the public area of her house, where visitors might appear, without the permission of her husband. Children started their education at home, learning their letters and numbers and some music from their mothers. Boys usually began attending schools at age seven. These were private institutions that included rigorous physical education, since at age eighteen all boys began military service in the hoplite infantry.

Girls began another kind of service even earlier. From the time of her first menstruation a girl was considered marriageable; arranged marriages frequently happened as early as age fourteen, the idea being to take maximum advantage of her fertile years. "We have prostitutes for pleasure," wrote one Athenian, "concubines for company, and wives for producing heirs and maintaining the household." But even if few Greeks wedded for love, affectionate marriages certainly existed. Take two representative gravestone inscriptions:

> Here by this busy road lies Aspasia, a worthy wife now dead. Her husband Euopides put up this monument for her in memory of her good disposition; she was his consort. (Chios, 5th century BCE)

---

[3]   Socrates never went drink-for-drink against Milo of Croton, a 6th-century BCE Olympic athlete who reportedly ate twenty pounds of meat daily—which he washed down with two gallons of wine.

The woman buried here cared neither for clothes nor money in her lifetime, but only for her husband and for maintaining an upright reputation. Dionysia, your husband Antiphilus inscribes your tomb in return for the youthful years you shared with him. (Athens, 4th century BCE)

From the time of her wedding, a woman all but disappeared into her husband's house, seldom going into public, and devoting her days to childrearing and weaving. Greek culture abhorred idleness, and since most households—even relatively poor ones—had slaves to do the bulk of domestic labor, married women traditionally kept busy at the loom.[4] A healthy wife might expect to have ten pregnancies in her lifetime, although it remains unclear how many miscarriages she might suffer or how many of her children might die in infancy.

Wives governed their households—watching over their children, planning menus, caring for household items—but slaves performed most of the domestic chores. Classical Greece lived off slave labor, but slave populations in the ancient

Penelope and Telemachus   While seated at her ever-present loom, Penelope and her son ponder the whereabouts of the long-absent Odysseus.

---

[4]   Odysseus's wife, Penelope, who spent twenty years at her loom while patiently waiting for her husband to return from his wanderings, was an iconic image.

world were not self-perpetuating. The conditions of their lives were so harsh that their mortality rates exceeded their birth rates. The Greeks thus constantly needed fresh supplies of slaves to continue their lives of democratic freedom. Apart from domestic work, most slaves were used in farm labor and menial shopwork. The least fortunate of the male slaves were put to work mining or as oarsmen in Greek ships; the least fortunate of the females were the forced sexual partners of their male owners.

Two groups of women formed important exceptions to these constraints. Rural women regularly appeared in the towns, where they sold their produce in open-air markets. And companies of priestesses were important figures in various religious rites and festivals—especially the women known as *maenads*, the ecstatic followers of the god Dionysius, whose cult figured large in the development of Greek tragedy.

THE INVENTION OF DRAMA

What epic and lyric poetry were to the Archaic Age, stage drama was to the Classical—its characteristic and most powerful expression. Theater was more than an art form; it was a public rite and a civic obligation. Athens led the way, although the other major cities soon staged tragedy festivals as well.

Tragedy

Tragedy was the most distinctive form of public theater. The first tragedies we know of were staged in the time of Cleisthenes in the 6th century BCE—indeed, it is possible that the development of tragedy was one of Cleisthenes's civic reforms discussed in chapter 4—but the genre possibly dates to even earlier. The earliest complete plays that have come down to us are seven dramas by Aeschylus (525–456 BCE), often described as the father of tragedy. Although tragedy's actual origins are uncertain, it likely began with the choral odes sung by crowds to Dionysius—the god of wine, of passionate feeling, of life force—at the spring festival held in his honor in Athens. A latecomer to the Greek pantheon, Dionysius was a potent but disruptive force, one who promised his followers a transformative experience, a sense of moving out of oneself (ecstasy—from Greek *ek stasis*, meaning "out of nonmovement").

This was an unnerving development. Greek religion had always been passionately adhered to without ever being essentially emotive. Gods and goddesses often had, and played, favorites among human beings. Athena's protection of Odysseus comes to mind, as does Hera's guardianship over women in childbirth. Yet they seldom felt or showed any actual emotion toward humans except for episodic wrath. People offered prayers and sacrifices to the Olympian deities, but the relationship between the faithful and the deities was more contractual than intimate. Wanting a good grain crop, they prayed to Demeter, who granted the wish or not depending on whether she liked their offerings. Wanting safe passage at sea, they prayed to Poseidon. The cult of Dionysius was different. People turned to him not for favors but for spiritual elation and passionate release. His most passionate followers were the maenads, women who wore animal skins and brandished torches while celebrating the god's power in dance and song. At the peak of their frenzy, groups of maenads would sometimes attack wild animals with their bare hands and tear them apart. At the climax of *The Bacchae* by Euripides (d. 406 BCE) a group of them claw and tear apart a man before eating his flesh.

The German philosopher Friedrich Nietzsche (1844–1900) famously attributed tragedy to the Greek world's efforts to rein in the raw emotional power of the Dionysian cult. By sublimating these choral celebrations into a carefully managed public theatrical rite, he argued, the leaders of Athens created tragedy, a genre that provides a cathartic release of elemental passions within a strictly controlled setting. Nietzsche got many details wrong in his analysis, but his *Birth of Tragedy out of the Spirit of Music* (originally published in 1872 and revised in 1886) remains one of the most stimulating books ever written about ancient Greece.

Certain norms governed the practice, one of the most important being that tragic playwrights were expected not to compose original stories but to draw from a store of well-established popular legends and folktales. Sophocles (ca. 496–406 BCE) was not the only playwright to write a tragedy about Oedipus; rather, his great work is simply the best-known version. To the Greeks, it simply

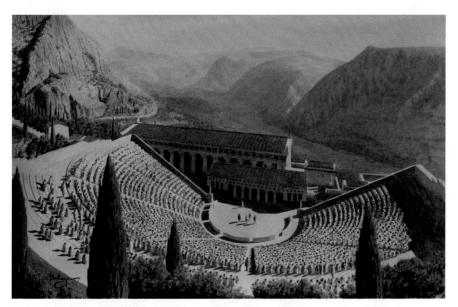

The Amphitheater at Delphi   Ancient Greek amphitheaters were very large, open-air structures that took advantage of hillsides for their terraced seating. This example dates to the 4th century and is set on the slopes of Mount Parnassus—sacred to the gods in Greek mythology—above the temple of Apollo at Delphi.

required more artistry to captivate an audience with a story they already knew than to rely on an original plot—the ancient stage equivalent of a computer-generated special effect in today's movies. One can be startled by such a thing, even impressed, but not emotionally moved. Euripides (ca. 485–406 BCE) was often criticized for his use of innovations—original or little-known stories, unexpected plot twists, surprise endings—although most people granted his brilliance with language and characterization. (Socrates reportedly once asserted that Euripides was the only playwright whose works were worth the walk to the theater.) Every major polis staged tragedies as a ritual of religious observance. Athens was the center of theatrical culture, with its annual festival called the Dionysia, for which playwrights submitted trilogies of new tragic plays, plus a burlesque piece called a satyr play and a comedy, usually political in nature. A civic council selected the most promising plays and produced them for the festival, at which attendance was required of all adult male citizens. At the end of the festival, the audience selected the best tragic trilogy of the year, and its author was granted awards and high honor.

Tragedy aimed to inspire both fear and empathy, which it accomplished by showing the relentless nature of fate and exploiting the paradox that people take pleasure in observing the suffering of others—a paradox made doubly ironic by the world's indifference to human pain. To the Greeks the cardinal sin was **hubris**—the excessive pride that leads people to think that they are in control of their own lives—because the hard reality is that our fates are fixed. Greek morality consisted of recognitions: of our obligations, our limitations, the futility of our aspirations, and our helplessness against the world's indifference. For the Greeks, we cannot alter what the world does to us, but we can control how we respond and adapt to our fates.

In the tales of the Theban ruler Oedipus, for example, the hero believes he has escaped the fate decreed for him at birth—namely, that he would kill his father and marry his mother. Then he discovers that he has done precisely that. Horrified by the revelation, he blinds himself and spends the rest of his life as a wandering beggar. In *Oedipus at Colonnus* the playwright Sophocles has the chorus sing a sorrowful ode as the blind beggar sits in despair:

> What foolishness it is to desire more life, after one has tasted
> A bit of it and seen the world; for each day, after each endless day,
> Piles up ever more misery into a mound. As for pleasures: once we
> Have passed youth they vanish away, never again to be seen.
>
> Death is the end of all.
> Never to be born is the best thing. To have seen the daylight
> And be swept instantly back into dark oblivion comes second. *(lines 1211–1238)*

Such misery is not a matter of life being fair or unfair; life is simply life, and we ought not to resist or bemoan it. "Let weeping cease, then," sings the chorus in *Oedipus at Colonnus*'s last lines, "and let there be no mourning. These things are in the hands of the gods." Happiness in life is possible, but it is not a birthright. A gloomy outlook, but a necessary one, to the Greeks: only by facing this hard reality can we truly have courage, and only thus can we accept both the good that happens and the evil that comes to us. Tragedy humbles us and reminds us to be thankful for small blessings.

Comedy, on the other hand, indulged not only the desire for merriment but also the urge to make fun of someone. We know of comic playwrights from many *Comedy* poleis, but the overwhelming number of surviving plays and fragments come from Athens. The earliest comedy writers, like Aristophanes (ca. 446–386 BCE), emphasized political satire. Eleven plays of his survive (of thirty that we know of), most of which skewer Athens's leading politicians, generals, and social leaders. Poets, playwrights, and philosophers receive their share of ridicule too. Much of the humor is coarse. In *The Acharnians*, for example, Aristophanes makes fun of two poets he disliked by staging a scene in which they both appear on a dark street one night. The first fellow, fearing that he is going to be mugged by an attacker, defends himself by hurling a rock—but he misses his attacker and hits the other poet in the face, and it turns out that what he threw was not a rock but a large turd.

Aristophanes's most famous play is perhaps *Lysistrata*, which is a bitingly satirical piece about the conduct of the Peloponnesian War. The title character stages her own form of protest against the never-ending war by persuading the Athenian women (wives and hetairai) to join in a sexual boycott until the men come to their senses and negotiate an end to the conflict. The play abounds in rapid-fire, crisp dialogue and clever sexual puns. It also includes crude but funny set-pieces that portray the increasingly frustrated men as they stagger across the stage, groaning with gigantic prosthetic erections and begging their wives to come back to bed.

Comedy after Aristophanes became somewhat tamer, in that it aimed its barbs less at specific real individuals and more at generic personality types—the braggart soldier, the clever servant, the shrewish wife, the coquettish maid. Few of these plays survive, and we owe most of what we know of them to later Greek writers who made reference to them.

THE PELOPONNESIAN DISASTER

A war with Sparta ended Athens's Golden Age. Lasting longer than any previous war in Greek history, this twenty-seven-year conflict is called the **Peloponnesian War** (431–404 BCE) because it matched Sparta's Peloponnese-based alliance against Athens and the Delian League. The result would leave Greece in ruins.

Trying to make sense of the war, in turn, would inspire new Athenian contributions to history, medicine, mathematics, and philosophy. Like the figures in the great tragedies for which they were famous, the Athenians brought their misfortune on themselves—and indeed on all of Greece—by their hubris. The most famed democracy of the ancient world turned itself into a grasping despotism and in effect willed its own demise. In the contest between values and greed, values lost.

Origins of the War

Athens had learned neither humility nor gratitude after the Persian Wars. Heady with pride and headstrong with determination to retain leadership in Greece, the Athenians spent most of the 5th century BCE bullying the city-states they had helped to defend against Darius and Xerxes. At first, no one dared to question them. When the Athenians began to withdraw funds from the Delian treasury to build up and beautify their own city, only Sparta (and its closest ally, Corinth) complained about Athenian hypocrisy. Through the 470s and 460s BCE, however, several cities grumbled openly about Athens treating them like colonies—to which Athens responded by attacking and colonizing them outright (see Map 5.1).

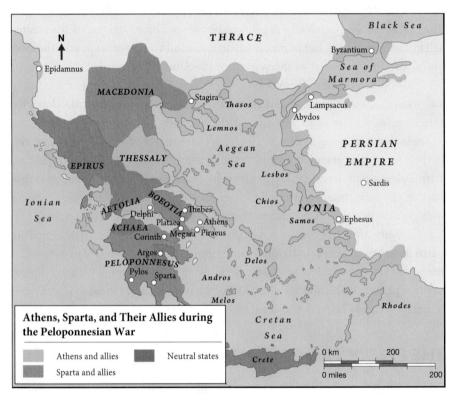

MAP 5.1   Athens, Sparta, and Their Allies during the Peloponnesian War   It took some time for the alliances to take shape, and many diplomatic shifts and adjustments occurred during the two decades before the start of the war in 431 BCE. Directly or indirectly, the war affected every polis in Greece.

Athenian garrisons were established across Greece, and corps of Athenian officials were set in charge of polis after polis. If they ever questioned their entitlement to an empire, no evidence of it survives. By 440 BCE Pericles had established a peace treaty with Persia so that he could set his sights on Sparta and Corinth, the last barriers to Athenian control of all of Greece. After several more years of provocations and last-minute resolutions, open war between Athens and Sparta erupted in 431 BCE.

Sparta's hoplite army was superior to that of Athens, but the Athenian navy ruled the sea. There were surprisingly few pitched battles in the first years of the *Course of* war; instead, the Spartans laid a protracted siege of Athens by land, while the *the War* Athenian ships established a blockade that kept food and goods from reaching Sparta by sea. The stalemate favored Athens until an epidemic of typhus struck the city in 429 BCE and killed roughly one-third of the population, including the aged Pericles.

Military command in Athens was henceforth contested by a series of ambitious figures, none of whom was more devious and brilliant than Alcibiades (ca. 450–404 BCE), one of the last members of an ancient aristocratic family. In a game of brinksmanship with a political rival, Alcibiades urged Athens to send an army to Sicily to help a colony that had requested aid against a local rival of its own. This campaign, known as the Sicilian Expedition (415 BCE), turned out to be a military disaster for Athens, which prompted Alcibiades to flee the city and join Sparta. For three years he led Sparta's forces effectively against his old polis, turning the tide of the war, until rumors that he had an affair with another Spartan leader's wife forced him to flee again (412 BCE)—this time to Persian-controlled Anatolia. According to Thucydides, Alcibiades advised the Persians to focus their efforts on weakening both Athens and Sparta, rather than aiming at one or the other. Sound advice, but Thucydides goes on to insist that Alcibiades was actually using his influence at the Persian court to plot his own return to Athens's good graces, which he achieved the following year—although he took care not to press his luck by entering the city and wisely joined Athenian troops stationed afield instead.

Meanwhile the Spartans struck a deal with the Persians, who agreed to provide them with a fleet of their own triremes. The Spartans themselves knew little of sailing, but there were enough enemies of Athens around by now to fit out a navy. In 411 BCE Alcibiades led an Athenian naval force to two quick victories over the Spartans. At this point, Athens seemed poised to bring the war to a successful conclusion, but the Persians, irked by Alcibiades's connivances, replenished Sparta with money, men, and ships, and by 407 BCE the new naval force challenged Athenian invincibility, which effectively assured a Spartan victory. In 404 BCE the Spartan army entered Athens itself, and the war was over. Alcibiades fled once more to Anatolia, hoping to persuade the Persians to equip him with an army he could use to drive the Spartans out—but he was quickly murdered under circumstances that are not entirely clear.

With the long Greek catastrophe finally over, Corinth and Thebes both demanded that the Spartans level the city of Athens and enslave its entire population. But the Spartans demurred. Instead, they pulled down Athens's fortifications, scuttled its fleet, installed a committee of thirty antidemocratic Athenians—the Thirty Tyrants—to govern the defeated city, and, ever concerned about another helot uprising, returned to Sparta as fast as they could. In their brief time in power (eight months over 404–403 BCE), the Thirty Tyrants reportedly exiled or killed more than fifteen hundred Athenians whom they deemed political enemies and confiscated their money and property. Outraged at the Tyrants' violence and greed, citizens who wanted to restore democracy banded together to regain control of Athens, which they accomplished with the help of the Spartan leader Pausanias (d. 395 BCE). (Sparta's clemency arose from the conviction that despite the sorrows caused by Athenian hubris, the city's democratic principles should be restored in honor of Athens's role in winning the Persian Wars.) The democratic rebels defeated the forces of the Thirty Tyrants in a series of bloody street fights.

Consequences of the War   Athens never recovered from its defeat, however, nor did Greece from the general ruin. A pallid democracy was restored in 401 BCE, but with its imperial revenues lost and most of its territories scorched, the Athenian economy remained constricted. Sparta shied away from playing any larger role in Greek affairs and focused on suppressing any helots who may have been encouraged by the disaster to attempt rebellion. This made Greece a tempting target for a resurgent Persia, which soon began to ponder another invasion. As it happened, someone else beat them to the punch.

Catastrophes can have beneficial effects. By their very completeness, catastrophes inspire a willingness to rethink old assumptions. The collapse of Greece in the Peloponnesian War led a number of brave individuals to make deep and serious inquiries into the nature of politics, the weakness of human will, the causes of greed, the quest for justice, and the desire to believe that the world makes sense. These issues had long been essential concerns of Greek cultural and intellectual life but had been examined and explored more in artistic genres such as poetry and tragedy. The intellectual life of post–Peloponnesian War Greece had a more analytical and scientific quality.

ADVANCES IN HISTORICAL INQUIRY

Herodotus (ca. 484–425 BCE), we saw earlier, had given an exciting new direction to this inquiry when he all but invented historical writing with his *History of the Persian Wars.* Previous historical writing—with the partial exception of the historical books in the Hebrew Bible—had consisted largely of propagandistic narratives, lists of deeds, blowhard memorials, and the occasional funerary inscription. Herodotus was the first to gather information firsthand, to organize it systematically, and to present it critically. His successor Thucydides (ca. 460–395 BCE) extended Herodotus's methods and created something entirely original.

Thucydides's *History of the Peloponnesian War* is an astonishing achievement in many ways. Recognizing, as he writes in the book's stately preface, that "the war, when it began, would be great and important beyond any previous war," Thucydides dedicates himself to following it in detail. Before writing, he conducted interviews, reviewed documents, and checked contradictory accounts, paying attention to technological and logistical details with the thoroughness of a general preparing for battle. For Thucydides, the Peloponnesian War was the first ideological war in Western history—a conflict not merely between political states but between states of being. Athenian greed and hubris, and Spartan envy and suspicion, tell only part of the tale. Thucydides digs deeper and presents both sides as acting out of different conceptions of freedom.

Thucydides

Freedom, of course, is a relative quality; one defines it in terms of what one is free *from.* To militaristic Sparta, freedom meant freedom from chaos and unpredictability; to hyperambitious Athens it meant freedom from restraint in the pursuit of its desires and perceived rights. Thucydides sees a measure of truth in each point of view but is too committed to political realism to cast his vote entirely for one side or the other. In fact, the casting of votes is itself something Thucydides believes little in. Rather, he identifies as Athens's greatest weakness not its selfishness and hypocrisy but its commitment to democracy. Thucydides argues that democracy, despite its theoretical appeal, is doomed to fail because it is based on a lie—namely, the notion of human equality. To drive his point home, Thucydides composes a handful of brilliant set-pieces, either wholly fictitious events or highly imaginative reconstructions of speeches, dialogues, and debates. One of the best known is "Pericles's Funeral Oration" of 429 BCE, which Pericles delivered at Athens's annual public funeral for their war dead. He opens with praise for the city's forefathers:

> It is a good and proper thing, as we gather to lament those who have died, to begin by speaking of our ancestors and paying tribute to their memory. They inhabited this land from time immemorial, and as a result of their valor it has been handed from generation to generation, to this present day, leaving us the possessors of a free state. But as deserving of praise as those ancestors are, how much more so our own fathers whose

struggles added so greatly to this inheritance, leaving us, their sons, in possession of a great empire!

Then Pericles moves on to praise the glories of Athens's government:

> Our form of government is without parallel or peer in the institutions of others. We do not copy our neighbors but serve as an example to them. We are a democracy, it is true, since the power to govern is in the hands of the many rather than of the few; but while we maintain equal justice for all in private matters, we recognize the claims of excellence. When one of our citizens distinguishes himself in some way, we raise him to public service—not as a matter of privilege but as a reward for his merit. Poverty is no obstacle; any man, no matter how obscure his condition, can render his polis good service.

After praising Athenian cultural attainment, military might, and hospitality, Pericles sums up by declaring:

> Athens is the school of all Greece, and every Athenian, it seems to me, is alone equal to any challenge in any sphere of action, so happily versatile is he. This is no simple boast, thrown out for this special occasion. It is simple fact, as proven by the power of the great society created by those abilities. . . . These men whom we commemorate today died in a manner fitting for Athenians. We, their descendants, must resolve to be as steadfast in the field as they were. . . . Heroes have the whole earth for a tomb. Even in far-distant lands where columns bear inscriptions [of their deeds], there lives enshrined in every heart a record that needs no epitaph to preserve it. So let us take these heroes as our models, and, knowing that happiness comes from freedom and that freedom comes from valor, let us never shrink from the dangers of war.

Thucydides's history breaks off suddenly, in Book 8, with the battle of Cynossema in 411 BCE, a minor victory for Athens over the new Spartan naval force, leaving the last seven years of the war untreated. The work is clearly unfinished, although historians disagree about why the book was never completed. (Fortunately, the last years of the war are fully detailed in the *Hellenica* of Xenophon, a later Athenian historian, ca. 430–356 BCE.) It seems certain that a ninth book was intended, to reflect the nine-book structure of Herodotus's *Persian Wars*, but Thucydides completed enough of his masterpiece to leave the Greek tragedy dissected and exposed with un-matched and gimlet-eyed skill.

MEDICINE AS NATURAL LAW

Just as Thucydides gave clear-eyed diagnoses of Greek political decline, Hippocrates of Kos (ca. 460–370 BCE) divorced illness and disease from superstitions and religious beliefs. In the process, he made human suffering—or, at least, one type of human suffering—a feature of the natural world. His separation of physical health from religious issues also makes him the founder of Western medicine.

Earlier traditions, as in Egypt and Babylon, had built up an understanding of how to treat various maladies, but knowledge of how the body works, how *Hippocrates* diseases function, and why any given remedy works (or does not) remained mysteries. Such things were attributed to astral influences, spells cast by demons, and the whims of the gods. Hippocrates was the first to study medicine systematically to work out the processes by which various herbs and treatments produced their effects. He and his successors compiled the *Hippocratic Corpus*, seventy volumes that discuss maladies (such as epilepsy, the "sacred disease") as natural phenomena rather than divine curses. He was the first to categorize diseases and therefore to produce a preliminary sketch of a natural structure. Acute, chronic, endemic, and epidemic were the first categories, followed by subcategories according to organs and bodily systems.

One of the best-known parts of the *Hippocratic Corpus* is the oath to be sworn by all physicians, marking the official start of their careers. The original form of the **Hippocratic oath** goes as follows:

> I swear by Apollo, Asclepius, Hygeia, and Panacea, and do bear witness before all gods and goddesses that I will remain true to the following oath, to the best of my ability and judgment:
>
> that I will hold as dear to me as my own parents the man who taught me this art [of medicine], will live with him, and if necessary will share my possessions with him;
>
> that I will regard his children as my own brothers, and will teach them this same art;
> that I will prescribe health regimens for the good of my patients to the very best of my ability and will never intentionally do harm to anyone; . . .

that I will preserve the purity of my life and my practice; . . .

and that I will always preserve the confidentiality of anything I learn about my patients and their households in the practice of my profession, not permitting anything to be spread about.

To the extent that I faithfully keep this oath, may I live my life and practice my art enjoying always the respect of all men; but if I fail to do so, and if I violate this oath, may the opposite be the case.

The Hippocratic oath has been modified numerous times, but it remains a rite of passage for most practitioners of medicine in the Greater West.

The significance of Hippocrates's work lay not only in its contributions to medical science. He also regarded human beings as part of the natural landscape—capable of, and responsive to, rational analysis. He severed medicine from religion and allied it with philosophy.

THE FLOWERING OF GREEK PHILOSOPHY

Philosophy was the area of the Greeks' greatest and most enduring achievement. Much had happened in this field since the Milesians discussed in chapter 4.

The Pythagoreans   A group of philosophers known as the **Pythagoreans**—named after their founder, the Ionian Greek thinker and mathematician Pythagoras (570–495 BCE)—had directed philosophy away from the early Milesian focus on primal essences. The Pythagoreans sought instead to identify the rational ordering of those essences, the laws that governed their interaction; hence their focus on mathematics. Heraclitus of Ephesus (mid-5th century BCE), for example, tried to explain the world's obvious diversity and changeability as a rational patterning and repatterning of opposing forces (hot/cold, light/dark, wet/dry, etc.). If closely observed, even the infinite progressions of a child's kaleidoscope follow a rational pattern. Hence such conclusions as: "We step and yet we do not step into the same river twice; we are and we are not." "A road goes uphill and downhill at once—it is the same road." "No god or man made the world. It is the same for all, always was, is, and will be, an eternal fire eternally kindled and extinguished in equal measures."

Zeno of Elea (ca. 490–420 BCE) introduced a number of mathematical paradoxes that seem to presage Einstein's theories about time–space continuums. Imagine, for example, that an archer unleashes an arrow at a target. In any one instant of time, the arrow is moving neither to where it is nor to where it is not. It cannot move to where it is not because no time elapses for it to move there; it cannot move to where it was because it is already there. In other words, at every instant of time there is no motion occurring. If everything is motionless at every instant and time is composed of instants, then motion is impossible. Another Pythagorean, Empedocles of Acragas (ca. 490–430 BCE), undercut Heraclitus's argument about the interplay of opposing forces. Empedocles observed that such coming into existence and passing from existence of new substances makes no sense, since it would necessarily mean the coming into existence and passing from existence of nonexistence itself. Instead, Empedocles posited not one all-encompassing element of nature but four: fire, air, earth, and water. This theory of the four elements would become standard philosophical thought for the next two thousand years.

A second group of thinkers called the **Sophists** also had their day. Few of their names have come down to us, but in any case the Sophists specialized in *The Sophists* packaging ideas rather than in producing anything original. Their emphasis lay in rhetorical skill rather than in genuine investigation: in the bustling economic scene of classical Athens, they aimed to help enterprising people to prosper. The Sophists' closest modern-day analog would be the motivational speakers, investment gurus, and leadership coaches of cable-television specials and expensive weekend seminars. They traveled from city to city, offering paid instruction in everything from public speaking and career guidance to introductory surveys of exciting "useful knowledge" from around the world. These activities are easily mocked as derivative and shallow, and the Sophists have come in for more than their fair share of criticism over the centuries. (Indeed, the modern meaning of "sophistry" is plausible but deceptive argumentation.)

In the wake of the Peloponnesian War arose a trio of the most influential and impressive philosophers in history, whose lives, written works, and the schools they established changed Western intellectual culture forever. These three individuals—Socrates (469–399 BCE), Plato (ca. 427–347 BCE), and Aristotle (384–322 BCE)—permanently altered the direction and scope of philosophy. For the subsequent fifteen hundred years, Western science, religion, and politics, as well as philosophy itself, followed the intellectual trajectories they established.

Socrates, who left no writing of his own, is the most enigmatic of the three. At *Socrates* least partially trained in the Sophist tradition, he pulled philosophical inspection *and the* away from the theoretical model making of the Milesians and Pythagoreans and *Meaningful* insisted that it pursue questions that actually matter to any thinking individual *Life* who wants to live meaningfully. Geometrical schema are fine, Socrates felt—but what good are they for answering questions like What is the right way to live?, How can one know anything for certain?, What is love?, or What is justice? Socrates's signal achievement was to make philosophy a practical urgency—"to pull philosophy back down from the sky," as the 1st-century BCE Roman writer Cicero put it. Ethics and politics (by which he meant communal ethics), not cosmology and natural science, should be the essential concerns of philosophical inquiry, he insisted, or else why bother?

Reputedly the ugliest but most charming man in Athens, he married a woman named Xanthippe, had a family, worked as a stonemason, fought in the Athenian army, and participated in municipal government. At the age of seventy he was arrested on charges of impiety and corrupting the youth of the city; after an eventful trial he was convicted and sentenced to death by poison—a fate he reportedly accepted with calmness and grace. The charges against him may well have been politically motivated, or at least partly so. Like Thucydides, Socrates criticized democracy as an irrational political system based on the mistaken concept of human equality, and he had close friends among leading antidemocratic figures in Athens. The charge of impiety rested on his claim to be inspired by a "divine spirit" (*daimonion*). The corruption charge asserted that he intentionally urged his pupils to question the values handed to them by society.

Socrates founded no formal school but inspired so many later thinkers that he may be the single most influential figure in Greater Western philosophy. Certainly he set the terms of debate, for from his own time until the 19th century ethics and politics remained the central topics of inquiry. Only with the work of Karl Marx and Georg Friedrich Hegel—both mid-19th-century writers—did

The Death of Socrates Jacques-Louis David (1748–1825) was the chief proponent of French classicism. This 1787 painting shows Socrates—arguing to the very end—as he prepares to drink a cup of poison while his friends and disciples mourn. The seated figure with his hand on Socrates's knee is Plato.

philosophy turn from these concerns toward the kind of philosophy dominant today. They helped make philosophy the study of the systems (economic, ideological, and linguistic) that restrain, shape, and perhaps control our thinking and lives.

Almost all that we know of Socrates's life and thought comes from four sources: the dialogues of his greatest pupil, Plato; the essays of another pupil, the historian Xenophon mentioned earlier; a few scraps of commentary by Aristotle (Plato's student); and a hilarious caricature of him in Aristophanes's comedy *The Clouds*. Together, they present a coherent although not conclusive portrait of the man whose misfortune was to reach his greatest fame when a sore and humiliated Athens was least inclined to tolerate criticism of its democratic greatness.

Socrates is associated more with a method than with a set of ideas. The **Socratic method** consisted of patient and thorough questioning, rather than the assertion of observations or deductions. A consistent pattern emerges in all his appearances in his pupil's dialogues. When asked, for example, to describe the best political system, he begins by asking what we mean by Justice—the quality that all political life aims to supply. Only by understanding the terms we use, Socrates insists, can we begin a proper inquiry. Nothing can be assumed if we wish to seek true understanding. Usually his interlocutors, turned in every direction by his clever questioning, end up admitting that they have no idea how to define anything, and Socrates declares that true philosophical inquiry can therefore at last begin. What the prosecutors at his trial failed to grasp was that Socrates did not doubt that Justice (or Love, or Being, or Truth, or Goodness) exists. He was merely willing to entertain such a doubt as a stimulus to thinking about it.

Despite his charisma and brilliance, or perhaps because of them, he was a terribly annoying man. Think of a conversational bully who delightedly dismantles the ideas of others but never fully offers ideas of his own to replace them. In *The Republic*, Plato's longest and most intricate dialogue, Plato presents Socrates tearing to shreds the ideas of four different characters regarding the nature of Justice. Then, when asked to offer his own definition, Socrates spends the next six books of the dialogue discussing the ideal form of government—but without ever offering his own convincing definition of what Justice actually is. In the end he wins by exhausting his opponents, not by defeating them. Nevertheless, Socrates set philosophy on a new course, one pursued avidly by his most brilliant student, Plato.

Plato came from a wealthy, aristocratic family. Brothers, half-brothers, and cousins populate many of his dialogues—presumably an indication of his pride *Plato* in his kin. He received an excellent education in mathematics, music, literature, *and Ideal* gymnastics, and philosophy, all of which are discussed and cited extensively in *Forms* his writings. He seems, unlike his teacher, never to have had a profession apart from teaching in the **Academy**, the school he founded when he reached the age of forty. As the Peloponnesian War drew to its close, he thought of taking an active role in politics, but he was enraged at the ham-fisted rule of the Thirty Tyrants. When the restored but nearly impotent democracy sentenced Socrates to death, Plato all but washed his hands of active public life. He took refuge at Megara for a while and traveled to Sicily and southern Italy. Returning to Athens around 385 BCE, he established the Academy, took on pupils, and began to lecture and compose his dialogues.

The period from 385 to 360 BCE were the years of his greatest productivity and originality. He peopled his dialogues with artists, politicians, poets, Sophists, and orators from the Athenian scene. References to poets and playwrights, often

Plato's Academy   This Roman mosaic from Pompeii (ca. 100 BCE) imagines a scene at Plato's Academy. A half-dozen philosophers, including Socrates (shown rubbing his chin), gather around Plato. Unlike his student Aristotle, who famously paced constantly while lecturing, Plato, a high aristocrat, enjoyed his leisure. Here he rests against a tree while examining a scroll.

including quotations, appear in almost every dialogue, as do many of the writers themselves. In the last dozen years of his life, 360–347 BCE, perhaps tiring after long labor, he began to outline and dictate in rough form his dialogues to his students, who then fleshed them out in a more turgid, "academic" style. The extraordinary literary polish of the middle years gradually disappeared, although his mind remained as sharp as ever. He became increasingly conservative as he aged, however, and by the time he wrote *The Laws*, one of his last works, he was deeply embittered by the world's foolishness.

Most of Plato's dialogues repeat a pattern. Socrates encounters a group somewhere in or near Athens and joins their conversation. It might be at an evening entertainment, along a road to a temple, sitting in a town square, or chatting in a portico. Picking up on an apparently offhand comment by one of the group, Socrates begins to probe his fellows' attitudes, language, convictions, and assumptions until they admit hopeless befuddlement and beg Socrates to set them aright. Socrates sometimes obliges but just as often demurs: the dialogue functions not as a means to a dogmatic conclusion but as an invitation to the reader to continue the discussion. Plato's earliest dialogues, most historians agree, present a historically accurate portrait of Socrates's own philosophy. As the years went on, however, he increasingly used Socrates as a literary device, a mouthpiece for his own ideas.

Plato begins with an observation: the world we observe with our senses is pale and imperfect—defective, jumbled, and filled with apparent contradictions. And yet we intuit order within it. We see parts of things; we intuit whole things. We observe, for example, two chairs. They may vary widely in size, shape, color, and material, and yet we know that they are both indeed chairs. They possess some quality, an ineffable "chairness," that determines their identity. Plato's philosophy argues that "chairness" really and truly exists; it is an example of what he terms the **Ideal Forms**. Where does it exist? Perhaps in a parallel universe or as an idea in the mind of God. Who can say? The point is that it does exist and that everything we perceive as a chair possesses it. Thus to Plato our world should be thought of as a pallid reflection of the world of Ideal Forms, a corrupt descendant filled with flawed and partial representations of the Forms. Plato's dialogues can be thought of as a series of discussions, each about a particular abstract Form— Love, Beauty, Goodness, Art, or Justice—because we can only understand our world in relation to the Forms it so imperfectly represents.

Plato insists that we can in fact understand the Ideal Forms because of the dual nature of human beings: we are not merely animated flesh but eternal souls temporarily housed in physical bodies. Each soul carries deep within itself an instinctive knowledge of the Ideal Forms, a memory of ultimate reality as yet lacking a clear shape. That is why we feel we know what chairness is, although we struggle to express it in words. Plato's philosophy is essentially romantic and mystical. It yearns for and aspires to an ineluctable perfect state of existence that seems as though it should be within our grasp. If only we can keep talking, if only we can remain willing to strip away untested assumptions, if only we can help one another along the way, we will eventually attain the true meaning of the Ideal Forms that constitute ultimate reality.

No other writer comes close to Plato's skill at portraying philosophy as a kind of pilgrimage, a journey toward a salvation that can be attained only with other people. There are no solitary revelers in Plato's world. Each of his dialogues ends differently, in terms of whether a true understanding of any particular Form is attained. Yet they all end with a warm feeling of community, of something special having been shared. It is the process of philosophy as much as the ideas attained by it that Plato portrays so lovingly and unforgettably.

Aristotle and the Pursuit of Happiness

Aristotle was Plato's most distinguished pupil and has a good claim to be among the most influential thinkers in Greater Western history. A tireless worker, he threw himself into the study of everything from ethics and metaphysics to botany and poetics. Ancient sources credit him with as many as two hundred separate treatises, some of great length. Roughly thirty treatises survive, perhaps more and perhaps fewer, depending on the debated authenticity of a handful of texts.

Two 4th-Century BCE Busts Portraying Plato and Aristotle   By tradition, Aristotle is always shown with a shorter beard than his teacher's.

Despite their unflagging brilliance, however, most of the texts consist not of Aristotle's own writing but of lecture notes later collated and stitched together (according to tradition by his son, Nicomachus). If his lectures were in fact like these composite transcripts, Aristotle was a remarkable but dull teacher. The contrast with Plato's dialogues could hardly be any stronger. Plato was an artist of the highest order; his dialogues have polish, wit, sharp characterization, and narrative drive. They manage the neat trick of expressing complex ideas with such clarity that anyone can grasp them. Aristotle, by contrast, comes across as an astonishing but long-winded teacher struggling to convey an enormous, unwieldy body of knowledge.

The ideas that come through are vital, however, although his range makes it difficult to present them in a systematic way. The key to Aristotle lies in his method: unlike his teacher (but much like his own father, a physician), Aristotle begins not with the theoretical examination of the Ideal Forms but with intense scrutiny of the tangible natural world. He accepts the notion of the Ideal Forms, or claims to, but he believes that their essential elements appear physically within each object. Existence consists of the continual interplay of Ideal Form and earthly matter—rather like the way our genetic coding continues to affect our physical development throughout our lives. Aristotle, then, offers a compromise between Plato's idealism and the rough materialism of the Milesians.

Moreover, Aristotle asserts that the continuous nature of the interplay of forces drives the universe forward toward a goal. Everything is in a state of becoming. A seed is on its way to becoming a seedling, then a plant in full flower, then a withering husk, then a decayed nutrient for another seed. Each existing thing, whether animate or not, plays a role in the unstoppable push forward to new life. Since we ourselves are part of this impetus of birth, life, and decay, we can take solace in knowing that our existence is ennobled with purpose. Every existing thing, he says, has a **telos**—an intrinsic purpose, a necessary role in the cosmic drama. The telos of an animal embryo is to become that animal; that of teeth is to chew food. For Plato, the physical world is a flaw and a hindrance to our understanding. Aristotle instead sees the world as a process—a march forward into ever new being (and hopefully, but not necessarily, ever better being).

But do human beings have a telos? If so, is it a general telos applicable to the whole species, or is it unique to each nation or even each individual? Aristotle wrestled with these questions over and over. If human life is teleological, is that not the same as saying it is fated or even predetermined? Are we in control of our own destinies, and if not, then what sound basis can there be for morality? Aristotle's answer is characteristically complex. He begins with the observation that ethics is a practical science, not a theoretical one. The point of it is to learn how to act and live a well-ordered life, not to gain some abstract knowledge about the nature of goodness for its own sake.

Most people, he says, would agree on most ethical propositions: that happiness is better than sadness, that pleasure is preferable to pain, that courage is superior to fearfulness. We all might disagree on specifics regarding those virtues; some of us, for example, might take greater pleasure in being renowned for beauty than for intelligence. What interests Aristotle is the relationship between ethical values. Is courage of greater or lesser value than loyalty? Is it more important to be temperate in one's desires or to be well liked? Whatever their relative standings, he insists that happiness (*eudaimonia* in Greek—meaning "being in accordance with the spirits," literally, or "living well," colloquially) is the supreme virtue, toward which all other virtues point. To Aristotle happiness must entail something intrinsic to human beings as a species. This something that we possess or experience that no other creatures can, he says, is our capacity for rational thought. If we follow the use of reason, if we cultivate it as a means of life, we can and will attain happiness. Whether we are happy has little to do with the contingency of world events and is the product of our own choices—choices in our actions and in how we react to the world. In this way, individual free will is preserved, as is the notion of a human telos. In other words, our telos is to pursue happiness, but whether we achieve it, or the way in which we achieve it, is up to us.

Plato and Aristotle were both interested in politics, although only at a distance. Two of Plato's dialogues—*The Republic* and *The Laws*—describe a vision of an ideal society, one in which an oligarchy of highly educated guardians or a monarchy led by an enlightened philosopher-king would oversee the day-to-day governance of society. Most people are neither capable of nor interested in governing their own affairs and are happy to leave the work of running the world to their superiors. This ideal system is clearly a response to the failures of Athenian democracy. But whether Plato himself believed in it is unlikely, because such a system assumes that properly educated rulers will never be corrupted by power, an assumption that cannot be made of the imperfect world in which we live.

Like Plato, Aristotle thought that democracy was a bad system because it did not restrict decision making to the most educated citizens. Unlike his great teacher, however, Aristotle believed in the implementation of good government—even to the point of writing constitutions for various poleis—although he had no direct involvement in political life that we know of. After Plato's death around 347 BCE, Aristotle left Greece altogether and lived in Asia Minor for four years. In 343 BCE King Philip II of Macedonia (r. 359–336 BCE) invited Aristotle to come to Pella, the capital of Macedonia, and tutor his teenage son. Aristotle took the job, in a kingdom to the north of Greece inhabited by a tribe who spoke a language of disputed relation to Greek. There he spent eight years teaching the lad, and then in 335 BCE he returned to Athens and established his own school, the **Lyceum**, where he spent the rest of his life teaching his empirically based, life-guiding philosophy.

The lad he tutored in Pella most definitely took an interest in politics. His name was Alexander.

THE RISE OF MACEDONIA AND THE CONQUESTS OF ALEXANDER THE GREAT

In its bloody, insurrection-filled past, Macedonia also had suffered in the invasions by Darius and Xerxes. The Greeks themselves regarded the Macedonians as barbarians—or at the very best as poor backward cousins. Whereas Greece prospered during the Periclean age, Macedonia remained ignored and reviled. But the self-destruction of Greece during the Peloponnesian War gave Philip II (r. 359–336 BCE), and then his son, dreams of glory.

Alexander the Great (r. 336–323 BCE) was the greatest conqueror of the ancient world. He took over from his father, Philip II, rule of a semi-Hellenized *Macedonian* kingdom when Philip was assassinated in 336 BCE. Philip had been an ambitious *Power* commander and seems to have had designs on conquering Greece from early on; he also pushed northward into the central Balkans. The strength of the Macedonian forces owed much to the extensive gold mines discovered in the Pangaion Hills in the southern Balkans, which enabled Philip and Alexander to raise, train, and equip an exceptionally effective army. In 347 BCE, when he was ready to make his attempt on Greece, Philip reportedly sent a herald to Sparta with a warning: "If I win this war, you will be my slaves forever." According to the legend, the Spartans sent back a terse one-word reply: "If." Philip never made it to Sparta or Athens, but he did advance as far as Thebes and Corinth before being murdered by one of his bodyguards (whose motives remain unclear).

By 334 BCE, two years after Philip's death, Alexander was firmly in control of all of Greece and had already determined to advance eastward against the Persian Empire. And that was just the start.

When Alexander succeeded to the Macedonian throne in 336 BCE, Greece could not stand in the way of his territorial ambitions, since all the poleis were in *The Rule of* such weak condition. In turning his sights to Persia, Alexander's thinking was *Alexander* sound. The conflict between Greece and Persia had never been settled definitively. Internal discord and political strife had followed the defeat of Xerxes's forces in 479 BCE, but by the time of the Peloponnesian conflict Persia was already trying to manipulate the outcome in Greece to prepare the way for another attempt. Alexander simply recognized, correctly, that Greece would never be free of the

Alexander the Great   This detail from a large floor mosaic in Pompeii depicts Alexander at the battle of Issus (333 BCE). He appears in the thick of the fighting, eyes fixed on the Persian emperor Darius. Alexander frequently went into battle without a helmet, confident in his destiny to conquer the whole of Persia. He is clean-shaven, a relative rarity for his time, and wears an image of the monster Medusa on his breastplate—the better to frighten his foes.

Persian threat. He decided to settle the matter once and for all by reversing the scales and sending his Greek army to topple the throne in faraway Persepolis.

The narrative of Alexander's campaigns is well documented (see Map 5.2). In 334 BCE he took Asia Minor; within two more years he had conquered the Holy Land and Egypt. By 331 BCE he had advanced through Syria and met the main Persian army at Gaugamela, not far from the ancient Assyrian city of Nineveh along the upper Tigris, and slaughtered it.[5] He then marched to Persepolis, deep into today's Iran, and in 330 BCE he destroyed the capital. Determined to press on until every last vestige of Persian power was defeated, Alexander spent five more years on campaign through the territories of Parthia and Bactria (today's eastern Iran and Afghanistan) and then down the Indus River valley, where his astonished men encountered Indian war elephants. Alexander still wanted to press on and take India, but his exhausted men threatened to mutiny, and so in 325–324 BCE he reluctantly led his forces back west to

---

[5]   After the battle of Gaugamela, the Persian emperor Darius III fled into the nearby hills, where a local tribal chieftain murdered him. This ended the empire founded in the 6th century BCE by Cyrus the Great.

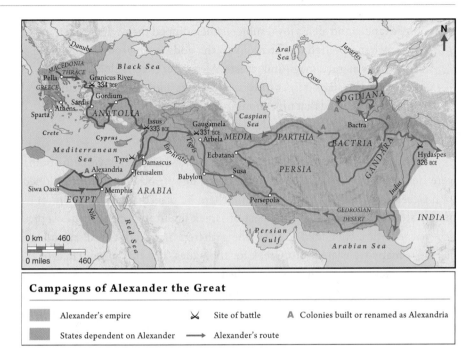

Campaigns of Alexander the Great

▨ Alexander's empire	⚔ Site of battle	▲ Colonies built or renamed as Alexandria
▨ States dependent on Alexander	⟶ Alexander's route	

MAP 5.2 Campaigns of Alexander the Great   Alexander's stunning conquest was mostly complete by 330 BCE.

the city of Babylon. It was the most stunning military adventure of the ancient world, an unparalleled feat.

But it is one thing to conquer vast territory and quite another to create an empire. Alexander's long-term plans are unknown, because in 323 BCE he took ill and died at the age of thirty-three. By the time he was halfway through his conquests, however, he had already instituted a profound change in his army by admitting large numbers of Persian soldiers and officers, who underwent training in Hellenic tactics, learned a simplified version of the Greek language (called *koiné*, or "common speech"), and wore Greek dress. Alexander's kinsmen nearly revolted at what they regarded as a treacherous "Persianization" of their ranks, but in a dramatic showdown at Opis, an ancient Babylonian city near the Tigris, Alexander regained their trust. As described later by the writer Arrian of Nicomedia (d. 160 CE) in his *History of Alexander,*

> To commemorate the restored harmony of his troops, Alexander of-fered sacrifice to all the gods he customarily honored, and hosted a great banquet, at which he made a point of sitting among his Macedonian con-tingent. The Persians, though, were placed immediately beside them, and right next to the Persians were the officer of other conquered peoples.

Alexander and all his loyal subjects then dipped their wine from the same bowl and poured out libations to the gods, each group following the lead of its augurs, magi, and priests. Alexander prayed aloud that the Greeks and Persians might rule together harmoniously in a single empire. It is reported that nine thousand men attended this banquet, and that every one of them repeated his prayer.

He had taken care to establish in his wake a sprawl of Greek-style cities. Some were newly built, most notably Alexandria in Egypt; others were refashioned with Greek institutions and laws. Within them he placed a loose network of libraries stocked with copies of the best of Greek literature, science, philosophy, and mathematics. He added to these the gathered manuscripts of Persian high culture—many translated into Greek for the widest dissemination. He also arranged (in fact, ordered on penalty of death) for his leading officers to divorce their Greek wives and to take Persian ones instead. It is unclear whether Alexander consciously intended by this to create a pluralistic society. Perhaps he intended simply to develop a new aristocracy, one that identified itself with a new race of his own manufacture. He certainly was impressed by, and attuned to, the eastern custom of deifying kings. In either case, he was developing a cosmopolitan social order.

THE HELLENISTIC WORLD

The eastern Mediterranean traditions had included the Greek, Egyptian, and Hebrew traditions. The Persian and Babylonian traditions had included those of the Mesopotamian valley and the eastern lands that had absorbed and assimilated them. As Alexander's vast battlefield settled into relative peace, a single Hellenistic civilization embraced and absorbed them all. This was the Hellenistic Age (323–30 BCE), and it lasted until the Romans came in the 1st century BCE and instigated a new era.

The Hellenistic Kingdoms

The political narrative of the time is not particularly enlightening. Many wars and palace coups came and went, but none in service of a significant new idea. In general terms, Alexander's enormous war zone split quickly into a quartet of separate kingdoms, each governed originally by one of his leading generals: Ptolemaic Egypt, Seleucid Asia, Attalid Anatolia, and Antigonid Greece.[6] Because the new rulers and settlers came from throughout Greece and not simply from a single city like Athens, the Hellenistic world had a broad degree of cul-

---

6   Take the -ic and -id endings off the dynastic adjectives, add -us (or -os, if you are a Hellenic purist), and you will have the names of the first succeeding generals.

MAP 5.3 The Hellenistic World, ca. 200 BCE Divided into four separate kingdoms, the Hellenistic world was noteworthy for its vibrant urban life, its dissemination of Greek culture and values, and its splendid libraries. Rural life remained impoverished, however, and court life seethed with conspiracies and betrayals.

tural cohesion. The single dialect of koiné Greek came into general usage throughout the territories—this was the Greek in which, ultimately, most of the Christian New Testament was written. In all four kingdoms the governments were tightly centralized, and efficient tax collection led to the building up of vast treasuries (see Map 5.3).

Apart from supporting their armies, the main expenditure of the governments was the construction of more and more cities and their supporting infra- *Urban* structures. Manufacturing and commerce were the hallmarks of Hellenistic life, *Expansion* and these required a solid and expansive urban base. At least three hundred new cities were founded in this era, and hundreds more received huge injections of money to improve their infrastructures. Within a century of its construction, the city of Alexandria had a half-million inhabitants; Seleucia had a quarter million. The Seleucids poured money into refurbishing their Mediterranean harbors and extending their roadways into India. The Ptolemies in Egypt hired geographers and cartographers to search out and map new overland trade routes into Arabia, Ethiopia, and Nubia. The Antigonids invested in canals and a vastly

Cleopatra   Cleopatra VII Thea Philopator (r. 51–30 BCE) was the last pharaoh to rule ancient Egypt. Renowned for her youthful beauty, she dazzled more with her charisma and wit. According to the much later Greek philosopher and biographer Plutarch (46–120 CE), she could speak nine languages. She presented herself to the Egyptians as the reincarnation of the goddess Isis.

expanded fleet of ships that was able to trade with Spain and Britain (important sources of silver and tin, respectively). The Attalids, who ruled the smallest of the successor-states, made a strategic alliance with the Roman republic to check the expansionist aims of the Antigonids. Their capital, Pergamum, had an amphitheater that could seat ten thousand and a library that contained 200,000 volumes.

Not everyone prospered. Farming remained the occupation of the great bulk of the population, and farmers generally lived in poverty throughout the Hellenistic years. Poor crop yields were not the cause. Farmers steadily produced abundant quantities of foodstuffs, and the proliferation of cities meant the increased, and increasingly easy, availability of markets. Rather, intentionally harsh tax policies in all the Hellenistic kingdoms kept small farmers poor. Two motives prompted such exploitation: a desire to promote the development of the urban economies and a perverse belief that abject poverty would keep the agrarian population incapable of rebellion. Hellenistic splendor thus resulted less from a general prosperity than from the intentionally inequitable distribution of wealth.

The Arts under Royal Support   Among those who benefited, at least financially, were writers and artists. Hellenistic monarchs became the supporters of scholarship and the arts on a vast scale, competing with one another to lure the best and the brightest to their capitals. Scholars and artists focused on gathering and assimilating the intellectual and cultural traditions of their various populations. The promotion of libraries was key here. Translations, commentaries, histories, and encyclopedias were the most characteristic cultural productions of the age. Explorers sent out by the four monarchies traveled to the Caspian, Black, and Red seas and came back with exciting travelogues describing new geographies, cultures, and technologies. The most adventurous Hellenistic Greek explorer of all was Pytheas (d. ca. 306 BCE), who ventured as far as central Norway. He was the first writer to describe the phenomena of the northern lights and the Arctic snow cap.

Non-Greeks who also ventured far and related their discoveries in koiné Greek included a Babylonian priest named Berosus (d. ca. 270 BCE), who wrote a history of his people and translated several astronomical works into the new common tongue. Manetho (d. ca. 270 BCE), an Egyptian, wrote a comprehensive history of his homeland too, in which he created the system of periodization still used today regarding Egypt's Old, Middle, and New Kingdoms, with their various Intermediary Periods. Others explored as far south as today's Ethiopia and Kenya and as far east as India.

The fortunes acquired by those in trade and industry, as well as in government, meant a widespread demand for decorative arts—statuary, jewelry, frescos and mosaics, tapestries—to adorn the homes and villas of the well-to-do. The preferred styles were more ornate, as with the exaggerated naturalism of statues like that pictured here of Laocoön and his sons.

In drama, playwrights turned to lighter fare than the Classical tragedians had produced. Working in politically repressive regimes, they aimed simply to entertain the masses with escapist comedies featuring stock characters—shrewish wives, clever slaves, braggart soldiers, and the like. The best of the writers of this so-called New Comedy was Menander of Athens (ca. 341–290 BCE), who wrote more than one hundred comedies, only one of which survives whole. He holds the distinction of being the only Greek playwright to be quoted in the Christian New Testament, when St. Paul warns his newly converted companions to avoid socializing with sinful people: "Bad company corrupts good morals."[7]

Laocoön and His Sons   In mythology, Laocoön was a priest in the cult of Poseidon who offended the sea god by marrying and, according to rumor, daring to make love to his bride in a temple dedicated to the deity. This sculpture shows Laocoön and his sons being attacked by two sea serpents sent by Poseidon. It was carved in the 1st century BCE, probably on the island of Rhodes, and housed in Rome. After going missing for many centuries, it was excavated in 1506. It now stands in the Vatican Museum as an iconic example of Hellenistic sculpture's emphasis on movement and gesture.

But it was in the sciences that Hellenistic intellectual life really shone. *Scientific* Scholars were able to bring together the Greek, Egyptian, and Persian traditions in *Innovation* everything from astronomy and geometry to mathematics, medicine, and physics. The wide availability of libraries and laboratories—both of which were considered "must-have" accessories of the well-to-do—sparked many new abstract and practical advances, word of which spread rapidly. Aristarchus of Samos (ca. 310–230 BCE) and Eratosthenes of Cyrene (ca. 285–194 BCE) were the preeminent

---

[7]   1 Corinthians 15.33.

astronomers. Between them, they proved, by applying Greek mathematics to Babylonian astronomical tables, that the earth and other planets revolved around the sun, and they calculated the circumference of the earth to within 200 miles.

In geometry, Euclid (ca. 330–270 BCE) led the way. *The Elements of Geometry* became the basic textbook for teaching the subject for fifteen hundred years. In medicine, figures like Herophilus of Chalcedon (ca. 335–280 BCE) introduced (briefly and on the sly) the practice of human dissection, from which he determined the role of the heart in transmitting blood through the arteries—a bit of knowledge quickly lost until it was rediscovered by the English physician William Harvey in the 17th century CE. Archimedes of Syracuse (287–212 BCE)—the physicist famous for shouting "Eureka!" ("I've got it!") and running naked through the street—determined the law of specific gravity, devised the first compound pulley, and invented the hydraulic screw propeller.

Philosophy for a New Age

In philosophy, thinkers turned away from both the abstract idealism of Plato and the empiricist realism of Aristotle. Instead, their works assumed that the human quest to understand the meaning of life and the nature of reality was pointless, either because no such meaning or reality exists or because human intellect is powerless to comprehend them. Four major schools of philosophy predominated: **Skepticism**, **Cynicism**, **Epicureanism**, and **Stoicism**. The first two differed from one another mostly in matter of degree. Skeptics like Pyrrho of Elis (ca. 360–270 BCE), Arcesilaus (ca. 315–241 BCE), and Carneades (ca. 214–128 BCE) emphasized the flaws inherent in human intellect. Since all our knowledge of the world derives from our senses and all of our senses can be deceived (as in optical illusions), then it is impossible for our minds to attain 100 percent certainty about anything. Cynics went even further to assert that only our natural instincts can possibly be deemed right and true—and thus the laws, morals, and customs that organize civil society must be rejected as shams. They made a point, therefore, of exposing what they regarded as the hypocrisy of civic life: by arguments when possible and by crude actions when necessary. The most famous early Cynic, Diogenes of Sinope (d. 323 BCE), at least once expressed his rejection of social conformity by defecating and masturbating in public. When asked why he customarily carried a lamp everywhere he went, even in the daylight, he would respond that he was seeking a single honest man. "Man has misconstrued every gift bestowed on him by the gods" was one of his maxims.

The Epicureans and Stoics, by contrast, were more moderate, disciplined, and pragmatic. *Of course* the world is beyond human comprehension, they asserted, but that is exactly where we need to start thinking the hardest, not stop in despair. "Any philosophy that does not relieve human suffering is worthless," according to

Zeno of Citium (d. 262 BCE), the founder of Stoicism. Relief from suffering was the central thrust of these two schools. The Epicureans' philosophy was not, as is widely assumed, to devote themselves to simple hedonism—to wine, women, and song, as the phrase goes—but rather to devote themselves to the avoidance of suffering. As Epicurus himself (d. 270 BCE, after whom the school is named) wrote to a friend,

> When we say that pleasure is the goal of life, we do not mean excess or sensuality; that is what others think about us, out of sheer ignorance, prejudice, or deceit. By pleasure we mean simply the absence of suffering in the body and of anguish in the soul. A pleasurable life comes not through endless bouts of drinking and revelry, not through sexual delight or the enjoyment of fine fish and other delicacies at the table. No, it comes from sober reasoning, from seeking out the true principles behind every choice and selection, and from rejecting every false belief that brings agony to the mind.

This "scaling down" of philosophical aims from Plato's search for Ideal Forms can be viewed as a decline, but as an expression of concern for the everyday human struggle to survive in a harsh world, the pragmatic turn of Hellenistic philosophy is deeply humane.

THE MACCABEAN REVOLT

In the second century BCE the Hellenistic monarchies grew increasingly unstable, which inspired a wave of palace coups and popular uprisings. The most significant of the latter was the rebellion of the Jews in Seleucid Palestine. The relative atmosphere of tolerance in Hellenistic times might have provided the Jews a respite from oppression, but the eastern-inspired custom of deifying monarchs—which Alexander the Great had originally encouraged—meant that the Jews would never be docile subjects.

The Revolt of the Maccabees (167–142 BCE) originated with a contested succession to the Jerusalem high priesthood during the reign of the Seleucid king Antiochus IV (r. 175–164 BCE). Two main contestants emerged: Jason and Menelaus, whose very names suggest the degree of Hellenization that took place even in the Holy City. Neither was a paragon of virtue.

Jason paid Antiochus a large bribe to win the post, which left Menelaus with no choice but to offer an even larger one, but Menelaus did not have enough cash on hand, so he broke into the Temple treasury and stole some golden vessels. Although it assured him the high priesthood, Menelaus's theft outraged the people, and the city erupted in riot. Antiochus invaded the city and established a garrison of his Syrian soldiers on the Temple Mount. These soldiers, consisting of followers of both the Greek and the Zoroastrian religions, demanded some sort of accommodation for their religious rites—and Antiochus (with Menelaus's consent as high priest) allowed pagan altars to be set up within the Temple.

Maccabean Triumph

This perceived act of profanity triggered a full-scale Jewish rebellion against Seleucid rule. The leaders of the rebellion were a family called the Hasmoneans, but the rebellion itself took its name from that of the eldest Hasmonean son, Judas Maccabeus. The revolt is a great heroic episode in the history of the Jews and their most significant military victory until the establishment of the modern state of Israel in 1948.

The odds were certainly against them, given the size and strength of the Seleucid forces, but the Jewish rebels showed remarkable tenacity. (A story from their retaking of the Temple itself, in 164 BCE, is the origin of the celebration of Hanukkah.) The surprised and exhausted Seleucids gave up the fight in 142 BCE and granted Judea independence. The Hasmoneans would remain in power until they were replaced by the Herodians in 40 BCE, a dynasty of puppet-kings under Roman control.

Changes in the Hebrew Canon

Despite the heroic nature of the revolt, however, the main Jewish texts that record its history, the books known as 1–2 Maccabees, were not admitted into the Hebrew canon. The ostensible reason for this—that they may have been written directly in Greek and hence lacked a Hebrew source/counterpart—only partially explains their omission. The Greek Septuagint Bible, including 1–2 Maccabees, remained in widespread use in the Jewish world for three hundred years: Jewish communities from North Africa to Mesopotamia used it, as did numerous communities within Palestine itself. The great Jewish philosopher Philo of Alexandria (d. 50 CE) used it. Rabbinical scholars drew on it in establishing new legislation. Syrian Jews used it to prepare their own translation of the Bible into vernacular Syriac (the Peshitta). For the rest of the Hellenistic period, and for at least two hundred years beyond, the Greek Septuagint was widely accepted canon in the Jewish world. The spread of Christianity in the first two centuries CE, however, altered Jewish attitudes toward their Greek Bible. Because Christians also used the Septuagint, it became tainted in Jewish eyes.

Returning to the Hebrew canon was a way of asserting the Jews' difference from the Christians, indeed, their independence from them. Hence they began to reconstitute the Hebrew text. The process of producing this version—by compiling old manuscripts, collating excerpts from older liturgical material, and at times even reconstructing the text from memory—resulted in the Masoretic text, the definitive Hebrew-language canon still in use today. Although still revered as part of the Jewish literary tradition, 1–2 Maccabees lost its canonical status. To disassociate themselves from the upstart new sect, the Jews cut themselves off from the biblical version that most of them used. In the process, they decanonized the books that record the last great triumph of their ancient era.

◆

The Hellenistic period was one of stark contrasts, when economic instability, extensive poverty, and authoritarian rule existed alongside great prosperity, astonishing scientific advances, and flourishing cosmopolitan culture. It bridged the gap between the tastes, customs, and values of Classical Greece and those that would be more characteristic of Rome. It was Hellenistic art and architecture, Hellenistic city planning and civic culture that the Romans strove to emulate, not those of Periclean Athens. The example set by Alexander, in particular, was one that the Romans would model, and the economic and political infrastructures that were put in place after his conquests would form the framework of Roman imperial government.

WHO, WHAT, WHERE

Academy	hubris	Skepticism
Alexander the Great	Ideal Forms	Socratic method
Cynicism	Lyceum	Sophists
Delian League	Peloponnesian War	Stoicism
Epicureanism	Pericles	telos
Hippocratic oath	Pythagoreans	tragedy

SUGGESTED READINGS

Primary Sources

Arrian. *The History of Alexander.*

Thucydides. *The Peloponnesian War.*

Xenophon. *Hellenica.*

Anthologies

Cohen, S. Marc, Patricia Curd, and C. D. C. Reeve. *Readings in Greek Philosophy: From Thales to Aristotle* (2011).

Irby-Massie, Georgia, and Paul T. Keyser. *Greek Science of the Hellenistic Era: A Sourcebook* (2002).

Lefkowitz, Mary R., and Maureen B. Fant. *Women's Life in Greece and Rome: A Source Book in Translation* (2005).

Tracy, Stephen V. *Pericles: A Sourcebook and Reader* (2009).

Studies

Bagnall, Nigel. *The Peloponnesian War: Athens, Sparta, and the Struggle for Greece* (2006).

Beard, Mary. *The Parthenon* (2010).

Bosworth, A. B. *The Legacy of Alexander: Politics, Warfare, and Propaganda under the Successors* (2005).

Briant, Pierre. *Alexander the Great and His Empire: A Short Introduction* (2010).

Briant, Pierre. *From Cyrus to Alexander: A History of the Persian Empire* (2002).

Burn, Lucilla. *Hellenistic Art from Alexander the Great to Augustus* (2005).

Connelly, Joan Breton. *Portrait of a Priestess: Women and Ritual in Ancient Greece* (2009).

Connelly, Joan Breton. *The Parthenon Enigma* (2014).

De Ste. Croix, G. E. M. *Athenian Democratic Origins, and Other Essays* (2005).

De Ste. Croix, G. E. M. *The Origins of the Peloponnesian War* (2002).

Dillon, Matthew. *Girls and Women in Classical Greek Religion* (2002).

Grabbe, Lester L. *A History of the Jews and Judaism in the Second Temple Period* (2006–2008).

Green, Peter, and Eugene N. Borza. *Alexander of Macedon, 356–323 BC: A Historical Biography* (2013).

Hanson, Victor David. *A War Like No Other: How the Athenians and Spartans Fought the Peloponnesian War* (2006).

Hanson, Victor David, and John Keegan. *The Western Way of War: Infantry Battle in Classical Greece* (2009).

Hölbl, Günther. *A History of the Ptolemaic Empire* (2001).

Humphreys, S. C. *The Strangeness of Gods: Historical Perspectives on the Interpretation of Athenian Religion* (2004).

Jonker, Louis. *Historiography and Identity (Re)Formulation in Second Temple Historiographical Literature* (2010).

Kagan, Donald. *The Peloponnesian War* (2003).

Navia, Luis E. *Socrates: A Life Examined* (2007).

Neils, Jenifer, and John H. Oakley. *Coming of Age in Ancient Greece: Images of Childhood from the Classical Past* (2003).

Reeve, C. D. C. *Philosopher-Kings: The Argument of Plato's "Republic"* (2006).

Romm, James. *Ghost on the Throne: The Death of Alexander the Great and the War for Crown and Empire* (2011).

Roochnik, David. *Beautiful City: The Dialectical Character of Plato's "Republic"* (2008).

Roochnik, David. *Retrieving the Ancients: An Introduction to Greek Philosophy* (2004).

Saxonhouse, Arlene W. *Free Speech and Democracy in Ancient Athens* (2008).

Shanske, Darien. *Thucydides and the Philosophical Origins of History* (2009).

Sourvinou-Inwood, Christiane. *Tragedy and Athenian Religion* (2003).

Thomas, Carol G. *Alexander the Great in His World* (2007).

Warren, James. *Presocratics: Natural Philosophers before Socrates* (2007).

Weinfeld, Moshe. *Normative and Sectarian Judaism in the Second Temple Period* (2005).

Weinfeld, Moshe. *The Place of the Law in the Religion of Ancient Israel* (2004).

Weinfeld, Moshe. *Social Justice in Ancient Israel and in the Ancient Near East* (2000).

Zuckert, Catherine H. *Plato's Philosophers: The Coherence of the Dialogues* (2009).

For additional resources, including maps, primary sources, visuals, web links, and quizzes, please go to **www.oup.com/us/backman.**

CHAPTER 6

Empire of the Sea: Rome

753 BCE–212 CE

The Romans believed themselves descended from the noble Trojans who had lost their city to Homer's Greeks. They may not have known their own true origin or they may simply have desired a better one. According to their legend, Aphrodite, the Greek goddess of love, fell head over heels for Anchises, a member of the younger branch of the Trojan royal family. Two things resulted from their tryst: a son named Aeneas, and the infliction of blindness on Anchises when he was caught boasting of his sexual escapade to some other soldiers. (Aphrodite's father, Zeus, hurled a lightning bolt from atop Mount Olympus and hit him in the eyes.) After the Greeks had set Troy ablaze, the story went on, Aeneas carried his blind old father on his back through crumbling ruins and flaming timbers to safety. Aeneas's postwar travels then took him into the central Mediterranean, where he learned of a prophecy that he would found a great new kingdom in central Italy, at a place called Latium.

ROME AND THE MEDITERRANEAN

The Roman Forum A forum was a marketplace or town square, and every Roman city had one. As a natural meeting place, a forum was frequently a site of popular political gatherings. The great forum in Rome was the venue of speeches and rallies, triumphal processions, criminal trials, and, occasionally, gladiatorial contests.

After a series of adventures Aeneas did indeed reach Latium and brought the region under his control. But he did not found the city of Rome itself. That was the work of two much later descendants of Aeneas, the twin brothers Romulus and Remus, who, also according to the legend, laid the city's foundations in 753 BCE and established a dynasty. Its kings ruled until a rebellion in 509 BCE overthrew the monarchy and established a republic.

Whatever the story or precise date of Rome's founding, Romans themselves valued practicality and dutifulness above all other virtues. But even pragmatists sometimes like to fantasize about noble ancestors and destined greatness. These spoke, too, to Rome's image as a republic of virtue, even as internal struggles put in doubt the Republic's very survival. And indeed, Rome achieved its golden age under an emperor, Augustus, and as an empire linked by the Mediterranean Sea.

ANCIENT ITALY AND THE RISE OF ROME

Links to Ancient Heroes

Their imagined link with Greece's heroic age mattered much to the Romans. On the practical level, an illustrious genealogy and a prophetic fate helped to legitimate, in their own eyes at least, the Romans' lording it over the other tribal and ethnic groups of central Italy. Surrounded by aggressive societies like the Etruscans and Sabines to the north and east and the Aurunces, Hernici, Marses, and Volscii to the south, the Romans were a warlike people from the first, continually forced to defend their own territory and conquests against other invaders.

Rule by Kings

On a deeper level, the Romans craved a linkage with ancient heroes because their early history boasted none of their own. Tradition told of seven monarchs who began Rome's rise in the world. These kings, who supposedly ruled from the founding of the city to the founding of the Republic (753–509 BCE), were for the

CHAPTER TIMELINE

750 BCE	650 BCE	550 BCE	450 BCE	350 BCE

- 753 BCE Legendary foundation of Rome
- ca. 753–509 BCE Roman monarchy
- 509–31 BCE Roman Republic
- ca. 450 BCE First Roman law code (Twelve Tables)
- 387 BCE Gauls sack Rome
- 367 BCE Election of the first plebeian consul

most part a competent group, but none of them would have made a suitable hero in an epic poem. (The regnal dates given in Table 6.1 are traditional but should not be regarded as factual because our knowledge of early Rome derives from archeological remains and sources that date to centuries later. In 387 BCE a Gaul army sacked Rome and burned down the municipal archives.)

Despite the individual kings' variable accomplishments, the period of monarchy did produce Rome's most famous and enduring government body: the **Senate**, a group of distinguished men chosen as the king's personal council. The Senate played the same role—advising government leaders—for a thousand years as Rome changed from a monarchy to a republic and back to a monarchy (the empire). It was always a Roman value that one should make important decisions only after consulting with advisors, never on one's own.

The early Greeks had the stimulus of continual contact with the other peoples of the eastern Mediterranean, but the Romans were in a different situation altogether: Italy, geographically speaking, faces westward (see Map 6.1). The Apennine mountain chain runs down the eastern edge of the peninsula, forming an imperfect but still significant natural barrier to approach from the Adriatic Sea. Moreover, most of Italy's abundant and fertile agricultural plains, as well as most of its natural harbors, stretch down the western coast. And apart from the great Po River complex that runs eastward across the northernmost part of the

250 BCE	150 BCE	50 BCE	0	200 CE

- 264–146 BCE **Punic Wars between Rome and Carthage**

- 146 BCE **Third Punic War leaves Rome undisputed master of the Mediterranean**

- 133–31 BCE **Civil wars and political struggles**

- 91–88 BCE **Social War between Rome and rest of Italy**

- 73–71 BCE **Slave rebellion led by Spartacus**

- 49–45 BCE **Civil war, with Julius Caesar the victor**

- 44 BCE **Caesar assassinated**

- 31 BCE **Octavian (the future Augustus) defeats Marc Antony at Actium; beginning of Roman Empire**

- 212 CE **Roman citizenship extended to all free peoples living in the empire**

- 31 BCE–14 CE **Reign of Augustus**

- 96–180 CE **Reign of the "Five Good Emperors"**

TABLE 6.1 **Rome's Kings**

Romulus (r. ca. 753–715 BCE)	Formed the Roman army into its distinctive shape of individual legions, each composed of six thousand infantry and six hundred cavalry. But he is perhaps best remembered for the mass kidnapping of thousands of Sabine women to provide wives for his troops.
Numa Pompilius (r. ca. 715–673 BCE)	Established the priesthood of the Vestal Virgins and abandoned the old lunar calendar for a solar one.
Tullus Hostilius (r. ca. 673–642 BCE)	A bloodthirsty warrior who, according to legend, so neglected the gods that on his deathbed, when he cried out to be saved, Zeus blasted him with a thunderbolt that turned his palace and his body instantly to ashes.
Ancus Marcius (r. ca. 640–616 BCE)	Built the first bridge across the Tiber River and founded the port at Ostia, thus connecting Rome to the sea. Also established Rome first's saltworks.
Tarquinius Priscus (r. ca. 616–579 BCE)	An Etruscan, he doubled Rome's size by conquering the Etruscans and used the booty he won to finance construction of the Roman Forum and the Circus Maximus. He also built Rome's sewer system.
Servius Tullius (r. ca. 579–535 BCE)	The second king of the Etruscan dynasty, he made socioeconomic status the determinant for voting rights, built the great Temple to Diana, and was murdered by his daughter and her husband, Tarquinius Superbus.
Tarquinius Superbus (Tarquin the Arrogant) (r. ca. 539–509 BCE)	A violent, loutish Etruscan dynast whose excesses led to his expulsion from Rome and the permanent overthrow of monarchy in 509 BCE.

peninsula, almost all of Italy's rivers flow westward. The only parts of Italy easily accessible to the Greeks were the southern third of the peninsula and the island of Sicily, where we find Greek settlements established as early as the mid-8th century BCE—the time of Homer. For these reasons the earliest **Latins** (the name given to the people who settled the region of Latium) had the greatest degree of commercial and cultural contact not with Greece but with Etruria, an advanced society to the north with whom they had close but uneasy relations.

The Etruscans   The **Etruscans** were a literate people who left behind a considerable body of writing (especially inscriptions). However, since their language is poorly understood, all that we know of them derives from archeological remains plus whatever the Romans and others wrote about them. They were excellent metalsmiths and builders; the Romans appear to have learned the techniques of building arches

MAP 6.1 Ancient Italy Italy's Apennine Mountains and the westward-flowing rivers that emerged from them shaped much of the peninsula's early history. Most towns and villages were oriented to the west, into the Tyrrhenian Sea, and to the south, into the central Mediterranean. Only a few towns faced east, into the Adriatic.

from them. The Etruscans also introduced the Romans to the blood sport of gladiatorial contests. Such contests originated as an aspect of funeral observances, an offering made in honor of the deceased, and were extremely popular. The Roman historian Livy (Titus Livius, 59 BCE–17 CE) describes a plethora of such games in 174 BCE. Titus Flamininus was a Roman general who would later play a big role in the conquest of Greece:

> Many gladiatorial games were held in that year; most of them were unremarkable, but one really stood out from the rest—namely, the games staged by Titus Flamininus to commemorate the death of his father. These games lasted four days, including the public food distribution, the general banquet, and the handful of theatrical performances that accompanied them. The high point of the festivity, of course, was the three-day contest in which seventy-four gladiators (a high number, in those times) fought.

Wrestling Match   In this Etruscan fresco from around 500 BCE from the Tomb of the Augurs at Tarquinii, two men wrestle over three metal cauldrons, which are probably the prizes of their contest. The cloaked figure to the left carries a curved staff known as a *lituus*, which was a mark of the priests known as *augurs*, or diviners. One of the chief ways to prophesize the future was to define a field of vision with a lituus and then observe within it the behavior of birds. Here, the cloaked figure seems to be supervising the contest, while the lituus and the birds flying over the combatants may indicate that he was seeking to foretell the result.

The Etruscans influenced the Latins in two profound ways: morals and religion. If we can credit the stories told about them by the Romans and Greeks, the Etruscans were well off and enjoyed their prosperity to the hilt. They held sumptuous feasts twice daily—with both male and female guests reclining on pillowed couches, in richly decorated homes, and imbibing flowing rivers of wine. Descriptions of these feasts fill many disapproving Latin and Greek pages—because the Romans, making a virtue of their own relative want, disdained luxury as self-indulgence. They never aspired to Spartan levels of austerity, but they placed a high value on frugality and self-discipline. Moral strength demanded sacrifice, as they saw it, and the placing of the common good before individual desire. In this way, the Etruscans taught the Romans by negative example.

In religion, however, their influence was direct and positive. The Etruscans practiced divination, or the reading of prophetic signs in certain natural phenomena—the shape of a slaughtered animal's liver, the blood splatter of a beheaded chicken, the rumbling sound of thunder or the groaning of a volcano, or the flight pattern of a group of birds. Divination was common throughout early Italy, but the Etruscan diviners (*haruspices*, in Latin) were considered the best.[1] The Romans adopted their practice and remained dedicated believers in it for many

---

[1]   Livy wrote, "When it came to signs and omens regarding public life, Roman custom was to consult nobody except Etruscan haruspices" (*History* 1.56).

centuries. Roman religion never fully recognized the haruspices as priests, but Roman society turned to them before any undertaking and took their warnings with the utmost seriousness.

FROM MONARCHY TO REPUBLIC

The Roman social elite's hatred of its Etruscan king motivated the creation of the Republic. In 509 BCE, the son of Tarquin the Arrogant raped a virtuous Roman matron Lucretia, who committed suicide to preserve her honor. Lucretia's kinsmen and friends overthrew Tarquin and established a form of government so new that they could label it only vaguely: **res publica**, "the public thing." Its constitution—mostly unwritten—changed numerous times over the centuries but remained based on the crucial idea of the separation of powers. In contrast to the ancient Athenians, who placed legislative authority in the single body of the popular assembly, the Romans erected an elaborate system of checks and balances between distinct institutions that prevented any single individual or group from amassing too much power. The Senate was the dominant body, composed of members of Rome's leading noble families, but its work was complemented by a number of legislative assemblies and executive magistracies. Most magistrates served one-year terms, so campaigning and deal making were more or less constant. Since different social groups were involved in the different offices, prudence dictated that families and classes would form alliances that would compete for choice political positions and to pass legislation.

In all, the early Republic functioned much in the spirit of Aristotle's ideal city-state, a smallish, organic society whose government involved all the leading figures of the city in a constantly changing network of mutually dependent relationships. Roman social hierarchy divided the population into three groups: the **patricians**, aristocrats who could trace their lineage to the members of the first Republican Senate established in 509 BCE; the **equestrians,** aristocrats of a lesser order who according to tradition originated as the earliest Roman cavalry; and the **plebeians**, all other free citizens. Initially, the patricians held the upper hand against the plebeians, but within two generations the so-called Struggle of the Orders had progressed to the extent that the Republic promulgated—sometime around 450 BCE—its first written law code. Known as the **Twelve Tables** (the name derives from the original dozen wooden slabs on which the code was written and set in public), it formed the basis for all subsequent Roman jurisprudence. It survives only in fragments, but the outline of its contents provides a good sense of its scope (see Table 6.2). The Tables marked the first significant concession to the plebeians; others would be demanded and gradually won over the next two centuries.

The Tables regarded property rights as the paramount concern of society.
The Twelve Indeed, the internal struggles of the first hundred years of the Republic centered
Tables on opening more avenues of government to the enterprising plebeian class, whose
strength came from their prosperity rather than noble lineage. In part, property
issues featured so prominently in the laws because a debtor's creditor could legally sell him into slavery, under certain circumstances. The Tables, therefore,
defined those circumstances. What mattered in this regard were the size and
length of the debt and the social status of the people involved. Roman law ultimately recognized a hierarchy of six distinct social classes. Interestingly, these
distinctions originated as a means of determining the amount and type of military service owed by each citizen; military needs, not economic roles, shaped the
foundational social structure.

TABLE 6.2 **The Twelve Tables**

	Table Topic	Number of Laws	Sample Laws
I	On summonses to court	10	When anyone summons anyone to appear before a judge's tribunal, the latter must appear immediately and without delay. [No. 1]
II	On judgments and thefts	11	If anyone commits a theft during daytime and is caught in the act, he is to be scourged and handed over as a slave to the person from whom he stole. If the thief is [already] a slave, he shall be beaten with rods and hurled from the Tarpeian Rock. If he has not yet reached puberty, the praetor shall decide whether he should be scourged and released, as reparation for the theft. [No. 5]
III	On property that is lent	10	Anyone who charges more than [10 percent] interest per year on a loan shall pay quadruple the amount [of the loan] as a penalty. [No. 2]
IV	On the rights of fathers, and of marriage	4	A father shall instantly put to death any newborn son who is a monster or is born with a nonhuman form. [No. 3]
V	On estates and guardianships	7	When no legal guardian has been appointed for an insane person or a spendthrift, his nearest male relative shall take charge of his [inherited] property. [No. 7]
VI	On ownership of property	10	A woman who has lived for an entire year with a man, provided that she has never stayed away from him for three successive nights, shall pass into his control as his legal wife. [No. 5]
VII	On crimes	17	Anyone who commits perjury shall be hurled from the Tarpeian Rock. [No. 12]

VIII	On the laws of real property	9	A space of two and one-half feet must be left between neighboring buildings. [No. 1]
IX	On public law	7	Anyone who organizes a nighttime assembly within the city of Rome shall be put to death. [No. 6]
X	On religious law	18	An oath shall have the greatest possible legal force and effect for the purpose of maintaining good faith. [No. 1]
XI	Supplement to Tables I–V	2	No widowed member of the senatorial order, if he is a father, shall contract a [second] marriage with a member of the plebeian order. [No. 1]
XII	Supplement to Tables VI–XII	3	If a slave should commit theft or vandalism, with the foreknowledge of his master, then the master shall be handed over to the victim [of the crime] in reparation for the harm done by the slave. [No. 3]

At each level of the hierarchy the essential social unit was the *familia*, a broader institution than "family." A familia consisted of an entire household and included the various aunts, uncles, nephews, nieces, cousins, close friends, clients, concubines, attendants, and house servants who lived under the same roof. It was firmly patriarchal, like the society as a whole. The male head of the household—the **pater familias**—held complete authority over the entire familia and was, legally speaking, the sole possessor of its property. Moreover, the pater familias possessed a legal right known as *patria potestas* ("paternal power," the subject of the fourth of the Twelve Tables), which gave him the right of life and death over his family. Several passages in the Twelve Tables delineate the extent of paternal power: *Paternal Power*

> To any father is given the power of life and death over his children. . . . A father has the power to sell any child of his into slavery, but if a child is sold three times by his father, he shall be free of his father after the third time. . . . In order to repudiate a wife, a husband shall simply say to her, "Manage your [dowry] property for yourself," take away her keys to the house, and expel her.

The father's authority was absolute and not to be questioned. Women were not property (except for slaves, of course) but had restrictions on their social actions. Roman law required a woman to have a legal guardian—usually her father or husband, but another male relative was possible—to conduct important public business like selling a property. Upper-class women often played influential roles in society; frequently well educated and socially connected, aristocratic women *Roles for Women*

Pater Familias   An upper-class Roman, identifiable by the robe he wears, is shown holding the busts of his ancestors, probably his father and grandfather. Deceased parents became the household gods of Roman families, and processions with these busts were a common ritual at festivals.

hosted formal dinners at which senatorial business was discussed, political allies and clients were courted, and prominent poets and scholars were patronized.

A unique subset of prominent women in Roman life was the tiny company of Vestal Virgins—six priestesses who presided over the cult of Vesta, the Roman goddess of the hearth. The Vestal Virgins were selected at a young age (usually between the ages of six and ten) and served terms of thirty years. Provided that they performed their temple duties unfailingly, they had complete legal independence, could own property, and received considerable honor. They were present at most public celebrations and at the dedication ceremonies of new public buildings. The Vestals's most important task was to preserve the Sacred Fire in the temple, which provided the source for all hearth fires in the city. As ritual guardians of the hearth the Vestals therefore served as the protectors of the Roman familia itself. After completing her service, a Vestal Virgin could marry if she wished, although if she did she then fell under the guardianship of her husband, who gained enormous prestige from having so renowned a wife.[2]

Among the plebeians, a woman's status and activity depended in large part on the kind of marriage she had, since Roman customs recognized different types of marriages. In one type, a wife remained under the patria potestas of her father even after her wedding, which meant that (with her father's permission) she could control her own property within the marriage independent of her husband. More frequently, a wife was under the patria potestas of her spouse. Another form of bond was concubinage, in which a man had a publicly recognized

---

[2]   If a Vestal Virgin made the grave mistake of losing her virginity while serving the cult, she was punished by being buried alive in a chamber stocked with two or three days' provisions. As described by the Roman author Plutarch (ca. 50–120 CE), "There is no sight more dreadful than this. Indeed, Rome never experiences a day more filled with gloom. When the litter [carrying the offending priestess] arrives at the spot . . . the *pontifex maximus* [head priest] murmurs some obscure prayers, stretching out his hands to the gods. Then, the awful moment having arrived, he takes the priestess, who is completely shrouded [like a corpse], and guides her to the ladder that leads down to the chamber, before himself turning away from her, along with the other priests present. When she has descended the ladder, it is drawn up. The chamber is then quickly buried with an enormous quantity of dirt thrown down from above, until the earth is level with the rest of the embankment. Such is the punishment for those Vestals who forsake their chastity."

relationship with another woman (his concubine). Legally speaking, concubines were not regarded as wives but as socially acceptable partners to a married man, entitled to polite treatment in society. A woman could not be married to one man while being a concubine to another because that would constitute adultery. A Roman man, in contrast, could have sexual relationships with any female slave in his familia.

The Romans saw justice in these arrangements, since it was the fathers' and husbands' responsibility, ultimately, to preserve the honor of the familia. Without it, a family could not hold its place in society.

THE REPUBLIC OF VIRTUE

Honor means different things to different people. Etymologically, it derives from the Latin word for "burden" (*onus, oneris*), reflecting the toil and struggle one must maintain to achieve it. To the Romans, honor consisted of playing one's appointed role in the familia and in the Republic. A father's honor lay in preserving his family's economic, social, and moral well-being. The Republic helped by implementing the office of **censor**, one that quickly became the most prestigious and feared of all the Roman magistracies.

The best-known censor is Cato (234–149 BCE), the subject of one of the popular biographies written by Plutarch (c. 50–120 CE), a Roman author and philosopher working centuries after Cato's censorship. According to Plutarch's *Life of Cato the Elder,*

Censoring the Public

> The office of censor, one might say, towered above every other civic honor and was in fact a perfect climax to a political career. Its powers were many and widespread, and included the authority to inspect the lives and morals of the citizens. The people who created the censorship believed it right not to leave people free to act as they wished without others' seeing and judging them—not in marriage, the begetting of children, the workings of everyday life, or socializing with one's friends. In fact, they deemed these to be the very aspects of a man's life where he shows his truest character. (ch. 16)

Plutarch then goes on to describe Cato's most famous exercise of censorial power. A prominent senator named Lucius Quinctius had conducted an unseemly relationship with a handsome young lad. Once, when the two were reclining together after a dinner that included too much wine, the young lad declared that he loved Lucius so much that he had run to his house when summoned, although he had been watching his first gladiatorial combat ever and had been looking forward to seeing a man slaughtered. Lucius, ever the attentive lover, then ordered a convicted criminal beheaded in front of his beloved to make up for what the lad had missed. Cato, horrified, stripped Lucius of his senatorial rank.

The censor had three specific duties: to maintain the census (the official list of all citizens of Rome, their property, and their legal class), to administer the finances of the state for all public works, and, most ominously, to preserve public morals. The censors could reward or punish an individual, or even an entire familia, by entering notations in the official census about the person's moral health. A black mark in the census imposed a moral stain called infamy (*infamia*), which meant the loss of the right to vote or participate in public life, the loss of admission into proper society, the ruin of any hopes to establish suitable marriages for one's children, and a permanent demotion in social status. Hence Romans considered it essential to observe, and to be seen to observe, the moral standards demanded by society.

What ethical crimes earned the censor's black mark? Most had to do with a failure to exercise proper leadership of the familia: a lifestyle of excessive luxury; neglect of one's crops; overindulgence of one's wife and children; failure to observe norms regarding marriage, inheritance, or divorce; cruelty to slaves; failure to take care of one's clients; commercial fraud; or participation in disreputable trades like acting or prostitution.

Daily Life and Religion

The Romans valued simplicity. Clothing, although coded to distinguish social classes, was unelaborate. Diets consisted of bread, simple vegetable dishes, fruits, and roasted meat, plus wine, invariably cut with water. Houses were simple structures turned inward to face a central open courtyard; poorer families resided in multiunit apartments that were based on the same design. Education in the early Republic was minimal except for those of senatorial or equestrian rank, and it took place entirely in the home. Boys received the basics of reading, writing, and arithmetic; were filled with moral tales of figures from Roman history; and began physical training as a preparation for military service. Girls, on the other hand, were instructed in home crafts like spinning, weaving, and sewing. Economic life centered on farming and local handcrafts, and much of the trade was by barter; in fact, the Republic did not even have a standard coinage until the early 3rd century BCE, when the geographic expansion of the Republic made a single coinage necessary.

Roman religion was polytheistic and animistic, focusing on a multitude of gods and spirits. The well-known deities of Jupiter, Venus, Mars, and the rest bore close resemblance to the Olympian gods and goddesses of the Greeks, and in later centuries the Romans emphasized the union of their mythologies. But for most Romans the smaller local divinities took precedence, especially the spirits of family ancestors known as the "household gods" (*lares familiares*), the daily worship of whom was the responsibility of the pater familias. These spirits watched over the household and the family property. Family ancestors continued to care for their descendants, and so prayers of dedication, thanksgiving, and respect were given to them always.

Religious life demanded constant, dutiful observance, following precise formulas of wording, gesture, and offering. Any mistake or omission rendered the ritual null and void. Since the Romans believed their well-being depended on the care of their spirit gods, observation of proper ritual was a matter of crucial significance. Religion was not a source of joy or spiritual exaltation but rather a moral responsibility. It is not accidental that the characteristic descriptor of Rome's legendary ancestor, Aeneas, was the Latin adjective *pius*—not "pious," but "dutiful."

SIZE MATTERS

The institutions, practices, and civic values established by the early Republic faced a dramatic challenge when the Republic began to expand. By 387 BCE the *Territorial* Roman Republic's might had extended only through a sweep of territory roughly *Expansion* 30 miles from the city. The increased area brought with it an increased popula- *and Social* tion, which Rome incorporated under its constitution. Conquered landowners *Conflict* and shopkeepers kept their property and legal rights, but now, as Roman plebeians, they paid taxes to the Republic. The Republic in turn used the additional revenues to connect towns with networks of roads and to bring freshwater into them with systems of aqueducts.

The larger the Republic grew, the more concessions it had to make to the plebeians who made up the bulk of the population. Two **consuls** served each year, sharing executive power. As early as 400 BCE plebeians had won the right of eligibility to the lower magistracies, and by 367 BCE the plebeians had forced passage of a law requiring that one of the two consuls be a plebeian. Soon the plebeians demanded a greater voice of their own in government, and the Republic responded by creating a plebeian council (*concilium plebis*) that played an advisory role. After the next wave of conquests, however, which extended the Republic's power through all of central Italy, the decisions of the plebeian council were made binding even if disapproved by the Senate.

The rise in power of the lower orders appeared to increase the representative nature of the Republic, but the patricians offset this by strengthening their ties with individual clients among the plebeian leaders. Moreover, the complex series of checks and balances among the various assemblies and magistracies prevented any single group from monopolizing power. The Greek historian Polybius (ca. 200–117 BCE) was a great admirer of the Republic and among the first to

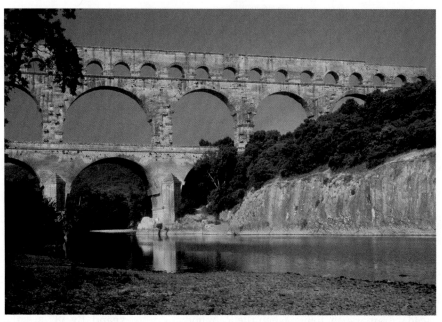

Roman Aqueduct   The Romans excelled in building aqueducts—complex delivery systems of tunnels, channels, bridges, and fountains to transport freshwater from remote sources. Shown here is one of the best-preserved examples, the Pont du Gard near Nimes (ancient Nemausus) in France, constructed in the late 1st century BCE. Built of stones fitted together without clamps or mortar, the span soars 160 feet high and 875 feet long, carrying water in a channel along its topmost level from 35 miles away.

champion Rome as the natural successor to the Hellenistic world. He wrote, "The result of this ability the various classes have to help or hinder each other mutually is to create in effect a unified government that can respond to any emergency; it is impossible to find a constitution better than this" (*Histories* 6.18).

The conquest of territory gained momentum throughout the 3rd century BCE. It is not clear how much of this resulted from intentional expansionism and how much from successful defensive strategies. However it occurred, by 265 BCE the Romans were in control of nearly the whole of the Italian peninsula and with their command of the westward-facing harbors were poised to move out into the sea-lanes. But there was a problem, because most of the western Mediterranean then lay under the control of Carthage. This wealthy North African city had been founded as a Phoenician colony in the 9th century BCE and came to oversee a vast commercial empire. Carthage had more money, more military power, and more naval experience than Rome. Carthage was also closer to the island of Sicily than Rome was, and Sicily, much of it held by Carthage, mattered enormously: it was one of the three greatest grain-producing regions in the ancient world, the other two being Egypt and Anatolia. If all of Sicily fell into Carthaginian hands, Roman Italy would be hard-pressed to feed itself (see Map 6.2).

The Western Mediterranean, ca. 264 BCE

Rome   Carthage

ATLANTIC

OCEAN

GAUL

Rhône

Ebro

Po

Marseilles

Adriatic Sea

IBERIAN

PENINSULA

Corsica

ITALY

Rome *LATIUM CAMPANIA*

Saguntum

Sardinia

*Balearic
Islands*

Panormus   Messana

Carthage

Sicily

Tunis   Acragas/   Syracuse

NUMIDIA   Agrigentum

Zama

MAURETANIA

*Mediterranean
Sea*

0 km   400

0 miles   400

A   F   R   I   C   A

N

MAP 6.2   The Western Mediterranean in the 3rd Century BCE   The foundations for the later Roman Empire were laid in the western Mediterranean, where Roman forces defeated and supplanted the Carthaginians in the three Punic Wars.

Neither Rome nor Carthage saw any workable way for them to share control of the Mediterranean, and consequently they never really tried. Rome had two factors in its favor: the solid loyalty of the peoples they had incorporated into the Republic and its mastery of a new technique of naval warfare. By dropping a series of large spiked planks onto the deck of an opposing ship, they could affix it to the Roman vessel, which allowed their soldiers to cross over and fight an infantry battle on the high seas. Between 264 and 146 BCE Rome fought three bloody wars with Carthage, won each time, and ended up as the master of the entire western Mediterranean basin. These became known as the **Punic Wars** (the name coming from the Latin word for the Carthaginians—*Poeni*—that is, Phoenicians): the first being a war for Sicily (264–241 BCE); the second being a war for control of Spain (218–201 BCE); and the last being an assault directly on North Africa (149–146 BCE), which ended with the complete destruction of Carthage and the sale into slavery of every Carthaginian who survived the carnage.

The Punic Wars

The Punic Wars marked a crucial turning point in Roman history. The first war, fought for control of grain-rich Sicily, required the Republic to develop naval forces. Up to this point the Romans had been a land-based society, with ample commercial fleets but little in the way of military capabilities at sea. With the experience gained in wresting Sicily from Carthaginian control, the Romans quickly moved around 240 BCE to seize Sardinia and Corsica and add them to its realm. With the struggle to control the Mediterranean thus leaning in favor of Rome, Carthage spent the next two decades developing its interests in eastern Spain; Rome countered by extending its reach into northern Italy and coastal France. The inevitable clash came in 218 BCE when hostilities with Carthage were renewed. This second war's most famous chapter was the surprise invasion of Italy by Carthage's young general (and heir to the throne) Hannibal (247–182 BCE), who crossed the Alps with a force of twenty-five thousand infantry and eighteen war elephants. A Roman force under the command of Scipio Africanus (237–187 BCE) conquered Carthage's Spanish territories and advanced into North Africa, which cut off Hannibal's supplies and forced his withdrawal in 204 BCE. In battle against Hannibal at Zama, just outside Carthage, Scipio defeated the young general, who fled into exile, thus ending the Second Punic War. The third war arose from Rome's desire simply to complete the vanquishing of its rival. Already in possession of Carthage's Mediterranean holdings, the Romans chose to bring matters to a close by destroying the city that had caused them so much trouble. Carthage was burned to the ground and all its inhabitants enslaved.[3]

But that hardly ended matters. Off in the east, King Philip V of Macedonia (r. 221–179 BCE) had supported Carthage in its second war with Rome, which prompted the Republic to declare war on him in 200 BCE. Philip surrendered in 197 BCE, and Rome freed the Greek poleis that had been under Philip's control and then withdrew. But when the Seleucid emperor Antiochus III (r. 223–187 BCE) moved his army into newly liberated Greece, the Romans returned (191 BCE), drove him out, and pursued him across Anatolia. Ironically, the Romans' decisive victory over Antiochus took place at Thermopylae, the site of the heroic stand of the Spartan forces against the victorious Persian army of Darius. According to the Greek historian Appian (95–165 CE), the Romans lost only two hundred men at Thermopylae, compared to the Seleucids, who lost ten thousand. So began Rome's expansion into the eastern Mediterranean. By the end of the Third Punic War Rome had seized all of Greece and most of Anatolia. In 146 BCE Rome stood as the undisputed master of the whole sea (see Map 6.3).

The problem was that the Romans had not exactly planned for their success. Their political system, designed to govern a compact land-based republic,

---

[3] The oft-told tale of the Romans' plowing the Carthaginian fields with salt to ruin the soil and prevent anyone from resurrecting the city is untrue.

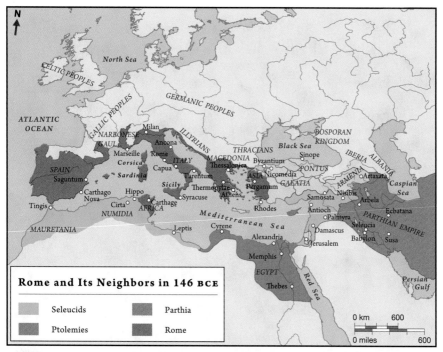

MAP 6.3   **Rome and Its Neighbors in 146 BCE**   The end of the Punic Wars in 146 BCE left Rome as the dominant force in the Mediterranean world.

unexpectedly found itself in awkward possession of a vast, scattered, sea-based empire. What to do? In the absence of an imperial plan, the Republic simply handed over the conquered lands to the generals who had taken them, thus out-sourcing the expense of maintaining the armies and running the provinces.[4] These generals were thus able to amass vast personal fortunes, and they promptly used these to fund further campaigns and to buy influence with the various coun-cils, assemblies, and magistrates back in Rome. To prevent civil servants from being corrupted by bribes, the Republic developed the tradition of assigning the leading magistrates, after their terms of office were complete, to provincial gover-norships. This got them out of the city and away from the avenues of power, but it also gave them the means to raise fortunes of their own so that they could reenter Republican politics with full coffers.

Stresses on the Republic

In other words, the Republic tried to combat corruption by spreading the corruption around. This revolving-door movement from central government to provincial leadership and back again proved immensely profitable to the forty or

---

[4]   Roman armies were organized into units called legions, which were in turn composed of three forces: cavalry, heavy infantry, and light infantry (auxiliaries). The size of legions varied considerably over time. Through most of the Republican period, a typical legion had three hundred cavalry and forty-two hun-dred heavy infantry, with highly changeable numbers of auxiliaries.

Bread and Circuses   The Circus Maximus ("Giant Track," literally) in Rome was, like the forum, a site for popular gatherings. Athletic contests of all sorts (especially chariot races) took place here, and the Circus also was a venue for food distributions. Most of the public games held here were associated with religious festivals.

fifty families who monopolized the process. It also caused terrible hardship and turmoil for the bulk of the people.

The Punic Wars had left many of Italy's farms physically and financially ruined, the victims of rampaging soldiers, neglect, or cheap imports of grain that knocked Italy's farmers out of the market. Many thousands of small landholders therefore sold their lands to the rich, who established vast plantations—known by the Latin term of **latifundia**—that specialized in commercial crops like olives and grapes. With so many slaves available because of the wars, there were few employment opportunities for the displaced rural classes, who flooded into towns and cities.

The population of Rome itself increased to unheard-of levels: from somewhere around 100,000 before the First Punic War (264–241 BCE) to easily five times that figure a little more than a century later. By the beginning of the Common Era, the city held well more than a million people within its borders. The government distributed "bread and circuses"—that is, food and entertainment—to keep the crowds quiet, but clearly something needed to be done. By the mid-2nd century BCE, voices in government were crying out for dramatic reform of the constitution as the only way to prevent the Republic from collapse. But what form would such reforms take?

CAN THE REPUBLIC BE SAVED?

From 133 to 31 BCE the Roman world suffered through a brutal series of internal wars and political struggles. Although the names kept changing, the basic issues at stake and the remedies proposed for them did not. The fundamental issue was whether the Republic could, or even should, be saved. Did an empire require a different form of government altogether, and if so, then what form should that government take? But other issues loomed large too. Should the military be reformed to allow broader participation by the people? What, if anything, should be done about the enormous inequities in wealth (and therefore in social and political power) that had resulted from Rome's rapid acquisition of so many new territories? Should a path to citizenship be opened to the newly conquered peoples at both ends of the Mediterranean—and if so, how broad and level should that path be? Conservative politicians wanted to preserve the constitution at any cost; they believed that traditional Roman values and virtues, if earnestly retained, could make the Republican framework work for the whole Mediterranean sprawl. Reformers, on the other hand, were convinced that the Republic was dead, or dying, and that hard-headed realism demanded sweeping change—although not increasing democracy. Calls to alter the constitution in favor of one social class or another met with fervent opposition from those demanding a different change or no change at all. The conflicts were fought in stages: between the Gracchi brothers and the Senate (133–122 BCE); between parties led by Marius and Sulla (86–82 BCE); then again by groups loyal to Julius Caesar and Pompey (52–44 BCE); and finally between the factions led by Octavian and Marc Antony (42–27 BCE).

With the Gracchi, the specific issue was economic: What should be done about displaced poor farmers? The Gracchi brothers, Tiberius (162–133 BCE) and *The* Gaius (152–121 BCE), championed a land redistribution plan that most in the *Gracchi* Senate—wealthy landowners who stood to lose from this legislation—would not tolerate. When efforts at a political resolution failed, the elder brother Tiberius was assassinated in 133 BCE. Gaius took up his brother's cause, but he too lost to his opponents—and committed suicide in 122 BCE. Gaius had proposed granting Roman citizenship to all of the Republic's Italian allies, which would have blocked the patricians' efforts to confiscate their landholdings.

Marius (157–86 BCE), a war hero who had served several terms as consul, altered a long-standing policy regarding military recruitment. Admission to the *Marius* army had earlier required the ownership of land—the idea being that those with *and Sulla* a vested interest in the Republic would make the most loyal and effective fighters.

But Marius saw how the vast numbers of displaced farmers, and their replacement with large slave-driven latifundia, meant that there were fewer landholders from whom to draw the number of soldiers needed to defend the state. After all, Rome now controlled an empire 3,000 miles from end to end. So he dropped the land-ownership requirement altogether and opened the ranks to anyone who was capable, interested in serving, and willing to swear loyalty to him as commander in chief. Other generals, in that age of semiprivatized armies, were free to follow suit. Those opposed to him, led by a patrician named Sulla (138–78 BCE), feared that admitting the lowest orders into public life would weaken the Republican spirit of the army.

The Republic dispatched Marius and his new army to North Africa in 107 BCE, where a local ruler named Jugurtha was stirring up opposition to Rome, and in 102 BCE sent him against a marauding group of Germans bent on invading Italy. Two years later, in 100 BCE, Marius retired from politics and moved to the east, hoping to spend his last years in peace. So much for planning. Throughout the 90s BCE Rome's Italian allies pressed their demands for citizenship in the Republic and their fair share in its seized lands and booty. These allies (*socii*, in Latin) finally formed an army of their own and decided to march on Rome, which triggered what is called the Social War (91–88 BCE). Marius was soon called out of retirement to help put down the rebels—after which he again withdrew.

At this point the patrician Sulla, elected consul in 88 BCE, was commissioned by the Senate to lead an army against a provincial rebellion in Anatolia, but the Plebeian Assembly appointed Marius to the post instead, which turned the two rivals (and their respective supporting factions) directly against one another. Sulla's forces purged both the Senate and the Assembly of his opponents, then marched off to Anatolia; Marius then entered Rome while Sulla was away and regained control, taking up his seventh term as consul—only to die soon thereafter. After Marius's death and his own victories in the east, Sulla seized control of Rome (82 BCE), had himself appointed dictator, and spent three years restoring the Senate's supreme position over the Plebeian Assembly—largely by proscribing anyone who opposed him.[5] The Republic lurched from one political extreme to another.

Caesar and Pompey The effect of Sulla's dictatorship was to empower the aristocracy and weaken the power of the plebeians. Soon, however, new leaders emerged to espouse the people's cause, once again using the army as their tool of influence. The most prominent of these military men were **Julius Caesar** (100–44 BCE) and Pompey (106–48 BCE, called "the Great" after his service to Sulla in 82 BCE).

---

[5]   Proscription was the formal proclamation, as well as condemnation of "enemies of the state." Individuals whose names appeared on proscription lists could be killed by any citizen—who could then confiscate the victim's wealth and property. Sulla proscribed three thousand individuals during his dictatorship.

Initially they cooperated on a plan to "restore the Republic" by forming an alliance with Marcus Crassus (ca. 115–53 BCE), but this alliance—a *triumvirate,* meaning "rule of three men"—soon dissolved into open rivalry between Caesar and Pompey, both headstrong, powerful egoists. Ostensibly, Caesar was the radical reformer, whereas Pompey was supported by the conservatives in the Senate. In reality they both probably wanted the same thing—namely, to run the empire as an empire. The centuries-old system of checks and balances among governmental assemblies and offices made efficient administration impossible. And Caesar and Pompey (whose backgrounds were as decidedly undemocratic military commanders) each wanted to institute a streamlined single-command administration. Caesar's power base was in the west; he had conquered Gaul. Pompey had made his name and fortune fighting in the east. Matters came to a head in 52 BCE when the Senate appointed Pompey as sole consul and declared Caesar an enemy of the state. War ensued.

In 49 BCE Caesar drove Pompey from Rome; Pompey fled east to raise more troops. Caesar caught up with him in Greece the following year and, in a battle at Pharsalus, defeated him. Pompey escaped from the battle but was later captured and assassinated by the Egyptian queen, Cleopatra (r. 51–30 BCE, the last active pharaoh Egypt ever had), who was allied with Caesar and in fact later became his lover and bore him a son. Caesar returned to Rome and became sole ruler. In 46 BCE he took the title of dictator. Two years later, after he had declared himself dictator for life, he was murdered by a group of nobles who feared that he was going to institute a monarchy. The Republic was essentially over (see Map 6.4).

Dreams of keeping a workable Republic died hard, however. When the civil struggle entered its final phase, between rival politicians and generals Marc Antony (83–30 BCE) and Octavian (63 BCE–14 CE), many still thought the old constitution could be restored. Antony soon left for Egypt to get support from Cleopatra, with whom he was in love. When Octavian—who was both Julius Caesar's grandnephew and his adopted son—finally defeated Marc Antony at the battle of Actium in 31 BCE, Octavian not only put an end to the strife but also added Egypt to the empire. After more than three thousand years of self-rule, Egypt was now another province in Rome's empire. Octavian's power was consolidated. *Octavian and Marc Antony*

Taking the title **Princeps Augustus** (meaning "first in honor"—his name being the first one on the list of Roman citizens kept by the censors), Octavian instituted a new chapter in Rome's history, the principate, and inadvertently gave himself a new name: **Augustus**. Recognizing the utility of maintaining a Republican image, Augustus ruled the empire as an emperor but steadfastly maintained the fiction of representative government, portraying himself merely as the person who put into action the decrees made by the Senate. By appearing to play by the old rules *The Principate*

MAP 6.4 **The Roman World at the End of the Republic, 44 BCE** By the time of Julius Caesar's assassination in 44 BCE, the territory that would be the Roman Empire was almost complete.

and to uphold traditional values, Augustus reinvented the political system. His reign (31 BCE–14 CE) was unusually successful. The Roman Empire had begun.

ROME'S GOLDEN AGE: THE AUGUSTAN ERA

Augustus and all his successors as rulers of Rome held the title of **imperator**, usually translated as "emperor" but which in Republican times was the term for a victorious general, especially one granted the right to a triumph.[6] This was an official recognition of exceptional military achievement, in which the triumphant general was allowed to parade his troops within the city limits amid songs, prayers, speeches, and festivities. At all other times the army was forbidden to cross the city limits (a line called the *pomerium*) and enter Rome itself. The only organized fighting force permitted within the pomerium was the imperator's personal bodyguard corps—the Praetorian Guard, which also functioned as a police force.

---

6 *Imperium* ("command") was the constitutional authority to command obedience—specifically from the military. Different magistracies held different degrees of imperium. All consuls held imperium during their term of office. But the Republic could assign *imperium maius* ("superior command") to individuals on a case-by-case basis.

The early emperors scrupulously avoided anything that smacked of monarchy: their homes were comfortable but not palatial; they wore simple dress; they walked the streets of Rome, took part in public debates, and attended religious services. Even their constitutional and honorific titles had Republican roots. With the exception of aberrant moral monsters like Caligula (r. 37–41 CE) and Nero (r. 54–68 CE), the early emperors cultivated auras of humility, honoring Republican traditions even while exercising central command. Caligula and Nero have been accused of nearly every imaginable vice: incest, theft, graft, torture, murder, prostitution. Caligula reportedly grew insane in office, insisting, for example, on his favorite horse's ordination as a priest, which he then tried to appoint to a consulship. Nero famously allowed the Great Fire of Rome to blaze for days without doing anything about it, then blamed the Christians for it and staged a bloody persecution of them that resulted in thousands more deaths. After nearly two hundred years of civil strife, most Romans were willing to accept autocracy so long as the autocrats kept the peace, promoted prosperity, and did not flaunt their power.[7]

To accomplish those goals, the emperors needed to control the army, facilitate urban growth, and help to integrate the hundreds of ethnic groups who lived within the empire. First, the army needed to be professionalized. In *Professionalization* Republic times, soldiers had been essentially the paid employees of *of the Army* the generals who commanded them. Caesar had conquered Gaul, for example, largely to acquire a fortune. Later, when Caesar clashed with Pompey for control of the government, he used a portion of his vast wealth to lure many of Pompey's defeated soldiers to join his army; when Octavian/Augustus defeated Marc Antony at Actium, the same held true for him. Augustus's immediate concern on starting his reign as imperator was to shrink the gargantuan army he had inherited. Hence he commandeered all of Egypt as his personal domain and used the money available through it to offer pensions and award estates to more than a quarter-million soldiers. This action reduced the army to a manageable twenty-eight legions. Soldiers henceforth received their pay, according to a set scale, directly from Rome itself instead of from the generals.

Given the size of the empire, most government had to be local—which meant *Urban* that western Europe had to be urbanized. Municipal traditions in the east were *Growth* widespread and strong, but the west (meaning North Africa, the Spanish peninsula, and virtually all of Europe north of the Alps) remained overwhelmingly rural. Most of Europe itself, moreover, consisted of a vast, dense forest in which the tribal inhabitants had established a sprawl of occasional clearings. To bring order to this world, the Romans began to build cities and a network of roads to

---

[7]   Caligula was murdered by members of his own bodyguard. Nero, who fancied himself a great artist and athlete, was politically inept as well as a murderous brute. He committed suicide before the group of soldiers planning to kill him could reach him.

connect them. Most inland cities began as military encampments that settlers refilled after the soldiers had moved on. The officials placed over these new settlements administered their surrounding districts, maintained the roads, and established all the public buildings needed to foster Roman civilization: temples, theaters, bathhouses, market squares, courts. So long as they maintained order, kept the population reasonably peaceful, and avoided blatant corruption, most municipal leaders, and later the provincial governors who represented the next higher stage of the imperial bureaucracy, enjoyed considerable freedom of action. In this way the empire operated more as a confederation of semi-independent city-states and provinces than as a monolithic empire taking orders from an autocratic central regime.

Social Integration   Many elements of Roman life contributed to social integration. The twin religious policies of toleration and syncretism played particularly important roles. Polytheisms, generally speaking, accommodate one another easily. My belief in one river god does not necessarily threaten your belief in another: two different rivers, two different deities—and hence there is no need for one religion to challenge or usurp the other. It is even possible that the two are the same god manifested and understood differently in different places. When the Romans absorbed first Greece and then the rest of the Hellenistic lands, they identified similarities between their faiths. The Greek thunder god Zeus approximated the Roman sky god Jupiter; Aphrodite paired with Venus; Athena resembled Artemis. Such parallels were not coincidental. As we have seen, polytheisms originate as attempts to explain natural phenomena: storms at sea happen because the sea god is angry about something, for example. And since Mediterranean societies confronted the same major phenomena, the divine powers they used to explain them bore certain similarities. By encouraging the Mediterranean peoples to recognize the same gods and goddesses, the Romans fostered a single, multiethnic civilization.

However, only the higher Greek divinities—the gods and goddesses of Mount Olympus—were merged in this way. Daily religious observances for most Roman people still focused on local deities and ancestral worship. This led the emperors to inaugurate communal ruler worship. The custom began as a civil recognition of the deification of late rulers; thus Augustus promoted the deification of the assassinated Julius Caesar, and his successor Tiberius (r. 14–37 CE) championed the deification of Augustus. Deceased rulers were to be regarded as universal "household gods"—symbolically, a pater familias to the entire empire. Soon enough, however, the notion arose of recognizing the divinity of the living emperor. By encouraging, and then by requiring, subjects to worship emperors (past or present) as divinities, the Romans tried to keep a degree of common religious practice among the people so as to counteract the forces that pulled them apart. It did not matter whether anyone actually believed in the emperor-god. It

The Ara Pacis This procession of senators and high priests appears on a side wall of the Ara Pacis, the "Altar of Peace" in Rome, commissioned by the Senate to honor Augustus and consecrated in 9 CE. As a whole, the Ara Pacis reflects the Augustan vision of Roman civil religion.

mattered only that they were willing to participate in a public, communal ritual once a year in which thanks were given to the divine ruler for his guidance. Dutiful observance, not sincere conviction, was both the goal and the spirit of the requirement. A cohesive civil society, not spiritual enlightenment, was the aim.

THE SEA, THE SEA

The Mediterranean Sea—"Our Sea" (*Mare nostrum*) to the Romans—was the essential infrastructure holding the empire together (see Map 6.5). Physically, the sea consists of two deep basins separated by an underwater ridge between Sicily and Tunisia, with narrow straits at either end. (The Strait of Gibraltar connects it with the Atlantic Ocean to the west, and the Dardanelles links it to the Black Sea to the northeast.) With a surface area of nearly a million square miles, it stretches 2,200 miles from west to east and nearly 1,000 miles at its greatest north–south expanse. Water enters the sea through the two straits and from a handful of rivers—the Nile in Egypt, the Ebro in Spain, the Rhône in France, and the Po in Italy. However, the warm climate causes faster than usual evaporation, which in turn causes the Mediterranean's relatively high salinity—hence the proliferation of salt deposits around the coastline.

MAP 6.5   The Mediterranean: Greek and Roman Perspectives Compared   Whereas the Greeks established hundreds of colonies abroad, the Romans recognized that their central position in the Mediterranean was an ideal site from which to create a network of links with all the peoples of the sea. Adapted from Malkin, Irad, *A Small Greek World: Networks in the Ancient Mediterranean* (2011).

Despite those million square miles of surface area, however, the Mediterranean is not large enough to have a significant tide. Ships can thus set sail at almost any hour of any day, a significant advantage for the trading cities that surround it. The Mediterranean's temperate climate results from its fortunate geography, and its smooth waters are a consequence of the relative narrowness of the Strait of Gibraltar: most North Atlantic storms cannot pass through the strait and instead are diverted up the western coastline of Europe. (This is one reason why it rains so much in England.)

Given these inviting conditions, ancient sailors had a relatively easy time crossing the Mediterranean. Moreover, the many islands and jutting promontories like the Italian and Greek peninsulas meant that sailors could ply the sea-lanes without ever losing sight of land, which helped them to reach faraway ports without getting lost. The ancients steered by landmarks rather than by the stars. Peoples as far apart as eastern Spain and the Holy Land could be in

Mediterranean Trade Routes

regular and reliable contact with one another, buying and selling wares, sharing ideas, and establishing permanent relationships. And in fact they needed such contact, because none of the coastal societies was economically self-sufficient. Mountains ring most of the eastern Mediterranean basin, and the Sahara Desert stretches along its southern expanse. In many places the mountains reach almost to the coast. Cut off from their agricultural hinterlands, coastal societies could not produce all the foodstuffs and material goods they needed to survive, and therefore they needed to trade with one another to stay alive. The natural qualities of the sea made this trade possible virtually year-round—even for bulky, heavy commodities.

The Romans recognized that their central position in the Mediterranean was an ideal site from which to create a network of links among all the peoples of the *Rome* sea. With Carthage in ruins, no rival stood in Rome's way. But lust for power was *Takes* not the only motive behind Rome's expansion—and may not even have been the *Charge* most prominent one. Rather, the Roman value of practicality likely played an important role. The Mediterranean linked hundreds of coastal societies; a ship sent out from Rome could reach Barcelona in only three days, Alexandria in ten. And these societies shared similar agricultural methods (the terracing of arid hinterlands, widespread use of irrigation systems), similar diets (grains, fish, olive oil, and wine), and similar social organizations (tradesmen and merchants playing the lead, rather than large landholders). If we think of the Mediterranean as a single entity, then the attraction of uniting them under a single administration becomes clear: with a single currency, single law, single tariff code, and single system of weights and measures in place, goods, capital, and services will move with optimal efficiency, raising everyone's standard of living.

Experience within Italy had convinced the Romans that people will put up with the loss of political freedom if they can still prosper economically, *Romanization* whereas policies of inclusion of subjected peoples within the dominant society will go far to relieve civil unrest. When attempting to secure a new territory, the regime begun by Augustus therefore took care to "Romanize" its institutions and trade, reinstall local rulers as representatives of the empire, and then withdraw. Since travel by sea was so quick by ancient standards, the Romans seldom had to occupy the lands they conquered. Word of any rebellion would reach the imperial court quickly, and a fleet could be dispatched long before the rebellion had a chance to take root. In other words, a town or district newly added to the Roman Empire could conceivably never see a Roman soldier again, as long as the laws were obeyed, the taxes paid, and things kept quiet.

Loading Grain on a Transport Ship   A worker here pours grain into a barrel; once full, the barrel would be rolled into the cargo area below deck. The name of the ship—*Isis Giminiana*—is given at the far left. The ship's master (*magister*) is Faurales, and the merchant is Abscanius. Two other workers haul sacks of grain up the gangplank at the right. This ca. 200 CE fresco comes from Ostia, a port city at the mouth of the Tiber River in central Italy.

While adding territories to its empire, Rome's army also provided a tool for social engineering. Taking further Alexander the Great's policy of cultural integration, the Romans opened the army to recruits from every part of the empire—enrolling Celts, Dacians, Illyrians, Libyans, Phoenicians, and Syrians alike, plus many others. In turn, their combined military experience helped bring Roman culture to the provinces. Non-Roman recruits received three meals a day and a regular salary, traveled from one end of the empire to another, and helped to keep the peace and serve the common cause. Along the way they learned Latin, acquired the basics of Roman law and morals, and practiced Roman civic religion. The empire's goal was to break down each soldier's sense of particular ethnic affiliation and replace it with a new identity, one based on membership in a larger, interconnected society. After twenty years of service, each soldier received either a cash pension or the grant of an estate and could enjoy all the fruits of citizenship.[8] The estates awarded were large, prosperous, and never in the individual soldier's original homeland. Having created a "Roman"—that is, someone whose self-identity and personal allegiance went beyond mere ethnicity, someone who participated in an idea of human unity—the last thing the government wanted was to restore him to his place of birth. In this way, the army used to fullest effect the Mediterranean, Mare Nostrum, to integrate the peoples of the empire, redistribute them, and cement the idea of "Romanness."

---

[8]   Citizenship was a prerequisite for joining the army. But noncitizens could enlist in the auxiliary forces and earn citizenship after retirement—to be passed on to their sons.

The emperor was the commander in chief of all the legions. In practice, however, the regular command of each legion was given to an imperial representative known as a **legate** (*legatus*), whom the emperor selected from the members in the Senate. In smaller provinces that required the presence of only one legion, the legate also served as the provincial governor. In larger provinces, two or more legions were assigned; a separate legate was assigned to each legion, but the provincial governor served as a superior commander to each legate. In this way, senators endorsed imperial power, while the throne made a point of recognizing senatorial privilege. Even more important, Rome placed senators in positions in which their status was publicly seen. The fiction of Republicanism was thus given continual attention, even as true control of the army remained centralized in the emperor's hands.

ROMAN LIVES AND VALUES

The first two centuries CE are known as the era of the Roman Peace, or **Pax Romana**. Like all historical labels it represents only a partial truth, and although most of the *Pax* empire experienced a sustained tranquility, there was more than enough discontent *Romana* around to keep the soldiers busy. Consider the rebellion in England in 60 CE led by Boudicca, the widow of a Briton tribal king. Some Roman soldiers had plundered the dead king's home, tied up and flogged Boudicca, and made her watch as they raped her daughters. After the attack, Boudicca rallied the Britons to drive the Romans from England. As the senator and historian Tacitus (ca. 56–120 CE) narrates it:

> Then a horde of Britons surrounded [the Roman garrison at Camulodunum—modern Colchester] and ransacked and set the town all ablaze, forcing the garrison to take refuge in the temple [to the divine emperor Claudius]; this temple was stormed after a two days' siege. Rome's ninth legion, under the command of Quintus Petulius Cerialis Caesius Rufus, tried to relieve the town but was first stopped, then routed, by the victorious Britons, who massacred the entire infantry. . . . [Boudicca's troops] delighted in plunder and scarcely gave a thought to anything else, for they continually passed right by Roman encampments and garrisons and headed straight for whatever targets had the most loot and the least protection. The Roman and provincial dead in those places is reckoned at seventy thousand, for the Britons had no interest in taking or ransoming prisoners or exchanging prisoners. All they wanted was to slit Roman throats or put nooses around them, to put Romans to the torch or to crucify them. . . . Boudicca circled her soldiers in a chariot in which her daughters rode with her, and cried out: "Britons! You are accustomed to female commanders in wartime. I am the daughter of accomplished warriors, but

> I am not now fighting for wealth or for a realm. Rather, I fight simply as an ordinary woman who has lost her freedom; I fight for the wounds done to my body and for the outrage done to my daughters. Roman malice knows no bounds—they murder old men and rape young girls. May our gods grant us the revenge we deserve!" (*Annals* 14.32–35)

It took eleven years for the Roman army to put down Boudicca's revolt—although they never managed to capture Boudicca herself. Following the defeat of her army, Boudicca killed herself by drinking poison.

Even so, for all the signs of discontent, no ancient society experienced anything close to the prosperity and social stability of the empire during the two centuries of the Pax Romana. Cities multiplied and grew, rights of citizenship were continually extended to more and more people, and piracy in the Mediterranean—which had been widespread throughout the Hellenistic Age—came to an end. Literacy spread, and something close to a regular system of justice ordered everyone's lives. In 212 CE, under Emperor Caracalla (r. 198–217 CE), every person in the empire who was not a slave was declared a citizen. The elaborate commercial networks allowed each region of the empire to specialize in producing what it did best (see Map 6.6).

MAP 6.6   Trades in the Roman Empire   Bustling trade routes helped to consolidate Roman rule over the far-flung empire.

Two significant economic weaknesses remained, however. First was reliance on slave labor. Slaves comprised as much as 20 percent of the empire's population, so labor-intensive activities—agriculture and mining in particular—were vulnerable to labor shortages. In the ancient world, the mortality rates of slave populations usually exceeded their birth rates, which meant that societies dependent on slave labor continually needed to add new slaves to the mix just to stay even. As long as the empire kept conquering new territories—and thus acquiring new slaves—the problem was held at bay, but only temporarily. The second weakness was the fondness of the wealthiest Romans for Asian luxury goods like silk and spices, which they purchased in large quantities. This passion drained gold and silver reserves from

Roman Women   Wall painting from Herculaneum, near Rome, 1st century CE, depicting a set of ladies being groomed by a servant hair dresser.

the Roman economy. Until about 200 CE, mines were able to keep up, but productivity declined quickly thereafter, which raised the danger of currency devaluation. But during the Pax Romana years, these were only potential weaknesses; for the time being, abundance and comfort were the hallmarks of Roman economic life.

The Romans adopted many of the great Greek intellectual and artistic achievements, but popular prejudice of the time regarded Greek culture as effete. They saw it as too inclined to luxury, idleness, and pleasure, especially when compared to the manly self-discipline and pragmatism that they liked to think was the essence of Romanness. Some of this is simply the swagger of the victor, but it would be a mistake to dismiss it outright. Roman culture valued a sense of duty— to the familia, to the household gods, to one's city, and finally to the empire. A good life was a life of virtue, of owed service duly performed. These were the values the Romans brought with them into the eastern Mediterranean, where they encountered the two dominant philosophies of the Hellenistic era, Epicureanism and Stoicism (see chapter 5).

Of the two, Stoicism appealed more to the Romans. Among philosophers the most prominent Roman Stoics were the tragedian, essayist, and statesman Seneca *Roman* (4 BCE–65 CE) and the former slave turned moralist and teacher Epictetus *Stoicism* (55–135 CE). Seneca dedicated many years of his life to serving the empire, even taking on the thankless task of tutoring the teenaged Nero. In the year 65 CE Nero accused Seneca of complicity in an attempt to murder him and ordered his former teacher to commit suicide. Seneca complied by slitting his wrists, but his blood flowed so slowly that he never lost consciousness. He drank poison next, but it too failed to kill him. Finally Seneca immersed his slashed arms in a hot bath. The warmth opened his veins, the blood ran out, and at last he died. His protracted death brings to mind such Senecan statements as "Act toward men as though God were always watching; speak to God as though men were always listening" and "You can tell a man's character by how he receives praise" (*Epistles* 2.2 and 52.12, respectively).

In contrast to the aristocratic Seneca, Epictetus led a life of poverty and austerity. Born lame and into slavery, he nevertheless learned some philosophy from a local teacher after his owner moved to Rome and granted Epictetus his freedom. He went on to teach philosophy himself. In 93 CE he moved back to Greece and set up a school. His most memorable passage comes from his *Enchiridion* (*Handbook*):

> In life, you ought always to behave as you would at a formal banquet. A dish is being passed around and it comes to you—so reach out your hand politely and take a modest helping, and then pass the dish along without delay. If a dish does not come your way, don't act out your longing for it by stretching out your hand for it. Just wait until it comes to you. This is how you should act regarding everything in life—including children, wife, career, and wealth. (ch. 15)

Stoic ethics conformed to Roman morals in the broadest sense—with their emphasis on duty, forbearance, self-discipline, and concern for others. Above all, one ought to serve Rome, praise Rome, live for Rome—because only in the empire and its vision of the unification of all societies in a single working whole can the harmony of the world be attained. Here is how the Roman poet Virgil (70 BCE–19 CE) described the empire's destined mission:

> Others shall cast their bronze to breathe
> with softer features, I well know, and draw
> living lines from the marble, and plead
> better causes, and with pen shall better trace the paths
> of the heavens and proclaim the stars in their rising;
> but it shall be your charge, O Roman, to rule
> the nations in your empire. This shall be your art:
> to lay down the laws of peace, to show mercy
> to the conquered, and to beat the haughty down.
> (*Aeneid* 6.1012–1028)

For at least 150 years after Augustus, Romans did this rather well. Dividing society between *honestiores* ("the better people") and *humiliores* ("the

*Imperial
Administration*

lesser people"), they provided a reliable infrastructure for urban life and a consistent form of justice for each. The honestiores consisted of the senatorial and equestrian classes, municipal officials, and army veterans, and their status entitled them to immunity from torture, lesser criminal fines, and, in capital crimes, exemption from crucifixion. (Like Seneca, honestiores condemned to death were allowed to commit an honorable suicide rather than face the intentionally humiliating and agonizing death by crucifixion.) The humiliores consisted of everyone else in the empire apart from the slaves—who, in terms of the law, were counted as property rather than people. People were expected to obey the law, pay their taxes, participate in public religious rites, and hold to the ethical duties of family care and public service; if they did so, the empire largely left them alone. Even in the prosecution of crime, Roman tradition was to allow matters to be resolved with as little state involvement as possible.

Most civil cases were tried without any public officials whatsoever. A plaintiff filed a complaint with a local magistrate called an *aedile* who maintained a list of individuals in the vicinity who held Roman citizenship. Any citizen accepted by the plaintiff and defendant could serve as judge. The aedile's role was limited to making sure the temporary judge understood the basics of the law as it pertained to the type of case he was judging. The judge's decision was then entered in the municipal records, and the matter was closed.

Taxes were collected by a tax-farming system. The imperial court determined its budgetary needs for the year and then apportioned the revenues owed by each province, district, and city to meet that need. Local officials, who presumably understood the economic realities of their own territories better than administrators back in Rome did, then collected taxes accordingly as they thought most fair and effective given local conditions. If they gathered more than they were required to send to Rome, they kept the surplus (public officials did not receive salaries); if they failed to meet their tax obligation, they were expected to make up the deficit out of their personal funds. Officials also paid for local public works out of their personal funds—roads and aqueducts, maintaining harbors and sewers, and so on. Personal profit from public taxation, therefore, was not frowned upon. In fact, some profit was necessary if the officials were to be held liable for years of deficit. What sounds like an invitation to abuse actually worked fairly well. If an official collected so much tax that the people began to grumble, Rome would hear of it quickly enough and deal with the overaggressive governor.

The system was sufficiently effective to survive even disastrous reigns like those of Caligula and Nero, whose well-known personal licentiousness went down poorly with most Romans precisely because such indecency was so very un-Roman. Domitian (r. 81–96 CE), an obsessively controlling personality, left most of the Senate disaffected by his failure to maintain the Augustan fiction of

Republican rule, but he did leave the treasury with a surplus despite an ambitious building campaign and several expensive military ventures.

HEIGHT OF THE PAX ROMANA: THE "FIVE GOOD EMPERORS"

The high point of the Pax Romana came during the reigns of the so-called Five Good Emperors: Nerva (r. 96–98 CE), Trajan (r. 98–117 CE), Hadrian (r. 117–138 CE), Antoninus Pius (r. 138–161 CE), and Marcus Aurelius (r. 161–180 CE). This was the time of the empire's greatest physical expanse and its greatest prosperity, but what really made these emperors so "good" was that they returned to the Republican fiction, giving the Senate its due respect while exercising autocratic control. Moreover, each of the five had the decency not to have a surviving heir, which allowed the Senate to appear to be the deliberative body for the selection of the next emperor. In reality, each of the five adopted his most capable general, who then became his successor after carefully going through the motions of a supposed senatorial election.

Thamagudi, Modern Timgad, Algeria   Founded by the emperor Trajan in 100 CE, Thamagudi boasted a theater, a forum, and streets paved in a checkerboard pattern.

The rulers appointed the provincial governors, district officials, and municipal chiefs who then administered the empire locally. Most came from the class of urban elites known as the **curiales**. Their chief duties were to provide justice, collect taxes, maintain roads and waterways, and keep the cities and harbors in good repair. Given the Roman means of tax gathering, these civil servants could acquire great wealth, but their sense of civic-mindedness obliged them to make up for public deficits personally. They were expected to use their own funds to provide public entertainments, food distributions, and religious ceremonies in honor of the emperors. That so many curiales did so provides an index of the strength of Roman public spirit.

◆

During the Pax Romana, in sum, the Stoic and dutiful ethos cultivated by the Romans helped them to create a remarkably stable and proud society. They saw themselves as the heirs to the Greek and eastern worlds, and they eagerly absorbed whatever in those traditions had practical value. Yet they also regarded themselves as morally superior, less inclined to luxury and ease, and dedicated to strong virtues and a hardheaded sense of pragmatic living. Those given to other values were the objects of scorn. For example, the Jews, who refused to Romanize or to serve in the army, were reviled although the Romans respected the antiquity of their traditions. Marcus Aurelius, author of the popular work known as the *Meditations*, described the secret of the Stoical Roman soul and its superiority to a new spirit that had appeared on the scene:

> A beautiful soul is one that is equally ready at any given moment to relinquish the body and give itself over to extinction and annihilation, or to continue living. Such preparedness must be the result of conscious judgment reached through reason and with dignity if it is to persuade anyone else; it must never result from obstinacy or with soul-killing display—as it does with the people called Christians. (*Meditations* 11.3)

WHO, WHAT, WHERE

Augustus	Julius Caesar	plebeians
censor	latifundia	Princeps Augustus
consul	Latins	Punic Wars
curiales	legate	res publica
equestrians	pater familias	Senate
Etruscans	patricians	Twelve Tables
imperator	Pax Romana	

SUGGESTED READINGS

Primary Sources

Epictetus. *Handbook.*

Julius Caesar. *The Civil War.*

Julius Caesar. *The Gallic War.*

Livy. *History of Rome.*

Marcus Aurelius. *Meditations.*

Plutarch. *Parallel Lives.*

Polybius. *The Histories.*

Seneca. *Epistles.*

Suetonius. *The Twelve Caesars.*

Tacitus. *Annals.*

Tacitus. *The Histories.*

Virgil. *The Aeneid.*

Source Anthologies

Beard, Mary, John North, and Simon Price. *Religions of Rome* (2005).

Cherry, David, ed. *The Roman World: A Sourcebook* (2001).

Kraemer, Ross Shepard, ed. *Women's Religions in the Greco-Roman World: A Sourcebook* (2004).

Lefkowitz, Mary R., and Maureen B. Fant, comps. *Women's Life in Greece and Rome: A Source Book in Translation* (2005).

Mellor, Ronald, ed. *The Historians of Ancient Rome: An Anthology of the Major Writings* (2004).

Shaw, Brent D. *Spartacus and the Slave Wars: A Brief History with Documents* (2001).

Warrior, Valerie M. *Roman Religion: A Sourcebook* (2001).

Studies

Aldrete, Gregory S. *Daily Life in the Roman City: Rome, Pompeii, and Ostia* (2009).

Beard, Mary. *The Roman Triumph* (2009).

Beard, Mary, John North, and Simon Price. *Religions of Rome* (2005).

Boatwright, Mary T. *Hadrian and the Cities of the Roman Empire* (2002).

Carcopino, Jérôme. *Daily Life in Ancient Rome: The People and the City at the Height of the Empire* (2008).

Eck, Werner. *The Age of Augustus* (2007).

Everitt, Anthony. *Augustus: The Life of Rome's First Emperor* (2007).

Fraschetti, Augusto. *The Foundation of Rome* (2005).

Goldsworthy, Adrian. *Caesar: Life of a Colossus* (2008).

Goldsworthy, Adrian. *The Complete Roman Army* (2011).

Goldsworthy, Adrian. *The Punic Wars* (2000).

Grubbs, Judith Evans. *Women and the Law in the Roman Empire: A Sourcebook on Marriage, Divorce, and Widowhood* (2002).

Haynes, Sybille. *Etruscan Civilization: A Cultural History* (2000).

Holland, Tom. *Rubicon: The Last Years of the Roman Republic* (2005).

Horden, Peregrine, and Nicholas Purcell. *The Corrupting Sea: A Study of Mediterranean History* (2000).

Lendon, J. E. *Empire of Honour: The Art of Government in the Roman World* (2001).

Meijer, Fik. *The Gladiators: History's Most Deadly Sport* (2007).

Milnor, Kristina. *Gender, Domesticity, and the Age of Augustus: Inventing Private Life* (2005).

Mouritsen, Henrik. *Plebs and Politics in the Late Roman Republic* (2001).

Reydams-Schils, Gretchen. *The Roman Stoics: Self, Responsibility, and Affection* (2005).

Rives, James B. *Religion in the Roman Empire* (2007).

Schultz, Celia E. *Women's Religious Activity in the Roman Republic* (2006).

Seager, Robin. *Pompey the Great: A Political Biography* (2002).

Seager, Robin. *Tiberius* (2005).

Southern, Pat. *The Roman Army: A Social and Institutional History* (2007).

Speller, Elizabeth. *Following Hadrian: A Second-Century Journey through the Roman Empire* (2004).

Strauss, Barry. *The Spartacus War* (2010).

Williamson, Callie. *The Laws of the Roman People: Public Law in the Expansion and Decline of the Roman Republic* (2005).

For additional resources, including maps, primary sources, visuals, web links, and quizzes, please go to **www.oup.com/us/backman.**

CHAPTER 7

The Rise of Christianity in a Roman World

40 BCE–300 CE

THE EARLY CHRISTIAN WORLD

The story fascinates, thrills, comforts, angers, and embarrasses at every turn, often all at once. It has touched everything from Western political ideas to sexual mores. Christianity began as an obscure reformist sect within Palestinian Judaism, at one time numbering no more than fifty or so believers. It went on, after three centuries of persecution by the Roman Empire, to become the world's most dominant faith.

The history of Christianity in the Greater West is complex, as is its legacy. One would be hard put to identify another idea, invention, school of thought, technology, or value system that has penetrated so far into the DNA of Western culture—and shaped so much of what is both good and bad in it. In this chapter we will see how Christianity arose, how it became a Roman religion, and how it absorbed such intellectual currents of the classical world as Stoic and Platonic philosophy. First, however, we must understand the

The Good Shepherd This wall painting, ca. 100–200 CE, depicts Jesus as the Good Shepherd. Note the heavily Romanized style: Jesus is beardless and wears a Roman tunic. The fresco is in the Catacombs of Saint Priscilla, under the city of Rome. Early Christians used catacombs (tunnels with underground rooms) as burial sites and meeting places for worship. It was much more common among the early Christian generations to portray Jesus as the Good Shepherd than to depict a crucifixion scene.

outlines of the Roman religion that provided the social and moral framework within which Christianity grew.

THE VITALITY OF ROMAN RELIGION

The fact of Christianity's triumph can blind us to the residual strength of traditional Roman religion. Roman cults continued to thrive for centuries, attracting new adherents and shaping both civic and personal lives by the millions. If anything, the empire's portfolio of *religiones licitae* ("legally approved religions") grew faster and stirred hearts deeper than Christianity could even hope to do. Moreover, Roman religion did not remain static but continued to develop new ritual traditions, emotional resonances, and intellectual sophistication. Rome embraced new deities by the score (including, of course, the deified emperors themselves) and built thousands of new temples across the empire. Traditional polytheistic Roman religion must be seen, in other words, as a vital, thriving, expansive, and energetic network of cults, not as a dusty relic patiently awaiting Christian conversion and enlightenment.

Growth of Emperor Worship

The expanding cult of the emperors is the most visible development in religious life. From the moment that Augustus dedicated the first temple to the deified Julius Caesar in 29 BCE, the veneration of Rome's leaders became one of the most important public rituals. The practice was intended to unite the people in

CHAPTER TIMELINE

100 BCE	50 BCE	0	50 CE	100 CE

- 40 BCE **Beginning of Herodian dynasty in Judea**
- ca. 5 BCE **Birth of Jesus**
- ca. 25 CE **Jesus begins his ministry**
- ca. 27 CE **Jesus crucified in Jerusalem**
- ca. 42–67 CE **Missionary journeys of Paul**
- 64 CE **Great Fire of Rome: Nero blames Christians**
- 64–305 CE **Intermittent brutal Roman persecutions of Christians**
- 66–70 CE **Great Jewish Revolt**
- ca. 126 CE **Pantheon built in Rome**

an act of thanksgiving for the blessings of the Pax Romana. The political motive behind emperor worship is obvious, but that does not mean emperor worship was insincere. In most ancient religions, divine forces permeated the physical world and caused or affected most natural phenomena, and the gods themselves wandered through our world at will and spoke to people through signs and oracles. Classical folklore and literature are full of tales of humans venturing into the afterworld, too: Odysseus and Aeneas are primary examples. So the idea that a living human ruler could be imbued with divine qualities was not out of the question, no matter how self-serving such a notion might be.

In the first three centuries CE, nearly half of all the state temples erected were dedicated to deified emperors living or dead. Statues of them were frequently added throughout the empire to temples that were already dedicated to another god or goddess. Emperors also imported into the capital city gods from regions around the empire that were associated in some way with the personal history of the ruler. Septimius Severus (r. 193–211 CE), for example, built a massive new 140,000-square-foot temple in the heart of Rome in honor of Bacchus and Hercules, the Roman variants of the Greek god and Greek hero, Dionysus and Herakles. Both figures were familiar, but their unique pairing was the cultic practice of Septimius's hometown in North Africa. It highlighted the emperor as the living embodiment of cultic and civic unity—the linchpin holding together the whole fabric of the Pax Romana.

| 150 CE | 200 CE | 250 CE | 300 CE | 350 CE |

■ ca. 140 CE **Last books of the New Testament composed**

■ 161–180 CE **Reign of Roman emperor Marcus Aurelius**

The Pantheon   Construction of the Roman Pantheon was finished around 126 CE. The temple's dome, which weighs around five thousand tons, is the largest unreinforced concrete dome ever constructed. A circular opening at its top lets in a dazzling beam of light that moves around the walls, illuminating the shrines of the various Olympian deities.

The **Pantheon**, built by the emperor Hadrian (r. 117–138 CE), was an all-purpose temple dedicated, as its name suggests, to the whole roster of major deities within the empire. Consisting of a portico (or porch) with a colonnade of three ranks of granite columns, behind which rose a vast rotunda covered with a splendid concrete dome, it was—and remains—a stunning site. The Pantheon was consecrated as a Catholic church in the 7th century, named in honor of Santa Maria dei Martiri.

The imperial cult took great pains to absorb and authorize new cults in the provinces, so that religious life not only took on a unifying structure but also grew more varied while doing so. New cults arrived with every generation and every territorial expansion of the empire. The best known were the cults of Cybele (or Magna Mater—the "Great Mother"), Isis, Mithras, and Sol Invictus (the "Unconquered Sun"), but there were countless others. These cults had diverse and often obscure origins. The Mithras cult, for example, originated in Asia Minor but claimed descent from the ancient Persian religious figure of Zoroaster, whereas the cult of Isis—which had certainly begun in early Egyptian times—took on the shape that Rome absorbed in Hellenistic Greece. Diverse origins aside, these new cults had much in common; hence historians often refer to them as **mystery religions,** or religions of salvation. All of them promised answers to the ultimate questions of human existence and a framework for worship and belief in this world while waiting for the world to come.

Mystery Religions

Were these new mystery religions a reaction against the centralizing efforts of the emperors? If so, they failed. The embrace of the new practices by Rome revitalized imperial religion in the first three centuries CE. It encouraged believers to participate in civic rituals and filled their hearts and minds with hope and comfort. In 110 CE Pliny the Younger, then governor of Bithynia, on the southern coast of the Black Sea, wrote admiringly to the emperor Trajan (r. 98–117 CE) about the resurgence in traditional religion:

> It is now indisputable that temples long abandoned are being used frequently and that sacred rituals long forgotten are being observed again. The meat of sacrificial animals can be purchased anywhere one goes, too, whereas so long ago buyers of it could hardly be found. Judge from this how many peoples' lives can be reformed; all they need is a chance at repentance. (*Letters* 10.96–97)

Pliny's closing line suggests a new development in religious thought—the belief in, and the desire for, forgiveness of sins. Traditional religion stressed community with others in the present world more than the attainment of another, better life in a world yet to come. It privileged the ideas of civic virtue and ritual exactitude over ethical improvement, and it emphasized *doing* good instead of *being* good. In other words, instead of earning forgiveness of one's sins and whatever reward such forgiveness would entail, it stressed acting to unite the community.

Most of the provincial cults, like those of Isis and Mithras, did posit an afterlife to which repentant believers went. (The afterlives of the unrepentant or the nonbelievers were less clear.) Those who died in the cults' good graces could look forward to an eternal reward of some sort. A 3rd-century CE epitaph erected on the tomb of Aurelia Prosodos, an Isis worshipper, by her husband, Dioskourides, reads, "To the gods of the underworld, Dioskourides, husband of Aurelia Prosodos, the best and sweetest of companions, erects this memorial. Farewell my lady! May Osiris grant you a draught of cool water." In the Isis cult, the goddess' husband Osiris revived the worthy deceased with a drink from an underworld spring, which began their enjoyment of eternal peace and pleasure.

In another innovation, several of the new cults were text oriented. With the exception of the Hebrew scriptures, previous religious writings were by and large mere collections of set prayers and ritual formulas. Influenced by the Hellenistic spread of philosophical and literary inquiry and the textual frenzy of Second Temple Judaism, however, the new religions of the first centuries CE produced a new type of religious literature. These speculative, interpretive texts explored ideas about the relationship between the mundane and divine worlds, the nature of human life, and the purpose of human suffering. The gods of the provincial cults were not simply divine potentates demanding rote prayers and well-practiced rituals. Instead, they were benevolent beings who understood human difficulties and desired that people live upright and ethical lives—in most cases (Isis, Mithras) to attain an otherworldly salvation, but in others (some strains of Judaism, for instance) simply to pursue justice and morality for their own sakes. The new texts were not scriptures—that is, they did not have the canonical status of the Jewish and later Christian writings, nor did they fill the same sort of liturgical function. Instead, they explored the intellectual ramifications of their central conceits.

Mithras and Isis   Two of the most popular religious cults in ancient Rome were those of Mithras and Isis. The Romans believed worship of the god Mithras originated somewhere in Persia, but this cannot be confirmed. The crucial episode in Mithras's story was his slaying of a sacred bull, the scene depicted here. The cult of Mithras was open only to men and was most popular among the ranks of the army. The cult of Isis, by contrast, was the domain of women. She was the goddess of marriage, health, and wisdom (especially in the realm of dream interpretation).

In so doing, these texts dissociated philosophy from religion, a development that enriched both traditions. Philosophy received a new stimulus by focusing less on the nature of the universe and more on the human lives within it. In turn, religion became increasingly a thing to think about and not simply to perform. As the ancient Greek thinker Epicurus (341–270 BCE) had famously put it, "Any philosopher's words that do not aim to relieve human suffering are pointless." The new provincial cults increasingly sought more than universal order and the submission to fate or divine desire. Instead, their followers desired solace, forgiveness, and the promise of a personal contentment. The Greater Western world entered the Common Era with a new attitude of spiritual and intellectual questing—an attitude that would shape the civilization of the next thousand years.

THE JESUS MYSTERY

Approximately 2 billion people today identify themselves as Christian; given a current world population of roughly 6 billion, Christians therefore comprise about 33 percent of the total. Islam comes in second place, with roughly 1.2 billion faithful (20 percent). Hinduism, with nearly 800 million adherents, ranks third

- Christian, 1,965,993,000
- Muslim, 1,179,326,000
- Hindu, 767,424,000
- Nonreligious, 766,672,000
- Buddhist, 356,875,000
- Tribal religion, 244,164,000
- Atheist, 146,406,000
- New religions, 99,191,000
- Sikh, 22,874,000
- Daoist, 20,050,000
- Jewish, 15,050,000
- Baha'I, 6,251,000
- Confucian, 5,067,000
- Jain, 4,152,000
- Shinto, 3,571,000
- Parsi (Zoroastrian), 479,000

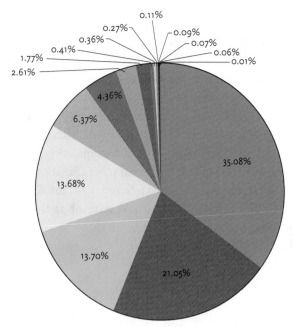

FIGURE 7.1   The World's Religions Today

(12 percent). Judaism, by contrast, makes up only about 0.20 percent of the world population, numbering a mere 15 million adherents. Jews, indeed, are almost statistically insignificant—an irony, given their remarkable place in the history of the Greater West (see Figure 7.1).

That development was neither rapid nor assured, however. Instead, Christianity spread with almost painful slowness and suffered repeated setbacks along the way. As late as 300 CE, if one could have surveyed the whole of the Roman Empire and then placed a bet on which religion in it was most likely to become the dominant religious force in the Western world, Christianity would not have been the pick. By that date, even after three hundred years of ardent evangelizing, teaching, bearing witness, and, as Christian tradition asserts, the performing of countless miracles by missionaries, Christians made up no more than 2–3 percent of the empire's population and possibly as little as 1 percent.

Moreover, biology, not conversion, accounts for the lion's share of whatever growth did occur in those years. Christians married other Christians and raised their children in the faith. Conversions did take place, however, and those who brought the gospel of Jesus to the "pagans" did so at the risk of their lives, a fact later Christians pointed to with pride. Christians had a significantly higher profile in the cities of the eastern Mediterranean than in other parts of the Roman world by 300 CE. Still, through vast stretches of the empire the very name of Jesus had yet to be heard, much less adored.

The New Testament and History

How a tiny sect thus grew to dominate Western culture is not easy to explain. Even after more than two thousand years, scholars are still trying to figure it out and still arguing about it. Two problems stand in the way. First, no one approaches the issue of historical Christianity—or any issue, for that matter—with absolute objectivity. Try as they might to remain detached, scholars are influenced by their personal convictions—even if the conviction is an ardent denial of belief. Second, our principle source for the history of Jesus's life and the careers of his early followers is the **New Testament**, which is a compilation of notoriously difficult texts written over a period of nearly a century. For Christians, the New Testament supplements the Hebrew Bible (usually referred to as the Old Testament) as holy scripture.

The canon of the New Testament as the modern world knows it did not become settled until the late 4th century. And its specific wording—reconciling variant readings and filling gaps—was not set until the early 5th century, a long time after the events it purports to relate. Twenty-seven texts comprise the New Testament (see Table 7.1):

- Four gospels (Matthew, Mark, Luke, and John), accounts of Jesus's life and teachings;
- A narrative of the actions of the original twelve apostles—the disciples hand-picked by Jesus to spread his teachings—immediately after Jesus's death;
- Seven authentic epistles (letters) by the later apostle Paul;
- Seven more epistles that tradition attributes to Paul but that he almost certainly did not write;
- Seven more epistles falsely accredited to four of the original twelve apostles; and
- The book of Revelation, a densely symbolic dream vision of the end of the world.

Not one of these twenty-seven works was written in Jesus's lifetime. Jesus himself wrote nothing and is never reported to have ordered his followers to write his teachings down. The earliest texts in the New Testament are the letters of Paul, who acknowledges that he never laid eyes on Jesus or heard him speak during his lifetime. The four gospels themselves, which provide the most detailed and precise information about Jesus, were not written until at least sixty years after his death. Nor were they necessarily written by the apostles whose name they carry. John's gospel, for example, was most likely written by a disciple of John—that is, by someone who learned about Jesus from John. Thus it likely represents John's understanding of who Jesus was and what he said and did, but few scholars believe that John himself wrote the gospel that bears his name. Hence the lateness of our

TABLE 7.1   **Books of the New Testament in the Order of Their Composition**

Year (CE)	Text	Author
50	1 Thessalonians	Paul
54–55	Galatians	Paul
55	Philemon	Paul
56	Philippians	Paul
56	1 Corinthians	Paul
57	2 Corinthians	Paul
57–58	Romans	Paul
(66–70: Jewish Revolt and Rome's subsequent destruction of the Second Temple)		
68–73	Gospel of Mark	? (attributed to Mark)
70–90	1 Peter	? (attributed to Peter)
80–85	Gospel of Luke	? (attributed to Luke)
80–85	Acts of the Apostles	? (attributed to Luke)
80–90	Colossians	? (attributed to Paul)
80–100	James	? (attributed to James, brother of Jesus)
85–90	Gospel of Matthew	? (attributed to Matthew)
85–90	Hebrews	? (attributed to Paul)
90–95	Gospel of John	? (attributed to the Beloved Disciple)
90–100	Ephesians	? (attributed to Paul)
90–100	2 Thessalonians	? (attributed to Paul)
90–100	1–2 Timothy, Titus	? (attributed to Paul)
90–100	Jude	? (attributed to Jude, brother of Jesus)
92–96	Revelation	? (attributed to John)
95–100	1–2 John	? (attributed to John)
120–130	3 John	? (attributed to John)
130–140	2 Peter	? (attributed to Peter)

closest written evidence of Jesus and his ministry. This lateness, combined with the many contradictions in the texts, leaves any effort to understand the rise of Christianity facing enormous challenges.

What are some of those contradictions? Many are simple discrepancies in chronology. The gospels of Matthew, Mark, and Luke, for example, all state that the Last Supper (Jesus's final meal with the full company of his twelve apostles, before his arrest by the Romans) took place during Passover, the Jewish holiday commemorating the exodus of the Hebrews from Egypt, whereas the gospel of John records that it occurred sometime before it. Others are flat-out contradictions of the historical record, such as Luke's famous setting of the scene of the birth of Christ:

> In those days a decree went out from Emperor Augustus that all the world should be registered. This was the first registration and was taken while Quirinius was governor of Syria. All went to their own towns to be registered. (2.1–2)

There is no evidence of a census of the entire empire under Augustus, however, only a handful of provincial censuses. Moreover, the only census of Judea that was performed when Quirinius was the governor of Syria took place in either 6 or 7 CE, which is at least a decade too late for Jesus's birth. Jesus was actually born between the years 7 and 3 BCE. The modern calendar, based on the number of years since the birth of Jesus, was invented in the 6th century by a Syriac monk who calculated backward from his own time, based on the reigns of Roman emperors, but in the process he made an arithmetical mistake—something easily done when working with Roman numerals—which explains how Jesus was actually born several years "before Christ."

Another set of contradictions in the New Testament are occasional tensions between the portrayals of Jesus's character in the gospels. Luke's Jesus, for example, shows a particular sensitivity toward women, whereas Matthew depicts a Jesus who shows hardly any interest in them at all—not even in his own mother. Mark's Jesus is a terse miracle worker who, apart from calling people to repent their sins, speaks mostly in oblique parables (short allegorical stories that indirectly convey moral lessons); John's Jesus, by contrast, is loquacious to an extreme and capable of both precise common-sense speech and sophisticated philosophical language.

A CRISIS IN TRADITION

Thus, although the basic outlines of Christian growth are fairly well known, the precise knowledge of how, when, and where the faith spread remain unclear and hotly debated. One rare point of agreement among scholars today is that the history of **Jesus of Nazareth** and the movement he founded must be understood in the context of Jewish tradition. Jesus was a Jew, as were all of his original followers, none of whom regarded their commitment to Jesus and his teachings as a denial of their Jewish identities. Indeed, they saw Jesus as the fulfillment of Jewish prophecy. In Jesus's own words, as recorded by Matthew,

> Do not think that I have come to abolish the law or the prophets. I have come not to abolish but to fulfill. For truly I tell you, until heaven and earth pass away, not one letter, not one stroke of a letter, will pass from the law until all is accomplished. Therefore, whoever breaks one of the least of these commandments, and teaches others to do the same, will be called least in the kingdom of heaven; but whoever does them and teaches them will be called great in the kingdom of heaven. (5.17–19)

These assurances might have quieted more Jewish concerns, however, if Jesus himself had been more strictly observant of Torah. Instead, he provoked widespread ire by performing work on the Sabbath, allowing his followers to call him the **messiah** ("anointed one," "Christ" in Greek), speaking scornfully of the Temple, and, most boldly of all, referring to himself as the Son of God. By Jesus's lifetime several Jewish traditions coexisted in uneasy dialogue with one another, but none of them was quite prepared for this.

The Hellenistic era had witnessed the rise of Jewish factions, divided primarily by two factors: commitment to Temple observance and the authority of the priests, *Jewish* on the one hand, and the new focus on rabbinical leadership and the "oral Torah" *Factions* (rabbinical law and its commentaries, later codified in the Talmud), on the other. Added to this mix was a potent new element: the belief in a coming *apocalypse,* or the world's imminent destruction with only the righteous saved. This apocalyptic faith resulted from the rising trend of exogamous marriage (or marriage outside of Judaism) and the exiled Jews' close contact with Zoroastrianism and its division of the world into two opposing forces, good and evil. The political scene contributed a number of factors as well. After the Maccabean revolt against the Seleucids, Judea was ruled by the Hasmonean and Herodian dynasties for a century, the last independent Jewish state until the 20th century (see Map 7.1). Although the era had helped foster a communal Jewish spirit, however, the Jews were sharply divided toward their dynasts. By long tradition Jewish kingship belonged solely to the lineage of the ancient ruler David, which made the Hasmoneans usurpers in the eyes of many. Struggles within later generations of the dynasty only confirmed their critics' opinion of them as imposters. Thoroughly Hellenized, the Hasmonean kings even bore Greek names rather than Hebrew ones. The line of Herod that replaced the Hasmoneans in 40 BCE was widely detested by the Jews, who regarded them (correctly) as puppets of the Roman state.

The kings tried to gain legitimacy by associating themselves closely with the Temple priests and their most important political allies, a party known as the

MAP 7.1   Judea in the Time of Jesus   Jesus did not travel far in his lifetime. The distance from his hometown of Nazareth to Jerusalem is roughly 65 miles. Except for his visits to the Temple in Jerusalem, he was seldom more than 20 miles from home.

Sadducees. These were one of three "philosophical sects" (*hairesis*) into which Judea was divided, according to the Jewish historian Josephus (37–100 CE); the other two were called the **Pharisees** and the **Essenes**. The Sadducees were an aristocratic party, the ideological descendants of the "Children of the Exile." They were reputedly strict upholders of Temple ritual, dedicated to the literal reading of scripture and the rejection of the oral Torah—"reputedly" because much of what is known of the Sadducees' thought comes from the testimony of writers hostile to them, including the authors of the four Christian gospels, as well as Josephus.

Opposing them were the Pharisees, the party more closely associated with the "People of the Land" and the rabbinical tradition. The most renowned figure believed to have been a Pharisee was the Babylonian scholar Hillel (110 BCE–10 CE, according to tradition), who is considered the central figure in establishing the core of the rabbinical law and its commentaries. The Pharisees generally were commoners (although, being urbanites, they regarded themselves as superior to the outlying rustics) and resisted Hellenization. They also held a number of religious beliefs that set them apart from other Jews—most notably, a belief in the immortality of the soul and the resurrection of the dead. They took the lead in advocating the arrival of a messiah, a savior of the Jewish people who would return them to freedom and safety. The Essenes, the third Palestinian sect mentioned by Josephus, are more difficult to identify. It is even possible that the name is a catchall term used by writers like Josephus to describe a host of minor Jewish sects that shared certain views. An ascetic community, they lived in isolated congregations and dedicated themselves to repentance and prayer in the hope of achieving mystical union with YHWH. The Essenes were the most eschatological sect within Judaism, meaning they were characterized by expectations of an imminent apocalyptic end of the world, although it is difficult to generalize how widely believed such ideas were.[1]

Jesus of Nazareth thus entered a Jewish world in high-voltage turmoil. When the Romans, led by Pompey the Great, conquered Judea in 63 BCE, they dismissed *Roman* and jailed the Hasmonean king and ruled in his name for twenty-five years, while *Rule* Pompey and then Marcus Crassus plundered the province mercilessly. In 40 BCE they installed the new dynasty, the Herodians. The Jews had mostly disdained the Hasmoneans, but they ardently hated the Herodians, and for good reason. Herod, named "king of Judea" (r. 37–4 BCE), was a brute who murdered anyone who stood in his way—which included two high priests, his brother-in-law, his mother-in-law, and even his wife. A lover of massive architecture, Herod built and rebuilt palaces, Roman temples, gardens, amphitheaters, hippodromes, baths, and fountains across Judea—including an ambitious restoration of the Jerusalem Temple itself. And he paid for it all with heavy taxation. Perversely, he ordered a golden imperial eagle to be installed over the gate leading into the restored Temple. When two rabbis complained of the blasphemy, Herod had them burned alive. Following Herod's death in 4 BCE, the emperor Augustus divided Judea into three provinces, one of which was administered by a Roman procurator; the other two went to Herod's sons, Herod Antipas and Philip. By the time Jesus began his ministry, sometime around 27 CE, Judea was crackling with religious rivalries and social–political tensions.

MINISTRY AND MOVEMENT

The gospels of Matthew and Luke relate a handful of episodes from Jesus's childhood and youth, but only become detailed when Jesus begins his ministry, around *Jesus and* the age of thirty. An early follower of **John the Baptist**, a Jewish revivalist *John the* preacher who prophesied the arrival of the messiah and urged his listeners to *Baptist*

---

[1]   The Essenes were probably the group whose collected writings, the Dead Sea Scrolls, were discovered at the Qumran caves near the Dead Sea in 1946.

King Herod and Jerusalem The southern wall of the Temple Mount is shown here. It is the entrance to King Herod's expansion of the Second Temple.

penance and passionate commitment to God, Jesus took up John's cause after his own baptism by John, most scholars believe. (The word *baptize* comes from the Greek *baptizein*, a verb meaning "to dunk" or "to plunge." Jewish tradition had long involved people giving themselves ritual baths of purification; John's innovation was to actively plunge the faithful into the water.) The gospels then relate how Jesus traveled throughout Judea, performing miraculous healings, driving out demon spirits, calling people to a revivified faith and universal love, and especially teaching them about the approach of "the kingdom of God." What he meant by this last point is by no means clear. Some of his followers (and his critics) understood him to be talking about Heaven itself, God's own dwelling place; others regarded the "kingdom" as a state of spiritual grace, a soulful enlightenment. To still others the kingdom was this world, the world we inhabit, but made just and perfect by a heavenly appointed ruler, a new King David—earthly life as it should be, in other words.

The differences matter. If the kingdom Jesus spoke of was indeed a paradise and an afterlife, then he was speaking the language of the Pharisees. If he meant a spiritual state, then he was appealing to the Essenes. If he intended an earthly kingdom marked by justice and order, then the Sadducees might have been the intended audience. And still other possibilities exist. As it happened, Jesus's oblique language could have been intended to appeal to everyone, which meant that it displeased and offended far more people than it attracted. In the life-and-death struggle of 1st-century Palestine, Jewish scholars on all sides were still fighting over the exact lettering of sacred texts, their meaning, and the purposes to which they were put. For them, Jesus's words often sounded so confusing as to be provocative:

> Then the disciples came and asked him, "Why do you speak to [the crowds] in parables?"
>
> He answered, "To you it has been given to know the secrets of the kingdom of heaven, but to them it has not been given. For to those who have, more will be given, and they will have an abundance; but from those who have nothing, even what they have will be taken away. The reason I speak to them in parables is that 'seeing they do not perceive, and hearing they do not listen, nor do they understand.'" (Matthew 13.10–13)

Jesus himself did not begin to preach and to baptize until after he learned that the detested Roman-installed governor of Galilee, Herod Antipas, had arrested and executed John the Baptist.[2] Jesus thus assumed leadership of a preexisting popular movement, but he quickly put his own stamp on it by summoning a corps of personal disciples, the **twelve apostles**, who spread the idea that Jesus himself was the long-promised messiah.[3] John's more general revivalist movement thus became specifically a Jesus movement, a sect dedicated to his unique ministry. Jesus traveled throughout Galilee, Samaria, and Judea proper—an area roughly 40 miles from east to west and roughly 80 miles from north to south—and preached the primacy of a passionate love of God over a formal observance of rituals. The desire and intent behind our actions, he seemed to say, matter more than the actions themselves.

Jesus and the Twelve Apostles

Jesus's message was forceful: If we harden our hearts against one another, we distance ourselves from "the kingdom of God"—by which he meant not only a heavenly hereafter but also a just and peaceful life on earth in spiritual

---

[2]   According to the Jewish historian Josephus, Herod Antipas killed John ("a good man who urged the Jews to be virtuous, to treat one another justly, and to worship the Lord") out of concern that he might raise a rebellion. In the gospel of Matthew (ch. 14) and the gospel of Mark (ch. 6), a different tale is told, with variants. John the Baptist had condemned Herod Antipas's marriage to Herodias, since she had previously been married to Herod Antipas's half-brother (confusingly also named Herod). At a banquet, the beautiful daughter of Herodias by her first marriage, named Salomé, performed a dance that so enchanted Herod Antipas that he offered her anything she wished—to which she replied that she wanted John the Baptist's head on a platter. Mark insists that Herodias told Salomé what to wish for; Matthew states that Salomé made the gruesome choice on her own. The gospel versions seem less likely than Josephus's barebones account. Presumably Mark and Matthew wanted to present a moral tale about the danger of female seductiveness.

[3]   Being twelve in number, the apostles provide a symbolic association with the Twelve Tribes of Israel. Of the gospel writers only Luke—who wrote the most fluent Greek—calls them *apostles*; Matthew, Mark, and John use the word *disciples*.

communion with one another. Our weakness is our vulnerability to sin, which makes us selfish, lustful, angry, and covetous. "Love your enemies," he urged, "[and] do good to those who hate you. Bless those who curse you, and pray for those who mistreat you." Love and forgiveness of others, he insisted, both express and inspire our love of God and guide us to the "kingdom of God."

When criticized for his inexact observance of Torah, Jesus replied that YHWH cares more for the sincerity in our hearts than for the mechanical precision of our rites. In this passage from Matthew, Jesus quotes two Torah verses:

> When the Pharisees heard that [Jesus] had silenced the Sadducees, they gathered together, and one of them, a lawyer, asked him a question to test him.
> "Teacher, which commandment in the Law is the greatest?"
> [Jesus] said to him, "'You shall love the Lord your God with all your heart, and with all your soul, and with all your mind.' This is the greatest and first commandment. And a second is like it: 'You shall love your neighbor as yourself.' On these two commandments hang all the Law and the Prophets." (22.34–40)

Jesus's own criticisms of the Pharisees and Sadducees display flashes of temper and a sharp tongue. It is small wonder that the leaders of the two groups grew irritated with him, locked as they were in a bitter struggle to lead the Jewish people and indeed to define the faith itself.

WHAT HAPPENED TO HIS DISCIPLES?

Jesus's popularity with the Jewish crowds is uncertain. Large numbers of people, perhaps even thousands at a time, regularly turned out to see him and listen to his teaching. However, many of those were mere curiosity seekers, wanting to observe one of his famous miracles, rather than true followers of his movement. To many Jews, and perhaps to most of them, he was an item in the short-term news cycle, the subject of gossip and debate, and nothing more; the evidence clearly suggests that he received only the passing attention of most Jews. Once started on his public ministry, Jesus gathered around him the twelve apostles, whom he charged with the missions of preaching, treating the ill, and exerting "power and authority over all demons" (Luke 9.1). But so long as Jesus himself lived and performed those duties, the apostles seem to have been companions more than anything else. After Jesus's death, they found their calling as the leaders and chief evangelists of the Christian communities—the story told in the book of Acts of the Apostles, which immediately follows the four gospels in the New Testament.

But it is worth noting that even Peter, the leader of the group, had moments of confusion about his mission.

What tipped the scales against Jesus in the Jewish community, ultimately, was the zeal of his disciples to have him recognized as the long-prophesied messiah. *Jewish* This, indeed, is the principal function of Matthew's gospel. Alone of the four *Rejection* gospel writers, Matthew aims specifically at a Jewish audience and focuses on de- *of Jesus* scribing those ideas and actions of Jesus that proved he was the long-promised savior. Echoes of the prophets can be heard everywhere. But there was a problem. Jewish tradition anticipated the arrival of an earthly savior, one who would create a safe, unified state for the Jews—in which justice would flourish and YHWH would be praised. Even as he embraced this designation as messiah, Jesus appeared otherwise; he was a savior of eternal souls, not the leader of a political revival. He did things no messiah was ever expected to do (such as to violate the Sabbath and speak disrespectfully of the Temple) and did *not* do the things that *were* expected of the savior. This combination made it all but impossible for most Jews to accept him in that role.

It is unclear whether Jesus's claim to be the messiah sufficed to warrant an ac- *Roman* cusation of blasphemy—the official complaint levied at Jesus by the Jewish head *Repression* council. In any event, Jesus's adoption of the title of "Son of God" set the seal on *and* Jewish rejection of him. Complaints about Jesus as a blasphemer mattered little to *Crucifixion* the Romans, however, who regarded Jewish religious disputes with disdain. More important to the Roman prefect, Pontius Pilate, was the popular talk among Jesus's supporters that he was the "King of the Jews." This smacked of treason against the Roman state because only the emperor had the right to designate a client-king within the confines of the empire. Pilate was notorious for his high-handed brutishness even before the issue of Jesus confronted him and more than once was rebuked for his harsh methods. When Pilate ordered Jesus to be crucified (likely in or around the year 27 CE), a sign bearing the words "Jesus of Nazareth, King of the Jews" was placed on the cross above his head.[4] It was Roman practice, when crucifying criminals, to identify their crime in this way. (The six thousand supporters of Spartacus who were executed along the Appian Way by Marcus Crassus in 71 BCE, for example, had the designation of "traitor" hung over their heads.)

Pontius Pilate's career as a Roman official with a taste for rough politics is well known. The Jewish philosopher Philo of Alexandria (20 BCE–50 CE) described him as a "rigid, stubborn, and cruel [administrator] who was known to execute lawbreakers even without a trial" (*Embassy of Gaius* 38.299). Josephus describes an incident when Pilate confiscated funds from the Temple and used them to

---

4   In Latin, the sign reads *Iesus Nazarenus Rex Iudaeorum*—hence the acronym INRI that appears frequently in images of the crucifixion.

Jesus and Pontius Pilate In this 6th-century mosaic from the church of St. Apollinaire in Ravenna, Christ is brought before the Roman prefect, Pilate, who is shown washing his hands. Jesus wears—inaccurately—a purple robe, symbolic of his kingship over all creation.

fund the construction of an aqueduct; when the Jews predictably gathered outside his court to complain, Pilate had secretly scattered dozens of armed soldiers, dressed as Jews, among the crowd. At his signal, the soldiers drew their swords and began attacking the Jews indiscriminately, killing several dozen protestors (*Antiquities* 18.3.2). Of Jesus's life and teachings, Pontius Pilate knew little and cared even less. All that concerned him was the maintenance of peace and order.[5]

After Jesus's death, the small cohort of people still faithful to him ran immediately into hiding, since the Romans were determined to stamp the sect out. Soldiers searched for them from street to street. Then, according to the New Testament, something extraordinary happened. Three days after Jesus was buried, groups of believers began to appear in the streets of Jerusalem proclaiming joyously that they had seen Jesus resurrected from the dead. In three days they had transformed, apparently as a group, from terrified fugitives hoping to escape capture into a company of bold, confident witnesses. They not only acknowledged their belief in Jesus but also broadcast it at every turn, even at the risk of death.

[5] One inscription survives that attests to the existence of Pontius Pilate; it was discovered in 1962 in the ruins of a Roman theater at Caesarea Maritima and is now on view in the Israel Museum in Jerusalem. It is a dedicatory inscription written in Latin, with the English translation, "Pontius Pilate, the prefect of Judea, had the Temple to Tiberius built and dedicated it to the august gods."

For the next few decades, until they themselves began to die in the 50s, 60s, and possibly 70s CE, those early disciples traversed the eastern half of the empire telling anyone who would listen about the transformative saving power of Jesus "the Christ" (the Anointed One, literally). Threats of popular violence or state persecution posed no barrier to them. They faced execution with stoic calm, according to both Christian and Roman reports, happy to embrace the **martyrdom** that would reunite them with their savior. Faithful Christians then and now have no doubt what caused the extraordinary transformation of that small group of disciples during those three days of hiding in Jerusalem; nonbelievers can only wonder. But one thing is clear: something dramatic happened to those people.

Something dramatic also happened to someone who was not there, in hiding, and was in fact helping the authorities to track down Jesus's followers: **Saul (Paul)** *Paul of* **of Tarsus** (ca. 5–67 CE). Saul was a passionately observant and argumentative *Tarsus* Pharisee from south-central Anatolia, a Greek speaker (*Paul* being the version of his Hebrew name in the broader society), and a Roman citizen. He studied Torah at Jerusalem in his youth with R. Gamaliel (d. ca. 50 CE)—revered as one of the greatest scholars of Jewish law in history—and acquired a solid background in Stoic philosophy. By his own admission, Paul never saw or heard Jesus but dedicated himself to persecuting his followers; he was present at, and likely participated in, the death by stoning of Stephen, the first Christian martyr, around 33 or 34 CE. Soon thereafter Paul set out from Jerusalem on the main road to Damascus, when he experienced a dramatic conversion after seeing a vision of the resurrected Christ. Paul mentions but does not describe this experience in any of his letters, but the book of Acts (written, according to tradition, by Luke) tells of it memorably:

> Now Saul, still breathing murderous threats against the disciples of the Lord, went to the high priest and asked him for letters to the synagogues in Damascus, that, if he should find any men or women who belonged to the Way, he might bring them back to Jerusalem in chains. On his journey, as he was nearing Damascus, a light from the sky suddenly flashed around him. He fell to the ground and heard a voice saying to him, "Saul, Saul, why are you persecuting me?" [Saul] said, "Who are you, sir?" The reply came, "I am Jesus whom you are persecuting. Now get up and go into the city and you will be told what you must do." The men who were with him stood speechless, for they heard the voice but could see no one. Saul got up from the ground, but when he opened his eyes he could see nothing; so they led him by the hand and brought him to Damascus.

After receiving baptism, Paul regained his sight and spent three years in the desert around Damascus, trying to understand the life-altering experience that had occurred to him.

Paul eventually dedicated himself to preaching Christian salvation to non-Jews, a mission that set him at odds with the apostles, most of whom regarded the message of Jesus as a mission meant solely for the Jews. The fact that Paul assumed the title of *apostle* for himself also rankled. He spent the remaining twenty to twenty-five years of his life traveling, preaching, and writing, until he was arrested by the authorities in Rome and executed in 67 CE. Paul's letters are the earliest of the New Testament texts, and they proclaim a powerful message of the hope that faith in the risen Christ offers to suffering humanity. Assuming that his letters are representative of the sum of his thinking, Paul shows no interest in anything that Jesus said or did during his lifetime. All that matters to Paul is the fact that Jesus was God incarnate and that he rose from the dead; Jesus's resurrection has defeated death, and our faith in this fact assures our own salvation. As he wrote,

> Now I am reminding you, brothers, of the gospel I preached to you, which you indeed received and in which you also stand. Through it you are also being saved, if you hold fast to the word I preached to you, unless you believed in vain. For I handed on to you as of first importance what I also received: that Christ died for our sins in accordance with the scriptures; that he was buried; that he was raised on the third day in accordance with the scriptures. (1 Corinthians 15.1–5)

It thus seems likely that the other New Testament texts were composed in part as a response to Paul's understanding of the Christian message, out of a conviction that Jesus's life mattered as much as his death. Paul's Jesus, in other words, should not become the default position. Other understandings of Jesus were just as important. Both literally and figuratively, those other understandings, it turned out, were all over the place.

CHRISTIANITIES EVERYWHERE

Whatever happened in Jerusalem to those first disciples, afterward they went out into the eastern Mediterranean determined to spread the message of Jesus. The problem, of course, was in agreeing on what that message actually was—and for whom it was intended. Was the Christian message intended for the Jews? For the Jews alone? For all people everywhere? There were factions in the early Christian movement supporting each of those views, plus others. Since Jesus and his initial disciples were all Jews, could non-Jews become his followers? And if they did, did they have to observe Jewish teaching and tradition, as the apostles themselves continued to do? If a non-Jew wanted to become a Christian, in other words, did he or she have to convert to Judaism first?

Questions like these abounded, causing many rifts to break out in the Christian movement, and the problems were exacerbated by the fact that no one had the universally recognized authority to settle such disputes as they arose. Peter was the leader of the original twelve apostles, but who should lead the movement after Peter's death in Rome in 64 CE? Peter's line of successors as **bishop** ("overseer") of the Christian community in Rome insisted that they were the heirs of Peter's own spiritual authority and hence were to be accepted as the supreme leaders of all Christians everywhere. But hardly anyone agreed with them. Why shouldn't the bishop of Jerusalem, the site of Jesus's Last Supper, crucifixion, and resurrection, take precedence? Others argued for the primacy of Antioch, the home of the first major Christian community outside of Jerusalem (see Map 7.2). Some insisted that Jesus's brother James (one of Jesus's four siblings—three brothers and a sister—mentioned in the gospels) had a hereditary right to lead the community. Still others argued that there should be no single leader at all and that guidance of the church should be left to a council of all the bishops together.

Until such matters could be resolved, the early Christians had no way to reconcile the differences in their beliefs. The apostles and early missionaries preached their messages in synagogues and market squares throughout the eastern Mediterranean, hoping to win as many converts as possible as quickly as possible, but these were the centers of ancient cultures that reached back two thousand years and more. Literacy was high because most of the people who heard Christian testimonies were versed in Hellenistic traditions. The missionaries, predictably, faced flurries of questions. Even those whose hearts were inclined to accept the new faith required some intellectual satisfaction before they were willing to commit:

- How can God be three separate beings—God, Jesus, and the Holy Spirit—and one indivisible being at the same time?
- If Jesus is "coeternal" with God, why is there no mention of him in the two-thousand-year tradition of Hebrew writings?
- If Jesus is the divine Son of God, how could he experience such human emotions as temptation, fear, and loneliness?

To crowds familiar with Hellenistic philosophy and the Hebrew scriptures, such questions were not easily ignored.

MAP 7.2   Early Christian Communities, ca. 350 CE   Christians were still a minority in the Roman Empire three hundred years after Jesus's death, but Christian communities had taken root in the eastern Mediterranean cities and started to expand into the countryside.

Because the apostles and other missionaries often disagreed on the answers to such questions, the communities of converts they established frequently believed different things. For the first three centuries after Jesus's death, in fact, it is inaccurate to speak of Christianity (with an uppercase "C"). What existed instead were many dozens of christianities (with a lowercase "c"), each with its own beliefs, liturgical traditions, and customs. There were communities of Christians who denied Jesus's divinity and believed good works were necessary for the salvation of some Christians but not for all. Others believed that Jesus had never in fact died but instead had gone into hiding. Some maintained that Jesus had passed along some body of secret knowledge, given only to a few initiates, that gave them the key to understanding that reconciled Christian revelation with Greek philosophy. Some insisted that Jesus had never actually existed in the flesh, and that what his disciples had seen and heard was a kind of hologram. Still others insisted that baptism was all that was needed to achieve salvation. The variant versions were, in all senses of the word, difficult to reckon.

ROMANS IN PURSUIT

Whatever their theological differences, most early Christians practiced their faith in secret, gathering in homes, in remote spots outside the city, in caves, or in warehouses—wherever they might escape notice. They needed to do so because Roman authorities were still in active pursuit of them, for two good reasons. First, to the Romans religion was a public affair, a means of uniting society in the observance of shared rituals. In contrast, Christians largely withdrew from society and taught, as far as the Romans understood it, that the affairs of this world are meaningless, the only meaningful reality being one's eternal existence in the heavenly kingdom yet to come. Christians seldom served in the army and refused to perform sacrifices to the emperor, which called into question their political loyalty. To the Stoic Roman mind, engagement in the affairs of the world was a duty and a sign of virtue; to devalue the affairs of the world seemed not ascetic but immoral. Moreover, Christians still spoke of their departed Jesus as a king, and as far as the Romans saw it, loyalty to a dead traitor was as bad as loyalty to a live one. Worse still, the Christians were said to practice ritual cannibalism by taking the Eucharist, or Holy Communion, in accordance with Jesus's instructions to his disciples at the Last Supper. Indeed, the central purpose of their gathering together was to eat the physical remains of their god Jesus. Even if the Christians ate the body and drank the blood of Jesus only symbolically, in bread and wine, the idea was repulsive to Roman sensibilities.

The second thing that condemned Christians in Roman eyes was their relationship with Judaism. The Romans had no love for the Jews, who were arguably *Crushing the Jews*

Masada   Ruins of the Jewish fortress at Masada, where rebel Jews pursued by the Roman army made their last stand in the Jewish Revolt of 66–70 CE. The Dead Sea can be glimpsed in the background. Masada is today the site where Israeli recruits take their oaths of military service.

the most volatile and troublesome people in the empire, but grudgingly respected the antiquity of their religion. When the Great Jewish Revolt of 66–70 CE erupted, Rome responded with heavy force, crushed the rebels, destroyed the Second Temple, killed untold thousands of Jews, and dispersed the rest once and for all. The slaughter was memorably fierce and was meant to be. In only a few years the Jews had passed from being, to Roman eyes, the residents of a hard-to-handle province to a despised race of stiff-necked ingrates and traitors. As the troops marched through Palestine in search of more Jews to kill or exile, they inevitably encountered groups of Christians who were eager to disassociate themselves from the Jewish majority. It is not a coincidence that the Christian gospels began to be written at this time, with their large servings of anti-Jewish language.

By the 70s and 80s CE the number of Christians who were not ethnically Jewish finally overtook the number who were. That itself required some redefinition of the relationship between the two faiths, but when the Jews became the leading active enemy of the Pax Romana, there was additional reason for the Christians to emphasize that they were not Jewish. The gospels make the case with unnerving thoroughness:

But when [John the Baptist] saw many Pharisees and Sadducees coming for baptism, he said to them, "You brood of vipers! Who warned you to flee from the wrath to come? Bear fruit worthy of repentance. Do not presume to say to yourselves, 'We have Abraham as our ancestor'; for I tell you, God is able from these stones to raise up children to Abraham." (Matthew 3.7–9)

After this Jesus went about in Galilee. He did not wish to go about in Judea because the Jews were looking for an opportunity to kill him. Now the Jewish Festival of Booths was near. . . . The Jews were looking for him at the festival and saying, "Where is he?" And there was considerable complaining about him among the crowds. While some were saying, "He is a good man," others were saying, "No, he is deceiving the crowd." Yet no one would speak openly about him for fear of the Jews. (John 7.1–2, 10–13)

Jesus said to [the Jewish leaders], "If God were your Father, you would love me, for I came from God and now I am here. I did not come on my own, but he sent me. Why do you not understand what I say? It is because you cannot accept my word. You are from your father the devil, and you choose to do your father's desires. He was a murderer from the beginning and does not stand in the truth, because there is no truth in him." (John 8.42–44)

Of course, to argue that one is not Jewish is not the same thing as to be anti-Semitic (anti-Jewish), but such an emphasis, repeatedly made over a sufficiently long time span, certainly opened the door to the evolution of a type of Jew-hatred. And as the christianities slowly spread around the Mediterranean, they continually had to repeat and refine their non-Jewishness: the diaspora of the Jews meant the side-by-side establishment of new Jewish communities in the cities as well. Wherever Christian communities took root, in other words, so too did new Jewish ones, and the efforts to explain themselves to the Romans began over and over again.

Persecution by the Romans was intermittent but brutal. Overall, many tens of thousands of Christians were arrested and killed during the first three centuries CE. The lucky ones were quickly executed; the others faced torture and humiliation before vast crowds in Roman forums. Popular resistance to Christians was ubiquitous and took many forms, from angry words to social ostracism to rough street violence, but persecution itself began in Rome as a deliberate policy before spreading, in the 2nd and 3rd centuries CE, into the provinces.

Persecuting the Christians

Catacombs of Saint Callisto, in Rome
The early Christians used underground crypts and rock chambers to bury their dead. The bodies were placed in niches like the ones shown here and then sealed. The catacombs became places of pilgrimage, and in this way the dead continued to be united with the living.

The first persecution occurred under Nero, during whose reign the first Christian communities were established in Rome under Peter and Paul. When the city experienced a catastrophic fire in 64 CE, Nero found the newcomer Christians to be a convenient scapegoat and contrived for them gruesome means of execution. He ordered hundreds of Christians to be covered in bloody animal skins, which made them the prey of packs of wild dogs; others were crucified; still others he had coated in paraffin and set alight as human torches. When the provincial governors took up the cause, they attempted to balance viciousness with some sense of fairness: Christians who converted back to Roman religion were forgiven, whereas those who remained Christian but held Roman citizenship were remanded to imprisonment in the capital. Only noncitizens who refused to renounce their Christian faith received the death sentence.

PHILOSOPHICAL FOUNDATIONS: STOICISM AND NEOPLATONISM

The Enduring Influence of Stoicism

Two philosophical schools offered alternatives to all the Roman and Christian faiths, even while contributing to their intellectual development: Stoicism and Neoplatonism. As we have seen, Stoicism dated back to Hellenistic times, well into the 3rd century BCE, but it received new life from Roman writers like Cicero and Seneca, who found in it the perfect expression of Roman values such as self-discipline, service to the community, and calm acceptance of divine law. Another burst of Stoic philosophy—a widespread and influential one, considering its source—came from Marcus Aurelius (r. 161–180 CE), the last of the "Five Good Emperors" discussed in chapter 6. His aphorisms, compiled in a book that he called "Notes to Myself" but is now known as the *Meditations*, appealed to many Romans and early Christians of the Pax Romana. (It helped that Aurelius wrote his book in koiné Greek, the same dialect used by the New Testament authors, which made his teachings more readily accessible to early Christians.) In line with earlier Stoic tradition, he believed the world is governed by an overarching sense of order and purpose, in service to which human lives play out. The only true happiness results from accepting one's limitations, keeping one's disappointments and frustrations in perspective, and performing one's duties to family, society, and the gods.

Aurelius's term for "order and purpose" is the Greek **Logos**, which resonated with anyone familiar with the gospel of John, where the word has much the same meaning.[6] The Logos, in the Stoic sense, gives not only a sense of the cosmos's purposefulness but also a measure of solace. It addresses the individual seeking both a place in the transient world and a permanent one in the divine world to come:

> The handiwork of the gods is replete with Providence, and the hand of Fate is not detached from nature. Rather, Fate spins and weaves the threads that Providence ordains. Everything flows from the home of the gods; more than that, a sense of needful purpose and well-being pervades the whole creation of which you are a part. Every part of the natural world contains and preserves an element of goodness that is given to it by the very nature of the world as a whole. . . . Take comfort in this thought, and live always by these doctrines. If you wish to face death with something other than mumbling confusion, give up your fascination with study, and let your heart be at rest and express simple gratitude to the gods for what they have done. (*Meditations* 2.3)

Marcus Aurelius   This bronze equestrian statue of the great emperor and Stoic philosopher is on display in Rome. Marcus Aurelius's reign, which ended in 180 CE, marked the high-point of the Pax Romana.

Stoicism offered more than a set of rules to follow or a group of ideas to adhere to. Some examples include: "No action is good if performing it causes you to violate a trust or behave shamelessly" (3.7). "Do not act as though you will live ten thousand years, for death is the fate that awaits you. Therefore, while you're alive and able, seek the Good" (4.17). "Do not hold life itself to be the only thing of value. Consider the infinite measures of time and space that lie behind you and before you; in the face of these eternities, what difference does it make whether you live for three days or three generations?" (4.50). "If a cucumber is bitter, throw it away; and if your path is full of briars, change direction. That is all you need to do. It is not for you to ask, 'Why do such things exist?'" (8.50). Stoicism cultivated the soul and urged people to perform spiritual exercises through daily reflection, prayer, and contemplation of the fact of mortality. The Stoics called these practices the

---

[6]   Meaning "word," literally, *logos* can also be seen in the suffix "-ology" that denotes so many English terms for science—like biology, geology, and meteorology.

discipline of *askesis*—meaning "peace of mind"—from which term the English word *asceticism* derives. Many early Christian leaders saw the compatibility between their religious beliefs and Stoic ethics and used the Roman notions to explain their faith.

The Platonic tradition also kept its appeal with polytheists and, increasingly, Christians, in an amalgam known as **Neoplatonism**. A series of Plato's disciples continued teaching at the Academy long after his death in 347 BCE, most of them *The Emergence* engaged in collecting, editing, codifying, and commenting on Plato's vast *of Neoplatonism* writings. A loose network of Platonist schools also spread across the Hellenistic lands, which ensured that Plato's philosophy and his way of doing philosophy would have the most wide-reaching influence in the centuries following his death. Plato's teaching of an Ideal Universe, from which our muddled and benighted cosmos derives, harmonized with many of the new provincial mystery cults and provided them with intellectual support. Many of the Neoplatonists were equally passionate in observing their traditional polytheistic convictions. In Plato they thus found an intellectualized version of their cults.

Plutarch (46–120 CE), a wealthy Greek who was an enthusiastic supporter of the empire, dedicated his life as a priest of the oracle of Apollo at Delphi. He also composed a shelf of stylized biographies, moral essays, literary criticism, and Platonic commentaries. His best-known and best-loved work is the series of *Parallel Lives*, in which he pairs eminent statesmen from Greek and Roman history. In these lively, intimate portraits of their respective virtues (or lack thereof), his concern is not with the details of political history but with the moral character of his subjects.

As he himself put it, he was interested in "the offhand occasion, word, or anecdote . . . that brings to light men's true tempers more than the story of any of their great battles, even those in which ten thousand men may have died." Nevertheless, Plutarch knew how to tell a good story. His narratives of the disastrous Athenian campaign to Syracuse and of Pompey's defeat at Pharsalus and subsequent death, for example, are gripping set-pieces. The *Parallel Lives* have been popular ever since Plutarch's own time. Roman society read them avidly, as did most Christian scholars at least until the 4th century. In the Renaissance, Sir Thomas North (1535–1604) produced the first version in English in 1597—although he cribbed it from a French translation since he knew no Greek.[7]

Plutarch's essays, by contrast, which medieval commentators grouped under the catchall title of *Moralia* ("Ethical Matters"), have never been as popular but give an indication of the breadth of his interests. They move from "Consolation to My Wife," written after the death of their infant daughter—"Sweet wife, let

---

[7]   William Shakespeare used North's Plutarch when composing his history plays *Julius Caesar, Antony and Cleopatra*, and *Coriolanus*.

us bear this pain with patient hearts. . . . Born after four sons, she was especially dear to you; and so dearly did you long for a girl that, when she finally came, I gave her your own name. . . . She had such a gentle spirit, marvelously kind"—to "On the Delay of Divine Justice," a dialogue that tackles the problem of why evildoers prosper. The dialogue ends with Plutarch telling a chilling parable about a scoundrel named Thespesius who lives only for pleasure and lies, cheats, and steals from everyone. He falls into a type of coma, and his admirers, thinking him dead, prepare to bury him. He wakes just in time and amends his behavior—having seen in his comalike state a vision of the punishments that await evildoers. Plutarch's message is that divine justice exists outside of time but is certain. Yet another essay, the speculative "On the Face of the Man in the Moon," attempts a cosmology—a system for explaining the origins and structure of the entire universe. In all, the *Moralia* unite a committed Neoplatonic philosophy with a common-sense search for the alleviation of suffering. Roman religion received a jolt of intellectual rigor in the works of writers like Plutarch, which helps to account for its continued vitality.

Many early Christians felt the attraction of that rigor as well. The Alexandrian theologian Origen (185–254 CE) used the Neoplatonic notion of *emanation*—the idea that the created world results from the outward-flowing essence of life from the eternal center of the Logos. In this way he explained the migration of souls from the Heavenly Divine and out into the created world. Origen supplemented this notion with the idea of spiritual return, a kind of undertow of purified souls flowing back toward the creating center. This idea did not originate with him; his younger contemporary Neoplatonic philosopher Plotinus (204–270 CE; a polytheist) had been elaborating the concepts of spiritual resurrection and return, as handed on to him by his own teachers, for years. But Origen was the first Christian thinker of note to explicate salvation in intellectual terms derived from a philosophical tradition.

Also Neoplatonic, but ultimately unorthodox from the Christian perspective, was Origen's denial of bodily resurrection. Origen is a unique figure in Christian history: he is regarded as one of the great Church Fathers, the first Christian philosopher of any note, yet most of his published ideas proved controversial and were formally condemned by later councils. He left behind an enormous body of writing; Jerome (ca. 347–430 CE), the later theologian who produced the definitive Latin version of the Bible (the Vulgate), credited him with nearly two thousand separate works. That is clearly an exaggeration. But even accounting for the texts later condemned and destroyed by church leaders, his surviving works are still voluminous.

Like the Roman cults, early Christianity received high-octane intellectual fuel injections from Stoicism and Neoplatonism. Both philosophies enriched it enormously by adding to Christianity's intrinsic emotional appeal a degree of sophistication that it had previously lacked. For the next fifteen hundred years Christian philosophers, scientists, mathematicians, and logicians were among the leading scholars in Western civilization and usually made up the majority of them. This was not necessarily because of the cultural hegemony of the Latin and Greek churches, but simply because the Christian faith itself invited, prompted, and demanded intense intellectual effort. It inspired a fascination with what is difficult and required its followers to acknowledge complex ideas about the nature of the world, human freedom, the meaning of suffering, and the purpose of existence.

Most notably, these early centuries of the Common Era introduced an emphasis on self-awareness, self-examination, and self-criticism. They urged the development of personal conscience and the constant striving for meaning and improvement, ideas that would mark Western culture indelibly. Such concerns had existed before, of course, but never with the same degree of emotional urgency and intellectual resolve. Western culture became marked by a kind of intellectual and spiritual restlessness, convinced that life has genuine meaning and purpose but never quite certain that it had discovered them. All the same, it was confident that the effort to find them was necessary and ennobling.

WHO, WHAT, WHERE

bishop	martyrdom	Pantheon
Essenes	messiah	Pharisees
Jesus of Nazareth	mystery religions	Sadducees
John the Baptist	Neoplatonism	Saul (Paul) of Tarsus
Logos	New Testament	twelve apostles

SUGGESTED READINGS

Primary Sources

Eusebius of Caesarea. *The History of the Church.*
The Gnostic Gospels.
Josephus. *The Antiquities of the Jews.*
Josephus. *The Jewish War.*
Marcus Aurelius. *Meditations.*

The Nag Hammadi Library.
The New Jerusalem Bible.
Philo of Alexandria.
Pliny the Younger. *Letters.*
Plutarch. *Parallel Lives.*

Anthologies

Ehrman, Bart D. *The New Testament and Other Early Christian Writings: A Reader* (2003).

Elliott, Neil, and Mark Reasoner, eds. *Documents and Images for the Study of Paul* (2010).

Warrior, Valerie M. *Roman Religion: A Sourcebook* (2001).

Studies

Boatwright, Mary T., Daniel J. Gargola, Noel Lenski, and Richard J. A. Talbert. *The Romans: From Village to Empire—A History of Rome from Earliest Times to the End of the Western Empire* (2011).

Brakke, David. *The Gnostics: Myth, Ritual, and Diversity in Early Christianity* (2011).

Brennan, Tad. *The Stoic Life: Emotions, Duties, and Fate* (2005).

Brown, Peter. *The Body and Society: Men, Women, and Sexual Renunciation in Early Christianity* (2008, orig. 1998).

Brown, Peter. *The Rise of Western Christendom: Triumph and Diversity, AD 200–1000* (2003).

Ehrman, Bart D. *Lost Christianities: The Battles for Scripture and the Faiths We Never Knew* (2005).

Engberg-Pedersen, Troels. *Cosmology and the Self in the Apostle Paul: The Material Self* (2011).

Ferguson, Everett. *Backgrounds of Early Christianity* (2003).

Fredriksen, Paula. *Augustine and the Jews: A Christian Defense of Jews and Judaism* (2008).

Fredriksen, Paula. *From Jesus to Christ: The Origins of the New Testament Images of Jesus* (2000).

Fredriksen, Paula. *Jesus of Nazareth, King of the Jews: A Jewish Life and the Emergence of Christianity* (2000).

González, Justo L. *The Story of Christianity. Vol. 1, The Early Church to the Dawn of the Reformation* (2010).

Jacobs, Irving. *The Midrashic Process: Tradition and Interpretation in Rabbinic Judaism* (2008).

Johnson, Luke Timothy. *Among the Gentiles: Greco-Roman Religion and Christianity* (2010).

Johnson, Luke Timothy. *The Writings of the New Testament: An Interpretation* (2010).

Lampe, Peter. *From Paul to Valentinus: Christians at Rome in the First Two Centuries* (2003).

Lieu, Judith M. *Christian Identity in the Jewish and Graeco-Roman World* (2004).

Luijendijk, AnneMarie. *Greetings in the Lord: Early Christians and the Oxyrhynchus Papyri* (2009).

MacMullen, Ramsay. *Romanization in the Time of Augustus* (2008).

Meier, John P. *A Marginal Jew: Rethinking the Historical Jesus*, 4 vols. (1991–2009).

Meier, John P. *The Vision of Matthew: Christ, Church, and Morality in the First Gospel* (2004).

Rasimus, Tuomas, Troels Engberg-Pedersen, and Ismo Dunderberg, eds. *Stoicism in Early Christianity* (2010).

Stark, Rodney. *Cities of God: The Real Story of How Christianity Became an Urban Movement and Conquered Rome* (2007).

White, L. Michael. *Scripting Jesus: The Gospels in Re-Write* (2011).

Wilken, Robert Louis. *The Christians as the Romans Saw Them* (2003).

Wilken, Robert Louis. *The Spirit of Early Christian Thought: Seeking the Face of God* (2005).

For additional resources, including maps, primary sources, visuals, web links, and quizzes, please go to **www.oup.com/us/backman**.

CHAPTER 8

The Early Middle Ages

300–750

The Greater West underwent a series of shocks from the 4th to the 8th centuries that gave a radically new direction to its development. Roman might had peaked in the late 2nd century, after which imperial control entered a holding pattern while internal squabbles dominated the political scene. Those squabbles centered on a constitutional problem: the empire had never established an orderly process for succession to the throne, which meant that the death of each emperor triggered some sort of contest for power. Compounding the internal strife, the western half of the empire fell victim to successive waves of Germanic settlers driven westward by population pressure and the advancing armies of Attila the Hun (r. 434–453) from central Asia. The Germanic peoples were immigrants and refugees more than invaders, but they were quick to draw swords when the Romans tried to check them at the Rhine and Danube rivers. The combination of internal confusion and external invasion led to Roman decline in the western empire, but also to the rise of a "new Rome" in the east—Byzantium. The Byzantine Empire, with its capital at Constantinople, developed as a strongly centralized and militarized state, in which the government's close relations with the Orthodox Church proved vital to each institution's success. In the Arab and Persian Middle East

THE EARLY MIDDLE AGES

Crown of King Recesvinth
The Visigoths, a Germanic people who in 410 stunned the Greater West by sacking Rome, were justly famous for their metalwork, and this crown (worn only in formal ceremonies) is one of their best-known pieces. It is made of gold encrusted with rock crystals, pearls, and sapphires.

new networks of tribal alliances and rivalries arose that challenged control of trade and pilgrimage routes, with violent results. As we will see in the next chapter, the interplay of these developments laid the groundwork for the rise of the Greater West's third great monotheism—Islam.

These four centuries are popularly known as the **Dark Ages** in western Europe, but most scholars refer to them as **Late Antiquity**.[1] Both labels are understandable. For much of the period from 300 to 700, western Europe was a dark place indeed, filled with poverty, famine and disease, nearly constant warfare, almost universal illiteracy, and a material standard of living that is horrifying to consider. Yet many of the institutional practices and cultural values of antiquity were still alive, if in beleaguered and benighted form. Further, for the Greek-speaking lands of the eastern Mediterranean, this was a heroic age when the achievements of the ancient world were fortified by the rapid development of Christianity. From their magnificent new capital city of Constantinople (modern Istanbul) on the Bosporus—the strait separating the Black Sea and the Mediterranean—the people of the Byzantine Empire achieved a level of wealth, power, and cultural glory that were never seen again in the Greater West.

---

[1]   The term **Middle Ages** denotes the thousand-year period between the founding of the Byzantine capital city of Constantinople (ca. 330) and the start of the Italian Renaissance around 1350. Many historians object to the use of "Dark Ages" for the early medieval centuries on the basis that the name is demeaning.

CHAPTER TIMELINE

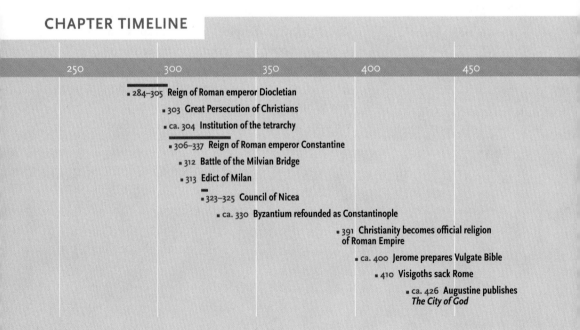

	250	300	350	400	450

■ 284–305 Reign of Roman emperor Diocletian

■ 303 Great Persecution of Christians

■ ca. 304 Institution of the tetrarchy

■ 306–337 Reign of Roman emperor Constantine

■ 312 Battle of the Milvian Bridge

■ 313 Edict of Milan

■ 323–325 Council of Nicea

■ ca. 330 Byzantium refounded as Constantinople

■ 391 Christianity becomes official religion of Roman Empire

■ ca. 400 Jerome prepares Vulgate Bible

■ 410 Visigoths sack Rome

■ ca. 426 Augustine publishes *The City of God*

THE IMPERIAL CRISIS

There is no mystery to the decline and fall of the western Roman Empire: a host of internal problems coincided with a wave of foreign invasions. Historians debate the severity of specific causes, or the relative rankings of various factors, but few serious scholars dispute that the combination of internal weaknesses and external pressures did the job. The real mystery is how the empire, despite such a host of problems, managed to survive into the 5th century.

Trouble first emerged in a major way with the death of Marcus Aurelius in 180. Aurelius had designated his son Commodus (r. 180–192) to succeed him, but Commodus was a poor ruler, a snarky, ill-mannered lout who threw tantrums when he did not get his way. He thought himself a great athlete, dressed in lion skins, carried a club, and demanded that people call him Hercules (the Roman name for the Greek hero Herakles). More than once he ordered the execution of senators and officials who opposed his wishes. The political atmosphere in Rome grew toxic in a way it had not been since the infamous reign of Nero. Commodus's death set off a civil war between a host of civil and

Commodus as Hercules The emperor Commodus (r. 180–192) loved to portray himself as a manly man, rather like Russia's Vladimir Putin today, and he regularly staged rigged athletic contests in which he emerged victorious. Here he has had himself sculpted as Hercules.

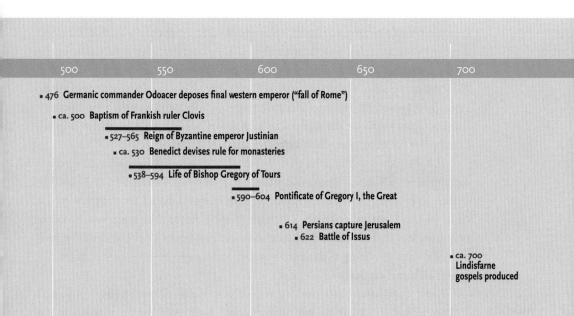

| 500 | 550 | 600 | 650 | 700 |

- 476 Germanic commander Odoacer deposes final western emperor ("fall of Rome")

- ca. 500 Baptism of Frankish ruler Clovis

- 527–565 Reign of Byzantine emperor Justinian

- ca. 530 Benedict devises rule for monasteries

- 538–594 Life of Bishop Gregory of Tours

- 590–604 Pontificate of Gregory I, the Great

- 614 Persians capture Jerusalem
- 622 Battle of Issus

- ca. 700 Lindisfarne gospels produced

Internal military officials, and this became the unfortunate pattern for nearly every impe-
Weaknesses rial succession throughout the 3rd century. The army accordingly grew in prominence as the sole bulwark against social unrest, which meant that power passed
almost exclusively to a series of generals, but since each successive general's claim
to legitimacy came only from having seized power by brute force, ambitious rivals
in the military in turn killed each one. In the sixty-seven years from 218 to 285,
there were as many as eighty-three claimants to the throne—only a handful of
whom died of natural causes.

Nonstop war undermined the economy by disrupting farming and commerce,
and the warmongering generals made matters worse by intermittently devaluing the
currency so they would have more coinage on hand with which to pay their troops.
But this triggered runaway inflation and drove hordes of laborers into the cities in
search of employment or alms, causing the urban centers to become choked with
homeless and desperately poor people. The smallpox virus then did the rest. By 300
the empire was reeling from disaster to disaster; the army was divided, decimated,
and demoralized; and the economy sputtered and wheezed like a dying engine.

IMPERIAL DECLINE: ROME'S OVERREACH

By cruel coincidence, this was when the imperial borders suddenly faced their
External most severe challenge with the inrush of the Germanic peoples along the Rhine–
Pressures Danube frontier and the renewed attack of the Persian Empire, which was then
under the aggressive Sassanid dynasty (224–651), in the east. The earliest Germans to arrive in large numbers, the Ostrogoths and Visigoths, advanced toward
Constantinople but were bribed with money and promises of assistance if they redirected their march into western Europe. They thereby spared the cities of the
eastern Mediterranean and moved instead into the underpopulated rural west, as
did most of the other Germanic groups that followed, but the Persians could not be
so easily disposed of. The lure of controlling the Holy Land and the Hellespont—
the linchpins between the European and Asian economies—proved too great,
causing the Persians to set their sights on outright conquest.

The Romans fought back valiantly but with little luck. The low point for them
came in 260, when the Persians captured the emperor Valerian (r. 253–260) in
battle. They held him as a slave, forcing him to kneel on all fours as a stepping
stool for the Sassanid ruler when he mounted his horse. The rapid succession of
emperors continued unchecked, the western provinces of the empire became
overrun with invading Germanic groups, and effective government from the
center all but disappeared.

Diocletian's A respite appeared with the long reign of a stern, no-nonsense emperor named
Reforms **Diocletian** (r. 284–305). He came from a long line of peasant farmers in the

MAP 8.1   Persian Ascendancy   This is the most famous of the Sassanid rock reliefs, not only because of its workmanship but because of the scene it portrays: the great victory of Shapur I (r. 241–272) over the Roman emperor Valerian (r. 253–260). Valerian was captured and executed, then skinned, stuffed, and mounted on the wall at Shapur's palace.

Roman province of Dalmatia (modern Croatia), had received only an elementary education but was raised with a deep belief in the rightness of the empire, and had sought a career in the army. A talented soldier, Diocletian rose quickly through the ranks and was popular with the soldiers he commanded. When the briefly serving emperors Carus (r. 282–283) and Numerianus (r. 283–284) died—according to several ancient sources, Carus being struck by lightning and Numerianus of a mysterious eye inflammation—the army overwhelmingly threw its support behind Diocletian. He faced enormous problems: a wrecked economy, a restive army, Germanic and Persian invasions, and a bloated, inefficient administration. His solutions were as blunt and direct as his personality.

The worthless currency that had triggered the inflation could hardly be helped. Europe's known gold and silver mines were largely tapped out by Diocletian's time, and without an influx of precious metals the fiscal crisis would continue. Diocletian addressed the problem by essentially withdrawing Rome's currency from circulation and returning the empire to a barter economy. Taxes were collected in kind (clothing, food, tools, manufactured goods, or whatever),

MAP 8.1   Diocletian's Division of the Empire, ca. 304   Diocletian divided the empire into two halves, each governed by an emperor (*augustus*) who was aided by an assistant ruler and designated successor (*caesar*).

and imperial soldiers were paid in the same. The debased coinage—once recaptured, melted, purified, and recast—eventually regained some of its value in Mediterranean trade, but a true money economy would not return to continental Europe until the 10th century.

Turning to the imperial army, Diocletian reformed it into separate civil and military divisions, with one force of "border troops" manning the Rhine–Danube frontier. This long line of fortified stations, together with a separate force of "palace troops," served as a roving field army that was under direct imperial command. Diocletian's border troops were essentially a form of civil militia made up of deputized residents, both Roman and German, of the frontier areas. The palace troops, the more professional fighting force, who were paid with real cash, were thus freed to concentrate on the struggle against the Persians to the east, with good results.

Last, Diocletian chose not to streamline the administration but to cut it into separate units, instituting a **tetrarchy** ("rule of four")—a new system whereby the empire was formally divided into two halves, east and west, with a separate emperor (*augustus* in Latin) for each (see Map 8.1). Diocletian appointed a fellow officer, Maximian, as augustus of the western half of the empire, retaining the wealthier eastern half for himself. Each augustus was assisted by a *caesar*, or junior emperor, who succeeded to the position of his augustus on that person's death or retirement and who then appointed a new caesar to assist him. At a stroke, Diocletian eased the bureaucratic burden on the central administration and provided a regular means for the selection of new augusti.

MARTYRDOM AND EMPIRE

Diocletian is chiefly remembered, however, for instituting in 303 the so-called **Great Persecution**, the longest and most vicious of the state attacks on Christians.

The Great Persecution

> In the nineteenth year of Diocletian's reign . . . in the month of April . . . near the time when Christians celebrate the Passion of the Savior . . . [imperial decrees] were promulgated that demanded the flattening of all Christian churches, the burning of all Christian books, the humiliation of all Christian leaders, and the imprisonment of all servants of Christ who refused to denounce their faith.

So wrote Eusebius of Caesarea (263–339), the most reliable chronicler of the Great Persecution, at the outset of his *History of the Church*. He then went on to describe, chapter by bloody chapter, the beating, flaying, decapitation, drowning, burning, rape, and mauling by animals of thousands of Christian martyrs.

Diocletian was less interested in annihilating the Christians than he was in persuading them to participate in civic celebrations of the imperial cult, however. After all, his own wife and daughter were reported to have been Christians. What mattered instead was the unraveling of social cohesion across the empire. For centuries Rome had been held together by a carefully cultivated public spirit, a sense of Romanness and the commitment to an ideal greater than parochial ethnic or religious concerns. Diocletian promoted the cult of emperor worship as a unifying force, a living symbol of everyone's participation in a world larger than themselves. The Christians' refusal to endorse the official cult, or even to give it empty lip service, seemed to strike at the very heart of the empire, and he therefore concluded that they had to be crushed into submission.

But that is not what happened, at least not with the majority of them. Many of the thousands whom Diocletian sent to their death accepted their fate with quiet resolve and even, if we can trust our sources, with some measure of happiness. Martyrdom, they felt, was a prize to be embraced. Reunion after death with the Christ whom they had served in life seemed too great a blessing to merit dreading the temporary unpleasantness that preceded it. Crowds eager for blood and tears

Medallion of Saint Mamai Saint Mamai, an early martyr popular with the Georgian people in the Caucasus, was thrown to the lions by the Romans in 275 CE. This 11th-century medallion depicts Mamai fearlessly astride a lion while brandishing a cross, symbolizing the victory over death won by Mamai and by all believers in Christ.

certainly saw all the blood they could want but, instead of tears, too often had to put up with hymns, prayers, and laughter.

Martyrologies—the narrative records of martyrs' sufferings—can seldom be taken literally. Their whole purpose is to glorify God by testifying to both the unimaginable sufferings endured by martyrs and the stoic, calm, and joyful spirit expressed by them even when caught in the lion's maw or pierced by the executioner's blade. The more gore, the better, and the more superhuman the acceptance of brutal death, the better still. Hence, when a Christian writer like Lactantius (ca. 240–320) penned his vivid chronicle *On the Deaths of Those Persecuted for Christ,* he found it easy to identify plenty of victims of Roman cruelty; the challenge lay in maintaining the fever pitch of his descriptions of the horrors they suffered. As with the history of Eusebius of Caesarea, after thirty pages of Lactantius's nonstop beheadings, eviscerations, poisonings, burnings, and beatings, one can sense the writer's rhetorical exhaustion—and there are still three hundred pages to go.

Nevertheless, even allowing for exaggeration in the sources, enough Christians accepted their martyrdom with such grace that the Romans who witnessed it were astonished. What was it about this religion that could enable someone to accept death happily, even eagerly? Was this something to envy, or was it simply insane? It is unclear how many Romans, if any, were sufficiently moved by the martyrs' behavior to convert to the faith. Yet it is certain that the Great Persecution got more people thinking about Christianity, and perhaps talking about it, than there had been before.

A CHRISTIAN EMPEROR AND A CHRISTIAN CHURCH

In 305, having done all that he could to save the empire, an exhausted Diocletian resigned from the imperial office (the only person to do so in Roman history) and returned to his homeland farm, dedicating his last years to his private passion: growing cabbages.[2] His mechanism for the orderly transfer of power failed in its

---

[2] Diocletian's passion for gardening is described by Lactantius, who became a close advisor of Diocletian's successor, Constantine the Great.

first attempt, however, and another civil war quickly engulfed the empire. When the smoke finally cleared a new emperor sat on the throne: **Constantine the Great** (r. 306–337), whose eventful reign changed everything—because he was the first Roman emperor to be a Christian.

According to the sources closest to the event, Constantine's conversion had occurred on the eve of the battle that would decide the civil war. A rival named Maxentius had also claimed the imperial title in 306; attempts to negotiate a power-sharing arrangement continually failed, and in 312 the two sides broke into open warfare. The conclusive battle took place a few miles north of Rome, at the Milvian Bridge. Reportedly, a heavenly voice spoke to Constantine in a dream and told him to embrace Christianity and to paint the cross on his soldiers' shields before the next day's battle. He did so, won the battle, became sole emperor, and committed himself to Christianity on the spot. The story seems too contrived to be true. It suggests, none too subtly, that the religion itself caused the military victory, although the soldiers can hardly have been believers. From this point on, it implies, imperial success could only come so long as the empire served the Christian God.

Constantine's Conversion

However the conversion occurred, it did in fact occur. Constantine's conversion must have been sincere, since there was no conceivable political advantage to gain from it. Christians, by the year 312, made up no more than 2 or 3 percent of the Roman population and may have constituted as little as 1 percent. Even if one considers only the urban population of the eastern half of the empire—that is, the geographic area and demographic group with the highest proportion of Christians—the new faith made up no more than 10 percent of the populace.

The impact of his conversion was immediate and dramatic. In 313 he issued the **Edict of Milan**, which legalized Christianity and guaranteed religious freedom for all faiths within the empire[3]:

Edict of Milan

> It pleases us to remove altogether the legal restraints issued heretofore regarding the Christians, any one of whom may henceforth practice the Christian faith, if he wishes, freely, openly, without molestation . . . and in free and unrestricted liberty of religious worship. . . . And moreover, in order to promote peace in our time, we grant to all religions [within the empire] the right of free and open observance of their faith.

---

[3] Too many historians confuse Constantine's Edict of Toleration (311) with the Edict of Milan (313). The earlier decree had simply ordered an end to the Great Persecution inaugurated by Diocletian. Christians had to wait two more years for their faith to be legalized.

Christ the Almighty   This mosaic from the church of Santa Prassede in Rome shows Christ on his heavenly throne, surrounded by his apostles and two martyrs, Prudence and Praxedis. From the 4th century on, the Good Shepherd iconography of Christ (see the illustration that opens chapter 7) gave way to images of Jesus as the mighty king of Heaven or the stern judge of the Last Day. The kinder, gentler Jesus did not become the norm again until the 12th century.

Constantine did more than legalize Christianity, however; he opened the imperial coffers in support of it. He ordered that public funds be made available to compensate individuals whose property and cash deposits had been confiscated for religious reasons. He poured money into building churches, training priests, promoting evangelical missions, copying sacred writings, and setting up Christian charitable houses. He granted Christians special tax privileges and showed personal preference for selecting Christians to serve in government offices. Not surprisingly, Christianity began to spread among the people of the east at a rate never before experienced.

Traditional Roman religion remained legal for several more decades, but the momentum was now decidedly in Christianity's direction. The years of struggle and persecution were over. By the end of the 4th century the majority of the eastern Roman population had embraced the new faith, and it became the official religion of the Roman Empire in 391, thanks to the emperor Theodosius I (r. 379–395).

Permitted at last by the Edict of Milan to practice their faith openly, Christians poured into the town squares to preach—and this is when the long-simmering problems of the "christianities" came into focus. To his dismay, Constantine found

Council of Nicea

that no two Christian groups worshipped in the same way, read the same canon, or recognized the same authority. Most accepted Jesus of Nazareth as the biblical messiah and Son of God, but many did not. Most believed that he had died on the cross and rose from the dead, but many did not. Most believed that he was physically present in the consecrated bread and wine of the Eucharist, but many did not. Constantine recognized that the christianities risked continued fracturing and internal fighting unless something was done. Accordingly, he summoned an ecumenical council—that is, a gathering to establish unity of faith—to meet at the eastern city of Nicea, ordering the leaders of every Christian community in the empire to attend. With one notable exception, the bishops all came. The council lasted for two years (323–325), passed dozens of resolutions, and symbolically capped its activity by issuing the **Nicene Creed**, which has stood ever since as the universal standard, the statement *par excellence* of Christian belief. The exact wording of the Creed has been revised numerous times over the centuries. Its opening text proclaims:

> We believe in one God,
> the Father, the Almighty,
> Maker of all that is, seen and unseen.
> We believe in one Lord, Jesus Christ,
> the only Son of God,
> eternally begotten of the Father,
> God from God, Light from Light,
> true God from true God,
> begotten, not made, consubstantial
> of one Being with the Father.
> Through him all things were made.
> For us and for our salvation
> he came down from heaven:
> and by the Holy Spirit was incarnate
> he became incarnate from the Virgin Mary,
> and was made man.
> For our sake he was crucified under Pontius Pilate;
> he suffered death and was buried.
> On the third day he rose again
> in accordance with the Scriptures;
> he ascended into heaven
> and is seated at the right hand of the Father.
> He will come again in glory to judge the living and the dead,
> and his kingdom will have no end.

Constantine regarded the newly standardized Christian Church as his own dominion. He had tradition behind him: in Rome the emperor had held the title of *pontifex maximus* ("chief priest"), which made him the leader of the entire pagan cult. The empire did not distinguish between political authority and religious authority, and Constantine saw no reason to alter the arrangement simply because the religion itself had changed. Taking the formal title of "thirteenth apostle," Constantine insisted that the emperor, so long as he himself was a Christian, was by that fact alone the supreme authority over the Christian Church.

Papal Claims to Power

This brought him into conflict with the bishop of Rome, Sylvester I (r. 314–335)—the one and only bishop who had refused to attend the Council of Nicea, since doing so would have implied a recognition of the emperor's authority over the church. (Sylvester did send a representative, however, to keep an eye on things.) Sylvester claimed for himself a title previously applied to many bishops: **pope** (from *pappas*, "papa"). His argument for supreme papal authority rested on Peter, the leader of the original group of apostles who had ended his days as the bishop of the Christian community of Rome; therefore, his successors as bishop of Rome should inherit the leadership of the church. The problem for those successors was that few Christians outside of Rome accepted their logic. Peter's original authority was beyond question, but after Peter's death (in 64 CE) the leadership of the community of bishops was an open question. Why should the bishop of Jerusalem not take precedence? Or the bishop of Antioch (the first city outside of Jerusalem to have a formally organized community)? Why should leadership not be left to a free election among all bishops? As it happened, most of the popes for the first thousand years of Christian history had little authority outside of their own city of Rome. Many were respected and even granted special honors, but few were obeyed. Starting with Constantine, the holders of the imperial title assumed their own supremacy over the church and exercised it.[4]

THE RISE OF "NEW ROME": THE BYZANTINE EMPIRE

Constantine made one additional epoch-making decision: in 324, in the midst of the Council of Nicea, he decided to abandon Italy and build a new capital city in the east. He chose the site known to the ancient Greeks as *Byzantion* (in Latin, *Byzantium*), on the promontory between the Sea of Marmara and the Black Sea. This was where Europe and Asia met, the nexus of east–west trade, and the strategic node for overseeing the administration of the eastern empire. By the 4th century it seemed clear that the western half of the Roman Empire was in severe

---

[4]   Pope Sylvester did the best he could, under the circumstances. He approved the legislation of the Council of Nicea, including the Creed, and simply reissued it under his own name.

decline. And although most people hoped for its survival, Constantine and his successors recognized that the eastern half of the empire was the more important half, being the virtual cradle of Western civilization. It was an urban, commercial, literate, and sophisticated world, newly given an additional sense of unity and purpose by its now-rapid assumption of a Christian character. The western half of the empire, in contrast, was weaker, poorer, ruder, agrarian, and ultimately expendable.

From the new capital built on the site of Byzantium, now renamed **Constantinople**, the rulers of the Byzantine Empire kept their eyes trained eastward, *Growing* vaguely acknowledging their links to the backward west but putting little effort *East–West* into propping up the crumbling administration there. The Byzantines regarded *Divide* their eastern empire as a "new Rome" purged of its pagan past and explicitly dedicated to creating a Christian realm. The new capital was formally dedicated on May 11, 330.

The Byzantine Empire of the 4th and 5th centuries wrapped around the eastern edges of the Mediterranean like a giant reversed letter C. It included all of today's countries of Libya, Egypt, Israel, Jordan, Lebanon, Syria, Turkey, and most of the Balkan states (see Map 8.2). Hundreds of ethnic groups resided within this zone, chiefly in the cities or within a day's journey of them. Since travel and communication were relatively easy, thanks to long-familiar sea-lanes and coastal roads, the government in Constantinople was able to retain centralized rule. The heart of the empire was the great Anatolian landmass, the center of

MAP 8.2   The Byzantine Empire in the Time of Justinian   Justinian and his wife and partner in rule Theodora waged war against the Germanic kingdoms in the west, aiming to reunite the empire and restore the imperial glory of the Augustan period.

grain production. Within a few generations, Byzantine society sloughed off its use of Latin and reverted to the Greek that had been the norm there until the arrival of the Romans.

The territory of Greece itself held a sentimental place in Byzantine hearts but was a relatively minor province in terms of economic and cultural life. The real nodes of energy apart from Constantinople itself were the coastal cities—Thessalonika, Ephesus, Antioch, Tripoli, and Alexandria—and a handful of inland cities like Jerusalem, Damascus, and Chalcedon. Manufacturing, trade, shipping, and finance were their lifeblood, but they also maintained hundreds of schools, academies, libraries, salons, and theaters that kept alive the classical traditions of literature, philosophy, and, to a lesser degree, science. In addition, the 4th and 5th centuries saw a frenzy of church building as Christianity at last sank its roots deeply into the culture.

The Byzantines' readoption of the Greek language represented a symbolic but also a practical turning away from the Latin-speaking west. Trade between east and west declined precipitously, since the west produced little that the east needed, apart from slaves. Beyond the disruptions and devastations caused by foreign invaders, the fundamental problem in the west was a dangerous imbalance in the distribution of wealth. Privileged families of senatorial and equestrian rank were often fabulously wealthy, but the laboring classes faced almost nonstop want and suffered repeated famines throughout the 4th and 5th centuries. Slaves, who represented as much as one-fourth of the western population by this time, fared even worse. "Many of the leading Roman families," wrote one chronicler in the early 5th century (Olympiodorus of Thebes, d. ca. 425), "have annual incomes equal to two tons of gold just from the rents owed on their properties, and if one factors in what they earn from the sale of their grain, wine, and other produce, another 1200 pounds of gold per year can be added to the sum." The lower orders scraped by on meager incomes, poor diets, and the ever-present dangers of debt. "Everywhere one turns one finds a carpetbagger," observed another writer (Libanius, d. 393), "in every territory, on every island, in every village, city, market, port, and backstreet. Everything is up for sale, including foster parents, nursemaids, servants—even the tombs of ancestors. Poverty, begging, and tears are everywhere to be found."

The "Fall of Rome"   The western empire continued to hobble along with its own augustus (who was decidedly subordinate to the augustus in Constantinople). But in 476 a German general named Odoacer put an end to the sham. He deposed the weakling ruler Romulus Augustulus (his name translates as "Little Emperor Romulus") and declared the western empire dead.

The Byzantine emperors occasionally showed some interest in influencing western matters by forming ties with several of the Germanic warlords who

thenceforth dominated Europe. **Justinian I** (r. 527–565) became the most *Reign of*
famous eastern emperor by reconquering much of southern Italy and the central *Justinian*
part of the North African coast in an ambitious effort to reconstitute the old
empire (see Map 8.2). His efforts failed in the end, however, since the economic
gains from the conquests never came close to offsetting the expense of the military effort. He scored more lasting achievements with his vast construction projects within the city of Constantinople, including his completion of the magnificent
church of Hagia Sophia ("Church of the Holy Wisdom") and his compilation of
the *Corpus Juris Civilis* ("Corpus of Civil Law").

A dozen years went into the making of the Corpus, which brought together, organized by topic, and provided commentary on centuries of legislation concerning every aspect of civic life from taxation to criminal law. It
created, in essence, a ready-to-use handbook for governing an entire society—
which is precisely the use to which it was put for centuries. The Corpus formed
the basis of all jurisprudence in Byzantium until the 15th century and provided a model for the development of the canon law of the Catholic Church. As
the foundation of all subsequent legal study in the Greater West until the
modern era, the Corpus did as much as anything else to form the legalistic
bent of our modern culture.

Unfortunately, Justinian's own place in modern culture is overshadowed by a
famously pornographic piece of propaganda written by Procopius of Caesaria (ca.
500–560), who served dutifully as Justinian's official biographer but also wrote,
and published anonymously, a *Secret History*—now, ironically, the only work of
his that anyone reads. The *Secret History* is wildly entertaining, to be sure, but it
says more about Procopius's own unstable personality than about the emperor
whose life it purports to tell. For example, he writes that Justinian

> was a fraud and a cheat. Hypocritical, cruelly two-faced, secretive; a
> practiced con artist who never showed any genuine emotion but could
> shed tears either of joy or sorrow, depending on the situation, whenever
> he perceived the need. A liar in every word—and not just in a haphazard
> way, but with real determination, affirming his schemes in writing and
> with the most solemn oaths, even in dealings with the public. But he
> regularly broke every agreement and pledge he ever made, like a con-
> temptible slave who stands by his lies until only the threat of torture can
> drive him to confess the truth. A faithless friend and a treacherous
> enemy, with a crazed lust for murder and plunder; quarrelsome, ex-
> tremely unruly, easily led to anything evil but stubbornly refusing any
> suggestion to do good. Quick to plot mischief and carry it out, but averse
> even to hearing a word of any noble action.

Hagia Sophia Universally acknowledged as one of the world's greatest buildings, the Hagia Sophia in Constantinople (modern Istanbul), constructed during the reign of Justinian (r. 527–565), is famous in particular for its enormous dome, supported by four giant pillars in the corners. The minarets were added under the Muslim Ottomans, who in the 15th century converted the church into a mosque. The internal view gives a sense of the massive interior and its brilliant play with sunlight.

But Procopius surpasses himself with his savage portrayal of Justinian's queen, Theodora, whom he describes as sexually insatiable, lewd, grasping, and venal. (One famous pornographic episode involves Theodora, a dozen soldiers from the imperial guard, lots of bondage, a loaf of bread, and a wild goose.) By other accounts it seems clear that Theodora was a difficult and divisive person, but Procopius's character assassination reads like the lurid ravings of an unbalanced man.

The stalling out of Justinian's military efforts turned into actual losses of territory by his immediate successors. Under emperors Maurice (r. 582–602) and Phocas (r. 602–610), Byzantium lost Egypt, Palestine, Syria, and parts of Anatolia itself to the Persians, who made another of their periodic efforts to control the western reaches of the Fertile Crescent. These were hard-fought campaigns that nearly brought Byzantium to its knees. Heraclius (r. 610–641) spent his entire reign in a life-or-death struggle to put the empire back on solid footing. But so much territory had been lost that he lacked the funds to pay his soldiers, a weakness that allowed groups of Avars, Bulgars, and Slavs to encroach on imperial lands in the Balkan region.

To combat the situation, Heraclius reorganized the army into a new system of **themes** (Greek *thema*, meaning "regiment" or "division"), which apportioned the *Heraclius's* lands of the empire to the military officers and gave them civil and economic juris- *Reforms* diction over the territories. The commanders then subdivided their zones into individual landholdings for each soldier serving under them. In this way, Heraclius stripped away the bloated, centralized imperial administration and replaced it with the army itself—which now, instead of receiving salaries from Constantinople, derived its own revenue from its landholdings and the fees it collected in return for its civic functions. It was a radical move, but one that dramatically improved military morale and effectiveness, since the soldiers henceforth had reliable sources of income and a personal stake in defending the empire from further attack.

Thus restructured, the Byzantine world achieved high degrees of prosperity and stability. Constantinople acted as the economic hub of the empire: *The Splendor of* all commerce passed through it. The city fiercely guarded its monopolies *Constantinople* on coinage, interest rates, weights and measures, and manufacturing standards, through which it exercised direct control of trade. In Justinian's time the Byzantines had learned how to cultivate silkworms and to spin the silk they produced, which allowed them to begin their own manufacturing of high-value silk cloth. The loss of market share felt by the silk traders from the Near East helped trigger a wave of wars against the Byzantines throughout the 7th and 8th centuries.

The splendor of the city was extraordinary, with hundreds of churches, fine palaces, theaters, baths, and bazaars (see Map 8.3). Most of the empire's cities suffered from Constantinople's dominance, since the capital drained commercial life from the provinces. Provincial cities continued, of course, but they became

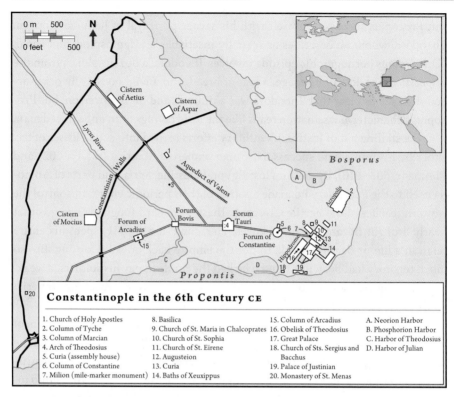

MAP 8.3   Constantinople in the 6th Century   Constantinople was the greatest city of the entire Middle Ages. Its only rivals in size, wealth, cosmopolitan culture, and architectural beauty were Cordoba (in Muslim Spain), Venice, and Baghdad.

more political and religious administrative centers than sites of industry and trade. This change had important social and cultural consequences for the old class of urban elites. The descendants of the Roman curiales, they had previously formed the backbone of intellectual and cultural life, but they gradually disappeared from the 7th century on. Those curiales had been chiefly responsible for cultivating and preserving classical learning, everything from Homeric epics to Athenian stage tragedies and the works of the great philosophers. But the narrowing provincial character of the cities resulted in a narrowing of urban education as well. Primary schooling remained available in most cities, but beyond this level the only education consistently available was religious—devotional writings, hagiographies (or lives of the saints), ecclesiastical chronicles, and the like. In other words, what the provinces gained in piety they lost in general intellectual sophistication. High culture throve only in the capital.

The Renewed Persian Threat

The Persians unleashed a new campaign into the Holy Land in 612 and two years later took Jerusalem. A rebellion against the Persians by the city's Christian inhabitants led to a brutal crackdown. For three days Persian soldiers smashed

Christian shops, homes, and churches until hardly a single Christian building was left standing by 614. A late Byzantine chronicler named Theophanes described it:

> In this year, the Persians conquered all of Jordan and Palestine, including the Holy City, and with the help of the Jews they killed a multitude of Christians—some say as many as ninety thousand of them. The Jews [from the countryside], for their part, purchased many of the surviving Christians, whom the Persians were leading away as slaves, and put them to death too. The Persians moreover captured and led away not only the Patriarch of Jerusalem, Zechariah, and many prisoners, but also the most precious and life-giving Cross.

Theophanes's account is not entirely reliable in its specifics, but it seems clear that a bloodbath occurred, and it was a harbinger of things to come. From the 7th century onward, a new tone of open hostility toward non-Christians entered much Christian writing, and military conflicts in the east took on qualities of religious revenge seeking. Up to this time, Christians generally had shown much more hostility to other Christians—the old problem of the many christianities—than they had shown to non-Christians. The 7th century marks a dark turning point in Christian relations with the world. The Byzantines, reformed and reenergized, launched a counteroffensive in 622. Heraclius chose a symbolic spot for his attack: he and the army set sail from Constantinople, sailed around Asia Minor, and landed at the Bay of Issus—the exact location from which Alexander the Great had launched his conquest of the ancient Persian Empire. From there, like Alexander, Heraclius scored victory after victory until he had regained virtually all of Syria, Jordan, and Palestine.

BARBARIAN KINGS AND WARLORDS

After Odoacer deposed the final Roman augustus in 476, the western Roman Empire was replaced by a parade of semistates ruled by thuggish clan leaders. Some of these warlords offered a modicum of administration and security. Most, however, dedicated themselves to pillaging whatever food and material wealth they could find—or to attacking rivals who had already stolen what they themselves had been plotting to seize.

A 6th-century monk in Celtic England named Gildas described village life in the aftermath of Saxon raids this way:

> Sadly, the streets of our villages are filled with the ruins of once-high towers that have been pulled to the ground, with stones pried from fences

> or left over from the smashing of sacred altars, with dismembered pieces of human bodies that are so covered with lurid clots of blood that they look as though the people had been run through a press, and whose only chance for any kind of burial is to rot in the ruins of collapsed homes; all the rest will simply fill the stomachs of ravenous beasts and birds. . . . To this very day not one of our villages is what it used to be. Instead, all lie desolate, routed, and ruined. (*On the Destruction of England*, ch. 24, 26)

Most of the people of western Europe, at least 90 percent of them, were reduced to subsistence farming. Probably one-half of all children born died before reaching the age of five, and one-half of all females who made it to marriageable age died before reaching the age of twenty-five, usually in childbirth. Tens of thousands of homeless refugees, and perhaps even more, roamed through the countryside at any given time, either having been driven from their homes by new waves of settlers, in flight from marauders, or in search of new territories where they could start afresh without rivals for the land. Meanwhile, the Mediterranean cities contracted into tiny hamlets—with sometimes a mere 10 percent of their former populations—and into corners of the settled urban area, leaving the emptied quarters to decay into ghost towns. Manufacture and trade beyond the immediate region became all but extinct (see Map 8.4). The sole exception was the commerce in slaves. (Slavery was ubiquitous in the ancient world and remained so in the early medieval centuries. By the 10th century, the church had developed to a point that it took action against the practice.)

Despite the miseries of the time, important aspects of Roman antiquity survived. Roman law remained in effect—inconsistently, to be sure, but not altogether forgotten. The Latin language continued as the dominant tongue in the west, and the barbarian kings did what they could to retain and emulate those elements of Roman tradition that they found useful. Intellectual life in the west was limited to the Christian monasteries that dotted the landscape from the 4th century on, but displayed real zest and ingenuity. Thus, although it was an age of poverty and chaos, it was a creative chaos. Ultimately it saw the amalgamation of the Roman, Germanic, and Christian cultures into the fascinating hybrid of medieval society.

One of the early chroniclers of the medieval era, Bishop Gregory of Tours (ca. 538–594), described the atmosphere memorably in the opening prologue to his *History of the Franks*:

> A great number of things keep happening—some good, some bad. The people of the various petty princedoms keep quarreling with each other in the fiercest way imaginable, while our rulers' tempers keep

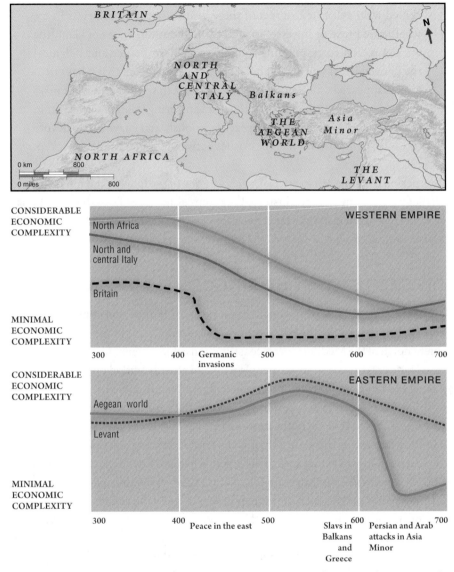

MAP 8.4 The Economy of Europe in the Early Middle Ages After waves of invasions and attacks, by 700 most of the people of western Europe were reduced to subsistence farming.

Adapted from Ward-Perkins, Bryan, *The Fall of Rome* (2006).

bursting into violence. Our churches are assailed by heretics, then re-taken in force by our Catholics; and whereas Christian faith burns hot in the hearts of many, it is no more than lukewarm in those of others. Church buildings are pillaged by faithless pagans as soon as they are gifted by faithful Christians. But no one has yet emerged who is a sufficiently skilled writer that he can record these events in a straightforward way, whether in prose or in verse. In fact, throughout the towns of Gaul [the ancient region corresponding roughly to modern France and Belgium] the knowledge of writing has declined to such an extent that it has virtually disappeared. . . . [And so] I have undertaken this present work in an effort to preserve the memory of the dead and bring them to the attention of those yet to come; but my style lacks all polish, and I have had to devote too much of my attention to the clashes between the good and the wicked.

This period from the 4th to 8th centuries was one of the longest and most dire and challenging eras in Western history. Our sources for it are few—because books seldom get written in active war zones—but enough evidence survives to provide a basic outline of what occurred. The picture is not pretty.

DIVIDED ESTATES AND KINGDOMS

The Germanic peoples who streamed into western Europe confronted innumerable challenges, not the least of which was the terrain. Most of the European continent north of the Mediterranean coastline consisted of dense forest. Newcomers faced bitter resistance from the people who had already settled open areas and so were forced to keep moving or to clear their own lands and begin farming from nothing. Moreover, various cultural traditions that had served the Germans well in the east served them ill in the more sedentary west.

Consequences of Settlement   One example is the early nomadic custom of dividing a man's estate equally between his surviving sons. This practice had provided for each new generation, because herds of animals could replenish their own numbers—but a western farm could not survive such division quite so easily. By the end of the second generation, if not earlier, the distributed lands were not sufficient to support a family. The most promising options, in such a case, were either to expand one's holding by clearing more forest at the perimeter (which worked in some cases, but in others seemed only to defer the problem) or to abandon the land altogether in search of new territory elsewhere. That move, however, exposed them to more hostilities, whether from previously settled peoples, other migrating bands, or warrior thugs. And once they found new places to settle, they faced the difficulty of clearing forests, digging wells, building homes, and beginning to farm, with only the wooden tools they had managed to bring with them. (Few common farmers had metal tools at this time.) Under such conditions, most of continental Europe remained stubbornly mired in poverty until the 9th century.

The transition to agricultural life had important consequences for Germanic women. In pastoral societies, the tending of flocks is the essential labor that supports the family; thus women can contribute equally as much as men. Primitive farm work, however, requires a degree of brute physical strength that usually only men can provide. Agrarian societies therefore often value men over women and boys over girls—an important marker in the evolution of gender hierarchies. In a farming world, the most important labor a female can offer to the benefit of society is to produce more sons. This is not to suggest that nomadic, pastoral societies are egalitarian in their gender roles, but the sparse evidence that survives of the Germanic peoples suggests that rigid, sizable, and permanent differences in the relative status of men and women emerged at the time of their transition to agrarian life. The Roman historian Tacitus (d. ca. 117) wrote that in ancient times Germanic women fought alongside the men in battle, regularly voiced their opinion in clan councils, and shared in inheritance rights. Moreover, at marriage the husband owed a dowry to the bride.

By the 5th and 6th centuries, all that had changed; most Germanic women and girls were largely housebound, preparing food and rearing children, with little voice in public matters and meager inheritance rights. Exceptions existed, of course. Visigothic law, for example, declared, "Let sisters succeed equally with brothers to the inheritance of their parents; and if a father or mother dies intestate, still let sisters and brothers both succeed to the inheritance of each parent in equal measure." But women's true value in Germanic society can be seen in the law of the Salian Franks, which decreed that anyone convicted of killing a female who was in her childbearing years owed a fine of 600 shillings, whereas anyone who killed a female past her fertile years owed only one-third that amount.

The problem of divided estates hobbled as well any sort of political development after 476: a warrior might turn himself into a king by forcing his will on *Clovis's* terrorized farmers, but he usually ended his life by dividing his kingdom among *Frankish* his heirs. One key example will suffice. A brutal warlord named Clovis, a member *Kingdom* of the Germanic group known as the Salian Franks, carved out a sizable kingdom for himself in what is today mostly France around the year 500 and made himself, briefly, the most powerful ruler in western Europe (see Map 8.5). When he died in 511 his realm was parceled out to each of his four sons: Theuderic, Chlodomer, Childebert, and Lothar. Theuderic, however, went on to have two sons of his own; Chlodomer had three. And although Childebert had only daughters (who could not inherit, according to Frankish custom), his younger brother Lothar made up for him by producing seven boys. In only two generations, therefore, a single kingdom had split into twelve autonomous principalities, each with its own officials, tax system, laws, courts, weights, and measures. Any chance of stable governance usually died out quickly in such circumstances, but there is little evidence that many of the warlords were interested in even trying to provide it.

MAP 8.5   The Frankish Kingdom, ca. 500   Around 500 the Frankish warlord Clovis established western Europe's largest new kingdom in what is today mostly France.

Clovis's realm proved an exception, for two reasons. First, his adoption of Christianity around 500 CE led to him being recognized as a defender of the church. An aura of ecclesiastical blessing hence clung to his line for generations to come. Second, the family he belonged to—the Merovingians—allied itself in the late 7th century with another warlord family, the Carolingians, who succeeded them and for a time, as we will see in chapter 10, united almost all of continental Europe. But even with the exception of the Franks, the political narrative of the early medieval era is grim.

Gregory of Tours fills the four hundred pages of his *History of the Franks* with tale after tale of savagery:

> This Rauching [another Frankish warlord] was extraordinarily vain—a man filled to bursting with pride, arrogance, and impertinence. He treated his servants as though he denied they were human beings at all. . . . For example, whenever a servant stood before him, as was usual, with a lighted candle while Rauching ate his meals, he would force the poor fellow to bare his legs and hold the lit candle between his knees until it burned

down to a stub. He would then demand that a new candle be lit, again and again, until the servant's legs were entirely scorched. If the servant cried out or tried to run, a drawn sword quickly stopped him, and Rauching himself would convulse with laughter as he watched the man weep. (5.3)

Gregory relates another tale about Rauching. Two of his servants fell in love and, knowing that he would forbid their union, ran to a local priest for protection. The priest negotiated on their behalf and extracted a promise from the warlord that "he would allow the couple to stay united forever." Once the pair were back at his stronghold, Rauching ordered a massive tree to be felled and its trunk split in two lengthwise, with each half hollowed out, as one would do in making a pair of canoes. Rauching then bound the servants together, encased them in the rejoined hollow tree trunk, and buried them alive in a deep trench, saying with a roaring laugh, "See? I haven't broken my promise. I haven't 'split them up'!" (5.3).

An 8th-century writer, Paul the Deacon, in his *History of the Lombards*, vividly described a different kind of horror—the prevalence of rape, and the efforts some women made to avoid it:

> [Lombard women] used to put the flesh of raw chickens under the band that held up their breasts; and this, once the summer heat had spoiled and putrefied it, gave off a horribly foul odor. Thus when the Avars [another invading tribe] tried to rape them they found that they could not bear the stench—and thinking that the smell was natural to these women, they ran away, cursing loudly that all Lombard women stink.

Neither Gregory of Tours nor Paul the Deacon was without bias, and their specific tales of horrors must be read with a critical eye, but the general picture they draw of a Europe in constant danger of falling apart is persuasive. Until a means was found to pass on undivided realms, little significant advance in government was possible. Most early Germanic kings and princes were itinerant; they traveled constantly, bringing whatever instruments of governance they had (records, copies of laws, accounts) with them. As often as not, individuals petitioning a ruler for justice had first to overcome a basic logistical problem: finding out where the king was and then going to him.

THE BODY AS MONEY AND WOMEN AS PROPERTY

Given these difficulties, little lasting political development took place. Rule was personal, not institutional. Customs varied enormously from "kingdom" to "kingdom," from tribe to tribe, and even from clan to clan. As the Germans gradually settled the land and interacted with the old Roman populace, how-ever, a degree of cultural assimilation occurred. Although easily 90 percent of the population remained illiterate, the old tribal customs that had been passed down orally for generations began to be written down in the 5th, 6th, and 7th centuries. These records provide our first nonliterary glimpses of Germanic values and practices.

Germanic Law Codes   Germanic law, overall, was constructed from the ground up, much like our modern system of torts, or claims of damages that result in legal rulings. Indi-vidual conflicts were dealt with as they arose and were judged by some sort of group consensus, and each case, once settled, provided a precedent for similar cases in the future. This ad hoc construction explains the somewhat random nature of the earliest written codes; they were the result of compiled specifics, not of ideological blueprints put into action. Nevertheless, some sense of consistent values emerges from the codes. In most of them, the issues of property, inheri-tance, marriage, and taxation are preeminent.

The most striking feature of Germanic criminal law was the apportioning of compensatory payments for the physical injury of another, a system called **wergeld**. In these brutal times, to harm or kill another man was quite literally to threaten the existence of his entire family, which depended on his labor for food production and on his strength for physical protection. Murder or assault thus threatened the family, which all too often responded to this sort of crime by de-claring a blood feud. Wergeld provided an alternative to endless vendettas. The system varied in its details from tribe to tribe, but the central idea remained the same: to compensate a victim, or his or her clan, by paying for the loss of a life or for an injury to a vital or nonvital body part. Every part of the body was assigned a monetary value—so much for an arm, an eye, a foot, and so on, right down to the fifth toe on either foot.[5]

Germanic law regarded women not as property but as legal minors regardless of their age, under the more or less permanent guardianship of their fathers and husbands. Among the Salian Franks, for example, a woman who married against her father's will forfeited her rights to any family property and could be put to death by any family member. Among the Burgundians, who settled in eastern France at about the same time, a man could divorce his wife at any time and for any reason, so long as he returned her dowry and paid an additional sum as inter-est. Any woman who tried to leave her husband was to be drowned in a swamp. One exception to this Germanic rule was the Visigoths, who settled in Spain in the 6th century. Visigothic custom allowed an unmarried woman over the age of twenty to be a free adult, legally responsible for herself.

---

[5]   Our own personal-injury insurance policies today follow the same general idea.

Early Medieval Germanic Culture   Dating from around 600 CE, this ring, found near Bergamo, Italy, evidently belonged to a noblewoman named Gumedruta, according to the inscription. The ring was used to affix wax seals to letters and official documents.

A girl was considered marriageable when she began to menstruate and was physically capable of bearing children; this usually happened around the age of fifteen. Within marriage, strict division of labor between the sexes was the norm. Although men did the plowing—an arduous task that generally required a man's physical strength—women performed most of the daily agricultural work from that point on: planting, weeding, fertilizing, and so on. Men focused on hunting, building, blacksmithing, felling trees, and clearing swamps. Men and women worked together to bring in the harvest, however.

A generation or two after settling in their respective parts of western Europe, most of the Germanic groups experienced a severe shortage of women. This happened for two reasons. First, relentless famine had forced the settlers to practice infanticide. In times of failed crops, which were many, this was an easy, if horrific, means of preserving the food supply. And since boys did the heavy labor, infant girls were the most frequent victims of infanticide. Second, many of those girls who survived childhood subsequently died in childbirth because the strains of pregnancy and delivery on malnourished teenagers commonly resulted in their death.

The shortage of women ironically caused an increase in their relative social value, according to a crude formula of supply and demand, which the law codes came to reflect. By the 8th century, Germanic women had many more legal protections and freedoms than before. In marriage, men began to owe dowries to their brides, not the other way around, to secure a mate; this dowry became in many cases the bride's own property that she controlled directly and in her own name. The custom also arose whereby a husband owed his bride a *Morgengab*, or "morning gift," after their wedding night, to compensate her for her lost virginity. These developments hardly made early medieval life significantly brighter, but they do illustrate some of the ways that Germanic culture adapted to its new circumstances.

CHRISTIAN PAGANISM

The most visible of the new circumstances was the Germans' gradual acceptance of Christianity. The traditional religion they had brought with them into the west was polytheistic and animistic: by offering prayers and gifts to the deities, they hoped to influence the workings of nature. Wotan and Thor were two of the most significant pagan gods, and they figured large in the tales of Germanic mythology. Wotan represented the forces of the Sun; Thor of Thunder and Lightning. Many of the German tribes encountered Christianity as early as the 4th century, as missionaries rushed westward to evangelize them. But the conditions of western Europe required missionaries to follow a different strategy than they had used in the cities of the eastern and central Mediterranean. Since continental Europe had no cities where the missionaries could address the hearts and minds of the multitude, they focused instead on the smallish number of Germanic rulers, princelings, and tribal warlords.

The Jelling Stone This 10th-century Danish runestone ("rune" refers to ancient Germanic scripts) is one of a series erected by King Harald Bluetooth (r. ca. 958–986), who is traditionally regarded as the first of his people to convert to Christianity. The stones commemorate that conversion and offer atonement for his parents' pagan hostility to the faith. "Bluetooth" wireless technology is named after Harald, for the simple reason that one of its founders was reading a novel about the king at the time that he founded his company. The company's logo consists of the runic version of the letters H and B.

Aided (the sources assure us) by stupendous miracles, the missionaries converted this upper echelon of leaders and urged them to order the conversion of their clans and tribes. Early medieval writers like Gregory of Tours and Paul the Deacon all relate fantastic tales of dramatic conversions of German rulers who then directed their victorious soldiers to receive baptism and join the cause of Christ. Of course, what usually happened in these baptisms—if anything happened at all—is that the rulers' subjects simply added Jesus to the long list of deities they continued to worship. This was sincere in its way, no doubt, but hardly reason to regard the people as Christian. Models of conversion from the top of society downward to the masses, usually either forced or enticed, can work, but they work slowly.

For many generations and possibly for centuries, medieval society was characterized by a curious, muddy amalgam of the two religions, which historians call "Christian paganism." When King Clovis ordered his followers to adopt Christianity by accepting mass baptism around the year 500, the Franks' conversion was real but incomplete. Jesus became for them a true deity but one of no more significance than the local forest god or one of their divine ancestors. Under these conditions, western Europe, in contrast to the Byzantine Empire, gradually produced a Christian religious culture that retained significant elements of pagan practice within it.

Christmas trees, for example, have nothing to do with the story of Jesus's birth. But the Germans had a tradition of honoring the tallest tree in each forest as the unique domicile of the forest's ruling deities, and so they would worship the gods by offering their tree-home various gifts, decorations, and songs of praise. This pagan ritual slowly acquired a Christian gloss until, by the 9th century, the popular incorporation of tree worship into Christian practice was complete. Another example is the popular celebration of bunnies and baskets of eggs at Easter—neither of which appears in any gospel version of the story of Jesus's resurrection. Germanic farmers owed a special tax to their tribal leaders at the onset of spring as an expression of gratitude for having helped the people to survive the perils of winter. Since theirs was a moneyless economy, they paid this tax with what they had at their disposal: baskets of eggs and springtime litters of bunnies.

CHRISTIAN MONASTICISM

The persistence of "Christian paganism" was indirectly abetted by the rise of Christian monasticism. Many religions have ascetic and contemplative elements to them, and Second Temple Judaism fairly bristled with them. For their first three hundred years, Christian missionaries were too busy in the streets and marketplaces of the eastern Mediterranean spreading the Word (usually just ahead of the Roman police) to focus on ascetic spirituality. Theirs was a call to action, not to meditation. But a Christian form of monasticism began in earnest in the 4th century. **Monasticism** rejected normal family and social life, along with the concern for wealth, status, and power. In their place, it favored a harsh life of solitude and spiritual discipline. What inspired this principled withdrawal from the world was, ironically, the gradual success of the Christian message itself.

When Constantine I announced his own conversion and issued the Edict of Milan in 313, Christianity's hour had finally arrived. And this was precisely the problem for many Christians. How could they prove to God, and to themselves, that they had the same heroic commitment to him that their ancestors had possessed, ancestors who had quite literally risked their lives every day for Christ? To be a Christian after 313 involved none of the risk, the danger, and the suffering that it had carried before. After the Edict of Milan, in fact, to be a Christian was easy, even fashionable.

For many faithful this proved intolerable, and so they intentionally sought out the loneliest, most rigorous, and most difficult way they could devise to love God—not out of spiritual masochism, but rather like athletes who push themselves to the limits of their ability in the pursuit of excellence. Men and women experiencing such desires went out into the deserts and forests, living in caves or on wind-blasted hilltops, exposed to the elements and wild beasts, scavenging for their food or begging it from passersby. Eventually, these ascetics began to live together in isolated communities where they tried to pattern their lives on those of the twelve apostles, as a sacred community united in their dedication to live by Christ's teachings.

Monasticism was extraordinarily popular in the 5th through 9th centuries, with hundreds of monastic houses established throughout the eastern and central Mediterranean, and it added a rich new element to a fast-Christianizing society. But when the movement arrived in western Europe, it had rather a different impact. There the trickle-down model of evangelization had created a religiously hybrid world in which Christianity was poorly understood and haphazardly practiced. When individuals with deep, resonant, and knowledgeable commitments to the faith entered monastic life, they helped to perpetuate Christian paganism by removing from society the very individuals most capable of correcting and deepening the Christian life of the masses.

Rule of Saint Benedict

Hundreds of monasteries and convents were established in the early medieval era, from Ireland to Hungary, from Spain to Poland, from Sicily to Sweden (see Map 8.6). Perhaps 90 percent of these houses organized their daily lives according to the **Rule of Saint Benedict**, a communal handbook written by Benedict of Nursia (ca. 480–547) to guide the monastery he had established at Monte Cassino in southern Italy. Benedict's Rule attracted so many adherents because it required relatively moderate discipline. Unlike the harsh regulations of other monastic communities, Benedict's Rule did not isolate monks and nuns from the outside world or deprive them of sleep, adequate food, or warm clothing. It also had a balanced focus on the monks' physical and intellectual, as well as their spiritual, well-being. Benedict's sister, Scholastica, is regarded as the founder of the Benedictine

MAP 8.6   **Monasteries in Western Europe, ca. 800**   Nearly every monastery and convent in western Europe was Benedictine at this time. New orders did not appear until the 10th century.

order for women.[6] Benedictine monks and nuns were required to spend several hours each day in physical labor and in study as necessary adjuncts to their central function of worship. The physical labor, which primarily involved some sort of farmwork for the monks and domestic labor for the nuns, helped to make each monastery self-sufficient. How could a community cut itself off from the world if it could not feed itself and produce its own tools, clothing, and shelter? Moreover, monasteries and convents frequently were located close together (and occasionally were administratively united), so the men and women could aid one another with specific tasks.

For the first time in Western history, physical work was seen as noble, even godly. But Benedict's insistence on study had the most immediate consequences

---

[6]   Once, after spending the day with his sister in prayer and discussion, Benedict rose to return to his monastery to sleep, in obedience to his Rule. Scholastica reportedly made a quick prayer for a thunderstorm—and God replied, forcing Benedict to stay behind, thus breaking his own Rule. Scholastica is still invoked by Catholics for protection from thunderstorms, although she should perhaps be invoked for stirring them up.

The Lindisfarne Gospels   Lindisfarne is a small island off the northeastern coast of England. In the early 7th century a monastery was founded there by an Irish missionary named Aidan (d. 651). Subjected to repeated attacks by Vikings, the monks abandoned the island in 875 and took with them all the monastery's treasures—including its famed manuscript of the four gospels, produced around 700. This is the opening page of the Gospel of Matthew.

for medieval Europe because monasteries virtually monopolized book production. Novice monks received a carefully designed education that taught them to speak, read, and write Latin, as well as the basic elements of arithmetic, geometry, astronomy, and music. This training required borrowing, copying, and commenting on the books of the western world's religious and secular learning. A constant stream of books thus flowed from monastery to monastery, creating western Europe's first libraries. We owe nearly the entire surviving corpus of classical Latin literature to the busy labor of copying and recopying by these monks. They preserved the poems of Virgil and Horace; the histories of Tacitus, Livy, and Suetonius; the speeches and letters of Cicero; and the plays of Seneca and Terence, among others. Once they had mastered the classical Latin literature, monks moved on to reading, copying, and commenting on the sacred Christian writings, preserving and extending the intellectual legacy of the faith. Until about 1100, nearly every single Christian scholar in western Europe either was a member of the Benedictines or had been educated by them.

Throughout Late Antiquity, or the early Middle Ages, monasteries were vital centers of Christian intellectual life, but they built on the foundations created by a group of scholars known as the Church Fathers. Some of these figures had monastic backgrounds; others were priests and bishops. Some wrote in Greek, others in Latin. Their work aimed at several goals: to explain Christianity to newcomers and strengthen the faith of those already in the church, to resolve the problem of the "many christianities," and to reconcile Christian faith with classical culture. Among the most important Latin Fathers were a monk, Jerome (347–420); a bishop, Augustine of Hippo (354–430); and a pope, Gregory the Great (r. 590–604); and among the Greek Fathers were Athanasius of Alexandria (ca. 298–373), Gregory of Nazianzus (ca. 329–ca. 389), and John Chrysostom (347–407)—bishops all. Jerome's greatest work was his translation of the Hebrew Bible and Greek New Testament into Latin. His version—known as the Vulgate Bible (from Latin *vulgatus*, meaning "the common tongue")—remains the official version of the scriptures in the Roman Catholic Church today. Augustine is remembered chiefly as a theologian whose masterpiece *The City of God* (ca. 426) forges a link between Christian and classical understandings of human development and history. Gregory, the first pope to have anything like the universal authority Peter's successors at Rome had always claimed, oversaw the first organized campaigns to evangelize the pagan Germans.

The Church Fathers

Of the Greek Fathers, Athanasius struggled mightily to protect the church from undue influence by the state, and he wrote a biography of the church's first monk, Antony of Egypt (d. 356). His *Life of Antony* became the model for all such hagiographies (lives of the saints), which were among the most popular literary genres of the entire Middle Ages. Gregory of Nazianzus is remembered not for a particular book (although he wrote many, chiefly exhortations to heretics to return to the church's teachings) but for his piety and dedication to putting his natural eloquence in service to God. "This is my gift to God; this is my treasure that I dedicate wholly to him. Everything else that I possessed in the world I gave up, at the command of the Holy Spirit . . . [which has been] my companion and counselor through all my life." John Chrysostom also had the gift of eloquence and is revered as one of the greatest preachers in the history of the Greek Orthodox Church.

◆

In fact, when western Europe began to emerge from the early Middle Ages, scholars and monks played a central role in the recovery. In the 8th century a new aristocratic warrior family rose to power in the northern Frankish territories. Resourceful, resilient, and ruthless, this family—the Carolingians—appointed themselves the would-be saviors of western Christendom and pursued the unification of Latin Europe with relentless focus and drive. The society they created would mark the first successful amalgam of Roman, Germanic, and Christian culture, and it laid the foundations for modern Europe.

We will pick up their story in chapter 10. For now, let us turn to the rise in the 6th century of the Greater West's third great monotheism, Islam.

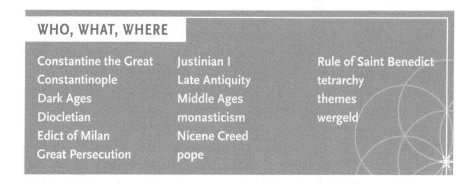

WHO, WHAT, WHERE

Constantine the Great	Justinian I	Rule of Saint Benedict
Constantinople	Late Antiquity	tetrarchy
Dark Ages	Middle Ages	themes
Diocletian	monasticism	wergeld
Edict of Milan	Nicene Creed	
Great Persecution	pope	

SUGGESTED READINGS

Primary Sources

Augustine. *The City of God.*
Benedict of Nursia. *The Benedictine Rule.*
Boethius. *The Consolation of Philosophy.*
Gregory of Tours. *History of the Franks.*
Jordanes. *History of the Goths.*
Paul the Deacon. *History of the Lombards.*
Procopius. *The Secret History.*

Source Anthologies

Evans-Grubbs, Judith. *Women and the Law in the Roman Empire: A Sourcebook on Marriage, Divorce, and Widowhood* (2002).

Head, Thomas, ed. *Medieval Hagiography: An Anthology* (2001).

Maas, Michael. *Readings in Late Antiquity: A Sourcebook* (2010).

Murray, Alexander Callander. *Gregory of Tours: The Merovingians* (2005).

Smail, Daniel Lord, and Kelly Gibson, eds. *Vengeance in Medieval Europe: A Reader* (2009).

Swan, Laura. *The Forgotten Desert Mothers: Sayings, Lives and Stories of Early Christian Women* (2001).

Studies

Ando, Clifford. *The Matter of the Gods: Religion and the Roman Empire* (2008).

Banaji, Jairus. *Agrarian Change in Late Antiquity: Gold, Labour, and Aristocratic Dominance* (2007).

Bassett, Sarah. *The Urban Image of Late Antique Constantinople* (2004).

Brown, Peter. *The Rise of Western Christendom: Triumph and Diversity* (2003).

Brubaker, Leslie, and Julia M. H. Smith. *Gender in the Early Medieval World: East and West, 300–900* (2004).

Curran, John. *Pagan City and Christian Capital: Rome in the Fourth Century* (2000).

Drake, H. A. *Constantine and the Bishops: The Politics of Intolerance* (2002).

Dunn, Marilyn. *Emergence of Monasticism: From the Desert Fathers to the Early Middle Ages* (2003).

Evans, J. A. S. *The Age of Justinian: The Circumstances of Imperial Power* (2001).

Geary, Patrick. *The Myth of Nations: The Medieval Origins of Europe* (2002).

Goldenberg, David M. *The Curse of Ham: Race and Slavery in Early Judaism, Christianity, and Islam* (2005).

Halsall, Guy. *Warfare and Society in the Barbarian West, 450–900* (2003).

Harmless, William. *Desert Christians: An Introduction to the Literature of Early Monasticism* (2004).

Heather, Peter. *Empires and Barbarians: The Fall of Rome and the Birth of Europe* (2010).

Herrin, Judith. *Women in Purple: Rulers of Medieval Byzantium* (2001).

Lawrence, C. H. *Medieval Monasticism: Forms of Religious Life in Western Europe in the Middle Ages* (2001).

MacLeod, Roy. *The Library of Alexandria: Rediscovering the Cradle of Western Culture* (2000).

McCormick, Michael. *Origins of the European Economy: Communications and Commerce, AD 300–900* (2001).

Pohl, Walter, Ian Wood, and Helmut Reimitz. *The Transformation of Frontiers from Late Antiquity to the Carolingians* (2001).

Smith, Julia M. H. *Europe after Rome: A New Cultural History, 500–1000* (2005).

Wickham, Chris. *Framing the Early Middle Ages: Europe and the Mediterranean, 400–800* (2005).

Wickham, Chris. *The Inheritance of Rome: Illuminating the Dark Ages, 400–1000* (2010).

Wood, Ian. *The Missionary Life: Saints and the Evangelisation of Europe, 400–1050* (2001).

For additional resources, including maps, primary sources, visuals, web links, and quizzes, please go to **www.oup.com/us/backman.**

CHAPTER 9

The Expansive Realm of Islam

30–900

The early history and development of Islam are as difficult to determine as the origins of Christianity. As with Christianity, Islam's earliest surviving records date to several decades after the death of the charismatic figure who founded the faith—in this case, the prophet Muhammad (ca. 570–632). Literacy came to the Arabs with the Qur'an itself, authored by God and transmitted by the Prophet, but not written in definitive form until long after Muhammad's death. Moreover, the first written collections of Muhammad's non-Qur'anic teachings—the *hadith*—did not appear until more than a century after his death and hence can be regarded as less than reliable evidence, by modern critical standards. But the authority of the Qur'an and hadith are beyond questioning for many devout Muslims, just as the authority of the gospels is undoubted by many Christians, a fact that complicates efforts to determine precisely what happened, when, and why.

THE ISLAMIC WORLD, ca. 900 CE

■ Sunni Muslim states   ■ Byzantine Empire
■ Shiite Muslim states

The importance of Islam in the development of Greater Western values cannot be questioned, however. Although it built on, and in some cases conformed to, cultural norms already established among the peoples of the Arabian peninsula, the Islamic revelation helped to define attitudes toward faith and reason, women and sexuality, law and the state, and warfare and tolerance that have lasted for centuries. The phenomenally rapid spread of Islam was a matter of ethnic

The Mosque at Cordoba One of the greatest mosques of the Middle Ages was built in the Spanish city of Cordoba. The mosque was constructed atop an earlier Christian church, and many of its magnificent columns were reclaimed from nearby Roman temples.

and military confrontation, to be sure. But it was also a complex interaction of cultural values and principles, an interaction in which the new faith adopted and absorbed as many preexisting characteristics as it suppressed, in the long march to regional dominance.

"AGE OF IGNORANCE": THE ARABIAN BACKGROUND

Geography and Climate

The Arabs had inhabited the peninsula that bears their name for many centuries. It is a forbidding place, roughly a million square miles in area, consisting of an arid central plateau that slopes from west to east and is surrounded by several deserts (see Map 9.1). Most notable are the rocky Syrian (Nefud) Desert in the north and the Great Arabian Desert (Arabic *Rub' al-Khali*, or "Empty Quarter"), which alone makes up one-quarter of the entire peninsula.[1] Two mountain ranges exist, one running parallel to the Red Sea coast on the southwest and the other stretching along the peninsula's southeastern coast, the site of today's country of Oman. Some water is available: several stretches of marshland dot the Red Sea coastline, and large aquifers run beneath much of the peninsula, but usually at depths too great to reach. Where the levels of sand and rock are not too extreme,

---

[1]   The sands of the Great Arabian Desert reach depths, in spots, of more than 1,000 feet. Daytime temperatures, moreover, can reach 130°F (55°C) in the summer.

CHAPTER TIMELINE

0	100	200	300	400

■ ca. 27–570 **"Age of Ignorance" (al-Jahiliyya)**

some natural oases and wadis—seasonal riverbeds—occur, and it is possible to dig wells.

But the essential geographical fact of premodern Arabia is that only 1 percent of the land could support agriculture and permanent human settlement. Division of the Arab peoples is thus a natural consequence of geography. The highland plateau accommodates the grazing of sheep and goats and is the traditional home of the nomadic Bedouin tribes; the fertile southwestern coastal zone is the abode of the Yemeni Arabs. Between those extremes, pre-Islamic tradition claimed that most of the peninsula's people are descended from two legendary ancestors: Qahtan and Adnan. Qahtan, according to the tradition, was the progenitor of the "pure Arab" people (*al-Arab al-aribah*) in the southern part of the peninsula, whereas Adnan fathered the "Arabized Arabs" (*al-Arab al-musta'ribah*) of the north. By the start of Islam in the 7th century, Qahtan and Adnan were reinterpreted as the offspring of Ishmael, son of the biblical patriarch Abram/Abraham through his concubine Hagar.

Whatever their origins, many Arab tribes were united by their language, of which each group possessed its own distinct dialect. Arabic is a Semitic language, *A Tribal* related to the tongues of the ancient Akkadians, Assyrians, Babylonians, and *Culture* Hebrews, and indeed, the Arabian peninsula is thought by many to be the point of origin of all Semitic-speaking peoples. Clan and tribal identities ran deep, and everything from the dialect one spoke to the headdress one wore to the lengthy

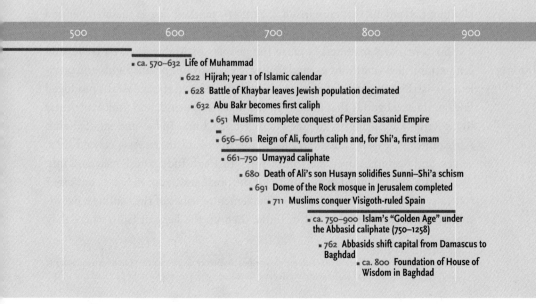

- ca. 570–632 Life of Muhammad
- 622 Hijrah; year 1 of Islamic calendar
- 628 Battle of Khaybar leaves Jewish population decimated
- 632 Abu Bakr becomes first caliph
- 651 Muslims complete conquest of Persian Sasanid Empire
- 656–661 Reign of Ali, fourth caliph and, for Shi'a, first imam
- 661–750 Umayyad caliphate
- 680 Death of Ali's son Husayn solidifies Sunni–Shi'a schism
- 691 Dome of the Rock mosque in Jerusalem completed
- 711 Muslims conquer Visigoth-ruled Spain
- ca. 750–900 Islam's "Golden Age" under the Abbasid caliphate (750–1258)
- 762 Abbasids shift capital from Damascus to Baghdad
- ca. 800 Foundation of House of Wisdom in Baghdad

MAP 9.1   Arabia in the 6th Century CE   Most of the Arabian peninsula was, and remains, uninhabitable. Intensely isolated yet dependent on connections with the world outside, the peninsula's peoples early on developed a wary, clan- or tribal-focused sense of identity and values. The revelation of Islam fostered a sense of Arab unity that helped end decades of tribal conflict.

chain of patronyms that comprised one's name marked one as the member of a particular group, with particular social standing.[2]

Trading Networks   Such markers mattered because the peoples of Arabia lived by trade, and long-established traditions existed that gave each group specific rights and privileges. Distributors rather than growers and manufacturers, the Arabs produced few commercial goods that interested the non-Arab world, and they made their living largely by bringing luxury goods from China, India, and sub-Saharan Africa into the eastern Mediterranean. The silk route across Asia carried silks, spices, and perfumes overland from China, through India and Persia, and into Byzantium and provided opportunity for the northern Bedouin tribes, but other routes existed as well (see Map 9.1). The Yemenite tribes of the southern peninsula brought goods by ship out of India, then up the Persian Gulf, where they

---

[2]   The dialects spoken by many of the southernmost tribes have more elements in common with the Semitic languages in Ethiopia than with the Arabic dialects found elsewhere throughout the peninsula.

were handed off to the tribes of the Najd plateau. Sabaean tribes along the Red Sea coastline carried gold and gemstones from Ethiopia northward to Syria and Palestine. The Arabs, acculturated to the harshness of the terrain and mounted on their camels, made ideal long-distance carriers. Their caravans stretched across the endless miles linking east and west, north and south. The Arabs lacked a developed maritime tradition, however; foreign merchants from Persia, India, and Ethiopia brought goods to and from the peninsula by sea.

Desert Transport Trains of camels brought Asian silks, spices, and gold to the Middle East and maintained the link between the eastern Mediterranean coast and the Arabian peninsula. Whenever possible, the caravans traveled at dawn and dusk, to avoid exertion during the blazing midday heat.

Arab historians termed the period before the advent of Islam the "Age of Ignorance" or "Age of Barbarism" (*al-Jahiliyya*). The simple absence of Islam suffices to merit the name, in Muslim eyes. Indeed, some writers used the term to embrace all of pre-Islamic human history, but most Arabs defined **al-Jahiliyya** more precisely as the *Red Sea* period from the death of Jesus around 27 CE to the birth of Muhammad in the *Wars* year 570 CE. Many of those intervening years were in fact particularly chaotic. Clashes arose between the Roman and Persian empires, between the Byzantines and the Persians, and between Christian sects, all to the north, and in the Red Sea, between the Yemenites of Arabia and the Abyssinians of Ethiopia, to the south. These struggles caused occasional but severe disruptions of the Arab trading networks, disruptions that often boiled over into violence between tribes and clans.

A little-known and underappreciated chapter in the history of these Red Sea wars provides an important vantage point from which to view the origins of Islam. In the late 4th century the Abyssinian king of Axum, in Ethiopia, converted to Christianity, and at virtually the same time one of the Arab kings in Himyar, in southern Arabia, converted to Judaism. Both rulers and their successors energetically promoted their new faiths in their respective realms, but in 523 the then-reigning Himyari king, named Yusuf, initiated a genocidal campaign against all the Christians in his realm, whether they were Abyssinian or Arab. The plight of the victims, as the news of the bloody massacres spread, elicited a sympathetic response not only from Christian Ethiopia but also from the Byzantine Empire and its rival, the Sasanid Persian Empire, all of whom saw the massacres as a justification to seize control of Arab trade routes and centers throughout the Near East. It is within this context—of a divided Arab peninsula that felt vulnerable to outside intervention even as it was exposed to religious monotheism—that we must examine the rise of Islam.

Muhammad before Revelation

Muhammad (ca. 570–632) belonged to the Hashim clan within the Quraysh tribe, a group that had long been associated with administering the great pagan shrine in the commercial city of Mecca. This shrine, called the **Ka'ba**, was a kind of Arab pantheon, an ecumenical temple to all the pagan deities of all the Arab peoples. Pilgrims from all over the peninsula came to Mecca to pray at the shrine and present offerings to the gods. These pilgrims, together with the merchants who frequented the city, made Mecca a particularly vibrant city with more cross-cultural contact than most Arab sites. A sizable Jewish community existed too, although there is no evidence of any meaningful Christian presence before Muhammad's lifetime. With Byzantium and Persia at war in the north and Arab-Jewish and Abyssinian-Christian armies vying for power in the south, an urge to promote pan-Arab cohesion took root and fostered a militaristic streak in Arab society, conditioned to regard the entire non-Arab world as a threat to its existence. The problem was: What could unite so disparate a sprawl of tribes and clans? The answer came in the form of a divine mission and the identification of the Arabs as a new Chosen People.

THE QUR'AN AND HISTORY

Born into poverty, Muhammad began his rise in the world when he went to work for a wealthy widow named Khadija and began to handle her commercial interests. After several years, he and Khadija married. Muhammad's trading activities brought him out of Arabia and perhaps as far north as Syria, long solitary journeys that suited his meditative temperament. At some point Muhammad made contact with Judaism and Christianity, although we do not know the specifics of what he learned or how.

The Prophet Muhammad and the Faith of Islam

In the year 610, at the age of forty, Muhammad received the first of a series of dazzling visions that continued for the rest of his life. They summoned him to a unique role—as the final prophet of the One True God—and they called on the Arab people to unite and bring God's message, as delivered through Muhammad, to all the nations on earth. This message was the **Qur'an**, a divine text inscribed on a golden tablet in heaven by God himself. In his mystical transports, Muhammad heard the heavenly text being read and repeated it aloud to his followers. (In Arabic, the book's title means "recital.")[3]

---

[3]   The Qur'an itself (7.157) describes Muhammad as *ummiya*, which means "unlettered." Although some commentators insist that the word means only that Muhammad lacked a formal education, most scholars interpret it to mean that he was functionally illiterate.

The core message of the Qur'an is that all religions are false except for belief in the One True God, called *Allah* in Arabic, who created all things and has ennobled human life with a divine purpose, which is to serve and worship him through a regimen of daily prayers and adherence to his laws. The Qur'an elaborates the "five pillars of faith": (1) bearing witness to the unity of God and the prophethood of Muhammad; (2) daily prayers while facing the direction of Mecca; (3) fasting during Ramadan, the ninth month of the Islamic calendar; (4) giving alms to the poor; and (5) for those physically able and with the financial means, the obligation to make a **hajj** (pilgrimage) to Mecca. Performance of the "five pillars" gave public expression to membership in the **ummah**, the community of the faithful. To the faithful, the merciful and compassionate Allah will grant the reward of eternal bliss in a garden paradise. The remainder of sinful mankind, by Allah's stern but just judgment, will enter eternal torment in a fiery hell:

> Praise be to Allah, Who hath sent His Servant the Book, and hath allowed therein no crookedness. (He hath made it) straight (and clear) in order that He may warn (the godless) of a terrible punishment from Him, and that He may give glad tidings to the believers who work righteous deeds, that they shall have a goodly reward, wherein they shall remain for ever; further that He may warn those (also) who say, "Allah hath begotten a son": No knowledge have they of such a thing, nor had their fathers. It is a grievous thing that issues from their mouths as a saying. What they say is nothing but falsehood! (Qur'an 18.1–5)

The Qur'an identifies Christians and Jews as the "People of the Book," who deserve a measure of respect but who also have a special obligation to recognize the completion of their revelational history in Allah's Prophet. Pagan polytheisms, however, deserve little patience:

> Those who disbelieve, among the People of the Book and among the polytheists, were not going to depart (from their ways) until there should come to them clear evidence—the Messenger from Allah, rehearsing scriptures kept pure and holy: wherein are books right and straight. Nor did the People of the Book make schisms, until after there came to them clear evidence. And they have been commanded no more than this: to worship Allah, offering Him sincere devotion, being true (in faith); to establish regular prayers; and to give *zakat* [a special tax for charity, one of the five pillars of the Islamic faith]; and that is the religion right and straight. Those who disbelieve, among the People of the Book and among the polytheists, will be in hell-fire, to dwell therein (for aye [ever]). They

are the worst of creatures. Those who have faith and do righteous deeds—they are the best of creatures. Their reward is with Allah: Gardens of Eternity, beneath which rivers flow; they will dwell therein for ever; Allah well pleased with them, and they with Him: All this for such as fear their Lord and Cherisher. (Qur'an 98.1–8)

Mankind's chief responsibility is therefore submission (*islam*, in Arabic) to Allah's absolute authority—and that duty gave its name to the religion, Islam. Among the virtues that Allah commands are modesty, charity, and sobriety. Moreover, he requires tolerance of Judaism and Christianity, Islam's revelational predecessors, but directs his faithful to eradicate stiff-necked pagans who reject Islam.

Muhammad preached to the crowds in Mecca soon after his first revelation, and as the revelations continued, his message became more refined. He came to describe Islam as the final and perfect phase of the relationship established by God in his covenant with the patriarch Abram/Abraham. The Arabs themselves, he preached, are descended from Abraham's liaison with his concubine Hagar, which produced their son, Ishmael. Islam thus stands in an evolutionary relationship with Judaism and Christianity. Jesus, the Qur'an proclaims, was in the line of prophets that began with Moses. The role of the prophets was to elaborate a better

An Early Qur'an   The Qur'an is, to all Muslims, the Holy Book of God, written by him in heaven on tablets of gold. The text came to earth by means of the Prophet's revelations. God allowed Muhammad to bear witness to the holy text and recite messages aloud to his followers. These passages were saved and memorized by the community, and after the Prophet's death in 632 they were compiled and transcribed. Pictured here is a fragment from an early North African Qur'an, written in Kufic script.

understanding of God's desires, and as the Jews continued to disobey and misunderstand, God continued to send prophets—including Jesus. The Christians, however, had also failed—in failing to live up to what God expected of them and in their shocking mistake of thinking Jesus was actually God. All this had inspired Allah to make one last, full, and perfect revelation through Muhammad and the revealing of the Qur'an.

The Qur'an is a holy text like no other and presents unique challenges to critical reading. Two difficulties stand out: the text's transmission and its (real or perceived) errors. First, its transmission. To devout Muslims, the Qur'an is a book written on gold tablets by Allah himself; it is the Word of God in a way that the Hebrew or Christian Bibles are not, since there is no human agency in its creation. Muhammad's mystical revelations—hundreds of them over the course of twenty-two years—presented him with various passages of this book, which he then recited to his followers, until the entire text had been passed on. The passages were memorized by his followers as they appeared, and Muhammad, by near-universal agreement, never committed any of the passages to ink. After Muhammad's death in 632, the Prophet's companions began to collect the memorized passages on various scraps of parchment and inscribed stone, which were ultimately collected into a single manuscript that was kept first by the Prophet's successor as leader of the Muslim community, Abu Bakr (r. 632–634), and later by one of the Prophet's widows, Hafsa bint Umar (d. 665). The sole manuscript eventually went missing, but not before a later leader of the community, Uthman (r. 644–656), arranged for an authorized copy to be made, thus establishing the definitive text—an exact duplicate, without error, of Allah's handwritten original in heaven.

The Qur'an as Historical Source

This leads to the second challenge posed by the Qur'an—its apparent errors. Mistakes in the Hebrew and Christian scriptures are numerous, of course, but can be explained as the results of human fallibility. Texts such as Paul's letters, after all, although divinely inspired, were written by a man sitting at a table (in Paul's case, usually in a prison cell). But how does one explain "errors" in a text that Allah did not inspire but actually wrote himself? The Qur'an, it turns out, is filled with anomalies. To begin with, how can we be certain that the authorized version prepared for Caliph Uthman correctly replicated the earlier, lost manuscript? Uthman's text introduced vowels to a text that had previously lacked them. Early Arabic writing, in common with other early ancient Near Eastern scripts, consisted only of the consonants within each word, leaving the reader to supply the vowels and punctuation out of context.[4] And if the text is indeed somehow

---

4   Try a simple example: *Rdng ths wrds s qt hrd.* Does this say "Reading these words is quite hard" or "Raiding those weirdos is [a] quiet herd"?

perfect, how does one explain the grammatical errors, skewed syntax, and fragmented sentences that abound in it? To this day, no standard critical edition of the Qur'an comparable to those made of the Hebrew and Christian Bibles has ever been published. Indeed, to many of the devout the very idea of such an edition is un-Islamic and possibly anti-Islamic, since it would be based on the assumption either that Allah is not the text's sole author or that Allah is capable of error. In either case, one is guilty of blasphemy.

Following the Qur'an, the most authoritative texts for Muslims are the collected non-Qur'anic teachings of the Prophet, known as the **hadith**. But several collections of these traditions exist, all compiled long after Muhammad's death, which further complicates their use as historical sources. The earliest surviving biography of the Prophet dates to well over a century after his death, too. So strictly speaking, there is no surviving contemporary Islamic evidence for Muhammad's life. By judicious use of the surviving much-later evidence—Qur'an, *hadith*, and biographies of the Prophet—we know much more about Muhammad, however, than we do about Moses or Jesus.

FROM PREACHER TO CONQUEROR

Muhammad preached that Allah had chosen the Arab people to bring Allah's message to the world and that this mission was therefore intended to bring an end to tribal strife. The people of Mecca, and especially the Quraysh leaders who owed their status to their role in traditional Arab religion, did not take kindly to

Muhammad's call to end the pagan cults. In 622, after twelve years of tense conflict, the Meccans drove him and his small company of believers from the city.[5] Muhammad then journeyed northward to Medina. This journey—the **Hijrah**—is commemorated by Muslims as the beginning of Islam's expansion and marks year 1 of the Islamic calendar. Medina, a commercial and cultic rival of Mecca, proved more receptive to Muhammad's teaching, and within two years Muhammad was in fact in command of the city.

Muhammad's
Conquests

Success in Medina inaugurated a discernible tonal shift in the spreading of the Islamic message, since from 624 on the Prophet was in possession of an army. The Qur'anic passages revealed in Medina have a more activist and determined tone than the earlier Meccan revelations, and later Islamic texts depict the Prophet from this point on as a conqueror as much as a preacher. Ibn Ishaq (ca. 704–768), Muhammad's first biographer, proudly relates how the

---

[5]   The ninth *surah* (chapter) of the Qur'an expresses Allah's anger at the pagan leaders in Mecca who, after befriending the Prophet, had turned against him, as the local power struggle worked itself out.

Prophet defeated the Jewish community at Medina, which had allegedly plotted against him:

> Muhammad issued an order that no one was to perform the afternoon prayer until after he had reached Banu Qurayza, and he sent Ali ahead of him, bearing the Apostle's banner. The soldiers rallied when they saw it, and Ali advanced as far as the town's fortifications. While camped outside the town, Ali heard some Jews say insulting things about Muhammad, which prompted him to turn quickly and rush to meet the Apostle on the road. He told him that he did not need to come any closer or deal with the miserable Jews.
>
> "Why not?" Muhammad asked. "Did you hear them slandering me?" And after Ali replied that he had done exactly that, the Prophet went on, "Once they see me they will stop."
>
> Then the Apostle approached the Jews' fortifications and cried out, "Listen, you animals! God has rejected you and brings His vengeance upon you!"
>
> The Jews surrendered. After confining them in Medina, Muhammad beheaded between six hundred and seven hundred of them, although some sources claim a number as high as eight hundred or even nine hundred.

Muhammad then began a series of rapid military ventures to defeat the Meccans and seize control of the entire peninsula—the first instances of a *jihad* ("struggle") of the sword, a holy war fought against those who persecute the Islamic believers. In 629, after five years of fighting, Muhammad was victorious. Once both Mecca and Medina were in his hands, Muhammad was able to bring most of the Arabian peninsula under his command before his death in 632. Given the sparse settlement of Arabia, the strategic key was to gain control of the handful of trade routes connecting the peninsula with the outer world. Muhammad understood this from his commercial travels. Once his Muslim forces were in a position to cut off the supply routes, the rest of the Arab tribes had no alternative but to surrender.

Before he died, Muhammad purified the Ka'ba in Mecca of its pagan trappings and rededicated it to Allah with a newly revealed truth: the large stone encased within the shrine had been sent to earth from heaven to show Adam and Eve where to build their first altar. Displaced by the Great Flood described in the Hebrew Bible, the long-forgotten stone was found by Abraham and his son Ishmael, who identified it and built a temple to house it, the first temple to Allah. The Ka'ba is that temple—and although what stands there now is a later, rebuilt temple, it still occupies the original site established by Abraham. It is thus the

Khaybar   The Khaybar oasis north of Medina was home to the largest Jewish community in Arabia, apart from the Himyari kingdom. After Muhammad led his community on the Hijrah from Mecca to Medina, in 622, he attempted to convert the Jews there, many of whom were members of a tribe known as the Banu Nadir. Jewish resistance to conversion led to tense relations with the Muslims, who were in possession of an army once Muhammad became the governor of the city. In 625 the Banu Nadir were expelled from Medina and made their way north to Khaybar. In 628 Muhammad attacked Khaybar and killed most of the Jewish population. The episode lives on in both Jewish and Islamic life. Palestinians today often shout "Khaybar! Khaybar!" when demonstrating against the Israelis. A rocket popular with the Islamist militant group Hezbollah has been popularly dubbed the "Khaybar II."

holiest site on earth to Muslims, who pray five times daily while kneeling in the direction of it. Muslims who make the required ritual pilgrimage (*hajj*) to Mecca walk in procession seven times around the Ka'ba. Those lucky enough to get next to the "House of Allah" (*Bayt Allah*, as it is known) will kiss the stone, which has the wondrous ability to absorb the believer's sins and render him pure.[6] The mosques built for communal worship by Muslims contain an inset wall notch (*qibla*) that points in the direction of the Ka'ba and provides the visual focal point for group prayers.

From the Prophet's sudden death in 632, Muslim leaders also kept an eye on the international scene, to prepare for the military expansion of Islam; Muhammad

---

[6]   According to Qur'anic tradition, the stone was originally a brilliant white in color but has absorbed so many sins over the centuries that it has turned black.

Completing the Hajj Pilgrimage (*hajj*) to Mecca is an obligation of every able-bodied Muslim. The endpoint of the pilgrimage is the sacred Ka'ba, the holiest site in Islam. Pilgrims perform a circular march (*tawaf* in Arabic) around the temple.

himself had clearly intended to advance northward into Palestine and Syria and was making plans to do so when he caught a fever and died. The long wars between Byzantium and Persia had exhausted both empires, and the time was right for the Arab advance. Muhammad had died without naming a successor, however. Most of the leading figures, known as the "Companions of the Prophet," threw their support behind Muhammad's father-in-law Abu Bakr, who took the title of **caliph** (*khalifah al-rasul Allah*, meaning "deputy of the Prophet of God").

Abu Bakr (r. 632–634) spent two years completing the conquest of Arabia and subduing Muslim groups who had rejected his succession (see Map 9.2). Upon his death, the Companions chose Umar (r. 634–644), an early convert, to succeed Abu Bakr. Umar directed his army northward, and within two years the Arabs had conquered Jerusalem, Antioch, and Damascus. Only one year later, in 637, Muslim forces took the Persian capital of Ctesiphon. According to Persian sources, the Arab soldiers were dazzled by the opulence of the capital and went on a looting spree. Taking care to send the required one-fifth of the booty to Caliph Umar, back in Medina, the army still netted enough for each soldier (reputedly eighteen thousand of them) to receive twelve thousand gold coins. Moreover, forty thousand Persian nobles were brought back to Medina as slaves.

Expansion under Muhammad's Successors

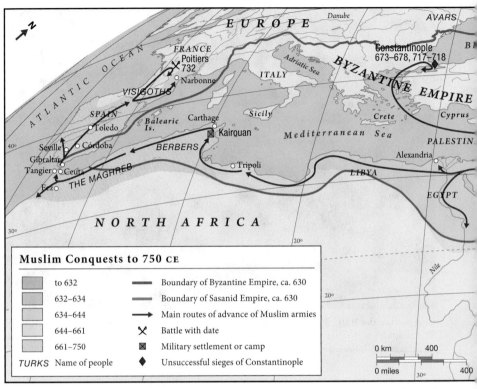

MAP 9.2   Muslim Conquests to 750   The Islamic Empire stretched from Spain to India, and until about 750 ethnic Arabs monopolized all positions of authority.

The rest of the Persian Empire surrendered to the Muslims by 651. Egypt had already fallen to the Arabs in 646—a crucial development that deprived Byzantium of a most important food source. It also triggered a quantum leap for the Muslims' development as a naval power: when the Muslims took Alexandria, Egypt's major port, two-thirds of the Byzantine imperial fleet happened to be tied up in the harbor. For a desert-dwelling people, the Arabs took to the sea quickly; this is why.

By 677 Muslim forces had reached the walls of Constantinople itself. The Byzantines drove the invaders off using a weapon called Greek fire—a naphtha-based compound that burst into flame when it came in contact with water. Undeterred, by 711 the Arabs had extended their conquests all along the coast of North Africa, had taken Sicily and the Balearic Islands, and had crossed the Strait of Gibraltar and seized Visigothic Spain. The Western world had never seen a military juggernaut like this: in 622 Muhammad and his small group of followers had been forced from their home in Mecca, yet within a hundred years those followers had conquered an empire that stretched from Spain to India, an area twice the size of that conquered by Alexander the Great (see Map 9.2).

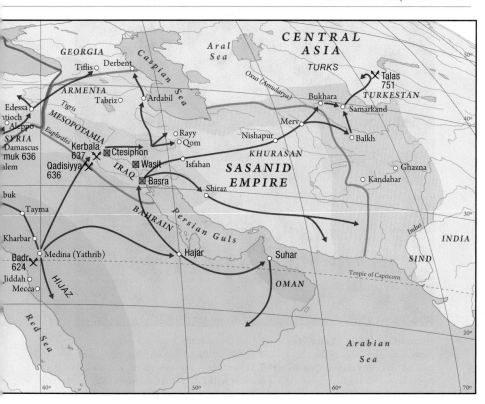

CONVERSION OR COMPULSION?

With their stunning victory over a much-weakened Persia and with their contain-
ment of a much-weakened Byzantium, there was no power on the scene capable of
halting or even slowing the Arab advance. Moreover, many people welcomed the
Muslims for the relief they brought from the ever-increasing taxes levied on them
by the Greeks and Persians to finance their wars with one another. Muslim attitudes to their new subjects took some time to work out, however.

The fraternal relationship among Judaism, Christianity, and Islam prevented
the Muslims from persecuting Jews and Christians. The Qur'an itself insists that *Attitudes*
"there is no compulsion in religion"—meaning that Jews and Christians cannot be *toward*
forced to accept Islam—since Allah's desire is for genuine conversion, not a terrified *People of*
acceptance of new faith to avoid execution. Caliph Umar (r. 634–644), in return for *the Book*
the surrender of the inhabitants of Jerusalem, had guaranteed the religious freedom
of the Jews and Christians residing there and had laid out the terms by which the
communities would live. This text, known widely as the Pact of Umar, formed the
model for the Muslim legal doctrine of the **dhimmi**, the "protected minorities"

Dome of the Rock   Completed in 691, the Dome of the Rock mosque in
Jerusalem is built upon the site, according to tradition, from which the Prophet
pushed off from earth during his mystical Night Journey through the heavens.
Apart from this tradition—which for Muslim faithful has Qur'anic authority
behind it—there is no evidence that Muhammad ever visited Jerusalem.

living under Islamic authority. The Jews and Christians, as People of the Book, deserved such treatment, in the hope that respectful handling by their Muslim rulers
would help them to see the superiority of Islam and thereby win their conversion.

Attitudes   The Persians fared less well. Although regarded by some early Muslim lead-
to the   ers as another People of the Book and therefore deserving of legal protection, the
Persians   Zoroastrian Persians were widely regarded as mere pagans. And most of the Arab
soldiers and clerics, citing Qur'anic authority, claimed the right to compel the
conversion of pagans, to destroy their temples and idolatrous art, and to set fire to
their sacred writings after a four-month grace period:

> But when the forbidden months are past, then fight and slay the
> pagans wherever ye find them, and seize them, beleaguer them, and lie in
> wait for them in every stratagem (of war): but if they repent and establish
> regular prayers and pay *zakat*, then open the way for them, for Allah is
> Oft-Forgiving, Most Merciful. (Qur'an 9.5)

Arab chronicles assert that the victorious Muslims never faltered in observing the dhimmi status of law-abiding Persians; Persian sources, on the other

hand, document widespread atrocities at the local level. Surviving legal records contain no reference to a single Muslim being prosecuted for violating the rights of a Zoroastrian. That may mean that no such violations took place, but it is more likely that such violations were never prosecuted.

By the early 8th century the Islamic Empire was an unqualified military success, but it consisted of a small group of ethnically Arab Muslims governing an enormous and overwhelmingly non-Arab and non-Muslim population. From the Atlantic coasts of Spain and Morocco to the Indus River valley in India, the Arabs ruled a polyglot mix of Romano-Hibernians, Visigoths, Berbers, Egyptians, Syrians, Jews, and Persians (to name only the most prominent groups). In much of the empire the Arabs made up less than 1 percent of the population. Subjects were encouraged to convert to Islam through positive appeals and by imposing restrictions on non-Muslim activities. The most important restriction, rigorously monitored, was a complete ban on any public expression of a non-Islamic faith or of any criticism of Islam.

Conversion brought with it membership in the ummah, immunity from non-*zakat* taxes, military and political preferment, and economic privileges, in addition to the innate spiritual blessings of the faith. Non-Muslims possessing dhimmi status had to pay a heavy poll tax (*jizya*). Beyond the ban to practice their faith or discuss it in public, they could not testify against a Muslim in a court of law and had to wear special items of clothing that identified their inferior status—usually a wide belt called a *zunnar*. Although Muslims could take dhimmi-status wives, their offspring were automatically regarded as Muslim. Islamic law forbade dhimmis to construct new houses of worship for themselves, and strict jurists denied them the right to fix older houses falling into disrepair, since such construction work would effectively constitute a public expression of their faith. As a result churches, synagogues, and Zoroastrian temples everywhere decayed until they were no longer safe for use, and the communities that had used them gradually ceased to worship as communities.

Given this combination of positive enticements to convert and restrictive discouragements to continue in their own faith, the subjects of the Arab empire gradually began to embrace Islam. Most Persians remained loyal to the Zoroastrian tradition, especially those who lived in the countryside. By 750, one hundred years after their defeat by the Arabs, perhaps 90 percent of Persians still practiced Zoroastrianism. To accelerate conversion, the Arab rulers offered cash payments to Persians who would attend Friday prayers and awarded new deeds to landowners who would convert and agree to pressure their tenant-farmers to adopt the new faith. Slaves were given their freedom in return for converting. The Persian chronicler al-Tabari (d. 923) famously described early Arab policy toward the Persians as "to milk them until they are dry, and then to suck out their blood." Nevertheless, the process was slow, and it was not until the 10th century that Islam became the majority religion throughout the empire.

THE ISLAMIC EMPIRE

From Muhammad's death in 632 until 750, the Islamic Empire was a military state focused on expansion of borders and the monopolization of military, economic, and political power by the Arabs who had received Allah's revelation. But as larger numbers of people embraced the new religion, voices arose that promoted a new understanding of the caliphate as a Muslim state rather than a specifically Arab one—that is, as a community based on religious rather than ethnic identification. As the early Christians had done in the 4th and 5th centuries, the Muslims of the 7th and 8th centuries reinvented their faith as a multicultural hybrid.

The Abbasid Caliphate

This process became formalized with the rise of a new dynasty, which seized control of the caliphate in 750: the **Abbasids**, who boldly abandoned the Umayyad capital of Damascus and built a new one far to the east—**Baghdad**, which remains the capital of modern Iraq. The move was as important, both symbolically and geopolitically, as Constantine's move from Rome to Constantinople.

The first 150 years, from 750 to about 900, of the Abbasid era (750–1258) is generally regarded as Islam's Golden Age. From their magnificent new capital at Baghdad the caliphs transformed Islam's original Arab culture. At the heart of Abbasid policy was the earnest, although cautious, welcoming of the involvement and traditions of the *mawali* ("clients," literally), the non-Arab Muslims. This new, open attitude was driven in part by simple pragmatism: by 750, ethnic Arabs were no longer the numerical majority of Muslims. Taken together, Berbers, Egyptians, Kurds, Persians, and Syrians greatly outnumbered the relatively small group of Arabs who still monopolized all positions of political, military, and religious authority.

Among the *mawali*, the largest single group by far were the Persians. The first wave of transformation under the Abbasids, therefore, was the intentional spread and promotion of Persian culture—the so-called Persianization of Islam. Administrative integration came first. Persia, of course, had long experience with administering a vast empire, going back to Cyrus the Great. Their tactic then had been a carefully controlled system of provincial governors called *satraps*; this same idea reemerged under the Abbasids as a network of new officials called *viziers*. A **vizier** (from Arabic *wazir*, meaning "helper" or "assistant") was the governor of a district and the personal representative of the caliph, a combination of administrator and ambassador.

To offset the danger of decentralizing imperial power, the Abbasids increased the number and extent of the state-owned estates (*sawafi*) within each province; overseeing these estates was one of the duties of the viziers. The Abbasids also increased the fiscal contributions owed by each province to Baghdad. With the new income, the Abbasids developed the city of Baghdad itself, improved the pay of the army, and continued developing the infrastructure that held the Islamic world together. Moreover, they withdrew from the viziers the authority to appoint local religious judges, or *qadis*, and monopolized control of all judicial appointments. Still, loss of authority proved inevitable. The viziers in Syria and Anatolia bore the brunt of continuing the offensive against Byzantium throughout the 9th and 10th centuries, a war they largely financed by themselves, which resulted in their increased autonomy from Baghdad and, ultimately, as we will see in chapter 10, the breakup of the Abbasid Empire into competing caliphates. Nonetheless, the Abbasids remained in nominal power until another conquering people, the Mongols, captured Baghdad in 1258.

SUNNIS AND SHI'A

The early Abbasid centuries may have been Islam's Golden Age, but they also witnessed a fundamental break in the Muslim world—the split between the Sunnis and the Shi'a. Caliph Umar died in 644, stabbed by a Persian slave who resented the Arab takeover. When the Muslim leaders met to select the next caliph, two main contenders vied for the position: Uthman ibn Affar, an early convert from the Umayyad clan among the Quraysh tribe, and Ali ibn Abi Talib, the Prophet Muhammad's nephew and husband of Muhammad's only surviving child, Fatima. Most of the community preferred Uthman, who subsequently became the third caliph (r. 644–656), the ruler who oversaw the production of the authorized text of the Qur'an. The disgruntled Ali did not have to wait long for his turn, however, since Uthman was murdered by a party of Egyptian rebels who saw no reason why Egypt's acceptance of the Islamic faith had to entail the country's political subjection to the culturally inferior Arabs.

Ali was elected to succeed Uthman, becoming the fourth caliph (r. 656–661), and he quickly established his capital at the fortified eastern city of Kufa, on the banks of the Euphrates River about 100 miles south of Baghdad. The move from Medina disappointed many Arab leaders, who felt it as an insult to their homeland and therefore transferred their allegiance to a kinsman of the slain Uthman, a figure named Mu'awiya who had served as the provincial governor of Syria and resided in Damascus, a heavily Arabized city. Tensions between Mu'awiya and Ali rose with each passing year and could well have broken out into full-scale civil war, except that Ali was murdered in Kufa in the year 661 by a local rebel. It is a complicated narrative filled with names that are unfamiliar to most readers, but one whose consequences were important.

In the short term, the caliphate would remain in Umayyad hands until 750. In the long term, however, this series of elections, rebellions, and murders triggered the schism between the Sunnis and Shi'a. (In Arabic *Shi'a* is the plural noun, *Shi'i* is the plural adjective.) The rift is both political and religious. **Sunni** Muslims regarded selection by the community as the sole legitimate means to

The Sunni–Shi'a Schism

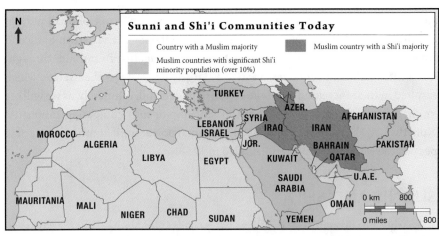

MAP 9.3   Sunni and Shi'i Communities Today   While communities of Shi'a can be found everywhere in the Muslim world, they have tended to concentrate in particular areas—most heavily in the Persian east (today's Iran and the southern regions of Iraq).

leadership of the Islamic world. The **Shi'a**, on the other hand, insisted that political and religious legitimacy could pass only to members of the Prophet's hereditary line. For them, Ali and his descendants via Fatima were thus forever the true successors to Muhammad. The Sunnis take their name from the *sunan* ("principles" in Arabic), the written and oral legacy of the Prophet's teachings and personal actions. The Shi'a (whose name derives from *shi'at Ali*, "the party of Ali") stress the divine appointment of the **imams**, the heavenly appointed heirs of Muhammad, whose words and judgments they regard as infallible. The Shi'a regard Ali as the first imam and the first true caliph, and consequently they reject most of the religious customs established under the first caliphs—Abu Bakr, Umar, and Uthman—and their Umayyad successors.[7]

The antagonism between Sunnis and Shi'a grew sharper as their traditions developed. By 800 the Shi'a comprised roughly a tenth of the Islamic world, and although Shi'i dynasties later rose to power in Egypt and parts of North Africa, the area of Persia that is now Iran quickly became and remained the heartland of Shi'ism (see Map 9.3).

The rift between Sunni and Shi'i Muslims widened and grew increasingly bitter with every generation. The dispute involved more than competing claims to inherit the Prophet's mantle as leader of the Islamic community. Rather, an explicitly religious element entered the tradition. The death in battle of the beloved Shi'i leader Husayn ibn Ali al-Shahid, Ali's son, in 680 had inspired the creation of a

---

[7]   Several denominations of Shi'ism developed in the early centuries, differing from one another primarily in the individuals each recognized as a true imam.

messianic narrative. Popular belief expected Husayn's return as the *Mahdi*—the "Guided One" who will emerge at the end of time and secure Islam's ultimate victory on earth. This belief now evolved into the Shi'i doctrine of the "hidden imam."

What differentiated the various sects of Shi'ism that emerged in Abbasid times was the number of true imams each group recognized, before the final imam went into hiding to await the moment of messianic return. The Shi'a, bound by their allegiance to Ali's descendants, thus incorporated the religious teachings and legal judgments rendered by those imams. In this way, their varying political programs transmuted into a web of traditions very much at odds with those of the Sunni majority.

The Abbasids were in a bind. To retain the support of the Islamic majority they had to champion Sunni orthodoxy, yet they owed their dynastic success to the backing they had received from the Shi'a. Moreover, the open bias they *The* showed for promoting Persians at court led to demands by other *mawali* groups *Abbasid* for similar treatment. The rulers embraced as many aspects of the various *mawali* *Response* cultural traditions as could be harmonized with Islamic teaching, whether Sunni or Shi'i. The Persians, for example, had an ancient custom of veiling of their women whenever they appeared in public. This was done not to denigrate women but to express ethnic pride: inferior non-Persian men had no right to look upon a Persian woman. The veil was a badge of honor, an expression of superiority. This Persian practice harmonized well with the Qur'anic demand for sexual modesty, and thus it became generally Islamized.

ISLAM AND THE CLASSICAL TRADITIONS

The Arabs' conquests exposed them to the Greater West's centuries-long intellectual, scientific, and artistic traditions, but they disdained any aspect of *Preservation* Zoroastrian learning and resented the Persians' embrace of Shi'ism. This *of the Latin* made the Arabs much more open to the Greco-Roman and Judeo-Christian *West's* intellectual legacy. The Arabs were new to literacy, however, and could not *Cultural* access the texts available to them in the countless libraries of the Near East *Legacy* and North Africa. Starting in the 8th century, groups of Syrian Christians— mostly scholar-monks—began to translate the writings of the ancient Greeks and Romans into Arabic for the benefit of their new rulers. Soon, scholars in North Africa, Sicily, and Spain became involved. Their activity was prodigious: within two or three generations the whole corpus of Western thought lay available for Muslim scholars to read. It included the mathematical and geometrical works of Euclid and Archimedes, the medical knowledge of Hippocrates and Galen, the historical texts of Herodotus and Thucydides, the books of the Hebrew Bible and the New Testament, and works of geography, astronomy, poetry, and

Veiled Women   This 17th-century fresco from Safavid Iran is a late rendering of an early episode in Islamic history. It shows a group of women mourning the dead during one of the expansionist wars of the first Islamic century (650–750 CE). The veiling of women, practiced by most Near Eastern peoples to some degree, was particularly associated with Persian culture, and it came to be the enforced norm within Islam after the Abbasid dynasty relinquished Arab Damascus and moved the capital east to Baghdad. The so-called Persianization of Islam then commenced. The Abbasids remained in power until the Mongols destroyed Baghdad in 1258.

law. Roman histories, legal texts, Stoic meditations, and technical treatises were available too. The leading Muslim scholars absorbed most of this knowledge eagerly, finding in it much that was of immediate practical value. Indeed, with the support of the caliph's court, scholars established a large library and institute for the study of classical texts called the "House of Wisdom" (*bayt al-hikma*).

As a rule, any text or genre of inquiry that could be reconciled with Islamic doctrine received a warm welcome. But the Greco-Roman philosophical tradition, specifically, was another matter altogether. Why would anyone look to pagans like Plato and Aristotle for answers to questions about the purpose of human life, the nature of truth, the definition of justice, or the understanding of morality? After all, all those answers were available in the Qur'an and the *hadith* and the body of Islamic law that grew out of them, the **shari'a**.

Numerous Islamic scholars did read Greek philosophy, however—especially the works of Aristotle. Al-Kindi (d. ca. 870), al-Farabi (d. ca. 951), Ibn Sina (d. 1037), al-Ghazali (d. 1111), and Ibn Rushd (d. 1198) all wrote brilliant commentaries on it. Al-Kindi was one of the first to argue that philosophy posed no difficulty for pious Muslims:

> Aristotle, the greatest of the Greek philosophers, wrote that "we should be grateful to the fathers of those who have contributed anything of truth, since they were the cause of the philosophers' existence." . . . How beautiful is his statement. We need feel no shame in appreciating the truth or in acquiring it from wherever it comes from—even if the truth comes from peoples and races far distant from us and far different from us. To the man who seeks truth, nothing is more important than the truth. Truth cannot be disparaged, and neither should be the one who speaks it or conveys it. Truth, indeed, diminishes no one and exalts all.

To the great bulk of Islamic society, however, philosophy was irrelevant, a brain-churning waste of time when one could be pondering the Qur'an and the judgments of Islamic legal scholars. Greek tragedy also fell on deaf ears among the Muslims because the idea of an inexorable fate other than the determination of the all-knowing Allah was anathema to them. Consequently, the great plays were neglected absolutely—never performed, never recopied, never commented on. The epic poetry of the Greeks and Romans also held no interest for Muslim readers, who preferred the stories of their own heroes, whose exploits they related in prose and verse—such as the great collection of tales called the *Shahnameh* ("The Book of Kings") by the Persian poet Ferdowsi (d. 1020)—and in histories. The Arabs especially excelled in historical writing, with figures like Ibn Ishaq (Muhammad's first biographer, d. 768), al-Waqidi (d. ca. 822), and al-Masudi (d. 956). It remains unclear, however, how much attention Muslim historians paid to classical writers like Herodotus, Thucydides, or Tacitus. Intrigued by what they read or heard about, the caliphs maintained two principal centers for this translation in the late 8th and throughout the 9th century, both located in Baghdad. One was led by the Arab scholar al-Kindi (d. ca. 870) and the other by the Syrian Christian physician Hunayn ibn Ishaq (d. ca. 873). Hunayn ibn Ishaq also made the first translation of the Septuagint version of the Bible into Arabic.[8]

Muslim writers excelled in two genres especially—histories and travelogues. Like the Romans before them, the Muslims explored the history and geography of their newly acquired territories both as a pragmatic measure (the better to govern them) and as propaganda (to illustrate the advantages brought by the arrival of

---

[8]   By the time of the Abbasid takeover in 750, fully 50 percent of all Christians worldwide lived under Islamic rule. As they became Arabized, it became necessary to translate the scriptures into Arabic. Hunayn ibn Ishaq, incidentally, is not the same Ibn Ishaq who wrote the biography of Muhammad.

Islam). Many of the histories focused on a particular tribe, city, or region, but ambitious writers like al-Baladhuri (d. 892) and al-Tabari (d. 923) composed massive chronicles of the entire empire. Among the most famous of Muslim travel writers was Ibn Fadlan (d. ca 950), who journeyed north into what is today Ukraine and western Russia; to him we owe the classic description of Viking burial customs. A genuine spirit of curiosity about other cultures informs his (and other writers') descriptions, but so too does a judgmental sense of Arab superiority:

> The Rus are the dirtiest creatures God ever made. They defecate and urinate anywhere, without shame. Like beasts, they do not wash their privates after sex and do not wash their hands after eating. After their travels they drop anchor (or, as with the ones I saw, tie up their ships along the shore of a river like the great Volga) and build large wooden huts for themselves on the shore. Each hut can hold between ten and twenty people. Inside, each man rests on a couch. They have lovely slave girls with them, whom they will sell to slave-merchants eventually, and each man has sexual intercourse with a slave girl whenever he wishes, even in front of his companions. Sometimes the whole company gets involved, each with his own girl, all in each other's presence. If a merchant happens along who wants to buy a girl, he simply looks on and waits for the man to be finished.

The al-Kindi school focused on philosophical, literary, and logical texts, whereas the ibn Ishaq school tended to emphasize the Greek scientific and medical writings. Muslim scholars showed little interest in the Romans, whose intellectual works they regarded as derivative of the Greeks, although they did admire the Romans' adeptness with technology. But for every eager scholar wanting to pursue Greek knowledge, dozens of suspicious clergy cautioned against the ideas of unbelievers. The early Christian communities had exhibited a similar hesitation toward pagan Greek learning, until figures like Augustine of Hippo showed that classical learning posed no intrinsic threat to Christian orthodoxy and could in fact help to clarify Christian ideas and beliefs. Resistance to the Greek tradition was as tenacious and passionate as the support expressed for it by scholars like al-Kindi.

The Challenge of Classical Greek Culture

Few of the great Muslim philosophers could read Greek; most depended on the translations made for the caliphal court. And like academics everywhere, some of them claimed more expertise than they actually had. Here is al-Kindi's thumbnail synopsis of Aristotle's *Metaphysics*:

> In the work called *Metaphysics* Aristotle sought to explain those things that exist yet do not possess matter; and how these things may co-exist with things that do have matter—and yet remain unconnected to

matter and separate from it. He sought also to affirm the Oneness of God (the Great and Almighty), to explain God's many beautiful names, and to explicate how God is the causal agent of everything in the universe, making everything perfect—for God is the God of the universe, governing everything in His complete and perfect wisdom.

But Aristotle never said anything remotely like this. Was al-Kindi a charlatan? Certainly not. Rather, he wished to deflate clerical concerns about the dangers in seeking knowledge from non-Islamic traditions. He therefore tried to deflect criticism by making Aristotle sound like someone who would surely have been a Muslim if only he had been lucky enough to live in Islamic times.

At other times al-Kindi felt free to express Aristotle's views clearly:

> There is nothing shameful in admiring, and even in acquiring, the Truth, no matter where It comes from. To the student of Truth there is nothing that matters except Truth, and Truth is never cheapened or lessened by the person who states it, not even if he comes from a distant land and belongs to a backward nation. Indeed, Truth belittles no one and ennobles all.

Those interested in Greek philosophy thus faced a twofold problem: to show how a pagan discipline could explain Islamic truth while preserving the authority of revelation. Does revealed truth need logical explication? Does logical explication undermine the authority of the revelation?

Islamic thinkers had started to wrestle with these questions even before their discovery of the Greek tradition. From Muhammad's death in 632, Muslims and would-be Muslims had tried to answer a number of fundamental questions about the faith—the kinds of questions that anyone intrigued by the faith might raise. Was the Holy Qur'an created, or had it existed in heaven from all eternity? If it was present from the Creation, then why did Allah bother with the partial and imperfect Jewish and Christian revelations? And why does the Qur'an's message appear to change? How can it call first for Arabs to embrace Islam for repentance of their sins and to foster pan-Arab unity when later it calls Arabs to bring the message of Allah to the entire world? Another group of questions centered on Allah's attributes. In stating that Allah sees everything, hears our prayers, speaks, has knowledge, exerts will, and wields power, does the Qur'an imply that Allah is anthropomorphic—a kind of eternal man? And a third set of questions asked whether Allah's omniscience implies that every human's destiny is predetermined. Do we have free will, or has Allah, in knowing our ultimate fates, effectively set our ultimate fates?

The practical and immediate need to confront these matters resulted in a body of ideas and disciplines known as **kalam** (literally "speech" or "word," but usually translated as "theology"). *Kalam* was not philosophy and did not aspire to be. Instead, it was a method of inquiry into a limited number of specific issues that needed resolution, and its goal was to ease Islam's acceptance by cultures with long-established traditions that privileged rational thought. Reason, of course, is a universal trait. But the value placed on reason, in preference to other ways of knowing, is a cultural one. As Islam developed and as questions about the fundamental nature of Allah, the Qur'an, and human free will were articulated, Sunni leaders resolved them by seeking a consensus among the community of scholars. This was the tradition known as *ijma'* ("consensus"), a principle that embraced the use of reason to resolve a religious question. But *ijma'* was not open-ended. Once the community's answer on any given question had been authoritatively expressed, the question was considered closed for all time. Tradition trumped any rethinking of any issue.

But the Christian-initiated translations of the Greeks posed another problem: as a result of the monks' work, Muslim scholars encountered real philosophy (*falsafah* in Arabic), or open-ended rational inquiry. In philosophy, the answer given to any question does not close the matter; rather, it invites continual reappraisal. Philosophy is therefore as much an attitude of mind as it is any particular body of ideas, and it does not attempt to produce a desired goal. The liberal

Truth Attainable by Rational Argument   In this scientific manuscript from 13th-century Persia, two great rationalists, Aristotle and his pupil Alexander the Great, lead a discussion of the medicinal properties of certain animal organs and secretions. The eighteenth chapter (*sura*) of the Qur'an discusses a wise ancient ruler who held dominion "from the rising of the sun to the setting of the sun"; commentators have associated this figure with Alexander since the 8th century.

atmosphere of the early Abbasid years allowed philosophy to bloom, as the caliphs al-Rashid (r. 786–809), al-Ma'mun (r. 813–833), al-Mu'tasim (r. 833–842), and al-Wathik (r. 842–847) encouraged new translations of and commentaries on the Western philosophical canon. They promoted as well the study of the philosophical and scientific traditions of Zoroastrian Persia and Buddhist India. In addition to the House of Wisdom at Baghdad, these caliphs also opened a second center for liberal studies at Basra, in Iraq.

Opinions varied on the acceptability of the new cultural injections, but for the moment the inclusionists won. Prominent among these was a group of scholars known as the Mu'tazilites ("the Dissenters"). The Mu'tazilites held widely varying views, but they shared a belief that whenever tradition and reason were in conflict, the scale tipped in reason's favor. Another way to describe the Mu'tazilites is as the party inclined to prevent *ijma'* from sealing off intellectual inquiry. For this reason alone, they were generally disliked and distrusted by most Sunnis, but what earned the Sunnis' real ire was the Mu'tazilite position on the "createdness" of the Qur'an. The caliph al-Ma'mun (r. 813–833), a strong Mu'tazilite sympathizer, even proclaimed this position the official doctrine of the state and required appointees to public office to swear allegiance to it. He triggered a violent revolt and died soon thereafter under suspicious circumstances.[9]

Islam's effort to absorb classical Greco-Roman culture was therefore a highly fraught business. Sunnis and Shi'a judged the issue from different vantage points and by different methods, and disagreements were many and wide within each group. For every inclusionist like al-Kindi and the Mu'tazilites, there were dozens of exclusionists who regarded the effort to harmonize their faith with classical Greco-Roman or Zoroastrian culture as pointless at best and dangerous at worst. In this way Islam extended the general tendency in the Greater West to pursue reform movements, whenever they were thought necessary, as efforts to restore a lost preexisting purity.

The dangers of cultural borrowing and intellectual innovation played a role in the development of the singular Muslim custom of spiritual concealment, *takiyya.* Interpreting the Qur'anic verse "Whether ye hide what is in your hearts or reveal it, Allah knows all" (3.29) in a somewhat generous way, Islamic jurists in both the Sunni and the Shi'i camps provided a justification for the intentional hiding of what one believes. Thus a Shi'i Muslim could pretend to be a Sunni, or vice versa, to protect oneself without incurring divine displeasure. For Shi'i Muslims *takiyya* grew in importance from a bitter necessity during times of Sunni persecution to a fundamental and obligatory duty, the denial of one's faith as an expression of it.

---

[9]   One tradition asserts that al-Ma'mun was resting by a river and asked some courtiers what he should eat. They just happened to have some dates at hand. He died on the spot, presumably poisoned.

WOMEN AND ISLAM

The expansion of Islam, like the spread of all world religions, profoundly affected the status and treatment of women. As with Christianity, Islamic teaching on women's roles and rights in society developed as a dialogue between the revealed truth of the faith and the traditional norms and values of each society into which the faith was introduced. The picture that emerges is complex. Women in the early Muslim world did not enjoy anything approaching equal rights with men—but neither did they in the Christian or Jewish worlds. Women's experiences varied depending on ethnicity, social class, economic status, educational level, and geographical location, all of which make accurate generalizations about Islam and women difficult to assert with any degree of fairness.

The Qur'an makes plain that women share equally in the primary responsibility of all Muslims to remain obedient to Allah's commands. In recounting the Creation story of Adam and Eve in the Garden of Eden, the Qur'an rejects the biblical tradition of identifying Eve as the temptress who seduces Adam into sin; rather, both share responsibility for their sin and an equal portion of the punishment. Nevertheless, the Qur'an emphasizes the comparative physical weakness of women and their concomitantly increased vulnerability in a harsh world. The entire fourth chapter (*sura*) of the Qur'an is dedicated to the topic of women. This *sura* was revealed to Muhammad, according to tradition, after the battle of Uhud in 625, the first military defeat suffered by the Muslims, one in which many Muslim soldiers died, leaving behind a large number of widows and orphans. Islamic law requires that widowed women receive a guaranteed portion of their husbands' estates and that divorced wives are entitled to having their dowries returned to them. In pre-Islamic times, neither provision was the norm. The Qur'an also asserts the right of women to give testimony in legal cases, although a woman's testimony is considered only half as worthy as that of a man, and to bring suit for damages in civil cases. These too were innovations in Arab tradition. This *sura* also permits a man to have as many as four wives, but it obliges him to treat each wife with equal respect. Polygamy was an ancient custom among the Arab tribes, and a man was previously allowed to take as many wives as he wanted, without any social requirements on how he treated them. The Qur'anic tradition therefore represented a reining in of the practice.[10]

On the Sunni side, some Yemeni and Bedouin tribes had long practiced a legalized form of concubinage. In *mut'a* (literally "pleasure" or "enjoyment"), a man married a woman for a prearranged period of time—a year, a month, a week, or

---

[10] Muhammad himself had a total of eleven wives (thirteen, according to some sources), but seldom more than four at any given time. His serial marriages may have aimed at ensuring the unification of the Arab tribes by forging alliances across Arab society.

even a single day—and paid her a prorated dowry in return for his "enjoyment" of her.[11] It is unclear how widespread the practice was in pre-Islamic times, but some evidence dates it to as early as the 4th century CE among the Bedouin and possibly even earlier among groups of Egyptian traders. Several later writers claimed that Muhammad himself had practiced it (al-Tabari, *Chronicle* 1.1775–1776). Many Sunni jurists rejected *mut'a* and the assertion that the Prophet had ever been involved in it. But from the time of the legal scholar al-Shafi'i (d. ca. 819), a compromise allowed it, provided that the term of the marriage did not appear in the written marriage contract. The Shi'a, in contrast, championed *mut'a* from the start (and still practice it widely today).

Above all, Islam demanded of women obedience and modesty—obedience to religious tradition and social norms of gender roles and modesty of dress, demeanor, and speech. To lesser extents, it demanded the same of men. As the very name of the faith makes plain, the most important value for men and women to aspire to is submission. Misogyny certainly existed, even throve, in medieval Muslim society, but it is not an intrinsic part of the Qur'anic call itself. Ethnic, tribal, and class-based prejudices both spawned and encouraged misogynistic practices and attitudes. Islam softened many such customs. Among the pre-Islamic Arabs, for example, no restrictions were placed on a father's right to control and discipline his wives or children. In its way, such a tradition resembled the Roman custom of patria potestas or the classical Athenian strictures regarding women. Restrictions on women's movement in public—whether veiled or not, whether accompanied by an adult male family member or not—predated Islam and probably originated in the exceptionally dangerous nature of movement through the peninsula. The Qur'an itself says nothing about the subject.

◆

Arab culture, and to a lesser extent Persian culture, was undoubtedly patriarchal and paternalistic. Islam tempered and softened the harshest elements within both worlds, but in its desire to adopt and adapt to the many cultures that it encompassed, the faith allowed as many of preexisting life practices to endure as possible. Whether one looks at early Islam's political, intellectual, or cultural development, one is left with the impression not of a new and ideologically zealous culture forcing itself upon preexisting societies, but of an intricate interplay between a developing corpus of religious principles and a complicated, heterogeneous world over which Islam—seemingly in the blink of an eye—suddenly held sway.

---

[11]   For a marriage of only one day, the marriage price could be as low as a handful of grain or dates.

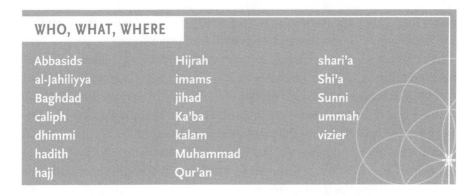

WHO, WHAT, WHERE

Abbasids	Hijrah	shari'a
al-Jahiliyya	imams	Shi'a
Baghdad	jihad	Sunni
caliph	Ka'ba	ummah
dhimmi	kalam	vizier
hadith	Muhammad	
hajj	Qur'an	

SUGGESTED READINGS

Primary Sources

Al-Bukhari. *The Hadith.*

Al-Kindi. *On First Philosophy.*

Ferdowsi. *Shahnameh (The Book of Kings).*

Ibn Fadlan. *Risala (Travels).*

Ibn Ishaq. *Life of the Prophet.*

The Qur'an.

Anthologies

Constable, Olivia Remie, ed. *Medieval Iberia: Readings from Muslim, Christian, and Jewish Sources* (2011).

Lopez, Robert S., and Irving W. Raymond, trans. *Medieval Trade in the Mediterranean World: Illustrative Documents* (2001).

McGinness, Jon, and David C. Reisman. *Classical Arabic Philosophy: An Anthology of Sources* (2007).

Renard, John. *Islamic Theological Themes: A Primary Source Reader* (2014).

Shinners, John, ed. *Medieval Popular Religion, 1000–1500: A Reader* (2006).

Studies

al-Khalili, Jim. *The House of Wisdom: How Arab Science Saved Ancient Knowledge and Gave Us the Renaissance* (2012).

Bennison, Amira K. *The Great Caliphs: The Golden Age of the Abbasid Empire* (2010).

Bowersock, G. W. *The Throne of Adulis: Red Sea Wars on the Eve of Islam* (2013).

Caswell, F. Matthew. *The Slave-Girls of Baghdad: The Qiyan in the Early Abbasid Era* (2011).

Cook, Michael. *Commanding Right and Forbidding Wrong in Islamic Thought* (2001).

Cotton, Hannah M., Robert G. Hayland, Jonathan J. Price, and David J. Wasserstein. *From Hellenism to Islam: Cultural and Linguistic Change in the Roman Near East* (2012).

Crone, Patricia. *God's Rule: Government and Islam—Six Centuries of Medieval Islamic Political Thought* (2005).

Crone, Patricia. *Meccan Trade and the Rise of Islam* (2004).

Crone, Patricia, and Martin Hinds. *God's Caliph: Religious Authority in the First Centuries of Islam* (2003).

Donner, Fred McGraw. *Muhammad and the Believers: At the Origins of Islam* (2010).

El Shamsy, Ahmed. *The Canonization of Islamic Law: A Social and Intellectual History* (2013).

Friedmann, Yohann. *Tolerance and Coercion in Islam: Interfaith Relations in the Muslim Tradition* (2003).

Goldenberg, David M. *The Curse of Ham: Race and Slavery in Early Judaism, Christianity, and Islam* (2005).

Griffith, Sidney H. *The Church in the Shadow of the Mosque: Christians and Muslims in the World of Islam* (2008).

Haider, Najam. *Shi'i Islam: An Introduction* (2014).

Hawting, G. R. *The First Dynasty of Islam: The Umayyad Caliphate, AD 661–750* (2000).

Hoyland, Robert G. *In God's Path: The Arab Conquests and the Creation of an Islamic Empire* (2014).

Kennedy, Hugh. *The Prophet and the Age of the Caliphates: The Islamic Near East from the Sixth to the Eleventh Century* (2004).

Khalek, Nancy. *Damascus after the Muslim Conquest: Text and Image in Early Islam* (2011).

Levy-Rubin, Milka. *Non-Muslims in the Early Islamic Empire: From Surrender to Coexistence* (2011).

Marsham, Andrew. *Rituals of Islamic Monarchy: Accession and Succession in the First Muslim Empire* (2009).

Mottahadeh, Roy P. *Loyalty and Leadership in an Early Islamic Society* (2001).

Turner, John P. *Inquisition in Early Islam: The Competition for Political and Religious Authority in the Abbasid Empire* (2013).

Young, M. J. L., J. D. Latham, and R. B. Serjeant. *Religion, Learning, and Science in the Abbasid Period* (2006).

Zadeh, Travis. *Mapping Frontiers across Medieval Islam: Geography, Translation, and the Abbasid Empire* (2011).

For additional resources, including maps, primary sources, visuals, web links, and quizzes, please go to **www.oup.com/us/backman**.

CHAPTER 10

Reform and Renewal in the Greater West

750–1258

In the middle of the 8th century, separated only by a year, two palace coups took place 2,000 miles from each other. Such events were commonplace in both realms and often involved blindings, beheadings, and poisonings—with at least one monarch ripped apart by having her limbs tied to four horses driven in four directions.[1] At first, perhaps, these two seizures of power did not seem remarkable. But each set its society on a new course of development and brought their worlds into direct and lasting conflict. One brought on the Carolingian dynasty that culminated in the reign of Charlemagne in western Europe; the other introduced the Abbasid caliphate based in Baghdad. Both would fundamentally shape the history of the Greater West.

THE GREATER WEST, ca. 1200

The centuries that followed witnessed much of the best and the worst of their societies' medieval era. They included unimagined prosperity, intellectual advance, artistic

Astrolabe A 12th-century astrolabe from Muslim Spain. The increase in maritime trade across the Mediterranean by 1000 owed a lot to technical innovations introduced by Muslim and Jewish scientists, many of whom worked in Spain.

---

[1] This unlucky individual was Brunhilde, a Visigothic noblewoman who married Sigebert, the king of Austrasia (a territory in the eastern reaches of today's France).

flourishing, religious revival, and political development—but also fiery hatred, social oppression, academic censorship, and xenophobia. They defined the broad division in Islam between Sunnis and Shi'a, still evident today, and the reinvention of Europe with feudal society and medieval cities. Perhaps most notoriously they included the Crusades in the Holy Land and also a new chapter in Jewish history.

TWO PALACE COUPS

The Abbasid Takeover

The first coup took place in Damascus in 750, when the Sunni family known as the Abbasids, members of the Banu Hashim clan, which traced its ancestry back to the great-grandfather of Muhammad, rebelled against the Umayyad rulers of the Islamic Empire. The Umayyad dynasty had never been popular. Despite building the shrine of the Dome of the Rock in Jerusalem and the Great Mosque in Damascus, they were seen (probably correctly) as more interested in power than in the faith. They only made things worse by reserving all positions of leadership in the empire for ethnic Arabs. Their prejudice led to severe economic and social trouble, as large numbers of Egyptians and Persians converted to Islam, abandoned their farms, and migrated to the cities, where they expected to receive preferment. The subsequent decline in agricultural production caused food prices to spike and imperial revenues to fall. The empire's cities swelled with disaffected

CHAPTER TIMELINE

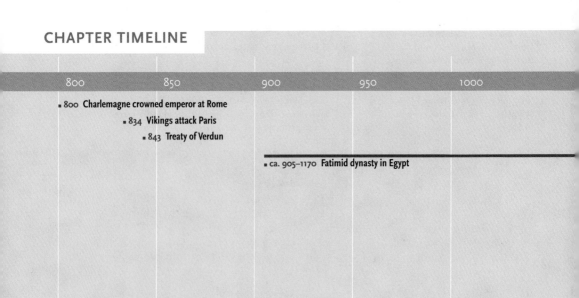

800	850	900	950	1000

- 800 **Charlemagne crowned emperor at Rome**
  - 834 **Vikings attack Paris**
  - 843 **Treaty of Verdun**

- ca. 905–1170 **Fatimid dynasty in Egypt**

populations, who found out the hard reality that membership in the *ummah*, the Islamic community, depended very much on the color of one's skin.

As unrest gained pace in the 8th century, the Abbasids, based in Khurasan, in northeastern Iran, began laying the groundwork for regime change. Although themselves Arab, the Abbasids championed a multiethnic vision of Islam. They cagily sought support among the Shi'a who had taken refuge in Iran with false promises of elevating their choice to the caliphal throne after the coup. Finally, in 750, they struck. Led by family patriarch al-Saffah ("the Slaughterer"), they routed the Umayyads on the battlefield, took control of the state, and promptly moved the capital eastward to their newly established city of Baghdad.[2] The Abbasids presided over the opening of the Islamic world to non-Arabs. Persians especially rose to prominence under the new regime, winning positions at court, in the provincial government, and in the Islamic schools. This began a sweeping process of cultural change, sometimes known as the "Persianization" of Islamic culture.

The second coup was much less bloody but no less epoch-making. The *The* Frankish warlord-kings who had held sway over northern Gaul since Clovis's *Carolingian* acceptance of Christianity around 500 were on the whole a sorry lot. These were *Takeover* the Merovingians, who fought incessantly, plotted even more, and showed no

---

[2] Al-Saffah invited the remaining Umayyads to a reconciliation dinner. Just as the first course was being served, his agents sprang from their hiding places, knives flashing. Only one Umayyad family member escaped.

1050	1100	1150	1200	1250

- ca. 1050 **Medieval agricultural revolution at its height**
- 1054 **Great Schism between Latin and Orthodox churches**
- 1066 **Norman conquest of England under William I**
- 1071 **Byzantines defeated by Seljuk Turks at Manzikert**
- 1077 **Holy Roman Emperor Henry IV does penance before Pope Gregory VII**
- 1095 **Pope Urban II calls First Crusade**
- 1096–1099 **First Crusade**
- 1100 **Banking industry emerges in Italy**
- 1122 **Concordat of Worms ends investiture conflict**
- 1135–1204 **Life of Maimonides, Jewish philosopher**
- ca. 1150–1212 **Reconquista of Muslim Spain**
- 1187 **Muslim reconquest of Jerusalem**
- 1204 **Crusaders of Fourth Crusade sack Constantinople**

persuasive interest in doing more with rulership than acquiring wealth and rooting out real or suspected rivals. From the mid-7th century on, they are known as the "do-nothing kings," whose ineffectiveness enabled local warlords and officials to usurp power for themselves.

The most successful of the usurpers was a family from northeastern Gaul known as the Carolingians. By the early 700s Pepin of Heristal was serving as a regional Merovingian official but was in reality an all-but-autonomous ruler. He passed his position on to his only, although illegitimate, son, **Charles Martel** ("the Hammer," d. 741), who added much of northwestern Gaul to the family domain and gave the name Carolingian (from *Carolus,* Latin for "Charles") to the dynasty. The secret to the Carolingians' effectiveness was a combination of vision, ruthlessness, and luck. The family early on developed a view of themselves as the self-appointed saviors of Christian Gaul and eventually of western Europe, destined like the biblical David to replace the rejected king Saul (that is, the Merovingian house) and establish a righteous and lasting realm.

For four or five generations the family advanced their dedication to uniting and strengthening western Christendom. One of the most dramatic events in this pursuit was Charles Martel's victory in 732 over Spanish Muslim forces that effectively stopped the Islamic advance into Europe. In 751 Charles Martel's son Pepin the Short completed the takeover of the Merovingian throne by persuading the papacy to recognize him as the true legitimate king of the Franks. The last Merovingian was deposed and the first Carolingian king enthroned.

THE CAROLINGIAN ASCENT

Pepin the Short (r. 751–768) became the king of the Franks by the acclaim of his people and the recognition of his title by Pope Stephen II (r. 752–757). He and his son and successor, Charlemagne (r. 768–814), stressed practical needs of stabilizing their realm and building an independent empire. The pope, for his support, gained in the Carolingian monarchy a military ally against the newest Germanic group to rip through Italy—the Lombards—and a tacit recognition that the Holy See was the arbiter of political legitimacy in Europe. Pepin and Charlemagne confirmed the pontiff's position as the secular ruler of the so-called Papal State, a wide swath of land across the middle of the Italian peninsula. With a strong ally and steady source of income, the papacy was able at last to exercise some genuine authority in the Christian world, although the precise nature and extent of that authority remained uncertain for many years.

There is something of an irony in the Carolingians' success. Genuinely pious and dedicated to the evangelization of barbarian Europe, they nonetheless owed *The Means:* their rise to power to their oppression of local churches. As early as the 720s, the *Ransacking* Carolingians had ransacked the monasteries in their domains to raise the reve- *the* nues they needed to pay their soldiers. Monasteries, after all, were the wealthiest *Monasteries* institutions in western Europe, possessors of large estates well run with collective labor forces. Their sacristies were often filled with valuable items bequeathed by pious neighbors. Some of them also held deposits of cash or valuables from ner- vous owners who feared leaving them in their own homes. Carolingian forces pre- sented the monasteries with a simple choice: these are barbarous times, and you can either give us your valuables to pay for our soldiers or you can be left alone to face certain annihilation by Germanic invaders or, even worse, the advancing Muslims. With their purses thus filled, the Carolingians' army swelled in size, enabling them to bring more and more of France under their authority. Charles Martel's great victory over the Muslims in 732, on the plain between Tours and Poitiers in midwestern Gaul, solidified the family's heroic status and justified (in their own minds, at least) their manhandling of the monks. As a source known as the *Chronicle of Saint-Denis* put it,

> The Muslims were marching to the city of Tours in order to destroy it, the Church of Saint Martin, and all the surrounding countryside, when Charles—that illustrious prince—opposed them at the head of his whole army. He set his soldiers in formation and fell upon the enemy as ferociously as a hungry wolf falls upon a stag, until, by the grace of Our Lord, he had slaughtered on the field 300,000 of the enemies of Christianity, including their king Abd ar-Rahman. This was how he came to be called Martel ["hammer"], for he struck down his foes on the field as though he were a hammer made of iron, or steel, or some other type of metal. And the most amazing thing of all was the fact that he lost only fifteen hundred of his own men that day.

Victory followed victory, and by the end of Pepin the Short's reign in 768, almost all of modern France lay under Carolingian control.

What distinguished the Carolingians from other warlord families was their genuine dedication to transforming the societies they ruled. Charles Martel and *The Goal:* Pepin the Short built nearly as many monasteries as they ransacked, and they es- *Christian* tablished scores of new churches and schools. Charlemagne is credited with hun- *Rule* dreds more. They supported missionary work among the Germanic peoples and at least attempted to develop an infrastructure of roads and bridges that would

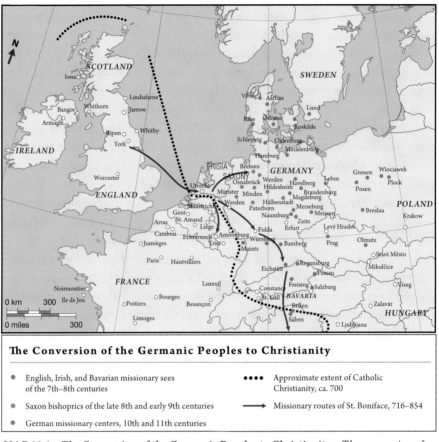

The Conversion of the Germanic Peoples to Christianity

- ● English, Irish, and Bavarian missionary sees of the 7th–8th centuries
- ● Saxon bishoprics of the late 8th and early 9th centuries
- ● German missionary centers, 10th and 11th centuries
- ●●●● Approximate extent of Catholic Christianity, ca. 700
- ⟶ Missionary routes of St. Boniface, 716–854

MAP 10.1   The Conversion of the Germanic Peoples to Christianity   The conversion of the Germanic peoples occurred over centuries. It was led by individual missionaries whose activities were approved, but not directed, by religious and political authorities.

connect villages and towns. The Carolingians were also distinguished by their stable succession pattern: for several generations in a row they produced a single heir who inherited the entire family domain, without the pressure to divide it among siblings.[3]

The greatest missionary of the age was **Boniface** (680–754), an Anglo-Saxon monk who spent forty years preaching to the Germanic peoples of the north, founding monasteries, churches, and schools with undiminished zeal (see Map 10.1). He had the ardent backing of the Carolingian court, "without which,"

---

[3]   The Carolingians did not rely on luck alone. They kept scores of mistresses and limited intimacy with their wives to the minimum needed to produce a male heir. Their method was not foolproof; in fact, several of the Carolingians did produce multiple legitimate heirs. Disease and warfare carried off most of them before political division occurred. In a few cases, a sudden assassination or imprisonment sufficed.

Boniface wrote in a letter to a friend, "I could neither administer my churches and defend my clergy nor continue the fight against idolatry." Charles Martel, in fact, created four dioceses in southern Germany in his honor (at Salzburg, Regensburg, Freising, and Passau) and appointed him metropolitan, or supreme administrative officer among a group of bishops, over all German lands east of the Rhine River. In return for this support, Boniface made sure that all the bishops he appointed, from the Low Countries to Saxony, declared loyalty jointly to the papacy and to the Carolingian ruler. The relationship between Rome and the Carolingians can be thought of as a partnership, although one in which the Carolingians had the dominant role.

CHARLEMAGNE

Following Pepin the Short's death, **Charlemagne** ("Charles the Great") spent forty years campaigning across Europe, expanding his realm into northeastern Spain, eastern Germany, Italy, Bohemia (part of today's Czech Republic), the Hungarian plain, and the northern reaches of the Balkans (today's Slovenia, Croatia, and Bosnia and Herzegovina). His great goal was to unite Latin Europe under a single government with a comprehensive legal system, a network of churches and schools, a reliable basic infrastructure, and a regularized system of weights and measures (see Map 10.2).

Charlemagne's energy was prodigious. According to Einhard's *Life of Charlemagne*, a biography written to order during the reign of Charlemagne's heir, Louis the Pious (r. 814–840), he also suffered from lifelong insomnia, which he inflicted on his courtiers:

> He habitually awoke and rose from his bed four or five times a night. He would hold audience with his retinue even while getting dressed or putting on his boots; if the palace chancellor told him of any legal matter for which his judgment was needed, he had the parties brought before him then and there. He would hear the case and render his decision just as though he was sitting on the bench of justice. And this was not the only type of business he would carry on at these hours, for he regularly performed any one of his daily duties, whether it was a matter for his personal attention or something that he could allocate to his officials. (ch. 24)

A pragmatic streak led the Carolingians to pursue a limited form of meritocracy; perhaps they had no real alternative. After all, the relentless traveling of the royal court exposed them to a parade of ineptitude. Everything from illiterate priests to judges with no knowledge of the law made the need for reform clear. Thus anyone

MAP 10.2 Charlemagne's Empire The Carolingian realm at its height reunited most of the European part of the western Roman empire.

with a useful skill could find service somewhere in the regime. Stable government required a central base of operations, and so Charlemagne built the first permanent capital of any Germanic ruler. To this capital at Aachen (Aix-la-Chapelle, on today's French–German borderlands), the court brought poets and theologians from Spain, historians and legal scholars from Italy, grammarians from Ireland, and biblical scholars from England. But they also scouted out skilled stonemasons, carpenters, metalsmiths, scribes, weavers, tanners, musicians, coopers, and herbalists. Social background usually took a backseat to the more important issue of ability.

Putting these scholars, artists, and craftsmen to work, Charlemagne's court inaugurated a cultural revival known as the **Carolingian Renaissance** (named *The* after the remarkable Italian Renaissance discussed in chapter 12). Under the di- *Carolingian* rection of an earnest Englishman named Alcuin (730–804), hundreds of monas- *Renaissance* tic scribes created whole libraries by producing copy after copy of the classical and Christian authors, grammarians explained the workings of Latin composition, and poets sang the glories of Carolingian rule in classical meters. Most of the Carolingian Renaissance consisted of a kind of cultural salvage operation— preserving, cataloging, copying, and distributing works of the classical and Christian past. But in that work they introduced a number of innovations, one of the most important of which was a new technique of writing.

INROMANTIMESTEXTSWEREWRITTENLIKETHISALLI-
NCAPITALSANDWITHOUTPUNCTUATIONORSPACESBE-
TWEENTHEWORDS

The Romans' practice had two aims: to save space on expensive writing surfaces and to support their practice of oral reading. (Most people will find the collapsed sentence above is easier to read aloud than silently.) Alcuin soon found that his army of scribes found Roman script too confus- ing (medieval monks, after all, were supposed to maintain silence unless addressed by a superior), which led to endless copying errors. Hence he broke with tradition and created a new way of writing—a script called Carolingian (or Caro- line) minuscule, which used upper- and lower- case letters and introduced spaces between words. Alcuin's inventions not only made it easier for scribes to produce reliable texts, but also re- sulted in a new way of reading that made it a pri- vate, silent pleasure rather than an oral, communal one.

The Carolingian Renaissance was a court- directed enterprise and as such it reflected and expressed the court's interests. Simply put, most of the works produced aimed specifically to strengthen either the Roman Catholic Church or the Carolingian dynasty. What they did not aim

Carolingian Miniscule Script   In order to minimize scribal errors and ease comprehen- sion, the Carolingian court introduced lower- case letters and word spacing. This 8th-century page is a table of contents for a manuscript of the Salic Laws.

to do was to distinguish between the authorities held by each—since such a distinction did not exist. In Carolingian eyes, all power belonged to the king.

Charlemagne's
Rule

Charlemagne viewed power and status as commodities that he alone possessed and could parcel out at will. He governed his vast realm by delegating local, provincial authority to a caste of counts (*comites* in Latin) who represented the king and exerted power in his name, but these were not hereditary positions. The title of count was a job description, not a designation of social class. Charlemagne could appoint the lowest-born peasant as count, if he wished, and that count's position of honor would be equal to that of any count who claimed an aristocratic background. Ability and loyalty to the throne were what mattered most. The court held several assemblies each year, to which various counts and other officials were summoned. A typical summons read like this:

> In the name of the Father, and of the Son, and of the Holy Spirit. Charles, the most serene, august, heavenly crowned, magnificent, and peaceful emperor, and also, by God's mercy, the King of the Franks and of the Lombards, to Abbot Fulrad.
>
> You are hereby informed that I have decided to convene my General Assembly this year in eastern Saxony at the place called Stassfurt, on the Bode River. I therefore command you to come to this place on the fifteenth day before the calends of July—that is, seven days before the Feast of Saint John the Baptist—with all your men suitably armed and at the ready, so that you will be prepared to head out from that place in any direction I choose. In other words, come with arms, gear, and all the food and clothing you will need for war. Let every horseman bring a shield, lance, sword, knife, bow, and supply of arrows. Let your carriage train bring tools of every kind: axes, planes, augurs, lumber, shovels, spades, and anything else an army might need. Bring also enough food to last three months beyond the date of the assembly, and arms and clothing to last six.
>
> I command, more generally, that you should see to it that you travel peacefully to the aforesaid place, and that as your journey takes you through any of the lands of my realm you should presume to take nothing but fodder for your animals, wood, and water. Let the servants belonging to each of your loyal men march alongside the carts and horsemen, and let their masters be always with them until they reach the aforesaid place, lest a lord's absence be the cause of his servants' evildoing.
>
> Send your tribute—which you are to present to me at the assembly by the middle of May—to the appointed place, where I shall already be. If it

should happen that your travels go so well that you can present your tribute to me in person, I shall be greatly pleased. Do not disappoint me now or in the future, if you hope to remain in my favor.

The counts owed their status entirely to the king's favor, not to any birthright of their own. Moreover, the king trained and sent out teams of *missi dominici* (literally, "dispatched royal agents" or "traveling lords"), who moved in regular circuits throughout the realm, reviewing comital records, holding open courts, and inviting the local populace to come forth with complaints about the job performance of the counts.

It was a system of government that was meant to evoke the ruling style of the

Charlemagne's Chapel at Aachen   Charlemagne had his palace chapel modeled after the church of St. Ambrose in Ravenna, Italy. Ravenna had been the de facto capital of the Roman Empire since the 3rd century, and of the western Roman Empire after the transfer to Constantinople in the 4th. His throne was placed at one end, the altar and a shrine to the Virgin Mary at the other.

ancient Roman emperors, seeking a balance of centralized aims and local needs. The Carolingians admired the Roman idea of getting their subjects to see themselves as part of a larger civilization, although in the Carolingians' case the larger civilization was Latin Christianity, not Roman polytheism. When building his palace complex at Aachen, Charlemagne ordered its chapel to be modeled on the Byzantine church of San Vitale that Justinian had built in Ravenna. And he had nearly identical marble pillars, stone columns, and glittering wall mosaics (and the appropriately skilled workmen) hauled north from Italy to do it.

IMPERIAL CORONATION

Charlemagne sought to elevate himself and his empire to the imperial dignity enjoyed by Byzantium. He made protection of the pope and Roman orthodoxy an essential component of his mandate. The culmination of his efforts took place on Christmas Day in the year 800, in Rome, when Pope Leo III (r. 795–816) placed a crown on Charlemagne's head and proclaimed him Augustus, the title of the first Roman emperor. The significance of the coronation was symbolic and also more than symbolic. The symbolic significance had to do with the date. The traditional Anno Domini system of dating (today designated instead as the Common Era)—that is, reckoning the years from the purported time of Jesus's birth—was then still a novelty. It had been created by a Syrian monk in the 6th century but had only become used in the west after the English scholar-monk Bede (d. 735) had promoted its use. By the time of Charlemagne's coronation, most literate people in Europe used the new system. Still, the bulk of the population probably still thought in terms of the old system (called annus mundi II) they had inherited from earlier times, and according to this system the year 800 was actually the year 6000.

Einhard reports that Charlemagne was surprised and incensed by the coronation. He would not have attended Mass even on Christmas if he had known what Leo was planning to do. But Charlemagne had been in Rome since early November, and the man who never slept would never have been caught in an unplanned coronation. More likely, some mishandled detail in the crowning ceremony caused his angry outburst. Regardless, Charlemagne probably took advantage of the calendrical quirk of the year 800/6000 to make his coronation signal the start of a bright new age in history.[4]

Message to Byzantium
However, the significance of his coronation was far more than symbolic: it sent a political message to Byzantium. Seeking support for their claims to political legitimacy, early medieval rulers like Clovis had frequently turned to the Greeks. The Byzantines, for their part, regarded the Latin westerners as ill-mannered and backward poor cousins, nominally members of the Christian family but hardly the sort of relatives one boasts about. Most Byzantines, in fact, regarded the loss of western Europe as a blessing in disguise. Charlemagne's coronation, however, changed everything. By assuming the imperial title, he effectively declared the Carolingian court independent of and equal to the Greek east. Moreover, by receiving the crown from the pope, the Carolingians established a way to pass on the imperial title in which the Byzantines had no role.

Constantinople was not pleased with this declaration of independence but was powerless to do anything about it. Compounding matters, the throne in Constantinople was occupied at the time by an unpopular ruler, Irene (r. 797–802), who had seized power by organizing a coup against her ineffectual son Constantine VI (r. 776–797). Charlemagne sent Irene an embassy and proposed marriage. If the marriage happened, his ambassadors urged, the eastern and western empires would unite, the growing rift between the Latin and Greek churches would heal, and the Christian world could mount a powerful joint offensive against Islam. Irene was inclined to accept, but she fell from power before she could give her answer. Her interest in marrying Charlemagne was the last straw

---

4   Think of Charlemagne at his coronation as almost like a modern politician who coordinates speeches and ribbon-cutting ceremonies to coincide with significant anniversaries.

for several Byzantine high officials, who seized Irene, cut off her hair, and forced her into a convent, never to emerge. Once in the convent, she seems to have accepted her fate with grace, seeing her life as a nun as a penance for her cruelty to her son. She died in 805. Charlemagne was so furious at this spoiling of his grand plan that he even formed a brief alliance with the Abbasid caliph in Baghdad, Harun al-Rashid (r. 786–809), to mount a two-pronged invasion of Byzantium. Nothing came of it—except that Charlemagne received, among other fine gifts from the caliph, the first elephant he had ever seen.

CAROLINGIAN COLLAPSE

Carolingian luck ran out after Charlemagne's death in 814. At his death, Charlemagne's crown passed to his sole surviving heir, Louis the Pious (r. 814–840), but Louis had few of his father's gifts. Studious and well-meaning, he nevertheless lacked charisma and quick wit. He was also intensely straitlaced and moralistic—hence his nickname—and banished from court all the dancing girls and mistresses who had made his father's sleepless nights less lonely. Even worse from the dynastic perspective, Louis was determined to make up for his father's sexual libertinism by remaining staunchly faithful to his wife. As a result Louis was survived by three sons.

In 843, shortly after Louis's death, these sons agreed to the **Treaty of Verdun**, which divided the empire into three parts: Charles the Bald received the western *Treaty of* part, Lothar the middle, and Louis the eastern part (see Map 10.3). Although of *Verdun* course no one knew it at the time, this treaty roughly defined the political contours of western Europe that exist today. Other than brief periods under Napoleon and Hitler, Europe would never again see as large a unified state as it had under Charlemagne.

After the Treaty of Verdun, the delicate sense of cultural unity across Latin Europe fostered by Charlemagne dissolved almost immediately into factionalism. The large-scale division of the empire was accompanied by decentralization of power at the local level. Nobles increased their authority in their own territories and built up groups of military followers who were primarily loyal to them, not to some distant king or emperor. Civil war became incessant, and Europe in the 9th and 10th centuries seemed likely to slip into another Dark Age.

Exacerbating the internal rot, new waves of invaders attacked Europe. Another nomadic group emerged from the central Asian steppe and marched into the *The* plains of eastern Europe below the Danube River. These were the Magyars, the *Magyars* ancestors of today's Hungarian nation. They were a localized threat, however, encroaching only on the easternmost former members of the Carolingian state, although the people of northern Italy also had some reason to fear them.

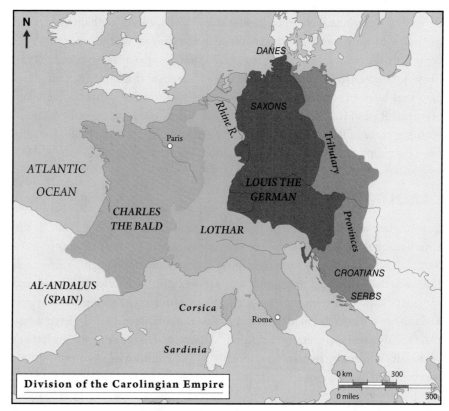

MAP 10.3   Division of the Carolingian Empire, 843   Charlemagne's three grandsons divided
the empire among themselves with the Treaty of Verdun. The treaty helped to confirm a lasting
political and cultural distinction between France and Germany.

The Vikings

A much greater threat came from the north—the Vikings ("sea raiders").
Their hordes had begun to beset Latin Europe as early as Charlemagne's time; as
the Carolingian state fractured, the invasions gained pace.

What made the Viking threat so severe was the unpredictable nature of their
attacks. Unlike the Magyars—a large, slow-moving land force—the Vikings
raided in smallish groups of perhaps two dozen fighters per warship. Those ships,
moreover, were designed to sail in as little as 3 or 4 feet of water, which meant that
the Vikings could move upriver. Most of Europe's rivers flow northward and
westward—opening directly on the Atlantic, the North Sea, and the Baltic Sea—
in other words, directly in front of the Vikings' approach. The attackers were thus
able to move with terrific speed and attack far inland. Viking warships attacked
Paris in 834, during the reign of Louis the Pious, and even sacked Seville, the
capital of Muslim Spain, about a decade later. There was no advance warning for
these raids. The Vikings simply appeared all of a sudden, attacked and pillaged,
and disappeared before any kind of defense could be mounted. And of course the

incessant civil war that followed the Treaty of Verdun only made the problem worse. Here is how a church council lamented the suffering of the time:

> Our cities are depopulated, our monasteries wrecked and put to the torch, our countryside left uninhabited. . . . Indeed, just as the first humans lived without law or the fear of God and according only to their dumb instincts, so too now does everyone do whatever seems good in his eyes only, despising all human and divine laws and ignoring even the commands of the Church. The strong oppress the weak, and the world is wracked with violence against the poor and the plunder of ecclesiastical lands. . . . Men everywhere devour each other like the fishes of the sea.

In the words of the Old Norse poet Snori Sturluson (1179–1241), the Vikings "were like mad dogs or wolves, biting the edges of their shields, / and were as strong as bears or bulls. They killed men everywhere / and nothing could stop them—not fire, not steel." No wonder that scattered figures across Europe, gathering crowds of frightened followers around them, began to proclaim the end of the world.

And then the Muslims came again.

THE SPLINTERING OF THE CALIPHATE

The multicultural vision and policy of the Abbasids outraged many and inspired a predictable backlash. "O Lord," cried one offended Arab elitist, "the sons of whores have multiplied so much—please guide me to another land where I need not deal with bastards!" And as it happened, many were guided away from the cosmopolitan empire. The last Umayyads had fled as far as Spain, where they officially seceded from the caliphate and declared an independent kingdom of their own in 756. Other regions soon followed suit: Algeria broke away in 779; Morocco in 789; Tunisia in 800; Khurasan (northeastern Iran and part of Afghanistan) in 819; Sind (roughly the territory of today's Pakistan) in 867; and Egypt, too, in 868, only to have its rebels overthrown and succeeded by a new dynasty called the Fatimids in 905. So too did numerous smaller princedoms. Thus the cultural glories of the Abbasid Golden Age came at the cost of the political shattering of the empire (see Map 10.4).

Many issues beyond concern about heretical ideas played into the disintegration. Other issues were ethnic pride and racial bias, a sense of unfair commercial and tax policies, and frustration over the perceived stalling out of strong jihad in favor of soft intellectualism. It is no coincidence that the splinter states became seedbeds for strict conservative reform movements, such as the Almoravids and the Almohads in North Africa and Spain. These sects, and others like them, called for halting what

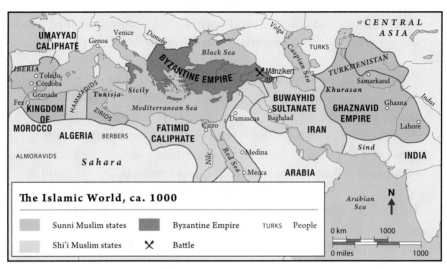

MAP 10.4   The Islamic World, ca. 1000   By the start of the 11th century, the political unity of the Abbasid caliphate was shattered.

they regarded as the cosmopolitan rot that had beset Islam. They demanded a return to the militarism, discipline, and order of the great conquering age of the Prophet and his Companions. Only by restoring the active spirit of jihad, the reformists asserted, could the great cause of bringing Islam to the world be fulfilled.

Increasing Muslim Hostility toward Jews and Christians

Two important developments coincided with the breakup of the Islamic Empire. First, internally, Muslims had become the majority in two or three generations. Conversion, coercion, and emigration had caused the Jewish and Christian populations to shrink. Most Muslims states still recognized the legal rights of their non-Muslim subjects as dhimmis. But it is one thing to live in tolerance with foreign communities that vastly outnumber one's own and quite another when one's own community has become the majority and the other groups suddenly appear as out-of-place foreigners. Acts of anti-Jewish and anti-Christian hostility grew increasingly common through the 9th and 10th centuries, especially in areas experiencing temporary economic troubles. They became common features, too, of the reformist movements of the age. This was popular violence rather than state-run persecution in most cases, although the victims may not have appreciated the difference.

Islamic State Efforts to Expand Commerce

Second, this fracturing of the caliphate coincided with the breakup of the Carolingian Empire. With western Europe entering another dark period, many of the splinter Islamic states saw an opportunity to expand commerce. After all, whether for dynastic, ethnic, or religious reasons, they tended to dislike one another intensely and preferred to trade with Christian Europe rather than with their Islamic neighbors, and hence the new wave of Islamic attacks on Europe in the 9th and 10th centuries, coinciding roughly with the Magyar and Viking invasions. By 850 Muslim forces had conquered Sicily, parts of southern Italy, and the Balearic Islands, and they had made successful raids on Sardinia, Corsica, and the cities of Marseilles and Rome. But the Islamic attacks were not campaigns of conquest. Rather, they were attempts to carve out zones of interest, economic trading posts, and certain resources. And, as often as not, they were competing with one another to create these zones. For example, the Aghlabids of Tunisia seized Sicily in part to make sure that the Rustamids of Algeria did not get it.

All these developments transformed European and Muslim relations, which had been characterized by violence, distrust, and suffering. When the smoke cleared, Latin Europe and the Islamic world were each profoundly different places than they had been before. In the following sections we will examine how the Christian and Muslim worlds reinvented themselves between the 10th and 13th centuries.

THE REINVENTION OF WESTERN EUROPE

European reinvention followed two main lines of development—in the north via a new network of lords and vassals, bound by feudal bonds, and in the south by the growth of cities, powered by trade. The church, beset by corruption of astonishing proportions, responded with a reform movement of its own that remade the institution and put Christian life on a wholly new trajectory. The combination of these reinventions—social, civic, and spiritual—led directly to some of the greatest achievements of the medieval era. They also paved the way for the Crusades.

Across continental western Europe the decay of the state and the pressure of foreign invasion drove farmers and their families to abandon their scattered homesteads and to take shelter in groups, under the protection of whatever strongman might exist in the district. Having little or nothing else to give in return for protection, they offered their labor. By this simple demographic shift, a society of individual farmers evolved into a new society based on **manors**—collective farms under the authority of lords. The lords owned the land and the major share of its annual yield, although the work was done by dependent farmers called **serfs**. Serfs were not slaves, although their daily lives differed little from slavery; lords could not buy and sell serfs as though they were mere property. Rather, serfs and lords were tied together by complex networks of mutual duties and rights. Serfs could not leave the manor, for example, or marry their offspring to someone from another manor, without their lord's permission. Lords were required to resolve disputes between serfs. The services owed back and forth made medieval manors like miniature communities, like agrarian states unto themselves (see Figure 10.1).

The peasants brought varied backgrounds to their collective work, including knowledge of techniques like crop rotation (planting fields with a different crop

The Manorial Order

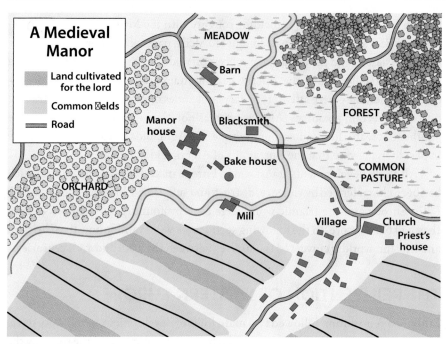

A Medieval Manor   This schematic rendering of a manor illustrates its self-sufficiency as an economic entity.

in each season, so as not to deplete the soil), the use of wheeled plows, and the invention of horseshoes (which allowed quicker and more agile horses to replace lumbering teams of oxen as draught animals). Crop yields nearly doubled as a result. By living and working collectively, sharing labor, skills, and resources, farming on manors became much more productive. Crop surpluses became the norm, and by about 950, the height of what some historians call an "agricultural revolution," western Europe became a food exporter for the first time in its history. It was largely to secure access to this food supply that the rump states of the broken Abbasid Empire began to compete for trading zones along the Mediterranean coast. And this trade allowed the new class of manorial lords to become rich—rich enough eventually to give up wooden manorial houses for stone castles.

But the manorial lords lacked any real political legitimacy. They were, in many cases, of questionable ancestry and social status, men to whom war refugees had fled in desperation. These warlords (the Latin term is *milites*) used a variety of strategies to legitimate themselves. One popular option was simply to invent aristocratic genealogies for themselves, claiming descent from the Carolingians. Another method was to form ties with other *milites*—a medieval equivalent of the modern practice of governments recognizing one another.

The Ties that Bound   In this scene from the Bayeux Tapestry (1067), the earl of Wessex, Harold Godwinson, swears his fealty to Duke William of Normandy.

By securing the support of other *milites* in the region, a warlord acquired at least a veneer of political authenticity.

These relationships between warlords had substance: some forms of military service, counsel, and economic assistance were invariably involved. Since each warlord differed in the amount of land or social recognition he commanded, these relationships slowly took on a hierarchical form, with a senior partner and a subordinate one—hence the terms **lord** and **vassal**, respectively. In forming a tie, a lord bestowed on the vassal dominion over a fief—that is, an allotted manor or manors—and the vassal in turn pledged in a public ceremony to serve the lord loyally. These public rites varied widely across Europe, but evidence suggests that often the lord handed over a clod of earth to symbolize the fief being bestowed. Since the Latin word for "fief" is *feudum*, these relationships came to be generally known as **feudal bonds**.

By about 1000, these connections had spread across much of northern Europe; by 1100 they dominated it. Manors and feudal relations helped create a new society based on land tenure and ties of personal loyalty. Serfs worked for a landlord in return for the security and primitive justice he provided, whereas *milites* were bound to one another as lords and vassals. Again, the system varied from territory to territory. The feudal networks in France, for example, were significantly more elaborate, hierarchical, and complicated than those in Anglo-Saxon England, which had never been part of the Carolingian Empire. When William, duke of Normandy, known to posterity as William the Conqueror (r. 1066–1089), seized the island in 1066 and parceled out the lands to his leading noblemen-vassals, he made it all but impossible for them to redistribute the land to vassals of their own. Germany added its own twist, as great lords created feudal relations with high-ranking churchmen—abbots and bishops. Since these men would presumably not be producing heirs, there was little danger of the feudal lands becoming hereditary holdings. German towns along the Baltic coast also developed a trading network that reached from Denmark to Sweden and northern Russia, a network that developed into a commercial cartel known as the Hanseatic League.

MEDITERRANEAN CITIES

Mediterranean Europe followed a different trajectory. By long-standing custom, social position there had depended less on controlling land than on participating in the public life of the community: merchants, financiers, civic officials, and professionals formed the backbone of southern European life. Urban life had declined during the long centuries of the Dark Ages—some cities had collapsed to the point where they had only one-tenth of the ancient population levels—but revived under the short-lived stability of the Carolingians. Food surpluses from the new manors gradually made their way into urban markets. The Muslim attacks of the 9th and 10th centuries forcibly (and probably unnecessarily) opened those markets to trade with North Africa; cities like Barcelona, Montpellier, Marseilles, Genoa, Pisa, and Venice were the first to establish permanent commercial relations with the Muslim countries, and as a result they witnessed a dramatic rise in their wealth and power (see Map 10.5).

Economic Powerhouses of Europe   The Mediterranean accordingly roared back to life, and from about 1000 to 1400 these cities were the economic powerhouses of Europe.[5] At the same time, the Byzantines' territorial losses to the Abbasids forced them to reorient their military and commercial attention northward into the Slavic Balkan lands and the territories around the Black Sea. As the Greeks gradually relinquished their control of the sea-lanes in the eastern Mediterranean, the Latin cities moved in aggressively. More cities joined in—Amalfi, Naples, Venice—and soon Latin Europe's commercial network, having expanded throughout the Mediterranean, spread around Spain, through the Gulf of Biscay, and into the North Sea. They brought lumber, minerals, wool, and metal ores to the manufacturing

---

5   In 1150, the annual commercial tax revenue from the city of Palermo alone was four times that from the entire kingdom of England.

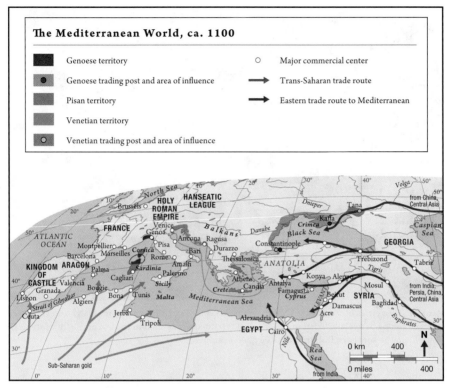

MAP 10.5   The Mediterranean World, ca. 1100   Control of trade routes and access to commercial centers played as great a role as religious rivalries in Mediterranean life.

centers along the coast, transporting eastern silks, spices, metalwork, and dyed cloth back to the west. Developments in ship design led to larger and swifter commercial vessels, capable of delivering larger cargoes at less cost. Meanwhile, the growing use of financial instruments like letters of credit, also known as bills of exchange, reduced the danger of carrying large amounts of cash. By the late 11th century, an embryonic banking industry had already emerged in Italy.

Mediterranean cities quickly became multiethnic emporia, much as they had been during the Pax Romana. A visitor to 12th-century Barcelona or Pisa, for example, would find the streets and markets crowded with merchants from Alexandria, Athens, Brussels, Lisbon, Palermo, and Tunis, as well as a dozen other places—with more than a sprinkling of Jews from all around the Mediterranean. The interaction among groups was regulated by complex systems of municipal and religious laws, ethnic customs, class privileges, and commercial traditions. Merchants of different ethnicities, cities, or social strata each had specific rights and privileges, negotiated with municipal governments. To keep straight who was who, Mediterranean cities began to use dress codes known as sumptuary codes to identify people. These sumptuary codes elaborately

Amalfi   The cities of the western Mediterranean saw a tremendous surge in wealth and vitality, as trade routes between Christian and Muslim territories reopened in the 9th and 10th centuries. Amalfi, on the southern Italian coast, is a good example.

regulated styles of dress, types of fabrics, headgear, footwear, numbers of buttons, and the sorts of decorative badges, pins, and scarves each person could wear. The idea was not to shame groups but to establish the rules of their engagement.

The communicative calculus could be elaborate: a Muslim cloth merchant from Famagusta (in Cyprus), for example, conducting business in Montpellier with a Christian member of the jewelers' guild from Marseilles was entitled to a specific set of legal rights. One had to know whom one was dealing with, or there was no deal. Moreover, since different groups often had different housing and dietary requirements, the custom quickly arose of segregating the cities: merchants from cities that did a lot of business with one another were awarded buildings, streets, or even whole neighborhoods to themselves. There they had special houses, butcher shops, alehouses, and worship sites so that each could live according to their own customs.

Most cities were governed by municipal councils and various administrative executives, usually drawn from the urban elites. This group consisted of local rural aristocrats, well-to-do merchants, the professional classes (bankers and lawyers, chiefly), and representatives of the leading artisanal and commercial guilds (professional associations, similar to modern cartels, that set prices and manufacturing standards within a given town).

THE REINVENTION OF THE CHURCH

The Catholic Church also reinvented itself in the post-Carolingian centuries. It needed reform badly, because many forms of corruption had taken hold by the 9th and 10th centuries, owing to the *milites*, the secular warlords in Latin Europe. Simply put, the warlords, to raise funds for their armies, revived the old Carolingian practice of ransacking their own churches and monasteries. Many simply plundered and ran off with the spoils, but others conceived of a longer-term strategy for tapping into ecclesiastical wealth: they expelled the clerical leaders (often by killing them) and sold the positions to their military and political underlings and supporters. By placing their clients in ecclesiastical positions, the warlords secured a set percentage of the churches' annual revenues. In turn, they rewarded their followers with fancy titles, accoutrements, salaries, and prestige. This abuse, known as **simony**, was rampant, from village churches and small monasteries to large episcopacies and even the papacy. Few religious houses avoided the onslaught.

The chronicles of the 10th and 11th centuries abound with abominable behavior by warlord lackeys in church positions. The nadir was reached in Rome. During a period remembered as the "Pornocracy" (904–984), the papacy was bought and sold numerous times among the leading families in Roman politics. Pope John XII (r. 956–963), who did not himself purchase the papacy but received it from his father, who arranged his election to the office as an eighteenth birthday present, was reported to have sold the bishopric of one town to a ten-year-old boy, as a birthday present from the boy's father.[6] The tradition of state control of the church dated back to the emperor Constantine and the Council of Nicea (discussed in chapter 8). The more recent tyranny of the Carolingians had been stark, but they never abused the church in the same way that the warlords now did. The fundamental reform required was to insist on the churches' freedom from secular control. *Libertas ecclesie!* ("Freedom for the church!") became the demand of the reformers.

The reform movement began at the grassroots level, on the new manors, where the problem of simony was felt most acutely. To the peasants, simony not only looked bad but also created a profound spiritual crisis. The Carolingians,

---

[6] John's favorite mistress, it was said, wore a papal crown, sat on a throne, and turned one wing of the papal palace into a whorehouse. He died in bed with a married woman.

after all, had struggled mightily to promote Christian education and to improve the quality of parish church life. As a result, by the mid- to late 10th century probably a clear majority of western peasants were meaningfully, knowledgeably Christian. And the one teaching they all knew was that they needed the sacraments to achieve salvation, especially baptism.

But does a "priest" who is a simoniac—who got his job only by buying the title from a warlord—actually have sacramental authority? Even if the "priest" does perform a Eucharist, are the bread and wine of that ceremony truly turned into the body and blood of Christ? And if not, is the ceremony of any value at all? If a peasant couple has a sickly infant whom they want to have baptized, is the baby truly baptized if the priest is a simoniac? The question was not theoretical: probably one-half of all children born in Europe at this time died before the age of five. Since Catholic doctrine maintained that only baptized Christians can be saved, the couple's baby would presumably suffer eternal damnation because of the illegitimacy of the priest's action. It gets more complicated, too: What if the priest in question had been properly trained for his vocation, but his ordination to the priesthood had been performed by a simoniac bishop? Or if that bishop's elevation to the episcopacy had been performed by a simoniac archbishop—perhaps by that ten-year-old boy appointed by John XII?

Outraged peasants understood one thing quite well: this problem existed because the *milites* had taken over the churches. Warlords no longer merely controlled the peasants' lives on the manors; their greed for church revenue now placed even the peasants' eternal souls in jeopardy. Demands for freeing the churches from the warlords' clutches therefore began on the manors, where the population could express collective complaint. These rallies for reform, called "Peace of God" assemblies, began as individual demonstrations. However, they multiplied in number, since peasants everywhere had essentially the same complaint and the same sole method of protest available to them. They thus took on the appearance of a movement—indeed, the first mass movement in Western history.

Movements need leadership. That leadership came from Latin Europe's bishops. The reawakening of Europe's cities had revived the episcopacies as well. Although defined as the spiritual descendants of the original twelve apostles, bishops had always been second-tier figures in the Latin Church. When more than 90 percent of the population lived in the countryside, churchmen in cities lacked prestige—especially since hardly any cities in continental Europe were of any real size.[7]

---

[7]   In Charlemagne's time, for example, the city of Paris was only 7.5 acres in area. In comparison, the university campus at which I teach, Boston University, is 75 acres in area.

Monasteries had always been the real centers of power in Latin Christianity, going back to the Benedictine order established in the 6th century. Most of the scholars drawn into the Carolingian court had been monks and abbots, and monastic wealth (when it was not plundered) was the largest accumulated treasure in most districts. As cities grew in size and number, the relative importance of bishops did too. And they seized on the Peace of God assemblies as a means to place themselves at the forefront of church reform. Bishops began to convene regional councils, schedule and organize assemblies, arrange for large-scale public masses, commission speakers, issue calls for specific *milites* to relinquish their strangleholds over their churches, and above all promote themselves as the leaders of church reform. The more success they had in winning their own churches' freedom, the faster they rose in popular estimation.

By the time the reform reached the papacy—the last part of the church to be reformed—the bishops were clearly the dominant power brokers. But as the bishops took center stage, so too did the pope—who was, after all, the bishop of Rome.[8] The second half of the 11th century was filled with diplomatic, rhetorical, and military wrangling between Rome and its rivals. Two issues stood out, among many: lay investiture and papal supremacy. Most political rulers by this time acknowledged (grudgingly, perhaps) that the church should appoint its own priests and bishops, but they wanted to retain their own role in the process by insisting that they, as the leaders of secular society, should invest (that is, formally bestow upon) all clergy with the lands and revenues that came with their offices. Even more important were the differences of opinion regarding the specific authorities and privileges assumed by the new, reformed papacy. What powers did the pope have, need to have, and ought to have? What limits should there be on papal power? This issue was especially important to the Eastern Orthodox churches, most of whose bishops were willing to recognize the pope as a "first among equals" but adamantly refused the notion of a papacy that ruled over all bishops (and by extension over the entire church). Rome's claim to supreme authority over all Christians rankled both the Byzantine emperor and the patriarch at Constantinople.

Half-hearted efforts at reconciliation came to an end in 1054, when the pope, Leo IX (r. 1049–1054), and the patriarch, Michael Cerularius (r. 1043–1059), angrily expelled each other from the church. This mutual excommunication initiated a formal break between the Latin and Orthodox churches that came to be known as the **Great Schism**. As the split between the Christian leadership

The Great Schism

---

[8]   At first, the overwhelming majority of popes came from monastic backgrounds. In the second thousand years of Christianity, more than 90 percent of popes were bishops before rising to the Holy See.

widened, Rome and Constantinople openly competed for the allegiance of new converts in eastern Europe and Russia. Leo spent much of his time as pope on the road, bringing the majesty of the office to the eyes of Europe's commoners for the first time, and his successor, Nicholas II (r. 1059–1061), created the College of Cardinals (cardinals being officially appointed advisors to the Holy See)—which subsequently acquired sole power to elect the next successor to Peter. The pontificates of Leo and Nicholas were, each in its own way, declarations of papal power.

The Gregorian Reform

Pope Gregory VII (r. 1073–1085), however, was the staunchest advocate of the primacy of the pope as the leader of all Christian peoples, so much so that the entire reform movement is commonly referred to as the **Gregorian Reform**. Within the church, Gregory campaigned to improve the moral and educational caliber of the clergy by holding the priesthood to high standards of competence and also—especially in matters of sexual behavior—to stringent standards of conduct. He also demanded strict conformity to the standard religious services authorized by the church hierarchy and the use of Latin as the universal language of Christianity. Thus, under Gregory VII, the movements for clerical reform and centralization of authority within the church merged.

Gregory demanded an end to **lay investiture**—the selection and appointment of church officials by secular authority—and secular control over church lands. In a deliberately public disagreement with the German emperor Henry IV (r. 1056–1106), Gregory challenged the emperor's authority to appoint bishops within his domains. The struggle for control of the church pitted the most powerful secular and sacred rulers of Christendom against each other. Gregory invalidated Henry's right to rule over his territories and encouraged the emperor's enemies among the German princes to rise against him. As rebel forces gathered, Henry was forced to prostrate himself before the pope and beg forgiveness.

The Investiture Conflict   Holy Roman Emperor Henry IV, facing rebellion from his nobles, pleads with Countess Matilda of Tuscany to help persuade Pope Gregory VII to end the conflict. Matilda dominated northern Italy at this time, and so long as she supported Gregory (which she did), Henry's troops could not advance to put pressure on the pope to relent. This image appears in an 11th-century manuscript of *The Life of Matilda, Countess of Tuscany.*

This was the tipping point in what has come to be known as the investiture conflict, and all sides recognized a need to find a compromise. In 1122 it was reached: the **Concordat of Worms**, signed in that year, reconfirmed the church's right to appoint its own clergy, but the secular rulers retained the right to bestow all the lands and revenues associated with those appointments. The great reform, everyone hoped, was finished.

THE REINVENTION OF THE ISLAMIC WORLD

From the 9th century onward, the political history of the Islamic world was exceptionally turbulent and complicated. The western rump states went through numerous shifts in dynastic rule (usually violently), oscillated between conservative and liberal efforts to reform their societies, and constantly redefined their relations with Latin Europe. In the central zone of the Near East, the arrival of yet another Asiatic group—the Seljuk Turks—in the early 11th century set off a chain reaction of wars, rebellions, and coups that destabilized the region just at the time when trade relations with Christian Europe were reopening. Farther to the east, a powerful resurgence of Turkic and Persian cultures brought enormous and lasting changes to the caliphate.

The westernmost Islamic states, from Spain to Libya, were centers of manufacture. Ceramics, textiles, glassware, and metalwork were the dominant industries, after agriculture. The ethnic Arabs who monopolized the political and military commands disdained agriculture; slaves performed much of the labor, along with most of the menial tasks in urban life. Sub-Saharan black Africans, acquired by Moroccan traders working down the coast, made up much of the slave population. Tax records from the city of Cordoba attest to eight thousand black slaves in that city alone in the early 11th century. Apart from the great cosmopolitan city of Cordoba—the home of the Great Mosque and a palace library filled with more than 400,000 volumes—the western states of Spain and across North Africa were not renowned as centers of intellectual life.[9] In the 9th and 10th centuries the rulers remained focused on spreading the faith among their subjects. Islam became the majority religion across North Africa by the early 11th century, which coincided with the rise of new dynasties made up of ethnic Berbers, who regarded the long Arab monopoly as a failed enterprise. These new dynasties—in Morocco, Algeria, Tunisia, and Libya (then called Tripolitania and

Western States

---

[9] One notable exception was the brilliant Andalusian philosopher Ibn Rushd (1126–1198, better known in the West as Averroës). In his lifetime, however, Ibn Rushd was widely regarded with suspicion for his eager embrace of Aristotelian rationalism. He was constantly driven from court to court, city to city, by those opposed to his openness to non-Islamic tradition.

Cyrenaica)—were frequently characterized by martial jihadist campaigns to "purify" society of elements not sufficiently Islamic. Popular attitudes to resident Christians and Jews hardened noticeably.

Islamic Heartland

In the Near Eastern heartland the contest between established Arab leaders and the newly converted Turks provided the chief political narrative (see again Map 10.4). This was by far the most ethnically, linguistically, and religiously diverse region in the Islamic world: Arabs, Syrians, Persians, Turks, Kurds, Berbers, Copts, Jews, Armenians, and a dozen others were all on the scene, representing every Islamic, Christian, and Jewish sect. Although technically part of the Abbasid caliphate, most of the Holy Land region in the 10th and 11th centuries consisted of a sprawl of independent principalities. Clashes across ethnic and religious lines were common, but the region retained its commercial vitality as the linchpin between the Mediterranean and the Silk Road economies, with Jerusalem and Damascus the most important cities. Industry, commerce, and finance—all urban phenomena—were the most important elements in the economy, and each group in each community carefully guarded its traditional rights and privileges. Schools and libraries were numerous but chiefly sectarian. Most of the population managed a stable way of life, although trouble usually arose when local dynasties changed, which provided opportunities for extremist groups in all sects to flex their muscles and carve out areas of dominion for themselves.

The eastern realm of Islam centered on the capital of Baghdad but reached all the way to India. So vast an area was difficult to administer, and so challenges to Abbasid rule were constant—which led the Abbasids to turn to the Asiatic Turks as military allies just as they had earlier turned to the Persians. The Abbasids carefully promoted and paid honor to the cultural traditions of their allies. They embraced the spread of the Persian and Turkish languages; they employed Persian and Turkish elements in their architecture and pictorial arts; and they encouraged Persian and Turkish literary and scientific traditions. Perhaps most significantly, they aided the spread of the spiritual tradition of **Sufism**, a mystical form of Islam that emphasizes personal experience of the divine over obedience to the Qur'an and Islamic law. This was the most culturally "open" territory in the Islamic world, but it is worth noting that this openness resulted as much from political pragmatism as from a generosity of spirit. The flowering of intellectual life and artistic culture centered on Baghdad was the glory of the age, until it came to a fiery end when the Mongols demolished the city in 1258, slaughtering more than 300,000 people in twelve days and burning hundreds of libraries, temples, hospitals, palaces, and art collections in the process.

THE CALL FOR CRUSADES

Between 1096 and 1291 Latin Europe undertook a series of large-scale military campaigns to win back the Holy Land, which had been under Muslim control since 639. Numerous small-scale efforts continued after that but amounted to little. Nonetheless, the Crusades changed societies and regimes throughout the Mediterranean.

The Crusades are unique in European history because they are the only wars that were formally sanctioned and blessed by the church. To take part in them was considered not only morally justifiable but also a positive spiritual action. These wars, the church proclaimed, pleased God and made one a better Christian—to the point that if a soldier died on a crusade, he was assured forgiveness of all his sins and eternal salvation (assuming that he had had a penitent heart and pure motives). The church called for crusades, preached them from the pulpit, formally inducted their leading fighters, and arranged their financing. As enthusiasm for crusades to the Holy Land waned in the 13th century, the Crusades' mechanisms of preaching and finance were brought to bear on conflicts elsewhere in Europe.

Although a new phenomenon, the Crusades were nevertheless a product of the centuries that had preceded them. If one disregards the religious motive that lay behind them, the Crusades appear as simply another chapter in the centuries-old struggle for control of the eastern Mediterranean shorelands. These lands offered access to both the European economy, centered on the sea, and the overland Asian economy composed of the great silk and spice routes. Its geographical location made the Holy Land valuable long before it became holy. The Phoenicians and the Hittites had fought over it. So had the Egyptians and the so-called Sea Peoples, the Hebrews and the Canaanites, and the Persians and the Greeks. The Romans came next, then the Persians again, the Byzantines after that, and then finally the Arabs under Muhammad. And the litany of conflicts continued after the Crusades ended. In short, the Crusades had a larger context of Greater Western struggles that involved many more factors than religion alone. Yet the religious factor is what makes the Crusades unique. To find ways to justify warfare is one thing, but how did the Latin West ever develop the idea that Jesus wanted his followers to kill Muslims?

Part of the answer lies in the great Gregorian Reform effort, in which intellectual reform was as important as institutional renewal. At the many councils *The* convened during the 10th and 11th centuries, the church debated, among many *Christian* other things, the theology of warfare. Under what conditions, if any, may a Chris- *Explanation* tian legitimately use physical violence? Jesus had preached "Blessed are the peacemakers" and had accepted his own torture and death, but did that necessarily imply that Christians must never use any kind of force? Did the bravery of the martyrs of the first Christian centuries require all Christians to forego self-defense when attacked? If one sees a criminal brutally assaulting a woman, is one committing an un-Christian act by beating him into submission?

Such questions were not hypothetical. Latin Europe was overwhelmingly Christian by the late 11th century, but it was also a society organized for warfare—a secular hierarchy of warlords in the north and an aggregation of maritime cities, each with its own militia, in the south. The reformed church needed to find ways to manage and restrain conflicts. One method it employed was the Truce of God, a solemn ban on warfare on holy days and on assaulting pilgrims. Those who violated the Truce were excommunicated. Christian warfare was acceptable, the church decreed, only if it met three criteria: it must have a just cause, it must be fought in a just way, and it must be declared by a just authority.

By 1096, many Europeans believed that warfare against Islam was indeed a just cause. After enduring centuries of persecution under the Romans, Christians in the Holy Land, across North Africa, and throughout the Mediterranean faced conquest by the followers of Muhammad. In creating the great Islamic Empire, after all, Muslim armies had killed hundreds of thousands of Christians and Jews. Under the early caliphs there had been a concerted effort to protect the empire's dhimmis, but as the years went by and Muslims gradually became the majority group within the overall population, hostilities toward Christians and Jews increased. As Islamic unity then shattered into a maze of ethnic, sectarian, and dynastic rivalries, popular willingness to tolerate the non-Muslims in their midst only declined. The 10th and 11th centuries saw repeated popular attacks on Christians and Jews and sporadic state-run persecutions.

The popularity of pilgrimage as a Christian devotion complicated matters further. For centuries waves of pilgrims had ventured from Europe to the Holy Land—with Muslim blessing—to worship at the sites associated with Christ. Pilgrimage, however, is by its very nature a public display of faith and therefore at odds with dhimmi law. Muslim ire focused on the European pilgrims traveling through their lands, less so on their own Christian subjects, and those pilgrims began to experience bitter street-level harassment and violence. Soon enough, however, intolerance of the dhimmis themselves took root in many places. Islamic reform groups like the Almohads and Almoravids in Spain and North Africa made no secret of their determination to crush the Christians and Jews living among them. In 1009 the Egyptian ruler al-Hakim (r. 996–1021) demolished the Church of the Holy Sepulcher in Jerusalem (the church built over what is believed to have been Jesus's actual tomb) and ordered every church and synagogue in his realm similarly destroyed. Christians across Europe were horrified but not altogether surprised. To take up arms against such attacks therefore seemed to satisfy the requirement of a just cause.

Church of the Holy Sepulcher   What the crusaders were after: the tomb of Christ at the Church of the Holy Sepulcher in Jerusalem. The present chapel structure was built in the 13th century. Earlier buildings were damaged or destroyed by various attackers, the most notable being the Egyptian caliph al-Hakim in the early 11th century.

But it was the Seljuk Turks whose arrival near the holy sites in the 1060s and 1070s did the most to interrupt the passage of pilgrims. The Abbasids had long courted the Turks, whose military might was considerable, and hoped to use them against Shi'i princes in Syria, Palestine, and Egypt who refused to obey Baghdad. The Turks were new to Islam and burned with the zeal often found among recent converts. With the caliphs' blessing they marched westward, defeated the Byzantine army at Manzikert in 1071, and spread throughout Anatolia, setting up an independent state. But many of the nomadic warriors refused to settle down and raided the Arab-led states to their south. The threat to the splinter states inspired them to crack down on their dhimmis in a show of force. The age demanded an expression of rigorous jihad, and it got it.

THE CRUSADES

There were eight major crusades, and all except the First Crusade ended in failure. The soldiers of the first campaign conquered the Holy Land in 1099 and carved four separate states out of it (see Map 10.6). These became nominally Christian

MAP 10.6   The Crusades   The First and Second Crusades took the land route from western Europe to the Holy Land, since the difficult pilgrimage was intrinsic to the religious zeal that drove the campaigns. The Third Crusade used a combined land and sea approach. All crusades to the Holy Land thereafter were exclusively maritime affairs.

states, although the overwhelming bulk of their populations were Muslims, Jews, and non-Latin Christians.

Despite their violent creation, however, the states quickly developed internal policies that granted as much autonomy as possible to the native groups. The crusaders turned into surprisingly lenient rulers, as evidenced by the contemporary chronicler Ibn al-Athir's (1160–1233) claim that thousands of Muslims and Jews migrated to the crusader states because they found life under the crusaders' rule preferable to life under the warring Arab and Turkish warlords. (It was for this claim, presumably, that the terrorist group ISIS desecrated al-Athir's tomb in Mosul, Syria, in June 2014.) Christian trade with Muslims continued in the Mediterranean cities throughout the Crusades—and in fact increased steadily. Muslim sources of the age never present the struggles for the Holy Land in religious terms, and the Christian conquest of Jerusalem in 1099 triggered no groundswell of outrage outside of Palestine itself. For two centuries, outraged resistance to the crusaders' control of the Holy Land was found only in the immediate area; contemporary evidence suggests that the Islamic world as a whole was more concerned with the arrival of the Turks (11th–12th centuries) and the approach of the Mongols (12th–13th centuries).

No kings were involved in the First Crusade (1096–1099), which may be one reason why it alone was an unqualified success. Led by a handful of French and Flemish *The* noblemen, the crusaders marched to Constantinople, where the wary Byzantines gave *Course* them fresh supplies and urged them to head as quickly as possible to Anatolia. Turkish *of the* cavalry harassed them repeatedly for months, picking off thousands of soldiers while *Crusades* avoiding pitched battle, until the crusaders made it to Antioch, where they regrouped before their further push southward. Finally in 1099, after they had been on the way for three years, they reached Jerusalem, which they took after a month-long siege.

The Second Crusade (1147–1149) came two generations later, when King Louis VII of France, determined to stop local incursions against the crusader-held territories, led a disastrous campaign that ended with his failed siege of Damascus, after which he led his troops home in shame. The Third Crusade (1189–1193) was perhaps the most dramatic. It was led by King Richard the Lionheart of England (r. 1189–1199), King Philip Augustus of France (r. 1180–1223), and Emperor Frederick Barbarossa of Germany (r. 1155–1190). Their opponent was Salah ad-Din (better known in the west as Saladin), the ethnically Kurdish sultan of Egypt and Syria (r. 1174–1193) and founder of the Islamic Ayyubid dynasty. The bulk of the fighting consisted of grueling face-to-face battles. Finally the two sides struck a deal that gave the Muslims control of Jerusalem but guaranteed Christians and Jews the right to visit the city.

That truce unfortunately vanished only a few months after the crusade's end, when Saladin unexpectedly died. Only one of the subsequent crusades ever made it to the Holy Land. The Fourth Crusade (1202–1204) got diverted to

The Siege of Antioch   William of Tyre's *Histoire d'Outremer* ("History of Events across the Sea") is one of our best sources for the first two crusades and the internal life of the crusader states between wars. Here the 1098 siege of Antioch—the most strategically important battle of the First Crusade—is depicted. After taking Antioch, the crusaders had a regional base that could be resupplied by sea.

Constantinople (which the crusaders seized and held for the next seventy years). The Fifth (1217–1221), Seventh (1248–1254), and Eighth (1270) crusades all focused on Egypt and North Africa. Only the Sixth Crusade (1228–1229), led by the joint Sicilian king and German emperor Frederick II (r. 1220–1250), produced a qualified success when Frederick managed to negotiate the surrender of Ayyubid control over the Holy Land.

A separate and special case of the crusades was the Spanish Reconquista (711–1492). The Muslim armies that seized Spain in 711 retained control of about 80 percent of the peninsula. The northernmost tier remained in Christian hands, although this territory were divided among a half-dozen different royal families. Muslims' treatment of their Christian subjects initially was harsh but generally followed the strictures established for dhimmi communities. By the late 10th century, however, as the majority of the population became Muslim, patience with the Christian minority ran out and open persecution, though still intermittent, became increasingly common, which led the northern territories to begin attempts to regain control of the peninsula—which they finally accomplished in 1492. The Reconquest was not a continuous victory march southward, however. The border between Christian Spain and Muslim Spain fluctuated considerably, and individual territories were conquered, lost, reconquered, and lost yet again numerous times. Only some of the campaigns were technically crusades, recognized and supported by the church; most were undertaken, and regarded, as local efforts to extend royal prerogatives.

The Impact of the Crusades   Although a largely failed enterprise, the Crusades had a lasting impact on the Greater Western societies. Europe's kings henceforth showed renewed interest in controlling the churches within their realms; the Mediterranean states, having benefited from transporting and supplying the crusading armies and Christian outposts in the Holy Land, now commanded the sea-lanes throughout the entire basin. Medieval literature explored new settings and techniques after exposure to Islamic traditions. The "framed-narrative" technique in the wildly popular *Tales* *of the Arabian Nights* (in which a series of individual stories are linked by an overarching single story) provided the model for European works like *The Decameron* of Giovanni Boccaccio and *The Canterbury Tales* of Geoffrey Chaucer. And the complexity of financing the Crusades inspired advances in banking techniques across Europe.

Caught between crusaders from the west and Turks from the east, the Byzantines survived by playing one side off the other. They no longer had the military might to assert themselves and became adept at diplomatic manipulation, acquiring for themselves a reputation for trickery and unreliability. The crusaders came to despise the Byzantines as much as the Muslims, which explains the wild violence unleashed when the soldiers of the Fourth Crusade (1202–1204) sacked Constantinople.

TURKISH POWER AND BYZANTINE DECLINE

The crusader era witnessed dramatic change in the Middle East. First, the arrival of the Turks upset and ultimately overthrew the Arab rulers of the Middle East. In their place, the Turks created an independent state in Anatolia, called the Sultanate of Rum, and a second Turkish-dominated state in a reunited Egypt and Syria, called the Mamluk Empire (see Map 10.7). The Mamluks (Arabic for "slave") originated as an elite bodyguard unit for the Abbasid caliphs. Their name derives from the Turkish practice of kidnapping and enslaving Christian children throughout the Middle East, forcibly converting them to Islam, and putting them through an extraordinary military discipline and training. These slave-soldiers were thus culturally Turkish (by forced adoption) and were independent of the tribal loyalties of the regular Muslim armies.

Nominally subject to the caliphs in Baghdad, the Mamluk Empire and the Sultanate of Rum comprised the center of Islamic power. In 1258 Abbasid power disappeared entirely when the Mongols destroyed Baghdad; the Mongols' own self-proclaimed drive for world domination ended when they were decisively defeated themselves by the Mamluks only two years later. Turkish hegemony over the Islamic world would last in one form or another until the early 20th century.

In the second major shift that the Middle East experienced during the crusader era, the Byzantine Empire effectively ceased to exist as a world power. After the crusaders wrecked Constantinople in 1204, they held on to the empire for more than seventy years, parceling it out to themselves as fiefdoms. For three generations the usurpers plundered Byzantium and all its holdings, determined to crush the Orthodox Church and replace it with Roman Catholicism. By the time they were driven out, in 1278, the empire was in tatters and lived on only as a weak confederation of four minor states. Through diplomatic maneuvers, it managed to

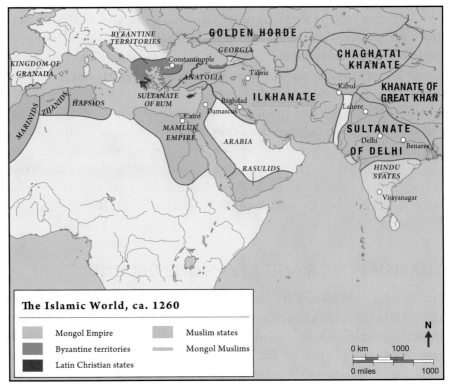

MAP 10.7   The Islamic World, ca. 1260   The Mongol conquest of Baghdad in 1258 was the greatest single military disaster ever visited on the Islamic world. More Muslims were killed in the Mongol advance than were killed in all of the Crusades combined.

survive until its final defeat by the Ottoman Turks in 1453, but for much of its last two centuries the Byzantine Empire consisted of little more than the city of Constantinople itself.

JUDAISM REFORMED, RENEWED, AND REVILED

Scattered by the Romans in 70 CE, the Jews of the Diaspora were left stateless, exiled from their homeland, hounded by Christian evangelists, and still subject to persecution by the Romans. Yet the Jews survived—by adapting imaginatively to the societies where they lived while holding to the core of their traditions. As a Mediterranean people, they had dispersed, predictably enough, around the sea basin (see Map 10.8). In most places local laws forbade them to own farmland, and hence the Jews of the Diaspora became even more heavily urbanized than they had been before. Life in cities, moreover, offered them a measure of safety, since they tended to live as discrete communities.

MAP 10.8 Principal Centers of Jewish Settlement in the Mediterranean, ca. 1250 By the 13th century Jewish life was more urbanized than ever before.

In their own designated neighborhoods, they could have at least limited security and autonomy.

The class and sectarian rifts that had characterized life in Judea in Christ's time ceased to have meaning. They were all exiles now, and the Temple was no more. The rabbinical strain of Judaism that traced its roots to the Babylonian Captivity hence became the norm for Jewish life. In city after city, Jews established their synagogues and schools, their butcher shops and eateries, and settled into lives as merchants and professionals.

As during their first exile in Babylon, the Jews quickly found that life as a religious minority presented challenges not addressed in the Torah. How does one live a Jewish life in a non-Jewish world? The rabbis set to work gathering, sifting, organizing, and commenting on the decisions handed down by earlier religious judges. At the same time, new judgments were being rendered from one end of the Mediterranean to the other. These judgments and the precedents on which they rested were studied at the great rabbinical academies and eventually codified in the **Talmud**. It had two parts—the *Mishnah* (the collected rabbinical laws, compiled around 200) and the *Gemara* (commentaries on the laws compiled around 500). Together, they formed the central pillar of medieval Jewish life. There were competing versions—one produced by scholars in Babylon (where the rabbinical tradition dated to the 6th century BCE) and another in Jerusalem.[10] Although both are considered valid, when the word *Talmud* is used, it generally refers to the Babylonian version.

Throughout the Middle Ages, most rabbis in Europe received their training at the academies in the Levant, either in Jerusalem or in Baghdad. An important new chapter of Jewish history began with the Carolingian collapse in the late 9th century, however. A number of late Carolingian princes, hoping to ignite some local manufacturing and commercial activity, invited Jewish communities to relocate from the Mediterranean and to settle permanently in northern Europe. They offered various enticements—legal autonomy under Carolingian protection, advantageous tax schedules, housing allowances, and so on. Once such guarantees were in place, scores of Jewish families, companies, and social networks migrated to the north and settled in the small towns that dotted the Rhine River valley and along the Seine.

For example, in 1084, shortly after arranging the legal founding of Speyer as a municipality, its lord, Bishop Rudiger, issued the following charter:

> In the name of the Holy and Indivisible Trinity, I, Rudiger, by the grace of God bishop of Speyer, having completed the task of establishing Speyer as a legally recognized city, determined to increase the city's honor a thousand-fold by bringing a community of Jews to live permanently within it; and so I invited in Jews from abroad and from Jewish communities in other towns. Moreover, I enclosed them within a fortified wall, lest they be too easily harmed by the rioting common people. . . . I gave them license and privilege to work at money changing according to their desire . . . and I bestowed upon them, from the Church's holdings, a burial ground for their own possession and use. . . . As much as I am the ruler of Speyer's [Christian] residents, so is the archisynagogos [rabbi] for the Jews [therein]: he has power to judge all disputes and petitions brought before him. . . . In general, I have granted to the Jews of Speyer—as a crowning grace to my benevolence—statutes of such benefit to them as to be unequalled anywhere in Germany.

As decades passed, these small communities prospered and grew.

---

[10] Although called the Jerusalem Talmud, it was actually compiled by scholars in and around the city of Tiberias, along the western shore of the Sea of Galilee.

Jewish Synagogue and Christian Church   During the centuries-long Christian reconquest of Spain from Muslim control, many towns and villages changed hands numerous times. Mosques were turned into churches, then back into mosques, then again into churches, over and over. Synagogues were also built, taken over, handed back, and reclaimed for another repeatedly. This 13th-century building in Toledo, in central Spain, was a mosque that was eventually converted into the church of Santa Maria la Blanca. Skilled craftsmen of all faiths found work in the near-constant renovation. In a handful of Christian churches in Spain, the vine-tracery patterns carved on arches by Muslim stonemasons turn into Arabic lettering and spell out the creed: "There is no God but Allah, and Muhammad is his Prophet."

Although they remained in contact with the Mediterranean communities, northern Jews soon began to follow a different path of development from *Different* southern Jews. These different paths ultimately resulted in the formation of *Paths of* two distinct Jewish cultural traditions—that of the Ashkenazim in the north *Development* and the Sephardim in the south. The Ashkenazim were the most geographically remote from their homeland, surrounded by hostile Christians who rejected the late Carolingians' courting of Jews. They therefore turned inward, developing a brilliant conservative culture that focused on preserving Talmudic tradition at all cost. The Sephardim, comfortably Mediterranean, were in constant contact with Arab, Greek, and Latin cultural developments, and they participated more directly in intellectual exchange and changes in cultural norms. The stark contrast between Ashkenazic and Sephardic Judaism became apparent when groups from both traditions migrated back to the Holy Land when it was under crusader control. They wore different styles of clothing, followed different liturgies and rituals, and spoke different vernaculars.[11] Providing separate synagogues, butcher shops, markets, and housing for both communities challenged the ingenuity of the crusader-state regimes and led to near-constant low-grade social friction.

North or south, east or west, medieval Jews lived in their separate districts in the cities. And these districts were frequently encircled by protective walls both to mark the territory of Jewish autonomy and to protect the Jews from angry Christian mobs. (The local rabbi possessed the key to the gate.) The church insisted that the only proper Christian response to the Jews was tolerance and coexistence—and that it was the church's special responsibility to protect the Jews. As Pope Innocent III (r. 1198–1216) put it in 1199,

> No Christian may use violence in order to force a Jew to receive baptism . . . for no one who has not willingly sought baptism can be a true Christian. Therefore let no Christian do a Jew any personal injury—except in the case of carrying out the just sentence of a judge—or deprive him of his property, or transgress the rights and privileges traditionally awarded to them. Let no one disturb the celebration of their festivals by beating them with clubs and hurling stones at them; let no one force from them any services which they are not traditionally bound to render; and we expressly forbid anyone . . . to deface or violate their cemeteries or to extort money from them by threatening to do so.

But a declaration like this is usually a tacit recognition that such crimes did occur—which they did, frequently. Popular violence against Jews was a constant element of medieval life. Almost without exception, a papal call for a crusade to the Holy Land triggered a popular uprising against the Jews. Most infamously, in 1096 rabid crowds murdered hundreds of Jews in the German cities of Cologne, Mainz, and Worms. In the aftermath of these slaughters, the church took measures to prevent anti-Jewish violence whenever it summoned a crusade, but those measures usually failed. Official forms of persecution existed too. In the French city of Toulouse, for example, a representative of the Jewish community was required to stand on the steps of the Christian cathedral every year on Good Friday and be publicly slapped in the face by the bishop.

Despite the harsh circumstances confronting them, the Jews of the 9th to 13th centuries flourished. Their communities benefited from the economic

---

[11] The southerners spoke early forms of Ladino, related to Old Spanish. The northerners spoke early forms of Yiddish.

growth of the era, which they had helped to produce. Their synagogues and schools brimmed with life, and many Jews played important roles in Christian society as advisors, teachers, translators, and intermediaries. Two of the greatest Jewish thinkers of all time emerged at this time too: Rashi (1040–1105) and Maimonides (1135–1204). Rashi, an Ashkenazic Jew, lived in northern France and is regarded as the supreme commentator on the Torah. To the present day, printed editions of the Talmud include Rashi's line-by-line commentary on each page. Rashi's commentaries on the Hebrew Bible were important not only to Jewish scholars but also to certain Christian ones, since his mastery of biblical Hebrew clarified hundreds of passages that had frustrated textual scholars for centuries. Later Franciscan commentators like Nicholas of Myra had a special affinity for his writings. Maimonides, by contrast, was Sephardic, having grown up in Seville. The arrival in Spain of the Almohads, one of the brutal Sunni reformist sects, made life there untenable, so Maimonides traveled throughout the Mediterranean. He settled at last in Cairo, where he worked as a physician during the day and spent his nights writing legal texts, medical treatises, biblical commentaries, and philosophy. His two major works were the *Mishneh Torah*—an enormous compilation of Jewish law, with commentary— and the *Guide for the Perplexed*, a brilliant but difficult analysis of the relationship between reason and faith.

◆

These centuries witnessed the cultural maturation of Christian Europe and the Islamic Near East as the two faiths developed most of the institutions, traditions, and value systems that would characterize them into the modern age. In each case, that maturation emerged from the complex interplay of religion, ethnic and social customs, and the intellectual legacies of the ancient world. Jewish ideas and values developed as well, coalescing into the dominant strains that carried Jewish life into the early modern era.

WHO, WHAT, WHERE

Boniface	feudal bonds	serfs
Carolingian	Great Schism	simony
Renaissance	Gregorian Reform	Sufism
Charlemagne	lay investiture	Talmud
Charles Martel	lord	Treaty of Verdun
Concordat of Worms	manors	vassal

SUGGESTED READINGS

Primary Sources

al-Baladhuri. *The Origins of the Islamic State.*

Benjamin of Tudela. *Itinerary.*

Einhard. *The Life of Charlemagne.*

Ibn al-Athir. *The Universal History.*

Ibn al-Haytham. *The Advent of the Fatimids.*

Maimonides. *The Guide for the Perplexed.*

Rashi. *Commentary on the Torah.*

al-Tabari. *The History of al-Tabari.*

Theophanes. *The Chronicle of Theophanes the Confessor.*

Anthologies

Allen, S. J., and Emilie Amt, eds. *The Crusades: A Reader* (2003).

Constable, Olivia Remie, ed. *Medieval Iberia: Readings from Muslim, Christian, and Jewish Sources* (2011).

Dutton, Paul Edward, ed. *Carolingian Civilization: A Reader* (2004).

Lopez, Robert S., and Irving W. Raymond, trans. *Medieval Trade in the Mediterranean World: Illustrative Documents* (2001).

Shinners, John, ed. *Medieval Popular Religion, 1000–1500: A Reader* (2006).

Studies

Bachrach, Bernard S. *Early Carolingian Warfare: Prelude to Empire* (2000).

Beckwith, Christopher I. *Empires of the Silk Road: A History of Central Eurasia from the Bronze Age to the Present* (2009).

Chazan, Robert. *God, Humanity, and History: The Hebrew First Crusade Narratives* (2000).

Chazan, Robert. *The Jews of Medieval Western Christendom: 1000–1500* (2007).

Christie, Niall. *Muslims and Crusaders: Christianity's War in the Middle East, 1096–1382, from the Islamic Sources* (2014).

Constable, Olivia Remie. *Housing the Stranger in the Mediterranean World: Lodging, Trade, and Travel in Late Antiquity and the Middle Ages* (2003).

Cook, Michael. *Commanding Right and Forbidding Wrong in Islamic Thought* (2007).

Crone, Patricia. *Meccan Trade and the Rise of Islam* (2004).

Crone, Patricia, and Martin Hinds. *God's Caliph: Religious Authority in the First Centuries of Islam* (2003).

Davidson, Herbert A. *Moses Maimonides: The Man and His Works* (2004).

Friedmann, Yohanan. *Tolerance and Coercion in Islam: Interfaith Relations in the Muslim Tradition* (2003).

Griffith, Sidney H. *The Church in the Shadow of the Mosque: Christians and Muslims in the World of Islam* (2008).

Heather, Peter. *Empires and Barbarians: Migration, Development, and the Birth of Europe* (2009).

Hillenbrand, Carole. *The Crusades: Islamic Perspectives* (2008).

Jotischky, Andrew. *Crusading and the Crusader States* (2004).

Kennedy, Hugh. *The Prophet and the Age of the Caliphates: The Islamic Near East from the Sixth to the Eleventh Century* (2004).

Khamis, Ulrike al-. *Early Capitals of Islamic Culture: The Art and Culture of Umayyad Damascus and Abbasid Baghdad, 650–950* (2014).

McCormick, Michael. *Origins of the European Economy: Communications and Commerce, AD 300–900* (2002).

Moore, R. I. *The First European Revolution, c. 970–1215* (2000).

Peri, 'Oded. *Christianity under Islam in Jerusalem: The Question of the Holy Sites in Early Ottoman Times* (2001).

Ray, Jonathan. *The Sephardic Frontier: The Reconquista and the Jewish Community in Medieval Iberia* (2008).

Tolan, John V. *Saracens: Islam in the Medieval European Imagination* (2002).

Tyerman, Christopher. *God's War: A New History of the Crusades* (2009).

Wickham, Chris. *Framing the Early Middle Ages: Europe and the Mediterranean, 400–800* (2007).

Wickham, Chris. *The Inheritance of Rome: Illuminating the Dark Ages, 400–1000* (2009).

For additional resources, including maps, primary sources, visuals, web links, and quizzes, please go to **www.oup.com/us/backman.**

CHAPTER 11

Worlds Brought Down

1258–1453

The 13th and 14th centuries were an age of unparalleled achievement and trauma. The earliest signs of a recognizably modern European world appeared—parliamentary government, an embryonic form of capitalism, universities, the emerging primacy of science, and the spread of literacy and vernacular culture. Modern technologies like mechanical clocks, eyeglasses, magnetic compasses, and paper mills came into use. So too, however, did violent practices like the inquisition against heretics and the persecution of Jews. The Catholic Church assumed the basic institutional form it has today, but it also witnessed an extraordinary wave of popular mysticism and lay evangelism. Some even feared that lay revelation would displace the Church as the mediator between God and man. Interest in science surged, in the confident belief that the cosmos was a rational structure whose deepest secrets could be discovered. At the same time, the greatest scientific mind of the age, English friar and scholar Roger Bacon, warned that the Antichrist, fast approaching, would appear

THE GREATER WEST, 1453

A World Turned Upside Down
Pictured here is the battle of Crécy (1346), the first great battle in the Hundred Years' War. The English are on the left, with infantry longbowmen shown—inaccurately—in the front lines. Confronting them are the mounted knights of France. Much bloodshed ensued, ending in a surprise English victory. Similar slaughter occurred at Poitiers (1356) and Agincourt (1415), although the war ended, in 1453, with the French victorious.

in the guise of a scientist. Economically, Europe finally overtook the Islamic world in wealth and ingenuity, yet its very success carried within it the seeds of catastrophe. It also contributed to a growing willingness of society to ignore the teachings of the Church.

The Islamic world similarly shone, even as it split permanently into distinct civilizations. The Mongols brought the caliphate to a sudden and savage end, but their equally swift withdrawal from the scene opened the door to new Muslim conquests, eastward into India and across the Red Sea into sub-Saharan Africa. Two new powerful Islamic states emerged—the Mamluks in Egypt and Palestine and the Ottoman Turks in Anatolia and Syria. Sectarian differences continued, but the urgency of the conflicts between them abated. However, the Sufi movement, which the advance of the Turks westward had accelerated, remained a challenge for Islamic society. The Ottomans' sack of Constantinople in 1453 put an end to the long-exhausted Byzantine Empire, and their subsequent advance into southeastern Europe brought the entire Greater West into a new alignment, with the Turkish superstate now serving as a bridge between Christian Europe and the Middle East.

It is important to consider these two centuries together because the ways in which societies responded to the shared horrors of the 14th century—a perfect trifecta of famine, war, and plague—were largely shaped by what had happened in the 13th.

CHAPTER TIMELINE

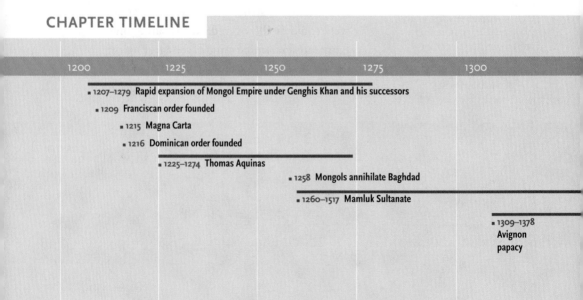

1200	1225	1250	1275	1300

- 1207–1279 Rapid expansion of Mongol Empire under Genghis Khan and his successors
- 1209 Franciscan order founded
- 1215 Magna Carta
- 1216 Dominican order founded
- 1225–1274 Thomas Aquinas
- 1258 Mongols annihilate Baghdad
- 1260–1517 Mamluk Sultanate
- 1309–1378 Avignon papacy

LATE MEDIEVAL EUROPE

Latin Europe's history had been shaped by two opposing waves of development. The dual economic and cultural engine of the Mediterranean region spread its influence northward, bringing elements of cosmopolitan urban life, intellectual innovation, and cultural vibrancy into the European heartlands. Political leadership, however, came from the north, as the monarchies of England and France and the Holy Roman Empire pushed their boundaries southward, drawn by Mediterranean commerce and the gravitational pull of the papal court. The cross-fertilization of north and south benefited each and fostered Europe's ability to reform and revitalize itself. In the Muslim world, by contrast, innovation came largely from outside, in the dominance of Islamicized foreign rulers—the Ottoman Turks and their ethnic cousins, the Mongols and Tartars.

Feudal England, France, and the Holy Roman Empire were the leading powers of the age. Their kings and princes dominated the political scene, and their soldiers provided the overwhelming bulk of the crusaders. From the 11th to 13th centuries, they continually extended their power southward to reach the Mediterranean. The Holy Roman emperors had claimed sovereignty over northern Italy since the 10th century. The apex of German might in Italy was reached around 1200, when the new Hohenstaufen dynasty acquired by marriage the throne of the kingdom of Sicily and Naples. France's Capetian dynasty, which came to power in 987 with little more than the city of Paris to its credit, engaged

Political Power

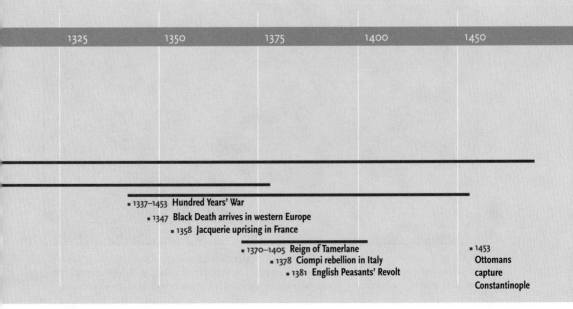

1325   1350   1375   1400   1450

- 1337–1453 Hundred Years' War
- 1347 Black Death arrives in western Europe
- 1358 Jacquerie uprising in France
- 1370–1405 Reign of Tamerlane
- 1378 Ciompi rebellion in Italy
- 1381 English Peasants' Revolt
- 1453 Ottomans capture Constantinople

in five generations of aggressive diplomacy: through marriage, it brought more and more of central and southern France into the family domain. By the reign of Louis VII (r. 1137–1180), its control reached as far south as the Pyrenees, although it still lacked a Mediterranean outlet—which finally came with the Albigensian Crusade waged by Philip IV (r. 1180–1223) against the Cathar heretics in southern France and the marriage of Louis IX (r. 1226–1270) to Margaret of Provence. England's monarchs had pursued similar aims. At its zenith, in the reign of Henry II (r. 1154–1189), the royal domain included England, Normandy, Brittany, Maine, Anjou, Gascony, and Aquitaine. As Henry's successors—Richard the Lionheart (r. 1189–1199), John (r. 1199–1215), and Henry III (r. 1215–1272)—gradually lost control of the French territories, they compensated by opening a strategic offensive in the Mediterranean marriage market.

The countervailing wave was the northward spread of Mediterranean urban institutions and commercial techniques. Cities proliferated in the 12th and 13th centuries across feudal Europe and brought with them Roman law, notions of municipal citizenship, representative government, commercial and artisanal guilds,

MAP 11.1   Europe in 1300   By 1300 the politically dominant kingdoms of northern Europe had extended their borders to the economically dominant Mediterranean region. Venice retained control over most of the eastern sea, while Barcelona and Genoa held sway over most of the western sea.

schools and universities, and even Mediterranean dress codes. These eased the interactions of the increasingly polyglot and ethnically varied cities (see Map 11.1).

The church, too, reached the zenith of its worldly power. The Gregorian Reform discussed in the preceding chapter (named after Gregory VII, r. 1073–1085) had *Papal* resulted in a sturdy, hierarchical organization—of priests, bishops, archbish- *Authority* ops, and, at the summit, the Holy Pontiff, the pope. Popes like Innocent III (r. 1198–1216) and Gregory IX (r. 1227–1241) exercised a degree of worldly power that no earlier popes had ever had. The new papacy based its authority on a principle called *plenitudo potestatis*—literally "fullness of power" but better translated as "ultimate jurisdiction"—which stressed the church's responsibility toward the world. On the Day of Judgment, it argued, every person must stand before God and be held responsible for his or her sins, but the church must also be held accountable for God's judgment. Did your priest teach you the proper doctrines and morals? Did he help guide you through life's challenges and temptations? Did he nourish you with the sacraments? Since the clergy bear some responsibility for every person's ultimate fate, the church must have a right to pronounce on the doings of our lives, particularly those with a moral component. *Plenitudo potestatis* did not assert the church's right to control individual lives, only its right to be heard.

SCHOLASTICISM

Through its bishops, the church oversaw the universities of Europe (see Map 11.2). This was the great age of **scholasticism**—really a curriculum rather than a philosophy. Scholastic learning was based on the conviction that the whole of the cosmos was rationally ordered: God, having created man as a rational creature, has given him the ability, but also the responsibility, to determine the universe's operation. Not surprisingly, the rediscovered works of Aristotle took center stage, since his inductive method proved most amenable to the study of nature. Scholastic writers specialized in a type of encyclopedia called a *summa*, which attempted to summarize all existing knowledge on a given topic. Many of the scholastics were members of the Dominican or Franciscan orders (discussed later in this chapter) and taught in universities. On the whole, they believed in the human capacity to discover truth in all areas of human experience. Apparent inconsistencies in human knowledge are merely imperfections in our own understanding, not flaws in nature.

No one will ever award Albertus Magnus (1193–1280)—or his brilliant pupil Thomas Aquinas (1225–1274)—prizes for prose style. They wrote in an *Thomas* annotated outline form: lists of questions followed by lists of answers, with *Aquinas* subsections, objections, and counterassertions inserted wherever deemed

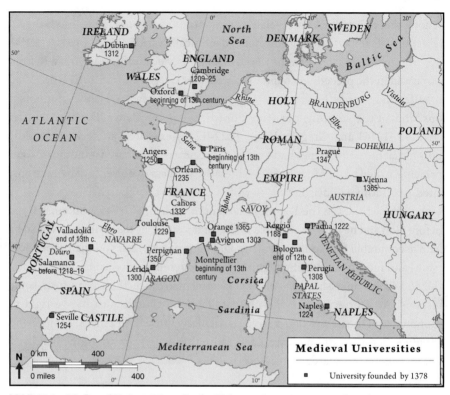

MAP 11.2   Medieval Universities   By the 12th century, universities eclipsed monasteries and cathedral schools as the most prestigious centers of learning in Latin Christendom. They attracted students—all male—from many lands and helped to forge a common elite culture across most of Europe.

appropriate. One might be reading lines of code for a computer program. For them, elegance lay in the thought behind the words, not in the words themselves. Indeed, any stylistic flourishes that drew attention away from the ideas undermined the force of the argument. True beauty lay in the perfectly rational ordering of God's creation and in the perfectly rational representation of it in words. Here, for example, Aquinas argues that the soul does not die when the body does:

> If the destruction of the body means the destruction of the soul, then it must follow that any weakening of the body entails a weakening of the soul. But in reality, if the soul is weakened in any way by a weakening of the body, that is only coincidental . . . and if our understanding flags or falters because of fatigue, injury, or weakness in the body—this is not necessarily fatigue, injury, or weakness in the understanding itself but only in those bodily faculties that the understanding utilizes. (*Summa contra Gentiles* 2.79)

The prose is bloodless (even more so in the original Latin). The point of it is to strip away rhetorical effect so that the beauty of God's Truth—in this case, the eternality of the human soul—can shine through, like sunlight through a windowpane.

Scholasticism represents a powerful moment in the history of Western culture, when it seemed possible to understand everything. The cosmos appeared to work with a formal perfection, and the limits of the human intellect seemed boundless. But unlike the distant and indifferent Creator of the deists of a later time, the God of the scholastics was present, active, brilliant, and benign—an artist and scientist. The rational mind, Aquinas and others insisted, is not a tool but a beautiful gift through which we can perceive all the divine and hidden harmonies of life. This confidence overflowed into other areas of medieval life, like the creation of literary masterpieces like Dante's *Divine Comedy* (written between 1313 and 1321), in which the poet crafts his own salvation via a journey through an afterlife (Hell, Purgatory, Paradise) of his own design, and the construction of soaring Gothic cathedrals. Marked by pointed arches, ribbed vaulting, flying buttresses, and stained-glass windows, Gothic churches appealed to the senses in the way that Thomas Aquinas's *Summa* appealed to human logic and reason: both were designed to lead people to knowledge that touched the divine. It would be a long time before the European world was again so self-confident.

In science the most brilliant and divisive figure was Roger Bacon (1214–1292), a sharp-tongued English Franciscan who delighted in disparaging the "idiot jackasses" *Roger Bacon*

he found in the leading universities. Bacon was convinced that the natural world formed a perfect enactment of God's grand design, but that the beauty of the whole could only be perceived after one had mastered all of the individual sciences. He threw himself with gusto into learning Arabic, Greek, and Hebrew and the scientific and philosophical traditions within them, as well as every science from astronomy to zoology; then he set himself to write a grand synthesis—a kind of *summa scientifica* that would encompass the entire natural world as an organic whole, divinely created and rationally ordered. Because of his brashness, his Franciscan order placed Bacon under house arrest and forbade him to write, but not until he had penned a prospectus for the project, a lengthy book known as the *Opus maius* (*Major Work*).

Interior of Sainte-Chapelle, Paris   The stained-glass windows of Sainte-Chapelle (1246–1248) are a fine example of the vibrancy of Gothic art. The pointed arches and ribbed vaulting of the Gothic style can be seen clearly.

Whether in philosophy, science, medicine, law, or any other intellectual field, the central assumptions of the scholastic writers of the late Middle Ages were that the world made sense; that it was rationally ordered; and that all its various truths, once learned, were in harmony with one another. The "unity of Truth" is how they described it. And God, who gave man the gift of reason, intended for him to discover it.

MYSTICISM

In apparent contrast to the intense rationalism of the scholastics, mysticism, or the experience of direct contact with God, was also among the central aspects of the age. It was hardly a new phenomenon. The voices that had sent Abraham on his first wanderings in the Holy Land, the burning bush on Mount Sinai through which Moses heard God's commands, the warnings of the biblical prophets—all these were God's piercing of the veil between the divine world and our own. In the early Christian era, Church Fathers like Jerome and Augustine reported mystical revelations. God spoke to the masses countless times through the miracles of the saints. What was unique about the mystical experiences of the late Middle Ages was their sheer number. Many hundreds—even thousands—of people claimed to have experienced God, in the form of either visions or otherworldly voices. They included austere Carthusian and Cistercian monks and nuns (two relatively new monastic orders discussed later in this chapter) and courtly poets, but also everyday peasants and town dwellers—school teachers, lawyers, shop-keepers, midwives, government officials, children, and the elderly.

Some people had single life-altering visions; some had repeated experiences; others had literally hundreds of powerful, stirring episodes of contact with the divine. These revelations centered on Christ. People heard Christ, saw Christ, spoke with Christ, embraced Christ, and kissed Christ. Moreover, the Christ whom they encountered was not the stern, lordly King of Heaven and Judge of the Last Day (the most common images of Christ in early medieval art). Rather, he was the gentle, caring Christ who suffered and died out of his love for all mankind. One mystic, an Englishwoman named Margery Kempe (1373–1438), speaking in the third person, describes how, on a pilgrimage to Jerusalem,

> [she] wept and sobbed as plenteously as though she had seen Our Lord with her bodily eye, suffering His Passion at that time. Before her in her soul she saw Him verily by contemplation, and that caused her to have compassion. And when they came up on to Mount Calvary [the hill outside Jerusalem where Jesus was crucified], she fell down because she could not stand or kneel, and rolled and wrestled with her body,

spreading her arms abroad, and cried with a loud voice as though her heart would burst asunder; for, in the city of her soul, she saw verily and clearly how Our Lord was crucified.

After she returned to England, the sightings continued:

> When she came home to England, [the visions] came seldom at first, as it were once a month, then once a week, and afterwards daily; and once she had fourteen [visions] in one day, and another day she had seven, and so on, as God would visit her, sometimes in church, sometimes in the street, sometimes in her chambers, sometime in the fields, whenever God would send them, and she never knew the time nor the hour when they would come.

Two aspects of the mystical exaltations stand out. First, people experiencing contact with God did not come away with new insights into theological mysteries or dramatic new interpretations of scripture. They did not know how to live better or make the world a safer and more prosperous place. Time after time, they described their experiences simply as intense waves of emotion. They felt an overwhelming sensation of God's love—as though God wanted only to remind people that He had not forgotten them. He sees their suffering and wants to reassure them that they are loved. An account from another Englishwoman, Julian of Norwich (1342–1416), reads:

The Message of God's Love

> I have begged repeatedly to understand what God meant by these visions ever since I had them. Finally, after more than fifteen years, I received the answer, for I heard in my soul the following words: "Would you like to know the Lord's message in all this? Then learn this well: Love was His message. Who showed this message to you? Love did. What did He show you? Love. Why did He show it to you? Out of Love. Hold on to this idea and you will forever grow in your knowledge and understanding of Love; otherwise you will never know or learn anything."
>
> And this is how I learned that Love was Our Lord's message. I saw with certainty that even before God created us He loved us, and that His Love has never slackened, and that His Love shall endure forever. All the works He has done have been done out of this Love; in this Love He has created all things for our good use; and in this Love our lives are everlasting. We began to exist at the moment of our creation, but the Love that made us was in God from the beginning of time. Our truest beginning is therefore in His Love, and all of this we shall see in God, without end.

*Women
Mystics*

Second, mysticism privileged women. Vastly greater numbers of women reported experiencing this sort of contact than men did, and it seems likely that even greater numbers of women experienced the visions without reporting them. Hildegard of Bingen (1098–1179) was a noble-born German abbess who dramatically described her visions in prose, painting, and music. Hadewijch of Flanders (d. ca. 1245) composed a long sequence of poems and letters that described her own "mystical marriage" to Christ in the vocabulary of courtly love. Julian of Norwich, quoted above, was an educated commoner who at the age of thirty had sixteen separate visions. As a result, she became a recluse and devoted the rest of her life to puzzling out what had happened to her. Her *Revelations of Divine Love* is one of the most moving of all mystical books. Catherine of Siena (1347–1380) started seeing visions in early childhood. For several years she hid from the world, a recluse in her crowded family home (she was the twenty-second of twenty-four children), but at the age of twenty she dedicated herself to social reform and became a tireless advisor to princes and popes. Her visions continued throughout her life.

Hildegard of Bingen Hildegard was a beloved abbess, a renowned mystic, and perhaps the first multimedia artist. When, in her late thirties, she admitted to her brother (who was a priest) that she had started having visions as a child and in fact still had them, he urged her to write. She wrote several books in which she tried to put her experiences into words. When she decided that her writings were inadequate, she put down the pen and took up a brush, composing dozens of ecstatic, expressive paintings. When that too proved insufficient to her, she composed music in the hopes that here at last she could describe what it feels like to be in God's intimate presence. Much of her music survives and is available on recordings. In the image presented here, she begins to write. The manuscript from which this image was photographed was destroyed in World War II.

Although many mystics criticized contemporary problems in the church, none saw themselves as rebels against it. In fact, most took special care to champion orthodox doctrine. But the sheer number of late medieval mystics suggests a grave dissatisfaction with the church and the world.

THE GUILD SYSTEM

The mystical exaltations may have had something to do with the economic vibrancy of the late Middle Ages. The medieval economy had grown at an impressively steady rate since the late 11th century. Fueled by agricultural surplus and the reopening of commercial ties with the Islamic world, it saw advances in financing, manufacturing, and shipping. But not everyone was pleased with this embryonic form of capitalism. The church, itself among the wealthiest of institutions, had a conflicted relationship with it because capitalism functioned on the use of credit. Credit—that is, the loaning of money at interest—was morally suspect to many churchmen, since it entailed profiting from someone else's need. The very success of the economy raised the potential danger of materialism. The more money, possessions, property, and investments people had, the church feared, the more time they would devote to their management. God does not care about the value of our possessions, the church counseled, but about the value of our lives. Wealth is indeed better than poverty, but it is not intrinsically good.

That did not stop people from pursuing wealth by an impressive array of new techniques. Among the most important innovations was the guild system. A medieval **guild** somewhat resembled a modern trade association or cartel: it set prices, quality standards, methods and volume of production, and wages paid to workers. It also assigned market shares to individual artisans or merchants. Each city had its own guilds, usually one for each artisanal industry (such as brewing, weaving and dyeing, or metalwork) and another set for the commercial companies (finance, trading, shipping) that brought the goods to market. Guilds played important roles in urban life, funding charities, schools, and hospitals. Among the bylaws of the wine and beer merchants' guild at Southampton, England, in the 13th century, for example, was this provision:

> Whenever the guild is in session the lepers at [the hospital of] La Madeleine shall receive in alms from the guild eight gallons of ale, as shall the sick in [the hospitals of] God's House and Saint Julian's. The Franciscans shall receive eight gallons of ale and four gallons of wine; and sixteen gallons of ale shall be distributed to the poor from whatever spot the guild meets at. . . . If any guild member should fall into poverty and cannot pay his debts, and if he is unable to work and provide for himself, then he shall receive from the guild one mark [of silver] every time the guild meets in session, in order to relieve his suffering.

Guilds not only complemented but also at times nearly replaced the charitable functions of the church. The reach of the church in the late Middle Ages was extensive. It orchestrated crusades, ran and policed the universities and cathedral schools, oversaw the workings of the marketplace, judged the activities of Europe's bedrooms, excommunicated kings and princes, warred with them on

Two Master Craftsmen The Italian sculptor Nanni di Banco (1383–1430) carved this relief of a stonemason and a woodcarver in honor of the Florentine builders' guild.

occasion, and staged councils to determine ever-finer details of canon law. Many feared it had lost sight of its central mission of ministering to the people. This was the impetus behind the founding of the mendicant orders, groups dedicated to assisting the clergy in the performance of their evangelical mission. These orders grew rapidly in number, size, and popularity, and their astonishing success can be attributed to two principle factors—their unique dedication to serving the common people and the fact that they, unlike the clergy they assisted, opened their membership to women.

THE MENDICANT ORDERS

Franciscans and Dominicans

The two leading **mendicant orders** were the Franciscans and the Dominicans. The Franciscans, established in 1209 by St. Francis of Assisi (1181–1226) and approved by Pope Innocent III, dedicated themselves to preaching and service to the urban poor. They begged for alms and food and donated whatever they collected to the destitute. They preached Francis's simple message of love, forgiveness, and charity.[1] People flocked to them wherever they went. The Dominicans, on the other hand, aided the church's teaching mission. From the church's perspective, too many faithful, especially in the countryside, still lacked proper religious instruction and so drifted into heresy. Heresies, in fact, enjoyed something of a golden age in the 13th and 14th centuries. Dominic de Guzmán (1170–1221), an earnest Spanish cleric, established the order named after him (officially known as the Order of Preachers) in 1216 in the hopes of bringing the heretical back into the Catholic fold. He viewed heresy as the product not of human evil or of Satanic mischief but of the church's failure to provide appropriate religious education. In response, the Dominicans established schools across Europe, debated heretical ideas, and preached tirelessly.

Catharism and Lollardy

The two most prominent heresies were Catharism and Lollardy, and both were profoundly critical of the church (see Map 11.3). The Cathars posited two separate and equal gods, one absolutely good and the other absolutely evil. Trapped in the cosmic war between them, humans were condemned to a miserable cycle of reincarnation. To the Cathars the physical universe was the creation of the evil deity; our souls, by contrast, were created by the good god. We therefore participate in the cosmic struggle by overcoming our own physicality, the demands of the flesh, and the human concern for material wealth. Once we have achieved the appropriate spiritual state, we break the cycle of reincarnation and our souls are released

---

[1]   Francis of Assisi, whose name Cardinal Jorge Bergoglio took when he was elected pope in 2013, was revered not for the brilliance of his thought but rather for the dedication with which he endeavored to live simply in imitation of Jesus's earthly life.

MAP 11.3   **Medieval Heresies, ca. 1200–1350**   Heretical ideas could be found almost anywhere, but individual groups of heretics tended to conglomerate in particular areas. The Lollards resided chiefly in England, while the Cathars predominated in southern France and parts of northeastern Spain.

from our bodies in a spiritual exaltation that tips the cosmic scale in favor of the universal good. The Lollards were almost dull in comparision.

Lollards condemned church corruption and worldliness. They believed in the right of nonpriests to preach, and they taught that to live according to the spirit of Christ is more important than to follow the many letters of the church's laws. The Lollards had no common body of doctrines; they shared instead a general anticlericalism toward Rome, whose obvious wealth and involvement with earthly matters corrupted its spiritual authority in their eyes.

The Dominicans confronted these and other groups with relentless preaching and arguing. Dominicans were confident that the errant had only to hear *Inquisition* Christian truth properly presented and they would return to the church's embrace confidently and with gratitude. Of course, it did not always work out that way, which led to the development of a sterner educational tool—the inquisition. The **inquisition** began as a pedagogical program to counter heresy: determine what an individual or group actually believed and then demonstrate its errors.

Its origin lay in a principle of ancient Roman law similar to our modern "probable cause" hearings. According to this principle, certain crimes are so detrimental to society that the state has a right, indeed a responsibility, to investigate pre-emptively if there is a reasonable likelihood that the crime might be in the offing. Heresy fell into this category because it imperiled the soul not only of the heretic; any innocent bystander might succumb.

Like other interrogation methods used in medieval times, inquisition did not shy away from using physical force. But the Inquisition (with an uppercase I) of popular legend and Hollywood films, with black-hooded sadists plying red-hot pincers in dank dungeons, largely came later, during the 15th and 16th centuries. Nevertheless, medieval inquisitions used enough coercion and manipulation to earn a dark reputation. The Dominican friars became especially associated with inquisition, although the overwhelming majority of them dedicated themselves to teaching, preaching, and peaceful ministry.

EARLY REPRESENTATIVE GOVERNMENT

Modern democracy has its immediate roots in the parliamentary tradition created by late medieval society. By 1300 nearly every state in Latin Europe, large or small, had some sort of representative assembly that possessed genuine power, usually by means of controlling the king's or prince's access to tax revenue.

Noble advisory councils were nothing new. But the late medieval addition of representatives of the common people signified the real breakthrough. The governments' need for revenue drove the issue but does not explain it entirely. Since Europe's nobles and churches remained exempt from taxation, the king's only recourse for new revenues was to tax the free commoners in the cities. The urban classes responded positively, for the most part, provided that the king granted them in return a voice in the formation of government policy. By 1100 such commoners' councils held an advisory role in government, but by 1300, when the urban manufacturing and commercial sectors represented the bulk of their realms' collective economic output, the urban classes had expanded their advisory role into power to initiate legislation for the king and the authority to veto the king by controlling his purse.

The English Parliament   The transition was not always smooth. Constraints on royalty in England included the signing of the Magna Carta in 1215 and the Provisions of Oxford in 1258, and both came about after high drama and much strong-arm maneuvering. The **Magna Carta** is principally a conservative document in which the king confirmed the long-standing rights and privileges of England's nobles. But it did contain one important innovation—an explicit recognition that the king is not above the law. The Provisions of Oxford was the first formal document to enshrine the idea that royal rights were limited and that other facets of government, under the control of the lower orders, possessed constitutional authority. England's governing body came to be known as the **Parliament**, and it consisted of two bodies—the House of Lords and the House of Commons. (The nobles insisted on separate buildings, so that they would not have to mingle with the commoners.)

In France, the Capetian kings from Louis VIII (r. 1223–1226) on were hobbled not only by their feudal obligations to the nobles but also by their practice of awarding land grants (*apanages*) to the younger sons of each Capetian generation. As consolation prizes for not inheriting the crown, apanages were independent provinces that required their holder to perform no service to the throne. The Capetians therefore had even greater need to seek the financial assistance of the urban populace, which they did by developing the French parliament—the **Estates General**.

The French Estates General

The German case was more complicated. Frederick II (r. 1212–1250) had inherited the Holy Roman Empire from his father and the Kingdom of Sicily (which included southern Italy) from his mother and frankly had little interest in his German lands at all. His southern realm was wealthier and more cosmopolitan. Frederick encouraged urban growth within Germany but also issued, in 1231, the Constitutions in Favor of the Princes of Germany, which severely curtailed the power of those cities and indeed of his own feudal claims to privilege. He gave up a strong German monarchy in return for the German princes' leaving him alone to pursue his own goals in the Mediterranean. Nevertheless, his actions helped solidify the gains made in establishing the German parliament—known as the **Diet**.

The German Diet

By 1250 or thereabouts, the balance between the authority and status of the commoners and that of the nobles was changing dramatically. The warlords (*milites*) had easily justified their emergence in the 11th century, with their monopoly on political power and privileged status. Three struts bolstered their authority: economic wealth, literacy, and military service. They generated through their manors the largest portion of economic production in the realm. They alone could perform government service, since they had a virtual monopoly, among the laity, on literacy, and they provided the dominant and most effective military service. But the rise of the urban economy had shifted economic dominance within Europe to manufacturing and commerce instead of agriculture, and the spread of literacy among city dwellers had opened up civil service to commoners. Government became professionalized, in other words, and men of noble birth began to shun the lesser offices of civil administration. That left room for commoners to enter and replace them. As the struts that legitimated noble authority gradually disappeared, voices began to murmur darkly about unjustified privilege.

Threats to Noble Authority

THE WEAKENING OF THE PAPACY

Confrontation at Anagni

Pope Boniface VIII (r. 1294–1303) had begun his pontificate with a splendid jubilee that brought as many as a million pilgrims into Rome, but papal stature had declined precipitously since then. Boniface, a rock-ribbed papal triumphalist, had provoked widespread ire by his insistence that "it is absolutely necessary to every single human being's salvation that he be subject to the Roman pontiff"—a declaration that he meant most literally. The claim was not new, but Christians everywhere chafed at the tone. Philip IV of France (r. ca. 1285–1314), who understood Boniface's claim as undermining his own desire to tax the French clergy, responded by issuing an arrest warrant for the pope, accusing him of everything from murder and bribery to devil worship and sodomy. When Philip's soldiers hunted down Boniface at his vacation residence in the central Italian town of Anagni, they slapped and beat the old man mercilessly (Boniface was then nearly seventy). Boniface's humiliation demonstrated the limits of papal control, and he died within days.

The Avignon Papacy

More troubles followed in quick succession. In 1305 the College of Cardinals met in Rome, after the death of the briefly reigning Pope Benedict XI (r. 1303–1304), and elected a Frenchman to the Holy See, who took the name Clement V (r. 1305–1314). Clement proved so unpopular with the crowds in Rome, however, that he had to flee the city in fear of his life; he and all the cardinals who had voted

The Papal Palace at Avignon   Political conflicts in Rome forced the papal court to flee the city and take refuge in Avignon in southern France from 1305 to 1378. The palace they constructed is more forbidding than welcoming, a symbol of a church under siege.

for him took refuge in southern France, where they built themselves an immense palace whose imposing walls and thick gates reflected the defensive posture of the papacy.

From 1305 until 1378 the papal court stayed behind those walls. This era is thus known as the **Avignon Papacy**. All five popes of those years were Frenchmen, and none of them is remembered with much admiration. For decades their chief concerns seems to have been manipulating international politics so that they could be restored to Rome and insisting on papal rights to complete obedience by the faithful. Decrees and demands flowed endlessly from the palace gates, but the popes themselves were all but absent from Christian life.

NOBLE PRIVILEGE AND POPULAR REBELLION

The word *chivalry* derives from the French word for horsemanship (*chevalerie*) and originally denoted skill at mounted shock combat: heavily armored knights *The Code* astride thundering warhorses, bearing swords, lances, maces, and flails. Knights *of Chivalry* proved their worth at tournaments, fighting other knights in all-too-real contests in which many were killed. They sought not merely renown but also position as a vassal to higher lords in search of loyal underlings. *The Song of Roland*, a popular epic poem written down around 1100, depicted its hero as the very summit of knightly perfection—an unsurpassed warrior loyal to his lord but to little else. The fictional Roland exhibits no qualities other than his usefulness on a battlefield. By 1200, however, a significant change had occurred, and the ideal knight portrayed in literature was more a figure like Sir Lancelot, Sir Galahad, or Saint Perceval of the Arthurian legends. All were still champion fighters, but they were also models of **chivalry** in a new sense—comportment, noble demeanor, learning, and piety. They were sensitive to music and art and, above all, were chivalric lovers of virtuous noblewomen.[2]

An Italian-born French writer named Christine de Pizan (ca. 1364–1430) is one of our best sources regarding chivalry. She was Europe's first female professional writer, having turned to her pen as her only means of support after the death of her nobleman husband in 1390. Over the next forty years she produced hundreds of poems and many volumes of allegorical tales, biographies, translations, literary criticism, and commentaries on politics, religion, and society. Throughout it all her central theme was the failure of society to value women appropriately. The cult of chivalry, as she saw it, helped to smooth the rough edges of aristocratic behavior toward women, but this gain came at the cost of turning

---

[2]   Lancelot's mistake was not in loving Arthur's queen, Guinevere, but in loving her with the wrong kind of love, adultery.

women into adored figurines—angels on pedestals. Worse still, Christine suspects that for all their showy declarations of courtly love, most men are still motivated by mere lust. At the end of her most famous book, an allegory called *The City of Ladies,* she urges her readers to "chase away all lying flatterers who use every trick and stratagem they can think of to get that which you should preserve above all—your honor and reputation. Oh ladies! Run away from their foolish declarations of love! Run, for Heaven's sake! Run! Nothing good can come of their tricks."

Over the course of the 13th and 14th centuries, as aristocrats sought to maintain leadership of society, chivalry took on newer and more symbolic roles. Coats of arms, for instance, which had originally served the practical purpose of identifying battlefield participants, began to adorn everything a nobleman owned, from tableware and fireplace masonry to goblets, gloves, and stationery. Aristocrats not only patronized musicians and poets but also now endowed colleges, scholarships, chapels, and hospitals and emblazoned them all with their names and heraldic signs. Genealogy became a passion of the elite, and its results (often fanciful) were published in books and embroidered on tapestries. Songs, tales, and histories enumerated their elevated sensibilities. Commerce and trade were denigrated as beneath the dignity of a lord. The noble class felt the need to emphasize at every turn the chasm that separated it from commoners: the nobles were not different because they were privileged, they seemed to say, but were privileged because they were different. And the difference was essential, not functional.

A Noble Warrior?   Mounted shock combat—that is, armored knights atop armored warhorses—was the premier technique of warfare in the Middle Ages. The *Manesse Codex,* from which this image is taken, is a famous compilation of German chivalric poetry dating to about 1300. The knight shown here is not drawn to life (where are his weapons?) and should be regarded only as representative of the noble grandeur of chivalrous knighthood.

But the military role of the knightly class remained and sufficed to maintain the hierarchy. So long as mounted shock cavalry remained the premier fighting force, commoners might complain about abuses of privilege, but not about the very idea of privilege. In contrast, popular rebellions of the late Middle Ages— the three best known are the Jacquerie uprising in France (1358), the Ciompi Rebellion in Italy (1378), and the Peasants' Revolt in England (1381)—shared a common element: they questioned the very order of medieval society, not merely the abusive actions of a few elites within it. None was ultimately successful, but they gave powerful expression to the resentment of the commoners against continuing noble privilege.

An anonymous poet of the time asked,

> When Adam delved and Eve span,
> Who was then the gentleman?

Although simply phrased, it was a radical question: When God created the world in all its original perfection, were there any "gentlemen"? Any privileged few who lived off the labor of the many? If not, then the existence of them now must be a distortion of God's original intent, which could be no other than the equality of all mankind.

The couplet was referred to in a sermon delivered by one of the leaders of the **English Peasants' Revolt**, a Lollard priest named John Ball (1338–1381). The story is retold in the *Historia Anglicana* of Thomas Walsingham (d. 1422):

The English Peasants' Revolt

> *When Adam dalf, and Eve span, who was thanne a gentilman?:* From the beginning all men were created equal by nature, and that servitude had been introduced by the unjust and evil oppression of men, against the will of God, who, if it had pleased Him to create serfs, surely in the beginning of the world would have appointed who should be a serf and who a lord.

Ball ended by recommending

> uprooting the tares [weeds] that are accustomed to destroy the grain; first killing the great lords of the realm, then slaying the lawyers, justices, and jurors, and finally rooting out everyone whom they knew to be harmful to the community in future.

In the 14th century several simple, inexpensive technologies developed in weaponry, which knocked the third and final strut—military protection—out from under aristocratic claims to justified privilege. The two most significant weapons were the longbow and the crossbow, which appeared first in Wales and

Innovations in Weaponry

Scotland, where they were used to repulse the English armies of King Edward I (r. 1272–1307), and possibly even before that. Prior to this time, bows were largely used by noble cavalry. The physical challenge of sitting astride a broad warhorse while fully armored, however, meant that knights' bows were relatively short in length and hence of limited power and range. The Welsh and the Scots, however, hit upon the idea of turning bows into infantry weapons instead, which allowed them to increase the length of the bow significantly. Longbows—familiar today as "bows and arrows"—were often a full 6 feet long, and their arrows could pierce a suit of armor at a distance of 200 yards.

The crossbow was the medieval equivalent of a sawed-off shotgun, and it shot thick metal darts called *quarrels*. A ratcheted steel gear, turned by a steel crank, drew the bowstring; once released, the quarrel likewise could pierce plate armor and even shatter the bones it protected.[3] Crossbows date back to Alexander the Great. The late medieval weapon, however, used a steel, not wooden, bow piece, which gave it tremendous force and required the crank to arm it. The crossbow was designed for close-range killing and holds the distinction of being the first weapon ever banned by the Catholic Church—not for its deadly force per se but because it allowed the unthinkable: with it, commoners could kill noblemen almost at will. This was more than social inversion, the church declared; it was an intrinsically immoral attack on God's ordering of society.

THE HUNDRED YEARS' WAR

The **Hundred Years' War** (1337–1453) was the longest (although not continuous) war in Western history—and almost the longest in preparation. England and France had experienced fierce tensions and rivalries since 1066, when, as we saw in chapter 10, William the Conqueror crossed the English Channel with his army and conquered England. From this time on, the English kings, as kings, were autonomous sovereigns but, as dukes of Normandy, also vassals of the throne in Paris. French kings were thwarted whenever they tried to curb the ambitions of their Norman vassals, however. And when the Norman kings managed to acquire even more French territories through strategic marriages—such as the marriage of Henry II (r. 1154–1189) to Eleanor of Aquitaine—the vassals stood more powerful and respected than the lords.

Origins and Course of the War   Matters came to a head when England's king Edward III (r. 1327–1377) claimed the French throne for himself in 1337. Legally, his claim was correct, because he was married to the last remaining Capetian heir of France's king

---

[3]   In Spain, the crossbow may have been used as a surgical tool. A quarrel embedded in a soldier's bone could be removed by tying it to a quarrel shot by a crossbow in the opposite direction.

al-Musta'sim (r. 1242–1258), rolled up in a Persian carpet and then trampled by Mongol horsemen.

A contingent of Mongol soldiers then pressed farther westward as far as Damascus but were finally repulsed in 1260 at 'Ayn Jalut, near Nazareth, by a Mamluk army coming out of Egypt. The Mongol realm reached its greatest extent in 1279, when Kublai Khan, one of Genghis's numerous grandsons, conquered southern China. By then the Mongol Empire covered some 12 million square miles of land, nearly one-quarter of the Earth's land surface (see Map 11.6).

At the height of their power the Mongols controlled an almost unimaginably vast empire, from Beijing to the Euphrates River and from Moscow to the Arabian Sea. In their wake, they left behind vast numbers of dead. In China alone, census records show that the population in 1200, before Genghis Khan's invasion, stood around 120 million people; in 1300 it figured only 60 million. Ibn Battuta (d. 1378), the famous Spanish Muslim traveler, reported that Persia's population fell from 2.5 million in 1220 to a mere 250,000 in 1260. Some estimate that fully half of Russia's population died as a result of the Mongol conquests. Fra Giovanni

MAP 11.6 The Mongol Conquests The Mongol conquests were among the bloodiest in human history. Within China alone, the Mongols under Genghis Khan killed 20 million people. His successors did their best to equal those numbers as they tore through central Asia, Russia, Persia, and the Middle East.

di Pian Carpini, an eyewitness to the destruction of the Russian capital city of Kiev, described it this way:

> When the Mongols launched their next attack, upon Russia, they caused enormous destruction, leveling many cities and fortresses and butchering countless men. They besieged Kiev, the capital, for a long time—and when they finally took it they put to death nearly everyone living in it. When my companions and I traveled through that area, we saw the skulls and bones of innumerable corpses lying everywhere on the ground. Kiev at one time had been a large and densely populated city, but now it hardly exists at all—a mere two hundred homes still stand, and every one of their inhabitants has been reduced to slavery. (*History of the Mongols*)

Mongol Rule

The Mongols had little interest in actual governance; they left most of the peoples under their control free to live according to their traditional laws and customs, provided that they sent taxes and tribute whenever asked and obeyed without question any new law that the khans decreed. The Mongols understood the significance of trade, however, and were scrupulous about awarding and enforcing safe-passage guarantees to merchants (who paid handsomely for them). Beyond this, however, they showed no real concern for administration, relying instead on massive violent retribution against any group who resisted Mongol authority to keep peace and order. Time and again, they slaughtered entire towns and villages, punishing collectively any infraction committed by anyone. Merchants and travelers moving across Asia commented repeatedly on the tranquility and order they saw everywhere throughout the Mongol-controlled continent, but as Fra Giovanni recognized in the ruins of Kiev, the tranquility was really the paralysis of brutalized people.

IN THE WAKE OF THE MONGOLS

Mongol Successor States

The Mongols began to fight among themselves after the death of Genghis's grandson Kublai Khan (r. 1260–1294), and the enormous territory they held broke into a number of smaller although still considerable states. The most important of these were the Khanate of the Golden Horde, which dominated the southern Russian steppe; the Il-Khanate, which ruled over most of the previously Persian-controlled part of the Islamic Empire; the Chagatai Khanate, which controlled central Asia; and the Yuan dynasty in China, which held nominal leadership over all the Mongol realms from its capital in Beijing (see Map 11.7).

Numerous Western states and individual rulers attempted to forge some sort of peaceful relations with the Mongols. Louis IX of France famously sent an

Philip IV (r. 1285–1314). However, the French court, which recognized Philip VI (r. 1328–1350) of Valois as king (the Valois took over when the Capetians had no male heir), would have none of it, and the war began. On again, off again, the Hundred Years' War left the French countryside ravaged and its people dispirited (see Map 11.4). The English, who were vastly outnumbered, avoided pitched battles and instead sent innumerable small raiding forces, armed with longbows and crossbows, which could pierce the French suits of armor and render mounted knights ineffective. Their mission was to vandalize as much French territory as possible, terrorize the people, and then return to England before the French could muster their enormous feudal army.

At stake was not simply dynastic territorial rights but an entire way of life. As one chronicler described an early English victory, at the battle of Crécy in 1346,

> The English [longbow] archers stepped forward and shot their arrows with great might—and so rapidly that it seemed a snow-blizzard of arrows. When these arrows fell on the Genoese [one of France's allies at the time]

MAP 11.4 The Hundred Years' War During the Hundred Years' War, English kings contested the French monarchy for the domination of France. For many decades the English seemed to be winning, but the French monarchy prevailed in the end.

and pierced their armor, they cut the strings of their own weapons, threw them to the ground, and ran. When the king of the French, who had arrayed a large company of mounted knights to support the Genoese, saw them in flight he cried out, "Kill those blackguards! They're blocking our advance!" But the English kept on firing, landing their arrows among the French horsemen. This drove the charging French into the Genoese, until the scene was so confused that they could never regroup again. . . . [When the slaughter ended,] it became clear that the French dead numbered eighty banners [flag-bearers], eleven princes of the realm, twelve hundred knights, and thirty thousand commoners.

Joan of Arc and France's Victory

The war ended with an improbable French victory, led by a charismatic peasant girl named **Joan of Arc** (ca. 1412–1431), who claimed to have received messages from Heaven telling her to drive the English from France. Unlike most mystics of her time, however, Joan received concrete messages outlining what was expected of her: to take control of the French army, inspire the French soldiers, and drive the English from the land. The French army briefly rallied under her leadership and scored several victories, until Joan was captured in battle and executed by the English in 1431. Shortly thereafter, the Burgundians, who had been allied with England against the French, reversed course and sided with the French. With their newly combined forces, the French and Burgundians drove the English from the land, and in 1453 a permanent peace was settled. The first death knell of the feudal aristocracy had been sounded, however, despite the victory.

Joan of Arc   This early image of Joan of Arc shows her in armor but without her hair cropped. Joan cut her hair short in a conscious effort to appear manly; after her capture, this gender-bending display was used as evidence of her supposed witchcraft and heresy. In reality, Joan's ease at cutting across social boundaries—a commoner, leading an aristocratic army—unnerved people as much as her violation of gender norms did. She was only nineteen when she was put to death.

THE PLAGUE

Another even more dire death knell sounded for the whole Greater Western world in late 1347, when a fleet of Genoese merchant ships returning from the Black Sea arrived in the harbor at Messina, Sicily. Aboard the vessels was a pack of rats carrying the bubonic plague. This disease originated in eastern Asia and had worked its way westward along the trade routes; the violent advance of the Mongol army under Genghis Khan (ca. 1167–1227) and his successors probably sped matters up considerably. Since the disease had never existed before in the west, the people had no biological means of fighting it off, and it took several centuries for the necessary antibodies to develop among the populations at large. Waves of the plague—known popularly as the **Black Death**—therefore returned to the Near East and Europe until well into the 18th century.

This was the single worst natural disaster in Greater Western history, killing as many as 50 million people in less than three years—roughly one-third of the European and Muslim populations (see Map 11.5). A Sicilian eyewitness, Michael of Piazza, recorded the following:

Reactions to the Black Death

> At the start of November [in 1347] twelve Genoese galleys . . . entered the port at Messina. They carried with them a disease so deadly that any person who happened merely to speak with any one of the ships' members was seized by a mortal illness; death was inevitable. It spread to

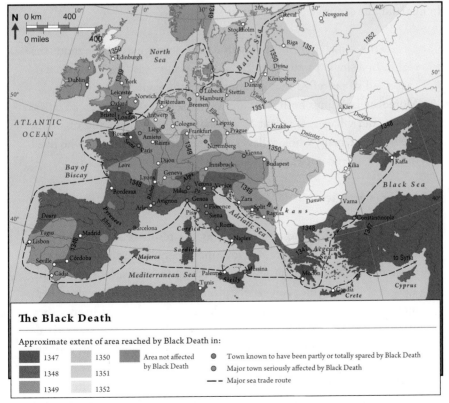

The Black Death

Approximate extent of area reached by Black Death in:

- 1347
- 1348
- 1349
- 1350
- 1351
- 1352
- Area not affected by Black Death
- ○ Town known to have been partly or totally spared by Black Death
- ● Major town seriously affected by Black Death
- – – Major sea trade route

MAP 11.5   The Black Death   From Sicily, the plague spread outward in concentric circles. Its waves of death needed only two years to kill more than 20 million people in Europe alone.

everyone who had any interaction with the infected. Those who contracted the disease felt their whole bodies pierced through with pain, and they quickly developed boils about the size of lentils on their thighs and upper arms. These boils then spread the disease throughout the rest of the body and made its victims vomit blood. The vomiting of blood normally continued for three days until the person died, since there was no way to stop it. Not only did everyone who had contact with the sick become sick themselves, but also those who had contact only with their possessions. . . . People soon began to hate one another so much that parents would not even tend to their own sick children. . . . As the deaths mounted, crowds of people sought to confess their sins to priests and to draft their wills . . . but clergy, lawyers, and notaries refused to enter the homes of the ill. . . . Franciscans, Dominicans, and other mendicants who went to hear the confessions of the dying fell to the disease—many of them not even making it alive out of the ill persons' homes. (*History of Sicily*)

In England, the canon Henry Knighton wrote,

At the same time sheep began to die everywhere throughout the realm. In a single pasture one could find as many as five thousand carcasses, all so putrefied that no animal or bird would go near them. . . . Moreover, buildings both large and small began to collapse in all cities, towns, and villages, for want of anyone to inhabit them and maintain them. In fact, many whole villages became deserted; everyone who lived in them died and not a single house was left standing. (*Chronicle*)

In Paris, French writer Jean de Venette described a popular reaction to the crisis:

Some said that the pestilence was the result of infected air and water, . . . and as a result of this idea many people began suddenly and passionately to accuse the Jews of infecting the wells, fouling the air, and generally being the source of the plague. Everyone rose up against them most cruelly. In Germany and elsewhere—wherever Jews lived—they were massacred and slaughtered by Christian crowds, and many thousands were burned indiscriminately. The steadfast, though foolish, bravery of the Jewish men and women was remarkable. Many mothers hurled their own children into the flames and then leapt in after them, along with their husbands, in order that they might avoid being forcibly baptized. (*Chronicle*)

MAP 11.7   The Mongol Successor States   The Mongols were warriors, not statesmen, and their vast conquests quickly broke up into a patchwork of separate khanates held together by brute force—much as had occurred in the wake of Alexander the Great's conquests in the 4th century BCE (see Map 5.3).

emissary to Batu Khan (r. 1227–1255), khan of the Golden Horde, congratulating him on his conquests and offering to bestow those lands on him officially in return for Batu's conversion to Christianity, pledge to become Louis's vassal, and payment of an annual tribute. Batu responded that he would teach Louis a lesson by burning Paris down around his ears.

Nonetheless, because the Mongols were willing to deal with Westerners, one effect of their conquests was to open China to European travelers for the first time. The most famous of these travelers was Marco Polo (1254–1324), a Venetian merchant who claimed to have spent twenty years in the court of Kublai Khan—"claimed" because not all scholars agree that Marco Polo actually made it to China. Nonetheless, the account of his travels stimulated other Europeans to seek out the fabulous riches of the East. Christopher Columbus's copy of *The Travels of Marco Polo* still survives.

Among the first travelers from the West were teams of Franciscan missionaries sent by the church with the optimistic charge of converting the great khans to Christianity. One of these was Fra Giovanni di Montecorvino (1247–1328), who

The Opening of China to the West

A Mongol Passport The court of the Mongol ruler Kublai Khan (r. 1260–1294) issued this engraved safe-conduct pass, which guaranteed its bearer safety while traveling through the Mongol lands. The inscription reads: "By the strength of Eternal Heaven, an edict of the khan. He who has not respect [for the bearer of the passport] shall be guilty."

established a church at Beijing, built a Christian school for 150 slave children he had purchased and manumitted (freed), and translated the Psalms and the whole of the New Testament into Tartar for them. He sent back to Rome an extraordinary letter:

I, Fra Giovanni di Montecorvino, set out from the city of Tauris, in Persia, in the year of Our Lord 1291 and made my way to India, where I remained for thirteen months . . . and baptized about a hundred people. . . . I then continued my journey until I made it all the way to [China], the realm of the Great Khan who rules over the Tartars and to whom I presented the letter of our Holy Father the Pope, inviting him to adopt the Catholic faith of Our Lord Jesus Christ. The Khan is too set in his idolatrous ways to change, although I must record that he has extended great friendship to us Christians in the years I have been living here in his realm. . . . I have built a church in [Beijing], where the Khan has his chief residence, . . . and in this church I have baptized some six

Papal Gift to the Great Khan This is a copy of a now-lost original painting by Zhou Lang in 1342, depicting the arrival of a gift horse from Pope Benedict XII (r. 1334–1342) to the last Mongol ruler of China, Shundi (r. 1333–1370). The gift was brought to the Chinese court by a Franciscan emissary named Fra Giovanni di Marignolli (ca. 1290–1360).

The Spanish Muslim writer Ibn Khaldun (1332–1406) summarized the ruin this way:

> It was as though humanity's own living voice had called out for oblivion and desolation—and the world responded to the call. Truly Allah inherits the earth and all things upon it. (*Muqaddimah*)

People tried every medicine, folk cure, and prayer they knew, all to no effect. In several instances townsfolk, who knew that the disease had something to do with rats, intentionally burned their entire towns to the ground to drive the rats away, but this of course only accelerated the spread of the contagion. By the time the plague had spread its way through nearly every corner of Europe, North Africa, and the Near East, it had left behind piles of corpses so massive that people hardly knew what to do with them. Scores of "death ships" bobbed directionless on the seas, every person on board dead, with the victorious rats silently gnawing on their remains.

The consequences of the catastrophe were innumerable. The fatalities, coupled with the fear of interpersonal contact, halted agricultural and industrial production and severed all commercial ties. The death of so many farm animals had equally long-term effects: wool and dairy production all but ceased, and the loss of oxen and horses as draught animals meant that farming would be slow to restart. Once the immediate crisis passed, twin spirals of inflation and recession followed. Urban workers who had survived could demand higher wages for

Consequences of the Crisis

Burying Plague Victims This page from the *Annals* of Gilles de Muisit, late 14th century, shows crowds in Tournai (Belgium's oldest city) struggling to bury all the dead left in the Black Death's wake.

their labor, and this, combined with the general scarcity of goods, triggered rapid increases in prices. Rural workers faced a different problem. So many people had died that even decreased food production met local needs—and hence food prices dropped precipitously. When rural workers demanded lower rents for their work on the land, the landlords could hardly refuse. But the collapse in crop prices hurt the farmers more than the decreased rents helped them. So in general terms, urban workers who survived the Black Death profited from the decimation, whereas rural workers were driven even deeper into poverty.

Each return of the Black Death over the centuries left new iterations of the same miseries in its wake. No epidemic ever reached the hopeless severity of the first wave, but fear of the plague haunted the Greater West for many generations.

THE MONGOL TAKEOVER

The 13th and 14th centuries witnessed the near-complete takeover of the Islamic world by a new wave of foreign conquerors, who dominated Muslim life for the next three hundred years, reconfiguring its map and introducing new cultural and social elements into Islamic identity. Leadership of Islam had long been monopolized by two groups, the Arabs and the Persians. Although often in tension with each other, they had nevertheless worked out some sort of creative cultural compromise. The arrival of two groups of newcomers, however, renewed cut-throat competition between the Muslim states. Neither group was monolithic. Instead, each was a compound assemblage made up of numerous tribes and clans linked by language: the Mongols and the Turks.

Rise of the Mongols

The most destructive of the invaders were the **Mongols**, who began moving westward in the 12th century. No one knows the precise origin of the Mongols. Ancient Chinese records trace them back to a group they called the Donghu (3rd century BCE), which was actually a confederation of various peoples speaking related dialects of an early version of the Mongolian language. But some scholars claim to see elements of early Turkish dialects in the Donghu as well. Certainly the Mongols, as they spread across Asia, maintained continuous contact with Turkish-speaking groups and absorbed elements of Turkish culture. As the two groups gradually merged, they became known in the west as the *Tartars* (a word that derives from the Latin *Tartarus*, "hell").

Nomadic peoples of the steppes found it natural to form occasional alliances and confederations—and to disband them just as casually. When gathered, these armies were often of considerable size. Fighting on horseback, they moved quickly and specialized in lightning strikes on other nomadic groups and small population centers. Siege machinery was largely unknown to them, which allowed fortified cities to withstand their assaults. The Mongols were a diverse group of tribes along the northern and northwestern borders of China, and the Chinese themselves had been traditionally among the Mongols' favorite targets for raiding. Centuries of such attacks had prompted the Chinese to build the Great Wall, a series of fortifications made of stone, brick, pressed earth, wood, and other materials. Although not impregnable, the wall repulsed attackers and migrants alike with sufficient success that it was a major reason for the seemingly endless waves of invaders and nomads who moved westward across Asia and into the Western world.

Under their brilliant but brutal commander Temüjin (ca. 1167–1227), the Mongols forged another of their periodic confederations. Better known by his title of **Genghis (Chinggis) Khan**, or "Universal Ruler," he broke through the wall in 1207 and subdued the northern half of China. The Chin emperor surrendered in 1214 and awarded Genghis Khan an enormous tribute payment of gold and silver coins, which sources say required three thousand horses to carry. At this point Genghis might have stopped his conquests, because in diplomatic records he referred to himself as the "supreme emperor of the east" and wrote to the Abbasid ruler in Khwarezmi (in modern-day Iran) as the "supreme emperor of the west." The arrogant al-Nasir (r. 1180–1225) rejected Genghis's peace offering, however, and slaughtered all 450 members of the diplomatic embassy he had sent. This called for revenge, and in 1219 Genghis Khan moved westward and quickly crushed what was left of the Abbasid state. *Conquests under Genghis Khan*

Genghis left local rulers in place, so long as they swore unquestioning obedience to him, and he installed Mongol tax collectors in each region to ensure a flow of revenue into his coffers. Some towns rebelled and slew these Mongol officials as soon as Genghis had moved on, which prompted the great khan to return in wrath and annihilate entire populations. Once he was even reported to have ordered the killing of every living creature in a city, including its domesticated animals. Ali ibn al-Athir (1160–1233), the great Kurdish historian, described the Mongols memorably in his *Universal History*:

> Even Antichrist, though He strike down all those who oppose him, will spare those who follow Him—but these Mongols spared no one, not even men, children, or women; they even ripped open the stomachs of women who were pregnant and killed their unborn children. . . . These people came out of the lands of China and attacked cities . . . in Turkestan . . . and advanced on Samarkand, Bukhara, and other sites in Transoxiana. One of their armies made it as far as Khurasan and continued their campaign of conquering, pillaging, and ruining until they reached . . . the borders of Persia, Azerbaijan, and Iraq, . . . all of which they destroyed and wholly depopulated, except for a small remnant, in less than a year's time.

Coming as it does near the end of the *Universal History,* ibn al-Athir's passage denotes the apocalyptic role he saw the Mongols to be playing. Surely the end of the world was nigh if such malevolent power as the Mongols possessed could roll over the world at will. Had he lived another quarter century, ibn al-Athir would have seen his worst imaginings realized.

Expansion under Genghis's Successors

The Mongol conquests were far greater than those achieved by any earlier people, or by any people since Genghis Khan died in 1227, and after a bitter fight among brothers he was succeeded by his third son, Ögedai (r. 1227–1241), who continued to push the borders of the Mongol-dominated realm farther west until they reached Anatolia. Another branch of his army, moving north of the Black Sea, threatened Hungary and even reached northward to the Baltic Sea and southward to the Balkans. Under Hulagu (r. 1256–1265), a general under the command of his ruling brother Möngke Khan (r. 1251–1259), the Mongols annihilated Baghdad in 1258. According to Muslim sources, as many as 300,000 people were killed in a two-week-long orgy of slaughter. The Mongols destroyed the royal library (one chronicle reports that the Tigris River ran black from the ink of all the books hurled into it) and burned dozens of mosques, schools, and hospitals. At the end, Hulagu had the Abbasid caliph,

The Siege of Baghdad The Mongol conquest of Baghdad in 1258 ended the caliphate, the main political institution of the Islamic world since the death of Muhammad. This illustration of the siege of Baghdad from a 15th-century Persian manuscript shows the last Abbasid caliph, al-Musta'sim (r. 1242–1258), submitting to the Mongol khan Hulagu (r. 1256–1265).

thousand people, as near as I can reckon.... I believe it is possible that, if I had had two or three comrades to aid me, the Khan himself might have been baptized by now, and for this reason I beg that if any friars are willing to come this far and dedicate themselves to so great a task ... then they will come....

It has been twelve years since I had any news of the papal court, our Franciscan order, or the general goings-on in Europe. Two years ago a fellow from Lombardy came here—a surgeon—and spread the most vicious rumors about the papal court and other matters [Fra Giovanni refers here to Boniface's humiliation by Philip IV at Anagni], but since these blasphemies are too horrible to be true I beg to hear the truth and pray that my fellow Franciscans, to whom I address this letter, do all they can to bring my request to Our Holy Father the Pontiff.... As for myself, I have grown old and gray; even though I am only fifty-eight, toil and trouble have aged me. I have acquired a working knowledge of the language and script used by the Tartars, and have already translated the New Testament and the Psalter for them.... To the best of my knowledge there is no king or prince anywhere in the world who can compare to the Great Khan in terms of the vastness of his realm, the number of his subjects, or his wealth. But here I must now stop.

[Beijing], the eighth of January, in the year of Our Lord 1305.

Two years later, Pope Clement V (r. 1305–1317) appointed Giovanni the archbishop of Beijing and sent him the assistants he had requested.

PERSIA UNDER THE IL-KHANS

The Mongols were themselves shamanistic, meaning that they followed tribal spiritual leaders who were in contact with the spirit world and worked as miracle healers. The Tartars who succeeded them were generally tolerant of other religions and did little to hinder the development of either Christianity or Islam. There were, of course, exceptions. One early emir (prince) of Il-Khan Persia (modern-day Iraq and Iran), Nawruz (d. 1297), issued a decree:

> All [Christian] churches shall be torn down, their altars destroyed, and all celebrations of the Eucharist shall cease; moreover all hymns of praise and ringing of bells to call Christians to prayer shall be abolished. I decree too that the leaders of all Christian and Jewish congregations shall be killed.

Il-Khan Rule and Culture

But although several prominent Mongols did convert to Christianity, Islam was far more successful in spreading its message among not only the Mongols themselves but also their tributary peoples. Since the arrival of the Seljuk Turks in the 11th century, a significant number of Muslims were Turkish speaking. This gave the Muslims a considerable advantage in proselytizing, because the long history of interaction between the Turks and Mongols had fostered widespread understanding of their respective languages. Moreover, groups of Turks had traditionally been among the Mongols' chief steppe allies in the occasional confederations of tribes that formed and dissolved over the centuries. Mahmoud Ghazan (r. 1295–1304), ruler of the Il-Khan kingdom in Persia, converted to Shi'a Islam—probably as a political move. (Rumor had it that he continued to practice shamanism privately.) He then declared Islam the official religion of the state.

A few cultural and intellectual highlights stand out in the Il-Khan period. Rashid ad-Din Hamadani (1247–1318) was a physician and historian; his encyclopedic *Jami al-Tawarikh* (*Compendium of Chronicles*) is one of the greatest of medieval world histories. Hafez Shirazi (1325–1390) is perhaps the best loved of all Persian poets to the present day; his lyrical verses praise the beauty of the human form in language reminiscent of religious mysticism. Scholars in Il-Khan Persia also translated Chinese medical texts, and artists perfected blue-and-white ornamental tile work.

The Il-Khan rulers never enjoyed much popularity with the peoples of Iraq and Iran, however. Turkish gradually replaced Mongolian as the official court language, and Turks and Mongols held the supreme political and fiscal offices. Ethnic Persians, however, continued to make up the bulk of the civil administration throughout Iraq and Iran. Too much of Il-Khan policy was aimed at diverting wealth into Mongol hands for there to be any popular base to their power. After 1335 there

Tamerlane on His Throne   There is no universal Islamic prohibition against representational art; rather, there is a general, ethnically Arab aversion to it. The Persian and Turkish artistic traditions embraced representational art from the start. Here we see Tamerlane (r. 1370–1405) receiving an audience of nobles and courtiers on the occasion of his accession to the throne in Samarkand, in eastern Iran. This image comes from the *Zafarnama* ("Book of Victory"), a history of Tamerlane by Sharaf ad-Din Ali Yazdi, a 15th-century Persian writer.

were no more Mongols in charge, since the Il-Khan line died out; this triggered a long series of civil wars between petty emirs. Adding to Persia's troubles, a new dynasty in China—the Ming—came to power, conquered Mongolia, and cut off the silk routes across central Asia. Persia's economy consequently went into a tailspin.

Another Tartar warlord, around 1400, named Timur the Lame, or **Tamerlane** (r. 1370–1405), briefly terrorized Iraq and Iran while trying to reestablish Tartar supremacy. Historians often refer to him as the final Mongol emperor. Tamerlane cut a huge swath of destruction: Baghdad, Delhi, Isfahan (where he notoriously ordered forty thousand citizens beheaded and had a pyramid made of their skulls), Aleppo, Damascus, and Iznik. He burned mosques, schools, and libraries everywhere he went, ordered all Christian churches torn down, and rounded up all the most skilled artisans and deported them to his own capital at Samarkand, where they were forced to finish their lives constructing palaces and monuments in his honor. No one mourned his passing, and it would take many generations for Iraq and Iran, already smarting from earlier Mongol atrocities, to recover from the damage he had inflicted on them.

Reign of Tamerlane

The Mamluk Sultanate

A NEW CENTER FOR ISLAM

The Turkish-led Mamluk Sultanate largely escaped the catastrophic violence of the Mongols. And so it became, for 250 years, a stronghold of western Islamic civilization. Stretching from modern-day Libya and Egypt on the African coast to northern Syria, the Mamluk Sultanate centered on the great cities of Alexandria, Cairo, Jerusalem, Damascus, Antioch, and Aleppo (see Map 11.8). It lasted through two distinct periods: the Bahri (1250–1382) and the Burji (1382–1517).

The **sultan** was a military officer, a general in chief, and the position was therefore determined by the army. Most sultans in fact gained office by selection

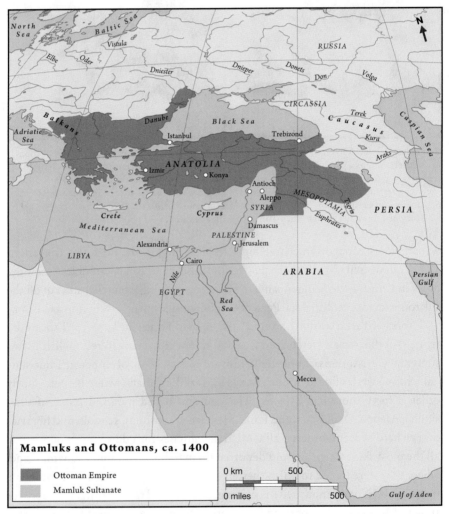

MAP 11.8   Mamluks and Ottomans, ca. 1400   With the Tartars entrenched farther to the east, the Mamluks and Ottomans divided the western Islamic world between them.

from the leading generals. A few sultans did attempt to pass their position on to their sons, but usually the heirs were ousted by rival generals. The Bahri and the Burji were both foreigners to the region. The Bahri sultans were Kipchak Turks, an ancient people who had originated in Siberia and slowly migrated westward, reaching the Middle East around 1050, where they found employment in the highly disciplined ranks of the Mamluk soldiery. The Burji, by contrast, were ethnic Circassians, an obscure group from the Caucasus Mountain region who spoke Turkish in addition to their ancestral Adyghe language. (The name *Circassian* comes from the Turkish for "people from the Caucasus.") Both periods were characterized by short-lived sultanates: twenty-seven reigns in the Bahri era (an average of four years apiece) and twenty-six in the Burji (an average of a little more than five years apiece).

Islam had been an international multiethnic religion since the late 7th century, but political, religious, and social authority had been monopolized for more than six hundred years by just two groups, Arabs and Persians. The rise of the Mongols and Turks not only shattered those monopolies but also drove the long-ruling societies into secondary status in their own homelands. They would not fully emerge from the political shadows until the 20th century. Moreover, Mamluk rule, occasioned as it was by military force, relied on force to sustain itself.[4] The atmosphere of violence both colored and contributed to a sense of failed jihad. The crusaders had been driven from the Holy Land in 1291, it is true, but Islam as a geopolitical force was in retreat. The Christian Reconquista in Spain gained pace through the 13th and 14th centuries, and the survival of Constantinople continued to rankle because Muslims had been trying to take the city for nearly seven hundred years. The great capital city of Baghdad had also been flattened. And the advance of the Mongols, some of whom had nominally converted to Islam, did nothing to slow the spread of Orthodox Christianity among the peoples of Russia and the Balkans, whom they dominated politically for several centuries.

In the Mamluk state, therefore, a concerted effort to restore a strong, authoritarian Islam continued. This was ironic, since many of the Mamluks—from some of the sultans down to the common soldiers—were Muslim in name only. Many soldiers never even bothered to learn to speak Arabic and regarded Arabs and Egyptians alike with disdain. In this regard, they resembled the supposedly Muslim Il-Khan ruling class in Persia, and, being largely uncommitted to religion in general, they thereby acquired reputations for religious tolerance that are not quite deserved.

---

[4]   More than half of the Mamluk rulers were assassinated or executed after mostly sham trials. More than half of the remainder were forcibly deposed or resigned under threat of deposition.

The greatest of the Mamluk rulers was the first: Baibars (r. 1260–1277), who famously crushed the Seventh crusade led by Louis IX, defeated the Mongols at 'Ayn Jalut in 1260, and recaptured the city of Antioch in 1268—a victory that sealed the ultimate defeat of the remaining crusader states. He also perfected what became the distinctive Mamluk system of granting lands to officers and soldiers in return for their military service. Rather like the network of feudal relations in Latin Europe, only stripped of Europe's complex system of social and constitutional obligations, this system left common farmers at the mercy of their Mamluk overlords. By 1300 or so, fully one-half of whatever revenues each lord raised was owed to the sultan, which guaranteed him sufficient funds to keep adding new slaves to the army. Fortunately for the sultan, much of the spice trade from east Asia had been rerouted to avoid the Mongols and

Mamluk Decorative Lamps   These lamps date to the first half of the 14th century and are made of enameled glass. They were produced in the Mamluk Empire, which then was composed of Egypt, Palestine, and Syria. The inscription reads that they were created in honor of Sultan Badr ad-Din al-Hasan, who ruled the area at the time when the Black Death hit.

came instead by ship around the Arabian peninsula and up through the Red Sea, thus entering Egyptian markets directly. Therefore, the Mamluk Sultanate remained extraordinarily wealthy, although the bulk of the wealth was monopolized by the ruling elite.

With so much wealth at their disposal, the Mamluk sultans did more than expand their armies: they also patronized art in intentionally showy but often brilliant ways. Sumptuously woven textiles and carpets became a hallmark of their courts (and highly prized commodities among the European well-to-do). Their palaces were showcases for decorative glass, enameled lamps and statuary, exquisite ironwork, and libraries filled with books of fabulously ornate calligraphy and jeweled bindings. Moreover, the Mamluks built scores of new mosques and madrasas (religious schools) and bestowed lavish endowments on them. The Mamluks had a particular enthusiasm for Sufism—which, as discussed in chapter 10, the bulk of Sunnis had difficulty reconciling themselves to—and brought hundreds of Sufi masters and thousands of Sufi texts into their realm.

In a conservative reaction against Mamluk ostentation and support of Sufism, the most vigorous intellectual life under the Mamluks was found among the *Conservatism* Arabs, Egyptians, Kurds, and Syrians who smarted under the new regime. The *and Reaction* most influential thinker of the era was Ibn Taymiyyah (1263–1328), a prolific legal scholar whose works urged a return to the stripped-down essentials of Islam, insisted on conservative readings of the Qur'an and *hadith*, and raged against the dangerous influence of Sufism. (One of his favorite words to describe Sufism was *bid'a*—"reckless innovation" or even "newfangled nonsense.") Taymiyyah insisted on the Qur'an's absolute authority and rejected any efforts to interpret its meanings apart from the most literal and exact. Although trained in *kalam* (theology) and philosophy, he rejected speculative thought as fundamentally un-Islamic and called for all Muslims to adhere to jihad against all the enemies of the faith—among whom he included the Mongols and the Shi'a. He also called on Muslims to reject the cult of Islamic saints, which he regarded as an impious absorption of Christian practice.[5] And perhaps most significantly for later centuries, he ardently championed the restoration of ethnic Arab leadership over international Islam.

The Black Death decimated the Islamic world just as it did the European world, and the Mamluk Sultanate never fully recovered from the blow. In Cairo alone, as many as forty thousand people perished. When the Burji regime replaced the Bahri in 1382, they made factionalism even worse by purging the Turkish elite and installing their Circassian fellows, through whom they ordered

---

[5]   "Many of these saints' venerators do not even know that this is a practice derived from the Christians. May Christianity and its followers be accursed!" (*Kitab Iqitada*).

even heavier taxation of the common populace. The Burji likewise earned well-deserved reputations for graft and corruption that further alienated them from their subjects in Egypt and Syria. But so long as the Mamluk military machine stood supreme, there was little anyone could do about them.

By 1500, however, two things had occurred that brought Mamluk power to an end. First, Portuguese explorers had rounded the African continent and interjected themselves into the spice and silk trade coming out of India, thus depriving the Mamluks of desperately needed revenue. Second, the Ottoman Turks, whose enthusiastic embrace of gunpowder and cannons gave them a clear tactical advantage over all rivals, challenged Mamluk control of Syria and Palestine with an assault on Aleppo. This gained, the Turks pressed farther southward, taking all of Syria in less than a year and in early 1517 capturing Cairo itself, putting an end to the Mamluk era. The establishment of Ottoman power inaugurated Islam's modern era.

THE OTTOMAN TURKS

The **Ottoman Turks** (tribal cousins of the Seljuk Turks of two centuries earlier) had arrived in force in the late 13th century, under their charismatic leader Osman (r. 1281–1324). No one would have predicted it, but the Ottoman regime gave the Islamic world its lengthiest, most stable, and most prosperous rule. To a certain extent, they had the Mongols to thank for that. The Mongols' devastation had been so vast, and their extortion of wealth afterward so extensive, that Iraq and Iran required at least a century to recover. Meanwhile, the realm of the Seljuk Turks, who had dominated most of Anatolia since their victory over the Byzantines at Manzikert in 1071, had broken up into a sprawl of warring principalities, which the Ottomans were then able to pick off one at a time. The turning point was a severe defeat inflicted on the Seljuks by the Mongols in 1243 at Köse Dağ in northeastern Anatolia.

Ottoman Expansion and Consolidation
In 1453 the Ottomans under their leader **Mehmed II** (r. 1451–1481) achieved what Muslim armies had dreamt of since the 7th century—the conquest of Constantinople, capital of Byzantium. Only the Mamluks, far to the south, rivaled the might of the Ottomans (see Map 11.8). By 1500 even the Mamluks were in retreat, leaving the Ottomans as undisputed leaders of the Islamic world, a position they held until they finally fell from power in the aftermath of World War I. Through most of its long history, the Ottoman Empire comprised most of North Africa, the Hijaz (that is, the western coastal strip of Arabia including the holy cities of Mecca and Madina), Palestine, Mesopotamia, Syria, Anatolia, the Balkans, Hungary, and the Crimea. This was an area larger than the Byzantine Empire had ever been.

They had the advantage of arriving on the scene in the late 13th century when everyone else but the Mamluks were weakening. Under the Seljuks, much of the Greek Orthodox and Armenian Christian populations had been driven off the land by the Turkish leaders' need to award land parcels to their soldiers. Unattached Turkish frontier warriors and mercenaries (called *ghazis*, in Turkish) made things worse, massacring and enslaving Christians in roughly equal numbers in the 12th and early 13th centuries. Famines and disease took care of much of the

THE OTTOMAN EMPIRE AT ITS GREATEST EXTENT

rest. By the time the Ottomans came to power, the Turks' scorched-earth policies had emptied most of the Anatolian countryside. Many of the displaced Christians relocated to the Balkan and Black Sea territories, where the Byzantines still exercised some control, whereas town dwellers preferred to emigrate into Latin Europe, especially Italy. Those Christians who remained faced punitive taxation and various forms of social discrimination, and occasionally some entire villages converted to gain a sounder footing under the new regime. By 1300 Anatolia was overwhelmingly Muslim, and the Ottomans responded by building hundreds of new mosques, madrasas, and hospitals—even temporary housing for new converts, as a means of instructing them in Islamic customs.

The Ottomans had an even stronger enthusiasm for Sufism than the Seljuks had, and they consequently brought in Sufi preachers in huge numbers. The Sufis bore special responsibility for converting the remaining Christians, which they did by emphasizing a kind of religious syncretism not seen since Roman times. Sufi sermons drew direct parallels between the biblical twelve apostles and the twelve Shi'i imams; others presented Allah, Muhammad, and Ali as an Islamic Trinity. The way had been prepared for these preachers by earlier figures like the great Sufi poet Jalal ad-Din Muhammad Balkhi (1207–1273), better known in the West as **Rumi**, who penned thousands of verses, a number of sermons, and a famous collection of letters. Although he was a strict Muslim, Rumi's poetry frequently aimed at an ecumenical appeal:

> In search of Allah I ventured among the Christians and looked upon the Cross,
> But I did not find Him there;
> I entered pagan temples and looked upon the idols,
> But I did not find Him there.
> I explored the mountain cave at Hira [the site of Muhammad's first Qur'anic revelation]
> And even went as far as Kandahar, but I did not find Him there.
> So I made up my mind to climb to the top of Mount Caucasus,

> But there I found only a phoenix's nest.
> Turning around, I set out for the holy Ka'ba, the refuge of young
>   and old,
> But I did not find Him even there.
> Trying philosophy next, I looked for insight in the writings of Ibn Sina,
> But I did not find Him there....
> Finally, at last, I looked in my own heart, and found Him;
> He had been there all along. (Quatrain 1173)

Rumi's writings champion Islam without disparaging other faiths. His approach seemed too gentle to many of his contemporaries, especially those Sunnis who were ill at ease with Sufi emotionalism. Yet the beauty of his poetry secured him an avid readership that lasts to the present day. Another Turkish poet, Yunus Emre (1240–1321), likewise excelled at combining the language and imagery of mystical spirituality and earthly delight. The appearance of such poets, and their immediate and enduring popularity, parallel the European development of its vernacular literatures.

The unsettled nature of much Muslim life, as the Il-Khans plundered Iraq and Iran and as the Muslims in Spain confronted the Reconquista, meant a continuous flow of immigrants into the Ottoman lands. Judges, theologians, engineers, and civil bureaucrats, as well as farmers and artisans, poured into the region in large numbers. This influx of skilled labor and administrative talent enabled Ottoman society to stabilize quickly as a developed economic and political entity. And the Byzantine collapse opened Thrace, Macedonia, and the Balkans to Turkish expansion too. Under Murad I (r. 1359–1389) the Turkish army added most of Bulgaria to the Ottoman domain as well, although Murad himself died shortly thereafter in battle against the Serbs at Kosovo. In formalizing the peace accord after the fray, a prominent Serb princess married Murad's son and heir, Bayezid I; the union was reportedly an unusually happy one. Even more significantly, Serbian forces promptly joined up with Bayezid and helped him to attack Bosnia, Herzegovina, and parts of Hungary.

The stronger the Ottomans became, however, the more suspicious of them the Mongol Il-Khans in Persia and the Mamluks in Egypt grew. The popularity of Sufism among the Turks, and its sometimes troubling ecumenical traces, added to the popular hostility toward them. Bayezid I (r. 1389–1403) went so far as to name his first three sons Musa (Moses), Issa (Jesus), and Mehmed (Muhammad), which was beyond the pale in most Sunni eyes. When the Ottoman rulers, mimicking the Mamluks, formed their own personal bodyguard of slave-soldiers, called **Janissaries** (after the Turkish *yeniçeri*, meaning "new soldier"), they conscripted Greek Christian boys to supplement Turkish recruits, a practice known

The Conquest of Constantinople   This fresco on the outer wall of a Byzantine church, painted around 1537, depicts the 1453 siege of the city led by Sultan Mehmed II (r. 1451–1481). The massive cannons used by the Ottomans to break the defenses had been forged in Hungary by the ironworkers' guild, in hopes that the Turks would settle for Constantinople and leave the Hungarians alone. They were wrong.

as *devshirme*. Although these boys were raised as Muslims, the Mongols and Mamluks used the makeup of the Janissary corps as further evidence of the Ottomans' weak commitment to Islam and justification for their own attacks on the state.

Despite those attacks, the Turks entered the 15th century as the clear leaders of international Islam. Turkish replaced Arabic and Persian as the language of diplomacy, and ethnic Turks filled the upper ranks of the civil and military hierarchies. When Constantinople was finally taken in 1453, it was renamed Istanbul ("the city") and established as the new capital of the Turkish state. The choice was doubly symbolic: not only did the Islamic world itself now stand triumphant over the Byzantines, but also the Ottomans, unlike all earlier Muslim leaders, took up residence in the very city that straddled Asia and Europe. Islam would henceforth be a civilization on two fronts, facing both east and west, rooted in the faith that arose from Arabia but as much involved in Western ways as in Eastern. It was no coincidence that what enabled the great sultan Mehmed II to finally achieve the conquest of Constantinople was his use of massive cannons that had been forged for him by engineers in Hungary. It was an Eastern army with Western technology.

The New Capital of Istanbul

The dominant spirit of the age, before the catastrophes of the 14th century, was a willingness, a confident willingness, to question the values of society and state—not necessarily to challenge or undermine them but to express a conviction in progress, a belief that human experience and understanding not only change but also move forward with time. When that faith in progress confronted the devastations of the 14th century, however, the collapse of old certainties left behind it an overwhelming sense of loss and bewilderment. No one could have predicted that the crises of the 14th century would spark one of the greatest periods of cultural achievement in European history, the Renaissance.

WHO, WHAT, WHERE

Avignon Papacy	Hundred Years' War	Ottoman Turks
Black Death	inquisition	Parliament
chivalry	Janissaries	Rumi
Diet	Joan of Arc	scholasticism
English Peasants' Revolt	Magna Carta	sultan
Estates General	Mehmed II	Tamerlane
Genghis (Chinggis) Khan	mendicant orders	
guild	Mongols	

SUGGESTED READINGS

Primary Sources

Anonymous. *The Secret History of the Mongols.*
Alighieri, Dante. *The Divine Comedy.*
del Carpine, Giovanni Pian. *History of the Mongols.*
Froissart, Jean. *Chronicles.*
Ibn Battuta. *Travels.*

Ibn Khaldun. *The Muqaddimah.*
Ibn Taymiyya. *Following the Straight Path.*
Ibn Taymiyya. *The Goodly Word.*
Kempe, Margery. *The Book of Margery Kempe.*
Pizan, Christine de. *The Book of the City of Ladies.*
Rumi. *Complete Poems.*

Anthologies

Aberth, John. *The Black Death: The Great Mortality of 1348–1350; A Brief History with Documents* (2005).
Avery, Peter. *The Collected Lyrics of Hafiz of Shiraz* (2007).
Dean, Trevor, trans. *The Towns of Italy in the Later Middle Ages* (2000).
Doss-Quinby, Eglal, Joan Tasker Grimbert, Wendy Pfeffer, and Elizabeth Aubrey, eds.

and trans. *Songs of the Women Trouvères* (2001).
Massoud, Sami G. *The Chronicles and Annalistic Sources of the Early Mamluk Circassian Period* (2007).
Murray, Jacqueline, ed. *Love, Marriage, and the Family in the Middle Ages: A Reader* (2001).

Studies

Aberth, John. *From the Brink of the Apocalypse: Confronting Famine, War, Plague, and Death in the Later Middle Ages* (2001).

Allsen, Thomas T. *Culture and Conquest in Mongol Eurasia* (2001).

Amitai-Preiss, Reuven. *Mongols and Mamluks: The Mamluk–Ilkhānid War of 1260–1281* (2005).

Arnold, John. *Inquisition and Power: Catharism and the Confessing Subject in Medieval Languedoc* (2001).

Beckwith, Christopher I. *Empires of the Silk Road: A History of Central Eurasia from the Bronze Age to the Present* (2010).

Blumenfeld-Kosinski, Renate. *Poets, Saints, and Visionaries of the Great Schism, 1378–1417* (2006).

Cahen, Claude. *The Formation of Turkey: The Seljukid Sultanate of Rūm; 11th to 14th Century* (2001).

Clark, Victoria. *Why Angels Fall: A Journey through Orthodox Europe from Byzantium to Kosovo* (2000).

Cohn, Samuel K., Jr. *Lust for Liberty: The Politics of Social Revolt in Medieval Europe, 1200–1425; Italy, France, and Flanders* (2006).

Dunn, Alastair. *The Peasants' Revolt: England's Failed Revolution of 1381* (2004).

Dyer, Christopher. *Making a Living in the Middle Ages: The People of Britain, 850–1520* (2003).

El-Cheik, Nadia Maria. *Byzantium Viewed by the Arabs* (2004).

Finkel, Caroline. *Osman's Dream: The History of the Ottoman Empire* (2007).

Goffman, Daniel. *The Ottoman Empire and Early Modern Europe* (2002).

Imber, Colin. *The Ottoman Empire, 1300–1650: The Structure of Power* (2009).

Inalcik, Halil. *The Ottoman Empire: The Classical Age, 1300–1600* (2001).

Inalcik, Halil, and Donald Quataert, eds. *An Economic and Social History of the Ottoman Empire* (2005).

Komaroff, Linda, and Stefano Carboni. *The Legacy of Genghis Khan: Courtly Art and Culture in Western Asia, 1256–1353* (2002).

Leopold, Antony. *How to Recover the Holy Land: Crusading Proposals of the Late Thirteenth and Early Fourteenth Centuries* (2000).

Liu, Xinru. *The Silk Road in World History* (2010).

Pegg, Mark Gregory. *The Corruption of Angels: The Great Inquisition of 1245–1246* (2001).

Rouighi, Ramzi. *The Making of a Mediterranean Emirate: Ifrīqiyā and Its Andalusis, 1200–1400* (2011).

Rubin, Miri. *Gentile Tales: The Narrative Assault on Late Medieval Jews* (2004).

Sumption, Jonathan. *The Hundred Years War* (2000–2011).

For additional resources, including maps, primary sources, visuals, web links, and quizzes, please go to **www.oup.com/us/backman**.

TEMPLA DOMVM EXPOSITIS·VICOS FORA MOENIA PONTES:
VIRGINEAM TRIVII QVOD REPARARIS AQVAM.
PRISCA LICET NAVTIS STATVAS DARE COMMODA PORTVS:
ET VATICANVM CINGERE SIXTE IVGVM:
PLVS TAMEN VRBS DEBET·NAM QVAE SQVALORE LATEBAT:
CERNITVR IN CELEBRI BIBLIOTHECA LOCO.

CHAPTER 12

Renaissances and Reformations

1350–1563

Pope Sixtus IV Sixtus IV (r. 1471–1484) is remembered for building the Sistine Chapel, establishing the Spanish Inquisition, and developing the Vatican Library. Record collection had long been professionalized in the papal court; in fact, references to standing administrative offices with bureaucratic support date back to the 6th century, but a formal library was another matter. Sixtus saw the need for a centralized permanent collection of the church's manuscripts. Pope Nicholas V (r. 1447–1455) was the library's actual founder, but Sixtus greatly expanded and reorganized it and also made it available to scholars. Sixtus was a Franciscan, one of the last of his order to hold the papacy, but quickly became enamored of the pomp and splendor of the Renaissance court. He appointed a half-dozen of his nephews to the College of Cardinals, including Giuliano della Rovere—the tall figure in the center—who later became Pope Julius II (r. 1503–1513), the target of Erasmus's great satire *Julius Excluded from Heaven.*

The Renaissance, the period in Europe roughly from 1350 to 1550, is one of the few eras in Greater Western history that named itself. The cultural elite of the time believed they were living in an age of self-conscious revival. They were bringing back to life the ideas, moral values, art, and civic-mindedness that characterized, they believed, the two high points of Western culture: Periclean Athens and Republican Rome. One of the first to use the term was the Italian writer, painter, and architect Giorgio Vasari (1511–1574). After a thousand years of medieval barbarism, Vasari claimed, Italian artists and thinkers had bravely restored the lost perfection of art and philosophy as known to the ancients. An earlier Renaissance writer on education, Pier Paolo Vergerio (1370–1444), insisted that only the study of the classical liberal arts could lift society from the moral and spiritual decay of the medieval era. "Only

THE GREATER WEST, ca. 1550

those liberal arts," he proclaimed, "are worthy of free men; they alone can help us to attain virtue and wisdom . . . [and fill in the gaps in our moral knowledge] which the ignorance of the past centuries has intentionally created."

Una rinascità was a "rebirth" of classical values that gave fresh hope and creative energy to Europe. It also led to the greatest eruption in Greater Western religion since the birth of Islam—the Protestant Reformation.

REBIRTH OR CULMINATION?

Not everyone in the Renaissance shared Vasari's and Vergerio's sense of the near-mythic magnificence of antiquity, and it took some time for the French version of the word *rinascità*, *renaissance*, to catch on. It did not acquire positive connotations until the English writer John Ruskin (1819–1900) used it in his famous study of architecture, *The Stones of Venice* (1851): "This rationalistic art is the art called Renaissance, marked by a return to pagan systems" (1.1.23). Most of Vergerio's and Vasari's contemporaries were simply grateful to have been born after the filthy muddle of the Middle Ages. Francesco Petrarch (1304–1374), usually regarded as the father of humanism and the first Renaissance writer, expressed this nostalgia for the deep past of Rome and Athens. In an open letter written toward the end of his life, called the *Letter to Posterity*, he recalls his youthful studies:

CHAPTER TIMELINE

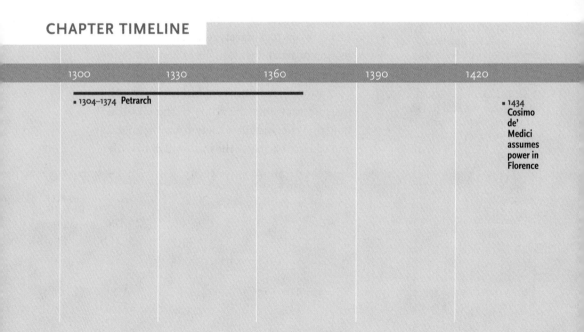

1300	1330	1360	1390	1420

- 1304–1374 **Petrarch**

- 1434
Cosimo de' Medici assumes power in Florence

I had more of a well-rounded mind than a keen intellect, and was naturally inclined to every type of virtuous and honorable study but especially to moral philosophy and poetry. After a while, it is true, I began to neglect poetry in favor of sacred literature, in which I soon found a buried sweetness that I had previously acknowledged to be there but only in a perfunctory way; now however I found its sweetness so great that poetry became a mere afterthought for me. Out of all the subjects that intrigued me, I fixed especially upon antiquity—for the truth is that our own age repels me and has always done so. Indeed, were it not for the love of those I hold dear, I would rather have been born in any age but our own. I have spent most of my life thinking about other eras, in fact, as a way of ignoring my own, and that is why I have always loved the study of history.

However, the Renaissance—or the early part of it, anyway—shared more with its preceding age than it wanted to admit. The three elements most characteristically associated with the Renaissance—classicism, humanism, and modern statecraft—represent no essential break with medieval life at all. They may in fact be thought of as the culmination of medieval strivings.

The cult of classical learning and literature had its origins in early Christian monastic life. Novice monks had long been directed to study the Roman poets *Classicism* Virgil and Horace, the historians Suetonius and Sallust, and the playwrights Terence and Seneca. It was their means to learn Latin before being granted access to

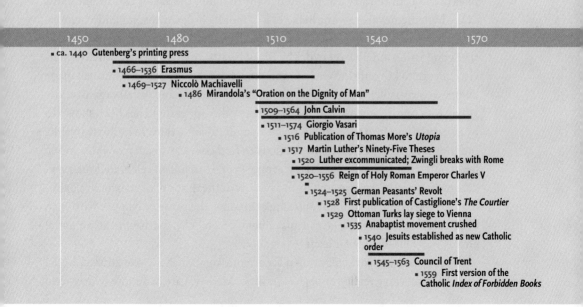

1450   1480   1510   1540   1570

- ca. 1440 **Gutenberg's printing press**
- 1466–1536 **Erasmus**
- 1469–1527 **Niccolò Machiavelli**
- 1486 **Mirandola's "Oration on the Dignity of Man"**
- 1509–1564 **John Calvin**
- 1511–1574 **Giorgio Vasari**
- 1516 **Publication of Thomas More's *Utopia***
- 1517 **Martin Luther's Ninety-Five Theses**
- 1520 **Luther excommunicated; Zwingli breaks with Rome**
- 1520–1556 **Reign of Holy Roman Emperor Charles V**
- 1524–1525 **German Peasants' Revolt**
- 1528 **First publication of Castiglione's *The Courtier***
- 1529 **Ottoman Turks lay siege to Vienna**
- 1535 **Anabaptist movement crushed**
- 1540 **Jesuits established as new Catholic order**
- 1545–1563 **Council of Trent**
- 1559 **First version of the Catholic *Index of Forbidden Books***

the scriptures and the patristic literature (the texts of the Church Fathers). The works of Aristotle, Ptolemy, Galen, and Euclid, moreover, had dominated university education from the start. But the great scholars of the Renaissance broadened this core canon by seeking out long-lost manuscripts; virtually anything by a classical author was of interest. Petrarch himself unearthed Cicero's *Letters to Atticus*, lying unused and unknown on a dusty library shelf in Verona for centuries, and brought out a new edition of it.

What distinguished the Renaissance approach to the classics was a passionate conviction that they contained all that humans have best thought and best expressed. It was simply impossible not merely to be educated but also to be a complete, satisfied, and accomplished human being without knowing the wisdom of the ancients. Pier Paolo Vergerio described the classical canon as "the only literature whose study helps us in the pursuit of virtue and wisdom, and brings forth in us those most sublime gifts of body and mind that ennoble men's spirit and that are properly regarded as second only to virtue itself as our most dignified attainment." Renaissance scholars traveled through scores of libraries and archives, sifted through piles of manuscripts, corrected the minutest scribal errors, and commented prolifically on the cultural context and multiple meanings of a writer's text. Moreover, these scholars put their learning to use in original works of their own, in every genre from poetry to stage drama, epistles to essays, histories to philosophical treatises.

Humanism The concern in this period to develop human potential, to value the particular, and to assert the inherent dignity of each person is called **humanism**. The idea itself was not new, but the degree of emphasis placed on it was. The catastrophes of the 14th century had inspired many to doubt the values and assumptions of the high medieval era—the belief in a rationally ordered cosmos and a benevolent deity, the naturalness of a hierarchically structured society, the conviction that good will triumph over evil. The Black Death, after all, had shown no apparent concern to kill only the wicked, and the other calamities of the time had made people grow suspicious of accepted systems of thought and social organization. What does one do when everything a society takes for granted has been shown to be a sham? The world is a perilous place, denying all efforts to create anything like order or meaning. The best one can do is to find comfort, beauty, or value in the broken shards of the world scattered at one's feet. Humanism celebrated such specific pleasures: the precise arch of an eyebrow or the drape of a garment in a painting, the warm hue of sunlight entering a window, the sense of balance within an enclosure created by the artful placement of objects, the beautiful potential energy in a tensed coil of muscle.

A focus on the particular called for a representational art, one attuned to the hard but transitory reality of objects in time. Medieval art had more widely used symbolic and allegorical representations. Starting with the Florentine painter Giotto di Bondone (1267–1337)—a generation before Petrarch—artists strove for a more naturalistic, three-dimensional style of depiction. By the early 1400s linear perspective was introduced in painting, heightening the senses of depth, solidity, and realism the artists evoked. The 1427 fresco of the Holy Trinity painted for the church of Santa Maria Novella in Florence by Masaccio (1401–1428) marked the maturity of the new techniques.

Scholars in the Renaissance still wrote in Latin, although most of the creative literature of the age was in the vernacular, or local languages. This too reflected medieval practice, but for a different reason. In the Middle Ages, scholarship was written in Latin because it was the common tongue of the learned. Physicians in Spain

The Holy Trinity (in Perspective) The Italian artist Tommaso Masaccio (1401–1428) painted this masterwork in the church of Santa Maria Novella in Florence. It is among the first Renaissance paintings to employ linear perspective, in which parallel lines are represented as converging so as to give the illusion of depth and distance. Above Christ's head appear the Holy Spirit, in the form of a dove, and the head of God the Father. The man and woman shown in the lower corners are presumably the patrons who commissioned the work. Their clothing suggests that they were commoners rather than nobles.

could communicate with physicians in Hungary or Denmark; mathematicians in England could be read in Portugal or Poland. In the Renaissance, however, scholars wrote in Latin (or sometimes in Greek) out of a conviction in the intrinsic superiority of the classical languages. Latin and Greek, in the "pure" forms used in ancient times, were seen as uniquely capable of expressing complex thought. Hence scholars sought to take the living Latin and Greek they had inherited and purge them of what they considered barbarisms and corrupt usages. Words, phrases, and grammatical constructions that came into use in the postclassical era were avoided in the effort to return to the purity of ancient Latin. The results were disastrous and effectively killed Latin as a living language. Imagine a demand today to make Shakespearean English the only form of English worthy of public discourse.

The most famous of Renaissance descriptions of humanism came from Giovanni Pico della Mirandola (1463–1494), a young man of great and varied learning. His "Oration on the Dignity of Man" (1486) lays out the fundamental elements of the movement:

> I read somewhere of a Muslim writer named Abdullah who, when asked to identify the most wondrous and awe-inspiring thing to appear on the world's stage, answered, "There exists nothing more wondrous than Man." . . .
>
> But when I began to consider the reasons behind these opinions, every particular of their arguments for the magnificence of human nature failed to persuade me.

The unconvincing arguments include man's existence as a rational creature or as master of the physical world. What strikes Pico della Mirandola as the essential and glorious point about humans is rather something else: to us alone has God given the freedom and ability to be whatever we want, to become whatever we desire, and to achieve whatever we wish. A flower has no choice but to bloom, wither, and die; a stone may serve as a building block, a projectile, or a hindrance in the road, but it has no destiny of its own, no yearning to become something. Humans alone, he insists, are free to be whatever we wish to be:

> You alone, being altogether without limits and in possession of your own free will, . . . have it within you to establish the limits of your own nature. . . . Alone at the dark center of his own existence, yet united with God, Who is Himself beyond all created things, Man too exists beyond every created thing—and who can help but stand in awe of this great Fate-forger? Even more: How is it possible for anyone to marvel at any-thing else?

To describe man as, essentially, his own creator was to flirt with heresy—and Mirandola did in fact run afoul of the church. Consequently he issued a number of corrections and retractions and announced his interest in becoming an obedient monk. He died suddenly at age thirty-one, however, poisoned by an enemy who had slipped arsenic into his wine. His fate should not distract us, however, from recognizing the fundamentally religious nature of humanism. Humanism was not a secular philosophy. It sought to define the place of humanity in God's divine plan, to parse the relationship between man and God, and so to glorify both.

The third major element of the Renaissance was statecraft. The concept of a

Statecraft   state is a relatively modern one. A state as a thing in itself, independent of the people who comprise it and following its own norms and rules, requires a degree of abstraction. Earlier notions of government had regarded the state as a network of personal relationships, but not necessarily as a distinct object. It had the king at the center, with his web of obligations and privileges to his nobles, his commoners, and the church. Exceptions to this model existed, of course, but until the 13th century they were in the minority.

Renaissance theorists and power brokers, taking their cue from late medieval writers like Brunetto Latini (1220–1294) and Marsiglio di Padova (1275–1342), thought of the state in a new way. The political state was a thing, a part of the natural world, and it functioned according to rules. Political leaders who understood this governed most effectively because they could direct the state by means of its own internal logic. Statecraft therefore involved understanding systems of law, taxation, and economy. It involved the intricacies of diplomacy and negotiation, the mechanisms of crowd control, the manipulation of public opinion, and the knowledge of when to deceive or to exert force. Idealism had no part in it, and

The Ambassadors   This powerful painting by Hans Holbein the Younger (ca. 1497–1543), *The Ambassadors*, depicts a French nobleman dispatched to London on a diplomatic errand, together with his friend, a French bishop. Together they represent the active and the contemplative modes of life, with objects representing knowledge, power, and art in the background. The diagonally oriented object in the foreground, when looked at obliquely, is a skull representing death.

politics became a hard science rather than an expression of personal desire. For that very reason, however, it offered the perfect site for educated men of the Renaissance. Conscious of their abilities and dedicated to the ancient Roman virtue of civic-mindedness, they could take their proper place within the world by mastering its rules and methods.

THE POLITICAL AND ECONOMIC MATRIX

Renaissance Roots in Urban Italy

Europe needed men of ability, Italy especially. Italy was by far the most developed urban society in Europe, followed closely by southern France and eastern Spain, yet its political scene was a mess. The northern city-states, where the Renaissance began, had long been under the leadership of the Holy Roman emperor, at least in name. Since the 10th century Holy Roman emperors had brought armies over or around the Alps, intermittently but repeatedly, to reassert their claims—and most of Italy's city-states opened their gates, bowed deeply, and paid their ritual and financial tribute. But once the armies were safely back in Germany, the Italians instantly returned to their independent republican ways.

By the start of the Renaissance many northern Italians wanted to end permanently the imperial claims over their territories. Others, however, saw some utility in the on-again, off-again imperial connection and so opposed autonomy. This scenario, in which the papacy became deeply involved, led to strife between and within each of the city-states. By the time of the 14th century's disasters, northern Italy was a mercenary's dreamscape. Wars large and small, palace coups, assassinations, plots, pillagings, enforced exiles, and institutional corruption had spread everywhere (see Map 12.1).

Political Transformation of Italian City-States

A unique feature of the Italian scene, however, helped pave the way for the Renaissance. Italian nobles tended to live within the cities, although their rural estates were distant, and hence they played an active role in urban culture that nobles in northern Europe did not. That included both established lineages and wealthy commoners whose riches had helped them purchase aristocratic titles. Moreover, the elitist bias against trade and commerce that characterized northern European aristocratic society was much less virulent in Italy. Hence, by 1400, ties (usually volatile) had developed between the urban aristocrats and the mercantile and banking families of the burgher class. This connection allowed the upper classes to usurp republican government and to institute direct, often-tyrannical control over the city-states. Most who did so, imitating the 1st-century emperor Augustus, maintained the fiction and rituals of republican government while establishing despotic rule.

Most city-states thus had actual, if barely functioning, republican governments between 1350 and 1450 (the first half, roughly, of the Renaissance) but oligarchic

MAP 12.1   Renaissance Italy   The political map of Renaissance Italy differed little from that of medieval Italy: a large Kingdom of Naples in the south; the perennially embattled Papal States in the center, and a sprawling matrix of city-states in the north. Most humanistic activity took place in the north and in the court cities of Rome and Naples.

governments from 1450 to 1550 (the second half). In Florence, for example, the Medici family, which had risen through the ranks in banking and textiles, came to political prominence shortly after 1400. Through three generations—under Cosimo de' Medici (r. 1434–1464), Piero de' Medici (r. 1464–1469), and Lorenzo de' Medici (r. 1469–1492)—they governed a pretend republic. In 1531 the family became the hereditary dukes of Florence (later elevated to the status of an

The Medici and the Magi   Wealth has its privileges, among which has been the tradition of artists inserting portraits of their patrons into their religious paintings. Usually this was done by placing the patron somewhere within the frame of the original biblical story, but with this painting of the Three Magi coming to worship the child Jesus, the Renaissance master Benozzo Gozzoli (1420–1497) has gone one step further by portraying Cosimo de' Medici and his family members as the guides who brought the Magi to the infant Jesus. The imposition is apt, since the gifts brought by the Magi (gold, myrrh, and frankincense) were symbolic of the finance and spice trades that brought the Medici their enormous wealth.

archduchy) and placed three family members on the papal throne during the Renaissance—Leo X (r. 1513–1521), Clement VII (r. 1523–1534), and Leo XI (r. 1605). In Milan, the famous Visconti and Sforza families followed similar trajectories, with the Visconti family taking the ducal title in 1369 and holding it until the family line died out in 1447. At that point the Sforza family (of peasant origins, with several generations of mercenary soldiers thrown in) took over and governed by fiat until 1535. The d'Este family in Ferrara, who had led local politics since 1264, won a ducal title in 1452 (and another in 1471) and held on to power until 1597; likewise the Gonzaga family in Mantua, where they ruled without stop from 1328 to 1708.

The concentrations of wealth and power in these city-states, and in others like them, made possible elaborate systems of patronage, which gave a tremendous boost to intellectual and artistic life.

A Culture of Consumption   Again like Augustus, Renaissance oligarchs put their resources to work in the public sphere. They commissioned scores of palaces, chapels, public fountains and market squares, mausoleums, fortifications, libraries and museums, schools, and hospitals. All were done in the newest styles and were richly decorated with paintings, sculptures, frescos, and tapestries—and they provided hundreds of opportunities for scholars, artists, and architects. Art was not for art's sake alone in the Renaissance: it expressed humanist values and aesthetics while serving to elevate the civic spirit and also promoted the glory and wisdom of the patron whose support made the art possible.

The depressed economy contributed as well, since labor costs were comparatively low. The building frenzy of the 14th and 15th centuries therefore represented a jobs program: it bolstered support for the regimes by putting people to work. Manufacturing still limped along, since the shrunken population meant a decreased need for most goods; the demographic recovery was slow across Europe. The city of Toulouse, for example, had numbered thirty thousand in the early 14th century, and by the early 15th it had only eight thousand. Within Italy,

Genoa had lost more than one-third of its population; Bologna and Milan had each lost half; Florence had lost three-fourths. Many towns did not regain their 13th-century populations until the 20th century. Moreover, the ongoing struggles against the Ottomans, who pressed their frontiers to the gates of Vienna, interrupted trade with Asia. Even with such drastically reduced numbers, the drift of the rural poor into the cities ensured a constant labor surplus. Labor costs therefore were cheap, making the vast construction projects of the Renaissance possible.

The rich are with us always. Even in a depressed economy, concentrations of capital exist and often grow, so long as the possessor is lucky or clever (or corrupt) *Economic* enough to seize the opportunities. In the Renaissance, those opportunities ex- *Inequality* isted, especially in finance and armaments. With so much construction to perform and so much war to wage, those with capital were able to lend it at handsome rates of interest. Meanwhile, manufacturers found markets always in search of weaponry and construction equipment. Venice's Arsenal—its shipbuilding factory— employed three thousand laborers at the start of the 15th century. Tax records from that time show that two-thirds of the city's merchants made at least 6,000 ducats per year, and one-half of those fortunate merchants actually made well over 12,000.[1] Seven merchants actually had annual incomes of more than 140,000 ducats. Such severe inequities in the distribution of capital ensured that rents and wages worked in favor of the elite. So did the power of the guild leaders and urban nobles. In Milan, a mere 5 percent of the population controlled one-half of the city's wealth. No wonder they had the ability to commission palaces, endow museums and libraries, dress in expensive silks and furs, and commission such splendid works of art. The Renaissance, for all its cultural glories, was a miserable time to be a poor farmer or a simple workman—which is precisely what the overwhelming majority of people were.

THE RENAISSANCE ACHIEVEMENT

Art and intellectual life tend to thrive when supported. The cult of patronage— that is, the eager support of painters, sculptors, poets, and scholars as a sign of one's sophistication—and the appreciation of individual talent gave a tremendous impetus to new forms of expression and the pursuit of knowledge. The influx of scholars and artists from the east also contributed as the Ottomans closed in on the remnants of Byzantium. One Sicilian humanist, Giovanni Aurispa (1376–1459), rushed to Constantinople in the years leading up to the Turkish

---

[1]   A Venetian ducat of that time was minted of roughly 0.125 ounces (one-eighth of an ounce). An approximate contemporary estimate of the value of 6,000 ducats would be about $1.2 million.

A Renaissance Print Shop   The printing press made written materials available to the population on a vast scale, but printing was nevertheless a slow and laborious process. In this scene two workers are setting type in a frame, while in the front, to the right, another worker fixes the type in place and inks it before placing it in the press. The worker in the front, to the left, carefully peels a printed sheet from its frame. This woodcut was created by the Swiss artist Jost Amman (1539–1591).

siege and came back with more than two hundred manuscripts that might otherwise have gone up in flames. Copyists were hired by the hundreds in every city to get texts like these reproduced and circulated. By 1400 Florence had opened the first lending library in Europe; one could actually borrow books and bring them home rather than have to read them on site, as before. The invention of the printing press by Johannes Gutenberg around 1440 allowed books to pour over Europe like a tide. Aldus Manutius (1450–1515) was the most celebrated of humanist publishers; his printing house in Venice produced editions of well over a hundred Latin and Greek texts before his death.

Vernacular literature also began to appear in print. This is important because most of the truly memorable literature produced in the Renaissance was in the

The Triumph of Vernacular Literature

common, not the learned, tongues. Petrarch's great sequence of sonnets and other poems to his beloved Laura—the *Canzoniere* (*Song Book*)—have proved enduringly popular, whereas his Latin epic poem about the Roman general Scipio Africanus—called *Africa*—is turgid and lifeless. Much better is Ludovico Ariosto's (1474–1533) immense, and immensely entertaining, mock-epic *Orlando Furioso* (*Crazed Roland*). It tells of the mad adventures of Charlemagne's knight Roland, who loses his mind when his beloved Angelica falls in love with a Muslim prince and moves to China. Roland promptly turns into a one-man juggernaut, rampaging through Europe, Asia, and Africa and destroying everything in sight. Giovanni Boccaccio (1313–1375) wrote the first Italian novel—called *Filocolo* (*The Love Afflicted*, 1336)—but is best remembered for his collection of thematically linked short stories called *The Decameron* (*Ten Days*, 1353), in which ten friends escape from plague-ridden Florence into the countryside and entertain themselves by each one telling a story to the rest every day for ten days.

Not many Renaissance stage plays have lasted; only two are still widely read and produced today. Pietro Aretino (1492–1556), known in his lifetime as the "Scourge of Princes" for his scathing wit and willingness to blackmail the prominent when short of funds, wrote several brilliant bawdy comedies. His best play, a comedy called *La Cortigiana* (*The Woman Courtier*), tells of an upright wealthy citizen from Siena who receives an appointment as a papal cardinal. Traveling to Rome for his installation, he sees a beautiful young woman sitting at a window and decides he must have her as a mistress. The comedy ensues when a scheming con artist tries to teach the elderly man how to flatter and entice the young beauty—all the while pursuing a plan of his own.

The other great Renaissance comedy is *La Mandragola* (*The Mandrake Root*), by Niccolò Machiavelli (1469–1527). The play, which appeared in 1518, tells of another upright elderly man, Nicia, newly married to a stunning but sexually shy beauty named Lucrezia. Unable to convince his bride to sleep with him, the foolish husband confides in a dashing young ne'er-do-well named Callimaco, who, desiring Lucrezia for himself, hatches a plot. He tells Nicia that he has learned, through careful study of ancient Greek scientific manuscripts, of a potion made from mandrake root. When given to a woman, it instantly enflames her with a lust that cannot be denied. The drug has an unfortunate side effect, however: the first man to have sex with the woman will die immediately afterward. Nicia declares that he wants Lucrezia, but not enough to die for it. Callimaco then announces—tremblingly, hesitantly—that he himself suffers from an unspecified mortal illness and has only a few days to live. So great is his admiration for Nicia and his desire to perform a useful service before he dies that he volunteers for the suicide mission.

La Mandragola surprises most people who read or watch it. They usually come to the play knowing Machiavelli from another work of his, a small politi- **Machiavelli's** cal treatise called *The Prince*. In 1499 the people of Florence had overthrown the **The Prince** Medici oligarchy and restored republican government. Machiavelli, a Florentine, loved and served its republic with passionate dedication for thirteen years, from 1499 to 1512—as a diplomat, civil servant, and military overseer. Late in 1512, however, a counterplot restored Lorenzo de' Medici to power. Machiavelli was dismissed, arrested for conspiracy, tortured, and ultimately released. In retirement at his country estate, he then gave himself over to study and writing.

The Prince, although he never published it, was the first thing Machiavelli wrote after his release from prison. (He wrote it in a matter of weeks, then circulated it among a small circle of friends and dedicated it to Lorenzo de' Medici—probably in hopes of winning a position in the new government.) It is a notorious book, praised by some for its clear-eyed realism about how political power actually works and vilified by others as little more than a how-to manual for thugs. Society, Machiavelli argues, benefits more from stable order than from benevolent instability. Therefore, a prince's first responsibility is to secure his own power, even if the exercise of that power is unjust. Ruthlessness should not be pursued for its own sake, but a wise prince will never rule it out altogether. A prince ought always to maintain an upright public appearance, but behind the scenes he should use any means at his disposal—including lying, cheating, stealing, or killing—to maintain power. Although *The Prince* never uses the phrase, its essential message is that in politics the end justifies the means.

Once the book was published, five years after Machiavelli's death, people read it with a shudder of horror. Machiavelli's defenders point to the chaotic state of Italian politics at the time, with French, German, and Spanish invaders at every turn. *The Prince*, they suggest, is simply a plea for a no-nonsense messianic figure who would restore Italian liberty. Perhaps. Machiavelli's letters, however, show that he was a man of republican Florence, first, last, and always. He would have been delighted to see Ferrara, Mantua, Milan, Pisa, or Venice crushed by a foreign army if that were to Florence's gain. Complicating matters, he dashed off *The Prince* in a few weeks. Machiavelli then spent four years (1513–1517) composing his major work, *Discourses on Livy*, which elaborates a complex and passionate argument on the superiority of republican government to any other type of political organization. Because no one except specialist scholars ever reads the *Discourses*, it has escaped popular notice that it demolishes nearly every idea put forth in *The Prince*. "No properly run republic should ever find it necessary to overlook the crimes of any given citizen because of his supposed excellence.... Governments of the people are superior to any government by a prince" (1.24, 1.58).

Less controversial were Marsilio Ficino (1433–1499) and Baldassare Castiglione (1478–1529). Ficino was a celebrated philosopher who spent his career at the Medici court. He had mastered classical Greek as a young man and became a devout exponent of Neoplatonism. His greatest achievement, in fact, was a translation into Latin of the entire corpus of Plato's writings. Until its publication in 1484, Plato had hardly been known in Latin Europe, and Western intellectual life had been long dominated by Aristotle. Ficino's other major works include a long treatise, *On Platonic Theology*, which explicates Christian doctrine on the immortality of the soul using Platonic ideas. He argues that the unique, characteristic destiny of the human soul is to investigate its own nature, but such investigation inevitably results (at least temporarily) in confusion and misery. Hence the ultimate goal of the soul is to rise above physicality, to become disembodied, and to achieve union with the divine. As a hybrid philosophical and mystical treatise, it is a stunning exercise. Ficino was the tutor of many Neoplatonists, most famously of Giovanni Pico della Mirandola, the author of the "Oration on the Dignity of Man."

Castiglione's The Courtier

Castiglione came from an ancient noble family near Mantua and spent his entire life in the circle of social and political elites. He served as a personal aide and confidante to the marquis of Mantua and then to the duke of Urbino and spent several years in Rome as an ambassador to the papal court, then several more as papal envoy to the royal court of Spain in Madrid. He is remembered primarily for *The Courtier* (1528), which is a kind of memoir written in the form of a fictional philosophical dialogue. In it he laments the passing of the

Renaissance's golden era, when humanism was at its height. By 1500 Italy was overrun by ambitious foreigners, and courtly life as Castiglione had known it (or at least as he chose to remember it) had declined into a tawdry arena of power grabbing, money grubbing, and social climbing. He depicts fictionalized versions of the companions of his youth—elegant, charming, cultivated, effortlessly superior to everyone—who spend four evenings in an extended conversation about the qualities of an ideal courtier.

To Castiglione the courtier is above politics: he graciously advises any figure deemed worthy of attention but does not advocate any particular political philosophy. This marks a shift from the original ideal of humanism, which expected a passionate civic spirit from its adherents. Castiglione's figures expound on the need for courtiers to appreciate music and poetry; to excel at dancing, sports, and refined conversation; to understand the importance of fashion as well as affairs of state. In short, courtiers should exist beautifully, all the while exuding an air of nonchalance and unpracticed elegance. *The Courtier* was extraordinarily popular, going through more than one hundred editions between its appearance in 1528 and 1616. Its significance lay in its elegiac mood: at a time when many of Europe's nobles were being displaced from political life, Castiglione consecrated for them the qualities that lifted them forever, in their own minds, above the common rabble.

CHRISTIAN HUMANISM

As the ideas and values of the Renaissance spread outward from Italy, they took on new styles, concerns, and emphases. Ultimately, if indirectly, they led to the shattering of the religious unity that had marked Latin Europe since the advent of Christianity.

It took some time for humanism to catch on in the north. The prolonged agony of the Hundred Years' War in England and France certainly impeded the spread of the new learning. So did the resistance of the universities of Paris and Oxford—both strongholds of Aristotelianism. As for Germany, intellectual life there had long been centered in the royal and aristocratic courts. By this time Germany had fractured into hundreds of principalities (nominally under the authority of the Habsburg dynasty, but effectively autonomous), and its relatively few universities did not rush to embrace new ideas.[2] When humanism did finally begin to take root throughout Europe, around the year 1500, it developed along a variety of trajectories; especially significant among them was a kind of humanism that came to be known as **Christian humanism.**

---

[2]   Munich did not acquire a university until 1472. Even then, the university was at Ingolstadt, several miles away.

The Four Holy Men   "A panel on which I have bestowed more care than on any other painting" is how the German Renaissance master Albrecht Dürer (1471–1528) described this powerful group portrait, completed in 1526. It depicts, from left to right, St. John the Evangelist, St. Peter (holding his ever-present key to paradise), St. Mark, and St. Paul the Apostle (who carries a copy of the Bible and a sword, the latter being a reference to his martyrdom). Dürer was a passionate supporter of the Lutheran Reformation, and the bottom portion of each panel (since lost) bore passages from Luther's German translation of the scriptures.

Like early humanism, Christian humanism rejected scholastic system building and looked to the past for new models of thinking and behavior. However, Christian humanists showed a strong preference for texts and traditions that contributed specifically to religious faith. Their goal was not to become better all-round individuals, but better Christians. Consequently, they focused less on the writings of the ancient philosophers and poets and more on the early writings of the Christians—especially the New Testament itself. In the visual arts, Christian humanists showed little interest in depicting classical pagan themes; rather, painters and sculptors avidly adopted Renaissance techniques to produce striking new presentations of biblical imagery. The Christian humanists were passionate reformers, dedicated to promoting Christian education and practical piety through the preparation of newer and better texts.

The Christian humanists were not yet anti-Catholic, only anticlerical. The shortage of priests had always been more dire the farther north one traveled in Europe, with exceptions in cities like Paris, London, and Mainz, but the problem had been persistently acute since the Black Death. Clergy at the grassroots level were in painfully short supply, and those who were available were often poorly trained. Hence northerners had developed strong traditions of lay piety. They focused less on the church's sacramental life and more on the simple reading of scripture, the singing of hymns, and communal prayer. Religious fraternities and sororities abounded, offering many a life of organized piety, education, and moral rigor that deemphasized ecclesiastical dogma and ritual.

The Brethren of the Common Life   The best known of these organizations was the Brethren of the Common Life, established in Holland in the late 14th century; its reputation for pious simplicity and educational excellence spread quickly across Europe. The Brethren community preached what they called the "new devotion" (*devotio moderna*), based on the idea of replicating in one's own life the actions and attitudes of Jesus, rather than the formal doctrines and disciplines of the church. An early member of the Brethren, Thomas à Kempis (1380–1471), wrote *The Imitation of Christ*, which went on to become the most widely read and frequently translated Christian devotional book in Europe. But the most famous alumni of the Brethren were Desiderius Erasmus and Martin Luther.

ERASMUS: HUMANIST SCHOLAR AND SOCIAL CRITIC

Erasmus (1466–1536) was arguably the greatest of all humanist scholars, admired for the breadth of his classical learning, his quick wit and generous spirit, and the elegance of his writing. The illegitimate son of a Dutch priest in training and a physician's daughter, he grew up in Rotterdam and received his primary education at home. In 1483, however, both of his parents died in a new outbreak of the plague. Supported by the Brethren of the Common Life, Erasmus entered a series of monastic and lay-fraternal schools, where he was unhappy with the communities' frequently dour discipline but delighted in their extensive libraries. In 1492, brilliant but penniless, he took monastic vows, entered an Augustinian house, and was soon ordained to the priesthood. He hated monastic life, however, and thought most of his fellow monks joyless and haughty automatons. Fortunately, a bishop from Cambrai, not far away in northern France, heard of Erasmus's brilliance and took him on as a personal secretary in 1495. The bishop urged Erasmus to pursue more formal study and sent him to the University of Paris.

Once he had finished his degree, Erasmus set out for England, where he had been invited to lecture at the University of Cambridge. Freed from the bishop's service, Erasmus spent the rest of his life as an itinerant scholar, lecturing at various universities and visiting one noble court after another. Chronically short of funds, he was offered many lucrative academic posts throughout his life but declined them all, preferring his freedom. He also rejected several offers to be appointed a Catholic bishop and two nominations to the College of Cardinals. He studied and wrote constantly, even while traveling. In fact, he claimed to have written much of his most famous work, *The Praise of Folly* (1509), while on horseback during a trip to England to visit his friend and fellow humanist Thomas More. He died in Basel, Switzerland, in 1536.

Despite such an unsettled life, Erasmus produced an astonishing amount of writing. His letters alone fill eleven fat volumes in their standard edition. He wrote in three distinct voices. His most popular works were witty satires like *The Praise of Folly* that aimed to entertain people while pointing out society's flaws and foibles. A personified figure of Folly here delivers a monologue on the crucial but unappreciated role she has played in human history. Everyone from kings and princes to peasants and peddlers, she claims, owes something to her for the simple reason that humans all prefer foolishness to common sense. Every page of history proves her

Erasmus the Satirist

Erasmus of Rotterdam Given the fact that he was the most traveled, best-connected, and most highly regarded religious scholar in Europe, there are surprisingly few contemporary portraits of Erasmus, the man who made a heroic last-ditch effort to reform Catholic Christianity before Martin Luther's break with Rome. This portrait, by fellow Dutchman Quentin Metsys (1466–1530), captures the quiet determination of the man. Despite his gift for satire and enjoyment of good (and sometimes bawdy) humor, Erasmus dedicated long years of work to exposing problems within the Catholic Church and promoting a spiritual rejuvenation that would keep all Christians within the arms of the church. His failure marks an important turning point, since most of the great reforms in the church in earlier centuries had been inspired from without. From Erasmus's time to the present, Catholic reform has been largely driven from within the institutional leadership.

point. In works like this, or his popular *Colloquies* (1518), Erasmus lampoons pedantic teachers, hypocritical clerics, greedy landlords, shrewish wives, petulant youths, preening nobles, untrustworthy merchants, and others with a wit that is pointed but almost never mean-spirited.

Erasmus's most notorious satire, though, is a prickly piece called *Julius Excluded from Heaven* (1513), a lengthy sketch depicting a confrontation at the Gates of Heaven between the recently deceased Pope Julius II (r. 1503–1513) and St. Peter. Julius is drunk when he arrives and tries to unlock the gates with the key to his private money chest. Asked to account for his many sins, ranging from murder to sodomy, Julius replies that his sins were all forgiven "by the pope himself"—meaning, of course, Julius himself. When St. Peter refuses to admit Julius into heaven on account of his excessive concern for worldly power and war making, the pope throws a fit, threatens to excommunicate Peter, and announces that he will raise an army to burst through the gates and take Paradise by force.[3]

Erasmus the Educator

In his second voice, Erasmus composed a long series of moral polemics, earnest in tone yet intended for a general audience. In these books—like *Handbook of the Christian Soldier* (1503), *Education of a Christian Prince* (1516), and *The Complaint of Peace* (1517)—he condemns empty religious formalism and urges people to seek out the vital spirit of Christ as depicted in the Bible. They should live simply, honorably, peaceably, and with sincere conviction. Both these serious and his satirical works were immensely popular: it has been estimated that by Erasmus's death in 1536 some 15 percent of all the printed books purchased in Europe had come from his pen.

In his third voice, Erasmus toiled at the most detailed and exacting textual scholarship—revised and annotated editions of the writings of the Latin Fathers

---

[3] At one point the pope complains to St. Peter, "You would not believe how *seriously* some people take little things like bribery, blasphemy, sodomy, and poisoning!"

Ambrose (d. 397), Jerome (d. 420), and Augustine (d. 430). He followed these *Erasmus* projects with his masterpiece, a new critical edition of the Greek New Testament *the* (1515), whose fifth and final version appeared in 1535. Known as the Received *Scholar* Version (*Textus receptus*), it was used by most early translators of the New Testament into English and other vernaculars. These works had a much smaller readership, understandably, but he regarded them as his chief legacy to the world.

MARTIN LUTHER: THE GIFT OF SALVATION

Among those who used Erasmus's New Testament as the basis for a vernacular translation was **Martin Luther** (1483–1546), the German monk whose agonized quest for salvation triggered the break with the church known as the **Protestant Reformation**. Like the humanists who sought to restore ancient morals, Luther sought to re-create what he believed to be Christian belief and practice as they had existed in the apostolic church. He saw himself as a restorer, not a revolutionary, a liberator rather than an insurrectionist. A brilliant biblical scholar, Luther had the gift of expressing his ideas in clear, forceful language that ranged easily in emotional pitch from exquisite descriptions of God's loving kindness to the coarsest verbal abuse of his foes (who consisted of anyone who disagreed with him). His charisma, energy, and passionate feeling were immense; he needed such powerful drive because his ultimate goals—once he decided that compromise with Rome was impossible—were nothing less than the complete overthrow of Catholic tradition and the resetting of the Christian clock, so to speak, fifteen hundred years back.

Luther was born—proudly—of modest, laboring stock in northern Germany. His hardworking parents instilled piety and order in him from an early age, and when it came time for his education they sent him to a school run by the Brethren of Common Life. Hoping to establish his son in a legal career, Luther's father then sent him to the University of Erfurt, but Martin was drawn instead to theology and the classical languages. In 1505, aged twenty-two, he shattered his father's hopes by taking vows as an Augustinian monk. A mere two years later he was ordained a priest.

His vocation brought him no peace, however. Belief in God tormented Luther because he could see no way to please Him. God's majesty was so immense, so *Crisis of* vast, and so inconceivably great that Luther found it impossible to believe that *Faith* anyone could merit salvation. No one deserves to be saved, he believed, for the simple reason that no one can deserve to spend eternity in God's presence. How can anyone possibly claim to merit that? And yet that was precisely what Christian tradition told him to pursue—a life of prayer, repentance, good works, and devotion that would earn him the salvation Christ had promised to everyone who did so. Luther observed his monastic discipline with fanatical determination, even to the point where his abbot feared for his sanity. And yet the fear that nothing he did could possibly justify his standing before God never left him. So sharp grew his agony, he later wrote, that he began to despise God for having created a game that we cannot win—and then punishing us with eternal torment for losing it:

> Even as a blameless monk I still felt certain that in God's eyes I was a miserable sinner—and one with a very troubled conscience—for I had no reason to believe that God would ever be satisfied by my actions. I could not love a righteous God who punished the unrighteous; rather, I hated Him. I was careful never to blaspheme aloud, but on the inside, in the silence of my heart, I roiled and raged at God, saying, "Is it not enough for You that we, miserable sinners all, are damned for all eternity on account of original sin [the notion that, as a result of Adam and Eve's misbehavior, all human beings come into the world with a moral stain upon them from birth]? Why do You add to our calamity by imposing the Ten Commandments on us as well? Why add sorrow upon sorrow through the Gospel teachings, and then in that same Gospel threaten us with judgment and wrath?"

Epiphany in 1513

But then came the breakthrough. Having been sent by his exhausted abbot to teach theology at the University of Wittenberg, Luther, in 1513, was preparing lecture notes on St. Paul's epistle to the Romans, a text he had read countless times before, when suddenly a new insight flashed through his mind:

> I pondered these words night and day until, at last, God had mercy on me and gave me to understand the connection between the phrases "The justice of God is revealed in the Gospel" and "The just will live through faith" [Romans 1.16–17]. I suddenly began to understand that God's justice—that is, the justice by which a just person may live forever—is a gift of God won by faith. . . . All at once I felt reborn, as though I had entered Paradise through gates thrown wide open, and immediately the whole of Scripture took on a new meaning for me.

In other words, *of course* God knows that we do not "deserve" salvation. But salvation is God's gift to us, and He simply wants us to have it anyway.

After this revelation, he tells us, the rest of the scriptures' meaning lay open to him, as though he were reading the words for the first time. To be righteous in the eyes of God, one did not have to confess one's sins to a priest, give alms to the poor, or perform ritual devotions like pilgrimages or vigils. One did not have to follow rites like reciting of the rosary or abstaining from meat on Fridays. One

Martin Luther and Katherina von Bora   The German painter Lucas Cranach the Elder (1472–1533) produced this dual portrait of the great Protestant reformer and his wife; this painting, in fact, may have been produced in honor of their betrothal. (Cranach was present at the ceremony.) Their marriage was an unusually happy one, perhaps the only thing in Luther's life that never caused him any agony.

attains righteousness simply by having faith in Christ; one must simply accept the salvation He offers as an unmerited gift. This idea became canonized in Luther's understanding of **justification by faith alone** (*sola fide* in Latin). It results not from our merit but from God's grace alone, as expressed uniquely through Christ's sacrifice on the cross. Moreover, everything that God requires of us is expressed not through the teaching authority and tradition of the church but through the words of scripture alone. Anything beyond biblical teaching is superfluous to salvation at best and an impediment to it at worst. Few of these ideas were new. In fact, many of them had been enunciated centuries earlier by Augustine (d. 430), the founder of Luther's own monastic order. But Luther carried them to a degree far beyond Augustine or any other theologian.

LUTHER'S REBELLION AGAINST THE CHURCH

Luther's theology offended the church because it made the church irrelevant. From the time of the Gregorian Reform in the 11th century, the Catholic Church had developed its theology of salvation with itself as the irreplaceable intermediary between God and humanity. The church and the believer worked together to effect salvation, through teaching and ministry, the sacraments and pious action. The relationship was not a crude contract, although many saw it that way and had been making similar complaints since at least the second half of the 14th century.

Anti-Catholic Propaganda   This anonymous woodcut of 1520 by a German satirist depicts the devil (complete with wings and clawed feet) sitting on a letter of indulgence and holding a money collection box. The devil's mouth is filled with sinners who presumably bought letters of indulgence in good faith, thinking they had been absolved from their sins. Illustrations such as this, often printed as broadsheets and sold very cheaply, clearly conveyed criticism of the church to people who could not read.

What prompted Luther's rebellion against the church was not merely his new understanding of scripture—because it was not, after all, new. Rather, it was his ire over the church's practice of selling **indulgences**, a monetary donation to the church as a means to satisfy some of the requirements for the forgiveness of sin. A quick theological aside: from the 12th century on, Catholic doctrine had understood penance for sin to have the four elements of contrition, confession, absolution, and satisfaction. One first has to repent honestly for what one has done; second, one must confess the sin fully to a priest; third, one receives absolution from that priest if the confession is sincere and genuine; and fourth, one must then make some sort of restitution for what one did. An indulgence—earned by some explicit act of charity or devotion—was a way of meet-

Indulgences for Sale   ing the fourth demand. A special donation to the church was one way of earning an indulgence. Hence, although it was not an act of "purchasing forgiveness," it certainly could look like one—especially if the process was abused. And it was, egregiously, in Luther's time.

Many people had criticized the practice, including Erasmus. The Renaissance popes, as involved as ever in Italian politics, had waged wars against various despots, had tried to resist the advancing Ottoman Turks, and had expanded the church's network of universities across Europe. As a result, they were in constant and desperate need of funds, and many turned to the offering of indulgences as a reliable means of raising cash. An enormous campaign spread throughout Germany and Italy to raise funds for the construction of the huge new St. Peter's Basilica in Rome. In 1517 Martin Luther, just recently released from his spiritual tortures, witnessed the abusive and predatory selling of indulgences in both regions and was outraged. The symbolic starting point of the Protestant Reformation was not his biblical epiphany in 1513 but his **Ninety-Five Theses** of 1517—a manifesto condemning the theology of indulgences.

The Ninety-Five Theses   The Ninety-Five Theses are simply a list of assertions that Luther declares himself prepared to argue—the arguments themselves are not part of the text. This sort of bulletin of ideas was a common practice in universities of the time.

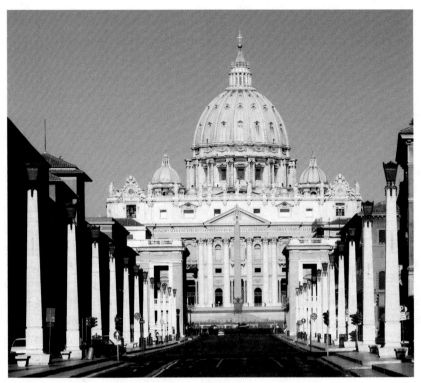

The Basilica of St. Peter in Rome   Four Italian artists share the bulk of the credit for this late Renaissance masterpiece of architecture and art: Donato Bramante (1444–1514), Michelangelo Buonarroti (1475–1564), Carlo Maderno (1556–1629), and Gian Lorenzo Bernini (1598–1680). It is the largest church in Europe, and it took 120 years to complete its construction and decoration. By centuries-old tradition, its altar is built over the site of St. Peter's tomb.

Like the modern custom of publishing the prospectus of one's doctoral dissertation, it invited argument and discussion. He got it. Pope Leo X (r. 1513–1521) spent three years examining Luther's position and finally responded with a papal bull on June 15, 1520, called *Exsurge Domine* ("Arise, O Lord"). He condemned forty-one of the theses as heretical, and he gave Luther sixty days to withdraw the offending statements. Luther answered by publicly burning his copy of the bull on December 10, exactly sixty days after it was issued. After this, there was only one action Leo could take: On January 3, 1521, the pope excommunicated Luther and banned his writings. Enforcement of that ban, however, was a matter for civil authorities, and consequently Luther was ordered to appear before an imperial court (diet) in the German city of Worms. Luther appeared but boldly refused to recant anything he had written; he then fled the scene at night, before the diet passed sentence on him. A powerful German prince—Frederick III of Saxony (r. 1483–1525)—gave him refuge. From this point on, little effort was made to mend fences. Disaffected Christians across Germany flocked to Luther's message by the thousands and then by the tens of thousands. Within a few years the religious unity of Christian Europe was permanently sundered.

Earlier, in 1520, Luther's *Address to the Christian Nobility of the German Nation* had laid out his vision for the organization and administration of his reformed church. Since there was no supreme spiritual authority—each believer needing only his or her Bible and conscience—Protestant churches needed only secular administration and guidance. For that, Luther turned to the princes. A prince who formally broke with Rome and converted to Lutheranism was entitled, Luther wrote, to confiscate the Catholic ecclesiastical lands, properties, and wealth within his principality and to lead the administration of the new reformed churches. The temptation was great, but most princes feared that seizing the extensive holdings of the churches and monasteries would cause the Holy Roman Emperor Charles V to rush to Catholicism's defense. Hence, although most of the nobles converted to Lutheranism, they hesitated to start plundering.

"The Pope is the Antichrist, and the Catholic Church is the most unruly of all crooks' lairs, the most brazen of all brothels, and the Kingdom itself of Sin, Death, and Hell," Luther wrote in a late book titled *On the Roman Papacy: An Institution of the Devil*. Pope Leo, for his part, dismissed Luther as "a German drunkard who will mend his ways once he sobers up." With so much at stake in terms of geopolitics, it is not surprising that the rhetoric of the religious dispute became feverish. Catholics and Protestants at all levels of society hurled abuse at each other.[4] Erasmus and Luther, for a while, had maintained a civilized debate in print over theological issues like free will, the workings of divine grace, and the interpretation of scripture. (The two men never met personally.) Other than that, however, most of the religious battle was in poisonous language. When large numbers of German peasants were persuaded by radicals to rise up in arms against their landlords in 1524 and 1525 in a rebellion known as the **German Peasants' Revolt**, Luther responded savagely. Whereas the peasants had been stirred by Luther's insistence on the dignity of all believers, he called on the princes to take bold action.

Luther and the German Peasants' Revolt

If his aim was to scare the peasants into submission, *On the Thieving, Murderous Hordes of Peasants* was a brilliant success:

> Therefore every one of you [German princes] who can, should act as both judge and executioner. . . . Strike [the peasants] down, slay them, and stab them, either in secret or in the light of day . . . for you ought always to bear in mind that there is nothing more poisonous, dangerous, or devilish than one of these rebels. . . . For baptism frees men's souls

---

4   Although they came to be known as *Protestants* ("those who protest"), Luther and his followers called themselves *Evangelicals*.

alone; it does not liberate their bodies and properties, nor does the Gospel call for people to hold all their goods in common. . . . Fine Christians these peasants are! There can hardly be a single devil left in hell—for I do believe they have all taken possession of these peasants, whose mad ravings are beyond all measure. . . . What a wonderful time we live in now, when a prince can better merit heaven by bloodshed than by prayer!

Most of the rebels, denied Luther's expected support, laid down their weapons at once. The rest were quickly defeated in a battle at Frankenhausen in May 1525, and the revolt ended. The rebel leader, an apocalyptic firebrand named Thomas Müntzer (1488–1525), was executed. The cost of victory was high, however. As many as 100,000 people lost their lives.

After this, the "Protestantization" of Germany gained pace, as the princes now rushed to support Luther's program and seize church lands and treasuries. Sincere religious conviction undoubtedly motivated them, but political and economic factors obviously were also at play. By formally adopting the Lutheran cause, princes acquired—with Luther's own blessing—the authority to appoint pastors to the new churches. This effectively placed the nobles in charge of the entire institution. Freed from having to meet their former fiscal obligations to Rome or to recognize the authority of ecclesiastical courts, the princes likewise ensured the obedience of the new Lutheran churches to noble demands. The policies they developed came to be summarized by the phrase, "The religion of the ruler determines the religion of the land" (*Cuius regio, eius religio*). And most of the princes promoted the new *religio* to strengthen their grip on the *regio*.

Protestantism Spreads and Divides

The Catholic–Protestant rift thus became an unbridgeable chasm. What began as an in-house theological dispute took on more and more political and social elements with every passing year. Two interconnected issues now took on special significance: the constitutional arrangement within Germany and the threat posed by the Turks.

For two centuries the four hundred or so German princes had enjoyed independence from imperial control, while the Habsburgs went about adding to their domain in eastern Europe and marrying available heiresses throughout the continent. When Charles V (r. 1520–1556) came to the throne, he inherited, by a genealogical quirk, several lines of the Habsburg family legacies. These territories, when considered in the aggregate, put him in the sudden and unexpected position of having the German princes surrounded (see Map 12.2).[5]

Charles V Comes to Power

By constitutional tradition, Charles had no cause to take advantage of his position by imposing his rule on the princes. However, since he was, as Holy Roman emperor, the leading royal defender of Catholicism, he considered

MAP 12.2   The Domains of Charles V, 1520   Charles V (r. 1520–1556) inherited several lines of Habsburg family territories, with the result that he dominated the continent.

seriously his obligation to combat the Protestant heresy. The princes, for their part, had good reason to support Luther: he had essentially given them control of the churches aligned with his movement.

The Turkish Threat

The Turkish threat was complicated. Ottoman forces had driven deep into Europe after taking Constantinople in 1453, in the hope of weakening Christendom generally and stopping Habsburg advances specifically. Charles V, naturally, spearheaded the effort to hold them at bay. But many Protestant princes hoped to form an alliance with the Ottoman sultan, Suleiman the Magnificent

---

[5]   His formal title(s), used on all his official records, ran as follows: "Charles, by grace of God the elected Holy Roman Emperor, forever August, King in Germany, King of Italy, Castile, Aragon, León, both Sicilies, Jerusalem, Navarra, Granada, Toledo, Valencia, Galicia, Majorca, Sevilla, Sardinia, Cordova, Corsica, Murcia, Jaen, the Algarves, Algeciras, Gibraltar, the Canary Islands, the Western and Eastern Indies, the Islands and Mainland of the Ocean Sea, etc. etc., Archduke of Austria, Duke of Burgundy, Brabant, Lorraine, Styria, Carinthia, Carniola, Limburg, Luxembourg, Gelderland, Athens, Neopatria, Württemberg, Landgrave of Alsace, Prince of Swabia, Asturia and Catalonia, Count of Flanders, Habsburg, Tyrol, Gorizia, Barcelona, Artois, Burgundy Palatine, Hainaut, Holland, Seeland, Ferrette, Kyburg, Namur, Roussillon, Cerdagne, Zutphen, Margrave of the Holy Roman Empire, Burgau, Oristano and Gociano, Lord of Frisia, the Wendish March, Pordenone, Biscay, Molin, Salins, Tripoli and Mechelen, etc."

(r. 1520–1566), who had come to his throne at roughly the same time as Charles V came to his. Such a pact, they hoped, would leave Charles as the surrounded party and thereby neutralize his power. Diplomatic relations between Protestant rulers and Suleiman were extensive. The Turks had large numbers of Jews and Christians living within the European part of their empire, and for the time being, at least, they treated them with the tolerance required by dhimmi law. Dhimmi law did not protect Christian and Jewish buildings, however, as Suleiman's forces advanced through southeastern Europe. When the Turks overran Buda, the capital of Hungary, they delighted in destroying churches and synagogues throughout the city. Indeed, they set aflame a collection of Renaissance art as rich as anything in Florence or Milan.[6]

Turkish Atrocities   Throughout the 16th and 17th centuries the Ottomans made repeated efforts to expand their control in southeastern Europe, twice getting as far as the gates of Vienna. This woodcut depicts popular fears of Turkish savagery. "Such amusements are common in all wars," warned Erasmus in 1530, when this image was published. The Turks did commit atrocities like those shown here, but no more so than what European Catholics and Protestants inflicted on one another (and what both sometimes inflicted on the Jews) throughout the religious wars of the 16th and 17th centuries.

Suleiman's advance compelled Charles to mobilize his forces, but since the Turks were not yet threatening Habsburg lands directly, Charles bided his time. The Lutheran princes kept negotiating with Suleiman to keep the pressure up. An alliance did not happen in the end, but Suleiman concluded that Charles was too weak to offer any real resistance and so launched a fresh attack in 1526 and quickly took most of Hungary. After a brief pause he advanced his army as far as Vienna, to which he laid siege in 1529. At this point even the Protestants were worried. Luther published in that same year the pamphlet *On the War against the Turks*, in which he called for a united European front against the Ottomans yet rejected as un-Christian the notion of a crusade. Suleiman's siege failed, however, and the Turkish advance was temporarily stopped.

THE REFORMATION GOES INTERNATIONAL

Like other reformers before him and since, Martin Luther believed that those who joined him in rebellion would agree with his proposals for the future. But things seldom turn out that way. People, it seems, unite more easily in opposition

---

[6]   Buda—supposedly named after Bleda, Attila the Hun's older brother—was much later incorporated with the small nearby town of Pest to become today's Budapest.

to a present evil than they rally around a new vision of future good. With its spread beyond Germany, especially in the legacy of John Calvin, Protestantism in fact thrived on divisions.

When Luther began his revolt, many among the pope's advisors recommended immediate and dramatic action. Luther, after all, seemed intent on tearing down the entire Catholic tradition. However, just as many others counseled a quietist approach. Once Luther validated the idea that people can interpret the scriptures for themselves, they pointed out, people would soon disagree with Luther's interpretations as much as they disagreed with Rome's. The rebellion would then splinter into countless factions and soon disappear under its own dead, fractured weight.

Each group of advisors was half right. At the start, Luther saw his actions as a much-needed campaign to correct flaws in Catholic belief and practice, not as a drive to destroy the church. He was a reformer, not a revolutionary. Dramatic counteraction was indeed called for, but not in the urgent sense recommended by the alarmists. As for the second group, they saw correctly the coming splintering of the reformers into rival groups, but their assumption that division meant failure was wrong. They had severely underestimated the intensity of anticlerical feeling—and the deep resentment of the church's abuses and failings. By the time they realized their mistake, it was too late. Luther and his followers had flooded Germany with polemical pamphlets, sermons, hymnals, catechisms, and above all the Bible itself in translation.

It took a generation, more or less, for Luther's ideas to catch on outside of Germany. His basic ideas were known. How could they not be, considering the enormity of the scandal he had caused? However, Luther wrote most of his works in German—since vernacular scripture reading and vernacular worship were so central to his theology. And translators did not rush to bring his works into other tongues. Luther had taken care to produce a number of pamphlets and broadsides in Latin to encourage the spread of the revolt. His ongoing debate in print with Erasmus—the most revered scholar in the Christian world—also kept his program in the spotlight. Still, when Protestantism did start to spread, it did so on the heels of the spread of Christian humanism. Many saw that intellectual effort as preparation for the spiritual regeneration coming out of Germany.

Not all Christian humanists were, or became, Protestant. Many of the most famous, in fact, remained staunchly Catholic. What contributed to the spread of Protestantism was not humanism itself but rather the dialogue between Renaissance and Reformation. It was the spirit of questioning, of returning to ancient sources. Many heard that dialogue and clung ever-more fiercely to the Catholic tradition. Many others, however, who might otherwise never have thought it possible, heard in the debate a calling to a wholly new, and newly holy, path.

Scholars and Activists

The best of the Christian humanist scholars were all dedicated Catholics: Guillaume Budé (1467–1540), Jacques Lefèvre d'Étaples (1455–1536), Cardinal

Francisco Ximénez de Cisneros (1436–1517), and Joan Lluís Vives i March (1493–1540). Other writers—primarily Protestants like Ulrich Zwingli (1484–1531) and John Calvin (1509–1564)—remain better known and were more historically significant because of their activities in the world. But pure scholars should have their due, too.

Budé was a classical linguist, one of the finest Greek scholars of his generation. Supported by the French royal court, he produced a Greek lexicon that remained the standard for scholars for nearly two hundred years. He also founded the school that later became the Collège de France and the library that ultimately grew into the Bibliothèque Nationale, both in Paris. Lefèvre, also a royal favorite, was an industrious writer of biblical commentaries as well as editions and translations of patristic texts. In 1530 he published the first ever translation of the entire Bible into French.

Cisneros held immense power in Spain: he was the archbishop of Toledo, was twice the regent for the crown, and served as Grand Inquisitor at the high point of that institution's power in Spain. As a statesman Cisneros was blunt and direct to the point of cruelty. He ordered the forced baptism of the Muslims of southern Spain and the burning of Arabic manuscripts in the library at Granada. As a scholar, however, he was patient in the extreme: he spent fifteen years producing the *Complutensian Polyglot Bible*—an impressive work that reproduced, in parallel columns, the best texts then available of the entire Bible in Aramaic, Greek, Hebrew, and Latin.

Lluís Vives, a much more sympathetic figure, dedicated long years to social reform as well as to reform within the Catholic Church. He was an earnest champion of education for women and welfare for the poor. The fourth-generation son of a *converso* family—that is, a Spanish family that had once been Jewish—he witnessed the Inquisition's execution of his father, grandmother, and great-grandfather.[7] And

Polyglot Bible   A page from the *Complutensian Polyglot Bible* (1514–1517) published by Cardinal Francisco Cisneros, one of the great humanistic achievements of the Renaissance. The three main columns present the biblical text in Hebrew, Latin, and Greek, while underneath are printed passages in Aramaic, where they survive, and alternative readings. The Complutensian edition was used extensively by the English translators who produced the King James Bible (Authorized Version) in 1611.

---

[7]   As we saw in chapter 11, scholars use *inquisition*, with a lowercase *i*, to refer to the inquisitorial process in the Middle Ages. Uppercase *Inquisition* is reserved for the Renaissance, when what had been a legal process turned into a formal institution.

although he never wavered in his Christian commitment, he left Spain as soon as he could and never returned. After studying in Paris, he became a professor of philosophy at Oxford and spent his time between Oxford and the royal court in London, where he served as private tutor to the Tudor family.

Zwingli

Among the Protestant humanists, the most influential were Ulrich Zwingli and John Calvin. Zwingli left behind more than twenty volumes of writings—sermons, biblical exegesis, topical essays, some poetry—but little of this is read by anyone other than specialists. His impact was in the world of action rather than thought. He was born to a Swiss farming family and received a good although unremarkable education. In 1498 he enrolled at the University of Vienna but was expelled for reasons no one has ever discovered. He was ordained a priest and spent several years as a military chaplain. A crisis of conscience, however, led him to withdraw from his post and take up duties as a simple parish priest in a small village in Switzerland. This position gave him ample time for self-education, and in a few years he had mastered Greek and acquired a usable knowledge of Hebrew.

By 1516 personal study of the scriptures had inspired Zwingli to doubt the value of much Catholic doctrine and ritual, but he was too timid to admit his opinions publicly until Martin Luther published the Ninety-Five Theses. Zwingli then dedicated himself to the twin goals of supporting Luther's Reformation and securing Switzerland's independence from French, Italian, and imperial meddling. He formally broke with Rome, and by 1522 most of the German-speaking cantons of Switzerland had done the same and had placed themselves under Zwingli's leadership. He moved to Zurich, which became second only to Luther's Wittenberg as the unofficial capital of the Protestant movement.

Zwingli's brand of Christianity differed from Luther's in a number of specifics. In fact, Zwingli, who did not meet Luther personally until 1529, is one of the first examples of a Protestant who broke away from the movement's founder. He died in battle against armies from the Catholic southern portion of Switzerland, and the embryonic church he had created became subsumed by the new church created by John Calvin.

The Anabaptists

A brief but violent interlude, however, preceded Calvin on the scene. Several dozen radical members of Zwingli's church at Zurich quit Switzerland and took up residence in exile at Münster, in northwestern Germany. Disgusted by what they considered the immoral joining of Protestant religion with secular government (Luther and the German princes, Zwingli and the Swiss town councils), they established themselves as an apocalyptic sect known as the **Anabaptists**. Their name means "rebaptizers" because the group rejected infant baptism as meaningless by itself and called for a second baptism in adulthood. They also embraced a literal reading of scripture, polygamy (although the extent of this is still debated), and the imminent approach of Christ's Second Coming. The sect came under the charismatic leadership of Jan van Leiden (1509–1536), who proclaimed himself the successor to the King David of biblical times and his Münster church as the reincarnation of the Jerusalem Temple. Zwingli and Luther both denounced the group, as did all the Catholic rulers of the time. Persecutions followed as Münster was stormed by the Catholic prince (and bishop) of the city, the Anabaptists were tortured and executed, and their sympathizers across Europe were arrested.[8]

By the time John Calvin established his own Reformed Church in Geneva, the conflict between rival Christianities had moved well beyond a war of words. Most of the Scandinavian territories (Finland was the exception) had declared for Lutheranism by the end of the 1520s. Lutheranism had also sunk deep roots in northern Germany and parts of Poland, Hungary, and the Low Countries. England was, for the time being, still staunchly Catholic, although Henry VIII's (r. 1509–1547) marital woes led him in 1534 to break with Rome and establish the Church of England, as we will discuss further in chapter 14 (see Map 12.3).

CALVIN: PROTESTANTISM AS THEOLOGY

At first glance, **John Calvin** seems an unlikely revolutionary. Quiet, reserved, and intensely bookish, he studied (under pressure from his father) for a legal career at the University of Bourges, where he fell under the spell of humanist classicism. At about the same time—somewhere around 1530—he had an evangelical conversion that changed his entire life. He described the event in the introduction to his later *Commentary on the Psalms*:

> All at once, God overpowered my mind, which at that point was far more incorrigible in such matters than one might expect in one so young, and opened it [to the Truth]. Having been given this sampling of, this introduction to, true godliness, I instantly burned with such a passion to have better knowledge of it that, even though I never abandoned my other studies entirely, I pursued them with much less drive than before.

If his account is accurate, his was an intellectual rather than mystical conversion, although it was no less passionate for that. True to his bookish nature, he

---

8   Crushed by its enemies, the Anabaptist movement disappeared. The Mennonite church, founded by Menno Simons (1496–1561) of Holland, is a late offshoot that still survives.

MAP 12.3   The Protestant Reformation, ca. 1540   By 1580, the reformation of the Church had spread rapidly across northern and central Europe, but it was never a uniform movement. Reform was always at a local level. Italy and Spain remained predominantly Catholic. France, the Low Countries, southern Germany, and central Europe were hotly contested, but England, Scotland, northern Germany, and Scandinavia were decisively Protestant by the end of the 16th century.

turned almost immediately to writing the first edition (1535) of his main work, *Institutes of Christian Religion,* which he continued to revise until his death. (Its final and definitive editions appeared in 1559 in Latin and in 1560 in French.)

The *Institutes* was the first work to lay out the emerging theology of Protestant Christianity in a systematic, logical, organized way. Here is a representative passage on how the Reformed Church uses discipline:

Calvin's Institutes of Christian Religion

> It is necessary, likewise, to distinguish between different kinds of sins, for some are only minor infractions whereas others are enormous and enormously wicked crimes. In order to correct the latter, mere warnings and reproofs do not suffice, and one must resort to sterner measures—as Paul shows [1 Corinthians 5.1–5] when he does not allow himself to rest content after having condemned the man of Corinth who had committed incest, but immediately excommunicates the man after his conviction for the crime. Now we begin to see how the spiritual authority of the Church, which corrects sins according to God's Word, preserves our health, orders our lives, and establishes bonds of unity among us; for whenever the Church banishes from the community those guilty of adultery, fornication, theft, robbery, sedition, false witness, or any other crimes of that sort, or when it banishes those stubborn people who criticize God's Holy Judgment, even after having been admonished for lesser sins, it [the Church] exercises no unauthorized rational power but only the jurisdiction that God Himself has given it. . . . Anyone who believes that the Church could even exist without this power to discipline is sorely mistaken—for how could we do without the very thing that God saw fit to give us? The reasons why this is necessary will be made clear in its action. (4.12.4)

Martin Luther, like his model St. Augustine, had been far too impulsive and emotive a writer ever to write anything like this.

Calvin shared Luther's central, defining notion of an infinitely majestic, all-powerful, and all-knowing God whose transcendent might and will are in absolute control of the entire cosmos. But Luther softened this commanding image by emphasizing the infinitely merciful, because unmerited, love that God feels for us. Calvin stressed instead the unfathomable mystery of God's justice. Since He is all-knowing, argued Calvin, God has known since the moment of Creation which human beings are to be saved and which are to be damned—and these fates are sealed absolutely by the sheer force of God's will. There is nothing any human being can do to alter his or her fate. All is predestined and beyond our capacity to understand. Does this concept of **predestination** mean that many apparently "good" people will be punished in hell while many apparently "bad" people will be rewarded in heaven? Yes, it does, but this, to Calvin, is simply the consequence of our complete inability to understand God's purpose, rather than

The Concept of Predestination

a sign of God's supposed hypocrisy. We must remain faithful to the belief that God's ways are ultimately and supremely just, even if we cannot comprehend them. In essence, what Calvin called for was an attitude of radical humility before God, an absolute submission of the soul to the Almighty's wisdom, power, and righteousness.

But this is not an attitude of passivity. It is precisely because we cannot know whether we are among the *Elect*—his term for those predestined for salvation—that Calvin demands of his followers the strictest possible adherence to moral standards. To the Elect, he writes, good ethical behavior will come naturally and *Spread of* be the sign of their chosen status. To those who are not elected, their moral be-*Calvinism* havior will not affect their ultimate fate in the slightest—but they therefore have all the more reason to live according to a godly standard. The joy of such a life is in fact the only meaningful pleasure they will have before confronting the eternal torments of hell. Membership in good standing in the Reformed Church—Calvin's name for the branch of Christianity he established—is a likely indicator that one is among the Elect. Membership in the despised Roman Catholic Church or the Orthodox Church is as likely an indicator that one is not. But although being a Calvinist immeasurably improved one's odds of salvation, it alone determined nothing. The central concern of life therefore should not be the destiny of our individual souls but the fulfillment of God's purpose on the entire earth.

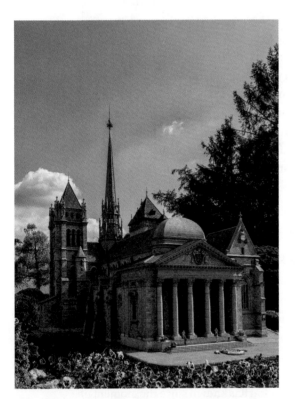

Calvinist Churches: Geneva   This church, dedicated to St. Peter, contrasts sharply with the audacious grandeur of the Vatican basilica. Sometimes referred to as the "adopted home" church of the Swiss reformer John Calvin, it is, stylistically, a hodge-podge, with structures and elements from every century since the 12th. The interior is shorn of decoration apart from the architectural elements: no mosaics, frescos, paintings, or sculptures; nothing to distract the worshipper from the Word being preached from the pulpit.

Calvin's teachings found receptive audiences all around Europe. Apart from its success in Switzerland, Calvinism became the dominant creed in Holland (where it became known as the Dutch Reformed Church), in Scotland (where it was called the Presbyterian Church), in parts of France (where Calvinists were called Huguenots), and in parts of England (where they were ultimately called Puritans). The theocratic state he established in Geneva earned a well-deserved reputation for severity, but Geneva also earned a reputation for modest, honest, and godly behavior. Calvinist communities emphasized simplicity and austerity in worship. Anything that smacked of Catholic ritual or hierarchical structure was eschewed. Instead, churches were communities of equals—joined together in prayer, scriptural reading, hymn singing, and listening to sermons. How can there be a pecking order among the Elect? Sermons indeed form the centerpiece of Calvinist worship, since they are by nature ruminations on scripture. Calvin himself was too gifted a scholar to insist on only literal readings of the Bible, although he tended to seek out symbolic or other interpretations only after considering the literal first.

Still other reformers and groups branched off to form new denominations, but these were considerably smaller in size and tinged with elements of ethnic or national rebellion. Lutheranism and Calvinism were the two with the greatest international appeal, and by 1550 they had torn the religious fabric of Europe asunder. Only in the late 20th century, in the aftermath of two World Wars and the Holocaust, would there arise serious efforts to reconcile the fissures in Christianity.

THE GODLY SOCIETY

Although they were intent on religious reform, Luther, Calvin, and the other Protestant leaders did not think of themselves as social reformers. Indeed, as we have seen, when radicals like Thomas Müntzer, leader of the German Peasants' Revolt, interpreted Luther's theology as a call to social rebellion, Luther called for the rebels' extermination. The reformers, in fact, relied on existing social and political structures for their vision of a new Christendom: from feudal princes in Germany to urban elites in Switzerland, the existing social models provided the backbone of the Protestant campaigns.

And a strong backbone was needed, according to Luther, Calvin, and others. Human nature was too depraved, too ensnared in its own sinfulness, to be trusted. *The* Figures of authority were needed to provide discipline. Protestant theology *Patriarchal* championed the notion of the "priesthood of all believers"—meaning that each *Order* individual could discern the teachings of the Bible for him- or herself. But only strong and demanding leaders could make sure that people lived according to the truths they read in scripture. Hence Luther granted power to the German princes to enforce the teaching of the new Lutheran churches within their domains. Calvin established the town councils of the Elect to supervise, judge, and punish the Reformed citizens of Geneva and elsewhere.

Both men wrote extensive commentaries on the following passage from the New Testament:

> Let every person be subject to the governing authorities, for there is no authority except from God, and those authorities that exist have been instituted by God. Therefore whoever resists authority resists what God has appointed, and those who resist will incur judgment. For rulers are not a terror to good conduct, but to bad. Do you wish to have no fear of the authority? Then do what is good, and you will receive its approval; for it is God's servant for your good. But if you do what is wrong, you should be afraid, for the authority does not bear the sword in vain! It is the servant of God to execute wrath on the wrongdoer. Therefore one must be subject, not only because of wrath but also because of conscience. (Romans 13.1–5)

The Patriarchal Family   Since sinfulness is present in us from birth, disciplined authority needed to be as much a cornerstone of parenting as was love itself. Hence Protestant social ideology called for the patriarchal family as the fundamental unit of godly society. In that family, the man stood as the undoubted leader, charged with the protection and care of the whole household. The mother was subject to her husband's authority and given the special task of beginning the moral and spiritual

The Patriarchal Family   Cornelius Johnson (1593–1661) was a popular portraitist among the English aristocracy of the 17th century. This painting from 1640 shows Arthur, 1st Baron Capell (1604–1649), together with his family, posing before their formal garden. Note that of the three females in the picture (his wife in the center and his two daughters at the right), Lady Elizabeth Capell is looking respectfully at her husband, daughter Mary is gazing at her baby brother, and daughter Elizabeth is looking shyly to the right; only the males in the picture look directly at the viewer.

education of their children. Luther and Calvin here drew on Paul's epistles: "Wives, be subject to your husbands as you are to the Lord. For the husband is the head of the wife just as Christ is the head of the church, the body of which He is the Savior. Just as the church is subject to Christ, so also wives ought to be, in everything, to their husbands" (Ephesians 5.22–24).

Husbands and fathers exercised their authority in a variety of ways. Physical discipline was permitted within certain limits, but men were expected above all to lead by setting examples of rigorous and godly behavior. To help them, most Protestant denominations offered some form of personal and family counseling. They also emphasized Bible reading within all family devotions. But since the godly family was the basic unit of godly society, the society itself had an intrinsic right to step in and exert authority when a parent failed. Public shaming, social ostracism, banishment from church life, and imprisonment were widely practiced.[9]

In the godly society, sexual morality played an important role. At least in their first two or three generations, Protestant Christians placed a significantly sharper and more constant focus on sexuality than did their Catholic peers. Chastity before marriage and fidelity within it remained the moral ideal for all Christians, but Catholic Europe had long allowed a certain liberality in sexual matters, especially for men. Prostitution, although regulated, had been legal throughout Europe for centuries, for example, and no social stigma fell on the men who frequented prostitutes.[10] One way that Protestants sought to curb prostitution—apart from simply closing down the brothels—was through early marriage. With access to legitimate sexual release, they believed, men would not be tempted to resort to illegitimate means.

Sexual Morality

---

9   The Scottish reformer and founder of the Presbyterian tradition, John Knox (1514–1572), wrote a vitriolic treatise called *First Blast of the Trumpet against the Monstrous Regiment of Women* (1558). The tract takes aim specifically at England's Queen Mary and her heavy-handed efforts to restore Catholicism in the realm (discussed in chapter 14), but its general attitude regarding women's biblical call to subservience to men is clear. "To promote a woman to bear rule, superiority, dominion, or empire above any realm, nation, or city, is repugnant to nature; contumely [an insult] to God, a thing most contrary to His revealed will and approved ordinance; and finally, it is the subversion of good order, of all equity and justice. In the probation of this proposition, I will not be so curious as to gather whatsoever may amplify, set forth, or decor the same; but I am purposed, even as I have spoken my conscience in most plain and few words, so to stand content with a simple proof of every member, bringing in for my witness God's ordinance in nature, His plain will revealed in His word, and by the minds of such as be most ancient amongst godly writers. And first, where I affirm the empire of a woman to be a thing repugnant to nature, I mean not only that God, by the order of His creation, has spoiled [deprived] woman of authority and dominion, but also that man has seen, proved, and pronounced just causes why it should be. Man, I say, in many other cases, does in this behalf see very clearly. For the causes are so manifest, that they cannot be hid. For who can deny but it is repugnant to nature, that the blind shall be appointed to lead and conduct such as do see? That the weak, the sick, and impotent persons shall nourish and keep the whole and strong? And finally, that the foolish, mad, and frenetic shall govern the discreet, and give counsel to such as be sober of mind? And such be all women, compared unto man in bearing of authority. For their sight in civil regiment is but blindness; their strength, weakness; their counsel, foolishness; and judgment, frenzy, if it be rightly considered."

10   Men had tended to put marriage off until they were established in a trade, which could take until their thirties.

The era also witnessed new efforts to combat homosexuality. Same-sex eroti-cism had been regarded as a sign of weakness since Roman times. Christianity added the notion that the activity was immoral since it denied the procreative function that was sexuality's whole intent and purpose. Until the 13th century, however, homosexuality was not a criminal offense. By 1260 in France, homo-sexual acts became punishable by death. Comparable measures were instituted across Europe, at both the national and the local levels, although it remains un-clear how often such laws were enforced. Hostility to homosexuality increased with the need to rebuild the population after the Black Death as well. Although Renaissance classicism brought more liberal attitudes, in Florence alone more than fifteen thousand people were arrested for sodomy between 1432 and 1502 (although not all were convicted). The Spanish Inquisition arrested more than fifteen hundred people on charges of homosexual acts between 1540 and 1700.

Protestantism's emphasis on biblical truth (*sola Scriptura*) sharpened antiho-mosexual sentiments significantly, although formal condemnations came mostly at the local levels of government.[11] One notable exception was England's "Buggery Act," passed in 1533 under King Henry VIII, whose break from Rome we will examine in chapter 14. The act remained in force until 1861, when the death pen-alty it called for was replaced by a sentence of life imprisonment.

> Forasmuch as there is not yet sufficient and condign [deserved] pun-ishment appointed and limited by the due course of the Laws of this Realm for the detestable and abominable Vice of Buggery, [whether] committed with mankind or beast: May it therefore please the King's Highness, with the assent of the Lords Spiritual and the Commons of this present parliament assembled, that it may be enacted by the authority of the same, that the same offence be from henceforth adjudged a felony, and that such an order and form of process therein to be used against the offenders as in cases of felony at the Common Law; and that the offenders being hereof convicted—by verdict, confession, or outlawry—shall suffer such pains of death, and losses and penalties of their goods, chattels, debts, lands, tenements, and [inherited properties], as felons do according to the Common Laws of this Realm; and that no person offending in any such offence shall be admitted to [the king's] clergy; and that Justices of the Peace shall have power and authority within the limits of their commissions and jurisdictions to hear and determine the said offence, as they do in the cases of other felonies.

---

[11] Just six passages from the Bible explicitly condemn homosexuality, and two are simply New Testament restatements of Old Testament proscriptions. The scriptures record no direct teaching from Jesus.

What makes any type of sexual activity a crime against the state instead of a matter of personal morality? In Protestant Europe, where the state had become the administrative head of the religious community, a sin against public morals was also a crime against civil society. Hence homosexuality—along with adultery, masturbation, foul language, gambling, and drunkenness—required a civil response. Sixteenth-century Protestants read the Bible as mandating the two-parent, heterosexual, married, nuclear family. Any sexual activity outside that norm was in essence a threat to the godly state.

THE REBIRTH OF SATIRE

A literary genre that thrived outside the norms of taste was satire, which roared back to life in the 16th century. The conjunction of increasing literacy rates and the mass availability of printed texts generated a demand for literary entertainment unlike anything the Western world had experienced before. Not that the love of storytelling was itself new, but oral tradition could now give way to print on paper. Reading became a common pleasure of everyday life, no longer the reserve of scholars and monks. Printing houses across Europe poured out a steady stream of poetry, histories, stage dramas and comedies, travelogues, essays, memoirs, popular science tracts, and collections of letters and speeches.

Not everyone in Europe was reading Erasmus, Luther, and Calvin constantly—which is probably a good thing. In addition to Machiavelli and Aretino, three European writers stand out in the first half of the 16th century: Thomas More, Ulrich von Hutten, and François Rabelais. They could hardly have been more different in their personalities and life stories, but the most famous works of all three were satires.

Satire had been one of the most popular literary genres among the Romans. The English word *satire*, which appeared for the first time in 1509, in fact derives from Latin *satura* (denoting a witty poem that ridicules vice). "Satire is all ours," once bragged Quintilian (36–96 CE), Rome's greatest literary scholar. But satire had all but disappeared during the Middle Ages. Levity about the world's idiosyncrasies and human foibles did not appeal much to the monks who established the classical canon in their scriptoria. With the rise of classical humanism, however, satire returned as a favorite literary genre. There were, after all, plenty of people to ridicule: warmongering popes, fey aristocrats, affected scholars, grasping financiers, humanistic despots, self-absorbed artists.

Erasmus helped to revive prose satire with his *Praise of Folly*, and satire in prose, in fact, became the preferred style in the 16th century. His close friend Thomas More (1478–1535) penned a popular book called *Utopia*

Thomas More's Utopia

Utopia   This woodcut by Ambrosius Holbein (ca. 1494–1519)—older brother of the famous artist Hans Holbein (ca. 1497–1543)—was the frontispiece for a 1518 edition of *Utopia*. Against a backdrop of the fictional island, Raphael Hythlodaeus describes the Utopian way of life to More.

(1516).[12] It consists of two parts, the first being an imaginary discussion between More and a traveler-adventurer named Raphael Hythlodaeus on the various ills then besetting Europe. High on the list are pervasive poverty, religious intolerance, the failure of systems of justice, and the propensity to war. In the second part, Hythlodaeus describes for More his travels to a "perfect society"—a far-distant island in the Atlantic named Utopia (which is an Anglicized version of the Greek phrase "no place").

Utopia is a crescent-shaped island, 200 miles across, in which the population lives in scattered communities of about seventy-five thousand each. All goods are held in common; citizens take turns, in two-year shifts, farming the land and working at artisanal crafts; medical care and primary education are free and available to all. There are no lawyers; all wives are subservient to their husbands, to whom they must confess their sins once every month; and the penalty for pre- or extramarital sex is enslavement. There are a lot of slaves, consequently, who do most of the hard labor. Although meant as a satire, there is nothing in *Utopia* to make a modern reader laugh, because More was largely humorless. (According to a family memoir, he laughed at court jesters when they made pratfalls, but at little else.) *Utopia* remains a valuable book, however, not least for the insight it provides into its author's mind.

Hutten's Letters of Obscure Men

Far more successful as satire is the fictitious *Letters of Obscure Men* (1517) by Ulrich von Hutten (1488–1523), a swashbuckling imperial knight and occasional humanist writer. In 1515 the Duke of Württemberg killed a beloved cousin of Hutten whose wife he had designs on. Hutten responded by publishing blistering Latin poems that ruined the duke's reputation and led ultimately to his overthrow. They made Hutten famous, and in 1517 Maximilian I (r. 1493–1519) appointed him the poet laureate of the German Empire. In that same year, Hutten became a passionate supporter of Martin Luther and coauthored, with his humanist friend Johann Jäger (1480–1539, who used the pseudonym Crotus Rubeanus), the *Letters of Obscure Men*.

---

[12]   More is best known as the royal chancellor who refused to recognize Henry VIII's annulment of his marriage to Catherine of Aragon and opposed the king's plan to establish a national church under royal control that would deny the supremacy of the pope (discussed in chapter 14). He paid for his opposition with his head.

Filled with clever wit and broad, coarse humor, the *Letters* purport to be addressed to a prominent nobleman by fanatical Catholic monks and friars regarding why it is necessary to burn Jewish books like the Talmud and anti-Christian polemical literature. The diatribe is in reference to a real event: the dispute, several years earlier, between the famed humanist scholar Johann Reuchlin (1455–1522) and a group of zealous Catholic Inquisitors who had argued for the same cause. (The title echoes the *Letters of Notable Men* that had passed between Reuchlin and his adversaries.) The *Letters* were written in intentionally bad Latin, making much of their humor impossible to convey in English. Reading them, it is clear that Hutten never lost his hatred of Catholic monks, who might well respond to Protestantism and satire with book burnings, and this book is a settling of old debts. He gives his monks outrageous names like Brother Goatmilker and Brother Shitshoveller, attributes every sort of lechery to them, and describes them nervously defecating under their robes during public debates. His aim is less to defend the Jews (although he was indeed an opponent of the book burnings) than to ridicule the pretensions and hypocrisy of the Catholics. The aristocrat who receives the letters—a real figure in Hutten's time—also comes in for a lambasting. The monks sordidly declare their passionate relations with his wife.

The best known of the three satirists was François Rabelais (ca. 1494–1553). Born to a wealthy country lawyer, he received a sound education before entering *Rabelais* the Franciscan order sometime around 1510 and becoming a priest about a decade later. He traveled to libraries around France and earned a reputation as a first-rate classical scholar, but in 1524 he suffered the indignity of having his Greek books confiscated by one of his superiors, who thought they might lead to heresy. Rabelais successfully petitioned Pope Clement VII (r. 1523–1534) in 1524 for release from his Franciscan order and to be allowed to join the Benedictines. Through his new order he studied medicine in Paris. However, since he disliked Benedictine life too, he broke his vows and moved to the University of Montpellier to continue his medical training. He finished in record time, quickly sired two children with a local widow, and then moved on to practice medicine in Narbonne and Lyons.

In 1532 Rabelais published a brief satirical novel, *The Horrible and Terrifying Words and Deeds of the Renowned Pantagruel, King of the Dipsodes*. When this proved unexpectedly popular, he followed it with three more volumes that continue Pantagruel's adventures while also providing, in another volume, the backstory of Pantagruel's father, Gargantua. The five books are now published together as a single work, *Gargantua and Pantagruel*. (A supposed sixth book, written by an opportunistic forger, appeared in 1564, eleven years after Rabelais's death.) Gargantua and Pantagruel are giants—enormous, misshapen, driven by inexhaustible appetites of body and mind, and delighting in broad scatological humor—and the same can be said of *Gargantua and Pantagruel* the novel, a vast, loose-jointed sequence of episodes in the protagonists' lives. The closest it comes to offering a coherent story is a lengthy rambling narrative in Books 3 and 4 about their efforts to help a friend. (Another giant, named Panurge, wishes to locate an oracle known as the Sacred Bottle for help deciding whether to marry a girl whose fidelity is uncertain.) Although lively, the novel is shapeless, repetitive, and overlong.

What was its purpose? Rabelais certainly wanted to entertain his readers and make them laugh. "Mirth is my theme, and tears are not, / For laughter is man's proper lot" is the famous ending couplet of Rabelais's verse preface. *Gargantua and Pantagruel* and *Letters of Obscure Men* are the only truly funny books written in that unfunny century. Being satire, the laughs they raise come at someone's expense; we laugh because someone is being ridiculed. Both books have numerous targets, but they share one in particular, the Catholic clergy. Whereas Hutten attacks them from the Protestant side, Rabelais offers a Catholic in-house attack.

The wounds he inflicts, however, result not from rapier wit but from a heavy two-handed broadsword. He mocks dry-as-dust scholastic theologians and pompous overfed monks by exaggerating their flaws a hundredfold. He lambasts puritanical morality by having his heroes indulge in orgies of food, sex, and drink that would make a Roman emperor blush. Bodily functions stain every page. In one early passage (1.17), Gargantua caps off a drinking binge by untying his codpiece and urinating so much he floods the entire city of Paris, "drowning 260,418 people, plus women and children."

Still, the book's verbal energy is extraordinary. Rejoicing in his freedom from church Latin, Rabelais pours words onto the page in a kind of vernacular euphoria. The novel is a hymn to the French language and a celebration of human freedom: freedom to think, to scoff, to lust, to indulge in manic excess, to coin words, to imagine outrageous scenes, to offend, to risk boredom, and to delight in whimsy. Ultimately, it is about the freedom to hope for a better world than the one we live in. As a work of art it has failings, but as the expression of an irrepressible spirit it can never cease to fascinate. And that spirit is humanism.

CATHOLIC REFORM AND THE COUNCIL OF TRENT

Whether it followed a humanist line or another, Catholic reform was certainly needed, and figures like Erasmus and More spent their lives calling for it. Even the most worldly of Renaissance popes recognized that many of the faithful were put off by the church and its cumbersome institutions. The problem was how to find reforms that would please everybody. Through much of the 14th and 15th centuries, when the Holy See was a political football of the Italian nobility, a movement arose to strengthen the role of general councils in ecclesiastical governance. The popes, many of them more concerned with their personal fates than with the office they held, opposed this "conciliarism" vehemently, but the resulting deadlock only aggravated the problems that both sides were supposedly trying to address. The success of Protestantism produced urgent calls for a general council; papal dithering only made the calls more insistent. But then, surprisingly, the Protestant juggernaut stalled. By 1540 every state in Europe that would become Protestant had done so; no new national-scale conversions were won by any of the major Protestant branches (see Map 12.3).

Beginning with Pope Paul III (r. 1534–1549), the court in Rome finally took the lead in bringing on reform. He appointed a commission of high-ranking clerics to investigate church abuses; this commission's final report, published in 1536, laid bare scores of problems in the administration of the papal court, the actions of the bishops, and the shortcomings in parish life. In 1537 Paul issued a bull condemning the enslavement of the indigenous peoples of the New World (discussed in the next chapter); in 1540 he confirmed the formation of the Society of Jesus, or the Jesuits, a teaching and missionary order; and in 1542 he authorized the creation of the Holy Office—that is, the Roman Inquisition. Last, after securing guarantees that its proceedings would be subject to papal approval, he called for a full ecumenical council to study and propose solutions to the general reform of Catholic life, which has come to be known as either the **Catholic Reformation** or the **Counter-Reformation**. This **Council of Trent**, which convened (with a few intermissions) from 1546 to 1563, was the most important assembly of its kind until the Second Vatican Council of 1963–1965.

Although the religious revolt in northern Europe was obviously its trigger, the Council of Trent was more than a response to Protestantism; efforts at reform *The* had begun long before Luther appeared on the scene. Nevertheless, the Council's *Plan for* initial actions offered no hint of compromise but rather highlighted the differ- *Renewal* ences between what it regarded as Catholic truth and Protestant lies. If anything, they asserted the Catholic position with even more force than before. The problems confronting the church, the Council believed, were not with doctrine itself but with the ways in which doctrine was taught to the people. The changes most needed were therefore in leadership and organization.

Paul III's successor, Pope Julius III (r. 1550–1555), devoted himself to personal pleasure—in particular, his infatuation with an illiterate, fourteen-year-old street beggar named Innocenzo. Julius moved Innocenzo into the Vatican palace, awarded him several wealthy benefices, appointed him the abbot of the monastery of Mont Saint-Michel, and made him a cardinal. Julius, thankfully, was around for only a few years, and the popes who succeeded him pressed the Council to reach even further in its ambition: Paul IV (r. 1555–1559) and Pius IV

Catholic Reform   Pope Paul III (r. 1534–1549), in an oil portrait by the great Venetian artist Titian (Tiziano Vecellio, 1490–1576), called for the Council of Trent (1545–1563), whose pomp and circumstance are also on display here. Initially summoned in 1537 to lay out the plan for the Catholic Reformation, the Council was delayed for financial and bureaucratic reasons; it finally met, ironically, when Martin Luther had taken to what was to become his deathbed.

(1559–1565).[13] The Council ordered a streamlining of the church bureaucracy, outlawed ecclesiastical pluralism (the practice of a single individual holding appointments to serve in multiple parishes or dioceses), and heightened the responsibility of bishops to oversee the life of their provinces. Most important of all, it charged them with improving the education of their clergy and of the flocks they served. To assist them, the church helped to build hundreds of new parish schools to train teachers. At the higher levels, the church increased the funding for universities and reorganized curricula.

THE SOCIETY OF JESUS

Several new ecclesiastical orders joined the campaign and dedicated themselves specifically to education: the Ursulines ("Company of Saint Ursula"), founded in 1535 and papally approved in 1544, created a network of schools for girls across Europe and soon in the New World. More famous still was the Society of Jesus, commonly called the **Jesuits**, found by St. Ignacio de Loyola (1491–1556) in 1540. "A Society founded for a single, central purpose—namely, to strive for the defense and propagation of the Faith, and for the progress of souls in Christian life and doctrine," the Jesuits dedicated themselves to preaching and teaching at all educational levels, although historically they have tended toward higher education. Founded as they were by a former soldier—Loyola, a Spanish noble and career military man, experienced a conversion while recuperating from severe battle wounds received in 1521—the Jesuits formed a compact and highly

---

[13] Julius is the last pope known to have been sexually active and explicitly homosexual.

centralized organization. They took vows of poverty, chastity, and absolute obedience to their superiors, especially to the pope, and became the church's most successful tool in bringing Christianity to the outside world.

Within ten years of their founding, the Jesuits had established mission schools in India and Japan, and by 1600 they had extended their reach into South and North America and into sub-Saharan Africa. And since the Council of Trent particularly emphasized the doctrinal point that for Catholics, unlike Protestants, doing "good works" was an essential requirement of Christian living, the reformed church stepped up its involvement in charitable work among the world's poorest peoples.

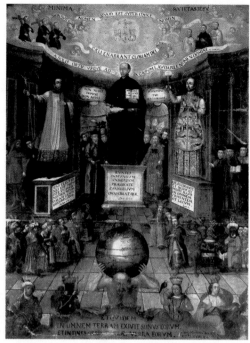

Jesuit Missionaries   The Jesuits were pivotal in revitalizing the Catholic Church's evangelical and educational missions. In this 18th-century painting from Lima, Peru, the order's founder, St. Ignatius Loyola, appears in the center, flanked by two loyal followers, St. Francis Borja and St. Francis Xavier. At the bottom, figures representing Africa, Asia, North America, and South America bear witness to the extent of Jesuit missionary activity.

The combined efforts of these new orders, especially in their conflation of schoolroom teaching and service, helped gain many converts in the New World. They even returned many Protestant believers in southern Germany, parts of Bohemia, and throughout Poland–Lithuania to Catholicism.

The Jesuit Mission: Education and Conversion

Education required books, however, and education in the Catholic faith faced a potential obstacle: non-Catholic books were easily available too. The post-Trent church confronted the problem—or thought it had done so—by producing an *Index of Forbidden Books*. The first version of the *Index*, promulgated in 1559, was regarded as too severe in its strictures, and a revised and slightly moderated version appeared in 1564. The *Index* was continually updated over the centuries, with more than forty editions published between 1564 and its eventual suppression in 1966, making it the longest institutionalized censorship in Greater Western history. It was also, arguably, the least effective, since few of the condemned books ever went out of print. In fact, the *Index* represented a perfect shopping list for individuals who wanted to read materials officially denied them. True, 90 percent of the books ever placed on the list were dense theological treatises that non-Catholics or lay Catholics were unlikely ever to read in the first place. Even so, the 1564 *Index* singled out quite an impressive list of writers. It condemned the works of Pietro Aretino, John Calvin, Nicolaus Copernicus (the Polish astronomer who developed the heliocentric model of the universe, in which the sun, not Earth, is the fixed center), Desiderius Erasmus, Henry VIII of England, Martin Luther, Niccolò Machiavelli, François Rabelais, and William Tyndale (an early translator of the Bible into English). Also forbidden were the Qur'an and the Talmud. Later editions added the humanist *Essays* of Michel de Montaigne and the scientific writings of Johannes Kepler and Galileo Galilei.

Jesuit training emphasized all-round education, so that Society members would be prepared for any educational or missionary challenge thrown their way. Even today, the training of a Jesuit takes up to thirteen years. Although grounded in classical humanism, Jesuit education branched off into mathematics and astronomy. Several of the leading scholars of the age were Jesuits. Christoph Scheiner (1573–1650) was a German astronomer who discovered sunspots independently of Galileo; he also wrote one of the first treatises on the physiology of the human eye. Alexius Sylvius Polonus (1593–1653) was a Polish astronomer like Copernicus and specialized in the design of ever-more refined telescopes. Although primarily an engineer, he nevertheless used his instruments, mastery of mathematics, and Copernican theory to compose a new work on the design of the solar calendar.

Another influential Jesuit, Carlo Borromeo (1538–1584), was no scholar but dedicated his career to promoting a better-educated clergy. Coming from a wealthy aristocratic family (his mother was a Medici), he used his personal fortune and the large income from his position as archbishop of Milan to found numerous colleges and seminaries. He also established the Academy of the Vatican Nights, an informal symposium to keep church leaders informed of the newest learning.

WHAT ABOUT THE ORTHODOX EAST?

The 15th and 16th centuries were a time of neither renaissance nor reformation for the Orthodox world. The central fact of Orthodox life in this era was conquest by the Ottoman Turks, followed by efforts to adapt to Muslim rule. From about 1350 on, thousands of scholars, artists, soldiers, farmers, officials, and other refugees from Byzantium fled into western Europe. Apart from these scattered communities, the only part of the Orthodox world that remained uncontrolled by the Ottomans, once Constantinople fell in 1453, was Russia. The Turkish court eventually awarded its Orthodox subjects the status of a *millet* (Arabic for "nation"), which meant that the community governed its own internal affairs in accordance with its own laws and customs. But since Islamic law defined its subject communities by faith rather than ethnicity, the immediate impact of millet status was to strengthen the authority of the Orthodox Patriarch of Constantinople, who henceforth held sway over the previously autonomous Albanian, Arab, Bulgarian, Georgian, Greek, and Serbian Orthodox churches. All the traditional restrictions on subject Christians remained in place.

Ottoman policies toward its subject Christians were moderately tolerant. Forced conversions to Islam were forbidden by law but occasionally occurred; notably, individuals who did convert but then returned to Orthodoxy, or whose children returned to it, were customarily given three opportunities to recant their apostasy, after which they were killed (if male) or imprisoned (if female). The practice of *devshirme*—whereby Christian children were stolen from their families, raised as Muslims, and sent through the rigors of specialized military training to become Janissaries—continued unabated. Indeed, it accelerated through the 16th century. The Ottoman sultans relied on these slave-soldiers, who were under their direct authority, to provide a check on the ambitions of Turkish nobles. Hostilities between the Ottoman state and Europe, however, meant that Orthodox Christianity experienced none of the innovative influences of the Renaissance, Protestant Reformation, or Catholic Reformation. The ideas and values of Renaissance humanism—whether Christian or otherwise—made no inroads in the east; neither did the Protestant reformers show much interest in intellectual or religious exchange with the Orthodox. Martin Luther, fearing Turkish advances into central Europe, approved of a military campaign against the Ottomans but explicitly rejected the idea of a crusade. "Christian warfare," he insisted, was an oxymoron.

It may have been an oxymoron, but it was about to become Europe's reality. The hopeful and confident humanism of the Renaissance gave way to one of the bitterest and most violent periods in Europe's history: the era of the Wars of Religion (ca. 1524–1648), which left millions dead across the continent.

The Reformation was, like the Renaissance, a movement with its eyes on the past. Only by returning to the pure values and practices of an earlier era could society set itself on the right path for development and growth. There was something to be said for the backward glance, but at the same time a number of startling discoveries were about to change everything in Greater Western life: new worlds, new civilizations, new political and economic alignments, new ideas about the cosmos, and new understandings of the fundamental structure of nature were about to challenge every assumption and institution of society. It is an irony of the age that the Greater West entered the 16th and 17th centuries with its eyes on the past as it raced headlong into the future.

WHO, WHAT, WHERE

Anabaptists	German Peasants'	justification by faith
Catholic Reformation/	Revolt	alone
Counter-Reformation	humanism	Martin Luther
Christian humanism	indulgences	Ninety-Five Theses
Council of Trent	Jesuits	predestination
Erasmus	John Calvin	Protestant Reformation

SUGGESTED READINGS

Primary Sources

Boccaccio, Giovanni. *The Decameron.*

Calvin, John. *Institutes of Christian Religion.*

Cellini, Benvenuto. *Autobiography.*

Erasmus of Rotterdam. *Julius Excluded from Heaven.*

Erasmus of Rotterdam. *The Praise of Folly.*

Hutton, Ulrich von. *Letters of Obscure Men.*

Luther, Martin. *Address to the Christian Nobility of the German Nation.*

Luther, Martin. *The Freedom of a Christian.*

Luther, Martin. *Table Talk.*

Machiavelli, Niccolò. *Discourses on Livy.*

Machiavelli, Niccolò. *The Mandrake Root.*

Machiavelli, Niccolò. *The Prince.*

Rabelais, François. *Gargantua and Pantagruel.*

Vasari, Giorgio. *Lives of the Artists.*

Anthologies

Black, Robert, ed. *Renaissance Thought: A Reader* (2001).

Janz, Denis R., ed. *A Reformation Reader: Primary Texts with Introductions* (2008).

King, John N., ed. *Voices of the English Reformation: A Sourcebook* (2004).

Wiesner-Hanks, Merry. *The Renaissance and Reformation: A History in Documents* (2011).

Studies

Baylor, Michael G. *The German Reformation and the Peasants' War: A Brief History with Documents* (2012).

Benedict, Philip. *Christ's Churches Purely Reformed: A Social History of Calvinism* (2002).

Bolzoni, Lina. *The Gallery of Memory: Literary and Iconographic Models in the Age of the Printing Press* (2001).

Caffiero, Marina. *Forced Baptisms: Histories of Jews, Christians, and Converts in Papal Rome* (2011).

Diefendorf, Barbara B. *From Penitence to Charity: Pious Women and the Catholic Reformation in Paris* (2006).

Eisenstein, Elizabeth. *The Printing Revolution in Early Modern Europe* (2005).

King, Ross. *Machiavelli: Philosopher of Power* (2009).

Levi, Anthony. *Renaissance and Reformation: The Intellectual Genesis* (2004).

MacCulloch, Diarmaid. *The Reformation: A History* (2005).

Martines, Lauro. *Strong Words: Writing and Social Strain in the Italian Renaissance* (2001).

Mazzotta, Giuseppe. *Cosmopoiesis: The Renaissance Experiment* (2001).

McGrath, Alister E. *Reformation Thought: An Introduction* (2001).

Muslu, Cihan Yüksel. *The Ottomans and the Mamluks: Imperial Diplomacy and Warfare in the Islamic World* (2014).

Nauert, Charles G., Jr. *Humanism and the Culture of Renaissance Europe* (2006).

Oberman, Heiko A. *Luther: Man between God and the Devil* (2006).

O'Malley, John W. *Trent and All That: Renaming Catholicism in the Early Modern Era* (2000).

Ozment, Steven. *The Serpent and the Lamb: Cranach, Luther, and the Making of the Reformation* (2012).

Parks, Tim. *Medici Money: Banking, Metaphysics, and Art in Fifteenth-Century Florence* (2006).

Pettegree, Andrew. *The Book in the Renaissance* (2011).

Pettegree, Andrew. *Reformation and the Culture of Persuasion* (2005).

Randall, Michael. *The Gargantuan Polity: On the Individual and the Community in the French Renaissance* (2008).

Stjerna, Kirsi. *Women and the Reformation* (2008).

Taylor, Barry, and Alejandro Coroleu. *Humanism and Christian Letters in Early Modern Iberia, 1480–1630* (2010).

Wiesner-Hanks, Merry E. *Women and Gender in Early Modern Europe* (2008).

For additional resources, including maps, primary sources, visuals, web links, and quizzes, please go to www.oup.com/us/backman.

FRANCISCI

DE VERULAMIO,

Summi Angliæ

CANCELARII,

Instauratio

magna.

Multi pertransibunt & augebitur scientia.

Sin Bischofsiabri

LONDINI
Apud Joannem Billium
Typographum
Regium.

CHAPTER 13

Worlds Old and New

1450–1700

In the 13th century a Franciscan scholar from England named Roger Bacon (1214–1294) gleefully tore into everyone around him who thought of themselves as scientists. He could, and did, find fault in anyone. Phrases like "damned fools," "ignorant asses," "inept buffoons," and "miserable idiots" pepper his writings in his own colorful Latin. Science, he argued, had been for too long a prisoner to philosophers who never thought to test their abstractions against the evidence of their senses. When a renowned scholar like Albertus Magnus (ca. 1200–1280) came to lecture at the University of Paris and was received "like a second Aristotle," Bacon reacted bitterly: "Never before in the history of the world has there been committed a[n intellectual] crime as perverse as this."

Bacon did not oppose grand theories in themselves. Rather, he believed that the only valid way to reach them was through observation. "Experimental science is the Queen of All Sciences, the goal of all our speculation," he wrote in his *Opus Maius* (*Major*

THE AMERICAS IN 1600

ATLANTIC OCEAN

PACIFIC OCEAN

■ Spanish
■ Portuguese

The *Novum Organum* Francis Bacon was no scientist but an evangelist for science. By strict application of scientific methods, he believed, humanity could return to the state of perfect comprehension of and unity with the natural world that was lost with Adam and Eve's expulsion from Eden. The *Novum Organum* (*New Instrument*), published in 1620, laid out his vision for the method of attaining this true knowledge of the world. The frontispiece reprinted here shows a ship about to head out bravely into uncharted waters. The Latin inscription below quotes from the biblical book of Daniel: "Many will go, back and forth, and knowledge will be increased."

Work). But even that was not sufficient. One had to master all the sciences—including mathematics, optics, astronomy, botany, and physics—before one could even begin to theorize about any one of them. Bacon spent many years achieving just that mastery, as well as learning Greek and Hebrew (and possibly a smattering of Arabic), to reach the grand synthesis that he believed only he could achieve. In the end, however, struggles within the Franciscan order forced Bacon into house arrest and silence; he never had the chance to elaborate his grand Theory of Everything.

In the late 16th century Sir Francis Bacon (1561–1626) earned fame for his brilliance in law and philosophy, and he cultivated friendships among England's most wealthy and privileged people. Bacon (of no known relation to his medieval namesake) could, and did, flatter anyone. Bacon spent his last five years on the philosophical work that had always fascinated him. He planned a massive, comprehensive work to be called the *Great Instauration*—meaning the refounding of the entire Western intellectual tradition—but completed only a handful of discrete books that were to form parts of the whole. His *Novum Organum* (*New Instrument*) in 1620 reworked Aristotelian logic, whereas *The New Atlantis* (published in 1627, after the author's death) was a utopian fantasy. He envisioned, like Roger Bacon had done several centuries earlier, a grand masterwork, a complete synthesis of human intellectual understanding. His focus, however, was on the process of analysis rather than on the gathering of data or the testing of

CHAPTER TIMELINE

1480	1500	1520	1540	1560

- 1492 Columbus reaches the Americas
- 1494 Treaty of Tordesillas
- 1498 Vasco da Gama reaches India
- 1519–1521 Cortés's army conquers Aztec Empire
- 1519–1522 Magellan's fleet circumnavigates the globe
- 1531–1533 Pizarro's army conquers Inca Empire
- 1543 Copernicus, *On the Revolutions of the Heavenly Sphere*

hypotheses. Given facts A and B, what conclusions or assumptions can we validly draw from them—and how can we distinguish the valid from the invalid?

Both Bacons addressed the same problem, although from different angles: What are the intrinsic flaws in human thinking? What errors stand between us and Truth, and how can we overcome them? The world overwhelms us with data, impressions, facts, and observations, and our history overwhelms us with ideas, theories, opinions, and conjectures. We need a clear guide to dealing with all this input. How can we know that we are thinking properly?

The urgency of the question became all the more acute with the European discovery of the Americas in the late 15th century. How could all the holy books, the classical authors, the medieval theorists, and the brilliant minds of the Renaissance not have known about the existence of this "New World"—two entire continents filled with peoples, languages, religions, value systems, and traditions of which the Greater West was ignorant? If the best minds of the past four thousand years were of no help, then what would equip the people of the 16th and 17th centuries to come to grips with all of this new information? This shock to the system of Western thinking helped to spur a vibrant, even dizzying, new wave of scientific and philosophical advances known as the **Scientific Revolution** (roughly 1500–1750)—a period marked not only by a parade of new discoveries and ideas but also by intrinsic changes in the way of thinking about the physical universe that has since come to characterize Western views and values.

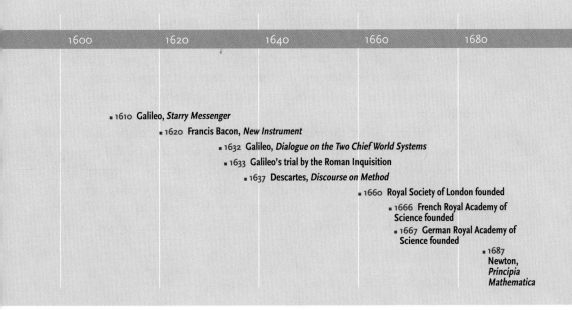

1600   1620   1640   1660   1680

- 1610 Galileo, *Starry Messenger*
- 1620 Francis Bacon, *New Instrument*
- 1632 Galileo, *Dialogue on the Two Chief World Systems*
- 1633 Galileo's trial by the Roman Inquisition
- 1637 Descartes, *Discourse on Method*
- 1660 Royal Society of London founded
- 1666 French Royal Academy of Science founded
- 1667 German Royal Academy of Science founded
- 1687 Newton, *Principia Mathematica*

The Scientific Revolution was not a rejection of tradition, unlike Renaissance humanism, but a new phase in its development. The astonishing discoveries of the age placed science at the center of intellectual life in a way that was unique to the West. Fields like mathematics, medicine, and astronomy had always played important roles in intellectual culture. Plato's Academy had expected everyone to master geometry before even beginning philosophical study. However, in the 16th and 17th centuries explorers and scientists did more than discover new continents, redraw the map of the world, place the sun at the center of the cosmos, discover the universal law of gravitation, and witness the Islamic retreat from science. They also came to define intellectual life and establish the standards by which it developed and was judged. The story from Bacon to Bacon helps to explain why.

EUROPEAN VOYAGES OF DISCOVERY

For more than four thousand years the entire known world had consisted of three continents: Europe, Africa, and Asia. From the start, the peoples of the Greater West had shown more restlessness and curiosity about the world than any other ancient culture. Phoenician travelers, beginning around 1200 BCE, had journeyed beyond the Straits of Gibraltar and into the Atlantic. The Greeks had circumnavigated the British Isles by 300 BCE, and by 100 CE the Romans had made contact with merchant-explorers from China. The latter ventured as far as the Euphrates River shortly after the time of Constantine the Great, around 360 CE, although much later the Ming dynasty closed China off from the outside world.[1] The first Christian missionaries had reached China well before the western Roman Empire fell in 476. Viking raiders had spread out through the Baltic, North, and Mediterranean seas and had reached a corner of North America by the 10th century. The Muslim Arabs, followed by the Persians and Turks, had carved out vast realms on all three continents and developed techniques to map the new territories. European stirrings in the Atlantic were thus only the latest phase in a centuries-long tradition of restlessness.

Portugal Takes the Lead

The Portuguese led the way. As early as 1415 their ships made contact with the coast of western Africa, down the expanse of what is today the country of Morocco. With the enthusiastic support of Prince Henry the Navigator (1394–1460), Portuguese fleets sailed next to the Azores and the Canary Islands. By 1445 they had reached the westernmost part of the continent, at today's neighboring states of Senegal and Gambia. In the 1460s they began to curve eastward

---

[1]   Under their great admiral Zheng He (1371–1435), Chinese fleets made it as far as the mouth of the Persian Gulf, to the Horn of Africa, and probably even up the Red Sea to Jiddah, not far from Mecca.

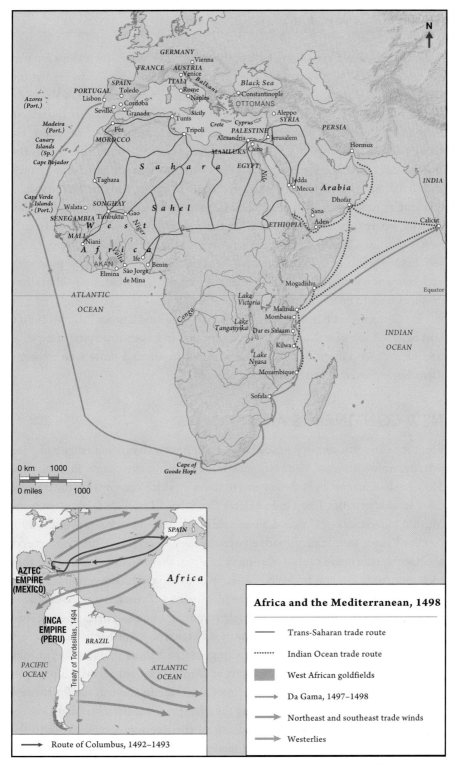

Africa and the Mediterranean, 1498

——	Trans-Saharan trade route
········	Indian Ocean trade route
▨	West African goldfields
—→	Da Gama, 1497–1498
—→	Northeast and southeast trade winds
—→	Westerlies
—→	Route of Columbus, 1492–1493

MAP 13.1 Africa and the Mediterranean, 1498 Only six years after Christopher Columbus, sailing for Spain, reached the Americas, the Portuguese explorer Vasco da Gama made landfall in India.

453

under the massive overhanging bulk of the Saharan expanse. Their ships crossed the equator in 1474, and in 1488 they reached the Cape of Good Hope at the southern tip of Africa. Ten years later, in 1498, under the command of **Vasco da Gama** (ca. 1460–1524), the first European fleet made landfall in India (see Map 13.1). These were journeys of exploration and trade, not of conquest. Da Gama told the local ruler in Calicut, the center of the spice trade, that he was the ambassador of the king of Portugal—the ruler of many lands and a man of such wealth that no one in this part of the world could compare, and that for sixty years this king's predecessors had dispatched ships to explore the seas in the direction of India, where they had heard that Christian kings like themselves lived. To connect with these Christian monarchs was the sole aim of their explorations, not to seek luxury goods or precious metals—because the kings of Portugal possessed such tremendous wealth as to make them uninterested in whatever gold or silver or spices were to be found in India or any other place.

Da Gama meant hardly a word of this, of course, and it is doubtful his Indian host believed any of it. Christian missionary zeal and a genuine spirit of exploration for its own sake motivated those who put to sea and those who financed them. So, however, did an expectation of profit.

NEW CONTINENTS AND PROFITS

From the early 9th century sub-Saharan gold, spices, slaves, and ivory had been prized commodities in Mediterranean trade. Muslim merchants in Spain and Morocco had first brought these items to Europe, which accounts for the tremendous wealth of cities like Granada and Cordoba. (Tax records show that the Muslim inhabitants of Cordoba alone held six thousand black slaves in the 10th century.) These were luxury goods enjoyed by the elites. When Christian forces of the Reconquista drove the last Muslim rulers from Iberia in the 15th century, they took over control of this trade and determined to expand it. The commodities exchanged for these luxury items were predominantly textiles, metalwares, glazed pottery, glass, and paper. Not surprisingly, some of the coastal African peoples had embraced Islam in the intervening centuries, but this posed no bar to trade. Money mattered, not faith. When Vasco da Gama reached India in 1498, he mistook Hinduism for a quaint Eastern version of Christianity but identified precisely every spice and precious stone in the markets. Once in Calicut, the Portuguese quickly established trading posts along the whole southwestern Malabar Coast of India. Within twenty years they had spread their commercial network to the Malay Peninsula, the Indonesian archipelago, and the Moluccas (Spice Islands); within another two decades, they had reached China and Japan. Their first permanent trading post in China, at Macao, was established in 1555 (see Map 13.2).

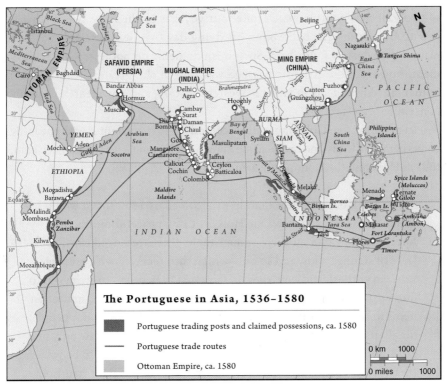

MAP 13.2   The Portuguese in Asia, 1536–1580   While the Spanish predominated in the New World, the Portuguese established themselves as the leading European commercial power in Asia in the 16th century.

Christopher Columbus's innovation in 1492 was to propose reaching Asia by sailing directly westward rather than circumnavigating Africa to the south. Although an Italian from Genoa, **Christopher Columbus** (1451–1506) sailed under the Spanish flag of Ferdinand and Isabella. Such international arrangements were common, so it is no wonder that just about every state ever associated with the first European to reach the Americas claims him as a native. To his fellow Italians he is Cristoforo Colombo, to the Spanish he is Cristóbal Colón, streets and squares in Barcelona commemorate Cristòfor Colom, and the Portuguese proudly recall Cristóvão Colombo.[2]

Christopher Columbus Discovers a "New World"

Every educated person in Europe and the Near East since the 12th century had known that the world was round. Columbus was unprepared for the size of the globe—thus the length of his historic journey, but not the fact of it. And then he ran into an unexpected roadblock, the Americas. Columbus never realized that the Caribbean islands he had landed at were in fact the outer islands

---

[2]   The English explorer John Cabot, who carried the Tudor flag as far as Newfoundland in 1497, was actually another Italian—Giovanni Caboto (1450–1508), from Venice.

of two vast new continents. Despite four voyages to the New World (that is, new to Europeans), he believed to his dying day that he had sailed to islands just off the coast of south Asia. Such misjudgments do not lessen his achievement, however. The Atlantic passage was one of the greatest technical and human-adventure feats in Greater Western history, and it had earth-changing consequences.

In his ship's log, Columbus duly recorded his first encounter with the indigenous people of the island that became known as *Hispaniola* (the "Spanish Island," today's Haiti and the Dominican Republic):

> When it became clear that they welcomed us, I saw that it would be easier to convert them to Our Holy Faith by peaceful means than by force, and so I offered them some simple gifts—red-dyed caps, necklaces of strung beads, and so on—which they received with great pleasure. So enthusiastic were they, in fact, that they began to swim out to our ships, carrying parrots, balls of cotton thread, spears, and other items to trade. . . . Still, they struck me as an exceptionally poor people, for all of them were naked—even the women, although I saw only one girl among them at the time. Every one of them I perceived to be young (that is, under the age of thirty), finely shaped and with handsome faces. . . . They appear to own no weapons and to have no knowledge of such, for when I showed them our swords they reached out and grabbed them by the blades, cutting themselves unexpectedly. . . . When I inquired, by pointing, about the scars visible on some of their bodies, they made me to understand, also by pointing, that people from another island had attacked them and tried to carry them off as slaves, but they resisted. . . . Overall they struck me as being clever, and I believe they would make good servants and could easily become Christian, since they have no religion of their own. They learned quickly to repeat the handful of words we taught them. If it please God, I intend to bring six of them home to Your Majesties, so that they might be taught to speak our language. Apart from the parrots, I saw no animals of any kind on the island.

Columbus's log entry reflects his disappointment in the poverty of the people. Expecting the vast riches of Asia's silk and spice trade, he found instead naked islanders—whom he mistakenly named "Indians"—with nothing but ready smiles and a number of parrots. On subsequent journeys he discovered more of the natural wealth available, and his enthusiasm recovered noticeably. In 1494 the monarchs of Spain and Portugal signed the Treaty of Tordesillas, which divided the lands of the newly expanded world between them: Spain laid claim to all the lands west of the meridian (north–south line) 1,300 miles west of the Cape Verde Islands, whereas Portugal held rights to all the new lands east of it. The treaty thus granted Portugal dominion over what became Brazil but left the rest of the New World to Spain; Portugal, in return, was spared Spanish competition in the Indian Ocean and South China Sea. Within a few years other adventurers had reached both the North American and the South American mainlands, and by 1507 at least one mapmaker—German cartographer Martin Waldseemüller (1470–1520)—began to appreciate that two entirely new continents had been found. On his revolutionary map, the *Universalis Cosmographia* ("World Map") of 1507, Waldseemüller named the new continents *America*, after the Italian cartographer Amerigo Vespucci (1454–1512), whose explorations and navigational charts he used in compiling his map.

The First Published Image of the New World
Christopher Columbus's first report to the Spanish kings of his discovery was published in Basel in early 1494; printed here is one of the illustrations that accompanied the Latin text. It shows Columbus arriving on the shore of "the island of Hispania" in a small landing craft. He offers a goblet as a peace offering to the inhabitants, who appear to be uniformly naked, male, and beardless, gathered at the shore to meet him.

News of Columbus's discovery spread quickly across Europe, and soon wave after wave of explorers and adventurers set sail. In 1513 the Spanish admiral Vasco Núñez de Balboa (1475–1519), standing atop a hill in what is today's nation of Panama, became the first European to see the Pacific Ocean. Only six years later Ferdinand Magellan (1480–1521) set out to circumnavigate the entire globe, an astonishing feat that took three years and claimed the lives of 262 of his initial crew of 280, including his own. Tales of the wealth available in the New World and in Asia set off a fiercely competitive wave of explorers, soldiers, and government representatives eager to stake out their claims (see Map 13.3).

Rise of the Atlantic Commercial Economies

Geographic location gave an immense advantage to the Atlantic seaboard nations of Europe: Portugal, Spain, France, the Low Countries, and England. The Mediterranean states, which had lived by maritime trade since 3000 BCE, were shut off from the New World bonanza since they could not pass the Straits of Gibraltar—which the Atlantic states (first Spain, and later England) had quickly sealed off like plugging a cork in a bottle. Left to trade with Asia only through the Ottoman-controlled land routes, they began a long and slow commercial decline. This resulted in a fundamental change in the structure of the European economy,

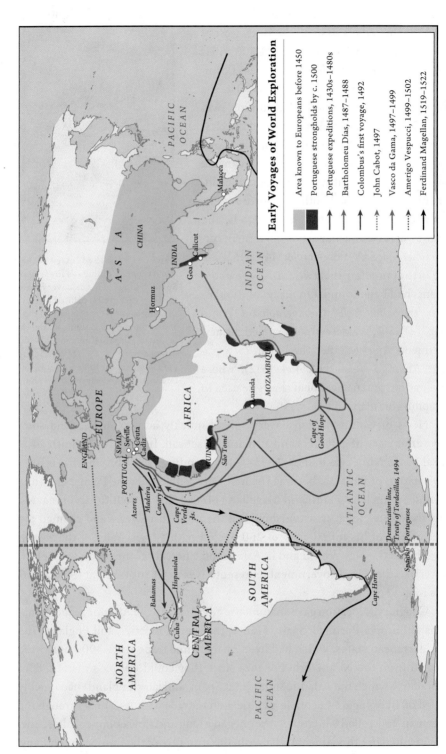

Early Voyages of World Exploration

- Area known to Europeans before 1450
- Portuguese strongholds by c. 1500
- Portuguese expeditions, 1430s–1480s
- Bartholomeu Días, 1487–1488
- Colombus's first voyage, 1492
- John Cabot, 1497
- Vasco da Gama, 1497–1499
- Amerigo Vespucci, 1499–1502
- Ferdinand Magellan, 1519–1522

MAP 13.3   Early Voyages of World Exploration   In a remarkably short period of time, the Portuguese and Spanish went from exploring the eastern Atlantic to circumnavigating the globe.

and by 1600 economic dominance had shifted away from the Mediterranean. The Atlantic states entered the 17th century as the economic and political power-houses of Europe.

The sudden and massive influx of gold from the New World triggered the rise of the Atlantic commercial economies. This gold was seized chiefly from the Aztecs and Mayans of Central America and the Incas of what eventually became Peru and Bolivia. Credit for these seizures belongs above all to the bands of **conquistadores** ("conquerors") led by Hernán Cortés (1485–1547), who in 1519–1521 subdued the Aztecs, and Francisco Pizarro (1471–1541), who vanquished the Incas in 1531–1533. The conquerors' forces were astonishingly few in number: Cortés commanded an army of no more than five hundred conquistadores, and Pizarro had only about two hundred—although both men benefited from assistance by tribes hostile to the Aztec and Inca overlords. The Europeans' technological advantage is obvious: supplied with firearms, they could mow down the spear-carrying natives with relative ease. But their victory was made incalculably easier by an inadvertent biological warfare that preceded them on the scene.

The Conquest of Mexico   This painting, from the second half of the 17th century, illustrates the dramatic conquest of the Aztec capital of Tenochtitlán (today's Mexico City) by Hernán Cortés in 1519. The Aztec Empire had long been the most powerful (and violent) of the New World kingdoms. Cortés, shown astride his horse in full armor in the foreground, began his campaign with only a few hundred soldiers—although he picked up many native conscripts on his way to Tenochtitlán. By 1521 Cortés had conquered the once-great empire. With the addition of "New Spain" (Mexico) and Pizarro's conquest a decade later of the Peruvian highlands, the Spanish Empire became the largest in the world.

Smallpox Victims   The protracted isolation of the peoples of the Americas from the rest of the world made them vulnerable to a battery of diseases that European colonists brought with them: the breath of a Spaniard was said to be sufficient to kill. These 16th-century illustrations, drawn by a native Mexican artist, depict smallpox victims. In the upper-left panel a doctor attempts to treat his patient. Undoubtedly he failed.

CONQUEST AND EPIDEMICS

Separated by a vast ocean, the peoples of Europe and of the Americas had been exposed to different types of bacteria and viruses and had consequently developed different biological responses to them. The sailors who landed with Columbus on Hispaniola brought with them the viruses for smallpox and measles. Neither disease had ever existed before in the New World, so they ran unchecked with horrifying effect. On Hispaniola alone, the indigenous population, which an early Dominican missionary (Bartolomé de Las Casas, 1484–1566) had estimated to be 3 million strong in 1492, fell by 1538 to a mere five hundred: a loss greater than 99.99 percent. In the opposite direction, some Europeans contracted a form of syphilis in the New World that seems never to have been present before in Europe. Within a few years, 5 million Europeans had died of it. Yet the impact on the New World was far greater. Cortés was able to conquer Mexico by 1521 with only six hundred men at arms because 90 percent of the Aztecs had already been obliterated by smallpox by 1520.

A Franciscan missionary, Toribio de Benavente Motolinia (1484–1568), described how the natives "did not know how to treat the disease . . . and consequently died in whole piles, like bedbugs. In many places, in fact, entire households died all at once, and since it proved impossible to bury so great a number of corpses, our soldiers simply pulled down the houses over these people, letting their own homes serve as their tombs." Motolinia wrote that when Cortés led his men in triumph through the Aztec capital of Tenochtitlan the soldiers could traverse the entire city stepping only on the corpses of smallpox victims, without ever once setting foot on the ground. Pizarro found similar circumstances favoring him when he stormed through Peru and Bolivia. Even a century later, in far-off Massachusetts Bay, smallpox and measles erased nine-tenths of the Native American population between 1617 and 1619.

Since the late 20th century historians have used the term **Columbian Exchange** to describe the momentous interactions between the Old and New Worlds initiated by Columbus's landfall in the Americas.[3] From men to animals

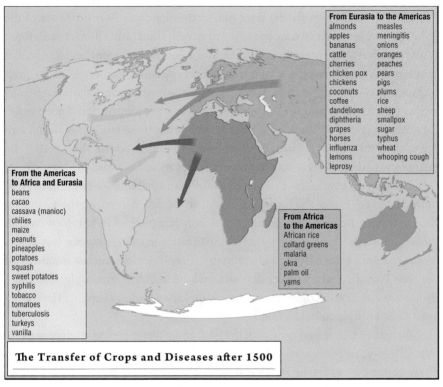

From Eurasia to the Americas

almonds	measles
apples	meningitis
bananas	onions
cattle	oranges
cherries	peaches
chicken pox	pears
chickens	pigs
coconuts	plums
coffee	rice
dandelions	sheep
diphtheria	smallpox
grapes	sugar
horses	typhus
influenza	wheat
lemons	whooping cough
leprosy	

**From the Americas
to Africa and Eurasia**

beans
cacao
cassava (manioc)
chilies
maize
peanuts
pineapples
potatoes
squash
sweet potatoes
syphilis
tobacco
tomatoes
tuberculosis
turkeys
vanilla

**From Africa
to the Americas**

African rice
collard greens
malaria
okra
palm oil
yams

The Transfer of Crops and Diseases after 1500

MAP 13.4   The Transfer of Crops and Diseases after 1500   The interchange of plants, animals, and microbes between the Old and New Worlds permanently altered demographic patterns, technologies, cultures, and cuisines on both sides of the Atlantic.

and from plants to microbes, the movement of life-forms across the Atlantic Ocean dramatically and permanently altered ecologies, societies, and cultures. Europeans introduced horses, chickens, cows, pigs, and goats to the New World (but also rats) and brought back to Europe minks, llamas, and turkeys. Within two centuries of 1492 they also brought apples, carrots, coffee, garlic, lettuce, oats, rye, and wheat to the Americas and sent the first avocados, blueberries, chili peppers, cocoa beans, cotton, potatoes, tobacco, tomatoes, and zucchini to Europe (see Map 13.4). (Tomatoes, however, were long believed to be poisonous and were valued only as a decorative species; there was no marinara sauce in Italy until the late 19th century.) Many of these exchanges were beneficial to both sides of the Atlantic. At the microbial level, however, a different story played out. Among European and African diseases transferred to the New World were not only smallpox and measles but also diphtheria, influenza, malaria, typhus, and yellow fever, among others.

The Columbian Exchange

---

[3]   Historian Alfred W. Crosby coined the phrase in his pioneering work, *The Columbian Exchange: Biological and Cultural Consequences of 1492* (1972).

European Exploitation   Such unintended suffering does not excuse the outright brutishness of the Europeans in the Americas. In sailing to Africa, India, and China, the Europeans had shown no interest in conquest and colonization since they were able to acquire what they wanted—nonperishable luxury goods—by simple trade. Their technological advantage, in military hardware, over the sub-Saharan Africans was as great as it was over the indigenous American peoples, but it did not prompt them to slaughter millions of Africans and seize their lands. Smallpox and other epidemic diseases changed everything, though, because they caused the Europeans to develop almost instantly a different attitude toward the New World: here lay two vast continents that were, in effect, uninhabited—or near enough to uninhabited to inspire the Europeans to finish the job. Moreover, the success of the Protestant Reformation accelerated European interest in the New World. Protestant leaders saw not only an opportunity for evangelization but also a means to finance their struggles back home. The coincidence of the discovery of the New World's gold and silver deposits, and the bubbling over of the Catholic–Protestant rift into outright war in the 1540s (discussed in chapter 14), was too great to be entirely coincidental.

Once they had seized control of the gold and silver mines, the Europeans set to the large-scale production of cash crops like cotton, sugar cane, and tobacco. These commodities fetched high prices, retained consistent demand, and traveled well across the long distance from New World to Old. The annihilation of the local populace presented a problem, however, since all three crops were exceptionally labor intensive in their production. Without a large infusion of people to work the land, producing these crops was out of the question. There were only two ways to put people on the land in the numbers needed: settlement and slavery.

THE COPERNICAN DRAMA

Science interested few people during the Renaissance; at best it formed a minor hobby for some. Like the classical Romans they emulated, Renaissance thinkers showed a keen interest in applied technology but spent little time on pure science, that is, the direct observation, investigation, and theoretical explanation of natural phenomena. One partial exception was the great artist Leonardo da Vinci (1452–1519), whose curiosity about the natural world and eye for observation inspired him to make intricate drawings of human anatomy, various forms of plant and animal life, and types of machines. The only other Renaissance figure who may qualify as a scientist was the Swiss physician Philip von Hohenheim, better known by his nickname of Paracelsus (1493–1541). His understanding and practice of medicine was thoroughly medieval, although he did some pioneering experimentation with various chemicals and minerals in the treatment of disease. His most significant discovery was the development of laudanum—a tincture of opium dissolved in alcohol that was used to treat a host of maladies until the early 20th century.

The rise of pure science—or the "new science"—began with developments in astronomy. Astronomy had formed a key component of Western science and *Origins in* philosophy from the beginning, going back to the ancient Greeks. The geocen- *Astronomy* tric model of the universe handed down for two thousand years posited a static Earth at the center, with the sun and other "moveable stars" (the planets) swirling about it in perfect circular orbits. The unmoving "fixed stars" comprised bright points on the ceiling of Creation. The universe was thus a single, finite, enclosed entity with the Earth—Nature's masterpiece—at its center. Christians, to the extent they thought about such things at all, saw no reason to challenge the geo- centric model and indeed felt that it contributed to the Christian view of human- ity as God's supreme creation. Science was religion's handmaiden. God created the universe, in fact, to provide humans with a home. To study the workings of the natural world, therefore, was to most Christians a way of praising God and

strengthening faith by deepening our appre- ciation of God's Creation. Throughout the Middle Ages, in fact, the church was the pri- mary institution, and often the only one, promoting the study of science. When West- ern science revived in the 16th century, it did so once again hand in hand with Christian faith. It is a modern conceit that science ad- vanced only when it divorced itself from reli- gion; that divorce became finalized only in the 19th century. The Scientific Revolution therefore must be understood as an offshoot of religious history.

Flaws in the geocentric model were evi- dent from the start. Even to the naked eye, the movement of the planets across the night sky is irregular: the transit of Venus (the ap- pearance of Venus as a small black disk moving across the face of the sun caused when Venus passes between the Earth and the sun) is just one such irregularity. If the planets all move in ever-widening perfect concentric circles around a stationary Earth,

Drawing of a Fetus   Leonardo da Vinci (1452–1519) performed as many as three dozen human dissections in his lifetime (he also dissected several cows and monkeys), which gave him unpar- alleled knowledge of the body. He prepared over two hundred detailed drawings for publication as a book on anatomy. As shown in this drawing of a fetus, he also wrote extensive notes. This image reveals as well da Vinci's use of "mirror writing," which he used not for any secret purpose but simply because he was left-handed and found it easier to write this way without smudging the page.

how could the orbits of Venus and the sun intersect in this way? Over the centuries astronomers had come up with scores of intricate arguments to explain away the inconsistencies of the geocentric model, but with each new refinement the system seemed less and less viable.

Copernicus's Theory of Heliocentrism

Sometime around 1510 the German Polish clergyman and astronomer **Nicolaus Copernicus** (Mikołaj Kopernik in Polish) began to develop a different model that resolved many of the irregularities. This **heliocentric** model posited that the sun was the fixed center, and the Earth was one of the planets in orbit around it. By 1514 he carefully circulated his findings among a handful of friends. They spent years gathering more precise observational data, and Copernicus continued to refine his hypothesis. His book, *On the Revolutions of the Heavenly Spheres*, was not published until 1543, the year of his death.

Copernicus had feared the book would set off a firestorm within the Catholic Church, but it did not. As early as 1536 a scientifically inclined cardinal, Nikolaus von Schönberg (1472–1537), had already written to him, encouraging his work:

> It was several years ago that I first heard of your skills, about which so many people were constantly speaking, and first developed such high regard for you. . . . What I learned was that you had not only mastered the knowledge of the ancient astronomers but had in fact created an entirely new cosmology according to which the Earth moves [in orbit] while the sun actually holds the most fundamental or central place in the universe. . . . At the risk of intruding upon your activities I want to urge you, with the utmost seriousness, to make these discoveries of yours known to scholars, and please to send me (as soon as is feasible) your writings on the workings of the universe, together with your data tables and anything else you may have that pertains to this important matter.

More criticism came from Protestant leaders, for whom the explicit teachings of scripture carried more weight. Luther himself is often said to have condemned "that damned fool Copernicus" for challenging the authority of scripture. (In reality, there is little evidence that Luther was fully aware of Copernicus's work.) Church condemnation did come, but not until some six decades later, when the debate had shifted, as we shall see, to Galileo's elaborations of the heliocentric theory and his claims for the scientific process that propounded it.

Copernicus had prepared for some resistance. In the preface to his book, he directly addressed the then-reigning pope, Paul III (r. 1534–1549). His book, he said, offered a simple hypothesis, an explanation of planetary movements that accommodated the available data far better than any permutation of the geocentric model. He closed with a dignified appeal to the church's concern for scholarly truth:

I have no doubt that our most skilled and talented mathematicians will concur with my findings, so long as they are willing to investigate, with all the honest seriousness that scholarship requires, the arguments I have set forth in this book in support of my theories. But still, in order that everyone, both the learned and the non-learned, may see that I hide from no man's judgment, I have decided to dedicate these findings of mine to Your Holiness, rather than to another, for even in this remote part of the world where I reside Your Holiness is regarded as preeminent in dignity for the position you hold, for your love of learning, and even for your interest in mathematics. . . . And if there should be any amateurs who (not letting their ignorance of mathematics stand in the way of a chance to pass judgment on such matters) presume to attack my theory because it contradicts some passage of Scripture that they misinterpret for their own purposes, I simply do not care; in fact, I dismiss their opinions as mere foolishness. . . . Mathematics is written for mathematicians. . . . I leave it to Your Holiness and all learned mathematicians to judge what I have written.

What follows, in other words, is a set of mathematical proofs subject only to the critical review of mathematicians. He makes no theological or even astronomical

Nicolaus Copernicus   This portrait of the great astronomer Nicolaus Copernicus (1473–1543) intentionally emphasizes his Catholic piety. Shown also is a page from his book *On the Revolution of the Heavenly Spheres* that illustrates the foundational discovery of the Scientific Revolution, Copernicus's heliocentric (sun-centered) model of the universe.

claims, but argues only that his model conforms to the available data more precisely than did earlier models.

Kepler's
Laws of
Planetary
Motion

Word of Copernicus's work spread quickly around Europe, and a number of scholars elaborated on the heliocentric theory. The Danish astronomer Tycho Brahe (1546–1601), for example, devoted his career to making ever-more precise chartings of planetary movements and stellar positions. This improved data made possible the next major leap in astronomy, when Brahe's German pupil Johannes Kepler (1571–1630) formulated three famous principles that came to be known as *Kepler's laws of planetary motion*. These laws hold that the planets move in ellipses around the sun, that they move at non-uniform speeds, and that the velocity of each planet throughout its orbit is in direct proportion to its distance from the sun at any given moment. Kepler had fought a childhood battle with smallpox that had left him very nearsighted; unable to gather his own observational data, he used the mountain of astronomical tables and star charts left behind by his teacher. With these, he validated his model with a mathematical precision that few of his contemporaries could equal or even understand. Even Galileo initially ignored it.

GALILEO AND THE TRUTH OF NUMBERS

Galileo Galilei (1564–1642) was a genius in astronomy, mathematics, and physics, as famous in his day as Albert Einstein was in the 20th century. His achievements in any one of those fields alone would warrant his being remembered.[4] Trained in mathematics, which he later taught at the University of Padua, he learned astronomy largely on his own and with the use of his telescope. In *The Starry Messenger* (1610), the first report of his astronomical discoveries, he describes the most significant of them: the moons of Jupiter. The force of this discovery is often difficult for modern readers to appreciate. The geocentric model made no allowance for smaller bodies in orbit around the planets. Everything, in the classical view, orbited the Earth. Yet here was direct evidence against it.

The elaborate mathematical arguments of Copernicus and Kepler were easily ignored. By the astronomers' own admission, they were nothing more than conjectures, a way to make the numbers fall into neater computational alignment. Few people then alive even understood them. But Galileo's discovery was as solid and incontrovertible as the New World continents that Christopher Columbus had run into in 1492. Anyone with the telescope he developed—and Galileo himself sold them, as a business venture, on the side, as well as giving them to people whose patronage he sought—could look up in the sky and see Jupiter's moons

---

[4] Galileo was a skilled tinkerer too, renowned for his redesign of the telescope (invented by Hans Lippershey, of the Netherlands) and of the geometric compass (used by surveyors and artillerymen).

for themselves. Galileo's findings were confirmed by none other than Christopher Clavius (1538–1612), the most prominent expert in mathematics and astronomy in the church, and the city of Rome gave Galileo a triumphant welcome in 1611.

Yet in 1633, only twenty-two years later, he was arrested and forced to recant. What had changed? Two factors principally, and Galileo shares in the blame for the first. In 1623 he published a treatise on comets in which he made a crucial mistake: he argued that comets were not physical objects but only optical illusions—tricks of refracted sunlight. Moreover, in putting forth this (wrong) hypothesis, he went out of his way (not unlike Roger Bacon) to insult astronomers who had asserted (correctly) that comets were in fact fiery solid bodies passing through the solar system far beyond the orbit of our moon. Several of those astronomers, however, were highly regarded clerics who taught at the church's college in Rome, and the papal court was in no mood to countenance such outright rudeness. Several years earlier, in 1616, the church had condemned the heliocentric model as contrary to scripture, and Galileo was given a friendly warning to refrain from promoting or teaching Copernicanism. He complied, for the most part, but the offensive passages in his new treatise on comets called for some sort of response. *Rising Tensions between Science and Religion*

If Galileo's first problem was scientific and political, his second concerned scripture. What happens when scientific conclusions and biblical statements are in conflict? In a letter to the Grand Duchess Christina, published in 1615, he argued that the Bible should be interpreted in a way that makes it compatible with scientific findings. Here he invited a debate that Copernicus and Kepler had studiously avoided. They had presented heliocentrism as a mathematical theory only. Although aware that it contradicted scripture, they offered no opinion about which form of truth was preferable. Galileo, however, brought the Copernican claims into direct open conflict with scripture—and he made it clear that in his mind the Bible had to accommodate science, not vice versa.

Galileo Galilei by an Unknown Painter   Galileo was an accomplished musician (he played the lute) as well as a world-class astronomer, engineer, mathematician, and physicist. Never married, he had three children by his live-in companion, Marina Gamba (d. 1612), and was a caring, if distant, father. His daughter Virginia (1600–1634) became a nun, took the name Sister Maria Celeste, and consulted with her father on many of his researches. They are buried together in the Basilica di Santa Croce in Florence.

Science and religion in the Greater West had always known tension, but the strain was proof of their close relationship. Apart from Jewish and Muslim scholars, every European scientist of any note since the fall of the Roman Empire had been a sincere

Christian, often at odds with the church but always identifying with it. Copernicus and Galileo were both devout Catholics, and Brahe and Kepler were pious Protestants. And every Jewish and Muslim scientist had been a devout, if sometimes unorthodox, believer. The first identifiable atheist—that is, one who expressly and openly denied the existence of any deity whatsoever—in Greater Western history was not a scientist at all but a German seminary dropout. Matthias Knutzen (1646–1675) published three pamphlets in 1674 denying "God, any Authority from On High, and all sects and their ministers." All that is needed to live a moral life, he wrote, is "to harm no one, live honestly, and give each person his due. . . . There is only this one life, after which there is neither any reward nor any punishment."

Scripture, Galileo implied, allows room to maneuver; science, however, does not. The church's position—and, to include the Protestants, the churches' position—was that two thousand years of tradition should not be overthrown because of some opaque mathematical formulas that relatively few people understood properly. The problem, essentially, came down to **epistemology**, or the study of the nature of knowledge itself. What exactly does it mean "to *know* something"? At what point can mere humans justifiably declare that a given statement is universally true?

INQUISITION AND INQUIRY

As we know from chapter 11, "Inquisition" is a historical term, a word denoting a specific phenomenon of the past. One could even call it a technical term, since it describes a precisely defined and regulated judicial process established by the Catholic Church in 1184. That process evolved over time, naturally, but even into the 19th century the word referred to a special type of investigation, conducted by ecclesiastical or secular authority, for the sake of public safety. But *Inquisition* is also a popular term, loosely used to describe almost any process or institution that one deems profoundly unfair.

The Inquisition of the early modern era differed significantly from its medieval forebear. Pope Lucius III (r. 1181–1185) had established the inquisition as a way of stopping the unjust execution of people for dissident religious beliefs. False beliefs within Christianity were a sin against the church but also a crime against the secular medieval state, and in the 12th and 13th centuries the aristocratic courts of Europe were quick to act against heretics—convicting them, killing them, and confiscating their property. The church took a dim view of heresy but championed the idea of intellectual free inquiry. Lucius's decree of 1184 helped to codify a strict, narrow definition of actionable heresy and brought state exercise of authority over heretics under the church's jurisdiction. As brutal and backward as the medieval inquisition is to modern sensibilities, it is important to note that the number of people killed for dissident Christian beliefs across Europe actually declined—and sharply—after the inquisition's establishment.

Nonetheless, ugly is ugly, and even without the use of physical torture (and most medieval inquisitions never resorted to it) the threatening nature of the inquiry was obvious and coercive. That ugliness grew in the early modern era when the Inquisition was officially taken over as an institution of government. In the 16th and 17th centuries the monarchical states in France, Portugal, and Spain assumed control of it—as did the lesser princes in Germany, Italy, and the Low Countries—and used it to terrorize dissidents and control political opponents. Churchmen actively colluded in the process, certainly, but the notorious Inquisition of the time was as much an indicator of the loss of church power as it was an index of religious and intellectual intolerance. *Government Takeover of the Inquisition*

Although some supported the idea, the Inquisition was not the weapon of choice for dealing with the Protestant Reformation. The Protestants, after all, declared their own separation from Rome and hence no longer came under the church's jurisdiction; later, as we saw in chapter 12, the policy of *cuius regio, eius religio* ("the religion of the ruler determines the religion of the land") granted a certain degree of toleration across the Catholic–Protestant divide. The Inquisition instead focused on two principal targets: false converts from Judaism and Islam and advocates of the new science. The issue of false converts was a complex one, arising from financial envy, racial prejudice, and unease about aristocratic stature. The conversion of nonbelievers to Christianity had been a desire central to Christian aspirations since the dawn of the religion, but fanatical worries arose from the 15th century onward that many of Europe's converts were converts in name only—people who publicly proclaimed their Christianity but privately retained their Jewish or Muslim practice. Such suspects were referred to as *crypto-Jews* and *crypto-Muslims*. *Targets of Inquisition*

The concern was not merely that they were religious frauds but that there was something evil intrinsic to their makeup. Some element in their collective bloodlines, it was feared, permanently tainted their Christianity and kept them from a genuine and full commitment. That would have been bad enough for most of the bigots of the time, but what made matters even worse was the upward social mobility of the professional classes of the Renaissance and Reformation eras. Noble families in economic decline often married wealthy, ambitious urbanites from the rising merchant economy. For them, the danger of exposing their pure noble blood to the supposedly inferior and possibly diseased elements in Jewish or Muslim blood set off a clamor of concern. Crypto-Jews and crypto-Muslims, in other words, were perceived as a threat to noble security and privilege as much as a threat to faith.

Expulsion of the Moriscos from Spain   This painting by the 17th-century Spanish artist Pere Oromig depicts the expulsion of the Moriscos (suspected crypto-Muslims) from the coastal town of Vinaròs, in eastern Spain, in 1609. Moriscos comprised nearly one-third of the population of this part of Spain at the time.

The other major class of Inquisitorial victims, the proponents of the new science, are more difficult to generalize about. Their names have become *causes célèbres* over the centuries. Giordano Bruno (1548–1600), a Dominican friar, mathematician, and cosmologist, provides the most dramatic example. Bruno had little training in science but much amateur enthusiasm for it. Seizing eagerly on Copernican heliocentrism, he soon went further—without any good scientific basis for doing so. He argued that the universe is infinitely large, that the fixed stars were suns like ours with planets of their own in orbit around them, and that life on these planets is a likelihood. Thus he denied the special nature of human beings as part of God's Creation, which was tantamount to denying the special role of Christ as the universal savior. Bruno's admirers over time have given him too much credit: he spun out so many ideas about science that the chance of at least some of them turning out to be true was high. But although he was not a scientist in the sense that Galileo was, he too fell victim to the Inquisition. The court followed its usual tactic of delay, negotiation, and appeal; if Bruno would have only agreed to keep a low profile for a few years, he might well have been given his freedom. But he refused and was executed in a public square in Rome, with his ashes dumped into the Tiber River.

The Trial of Galileo   The most famous case of all is that of Galileo. Two inquiries into his science occurred, one in 1616 and another in 1633. The 1616 tribunal, led by

Cardinal Robert Bellarmine (1542–1621)—a Jesuit who, like most Jesuit astronomers, accepted Galileo's work up through *The Starry Messenger* (1610)—reiterated the church's partial condemnation of heliocentrism and, as we have seen, let Galileo go with a warning. Copernican theory could continue to be discussed and investigated, so long as it was presented only as a mathematical hypothesis instead of as incontrovertible truth. Sixteen years later, having won further fame with his discoveries in optics, physics, and the study of tides, as well as his mathematical theory of infinite sets, Galileo breached his 1616 agreement. In his *Dialogue on the Two Chief World Systems* (1632), he argued openly for the heliocentric model as the indisputable truth. The new treatise was written in the form of a dialogue between geocentric and heliocentric astronomers, and although Galileo was careful to make the heliocentrists capitulate at the end, he nevertheless made the old-style astronomers look foolish. Even worse, he named the spokesman for the traditionalists Simplicio ("Simpleton"). He should have known better. When Inquisitors petitioned to place Galileo on trial, an irritated Pope Urban VIII (r. 1623–1644) allowed them to proceed.

As Galileo learned, tone matters. The church had promoted scientific work for centuries and had a tradition of accepting ideas and discoveries not immediately reconcilable with doctrine. It understood that knowledge proceeds by probing, doubting, and testing. What matters is patience and humility. Galileo had sufficient patience but lacked humility when it came to his work. Other Catholic scientists of the era presented new findings every bit as jarring to traditional sensibilities as Galileo's but described them as discoveries in progress rather than indisputable truths. A German named Athanasius Kircher (1601–1680) was a pioneer of microbiology and linguistics.[5] An Italian physicist named Francesco Maria Grimaldi (1618–1663) made the first observations that led to the wave theory of light; he also compiled the first map of the lunar surface that described its geological features in detail. These men understood scientific research as a never-ending process, a slow groping toward truth, but one that can never declare final success. The infinite complexity of the universe precludes such hubris. But Galileo effectively altered the rules or at least claimed that the rules were alterable and that pure truth—final and complete—was attainable. His revolutionary breakthrough was not heliocentrism in itself but the argument that science justifies itself, ratifies itself. Biblical authority and intellectual tradition mean nothing in the face of empirical data and rigorous mathematical logic. The separation of science from religion, to Galileo, was not a divorce. It was an annulment.

---

[5]   Kircher was the first to describe microbes, and he correctly identified ancient Egyptian hieroglyphics with the Coptic language. He also wrote an entire encyclopedia of the Chinese language.

Hence the Inquisition's action against him arose from the complaint that Galileo had broken a contract with the church as much as from his scientific views. The formal judgment rendered by the tribunal reads as follows;

> Seeing that you, Galileo, . . . were denounced by this Holy Office in 1615 for asserting the truth of the false doctrine, maintained by some, that the sun is the unmoving center of the universe and that the Earth moves in orbit around it . . .
>
> And seeing that . . . it was agreed that if you refused to stop [proclaiming this theory as decided truth] this Holy Office could order you to abandon the teaching altogether . . . and that you could therefore be subject to imprisonment . . .
>
> And seeing that . . . your *Dialogue on the Two Chief World Systems* has recently been published . . . in which you try to give the impression that the matter is still undecided, calling it only "probable" . . . and that you confess that numerous passages of the book are written in such a way that a reader could in fact draw the conclusion that the arguments for [heliocentrism] are irrefutable . . .
>
> We conclude, proclaim, sentence, and pronounce that . . . you have made yourself strongly suspected of heresy.

The Trial of Galileo   Galileo's endorsement of Copernican heliocentrism was not the reason for his trial and condemnation by the Roman Inquisition. The church itself, after all, had used the Copernican model when it reformed the calendar in 1582. Rather, at stake was Galileo's insistence that in any disagreement between scripture and science, science must win out; indeed, the assertions of scripture in such matters were simply irrelevant.

His punishment was house arrest and penance, and the Inquisition ordered his *Dialogue* to be burned. Galileo agreed and spent his last years in quiet work.[6] In 1638 he published his last major work, the *Discourses on Two New Sciences*, which treats problems of motion, acceleration, and mathematical theory. His trouble with the Inquisition was clearly related to, but not solely composed of, his belief in heliocentrism itself; rather, the immediate issue was his breaking of a sacred vow.

The more general and important issue, however, was in the debate about Truth itself. The case of Galileo and the Inquisition marks an important turning point in intellectual history—the rise of a belief in *quantification*. If the numbers in Theory A work more precisely and consistently than the numbers in Theory B, this belief asserts, then Theory A is for that reason alone accepted as true. But is that really the case? Numbers are powerful things, but they are not necessarily the surest (much less the only) route to Truth, and the Inquisition insisted on the point. Anyone who has ever argued that their scores on standardized exams do not reflect the reality of their knowledge and skills is holding to a position consonant with that of the Inquisition. Right or wrong, the Inquisition trusted God's Word more than it trusted mathematical formulas.

THE REVOLUTION BROADENS

It is unclear how much all of these discoveries and debates mattered outside the walls of academia and of the church. To a 17th-century peasant shoveling manure out of a cow stall, it probably did not matter whether that manure was at the fixed center of the universe or if it was in orbit around the sun; all he cared about was getting it out of the barn before the landlord came to punish him for not keeping up with his duties. But discoveries in other fields mattered a great deal at the time because of their immediate practical value. Increasingly, too, they mattered because of ethical tensions as older taboos declined, especially in regard to Islam.

In medicine, the English physician William Harvey (1578–1657) identified the circulation of blood in the human body via the intricate system of heart, veins, *Advances in* and arteries (see Table 13.1). The existence of internal organs and tissues came as *Medicine,* no surprise, but physicians had never understood their individual functions or *Chemistry,* their working together as a system. Harvey's work opened the door to compre- *Physics,* hending the human body as an integrated organism. In chemistry, the Anglo- *and Biology* Irish pioneer Robert Boyle (1627–1691), extrapolating from the atomic theory inherited from ancient Greece, described the molecular structure of compounds.

---

[6]   The legend that Galileo, at his verdict, muttered under his breath, "Even so, it [Earth] moves" is most likely false. The first instance of it appears in a fanciful Spanish painting after his death.

In physics he both determined the role of air in the propagation of sound and de-rived *Boyle's law,* which states that the volume and pressure of a gas at constant temperature vary inversely. These discoveries helped in deriving new chemicals and stabilizing air pumps. In biology the English natural scientist Robert Hooke (1635–1703) employed a compound microscope to discover the cellular structure of plants, which, when studied over time, gave hints of the actual process of growth. Organic life, Hooke was the first to assert, is an ongoing process of growth and decay according to natural principles. By analyzing fossils he came close to devel-oping a full-blown theory of evolution almost two hundred years before Darwin.

TABLE 13.1   **Major Works of the Scientific Revolution, 1500–1700**

1543	*On the Revolutions of the Heavenly Spheres*	Nicolaus Copernicus (1473–1543)
1543	*On the Makeup of the Human Body*	Andreas Vesalius (1514–1564)
1600	*On the Magnet and Magnetic Bodies*	William Gilbert (1544–1603)
1609	*The New Astronomy or Celestial Physics*	Johannes Kepler (1571–1630)
1610	*The Starry Messenger*	Galileo Galilei (1564–1642)
1614	*The Wonderful Law of Logarithms*	John Napier (1550–1617)
1619	*The Harmonies of the World*	Johannes Kepler
1620	*New Instrument*	Sir Francis Bacon (1561–1626)
1628	*On the Motion of the Heart and the Blood*	William Harvey (1578–1657)
1632	*Dialogue on the Two Chief World Systems*	Galileo Galilei
1637	*Discourse on Method*	René Descartes (1596–1650)
1653	*On the Arithmetical Triangle*	Blaise Pascal (1623–1662)
1658	*The Spirit of Geometry*	
1660	*New Experiments Physico-Mechanical*	Robert Boyle (1627–1691)
1661	*The Skeptical Chymist*	
1665	*Micrographia*	Robert Hooke (1635–1703)
1687	*Principia Mathematica*	Sir Isaac Newton (1642–1727)

All this points to an important development. If Galileo had effectively re-moved God from the workings of the physical cosmos, the scientists who fol-lowed him began to discover the structures that took the place of Providence. However useful these discoveries might have proved, could they compensate for the loss of a divine purpose in life? When one takes away the idea that the uni-verse functions, however mysteriously, according to a heavenly plan, then one risks the fear of a random, meaningless existence. The English poet and cleric John Donne (1572–1631) described this feeling of loss and confusion in "An

Anatomie of the World" (1611), written for an aristocratic patron on the anniversary of the death of his wife:

> And new philosophy calls all in doubt,
> The element of fire is quite put out,
> The sun is lost, and th'earth, and no man's wit
> Can well direct him where to look for it.
> And freely men confess that this world's spent,
> When in the planets and the firmament
> They seek so many new; they see that this
> Is crumbled out again to his atomies.
> 'Tis all in pieces, all coherence gone,
> All just supply, and all relation;
> Prince, subject, father, son, are things forgot,
> For every man alone thinks he hath got
> To be a phoenix, and that then can be
> None of that kind, of which he is, but he.
> This is the world's condition now.

The poem expresses above all the pain that follows a great personal loss. Yet it also captures the dread of a shapeless and unintelligible universe that was felt so

Sic Transit Gloria Mundi   "Thus passes the glory of the world" is the cautionary message of this 1655 painting from Spain. A sleeping nobleman dreams of wealth, power, knowledge, art, beauty, and military prowess, while a skull joins the worldly objects on the table and an angel enters the dream, holding a banner that reminds the viewer that death is the end of all things.

widely at the time. "The world's condition now" seemed one of decay and doubt; ordered existence is so jumbled and out of joint that one does not even know "where to look for it."

It is a powerful poem that should be read whole. Not all scientific discoveries, it asserts, are advances, because they come at a cost. Take the discovery of the circulation of blood. This breakthrough occurred not simply because William Harvey happened to come along and figure it out. It became possible only with the dissection of human bodies—corpses, mostly, but not all.

THE ETHICAL COSTS OF SCIENCE

Deep cultural taboos against the desecration of the body had forbidden dissections for millennia. These taboos predate Christianity and even Judaism. The elaborate funeral rites of the Egyptians and Mesopotamians, with their careful cleansing and wrapping of the body, the incantation of prayers and hymns, the presentation of offerings, the ceremonial burial or burning of the remains under the guidance of priests—all these document a powerful impulse to treat the dead with decorum. At the end of Homer's *Iliad*, Achilles drags Hector's dead body behind his chariot as he circles Troy. For Achilles it is a moment of triumph; for the reader or listener, it is a moment of moral horror: How can the great Greek hero behave so monstrously? Does Achilles even deserve to be called a hero? To an ancient audience, the scene cast doubt on all that had gone before.

Changing Attitudes toward Human Dissection   William Harvey was able to make his great discovery because, by the 17th century, many Western states had come to believe that certain individuals *deserved* to have their bodies desecrated; it was a final supreme punishment for the evil and worthlessness of their lives. After Harvey's breakthrough, detailed knowledge of the operation of the internal organs followed quickly, but these advances required a new horror: the careful cutting open of people while they were still alive. Harvey himself participated in some of this. Victims of these procedures spent weeks, and sometimes months, in constant agony.[7]

Who were these miserable people? It varied from state to state, but in general the possibility of dissection after death awaited anyone convicted of murder, treason, or counterfeiting. Theft too opened the door to the cutting table, if the person one stole from was well connected. (Heretics and witches did not need to fear the dissector's knife; they were burned at the stake. Besides, it was assumed that they were unnatural and so would not contribute to the understanding of normal human physiology.) A hardness of heart toward certain sectors of society had to

---

[7]   Physicians would make strategically placed incisions, then peel away layers of skin and muscle, to observe, for example, the full process of digestion from stomach to bowel.

Two Views of Human Dissection   The great Dutch painter Rembrandt van Rijn (1606–1669) offers a dignified portrayal of the start of a lesson on human anatomy; at this time, religious and civil law permitted a handful of dissections of human cadavers to be performed, under strictly regulated conditions. By contrast, the later satirical drawing by the English artist William Hogarth (1697–1764), part of a series called "The Progress of Cruelty," shows a considerably more careless and cavalier approach, after British law permitted the dissection of those convicted of felonies. Hogarth undoubtedly exaggerates the horrible scene for effect. But partial dissections were in fact occasionally done on individuals who were, as in Hogarth's picture, still alive.

exist before Harvey could make his discovery. Many people felt a concern that scientific knowledge can come at too high a price, ethically speaking, for the benefits it brings.[8]

But the picture becomes cloudier the more we look at it. Dissections actually were fairly common in the Middle Ages in the Mediterranean regions of Europe and in the Middle East. In Muslim Spain a physician named Ibn Zuhr (1091–1161) performed dissections for research and several autopsies. He was in fact the first physician to deny that the human body was composed of four humors—although he found few people who believed him—and he invented the medical procedure now known as tracheotomy. A personal physician of the sultan Saladin himself, al-Baghdadi (1162–1231), anatomized the corpses of a famine that struck Egypt in 1200, where he had traveled to meet the great Jewish scholar Maimonides.

In Christian Europe decrees forbidding the dissection of human remains for the purpose of transporting them whole to a distant burial site appeared as early

---

[8]   Even today, people today seldom stop to wonder where the thousands of cadavers used each year in our medical schools come from. Individuals who donate their bodies to science make up only a fraction of the bodies used. The rest are the unclaimed remains of America's homeless population, donated by our county morgues. Practices vary from state to state in the United States. Illinois, for example, requires county medical examiners to keep unclaimed bodies for sixty days before releasing them to medical schools; Maryland requires a wait of only fourteen days. Medical examiners in New York, however, are allowed to release unclaimed cadavers within twenty-four hours.

as the 1160s, but these were not prohibitions of dissection generally. When in the Third Crusade (1189–1193) the German emperor Frederick Barbarossa (r. 1152–1190) drowned in a river in Anatolia, his troops, wanting to bury him in Jerusalem, tried to preserve his body in vinegar. The human body, it turns out, does not pickle well, and as Frederick decomposed, the crusaders buried his flesh, organs, and bones in three separate sites. By 1300, in fact, dissections for the teaching of anatomy were standard in the leading medical schools, such as the University of Montpellier. At the University of Bologna, another center for medical research and teaching, dissections were performed annually from 1315 on and were made available to the public. It was only in northern Europe that human dissections were both taboo and illegal, and those countries had a less developed scientific tradition. England forbade human dissections until the 16th century, and even after authorizing them on criminals, the law permitted a total of only ten per year throughout the kingdom.[9]

THE ISLAMIC RETREAT FROM SCIENCE

The ethical cost of science detached from religious faith may not have troubled the Muslim world in the same way as it did the Christian West. At least it seems that way, because science had largely disappeared from Muslim intellectual culture, displaced by legal and theological studies, historical writing, and poetry. From the 7th to the 11th centuries the Islamic world had excelled in every science—medicine, physics, astronomy, mathematics—on both the theoretical and the practical levels, leaving Latin Europe and the Orthodox East far behind. By 1200, however, the Latin West had taken the lead. Undoubtedly, the Mongols' wholesale destruction of the great Islamic libraries, observatories, and universities deserves a heavy share of the blame. But although books and laboratories may burn, their demise does not explain the death of a certain type of curiosity about the world. The simple fact is that, with a few exceptions, Islamic scholars and their patrons from the 14th century onward valued scientific knowledge less than they had done in earlier centuries. Throughout the Renaissance period in western Europe, much of the Islamic world was too engulfed in warfare and internal strife to continue supporting scientific academies and observatories. The arrival of the Ottomans and Mongols, the rise to power of the Safavids in Persia, and the political recalibrations all three caused instead inspired philosophical and historical pursuits in the effort to redefine the very nature of Islamic identity.

---

[9]   The British Murder Act of 1752 finally allowed the bodies of executed murderers to be available for dissection. France, Germany, and the Low Countries allowed the anatomization of anyone convicted of gross felonies.

The popularity of Sufi mysticism remained problematic too. Their affinity for Sufism set the Ottoman Turks at odds with the more staid Arab majority *Ibn Taymiyya's* they governed. Urged on by heavyweight scholars like Ibn Taymiyya (1263– *Fundamentalist* 1328), Arab religious leaders in the early Ottoman centuries again placed *Movement* the *umma* ("community") at the center of Sunni life. In this conservative view, the traditions of the Qur'an, hadith, and sunnah were paramount, and all forms of speculative theology and metaphysical innovation were denounced. Ibn Taymiyya's career, together with those of his acolytes, can in fact be thought of as a small-scale Islamic analog to the Protestant Reformation:

- It demanded a strict return to the authority of early texts.
- It called for stripping away every aspect of religious life not specifically called for in those texts.
- It condemned as heretics all who disagreed with its followers or who used their ideas for other purposes.
- It was openly hostile to all forms of monastic life and to the cults of popular saints.
- It considered the earliest religious community (the Companions of the Prophet) the most perfect in its observance of confessional life.

All of these traits were shared by the Sunni and Protestant reformers.[10] Ibn Taymiyya's party attacked Sufism as fundamentally un-Islamic, since it emphasized ecstatic union with God over strict observance of his laws. This conservative element in Islam, centered on the Great Mosque in Damascus, dominated the curricula in the madrasas from the 14th through 16th centuries and kept the schools' focus intently on the Qur'an, hadith, and sunnah. Their goal was to produce pious and obedient Muslims, not to advance learning. Memorization of the traditional canon, not the pursuit of new knowledge, was the goal.

Another important reason why the Scientific Revolution posed a particular problem for scientifically inclined Muslims was because of its overthrow of the *The* classical Greek tradition. Islamic science had relied as heavily on Greek founda- *Decline of* tions as medieval European science had done. A physical universe without any *Islamic* rational ordering or, even worse, one that functioned entirely by its own internal *Science* mechanisms independent of a divine will, ill suited Muslim habits of thought. The *and Its* only scientific figure of real note in the Islamic world during this period was Taqi *Critics* ad-Din (1526–1585), who was a highly skilled engineer rather than a true

---

10   In modern times Taymiyya inspired Muhammad ibn Abd al-Wahhab (1703–1792), the founder of Wahhabism, the official doctrine of Saudi Arabia.

scientist. In 1577 he designed an astronomical observatory in Istanbul for the Ottoman ruler Murad III (r. 1574–1595), who wanted it to predict the success or failure of his political schemes. When Taqi ad-Din confidently predicted victory in Murad's planned offensive against Safavid Persia, only to have those predictions proven wrong when a new outbreak of bubonic plague hit the city once the campaign was begun, the sultan ordered the observatory torn down in 1580.

The decline of Islamic science did not go unnoticed. The great scholar Mustafa Katip Çelebi (1609–1657) bemoaned the shortcomings of his age:

> There are so many ignorant people ... their minds as dead as rocks, paralyzed in thoughtless imitation of the ancients. Rejecting and belittling all new knowledge without even a pause to give it any consideration, they pass themselves off as learned men but really are just ignoramuses who know nothing about the world or the heavens.... The [Qur'anic] admonition—"Have they not contemplated the kingdom of Heaven and Earth?" [7.184]—means nothing at all to them, and they seem to think that to "contemplate the Earth and sky" means to stare at them like a cow.

He was not alone in his complaint. Even one of the Muslim emperors of Mughal India, Muhi ad-Din Muhammad Aurangzeb (r. 1658–1707), lamented the fall in intellectual stature of Islam. In a diatribe against one of his early tutors, he harshly condemned what passed for education in the Muslim world:

> And what were some of the things you taught me? You taught me that France was a small island whose greatest king had previously been the king of Portugal, then of Holland, and then of England! You taught me that the kings of France and of Spain are just like our own petty provincial princes! ... God be praised! What impressive knowledge of geography and history you had! Wasn't it your duty to teach me about the ways of the world's nations—their exports, their military might, their methods of warfare, their customs and religions, their styles of government, their diplomatic aims? ... Instead, all you thought I needed to know was Arabic grammar and law, as though I was a [religious] judge or jurist.... By the time my education was finished I knew nothing at all of any science or art, except how to toss off some obscure technical terms that no one really understands!

Throughout much of the Ottoman Empire, frustration at the increasingly arid curricula of the madrasas drove the more creative minds on to new schools known as *khanqas*, where the emphasis was on Sufi mysticism. Poetry, music, and metaphysical writing formed the core of this schooling, much of it powerfully imaginative and emotive. (Graduates from the *khanqas* frequently celebrated the completion of their studies by hurling the textbooks from their madrasa years into wells.) But science was still ignored. Memorization and transmission trumped exploration at every turn, leaving the European world unchallenged in its pursuit of scientific truth.

THINKING ABOUT TRUTH

Having severed its connection with the religious intellectual tradition, European science needed new standards. That included Standards of practice, criteria for determining the quality of evidence and argument, and principles for defining scientific truth. Without such agreement, scientific progress would be fitful at best, permanently hobbled at worst. Suppose one conducts an experiment several times and each time achieves the same result. At what point may one legitimately conclude that this result is *always* the result—the natural and inevitable result of that experiment? Five times? Five hundred times? Five thousand times? When does it cease to be a mere result and become a conclusion? When does a general conclusion become an accepted scientific theory, and when does it finally become—the Holy Grail of research—a law of nature? Starting with Galileo and those who supported him, science had sloughed off its ancient standards and criteria but had yet to agree on new ones to replace them. Even science, it turned out, needs a philosophy—or, as the new scientists put it, a method.

The 17th century was replete with efforts to establish this method, as new findings emerged from laboratories and lecture halls across Europe (see Map 13.5). Europe's monarchies gave enthusiastic support to scientific efforts. One of the first acts passed under England's King Charles II (r. 1660–1685) was to confirm the founding of the Royal Society of London for Improving Natural Knowledge (1660, commonly known as the Royal Society), the oldest scientific academy still in existence.[11] Six years later (1666) Louis XIV established the French Academy of Sciences (*Académie des Sciences*), and one year after that Germany's King Leopold I (r. 1658–1705) chartered the German Royal (now National) Academy of Science (*Akademie der Wissenschaften*). With such support behind them, scientists across Europe made startling advances. Two of the most significant figures in this effort were Sir Francis Bacon and René Descartes. They represented the essential halves of the **scientific method**: inductive reasoning

---

[11] The Latin epigram to the coat of arms granted to the Royal Society reads *Nullius in verba*: "Take no one's word on anything."

MAP 13.5   Centers of Learning in Europe, 1500–1700   Europe's rulers invested heavily in scientific research in this period; the Islamic world's rulers did not. Thus came to an end the long-established lead held by the Muslims over Christian Europe in scientific sophistication.

through observation and experimental research and deductive reasoning from self-evident principles. Isaac Newton subsequently made their ideas the foundations for mathematically precise scientific laws.

Francis Bacon and the Promotion of the New Science

Sir **Francis Bacon** (1561–1626) we have already met. As the son of a career courtier, he grew up in high society, learned its manners, and became accustomed to its privileges. (His father, Sir Nicholas Bacon, had been the Lord Keeper of the Great Seal to Elizabeth I.) He worked as a lawyer and held a seat in Parliament. In 1589 he finally gained his first position in the royal administration and worked his way up, until, in the reign of James I (r. 1603–1625), he made it to the top of the ladder, serving as Lord Chancellor and—a last plum—in his father's old position as Keeper of the Great Seal. But Bacon had expensive tastes. Even with all his income, he built up enormous debts, which may or may not have led to his taking bribes. Scandals swirled around him for several years as enemies and creditors colluded to bring him down. In 1621 he finally fell from power in disgrace. Although he was allowed to keep his properties and aristocratic titles, he was barred from all political life and from most of privileged society.

A profoundly cautious man, except when it came to his spending habits, he advocated an uncompromising empirical and incremental approach to all knowledge, the gradual acquisition of discrete fact after fact, observation after observation, all of them subjected to repeated testing to ensure their accuracy, until one has finally assembled enough data to hazard a general hypothesis. Mankind is prone to drawing hasty assumptions, he argued, and the only antidote is the patient accumulation of tested and retested facts.

Francis Bacon   This 1617 portrait by Flemish painter Frans Pourbus shows Sir Francis Bacon (1561–1626) in all his finery, before his fall.

Roger Bacon, the medieval Franciscan (again, only intellectually related to Francis, as far as we know), had already identified four barriers to intellectual progress, errors so common as to be nearly universal:

> There are, in fact, four distinct impediments along the pathway to Truth—stumbling blocks, if you will, that get in the way of every man, no matter how learned he may be, and frustrate anyone who strives to reach the Truth. These impediments are: first, the precedents established by ill-equipped earlier authorities; second, long-established customs; third, the passionate sentiments of the ignorant masses; and fourth, our own habits of hiding our ignorance by the ostentatious display of what we think we do know.

Francis Bacon likewise identified four problems, which he called "illusions" (*idola* in Latin). Here he located the source of error in human nature, our own habits of thinking, the words we use, and tradition. Although the correlation is not exact, he clearly had the earlier Bacon in mind:

> There are four types of illusions that bedevil the human mind— illusions to which, in order to keep them distinct, I have attached particular names. These are the illusions of the tribe, illusions of the den, illusions of the marketplace, [and] finally illusions of the theater....
>
> The *illusions of the tribe* are the fallacies inherent in human nature, ... [above all] the human tendency to consider all things in relation to itself, whereas everything that we perceive via our senses and reason is actually just a reflection of ourselves, not of the universe. The human mind resembles nothing so much as a flawed mirror, and like such a mirror it imposes its own characteristics upon whatever it reflects, and distorts and disfigures it accordingly.

The *illusions of the den* are the fallacies inherent in each individual. Every mind possesses—in addition to the fallacies common to all men everywhere—its own individual den or cavern whose qualities intercept and corrupt the light of Nature as it receives it. This may result from each person's individual and unique disposition, from his education, his interaction with others, or his reading. . . .

There are also what I call the *illusions of the marketplace*, the illusions created by the daily interactions and conversations we have with each other—for we speak through language but words have been formed arbitrarily . . . and they throw everything into confusion. . . .

Finally, the fallacies I call the *illusions of the theater*. By this term I mean those mistakes that creep into men's minds from the teachings of different philosophies and from erroneous arguments. We must regard every philosophical system yet designed or imagined as nothing more than a play that has been staged and performed—a charade, in other words.

He saw scientific thinking as the careful piling up of individual bricks of knowledge to create a solid edifice. But Bacon himself never did any actual science; a wealthy aristocrat and career administrator, he was accustomed to telling other people how to do their jobs. Descartes, on the other hand, practiced what he preached.

Descartes and the Quest for Truth

René Descartes (1596–1650) received a good Jesuit education as a youth, but when he left school in his native France he was, he wrote, "filled with so much doubt and false knowledge that I came to think that all my efforts to learn had done nothing but increase my ignorance." In November 1618 he met he met a gifted Dutch mathematician named Isaac Beeckman (1588–1637), and for entertainment they invented mathematical problems for each other. From this sort of play Descartes came to realize that geometric forms like lines and curves, when marked on a graph, could be described by algebraic formulas. Thus was born analytical geometry, a discovery that set the trajectory for Descartes's intellectual life. As he began to elaborate on his original finding in 1619, he all but disappeared for nine years—moving from city to city, from France to Italy to the Netherlands, never telling anyone his addresses (which he changed regularly anyway) and gradually selling off the properties he had inherited from his parents. "To live well, live in secret" became a favorite personal motto. He emerged from self-exile in 1628 in the Netherlands, where he remained for twenty years, although still moving frequently. He moved to Sweden in 1649 at the request of its queen, who appointed him her tutor, but he soon caught pneumonia and died in February 1650.

Descartes's greatest achievements were in mathematics and philosophy.[12] The invention of analytical geometry, apart from its inherent value, made possible the later discovery of calculus and mathematical analysis (differential equations and the like). His best-known work, however, remains the *Discourse on Method* (1637), which he wrote as an introduction to a volume of several scientific papers. In it he presents not only his own working method as a scientist but also a creed, a set of principles that guide one to true knowledge, a hybrid of science and philosophy.

In the *Discourse* he vows "never to accept something as true which I did not distinctly know for myself to be true." Rather than encourage skepticism and doubt, however, Descartes advocates passionately for certainty. Doubt is not a philosophy but merely a tool—and Descartes detested thinkers like Michel de Montaigne (1533–1592), the author of the famous *Essays*, who seemed to him to regard skepticism as the end point of human endeavor. For Descartes, doubt is the point at which one needs to start thinking the hardest. But what does "knowing" consist of? And what, precisely, is truth?

Descartes begins with a distrust of the senses. The data we gather about the world through our senses cannot be fully trusted for the simple reason that our sense perceptions are imperfect. Optical illusions are common; people often hear sounds or voices that are not actually present or fail to hear those that are. Individuals who have lost a limb frequently report feeling an itch on a part of their body that is no longer there. Knowledge based on sense data therefore can never be entirely trusted, since it depends on a flawed system of observation—a fact that undermines the very foundation of experimental science. One can try to validate one's data by performing an experiment numerous times and gathering the data with scrupulous repetitive care. Nonetheless, logically speaking there is no absolute certainty that an experiment that repeatedly renders a particular result after 5 million consecutive attempts may not suddenly give a different result on the 5-million-and-first.

True and absolute knowledge, if attainable at all, must therefore derive from a different source than empirical observation. For Descartes that source is logic. Logical thought is itself an absolute reality, or, as he famously put it, "I think, therefore I am" (*Cogito ergo sum*, in Latin). I can doubt everything I see, everything I hear, everything I touch, smell, or taste. I can even doubt whether I am alive. But even in the absence of all sense data, my thinking mind—all by itself—knows that I am doubting, knows that I am thinking about thinking, and therefore I know absolutely that I exist (see Figure 13.1).

---

[12] Descartes also made numerous advances in optics, meteorology, physics, and even physiology. As a young man, he dissected cows.

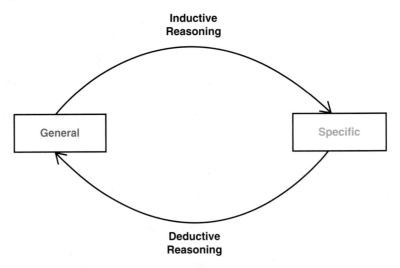

FIGURE 13.1   Inductive versus Deductive Reasoning

"Congratulations," one might say. "You exist. So what?" But Descartes's insight contains the germ of a revolution in scientific and philosophical thought. Absolute truth, he argues, is theoretical instead of physical, and the theoretical expression of physical reality is ultimately more real than any physical manifestation of it. Consider, for example, a circle. One can express the idea of a circle by drawing one on a piece of paper, but also by describing it in words: "A figure in two dimensions made up of all the points equidistant from a single central point." The description in words is one level of abstraction above the physical drawing on paper. But one can move to an even higher level of abstraction by describing a circle in algebraic notation, as a mathematical formula. This, to Descartes, is an absolute truth, because this formula will describe all circles, in every place and throughout all time. If scientific investigation seeks to understand the truth about circles, it must work at this abstract level. Only here can absolute truth exist and be understood.

Descartes described an entire universe guided by an immense, internally consistent, and utterly logical set of laws and formulas that the human mind can grasp—and this way of thinking has dominated Western scientific life ever since. Scientific research of every type—whether in physics, chemistry, microbiology, astronomy, medicine, or any other field—begins with an assumption that everything operates according to a set of natural laws. The goal of research is to peel back the visible covering of the universe and see the logically cohesive structure underneath. It may be a coherent structure of unimaginable complexity, but we do not doubt that it is there and that it makes rational sense.

John Donne had complained that the universe is "all in pieces, all coherence gone." Descartes was the first to argue convincingly that another type of system, based on fixed and unalterable natural laws, can take the place of biblical and classical authorities—and that humans can figure those laws out. Just as the human mind exists within but also beyond the body, the abstract laws of nature exist within and beyond the physical universe. They guide it, shape it, drive it, and ennoble it with purpose.

NEWTON'S MATHEMATICAL PRINCIPLES

The first person to deliver on Descartes's promise was Sir **Isaac Newton** (1642–1727), the greatest scientist in Western history before Albert Einstein (1879–1955). Born into an English farming family, from an early age he enjoyed tinkering with machines, a hobby he continued throughout his life.[13] He earned a bachelor's degree in 1664 from Cambridge University in classical studies, but by that time Newton had already started to teach himself mathematics and physics by reading the works of Descartes. When the plague swept through England, he withdrew to his family's rural home, where he began his work in optics and in the calculation of infinite series. The first resulted in his discovery that light can be broken into the spectrum of colors and has the properties of a wave, and the second resulted in his discoveries of integral and differential calculus. Within two years he had become the leading mathematician of his age and earned a prestigious professorship at Cambridge, where he remained for thirty years. He spent his last thirty years in London serving as master of the Royal Mint and president of the Royal Society.

Newton's greatest achievement was his *Philosophiae Naturalis Principia Mathematica* (*Mathematical Principles of Natural Philosophy*), published in 1687. It is not light reading. Newton was a moody, obsessive loner who loathed being disturbed in his work, especially by people who could not understand the complexity of his thinking—which was just about everyone. Only three hundred copies of the first edition of the *Principia* were printed, which was probably well more than the number of people capable of making sense of it. Newton insisted on having empirical data as the basis for his high-flying mathematical formulations, and hence the *Principia* skips from topic to topic, wherever there are sufficient data to begin computing. Nevertheless, the variety and number of topics Newton addresses add up to a comprehensive theory about the physical world.

Its fundamental and astonishing idea is the theory of universal gravitation. What prompted Newton's thinking was the question of why, if things like apples fall to the ground, the planets do not also fall to the Earth's surface. There is evidently nothing holding them in orbit in the sky. Physical theory had been *The Theory of Universal Gravitation*

---

[13]   Newton invented the reflecting telescope—one that uses a curved mirror rather than a second lens to focus captured beams of light.

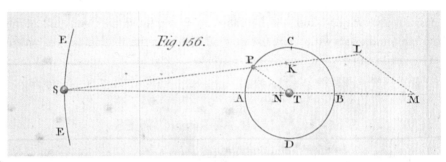

The Geometry of Gravity   Sir Isaac Newton's *Principia Mathematica* (1687) was the closest thing the world had yet seen to a scientific Theory of Everything and dominated the field of physics until the start of the 20th century. This image (Figure 156) illustrates his thoughts on the gravitational interaction of three bodies: a central and fixed star, represented by the letter T, and two planets in orbit around it, P and S.

based for centuries on the belief that motion was an intrinsic quality of all matter. Water flows because that is what water does; the atoms that propel our bodies forward are in constant movement because movement is life itself. Death, in this view, is a cessation of natural movement. Newton argued instead that motion results from the interaction of objects, and he showed that the interaction can be calculated precisely by taking into account their mass, velocity, and direction of motion. In this way he developed the physical concept of force. But he then complicated matters by introducing another idea—what he called the "weight" (*gravitas* in Latin) or attraction that all physical objects feel toward one another whether they are in a static or dynamic state. Thus was born the idea of gravity.

In his descriptions of gravity, which he further showed to be determined in permanent ratios according to mass, distance, and force, he produced a comprehensive explanation for physical actions as simple as an apple's fall from a tree and as complex as the elliptical orbits of the planets in the solar system. Descartes had shown the logical necessity of a universal set of natural laws governing all matter. Now Newton provided the mathematical formulas that those laws consisted of. The universe was not only internally coherent according to a single, although undeniably massive, set of laws, but also those laws were knowable, calculable, and provable. When Newton died in 1727, he was given a hero's funeral and buried in the royal church of Westminster Abbey.

◆

The immediate impact of the Scientific Revolution was moderate, but it changed Greater Western culture profoundly. The universe became in the popular mind less of a divine and glorious mystery and more of a fascinating mechanism, with all that is good and bad in that transition. The new tenets included the belief in a rational explanation for everything we experience, the considered reliability of an idea that is based on quantifiable evidence, and the habit of privileging the demonstrably logical over the intuitive. All came increasingly to characterize much of European thought. Not coincidentally, European society, being open to the exploration of the world and the exploitation of its potentialities, became poised to emerge as a global power.

Not that sounds of alarm were not raised. When the Royal Society, England's premier institution for the promotion of science, was established in London, some warned that it was nothing short of the beginning of a Satanic apocalypse. One prominent Anglican clergyman, Robert South (1634–1716), denounced the members of the society in a sermon in 1667 as:

> the profane, atheistical, epicurean rabble ... who have lived so much in the defiance of God . . . a company of lewd, shallow-brained huffs [blowhards] making atheism and contempt of religion the sole badge of wit, gallantry, and true discretion. . . . The truth is, the persons here reflected upon are of such a peculiar stamp of impiety, that they seem to be a set of fellows got together, and formed into a diabolical society, for the finding out new experiments in vice.

Developments in the Christian West and the Islamic West now sharply diverged. Europeans came increasingly to view the world as knowable, explorable, and understandable. In fact, it became something that they could dominate. At the same time, the Islamic world took a pronounced inward turn, eschewing science and exploration in favor of a reexamination of traditional values. Neither path was intrinsically right or wrong, but both resulted from conscious cultural choices and as the expressions of value. The consequences of those choices would be felt for centuries to come.

WHO, WHAT, WHERE

Christopher Columbus	Galileo Galilei	scientific method
Columbian Exchange	heliocentric	Scientific Revolution
conquistadores	Isaac Newton	Vasco da Gama
epistemology	Nicolaus Copernicus	
Francis Bacon	René Descartes	

SUGGESTED READINGS

Primary Sources

Bacon, Francis. *Novum Organum (New Instrument)*.

Descartes, René. *Discourse on Method*.
Galilei, Galileo. *The Starry Messenger*.

Anthologies

Donnelly, John Patrick, ed. and trans. *Jesuit Writings of the Early Modern Period, 1540–1640* (2006).
Finocchiaro, Maurice A., ed. and trans. *The Essential Galileo Galilei* (2008).

Hellyer, Michael. *The Scientific Revolution: The Essential Readings* (2008).
Jacob, Margaret. *The Scientific Revolution: A Brief History with Documents* (2009).
Mayer, Thomas F. *The Trial of Galileo, 1612–1633* (2012).

Studies

Biagioli, Mario. *Galileo's Instruments of Credit: Telescopes, Images, Secrecy* (2007).
Bireley, Robert. *Religion and Politics in the Age of the Counterreformation: Emperor Ferdinand II, William Lamormaini, S. J., and the Formation of the Imperial Policy* (2011).
Blackwell, Richard J. *Behind the Scenes at Galileo's Trial* (2006).
Brooke, John, and Ian Maclean, eds. *Heterodoxy in Early Modern Science and Religion* (2006).
Crosby, Alfred W. *The Columbian Exchange: Biological and Cultural Consequences of 1492* (2003, orig. 1972).
Crosby, Alfred W. *Ecological Imperialism: The Biological Expansion of Europe, 900–1900* (2004, orig. 1986).
Dallal, Ahmad. *Islam, Science, and the Challenge of History* (2012).
Dear, Peter. *Revolutionizing the Sciences: European Knowledge and Its Ambitions, 1500–1700* (2009).
Evans, Robert J. W., and Alexander Marr. *Curiosity and Wonder from the Renaissance to the Enlightenment* (2006).
Feingold, Mordechai. *The Newtonian Moment: Isaac Newton and the Making of Modern Culture* (2004).
Gaukroger, Stephen. *The Collapse of Mechanism and the Rise of Sensibility: Science and*

the Shaping of Modernity, 1680–1760 (2011).
Gaukroger, Stephen. *The Emergence of a Scientific Culture: Science and the Shaping of Modernity, 1210–1685* (2006).
Gaukroger, Stephen. *Francis Bacon and the Transformation of Early-Modern Philosophy* (2001).
Godman, Peter. *The Saint as Censor: Robert Bellarmine between Inquisition and Index* (2000).
Henry, John. *Knowledge Is Power: How Magic, the Government, and an Apocalyptic Vision Inspired Francis Bacon to Create Modern Science* (2004).
Hessler, John W. *The Naming of America: Martin Waldseemüller's 1507 World Map and the Cosmographiae Introductio* (2008).
Hessler, John W. *A Renaissance Globemaker's Toolbox: Johannes Schöner and the Revolution in Modern Science, 1475–1550* (2013).
Jardine, Lisa. *Ingenious Pursuits: Building the Scientific Revolution* (2000).
Lindemann, Mary. *Medicine and Society in Early Modern Europe* (2010).
Mayer, Thomas F. *The Roman Inquisition: A Papal Bureaucracy and Its Laws in the Age of Galileo* (2013).

Park, Katharine. *Secrets of Women: Gender, Generation, and the Origins of Human Dissection* (2010).

Park, Katharine, and Lorraine Daston. *Early Modern Science* (2006).

Saliba, George. *Islamic Science and the Making of the European Renaissance* (2011).

Shapin, Steven, and Simon Schaffer. *Leviathan and the Air-Pump: Hobbes, Boyle, and the Experimental Life* (2011, orig. 1985).

Shea, William R., and Mariano Artigas. *Galileo in Rome: The Rise and Fall of a Troublesome Genius* (2003).

Spiller, Elizabeth. *Science, Reading, and Renaissance Literature: The Art of Making Knowledge, 1580–1670* (2004).

Tutino, Stefania. *Empire of Souls: Robert Bellarmine and the Christian Commonwealth* (2010).

For additional resources, including maps, primary sources, visuals, web links, and quizzes, please go to **www.oup.com/us/backman.**

CHAPTER 14

The Wars of All Against All

1540–1648

The conflicts that divided Christianity were wars of words in Luther's and Calvin's time, but within a generation of their passing the words gave way to gunpowder. These wars were Europe's first in which mass armies and modern weaponry were the new norm, and the exponential increases in troop numbers and firepower resulted in carnage on a scale previously unimaginable. In 1066, Duke William of Normandy conquered all of England with an army of ten thousand soldiers; in 1632 nearly nine times that number of Protestant and Catholic

THE GREATER WEST, 1648

forces fought in a single battle at Alte Veste, near the German city of Nuremberg. Between 1540 and 1648 as many as 10 million soldiers and civilians were killed in religiously inspired wars from Britain to Bohemia and from Sweden to Serbia. The first blows landed in France and Holland, where civil dissension combined with religious difference and rivalry for New World riches to create a toxic brew of hatred. In England, by contrast, the ultimate adoption of Protestantism in fact signaled the end of an even longer civil war and the start of a golden age.

The Triumph of Death
Painted around 1562 by Dutch master Peter Bruegel the Elder, this picture represents the horrors of the warfare then starting to reengulf western Europe—the Wars of Religion. The "Triumph of Death" motif dates to the 14th century, when the Black Death poured over the entire Greater West. Bruegel gave it new life in this savage depiction of hell on earth. "About suffering they were never wrong/the Old Masters," wrote Englishman W. H. Auden in his great poem, "Musée des Beaux Arts" (1938).

It took the Thirty Years' War in Germany (1618–1648), however, to embroil all of Christian Europe.

Although often referred to as the "Wars of Religion," the wars that wracked the Greater West in the 16th and 17th centuries enmeshed religious antagonisms with economic, social, and political conflict. A more accurate term might come from English philosopher Thomas Hobbes (1588–1679): "the war of all against all." The brief but bloody German Peasants' Revolt of 1524–1525 served as a prologue because it not only displayed the interaction of religious, economic, social, and political factors characteristic of the later conflicts but also spotlighted the enormous devastation wreaked on ordinary people during this period.

The war of all against all affected everyone from princes to peasants. It led to the toppling of Spain as the dominant European power and the rise of England and the Netherlands. It also included war within state boundaries, from the frenzied pursuit of "witches" to the increased persecution of Jews. The religious wars in Europe had their brutal analog in the Middle East as well, in the dynastic and territorial wars between the Ottoman Turks and the Safavid Persians, struggles with their own bitter elements of religious dissent and revolution. The most spectacular development in the Muslim world was the forced conversion of the Persians from Sunni to Shi'i Islam as a means of strengthening a distinct Iranian identity.

CHAPTER TIMELINE

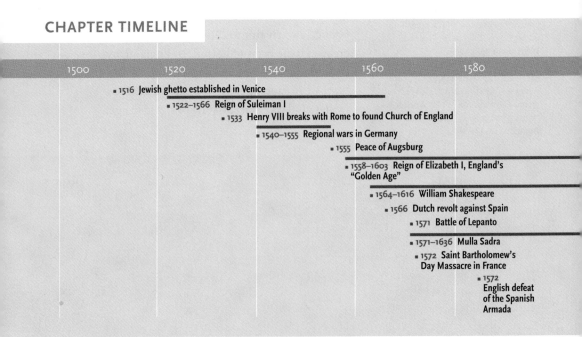

1500	1520	1540	1560	1580

- 1516 Jewish ghetto established in Venice
- 1522–1566 Reign of Suleiman I
- 1533 Henry VIII breaks with Rome to found Church of England
- 1540–1555 Regional wars in Germany
- 1555 Peace of Augsburg
- 1558–1603 Reign of Elizabeth I, England's "Golden Age"
- 1564–1616 William Shakespeare
- 1566 Dutch revolt against Spain
- 1571 Battle of Lepanto
- 1571–1636 Mulla Sadra
- 1572 Saint Bartholomew's Day Massacre in France
- 1572 English defeat of the Spanish Armada

Moreover, the Greater West's religious realignments took place within the context of increasing international competition and belligerence. So wrenching were the changes, greeds, and hatreds of the age that many of the fundamental values of civilization came into doubt—a crisis that led scholars, writers, and artists to reconsider what, if anything, they could still believe in.

FROM THE PEACE OF AUGSBURG TO THE EDICT OF NANTES: FRENCH WARS OF RELIGION

The Protestant movement was only seven years old when the German Peasants' Revolt erupted in 1524, but it had already progressed far enough to shred permanently any sense of Christian unity. Encouraged by Luther's open approval, the Protestant nobles had responded in force and crushed the rebellion ruthlessly. The experience sharpened more antagonisms than it resolved, however, and, as we saw in chapter 12, set the stage for battle with the Holy Roman Emperor Charles V (r. 1520–1566). The Catholic nobles in southern Germany—none of whom had stood up to support the peasants—feared the aroused might of their Protestant peers and looked to Charles to restore order.

But although they hoped for Protestantism's defeat, the Catholic princes were wary of Charles's ending up with more power in Germany as a result. When Charles finally began military action in the 1540s, support from the Catholic

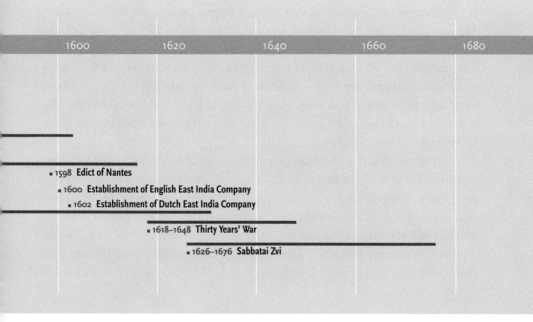

1600   1620   1640   1660   1680

- 1598 Edict of Nantes
- 1600 Establishment of English East India Company
- 1602 Establishment of Dutch East India Company
- 1618–1648 Thirty Years' War
- 1626–1676 Sabbatai Zvi

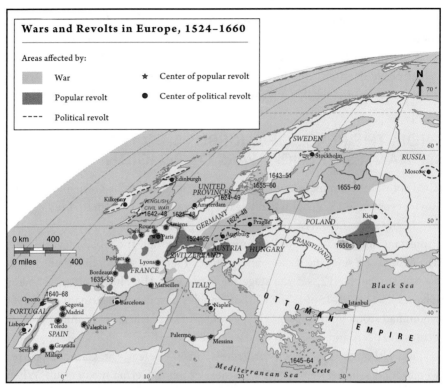

MAP 14.1   Wars and Revolts in Europe, 1524–1660   The 16th and 17th centuries in Europe saw a nearly constant series of violent clashes that were political, social, economic, and religious in nature.

princes was at best occasional and at worst verged on treason. For this reason, the war quickly degraded into an inconclusive series of advances and defeats. Finally, when it appeared certain that neither side could gain a clear victory, Charles and the Lutheran princes agreed to a compromise settlement. Known as the **Peace of Augsburg** (1555), it granted Lutheranism legal recognition and established the principle of *cuius regio, eius religio*—the religion of the ruler determines the religion of the land—with certain guarantees offered to ensure the rights of the religious minority.

Any hopes that the Augsburg compromise might serve as a model for other countries faded with the first test, when in 1562 France became embroiled in a religiously charged civil war that raged for more than three decades (see Map 14.1). The problem was that the Augsburg treaty had recognized the legal validity of Lutheranism but had not done so for Calvinism (since Calvin's version of Christianity had a negligible presence in Germany). And Calvin, who lived across the Swiss border, in Geneva, longed to secure legitimacy for his followers back in France, known as **Huguenots**.[1] By 1562 nearly one-fifth of the French population was Huguenot—primarily in the southern and eastern parts of the realm.

Calvin's chance came in 1562, when control of the French monarchy came up for grabs. The teenaged King Francis II had died in 1560 after only one year on the throne, leaving his even younger brother, Charles IX (r. 1560–1574), to succeed him. The question of the regency—that is, of someone appointed to run the government on Charles's behalf until he came of age—exposed political rivalries and religious antagonism as well. Each of the two leading noble families had ties to royalty, but one was Catholic and the other Huguenot. The Catholic faction was led by the duke of Guise, whereas the prince of Condé and Henri de Navarre led the Huguenots. The queen mother, Catherine de' Medici (d. 1589), a relation of the Florentine family who was closely aligned with the papacy, formed yet another faction of her own. Although essentially a court conflict among aristocratic rivals, the war quickly engulfed the whole population. The leaders of each faction appealed to the masses and turned a dispute over the *roi et loi* ("king and law") into a fight over *foi* ("faith"). Mob violence determined the course of the war almost as much as the actual armies did, because Catholics and Huguenots everywhere attacked each other. They ransacked each other's churches and plundered each other's shops and households. Clergy on both sides urged the fight onward.

The war's grimmest episode was the **Saint Bartholomew's Day Massacre**, a week-long orgy of violence that began as an assassination plot and turned into a mass riot (August 24–29, 1572). The Huguenot leaders had come to Paris to celebrate the wedding of Henri de Navarre, the Huguenot leader, to Marguerite de Valois, sister of the French king, Charles IX (r. 1560–1574). This marriage was intended to ease relations between Catholics and Protestants by uniting their causes in the royal family, but the attempt at a truce was undone by Catherine de' Medici, whose Catholic faction plotted to kill the Protestant leaders. News of the murders spurred mobs to action, and soon crowds in other cities had joined in. When the killing finally ended, thousands of Protestants lay dead, the victims of shooting, strangling, knifing, and drowning. In addition to Paris, massacres took place in Angers, Bordeaux, Bourges, Gaillac, La Charité, Lyons, Meaux, Orléans, Rouen, Saumur, Toulouse, and Troyes—all cities that had reverted to Catholic rule. The killings sparked Protestant fury, and the Huguenots redoubled their efforts to bring down the royal house, aided now by sympathetic

The Saint Bartholomew's Day Massacre

---

[1]   The origin of this term is uncertain. In 16th-century French the slang word *eiguenot* (meaning "a confederate or ally") may have contributed to *Huguenot*, but it is possible that the word refers in some way to King Hugh Capet (*Hugues*, in French), the 10th-century monarch whom certain Protestant writers had described as a king noteworthy for his tolerance.

Saint Bartholomew Day's Massacre   On August 24, 1572, a plot to assassinate leaders of the Huguenot faction in Paris inspired a terrifying wave of mob violence by thousands of the city's Catholics against their Protestant neighbors. Some estimates put the number of Protestants killed in the riot as high as thirty thousand. The original target of the assassination plot, Gaspard de Coligny, the military leader of the Huguenots, can be seen hanging out of a window to the right. (He was only wounded, but was subsequently executed.) Catherine de' Medici is at the far back, center-left, emerging from the royal palace (the Louvre) and examining a pile of Protestant corpses. The only surviving work of French Huguenot painter François Dubois (1529–1584), this is the best-known depiction of the Saint Bartholomew Day's Massacre.

Protestants from Germany and the Netherlands. Catholic Spain responded in turn by sending its troops into southern France. France's civil war threatened to engulf all of Latin Europe.

Reign of Henri IV

The whole miserable struggle ended when the next French king, Henri III (r. 1574–1589), was murdered—ironically, by an unstable fanatic (Jacques Clément, disguised as a priest) who felt the king was insufficiently Catholic.[2] Soon afterward, Prince Henri de Navarre, married to Princess Marguerite, acceded to the throne. Although the Protestant champion, Henri made the cool calculation that France, being 80 percent Catholic, had to have a Catholic king. "Paris is worth a Mass," he reportedly declared, and then announced his conversion to Catholicism. It took several years to convince the Catholics of his earnestness and to mollify the disappointment of the Protestants. In the end, however, he won the

---

[2]   Jacques Clément was killed immediately by the king's bodyguards. When he learned of the regicide, Pope Sixtus V (r. 1585–1590)—also an unstable fanatic—praised Clément as a martyr and tried (unsuccessfully) to have him canonized. In his brief pontificate Sixtus ordered so many executions of criminals (including any priest who broke his vow of chastity) and political enemies that it was said there were more heads displayed on pikes in the city of Rome than there were melons on sale in the markets.

support of both and began a long reign that is widely regarded as one of the high points of French history—as Henri IV (r. 1589–1610). In 1598 he promulgated the **Edict of Nantes**, which guaranteed religious freedom, under certain restrictions, throughout the realm. This edict, together with the Peace of Augsburg, established a legal right to believe as one wished—but in both cases freedom of religion was technically imposed on the people by the king, rather than arising from a demand from the populace. In other words, religious freedom was a power of the monarch, not a right of the people. For a brief spell the Continent had achieved peace, but it had not attained tolerance nor even embraced the very idea of it.

STRIFE AND SETTLEMENT IN ENGLAND

Meanwhile, a different sort of religious settlement evolved in England. There a civil war known as the War of the Roses (1455–1485) had erupted soon after England's humiliating defeat by the French in the Hundred Years' War (1337–1453), as various factions fought to shift the blame for England's loss and to win the throne.[3] The War of the Roses never involved large numbers of commoners, but it decimated the English nobility. When it ended in 1485 a relatively minor aristocrat named Henry Tudor became king, largely by default. Ruling as Henry VII (r. 1485–1509), he understood that he could make no elaborate claims of distinguished lineage or heavenly favor—and he wisely did not attempt to do so. He governed modestly and frugally, making sure not to upset the delicate truce he had worked out with Parliament. Henry was quick to recognize the potential of the New World discoveries, however, and he invested heavily in developing England's meager maritime capability. It was Henry who commissioned the voyage in 1497 to North America of the explorer we met in chapter 13, John Cabot (Giovanni Caboto).

When his son Henry VIII (r. 1509–1547) came to the throne, the kingdom had begun its climb to wealth and power on the international stage. Portraits of Henry VIII convey an aura of swagger, of manly vitality and newfound wealth altogether absent from portraits of his cautious father. They differed not only in personality but also in royal self-regard. Henry VIII's portraits exude self-confidence and more than a touch of the gaudiness of the *nouveau riche*—for "newly rich" is precisely what the Tudor monarch was becoming. His marriage in 1509 to Catherine of Aragon, the daughter of the king of Spain and the widow of Henry's brother, was a corporate merger of the two leading Atlantic seaboard powers. It promised to secure England's new dominant position in Europe for generations to come.

---

[3]   The War of the Roses took its name from the white and red roses on the respective heraldic badges of the noble houses of York and Lancaster.

Establishment of the Church of England

But then came the "King's Great Matter." Catherine, a pious, loving woman with a frail physique, had produced several sickly children, and only one—a daughter, Mary—had survived infancy. By 1527, after eighteen years of marriage, it seemed likely that Catherine would not produce the male heir Henry so desperately needed. Further, he had fallen in love with Anne Boleyn, a lady at court and a supporter of the Reformation. He decided to ask the pope to annul the marriage on the grounds that it had never been valid and, indeed, had violated divine law. [4] This move offended Rome (especially since the marriage had happened only by means of a special papal grant in the first place), the royal house of Spain (since their princess was being publicly humiliated), and the German emperor (since Charles V was Catherine's nephew and was already smarting from his losses to the Lutherans in his realm). Prior to this succession crisis Henry had shown no interest in the Protestant Reformation and had even published a treatise against Luther in 1521 that earned him the title of "Defender of the Faith" from a grateful Pope Leo X (r. 1513–1521). But the desire for a male heir and for Anne Boleyn trumped Henry's regard for Rome. After much dramatic although failed diplomacy, he decided in early 1533 to break with the Catholic Church and establish the **Church of England**, or Anglican Church. It was a Protestant church with the monarch as its supreme head.

In creating the Church of England, however, Henry did more than establish yet another form of Protestantism; he brought England directly into the turmoil raging across Europe. Yet another version of Christianity was arguably the last thing Western culture needed at the time. Worse, it set the two 16th-century powers leading the exploration of the New World and the new international economy at direct odds with one another. England and Spain, briefly united in Henry's marriage to Catherine and on the brink of becoming a joint superpower, instead remained bitter rivals through the rest of the century. Henry's action did result in an enormous increase in royal income, however. He ordered the suppression of every Catholic monastery in the realm and seized all their holdings—which may have amounted to one-fifth of the real estate in England and Wales. The Tudors used this wealth, along with their New World riches, to buy support in both houses of Parliament. Hence, too, the elaborately bejeweled and befurred portraits of the king.

Escalation of Religious Strife

At Henry's death in 1547, the throne passed briefly to his son Edward VI (r. 1547–1553). Only ten at his accession, Edward never emerged from the shadow of the regency council established for him. The steps made to eradicate Catholicism were undone when Edward fell ill and died, and the throne passed, after some intrigue, to his elder half-sister, Mary (r. 1553–1558). Mary, as the daughter

---

4   Leviticus 20.21 condemns marriage with one's brother's widow and warns that such illicit unions "will be childless."

of the scorned Catherine of Aragon, was resolutely Catholic and determined to restore Catholicism. Her reign has entered popular memory as a nightmare of religious violence, earning her the nickname of "Bloody Mary." In reality, she was quite popular at first, especially with the many Catholics who still remained in the kingdom. Even many Protestants sympathized with her after her father's break with Rome. But her decision to marry Prince Philip of Spain in 1554 changed matters and dispelled any hopes that a peaceful religious settlement might be reached.

A wave of political purges and religious persecutions marked Mary's last three years on the throne, with roughly three hundred Protestant leaders hunted down as enemies of the crown and killed. Their stories were told— with more love for sensational detail

Henry VIII of England   Henry VIII (r. 1509–1547) commissioned German artist Hans Holbein the Younger to execute several portraits of the king. This one shows Henry in 1540, confident of his powers. It may have been a wedding gift for his fifth wife, Catherine Howard. Henry famously had six wives before he died. The first, Catherine of Aragon, had given him Mary (r. 1553–1558); the second, Anne Boleyn, produced another daughter, Elizabeth (r. 1558–1603); and the third, Jane Seymour, gave birth to his only son, Edward VI (r. 1547–1553). Wives four and five, Anne of Cleves and Catherine Howard, gave him nothing but misery, and number six, Catherine Parr, brought genuine affection and comfort to his last years.

than for historical accuracy—by John Foxe (1516–1587) in his *Book of Martyrs*, first published in 1563 (with the melodramatic subtitle *Actes and Monuments of These Latter and Perillous Days, Touching Matters of the Church*). The work is enormous, longer even than the Bible. And for a while it had nearly as much authority over English Protestants; a decree in 1570 ordered that a copy of it be placed in every (Anglican) cathedral church in England.[5]

Mary died childless, and the crown passed to her half-sister, **Elizabeth I** (r. 1558–1603), during whose reign England reached the apogee of international power and prestige. At home, Elizabeth secured in 1563 a religious settlement that established the Anglican Church as the official faith, with the monarch as its supreme leader. This compromise, known as the Thirty-Nine Articles of Religion, was a hybrid of Catholic ritual and Protestant theology, and it eventually proved amenable to a majority of her subjects. Elizabeth's settlement placed

England's "Golden Age" under Elizabeth I

---

[5]   Until the start of the 19th century, the three most widely disseminated books in England and America were the Bible (Authorized Version); English writer and preacher John Bunyan's (1628–1688) *The Pilgrim's Progress*, a Christian allegory first published in 1678; and Foxe's *Book of Martyrs*.

Elizabeth I of England   The English artist George Gower (1540–1596) is believed to have painted this striking "Armada Portrait" of England's greatest queen. In her later years Elizabeth's royal outfits were even more lavish and outlandish than those of her father, Henry VIII, and in images like this one the effect was nearly iconic.

legal restrictions on Catholic holdouts, but she was even sterner with the more radical wings of the Protestant movement, especially the Puritans—strict Calvinists who opposed all vestiges of Catholic ritual in the Church of England and who began to see the New World as a more inviting place to live.

Elizabeth increased England's involvement in the new Atlantic economy, which brought her into direct conflict with Spain. She promoted the piracy campaigns of Sir Francis Drake (1540–1596) against the Spanish fleets returning from the New World, laden with gold and silver. She also underwrote further exploration of North America. Given the already tense relations between England

THE SPANISH ARMADA

and Spain, Elizabeth's actions were sure to cause further trouble—which came in 1588 when Philip II (r. 1554–1598) sent his famed Armada (Spanish for "fleet") of 130 massive warships to invade England. After trapping the Spanish in the English Channel, the smaller but lighter English fleet scattered the Armada by sending blazing fireships into its midst. More than half of the Spanish vessels were destroyed or put out of commission. Many ships were wrecked by storms as they tried to return to Spain by rounding the coasts of Scotland and Ireland. The defeat of their "Invincible Armada" shocked the Spanish, whereas Protestants throughout Europe rejoiced. After 1588 England's involvement in the hornets' nest of Continental politics would become only more intense.

The defeat of the Spanish Armada marked the high point of Elizabeth's popularity. Commonly regarded as England's Golden Age, the Elizabethan period was characterized by a heightened sense of national identity that victory over Catholic Spain confirmed. The rapid growth in the popularity of staged plays confirmed this national pride, since plots taken from England's history proved especially popular with audiences. One of the earliest such plays was *The Famous Chronicle of King Edward I* (1592) by George Peele (1556–1596), which proved so popular that Christopher Marlowe (1564–1593) was inspired the following year to pen *Edward II*. Marlowe died soon after completing it, but his friend and rival William Shakespeare (1564–1616) carried on the tradition with a series of dramas focused on the line of kings that preceded the Tudor dynasty: Richard II, Henry IV, Henry V, Henry VI, and Richard III, among others. Shakespeare also penned comedies and tragedies—perhaps the greatest in each genre being *A Midsummer Night's Dream* (1595), *Twelfth Night* (1601), and *Measure for Measure* (1604) among the comedies and *Hamlet* (1601), *Othello* (1604), *Macbeth* (1605), and *King Lear* (1606) among the tragedies.[6]

Elizabethan Drama

DUTCH ASCENDANCY AND SPANISH ECLIPSE

Spain was also fighting at the time against the Netherlands, which had formed part of the Habsburg Empire. Smarting under Catholic rule, the staunchly Calvinist Dutch revolted against Philip II in 1566. They fought over religion, of course, but even more important was the money to be made in the New World. The Dutch, who had involved themselves in overseas exploration from the start— many Dutch sailors and officers manned the early Portuguese voyages into the Indian Ocean and South China Sea—resented having to send a portion of their earnings to Madrid, and they therefore sued for independence. Formal recognition of an independent Netherlands had to wait until 1648, although the Dutch had achieved de facto freedom from Spain by 1581.

Revolt of the Netherlands

England was happy to see Spain lose to the Netherlands and so gave the Dutch whatever overt and covert assistance they could afford.[7] The benefits proved obvious. With Spanish naval might curtailed, England established its East India Company in 1600. The Dutch founded their own East India Company in

---

[6]   The precise chronology of Shakespeare's plays is uncertain and still hotly debated by scholars even after four hundred years of study. The dates assigned here are estimates.

[7]   The playwright Christopher Marlowe served briefly as a spy for Elizabeth in Holland.

1602, leaving the Netherlands and England as the two most prominent European trading nations in the Americas. Both were chartered joint-stock companies that enjoyed lucrative monopolies over specified commodities coming from specific locations; such companies were allowed to operate without much government control in the areas chartered to them. In North America, England built its first settlement in Virginia in 1607, and the Dutch colonized the southern portion of the island of Manhattan in 1612. Spain thus entered the 17th century in a state of severe economic decline, whereas England and the Netherlands succeeded it as rising powers.

THE THIRTY YEARS' WAR

Origins and Course of the War

Economic rivalries, political aspirations, and religious conflicts culminated in the last and bloodiest of the so-called Wars of Religion: the **Thirty Years' War** (1618–1648), which began as a conflict between Protestants and Catholics in Germany but ultimately involved nearly all European powers and desolated lands and peoples across central Europe. Since the death of Charles V in 1558, the Habsburg rulers had generally tried to achieve a peaceful accord with and between their various Protestant and Catholic subjects. Policies changed, however, during the political maneuverings that led to the reign of Ferdinand II (r. 1619–1637), an archly conservative Catholic who was determined to eradicate Protestantism within the Holy Roman Empire. Rebellions by his Protestant subjects in Bohemia set off a chain reaction, and soon full-scale war across Germany, Austria, and Bohemia began. The war dragged on for decades in part because the Atlantic states profited from it: so long as the Germans remained mired in civil strife, they could not interfere with or compete against the English, Dutch, French, and Spanish, who were busy plundering North and South America.

All of the fighting took place in German territories, but it involved nearly every state in the Greater West. Its effects were devastating: roughly one-fifth of the entire German population died. France and England each sent assistance to both sides of the conflict. When the Protestants were winning, they aided the Catholics, and when the Catholics were winning, they supported the Protestants. The Dutch assisted whichever side promised to help them maintain independence from Spain. Denmark entered the conflict with the aim of seizing northern German territory for itself. The king of Poland joined the fighting to defend the Catholic faith and to claim the throne of Sweden. The Swedes, for their part, fought to defend Protestantism—and to gain a military alliance with Orthodox Russia against Catholic Poland. International involvement became near universal when the Ottoman sultan Osman II (r. 1618–1622) invaded Catholic Poland with 400,000 infantry and later found himself being attacked by

Ceux que Mars entretient de ses actes meschans   Ils les font prisonniers ils bruslent leurs villages,   Sans que la peur des Loix nonplus que le deuoir,
Accommodent ainsi les pauures gens des champs   Et sur le bestail mesme exercent des rauages,   Ny les pleurs et les cris les puissent esmouuoir.

The Horrors of War   In 1633 the French printmaker Jacques Callot (1592–1635) published his most famous series of prints—made in collaboration with his friend, French engraver Israel Henriet (1590–1661)—entitled "The Miseries and Misfortunes of War." Shown here is the seventh plate in that series (of seventeen), depicting soldiers ransacking a rural village during the Thirty Years' War. Scenes like this occurred across Europe during that conflict, which ended with 8 million dead.

Protestant forces coming out of Germany. By 1648, after more than 7 million military and civilian casualties, with still no clear victor in sight, the nations of Europe were exhausted—physically, economically, and morally—and agreed to a set to accords known as the **Peace of Westphalia** that finally put an end to the carnage.

As with the Hundred Years' War between England and France, the significance of the Thirty Years' War lay more in how it was fought than in the bleak *Mass* narrative of which side won which battle in any given year. This was the first war *Armies and* in which most of the fighting used modern weapons based on gunpowder. Armed *Modern* commoners now formed the overwhelming bulk of the armies, marching in for- *Weaponry* mation, with lines of muskets flanked by cumbersome but mobile artillery. Under the command of cavalry officers still drawn from the upper classes, the armies were larger than any that had taken the field before. At the first battle of Nördlingen in 1643, for example, close to fifty thousand soldiers took part, and ten thousand lay dead on the field by battle's end. Only two years later a second battle was fought on the same site, with thirty thousand soldiers entering the fray and only twenty thousand coming out alive. Similar levels of slaughter took place at Khotyn in 1620, at Breitenfeld in 1631, at Lützen in 1632, at Breda in 1634, at Jankau in 1635, and at Lens in 1648. Corpses rotted by the tens of thousands in fields all across central and eastern Europe.

Among the most vivid testimonies to the war's savagery is a remarkable novel by Hans Jakob Christoffel von Grimmelshausen (1621–1676). Kidnapped *Grimmelshausen's* by German Hessian soldiers when he was only ten, he was captured in The Adventures of battle and redrafted into military service by several armies until the war's a Simpleton end in 1648. His novel, *The Adventures of a Simpleton*, appeared in 1668 and tells of a young boy who, like von Grimmelshausen, is pressed into service and witnesses unspeakable horrors. An early scene sets the tone:

> At first I did not intend to force you, gentle reader, to accompany these soldiers to my father's homestead, for I know what evil things are about to happen there; but the nature of my story requires me to leave some record of the brutal acts performed, time and again, by those involved in the war here in our Germany.... After stabling their horses, the soldiers all set about their appointed tasks, the sum of which was the utter ruin and desolation of our farm. Some began to slaughter all of our animals and set them stewing or roasting, so that it appeared as though they were preparing a jolly feast; but others ransacked our house from top to bottom.... Whatever they did not want to cart away they tore to pieces. A few started to thrust their swords into the haystacks and bales of straw, to find any hidden sheep or swine they could add to the slaughter.... Our maid Ursula, shame to tell, was dragged into the stable and so roughed up that afterwards she refused to come out. Then they took one of our hired workmen and stretched him out flat upon the ground, and, prying his mouth open with a bit of old wood, they dumped a slop-bucket full of shit and piss down his throat. They called this a "Swedish cocktail."

After rounding up other farmers in the neighborhood, the soldiers began interrogating them:

> First they took the flints out of their pistols, jammed the farmers' thumbs into the opened space, and used the pistols as thumbscrews to torture them as they would witches. One poor fellow, even though he had confessed to no crime at all, they thrust into the oven, and lit it. They wrapped a rope around another fellow's head and twisted it with a piece of wood until blood gushed from his mouth, nose, and ears.... I cannot report much about what happened to the women, young girls, and maidservants of the district, for the soldiers prevented me from seeing it; but I remember hearing pitiful screams coming from each corner of our house.

Much of the novel's horror comes from Grimmelshausen's identification of the soldiers simply as *soldiers*. He often does not differentiate among Bavarians, Saxons, Austrians, Swedes, Dutch, French, Spaniards, Danes, Poles, Hungarians, Serbs, Lutherans, Calvinists, or Catholics. They are all the same: there are no meaningful sides to the conflict, and the war is its own repellent cause and justification. But the novel offers more than scenes of savagery. Simpleton runs away from the army and finds his way through a dizzying series of unpredictable adventures. He turns himself into a populist highwayman à la Robin Hood; he hides by impersonating a woman; he takes the place in high society of an aristocrat; he becomes a con artist and a religious pilgrim. He voyages to a fantastic underwater realm inhabited by mermen. In the end, he denounces the world as irredeemably corrupt and becomes a hermit. At turns hilarious and horrifying, the novel depicts a treacherous world without order. To search for simple human decency and the tiniest bit of stability in life is to seek the impossible.

Grimmelshausen wrote several other novels, each a sequel to his first, usually narrated by a minor character from *Simpleton*. The series recalls Geoffrey Chaucer's *Canterbury Tales* in its shifting kaleidoscope of experiences and views. The greatest German novel before Goethe, *Simpleton* has never been surpassed as a depiction of war as collective insanity. An additional aspect of that insanity consists of Simpleton's repeated encounters with a dreaded element of European life in the 16th and 17th centuries—witches.

ENEMIES WITHIN: THE HUNT FOR WITCHES

Popular belief in witchcraft had roots in pre-Christian classical, Germanic, and Celtic culture. Ancient and medieval attitudes toward witches differed from those of the early modern era, however. Earlier Europeans had held that some individuals are simply born with an intrinsic ability to summon supernatural forces at will, which they can use for good or ill. In contrast, people of the 16th and 17th centuries developed the belief that magical powers resulted from an explicit and conscious contract made between the witch (who could be male or female) and the devil, Satan. They believed witchcraft was intentional—a power that an individual chose to acquire—rather than an innate, although freakish, ability possessed from birth. And that made popular fear of it all the stronger, especially given the era's heavy emphasis on human weakness and sinfulness. If people could be so easily coaxed into a pact with Satan, then witchcraft could conceivably take over rhw world and bring about its ruin. A witch was not merely someone "possessed of powers" but someone actively engaged in evil, and the danger he or she represented required immediate action.

That action consisted of arrest, trial, torture, and execution on a scale that is difficult to comprehend. Campaigns against witches increased in number markedly toward the end of the 15th century but became frenzied after 1560, once Europe's religious disputes turned violent. From 1560 to 1670, nearly 200,000 people across Europe were accused of witchcraft and subjected to judicial persecution or mob violence (see Figure 14.1). Roughly

Links between Persecution of Witches and Wars of Religion

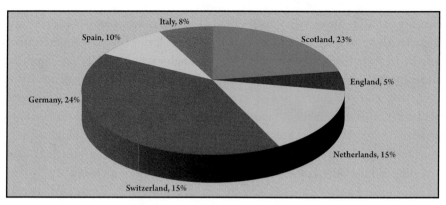

FIGURE 14.1   Witchcraft Trials, 1450–1750

one-quarter of them were executed. Those who confessed and repented—which required identifying other witches and agreeing to testify against them—were briefly imprisoned, frequently marked by a tattoo, fined, and released, to be socially shunned for the rest of their lives. And although there seems to be no substantial difference between the frequency of Protestant and Catholic prosecutions of witchcraft, it does appear that the Protestant–Catholic divide played a role: witchcraft mania struck most ferociously where Protestants and Catholics were most equal in number and hence locked in protracted conflict. Accusations of witchcraft seldom crossed confessional lines, however. Catholics and Protestants generally did not accuse the other group but instead members of their own denominations; in fact, they frequently shared information about supposed witches, seeing them as a threat to both groups. The witches who appeared in stage dramas like William Shakespeare's *Macbeth* were realistic characters to audiences, in addition to the symbolic role they played. Germany and Scotland had the most witchcraft trials per capita, but in the end, no country was immune to witchcraft mania.

Targeting Women

Neither was either sex: both men and women were believed capable of selling their souls to Satan. Nonetheless, at least three-quarters of those arrested for witchcraft, and nearly 90 percent of those executed for it, were women. (Ireland was the sole exception: roughly 90 percent of its prosecuted witches were male.) Popular assumptions about women's nature—as emotional, impulsive, passionate, demanding creatures—fueled the phenomenon. Women were regarded as generally weaker than men, but especially in regard to sex. Ideas about sexuality, derived from ancient Greek medicine, held that female lust, once aroused, was insatiable.[8] Only a demonic lover like Satan, it was assumed, could satisfy a

---

[8]   Many of the constraints placed on women—such as limiting their appearance in public or regulating their dress—were justified as protecting them from their own inability to control their passions.

woman's sexual longing—and that was precisely the appeal used by the devil to ensnare his victims. Men who became witches were generally assumed to have been enticed into it by women who had already given themselves over to satanic lust.

In this way, the witchcraft craze accords with the period's concern with sexuality in general. Ironically, the era's emphasis on early marriage was directly related to its fear of unchecked sexuality. It valued women as the "godly wives and mothers" responsible for their children's moral education, the dutiful subjects of their husbands, and the preservers of sacralized domestic life. A force as powerful and unpredictable as a woman's body needed to be firmly controlled—or else all hell, literally, could break loose.

Burning Witches   This broadsheet from October 1555 announces the burning of convicted witches in the small village of Derneburg, in lower Saxony. In the background, someone is being beheaded, while flames engulf the interior of the building on the right. A child seems to have been flung to the ground in the doorway.

THE JEWS OF THE EAST AND WEST

The era was cruel to Jews as well. Late medieval hostility to Jews had resulted in a series of expulsion orders, first from England (1290), then from France (1306) and Germany (numerous times), and finally from Spain (1492) and Portugal (1497). Forced from one territory to the next, the Jews gradually concentrated in the Netherlands, Italy, North Africa, and the Ottoman Empire, where the Ashkenazic and Sephardic traditions of Judaism, introduced in chapter 10, once again confronted each other (see Map 14.2).

For the host countries, the sudden increase in the Jewish populations aggravated social tensions and led many to segregate the Jews into separate districts. Regulations like these had been common since the 12th century. The surge in Jewish numbers within those districts, however, frequently led to new legislation limiting the Jews' freedom to move and act within the larger community. Venice established the first modern **ghetto** in 1516, but other European cities were quick to follow. (The word *ghetto* likely derives from the Italian *borghetto*, meaning a "small borough" or "precinct.") Life in these communities was often difficult, since Jews from many backgrounds were thrust shoulder to shoulder within a larger social context of economic decline and Christian hostility. The economic

MAP 14.2   Expulsions and Migrations of Jews, 1492–1650   Exiled Jews fled in all directions, but considerable numbers favored moving northward into the Netherlands and eastward into the Ottoman Empire.

decline occurred largely because of the shift of economic power from the Mediterranean—where the Jews had taken refuge—to the Atlantic seaboard. Only those Jews who had migrated to the Netherlands moved into a society of economic growth.

In the Ottoman state, which, after 1515, included the Holy Land, Jewish refugees from Europe generally received a cordial welcome from the Ottoman rulers Bayezid II (r. 1481–1512) and Selim I (r. 1512–1520), who encouraged Jews to settle in the Holy Land.[9] Many Jews, on arriving, expressed surprise at the squalor into which the cities had fallen. An Italian refugee, Rabbi Obadiah of Bertinoro, sent a letter back to a friend in which he estimates there being "only about seventy [Jewish] households in all of Gaza," whereas in Hebron he found "only twenty households . . . half of them coming from Spain and just recently arrived."

---

[9]   Spanish Jews set up the first printing press in the Ottoman state. Two Sephardic Jews, Joseph Hamon (d. ca. 1540) and his son Moses Hamon (d. 1567), served for a total of thirty years as personal physicians to the sultans.

In Jerusalem itself he found "only seventy households left, all of them poverty-stricken and with no means of support. . . . Anyone who has food to last a year, or the means to procure it, is considered wealthy here."

Not surprisingly, as most Jews' social and economic lives grew shaky in the 16th and 17th centuries, many found solace in new messianic movements. *Messianic* In Italy, led by charismatic adventurers like Solomon Molcho (1500–1532) *Movements* and David Reubeni (1490–1541), and in the Ottoman Empire, inspired by rabbis Isaac Luria (1534–1572) and Hayyim Vital (1543–1620), thousands of Jews believed in the imminent arrival of the long-promised messiah. These four figures, and others like them, preached a message of intense spiritual and social reform to prepare for the restoration of David's kingdom (discussed in chapter 3). These movements involved a minority of the Jews, but they were popular enough to make the rulers of their host countries concerned about the potential for social unrest.

Reubeni was an especially enigmatic figure, known today primarily through his diary, published in 1895. A curly-haired and heavily bearded dwarf, he had a striking appearance. He probably came from the large Jewish community at Cranganore in India, but at some point he traveled to Khaybar, in today's Afghanistan. In 1522 he appeared in Sudan, speaking to crowds about a large Jewish kingdom in the east, supposedly ruled by his brother Joseph. For some reason, Reubeni also claimed to be a direct descendant of the Prophet Muhammad. His life's aim was to create a military alliance between European royalty and his supposed royal brother to open a two-front war on the Ottoman Empire. In 1524 he went to Rome, entering the city while riding a white horse, and was received by Pope Clement VII (r. 1523–1534). With Clement's recommendation in hand, he approached the Portuguese king João III (r. 1521–1557), the rulers of Milan and of Venice, and finally the Habsburg emperor Charles V, each of whom promised some form of aid. Reubeni's habit of complaining to these rulers about their treatment of native Jews, however, turned them against him. Sometime around 1531 he was arrested in Italy and sent to Spain, where he was tried by the Inquisition. No official record of his trial or execution survives, but a later chronicle records that in 1541 "a Jew from India who had come to Portugal" was put to death by the Inquisition at Llerana in southern Spain.

When Sabbatai Zvi (1626–1676) came along and preached his own version of messianic deliverance, he found an enormously receptive audience. He *The* was from Smyrna (modern Izmir, Turkey). **Kabbala**, a mystical interpretation *Sabbatean* of scripture developed by rabbis, had originated centuries before. In 1648, *Cult* however, in fulfillment of a kabbalistic prophecy, Zvi declared himself the messiah and ultimately moved to Istanbul, where he converted a Jewish scribe who promptly forged an ancient-looking revelation document from the patriarch Abraham.

> I, Abraham, confined for forty years to life in a cave, spent a long time in pondering when the miraculous time of deliverance might come, when suddenly, a heavenly voice cried out: "A son named Sabbatai will be born to Mordechai Zvi in the year 5386 [1626]. He, the great Messiah, will humble the Serpent and take his seat upon my throne."

Armed with this, Zvi preached to Jews throughout the Ottoman lands—Istanbul, Athens, Alexandria, Cairo, Gaza, Jerusalem, Aleppo—and gained followers everywhere. Jews as far away as Italy, France, Germany, and the Netherlands joined the movement. At least one entire community, at Avignon, made preparations to quit the city and move with all their belongings to Jerusalem, to join the anticipated new kingdom.

Zvi went so far as to issue a universal proclamation to all Jews:

A Messiah on His Throne This page from a prayer book published in Amsterdam in 1666 shows Sabbatai Zvi (1626–1676) enthroned, with angels bringing him a heavenly crown. Note the lower image, which has him presiding over a table at which are gathered the representatives, presumably, of the Twelve Tribes of Israel. The Hebrew word in large print in the center of the image means the "restored harmony" expected to be provided by the messiah.

> Sabbatai Zvi, the first-born son of YHWH, and the Messiah and Redeemer of all the people of Israel, to all the sons of Israel, sends Peace. Since you have been thought worthy to behold the great Day of Fulfillment promised by YHWH through His prophets, all your sorrows and lamentations must end and be turned to celebrations, your fasts be turned into feasts, and your tears must cease. Rejoice, instead, with psalms and hymns! Let your days of sadness and despair become days of jubilation! For I have appeared!

As unlikely as it sounds, the proclamation generated enormous excitement throughout the international Jewish world. Zvi's portrait was printed in Jewish prayer books (frequently appearing next to images of King David). His initials were carved on synagogue walls and embroidered onto flags, and prayers for him were inserted into Jewish liturgies.

The speed of the Sabbatean cult's rise reflects the misery and difficulty of Jewish lives. Persecutions of the Jews grew in number and ferocity throughout the era, leading many to find hope only in a miraculous deliverance. Even a number of Christian groups welcomed the supposed messiah's arrival, although they were probably more excited by the idea of the Jews leaving Europe than they were about their liberation. But the Ottoman ruler Mehmed IV (r. 1648–1687) grew concerned about Zvi's popularity. Afraid that large numbers of Jews migrating to the Holy Land would push for its independence, he pressured Zvi to stop his activity. Zvi responded, on September 16, 1666, by suddenly announcing his conversion to Islam—for which Mehmed rewarded him with great wealth, a prominent position at court, and several new wives. To Jews everywhere, the blow was devastating, and the Sabbatean movement fell apart instantaneously.

Within Europe, most of the early leaders of Protestantism were surprised by the refusal of the Jews to convert to Christianity. For centuries, figures like *Escalating* Martin Luther believed, the Jews had bravely and correctly held out against the *Anti-* false teachings of the Catholics. "If I had been born a Jew," Luther wrote in *On* *Semitism* *Jesus Christ Having Been Born a Jew* (1523), "and if I had witnessed such idiots and buffoons [as the Catholics] trying to teach and administer Christian truth, I would as soon have turned myself into a pig as into a Christian." But surely, most reformers confidently felt, once the beautiful gospel truth was finally restored by the Protestants, the Jews would rush to accept it. Conversion would be their reward for enduring centuries of Catholic idiocy and persecution. "We will receive them with open arms, permit them to trade with us, to work with us, live among us, hear our Christian preaching, and witness our Christian way of life." When that failed to happen, the reaction was severe.

Luther himself penned many private letters to friends in which he railed against Jewish perfidy. He also expressed his wrath publicly in several viciously anti-Semitic tracts, the most notorious being *On the Jews and Their Lies* (1543):

> What ever shall Christians do with the damned, rejected Jews? We can hardly tolerate having them live among us as they do—for if we do, now that we know of their lies, hatred, and blasphemy, we will be complicit in their evil. We are powerless to convert them, but powerless too to put out the unquenchable fire of God's wrath, of which the prophets wrote. . . . Here is what I recommend. First, we ought to burn down their synagogues and schools, and bury underground whatever is immune to fire, so that no one ever again needs to see a single stone or cinder of them. . . . Their homes too should be set ablaze and destroyed. . . . Let all their prayer books and copies of the Talmud be taken from them, for it is by means of these that they propagate their idolatry, their lies, their foul cursing, and their blasphemies.

The tract goes on like this for more than a hundred pages. Luther may not have persuaded tolerant Christians to become otherwise—and it deserves pointing out that many Christians disagreed, in print, with Luther. Yet his uniquely authoritative position among Protestants probably encouraged and confirmed many anti-Semites in the bigotry they already had.

The early modern era, in sum, was marked by harsh religious tensions compounded by severe economic dislocations. Small wonder, then, that so many dispossessed Christians fled to the New World. Small wonder, too, that so many dispossessed Jews fled to the Old.

THE WANING OF THE SULTANATE

The Ottoman economy peaked under Suleiman I, who held the sultanate from 1520 to 1566. Suleiman, the contemporary of Charles V in Europe, is known in Europe as "Suleiman the Magnificent." In the Muslim world, he is called "Suleiman the Lawgiver" in recognition of his work codifying the great mass of legislation he inherited from his predecessors. He also made the imperial administration more efficient. As we saw in chapter 12, he was a successful warrior as well, extending Ottoman power to Hungary.

Economic Causes   With the growth of the Atlantic trade, however, the Ottoman economy gradually slowed and stagnated. Population increase both fueled the economy's peak under Suleiman and brought about the stagnation. When the economy was still expanding, immigration increased significantly. The arrival of the Jews formed only a part of this; a much greater factor was the influx of Muslims from Egypt and Syria and parts of Persia. Cities like Edirne, Trabzon, and Iznik grew by as much as 80 percent, while scores of cities grew by 40 to 50 percent. Rural villages increased in size and number by 30 to 40 percent over the 16th century. Much of this growth resulted from the flight of people from conflict zones between Ottoman and Safavid forces. Ultimately, overpopulation set in and was felt first in the countryside. Available farmland grew scarce, and local authorities responded by permitting the clearing of forests. Woodland, never abundant in much of the region, became even scarcer and contributed to a loss of commercial diversity.

Adding to the trouble was the influx of gold and silver from the New World, which led to spiraling inflation. In 1580, for example, it took 60 silver Turkish coins to equal 1 gold ducat (then the international standard currency of account), but only ten years later it required 120. By 1640 it took 250. Population growth and the concomitant increase in demand for goods and services also drove this "price revolution." The price of basic commodities like wheat increased by a factor of twenty between 1500 and 1600.

Istanbul   This painting from 1537 shows a bird's-eye view of the Ottoman capital of Istanbul. The picture still follows the medieval tradition of orienting maps with east at the top; a modern viewer needs to turn his or her head sideways to the left. The Hippodrome and the former Church of Hagia Sophia (renamed the Ayasofya Mosque and renovated to include two minarets) are the two largest structures visible.

As in Christian Europe, economic misery made religious and ethnic tensions worse. Popular resentment of ethnic and religious foreigners, especially of the Sufis and Shi'a, increased. Street violence between factions forced local officials to take more direct and heavy-handed actions to keep the peace. But this required money. Over the 16th and 17th centuries, therefore, the power of the Ottoman sultanate waned. Provincial governors and urban or district commanders first demanded the right to collect their own taxes and then used the revenue to finance their new political muscle.

The sultan's loss of fiscal and political power escalated the conservative trend in religion. Madrasas across the Ottoman state declared their opposition to any sort of speculative thought. Preachers condemned public morals for straying from the early texts.[10] Even the natural sciences, which had been one of the

Conservative Reaction

---

[10]   Especially popular targets for preachers were the new enthusiasms for coffee and tobacco, brought over from the New World.

glories of Islam in the medieval period, came under attack. When Murad III (r. 1574–1595) had an astronomical observatory built in 1579, local preachers—mostly Arabs—condemned it as an offense against Allah to attempt to unravel the secrets of the act of creation. As we saw in chapter 13, the observatory was quickly torn down.

NEW CENTERS OF INTELLECTUAL AND CULTURAL LIFE

The creative centers of intellectual and cultural life thus moved from the Ottoman Empire to Safavid Egypt and Persia. Cairo emerged as the vital site for scientific work. It was also the home of Ibn Khaldun (1332–1406), whose great *Muqaddimah* (*Introduction to History*) posited a new philosophy of history, based on the interplay of group identity and materialism—or the pursuit of worldly goods.

Illuminationism

Safavid Persia, by contrast, became the center for metaphysics, the branch of philosophy that examines the nature of reality. Its great achievement was a philosophical program known as **illuminationism** (*al-hikmat al-ishraq*). Illuminationism derived from the attempt to harmonize Islamic doctrine with classical Greek thought and the mystical elements of Zoroastrianism and hence to give Sufism a measure of intellectual respectability within the larger Muslim world. Elements of illuminationism date to the 12th century, but the theory was given its fullest and most brilliant expression in the work of **Mulla Sadra** (1571–1640), the greatest Muslim philosopher of the modern era. Mulla Sadra's most important book, *Transcendent Wisdom Concerning the Four Journeys of the Intellect* (1638), maps out four stages in the route to spiritual and philosophical enlightenment. He dissects the cognitive processes that lead from the understanding of the physical world to a consideration of the essence of God and the nature of the relationship of humans to the Creator. Illumination is both a divine blessing and a technique of enlightenment, an aspect of spiritual discipline.

Illuminationism was in fact a common feature of Greater Western philosophical thinking of the age, although European and the Middle Eastern thinkers arrived at it by different trajectories. In western Europe it is expressed in the philosophies of Baruch Spinoza (1632–1677) and Gottfried Wilhelm von Leibniz (1646–1716). Spinoza, a heretical Jew expelled by his Amsterdam synagogue, was also a heretical illuminationist. He argued for a highly original form of pantheism (the identification of God with the universe and its phenomena) that asserted that God was nature itself (*natura naturans*, in his posthumously published masterpiece, the *Ethics*) and that every facet of and occurrence in nature is a necessary consequence of God's existence. But the identification of God and nature should not elicit an attitude of wonderment and awe from human beings. To Spinoza, human life has no divinely ordained purpose, and the occurrences of nature possess no supernatural meaning; they simply *are*. The rational study of nature leads to no spiritual revelation, only to a rational understanding of God's manifestation within nature—which, Spinoza insisted, is illumination enough for anyone.

The radical nature of Spinoza's views is evident from the writ of *herem* (a form of excommunication in Jewish law) issued by his synagogue. Its central portion reads,

> The leaders of this holy community, long familiar with the evil ideas and actions of Baruch de Spinoza, have tried repeatedly and by numerous stratagems to turn him from his evil ways; but we have failed to make him mend his wicked ways—in fact, we hear fresh reports every day about the abominable heresies he practices and teaches, and the monstrous deeds he continues to perform. . . . And [therefore] we have decided that the said Baruch de Spinoza should be excommunicated and expelled from the people of Israel. . . . [Wherefore], in accordance with the will of the Holy One (may He be ever blessed) and of this Holy Congregation, and in the presence of the holy scrolls of the Torah, with their 613 commandments, we hereby excommunicate, cast out, curse and damn Baruch de Spinoza with the same form of excommunication with which Joshua condemned Jericho, with the curse with which Elisha cursed the boys, and with all the curses which are written in the Book of the Law. Cursed be Baruch de Spinoza by day and cursed be he by night; cursed when he lies down and cursed when he rises up; cursed when he goes out and cursed when he comes in. The Lord will not spare him; His righteous anger and wrath will rage against this man, and bring upon him all the curses written in the Law. May the Lord blot out his name from under heaven, and condemn him to separation separate from all the tribes of Israel with all the curses of the covenant as they are contained the Law.

The rest of the writ is nearly as vehement.

In contrast to Spinoza, the German philosopher Leibniz saw divine emanation everywhere. He rejected pantheism in favor of an idea to which he gave the awkward name of *monadology*: all forms of natural life are composed of fundamental units he called "monads," which contain within themselves all the qualities of the life-form they make up. The concept is difficult to grasp—and Leibniz himself had difficulty in expressing it—but may be thought of, for

Spinoza Baruch de Spinoza (1632–1677) was the greatest Jewish philosopher since Maimonides (1135–1204), although his ideas led to expulsion from his Amsterdam synagogue.

organic matter at least, as something akin to a particular life-form's unique genetic code. God himself, said Leibniz, is not present in nature, as Spinoza would have it, but his intent is present in the system of monads. The study of nature does not bring us, therefore, into God's presence, but it does illuminate for us the workings of His mind.

Mulla Sadra did not see God in creation like Spinoza; neither did he behold a divine intelligence in it like Leibniz. Rather, he saw a mystical unity in creation that parallels the unity of God Himself and draws the enlightened believer into a stronger desire for spiritual ascent, a return to the Oneness at the heart of all things. Sadra thus pulled together and harmonized Sufi mysticism, Shi'i doctrine, and Aristotelian rationalism:

> Philosophy is the process of perfecting the human soul by coming to a true understanding of things-as-they-are, which is achieved—when it is achieved at all—through rational demonstration rather than intuition or appeal to prior authority. By means of philosophy, we come to resemble our Creator, and this allows us to perceive and ascribe a rational order to His creation.

Most of Arab Islam during this period adhered to a staid and increasingly conservative form of Sunni Islam, eschewing scientific and metaphysical innovation in favor of rigid tradition. As early as the late 14th century Ibn Khaldun observed that most of the creative intellectual energy in the Islamic world came from non-Arabs. From the *Muqaddimah*:

> All the great grammarians have been Persian, . . . all the great legal scholars. . . . Only the Persians still write great books and dedicate themselves to preserving what is known. Thus, a saying attributed to the Prophet himself rings true: "If Knowledge was suspended from the highest ceiling in heaven, the Persians alone would get it." . . . All the intellectual arts, in fact, have long since been abandoned by the Arabs and become the sole preserve of the Persians.

The encouragement given to non-Arab Islamic and pre-Islamic traditions by the Ottomans thus stemmed from a sincere interest in promoting innovation and inquiry, but it also served a political purpose by providing a counterweight to the Arab-centric views holding sway from the Arabian peninsula through Palestine and Syria. It also provides another example of the interconnected nature of the cultural life of the Greater West.

WARS OF RELIGION: THE EASTERN FRONT

Christian Europe was not the only theater of conflict. Events in the Middle East, too, turned violent in the 16th and 17th centuries, thanks to a similarly toxic mixture of religious, economic, and ethnic enmity. Three large, multiethnic states dominated the Islamic world around 1500: the Ottoman Empire, the Mamluk Sultanate in Egypt and Syria, and Safavid Persia. Twenty years later only two remained, and they challenged each other for leadership of the Muslim world for the next two hundred years.

The Ottoman Turks and the Safavid Persians, heading up the Sunnis and Shi'a, respectively, were the standard-bearers of Islam. Ethnic Arabs held decidedly second-class status in both societies, and efforts to alter their position failed before the military might of the dominant regimes. Bayezid II (r. 1481–1512) and his son Selim I (r. 1512–1520) were anxious to continue the policy of aggressive Ottoman expansion and drove the Turkish army northward into the Black Sea, westward into the Balkans, southward toward Egypt, and eastward toward Persia. Bayezid even constructed a large naval fleet that defeated the Venetians in 1503 and left the Turks in command of the eastern Mediterranean sea-lanes. Bayezid had a more peaceful side to his personality, however, and took particular delight in managing the palace schools (sometimes even volunteering to examine students personally) and in fostering trade.

Selim—whose nickname Yavuz ("the Inflexible") describes his personality—began his reign with a near-paranoid fear of Persian designs on his realm and spent his first two years in power executing forty thousand suspected Safavid sympathizers in Anatolia. Non-Muslims fared better under these two than did non-Sunni Muslims. Nearly a quarter million Jews emigrated to the Ottoman realm after the European expulsions and settled in Anatolia and Palestine. Like many of their predecessors and courtiers, however, Bayezid and Selim practiced an eclectic form of Islam. It was formally Sunni but tinged with a passionate admiration for Sufism.

Just as tensions grew between the Ottomans and their Sunni Arab base, relations between the Ottomans and the Shi'i Safavids grew increasingly bitter. The *Ottoman–* Ottomans' economic stagnation worsened, whereas Safavid Persia not only *Safavid* carved out its own Islamic identity but also, as we have seen, challenged the very *Strife*

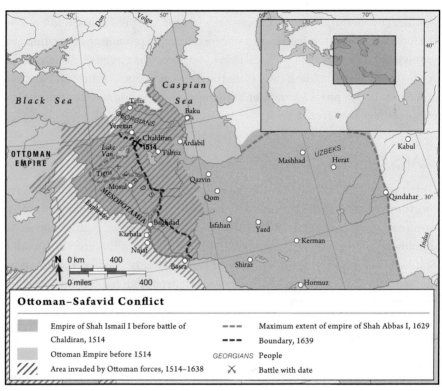

MAP 14.3 Ottoman–Safavid Conflict Struggles between the two great Islamic empires paralleled those among the states of Christian Europe in their virulent blend of political, religious, economic, and social factors.

notion that the center of Muslim civilization lay with the Arabs and Turks. The pulse of vital Islamic life, Persians insisted, had moved permanently eastward to Iran. The Persian shah (emperor) Ismail (r. 1501–1524), who believed himself divine, ordered the immediate conversion of all Sunnis in Iran to Shi'ism on penalty of death. And he made good on the threat by executing tens of thousands, confiscating their homes and goods, closing their mosques, and absconding with the funds for their schools. He also urged the Turkish people to overthrow the Ottomans. As a colorful warning to Bayezid II, Ismail had another political rival killed, the skin removed from his corpse and stitched around a life-size straw figure, and the "corpse" sent to Istanbul.[11]

Predictably, wars broke out between the two states and continued through the reign of Ismail's son and heir Tahmasp I (r. 1524–1576). Religious hatred intensified with each new reign (see Map 14.3). Ismail II (r. 1576–1577) played a

---

[11] Ismail kept his rival's skull—gold-plated and encrusted with jewels—and reportedly used it as a drinking cup.

role in Persia similar to that of England's Mary Tudor. He tried to force the realm to reconvert to Sunni Islam, but the purges and persecutions he ordered became so bloody that his closest supporters poisoned him after only two years on the throne. (Among other atrocities, he killed or blinded five of his brothers. Ismail died when someone put poison in his opium.) Occasional persecutions of Iran's Jewish and Christian communities broke out in the 16th century, but in the 17th religious relations improved significantly. In general, as the Shi'a became more firmly established and were less involved in strife with Sunni holdouts, they eased up on oppression of Jews and Christians. Moreover, many Jewish immigrants from farther west earned the shah's gratitude by introducing him to gunpowder and the casting of heavy artillery. The desire by rulers like Abbas the Great (r. 1588–1629) to increase Iran's export of silk textiles and Persian rugs also opened the way for Armenian Christians, long expert in the crafts, to thrive under Safavid rule.

Ottoman relations with Europe remained uneasy, especially with Habsburg Austria and Venice, their neighboring rivals for control of trade routes. The absence of a natural boundary between the Turkish and the Austrian realms kept mutual concerns for safety at a high level. And with the relative decline of Mediterranean trade compared with the Atlantic trade, control of the sea-lanes in and out of the Levant became all the more important. At the battle of Lepanto in 1571, an alliance of naval forces led by Venice and King Philip II of Spain defeated the Turkish fleet and decimated its corps of experienced officers. The so-called Long War (1593–1606) against Austria highlighted the need to modernize the Ottoman army with gunpowder weaponry, but resistance to Western technology among the Arab populace made this an unpopular development. *European Victories over the Ottomans*

Just as unpopular and destabilizing was the repeated phenomenon of women running the imperial government. The era of the 16th and 17th centuries in general—but especially the period from 1640 to 1670—is referred to as the **Sultanate of Women** (*kadınlar saltanatı* in Turkish; see Table 14.1). During the reigns of several weak sultans, such as Ibrahim I (r. 1640–1648), and several minorities, such as that under Mehmed IV (r. 1648–1687), the leading women of the imperial harem effectively controlled the government. Taking the title of "queen mother" (*valide sultan* in Turkish), these women ran the state, directed foreign policy, and oversaw the fiscal system. *Sultanate of Women*

What made matters worse, from the point of view of their disgruntled, mainly Arab, subjects, was the fact that most of these women were non-Muslim by birth, and their embrace of Islam was therefore suspect. (The Ottomans made a point of marrying as many Christian-born wives as possible, as a nod to their Christian subjects.) In the 16th century the most prominent sultanas were Nur-Banu and Safiye, who either ran or helped to run the Ottoman state in the years 1574–1583

TABLE 12.1 **Sultanate of Women**

Name	Years in power	Mother of	Wife of	Ethnicity
Ayşe Hafsa	1520–1534	Selim I	Suleiman I	Tatar
Nur-Banu	1574–1583	Selim II	Murad III	Venetian
Safiye	1595–1603	Murad III	Mehmed III	Venetian
Hatice	1617–1621	Ahmed I	Osman II	Serb
Kösem	1623–1648	Ahmed I	Murad IV and Ibrahim I	Greek
Turhan Hatice	1648–1683	Ibrahim I	Mehmed IV	Ukrainian

and 1595–1603, respectively. Both of Venetian descent, they restored relations with Venice after the battle of Lepanto and strengthened commercial ties between their empires. Two figures who especially stood out in the 17th century were Kösem, the Greek-born mother of Ibrahim, and her Turkish daughter-in-law Turhan Hatice, whose rivalry was as much personal as political and ended with Kösem's assassination in 1651.

ECONOMIC CHANGE IN AN ATLANTIC WORLD

After severe contraction in the late Middle Ages, Europe's population began to grow around 1500 and did so steadily for the next three hundred years, despite the carnage of the religious wars (see Figure 14.2). A gradual decline in outbreaks of plague accounts for much of this, but so does the tremendous improvement in the food supply. Famine has always been nature's principal method of population control. For the premodern world, steady growth in demographic numbers is a sure indicator of steady growth in the availability of food. Europe saw just such a steady growth from the 16th to 18th centuries, for two reasons. First, food exports to the Ottoman-controlled east declined. And second, as we saw in chapter 13, Europe was introduced to new crops from North and South America—the most important being corn (maize), beans, and potatoes. It is unlikely that these were brought back with the intention of introducing new foodstuffs. Rather, they were probably loaded on ships as victuals for those making the journey back to Europe. Most Europeans disdained corn (maize), which they thought inedible for humans; they prized it instead as

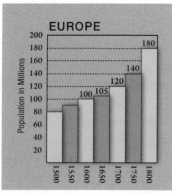

FIGURE 14.2   Population Growth in Europe, 1500–1800

animal fodder. Beans and potatoes, however, made radical changes in the European diet. By long-standing feudal custom, Europe's manors remained dedicated to grain production, but beans and potatoes quickly dominated the peasants' individual garden plots. Gradually, fields normally left fallow were also given over to the new crops, which helped replenish the soil. Their high yields made them popular, not as market crops but as staples of the peasants' own diets. By the 17th century peasant households were eating as many as two or three dozen potatoes a day—not the most satisfying of diets, but infinitely preferable to famine.

Increasing food supplies, however, could not halt the inflationary spiral of the "price revolution." Small landholders who could not keep up with their rents therefore risked sliding back in to debt bondage, and the manorial lords who lived off those rents faced severe potential drops in their own incomes as well. For many aristocrats, an answer to their trouble lay in the **enclosure movement**. By enclosing farmland—that is, by constructing a border of fences or thick hedgerows around it—landlords could evict their tenants, convert crop fields to meadows, and raise sheep or other herd animals instead. Their labor costs thus declined sharply, and the wool generated by their sheep was self-renewing. Moreover, the steady rise in human population meant a steadily growing demand for textiles. In this way landed nobles improved their incomes significantly, but at the expense of the evicted farmers. Lacking the funds to purchase new lands of their own, rural workers had difficulty supporting themselves.

Enclosure was not a new phenomenon, although it had been primarily a feature of British life rather than that of the Continent. Thomas More had described the consequences of land enclosure, albeit in satirical fashion, as early as 1516 in his *Utopia* (introduced in chapter 13):

> It's because of sheep. These animals, so naturally mild and so easy to tend, can now be said to have become uncontrollable devourers, consuming even the people themselves; they empty homes, devastate crop fields, and turn whole villages into ghost towns. Any place where sheep can be raised to produce fine and rich wool, the nobles, gentry, and even the abbots (those supposed "holy men"!), not content with their rents and yearly fees, and feeling that it is not enough to live in luxurious laziness and do no actual good in the world, but choosing instead to bring actual harm into it, enclose all the land for pasture and put an end to farming. They demolish homes and level villages. The churches they allow to remain, of course, but only so they can use them as sheepfolds. As though they did not waste enough [land] already on coverts and private parks, these fine people are now destroying every human dwelling and letting every scrap of usable farmland run wild. (Book 1)

Evicted farm families had few options. The younger men could enter the military or merchant marines, and the females could seek positions as domestic servants, but for many the solution lay in seeking new fortunes abroad. It was a difficult decision to travel thousands of miles from home, take up residence on a foreign continent, and begin the work of clearing the land afresh. But many chose to do so because of population rise and land hunger. The feverish religious hostilities of the time, too, provided ample reason to quit the Old World for the New.

◆

The 16th and 17th centuries, in sum, were not necessarily more religious or more filled with religious hatred than earlier periods in the history of the Greater West. However, religion became enmeshed in economic and ethnic rivalries on an unusually large scale and to a degree of fanaticism unlike anything that had existed before, with the possible exception of the medieval Crusades. Such antagonisms would not reach this fever pitch again until the 20th century.

WHO, WHAT, WHERE

Church of England	Huguenots	Peace of Westphalia
Edict of Nantes	illuminationism	Saint Bartholomew's
Elizabeth I	Kabbala	Day Massacre
enclosure movement	Mulla Sadra	Sultanate of Women
ghetto	Peace of Augsburg	Thirty Years' War

SUGGESTED READINGS

Primary Sources

Grimmelshausen, Hans Jakob Christoffel von. *The Adventures of a Simpleton.*

Mulla Sadra. *The Four Journeys of the Intellect.*

Anthologies

Diefendorf, Barbara B. *The Saint Bartholomew's Day Massacre: A Brief History with Documents* (2008).

Halperin, David J. *Sabbatai Zvi: Testimonies to a Fallen Messiah* (2007).

Kors, Alan Charles, and Edward Peters, eds. *Witchcraft in Europe, 400–1700: A Documentary History* (2000).

Pryor, Felix, comp. *Elizabeth I: Her Life in Letters* (2003).

Studies

Bonney, Richard. *The Thirty Years' War, 1618–1648* (2002).

Briggs, Robin. *Witches and Neighbors: The Social and Cultural Context of European Witchcraft* (1996).

Clark, Stuart. *Thinking with Demons: The Idea of Witchcraft in Early Modern Europe* (1999).

Dale, Stephen F. *The Muslim Empires of the Ottomans, Safavids, and Mughals* (2010).

Diefendorf, Barbara B. *Beneath the Cross: Catholics and Huguenots in Sixteenth-Century Paris* (1991).

Dursteler, Eric R. *Renegade Women: Gender, Identity, and Boundaries in the Early Modern Mediterranean* (2011).

Fairchilds, Cissie. *Women in Early Modern Europe, 1500–1700* (2007).

Goffman, Daniel. *The Ottoman Empire and Early Modern Europe* (2002).

Goldish, Matt. *The Sabbatean Prophets* (2004).

Greyerz, Kaspar von. *Religion and Culture in Early Modern Europe, 1500–1800* (2007).

Hartz, Glenn. *Leibniz's Final System: Monads, Matter, and Animals* (2006).

Holt, Mack P. *The French Wars of Religion, 1562–1629* (2005).

Israel, Jonathan I. *European Jewry in the Age of Mercantilism, 1550–1750* (1989).

Kamen, Henry. *Spain, 1469–1714: A Society of Conflict* (2005).

Kaplan, Benjamin J. *Divided by Faith: Religious Conflict and the Practice of Toleration in Early Modern Europe* (2007).

King, John N. *Foxe's* Book of Martyrs *and Early Modern Print Culture* (2006).

Kleinschmidt, Harald. *Charles V: The World Emperor* (2004).

MacHardy, Karin. *War, Religion, and Court Patronage in Habsburg Austria: The Social and Cultural Dimensions of Political Interaction, 1521–1622* (2003).

McCabe, Ina Baghdiantz. *A Global History of Consumption, 1500–1800* (2014).

Moris, Zailan. *Revelation, Intellectual Intuition, and Reason in the Philosophy of Mulla Sadra: An Analysis of the Al-Hikmah Al-'Arshiyyah* (2003).

Nadler, Steven. *Spinoza's* Ethics*: An Introduction* (2006).

Nadler, Steven. *Spinoza's Heresy: Immortality and the Jewish Mind* (2002).

Newman, Andrew J. *Safavid Iran: Rebirth of a Persian Empire* (2008).

O'Malley, John W. *Trent and All That: Renaming Catholicism in the Early Modern Era* (2000).

Parrott, David. *Richelieu's Army: War, Government, and Society in France, 1624–1642* (2001).

Peirce, Leslie. *Morality Tales: Law and Gender in the Ottoman Court of Aintab* (2003).

Pursell, Brennan C. *The Winter King: Frederick V of the Palatinate and the Coming of the Thirty Years' War* (2003).

Thomas, Hugh. *Rivers of Gold: The Rise of the Spanish Empire* (2004).

Van Zanden, Jan Luiten. *The Long Road to the Industrial Revolution: The European Economy in a Global Perspective, 1000–1800* (2009).

Wiesner-Hanks, Merry E. *Early Modern Europe, 1450–1789* (2006).

Wilson, Peter H. *The Thirty Years War: Europe's Tragedy* (2009).

For additional resources, including maps, primary sources, visuals, web links, and quizzes, please go to **www.oup.com/us/backman**.

CHAPTER 15

From Westphalia to Paris: Regimes Old and New

1648–1750

"Those who did not live in the 18th century before the [French] Revolution do not know life at its sweetest," declared the French career diplomat Charles de Talleyrand-Périgord (1754–1838). An egoist right to the tips of his aristocratic fingers, Talleyrand knew what he was talking about. The period of the Ancien Régime ("Old Regime"), from 1648 to 1789, was a time of unparalleled privilege and delight for the European upper aristocracy. The end of the Thirty Years' War in 1648 brought peace to once-warring states, freeing elites to concentrate instead on amassing wealth and power. Urban manufacturing and commerce had long since become the main engines of economic life, but the landed elite still enjoyed various rental incomes, judicial fees, annuities, ecclesiastical and governmental sinecures, and military

Teaching Manners Old Regime Europe placed profound importance on proper manners, one example being the publication of the first etiquette manuals for "proper" urban families. In this 1740 painting by Jean-Baptiste Chardin (1699–1779), a governess chides her charge for having dirtied his hat—presumably having dropped it on the ground during a tennis match.

THE GREATER WEST IN THE AGE OF ABSOLUTISM

- Peterhof
- Potsdam
- Schönbrunn
- Versailles

○ Palace built by absolutist monarch

revenues. That was more than enough for them to live in lavish comfort, especially given their most closely held privilege—exemption from paying taxes. A belief in absolute order spread throughout society, inspiring a demand for norms in the arts and even everyday life.

This was the Baroque Age, when fabulously ornate palaces, churches, summer residences, concert halls, libraries, museums, theaters, pleasure gardens, and private academies sprang up by the hundreds across Europe. Most were filled to bursting with paintings and sculptures and rang out with the music written to order by court composers and played by servant musicians—all for the enjoyment of the wealthy, powdered, perfumed, wigged, and brilliantly attired nobles. Their images, coats of arms, and marble-inscribed names bedecked everything in sight. The display sought not merely to impress but also to overwhelm the viewer with its expressive power. And that meant the power not of the architect, artist, or composer, but of the nobleman or woman whose authority and station made such glories possible. Europe's elites had always enjoyed their privileges, but never before on this scale.

The all-encompassing grandeur was designed to stun the people into a state of paralyzed awe. But such a display was possible only by means of a brutal hoarding of wealth. Few periods in Greater Western history ever saw a more intense concentration of power and wealth among the elites—or such widespread penury and suffering by the common people. The German poet Johann Wolfgang von

CHAPTER TIMELINE

1620	1640	1660	1680	1700

- 1642–1649 English Civil War
- 1643–1715 Peace of Westphalia
- 1648 Peace of Westphalia
- 1649 Charles I of England beheaded
- 1649–1660 Cromwell's rule in England
- 1651 Hobbes, Leviathan
- 1660 Monarchy restored in England
- 1670 Molière, *The Middle-Class Gentleman*
- 1675 Founding of Bedlam Asylum (England)
- 1683 Ottoman siege of Vienna repulsed
- 1688 England's Glorious Revolution
- 1689–1725 Reign of Peter the Great (Russia)
- 1701–1714 War of the Spanish Succession

Goethe (1749–1832) described Europe's peasant farmers as "caught between the land and the aristocracy as between an anvil and a hammer." Not a comforting image—especially when one realizes that Goethe did not make the observation out of sympathy for the commoners' plight but merely as a recognition of what was and needed to be.

Below this picture of serene Continental privilege, however, a different scene roiled. England suffered through a brutal civil war and Puritanical theocracy that ultimately gave way to an uneasy constitutional monarchy, whereas much of the Islamic world underwent another wave of religious reform that (true to the pattern) grew ever more conservative. As international trade grew and a new economic system came into being, Europe faced a new round of crises and war.

THE PEACE OF WESTPHALIA: 1648

By 1648 most of Continental Europe was exhausted by more than one hundred years of brutal religious warfare. Unable or unwilling to continue the carnage, all sides sued for peace. The **Peace of Westphalia** (1648) is an umbrella term for a collection of individual treaties that ended the hostilities. It rearranged political borders, created a framework of mutually agreed-on diplomatic principles, and established a network of recognized sovereign governments. More than one hundred delegations participated in the negotiations, which took seven years: sixteen

1720	1740	1760	1780	1800

- 1720 South Sea Bubble
- 1736 Fall of Safavid dynasty (Persia)
- 1740–1748 War of the Austrian Succession
- 1755 Samuel Johnson, *Dictionary of the English Language*
- 1756–1763 Seven Years' War

nations, sixty-six German imperial principalities, and twenty-seven nongovernmental interest groups (such as churches, corporations, and guilds). This was the
first general diplomatic congress in European history, and it provided a model for
subsequent international assemblies.

*Quest for
a Balance
of Power*

The peace dramatically revised the political map of Europe by splitting
some states, joining others, carving out new independent entities, and moving
many traditional boundaries (see Map 15.1). In so doing, it paid little attention
to preserving ethnic domains. The goal instead was to produce a balance of

MAP 15.1   Europe in 1648   The balance of power sought by negotiators of the Peace of
Westphalia depended especially on the fragmentation of the former Holy Roman Empire into
multiple states, while maintaining a strong Austrian–Hungarian empire as a bulwark against the
Ottoman rulers in Istanbul.

power between the states created by the Peace. If each new state was roughly equal in power to its neighbor, the thinking went, then wars would be less likely to break out between them. But to establish such a balance, the negotiators had to consider more than mere acreage; population density, economic and technological development, access to ports and rivers, and the availability of natural resources all had to be factored in. The resulting map created several new states (an independent Holland, Portugal, and Switzerland, for example) scattered among the larger territorial powers (Austria–Hungary, Bavaria, Brandenburg–Prussia, France, Poland–Lithuania, Spain, and Sweden). Moreover, countries now had a mechanism for creating alliances to check an ambitious neighbor. This eased tensions by allowing each state to control its own foreign policy in a meaningful way. Even small states like Switzerland or Holland had strategic strengths that made them valuable allies. Threatening to withdraw their support from an alliance could make even a large state like France or Spain reconsider its policies.

The Westphalia treaties also reaffirmed the principle of religious establishment—the idea that the ruler of each state could determine its offi- *Religious* cial religion (*cuius regio, eius religio*)—while guaranteeing the freedom of *Establishment* other faiths and denominations within certain prescribed limits. Strictly speaking, religious establishment meant more than a preference for any particular faith or denomination and was distinct from theocracy (government ruled by religious authority). Rather, it created a formal relationship between the state and the specific church. Religious establishment in the modern sense, in which the established church serves as an organ of the state, was a product of the Protestant Reformation: England established the (Anglican) Church of England in 1533, and the (Lutheran) Church of Sweden came into formal existence in 1536. Most of the states carved out by the Peace of Westphalia had in practice established churches, although few had the formal legal structures uniting church and state that England and Sweden did.

This sprawl of new or heavily revised territorial states left most monarchs without serious rivals for power. Where councils and parliaments had provided *The* a limited check on royal ambitions, few of these customs survived intact. The *Conditions* aristocracy remained wealthy, privileged, and secure in their control of the *for* agrarian countryside, but also unable to unite in opposition to royal aims. The *Absolutism* new states were professional bureaucracies—uninviting to most nobles, who found it more to their liking to remain in their baroque palaces and chateaux than to crowd into expensive cramped quarters in the busy capital cities. Moreover, individual rulers could now consolidate extensive, centralized authority over their common subjects, so long as they avoided using that power to threaten their neighbors. In other words, the alliances and guarantees that aimed to prevent a king from intimidating his neighbors actually helped him to tighten his grip on his own subjects. In this way the Peace helped to trigger the rise of royal **absolutism**, or a king's absolute power—not as a consciously deliberated policy, but rather as the unintended consequence of the quest for a balance of power.

THE ARGUMENT FOR TYRANNY

The argument for tyranny is a simple one, to its enthusiasts: it provides freedom. This may seem contrary to common sense, but the argument is sound. We define freedom by what we are free *from*. Many people, quite understandably, think of freedom as independence, as freedom from control. To others, however, true freedom consists of freedom from chaos. The restoration of order after a long period of anarchy can thrill people with a sense of regained liberty—the liberty of a reliable, well-regulated tranquility.

Restoration of Order

The argument is an old one. The Archaic and Classical Age Greeks celebrated their tyrants (*tyrannoi*, like Pisistratos) and wrote them into their constitutions as necessary correctives to democracy's occasional tendency to drive the cart into a ditch. The Roman Republic too allowed for constitutional dictatorship, a temporary although renewable grant of unlimited authority to revise the laws, reform government, and command the military. Julius Caesar had been a dictator—and a popular one until he appointed himself dictator for life, which made him effectively a king and all but assured his assassination. In times of crisis, as when an airplane is spinning out of control or a ship is foundering in a storm, the rights to individual self-expression and self-determination do not further the cause of rescue; there is no time to hold elections, seek consensus, and let everyone on board freely express their views about what to do. Instead, the argument goes, salvation requires a single firm hand on the controls and a single strong voice issuing commands to an obedient crowd. Tyrants can make mistakes, of course, but they at least have the potential of saving the ship or landing the plane. Noisy, messy democracy and respect for independence of thought and action in such a plight only guarantees a disaster.

The catastrophic wars of religion and civil wars before them, many now argued, were the result of liberalizing, mass-driven politics. Only a restoration of patriarchal society, headed by noble male authority, could save Europe from ruin. But this could not be done quietly or subtly. The aristocracy needed to parade its power, to boast of it, and to glorify it in everything it did. And the higher the aristocrat, the greater the need for spectacle. Kings, of course, needed to parade their glorious position more than anyone else. Privilege, in the age of absolutism, was not a consequence of power but the very essence of it. Jean Domat (1625–1696), a prominent French jurist and royal favorite, justified the ostentation:

> Law grants the sovereign many rights, one of which must be the right to public display of anything that gives evidence of the grandeur and majesty needed to express the authority and dignity of his high and wide-ranging office. . . . God Himself [after all] wants monarchs to augment the authority He has shared with them, in ways that promote the awed respect of the people, and this can be achieved only by the grandeur conveyed by the brilliance of their palaces.

The Peace of Westphalia did not institute absolute monarchy in any formal sense, but it did establish the conditions that made its rise likely. Some early indicators of royal dictatorship had emerged even before the Peace. In France the rapid concentration of power by the monarchy had begun under King Louis XIII (r. 1610–1643), whose chief minister—Armand-Jean du Plessis, Cardinal de Richelieu (1585–1642)— summed up the problems confronting the throne when he first came to power in 1624:

> The Protestants acted as though they shared the state with you, the nobles, as if they were your equals rather than your subjects, and the governors of the provinces as though they were monarchs of their own offices. These scenarios set a bad example, one so harmful to the kingdom that even Your most loyal courts were influenced by it and were driven—unreasonably—to

Cardinal de Richelieu

Richelieu   Armand-Jean du Plessis, Cardinal de Richelieu (1585–1642), was the sickly younger son of a low-ranking noble family, who grew to become the most powerful figure in the kingdom of France after the king himself. Richelieu believed firmly in the necessity of an absolutist monarchy; only a strong central monarch, ably guided and determined to exert his authority energetically, could maintain civil order. Richelieu's rapid rise in the church and the French government went hand in hand. Consecrated a bishop in 1608, he became France's secretary of state in 1616; in 1622 he was made cardinal, and two years later he was Louis XIII's chief minister—a post he held until his death.

build up their authority to the detriment of Your own. Might I add that every individual seemed to measure his worth by the boldness of his presumption, . . . each one deeming the privileges he held from You valuable only to the extent that they satisfied his greedy fantasies. . . .

Sure in the knowledge of how much good a king can accomplish when he puts his power to proper use, I, in my confidence, dared to promise Your Majesty that You would soon regain control of Your state and that before much time elapsed Your wisdom and courage, together with God's blessing, would put the realm on a new path. I swore to Your Majesty that I would spare no effort and would use whatever power it pleased You to grant me to ruin the Protestants, to break the stiff-necked pride of the aristocracy, to return all Your subjects to Your dutiful service, and to restore Your name to the high position it deserves in foreign lands. (*Political Testament*, ch. 1)

Richelieu accomplished all this and more with a mix of careful negotiation and heavy-handed intimidation. He neutralized most of Louis XIII's foes thanks to his network of domestic and international spies, his ability to charm, his willingness to bribe, and above all his ruthless conviction that only an all-powerful throne could keep France safe and strong. Richelieu's passion for order and security was as evident in his personal life as in his public policies, and in this regard he represents most of the values of the Age of Absolutism.

THE SOCIAL CONTRACT

Thomas Hobbes

Richelieu's dedication to a supremely powerful monarchy was instinctive, but more than one philosopher of the time reached a similar position by rational thought. None of these thinkers directly created absolutism as a political force, but they helped explain the sentiments that gave rise to it. The philosopher most closely associated with the theory of absolutism is Thomas Hobbes (1588–1679). Hobbes was not England's first philosopher, nor even its first political philosopher; he was, however, the first to write philosophy in English. A contemporary of René Descartes, with whom he corresponded, and Sir Francis Bacon, whom we also met in chapter 13, Hobbes spent most of his adult life as a tutor and secretary to the 2nd and 3rd Earls of Devonshire (both named William Cavendish, 1591–1628 and 1617–1684), which left him ample time to take advantage of their magnificent library. He had broad interests that included history, law, mathematics, and physics, as well as philosophy. Forced to spend time in exile in Paris after the arrest and subsequent execution of King Charles I in 1649 because of his strong royalist views, Hobbes returned to

London in 1651 with the completed manuscript of his best-known work, *Leviathan*.

Although his own life was comfortable, Hobbes's philosophy owes much to the violence and misery of his age. He emphasizes the instincts for self-preservation and self-regard that are natural to all people. Our polite, civilized behavior toward one another is an acquired attribute, one that masks and hopefully controls our baser passions for food, wealth, power, pleasure, and status. The problem, he argues, lies in the finite nature of the things we desire. Seeking always to satisfy ourselves, we unavoidably live in a state of constant competition with one another. "The war of all against all," as he memorably put it, corrodes our civilized veneer and leads us into periodic anarchies like the one Europe suffered after 1500. Moreover, people are unequal in specific abilities—some being stronger, others faster or more cunning or more agile—but in the long run these differences balance each other out. The war of all against all therefore becomes a permanent state, with

> no place for industry, because the fruit thereof is uncertain; and consequently no culture of the earth; no navigation or use of the commodities that may be imported by sea; no commodious building; no instruments of moving and removing such things as require much force; no knowledge of the face of the Earth; no account of time; no arts; no letters; and which is worst of all, continual fear and danger of violent death; and the life of man [is] solitary, poor, nasty, brutish, and short.

It is a pessimistic view of life—but an understandable one, given the agonies Europe had experienced since the discovery of the New World, the Protestant Reformation, the Wars of Religion, civil wars, the Inquisition, and witchcraft mania.

Hobbes sees only one way out of the misery of the state of nature: limitless sovereign authority. Only by transferring our innate rights of self-determination to a governing authority entrusted with absolute power over the people can we hope to free ourselves from chaos. Interestingly, Hobbes does not much care whether the absolutist government is a monarchy, an oligarchy, or a democracy. All that matters is that the government, whatever its form, has unquestioned power to compel obedience. Unlimited and indivisible power to legislate, adjudicate, execute, and enforce, in a single sovereign entity, is the only way to live an ordered, peaceful, and prosperous life. Of course it also fails to prevent the abuse of that power, but Hobbes counters this charge with two assertions. First, no absolute tyranny can ever be worse than absolute chaos. And second, a people's total submission to the sovereign authority will temper any possible inclination that authority might have to abuse its power.

The Social Contract   Thomas Hobbes's *Leviathan* is the first work of political science in English. The Latin verse at the top of this title page of the first edition (1651) reads: "There is no power on earth like Him" (Job 42.25).

Leviathan is a difficult book to read. Its archaic English—all four hundred pages of it—defeats all but the most determined readers. (I have modernized its spelling and punctuation in the passages above.) But it deserves attention. A darker yet more substantial work than Machiavelli's *The Prince* (discussed in chapter 12), *Leviathan* elaborates what later became known as **social contract** theory. This theory holds that when people decide to live in community they enter a covenant with one another, compromising their individual free wills in return for the benefits of society. Government, which bears responsibility for preserving social stability, may therefore legitimately assert its will on the community whenever it deems it necessary to do so. Renunciation of personal liberty, in other words, is the price of peace, but the truest form of freedom, Hobbes insists, lies in that very renunciation.

Richelieu and Hobbes were not the only 17th-century figures to argue for absolutism, but they are the most interesting. Both men were brilliant, moody, and pessimistic about human nature, and each worked diligently to bring their ideas to fruition—Richelieu in deed, Hobbes on the page. Had they met, they might have recognized each other as kindred spirits despite their religious differences. For all his worldliness, Richelieu was a devout Catholic, and scholars still debate whether Hobbes was an atheist.[1]

Each also had humane pursuits. Richelieu collected classical manuscripts (later donated to the Sorbonne, of which he was the chief executive), founded the Academie Française (the premier literary society in France), patronized painters and sculptors, and ardently promoted theater. Hobbes dabbled in mathematics and physics, published his own translations of Thucydides and Homer, and wrote a vivid history of the English Civil War. Still, both men shared unsettling and ominous views about human nature and the hard realities of life. Their influence

---

[1]   Can one be committed to Christianity while endorsing secular absolutism? Hobbes says yes, but was he just trying to avoid inflaming the still-smoldering religious antagonisms of his age?

was profound, and the fears they articulated were shared by many—fears that allowed absolutism to take root and flourish. For a while on the Continent, it even enjoyed popular support.

No one was a greater enthusiast for the authority of monarchs than Jean Bodin (ca. 1529–1596), a modest cleric who studied philosophy and law, became *Jean Bodin* an advisor to kings Charles IX (r. 1560–1574) and Henri III (r. 1574–1589), and turned himself into France's first great political theorist. But Bodin has suffered too frequently from historians' characterization of him as a "divine-right absolutist," which is a misreading of his work. His most significant publication—one out of a whole shelf of books—was *Six Books on a Commonwealth* (*Les Six Livres de la République*), which appeared in 1576 when Bodin was at the height of his career. Throughout this work he carefully distinguishes between a state and a government. A state, to Bodin, is an organic community of people united by faith, values, and cultural inheritance, whereas a government is a human creation, a mechanism for meeting the needs of a community; just as there can be various forms or iterations of a state, there are likewise various forms of government. Bodin advocated a combination of monarchy and democracy, a government in which the sovereign monarch determines the shape of the government while securing the rights of all his subjects to have access to magistracies and other offices regardless of social class or economic status. The king alone determines the law, but all citizens participate equally in it. The king himself must remain unbound by the laws he creates (*legibus absolutus*—"not bound by the laws"), which for Bodin is the very definition of sovereignty. The sovereign monarch answers only to natural and divine laws—but he must indeed answer to them, and hence his power is not "absolute" in the sense historians usually, and inaccurately, attribute to Bodin.

ABSOLUTE POLITICS

The dominant dynasties, and the most representative, of the Old Regime were the Bourbons in France, the Hohenzollerns in Brandenburg–Prussia, the Habsburgs in Austria and (a separate branch of the family) in Spain, and the Romanovs in Russia. A web of intermarriages that in some cases went back generations or even centuries connected the royal families to one another. Even so, ties of affection were minimal and always gave way to politics. Standing armies became arms of the state as royal families undertook vast building projects to display their majestic authority.

Despite the supposed "balance of power" established at Westphalia, France was the dominant Continental state in every way. With somewhere between 15 *France* and 18 million people, France around 1648 had twice the population of Spain and

Another Siege of Vienna   In 1683 the Ottomans once more marched against the Habsburg Empire (their earlier efforts having been in 1529 and 1532). The Turks had an army of nearly 100,000 soldiers. The Habsburgs called on their Polish and Lithuanian allies to join in the defense and carried the day. In this painting by the Flemish artist Frans Geffels (1624–1694), the Turks have launched their assault on the city. The Poles and Lithuanians have not yet appeared on the scene. According to legend, as part of the celebration over the Habsburgs' ultimate defeat of the Turks, the Viennese bakers' guild created a new pastry: the croissant, which was designed to mock the Islamic crescent, visible on the Turks' flag above the tent on the left. The powerful Ottoman forces were symbolically reduced to puff pastries.

three times that of England. With its superior resources concentrated among the upper orders, all of whom lavished funds on the arts, French culture flowered. Young King **Louis XIV** (r. 1643–1715) set immediately to increase the size of his army in the hope of matching France's cultural clout with its military muscle.

Brandenberg–Prussia   Brandenburg–Prussia, by contrast, was a surviving remnant of the old Holy Roman Empire, steeped in tradition and pride but for the moment a poor, defenseless, war-shocked ruin (see Map 15.1). Much of the worst fighting of the Thirty Years' War had taken place here, leaving large stretches of the countryside desolate and many towns depopulated. Economic development came slowly, and most commercial, technological, and institutional innovations appeared here one or two generations after they had taken root in England, France, or Holland.

Austria   Habsburg Austria had a long genealogy going back to the Middle Ages, but the traumas of the 17th century had left much of its land depleted and demoralized. The Ottoman Turks advanced on Austria almost as soon as the Westphalia agreements were signed; by 1683 they had reached Vienna, which they besieged for two months before giving up.[2] (Forces from Poland, Russia, Venice, and the

---

[2]   The Turks used the ancient temple of the Parthenon in Athens as their main munitions storehouse. When Venetian artillery units took aim on it, the temple was blasted into the ruin it is today.

papacy joined the subsequent Austrian counteroffensive.) The Turkish defeat reenergized Austrian pride, an emotional swell that led to a sharp improvement in economic and social stability. This was the era, post 1683, of Austria's climb as a cultural capital, especially the cities of Salzburg and Vienna; the first Austrian composer of note, Heinrich Ignaz Franz Biber (1644–1704), almost single-handedly turned Salzburg into a pilgrimage site for music lovers.

The background to the Romanov dynasty lay in the decades of famines, civil wars, and foreign invasions known as the Time of Troubles (1584–1613). The *Russia* most persistent invading force came from neighboring Poland–Lithuania, whose king tried to put a son on the Russian throne. In 1613 an army of nobles, towns-people, and peasants finally expelled the intruders and put on the throne a noble-man, Michael Romanov (r. 1613–1645), who established an enduring new dynasty. When **Peter I** (Peter the Great, r. 1689–1725) came to power in 1689 after a seven-year regency, he brought with him the style and techniques of auto-cratic rule that he had learned when traveling in the West. The Romanov dynasty would last more than three hundred years.

POLICE STATES

Autocracy is not conceptually difficult to grasp, since dictatorships follow a few set patterns of development. The regimes of the 17th and 18th centuries were *Rise of* above all police states. Raw military muscle and the willingness to use it both *Professional* secured and expressed their power. The king's army in France mustered merely *Armies* 20,000 soldiers in 1661; by 1700 it numbered 400,000. The Prussian army in the Thirty Years' War had consisted mostly of unreliable mercenaries, with the result that Swedish forces had ravaged the Prussian countryside almost at will. After 1648 the Prussian monarch began to assemble a professional standing army of his own. It began small: between 5,000 and 6,000 men. But by 1750 it had ballooned to 180,000. Control of the Austrian army was given to a professional military of-ficer from France, Prince François-Eugène of Savoy (1663–1736), who oversaw its transformation from a ragtag mixture of old feudal forces and mercenaries into a national institution with modern methods of supply, training, and command. After only a few years' work, he had increased the size and quality of the Austrian forces to such an extent that they drove 100,000 Ottoman Turks eastward from Austrian lands by 1687, after which he turned the army around and expelled a French force advancing from the west. Austria thus entered the 18th century with a professionalized army of nearly 100,000 men.

The transformation of the Russian military was even more dramatic. Long consisting of an informal conglomeration of semifeudalized noble cavalrymen known as *streltsi*, the army was disbanded and brutally purged of political rivals by Tsar Peter I in 1698. Peter was determined to bring Russia in line with Europe in terms of economic and political development and resolved to catch up with Europe by emulating it. He modeled his new army along French and Prussian lines, put his soldiers in Western-style uniforms, gave them Western weapons (muskets and artillery), and hired Western officers to train them.

These massive new armies drew from the lower orders of their respective societies for the rank and file; men from the urban and professional classes or the lower nobility dominated midlevel officer ranks. The highest ranks were still primarily the purview of the high nobility but tended to include only those for whom the military was a lifelong career. Only Prussia used a military draft; in every other country, volunteers served. And there was no shortage of volunteers. The king's army offered commoners three meals a day, regular wages, solid training, and the possibility of a pension after a certain number of years in service—things they had little or no chance of attaining on their own. These were "drum and bugle" armies, divided into companies that fought in formation using long, unbroken lines. Discipline was harsh and frequently brutal: beatings, fines, half-rations, and imprisonments were common. The penalty for breaking ranks was flogging. Executions were common too. In Austria, Prince François-Eugène often performed them himself on soldiers who failed to obey orders on the battlefield. Peter I once personally executed five soldiers accused of rebellion, after allowing others to prepare the way by torturing the men first.

Wars of Louis XIV   The Peace of Westphalia, however, was largely successful in maintaining a relatively stable Europe. Conflicts remained, a couple of them even large-scale matters, but Europe between 1648 and the start of the French Revolution in 1789 was a much more peaceful place than it had been in the 140 preceding years. Most of the wars of the era arose from Louis XIV's grandiose plans to create a greater France, or, more accurately, to secure a number of frontier regions that might buffer France from external attack: the War of Devolution (1667–1668), the Franco-Dutch War (1672–1678), the War of the League of Augsburg (1688–1697), and the War of the Spanish Succession (1701–1714). Louis came to regret his overreaching, although not until the end of his life. On his deathbed, Louis is reported to have advised his heir (his great-grandson Louis XV, r. 1715–1774), "I was too quick to start wars, and I kept them going out of vanity. . . . Be a peaceful ruler, and devote yourself above all to easing the suffering of your subjects."

The Cost of Security   Why then were such enormous armies created? With fewer foreign and civil wars to fight, what purpose did they serve? Monarchs put their soldiers to use policing their own populations. Soldiers marched the streets and plazas, stood in university lecture halls, observed church services, watched crowds entering and leaving theaters, patrolled the countryside, guarded government buildings, and monitored harbors. They guarded city gates, performed maneuvers in town squares, staffed prisons (one of the new inventions of the age), and inspected printing houses. Without such vast reserves of manpower, royal absolutism was unthinkable. Maintaining the military—paying salaries, providing weapons and uniforms, serving meals, offering housing, supporting pensioners—remained a central concern of every monarch of the 17th and 18th centuries. The costs even in peacetime were enormous; the occasional conflicts of the age drove the expenditures exponentially higher.

Old Regime monarchs also relied heavily on separate companies of royal commissioners and civil servants—called *intendants* in France and known collectively as the Directory in Prussia—who traveled through the provinces and inspected the handling of royal and administrative affairs. These commissioners held jurisdiction over all matters relating to public finance (whether collecting it or paying it out), public safety, and justice. They also formed part of the kings' extensive networks of intelligence gatherers. Drawn chiefly from the urban professional classes, commissioners served the king personally and did not hold public office, and hence they received their own salaries directly from the royal purse. They were expensive

Prussian Military Discipline   By 1750 the Prussian line infantry made full use of flintlock muskets and bayonets, as well as military drills, which involved the rotation of the front and rear lines after each salvo. "If my soldiers were to think, not one of them would remain in the army," Frederick II of Prussia (r. 1740–1786) is reputed to have said. This painting by Carl Röchling (1855–1920), a German artist known for his representation of historical military themes, shows Frederick's forces charging directly into the fire of the Austrians at the battle of Hohenfriedberg in 1745, which the Prussians won.

supervisors to maintain, since the kings not only paid their salaries but also equipped them with trappings appropriate to a representative of the king.

In Prussia, all government positions of high and middling rank were reserved for military personnel, which effectively excluded much of the traditional aristocracy from power. It also made the king's position all the more secure, since literally everyone who worked in his government received a salary directly from him. In return for their exclusion from government, the nobles received royal permission to reinstate serfdom (which had become largely obsolete by the end of the Middle Ages) on their estates.

SELF-INDULGENCE WITH A PURPOSE: THE EXAMPLE OF VERSAILLES

Expensive too were the grand building projects of the age. Palaces and churches decorated with baroque profusion arose by the score, year after year, as did lecture and concert halls, libraries and museums, scientific laboratories, and academies. Louis XIV, stung by rebellions and resistance in Paris, ordered construction of an immense palace complex at Versailles, 12 miles from the turbulent capital. Building began in the 1660s, but the project was so extensive that Louis and his court did not move from the Louvre to Versailles until 1682. And other rulers built their own imposing piles too.[3]

Versailles itself had been a small rural village of only a thousand inhabitants fifty years earlier. Louis's palace—known properly as the Château de Versailles—transformed the simple hunting lodge that had previously existed on the spot into a spectacularly vast edifice that housed the entire royal court. The château possessed well over a half-million square feet of floor space divided among seven hundred rooms, most of them magnificent. Thousands of paintings, drawings, sculptures, tapestries, and precious objects lined the walls and adorned every room. The effect on a first-time visitor is overwhelming—not so much for its genuine beauty as for the audacity of its grandeur.

Controlling the Nobles   Louis's decision to build a new home for his court was self-indulgent, but with a purpose. By creating a single space for the royal government and by demanding the constant attendance of France's aristocrats, Louis was able to keep an eye on the nobles and keep them under his sway. Louis never forgot that his reign had begun with an aristocratic rebellion against him. Called the **Fronde**, this rebellion (1648–1653) had not targeted Louis personally; the king was only ten years

---

[3]   Friedrich II of Prussia built the palace at Potsdam, just outside Berlin; Peter I of Russia built the vast Peterhof palace complex in the capital city he founded, St. Petersburg; the Habsburgs in Austria established the palace of Schönbrunn, just outside Vienna.

Versailles As awe-inspiring as it is, this image still shows only one-third of the palace built by Louis XIV to house his court. It was the seat of government from 1682 to 1789. Meant to show-case French culture, everything that went into building the palace was manufactured in France. The cost was beyond calculation. Even the chamber pots were made of silver—some of which Louis had to have melted and cast as coinage to help pay for his War of the League of Augsburg (1688–1697).

old when the trouble began.[4] Instead, the Fronde was a reaction against the royal finance minister Cardinal Jules Mazarin (1602–1661), the successor to Cardinal Richelieu, who had imposed a tax on judicial officials and sought to curtail a number of aristocratic privileges. It took five years to quell the rebellion, and Louis resolved to keep a constant watch over the nobles by requiring their presence under his own ornate new roof. To make his job easier, he had the palace lined with secret passages, one-way mirrors, and peepholes, and he maintained a large private staff to spy on the goings-on in every room. The Duc de Saint-Simon (1675–1755), whose keen-eyed *Memoirs* provides an irreplaceable view of life at court, summarized the key role of Versailles as a means of controlling the nobles:

> [Louis] loved splendor, grandeur, and opulence in everything and inspired similar tastes in everyone in his court, even to the point

---

[4]   *Fronde* is the French word for a slingshot—a favorite weapon of the Paris rebels, who used them to shatter the upper windows of the royal buildings.

where the surest way to earn a royal favor—perhaps the honor of receiving a word from him—was to spend extravagantly on something like a horse and carriage. . . . There was a sly political purpose in this, for by making conspicuously expensive habits the fashion at court (even making them a sort of requirement for people of a certain rank) he forced the members of his court to live beyond their means, which inevitably brought them to depend on royal favors in order to maintain themselves. But this [habit of indebtedness] turned out to be a plague that gradually infected the entire country, for in no time at all it spread to Paris, then to the army, and finally to the provinces, and now a man of any social standing at all is judged solely by the costliness of his daily habits and the extravagance of his luxuries. Such foolhardiness—the result of vanity and ostentation—has brought vast worry in its wake and threatens to result in nothing short of a national disaster and utter collapse.

This was prescient: the story of the French economy in the 18th century is one of constant and compounded indebtedness, a fiscal rot of staggering proportions that ultimately brought down the entire regime. For the present, however, the spending continued at an astonishing pace.

Louis XIV of France Louis ruled France for seventy-two years (r. 1643–1715), the longest reign in Western history. As the epitome of absolutist monarchy, he not only held sway over his kingdom but made France the leading state in Europe. This 1701 portrait by the French artist Hyacinthe Rigaud (1659–1743) shows the king at the height of his power. The curious draping of his royal robe is thought to be the result of royal vanity: Louis was widely reputed to be very proud of his shapely legs.

It is doubtful that Saint-Simon ever spoke so boldly to the king himself about the danger. A far braver man was François Fénelon (1651–1715), a Catholic priest appointed in 1689 as tutor to Louis XIV's grandson. As part of his teaching Fénelon composed a novel in 1694, *The Adventures of Telemachus*, which describes the travels and education of the son of the famed Greek king Odysseus. The novel mounts a stinging attack on the ideas of divine-right monarchy and absolutism. "Good kings are quite rare," it says at one point; "in fact, the majority of them are rather poor." It also denounces the pursuit of glory through war and the debilitating love of luxury. Fénelon's book became hugely popular across Europe and was translated into a half-dozen languages. Louis XIV hated it but recognized the good effect Fénelon's tutoring had on his grandson, a famously spoiled brat. Fénelon was brave enough to speak out in a 1694 letter to the king:

> Sire, for thirty years now Your ministers have broken every ancient law of this state, in order to increase Your power. They have infinitely increased both Your income and Your expenses, but in the process have impoverished all of France and have made Your name hated—all for the sake of the luxury of Your court. For the last twenty years these same ministers have turned France into an intolerable burden to her neighbors through bloody war. Wanting nothing but slaves, we now have no allies. And in the meantime, Your people are starving and rebellion is growing. You are thus left with only two choices: either to let the rebellion spread, or to resort to massacring the very people whom You have driven into desperation.

In 1696 Fénelon was appointed archbishop of Cambrai, but the following year was relieved of his position as tutor.

MERCANTILISM AND ABSOLUTISM

Supporting the absolutist regimes was a varied set of economic policies known collectively as **mercantilism**. For about 250 years, from roughly 1500 to 1750, this was the prevailing model for understanding and managing the economic life of northern Europe: England, France, and the Netherlands were the chief centers of mercantilist thinking, with Austria, Germany, Spain, and Sweden comprising a second tier. The Mediterranean economy also contained some mercantilist elements but was less dominated by them overall. Mercantilism, in general, defined economic wealth as tangible assets: the money in circulation, land and mineral resources, the available precious metals, the aggregate of physical goods that can be produced from nature's resources. Global wealth therefore is static. Since the Earth is not increasing in size, the amount of economically valuable material is fixed, and the aim of commerce is thus to maximize the amount of valuable assets in one's possession. The two most efficient means of doing so are to increase the amount of bullion in one's possession, either through mining precious metals or by appropriating the bullion of others, and to export more commercial goods than one imports. But either way, the world economy is a "zero-sum game"—meaning that one player's gain is equivalent to another player's loss. Wealth is thus a matter of distribution rather than creation.

Mercantilism in Theory

Mercantilism thus champions **protectionism**—the blocking of imports by tariff barriers, usually, and, if necessary, by law. The system, since it was based on the idea of artificially manipulating the distribution of

Mercantilism in Practice

wealth, also welcomed the awarding of monopolies by government (in return for sizable bribes and licensing fees), the fixing of prices and wages, the blocking of competition, and the imposition of high domestic taxes. In a world of finite wealth, the reasoning went, assets must be concentrated in a small number of hands. Only this could enable the grand expenditures such as those needed to defend the realm, administer the government, and maintain social order. Mercantilism, in other words, did not aim at the prosperity of an entire people, nor did it think that possible to achieve. Rather, its purpose was to concentrate wealth among as few individuals as possible. The absolutist regimes perfected their policies over the 17th and 18th centuries—and in the process drove their own subjects into the direst poverty. (It is worth pointing out, by way of illustration, that the economic policies of China in the late 20th and early 21st centuries likewise include many mercantilist elements.)

The classic statement in defense of mercantilism came from Thomas Mun (1571–1641), an English merchant and member of the board of directors of the English East India Company. He wrote *England's Treasure by Foreign Trade* in 1630, although it was not published until 1664. In it he argues, among other things, for the forced lowering of domestic wages. If the people of England cannot afford to purchase food, clothing, and other consumer goods, he points out, then the government will have larger amounts of those commodities available for export, which will bring more money into the royal purse.

Today we understand an economy to be an abstraction, an invisible system of interactions that more or less follows basic laws of the marketplace. In the early modern era, however, the idea of a system open to expansion or contraction was a foreign concept. Money, goods, land, and raw resources were things one could put in one's hand, feel the heft of, and know to be real. Producing, selling, and consuming goods are aspects of human agency, but the notion of "an economy" or "a market" as an autonomous thing that determines human action requires a conceptual leap, and few people in early modern Europe were capable of or interested in making such a leap. Merchants understood that a scarcity of goods—as when, for example, a drought results in decreased crop yields—meant that they could charge a higher price. However, they interpreted this not as a scientific "law of the market" but simply as a scenario they could exploit. When 16th-century Spain imported tons of gold bullion taken from the New World, the country expected to acquire enormous wealth. As we saw in chapter 14, what it got instead was an inflationary spiral unlike anything Europe had ever seen, the collapse of the currency, and the ruin of vast stretches of the peninsula. Compounding the problem, the Spanish rulers spent this money on a colossal scale—on palaces, museums, churches, artwork, and the army—rather than investing it in wealth-generating

Mercantilist Center   The town of Bristol was founded shortly before the Norman Conquest of 1066 and for a while was important chiefly as the launching place for English armies on their way to Ireland. The discovery of the New World raised its significance enormously, and by the 17th century Bristol was the second-largest and busiest port in the kingdom. Between 1600 and 1750 Bristol was the principal site from which English slave-traders shipped African slaves to the New World. This painting from around 1760 by an anonymous British artist shows the busy quay, where goods were loaded and unloaded.

industry.[5] But no one at the time, in Spain or elsewhere, would have agreed that there was any connection between the importation of New World precious metal and spiraling inflation. That, they would have insisted, makes as little sense as asserting that consumption of massive amounts of food could result in dramatic weight loss.

MERCANTILISM AND POVERTY

Mercantilism served two specific purposes. First, it generated impressive amounts of revenue for the leading merchants and financiers of the age, who benefited from monopolies, protectionist policies that banned foreign competition,

---

[5]   Spain did not fully recover as an economic power until the late 20th century.

and the relative decline of domestic markets—thanks to the poverty of the bulk of the population. With captive markets in overseas colonies, too, high prices could be demanded with impunity. Second, mercantilism produced enormous returns for the governments, which made money from bribes and monopoly licenses, high tariffs on imported goods, onerous taxation of the common people, and investment in the commercial activities of the leading mercantile firms. If mercantilism did not create prosperity for the nation, that was never its aim. All that mattered was the preservation of the state and the institutions it controlled.

Mercantilism had been at work in France and Spain since the 1530s, in England since the reign of Elizabeth I (r. 1558–1603), and in most of the rest of

Dutch Peasant Life   The Dutch painter Adriaen van Ostade (1610–1685) produced this 1647 etching of peasant life. The scene is less than idyllic but all the more realistic for that reason. Even in the Dutch Golden Age, most peasants lived hardscrabble lives.

Europe after 1648. Its effects were stark. In contrast to the baroque splendor of aristocratic palaces and ornate churches was the grinding poverty of the peasantry, village laborers, and local artisans and craftsmen. A French official's report on conditions among the rural populace of Normandy in 1651 paints a brutal picture:

> The most consistent food source here are the rats that the people hunt, so desperately hungry are they. They also eat plant roots that the farm animals will not touch. One can scarcely find words adequate to describing the horrors one sees everywhere. . . . This report, in fact, actually understates those horrors, rather than, as one might think, exaggerates them, for it describes only the tiniest fraction of the suffering in this district, suffering so dire that only those who have actually seen it can understand its scope. Hardly a single day passes in which at least two hundred people do not die. . . . I attest to having personally seen whole herds of people—men and women, that is, not cattle—wandering the fields between Rheims and Rethel, rooting in the dirt like pigs, and finding nothing edible, but only rotting fibers (and even these are only plentiful enough to feed half the herd), they collapse in exhaustion and have no strength left to continue searching for food. . . . The rest survive on a substitute for bread that does not deserve the name, made as it is from a mixture of chopped straw and dirt.

The question must be asked: Given such unspeakable suffering, why did people accept absolutist government—or at least not actively oppose it? The only answer is that things were even worse during the Wars of Religion. One can hardly exaggerate the bloody, murderous horror that plagued Europe before 1648.

DOMESTICATING DYNAMISM: REGULATING CULTURE

European culture, too, was subject to a form of absolutism, but not simply as an extension of royal power. The upper classes became obsessed with rule making and breaking. Rules of etiquette, standards of spelling and usage, norms for musical composition and visual art, academic curricula, domestic architecture, even the subtle social demands of fashion—all these multiplied under the pressure to conform. All came to express explicit standards of value, certainty, decorum, and taste. Such standards have existed in every age, but they have seldom dominated life as they did in Old Regime Europe.

The **baroque** style, which had emerged with the Catholic Counter-Reformation discussed in chapter 12, had emphasized dynamic energy and raw emotional power. Roughly half the paintings by Flemish artist Peter Paul Rubens

From the Baroque to Classicism

Ecstatic Divine Love   Gian Lorenzo Bernini (1598–1680) carved this ultimate statement of baroque sculptural style about 1650. St. Theresa of Avila was a Carmelite nun whose mystical revelations formed the backbone of her books of confessional and theological writings. Her best-known books are *The Way to Perfection, The Inner Castle,* and her absorbing autobiography. In this last book (actually the first one she wrote) she describes one of her visions, this one of a heavenly angel: "In his hand I saw a long spear of gold, from the point of which a small flame showed. It was as though he thrust it repeatedly into my heart, piercing my innermost parts; and whenever he pulled the spear out it was as though he drew my heart out as well, leaving me all on fire with love for God. The pain was so great it made me moan—and yet this great pain was so sweet that I wanted it never to end."

(1577–1640) glorify Catholic themes; most of the rest portray the magnificence of Europe's royals and high aristocrats. The great Spanish painter Diego Velázquez (1599–1660) likewise devoted roughly half of his output to portraits of the Spanish royal family, whereas the other half were split between Christian and classical themes.

In music, the baroque zenith was reached by the Italian father–son team of Alessandro (1660–1725) and Domenico Scarlatti (1685–1757), and Antonio Vivaldi (1678–1741). The Baroque Age in music experimented wildly with new forms of compositions, the most important being the cantata, oratorio, and opera—all of which combined vocal performance with instrumental accompaniment. One reason for the popularity of the cantata and oratorio was the fact that, by being largely musical settings of biblical verses, they could be played in Protestant and Catholic churches alike. Opera, in contrast, provided opportunities for a broader range of settings and themes; stories taken from classical literature were enduringly popular, but so too were operas drawn from contemporary drama and fiction. Most music lovers today rank Johann Sebastian Bach (1685–1750) as the greatest baroque composer. In his own time, however, this renowned German composer was considered just a good provincial musician, especially as an organist. A figure of *real* stature would have composed operas, which Bach refused to do.

Bach insisted that "all music should be for God" ("*Alle Musik soll für Gott sein*"). But as the baroque style spread across Europe, its focus shifted to glorifying the monarchies. What else stood between the people and Hobbesian chaos? The courts slowly replaced the dynamism of the baroque with the controlled

Camillus and the School of Falerii   This painting (ca. 1635) by the French master Nicolas Poussin (1594–1655) re-creates a famous scene in the history of the Roman Republic. Camillus was a great general who several times saved the early Republic from aggressors. In 396 BCE he led an army against the enemy cities of Veii and Falerii and defeated them. According to tradition, a schoolteacher from Falerii offered to hand over all the students in his care to Camillus, as slaves. Camillus instead ordered the schoolteacher to be executed as an example of the stern justice that a ruler must sometimes perform—a message likely to be approved of by the French court of Poussin's time.

formal tone of **classicism**. In the visual arts this was the age of Frenchmen Nicolas Poussin (1594–1665) and Charles Le Brun (1619–1690); in theater, of Spanish playwright Pedro Calderón de la Barca (1600–1681) and his French counterparts Pierre Corneille (1606–1684) and Jean Racine (1639–1699); in literature, of English writers John Milton (1608–1674) and John Dryden (1631–1700). The strictures of formal classicism eased in the 18th century, but the insistence on proper composition, content, and form continued.

The Absolutist Age also saw the first comprehensive dictionaries of the European languages. Bilingual dictionaries, the sort to help English speakers learn French, or vice versa, had existed since the invention of the printing press. But dictionaries as normative reference works for native speakers and writers were another matter altogether. Nearly two dozen hastily produced English dictionaries had been published between 1550 and 1750 in a rush to capitalize on the dramatic spread of literacy made possible by print. Only with

Regulating Language: The First Comprehensive Dictionaries

Samuel Johnson (1709–1784), however, was the extensive and definitive *Dictionary of the English Language* (1755) finally published.

Johnson's nine-year labor was a watershed event. A dictionary, after all, is a rulebook, one that asserts, for example, that the word *chair* is spelled C-H-A-I-R and in no other way—not chaar, chaire, chayr, chare, chaere, char, or any other phonetic estimation. Prior to the 17th century writers spelled words however they wished. As long as the reader understood what the writer was saying, what did it matter how individual words were spelled? (To date, for example, seven authentic signatures of William Shakespeare's have been found, and he spells his name differently each time.) A dictionary sets meanings and defines usage; it standardizes and regulates syntax. Johnson's *Dictionary* succeeded where earlier efforts had failed, and it remained authoritative until the publication of the complete *Oxford English Dictionary* in 1928. In France, a team of scholars produced the first installments of the *Dictionary of the French Academy* (*Dictionnaire de l'Académie Française*) in 1698, which did for the French language what Johnson did for English. The *Dictionary of the Academy "della Crusca"* (*Vocabolario degli Accademici della Crusca*) had appeared in Italy even earlier, in 1612, and the *Dictionary of the Spanish Language* (*Diccionario de la Lengua Española*) arrived in 1780.[6] The German language, by contrast, did not acquire a comparable dictionary until the Grimm brothers (of fairy-tale fame) published their *German Dictionary* (*Deutsches Wörterbuch*) in 1838.

THE CONTROL OF PRIVATE LIFE

Proper Manners

If language needed standardization and control, so much more did daily behavior. Norms of social behavior had long been determined by local custom. Books of etiquette date back to the Middle Ages, when treatises on "courtesie" were required reading for the higher nobility of the late 12th and 13th centuries. Generalized works of etiquette for the urban classes, however, became increasingly common in post-Westphalia Europe. Richard Brathwaite (1588–1673) published a trilogy of guides—*The English Gentleman, The English Gentlewoman*, and *Description of a Good Wife*—that established norms of behavior that lasted a hundred years; Boston schoolmaster Eleazar Moody's *The School of Good Manners* (1715) was an enormously popular guide for colonial parents who wanted to raise well-behaved children. In Italy, Baldassare Castiglione's *Il Libro del Cortegiano* (1528; in English as *The Book of the*

---

6   In Italian, *crusca* mean "bran." Hence the Academy of the Bran, metaphorically, was the institution that separated the bran (authentic and proper Italian words and usages) from the chaff (foreign words and corrupt usages).

Courtier in 1561) had established the norms for proper comportment in the Renaissance, but was overtaken in the 17th and 18th centuries by texts aimed at bourgeois society.

This is the society lampooned in the great comedy *The Middle-Class Gentleman* (*Le Bourgeois Gentilhomme*, 1670) by Molière (the pen name of Jean-Baptiste Poquelin, 1622–1673), whose very title is a part of the joke: a bourgeois commoner is attempting to behave with noble manners, as if one can become civilized by mimicking polite behavior! But a laughing matter in 1670 became serious business a generation later, as books on table etiquette, polite conversation, proper dress and comportment, and the rearing of well-behaved children grew in popularity. A French guide from 1729 helped explain the proper use of a new invention—the napkin[7]:

> When at table one ought always to use a napkin, plate, knife, spoon, and fork; in fact it is now considered to be utterly improper to be without any one of these.
>
> The proper thing is to wait until the highest-ranking dinner guest unfolds his napkin before unfolding one's own, but if everyone at table is a social equal, they should all unfold their napkins at the same time and without ceremony.
>
> It is poor manners to use the napkin to wipe one's face, and even poorer manners to wipe one's teeth; but the grossest behavior of all is to use the napkin to blow one's nose.

This text from 1729 signals change in its very title: *The Room: The Rules of Propriety and of*

Table Knife and Fork   Most Europeans had traditionally used only knives and spoons at table. Forks, though known since Roman times, were used only as kitchen tools, if at all. Renaissance Italy reintroduced the use of table forks, although it is unclear whether this resulted from the desire to emulate the Romans or to limit one's exposure to disease—since people attending dinners commonly carried their own knives and forks with them in a box. As a rule, the farther north and west from Italy, the slower the adoption of the fork. In Germany and England especially, forks were long considered effeminate affectations, and the people of the American colonies did not embrace them until the late 18th century. The knife and fork shown here were made in Germany in the 17th century.

---

7   Until the early 18th century, polite diners used the edges of the tablecloth to cover their laps and wipe their hands.

Christian Civility (La Salle: Les Règles de la Bienséance et de la Civilité Chrétienne).
And as for bodily comportment,

> Decency and modesty demand that one keeps covered all the parts
> of the body, except the head and hands, when in society. Moreover, one
> should take every care never to touch with one's bare hand any part of the
> body that must remain properly covered; if one absolutely must do so, it
> must be done with the greatest discretion. A polite person simply must
> become accustomed to suffering small discomforts without twisting,
> rubbing, or scratching. . . .
>
> When one needs to urinate, one should always withdraw to a private
> place—for it is permissible to perform natural functions (and this is true
> even for children) so long as one does it where one is not seen. It is never-
> theless altogether impolite to emit wind from one's body—either from
> below or above—even if it is done without any sound.

Contrast an English guide from 1619, written in verse:

> Let not your privy members be
> laid open to be viewed;
> it is most shameful and abhorr'd,
> detestable and rude.
> Retain not urine, nor the wind
> which do thy body vex;
> so [long as] it be done in secrecy,
> let that not thee perplex.

Guidebooks laid out rules for conversation, letter writing, dress, the issuing of invi-
tations, and behavior at occasions such as weddings, funerals, balls, and theaters.

Regulation reigned in other areas of life too. In music, most of the major com-
positional forms moved toward formal definition: fugues and sonatas initially
and eventually concertos and symphonies. Every opera had to have its text (li-
bretto) approved by state censors before it could be staged to make sure the plot
carried no subversive messages. Just as significantly, popular pressure gradually
demanded further norms in opera—such as the strict separation of comedy
(opera buffa) and tragic opera (opera seria), the use of plots from classical drama
or from French neoclassical theater, and the use of the Italian language.[8]

---

8 Women were forbidden to take the stage in regular theater productions. Opera, however, offered them the
   chance to perform alongside men.

The Teatro San Carlo in Naples   Built in 1737, then rebuilt after a fire in 1816, this is the oldest continuously used opera house in Europe. The original upholstery was blue; the red was installed after the fire. Seen at the center here is the royal box, where members of the Bourbon dynasty sat. It was designed specifically for the staging of operas, with the auditorium built in a U-shape and tiered; an orchestra pit, so as not to overwhelm the singers; and all the backstage areas and equipment needed for any theatrical production. Opera houses were expensive, and most of those built in the 17th and 18th centuries resulted from the patronage of royals and high aristocrats. The tiered balconies were the reserve of the upper classes, with the seats of the main floor opened to non nobles. Thus opera, by its very popularity, helped to maintain the social system by embodying the privileged hierarchy while allowing the commoners to share in the delight made possible by aristocratic largesse.

Aspects of domestic, even private, life became subject to innovative strictures, too. Societies were brought up on the idea of maintaining order at all costs. For most urban dwellers, living quarters by long tradition had been single open-space rooms above the workshop, tavern, or storefront in which they worked. The activities of private life were conducted communally. Over the 17th and 18th centuries, however, domestic architecture took on interior walls, even among those with modest incomes. The activities of daily life—sleeping, cooking and eating, tending to hygiene, and socializing—were to be performed in discrete rooms. It is no accident that the word *privacy* was coined in the 17th century; before then, neither the word nor the concept existed.[9]

The Birth of Private Life

Even the human body became subject to a kind of control. Common people throughout the Middle Ages and Renaissance had worn simple garments that

---

[9]   Shakespeare seems to have been the first person who used the word "privacy." It appears in his comedy *The Merry Wives of Windsor* and in his narrative poem *Troilus and Cressida*, both published in 1602.

sheathed the body, whereas the 17th and 18th centuries saw the general introduction of underwear of various types. Henceforth, everyday dress for both men and women involved undergarments—not just to provide warmth but also to support and control the body's movement. Regulations like these were not imposed by government but arose naturally in a culture that valued order above everything else.

As standards of expected behavior rose, manners improved, and aesthetic values became defined and codified. In turn, attitudes toward those who failed to observe the new niceties grew harsher. Aristocratic culture had always prided itself on the chasm that separated it from the dirty masses, but a sense of cultural elitism began to emerge among bourgeois Europeans at this time as well. As a result, efforts spread to instill better behavior among the lower orders, some of them altruistic, others not. Centuries-old peasant entertainments like carnivals (rural festivals that usually preceded Lent, the Christian season of fasting and penitence in preparation for the Easter celebration of Christ's resurrection) were discouraged from the pulpit and judicial bench alike. English Puritan ministers railed against the evils of taverns, dances, country fairs, and popular folk songs. Protestant ministers in Germany struggled to stamp out rural irregularities in communal worship.

In the cities, the urban poor were no longer objects of pity and almsgiving but were denounced in sermons, speeches, broadsides, and newspapers (another invention of the age) as lazy, deceitful, uncouth, and potentially dangerous. New institutions arose to deal with them: poorhouses, hospitals, and reformatories. These institutions performed the valuable services of removing the unsightly destitute from polite society and then either rehabilitating them by teaching them a craft or effectively imprisoning them. In 1676 Louis XIV went so far as to order every city in France to build and maintain a hospital for warehousing the worst off of the urban poor.

In England, people whose behavior violated basic norms but who had not broken the law frequently ended up in Bedlam. Although the hospital dates back to the 13th century, in 1675 it became the first asylum for the mentally ill.[10] The idea caught on, and asylums soon dotted the whole European landscape. So too did prisons. Prior to the 18th century, jails or dungeons were simply holding areas for those waiting until judicial punishment (execution, lashing, maiming, or a simple fine) was carried out. But after 1700 state after state preferred to remove criminals from society altogether, and lengthy incarceration became the punishment of choice. Those whose presence offended polite society became isolated, institutionalized, and removed from the scene.

---

[10] In 1725 Bedlam was divided into separate wings for those considered curable ("patients") and incurable ("lunatics").

ENGLAND'S SEPARATE PATH: THE RISE OF CONSTITUTIONAL MONARCHY

As we saw in chapter 14, England rose to the top tier of European nations in the second half of the 16th century. When Elizabeth I died in 1603, however, a constitutional crisis threatened to undo the internal stability of the realm and endangered England's position in the international economy. In response, the new Stuart dynasty asserted absolutist rule, but the effort ended in civil war. The causes of the English Civil War were similar to that of the Fronde in France: religious animosities, struggles for power among competing factions of aristocrats, and a fiscal system that could not keep pace with the increasing costs of government. But in England these conflicts led to the deposition and execution of a king, a radical experiment in representative government that quickly dissolved into autocratic rule and ultimately led to the establishment of a **constitutional monarchy** under conditions designed to safeguard Parliament's place in government, an arrangement that has endured to the present.

With the death of Elizabeth, who had never married, came the end of the Tudor dynasty. After some intrigue, the throne passed to James Stuart, the great-grandson of Henry VIII's sister. This marked the beginning of the trouble-plagued Stuart dynasty, which lasted, with interruptions, until 1714. Being Scottish, James I (r. 1603–1625) faced rude resistance from the start despite the legitimacy of his succession.[11] More than ethnic prejudice was at work in this, however, because James was a passionate advocate of royal absolutism. Before coming to power in England he had published a political treatise called *The True Law of Free Monarchies* (1598), in which he argued that since kingship existed "before any estates or ranks of men . . . [and] before any parliaments were held or laws made," it is therefore unnatural for a king's power to be checked in any way. Indeed, kings hold their authority by divine right. The argument is as weak as James's stubbornness was strong, and the struggle to balance royal ambitions and parliamentary rights ultimately characterized the history of the entire Stuart dynasty.

The Reign of James I

James restated his position in a speech to the English Parliament in 1610:

> The state of monarchy is the supremest thing upon earth, for kings are not only God's lieutenants upon earth and sit upon God's throne, but even by God himself they are called gods. There be three principal [comparisons] that illustrate the state of monarchy: one taken out of the word of God, and the two other out of the grounds of policy and philosophy. In the Scriptures kings are called gods, and so their power after a certain

---

[11]   James, who ruled as James VI in Scotland (r. 1567–1603), was the first to style himself the king of "Great Britain."

relation compared to the Divine power. Kings are also compared to fathers of families; for a king is truly *parens patriae*, the politic father of his people. And lastly, kings are compared to the head of this microcosm of the body of man. . . . I conclude then this point touching the power of kings with this axiom of divinity, that as to dispute what God may do is blasphemy . . . so is it sedition in subjects to dispute what a king may do in the height of his power.

Colossally vain, James I also had a tremendous fear of assassination. His childhood in Scotland had been filled with political deceits, palace intrigues, kidnappings, and murder plots.[12] The horror of his early years made him distrustful of those around him, and once in power in Edinburgh and London he resolved that institutions like parliaments, courts, and churches were mere service organizations of the monarchy rather than sharers of power. Although he had been raised a Catholic, James found that Anglicanism suited his self-regard because it identified the king as undisputed head of the church. His greatest achievement was his support for a new English translation of the scriptures intended specifically for his newly adopted church—the so-called King James Bible, known officially as the Authorized Version.

The seldom-read dedication to the King James Bible provides a good example of absolutist ideology. It begins,

> Great and manifold were the blessings, most dread Sovereign, which Almighty God, the Father of all mercies, bestowed upon us the people of England, when first he sent Your Majesty's Royal Person to rule and reign over us. For whereas it was the expectation of many who wished not well unto our Sion, that, upon the setting of that bright Occidental [western] Star, Queen Elizabeth, of most happy memory some thick and palpable clouds of darkness would so have overshadowed this land, that men should have been in doubt which way they were to walk, and that it should hardly be known who was to direct the unsettled State; the appearance of Your Majesty, as of the Sun in his strength, instantly dispelled those supposed and surmised mists, and gave unto all that were well affected exceeding cause of comfort; especially when we beheld the Government established in Your Highness and Your hopeful Seed, by an undoubted Title; and this also accompanied with peace and tranquility at home and abroad.

---

[12] In childhood, James had seen more than one family member cut down. He regularly wore a heavy dagger-proof tunic under his royal garments.

But among all our joys, there was no one that more filled our hearts than the blessed continuance of the preaching of God's sacred Word among us, which is that inestimable treasure which excelleth all the riches of earth; because the fruit thereof extendeth itself, not only to the time spent in this transitory world, but directeth and disposeth men unto that eternal happiness which is above in heaven.

Then not to suffer this to fall to the ground, but rather to take it up, and to continue it in that state wherein the famous Predecessor of Your Highness did leave it; nay, to go forward with the confidence and resolution of a man, in maintaining the truth of Christ, and propagating it far and near, is that which hath so bound and firmly knit the hearts of all Your Majesty's loyal and religious people unto You, that Your very name is precious among them: their eye doth behold You with comfort, and they bless You in their hearts, as that sanctified Person, who, under God, is the immediate author of their true happiness.

James fervently believed in mercantilism and followed its tenets to escape financial dependency on Parliament. Eager to increase English power in North America, he established the colonies at Jamestown (1607) and Plymouth (1620), in what would eventually become the states of Virginia and Massachusetts. He also tried, although unsuccessfully, to arrange a marriage between his son Charles and a Spanish princess. He awarded many monopolies and collected enormous licensing fees, which raised opposition from the gentry, but he compensated them by creating (and selling to the highest bidders, most of whom came from the gentry—wealthy commoners who had acquired landed estates, partially in an attempt to simulate the life of the aristocracy) an unprecedented number of new noble titles. James granted more than two thousand knighthoods, but the "baronetcy" was his signature invention: he happily bestowed this honor on anyone who would pay his asking

Divine Writ James I's greatest achievement was his support for a new English translation of the scriptures intended specifically for his newly adopted church— the so-called King James Bible, known officially as the Authorized Version.

price of ten thousand pounds. Many purchasers came forward. When James first came to the English throne in 1603 the House of Lords had fifty-nine members; when he died in 1625 the House had more than twice that number.

Civil War

When James's son Charles I (r. 1625–1649) became king, opposition to the Stuarts had grown to the point that Parliament openly demanded constitutional reforms. Charles had inherited his father's vanity and stubbornness, however, in addition to his titles, and had no intention of compromising royal prerogatives. Unfortunately for him, he also inherited England's involvement in the Thirty Years' War. Meeting commitments to numerous parties in that struggle placed ever-greater pressure on royal finances, but Parliament passed a Petition for Right (1628) that denied the crown additional taxes and restricted the king's judicial authority. The following year Charles summoned a new Parliament, immediately arrested nine of its leaders, and dissolved the assembly; no new Parliament met for eleven years, during which time Charles bullied new fees and levies from the provinces. By 1640 king and country were wholly estranged. When Charles, once more strapped for cash, did finally summon Parliament again later that year, the legislators prepared a "Grand Remonstrance"—a lengthy list of formal complaints about royal abuses of authority.[13] Charles's troops eventually stormed the Parliament but were resisted. England's Civil War (1642–1649) had begun.

The parliamentary forces were disorganized at first but soon came under the leadership of Oliver Cromwell (1599–1658), a strict Puritan in religion and a member of the gentry by social status. Without much military experience, he nevertheless rose quickly through the officer ranks. He was one of the three or four most powerful figures on the scene when the army defeated Charles in battle and took him prisoner in 1645. Few people wanted to abolish the monarchy altogether, and most hoped to force the king to some sort of compromise. When news came that Charles was in secret negotiations with Royalist sympathizers to launch a Scottish invasion of England, however, patience was at an end. Parliament placed Charles on trial for treason in 1648, and when the tribunal returned a guilty verdict, Cromwell was one of the signatories to the king's death warrant. Charles was publicly beheaded on January 30, 1649, the first time in history that a reigning king had been legally deposed and executed by his own government.

---

[13]   On the advice of the Anglican archbishop of Canterbury, William Laud (1573–1645), Charles tried to force the autonomous Protestant Church of Scotland into the mold of the Church of England—and got a Scottish invasion of England for his trouble. He needed funds for a defensive campaign; hence the new Parliament.

But the people who had opposed the monarchy soon found that, having removed the head of the state, they could not agree on a replacement. Dissension broke out almost immediately; after several tense weeks, Cromwell took over the government by general acclamation. Parliament declared England a Common-wealth, an English translation of the Latin *res publica*, and in 1653 Cromwell himself took the title of Lord Protector. But this radical experiment in representative government quickly dissolved into a thinly disguised Puritanical theocracy. New restrictions on Catholics (whom Cromwell hated) were instituted; the Anglican Book of Common Prayer was condemned. Cromwell's government forced the closing of theaters (places renowned for their encouragement of immoral life-styles, in the Puritans' judgment). On the other hand, he invited the Jews to return to England (they had been expelled in 1290 by King Edward I), in the hopes that their return would trigger the onset of the end of the world, as he believed was predicted in biblical prophecy. *Repression and Restoration*

Cromwell intended that his son should succeed him, but his death in 1658 only revived the prospect of civil war. With no one of Cromwell's energy and forcefulness to hold the kingdom together and with hostility between religious denominations so stirred up, fears arose that civil war was imminent. In 1660 a newly elected Parliament invited Charles I's exiled son, who had taken refuge in France and Holland, to return to England and restore the monarchy, as the only means to pacify and stabilize the realm. Charles II (r. 1660–1685), who has come down in English history as the "merry king" but in truth was as intelligent as carefree, agreed to certain limits on royal power and took the throne amid a general sense of celebration. After over a decade of government by dour Puritans, the people welcomed Charles's love of pleasure and laughter and his reopening of the theater houses closed under Cromwell.

But the party was short-lived. An outbreak of bubonic plague in 1665 and the Great Fire of London in 1666 destroyed much of the city and took tens of thousands of lives. Charles quickly adopted a more serious approach to his duties, although he never managed to keep his living expenses within the budget the Parliament had set for him. In 1672 he attempted to force through a royal declaration that removed all legal penalties from the practice of Roman Catholi-cism, but backed down when Parliament resisted. Doubts about Charles's own religious loyalty filled the rest of his years on the throne, fueled by his marriage to a Portuguese princess, Catarina de Bragança, who was unpopular with the English on account of her Catholicism and her lasting inability to learn English.

Charles had no legitimate heir, since his wife's pregnancies had all ended in miscarriages and stillbirths. On his death in 1685 the crown passed to Charles's brother James II (r. 1685–1688), who was openly Roman Catholic and determined *The Glorious Revolution* to introduce absolutism.[14] James's short reign was filled with dissension, since the Parliament refused to remove the legal strictures that limited Catholic rights. Even more worrisome was the new king's desire for a much larger standing royal army. England had traditionally never kept soldiers in uniform and on the public payroll during peacetime. James's proposal, moreover, appeared too much in line with the actions of the post-Westphalian monarchs across Europe and stirred the Parliament into dramatic action.

In 1688 a group of leading members of Parliament invited the Protestant ruler of Holland, Prince William of Orange, husband of James II's daughter Mary, to invade their realm and depose James, on the condition that they accept a bill of rights guaranteeing Parliament's full partnership in a constitutional government. William and Mary agreed. James initially thought he could defeat his daughter and son-in-law but soon realized otherwise, and so he fled the scene. He was soon captured by William's men, who, with William's consent, allowed him to escape to France—where he lived out his days in the court of Louis XIV. Since the coup proceeded without significant violence (James's soldiers deserted him en masse), it is known as England's **Glorious Revolution**. Without shedding a drop of blood, England had staged a successful revolution, brought down an unpopular monarch, and brought to power a popular royal couple dedicated to Protestantism and constitutional rule.

OTTOMAN ABSOLUTISM

Political developments farther east mirrored Continental Europe's trajectory into absolutist government; both the Ottoman and the Safavid empires increased the centralization of their administrations in the 16th and 17th centuries. Language and culture distinguished them as much as did political regimes. The Ottomans controlled the Arabic-speaking nations, and the Safavids governed the Persian speakers. Important religious distinctions existed as well, with Sunni Islam dominating among the Arab peoples and Shi'i Islam practiced by the bulk of Persian speakers. Although overwhelmingly Muslim, neither of these states was religiously monolithic because large Christian and Jewish populations continued to reside in them.

Measures to Maintain Power

Ottoman military encroachments on Europe had continued well into the 17th century, and, as we have seen, at least three times (1529, 1532, and 1683) their armies had advanced as far as Vienna. After 1683 the Turks were put on the

---

[14]   Charles II was received in the Roman Catholic Church on his deathbed. James II had formally converted to Catholicism while growing up on the Continent during Cromwell's rule.

defensive for the first time in their history, a position exacerbated by the ascendancy of European merchant fleets in the Indian Ocean (see Map 15.2). Since they had previously lost control of the eastern Mediterranean at the battle of Lepanto in 1571 (discussed in chapter 14), the new setbacks occasioned two new developments for the Turks. First, they gradually relinquished control over the farthest provinces of their empire—Morocco and Algiers, along the North African coast (called the Berber, or Barbary, Coast by Europeans), which henceforth became independent states.[15] Second, the Ottomans delegated more power to provincial governors, with a system of tax farming that assigned local fiscal control to leading families. These steps were not, however, a complete capitulation of authority. Turkish autocracy had always differed from European absolutism in a fundamental way. Since the 15th century the monopoly of power was held by the dynastic house of Osman rather than by any specific individual. The sultan in Istanbul, as leader of the royal family, held primacy of place over his relatives, but power was rightfully held by every representative of Osman's line. The empire's system of government was therefore an oligarchical absolutism, but was no less absolutist for that.

Like that of its Western contemporaries, Ottoman absolutism was based on military might. The most important component of the army was the large corps of Janissaries (introduced in chapter 11). These "new soldiers" (the literal meaning of the Turkish word *yeniçeri*) were formed of Christian children from the Balkans and the Caucasus who, under the practice of *devşirme,* were stolen from their families, forcibly converted to Islam, and pushed into military service— just as had been the practice centuries before with the Mamluk slave-soldiers. They were sworn to celibacy during their years in the army, granted pensions and the right to marry on retirement, and accorded exceptionally high social status. By the 17th century civil government was largely dominated by former Janissaries. At that time too the traditional practice of *devşirme* was abolished, as ethnically Turkish families sought to place their own children in the corps in hopes of social and political advancement. Given the relative decrease in their military activity after 1683, the Janissaries were increasingly used (again like their European counterparts) as domestic police forces. In this role they

---

[15]   To resist Spanish dominance in the western Mediterranean, these new states encouraged the "Barbary pirates" to attack ships on either side of the Strait of Gibraltar. More than money, the Barbary pirates sailed in search of Christians they could abduct and enslave. Men were taken as galley slaves; women and girls, after forced conversions to Islam, were sold as slaves to restock wealthy figures' harems; and the boys, similarly Islamized, were destined chiefly for military service. By 1700 more than a million men, women, and children had been captured and enslaved.

MAP 15.2 The Ottoman Empire in 1683 In early modern times the Ottomans developed one of the world's most extensive and lasting empires. What held the hugely diverse Ottoman Empire together was its flexible bureaucratic structure, which frequently rewarded faithful conquered subjects and allowed loose tributary arrangements at the fringes.

maintained order, quelled revolts, and represented the ever-watchful eye of the sultan and his family.

PERSIAN ABSOLUTISM

As we know from chapter 14, the Safavid dynasty in Persia had been established in 1501, with Shi'ism proclaimed the state religion. The Safavids had emerged from a heterodox Sufi order and regarded themselves as either the earthly representatives of the Shi'i hidden imam or the hidden imam himself. Given their religious origins, they were not likely to recognize any checks on their power—an analog to European notions of divine-right monarchy. To be prudent, from their capital at Isfahan (roughly 100 miles south of today's Iranian capital of Tehran), they complemented the religious basis of their claims to absolute authority by relying on the unwavering support of a large and potent army. Most of their army was composed of regular infantry units that served only as needed. More significant for maintaining the regime was a unique network of militant units known collectively as the *Qizilbash* (meaning "crimson" or "red-headed"). These companies—identifiable by the distinctive red-topped headpieces they wore (and from which they take their name)—regarded the Safavid ruler as divine. So great was their zeal that the Qizilbash customarily went into battle without any type of defensive armor. They were convinced that Allah and their Safavid lord's blessing would protect them from harm.[16]

Under the greatest Safavid shah, Abbas I (r. 1587–1629), the Persians recaptured Baghdad and established commercial ties with both the British and the Dutch East India Companies. Baghdad had never fully recovered from the devastation wreaked on it by the Mongols and may have held as few as fifty thousand people. An elaborate irrigation network had made the river valleys fertile since Sumerian times. Now that too lay in ruins, and most of Iraq had become a patchwork of scrubby pastoral zones loosely but violently controlled by rival tribes. But Baghdad itself still mattered as a forward defensive position against a renewed Ottoman offensive. Friendly ties with the East India Companies were vital, since conflicts over control of the sea-lanes had shifted commercial routes away from the Persian Gulf and toward the Red Sea, on the other side of the Arabian peninsula. The shift threatened to cost the Iranians considerable revenue.

Like the European monarchs, the shahs centralized their nation's wealth as much as they did its political power, and they spent as lavishly on themselves as

---

[16] The Qizilbash still exist as a distinct religious community in Afghanistan, Azerbaijan, Iran, and Pakistan. The third president of modern-day Pakistan, Agha Yahya Khan (1969–1971), was Qizilbash.

did Louis XIV. Magnificent palaces, pleasure gardens, libraries, astronomical observatories, and public adornments filled the cities. They built mosques and madrasas by the dozen and restored older centers of worship that had been damaged during the Mongol and Tatar years. In Iraq the holy shrines in the cities of Karbala and Najaf—dear to the Shi'a—were rebuilt and again became important sites of

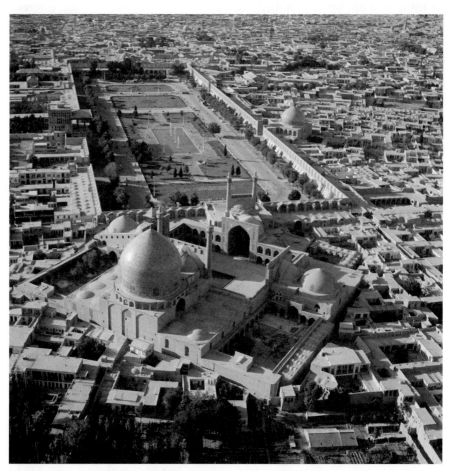

Isfahan Isfahan, in central Iran, was the capital of Safavid Persia from 1598 to 1736. Located on a high plain just east of the Zagros Mountains, its steep elevation—comparable to that of Denver, in the United States—makes for chilly winters and hot summers. Shown in this image is the Shah Mosque, built in 1611 and considered one of the great masterpieces of Persian architecture. The large square behind it (the Naqsh-e Jahan Square) was built to serve a purpose similar to that of the Château de Versailles—that is, it housed all the Safavid rulers' leading nobles and ministers of state, keeping them all in his direct sight. The mosque itself comes off the square at a unique angle, so that the towering entrance arch (called an *iwan*) and the central dome can both be seen from everywhere in the square. Visible to the right of the great dome is a smaller, lower dome that marks the "winter mosque"—a smaller, warmer site for use during the cold winters.

pilgrimage. Abbas II (r. 1642–1666) extended his realm northward into Afghanistan, taking the strategic city of Kandahar from the Mughal Empire in India, and ruled over a thriving and peaceable realm.

But the later Safavids gave in to the pleasures of their lavish lifestyle and spent more time enjoying themselves than governing, which led to the dynasty's *Rise of the* downfall in 1736. Decades of turmoil ensued until, in 1796, a new Persian dy- *Qajar* nasty took over—the Qajar—which held absolute power over Iran until 1925. *Dynasty* The founder of the new dynasty, Mohammad Khan Qajar (r. 1794–1797), had been castrated as a young boy by a rival for leadership of the Qajar tribe, an experience that likely contributed to his predilection for extreme cruelty and violence.[17] Mohammad was killed himself in 1797 by household servants whom he had ordered to be executed; after his assassination the Qajar shahs focused resolutely on maintaining their political power and the wealth that made it possible.

Yet they also distanced themselves from the theocratic ideology of the Safavids. Religious and legal authority thus devolved from the court-appointed officials (*qadis*) of earlier times to the caste of scholars in shari'a law produced by the madrasas. In the case of Shi'i Islam, these were predominately clerics who held the title of **mullah** ("guardian"—a position roughly analogous to a Jewish rabbi). Leadership of the mullahs fell to a higher office still, the **ayatollah** ("sign from God," literally). By 1800, Iran had evolved into a dual absolutist state: political and military might was monopolized by the secular state under the autocratic control of the shah, whereas religious authority remained the preserve of an elite corps of mullahs led by their clerical superiors, the ayatollahs.

INTERNATIONAL TRADE IN A MERCANTILIST AGE

Absolutist Europe and constitutional England formed the center of a vast network of international trade (see Map 15.3). It proved a hybrid of commercial, colonial, mercantilist, and capitalist practices. It also turned on new markets, sustained by slavery and domestic labor.

Starting with Sweden in 1664, Europe's leading countries created royal or national banks that quickly developed systems of credit to finance manufacturing, commerce, and development. Strict mercantilism demanded the use of

---

[17]   Mohammad once ordered the blinding of twenty thousand men in a city that resisted his authority. He also had the Georgian city of Tbilisi burned to the ground and its entire Christian population put to death in 1795.

MAP 15.3 World Trade Networks, ca. 1750   One of the most significant developments of the modern period was the permanent linking of the world's regions through trade networks.

precious-metal coins, and aristocratic Europe's demand for Asian luxury goods never abated. Hence there was a continuous drainage of gold and silver from *National Banks* the West, which led to the introduction of paper money. Released from *and Investment* dependence on actual bullion, the new national banks dramatically in-*Opportunities* creased loans, bonds, and other opportunities to invest. Credit now became available "on account," as promises to repay. National stock exchanges soon followed. Joint-stock companies like the British East India Company, the Dutch East India Company, and the South Sea Company benefited from the influx of investments. Their charters granted them monopolies on certain manufactures and trades, which allowed many to build impressive long-term returns. But investment opportunities were limited to those with excess capital, or wealth to invest, which was still a small percentage of the population. Mercantilist practices kept most laborers' wages at rock-bottom levels, and price controls and domestic taxes kept most skilled draftsmen from setting aside investment capital. As a result, most of the benefits of the international economy went to a small number of investors.

Investment was a new concept. The idea behind it—that capital itself, not people, can *do work*—is an abstraction that few fully understood. In purchasing stock, one is not buying a good or service, but rather the right to share in the profit generated by the future production and sale of those goods or services. Moreover, it takes money to produce goods and services, which usually means borrowing. In purchasing stock, one is also purchasing a share of a company's debt. Elaborate legal and financial arrangements can equally beguile and confuse those entering the investment market. The combination led frequently to speculative schemes, or "bubbles," that ruined thousands of investors.

The most famous crash was the South Sea Bubble of 1720. The South Sea *South Sea* Company had been formed in London in 1711 to trade with the Spanish colonies *Bubble* in North America. To finance its activities, the company purchased England's national debt (then some 50 million pounds, a substantial amount) in return for the right to exchange government bonds for shares in the company. Bondholders who despaired of the government's ability to redeem its bonds were thrilled by the possibility of New World riches and rushed to invest in the company. Soon a wave of speculation drove share prices to unprecedented heights, and the company encouraged the buying frenzy. It announced ever-more spectacular ventures that it intended to undertake, like the manufacture of a (nonexistent) machine that could remove salt from seawater—not to mention an ultrasecret "undertaking of great profit in due time to be revealed." Shares rose from 150 pounds each to more than 1,000 pounds before the inevitable crash came and investors were wiped out.

THE SLAVE TRADE AND DOMESTIC SUBJUGATION

Far more reliable investments than shares in the South Sea Company were New World agriculture and the slave trade that enabled it. Until the 19th century, when settlers moved westward across the Great Plains, the New World did not produce food for export. Crops like potatoes, beans, and corn (maize) had already been introduced into European farming and consequently were not shipped across the Atlantic.

But sugar cane, cotton, and tobacco did not grow well in Europe. Being non- *the Slave* perishable, they could also be transported overseas to generate enormous profits, *Trade*

Height of

but they were labor-intensive crops. The need for slaves thus grew, as did the demand for the crops they produced. Throughout the 18th century between 75,000 and 100,000 African slaves were shipped across the Atlantic annually, until the slave trade was finally abolished (by France in 1793, England in 1807). Exact accounting is impossible, but somewhere around 12 million sub-Saharan Africans were brought to the New World in chains. The greatest number of them went to the Caribbean islands, where they perished in horrifying numbers while working the sugarcane fields. Roughly a half-million were sent to what eventually became the American South (see Map 15.4).

The profits generated by slave-produced New World agriculture were enormous. England's colonial profits rose from 10 million pounds to 40 million pounds between 1700 and 1776. France saw its revenues increase from 15 million to 250 million *livres* in the same period. But the profits of the era were not distributed throughout society; they went to the highest social strata. Domestically, the rural economy was a ruin. As much as 20 percent of the European population lived in abject poverty.

Alcoholism and Disease   The introduction of maize and potatoes alleviated famine in Europe, but also raised a new danger—alcoholism. Crops no longer needed for food could be converted into distilled spirits, which provided the poor with an escape from the dreariness and hardship of their lives. Before, liquor distillation had primarily been a secret of monasteries. By now, however, the Protestant Reformation had advanced the knowledge of distillation across Europe. Gin became the hard liquor of choice among the poor, since it was so plentiful and cheap. By 1740, in England, gin production was nearly six times the nation's beer production— and all of it was drunk locally. The city of London alone had more than six thousand gin shops, which sold cheap gin in bottles with rounded bottoms (to encourage buyers to drain the entire bottle, lest they risk a spill on setting it down). When the government in 1736 tried to reduce consumption by imposing a heavy tax on gin, crowds took to the street by the thousands until they won a repeal of the tax.[18]

Those poor not killed off by drink often succumbed to disease, since the physical conditions in which the poor lived were appalling. In the district of Brittany, in northwestern France, dysentery killed 100,000 people in a single year (1779). Until about 1750, only one-half of all European children born lived to the age of ten, and only one-half of the females who made it to their tenth birthday

---

[18]   As liquor became a favorite item for governments to tax, people operated their private stills at night, so that the smoke produced would not be seen. That is why homemade liquor is known as *moonshine*. This usage of the word first appeared in 1782 in a London magazine.

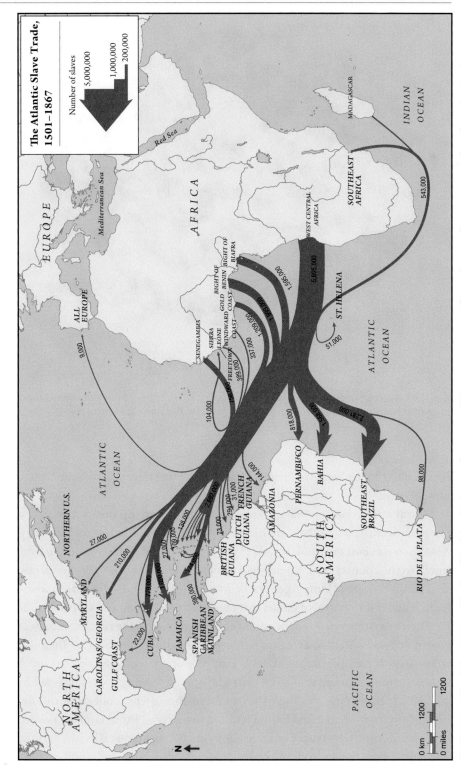

MAP 15.4 **The Atlantic Slave Trade** The Atlantic slave trade connected European ports to African slave-trading outposts and to plantations in the Caribbean, South America, and North America. The European countries bordering the Atlantic Ocean benefited most from this trade.

Cottage Industry In this example of cottage industry, an Irish family beats flax in order to expose the fibers contained within; once cracked open, the flax fibers are then soaked in water, removed, and spun by hand into linen thread.

survived until their fortieth. Pregnancy and childbirth were a death sentence for most of them.

Cottage Industry

Rural women became wage earners through the **putting-out system** of textile manufacture, which became increasingly widespread in the 18th century. Also known as **cottage industry**, this system transferred cloth production from towns to the countryside. Women had woven cloth for their families for centuries, but in the late Middle Ages textile production had shifted to cities, where it came under the control of guilds that regulated production and set prices. The putting-out system returned the center of cloth making to the rural economy, as new merchants sought to avoid the urban guilds and improve profits. These entrepreneurs typically purchased bulk quantities of raw wool and cotton, which they distributed throughout rural districts, often following routes claimed by competing entrepreneurs. Then they retraced their steps, collecting the finished cloth from women and taking it to urban markets. Rural families needed this work desperately. Wages remained low, but by assigning tasks like carding or spinning to their children, countrywomen were able to produce more finished cloth. Once redeemed, it often made the difference between life and death.[19]

THE RETURN OF UNCERTAINTY

Given the miseries of the age, the passivity of the people in the face of the excesses of absolutist society is striking. Even the most dramatic political action, like England's civil war and revolution, was undertaken by bourgeois and aristocratic factions. The underclass had seldom known prosperity and independence—and so had grown not to expect them. Disruptions could still spark them into action, as rebellions like the German Peasants' Revolt of 1524–1525 showed. Yet as long as absolutism kept the peace, as it generally did between 1648 and 1700, peasants complained of their lot but seldom rose up against it.

The reappearance of warfare after 1700 added just the uncertainty, insecurity, and violence needed to trigger mass unrest. First came the War of the Spanish Succession (1701–1714). When King Charles II, the last Habsburg king of Spain, died without an heir in 1700, France's Louis XIV and Austria's Leopold I—each of whom was married to a sister of Charles—greedily eyed the Spanish crown and its enormous overseas empire. Charles's will had named an heir to the throne: the grandson of his sister, the closest male relative available. But Louis hoped to win the crown for himself before the young man, Philip V, took power. Louis consequently invaded Spain; he also invaded the Spanish Netherlands, which brought him into a parallel war with England. The English army at this time was led by a career soldier named John Churchill, who defeated Louis's forces and brought the islands of Gibraltar and Menorca, plus France's New World territories of Newfoundland and Hudson's Bay, into England's possession.[20]

War of the Spanish Succession

A subsequent conflict was the War of the Austrian Succession (1740–1748), which arose when ambitious outsiders challenged Maria Theresa's succession to the throne because Salic law precluded royal inheritance by a woman. Several countries joined in this fray, less to advance claims of their own than to do anything they could to weaken the Habsburg family in general.

War of the Austrian Succession

But the largest and most devastating conflict of the age was the **Seven Years' War** (1756–1763), which pitted Great Britain, Brandenburg–Prussia, and some smaller German principalities against an alliance of Austria, France, Russia, Saxony, and Sweden (see Map 15.5). This last war arose, in general, in response to the changes made to the Westphalian "balance of power" by the earlier two

The Seven Years' War

---

[19]   Cloth was the leading commodity in this system, but not the only one. Leatherwork, soap and candle making, and even metalwork formed part of the cottage economy too.

[20]   His achievement resulted in his being created the 1st Duke of Marlborough, which raised the Churchills to the status of one of England's greatest noble families.

MAP 15.5   The Seven Years' War   In what historians often term the first worldwide war, the French and British fought each other in Europe, the West Indies, North America, and India. Skirmishing in North America helped to start the war, which became more general when Austria, France, and Russia allied to check Prussian influence in central Europe. The treaty between Austria and Prussia restored the status quo in Europe, but the changes overseas were much more dramatic. Britain gained control over Canada and India and was now the dominant naval power.

conflicts. England claimed that France was in illegal possession of numerous territories in North America and took preemptive action by seizing several of the disputed lands and a large number of French merchant vessels. Fast-militarizing Prussia, meanwhile, resented Austrian–Hungarian power in eastern Europe and provoked hostilities by forming an alliance with England. At this point, other kingdoms got involved, joining or forming new coalitions to try to maintain (or, in the case of Russia, to disrupt) the "balance of power" on the Continent. The result was seven years of Continent-wide war (1756–1763).

Together, these wars produced horrendous casualties. The Seven Years' War alone resulted in more than a million deaths. Cannon-fed sieges of cities and organized campaigns of arson marked the conflicts. Roused by the vast ruin of the countryside, the disruption of trade, the wasted expenditure, and the callous abuse of the peasantry, popular voices began to rise up and to demand change. Bread riots, calls for peace, and complaints over endless governmental deficits arose across Europe. Demonstrations against the treatment of the many by the very, very few erupted from Ireland to Austria and from Sicily to Sweden. The Treaty of Paris (1763) ended the immediate conflict by a complex formula of land reallocations, but few realms felt secure.

◆

Surely something could be done to restore order. As the century progressed, new voices arose, voices dedicated to the idea that change was possible, necessary, and within reach. The world was a dark place that needed new light and hope.

WHO, WHAT, WHERE

absolutism	Fronde	protectionism
ayatollah	Glorious Revolution	putting-out system
baroque	Louis XIV	Seven Years' War
classicism	mercantilism	social contract
constitutional	mullah	
monarchy	Peace of Westphalia	
cottage industry	Peter I	

SUGGESTED READINGS

Primary Sources

Bodin, Jean. *Six Books on a Commonwealth.*

Fénelon, François. *The Adventures of Telemachus.*

Hobbes, Thomas. *Leviathan.*

Molière. *The Middle-Class Gentleman.*

Richelieu. *Political Testament.*

Saint-Simon. *Memoirs.*

Tocqueville, Alexis de. *The Ancien Régime and the French Revolution.*

Anthologies

Beik, William. *Louis XIV and Absolutism: A Brief Study with Documents* (2000).

Gregg, Stephen H., ed. *Empire and Identity: An Eighteenth-Century Sourcebook* (2005).

Helfferich, Tryntje, ed. and trans. *The Thirty Years War: A Documentary History* (2009).

Wilson, Peter H., comp. *The Thirty Years War: A Sourcebook* (2010).

Studies

Anderson, Fred. *Crucible of War: The Seven Years' War and the Fate of Empire in British North America, 1754–1766* (2000).

Beik, William. *A Social and Cultural History of Early Modern France* (2009).

Bennett, Martyn. *Oliver Cromwell* (2006).

Bergin, Joseph. *Church, Society, and Religious Change in France, 1580–1730* (2009).

Brewer, John. *The Pleasures of the Imagination: English Culture in the 18th Century* (2013).

Brewer, John. *The Sinews of Power: War, Money, and the English State, 1688–1783* (2014).

Casale, Giancarlo. *The Ottoman Age of Exploration* (2010).

Clark, Christopher. *Iron Kingdom: The Rise and Downfall of Prussia, 1600–1947* (2006).

Cracraft, James. *The Revolution of Peter the Great* (2006).

Dale, Stephen F. *The Muslim Empires of the Ottomans, Safavids, and Mughals* (2010).

Fowler, William M., Jr. *Empires at War: The Seven Years' War and the Struggle for North America, 1754–1763* (2005).

Harris, Tim. *Revolution: The Great Crisis of the British Monarchy, 1685–1720* (2006).

Hufton, Olwen. *Europe: Privilege and Protest, 1730–1788* (2001).

Hughes, Lindsey. *Russia in the Age of Peter the Great* (2000).

Ingrao, Charles. *The Habsburg Monarchy, 1618–1815* (2000).

Jones, Colin. *The Great Nation: France from Louis XV to Napoleon, 1715–99* (2003).

Levi, Anthony. *Louis XIV* (2004).

Linebaugh, Peter. *The London Hanged: Crime and Civil Society in the Eighteenth Century* (2006).

Martinich, A. P. *Hobbes* (2005).

Matthee, Rudolph P. *The Politics of Trade in Safavid Iran: Silk for Silver, 1600–1730* (2006).

Newman, Andrew J. *Safavid Iran: Rebirth of a Persian Empire* (2008).

Ormrod, David. *The Rise of Commercial Empires: England and the Netherlands in the Age of Mercantilism, 1650–1770* (2003).

Prak, Maarten. *The Dutch Republic in the Seventeenth Century: The Golden Age* (2005).

Quataert, Donald. *The Ottoman Empire, 1700–1822* (2000).

Rowlands, Guy. *The Dynastic State and the Army under Louis XIV: Royal Service and Private Interest, 1661–1701* (2002).

Smith, Jay M. *Nobility Reimagined: The Patriotic Nation in Eighteenth-Century France* (2005).

Streusand, Douglas E. *Islamic Gunpowder Empires: Ottomans, Safavids, and Mughals* (2010).

Szabo, Franz A. J. *The Seven Years' War in Europe, 1756–1763* (2007).

Wheatcroft, Andrew. *The Enemy at the Gate: Habsburgs, Ottomans, and the Battle for Europe* (2009).

Whisenhunt, William B., and Peter Stearns. *Catherine the Great: Enlightened Empress of Russia* (2006).

Zagorin, Perez. *Hobbes and the Law of Nature* (2009).

For additional resources, including maps, primary sources, visuals, web links, and quizzes, please go to **www.oup.com/us/backman**.

CHAPTER 16

The Enlightened

1690–1789

The **Enlightenment** is a term coined in the second half of the 18th century to describe an array of intellectual and cultural activities of the 1700s. Most of these new ideas and pursuits, although not all of them, aimed to improve European life by setting its economic, political, religious, and social developments along paths dictated by reason and critical inquiry, rather than by tradition and faith. The **philosophes**—as the Enlightenment writers came to call themselves—both continued and broadened the Scientific Revolution by carrying over the scientific method of inquiry from the functioning of the natural world to that of the human one.[1] Their subject might be the mechanics of absolutist government, the growth of legal traditions, the development of moral codes, the workings of a national economy, or the functioning of the human mind or heart. Any field of human endeavor, when examined rationally, could be understood; and anything that could be understood could be improved.

THE GREATER WEST IN THE ENLIGHTENMENT

Enlightened Debate Moritz Daniel Oppenheim (1800–1882) painted this scene in which he imagines a gathering of Moses Mendelssohn (1729–1786), Gotthold Ephraim Lessing (1729–1781), and Johann Kaspar Lavater (1741–1801). As far as we know, this meeting never took place, but Mendelssohn was friends with both men. The painting represents the hoped-for harmony between Jews (Mendelssohn, in red), Christians (Lavater, in dark green), and secularists (Lessing, standing) that the Enlightenment tried to achieve.

---

[1] The term *philosophe* (French for "free thinker") came into general use during the 1740s. Before then, the writers preferred to call themselves *les Lumières* ("the Enlightened Ones").

At least it seemed that way for the first great figures of the Enlightenment, including John Locke (1632–1704), Pierre Bayle (1647–1706), Denis Diderot (1713–1784), and Adam Smith (1723–1790). And improvement was needed on all fronts. The suffering and uncertainty caused by the Seven Years' War made plain to Europe's intellectuals the moral bankruptcy of the Old Regime and the danger of arbitrary, unchecked authority. As people lost faith in the stability supposedly represented by absolutism, a new set of values emerged as the necessary bases for civil society: the importance of law, the fundamental dignity of human life, the need for freedom of thought, the value of religious toleration, the supremacy of reason over tradition and superstition. For different reasons, Voltaire (1694–1778) and Jean-Jacques Rousseau (1712–1778) pursued more skeptical approaches to Europe's value crisis—skepticism that they often directed at each other. Many Jewish writers saw the Enlightenment as an opportunity to secure a new place in European society. The leading Jewish philosophe, Moses Mendelssohn (1729–1786), confidently believed that the new values of the Enlightened could bring about civil harmony between Christians and Jews.

In the face of widespread poverty and its consequences, however, the Enlightenment had uncertain answers, and assessing its impact is by no means simple. The Enlightened writers and publicists had widely varying interests but also widely varying aims. Historians have traditionally emphasized the role of the reformist wing of the movement, those figures who wanted to address abuses and

CHAPTER TIMELINE

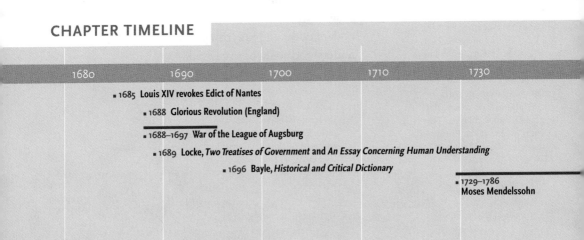

1680	1690	1700	1710	1730

- 1685 Louis XIV revokes Edict of Nantes
- 1688 Glorious Revolution (England)
- 1688–1697 War of the League of Augsburg
- 1689 Locke, *Two Treatises of Government* and *An Essay Concerning Human Understanding*
- 1696 Bayle, *Historical and Critical Dictionary*
- 1729–1786
  Moses Mendelssohn

excesses within existing society and government but without fundamentally replacing either. Another wing of the movement, however, was significantly more radical and sought either the destruction or the wholesale replacement of the values and institutions of the time. Whether moderate or radical, the men and women of the Enlightenment carried out the first major reform effort in centuries that aimed not to reestablish a supposed "golden age" of the past but to envision and create a wholly new world based on original ideas, practices, and values. They were, as a group, the most self-confident thinkers since the scholastic writers of the 13th century.

THE ENLIGHTENMENT ENTERPRISE

How could they be otherwise? Newton had proven that the universe is massively complex but rationally constructed; it functions according to a coherent system of natural laws. If the rational mind can decipher the workings of the universe, how hard could it be to figure out the supposed mysteries of human activity and behavior? Why not develop new modes of action that are more in accord with rational principles? And how could such a scheme fail to bring about a better and more progressive world, one stripped of contradiction, idiocy, superstition, and intolerance? The work of the philosophes, in the words of their greatest German representative, Immanuel Kant (1724–1804), would help humanity to grow "out

| 1740 | 1750 | 1760 | 1770 | 1780 |

- 1748 Montesquieu, *The Spirit of Laws*

- 1748–1793 Olympe de Gouges

- 1751–1772 Diderot, *Encyclopedia*

- 1759–1797 Mary Wollstonecraft
- 1762 Rousseau, *The Social Contract*
- 1764 Voltaire, *Philosophical Dictionary;* Beccaria, *of Crimes and Punishments*
- 1776 Smith, *The Wealth of Nations*
- 1779 Lessing, *Nathan the Wise*

of its self-inflicted immaturity." Its immaturity results from man's failure "to use his own rational intelligence instead of being led along by someone else. . . . Dare to learn! Anyone who persists in this immaturity, whether out of laziness or cowardice, makes it easy for others to think and act for him." These lines come from Kant's classic 1784 essay, "What Is Enlightenment?" The first stirrings of the movement arose in the 1690s, but its heyday was from 1740 to the outbreak of the French Revolution in 1789.

The philosophes did not pursue ideas for their own sake; a pragmatic impulse drove the whole enterprise. Their writings show the wide range of their interests as well as the sharpness of their wit. Consider just a sampler:

> From fanaticism to barbarism is but a single step.
> What a delightful comedy this world would be, if only we played no part in it.
>
> —*Denis Diderot*

> Generally speaking, errors in religion are dangerous; those in philosophy only ridiculous.
>
> —*David Hume*

> We call some actions vices simply because they are performed by ugly people.
> A book is a mirror: if an ass peers into it, don't expect an Apostle to peer back out.
>
> —*Georg Christoph Lichtenberg*

> [An author is] a fool who, not content with boring everyone around him during his lifetime, insists on boring generations yet to come.
>
> —*Baron de Montesquieu*

> As long as he is not actually insane, a man can be cured of every folly except vanity.
> Those who are slowest to make promises are those who keep them most faithfully.
>
> —*Jean-Jacques Rousseau*

> Theology amuses me so. In it we see human insanity at its fullest.
> [Optimism] is an obsession with saying "All is well" even when one is in Hell.
>
> —*Voltaire*

With a few exceptions—Kant and Scottish writer David Hume (1711–1776), most notably—their knowledge was broad rather than deep, and their passion for a concise turn of phrase resulted in annoyingly flippant remarks as well as brilliant quips. Yet the philosophes brought to most of their work remarkable talents for clarity and shrewdness and a dedication to practical reform. They wrote in many genres—essays, treatises, novels and stories, encyclopedia articles, letters, histories, poems, and stage dramas—to reach the widest possible audience. The philosophes may have been the most influential group of talented amateurs in European history, not only because of their influence on their own age but also because of the way they and their assumptions about human nature still affect us today.

LEARNING FROM OUR WORST MISTAKES

Whatever else historians mean by the term *Enlightenment*, they do not mean a coherent set of ideas. Like the medieval scholastics they resemble, the philosophes represent a method of thinking rather than a body of thought. Their efforts all originated in the conviction that the bulk of human misery results from the irrationality of our actions, traditions, beliefs, institutions, and values. Simply remove the uncritical and witless assumptions that guide our lives; replace them with finely reasoned alternatives that can be logically supported, measured, and calibrated; and then watch humanity create and enjoy a better, happier, and more productive life. The philosophes were not necessarily utopians. Indeed, one of the best-known pieces of literature produced by the Enlightenment—Voltaire's fable *Candide* (1759)—satirizes the utopianism that had spread among some of the movement's truest believers. And Hume, for all the geniality of his tone, should never be read by depressives. Yet the philosophes remained firm believers in human progress, the ability always to make life better.

Several factors triggered the Enlightenment, not the least of which were Louis XIV's decision in 1685 to revoke the Edict of Nantes, and the Glorious *Revocation* Revolution in England in 1688. The Edict of Nantes, originally promulgated in *of the Edict* 1598 by France's king Henri IV, had established the official policy of religious *of Nantes* toleration, and for nearly one hundred years this policy had preserved the peace between Catholics and Huguenots. Louis XIV knew little about religion (and was said by his sister-in-law never to have opened a Bible in his life), but he knew that he preferred a hierarchical Catholicism under royal control to a Protestant theology that privileged individual conscience over obedience to authority. At a stroke, Louis's decision to revoke the Edict stripped French Protestants of their legal rights. He seized the nearly one hundred cities that had been placed under Huguenot control by the Edict, drove their civic officials into exile, shut down their schools and churches, and banned all Protestant public activities. Forced to choose between conversion and banishment, approximately 200,000 French Protestants went into exile in Holland, England, and Brandenburg–Prussia. This renewal of persecution, coupled with fears about Louis's expansionist territorial aims, prompted the Holy Roman emperor Leopold I (r. 1658–1705) to cobble together a defensive alliance with England and the Netherlands, along with Sweden and several German principalities, called the League of Augsburg.

England's Glorious Revolution   Meanwhile, in England, Parliament forced the detested Catholic king James II from the throne in the Glorious Revolution of 1688. As we saw in chapter 15, the leaders of Parliament then offered the English throne to James II's Protestant daughter Mary, who had married the Dutch stadtholder, or chief magistrate, William III of Orange, on the condition that William and Mary accept the Declaration of Rights, which stipulated that all English monarchs were required to be Anglican, that freedom of speech was guaranteed, and that Parliament controlled

Persecution and Exile   The city of La Rochelle had long been a center of Huguenot life. After the Edict of Nantes was issued in 1598, direct persecution against French Protestants ceased but tensions remained. In 1622 the leaders of La Rochelle rebelled against King Louis XIII and were quickly put down; five years later, though, spurred on by English sympathizers, they rebelled again. This time Cardinal Richelieu came in person to oversee the siege of the city, which lasted fourteen months. Continued strife finally resulted in this scene from 1661, when three hundred Huguenot families were sent into exile. Louis XIV had risen to the throne in that year, and his intention to revoke the Edict of Nantes was well known.

the levying of taxes. William—Louis XIV's nemesis—was determined to lead the forces of the League against France. The War of the League of Augsburg began in 1688 and lasted for nine years. The Treaty of Rijswijk (1697) established a shaky peace, but the damage had been done: the horrors of the 16th and 17th centuries threatened to rise from the dead.

This specter of the return of religious intolerance, of vain saber rattling, and of the economic misery created by flat-out war sparked new efforts to rethink the attitudes of the age; hence the Enlightenment. Aristocratic and upper-middle-class readers had long enjoyed keeping up with new developments in science, but more and more thinkers were drawn to the critical investigation of human behavior. What is it that leads human beings, whether individually or communally, to act as they do? Is it possible to develop a science of humanity? And if we can understand ourselves better, can we learn to avoid our worst mistakes?

A NEW WORLD OF IDEAS

Freeing individuals from corrupt and irrational practices, whether in politics, the marketplace, or civic life, will lead to the improvement of society for the simple reason that most of the Enlightened regarded human nature as intrinsically good. Although based in self-interest, human behavior is also naturally social. We are equipped, in other words, with an ability to recognize in rationally chosen compromises an indirect means of satisfying our instinctive self-interest. We are naturally good and when given freedom to act will consistently choose the good for all. The Enlightenment lived on such hopes and convictions.

The movement drew writers from across Europe, but its geographic centers were Amsterdam, Edinburgh, Geneva, The Hague, Leiden, London, and Milan. Paris was not an important center of the Enlightenment until Voltaire brought the new thinking there in the 1740s, when the political atmosphere proved more amenable to reform. From these centers the writers of the Enlightenment poured forth a dazzling stream of ideas on every aspect of human life.

The inquiry began with the publication in 1689 of *Two Treatises of Government* and *An Essay Concerning Human Understanding*. The author of both works was the Englishman **John Locke** (1632–1704), commonly regarded as the first philosophe. Drawn initially to science, Locke studied medicine at Oxford University while reading philosophers like Descartes and Leibniz in his spare hours. In 1666 he met Lord Ashley, later the Earl of Shaftesbury, and joined his household as a general counselor. Locke provided medical care for the family, advised the earl on commercial and financial matters, arranged the marriage of the earl's heir, and oversaw the education of the Shaftesbury children. At one point Locke even performed a lifesaving operation on the nobleman. In 1672,

Locke and the Administration of the Commonwealth

when Shaftesbury became the Lord Chancellor of England, Locke was appointed to a secretarial position with the Board of Trade, an experience that seems to have sparked his interest in politics. When Shaftesbury fell from power in 1676, Locke moved to the Continent and spent the next decade living primarily in France and Holland, enjoying the support of various noble patrons, and working on the book that would become *An Essay Concerning Human Understanding.*

But politics interrupted his studies once again when a number of the figures busily planning the Glorious Revolution made contact with him in Holland. At their urging, Locke quickly produced *Two Treatises of Government*, which provided a philosophical justification for Parliament's dismissal of James II and its transfer of the crown to William and Mary. In the treatises he attacks the notion of absolutist monarchy. In its place, he sees all government as the expression of a social contract between the members of a community. This contract consists of recognizing that in choosing to live together, people tacitly agree to compromise their individual autonomy and to delegate to the government the power to adjudicate conflicts and administer the law.

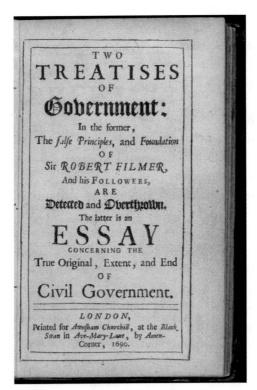

Two Treatises of Government   *Two Treatises*, published anonymously in 1690, is often regarded as the symbolic beginning of the Enlightenment. The authorship of John Locke (1632–1704) was widely known, though not officially claimed until later editions. The "Robert Filmer" mentioned in the subtitle was another political theorist (ca. 1588–1653) who had championed the divine right of kings.

But Locke, who spent his adult life among the propertied classes and enjoying their patronage, defined the central function of government as the administration of the commonwealth—which meant its property. He argued that all political rights begin with the "individual property interest"—that is, the ownership of property. Government is therefore legitimate only when it is composed of or chosen by individuals whose property comes under the state's jurisdiction. It is a moderate, limited form of democracy: only those people who own property, whether defined as land or commercial interest, have a rightful voice in determining the government's shape and activity. When a ruler such as

James II violates the social contract, the propertied classes may justifiably resist him and even, as proved necessary in this case, remove him from office.

Locke's dictum that civil rights consist primarily of the rights to "life, liberty, and property" was cribbed by future U.S. president Thomas Jefferson when he drafted in 1776 the American Declaration of Independence. But Jefferson altered Locke's position significantly, turning it into the better-known phrase "life, liberty, and the pursuit of happiness." Less well known is that Locke would probably have been horrified by the American revolutionaries, viewing them as rebels against the legitimate claims of the propertied men in England whom the colonists served.[2]

Locke's understanding of the social contract and the function of government stands in sharp contrast to Thomas Hobbes's argument in *Leviathan* (discussed in chapter 15)—the text to which Locke was implicitly responding. To Hobbes, the function of the state is to govern the people. Since we are all essentially equal in nature, our competing desires for self-fulfillment and self-preservation condemn us to constant competition, rivalry, and struggle, and government is therefore necessary to keep our hostile tendencies in check. Locke turns Hobbes's argument on its head: the essential role of the state is not to govern the people but to manage and administer its material wealth, or "property." The state does not decide who gets which property; that would go against Locke's conviction that the private ownership of property is an intrinsic human right. The state does, however, set the terms by which those who already possess property may keep it, transfer it, and manage it—all of which it does by establishing laws regarding the rights of ownership, by setting taxes on property, and by setting inheritance norms. And Locke goes a step further. Since the state's fundamental function is to administer the collective property of the nation, only those who possess that property have the right to participate in government. Government thus resembles a medieval guild, in which only those who engage in a particular craft or trade may set the rules for that craft's or trade's activities.

A French Huguenot refugee from Louis XIV's persecutions, **Pierre Bayle** (1647–1706), launched an internationally influential campaign against religious intolerance from his safe haven in the Dutch Republic. Born just before the Peace of Westphalia, he came to public attention in 1686 with an attack on Louis XIV's decision to revoke the Edict of Nantes, called *An All-Catholic France*, which he followed with *A Philosophical Commentary* in the next year. This latter work is a touchstone—the first major treatise in Europe's history to

Bayle and Religious Toleration

---

[2]   Locke's understanding of the property to which men were entitled included slaves. He purchased substantial amounts of stock in the Royal Africa Company (1671) and in the Company of Merchant Adventurers in the Bahamas (1672), both of which were deeply involved in the Atlantic slave trade.

champion the idea of religious toleration. The question, as Bayle frames it, comes to this: Is it ever right to compel a person to change his belief even if the belief he holds can be proven false? He insists that the answer is no, since the choice of belief must be regarded as an intrinsic individual human right. Although he presents an array of real and imaginary case studies to buttress his position, he never confronts head-on an obvious question: What if a given religious conviction is dangerous to society? Many Christians down the centuries have regarded the persecution of Jews as an essential element of their faith. Does the value we place on toleration require us to support such a conviction? Obviously not. Still, if Bayle's argument for religious tolerance was flawed, its influence was undeniable.

Bayle continued his scholarly efforts with his most accomplished work—the *Historical and Critical Dictionary*, a sprawling, eccentric encyclopedia that began to appear in 1697. Published in four fat folio volumes—more than three thousand pages—it is a wild collection of articles on topics ranging from ancient Greek philosophies to the erotica of Bayle's own time. Despite its massive size, the *Dictionary* was by far the biggest "bestseller" of all the philosophical works of Europe in the 18th century (see Table 16.1). It made, and still makes, delightful browsing, since Bayle allows himself to veer off on any tangent that holds his interest. Indeed, there are more tangents than text: more than 90 percent of the

TABLE 16.1 **Major Works of the Enlightenment**

1689	*Two Treatises of Government* *An Essay Concerning Human Understanding*	John Locke
1697–1702	*Historical and Critical Dictionary*	Pierre Bayle
1733	*Philosophical Letters of the English*	Voltaire
1748	*The Spirit of Laws* *An Enquiry Concerning Human Understanding*	Montesquieu David Hume
1751–1772	*Encyclopedia*	Denis Diderot
1759	*Candide*	Voltaire
1762	*The Social Contract*	Jean-Jacques Rousseau
1763	*Treatise on Toleration*	Voltaire
1764	*Philosophical Dictionary* *On Crimes and Punishments*	Voltaire Cesare Beccaria
1776	*The Wealth of Nations*	Adam Smith
1779	*Nathan the Wise*	Gotthold Lessing
1784	"What Is Enlightenment?"	Immanuel Kant

Dictionary consists of lengthy footnotes, addenda, marginalia, spin-off mini-essays, and sometimes even footnotes to footnotes.

But the fun has a serious purpose. Time and again, theodicy—the question of why evil exists—emerges as a central theme making the whole structure cohere. Bayle examines the question philosophically, historically, theologically, linguistically, in art and literature, as a practical matter of law, and even in a way that prefigures anthropology, the scientific study of human behavior. "Mankind is evil and miserable," he writes; "everywhere one looks there are prisons, hospitals, gallows, and beggars. History, one might say, is nothing but the narrative of man's crimes and sufferings." But why is this so, if the world was created for us by an omnipotent and loving God? Bayle returns to the question over and over, but in bits and pieces, as though the question is too horrifying to contemplate for too long. If God is all-loving, he argues, he would destroy evil if he could—and yet evil obviously exists, so one must conclude that God cannot stop it. Bayle will have none of this, since it concludes in essence that God is not God. Conversely, assuming that God could destroy evil if he wanted to, then he must not want to—in which case he is not all-loving. This too Bayle rejects. In the end, he suggests (although he never says so explicitly) that the question of evil has no rational explanation. The coexistence of an all-loving, all-powerful God and rampant, unremitting evil is simply a mystery that we must accept and acknowledge our inability to comprehend.

Yet this is not a failed exercise. Bayle's whole point is present here, although somewhat veiled. By his exuberant, continuous reexamination of the question, his implicit message is the fundamental and best argument for tolerance: the only proper human response to religious mystery is to recognize the inability of human beings to comprehend heavenly mysteries. No one can or should ever be so certain of his convictions that he deems it right to persecute those who disagree with him. We must tolerate, in other words, because we can never be sure.

Bayle is seldom read anymore, which is a shame. In his own time he was lauded as perhaps the greatest nonscientific mind in centuries. The German philosopher Gottfried Leibniz (1646–1716) described him as "one of the most brilliant men of our time, a man whose eloquence is as great as his intellect." Voltaire, in a generous mood, praised him as "the greatest master of logic who ever wrote." His influence on the later philosophes can hardly be overstated; and if he came to few positive conclusions in his work, that surely was part of his point.

Few of the Enlightened rejected religion absolutely. Many, however, subscribed to **deism**. Deists believe in a single, benevolent God who has created the cosmos but plays no active role in it. Like a divine clockmaker, he builds his machine, winds it up, and then leaves it to tick on its own. Deists like Hume, Voltaire, and Diderot insisted that the universe, from the moment of its creation, has operated solely according to rational principles. Since God plays no role in our lives, we owe him nothing more than a vague gratitude. More significantly, since God is unknowable, all dogmatic assertions are meaningless—which means that the teachings of all organized religions are without value. Churches—whether Catholic, Protestant, or Orthodox—have no right to command our obedience. A dual policy of religious freedom and of freedom from religious intolerance is essential to human progress. As Voltaire memorably put it in his popular *Philosophical Dictionary* (1764), "It is quite understandable that the fanatics of one sect want to wipe out the fanatics belonging to another, . . . but to have forced [someone like] Descartes to flee to Holland in order to avoid the wrath of the stupid . . . is an eternal shame upon our nation." At another place in the same work he defends deists as people "who do not claim to know how God punishes the wrong, or how He promotes the good, or how He forgives—for [the deist] is not presumptuous enough to boast that he knows God's nature; instead, the deist simply takes comfort in the knowledge that God is good and just."

Charles de Secondat, Baron de Montesquieu (1689–1755), was the most
Montesquieu prominent of the philosophes who were of aristocratic birth. Wealthy, well
and the Spirit educated, and happily married, he led a remarkably uneventful life, spend-
of Laws ing most of it at his lovely château near Bordeaux, not far from where the
great humanist Michel de Montaigne (1533–1592) had lived and composed his
Essays in the 16th century. **Montesquieu** gained fame with his first book, a satirical novel called *The Persian Letters* (1721), in which two fictional visitors
from the Safavid Empire entertain each other and their households back in
Persia, with letters describing their view of European customs in general but
French ones in particular. A typical skewering remark is "The people here [in
Paris] argue endlessly about religion, but even so, there appears to be a competition among them to see who can behave the most impiously." Next came a
lengthy historical essay on the cause of the decline of the Roman Empire (1734),
which he attributed primarily to the centralization and monopolization of
power in the imperial court.

Montesquieu's next and greatest work was *The Spirit of the Laws* (1748), a treatise in which he argues that laws and legal systems, unlike the great laws of Nature
that govern the cosmos, are human creations and hence can be neither infallible
nor immutable. Laws evolve through the interplay of specific peoples and cultures
and the circumstances of the world they inhabit. To be successful, laws must arise
from and respect "the people for whom they are framed . . . the nature and guiding
principle of each government . . . the very climate and soil of the country . . . the
main occupations of the people . . . their religious faith, their habits of thought,
their wealth, their total number, their commerce, manners, and customs."

Montesquieu warns that a single governing power, being unavoidably at a
distance from its subjects, cannot possibly establish a just and effective system of

laws and ultimately seeks only to preserve its own authority rather than serve society. His breakthrough assertion, therefore, is to demand the permanent separation of powers in government and to assign legislative authority to those figures who are closest to local traditions and needs. Doing so not only offers the best chance to develop a rational and sensible set of laws, he argues, but also best guarantees the stability of the government itself.

John Locke's concern for rational foundations quickly spread from government to economics, thanks to the pioneering work of **Adam Smith** (1723–1790), the Scottish philosophe widely cited as the "father of modern economics." Smith published his most influential work, *The Wealth of Nations*, in 1776 to prove the inevitable failure of closed-market mercantilism and the inevitable success of free-market economic policy—basic, as we will see, to modern capitalism. Mercantilism is wrong, he argues, for the simple reason that it is irrational: it assumes that people will passively accept their own poverty and oppression—all to support a regime that absorbs all available capital for its own ends. Smith endorses instead the concept of **laissez-faire** (French for "to leave alone"), in which the government neither controls nor intervenes in the economy. Laissez-faire economic policy, in contrast to mercantilism, is based on a rational view of human motivation. It allows people the freedom to make their own economic choices and to reap the rewards of their own success. But for this to happen, markets must have open competition and freedom from price fixing. He therefore warns against cartels—powerful monopolies or agreements between firms—quite as much as against interference by the state. "People of the same trade seldom meet together even for merriment or diversion, but that the conversation ends in some conspiracy against the public, or in some contrivance to raise prices." *Adam Smith and Free Markets*

Smith thus redefined the notion of a **market**. The word no longer meant merely a physical site where commerce occurs, but rather a pattern of human behavior. Commerce was now seen as following set laws, since all individuals, in any free economic exchange, will act rationally in their own best interest. And these laws are based on the economic choices people make from among a limited supply of goods, along with the competition between firms for buyers—in other words, supply and demand:

> The natural effort of every individual to better his own condition, when suffered to exert itself with freedom and security, is so powerful a principle, that it is alone, and without any assistance, not only capable of carrying the society to wealth and prosperity, but of surmounting a hundred impertinent obstructions with which the folly of human laws too often encumbers its operations.

To Smith, the laws of supply and demand serve as an "invisible hand" ensuring that individual interests are synchronized with those of the whole society. Free-market forces naturally will bring individual and social interests in line.

Beccaria and Rational Punishment

Rational self-interest also guided the investigations of Italian jurist Cesare Beccaria (1738–1794) into economics and law. His *Elements of Public Economy* (published posthumously, in 1804) anticipated some of Adam Smith's ideas on the need for economic policies that produced wealth for the entire populace by opening up markets to natural forces of competition, supply, and demand. His greatest work, however, is his study *On Crimes and Punishments* (1764). A system of criminal justice, he argues, should aim to promote social security and order rather than to seek revenge upon malefactors. It thus ought to consider the causes of crime as much as punishment for it. After all, he contends, it is preferable for society to prevent crimes from happening than to punish their perpetrators after they have occurred. Hence any just society will actively seek to eradicate poverty, which Beccaria sees as the principle cause of crimes against property. For crimes against humanity, the aim of a judicial system should be to rehabilitate criminals who are emotionally unbalanced and to teach them to understand themselves, the consequences of their actions, and the paths to personal improvement.

Punishment of crimes is necessary, Beccaria insists, but is more effective when it is imposed in a rational way. Toward that end, punishments should be only as severe as necessary to promote social order. Anything more severe, he argues, is tyrannical and merely provokes attitudes of resentment and hostility

An 18th-Century Scene from an Italian Prison   The prisoner in the center of the image is being drawn up in the *strappado*, a form of torture in which the victim's hands are tied behind his or her back and suspended in the air by means of a rope attached to the wrists, which usually dislocates both arms. By 1800 Beccaria's influence had helped to phase out such extreme punishment.

that make the criminal all the more likely to commit another offense. Punishments must also be consistently applied. The certainty of punishment, not the severity of it, deters crime more effectively.

Perhaps the most heroically energetic and resilient philosophe was the Frenchman **Denis Diderot** (1713–1784). Although he was far from the best *Diderot and* thinker or writer in the movement, he was undoubtedly the most important in *the Circulation* getting Enlightened ideas into print and into broad circulation. He had a won- *of the* derful ability to spot talent in others and was tireless in encouraging, prod- *Enlightenment* ding, supporting, and publishing new authors. He was the central force behind the great *Encyclopédie* (*Encyclopedia*), the vast compendium of all the new learning in science, philosophy, economics, law, technology, art, and religion produced by the writers of the age. Diderot was among the most utilitarian of the philosophes, a true believer in the cause of saving the world from tyranny, superstition, and ignorance. Here is how he himself put it, in the *Encyclopedia*'s entry on "Encyclopedia":

> The aim of an encyclopedia is to gather in one place the knowledge scattered all over the world; to display the general content and organization of that knowledge to one's contemporaries; and to pass this knowledge on to later generations—so that the achievements of the past may be useful to the future; so that our children, by so improving their own minds, may become more virtuous and more happy; and so that we may not perish without having proved a benefit to all mankind.... For we have long had need of a rational age [such as ours], in which men would no longer look to classical authorities for the truth, but to the study of nature itself.

Despite its size—thirty-five volumes of print and images—or perhaps because of it—the *Encyclopedia* (published 1751–1772) sold extremely well. Four thousand subscribers ordered copies before it was even in print. Thomas Jefferson purchased a set, and Empress Catherine of Russia (r. 1762–1796), hearing of Diderot's financial woes, purchased his entire library and hired Diderot, at a generous stipend, to be her "librarian" and guardian for the books.[3] But the *Encyclopedia* was not the only such effort; the 18th century, in fact, was a golden age for such enterprises. Just as 13th-century scholastics filled European libraries with *summas* on every topic, the Enlightened of the 18th gave birth to a glut of huge reference works: Pierre Bayle's *Historical and Critical Dictionary* (1697–1702) we have already met, but also Englishman Ephraim Chambers's *Cyclopaedia, or a Universal Dictionary of Arts and Sciences* (1728), Italian

---

[3]   The books were shipped to Saint Petersburg after Diderot's death in 1784 and are now a special collection within the Russian National Library.

Pages from the *Encyclopedia*   The *Encyclopedia* reflects the interest of Denis Diderot, widely shared by the philosophes, in technology for its own sake and as a tool for social reform. These illustrations depict scenes of sheet-glass manufacture and locksmithing.

Gianfrancesco Pivati's *Nuovo dizionario scientifico e curioso, sacroprofano* (*New Scientific and Curious, Sacred–Profane Dictionary,* 1744), German Johann Heinrich Zedler's *Universal-Lexicon* (1754), and the first edition of the *Encyclopædia Britannica* (1768), among other examples of this remarkable genre.[4]

VOLTAIRE AND THE LIMITS OF OPTIMISM

As it happened, the two most influential of all the Enlightened were considerably less optimistic than Diderot about the possibility of reforming society: François-Marie Arouet (1694–1778), who published under the pen name of *Voltaire,* and Jean-Jacques Rousseau (1712–1778). Both were prima donnas, desperate for attention and praise, but they differed profoundly in their origins, temperaments, aims, and styles.

Voltaire doubted the essential goodness of mankind, or at least of the lower orders of it. He believed in the possibility of human progress, but a progress firmly

---

[4]   Thomas Dobson's *Encyclopaedia* (1789–1798) was the first American encyclopedia. It copied much from the *Encyclopædia Britannica* and was soon replaced by the *Encyclopedia Americana.*

directed by a political and intellectual elite—of which he regarded himself and others like him as the indispensable leaders. Commoners, however, whether farmers in the countryside or laborers in the towns, he loathed as degenerate brutes incapable of rising above ignorance. Rousseau, on the other hand, came from those lower orders and held tightly to the conviction that goodness is the essential characteristic of all human beings. It is society itself, he argued, that corrupts the individual—especially the privileged classes with whom Voltaire was so comfortable. The power of the privileged, to Rousseau, derives from its enslavement and brutalization of the common man. Given these differences, it is no surprise to learn that the two men despised each other.[5]

Voltaire at Work   This portrait by Charles Corbet (1758–1808) shows Voltaire at his writing desk, with coat, scarf, and cap. The satisfied smile on his face was probably typical of this leading philosophe.

Born in Paris to a wealthy middle-class family, Voltaire was educated at the Jesuit Collège Louis-le-Grand, where he excelled in languages and law. After graduation, he took a job as secretary to the French ambassador to Holland. This might have been the start of a successful government career, but Voltaire's impulsive romantic entanglements and habit of poking sarcastic barbs at his social superiors kept getting him in trouble. He was imprisoned twice—once in the Bastille after publishing satirical verses about the prince regent—and released the second time only when he promised to flee the country. After an offhand witticism, a nobleman had Voltaire beaten by hired thugs—to which Voltaire responded by challenging him to a duel. But since Voltaire came from a lower social rank, his challenge enraged aristocratic society even more than the original insult had done. He fled to England in 1726, where he remained for three years.

The years he spent in England marked the turning point in his life. He moved easily through educated society and met many of the most prominent figures in England's political and intellectual life. He observed English law and government, studied Newtonian physics, and avidly read the works of John Locke. The culmination of his experience was witnessing the grand state funeral given to Isaac Newton. Returning to Paris, Voltaire published his *Philosophical Letters on the English* (1733), which instantly propelled him to the front ranks of the

---

[5]   Rousseau, who died on July 2, 1778, is said to have died happy since he had lived long enough to learn of Voltaire's death on May 30.

intellectuals of his time.[6] The *Letters* extol the rationalism of English life over the irrational, superstitious, and corrupt Continental world; he contrasts the modesty and gentleness of the Quakers with the rigid intolerance of the Calvinists, yet praises a constitution that permits both to practice their faiths freely despite the existence of an established Church of England. He marvels at the Quakers' absence of priests ("'We have none, my friend,' he replied, 'to our great happiness.'") and denounces the Presbyterians (who "wear the most severe expressions, . . . preach through their noses, and call [all other Christian denominations] 'whores of Babylon'"). He also praises the English for their judicial system, their open trade, and their dedication to promoting science.

The *Letters* were a sensation with the reading public, which is why the government ordered the book to be banned and copies to be burned. Voltaire went once again into exile, this time to a remote village, where he lived in the château of his mistress, the Marquise Emilie du Châtelet (1706–1749), an accomplished mathematician and physicist who taught Voltaire much of his science. (Her translation of Newton's *Principia Mathematica* is still the most widely used version in French.) For the next twelve years he poured out a stream of pamphlets, plays, histories, poems, scientific papers, essays, and letters that made him the most prominent philosophe of the age. (The standard edition of his complete works today fills almost two hundred volumes.) His two principal concerns were religious toleration and freedom of speech. Political freedom meant little to him, since the unwashed masses neither needed nor deserved it. Besides, their educated superiors would profit less from democracy than from Enlightened ideas put into efficient practice by an absolutist regime guided by philosophes such as himself.

The death of the Marquise at the age of forty-three in 1749 left Voltaire deeply mournful, and he sought a new chapter in his life in Berlin. He accepted an invitation to reside with, debate with, and act as counselor to Frederick the Great of Prussia (r. 1740–1786), the most rigidly absolutist ruler then in Europe. But Voltaire's air of self-satisfaction, his sarcastic gaiety, and his inability to resist challenging all forms of authority (even those he was in agreement with) led to a speedy falling out with the deeply serious-minded Frederick. After yet another brief imprisonment—this time in Frankfurt—Voltaire went to Geneva and lived there just long enough to make himself unwanted. He moved finally to a brilliant estate at Ferney, near the French–Swiss border, where he remained for the last twenty years of his life. It was at Ferney that he wrote his best-known work, the satirical novella *Candide* (1759).

The inspiration for the tale was a catastrophic earthquake that flattened the Portuguese capital of Lisbon in 1755, killing perhaps as many as sixty thousand

---

[6]   Shortly after returning to France in 1729, Voltaire shared in winning a lottery established by the French government. He was thus independently wealthy for the rest of his life.

people and demolishing almost 90 percent of the city's buildings.[7] The tragedy shocked Europe, and the suffering of the survivors challenged many people's confidence in the rational ordering of the world and the conviction that man can understand it. *Candide*, for all its characteristic humor, provides a first glimpse of the bitterness and pessimism that increasingly marked Voltaire's latter years. It also mercilessly satirizes the optimism of his rival philosophes—especially Rousseau, whom Voltaire regarded as vulgar, gullible, and naïve.

The novella tells of the title character and his thick-headed tutor Dr. Pangloss, whose fundamental teaching is that "everything is for the best in this, the best of all possible worlds." They stagger from one disastrous misadventure to an-

Sainte Vierge! s'écria-t-elle qu'allons nous devenir? un homme tué chez moi !

Candide   This drawing of a scene in Voltaire's *Candide* was created by Jean-Michel Moreau (1741–1814) , who provided many illustrations for Denis Diderot's *Encyclopedia*.

other, in the search for Candide's lost love, the beautiful but vacuous Lady Cunegonde, and for the mythical kingdom of gold, El Dorado. Candide and Pangloss suffer through wars, famines, plagues, imprisonments and tortures, earthquakes, shipwrecks, and slavery with stoic resolve. Experiencing nothing but evil, they cling to their belief that everything happens for a reason and toward some positive end. By the end, Candide concludes that the most anyone can do is to tend to whatever is within one's reach. In the face of the world's evils, one must "cultivate one's own garden." Pangloss, however, remains unenlightened and optimistic.

THE RADICAL THOUGHT OF ROUSSEAU

Jean-Jacques Rousseau (1712–1778), Voltaire probably would have said, was never enlightened to begin with. Born to a working-class family in Protestant Geneva, Rousseau was orphaned at an early age and led a hardscrabble youth,

---

[7]   Experts today reckon the severity of the Lisbon quake as 9.0 on the Richter scale. (The strongest earthquake ever recorded was 9.5, in Valdivia, Chile, in 1960.)

working at odd jobs and sleeping wherever he could. In constant poverty and ill health, he developed a bitter and nervous temperament. Even after he had achieved renown and a measure of wealth, he remained convinced that people were persecuting him. Almost entirely self-educated, Rousseau turned himself into a polymath by sheer will: he composed music, wrote novels, studied politics and philosophy, promoted new techniques of education, and acquired an amateur's knowledge of science. Brilliant but maladjusted, he spoke endlessly of his own virtue while complaining that no one understood him. He scolded everyone for their immorality, yet he had five children with his illiterate servant girl and placed each one in an orphanage. In his letters and his *Confessions* (completed in 1769 but not published until 1782, four years after his death), one of the most fascinating autobiographies ever written, he at once exaggerates his own sins and exonerates himself anyway. Bad as he was, he insists, others were worse. And then he pats himself on the back for his superior honesty.[8]

Yet this unstable misanthrope had a more profound influence on Western culture than any other figure of his time. At the heart of Rousseau's thinking was, ironically, an unshakable belief in the fundamental goodness, decency, and equality of people. All the corruption and evil of this world, he insists, is the fault of society—and not just the particular society of Old Regime France. It is the sheer fact of socializing, of living in community, that introduces injustice, pain, and unhappiness in human life. "Mankind is born free, and everywhere he is in chains." That is the memorable opening of *The Social Contract* (1762), one of his best-known works. To live in community means to relinquish one's freedom, to accept compromises of one's desires and will. We may gain a degree of civility in the process, but civilization itself plants the seed of corruption in our souls. And we see this corruption in the unfair hierarchies of wealth, privilege, and power that exist.

Jean-Jacques Rousseau   Allan Ramsay (1713–1784), a Scot, painted this portrait of Rousseau in 1766, when the great philosophe took refuge with David Hume (1711–1776) after his book *Emile* was condemned and the French government issued a warrant for his arrest.

---

[8]   *Confessions*, which is divided into two parts, carries the narrative to 1765. In the final pages he declares his intention to compose a third part "if ever I have the strength to write it." He never did write it, although he did find the strength to author three other works: *Considerations on the Government of Poland* (1771), *Rousseau, the Judge of Jean-Jacques* (1776), and *Reveries of a Solitary Walker* (1778).

Thus far, most of the Enlightened would agree. But Rousseau goes further. Simply redistributing wealth and influence, he says, will not solve anything. The real problem is the concern for wealth and power that civilized life creates. Rejecting the free-market economic theory of Adam Smith, Rousseau insists that the point of Enlightenment is to make people good, not rich. He similarly resists efforts like Diderot's to educate the masses in practical matters. To Rousseau, any philosophy that aims to help people enjoy material comfort and self-determination is wrongheaded, if not delusional. Human happiness, he insists, derives from a persistent pursuit of life's meaning. What is the good life, and what is happiness? Only by asking questions like these can we hope to achieve either. Even if we never discover the answers, the very search for answers will make us better and happier. In the end, it is the effort to retain our humanity in the face of the world's brutality that gives life meaning and makes it endurable.

Rousseau does take some concrete positions. He rejects Locke's argument that ownership of property establishes a political right, since everyone, rich and poor alike, has surrendered freedom in entering the social contract. The only legitimate form of government will embrace the mandate of the Enlightened majority—what he calls the General Will. But the General Will is infallible only when the people act selflessly and with properly Enlightened guidance. "The people are never corrupted but they are frequently deceived; this fact explains those occasions when the people appear to desire what is bad." As a believer in human goodness, Rousseau affirms that the General Will, properly expressed, must always be correct. It may not secure the highest economic yield (as Smith would ask), promote the best technical skills (with Diderot),

The Noble Savage   This handsome 1783 painting by Sir Joshua Reynolds (1723–1792) offers a romanticized portrait of a Tahitian native brought back to England by the explorer Captain James Cook (1728–1779). Jean-Jacques Rousseau (1712–1778) did the most to popularize the idea of the "noble savage"—that is, the non-European untainted by civilization's corrupting forces—but the notion was widespread before him. The idea—indeed, the very phrase—appears to have originated with the long verse-drama by the English poet John Dryden (1631–1700) entitled *The Conquest of Granada* (1672).

or crush religious superstition (with Voltaire). It simply expresses the deepest and truest desires of the people, which will always promote the well-being of all. Our natural altruism, our concern for others, can guide social life once we overcome our shortsighted individual desire. Provided that the law governing society derives from and expresses the General Will, the freedom of each individual consists of obedience to it. Rousseau thus championed a radical democracy that offended the aristocracy while rejecting rational progress, which offended most of the Enlightened.[9]

CAN WOMEN BE ENLIGHTENED?

In a word—no, according to the leading philosophes. The radical democracy advocated by Rousseau applied strictly to men. What they regarded as women's essential characteristic—their emotional nature—was simply incompatible with the cult of reason that they championed. Strict logic and empiricism leave no room for passion and instinct when trying to reform the world. Most of the philosophes were no more misogynistic than the rest of the society they wanted to change, but few of them took women seriously as thinkers—the principal exception was the Marquis de Condorcet (1743–1794).[10] Voltaire, a serial monogamist, treated the women in his life with genuine affection and respect; his fifteen-year affair with the Marquise du Châtelet was a true partnership in the Enlightenment cause. But Voltaire loved this accomplished mathematician and physicist for her genius and her uniqueness among women, never attributed the intellectual capabilities he saw in her to women in general, and never advocated for anything but traditional patriarchal society. In a letter to Frederick II of Prussia, Voltaire wrote that du Châtelet was "a great man whose only fault was being a woman."

Rousseau, true to his nature, was the opposite of Voltaire in this regard too. His relations with women were generally a toxic mixture of sensual delight, emotional distrust, and intellectual disdain. His shameful treatment of his servant-mistress speaks for itself. Ironically, among Rousseau's most popular books were two didactic novels, *Julie, or the New Héloïse* (1761) and *Emile, or On Education* (1762), in which he dramatizes his views on human nature, society, law, religion, education, and relations between the sexes. He calls for women to embrace what he regards as their natural sphere of domestic life, of loving

---

[9]   In subordinating individual desires to the General Will, Rousseau has sometimes been seen as the creator, in theory, of fascist totalitarianism.

[10] Condorcet, best known for his *Historical Sketch of the Progress of the Human Mind* (1795) and for his role in the tumultuous early years of the French Revolution, was a tireless champion of the rights of women. His major work in this regard was his 1790 essay, "On Admitting Women into the Rights of Citizenship." He was also a noted abolitionist.

service to their fathers and husbands, as caring nurturers of children. Admitting women into the public sphere, he warns in *Emile*, would have disastrous results: "Men would be tyrannized by women. . . . Considering the ease with which women arouse men's sensuality, men would be their victims in no time at all." Other philosophes were just as bad.

Despite such prevailing prejudices, women were critical to the success of the Enlightenment. Given the perils of censorship and imprisonment for disseminating antiabsolutist or irreligious views, many prominent women helped propagate the new ideas through large and regular **salons**—social parties filled with the leading writers and artists of the time, where new ideas were discussed, new works read aloud, and new discoveries shared. Although they were important cultural venues, the salons were unavoidably elitist. Most of the great hostesses— Marie-Thérèse Rodet Geoffrin (1699–1777), Julie de Lespinasse (1732–1776), and Suzanne Curchod Necker (1737–1794) in Paris and Elizabeth Montagu (1718–1800) in London, among others—were fabulously wealthy (usually by strategic marriage), and the gatherings themselves were sumptuous affairs where dozens of servants treated the assembled writers, philosophers, and artists to elaborate meals, fine wines, beautiful furnishings, and worshipful deference.

A Reading in the Salon of Madame Geoffrin   In this 1812 painting, French artist Anicet Charles Lemonnier depicts the best-known Parisian salon of the 1750s. Invited by the famed hostess Madame Geoffrin (the woman in blue on the right facing the viewer), a group of elite men and women gather to hear a reading of Voltaire's play *The Orphan of China* (1755). The bust is of the playwright and famous philosophe.

Still, a number of women made their own marks on the Enlightenment beyond the role of social enablers. Several had even made an appearance earlier, in the Scientific Revolution, where their efforts helped pave the way for the Enlightenment. Female scholars of the Scientific Revolution were generally members of the aristocracy, who were able to command respect by virtue of their social status. Margaret Cavendish (1623–1673) is an example. Privately tutored as a girl, she married the Duke of Newcastle and instantly became a leading figure in a rarefied world. She put her privilege to use by making her own penetrating research into scientific method—what we would today call the philosophy of science, rather than science itself. She corresponded with both René Descartes and Thomas Hobbes, wrote two impressive books (*Observations upon Experimental Philosophy*, 1666, and *Grounds of Natural Philosophy*, 1668), and was the first woman ever invited to attend a meeting of the Royal Society of London. Her contemporary in the central European province of Silesia, Maria Cunitz (1610–1664), was a commoner, although a well-to-do one who belonged to a prominent family of court-connected physicians. An astronomer, she composed her most important work—*Kind Urania* (1650), named after the ancient Greek muse of astronomy—while temporarily taking refuge with her family at a Cistercian monastery at Lubnice, in today's central Poland, during the Thirty Years' War. Enough women of private means engaged in science that a small subgenre came into existence of scientific works written (by men) specifically for a female readership.[11]

An important transitional figure between the Scientific Revolution and the Enlightenment is the English feminist writer Mary Astell (1666–1731), who condemned as a lie the notion that women were incapable of reason—but she as much criticized women for embracing that lie as she did men for propagating it. In *A Serious Proposal to the Ladies for the Advancement of Their True and Greatest Interest* (1694) and *A Serious Proposal, Part II* (1697), Astell called for women to awake from their passivity and decorum and to establish schools specifically for girls' education (*Part I*) and women's continuing education (*Part II*). "If all men are born free," she notably asks in *Some Reflections upon Marriage* (1700), "how is it that all women are born slaves?"

Moving into the 18th century, women again were deeply involved. Among the most influential was the French playwright, abolitionist, and political pamphleteer Olympe de Gouges (1748–1793). The daughter of a butcher and his shopkeeper wife, an unhappy marriage left de Gouges a widow at age eighteen. She moved with her small son to Paris, where she took on a series of wealthy

---

[11]   See, for example, Bernard de Fontenelle, *Conversations on the Plurality of Worlds* (1686), and Francesco Algarotti, *Newtonianism for Ladies* (1730).

lovers who introduced her to salon society. She began to write in the 1780s,
her first works being stage dramas that
depicted the horrors of the slave trade.
Subsequent dramas and essays called
for changes in the laws regarding marriage and divorce and culminated in
her most famous writing, a manifesto
entitled the *Declaration of the Rights of
Woman and the Female Citizen* (1791),
which played on the language of the
*Declaration of the Rights of Man and
Citizen* (1789), a fundamental document of the French Revolution (discussed in chapter 17). It opens with the
anthemic declaration that "The women,
daughters, and sisters who represent
the nation demand to be included in
the national assembly!" De Gouges grew frustrated with the French reformers'
lack of interest in equal rights for women, and she was ultimately executed by
guillotine in 1793.

Mary Wollstonecraft Painted in 1790 or 1791 by John
Opie (1761–1807), a popular English portraitist of the
time, this picture shows Wollstonecraft when she was in
Paris, still a passionate supporter of the Revolution. Her
disillusionment was soon to follow.

A *Vindication of the Rights of Man* and *A Vindication of the Rights of Woman* by
the English writer and reformer Mary Wollstonecraft (1759–1797) were published in 1790 and 1792, respectively, in London. Wollstonecraft was born into a
financially comfortable but emotionally fragile family (her father was a violent
drunk), and when she reached adulthood she dedicated her life to social reform.
She penned a number of novels and short-story collections, but came into her
own with the two *Vindications*. The first attacks the institutions of monarchy and
aristocracy, as the philosophes had done, but also the language and culture of
chivalry that surround them. The imposed inequality between the sexes, she
maintains, is simply the first instance and foundation of the idea of social division
with privileges reserved for some but not for others. Hence, she continues in the
second *Vindication*, any attempt to create a new society of liberty and equality
that does not grant those rights to women will inevitably fail of its own illogic.
Wollstonecraft was a divisive figure in her time, a result of what many regarded as
her scandalous personal life—she lived openly with her various lovers, even those
who were married. She spent her last years married to the novelist and political
writer William Godwin, by whom she had a daughter who grew to achieve her
own scandal-plagued fame as Mary Wollstonecraft Shelley (1797–1851), the
author of the novel *Frankenstein* (1818).

THE JEWISH ENLIGHTENMENT

The 18th century's promotion of reason and tolerance certainly appealed to Europe's Jewish populations. Many Jews supported the Enlightened goal of fighting superstition and ignorance, which were sources of anti-Jewish hatred. To secular Jews, an Enlightened world without religion would be a world without religious violence. And of violence they had had their fill.

As we saw in chapter 14, by 1500 hardly any Jews still resided in western Europe. Expelled from England (1290), France (1306), Germany (numerous times), Spain (1492), and Portugal (1497), many Continental Jews had migrated east. The confederation then known as the Polish–Lithuanian Union dates back to 1385. By 1600 it included what are today the nations of Poland, Ukraine, Belarus, Latvia, and Lithuania—and there the Jews enjoyed a welcome and a degree of tolerance that they had seldom known in the west (see Map 16.1). But matters changed when Poland became ensnared in political and social convulsions in the 17th century, including the so-called Polish–Swedish War (1600–1629) and the

MAP 16.1   Jewish Communities in Poland-Lithuania, ca. 1600   Poland had a long history of granting refuge to Jews exiled from Europe, Russia, and the Ottoman Empire. By 1600 as many as three-fourths of all Jews lived in Poland-Lithuania, where they represented roughly one-tenth the overall population.

Northern War (1655–1660).[12] Fleeing once more from oppression, several hundred thousand Jews returned to western Europe, whose nations gradually—and grudgingly—revoked their bans on Jewish presence.

Traditionally, most Jews had sought to secure a peaceful, although parallel, existence with Christian society. From their segregated communities, under the leadership of their rabbis, they had ventured out into the gentile world to conduct business. They could even engage, within limits, in the broader intellectual and social life—but returned at day's end to the community and its ritual life under the law. Jews had retained their distinctive identity for centuries, wearing traditional clothing, observing dietary restrictions, performing their mitzvahs, keeping their languages alive, and perpetuating the traditions of Jewish intellectual life. Now many Jews were determined to reestablish Judaism in the West, not as a separate, segregated society but as an integral part of the new progressive world.

The Hebrew term for enlightenment is **Haskalah**, the name of one of the two main developments in European Jewish history in the 18th century. The Haskalah movement accepted the idea of assimilation, or seeking to integrate Jews into the main European populace and culture. Moses Mendelssohn (1729–1786), a self-taught Prussian scholar who became one of Judaism's greatest philosophers, encouraged if not complete assimilation, at least a dignified integration with gentile society. Israel Jacobson (1768–1828), the German founder of Reform Judaism, deemphasized Jewish teachings that he regarded as merely ritual instead of moral or ethical. They recommended the decline of Jewish vernaculars like Yiddish and Ladino, which only kept Jews segregated from the European world, in favor of traditional Hebrew and the gentile vernaculars. Mendelssohn translated the entire Bible into German.

Haskalah

The Haskalah movement found widespread support among western European Jewish communities. The **Hasidim** occupied the other end of the spectrum and the other end of Europe. Founded by the Polish rabbi Israel ben Eleazar (1696–1760), also known as the Ba'al Shem Tov ("Master of the Good Name"), Hasidic Judaism represented a revivalist spirit rather than a new set of ideas regarding observant life. The Hasidim (literally, "the Pious Ones") decried Ashkenazic rabbinic Jewish life as too rule bound, soul deadening, and formulaic. At the same time, they found the mystical–philosophical Kabbalistic elements of Sephardic Judaism too foreign. What Rabbi Eleazar emphasized instead was a more vividly emotional and uplifting style of worship. Centered in the home instead of

Hasidism

---

12   In the Khmelnytsky Rebellion of 1648–1657 alone (also known as the Ukrainian War of Liberation), well over 100,000 Jews were slaughtered by rampaging Cossack troops seeking independence from Polish–Lithuanian control.

Jewish Enlightenment   Josef Johann Suss (1857–1937) painted this modern rendering of 18th-century Jewish scholars in debate. The figure in the center is a rabbi. The clothing and hats are typical of unassimilated central and eastern European Jews of the time.

the synagogue, the Hasidim adhered strictly to Jewish law but did so under the leadership of charismatic *zaddikim* ("holy men"), who led their congregations in joyous singing and dancing. The Hasidim maintained that sincerity of prayer, charity performed with warmth and eagerness, and sensitivity to God's ever-present reality are more pleasing in heaven than uninspired rituals. Eastern European Jews became known for the vitality of their worship and their communal lives. From these two developments—Haskalah and Hasidism—arose the Reform, Conservative, and Orthodox traditions of modern-day Judaism.

THE JEWS AND EUROPE'S AMBIVALENCE

European Christians were, as ever, ambivalent about the Jews. Most of the Enlightened favored integration—that is, incorporating the Jews into society at least in terms of law and governance—but were opposed to outright assimilation, an idea that raised the uncomfortable notions of intermarriage and socializing on equal terms. To anti-Semites, the Jews' willingness to assimilate raised suspicions of their supposed desire to attack Christian society from within. Frederick II of

Prussia issued an edict in 1744 that expelled all Jews from the city of Breslau, except for ten merchant and financial families. A similar enactment for the city of Berlin added that the few Jews who were allowed to remain in the capital could do so only on the condition that they refrain from marrying and bearing children. That was in 1750, the same year as when Maria Theresa of Austria evicted the Jews from the whole of Bohemia, only to invite them back, later, with the inspired idea of requiring them to pay a fee every ten years for the right to remain.[13] Nevertheless, numerous **Acts of Toleration** that offered full or partial constitutional rights to Jews were promulgated in country after country: Holland (1657), the British colonies (1665, 1740), Britain itself (1753), France (1781), Austria (1782), Spain (1789), and Hungary (1791).

But changes in law occur in advance of changes in popular opinion as often as they occur in response to them, and popular prejudices against Jews remained common across the Continent. The best hope for the future, many thought, therefore lay not in the conversion or assimilation of the Jews but in the promotion of tolerance as a secular, civil virtue applicable to all regardless of faith. This was the point of Baruch de Spinoza (introduced in chapter 14) when he wrote in his *Theological–Political Treatise* (1670), that all peoples, including the Jews, must surrender their self-appointed roles as the unique possessors of heavenly blessing, since "every man's happiness and true blessedness consists in enjoying the Good, not in indulging in the belief that he alone, to the exclusion of all others, is enjoying it. Anyone who thinks himself to be somehow more blessed and fortunate than his neighbors is therefore actually ignorant of both happiness and good fortune." Enlightened writers, notably Voltaire and Kant, ridiculed Judaism as a faith yet championed Jewish rights of full citizenship and had several Jews among their close friends.

The German playwright and philosopher Gotthold Lessing (1729–1781) wrote two plays that dramatized the plight of European Jewry—*The Jews* (1754) and *Nathan the Wise* (1779)—and presented (scandalously, for the time) Jewish characters who were more virtuous and kindhearted than their Christian neighbors. In the latter play, which takes place during the Third Crusade, there is a scene in which the title character tells the Muslim warlord Saladin a parable. A wealthy, powerful, and noble-spirited man possessed a beautiful ring that enabled its wearer to enjoy God's special love and favor and decreed that the ring shall be passed down the generations, with each owner giving it to the son he loved the most. After several generations, one owner decided that he loved all three of his sons equally and so had two exact replicas of the ring made. None of

---

[13]   In 1752, Maria Theresa promulgated a decree limiting all Jewish families to having a single son—or else face eviction.

the three heirs therefore knew for certain which ring was the original. In that situation, Lessing writes, the choices are stark: either the sons and their successors fight one another eternally, each certain that his own ring is the true one, or they decide to live together in peace in the hope that his ring is authentic and that its authenticity is proven by the excellence of its wearer's moral behavior. The parable is apt as a description of Lessing's hope for religious toleration and as a general expression of the spirit of the Enlightened. The only solution to religious strife, they maintained, is secular virtue.

THE UNENLIGHTENED

Competing ideas and tensions existed among the Enlightened about the lower orders of society as well, who still comprised the overwhelming bulk of the population. Some writers—Locke, Hume, Voltaire, and Kant especially among them—regarded the idea of radical democracy as sheer lunacy. But as poverty and its consequences spread, what was to be done? For Locke and Voltaire, to give common farmers and laborers a political voice equal to that of the educated and propertied was an offense to intelligence and good taste. (Voltaire was even known to order his servants to leave the room before allowing conversation on religion to begin. The lower orders, he felt, could never hope to understand his Enlightened ideas, so best not to inflame their ignorance by letting them overhear.) To Hume, distinction by birth was as fixed as distinction by race. Just as "there never was a civilized nation of any other complexion than white," so too the notion of the civilized mass of common people was unimaginable. As for Kant, the only political or civic freedom he could envision was one of freedom of the Enlightened from the tyranny of the brutish common folk. He wrote the following in his essay "What Is Enlightenment?" (1784):

> In truth, only a ruler with a large and disciplined army at his disposal can say, "Debate as much you wish, but obey me!" An ironical fact thus emerges—that the greater the degree of civic freedom, the more limited the freedom of the spirit; but a lesser degree of civic freedom allows the [Enlightened] mind to grow to the utmost it is capable of doing.

As for Voltaire, he wrote movingly in his great *Treatise on Toleration* (1763):

> It takes no great art, no specially trained eloquence, to show that all Christians should have tolerance for one another—but I am going one step further and asserting that all men should be regarded as brothers to

one another. What? A Turk, my brother? A Chinaman, my brother? A Jew? A Siamese? To which I respond: Yes! Absolutely! After all, are we not all children of the same Father, all created by the same God?

And yet Voltaire's personal letters and diaries, which fill 102 volumes in their standard edition, make plain that he despised Jews. Racial vituperation and caricature pour off their pages with numbing regularity. His anti-Semitism, like Martin Luther's in the 16th century, was certainly no worse than that of his contemporaries, yet his stature lent the prejudice a shameful degree of legitimation. His views of the lower orders were no less odious. He finds them ignorant, brutish, foul smelling, lazy, simplistic, and incapable of understanding or appreciating the noble work of the philosophes.

Few of the philosophes or those who read them felt any shame about disregarding the lowest levels of society. Millions of peasants lived on the edge of poverty and famine. Those who could not pay their rent were driven from the land. In France alone, throughout the 18th century nearly a quarter million peasants per year on average lost their farms and, having no place else to go, migrated into the cities. Across Europe, from Ireland to Poland, between 10 and 20 percent of all city dwellers were indigent laborers who depended entirely on charity for survival. The possibilities this raised for crime led local governments to build ever more workhouses, where the indigent presumably could earn their keep by doing low-grade manufacturing labor. In reality, nearly a quarter of them died within six months of entering the poorhouse.

The number of these institutions across Europe more than doubled from 1700 to 1789, with the bulk of that increase occurring after 1740. (The population of Europe increased by only 30 percent over the same period.) With these demographic shifts came new social problems. By 1789 nearly one-fifth of all childbirths in Europe occurred out of marriage, a key factor in which was the number of poor women who entered domestic service to the better-off. In the German principalities, the rate of out-of-wedlock births quadrupled from 1700 to 1800. Many novels of the era, such as the immensely popular *Pamela, or Virtue Rewarded* (1740) by English writer Samuel Richardson, narrate the drama of young girls in service at the mercy of their employers.[14]

Poverty grew more visible as it worsened, since the cities became choked with unemployed, starving crowds. The problem was exacerbated by disputes

---

[14] Nor were servant girls the only victims of lecherous rakes. Richardson's richest novel, *Clarissa*, tells of the repeated attempts to seduce the virtuous maiden (of good birth) of the title.

The Common Life   Louis Le Nain (1593–1648) was one of three French artist brothers, all of whom signed their works with only their family name, thus making it difficult to tell which brother painted which painting. The effort is further complicated by the brothers' similar subjects and style. Whether portraying a panel of city aldermen, a group of friends around a gaming table, or, as here, a peasant family listening to their grandfather play a song on his pipe, the Le Nain brothers show commoners' lives with dignity and grace.

over whose responsibility they were. Traditionally, Europe's poor had depended on churches, religious confraternities, guild-supported hospices, and almsgiving by those lucky enough to have money to spare. Caring for the indigent was generally not regarded as a responsibility of the state. But the numbers of the wretched, and the social ills associated with their condition, dramatized the need for radical new approaches.

Anglo-Irish novelist and satirist Jonathan Swift (1667–1745) offered an ironic one with his famous essay "A Modest Proposal" of 1729, to deal with the teeming swarms of orphan children in Ireland:

> I am assured by our merchants, that a boy or a girl before twelve years old is no salable commodity; and even when they come to this age they will not yield above three pounds, or three pounds and half-a-crown

at most on the exchange; which cannot turn to account either to the parents or kingdom, the charge of nutriment and rags having been at least four times that value.

I shall now therefore humbly propose my own thoughts, which I hope will not be liable to the least objection. I have been assured by a very knowing American of my acquaintance in London, that a young healthy child well nursed is at a year old a most delicious, nourishing, and wholesome food, whether stewed, roasted, baked, or boiled; and I make no doubt that it will equally serve in a fricassee or a ragout.

His point was satirical, but the essay raised few laughs. Swift's near contemporary Samuel Johnson (1709–1784), who compiled the *Dictionary of the English Language* discussed in chapter 15, among other influential works, wrote that "a decent provision for the poor is a true test of civilization" and opened his own home to a parade of the needy. Yet even he reserved his charity for the "deserving poor"—those who could not care for themselves because of physical or mental debility. Like most of his contemporaries, Johnson expected the unhandicapped poor either to fend for themselves or to accept misery as man's natural condition.

The philosophes, for the most part, failed to do much better. Rousseau, as we saw, argues that man's natural compassion is corroded by the competition for material goods. Economic and social privilege therefore legitimate and perpetuate one another. When Voltaire received a copy of the *Discourse*, he thanked Rousseau for his "newest attack on the human race." His characteristic sarcasm might be dismissed as lighthearted, but a note Voltaire wrote in the margin gives his real opinion away: "Here it is—the philosophy of a wretch who wants nothing more than for the rich to be robbed by the poor."

Yet the philosophes were not heartless. They spoke fervently against the injustices that made the lives of common peasants and laborers worse. Frenchman Gabriel Bonnot de Mably (1709–1785), for one, asserted the equality of all persons before the law, as well as the equality of their material needs—an early form of Communism. But they did not see elevating the lowest strata of society as important or even desirable. To most of the Enlightened, the uneducated laboring masses were simply a fact of nature, and no rational reform of society and civil life could change it. Even de Mably maintained that peasants were stupid and ignorant. They deserve sympathy, he argues, only because their poverty, which previously had been voluntary, had become institutionalized by absolutism. The philosophes, in sum, aimed at the rational reform of polite society. The great toiling bulk of humanity did not need liberty, wealth, and rights. They only needed better masters.

ASSESSING THE ENLIGHTENMENT

In the context of Europe's intellectual history, the significance of the Enlightenment can hardly be exaggerated. The philosophes generated new ideas, contributed enormously to culture, and inspired later generations to follow in their steps. But the Enlightenment had immediate cultural reverberations as well. With its full array of pamphlets, histories, encyclopedias, stage-plays, public lectures, and salons, it contributed to the development of the public sphere—that is, a common marketplace of ideas. Society talking to itself, debating its choices for the future. Such a development was a necessary precedent for the modern state.

Readers of the Enlightened were numerous and avid. The *Encyclopedia* appeared in thousands of private and public libraries all over France, as did its English, German, and Italian counterparts in those countries (see Map 16.2). Rousseau's *Emile*, like Voltaire's *Letters on the English* and *Philosophical Dictionary*, was known to tens of thousands. Lectures and public readings by Locke, Smith,

MAP 16.2 Subscriptions to the *Encyclopedia*, ca. 1780 Though expensive, Diderot's *Encyclopedia* sold widely. It consisted of 28 volumes—17 of text (over 70,000 articles) and 11 of plates (over 3000 illustrations).

Diderot, Beccaria, and others were enjoyed by untold numbers; and their ideas circulated through innumerable salon meetings. They fought against censorship by cleverly disguising their messages, by circulating to an extent under the governments' radar, by book smuggling across borders, and by the black market. But who exactly read these works and embraced their ideas, and what does that say about social and cultural change in 18th-century Europe?

Some of the Enlightened's most fervent readers and supporters came from the aristocracy itself. Indeed, a number of the leading philosophes were themselves noble born, such as the Baron de Montesquieu. But it is a mistake to give them too much credit here. By 1750 hereditary aristocrats made up a small portion of the European population, overall. Generally, the figure was 1–2 percent in England and France and increased as one moved eastward and southward through the Continent from there: 4–5 percent in Germany, 5–6 percent in Italy and in Austria–Hungary, 7–8 percent in Spain, and as much as 9–10 percent in Poland–Lithuania. Russia then provided a firm backstop with a return to a restricted 1–2 percent—although the bulk of these lived in western Russia's regions around Moscow and St. Petersburg, regardless of where their landholdings actually were.

Allowing for differences between countries, then, approximately 3–4 percent of the European population consisted of the hereditary aristocracy. The nobles found many of the philosophes' ideas worth investigating, but usually only those dealing with technical matters. It was one thing to improve agricultural yields, make mining more efficient, or develop better means to transport rural goods to urban markets. Beyond that, however, few dared or cared to venture. They expected legal privileges and monopolies, not open markets. Mercantilism and feudal privilege guaranteed their income, and the Enlightened ideas that attracted them most were the ones that could increase their profit margins.

Some nobles were drawn to Enlightened ideas about society, law, government, and religion—but they were few. In general, countries with a higher proportion of nobility (Italy, Austria–Hungary, Spain, Poland–Lithuania) also had more impoverished nobles—who, in turn, felt more threatened by change. Noble readers of the philosophes in those countries were few indeed. In England, France, and Germany, the nobles proved more willing to investigate Enlightened activity.[15] John Locke and David Hume owed much of their living to the patronage of society's greats. Immanuel Kant was revered by countless more Prussians than those who actually read and understood him. Diderot had a few noble

---

[15]   No fewer than 30 of the 160 author-contributors to Diderot's *Encyclopedia* were noble.

patrons who could be relied on to help him out of his legal troubles; and the Baron de Montesquieu and the Marquis de Condorcet actively participated in the Enlightened movement. But the overwhelming bulk of the aristocracy deeply distrusted more radical philosophes like Rousseau and tried hard to marginalize or imprison them.

The main audience for the Enlightened, then, was the middle class, or the **bourgeoisie** (from *bourgeois,* French for "city dweller")—especially its upper strata of people who earned their living in the professions—as doctors, lawyers, merchants, or local civil officials—or through investment in land, trade, or manufacturing. Many of these individuals were as wealthy as the hereditary aristocrats who shunned them, and the Enlightenment allowed them important roles in intellectual and artistic life that might elevate their place in society. Salons, learned societies, patronage of artists and composers, and support for theatrical companies were more than just means to promote the new learning. They also controlled its funding and shaped its development. John Locke's wealthy patrons, for example, influenced the development of his political thought, with its stress on property rights; it is impossible to imagine those patrons supporting Rousseau in the same way.

By 1700 this well-to-do bourgeoisie was large enough to support an ambitious campaign to spread Enlightenment ideas, values, and culture. The total population of France, for example, increased from roughly 22 million in 1700 to approximately 30 million in 1800—a gain of about 33 percent. But within that population the number of wealthy bourgeoisie increased 300 percent. Europe now had a highly developed urban culture. The greatest city of all was London, with just over a million people; Paris came next, with 600,000; the next tier was occupied by Berlin, Vienna, and Saint Petersburg, with about 200,000 each. Rome and Milan had slightly fewer, perhaps 150,000 each. Scores of smaller cities, too, had the wealth of the bourgeoisie to maintain universities, support scientific academies, offer lectures in public halls—and host private salons and establish Masonic lodges (see Map 16.3).

Masonic lodges date to the 17th century, perhaps starting in Scotland. They were essentially private clubs, whose members were sworn to secrecy about their activities.[16] For a nobleman, mingling in public with commoners was social suicide. As Freemasons, however, nobles could socialize with well-to-do commoners, either to arrange business dealings or to support programs such as the Enlightenment. Freemasonry was thus an 18th-century version of keeping a

---

[16] Freemasons derived their name from the medieval stonemason guilds. In earlier centuries, skilled craftsmen passed through stages of training—first as an apprentice, then as a journeyman (one who receives a day's wage), and then was "freed" to practice as a full-fledged members of the guild.

Urban Population of Europe in 1800

Percentage of population living in cities, by region:

- 0–1%
- 1–5%
- 5–10%
- 10–15%
- 15–20%
- 20–25%
- 25–30%

City with population of:

- ○ 8,000–40,000
- ◉ 40,000–200,000
- ● 200,000–400,000
- ■ over 400,000

The Growth of European Cities 1500–1800

Population
1,000,000
750,000
500,000
250,000
0

1500 1550 1600 1650 1700 1750 1800

— London — Amsterdam
— Paris — Lisbon
— Naples — Madrid
— Vienna — Venice

MAP 16.3 Urban Population of Europe in 1800 By 1800 city-dwellers—that is, people who lived in a town of at least 30,000—made up roughly 3% of the total population. That figure would rise dramatically in the 19th century.

private Facebook account. Here a controlled and closed circle of friends could stay in touch, trade ideas, and promote new projects.

The Catholic Church condemned **freemasonry** as evil. The church saw it as a conspiracy to destroy the divinely ordained institutions that kept the world in order. However, by 1750 Masonry had spread as far east as Poland and Russia and as far west as the

A Meeting of a Masonic Lodge in Vienna, 1790   The great Austrian composer Wolfgang Amadeus Mozart (1756–1791) was said to be a member.

American colonies, where figures like George Washington and Benjamin Franklin were members. In Paris alone, in the 1770s, there were well over ten thousand Masons. Through such stratagems as these, Enlightened ideas spread much farther than they could simply through book sales.

Most urban professionals clearly supported the scientific and aesthetic programs of the Enlightened. They favored breaking away from mercantilism and unleashing the free market—which is hardly surprising, since they were the ones most likely to benefit. They advocated Enlightened reforms in education as well, to promote science and technological development. None, however, spoke out in favor of public education for the masses. They desired instead vocational training for urban workers, with the elites in control of the curriculum, leaving higher matters like philosophy and political theory to leaders of the new society.

On political matters, the elites were divided. Enlightened absolutism seemed the best of all possible political worlds to many, and indeed many monarchs of the time avidly supported the philosophes, Frederick the Great of Prussia and Catherine the Great of Russia being the best examples. This group advocated a thorough reform and improvement of the current systems of governance, but not a revolution. But by the 1770s the pendulum was swinging in favor of a clean break with the past, a destruction of the Old Regime, and the creation of a new form of republic. This is also the decade in which Voltaire's reign as the supreme philosophe began to give way to Rousseau's. But the radical philosophes disagreed with their moderate colleagues mostly in degree. Both political programs were based on the rationality of the human world. Humans might be essentially good (to the radicals) or at least potentially good (to the moderates). Either way, they had it within their power to create happiness here on earth, if only they adapted their behavior to the laws of nature.

◆

Were the Enlightened truly the champions of the common man? Most of them did not pretend to be. They wanted a world based on merit and reasoned argument rather than inherited privilege. If they saw themselves as the unique possessors of that merit, they were simply being human. Rousseau, above all, radicalized the Enlightenment by speaking passionately to the lower orders. He came from them, and he urged them to disregard the fancy theories of the powdered and pampered salons. He especially despised Voltaire as a hypocrite. Voltaire died rich, yet a bitter man, because he was never granted the peerage he so desperately desired. Lauded by all as a champion of freedom, he had been shunted aside by a vulgar upstart from Geneva. When Rousseau cast the light of his reason on the Enlightened, he found them wanting, and he called on the masses to take their fates into their own hands. He was fortunate to have died in 1778 because he never saw the results of that call.

WHO, WHAT, WHERE

Acts of Toleration	freemasonry	market
Adam Smith	Jean-Jacques Rousseau	Montesquieu
bourgeoisie	John Locke	philosophes
deism	Hasidim	Pierre Bayle
Denis Diderot	Haskalah	salons
Enlightenment	laissez-faire	Voltaire

SUGGESTED READINGS

Primary Sources

Bayle, Pierre. *Historical and Critical Dictionary.*

Beccaria, Cesare. *On Crimes and Punishments.*

Diderot, Denis. *Encyclopedia.*

Hume, David. *An Enquiry Concerning Human Understanding.*

Locke, John. *An Essay Concerning Human Understanding.*

Locke, John. *Two Treatises of Civil Government.*

Montesquieu, Baron Charles de. *The Spirit of Laws.*

Rousseau, Jean-Jacques. *Confessions.*

Rousseau, Jean-Jacques. *Discourse on the Origins of Inequality.*

Rousseau, Jean-Jacques. *The Social Contract.*

Smith, Adam. *The Wealth of Nations.*

Voltaire. *Candide.*

Voltaire. *A Philosophical Dictionary.*

Source Anthologies

Hyland, Paul, ed. *The Enlightenment: A Sourcebook and Reader* (2001).

Jacob, Margaret C. *The Enlightenment: A Brief History with Documents* (2000).

Studies

Anderson, Fred. *Crucible of War: The Seven Years' War and the Fate of Empire in British North America, 1754–1766* (2000).

Berg, Maxine. *Luxury and Pleasure in Eighteenth-Century Britain* (2005).

Blanning, T. C. W. *The Culture of Power and the Power of Culture: Old Regime Europe, 1660–1789* (2002).

Blom, Philipp. *Enlightening the World: "Encyclopédie," the Book That Changed the World* (2005).

Buchan, James. *The Authentic Adam Smith: His Life and Ideas* (2006).

Dale, Richard. *The First Crash: Lessons from the South Sea Bubble* (2004).

Damrosch, Leo. *Jean-Jacques Rousseau: Restless Genius* (2007).

Doyle, William. *Aristocracy and Its Enemies in the Age of Revolution* (2009).

Fara, Patricia. *Pandora's Breeches: Women, Science, and Power in the Enlightenment* (2004).

Feiner, Shmuel. *Haskalah and History: The Emergence of a Modern Jewish Historical Consciousness* (2004).

Feiner, Shmuel. *The Jewish Enlightenment* (2003).

Goodman, Dena. *Becoming a Woman in the Age of Letters* (2009).

Goodman, Dena, and Kathleen Wellman. *The Enlightenment* (2003).

Groenewegen, Peter D. *Eighteenth-Century Economics: Turgot, Beccaria, and Smith and Their Contemporaries* (2002).

Hess, Jonathan M. *Germans, Jews, and the Claims of Modernity* (2002).

Hesse, Carla. *The Other Enlightenment: How French Women Became Modern* (2003).

Israel, Jonathan. *Democratic Enlightenment: Philosophy, Revolution, and Human Rights, 1750–1790* (2011).

Israel, Jonathan. *Enlightenment Contested: Philosophy, Modernity, and the Emancipation of Man, 1670–1752* (2006).

Israel, Jonathan. *Radical Enlightenment: Philosophy and the Making of Modernity, 1650–1750* (2001).

McMahon, Darrin M. *Enemies of the Enlightenment: The French Counter-Enlightenment and the Making of Modernity* (2001).

Munck, Thomas. *The Enlightenment: A Comparative Social History, 1724–1794* (2000).

Naimark-Goldberg, Natalie. *Jewish Women in Enlightenment Berlin* (2013).

O'Brien, Karen. *Women and Enlightenment in 18th-Century Britain* (2009).

Pearson, Roger. *Voltaire Almighty: A Life in Pursuit of Freedom* (2005).

Porter, Roy. *The Creation of the Modern World: The Untold Story of the British Enlightenment* (2000).

Saul, John Ralston. *Voltaire's Bastards: The Dictatorship of Reason in the West* (1992).

Straub, Kristina. *Domestic Affairs: Intimacy, Eroticism, and Violence between Servants and Masters in Eighteenth-Century Britain* (2005).

Sutcliffe, Adam. *Judaism and Enlightenment* (2003).

Zaretsky, Robert, and John T. Scott. *The Philosophers' Quarrel: Rousseau, Hume, and the Limits of Human Understanding* (2009).

For additional resources, including maps, primary sources, visuals, web links, and quizzes, please go to **www.oup.com/us/backman**.

DÉCLARATION DES DROITS DE L'HOMME ET DU CITOYEN

Décretés par l'Assemblée Nationale dans les séances des 20, 21 23, 24 et 26 août 1789, acceptés par le Roi

PRÉAMBULE

LES représentans du peuple François, constitués en assemblée nationale, considérant que l'ignorance, l'oubli ou le mépris des droits de l'homme sont les seules causes des malheurs publics et de la corruption des gouvernemens ont résolu d'exposer dans une déclaration solemnelle, les droits naturels, inaliénables et sacrés de l'homme afin que cette déclaration constamment présente à tous les membres du corps social, leur rappelle sans cesse leurs droits et leurs devoirs, afin que les actes du pouvoir législatif et ceux du pouvoir exécutif, pouvant être à chaque instant comparés avec le but de toute institution politique, en soient plus respectés; afin que les réclamations des citoyens, fondées désormais sur des principes simples et incontestables, tournent toujours au maintien de la constitution et du bonheur de tous.

EN conséquence, l'assemblée nationale reconnoit et déclare, en présence et sous les auspices de l'Être suprême les droits suivans de l'homme et du citoyen.

ARTICLE PREMIER

LES hommes naissent et demeurent libres, et égaux en droits, les distinctions sociales ne peuvent être fondées que sur l'utilité commune.

II.

LE but de toute association politique est la conservation des droits naturels et imprescriptibles de l'homme; ces droits sont la liberté, la propriété, la sûreté, et la résistance à l'oppression.

III.

LE principe de toute souveraineté réside essentiellement dans la nation, nul corps, nul individu ne peut exercer d'autorité qui n'en émane expressement.

IV.

LA liberté consiste à pouvoir faire tout ce qui ne nuit pas à autrui Ainsi, l'exercice des droits naturels de chaque homme, n'a de bornes que celles qui assurent aux autres membres de la société la jouissance de ces mêmes droits; ces bornes ne peuvent être déterminées que par la loi.

V.

LA loi n'a le droit de défendre que les actions nuisibles à la société, Tout ce qui n'est pas défendu par la loi ne peut être empêché, et nul ne peut être contraint à faire ce qu'elle n'ordonne pas.

VI.

LA loi est l'expression de la volonté générale; tous les citoyens ont droit de concourir personnellement, ou par leurs représentans, à sa formation; elle doit être la même pour tous, soit qu'elle protège, soit qu'elle punisse, Tous les citoyens étant égaux à ses yeux, sont également admissibles à toutes dignités, places et emplois publics, selon leur capacité, et sans autres distinction que celles de leurs vertus et de leurs talens

VII.

NUL homme ne peut être accusé, arrêté ni détenu que dans les cas déterminés par la loi, et selon les formes qu'elle a prescrites, ceux qui sollicitent, expédient, exécutent ou font exécuter des ordres arbitraires, doivent être punis; mais tout citoyen appelé ou saisi en vertu de la loi, doit obéir à l'instant, il se rend coupable par la résistance.

VIII.

LA loi ne doit établir que des peines strictement et évidemment nécessaire, et nul ne peut être puni qu'en vertu d'une loi établie, et promulguée antérieurement au délit, et légalement appliquée.

IX.

TOUT homme étant présumé innocent jusqu'à ce qu'il ait été déclaré coupable, s'il est jugé indispensable de l'arrêter, toute rigueur qui ne serait pas nécessaire pour s'assurer de sa personne doit être sévèrement réprimée par la loi.

X.

NUL ne doit être inquiété pour ses opinions, mêmes religieuses pourvu que leur manifestation ne trouble pas l'ordre public établi par la loi.

XI.

LA libre communication des pensées et des opinions est un des droits les plus précieux de l'homme; tout citoyen peut donc parler écrire, imprimer librement; sauf à répondre de l'abus de cette liberté dans les cas déterminés par la loi.

XII.

LA garantie des droits de l'homme et du citoyen nécessite une force publique; cette force est donc instituée pour l'avantage de tous, et non pour l'utilité particulière de ceux à qui elle est confiée.

XIII.

POUR l'entretien de la force publique, et pour les dépenses d'administration, une contribution commune est indispensable; elle doit être également répartie entre les citoyens en raison de leurs facultés.

XIV.

LES citoyens ont le droit de constater par eux même ou par leurs représentans, la nécessité de la contribution publique, de la consentir librement, d'en suivre l'emploi, et d'en déterminer la quotité, l'assiette, le recouvrement et la durée.

XV.

LA société a le droit de demander compte à tout agent public de son administration.

XVI.

TOUTE société, dans laquelle la garantie des droits n'est pas assurée, ni la séparation des pouvoirs déterminée, n'a point de constitution

XVII.

LES propriétés étant un droit inviolable et sacré, nul ne peut en être privé, si ce n'est lorsque la nécessité publique, légalement constatée, l'exige évidemment, et sous la condition d'une juste et préalable indemnité.

AUX REPRESENTANS DU PEUPLE FRANCOIS

CHAPTER 17

The French Revolution and the Napoleonic Empire

1789–1815

In the minds of many, the French Revolution of 1789–1799 is the prime divider of European history, the watershed event that announced the dramatic and bloody beginning of the modern age. Of the drama and blood there is no doubt. The Revolution overthrew monarchy, abolished aristocracy and the decayed remnants of feudalism, instituted representative government, spurred nationalism, and asserted the innate human rights of liberty, freedom of expression, and equality before the law. It proclaimed the beginning of a new era of enlightened independence. Along the way it also slaughtered hundreds of thousands of victims, triggered a continental war, terrorized into silent obedience the very people it purported to free, ruined fortunes, and crushed forms of religious and cultural life that had buoyed human spirits through centuries of deprivation and struggle.

It also led to an equally tumultuous and bloody aftermath that transformed the whole of Europe—and not just in the direction of liberty and modernity. The rise to power of Napoleon Bonaparte in France brought reform elsewhere, as he sought to expand the republic into an empire. Revolutionary principles advanced across Europe and beyond, even as Europe's monarchs struggled to halt the march of "liberty, equality, fraternity."

THE GREATER WEST, ca. 1800

NORWAY SWEDEN
GREAT DENMARK RUSSIA
BRITAIN PRUSSIA
PORTUGAL FRANCE AUSTRIAN
EMPIRE
SPAIN KINGDOM OTTOMAN EMPIRE
OF
NAPLES
EGYPT

The Declaration of the Rights of Man and Citizen This central document of the French Revolution was enacted by the National Assembly on August 26, 1789.

A REVOLUTION IN WESTERN HISTORY?

Much of the vocabulary of modern political life derives from the Revolution. Factions are described as "left," "right," "centrist," or "radical"; institutions promote their aims through "declarations" and "agendas," which their opponents dismiss as "propaganda." The "will of the people," not the privilege of the mighty, is the touchstone for political rectitude. Even the ideology of a faction, including those dedicated to "terrorism," derives from the language of the Revolution. So large does the Revolution loom in most Western minds that it is the first single political event given an entire chapter in most general histories of Europe—and yet most historians seem to be consciously unaware of that fact.

But other people disagree. Essentially, the Revolution changed little to nothing, they say. France began the year 1789 with a financially and morally corrupt political system. When the Revolution ended ten years later, with Napoleon in firm control of the state, France had simply replaced one autocratic regime with another. Much of France's subsequent political history, they argue, has consisted of a perpetual swing of the pendulum from one extreme to another: the French Republic (1792–1804), then Empire (1804–1814) and restoration of the monarchy (1814–1848), then Second Republic (1848–1852), then Second Empire (1852–1870), then Third Republic (1870–1940), then Vichy and Nazi-occupied France (1940–1945), then Fourth Republic (1946–1958)—which was followed, in the aftermath of the definitive collapse of empire with the loss of Algeria, by a Fifth Republic (1958–present).

CHAPTER TIMELINE

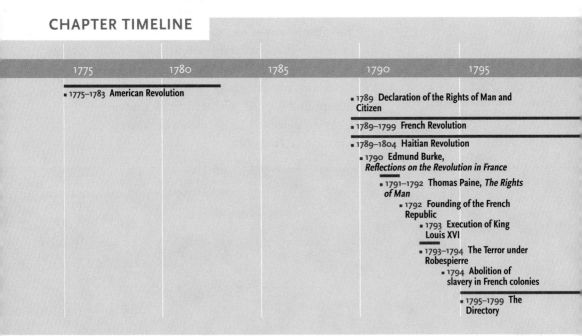

| 1775 | 1780 | 1785 | 1790 | 1795 |

- 1775–1783 American Revolution
- 1789 Declaration of the Rights of Man and Citizen
- 1789–1799 French Revolution
- 1789–1804 Haitian Revolution
- 1790 Edmund Burke, *Reflections on the Revolution in France*
- 1791–1792 Thomas Paine, *The Rights of Man*
- 1792 Founding of the French Republic
- 1793 Execution of King Louis XVI
- 1793–1794 The Terror under Robespierre
- 1794 Abolition of slavery in French colonies
- 1795–1799 The Directory

So was the French Revolution the single most important event in Western history, or was it an inconsequential spasm of violence inspired by values already long established? Or is the truth somewhere in between? Even in the eyes of its contemporaries, the Revolution appeared in widely varying guises. To the British statesman Edmund Burke (1729–1797), one of the founders of modern political conservatism, the Revolution showed only that the French people had proven themselves to be

> the ablest architects of ruin that had hitherto existed in the world. In that very short space of time they ha[ve] completely pulled down to the ground, their monarchy; their church; their nobility; their law; their revenue; their army; their navy; their commerce; their arts; and their manufactures. . . . [There is a danger of] an imitation of the excesses of an irrational, unprincipled, proscribing, confiscating, plundering, fero-cious, bloody and tyrannical democracy. . . . [In religion] the danger of their example is no longer from intolerance, but from Atheism; a foul, unnatural vice, foe to all the dignity and consolation of mankind; which seems in France, for a long time, to have been embodied into a faction, accredited, and almost avowed.

And yet the overthrow of the French monarchy led other Englishmen, like the young poets William Wordsworth (1770–1850) and Samuel Coleridge

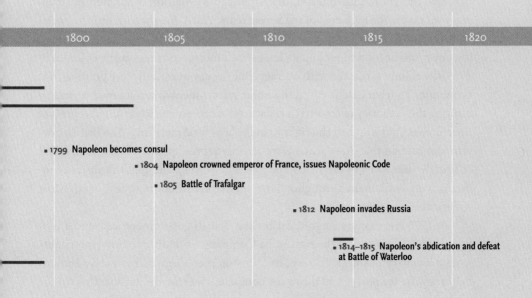

1800   1805   1810   1815   1820

- 1799 Napoleon becomes consul
- 1804 Napoleon crowned emperor of France, issues Napoleonic Code
- 1805 Battle of Trafalgar
- 1812 Napoleon invades Russia
- 1814–1815 Napoleon's abdication and defeat at Battle of Waterloo

(1772–1834), to race to the Continent to witness firsthand the creation of a utopian new world. As Wordsworth wrote in his great poem, *The Prelude* (published posthumously in 1850):

> Bliss was it in that dawn to be alive,
> But to be young was very heaven!—Oh! Times,
> In which the meager, stale, forbidding ways
> Of custom, law, and statute, took at once
> The attraction of a country in romance!
> When Reason seemed the most to assert her rights,
> When most intent on making of herself
> A prime Enchantress—to assist the work,
> Which then was going forward in her name!

Whether for the nobility of its aims or the ruthlessness of its methods, the Revolution still fascinates and impassions.

REVOLUTIONARY ROAD

Impact of the American Revolution

Coinciding with the waning years of the Enlightenment and the early years of the reign of Louis XVI (r. 1774–1792), the American Revolution had an enormous practical and ideological impact on France. French expenses to support the American colonists had helped to bankrupt the Crown, whereas the Enlightened ideals of liberty and equality provided heady inspiration for political reform.

Like the French Revolution, the American Revolution originated in struggles over taxes. The high cost of the Seven Years' War—fought with little financial contribution from the colonies—had doubled the British national debt, and when the government tried to recoup its losses with increased taxes on the colonies in 1765, the colonists reacted with outrage. But the key questions were political, not economic. To what extent could the home government assert its own power by limiting the authority of colonial legislatures? Accordingly, who should represent the colonies, and who had the right to make laws for Americans? The British government replied that Americans were already represented in Parliament, albeit indirectly (like most of the British people themselves), and that the absolute supremacy of Parliament throughout the empire could not be questioned. Most Americans felt otherwise.

In 1773 the dispute reignited after the British government awarded a monopoly on Chinese tea to the East India Company, excluding colonial merchants from a lucrative business. In response, Boston men disguised as native Indians held a rowdy "tea party" and threw the company's tea into the harbor. This led the

Parliament to extreme countermeasures. The so-called Coercive Acts closed the port of Boston, curtailed local elections, and expanded the royal governor's power. County conventions in Massachusetts urged that the acts be rejected, and other colonial assemblies joined the protest. In September 1744 the First Continental Congress met in Philadelphia, where the more radical members argued successfully against concessions to the Crown. Compromise was also rejected by Parliament, and in April 1775 fighting began at Lexington and Concord, a few miles from the revolutionary center of Boston. The fighting spread, and the colonists moved slowly toward open rebellion. The uncompromising attitude of the British government and its use of German mercenaries dissolved long-standing loyalties to the home country. Many "Loyalists" who wished to remain within the British Empire immigrated to the northern colonies of Canada.

On July 4, 1776, the Second Continental Congress adopted the Declaration of Independence. Written by Thomas Jefferson (who, as we learned in chapter 16, drew from the ideas and language of John Locke), it boldly listed the tyrannical acts committed by George III (r. 1760–1820) and proclaimed the sovereignty of the American states. It also universalized the traditional rights of English people, stating "that all men are created equal, that they are endowed by their Creator with certain unalienable Rights, that among these are Life, Liberty, and the Pursuit of Happiness." (The Declaration sidestepped the practice of slavery in the southern states, however, and indeed Jefferson himself was a slave-owner. Four of the first five U.S. presidents owned slaves, in fact, even during the years of their presidencies.[1]) By 1780, all thirteen states had adopted their own written constitutions.

On the international scene, the French wanted revenge for the humiliating defeats of the Seven Years' War. They supplied guns and ammunition to the rebels from the beginning—not from a desire to see democracy supplant monarchy but from a conviction that anything that undermined England's power indirectly favored France's. By 1777 French volunteers were arriving in Virginia, and a dashing young nobleman, the Marquis de Lafayette (1757–1834), became one of the most trusted generals of army commander and future president George Washington (1732–1799). In 1778 the French government offered a formal alliance to the American ambassador in Paris, Benjamin Franklin (1706–1790), and in 1779 and 1780 the Spanish and Dutch declared war on Britain. Catherine the Great of Russia helped organize the League of Armed Neutrality to protect neutral shipping rights, which Britain refused to recognize.

---

[1] The first presidents were George Washington (1789–1797), John Adams (1797–1801), Thomas Jefferson (1801–1809), James Madison (1809–1817), and James Monroe (1817–1825). Adams was the only one who never owned slaves. Four of the *next* five presidents were also slave owners, although not all during their years in office.

Marquis de Lafayette   The Marquis de Lafayette (1757–1834) was a precociously talented French military officer—he was commissioned at the age of thirteen—who traveled to America to help its rebellion against British rule. After the war ended, Lafayette returned to France in time to be elected to the Estates General of 1789. He helped to write the *Declaration of the Rights of Man and Citizen*. When radical factions took control of the National Convention in 1792, Lafayette fled to Belgium, where he was arrested and imprisoned for five years. Upon his release he returned to France, but refused to cooperate with Napoleon Bonaparte's government.

Thus by 1780 Great Britain was at war with most of Europe, as well as against the thirteen colonies. Outnumbered and suffering severe reverses, a new British government offered peace on generous terms. By the Treaty of Paris of 1783, Britain recognized the independence of the thirteen colonies and ceded vast territory between the Allegheny Mountains and the Mississippi River to the Americans. In 1787 the Federal Convention met in Philadelphia to draft the new Constitution of the United States.

Europeans who dreamed of a new era were fascinated by the American Revolution. The Americans had begun with a revolutionary defense against tyrannical oppression, and they had been victorious. They had then shown how rational beings could assemble to exercise sovereignty and form a new social contract. All this gave greater reality to the concepts of individual liberty and representative government and reinforced a primary Enlightenment ideal: that a better world was possible. No country felt the consequences of the American Revolution more directly than France. Hundreds of French officers were inspired by service in America, the Marquis de Lafayette chief among them. French intellectuals engaged in passionate analysis of the new federal and state constitutions. Perhaps most important, the war's expenses provided the last nail in the coffin for the French treasury.

Financial Crisis   The great German poet Johann Wolfgang von Goethe (1749–1832) may not have had France in mind when he stated that "revolutions are never the fault of the people, but of the government," but the judgment fits the French case—at least as an immediate cause. The Old Regime was in fiscal free fall from 1750 on—long before the French Revolution turned radical.

Wars with Spain, Holland, Austria, and Prussia had drained money from the treasury at an astonishing rate, but the losses simply made war even more necessary: the Crown, having already sucked every possible *sou* out of the domestic economy, needed more lands and people to plunder to maintain its place. Crop failures plagued the kingdom at midcentury too, driving rent payers into arrears and their landlords into still deeper debt themselves. When royal and aristocratic expenditures continued unabated, the result was a vast web of indebtedness. France had no national bank to regulate the fiscal rot, which forced the throne to live off short-term, high-interest loans from private sources. Then came France's considerable support of the American Revolution, financed by borrowed money. By the late 1770s fully 50 percent of the annual national budget went simply to paying the interest on the soaring national debt. Finance ministers came and went with steady regularity, some advocating fiscal restraint (a repulsive idea, to the court) and others supporting exuberant spending as a means of stimulating the economy. Heavier taxes were levied on the commoners to the point where massive protest loomed. No one seemed to know how to stop the downslide.

Louis XV (r. 1715–1774) had succeeded to the throne as a young child, and during the regency established for him (under the Duke of Orléans), much of the French aristocracy had worked tirelessly to secure and extend their privileges—especially exemption from having to pay most taxes. The right to remonstrate against royal legislation, which had been taken away by Louis XIV, was restored to the ancient aristocratic-led system of legal courts—the **parlements**—and aristocratic councils replaced royal bureaucrats at every level of government. Louis overturned these councils and restored royal bureaucrats when he reached majority age in 1723, but the parlements retained their right to remonstrate and became effective opponents of royal reform throughout the 18th century. In 1771 Louis deployed the army to dissolve the parlements, but his grandson, **Louis XVI** (r. 1774–1792), restored them in a bid for popularity on his accession in 1774.

The next decade witnessed a continued back and forth between king and aristocracy that would have been unthinkable in the days of Louis XIV, but the ever-increasing national debt emboldened people to attempt the inconceivable. Meanwhile, Enlightened ideas about economic and social reform gained support at court as a means of forestalling disaster. Amid cries of alarm over royal tyranny trampling the traditional liberties of the nobles, Louis XVI ordered a lifting of mercantilist policies restricting the grain trade, abolished the guild structure, and promoted religious toleration for France's 8 million Protestants. All of this was bad enough, as far as the aristocracy was concerned—but then Louis announced his support, in 1775, for a comprehensive land tax that would include the previously exempt nobility. The announcement sparked a firestorm of complaint.

Calls for such a tax were nevertheless repeated throughout the 1770s and 1780s as the only possible way to address the crisis. Further royal steps included abolishing serfdom, condemning the use of judicial torture, and reforming the prisons, but these measures—although generally popular—required new debt financing, which only added urgency to the call for the nobles to relinquish their tax exemptions. By 1787, amid bread riots by the peasantry and loud denunciations of royal abuses of power, a contentious aristocratic council demanded the reestablishment of the historical French legislative body known as the **Estates General**. This body, which had not met since 1614, had previously held jurisdiction over tax issues, and the nobles calling for it to convene rested their hopes in a simple statistical fact: the legislature, being made up of three orders (or Estates)—one for the nobility, one for the clergy, and one for the commoners—was sure to ratify the aristocracy's position supporting tax exemption because every single one of the eight thousand–plus ecclesiastical offices represented in the clerical estate was held by a member of the nobility. By tradition, each estate met and voted as a body. Thus, no matter how loud were the cries for reform from the **Third Estate**—the commoners, composed of the vast mass of peasants, some 75 percent of the population, and the working and middle classes of the cities— the abolition of the nobles' tax emption would lose by a two-to-one vote. Popular calls to change the custom of voting by order to voting by simple head count were hotly debated. The politically active commoners became known proudly as the *sans-culottes* ("without silk breeches"), to emphasize their distinction from the upper classes, who favored knee breeches and stockings; the commoners, being laborers, customarily wore long trousers.

The Three Estates   This French cartoon from 1789 depicts three fattened members of the privileged classes—an aristocrat, a bishop, and a judge—riding atop a naked, chained, and blindfolded commoner. The cartoon's message is clear: the Third Estate, despite its representation of the vast majority of the French population, is suppressed in a venal social order.

Prior to his reluctant calling of the Estates General, Louis XVI had agreed to double the number of representatives from the Third Estate, making those delegates equal in number to the other two orders combined, but he backed away from changing the voting system. Pamphleteers by the hundreds denounced this decision, which upheld the traditional privileges of the nobility and clergy. In the most inflammatory of all the pamphlets, *What Is the Third Estate?*, radical French clergyman Abbé Emmanuel-Joseph Sieyès

(1748–1836) answered his own question: everything. Comparing the nobility to parasites, he argued that they were not even part of the body politic. "The pretended importance, for public order, of having a privileged elite is nothing more than a lie, [for in reality] all the hard work on society's behalf is performed by the Third Estate. . . . And the fact that people of privilege have usurped every lucrative and honorable position in government is both a hateful injustice to the rank-and-file of the citizenry and a betrayal of the public interest."

In the spring of 1789 elections were held around France to select the Estates' delegates. Representatives of the commoners compiled detailed records of local grievances to be brought to Paris; these grievance notebooks *Formation* (*cahiers des doléances*) offer fascinating views of the attitudes and concerns of *of the* the common populace. An example comes from a small town on the river Orge, *National* not far from Paris: *Assembly*

> The order of the Third Estate of . . . Dourdan, filled with gratitude for the fatherly kindness of Our King Who deems it fitting to restore our rights and customs of old, and setting aside for the moment our present sufferings and debilities . . . begs Him to accept this statement of our grievances, complaints, and remonstrances. . . . This estate formally petitions:
>
> That no citizen should ever lose his freedom except according to the dictates of the law; . . . that no letters nor other writings sent through the public mail be the cause of the detention of any citizen, except in the case of treason or conspiracy against the state; . . . that the property of all citizens be respected as inviolable; . . . that every poll tax be abolished . . . and replaced by a tax on land and real property . . . and that the burden of this new tax be imposed equally on every class of citizen without distinction; . . . that the venality of civil offices be abolished; . . . that statutes limiting admission to officer status in the military to members of the nobility be rescinded; . . . that today's militia, which devastates the countryside, pulls workers away from their field labor, forces people into premature and ill-advised marriages [commoners could avoid being pressed into the militias by marrying], and subjects individuals to secret and arbitrary taxes, be abolished and replaced by a public, volunteer army. (*Archives parliamentaires de 1787 à 1860*, ed. Jérôme Mavidal and Èmile Laurent [Paris, 1862], ser. 1, vol. 3, pp. 250–254)

But as the representatives gathered at Versailles in May, the clerical and aristocratic estates pressed the king to bar the Third Estate representatives from

The Tennis Court Oath   Jacques-Louis David (1748–1825), the preeminent French artist of the revolutionary era, created this iconic painting of one of the Revolution's foundational events, the Tennis Court Oath sworn on June 20, 1789. In the center stands Jean Bailly, president of the new National Assembly, with the Abbé Sieyès seated next to him. In the foreground, a clergyman, an aristocrat, and a member of the Third Estate embrace in a symbol of national unity.

admission to the assembly, to which Louis assented. Outraged, the Third Estate's representatives took the revolutionary step of leaving the body and declaring themselves a **National Assembly** of "citizens" (*citoyens*) of France, not lowly subjects of a king. When the delegates found themselves locked out of their meeting hall on June 20, they moved to a nearby tennis court, along with a handful of sympathetic nobles and clergymen, including the fiery Sieyès. Here they swore an oath not to disband until France had a written constitution. With this **Tennis Court Oath,** the Revolution, which had begun as a revolt of the nobles against the demands of the king and people for a land tax, had become a movement to establish a constitutional monarchy that abolished aristocratic privilege (see Table 17.1).

Storming of the Bastille   At first Louis XVI appeared to agree to the National Assembly, but he also ordered thousands of soldiers to march to Paris. Fear spread that the king intended to quash this new government based on citizen consent. On July 14, 1789, crowds in Paris stormed the **Bastille**, a notorious prison where people could be incarcerated simply at the king's orders (although only a few individuals were held there at the time). The liberation of the Bastille—an event now commemorated each July 14 as the French national holiday—was the first instance of the people's role in revolutionary change.

TABLE 17.1   **Major Events of the French Revolution**

May 5, 1789	Estates General convene at Versailles
June 17, 1789	Oath of the Tennis Court
July 14, 1789	Storming of the Bastille
July–August 1789	Great Fear ravages the countryside
August 4, 1789	National Assembly abolishes feudal privileges
August 26, 1789	National Assembly issues Declaration of the Rights of Man and Citizen
August 1791	Austria and Prussia issue Declaration of Pillnitz
October 5, 1789	Women march on Versailles and force royal family to return to Paris
November 1789	National Assembly confiscates church lands
July 1790	Civil Constitution of the Clergy establishes a national church; Louis XVI reluctantly agrees to accept a constitutional monarchy
June 1791	Royal family is arrested while attempting to flee France
April 1792	France declares war on Austria
September 1792	National Convention abolishes monarchy and declares France a republic
January 21, 1793	Louis XVI is executed
February 1793	France declares war on Britain, Holland, and Spain
April–June 1793	Robespierre and allies organize the Committee of Public Safety
1793–1794	Reign of Terror darkens Paris and the provinces
October 1793	Marie-Antoinette is executed
February 1794	National Convention abolishes slavery in all French territories
July 1794	Robespierre is executed; Thermidorian reaction begins
1795–1799	Directory rules
1797	Napoleon defeats Austrian armies in Italy and returns in triumph to Paris
1799	Aided by disillusioned legislators, Napoleon overthrows the Directory and seizes power

Until July 1789 the Revolution had called merely for reform of the state, not its destruction. The new National Assembly wished to establish a constitutional monarchy based on Enlightened principles of individual rights and rational government, after all. But events in France would escalate into a movement that toppled the Old Regime and replaced monarchy with republic.

THE ENLIGHTENED REVOLUTION

Before drafting a constitution in 1789, the representatives of the National Assembly needed to confront growing violence in the countryside. As food shortages spread, peasants came to fear an aristocratic plot to starve the French people by burning their crops and barns. In many places, the **Great Fear** (historians' term for the rural panic that swept France during the summer of 1789) turned into peasant attacks on aristocrats and their noble manors. Alarmed by the unrest, on August 4 the National Assembly abolished what it called the feudal regime—that is, it freed the few remaining serfs and eliminated all special privileges in matters of taxation.

Declaration of the Rights of Man and Citizen

A few weeks later, on August 26, it issued the **Declaration of the Rights of Man and Citizen** as the preamble to a new constitution. In stirring words that evoked the American Declaration of Independence, it proclaimed that "Men are born and remain free and equal in rights." Indeed the emphasis on intrinsic human rights is the principal value espoused by the Declaration and the basis of all government. "Ignoring, neglecting, and disdaining the rights of man is the sole cause of public calamities and the corruption of government," it asserted. What are some of those rights? The Declaration granted freedom of religion, freedom of the press, freedom from unreasonable arrest, the right to property, equality of taxation, and equality before the law, but to men only. This was no oversight. As we saw in chapter 16, Olympe de Gouges would soon be inspired to issue her own "Declaration of Rights of Woman and the Female Citizen," declaring "Woman is born free and lives equal to man in her rights." (She was promptly arrested, charged with treason, and executed.)

The Declaration also established the principle of national sovereignty: the king derived his authority henceforth from the nation rather than from tradition. In October 1789, the market women of Paris, protesting the soaring cost of food, put this principle to the test. Accompanied by a few supportive men, they marched to the palace of Versailles 12 miles away and captured the royal family, bringing it to live "with the people" in the city. In so doing, they showed that monarchs existed to serve the people—and that kings ignored this new reality at their peril.

Consolidation of the Liberal Revolution

The National Assembly followed the king to Paris, and the next two years, until September 1791, saw the consolidation of the liberal revolution. The National Assembly abolished the nobility as a legal order and pushed forward with the creation of a constitutional monarchy, which Louis XVI reluctantly accepted in July 1790. In the final constitution, the king remained the head of state, but lawmaking power was placed in the hands of the National Assembly. New laws broadened women's rights to seek divorce and to inherit property, but women were not allowed to vote, let alone hold political office. The men of the National Assembly believed that civic virtue would be restored if women focused on child rearing and domestic duties.

The Women of Paris March on Versailles   The bread riots of late 1789 inspired the women of Paris—here accompanied by some citizen-militia—to march to the palace at Versailles to protest to the king. This protest (October 5) supposedly inspired the queen, Marie Antoinette, to quip "Let them eat brioche," when told that the women were demonstrating because they had no bread to eat. The anecdote appears in Rousseau's unreliable memoirs (*The Confessions*) and may well be his invention.

To rid the country of local aristocratic power, the National Assembly replaced the patchwork of historic provinces with eighty-three departments of approximately equal size with identical administrative and legal structures (see Map 17.1). All officials were elected; no offices could be bought or sold. (The departments are still the basic units of the French state today.) The jumble of weights and measures that had varied from province to province was reformed, preparing the way for the introduction of the metric system in 1793. Monopolies, guilds, and workers' associations were prohibited, and barriers to trade within France were abolished in the name of economic liberty. Thus the National Assembly applied the critical spirit of the Enlightenment in a thorough reform of France's laws and institutions.

The Assembly also imposed a radical reorganization on the country's religious life. In the name of religious toleration, it granted religious freedom to French Jews and Protestants. Motivated in part by the ongoing fiscal crisis, it nationalized the Catholic Church's property, used the lands as collateral to guarantee a new paper currency, and then sold them in an attempt to put the state's finances on a solid footing. But the Assembly was also motivated by Enlightenment rationalism and distrust of popular piety, so it went further: it established a national Catholic church with priests chosen by voters and forced the Catholic

MAP 17.1 Redrawing the Map of France, 1789–1791 Before 1789, France was divided into provinces named after the territories owned by dukes and counts in the Middle Ages. Many provinces had their own law codes and systems of taxation. Determined to install uniform administrations and laws for the entire country, the National Assembly divided the provinces into eighty-three departments, with names based on their geographical characteristics: for example, Seine-Inf, Seine-et-Oise, and Seine-et-Marne for areas containing the Seine River and Pyrénées-Orientales, Hte-Pyrénées, and Basses-Pyrénées for regions with the Pyrénées Mountains.

clergy to take a loyalty oath to the new government. The pope formally condemned these actions, and only about half of French priests swore the oath. Many sincere Christians, especially those in the countryside, were upset by these changes. The attempt to remake the Catholic Church, like the Assembly's abolition of guilds, sharpened the conflict between the educated classes and the common people that had been emerging in the 18th century.

Popular Response and Continued Disorder

Thus the new government failed to win active national support. Across France most peasant farmers and laborers did little more than seize the opportunity to destroy the local records that documented their obligations to landlords and then quietly return to their work. Rumors spread quickly of noble-backed gangs of thugs roaming the countryside seeking rebellion-sympathizing peasants to attack.

Continuing disorder in 1790 and 1791 made it clear that the French Revolution had failed to achieve unanimous consent, particularly as the nationalization of the Catholic Church unleashed religious antagonisms that transcended class boundaries. While working on the constitution of 1791, the National Assembly had become torn between factions advocating a constitutional monarchy to prevent social anarchy and those who, distrusting the king, advocated the creation of a republic. Louis XVI himself exacerbated this factionalism through a failed attempt to flee the country in June 1791: urged on by the bitterly unpopular queen, Marie Antoinette, who was in contact with her brother Leopold II of Austria,

Louis hoped to rally foreign support for counterrevolution. The members of the royal family were captured near the border at Varennes and brought back to the capital. Although the new constitution declared France a constitutional monarchy, after the widely denounced "flight to Varennes," Louis was little more than a prisoner of the National Assembly.

European rulers, who had at first welcomed the revolution in France as weakening a competing monarchy, soon realized that their power was also threatened. *Foreign* The shock of Louis XVI's capture led absolutist Austria and Prussia to issue the *Reactions* Declaration of Pillnitz in August 1791. This carefully worded statement declared *and the* their willingness to intervene in France in certain circumstances and was expected to prevent revolutionary excesses without causing war. *Beginning of War*

But the crowned heads of Europe misjudged France's revolutionary spirit. As part of the complicated negotiations in writing the constitution, the National Assembly was formally dissolved on October 1, 1791, with the renamed Legislative Assembly taking its place. The Legislative Assembly had new delegates and a different character. Most of the legislators were still prosperous and well educated, but they were younger and less cautious than their predecessors. Many belonged to a political group known as the **Jacobins**, who favored a republic over a constitutional monarchy. The new Legislative Assembly reacted with patriotic fury against the Declaration of Pillnitz. If the kings of Europe were attempting to incite war against France, then they would incite a war of people against kings. In April 1792 France declared war on Austria.

France's war against tyranny went poorly at first. Prussian forces immediately joined Austria against the French, whose military situation was dire: although France's army was large, more than two-thirds of its aristocratic officer corps had long since fled the country, leaving most of the military units leaderless. Even worse, most of those officers had joined the counter-Revolutionary forces. The road to Paris lay open.

THE REVOLUTION TURNS RADICAL

In this supercharged atmosphere, rumors spread of treason by the king and queen. In August 1792, a revolutionary crowd attacked the royal palace while the *The End of* king and his family fled for their lives to the nearby Legislative Assembly. Rather *French* than offering refuge, the Assembly imprisoned the king and called for a new National Convention to be elected by universal male suffrage. A new government came into power in September 1792. Called the National Convention, it promptly abolished the monarchy altogether and declared France a republic. Put on trial in December, Louis XVI was narrowly convicted of treason and condemned to death. The heir to the long French tradition of absolute monarchy met his end on

January 21, 1793, as "citizen Louis Capet," beheaded by the newly invented guillotine.

All members of the National Convention were republicans, and at the beginning, almost all were Jacobins. But the Jacobins increasingly divided into two bitterly opposed factions—the **Girondists**, named after a department in southwestern France that was home to several of its leaders, and the Mountain, so called because its members sat in the uppermost benches on the left side of the assembly hall (the source of the modern division of political ideology into "left" and "right"). The Mountain, led by **Maximilien Robespierre** (1758–1794), a passionate ideologue who believed that anything standing in the way of the Revolution had to be eradicated, quickly seized control of the government through its leadership of the innocent-sounding Committee for Public Safety. Robespierre and his committee believed fervently that the enemies of the Revolution would stop at nothing to undermine it and so began to purge the new government's ranks of Girondists and other individuals whose loyalty to the radical cause was suspect.

The Reign of Terror

The outbreak of proroyalist rebellion in the far west of France convinced Robespierre that all the achievements of the Revolution to date were threatened. In a shockingly brutal wave of violence in the name of the supposed purification of society—known as the **Reign of Terror** (1793–1794)—Robespierre's clique engineered the arrest of more than 300,000 French men and women in only nine months, some 40,000 of whom were executed. Defending the harshness of his methods, Robespierre later wrote:

> If virtue is the wellspring of popular government in times of peace, then virtue combined with terror is the wellspring of such a government in time of revolution: virtue (without which all terror is fatal) *and* terror (without which all virtue is impotent). For terror is nothing more than swift, sure, and inflexible justice—indeed, it emanates from virtue and is not so much an independent principle as it is a natural consequence of the general idea of democracy when applied to our country's most urgent needs. . . . Subdue the enemies of liberty by terror [if you must]! You are right to do so, as founders of our Republic. Government, in a Revolution, is a despotism of liberty against tyranny. (Report on the Principles of Public Morality, 1794)

Robespierre was writing in a context of catastrophic national emergency, with the Revolution endangered by foreign invasion, aristocratic plots, and internal dissension. To his mind, France's internal strife had to be quelled as quickly as possible to avoid annihilation. This radical view was deeply influenced by

Rousseau's idea of the general will. As we saw in chapter 16, Rousseau's unique interpretation of the social contract maintained that once agreement among citizens had created a state, that state acted with a higher wisdom with which truly loyal citizens could not disagree, especially in wartime. The "General Will" justified the Terror's mass executions and the suspension of individual rights and even free thought. The concept was one of the French Revolution's most powerful legacies, enacted not only by totalitarian regimes in the 20th century but also by democracies during times of stress.

Robespierre, who fell from power in 1794 and was himself guillotined, remains a divisive figure. Immediately after his death, his political enemies destroyed most of his papers and vilified him as a fanatical dictator—the portrait that long fixed his historical image. In the 19th century, however, groups representing the working-class French, then undergoing the horrors of the industrial revolution, revived his memory as a persecuted champion of the people. Although his methods were harsh, they argued, his goals of eradicating the inequitable distribution of wealth in society and of ensuring the availability of education and work for all were admirable.[2]

Although the pace of revolution slowed following the fall of Robespierre, the National Convention under his control had already enacted a number of radical changes aimed to "republicanize everything"—in other words, to effect a cultural revolution. It criminalized the practice of Christianity, replacing it with the Cult of Reason. Revolutionary festivals aimed to make the republic sacred included the Festival of Unity on August 10, 1793, which celebrated the first anniversary of the overthrow of the monarchy. The government adopted a new calendar to replace the Christian one: year 1 dated from the beginning of the republic in September 1792. Twelve months of exactly

The Guillotine Intended as a swift and hence humane means of execution, the guillotine, essentially a mechanical headsman, inadvertently became the central symbol of revolutionary fervor. Its first use was in 1792; the Reign of Terror ended with the beheading of Robespierre himself on July 28, 1794. Since estimates of the number of people guillotined during the Terror range from 15,000 to 40,000, and since most executions took place in Paris itself, a dedicated spectator could have seen an average of twenty-five to sixty beheadings a day. And in fact great crowds of observers did show up regularly—so many that entrepreneurial vendors printed and sold programs of the daily schedule of beheadings.

---

[2]   The British novelist Hilary Mantel (b. 1952) indeed presents a sympathetic portrait of Robespierre in *A Place of Greater Safety* (1992).

thirty days each received new names derived from nature—for example, "Thermidor" (roughly equivalent to mid-July to mid-August) recalled the heat (*thermal*) of summer. Instead of seven-day weeks, ten-day *décades* provided only one day of rest every ten days and pointedly eliminated the Sunday of the Christian calendar. Widely resisted from the start, the calendar remained in force for only twelve years, and indeed, most of the radical republican programs were rolled back in the period following Robespierre's execution known as the **Thermidorian Reaction** (from the death of Robespierre on 10 Thermidor, Year II—July 28, 1794). Far more enduring was the new metric system, eventually adopted by other countries in Europe and throughout the world.

Under Robespierre the National Convention also confiscated the property of all "enemies of the Revolution" and instituted a national military draft. The draft was necessary since Britain, Holland, and Spain had joined Austria and Prussia in the invasion of the country. Spain wanted to defend absolutism; England, which had executed its own King Charles I in 1649 and lived to regret it, hoped mostly to keep France preoccupied with a land war so that it could not challenge England's primacy in the international sea-lanes. Holland's involvement was defensive, since France had launched a surprise attack on it in 1795, to provide a counterweight to England and to round up many of the French nobles who had fled to that country.

Thus, although the Terror had ended in 1794, the revolution had not. The National Convention prepared yet another constitution in 1795, setting up a two-house legislature and an executive body—the Directory. Between 1795 and 1799, the republic endured in France, but it directed a war effort abroad that would ultimately bring to power the man who would dismantle the republic and launch his own revolution.

HOW TO JUDGE A REVOLUTION

Edmund Burke

Within weeks of the Storming of the Bastille in 1789, Edmund Burke, the British founder of modern political conservatism whom we met earlier in this chapter, began writing *Reflections on the Revolution in France*. Published in 1790, the book takes the form of a letter written to a friend and sets out Burke's reasons for believing that the Revolution would end in abject failure and misery. He may have predicted the carnage correctly, but had he truly known how to judge a Revolution? For Burke's sharpest critic, the English radical Thomas Paine (1737–1809), justice, not stability, is the true index of political legitimacy.

People, Burke argues, are inherently conservative—meaning that our natural instinct is to hold securely what we value and to desire to pass those things on to our heirs. These values include but are not limited to property and wealth: morals, religious beliefs, emotional connections, and notions of identity also constitute the human legacy and are worth keeping. But an impulse to conserve does not preclude change, he asserts. A stable society will always allow a degree of freedom and experimentation, and even encourage them, and will leave a path open for individuals to achieve on their own merits. Burke insists, however, that the fairest and strongest society will be one that evolves from, rather than breaks with, its past. "A spirit of innovation is generally the result of a selfish temper and confined views. People will not look forward to posterity, who never look backward to their ancestors."

Just as he argues that people are conservative by nature, Burke argues that inequality among people is not intrinsically evil. Indeed, it cannot be so, since it is natural. Some people are simply smarter than others; some run faster; some are more skilled with their hands; some are given to contemplation rather than action. Social and economic distinctions, therefore, are natural. A well-regulated society will not allow social inequality to be oppressive, he contends, and yet any society that does away with social inequality is itself oppressive. "Believe me, Sir, those who attempt to level, never equalize. In all societies, consisting of various levels of citizens, some description must be uppermost. The levelers, therefore, only change and pervert the natural order of things . . . Everything ought to be open, but not indifferently, to every man."

Burke suggests that we need to think in terms of degrees of freedom and model our government after the social structure that is natural to any given community. Gradual but constant evolution is the best guarantor of stability—and Burke shares Hobbes's notion (discussed in chapter 15) that government's primary function is to provide stability, not justice. He does not oppose justice as a principle, but he sees it as the consequence of a stable society rather than as a vague ideal to be pursued at any cost. In pursuing such heady although foggy-minded ideals as liberty, equality, and fraternity, Burke believes, the Revolution was doomed at its birth. Moreover, he concludes his *Reflections* with a prediction:

> When the leaders choose to make themselves bidders at an auction of popularity, their talents, in the construction of the state, will be of no service. They will become flatterers instead of legislators—the instruments, not the guides, of the people. If any of them should happen to propose a scheme of liberty, soberly limited and defined with proper qualifications, he will be immediately outbid by his competitors who will produce something more splendidly popular. Suspicions will be raised of his fidelity to the cause. Moderation will be stigmatized as the virtue of cowards, and compromise as the prudence of traitors, until, in hopes of preserving the credit which may enable him to temper and moderate, on some occasions, the popular leader is obliged to become active in propagating doctrines and establishing powers that will afterward defeat any sober purpose at which he ultimately might have aimed.

A revolution, in other words, *any* revolution, will always fail because those who lead it are united only in their opposition to what they have overthrown.[3] Once the work of creating a new government begins, unity will end. Former partners in revolution will become rivals in politics. To win out over each other, the rivals will keep offering the public increasingly generous, popular, and radical promises. Soon, angry accusations of being an "enemy of the revolution" will fly through the air, arrests and executions for treason will multiply, and riots will

France as a Storm-Tossed Ship   This 1796 British map fancifully depicts Revolutionary France as a ship in distress. Note the broken prow-mast and the cut-away anchor in the Bay of Biscay. Two aft-sails have become unmoored, and a storm brews ahead even while the ship founders on rocks at the bottom.

---

3   Burke had been a sympathetic supporter of the American Revolution—but because it had *not* been a revolution from his perspective, as the colonists had not sought to overthrow the British government. In Burke's eyes, the American fight for independence was analogous to a business division breaking away from its home corporation to become a separate entity.

ensue. The revolution will spin out of control until finally someone comes along who, to save the gains made by the revolution, restores order by force. That means "propagating doctrines and establishing powers" that will undermine the entire enterprise by creating a new version of the very order that the revolution overthrew. In other words, the revolution spins from Louis XVI to the Estates General, to the Girondists, to the Jacobins, to Robespierre and the Terror, to civil war, to Napoleon—from autocracy to autocracy. Burke published his book in 1790 before any of this happened, and he died in 1797 before seeing the end of the process, but he seems to have predicted each stage uncannily. He was not opposed to the core values behind the revolution—freedom of speech and assembly, the right to property, the belief in equality before the law; rather, he believed that revolution of any kind could never bring about the realization of those values.

Others saw the Revolution differently. In England, Thomas Paine wrote *The Rights of Man* (published in two parts, 1791–1792), in which he rebuts Burke's analysis. Paine had previously immigrated to America in 1774 as an enthusiast for the colonies' push for independence and stayed there until 1787, when he returned to London.[4] In 1792 Paine went to Paris to witness the Revolution firsthand and was elected to serve in the National Assembly although he could speak no French. Robespierre hated him and arranged for his arrest in 1793. Released the following year, Paine remained in France until he returned to America in 1802.

Thomas Paine

In *Rights of Man* Paine asserts that human rights are innate, granted by Nature rather than bestowed by government. Therefore, any state that restricts or subverts the rights of its citizens may be opposed and brought down:[5]

> It is a perversion of terms to say that a charter gives rights. It operates by a contrary effect—that of taking rights away. Rights are inherently in all the inhabitants; but charters, by annulling those rights, in the majority, leave the right, by exclusion, in the hands of a few. . . . They . . . consequently are instruments of injustice . . . The fact, therefore, must be that the individuals, themselves, each, in his own personal and sovereign right, entered into a contract with each other to produce a government: and this is the only mode in which governments have a right to arise, and the only principle on which they have a right to exist.

---

4 Paine published, anonymously, the pamphlet *Common Sense* in January of 1776, in which he rallied colonists to join the rebellion against Britain. Paine introduced few original ideas to the cause, but as a popularizer his influence was enormous. More than 100,000 copies of *Common Sense* were sold within three months of its publication; Paine donated all his royalties to George Washington, who had *Common Sense* read aloud to all his troops. As John Adams later wrote, "Without the pen of the author of *Common Sense*, the sword of Washington would have been raised in vain."

5 *The Rights of Man* was so popular and caused such scandal in London that Paine was tried in absentia for sedition against the crown.

He later takes a swipe directly at Edmund Burke:

> It appears to general observation, that revolutions create genius
> and talents; but those events do no more than bring them forward.
> There is existing in man, a mass of sense lying in a dormant state, and
> which, unless something excites it to action, will descend with him,
> in that condition, to the grave. As it is to the advantage of society that
> the whole of its faculties should be employed, the construction of
> government ought to be such as to bring forward, by a quiet and regu-
> lar operation, all that extent of capacity which never fails to appear in
> revolutions.

Government can retain its legitimacy, he insists, only by supporting the intrinsic rights of its citizens. It was in this spirit that Paine later grew distrustful of
Napoleon Bonaparte and ultimately abandoned France, calling the emperor "the
completest charlatan that ever lived."

Mary
Wollstonecraft
Another early supporter of the Revolution was Mary Wollstonecraft (1759–
1797), the English social reformer whom we met in chapter 16. With two passionate tracts, she also responded to Burke. *A Vindication of the Rights of Man* (1791)
and *A Vindication of the Rights of Woman* (1792) dismiss Burke's notion of liberty
as a smokescreen designed to protect the interests of the propertied classes, when
it is the rights of the lower orders that must be respected. She argues that traditional society has brutalized women and degraded them to a subhuman level,
leaving the only rational choice for reform to be the destruction of all existing
social mores and the political regimes that support them. The writers of the Enlightenment, she fears, and now the leaders of the Revolution in Paris, have woefully neglected the rights of women, and she appeals to them not to squander such
valuable partners in the struggle to reform society:

> I appeal to their understandings; and, as a fellow-creature, claim, in
> the name of my sex, some interest in their hearts. I entreat them to assist
> to emancipate their companion, to make her a help meet for them! Would
> men but generously snap our chains, and be content with rational fellow-
> ship instead of slavish obedience, they would find us more observant
> daughters, more affectionate sisters, more faithful wives, more reason-
> able mothers—in a word, better citizens.

Wollstonecraft too rushed to Paris to witness the Revolution, in 1793. Within
two years, however, she grew disillusioned with the violent turn of events and returned to England.

NAPOLEON

As internal decay and external threat increased, and the Revolution's very existence seemed threatened, the Directory summoned its most successful general to Paris to take control of the government, institute martial law, and restore order. His name was **Napoleon Bonaparte** (1769–1821).

Napoleon's Rise to Power

Actually, his name was Napoleone Buonaparte. Descended from a minor Italian baronial family, he was born and raised on the French-controlled island of Corsica. At the age of ten he moved with his family to Autun in east-central France and enrolled in an elementary military academy. Five years later he entered the elite École militaire in Paris, where he trained to be an artillery officer; in 1785 he received his commission as a second lieutenant in the French army. When the Revolution broke out in 1789, he was back in Corsica and soon was involved in the civil struggle there between factions loyal to the monarchy, to the Jacobins, and to Corsican independence. Napoleon supported the Jacobin cause from the start and soon earned the rank of lieutenant colonel. By 1793 he was back on the Continent and leading campaigns against France's foreign invaders. His early successes on the field and his publication of a pro-Jacobin pamphlet brought him to the admiring attention of the Committee on Public Safety, which promoted him to brigadier general.

Robespierre's fall in 1794 resulted in Napoleon's brief fall from favor, but when he fought off a royalist challenge to the Directory the following year, his restoration was complete. Awarded the position of commander of the interior, Napoleon led the war against the Austrians, who were invading France via Italy. His successes led to an ambitious 1798 campaign into Egypt, where the Directory government hoped that French occupation would weaken British trade by cutting the route to India.[6] Ultimately, the expedition failed, but the French occupation of Egypt lasted long enough for that largely Muslim country to experience Enlightenment-inspired legal reforms: the French abolished torture, introduced equality before the law, and proclaimed religious toleration.

With his army pinned down by British victory at sea, Bonaparte slipped out of Egypt and made his way back to France in October 1799. He soon learned from the Abbé de Sieyès that prominent members of the legislature were plotting against the Directory leaders. Years of upheaval and uncertainty had convinced these disillusioned revolutionaries that a strong military leader was needed to restore order. Together the conspirators and Napoleon organized a coup d'état. On November 9, 1799, they ousted the Directors and on the following day

---

[6]   In legend Napoleon used the Sphinx as a practice target for artillery. Its nose and beard were in fact broken off in the 14th century on orders of a Muslim cleric—outraged that local farmers, hoping to improve their harvest, had made ritual offerings to it.

Napoleon was named first consul of the republic. A new constitution consolidating his position was overwhelmingly approved in December 1799. Republican appearances were maintained, but Napoleon was the real ruler of France.

The Napoleonic Code

The record of his accomplishments is lengthy. After quelling France's internal conflicts and driving off its foreign invaders, Napoleon set himself to overhauling nearly every aspect of French civil life, problems he attacked with extraordinary energy and intelligence. His contemporaries, whether they admired him or hated him, marveled at his charisma and drive. "A man like me does not care if a million people die in pursuit of a goal," he once declared. (At the time, he meant it rhetorically; he later put the statement to the test on the battlefields, however.) Drawing on earlier Jacobin initiatives, he created the fairest and most comprehensive taxation system France had ever seen, abolished all feudal and local customs, and enacted a systematic law code for the entire country. Called the **Napoleonic Code** as a way to exalt the ruler's image, this civil law code of 1804 protected many of the gains of the French Revolution by ensuring equality of all male citizens before the law, universal male suffrage, property rights, and religious liberty. Napoleon then went on and constructed France's first system of national education, with primary and secondary schools (*lycées*) for boys in every major town; established a teachers' training college in Paris; and organized a network of military and vocational schools for young men drawn to specific professions.

Thus the Napoleonic Code benefited mainly the middle class, but Napoleon was too pragmatic to ignore the aristocracy and clergy. He invited the exiled nobles willing to swear loyalty to the new constitution to return to France, a shrewd maneuver that brought vast amounts of withdrawn treasure back into the realm, along with the talent pool of many experienced military and civil officials. Another practical compromise was Napoleon's decision to restore the legal recognition and practice of Catholic and Protestant Christianity; although personally an Enlightened deist, he saw the value of religion as an instrument of social cohesion. Although he guaranteed freedom of religious expression, he also arranged that all clergy received their pay directly from the central government, a move that kept Napoleon firmly in control of the churches.

Although he proclaimed himself a Republican, Napoleon did not permit all freedoms. He retained strict limits on freedom of speech and of the press, for example, which made it difficult for any individuals or parties to oppose his will or question his policies. (His defenders argue that Napoleon's restrictions were simply the standards of communications control to which he was accustomed from the army.) Embracing Rousseau's idea that women should raise the next generation of citizens but not be equal citizens themselves, he also denied political rights to women: they were not allowed to vote, to enter contracts, or to hold bank accounts, and they remained the legal dependents of their fathers and husbands.

Although he could be personally gallant toward the women in his private life (of whom there were many), he did not hesitate to state his opinion about the different positions of men and women in society. "A husband must possess absolute authority over his wife," he once declared, "and must have the right to say to her, 'Madam, you shall not go out of the house; you shall not go to the theater; you shall not pay a visit to such-and-such a person. And as for the children you bear—they are mine.'"

Napoleon relished his popular image as the savior of the Republic but he also believed in his unique personal authority. He had read much history in his school days and revered the Roman leader Octavian/Augustus, who had saved the Roman Republic by keeping its institutions and customs even while running them with an iron fist as the first Roman emperor. His vision for France was along those lines. To the tips of his fingers and the end of his days,

Napoleon Enthroned   This oil portrait by French artist Jean-Auguste Ingres (1780–1867) was first exhibited at the Paris Salon of 1806, where it met a chilly reception. Stiff and imposing, the figure of Napoleon holds the scepter of the Frankish ruler Charlemagne, founder of the Carolingian Empire (r. 768–814), in his right hand. A stylized version of the German imperial eagle appears on the carpet at his feet. In the background over his left shoulder is a shield representing the states of Italy. Nothing about this representation of supreme authority is subtle—which helps to explain its unpopularity with the viewing public.

Napoleon believed in France's destiny to lead all of Europe and in his own destiny *Imperial* to lead France in the effort. But that meant addressing the system of absolutism— *Coronation* because although it had been successfully stamped out in France, it still held sway in nearly every country in Europe, and each one of those regimes was determined to see France's Revolution fail. By 1804 he was ready to act. He arranged for an imperial coronation to be performed in Paris by Pope Pius VII (r. 1800–1823) himself, who blessed the imperial regalia before placing them on the altar. Napoleon then stepped forward, took them up, and crowned himself.

There would be no question of his subordination to Rome. He was his own man, the ruler of his own state. But an emperor by definition needs an empire. And so he conquered Europe.

THE RUSH TO EMPIRE

Napoleon's Revolutionary Conquests

As sheer narrative Napoleon's conquests make a riveting tale, full of dramatic, frequently startling, and occasionally moving episodes. In quick succession, between 1805 and 1812, he conquered the Netherlands, Bavaria, the Austrian Empire, northern Italy, the Rhineland Confederation, Saxony, Prussia, Poland,

MAP 17.2   Napoleon's Empire at Its Height   In 1809 Napoleon defeated the Austrian Empire, which extended his domain all the way to the borders with Russia and the Ottoman Empire. For the time being, a secret alliance with Russia kept the peace. Napoleon vowed to defend Russia against Turkish aggression, and Russia agreed to join Napoleon's commercial embargo against Britain. By 1812, however, he was ready to break the alliance and begin his campaign to bring down the tsar.

Spain, the Kingdom of Westphalia, and the Kingdom of Naples—nearly the whole of the Continent (see Map 17.2). A series of coalitions among various European powers against Napoleon had determined, more or less, the sequencing of these campaigns, but the general aim behind them was present in Napoleon's mind from the start. A desire to spread revolutionary ideals and values across Europe certainly played a part in this rush to empire, but so did a desire for glory. Napoleon's ego was as large as the continent he conquered, and many of the people of France shared his dream of domination. The French army was a truly national institution, being filled by conscription, and like the republic it fought for, it was organized as a meritocracy. Each victory on the battlefield therefore did more than score a military success; it validated the Revolution itself.

The French in fact followed each victory with another revolution, toppling each opponent's government, abolishing its centuries-old feudal privileges, rewriting its constitution and civil laws, dismantling its mercantilist practices and outdated tax codes, retooling its justice and educational systems, and establishing (often for the first time) freedoms of speech and worship. The justification for their work was simple: the nefarious and corrupt network of absolutist regimes that emerged in Europe after the 1648 Peace of Westphalia (discussed in chapter 15), would never allow the French Revolution to succeed and therefore had to be destroyed. Since it had been established as a system for controlling Europe, absolutism anywhere on the Continent would always conspire to undermine republicanism anywhere else, even if only to discourage its growth within its own domestic borders. The proof of this reality, to the French, lay in the unilateral invasions of their country as soon as the Republic had been established. The conquest of Europe after 1805 therefore was not aggressive imperialism but defensive (although preemptive) antiabsolutism.

Of course, it was easy to concoct such an excuse. Did the French truly believe it? Did Napoleon himself? Or was this mere after-the-fact rationalizing? This is the crucial issue for those who, from Napoleon's time to our own, try to form a judgment about the emperor. Admirers of Napoleon saw (and see) him as the bold man of action. To them, he brought down tyranny; in sweeping away absolutist traditions, he made possible the creation of a modern Europe based on individual rights and the championing of merit over inherited privilege. His detractors saw (and see) a power-mad glory-hound who simply replaced one form of tyranny with another. At most they grant him military genius and a remarkable gift for self-justification.

Across Europe, in country after country, Napoleon did dismantle the old order and attempted to install the new—although he was also careful to install a loyal member of his own family as the new king. We see a glimpse of his aims in a letter he sent in 1807 to his brother Jerome, whom he had just installed as the king of Westphalia—the very site of the formal birth of absolutism:

> My chief concern is for the well-being of your [new] subjects, not only as it affects your standing and my own, but also because of the impact it has on the whole condition of Europe. Do not listen to anyone who says that your subjects, being so long accustomed to servitude, will fail to feel gratitude for the freedoms you bring to them—for the common people of Westphalia are more aware than such individuals would have you believe, and your rule will never have a secure basis without the people's complete trust and affection. Quite simply, what the German people desire and pressingly demand is that men without rank but of genuine ability will have an equal claim upon your favor and advancement, and that every trace of serfdom and feudal privilege ... be done away with. Let the blessings of the *Napoleonic Code* and of public trials that use juries be the centerpiece of your administration. ... I want all your subjects to enjoy liberty, equality, and prosperity alike and to such a degree as no German people has yet known. ... Everywhere in Europe—in Germany, France, Italy, Spain—people are longing for equality and liberal government. ... So govern according to your new constitution. Even if Reason and the Enlightened ideas of our age did not suffice to justify this call, it still would be a smart policy for anyone in your position—for you will find that the genuine support of the people is a source of strength to you that none of the absolutist monarchs neighboring you will ever have.

The sentiments Napoleon expresses here suggest an idealism behind his conquests that would mitigate harsher conclusions about his character and rule. Even so, it is difficult to overlook the fact that his conquests came at the high cost of approximately 3 million battlefield deaths.

European Reactions   Reactions to Napoleon's revolutionary conquests ranged widely across the Continent. The absolutist regimes responded by sending their armies into France, but among the general population of Germans, Italians, Dutch, Spaniards, and even Russians there were many who cheered the French on. The German composer Ludwig van Beethoven (1770–1827) famously admired Napoleon and intended to dedicate his *Third Symphony* to him, until the imperial coronation in 1804 led him to tear the dedication page to shreds. The poet Johann Wolfgang von Goethe (1749–1832) was too conservative and elitist to support revolutionary egalitarianism; in fact, he served as an advisor to German forces fighting French troops in 1792 and 1793. Yet when he met Napoleon in 1806, he declared "*Voilà, un homme!*" ("Behold, a Man!") and accepted with pleasure the emperor's award of the Cross of the French Legion of Honor, which he continued to wear for the rest of his life.

Although Napoleon clearly fascinated his non-French contemporaries, and although many of them welcomed liberation from the absolutist regimes he toppled, most of them chafed against rule by Napoleon's revolutionary agents. The French conquests, in fact, helped trigger a rise in nationalistic fervor across Europe. Peoples humiliated by Napoleon's quick victories reacted by expressing a desire to unify and establish ethnically and culturally based states to forge their own destinies, rather than follow the path laid out for them by Napoleon.

THE CONTINENTAL SYSTEM

That path included replacement of mercantilism everywhere with a new set of economic policies that Napoleon termed the **Continental System**. This system had two aims. First, it sought to create an integrated Continental economy by establishing permeable borders for the transfer of goods, services, and labor across Europe: by encouraging freedom of movement while protecting property rights, the plan hoped to awaken a dormant entrepreneurial spirit. People no longer held in place by outdated customs would be free to seek opportunities wherever they might occur and thus create the truly meritocratic society Napoleon claimed to desire. *Economic Integration*

But the second aim of the Continental System was both its real purpose and the cause of its own failure: to bring about the collapse of Britain by imposing a strict trade embargo on it. Soon after proclaiming himself emperor, Napoleon had made several attempts at a naval attack on Britain, but these attempts had all ended in failure—most notably at the Battle of Trafalgar (1805), where a fleet led by Admiral Horatio Nelson spectacularly confirmed the naval supremacy that Britain had established during the 18th century.[7] The Continental System essentially closed all European ports to British shipping and redirected all Continental trade to markets within the continent itself. The overseas colonies of all Continental powers were likewise sealed off from British commercial contact. The hope was that Britain, unable to acquire sufficient raw materials for its industries and *Embargo against Britain*

---

[7] Although badly outnumbered by the combined French and Spanish forces, Nelson led his men to a decisive victory: half of the French–Spanish fleet was either destroyed or captured, with more than 13,000 casualties, whereas the British lost not a single ship and suffered only 1,600 casualties. Nelson himself, however, was shot and killed. His body was temporarily preserved in a barrel of brandy until the fleet returned to England. Afterward, he was given a funeral fit for a national hero.

denied access to its most significant markets, would weaken to the point of collapse, at which point Napoleon's administration could sweep into London and take over.

Failure of the Continental System   The system succeeded at neither goal. The embargo against Britain actually helped to turn the island into an economic superpower because it effectively removed all competition from England's aggressive expansion into global markets. Without any rivals on the scene, the British were able to extend their domination across southern and eastern Asia. France could hardly encourage Europeans to trade solely with other Europeans while their armies were tearing apart the countryside. Moreover, Napoleon needed capital to keep funding the war effort; this need for cash is what led to the sale of the vast French-held territories in the central part of what became the United States—the Louisiana Purchase (1803). England's dominance at sea, demonstrated in 1805 by the Battle of Trafalgar, became worldwide with Napoleon's ultimate fall in 1815. England proved able, in fact, to block most Continental shipping even along the European coastline, which forced the system's trade to proceed strictly over land, a much more costly enterprise.

The Treaty of Montefontaine   Also known as the Convention of 1800, this treaty ended hostilities that had broken out between the United States and France over merchant shipping and piracy in the Caribbean. This painting depicts the signing of the accord. With tensions between the countries resolved, the path lay open for the Louisiana Purchase of 1803, which effectively doubled the size of the territories controlled by the U.S. government.

Neither did the system work to generate an economically united Europe. The vast and complicated work of deabsolutizing the Continent—reallocating property, writing constitutions, instituting new civil law codes, creating school systems, revising tax structures—while pressing the military campaigns ever farther to the east, made it impossible to direct sufficient funds toward creating the new manufactures, supply lines, markets, currency exchanges, and tariff structures needed to make the System succeed.

The system did result in one significant change, however. By dismantling feudal ties and encouraging the freer movement of labor across Europe, Napoleon's policies accelerated the most important demographic shift of the early 19th century, the rise of **urbanism**. In 1800 only 2 percent of the Continental population lived in a city; by Napoleon's downfall in 1815 this percentage had doubled. (Some countries, such as Italy, had considerably higher degrees of urbanization. Others, such as Poland, were almost entirely agrarian.) This leap was made up not only of rural migration into cities but also of peoples migrating from one country into another. Polish former peasants appeared in German cities; Hungarian farm laborers took up residence in Austria and Italy; Spanish workers appeared in France. Many of these individuals, barred by language or ethnic prejudice from obtaining jobs in skilled trades, ended up as domestic laborers—cooks, maids, footmen, servants, gardeners. Those lucky enough to belong to the upper middle class (the bourgeoisie) thus became able for the first time to employ large corps of domestic staff, as the swelling of urban populations drove down the cost of such labor. By 1810 in Paris, for example, roughly one-fifth of the entire urban population worked in domestic service, and most of these were in service to bourgeois families rather than upper-class high society.

Urbanism and Its Consequences

Immigration on this scale produced profound social changes. For the bourgeoisie, the standard of daily living rose remarkably. Middle class women's lives changed because of the low cost of domestic labor. Freed from doing their own cooking, cleaning, house tending, and child rearing, they were able to indulge themselves in a more comfortable existence of leisure: tea parties, outings to museums, charitable work, and the enjoyment of music and reading increasingly filled the days of bourgeois women.

For the immigrants, their own family relations tended to break off, since it was predominantly individuals, not entire families, who moved into the towns to find employment. The cities thus swelled with isolated job seekers rather than cohesive family units. Young women unable to find work in domestic service or in other trades were therefore often reduced to prostitution as a means of survival. By 1815 Paris alone had more than thirty thousand active prostitutes, and London had twice as many. Young men unable to find work frequently drifted into illegal activities as well, and the dramatic rise in urban crime led to

Urban Workers "Street scenes" is the title of this illustration from an early 19th century German periodical published in Stuttgart, a city whose population more than tripled over the course of the century. Shown here, clockwise from upper left, are a milkmaid, fishmonger, coachman, fruit seller, organ grinder, and figurine seller.

the formation of modern police forces. Awareness of the rising troubles in the cities also inspired the governments of the early 19th century to begin compiling official statistics on population growth, degrees and patterns of poverty, the need for housing and urban infrastructure, the lack of education, and access to clean water and sewers.

Napoleon's wars, in the end, altered Europe's history as much as the Revolution had altered France's. The positive achievements or gains of the era may or may not be directly credited to the Revolution, but the absolute and irreversible clearing away of the Old Regime by Napoleon made those achievements possible. Europe after 1815 was an altogether different place from what it had been in 1789.

DOWNFALL

Napoleon's talents as a charismatic leader, military commander, administrator, and legal and social reformer were extraordinary, but so were his deficiencies. He had little understanding of naval warfare and less of economics. He trusted his own judgment over that of his advisers. He underestimated the extent to which ethnically based national identity mattered to the peoples of Europe. Worst of all, he had little curiosity about the things that did not directly interest him and so gave them insufficient attention. All of these weaknesses played a role in his ultimate military defeat and fall from power.

Early Miscalculations   The Continental System never worked. Indeed, as we have seen, it simply allowed the British to secure international markets in the Americas and Asia that proved so lucrative as to turn Britain into an economic superpower. Britain used its capital to invest in domestic infrastructure, such as networks of roads and canals, to facilitate further development. The Continent, subsumed as it was in war and reconstruction, could not match such investment. Until 1810 British goods slipped through the trade barriers and were readily available across Europe. Even the wasteful War of 1812 between Britain and America—fought over the issue of British searches of American vessels to make sure they were not trading with France—did not weaken the British position with respect to the Continent.

Napoleon also miscalculated when he overthrew the newly crowned Spanish king Ferdinand VII in 1808 and replaced him with his own older brother, Joseph Bonaparte. The dismantling of absolutism in Spain failed when Napoleon ordered the suppression of roughly two-thirds of the monasteries and convents in the realm and confiscated their property. The displaced Spanish nobility allied with the disenfranchised clergy to lead resistance against the invaders. Unable to defeat the Bonapartist forces in open battle, the Spanish fighters waged instead a guerrilla war that kept a large number of French troops (more than 300,000 of them) mired in an unwinnable conflict when they were sorely needed elsewhere in Europe. Small wonder that Napoleon complained of his "Spanish ulcer."

Meanwhile, family troubles added to his indigestion. Although an energetic womanizer, Napoleon dearly loved his wife Josephine; but like England's Henry VIII in the 16th century, Napoleon agonized over his wife's failure to give him a son. Convinced that he needed an heir to continue his life's work, he reluctantly arranged for a Parisian bishop to annul his marriage to Josephine in 1810, so he could remarry. (Pope Pius VII had refused to perform the annulment, which is why Napoleon turned instead to a local bishop—who, like all the French clergy, was on Napoleon's payroll.) He set his sights initially on the younger sister of Tsar Alexander I of Russia (r. 1801–1825), whose two daughters had recently died, leaving the succession to the throne in doubt; rather than invade Russia, then the last substantial absolutist state in Europe, Napoleon hoped simply to acquire it as a dowry. Alexander, however, refused the match although he was, at the time, Napoleon's ally in a grand (and delusional) plan: they hoped to drive the Ottoman Turks from Europe and carry the conquests of a unified Catholic and Orthodox Christendom as far as India.[8]

Alexander was a complicated character himself—emotional, idealistic, contradictory, and given to dramatic shifts of mood. His relations with Napoleon went from warm regard to implacable opposition of "the oppressor of Europe and the disturber of the world's peace." Yet he was dazzled by Napoleon's brilliance when they met, and he became unswervingly loyal in return for his help in bringing Finland and Poland under tsarist rule. The pact against the Turks soon followed. Alexander even insisted on his love for Napoleon after French forces had invaded Russia in 1812; only the French sacking of Moscow turned that love back to hatred.

---

[8]   The Russian writer Leo Tolstoy (1828–1910) provides extraordinarily sensitive portrayals of Napoleon and Alexander in his epic novel *War and Peace* (1869).

Charting a Disaster French civil engineer Charles Joseph Mainard created this striking image, known as a cartogram, in 1869. It grafts a chart onto a map, showing the depletion of Napoleon's army as the troops marched from Poland to Moscow and back. The constantly narrowing line represents the decline in French forces heading east (brown) and then returning west (black). The line below the main figure tracks the temperature of the brutal Russian winter. Edward Tufte (1942–), an American pioneer in the field of data visualization, describes Mainard's cartogram as the "best statistical graph ever drawn."

Napoleon married instead Marie-Louise, daughter of the Austrian emperor Franz II (r. 1804–1835), who soon gave him the son he so desperately wanted. The birth of this son (also named Napoleon) in 1811 signified an important change in people's perceptions of the emperor—even among the French. The destroyer of inherited privilege had himself produced an heir to whom he intended to pass on the government of all of Europe. Anti-Napoleon pamphlets began to circulate, and some government advisors began to urge the emperor to restrain

Imp. Lith. Regnier et Dourdet.

his ambition. One of those advisors, his former foreign minister Charles-Maurice de Talleyrand (1754–1838), even started to negotiate secretly with Franz II over how France might be governed should Napoleon fall from power.

In June 1812 Napoleon invaded Russia with an army of roughly 600,000 men—perhaps the largest single force ever mustered in European history to that *Invasion* time. Russia responded by avoiding direct clashes while maintaining a rearguard *of Russia* action, drawing the French farther and farther into the enormous landmass. In September Napoleon entered Moscow, after pounding through Russia's last defensive stand at the Battle of Borodino. He found the capital virtually deserted and two-thirds of it aflame. Hopelessly exposed and left unsupplied, the French marched back to Paris, hoping to return before the brutal Russian winter set in. Alexander's forces harassed the French enough to slow them down miserably, and the onset of winter did the rest of the damage. Only 40,000 of the original 600,000 made it back from Russia to France by November—a loss of more than 90 percent. Most of the dead had fallen victim to starvation, exposure, and exhaustion.[9]

Abdication and Defeat

Napoleon was able to hold on to power for two more years, but his position in Europe, and even in France, was never the same. Numerous countries came together in a coalition led by the Prussian Field-Marshal Gebhard Leberecht von Blücher (1742–1819), which inflicted several further defeats on Napoleon's depleted forces, ultimately forcing him to abdicate in April 1814. Imprisoned initially on the Mediterranean island of Elba, he escaped and returned to Paris, where he briefly seized control again of the government—a period that came to be called the Hundred Days, the length of time between Napoleon's escape from Elba and his final defeat. Napoleon was defeated for good by the combined armies of Britain and Prussia (commanded jointly by the Duke of Wellington and Field-Marshal Blücher) at the **Battle of Waterloo** in 1815. He was then imprisoned on the island of Saint Helena in the middle of the South Atlantic, more than a thousand miles from any mainland. He died on May 5, 1821, of the Spanish ulcer that had proved cancerous. No one doubts Napoleon's exceptional talents and charismatic energy, but few people accept uncritically his own judgment of himself. In the memoirs that he dictated during his seven years on Saint Helena, Napoleon wrote:

> [My] imperial government was a kind of Republic . . . [because I was] summoned to take control of the government by the voice of the nation itself. . . . There has never been, in fact, a king who was more truly a "people's sovereign" than I was. . . . If I were to return [to power] I would establish my empire once again upon the ideals of the Jacobins, for Jacobinism is a volcano that threatens all orders of privileged-based society. I could reproduce it easily even in Prussia . . . and with the power of Prussia at my disposal I could use [Jacobinism] as a club to smash Austria and Russia.

As for his capture and imprisonment, he wrote:

> My body is in the hands of wicked men but my soul is free. I am prouder here on Saint Helena than if I were sitting again on my throne, appointing kings and handing out crowns. . . . If I had succeeded

---

[9] Jakob Walter (1788–1864) was a German soldier assigned to Napoleon's army who later composed a memoir of his service in the Moscow campaign. Although lacking literary grace, the memoir gives powerful descriptions of the horrors of the long retreat through the winter. When the desperate soldiers took to slaughtering their own horses for food, Walter had to settle for catching the horses' blood in a pot—which he then boiled down into a semisolid and ate.

[by adding a reformed Russia to my empire] I would have been remembered as the greatest man ever to have lived. . . . [But my] martyrdom will strip away my reputation as a tyrant. . . . In time [I will acquire] a crown of thorns.

In the end, Napoleon showed little remorse. He believed above all in France's destiny to lead Europe and in his own destiny to lead France. To have achieved anything less would have been tragic, and to have failed to answer the cause of glory would have been worse than death. "Death, after all, is nothing," he declared; "but to spend one's life defeated and without glory is to die anew every day."

REVOLUTIONS IN THE COLONIES

ST. DOMINGUE ON THE EVE OF REVOLUTION, 1791

The revolution that produced so much upheaval in continental Europe transformed life in France's Caribbean colonies as well. News of the French Revolution spread to the Caribbean island of Hispaniola, where the sugar plantations and coffee farms enriched merchants, plantation owners, and sugar refiners—whites and free blacks alike—while slaves performed their punishing labor in often inhumane conditions. The western part of the island was the French colony of Saint-Domingue (modern Haiti). The eastern part of Hispaniola was Santo Domingo (modern Dominican Republic), a colony of Spain. Saint-Domingue was the wealthiest colony in the region, in part because the newly independent United States could now purchase sugar from French rather than British plantations, and it did so from Saint-Domingue. This thriving trade inspired investors and merchants in France to pour fast sums into expanding production there.

Widespread suffering made the Caribbean ripe for revolution, and in August 1791 slaves in northern St. Domingue organized a large-scale revolt. To restore authority over the slaves, the deputies in Paris granted civil and political rights to the free blacks—an action that infuriated white planters and merchants, who in 1793 signed an agreement with Great Britain, then France's enemy in war, declaring British sovereignty over Saint-Domingue. To complicate matters further, Spain, an ally of Britain in the war with France, offered freedom to individual slave rebels who joined the Spanish armies as long as they agreed to maintain the slave regime for the other blacks.

The Haitian Revolution

The few thousand French republican troops on Saint-Domingue were outnumbered, and fearing military disaster, the French commissioner freed all the slaves in his jurisdiction in August 1793. In February 1794 the National Convention

TOUSSAINT LOUVERTURE

"Black Napoleon"   Toussaint L'Ouverture (1743–1803) was the leader of the Haitian Revolution, the massive slave revolt (1791–1804) that overthrew the French colonial government of Saint-Domingue and created the independent Republic of Haiti.

abolished slavery and granted full rights to all black men in the colonies. These actions had the desired effect. One of the ablest black generals allied with the Spanish, the ex-slave Toussaint Bréda—later **Toussaint L'Ouverture** (1743–1803), meaning "the one who opened the way"—changed sides and committed his troops to the French. Toussaint remained in charge until 1802, when Napoleon sent French armies to regain control of the island. They arrested Toussaint and transported him to France, where he died in prison. With all blacks now uniting against any French takeover, however, the invaders suffered huge losses—some 50,000 of an army of 58,000—many of them from yellow fever. On January 1, 1804, the black generals who defeated the French proclaimed the independent republic of Haiti. Toussaint became a hero to abolitionists everywhere, a potent symbol of black struggles to win freedom.

◆

The years from 1789 to 1815 were exceptionally dramatic—on both sides of the Atlantic. But were they in fact the decisive turning point in Greater Western history? Burke obviously did not think so; but to his way of thinking, every turning point is a dead end that guides society back to its point of departure.

And does the question even matter? Most of Europe's major historians in the 19th century thought of the French Revolution as a bloody, unhelpful, and even sordid affair, whereas the American Revolution frankly did not interest them at all. As for Napoleon, the man himself fascinated people, but his achievements did not. "Bonaparte robbed the nation of its independence," wrote the French politician and writer François-René de Chateaubriand in 1848, "and after he was deposed, he was sent into exile . . . and died. When the news was announced at the door of the very palace from which the Great Conqueror announced so many funerals, it neither surprised nor interested anyone who walked by. What is there to mourn in his death?"

But it is clear that Napoleon catalyzed some of the most important achievements of the Revolution—the equality of male citizens before the law; the rights of personal freedom of thought, belief, and expression; the individual right to property; and the abolition of serfdom. He created Europe's first national system of public education. He established a fair and rational system of taxation. And then he brought those reforms to the nations he conquered. But in the process he created an imperial tyranny. His wars cost millions of lives. Among the French alone, perhaps 20 percent of all deaths that occurred between 1799 and 1815 resulted from his military actions. Among the many anecdotes preserved by those who visited Napoleon before his death is this prediction by the defeated emperor:

> War is becoming an anachronism. I fought in every corner of the continent because two social orders stood opposed to each other—the Old Regime, and the world that dated from 1789. They could not exist together, and in the end the younger destroyed the older. I know full well, in the end, that it was war that brought on my own downfall. My downfall, me—the very symbol and instrument of the Revolution and its values! . . . The world of the past was one of brute force, privilege, and stupidity, and every one of my victories was a triumph of the ideas of the Revolution. But sometime in the future, the victories will be won without cannon and bayonets.

WHO, WHAT, WHERE

Bastille	Great Fear	Reign of Terror
Battle of Waterloo	Jacobins	*sans-culottes*
Continental System	Louis XVI	Tennis Court Oath
Declaration of the	Maximilien Robespierre	Thermidorian Reaction
Rights of Man and	Napoleon Bonaparte	Third Estate
Citizen	Napoleonic Code	Toussaint L'Ouverture
Estates General	National Assembly	urbanism
Girondists	parlements	

SUGGESTED READINGS

Primary Sources

Bonaparte, Napoleon. *Memoirs.*

Burke, Edmund. *Reflections on the Revolution in France.*

Chateaubriand, François-René. *Memoirs.*

De las Cases, Emmanuel-Augustin. *The Life, Exile, and Conversations of the Emperor Napoleon.*

Paine, Thomas. *Common Sense.*

Paine, Thomas. *Rights of Man.*

Robespierre, Maximilien. *Virtue and Terror.*

Sieyès, Abbé de. *What Is the Third Estate?*

Walter, Jakob. *The Diary of a Napoleonic Foot Soldier.*

Wollstonecraft, Mary. *A Vindication of the Rights of Man.*

Wollstonecraft, Mary. *A Vindication of the Rights of Woman.*

Anthologies

Blaufarb, Rafe. *Napoleon: Symbol for an Age; A Brief History with Documents* (2007).

Dwyer, Philip, and Peter McPhee, eds. *The French Revolution and Napoleon: A Sourcebook* (2002).

Larsen, Anne R., and Colette H. Winn, eds. *Writings by Pre-Revolutionary French Women: From Marie de France to Elizabeth Vige-le-Brun* (2000).

Studies

Appleby, Joyce. *Inheriting the Revolution: The First Generation of Americans* (2004).

Bell, David A. *The First Total War: Napoleon's Europe and the Birth of Warfare as We Know It* (2008).

Birn, Raymond. *Royal Censorship of Books in Eighteenth-Century France* (2012).

Brown, Howard G. *Ending the French Revolution: Violence, Justice, and Repression from the Terror to Napoleon* (2007).

Censer, Jack, and Lynn Hunt. *Liberty, Equality, Fraternity: Exploring the French Revolution* (2001).

Cole, Juan. *Napoleon's Egypt: Invading the Middle East* (2007).

Desan, Suzanne, Lynn Hunt, and William Max Nelson. *The French Revolution in Global Perspective* (2013).

Doyle, William. *The Oxford History of the French Revolution* (2002).

Dubois, Laurent. *Avengers of the New World: The Story of the Haitian Revolution* (2004).

Dwyer, Philip G., ed. *Napoleon and Europe* (2003).

Dwyer, Philip G., ed. *Napoleon: The Path to Power* (2008).

Edelstein, Dan. *The Terror of Natural Right: Republicanism, the Cult of Nature, and the French Revolution* (2010).

Englund, Steven. *Napoleon: A Political Life* (2004).

Hanson, Paul R. *Contesting the French Revolution* (2009).

Hunt, Lynn. *Inventing Human Rights: A History* (2008).

Hunt, Lynn. *Politics, Culture, and Class in the French Revolution* (2004).

Israel, Jonathan. *A Revolution of the Mind: Radical Enlightenment and the Intellectual Origins of Modern Democracy* (2009).

Kates, Gary. *The French Revolution: Recent Debates and New Controversies* (2005).

Lawday, David. *The Giant of the French Revolution: Danton; A Life* (2011).

McPhee, Peter. *The French Revolution, 1789–1799* (2002).

McPhee, Peter. *Living the French Revolution: 1789–99* (2009).

McPhee, Peter. *Robespierre: A Revolutionary Life* (2012).

Middlekauff, Robert. *The Glorious Cause: The American Revolution, 1763–1789* (2005).

Mousset, Sophie. *Women's Rights and the French Revolution: A Biography of Olympe de Gouge* (2007).

Popkin, Jeremy. *You Are All Free: The Haitian Revolution and the Abolition of Slavery* (2010).

Rosenfeld, Sophia. *Common Sense: A Political History* (2014).

Scurr, Ruth. *Fatal Purity: Robespierre and the French Revolution* (2007).

Simonetta, Marcello, and Noga Arikha. *Napoleon and the Rebel: A Story of Brotherhood, Passion, and Power* (2011).

Tackett, Timothy. *When the King Took Flight* (2004).

Tackett, Timothy. *Becoming a Revolutionary: The Deputies of the French National Assembly and the Emergence of a Revolutionary Culture, 1789–1790* (2006).

Woloch, Isser. *Napoleon and His Collaborators: The Making of a Dictatorship* (2001).

For additional resources, including maps, primary sources, visuals, web links, and quizzes, please go to **www.oup.com/us/backman**.

THE HOME OF THE RICK-BURNER.

CHAPTER 18

Industrialization and Its Discontents

1750–1850

Humans have been tool users since the Neolithic Age. From the time of the first stone implements, the brute labor needed for subsistence was performed by men and women, and frequently children, holding tools in their hands. The Bronze and Iron Ages were in fact defined by tools.

The next major technological leap came with harnessing animals to larger tools like plows and wagons. By the Middle Ages both the waterwheel and the windmill captured the energy of the natural world, putting it to use in everything from milling grain to manufacturing paper. The Renaissance created tools of increasing sophistication such as the telescope and microscope, but as late as 1750 most goods produced in and consumed by the Greater West were overwhelmingly the results of handheld tools. This was especially true of food and textiles—the two commodities that humans consume the most over their life spans. Through the centuries, labor had become more efficient, and the West had learned new ways to use natural resources. But human

INDUSTRIALIZATION IN THE GREATER WEST, ca. 1850

SWEDEN
BELGIUM
UNITED KINGDOM
GERMANY
FRANCE
SWITZERLAND

Level of industrial output per capita (100=UK in 1900)
- 0–15
- 16–30
- 60–75

Increase in level of industrial output per capita 1830–1850
- ○ 50–100%
- ● over 100%

Home of the Rick-Burner The displacement of agricultural laborers by machinery led to a wave of riots in England in 1830 called "Swing Riots" (named after a fictitious "Captain Swing," a Robin Hood-esque figure who supposedly led the poor laborers). The rioters vandalized threshing machines and set fire to ricks (stacks) of hay. In this cartoon, a desperate farm worker broods over the sad fate of his family, while in the background a devilish spirit approaches him, bearing a lit torch.

labor, with all its limitations, still defined economic activity. Well into the 18th century, it required the labor of eight people, working twelve hours a day, to feed and clothe ten people.

The Industrial Revolution changed that forever. It also led to some of the most appalling conditions imaginable for body and mind for millions of people. Industrialization altered the landscape and the structures of urban life; it shifted economic power to a new class of bourgeois entrepreneurs, to whom it gave a degree of control over the working masses that would have made an absolute monarch envious. It changed how laborers felt about their crafts. It reshaped the relations between the sexes. And it ground millions of men, women, and children into wretched and seemingly permanent poverty. At the same time, however, it enabled Europe and eventually the United States to achieve extraordinary levels of economic growth and technical prowess.

The cultural movement known as Romanticism had its start during this period too. Inspired by the French Revolution and Napoleonic era as well as by the roaring rise of industrialization, Romanticism consisted of a radical revaluation of human life, its purpose, and its pleasure. It was as important a turning point in the history of values as was Renaissance humanism, and like its forebear, its roots lay in almost unimaginable human pain.

CHAPTER TIMELINE

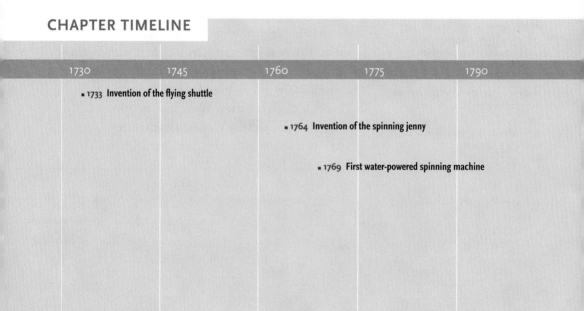

| 1730 | 1745 | 1760 | 1775 | 1790 |

■ 1733 Invention of the flying shuttle

■ 1764 Invention of the spinning jenny

■ 1769 First water-powered spinning machine

BRITAIN'S HEAD START

Starting in Britain in the second half of the 18th century, power-driven machines altered life profoundly, permanently, and absolutely. Industrialization created new economies, new cities, and new social relations, and it brought all of these changes on with startling speed. And the people of the time were quick to recognize the implications of mechanization.

The early English Romantic poets William Blake (1757–1827) and William Wordsworth (1770–1850) described the effects of industrialization on the human soul and the natural world as dire and ruinous. In a brief poem that serves as prologue to his epic *Milton*, Blake refers to an ancient legend that Jesus, in his youth, had visited England. Blake asks:

> And did those feet in ancient time
> Walk upon England's mountains green?
> And was the holy Lamb of God
> On England's pleasant pastures seen?
> And did the Countenance Divine
> Shine forth upon our clouded hills?
> And was Jerusalem builded here
> Among those dark Satanic mills?

| 1805 | 1820 | 1835 | 1850 | 1865 |

- 1818 **Creation of German Customs Union**

- 1819 **Peterloo Massacre, England**

- 1826 **Janissaries abolished in Ottoman Empire**

- 1830–1832 **Cholera epidemic sweeps across Europe**

- 1833 **Factory Act regulates work of children in Britain**

- 1850 **Britain crisscrossed by 6,000 miles of rail; population of London reaches 2.5 million**

Bring me my bow of burning gold:
Bring me my arrows of desire:
Bring me my spear: O clouds, unfold!
Bring me my chariot of fire!
I will not cease from mental fight,
Nor shall my sword sleep in my hand
Till we have built Jerusalem
In England's green and pleasant land.

The "dark Satanic mills" possibly refer to the massive grain mills that lay only a few miles from Blake's home in London, but in a larger sense they describe the smoke-billowing factories then spreading across all of England.

The first documented use of the phrase **Industrial Revolution** to describe a new economy driven by factories and a growing workforce appears in a letter written in 1799 by a French diplomat visiting England, who saw industrialization as a positive development. (He also claimed that the English had stolen the idea from the French.) Nevertheless, awareness of the changes brought by machine power was everywhere. As the German social scientist Friedrich Engels (1820–1895)

Dark Satanic Mills The painting *Coalbrookdale by Night* (1801) by Franco-British artist Philip James de Loutherbourg (1740–1812) has come to symbolize the birth of the Industrial Revolution in England. The Madeley Wood furnaces shown were owned by the Coalbrookdale Company, which was the first industrial firm successfully to use coke as a fuel. Coke is the residue from a controlled burning of coal with a restricted supply of oxygen; it burns at a significantly higher temperature and produces higher-grade metals in the smelting and refining processes.

wrote in *The Condition of the Working Class in England in 1844*, a sympathetic depiction of industrial workers' dismal lives, "An industrial revolution was a revolution which at the same time changed the whole of civil society."

Like so much of the Greater West's economic history, the basis of the Industrial Revolution lay in demographic change. Improvements in food production *Population* and advances in medicine (consequences of the discovery of the New World, the *Growth and* Scientific Revolution, and the Enlightenment) had combined to spur a persis- *Economic* tent increase in the European population ever since the 16th century; in the late *Dominance* 18th and early 19th centuries, however, the rate of increase grew dramatically. Larger domestic populations meant larger potential markets for manufactured goods. At the same time, Europe's international contacts meant increased opportunities to acquire raw materials and new targets for selling goods. The expansion of literacy, too, meant a more highly skilled labor force.

To take advantage of these conditions, one needed money—or access to it. It took financing to start private commercial ventures on a large scale. The absolutist mercantilist systems on the Continent had made that all but impossible. But when Napoleon demolished that system, national banks and stock exchanges came into existence, and financial markets could provide the capital, or funds for investment, needed. By 1815 most of Europe was ready to industrialize. England, however, had a fifty-year head start. Having avoided the burden of absolutism and left unaffected by the turmoil of the French Revolution and Napoleonic era, it had become a virtually unchallenged economic superpower.

England's population in 1780 had stood at roughly 8 million people; by 1850 it had grown to 18 million. By 1880 it had reached 26 million.[1] This created a large and constantly growing demand for goods like food, clothing, furniture, and housewares; it also provided plentiful cheap labor. According to the "Iron Law of Wages" made popular by the English economist David Ricardo (1772–1823), population growth always outpaces industrial productivity, and that fact drives labor wages down to subsistence levels—what he termed "natural wages." Cheap labor was the primary fuel propelling the industrial economy forward, and it remained so into the 20th century.

New technologies from the Scientific Revolution and the Enlightenment had dramatically improved crop yields. A single acre of farmland in 1750 pro- *Scientific* duced around 15 bushels of wheat, but by 1850 it produced 27 bushels. Careful *Agriculture* breeding of animals had resulted in sheep that in 1850 produced twice as much wool annually as they had done in 1750, and cows produced more milk as well. Higher productivity caused a decline in prices, which meant, theoretically, more

---

[1]   The engine of growth was the countryside, where improved medical care had lowered the mortality rate of children and mothers. The smallpox vaccine was available after 1790.

Agricultural Management   The English artist Thomas Weaver (1774–1843) painted this scene of Thomas Coke, 1st Earl of Leicester (1754–1842), inspecting a flock of sheep on his thirty thousand acre estate at Norfolk. Coke had enclosed most of his lands and encouraged the "scientific agriculture" of the time by experimenting with new types of feed and fertilizer and new techniques of animal breeding.

disposable income for the purchase of manufactured goods. England, in simple terms, had an active market economy in the 18th century, whereas the Continent would not until well into the 19th. In Spain, France, the German states, eastern Europe, and Russia, agricultural economies were still at the subsistence level. The overwhelming majority of the people (as many as 90 percent in some territories) ate what they produced and made their own clothes. In the absence of any "disposable income," or spending money, economic demand was nonexistent.

England had achieved its unique status by eliminating its small-scale farmers. Big landowners had driven most of their farmers off the land through a combination of increased rents, buyouts, and evictions; they then consolidated this land into large-scale holdings that they could farm more efficiently. Or they fenced off (enclosed) the land and gave up crop farming altogether, in favor of raising sheep and cattle for wool and dairy products. Acres of land that might have needed two hundred people to farm now needed only twenty to tend the herds and flocks. This decreased the landowners' labor costs while increasing their incomes. Instead of a countryside dotted with small farmers, England became divided among a small class of large landholders and a more numerous class of agricultural laborers who worked for wages.

Wage workers now used their incomes to purchase commodities that peasants had once made for themselves. Money had taken root as the foundation of *A Capitalist* the national economy. That new industrial economy is **capitalism**. It is a system *Economy* based on free markets—on the supply of and demand for money, goods, and services.

Clothing was, after food, the most important purchase most people made. Even today, textiles make up the second-largest commodity consumed worldwide. The growth of the population meant a need for more textile production. For England, which had been a mass wool producer since the Middle Ages, the new demand was especially for cotton—which was available from the southern United States. If enough American raw cotton could be brought to England, and if England could arrange its industrial capacity correctly, it could not only meet all domestic needs but also produce finished cloth for export. And political turmoil on the Continent left the English without any European competitors on the international market. The British had outlawed slavery in the 18th century, but that did not stop them from doing business with the slave-owning American South. American cotton and British wool formed the foundation of industrial expansion.

INNOVATION AND INFRASTRUCTURE

Social and cultural factors played a role too. First, by 1700 Britain was largely free from powerful guilds. Guilds had been central to the development of the medi- *Waning of* eval economy, but they were ill suited to a capitalist system, since their control of *the Guild* prices and production levels undermined the free play of supply and demand. In *System* Habsburg Austria, for example, if demand rose for a given commodity, then the guilds that controlled the commodity would not necessarily increase production. After all, a guild derived as much of its profits from government subsidies and membership fees as from commerce itself. Without an incentive to increase production, there was little reason to experiment with new technologies that might produce more goods more efficiently. England's remaining guilds were too weak and unimportant to check market forces.

Second, an entrepreneurial culture had taken root in England in the 17th century (as it had done in Holland too) that encouraged economic *An Entrepreneurial* growth. On the Continent, the nobility often believed that manu- *Culture* facture and commerce were "common" pursuits, beneath the dignity of an aristocrat. That class-based prejudice existed among the British also, but to a far lesser degree. So long as he conducted his business in a dignified and gentlemanly way, an English lord's reputation did not necessarily suffer—which made access to capital for industry easier. Moreover, the English constitution had developed in such a way as to center real power in the House of Commons, whose members largely were drawn from the bourgeoisie, the class most interested in promoting trade. The British legal system encouraged business by establishing the rights of property and allowing tradesmen to take out patents on the technologies they developed. Secure in the right to the rewards of one's own enterprise, manufacturers, financiers, and shippers were more willing and eager to innovate.

New Technologies

Although the manufacturing sector in England was spurred to new life, it quickly realized the limits of its means of production. Consider the textile industry. The putting-out system, which hired people to work in their own homes, had sufficed for a while, but the new demand for cloth far outpaced its ability to produce. Adding more carders, spinners, and weavers to the system helped, yet by 1750 a drive to find more efficient machines had begun. England by this time controlled a vast colonial empire whose many millions of subjects needed everything from clothes to furniture, beer to kitchen utensils, housewares to agricultural tools. Entrepreneurs had ample incentives to increase their output. Demand for goods like textiles, after all, was *elastic*: lower prices produced greater demand. Investment in new technology, such as the **flying shuttle** invented in 1733 by John Kay, increased rapidly. The flying-shuttle loom alone doubled a single weaver's ability to produce cloth. But now that weaving capacity had increased, there was incentive to increase the capacity of spinners to produce thread for the weavers. This led in 1764 to James Hargreaves's invention of the **spinning jenny**, a machine that could spin more than one spool of yarn at a time.

The most dramatic innovation, however, came in 1769 with the first water-powered **spinning machine**, which was quickly replaced by spinning machines and looms operated by **steam engines**. The application of steam power to textile production truly revolutionized the industry. Such machines, running continuously, day after day, could produce quantities of finished cloth previously unimaginable—and given the economies of scale, such production was highly profitable. They remained highly profitable too, although their productivity led to a decline in the price of the cloth. Early industrial factories driven by steam were immense, noisy, dangerous, and hot places that were miserable to work in; but the machines, if properly tended, never tired. By 1810 amounts of finished cloth that in 1750 had required more than two hundred skilled workers to produce needed only a dozen semiskilled machine operators. With factory cities fast filling with displaced farm populations looking for work, the downward pressure on wages made it possible for entrepreneurs to invest large sums in machinery while still reaping huge profits. These and other innovations changed completely the way large numbers of people worked and lived, and they shaped much of the rest of the 19th century.

A Comprehensive Transport System

The final ingredient necessary for Britain's launch of the Industrial Revolution was its development of the national infrastructure—the roads and waterways that brought the nation together. Without the ability to move

Spinning Machines   Quarry Bank Mill, in Cheshire, England, was the largest textile mill in Britain by 1830. Originally water-powered, the spinning machine (called the "mule") was driven by steam engine after 1810. Until the practice was outlawed in 1847, the Quarry Bank Mill relied heavily on unpaid, apprenticed child labor.

bulk quantities of raw materials into the new factories and to efficiently ship large inventories of finished goods out to market, the producers' innovations were all for naught. Here geography favored the British. Although large enough to support a population of tens of millions, Britain was yet small enough to make the idea of a comprehensive transport system seem feasible. Investments in coastal barges, and in expanding harbors to accommodate them, enabled the movement of coal—the chief fuel of industry—around the island. Smaller river barges allowed shipments to move up and down the rivers, and a new network of interior canals connected rivers to one another. By 1815 the British had constructed some 4,000 miles of canals, linking up their counties to such a degree that goods could be moved easily from any place in the realm to another. New networks of roads, and ultimately of railroads, completed the task, making Britain's physical infrastructure the most extensive and efficient in the world.

It had to be, given the enormous weight of the raw materials needed in the factories. Coal was available in enormous quantities, as was iron ore. Only the lack of means to move these resources efficiently had impeded their full use. Coal burns at a higher temperature than wood (the most common fuel in use before the 19th century), which made it more efficient in steam production. Moreover, the by-product of coal known as *coke* burns at an even higher temperature still, making it the fuel of choice for refining iron ore into usable iron and ultimately for producing steel. Britain's coastal and river barges moved coal and coke by the hundreds and thousands of tons. The development of wrought iron made it possible, in the 1820s, to move heavy freight overland by railcars driven by steam engines.

An English engineer, Richard Trevithick (1771–1833), developed the first steam engine capable of pulling a train. Trains themselves had been in use for well more than a century by that time, but they had been pulled along the tracks by teams of horses and had been used principally for transporting loads of coal from the mines. With the new steam-powered engine, freight could be moved anywhere affordably—so long as the tracks were in place. England thus began constructing an elaborate system of railroad tracks from mines and quarries to factories and markets all across the country. By 1830 a mere 100 miles of track existed, but within twenty years a network of more than 6,000 miles of track crisscrossed the country (see Map 18.1).

The unique combination of Britain's natural and cultural geography, its ability to inspire and capitalize on new technologies, and its legal and economic adaptability set the nation decades ahead of Continental Europe. Through the rest of the 19th century, however, it struggled to respond to the social problems created by industrialization, even while continuing to innovate and develop new technologies. Britain's challenge was to maintain its now dominant position in the world. In the wake of the tumultuous Napoleonic era, the rest of Europe would not industrialize—or develop industrialization's consequent problems—for another generation.

TRYING TO CATCH UP TO BRITAIN

Following Napoleon's downfall, the diplomats who redrew the political map of Europe at the Congress of Vienna in 1815 (discussed in depth in the next chapter) showed little enthusiasm for developing an industrial economy. More than anything, the statesmen, who represented more than two hundred separate states and princely houses, wanted to turn back the clock—if possible, all the way back to 1648 and the Peace of Westphalia (see Map 15.1). Most of the parties favored the restoration of monarchical governments across Europe, along with the economic and social programs that had traditionally supported them. Too much had changed, however, to allow that. Whatever their faults, Napoleon's conquests and his Continental System had freed people from serfdom and encouraged their migration to manufacturing and commercial centers—enough that the majority of the people wanted to move ahead into the new economic world opened up by Britain.

Industrializing Britain by 1850

Industries:

- ⬛ Textiles
- ⬛ Pottery
- ⬛ Copper mining and smelting
- ⬜ Tin mining and smelting
- ⬛ Iron extraction and smelting
- ◆ Lead mining
- ✳ Metalware and cutlery
- ⬛ Salt, soap, chemicals, and glass manufacture
- ⬛ Shipbuilding
- ⬛ Coalfield
- ⬛ Major port
- — Navigable river
- ⬛ Major canal
- ⬛ Major railway

MAP 18.1 Industrializing Britain by 1850   The British put to use all of their geographical and geological advantages in the march to industrialization: ports, rivers, coalfields. They quickly built national networks of roads, canals, and rails to link raw materials to factories and factories to markets and shipping hubs.

Differences between British and Continental Industrialization

Continental European industrialization differed from the British version in profound ways. First, Britain's commanding lead in international markets meant that Continental industry aimed instead to serve domestic markets. The European population, after all, was large enough to merit such attention, and by carefully assigning tariffs and import quotas, the Continental states could protect their newer industries from British competition. Second, the post-1815 states played even more central roles in industrialization than the government had done in England. The Continental governments not only built infrastructure but also invested directly in the fledging industries—especially in heavily capitalized industries like railroads—and in the building of factories. Third, important general differences emerged in the way each Continental country industrialized. Governments across Europe either made or purchased ships, weaponry, and other national-defense inventory on a large scale, but consumer manufacturing remained predominant. France, for example, tended to favor the production of luxury items like glassware, china, and fine housewares; in Germany specialty domestic commodities, such as linens, timepieces, tools, and kitchenwares, became their signal manufactures.

French Industrial Growth

Once again, demography and geography played important roles in the ways industrialization progressed. In France, for example, the population grew at a healthy rate, but considerably slower than its neighbors (see Figure 18.1). In 1700 the French population was somewhere near 20 million, and by 1850 it had grown to approximately 35 million, a steady but otherwise unremarkable growth rate of not quite 2 percent annually. Over the same period, Britain's population had leaped from 5 million to 20 million (a growth of nearly 5 percent per year), whereas Germany's had increased from 15 million to 34 million (about 3.5 percent per year). This meant that the need to increase food production that had driven the British rush to industrial production was lacking in France. Their traditional means of feeding themselves sufficed, which enabled the French to focus on luxury goods, niche markets that had smaller gross sales but higher profit margins.

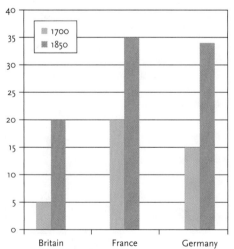

FIGURE 18.1   Population of France, Britain, and Germany, 1700–1850

This served France well from a social perspective because the maintenance of a traditional peasantry on the land had kept the urban labor pools from growing excessively large, as had happened in England. But it came at the price of France— once Europe's largest and most prosperous economy (although the wealth was hoarded at the highest levels)—becoming a second-tier commercial power.[2] Indeed, France's more measured industrial development resulted in generally less dire social disruptions compared to those suffered by the British and Germans, and the basic structures of much of French life in the countryside survived until the end of the 19th century.

The Congress of Vienna had consolidated Germany's three-hundred-plus inde- pendent territories to a mere three dozen larger entities. This augured well for *German* German industrial growth, especially given the rapidly expanding population, but *Industrial* the reigning conservative impulse after 1815 inclined each new state to adhere *Growth* strictly to its own laws and customs. Merchants wanting to move goods across terri- torial borders had to contend with multiple sets of tolls and tariffs, multiple laws and jurisdictional systems, and multiple currencies; few were willing to make the effort.

Germany therefore began to industrialize, although on a regional rather than a national level. The consequently lower levels of investment capital available meant that few entrepreneurs could afford expensive coal-fired machinery and had to rely on water-powered factories. This in turn meant that Germany's first factories were limited to areas in mountainous regions with access to fast-flowing streams, like Saxony and Silesia. Led by Prussia, a **Customs Union** (*Zollverein*) was created in 1818; by 1838 one-third of the German states had enrolled in the Union, creating not a full-fledged free-trade zone but a set of streamlined partner- ships. Members agreed to observe Prussian customs and regulations to promote industry. In this way, Prussian leadership in the move toward eventual German reunification can be seen decades before the political movement itself took root. The Customs Union hired British equipment and engineers to develop the German coal industry and to train them to build and maintain a railroad system. By 1850 nearly 4,000 miles of rail track had been laid in Germany, and industrial development had progressed to such a degree that one could say that industrial- ization brought about the unification of Germany.

Many European states failed to industrialize at all after 1815: Austria, Italy, the Netherlands (although not Belgium), Poland, Portugal, Russia, Scan- *Latecomers to* dinavia, and Spain. The reasons for this failure were unique to each terri- *Industrialization* tory, but most involved some combination of a lack of natural resources, a shortage of capital, and a disinclination of labor to adopt new skills and technologies.

---

2   French cities like Bordeaux, Lyons, and Montpellier, formerly bustling centers of trade, became quiet provincial towns.

In Austria and Spain, for example, geography worked against them. Fully two-thirds of the area of the Austrian–Hungarian Empire consisted of major mountain ranges that impeded infrastructural development. In Spain, the majority of the peninsula consisted of a hot upland plain, called the *meseta*, that was poor agricultural land, with few metal or mineral resources and little water.

In Italy—which after 1815 was still divided into more than a dozen small kingdoms and principalities—intense regional pride and a cultural disinclination to change frustrated efforts to unify and industrialize. Although agriculturally rich, and with long-established traditions of artisanal crafts and professional expertise (that is, financial, legal, and medical), few Italians valued the ideas of industrialized labor and mechanized production. What industrial production did exist, such as power-driven silk weaving in Lombardy, was performed on a part-time basis; seasonal female laborers simply filled in their days between the planting and harvesting of their crops. Even as late as 1861, in newly unified Italy's first-ever national census, Italian farmers outnumbered industrial workers three to one, and the majority of those laborers were women working part-time.

Railroad Development   Europe lagged behind Britain in railroad development, as in everything else, but did its best to catch up. In 1830, when England had established its first hundred miles of track, France had a mere 20 miles of track to

Italian Farm Workers   Italy was among the last of the western European countries to industrialize. These Italian farm workers, photographed sometime in the early 1900s, were still using oxen to pull their mower, long after other countries had introduced more modern techniques.

compare—and there was none anywhere else on the Continent. Belgium, how-ever, encouraged (like Britain) by its small size to construct a comprehensive rail system, by 1835 had established a network that covered the entire country. By 1850, however, things had changed. Germany, which by 1840 was funneling one-third of all its industrial investment capital into the railroads, had developed a grid of more than 3,600 miles of track, and France's rail line had grown to roughly 1,800 miles. Underdeveloped Austria, by contrast, had a mere 850 miles of track, and Italy had not even half of that amount (see Map 18.2). The general picture

MAP 18.2   Industrializing Europe by 1870   The late-19th-century unifications of Germany and of Italy (discussed in Chapter 20) added two more major industrial powers on the European scene, which left the nonindustrialized countries at a severe disadvantage. Large waves of immigration to the United States from Scandinavia, Poland, Ireland, Greece, and the Czech and Slovakian lands quickly ensued.

that emerges suggests that railways proved most successful when connecting areas already starting to industrialize, but they themselves were seldom enough to initiate industrialization. And furthermore, whereas industrialization greatly expanded national economies, the wealth it generated exacerbated rather than relieved social inequities.

TRYING TO CATCH UP TO EUROPE: THE OTTOMAN EMPIRE

The Muslim world after 1800, for the most part, had only one of the many elements that had been essential to trigger industrialization in Europe: a growing population. The other elements—investment capital, an openness to technical innovations, secure access to raw materials, a reliable transport infrastructure, flexible market economies, and a system of government amenable to entrepreneurialism—were in short or irregular supply.

Population Growth and Territorial Retreat Census records for the Ottoman state are spotty, although the general pattern seems clear: after a dramatic downturn in population during the 18th century, the 19th saw strong population growth, from roughly 7 million at the start of the century to about 20 million by its end. The growth was not evenly spread, however, with the lion's share of it happening in the empire's European provinces. (Generally speaking, the further east and south one traveled in the Ottoman Empire, the lower the population density.) This increase took place within a shrinking imperial geography, since Greece, the Balkans, Morocco, Algeria, and Tunisia had all broken away from Ottoman control by 1835 (see Map 18.3). As a result, the population density effectively doubled. Moreover, the political and social scene grew unsteady as the Ottoman Empire's hold over the western half of the Islamic world weakened.

Reform Efforts Historians, especially European historians, tend to portray the Ottoman state as in a gradual but nonstop decline after 1700. Certainly the defeat of their last great campaign to take Vienna in 1683 was a watershed, and subsequent territorial retreat against the Austrian–Hungarians and the Russians was disheartening for the Turks. Yet as late as 1750 the Ottomans were still the rulers, in terms of area, of the largest state in the Greater Western world. The empire showed great resilience and was open to many reforms. Indeed, the 18th and 19th centuries were marked, if anything, by continuous waves of reform as the rulers labored to address the myriad ethnic, religious, economic, and social problems confronting them. This was not blind flailing. Taking their cue from the great Spanish Arab scholar Ibn Khaldun (1332–1406), whose ideas inspired many of the enacted or merely proposed reforms (and whose famous book *The Introduction to History* [*Muqaddimah*] was translated into Turkish at this time), the Turks crafted a variety of reforms that would hold together the fabric of Islamic society. These considered the interplay between the unifying forces of religious allegiance, economic interdependence, and political tradition on the one hand and the polarizing forces of ethnic or tribal localism, social division, and technological underdevelopment on the other.

Numerous Turkish writers of the time, echoing the efforts of their Enlightened contemporaries in Europe, commented on the reform efforts emanating from the Istanbul court. One such writer was Sari Mehmed Pasha (d. 1717), the son of a grocer who rose ultimately to the position of imperial treasurer, who saw the fundamental problem in the empire as the blurring of distinctions between the Muslim ruling class and their tax-paying non-Muslim subjects:

> The admission of non-Muslims to the military ranks must be stopped, for nothing but trouble can result when those who are not descendants of cavalry officers are turned suddenly into cavalry officers. . . . Provincial town dwellers and farmers deserve to be protected, and their welfare increased by doing away with all [governmental] abuses; at the same time we should bend every effort to helping the people become prosperous—but it would be wrong to indulge the non-Muslims too much. (*The Book of Advice for Viziers and Governors*)

Such sentiments did not bode well for the Christians and Jews in the empire. And although Mehmed Pasha's opinions were not official policy, the unease in the empire frequently resulted in popular hostility against religious minorities.

Another watershed was Napoleon's 1798 invasion of Egypt. As we saw in chapter 17, the British soon drove away the French, but the event showed clearly how Muslim military might was falling behind that of Europe. Thereafter, periodic separatist movements arose throughout the Ottoman Empire and were usually encouraged by Russia and Austria–Hungary. These setbacks forced the Turks to invest time and money in rebuilding the military that they would otherwise have committed to developing their industrial capacity. They settled on a strategy of replacing their traditional patchwork system of administration—one that had ensured as much of each province's local customs as possible—and instead mandated a single system of law, granted citizen status to all, and abolished tax exemptions for privileged groups. In the early 19th century the ruler Selim III (r. 1789–1807), having witnessed the might of the French forces, tried to modernize the Turkish army along European lines but was stopped by a revolt of the Janissaries. His successor, Mahmud II (r. 1808–1839), took the drastic step of abolishing the Janissaries altogether

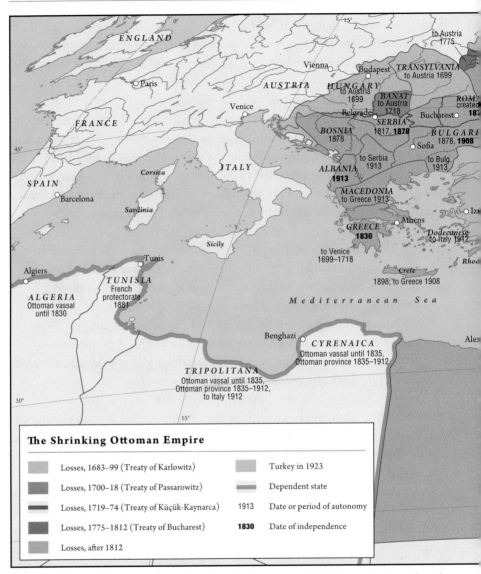

MAP 18.3   The Shrinking Ottoman Empire   The fracturing of the Ottoman Empire mirrored
that of the original Islamic Empire of the Middle Ages, with the western-most reaches of
North Africa breaking away first, followed by independence being declared along the southern
Arabian fringe.

in 1826. In their way, these reforms were progressive and echoed the egalitarian
sentiments then current in European thinking, but they were anathema to
much of the Muslim populace, most of whom angrily rejected the notion of
equal status before the law for their non-Muslim neighbors. Trading with non-
Muslims as equal partners was one thing; but standing as equals with them
before the law was another.

Ottoman trade with Europe took place through a group of trade agreements known somewhat ominously as **capitulations**. These agreements had previ- *Capitulations* ously been occasional arrangements that guaranteed Turkish and European *and Their* merchants access to one another's markets for a mutually agreed-on *Consequences* period of years. By 1815, however, most capitulations overwhelmingly favored the Europeans. In fact, they did little more than grant European traders the right to enter Ottoman markets at will—in return for vague European promises to aid the Ottomans diplomatically in their territorial disputes with Austria–Hungary

and Russia. Moreover, most capitulations ceded jurisdiction over all foreign traders and visitors to the foreigners' resident diplomats and granted jurisdiction over
foreigners whose home countries had no ambassador in Istanbul to whatever
countries did have diplomatic representation there. They even allowed selected
foreign governments to extend their own trading privileges to Christian and
Jewish subjects of the Ottoman state.

The net effect of these capitulations was twofold. First, the empire's Mediterranean trade fell almost entirely into the hands of the Europeans precisely at the
time when Europe began to industrialize. (Commerce in the Black Sea, Red Sea,
Persian Gulf, and Indian Ocean remained in Muslim hands and usually exceeded,
in annual revenue, the amount lost in the Mediterranean to the Europeans.)
Second, popular resentment of Christians and Jews, whether Ottoman subjects
or not, flared up significantly along with popular displeasure at what the empire's
Muslim subjects regarded as the ruling dynasty's weakness and corruption.

A French traveler through the Middle East at the end of the 18th century,
the count Constantin François de Chasseboeuf (1757–1820), summarized his
impressions of relations between the Turks' Muslim and non-Muslim subjects
this way:

> [Christian and Jewish merchants in Egypt] are confined to separate
> quarters where they live among themselves and have hardly any com-
> munication with the outside world; they dread such contact, in fact, and
> emerge from their neighborhoods as seldom as possible in order to avoid
> the insults thrown at them by the common people. . . . Living as they do
> in a kind of perpetual imprisonment, they are constantly fearful—that
> perhaps an outbreak of plague will force them to blockade themselves in
> their houses, or perhaps a revolt somewhere will cause their neighbor-
> hood to be plundered, or perhaps the leader of some Islamic faction will
> extort money from them.

His view of relations in Damascus was no better:

> Turks, in fact, never speak of the [Muslim] people of Damascus
> without mentioning that they are the biggest troublemakers in the whole
> empire. . . . But they are quick to add too that the Christians there are
> more vile and troublesome than anywhere else. . . . The Damascene
> Arabs, for their part, hate the Christians too, and this hatred is fomented
> by their continual contact with Mecca . . . for Damascus is the general
> meeting point for all Islamic pilgrims coming from the north of Asia, just
> as Cairo is for the Muslims coming out of Africa.

Even allowing for the traveler's ready stereotyping, the strain between communities is palpable.

Numerous efforts to revive the economy emanated from the court at Istanbul, but all failed. The Ottomans invested heavily in steamships, which increased the productivity of maritime trade, but were slow to develop railroads. Whatever rail lines they had in the 1800s were almost entirely limited to their European provinces; Anatolia, Palestine, and Egypt remained undeveloped in this regard. Farming methods did not undergo the transformative change they did in Europe, largely because most of the arable land remained in individual family farms and were never consolidated into the larger holdings necessary to make the expense of new technology bearable. Without a corresponding increase in production, rural society did not develop the market economy characteristic of Europe. In terms of manufacture, the empire never successfully freed itself of the guild structure, and hence incentives to increase production failed to materialize despite the continuing interest in Ottoman goods like silks, carpets, and textiles. The most notable change in the manufacturing sector of the 19th century was the increase in the percentage of women in the workplace, but their labor was mainly by hand. Mechanization was insignificant.

"Sick Man of Europe"

Industrialization Comes to the Ottomans   Pictured here is a late-19th-century silkweaving mill in Bursa, Turkey, where silk manufacture had been a specialty since the 16th century. Note the younger girls who tended the boiling basins where the older and more-skilled women extracted and cleaned the silk. Since Islamic tradition forbade, and generally still forbids, Muslim men to wear silk—they regard it as effeminate—silk cloth was primarily an export commodity, and a highly profitable one.

Without local market economies, access to investment capital, incentives to increase production, and a reliable infrastructure for transport, the empire could not industrialize and hence had no chance to catch up with the fast-growing European economy. As the "sick man of Europe"—as Westerners began to call the Ottoman state in the 19th century—Istanbul's hold over even its reduced empire continued to slip, prompting more efforts by the provinces to secede. The most famous and significant of these secessions was Greece's successful revolt in 1832, as we will see in the next chapter.

LIFE IN THE INDUSTRIAL AGE

Until the Industrial Revolution, the word *unemployment* did not exist in English. In earlier centuries the word *unemployed* had been widely used, but always in relation to an object instead of a person: a tool might lie unemployed on a workman's shelf; a workman himself, however, never "was unemployed." He was simply poor. The English writer Daniel Defoe (ca. 1660–1731), in his great historical novel, *A Journal of the Plague Year* (1722), described the ghostly emptiness of the London city streets with a reference to "coaches . . . left unemploy'd for five or six days"; yet people themselves, even the poorest among them, were seldom without work to do. Industrial society, however, was rife with unemployment. It indeed depended on it, because surplus labor kept wages down to a level that justified the capital risk of entrepreneurship. The coining of the word *unemployment* not only defined a state of being but also, knowingly or not, reduced the person afflicted with it to the status of a tool or unutilized object.

But unemployment was only one of the dire new developments created by industrialization. Hardly a single aspect of society remained unaffected. Everything from the role of the state to the structure of the family, from women's roles in society to the material standards of living, from the urban landscape to school curricula, and more, were altered in one way or another. Much of 19th-century history, in fact, can be read as a long effort to adapt to the changes brought on by the Industrial Revolution.

Unregulated Urban Expansion The easiest change to quantify is the increase in urban development—although the word *development* may be misused here. What occurred was largely the unchecked, uncontrolled, riotous, and blighted increase in the number and size of cities wherever the mechanization of labor took root. In 1800 Europe had a mere twenty-two cities with populations of 100,000. By 1850 that number had grown to forty-seven. The populations of cities both old and new likewise skyrocketed. By 1850 London's population stood at an astounding 2.5 million people, making it easily the largest city in Europe. Paris had roughly 1.5 million; Berlin and Naples each had a half million; Vienna held

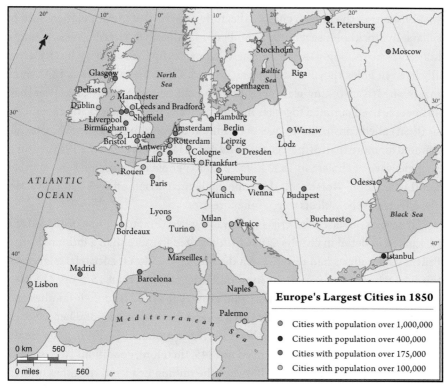

MAP 18.4 Europe's Largest Cities in 1850 Europe's cities grew rapidly in number and in size as industrialization spread, leading to miserable conditions for the poor, who lacked decent housing, public services, and work.

approximately 400,000; and Brussels held 250,000 (see Map 18.4). These leading cities had ballooned not only with industry but also with the financial and government administrations needed to manage it. There were lesser, although still large, centers—like Barcelona, Budapest, Hamburg, Lyons, Palermo, Rouen, and Stockholm. But even with these, the capacity to cope with such unprecedented increases in numbers failed miserably. For everyone except the reasonably prosperous—perhaps the top 15 percent of the urban population—living conditions ranged from the bad to the almost unendurable.

Workers, the unemployed, migrants, and their families were squeezed into filthy hovels with poor sanitation, little warmth, and inadequate supplies of fresh water to drink. Lacking any kind of sewage system, people relieved themselves in chamber pots and simply flung the refuse into the street.[3] Chemical smog and coal smoke filled the air; prostitution and violent crime were rampant. In the

Living and Working Conditions

---

[3]   By 1850, the ratio of urban inhabitants to flush toilets was still 200:1 in most industrial cities.

worker slums of the French city of Lille, fully one-third of the population lived in cellars. In Stockholm several thousand poor families, who lived primarily in the hilly areas surrounding the archipelago that makes up the center of the city, actually lived in holes they had dug in the ground. Census records from 1847 show that in one Irish working-class neighborhood in London, St. Giles, no fewer than 461 people lived jammed together in only twelve houses. Cholera and tuberculosis (then called consumption) were endemic and according to some estimates accounted for more than 50 percent of all deaths in factory cities in the 19th century. A single wave of cholera in 1832 killed 32,000 people in Paris alone and another 7,000 in London; worse still, the same epidemic carried off 250,000 in Russia. The effects of tuberculosis were even more dire.

The worst public health crisis of all was the Irish Potato Famine of 1845–1852 (discussed in detail in chapter 20), which resulted in more than a million deaths. British land policies had resulted in a disastrous situation for Irish farmers, two-thirds of whom (5 of 8 million) lived on farms of fewer than 15 acres. On such small holdings, the only crop they could grow that would feed their families and pay the rents they owed to their British masters was the potato—and hence the island's former agricultural richness was reduced to monoculture. When the potato blight (*Phytophthora infestans*) arrived in 1845, therefore, conditions were such as to maximize its destructiveness. Between the million dead and the other million Irish forced to emigrate, Ireland lost roughly a quarter of its entire population.

Local and national governments responded with housing codes, the expansion of sewage systems, and efforts to control crime, but were seldom able to keep pace with the misery. Factory workers, vulnerable to reduced wages created by the great abundance of labor, generally earned too little to support their families, and consequently women and children had to work too. In textile manufacturing, in fact, fully one-half of the pre-1850 labor force was made up of women and children as young as seven. Conditions for the workers were often dismal. Work-days were frequently twelve or even fourteen hours in length, and discipline could be brutal. An English woman who worked hauling carts of coal out of a mineshaft described her work this way to a Parliamentary panel investigating working conditions in the mining industry:

> I was married at 23, and went into a colliery [coal mine] when I was married. I used to weave when about 12 years old; can neither read nor write. I . . . make sometimes 7 [shillings] a week, sometimes not so much. I am a drawer [cart puller], and work from 6 in the morning to 6 at night. Stop about an hour at noon to eat my dinner; have bread and butter for dinner; I get no drink. I have two children, but they are too young to work. I worked at drawing when I was in the family way. I know a woman

who has [sic] gone home and washed herself, taken to her bed, delivered of a child, and gone to work again under the week. . . .

[When hauling coal] I have a belt round my waist, and a chain passing between my legs, and I go on my hands and feet. The road is very steep, and we have to hold by a rope; and when there is no rope, by anything we can catch hold of. There are six women and about six boys and girls in the pit I work in; it is very hard work for a woman. The pit is very wet where I work, and the water comes over our clog-tops always, and I have seen it up to my thighs; it rains in at the roof terribly. My clothes are wet through almost all day long. . . .

My cousin looks after my children in the daytime. I am very tired when I get home at night; I fall asleep sometimes before I get washed. I am not so strong as I was, and cannot stand my work so well as I used to. I have drawn till I have [worn the] skin off me; the belt and chain is worse when we are in the family way. [My husband] has beaten me many a times for not being ready [to have sex]. I [was] not used to it at first, and he had little patience. . . .

I have known many a man beat his drawer. I have known men take liberties with the drawers, and some of the women have bastards. (Parliamentary Papers, 1842, vol. 15)

The records of the parliamentary inquiries fill many hundreds of pages with similar testimony, all testifying to the brutal conditions in which factory workers worked and the often brutish treatment they received from their employers.

In France, factory workers were long required to carry a document called a *livret de circulation* ("travel booklet"), which was a kind of worker's passport. Foremen and superiors in a factory regularly wrote comments in an employee's *livret*, citing his or her mistakes, tardiness, poor attitude, breakages, or ill discipline. Applicants for factory jobs were required to produce their booklets for their prospective employers to review, and anyone who moved to another city to look for work had to present his or her *livret* to city officials and prospective employers.[4]

Apart from the demeaning nature of these conditions, industrial work also fostered economic and social dependency, since workers lived more or less at the mercy of their employers. Textile factories often provided housing for their unmarried female workers—the cost of boarding being deducted from their wages—which meant that many women literally spent their whole working lives

---

[4] Former convicts carried distinctive yellow *livrets*, to indicate their criminal pasts. Readers familiar with the 1862 novel *Les Misérables*, by Victor Hugo (1802–1885), will already know the difficulties confronting those who carried the yellow passport.

Working in the Coal Mines These engravings from *A Treatise on the Winning and Working of Collieries*, an 1852 report by mining inspector Matthias Dunn (1788–1869), show working conditions in the coal region of Midlothian, in Scotland. Above a boy pulls a loaded cart through a coal-mine shaft. Children sometimes started to work in the mines as young as age seven. Below a woman drags a heavy load of coal up a shaft, assisted by two small children (a boy and a girl) at the rear.

on the job site. Children sent to work in their youth ended up crippled and deformed, unable to care for themselves in their adult years. One observer of the child workers in the cotton mills, Lord Ashley, the Earl of Shaftesbury (1801–1885), left this vivid description:

> When I visited Bradford, in Yorkshire, in 1838, being desirous to see the condition of the children—for I knew that they were employed at very early ages in the worsted business . . . I asked for a collection of cripples and deformities. In a short time more than 80 were gathered in a

large courtyard. They were mere samples of the entire mass. I assert without exaggeration that no power of language could describe the varieties, and I may say, the cruelties, in all these degradations of the human form. They stood or squatted before me in all the shapes of the letters of the alphabet. This was the effect of prolonged toil on the tender frames of children at early ages. (Parliamentary Debates, 3rd ser., vol. 245)

All that was left for one thus ruined was to join the public welfare rolls. Given such wretched conditions, it is not surprising to learn that alcoholism became rampant—although it is a shock to discover that the problem was so extensive that in many cities the businesses staggered their scheduled paydays to minimize the number of drunks on the city streets at any given time. Neither is it surprising that workers and indigents alike began to riot. Labor strikes and demonstrations shook northern England as early as 1811. In France the silk-weaving center of Lyons erupted in worker rebellions in 1831 and again in 1834—the latter revolt resulting in several hundred deaths and the arrest, conviction, and deportation of approximately ten thousand city dwellers.

RIOTS AND REPRESSION

A riot over starvation wages by linen weavers in Silesia (then part of Prussia, today located in Poland) in 1844 gained such renown that the Romantic poet Heinrich Heine (1797–1856) commemorated their struggle in verse. "The Silesian Weavers" appeared in 1844, in the immediate aftermath of the revolt. Many of his poems were set to music by the German composers Franz Schubert and Robert Schumann. Karl Marx, the German thinker and activist whose anticapitalist theory we will explore in the next chapter, was also a fan. It is easy to see how lines like these, from "The Silesian Weavers," would appeal to Marx:

> Doomed is our king, the rich man's king,
> who remained unmoved by our suffering
> and snatched the last penny out of our hands
> before giving us over to his thuggish bands.

In England, the "Peterloo Massacre" occurred in 1819 when private militias hired by local factory owners showed up at a popular demonstration of workers held in Manchester's St. Peter's Field. Speakers there were calling for universal suffrage and secret ballots as the only means of forcing the government to address urban problems effectively. When the most popular of the speakers,

The Peterloo Massacre

a firebrand named Henry Hunt (1773–1835), began his speech, the militias swung into action:

> The commanding officer then approaching Mr. Hunt, and brandishing his sword, told him that he was his prisoner. Mr. Hunt, after enjoining the people to tranquility, said, that he would readily surrender to any civil officer on showing his warrant, and Mr. Nadin, the principal police officer, received him in charge. Another person, named Johnson, was likewise apprehended, and a few of the mob; some others against whom there were warrants, escaped in the crowd.
>
> A cry now arose among the military of "Have at their flags!" and they dashed down not only those in the cart, but the others dispersed in the field; cutting to right and left to get at them. The people began running in all directions; and from this moment the yeomanry lost all command of temper: numbers were trampled under the feet of men and horses; many, both men and women, were cut down by sabers; several, and a peace officer and a female in the number, slain on the spot. The whole number of persons injured amounted to between three and four hundred. The populace threw a few stones and brick bats in their retreat; but in less than

Cutting the Workers Down to Size This cartoon shows the private militia hired by factory owners putting down the labor strike at the Peterloo Massacre in 1819, in Manchester.

ten minutes the ground was entirely cleared of its former occupants, and filled by various bodies of military, both horse and foot. Mr. Hunt was led to prison, not without incurring considerable danger, and some injury on his way from the swords of the yeomanry and the bludgeons of police officers; the broken staves of two of his banners were carried in mock procession before him. The magistrates directed him to be locked up in a solitary cell, and the other prisoners were confined with the same precaution. The town was brought into a tolerably quiet state before night, military patrols being stationed at the end of almost every street. (Annual Register)

Unrest continued to grow throughout the century, giving rise to passionate debate over what to do about the myriad negative consequences of industrialization.

WOMEN AND CHILDREN LAST

Women were affected by industrialization in ways that men were not. Initially, women made up most of the workforce, at least in some industries: England's tex- *Women* tiles factories, in fact, notoriously hired women and children to a disproportion- *Workers* ate degree. Women and children made up as much as 75 percent of the labor force in some areas. On average, however, a woman received less than half the wages a man did in factory work. Working women in the 19th century also differed from their forebears in a significant way: they lived apart from their families. In rural areas, women had put in as many hours of daily labor as men had done, but since workplace and domestic space were the same, no fundamental division between work and family existed.

In urban factories, however, the female laborers were single girls or women who had left the family farm in search of work. Cut off from their traditional social units, they had to forge new connections in a strange and dangerous new urban setting. A married woman with one or two children was often able to rely on new friends or neighbors to help with childcare while she put in long hours at the factory. But as her family increased in number, it grew increasingly difficult for a married woman to keep working, no matter how badly the household needed her wages, and so she dropped out of the workplace.

Factory owners were quick to seize on the children themselves as replacement workers; children earned less than half of even the discounted wages of women, *Child* after all. It took the **Factory Act of 1833** to restrict and regulate—although not *Labor* ban—child labor in Britain. The act outlawed child labor for those under the age of nine, and it set a maximum limit of nine hours of work a day for children aged nine to thirteen. Restrictions on child labor on the Continent came even later.

Prostitution   The overwhelming surplus of labor that resulted from industrialization contributed to a dramatic increase in prostitution, as jobless women turned to it as their only way to survive. In this Parisian cartoon, middle-class customers leaving the Palais Royale encounter no shortage of women offering sexual service. It is estimated that Paris had as many as fifty thousand active prostitutes by 1850. London had eighty thousand.

Single women were vulnerable to sexual exploitation from demanding factory bosses, seducing boyfriends, or criminal attackers. Public health workers recorded that approximately one-third of all the babies born in any industrial city in England or France in the 1820s and 1830s were born out of wedlock. Throughout France, an average of thirty thousand newborns were abandoned at foundling hospitals and orphanages annually. Thousands more each year—although no one can know the precise number—were victims of infanticide. Prostitution formed another aspect of exploitation. Industrial cities swarmed with it: factory work and employment in domestic service to the wealthier families could absorb only a fraction of the working-class women packed into urban slums, so many of those with no other means to support themselves turned to sex work.[5] Paris had roughly thirty thousand streetwalking prostitutes in the 1830s; London had more than

---

[5]   The word *slum*, according to a popular although dubious folk etymology, emerged in the Industrial Revolution as a slang variant of the word *slime*, to describe the filthiness of the hovels into which workers were packed.

Workhouse   The St. Marylebone Parish Workhouse was established in 1730. By 1834 it had acquired several new and enlarged buildings. Refugees from the Irish Potato Famine drove its occupancy to over 2200. This photo dates to 1901, after a new wave of construction added two five-story blockhouses to the site. During World War I it also housed Belgian war refugees.

twice that number. Concerns about the spread of disease and the decline of morals rose accordingly.

To deal effectively with the social consequences of industrialization, Western governments began to create special bureaus for the collection of data: commissions on public health, on housing, on working conditions, on urban crime, on municipal codes and infrastructure, all appeared for the first time in the early 19th century, and the data they gathered form the basis of our understanding of the problems Europe faced as its economy mechanized. *Relief Efforts*

But the states were not the only institutions involved. Private charities, trusts, and societies formed by the hundreds, each usually dedicated to a particular urban problem.[6] Catholic religious orders established scores of hospitals, old-age homes, soup kitchens, and orphanages. In Paris, for example, the church-run Society of Saint Vincent de Paul formed in 1835 to provide clothing, food, and rudimentary education to workers and transients. Protestant groups instituted Bible-reading societies, evangelical gatherings, temperance societies (to fight the

---

6   London was the site of nearly five hundred relief organizations by 1850.

alcoholism rampant among the industrial poor), and workhouses, where the poor worked at menial jobs in return for room and board but no wages. In Scotland, the "Glasgow Young Men's Society for Religious Improvement"—a forerunner of to-day's YMCA—was formed in 1824 to provide healthy alternatives to urban crime, alcohol, and sexual license.

New Religious Denominations   Private religious groups inaugurated the idea of Sunday schools as places where young people could gather to study the Scriptures and sing hymns. Half of all British working-class children received reading instruction at Sunday schools. Among the many problems facing the slums was a dire shortage of places of worship. In industrialized Berlin, for example, the churches in the city, combined, could seat about 25,000 people on any given Sunday, but there were well over 800,000 people living in Berlin. Without churches, the faithful had to improvise. Some whole denominations emerged, either as completely new phenomena or as revitalized versions of older denominations, and most of them depended on a heightened emotionalism that responded to the desperate needs of the people. Among these new denominations were the Methodist, Quaker, and Baptist branches of Protestant Christianity. In the United States, itself beginning to industrialize in the North, some of the new denominations included the Latter-day Saints (the Mormons) and the Seventh-day Adventists; the second half of the 19th century saw the establishment of the Jehovah's Witnesses and the Salvation Army.

THE ROMANTIC GENERATION

Romanticism was the most pervasive and influential cultural phenomenon in the first half of the 19th century. Everyone agrees on that. What few historians can easily do, however, is state exactly what Romanticism was. Between 1899 and 1932 a brilliant Belgian historian named Henri Pirenne (1862–1935) published the massive seven-volume *History of Belgium*, and when he reached the 19th century and came to the topic of Romanticism, he briefly halted. A careful scholar, given to detail and precision, he indulged himself and came up with 152 separate definitions of it. Rather than compete with Pirenne, it may be better to back away from precision and describe **Romanticism**—vaguely, perhaps, but not inaccurately—as an intellectual reaction against the 18th-century Enlightenment ideals of order, discipline, and reason. To analyze human nature scientifically, the new generation felt, was to cheapen it by reducing people to machines. The human heart, in a clinical sense, can be studied as a matter of medical science—but the passions it houses are mysterious, darkly powerful, beyond reason.

We can see the Romantic temperament expressed most clearly in the arts, especially in literature. Compare the following lines of poetry from Samuel Johnson (1709–1784) and William Wordsworth (1770–1850). The differences between the poems are stark. First, Johnson:

The Romantic Values of Emotion and Instinct

> Where then shall Hope and Fear their objects find?
> Must dull Suspense corrupt the stagnant mind?
> Must helpless man, in ignorance sedate,
> Roll darkling down the torrent of his fate?
> Must no dislike alarm, no wishes rise,
> No cries attempt the mercies of the skies?
> Enquirer, cease, petitions yet remain,
> Which Heaven may hear, nor deem religion vain.
> Still raise for good the supplicating voice,
> But leave to heaven the measure and the choice,
> Safe in His power, whose eyes discern afar
> The secret ambush of a specious [false] prayer.
> Implore His aid, in His decisions rest,
> Secure, whate'er He gives, He gives the best.
> Yet when the sense of sacred presence fires,
> And strong devotion to the skies aspires,
> Pour forth thy fervours for a healthful mind,
> Obedient passions, and a will resigned;
> For love, which scarce collective man can fill;
> For patience sovereign o'er transmuted ill;
> For faith, that panting for a happier seat,
> Counts death kind Nature's signal of retreat:
> These goods for man the laws of Heaven ordain,
> These goods He grants, who grants the power to gain;
> With these celestial Wisdom calms the mind,
> And makes the happiness she does not find.
> ("The Vanity of Human Wishes," ll. 343–368)

Johnson's carefully measured, stately rhythms and strong rhymes bespeak order and stoic calm, even while the poem asserts the supreme need to reconcile the infinite longings of the heart with the world's harsh and finite realities. Happiness does not exist outside of ourselves, but we can attain something like it, the poem hints, by the calm acceptance of our limits, hopeful under the eye of a loving albeit mysterious God.

Wordsworth's poem, in contrast, follows a regular but less rigid metrical scheme, avoids rhyme altogether, and emphasizes throughout the world's sensuous delight:

> O there is blessing in this gentle breeze,
> A visitant that, while he fans my cheek,
> Doth seem half-conscious of the joy he brings
> From the green fields, and from yon azure sky.
> Whate'er his mission, the soft breeze can come
> To none more grateful than to me; escaped
> From the vast City, where I long have pined
> A discontented Sojourner—Now free,
> Free as a bird to settle where I will.
> What dwelling shall receive me? in what vale
> Shall be my harbour? underneath what grove
> Shall I take up my home? and what clear stream
> Shall with its murmur lull me into rest?
> The earth is all before me: with a heart
> Joyous, nor scared at its own liberty,
> I look about; and should the chosen guide
> Be nothing better than a wandering cloud,
> I cannot miss my way. I breathe again;
> Trances of thought and mountings of the heart
> Come fast upon me; it is shaken off
> That burthen of my own unnatural self,
> The heavy weight of many a weary day
> Not mine, and such as were not made for me. (Wordsworth, "The Prelude," 1.1–23)

The poet feels more than he thinks, exults rather than analyzes. He sets out from the hated City into the world of wild nature where he can breathe again, confident that he cannot fail to find his way.

Both poems are magnificent, but they work on the reader in different ways—and that difference is the result of Romanticism. Another pairing—this time in the field of music—might start with the floating melodic piano line that introduces the well-known chorale by Johann Sebastian Bach (1685–1750), "Jesu, Joy of Man's Desiring." Its lovely, long, regular run of eighth notes contrasts with the four-note blast that begins Ludwig von Beethoven's (1770–1827) *Fifth Symphony*. This is not to say that Bach's music lacks passion or that Beethoven's lacks structure (although many early critics and musicians complained of exactly that, when attempting to play Beethoven). Rather, these two passages of music affect the ear and stir the soul in different ways—intentionally. Bach's music is sublimely beautiful and moving—and yet one is always consciously aware of its cool, intricate structure. Beethoven's music can astonish us with its power—and yet part of its effect arises from the uneasy sense it inspires that Beethoven himself is at times barely in control of the surging passionate wave he is unleashing. Romanticism exalted, and exulted in, that sense of passionate abandon.

The Enlightened view of the world had resulted in the bloody French Revolution and, under Napoleon, millions of dead from Paris to Moscow. It was thus hard to justify maintaining its core tenets about the rational reform of society and the inevitability of progress. At the same time, Romanticism rejected the mechanized horrors of industrialism and the bourgeois values that championed it. Industrial capitalism, after all, gave every appearance of valuing commodities more than people, of regarding human beings merely as workers, consumers, and nothing more. For Scottish philosopher and historian Thomas Carlyle (1795–1881), as he expresses in his essay "Signs of the Times" (1829), it cheapened existence itself by quashing every humane value and attribute:

> Were we required to characterise this age of ours by any single epithet, we should be tempted to call it, not an Heroical, Devotional, Philosophical, or Moral Age, but, above all others, the Mechanical Age. It is the Age of Machinery, in every outward and inward sense of that word; the age which, with its whole undivided might, forwards, teaches and practises the great art of adapting means to ends. Nothing is now done directly, or by hand; all is by rule and calculated contrivance. For the simplest operation, some helps and accompaniments, some cunning abbreviating process is in readiness. Our old modes of exertion are all discredited, and thrown aside. On every hand, the living artisan is driven from his workshop, to make room for a speedier, inanimate one. The shuttle drops from the fingers of the weaver, and falls into iron fingers that ply it faster. . . . There is no end to machinery. Even the horse is stripped of his harness, and finds a fleet firehorse yoked in his stead. Nay, we have an artist that hatches chickens by steam; the very brood-hen is to be superseded! For all earthly, and for some unearthly purposes, we have machines and mechanic furtherances; for mincing our cabbages; for casting us into magnetic sleep. We remove mountains, and make seas our smooth highway; nothing can resist us. We war with rude Nature; and, by our resistless engines, come off always victorious, and loaded with spoils.

The Great Western Railway   First exhibited in 1844 by the British Romantic artist J.M.W. Turner (1775–1851), *Rain, Steam, and Speed—the Great Western Railway* hauntingly evokes the power and menace of industrialization.

The poem by Heinrich Heine quoted earlier, "The Silesian Weavers," imagines a group of women tending an industrial loom as they weave a death shroud for the German nation; witchlike, they weave a trio of curses into the cloth—denouncing God, the king, and the hellish industrialized country they have all become victim to. "O Germany, we're spinning out your pall / Weaving our triple curse through it all." To rebel against mechanization, utilitarianism, middle-class values, and bourgeois respectability was, in the early 19th century, a declaration of the freedom of the soul. To a lesser extent, Romanticism was also a nationalistic response against French predominance in the political and cultural spheres and hence a rebellion against the Napoleonic era.

The Romantic generation believed in *genius*—meaning by this word any individual's imaginative capacity, the passionate and spiritual instinct that allows us to feel connected to nature and to one another. The only true happiness people can attain in life, it follows, is to live in intimate harmony with our sensations and passions. This is not necessarily to promote hedonism; the desire to please and serve others can be as sincerely felt a passion as sexual lust. Indeed, most of the

Romantics believed that ethnic and cultural groups possessed a kind of collective genius—a shared spiritual intimacy that allows members of a race to understand one another intuitively.

This sense of cultural cohesion strongly influenced a development later in the century, nationalism (discussed in depth in the next chapter), when native groups broken apart artificially by the Congress of Vienna struggled to reunite. *Romanticism and* They sought a world of organic states brought to spiritual perfection by *Nationalism* their unique identities. The German Romantic philosopher Johann Gottlieb Fichte (1762–1814) put it thus, in his "Address to the German Nation" in 1806:

> Men who speak the same language are joined to each other by Nature herself, through countless invisible bonds, long before any human art begins; such men understand one another and can always make themselves understood with perfect clarity; they belong together, and they possess a single, indivisible nature. . . . Only when a [united] people is left to itself, so that it can create and develop in harmony with its own unique genius, and only when every individual within each group develops himself in accord with that shared genius—while also in harmony with his own individual genius—then, and only then, does the divine creative spirit manifest itself as it ought.

To remain in contact with the intuitive, passionate self—whether the individual or the collective self—was the only guarantee of a satisfying life to the Romantics. Reason is a tool to be deployed whenever needed, they felt, but it does not define humanity; to those who allow Reason to dictate their entire view of life and regard every activity and observation as an opportunity for analysis, the Romantics respond with an urgent alarm for people to wake up from their methodical dullness before they effectively turn into machines themselves.

◆

The dangers were many, and they threatened all of society. "Only the material, the immediately practical, not the divine and spiritual, is important to us," warned Carlyle. "The infinite, absolute character of Virtue has passed into a finite, conditional one; it is no longer a worship of the Beautiful and Good, but a calculation of the Profitable. . . . Our true Deity is Mechanism." Industrialization not only brought penury and suffering to millions at the bottom of the economic scale, but also cheapened everyone's lives by reducing them to a mechanical, bureaucratic, institutionalized monotony. When the machines take over, the Romantics urged, our souls die.

SUGGESTED READINGS

Primary Sources

Babbage, Charles. *On the Economy of Machinery and Manufactures.*

Carlyle, Thomas. "Signs of the Times."

Engels, Friedrich. *The Condition of the Working Class in England in 1844.*

Ricardo, David. *On the Principles of Political Economy and Taxation.*

Anthologies

Breckman, Warren. *European Romanticism: A Brief History with Documents* (2015).

Frader, Laura L. *The Industrial Revolution: A History in Documents* (2006).

Wu, Duncan, ed. *Romanticism: An Anthology* (2012).

Studies

Allen, Robert C. *The British Industrial Revolution in Global Perspective* (2009).

Berend, Iván. *History Derailed: Central and Eastern Europe in the Long Nineteenth Century* (2005).

Bilenky, Serhiy. *Romantic Nationalism in Eastern Europe: Russian, Polish, and Ukrainian Political Imaginations* (2012).

Burnette, Joyce. *Gender, Work, and Wages in Industrial Revolution Britain* (2008).

Clark, Gregory. *A Farewell to Alms: A Brief Economic History of the World* (2008).

Cohen, Deborah. *Household Gods: The British and Their Possessions* (2006).

Crump, Thomas. *A Brief History of the Age of Steam: The Power That Drove the Industrial Revolution* (2007).

Flanders, Judith. *Inside the Victorian Home: A Portrait of Domestic Life in Victorian England* (2005).

Griffin, Emma. *A Short History of the British Industrial Revolution* (2010).

Griffin, Emma. *Liberty's Dawn: A People's History of the Industrial Revolution* (2014).

Holmes, Richard. *The Age of Wonder: How the Romantic Generation Discovered the Beauty and Terror of Science* (2009).

Hudson, Pat. *The Industrial Revolution* (2007).

Landes, David S. *The Unbound Prometheus: Technological Change and Industrial Development in Western Europe from 1750 to the Present* (2003).

McLane, Maureen N. *Romanticism and the Human Sciences: Poetry, Population, and the Discourse of the Species* (2006).

Mokyr, Joel. *The Gifts of Athena: Historical Origins of the Knowledge Economy* (2004).

More, Charles. *Understanding the Industrial Revolution* (2000).

Perelman, Michael. *The Invention of Capitalism: Classical Political Economy and the Secret History of Primitive Accumulation* (2000).

Pollard, Lisa. *Nurturing the Nation: The Family Politics of Modernizing, Colonizing, and Liberating Egypt, 1805–1923* (2005).

Pomeranz, Kenneth. *The Great Divergence: China, Europe, and the Making of the Modern World Economy* (2001).

Richardson, Alan. *British Romanticism and the Science of the Mind* (2005).

Stearns, Peter N. *The Industrial Revolution in World History* (2012).

Sunderland, David. *Social Capital, Trust, and the Industrial Revolution, 1780–1880* (2007).

Swade, Doron. *The Difference Engine: Charles Babbage and the Quest to Build the First Computer* (2002).

Tekiner, Deniz. *Modern Art and the Romantic Vision* (2000).

Weightman, Gavin. *The Industrial Revolutionaries: The Making of the Modern World, 1776–1914* (2009).

Wrigley, E. A. *Energy and the English Industrial Revolution* (2010).

For additional resources, including maps, primary sources, visuals, web links, and quizzes, please go to **www.oup.com/us/backman**.

CHAPTER 19

The Birth of Modern Politics

1815–1848

The diplomats who convened at the Congress of Vienna (1814–1815) redrew the map of Europe, and in the effort they tried to turn back time by returning European politics to the familiar rule of kings. The high idealism of the French Revolution, they felt, had resulted in nothing to recommend it. In their minds, all it had done was to justify pillage across the continent in the name of foolish—because unrealistic—notions of freedom and equality. They feared the revolutionary virus and a country's capacity to wreak havoc on its neighbors, two dangers associated especially with France but now threatening all of Europe because of the dismantling of institutions and customs under Napoleon. Hoping to contain and eradicate both dangers, the diplomats in Vienna crafted a long series of decrees, treaties, and protocols. These agreements created a new balance of power among European nations by reconfiguring international borders and introducing a modest measure of constitutional government under royal leadership.

CIVIL UNREST IN THE GREATER WEST, ca. 1830–1840

The choices made at the Congress emerged in the dramatically changed context of England's rapid and unchallenged industrialization. Once released, the industrial genie could not be forced back into the bottle, which put the Congress members in the

Revolutionary Fervor This French illustration offers a joyous, optimistic vision of the rebellions of 1848, the most widespread revolutionary wave in European history. The peoples of Europe, joined together around their respective national banners, are achieving freedom from monarchy, as symbolized by the discarded crowns. In reality, reactionary forces regained control, and the revolts collapsed within a year.

difficult position of trying to restore old political and social traditions while promoting the radically new models of economic growth. Investment in industrial technologies was necessary—but was that the responsibility of the state or of individuals? Were the social troubles caused by industrialization the responsibility of the state too? If so, why? Who, ultimately, is responsible for the poor? Such considerations brought about the philosophical division between conservatism and liberalism, the two **ideologies**, or sets of beliefs regarding the social and political order, that would dominate most of European political development for the next two centuries. By midcentury, however, both of these positions were challenged by two new ideologies, socialism and its radical offshoot, Marxism. And none of these ideologies fully encompassed changes in family life and the budding rights of women. When everything has been called into question, as it was by the Napoleonic era's wiping clean the European slate, then every idea and value must be reevaluated in either the restoration of the old or the creation of the new. The 19th century was defined by this reevaluation.

CONSERVATISM IN POWER

The restoration of monarchies was the immediate and fundamental strategy of the diplomats. This is hardly surprising, since the royal families driven from power by Napoleon had spent the intervening years plotting their return.

CHAPTER TIMELINE

1770	1780	1790	1800	1820

- 1773–1859 Klemens von Metternich

- 1814 Joseph-Marie de Maistre, *Essay on the Generative Principle of Political Institutions*

- 1814–1815 Congress of Vienna

- 1818–1883 Karl Marx

- 1821–1830 Greek War of Independence

- 1825 Decembrist revolt in Russia

Complicating matters, however, was the fact that some of the dynasties created by Bonaparte—such as the new Duchy of Warsaw and the Kingdom of Piedmont–Sardinia—wanted to stay in power and had acquired a certain amount of popular support. Representatives of five major powers, the so-called Great Alliance, dominated the **Congress of Vienna** of 1814–1815: Austria, Britain, France, Prussia, and Russia. Further complicating matters was the new emerging political division that would take the form of liberalism versus conservatism.

Congress of Vienna

The leading figure of the Congress was **Klemens von Metternich** (1773–1859), an Austrian aristocrat and the chief diplomat for the Habsburg emperor. Metternich had been born in the age and social milieu of absolutism and aristocratic privilege, and throughout his long and active life he never wavered in his conviction that the people of Continental Europe were not ready for democracy. He did not disagree with democracy in principle, but he believed that a stable democratic society arose only from gradual, evolutionary change in political structures. The radical surgery represented by political revolution was guaranteed to fail and to bring misery to any society that attempts it. The issue for Metternich was not the desire of the powerful to maintain their status but the impatience of revolutionaries who believed they could pass over periods of organic growth. It is as impossible for a society to "fast-forward" into a condition that is ready to embrace democracy as it is for an

1830	1840	1850	1860	1890

- 1830 **Conservatives lose power in Britain; uprisings throughout Europe**
- 1832 **Reform Bill (Britain)**
- 1834 **New Poor Law (Britain)**
- 1838 **Beginning of Chartist movement**
- 1846 **Corn Laws repealed (Britain)**
- 1847 **Ten Hours Act (Britain)**
- 1848 **Rebellions throughout Europe; Marx and Engels,** *The Communist Manifesto*
- 1857 **Matrimonial Causes Act (Britain)**
- 1859 **John Stuart Mill,** *On Liberty*

individual to fast-forward from adolescence into mature adulthood. Metternich wrote in his *Memoirs*:

> The nature of Man is unchanging. The principal needs of any society are always and ever shall be the same; any differences that appear to exist between human societies are simply the result of the varying influences (different climates, different fertility of soil, existence as an island as opposed to a continental territory, etc.) that Nature has effected upon them. Such influences undoubtedly have consequences far beyond the fundamental material realities of life: they can establish and shape unique needs of the most advanced kind, and can even determine the laws of a society and influence the development of its religion. . . . It is true of institutions as well; their origins are frequently obscure, but they then progress through stages of evolution until they reach a developmental peak, only at last to decay. Like Man himself, and following the same natural laws, they have a period of infancy, then of youth, then of full adult vigor and intelligence, then of decline. But throughout this natural process they retain at all times two key elements that never relinquish or see a diminution of their everlasting power—namely, the dictates of religious and social morality, and the limits established by geography.

Conservatism thus values tradition and social stability above the wants or needs of the individual. As Metternich saw it, it was realism, pure and simple, a common-sense recognition that human life takes place within a physical and cultural geography to which it must adapt. Not all things are possible, and therefore to desire all things is impractical. Change is of course possible, but only when it comes about gradually.

The Liberal Opposition   Although the conservatives carried the day at Vienna and remained in power throughout Europe for much of the next thirty years, not everyone shared their dream of return to the past. In the first place, these others argued, the stable old order revered by conservatives had been neither stable nor ordered. The most wretched misery, confusion, and resentment had always roiled just beneath the surface of a society based on aristocratic privilege. It was merely that the aristocrats had paid no attention to any of it until the revolutionaries came and took their privileges away. Besides, a monopoly of privileges by social elites does not constitute a cultural tradition, at least not a tradition that is worth preserving. What the opponents of the Congress of Vienna wanted, therefore, was a new alternative, a society built on a different notion. **Liberalism**—as this opposing political view came to be called—assumed the intrinsic goodness of all people and

Diplomats at the Congress of Vienna in 1815   The Parisian court painter Jean-Baptiste Isabey (1767–1855) traveled to Vienna as part of the French delegation. There he executed portraits of each of the 23 participants; these studies eventually formed the basis of this famous group portrait. Metternich, who dominated the Congress, is the figure standing on the left. Given almost equal prominence in Isabey's patriotic composition is the French diplomat Charles Maurice de Talleyrand-Périgord, the figure seated at the right with his arm on the table, giving the impression that Talleyrand—who was representing a defeated France—enjoyed an equal part in negotiations. To a man, the diplomats were all members of their countries' aristocracies, and the treaties they produced reflected that fact.

argued that the people, if left to manage their own lives, would choose what is good, honorable, and fair. Liberals called therefore for civil liberties, equality under the law, the right to vote, and a free-market economy.

Conservatism and *liberalism* alike were newly coined words. The word *conservatism* appeared in English in a political sense for the first time in 1830 when it appeared in an article in the *Quarterly Review* by Irish statesman and Parliament member John W. Croker (1780–1857). The word *liberalism* was coined in 1819 by Anglo-Irish Romantic writer Lady Morgan (Sydney Owenson, 1783–1859), when she wrote admiringly of a friend that "he is worthy of a conversion to *Liberalism*."

Of course, more than just the vocabulary of politics was changing. The 19th century crackled with intellectual energy as people from Dublin to Istanbul, from Lisbon to Moscow, struggled to find new ways to order civic life. The profoundest and most intriguing drama of the age came not from the political struggles among monarchists, conservatives, liberals, socialists, and anarchists (to choose just five of the leading factions across the continent). It was the intellectual wrestling between the emerging new political traditions and developments in economics, science, philosophy, art, and religion. Like a child's kaleidoscope that changes shape with every turn of the wrist, the cultural landscape of Western civilization shifted, and was forced to shift, with every new development in the understanding of the world, the human heart, and the human mind. As with other creatively chaotic periods in history—the era of classical Greece or the Europe of the 14th and 15th centuries—the 19th century demanded the thinking through of everything afresh.

ROYALISM AND ITS OPPONENTS

The English educator Thomas Arnold (1795–1842) wrote in a letter to a friend in 1840 that "the principle of Conservatism has always appeared to me to be not only foolish, but to be actually *felo de se* [an attack upon itself]: it destroys what it loves, because it will not mend it." None of those who attended the Vienna congress would have agreed—or would have dared to say so, even if they did. One conviction dominated the assembly: only strong centralized governments, guided by noble traditions, served by professionalized bureaucracies, and backed by large national armies, could pull Europe back from the brink of disaster. But an entirely new and urgent issue presented itself, and it worked against the neoroyalist platform of the congress: the need to industrialize and to do so quickly. Industrialization required investment and entrepreneurship, and the people most interested in entering the new economy demanded something more—recognition of the rights of personal property, a role in shaping government policies, and a relatively free market. Capitalism in the new era existed to serve itself first. The government benefited only secondarily from taxation, which provided it with reliable revenue but without impeding innovation and economic growth.

Redrawing the Map of Europe

The Congress kept the two aims of strong monarchical government and an industry-friendly economy in sight, but did so to the exclusion of other considerations. When the diplomats put their pens to the map of Europe, they took into account royal desires, military capabilities, industrial resources, access to markets and harbors, and agricultural potential. The "Great Alliance" of the five major powers represented at Vienna swore to support one another:

> Any state which undergoes a change of government due to revolution by that fact alone ceases to be a member of the European Alliance.... And if on account of that change other states are threatened, the European Powers bind themselves, by peaceful means or if necessary by arms, to force the guilty state back into the bosom of the Great Alliance.

MAP 19.1   Europe after the Congress of Vienna, 1815   The Congress scaled back the boundaries of France to their status in 1790, ceded territory to Austria in western and northeastern Italy, and created the Kingdom of the Netherlands, a new German Confederation, and a new Kingdom of Poland ruled by Russia. The western part of Poland was ceded to Prussia.

All this produced a sprawl of states that were roughly equal to one another in military and economic potential (see Map 19.1). States thus existed in a balance of power that would discourage any one state from provoking its neighbor. To this extent the Congress succeeded. The rough parity of power achieved by its redrawn map kept Continental Europe free of conflict for fifty years. This period of international stability came to be called the **Concert of Europe.** It worked but failed to please.

However, the Congress failed, or refused, to consider a critical desire of the mass populations, the desire for nationalism. Most wanted to unite along ethnic lines and thereby create nations that expressed ethnic and national *genius*—the collective consciousness of a distinct culture. The lines drawn in Vienna dismembered such desires, and did so intentionally, for the simple reason that certain ethnic groups vastly outnumbered others. The Germans and the Poles, for instance, had to be forced into multiple states before any true balance of power could be achieved. The Polish people, therefore, were forced into an unnatural division, with their people dispersed between Prussia, Russia, and Austria–Hungary. The German territories remained just that—separate territories, dozens of them—lest they form a gravitational mass that would dominate all of its neighbors. The Italians too, politically disunited since the end of the Roman Empire, remained divided into a dozen principalities. Throughout the so-called Concert of Europe, nationalist reformers looked back at the Congress of Vienna as a gathering of callous reactionary elites parceling out the family silver to one another, whereas the legitimate desires of the people were crushed and forgotten.

Restoration of Royal Regimes   The policies of the new regimes were indeed conservative. They restored the royal families to power in Austria–Hungary, France, Prussia, Russia, and Spain; they also restored a dozen lesser princes to small buffer-zone states between the major powers. The returned monarchs quickly brought back all the elements of absolutism that they could get away with. Austria's Francis I (r. 1804–1835), for example, censored every medium of public communication and set up elaborate networks of spies and informants to stamp out any hint of radicalism.[1] France's Louis XVIII (r. 1814–1824) abolished the Estates General and established in its place a two-chamber legislature made up of a Chamber of Peers (the aristocracy) and the Chamber of Deputies. Membership in the latter was restricted to the wealthiest bourgeois, those most likely to inaugurate France's industrial development. Prussia's Frederick William III (r. 1797–1840) gained territories in the 1815 settlement, especially the early industrial centers of the Ruhr valley in the Rhineland and Westphalia, making Prussia for a while the leading German state in Europe. But he also cracked down sharply on any form of rebellion or demand for reform. Russia's tsar Alexander I (r. 1801–1825), who had symbolically led the defense of the country against Napoleon in 1812, died in 1825 without an heir, leaving the throne to pass to his brother Nicholas I (r. 1825–1855), a conservative autocrat. In Spain, Ferdinand VII (r. 1814–1833) nullified the liberal constitution drawn up in 1812 by the Napoleonic regime, reinstated the Inquisition, imprisoned the leaders of the Spanish Parliament, and declared a return to divine-right absolutism. England, of course, stood apart from the Continent and enjoyed its vast global supremacy in industrialized commerce; its central aim in the Concert of Europe was to support the Ottoman Empire, in the hope that a stronger Ottoman state would provide a check on the expansionist aims of tsarist Russia.

Popular opposition to conservatism resulted in numerous crackdowns. In 1817, for example, amid celebrations to mark the three hundredth anniversary of Martin Luther's rebellion against the Catholic Church, university students in Wartburg demanded a loosening of government controls over education. They ended up being chased and clubbed by police, and the governments of the German Confederation imposed strict new censorship regulations over student publications. They installed overt and covert surveillance networks on campuses

---

[1]   He was Francis I of Austria but had been Francis II of the now-defunct Holy Roman Empire.

Fighting for Greece   French artist Louis Dupré (1789–1837) was an eyewitness to the Greek struggle for independence from the Ottoman Turks. Here he portrays a Greek rebel hoisting the flag over fallen Turk fighters. The painting illustrates the linkage between Romantic passion and political nationalism.

everywhere, with commissioners whose job was to preserve the ideological stability of the universities.

Greek War of Independence In 1821, Greek patriots rose up against the Ottoman Turks, whose control over Greece had been reconfirmed at Vienna. When Tsar Alexander I sent troops to aid the rebels—Turkey's loss being Russia's gain—the conservative alliance pressed Russia to stop. All official aid to the Greeks was indeed halted, but by this point, under the influence of Romanticism, popular sentiment across Europe had swung strongly in favor of the Greek cause: Greece, after all, was the birthplace of Western civilization for the Romantic generation. When the English poet Lord Byron (1788–1824) popularized the Greek drive for independence with his own personal heroics, public pressure on the Ottomans and their conservative supporters increased; Greece subsequently won its independence in 1830.

The ruins of the Parthenon in Athens became a symbol of that struggle. Between 1801 and 1812 the former British ambassador to Greece, Thomas Bruce, the Earl of Elgin, under an agreement with the Ottoman government, removed a large number of statues and marble friezes from the Parthenon, shipped them to London (supposedly for safekeeping), and sold them to the British government. These "Elgin Marbles," once cleaned and secured in the British Museum, were enormously popular but controversial. The Greek government, formally established and internationally recognized as of 1830, denied Lord Elgin's supposed authorization to take the sculptures, insisting that any agreement reached under the former Ottoman government was invalid, and demanded the Elgin Marbles' immediate return to Greece. Nearly two hundred years later, they are still pressing their case.

Repression of Antiroyalists in Spain and Russia In Spain, the continued presence of antiroyalists inspired a new wave of repressive measures. These culminated, in 1823, with more than 200,000 French troops being sent into the country in defense of the Bourbon dynasty. In Russia in 1825, Nicholas I crushed a group of rebels known as the Decembrists, from their uprising on December 14 of that year. For many, the French revolutionary wave seemed quenched forever.

THE MORAL COMPONENT OF CONSERVATISM

Liberal-minded people, including historians, tend to portray conservatism as a reactionary movement. They see it as an effort by elites to retain their privileges at the expense of common people, common sense, and natural progress. There is something to be said for that view of the post-Vienna elites, but in the end it is neither accurate nor just. A core of strong ideas lay at the heart of conservatism, many of which can be traced back to Edmund Burke's *Reflections on the Revolution in France* (introduced in chapter 17), commonly regarded as one of the foundational texts of political conservatism. Another important source for conservatism was the *Essay on the Generative Principle of Political Institutions* (1814) by the French-Savoyard diplomat Joseph-Marie de Maistre (1753–1821).

More so than liberalism, conservatism has a philosophical basis, one that emerges from a central ethical question: How should people live? In particu- *Conservatism's* lar, how should people behave when living together? Conservatism recog- *Central Ideas* nizes the rights of individuals, but also the responsibilities that individuals have toward one another. It emphasizes the mutual duties that bind us together and create a cohesive society; in a conflict between individual desires and social requirements, the claims of society reign supreme. Those social claims may have any number of origins—cultural tradition, religious conviction, economic requirement, and political or social security among them—and any successful and legitimate government must work within the parameters established by them.

Conservatism thus values traditions, including religion, established norms of morality, and social continuity. Its ethical goal is the preservation of the group rather than the gratification of the individual. As its name suggests, conservatism *conserves* something, preserves it, and desires its continued existence: and the "it" is, in a word, tradition. Burke makes the following point:

> Government is a contrivance of human wisdom to provide for human wants. Men have a right that these wants should be provided for by this wisdom. Among these wants is to be reckoned the want, out of civil society, of a sufficient restraint upon their passions. Society requires not only that the passions of individuals should be subjected, but that even in the mass and body, as well as in the individuals, the inclinations of men should frequently be thwarted, their will controlled, and their passions brought into subjection. This can only be done by a power out of themselves. . . . But as the liberties and the restrictions vary with times and circumstances, and admit of infinite modifications, they cannot be settled upon any abstract rule; and nothing is so foolish as to discuss them upon that principle.
>
> . . . Society is indeed a contract. Subordinate contracts for objects of mere occasional interest may be dissolved at pleasure—but the state ought not to be considered as nothing better than a partnership agreement in a trade of pepper and coffee, calico or tobacco, or some other such low concern, to be taken up for a little temporary interest, and to be dissolved by the fancy of the parties. It is to be looked on with other reverence; because it is not a partnership in things subservient only to the gross animal existence of a temporary and perishable nature. It is a partnership in all science; a partnership in all art; a partnership in every virtue, and in all perfection. As the ends of such a partnership cannot be obtained in many generations, it

becomes a partnership not only between those who are living, but between those who are to be born. (*Reflections on the Revolution in France*)

Similarly, Joseph-Marie de Maistre emphasizes the organic nature of authentic political constitutions, which he sees as the by-product of social development rather than the creation of human minds:

> The more we study the role of human agency in the development of political constitutions, the more convinced we become that it plays the smallest of roles and is in fact a mere tool [of the larger social development]. To my mind there remains no reason to doubt the absolute truth of these four propositions: first, that the basic principles underlying all political constitutions exist prior to the laws themselves; second, that any [legitimate and enduring] constitutional law is, and must be, the natural development or sanction of a pre-existing, though unwritten, right; third, that the most essential, intrinsically constitutional, and fundamental rights are those which remain unwritten—and indeed cannot be put in written form without endangering the state; and fourth, that the inherent weakness and vulnerability of any constitution is directly proportional to the extent that it exists in written form. (*Essay on the Generative Principle of Political Institutions*)

Conservatism does not, on the whole, deny the need for change, but it is deeply skeptical of humans' ability to create entire new systems of religious belief, economic policy, political action, and social order. Such things, conservatives maintain, require time-tested, gradual development. As Burke had emphasized, revolutionary passions are ultimately self-defeating and leave misery in their wake. Napoleon's career was not one of tragic failure but of predictable failure, since what he had tried to accomplish was not natural. Conservatism appealed, and still appeals, to minds inclined to accept that the world has its own ways and that our abilities to reshape it to our liking are limited. The world as it actually exists is not egalitarian. Attributes like talent, intelligence, skill, beauty, wealth, and social position are simply not dealt out in equal measures to all people; hierarchies exist everywhere in nature and are, therefore, natural. Egregious abuses of privilege ought, of course, to be opposed. But opposition to hierarchy itself, and not just to its abuses, is unnatural, historically uninformed, and philosophically indefensible.

Reconciling Tradition with Industrialization   The conservative governments of the early 19th century hardly wished to halt the course of history. Rather, they wanted to ensure that the shock of industrialization did not obliterate all that was good and necessary in the European tradition. And there was no doubt about the need to industrialize. The

A New Institution but an Old Order   Irish statesman and member of Parliament John W. Croker is credited with coining the term *conservatism*. He also established a British institution that came to be closely associated with the ideology—the Athenaeum Club, whose elegant London quarters are shown here. Originally intended as a quasi-academic club—a club for men "of eminence in science, literature, the arts, and public service," according to house rules—it soon attracted British peers, Anglican bishops, and Cabinet members.

process had begun before the signatures were dry on the treaties signed in Vienna in 1815. But industrial capitalism seemed to conflict with the traditional society championed by the conservatives, since it valued individual enterprise and innovation. Capitalism depends on the freedom of capital and labor to move, the breaking of old customs and institutions, and the cool, calculating mentality of business— ledgers, inventories, market forces, interest rates, supply routes, tax incentives. The challenge was to achieve the economic benefits of industrial development without jettisoning the values—king, country, church, tradition—of the old order.

Consider, for example, the vast numbers of urban poor. Since the industrial economy profited from the enormous surplus of available labor, factory owners had no incentive to alleviate suffering—at least not until the social unrest created by their misery affected the workplace. The conservative governments recognized the need for public support for the poor, but tried to tailor these welfare programs in ways that would return the indigent to village societies. For example, 19th-century English conservatives supported the Poor Law, originally enacted in 1572. Under this law, a welfare recipient received a regular payment in the parish where he was born. The idea behind this plan was that the traditional networks of family, friends, church, and local squire would assume the responsibility of tending to his or her needs; the government's role was in essence to complement, but not to replace, traditional and natural methods of caring for the poor.

The moral component of conservatism had a powerful appeal. The role of government, as conservatives saw it, was to maintain and support a moral life, and they opposed efforts to insert the state into roles best left to individuals and the organic communities to which they belong. The obligation to aid the poor is immediate and personal, conservatives maintained: if I am aware of a family in my neighborhood who is in dire need of help, then I have a personal duty to come to its aid. To hold that the government ought to provide aid for all the indigent is foolhardy, because it is the most indirect, inefficient, and impersonal way of bringing assistance where it is needed. It is also morally wrong, since it means my passing along the problem to someone else. In its insistence on local solutions to local problems and on personal responsibility instead of government initiative, conservatism appeals to the desire for moral behavior and social connection.

THE CHALLENGE OF LIBERALISM

As strong as conservatism's appeal was, it lost ground to the steady opposing pull of liberalism. The second of the three main political traditions of the modern West (socialism being the third), liberalism regards the primary function of government to be the promotion of freedom instead of order. By 1830, as industrialization rushed ahead, the conservatives' hold on government weakened across Europe, and they even lost control in several nations. Rapid urbanization on the Continent made it difficult to contain and suppress the demands for social reform and political participation. These demands from the laboring population coalesced into the liberal alternative.

Liberalism's Central Ideas   True to its name, liberalism has proven more changeable than conservatism over the past two centuries, freely discarding some values while taking on new convictions, as conditions warranted. However, it has retained its fundamental dedication to freeing individuals from undue control. If conservatism rests on the foundation of preserving the best of society's past, liberalism, in general, seeks to liberate individuals from the strictures of inequality, injustice, and intolerance in the present. As written in a letter to a newspaper by the English philosopher John Stuart Mill (1806–1873), liberalism's answer to Edmund Burke, "A Liberal is he who looks forward for his principles of government; a [conservative] looks backward" (*Morning Star*, July 6, 1865). Compare a cutting comment from a prominent conservative periodical: "What lurking conspirator against the quiet of his native government . . . has failed to ask and receive the protection of our Liberals?" (*Blackwood's Magazine*, February 1828).

At least from the time of John Locke in the late 17th century (see chapter 16), liberals have asserted the fundamental equality and goodness of human beings:

> To understand political power right, and derive it from its original, we must consider, what state all men are naturally in, and that is, a state of perfect freedom to order their actions, and dispose of their possessions and persons, as they think fit, within the bounds of the law of nature, without asking leave, or depending upon the will of any other man.
>
> A state also of equality, wherein all the power and jurisdiction is reciprocal, no one having more than another; there being nothing more evident, than that creatures of the same species and rank, promiscuously born to all the same advantages of nature, and the use of the same faculties, should also be equal one amongst another without subordination or subjection, unless the lord and master of them all should, by any manifest declaration of his will, set one above another, and confer on him, by an evident and clear appointment, an undoubted right to dominion and sovereignty. (*Second Treatise of Civil Government*, ch. 2)

If people are individually good and equal, then the good society is achieved by leaving them alone as much as possible, to act freely. Any action by government that would curtail individual freedom, then, must be justified by extraordinary argument, since it upsets the natural good ordering of the world. To take the example of England's conservative Poor Law, liberalism finds it unacceptable. In tying the welfare recipient to his home parish, the law restricts his freedom of movement, his freedom to seek employment or education, and his freedom to determine his own fate. After British liberals came to power in 1830, they enacted the new Poor Law of 1834, so that welfare payments followed the recipient as he chose to move from one location to another, in search of work or for any other reason. It was a costlier and less efficient system of administration, to be sure— but it maximized the citizen's freedom to act.

Part of the difficulty for liberalism has been the very nature of freedom: it requires identifying what it is we are free from. The debate has infused political thinking ever since Thomas Hobbes made his arguments in favor of absolutism in the early 17th century (discussed in chapter 15). As formulated in the 19th century, liberalism meant above all freedom from control by government. From John Stuart Mill's classic work, *On Liberty* (1859), comes the following:

> [T]he strongest of all the arguments against the interference of the public with purely personal conduct, is that when it does interfere, the odds are that it interferes wrongly, and in the wrong place. On questions of social

morality, of duty to others, the opinion of the public, that is, of an overruling majority, though often wrong, is likely to be still oftener right; because on such questions they are only required to judge of their own interests; of the manner in which some mode of conduct, if allowed to be practised, would affect themselves. But the opinion of a similar majority, imposed as a law on the minority, on questions of self-regarding conduct, is quite as likely to be wrong as right; for in these cases public opinion means, at the best, some people's opinion of what is good or bad for other people; while very often it does not even mean that; the public, with the most perfect indifference, passing over the pleasure or convenience of those whose conduct they censure, and considering only their own preference. There are many who consider as an injury to themselves any conduct which they have a distaste for, and resent it as an outrage to their feelings; as a religious bigot, when charged with disregarding the religious feelings of others, has been known to retort that they disregard his feelings, by persisting in their abominable worship or creed. But there is no parity between the feeling of a person for his own opinion, and the feeling of another who is offended at his holding it; no more than between the desire of a thief to take a purse, and the desire of the right owner to keep it. And a person's taste is as much his own peculiar concern as his opinion or his purse.

Nineteenth-century liberals' desire for freedom from government intrusion is hardly surprising, given Europe's experience of hierarchy, privilege, and monarchical tyranny and considering that the strongest support for liberalism came from the new middle class, the bourgeoisie. Their newfound economic muscle depended precisely on individual freedom and the rights of property. Their position is easily expressed: so long as one does not harm others, one ought to be left alone to do what one pleases with one's own property. Society has no right to force an entrepreneur to manage his property in a certain way, just as the entrepreneur has no right to force his workers to accept low pay or miserable working conditions. Freedom of choice is all. A worker who does not like the pay or work-demands of any given workplace is free to walk away from it and pursue a better situation elsewhere. Better yet, he can cultivate his own entrepreneurial goals. Moreover, any worker who *is* willing to accept a job at low pay, harsh hours, and miserable conditions should be free to do so.

For this reason, 19th-century liberalism drew on the free-market economic theory of Adam Smith (discussed in chapter 16) to champion *laissez-faire* ("let it be") capitalism, or capitalism without government intervention: an unregulated economy was the only way to ensure the freedom of every individual to do as he saw fit. Hence 19th-century liberals opposed wage- and working-condition regulations, fought against high taxes, and resisted the idea of labor unions, even while they encouraged the free movement of the poor who received government assistance. That free movement, of course, is part of what guaranteed the vast surplus of labor that kept wages at rock-bottom levels.

The strict opposition of 19th-century liberals to government intervention differs from our understanding of liberalism today, but again, it reveals the ideology's fundamental commitment to the freedom of the individual. Liberalism has always tended to see the world as in constant flux, in contrast to the emphasis on time-honored customs and institutional structures found in conservatism. Since the world is continually changing, the only sensible way of managing it is to privilege meritocracy, opportunity, and innovation. Let creative minds create, without censorship; let individuals determine their own political fates, through free elections; let people with ideas and drive be free to exercise them and reap the benefits of their success, in free markets.

REBELLION AND REFORM

It was not the plight of the urban poor under industrial capitalism, therefore, that led to the political defeat of the conservative Tory party in Britain in 1830. Instead, it was the plight of the entrepreneurs, who wanted to free the new economy from what they regarded as the archaic paternalism of the aristocratic order. The solid middle class of the 19th century joined forces politically with another emerging group, skilled laborers—those whose technical expertise with new machinery allowed them to rise to higher wage levels. Together, they demanded greater clout through the extension of suffrage, the right to vote.

Liberal Reform in Great Britain

As we have seen, eighteenth-century British society was dominated by the landowning aristocracy, but that class was neither closed nor rigidly defined. Basic civil rights were guaranteed, but only about 8 percent of the population could vote for representatives to Parliament. The French Revolution then threw the British aristocracy into a panic for a generation, and after 1815 it was determined to defend its ruling position.

The first step in this direction began in 1815 with revision of the Corn Laws dealing with foreign grain imports. Fearing peace would bring a resumption of imports and lower prices for wheat, the aristocracy rammed through Parliament legislation that prohibited the importation of foreign grain unless the price at home rose to high levels. More broadly, the landed aristocracy opposed the new manufacturing and commercial groups who were insisting on a much greater place in the framework of political power and social prestige.

The conservative Tory party refused to reform representation in the House of Commons, however. About two-thirds of the members of the Commons owed

The New Voters   When the British House of Lords, in 1831, vetoed yet another draft of the Reform Bill that extended the vote to working-class men and re-drew the lines of the country's electoral districts, crowds of demonstrators took to the streets across the nation. The London protestors shown here are carefully presented as proud workers who are loyal to the monarchy.

their seats to the patronage of rich, titled landowners. In districts known as "pocket" or "rotten" boroughs, landowners used their power to return members of Parliament who would serve their interests. Liberals in the Whig party, the new industrial middle class, and radical artisans argued passionately against this system, their agitation peaking in the years 1830–1832. Only the fear of widespread rebellion allowed the Whig party to push through a reform package that directly challenged the Tories' hold on electoral politics.

The Reform Bill of 1832 eliminated the pocket boroughs and reallocated parliamentary seats for greater representation of the new industrial areas. It expanded the franchise to bourgeois men and substantial farmers, although only one in six men won the right to vote. Nonetheless, this reform brought British liberals and members of the middle class into a junior partnership with a landed elite that had ruled Britain for centuries.

The most significant example of liberal, middle-class power came in the repeal of the Corn Laws in 1846, a victory for laissez-faire economic policy. After Ireland's potato crop failed in 1845 and famine prices for food seemed likely in England, a minority of Tory aristocrats joined with the Whigs to revoke the laws to allow free imports of grain. England escaped famine and established a free-trade policy that lasted for nearly a century.

The following year, the Tories, who were competing with the Whigs for the support of the working class, pushed though the Ten Hours Act of 1847, which limited the workday for women and young people in factories to ten hours. This competition between a still-vigorous aristocracy and a strong middle class was a crucial factor in Great Britain's peaceful evolution in the 19th century.

In France, by contrast, it took yet another popular rebellion to pull the nobles from power. The reigning Bourbon king, Charles X (r. 1824–1830), had made *Continental* himself hated by dissolving the liberal-leaning parliament, ordering new elections, *Uprisings* and then rigging them so that only candidates he had preapproved could win. His timing was rotten, since France had just suffered through a miserable winter and shortages had doubled the cost of most foodstuffs. Spontaneous, angry food riots took place in most of the larger cities. Fearing revolutionary violence, Charles abdicated and passed the crown to his cousin Louis-Philippe (r. 1830–1848)—the last king France would ever have. He granted a new charter that doubled the number of Frenchmen who had the right to vote, but even this number still represented a mere 1 percent of the male population (compared to about 15 percent in Britain). The outlook for liberal reforms in France looked bleak.

Liberal-led rebellions broke out in 1830 in other parts of Europe too, although the protests failed to effect much real change. Factory workers in the German territories, for example, smashed industrial equipment and demonstrated in factory yards to protest their low pay and long hours. Disaffected Walloons—a French-speaking community named after their homeland, the Walloon region of Belgium—in the heavily industrialized Netherlands took to the streets and demanded better working conditions, recognition of their ethnic and linguistic identity, and a new constitution. University students and junior military officers campaigned for reform in Poland, seeking a reunification of all Polish people (divided by the Congress of Vienna among Prussia, Austria, and Russia) and a national constitution—to which Russia responded with an armed attack.

Spain's clash between conservatives and liberals was also violent. The restored Bourbon king, Ferdinand VII (r. 1813–1833), was a diehard absolutist who made only the mildest of compromises with constitutionalism. When he died without a male heir, the throne passed to his daughter Isabella II (r. 1833–1868), who at first seemed open to a modest reform program. Her claim to the throne was challenged, however, by her ultraconservative proabsolutist uncle, named Carlos—whose followers were therefore known as *Carlists*. The Carlists fought bitterly to restore divine-right monarchy, the authority of the Catholic Church, and traditional society, even at the expense of economic development. Wars with the Carlists hardened Isabella's attitudes, until in her later years she herself became a royal absolutist. Finally, in 1868, she abdicated the throne after some of her more reform-minded generals voiced their unhappiness against her drift into autocracy. She spent her last years in comfortable exile in Paris, but the struggle between Spain's conservative traditionalists and liberal constitutionalists continued into the 20th century with the bloody civil war of the 1930s (discussed in chapter 25).

What the reformers demanded throughout the 1830s and 1840s can be easily summarized: expanded suffrage, decreased taxes, confirmed property rights, deregulated trade and workplaces, and curtailed labor unionization. These issues served the bourgeoisie's interests. As the industrial economy developed, however, becoming more diversified and specialized, so too did the bourgeois class that promoted it. Usually only the great merchants, leading industrialists, and most prominent financiers had access to political power. The rest of the middle classes, from lesser merchants to lawyers and physicians and down to office clerks and school teachers, toiled away without any direct political influence.

Beneath the bourgeoisie was the great mass of the laborers, skilled and unskilled, working long, rigorously enforced shifts in the factories. These came to be known as the **proletariat**—a pejorative term that derived from the Latin and whose colloquial meaning was "those who smell." They were regarded as the lowest and most vulgar sort of humans, who contributed nothing to the betterment of society except the next generation of workers.[2] As reported in a news magazine of the time:

> The proletariat, which has not morally and physically any thing to lose, has allied itself to this revolutionary tendency. . . . This word, which has lately become familiar to all readers of German and French literature, signifies the lowest and poorest classes, those in fact who are totally destitute of property. (*The Daguerreotype*, October 16, 1847)

The bourgeois reformers aimed less at alleviating the proletariat's misery than at improving the efficiency of the economy. Limiting the workweek to a maximum of 70 hours for workers aged fourteen to nineteen, for example, reduced the number of jobless poor who received public assistance. Funds for welfare payments and housing subsidies were also redirected to workhouses, where the poor received room and board in return for long hours of unskilled drudgery.

The bourgeois were not necessarily heartless or grasping, and many of them donated generously to the poor. However, much like the early conservative political leaders, they believed that charity was a personal moral duty, not the rightful

---

2   The word *proletarius* in ancient Rome colloquially designated a "stunt cock," a slave whose sexual service gratified his male and female owners. Karl Marx (1818–1883), author of *The Communist Manifesto* (1848), adopted and popularized the word in its later Roman usage. After a wave of reforms instituted by the Roman general Marius (157–85 BCE), the *proletarii* formed the backbone of the Roman army—and the word gained a positive gloss.

function of civil government. Many hundreds of private charitable institutions were founded in the first half of the century: orphanages, hospitals, organizations like the YMCA and the Society for the Prevention of Cruelty to Animals, medical clinics, vocational schools (called *polytechnics*), athletic and hygienic programs, Sunday schools, musical societies, and lending libraries. The problems created by industrialism, however, far outstripped the ability of private, volunteer kindness to address them.

RESPONSES TO LIBERAL CAPITALISM

Angered by the slow pace and self-serving nature of liberal reform, the urban poor began to organize to demand swifter and more far-reaching reforms. In 1838 the *Chartism* London Working Men's Association drafted a "People's Charter," a petition that they circulated among laborers in city after city, ultimately collecting more than 6 million signatures. This became known as the **Chartist movement**, and it provided a model for labor protests across Europe. The Chartists made six essential demands:

1. Universal male suffrage
2. Annual elections
3. Secret ballots
4. Elimination of the requirement to own property to qualify for public office
5. Fair redistricting of electoral maps
6. Guaranteed salaries for those serving in government

Without the last, only the rich could afford to enter public service.

Chartism thereby helped to redefine liberalism. What society needed, the Chartists insisted, was not only personal freedom from undue governmental control but also freedom from the unjust control of people's lives by unfettered capitalism. Just as the power of government must be checked by constitutional restraints, lest it devolve into tyranny, so too does the industrial economy require regulation. Otherwise, it will become a system of economic slavery. It took several decades for the new ideas to flourish—starting with yet another round of protests, strikes, street riots, and violent clashes with states and industries.

The economic and social platform called **socialism** emerged in the 1820s and 1830s, as a way not of reforming liberal capitalism but of replacing it altogether. As *Socialism* with any ideology, socialism came in many varieties and still does today. But the different strands of socialist thought have all been variations on a single theme:

DESIGN

for a Community of 2000 Persons founded upon a principle
Commended by Plato, Lord Bacon and Sir Thomas More

EXPLANATION OF THE PARTS NUMBERED ON THE PLATE

1 Gymnasiums or Covered Places for Exercise, attached to the Schools and Infirmary.
2 Conservatory, in the midst of Gardens botanically arranged.
3 Baths, warm and cold, of which there are four for the Males, and four for the Females.
4 Dining Halls, with Kitchens, &c. beneath them.
5 Angle Buildings, occupied by the Schools for Infants, Children, and Youths, and the Infirmary; on the ground floors are Conversation-rooms for Adults.
6 Library, Detached Reading Rooms, Bookbindery, Printing Office, &c.
7 Ballroom and Music rooms.
8 Theatre for Lectures, Exhibitions, Discussions, &c. with Laboratory, Small Library, &c.
9 Museum, with Library of Description and Reference, Rooms for preparing Specimens, &c.
10 The Brew-houses, Bakehouses, Wash-houses, Laundries, &c. arranged round the Bases of the Towers.
11 The Refectories for the infants and children are on each side of the Vestibules of the Dining halls.
12 The Illuminators of the Establishment, Clock-towers, and Observatories, and from the elevated summits of which all the smoke and vitiated air of the buildings is discharged into the atmosphere.
13 Suites of adult sitting rooms and chambers.
14 Suites of Chambers, which may be easily and quickly made of any dimensions required; Dormitories for the Unmarried and Children.
15 Esplanade one hundred feet wide, about twelve feet above the natural surface.
16 Paved Footpath.
17 The Arcade and its Terrace, giving both a covered and an open communication with every part of the building.
18 Sub-way leading to the Kitchens, &c. and along which meat, vegetables, coals, &c. are conveyed to the Stores, and dust and refuse brought out.

New Harmony   Robert Owen (1771–1858) was a Welsh industrialist who used his fortune to promote a form of utopian socialism. Convinced that the root of modern suffering was the conflict between labor and machinery, Owen championed the eight-hour workday and employer-provided daycare. He came to America in 1825 with plans to develop an ideal worker community at New Harmony, Indiana. The plan for its physical layout and daily routine would look comfortably familiar to any Benedictine monk.

collective ownership and management of the major means of production within a society. The variations consist chiefly of different ideas about which industries ought to be socialized and the makeup of the collective ownership and management—a cooperative structure (like a medieval guild or modern cartel)? The state itself? Self-selected citizen ownership of equity?

Socialism began in France, although France trailed Great Britain in developing modern industry. French thinkers like Henri de Saint-Simon (1760–1825), François-Noël Babeuf (1760–1797), Charles Fourier (1772–1837), and Pierre-Joseph Proudhon (1809–1865) were acutely aware that the political revolution in France, the rise of laissez-faire economic policy, and the emergence of factory industry in England were transforming society. They argued that the central flaw of liberal capitalism is the very tendency toward profit seeking on which it is based. From a moral point of view, profit seeking caters to and encourages selfish individualism; still more fundamental, however, is the fact that the pursuit of capital inevitably becomes detached from the process of producing useful economic value. As one accumulates capital, in other words, one invests it in other ventures that will yield a positive return—but the positive return becomes one's sole concern, not the actual usefulness or even the desirability of the thing being invested in. When profit making becomes the very definition of economic good, socialists argue, an economy gradually becomes merely a race to hoard wealth rather than a means to provide all of society with its basic human needs.

In industrializing Britain, Robert Owen (1771–1858), a successful Welsh-born manufacturer, became one of the most influential socialists. In 1800 he bought a cotton mill in New Lanark, Scotland, and began to set up a model factory town, where workers labored only ten hours a day (thus prefiguring the Ten Hours Act by nearly half a century) and children between the ages of five and ten went to school rather than worked in the factory. Owen moved to the United States in the 1820s and founded a community named New Harmony in Indiana. The experiment collapsed after three years, a victim of internal squabbling. But from Owen's experiments and writings, such as *The Book of the New Moral World* (1820), would come the movement for producer cooperatives (businesses owned and controlled by their workers), consumers' cooperatives ("coops" in which consumers owned shares), and a national trade union.

THE REVOLUTIONS OF 1848

After more than two decades of discontent, urban workers and the homeless poor across Europe rose up in violent protest in 1848. With only a handful of exceptions—Britain, the Netherlands, Russia, and Scandinavia—every European government confronted mass rebellion of some sort. To some critics, the wave of uprisings looked suspiciously organized, but most regarded them as individual spontaneous bursts of rage, with each explosion giving encouragement to the next. Workers and the poor in every industrialized city, after all, faced the same problems. Demonstrators filled the streets and squares, blockaded roads, smashed factory windows and equipment, and looted and burned stores. Speeches and

MAP 19.2   Centers of Revolution, 1848   The revolutions of 1848 were so widespread because no country was prepared for the changes brought on by industrial development.

broadsheets proclaimed the end of political and economic elitism and called for the transfer of power to new governments chosen by full and open democratic processes. Regimes across Europe, fearing a revolution as bloody and destructive as had gripped France in the 1790s, responded with brute force, and by the time the dust settled, tens of thousands of rebels had been killed and hundreds of thousands had been driven into exile.

Coming as they did in the aftermath of several consecutive crop failures and growing concern of European-wide famine, these revolts frightened everyone. French political thinker and historian Alexis de Tocqueville (1805–1859) de- *France* scribed France as "a society cut in half—those who possessed no property were united in envy, and those who did possess anything were united in terror." The French king, Louis-Philippe, had forbidden public assemblies as early as 1835, in an effort to forestall political agitation. But in 1847 the leaders among the radical reformers organized a broad network of large-scale "private banquets," at which reformers plotted their moves and incited their audiences to increase their activity. The decision in January 1848 by the French premier François Guizot (1787–1874) to suppress these banquets triggered an uprising in Paris, which in turn triggered uprisings across Europe (see Map 19.2). Guizot declared himself "an unflinching enemy of universal suffrage—I regard it as the certain ruin of democracy and liberty."

Within a matter of days the protestors had forced Louis-Philippe to abdicate, and a new constitutional republic was established (the Second Republic, in France's back-and-forth political narrative between representative and centralized rule).[3] For the president of the new government, the Republican leaders chose Louis-Napoleon (r. 1848–1852), the nephew of the great emperor. He began modestly. In accepting the new post, he assured the assembly:

> I am guided by no ambition.... Having grown up in free countries and learned from the school of hard knocks, I will remain forever faithful to the duties [entrusted to me].... I vow to devote myself entirely, unreservedly, to strengthening this Republic by guiding it to develop wise laws, honest goals, and great and noble deeds, and my greatest honor will be to hand over to whomever succeeds me, after four years in office, a stable government, with its liberties intact and its genuine progress assured.

Only four years later, however, Louis-Napoleon declared the Second Republic dead, restored autocracy, and took the imperial title of Napoleon III (r. 1852–1870). Thus was born France's Second Empire.

In Italy, the uprisings took many forms. The northern city of Milan, rebelling against Austrian rule, began the year with a popular effort to give up smoking *Italian* tobacco since the taxes on it were so onerous. The no-smoking demonstration *States* worked too well, however: Austrian soldiers went on a retributive rampage and killed more than sixty people. Outrage over the imperial response triggered

---

[3]   Louis-Philippe fled to England in disguise, carrying a passport that identified him as "Mr. Smith."

unrest throughout the peninsula. In Rome, rebels assassinated the prime minister of the Papal State, causing Pope Pius IX (r. 1846–1878) to flee south, where he went into hiding with the temporarily exiled Duke of Piedmont and King Ferdinand II of Naples. Revolutionaries in Palermo succeeded briefly in forming a new government and issuing a constitution.

Germanic
Confederation

Uprisings throughout the German-speaking territories, including Habsburg Austria, were notable for their insistence on the unification of Germany into a single state. They did not achieve it, but the crowds in Vienna did manage to force Klemens von Metternich, the Austrian foreign minister, from office. Riots in Berlin resulted in the deaths of hundreds at the hands of Prussian soldiers. Despite promises from the Prussian king, Frederick William IV (r. 1840–1861), to introduce a liberal constitution, a conservative new legislature was put into place instead—one that proved the starting point for the career of a new military figure and diplomat, Otto von Bismarck (1815–1898), who, as we will see in the next chapter, would go on to become the most dominant European statesman of the second half of the 19th century.

The narrative of the revolutions of 1848 can easily become confusing, mainly because there were as many motives as rebels. Aristocrats feared the unbridled absolutism desired by Louis-Philippe of France and Francis I of Austria; industrial capitalists opposed the undermining of property interests through taxation and regulation; urban workers rebelled against inhumane work conditions and wretched pay; and the poor took to the streets to demand rescue from famine, crime, and disease. Europe's transition into a modern, developed industrial economy left everyone, it seemed, vulnerable and aggrieved. What brought on such a state of affairs? And how could a stable future be created from so much misery, distrust, and sheer rage? For the time being, most European states retreated into another brief era of law-and-order conservatism.

KARL MARX AND REVOLUTION

The first major figure to suggest an interpretation of this staggering era was a scholar-turned-journalist named **Karl Marx** (1818–1883). A German Jew, Marx had earned a PhD in philosophy from the University of Jena in 1841, but failed to win an academic position in Germany and turned to journalism. After he was accused of treason in 1844 for supposedly seditious criticisms of the government, Marx, who was then living in Paris with his young family, renounced his Prussian citizenship and made his way to London. While in Paris, Marx studied early socialist theory, economics, and the history of the French Revolution. He also began a lifelong intellectual and political partnership with Friedrich Engels (1820–1895), the German author of *The Condition of the Working Class in England* whom we met in the previous chapter. Early in 1848 Marx published **The Communist Manifesto**, coauthored with Engels, and shortly thereafter he returned to Germany to participate in the uprisings of that summer.

Marx came back to England in 1849, disappointed in the failure of the rebellions but confident in the eventual victory of reform. He had already laid out a general theory of history in a book called *The German Ideology* (1846), and he spent his remaining years refining his ideas and working to promote economic and social reform.

Karl Marx The works of Karl Marx (1818–1883) and Friedrich Engels (1820–1895) had little impact during their lifetimes but played a role in most of the major developments of the 20th century.

He had relatively little success in his own lifetime, either as a scholar or as a political activist, but he became arguably the single most influential political thinker of the 20th century. Only then were his ideas adopted—in severely reshaped form—by Communist parties around the world.

Marxism is essentially a theory about history, and like its creator, it is profoundly optimistic. Marxism provides the basis for, but is not identical with Communism, which is a form of socioeconomic organization in which private property is abolished, class structures are dismantled, and all wealth is held in common. One way to think of them: Marxism is the theory; Communism is the practice. Like Rousseau before him and the Romantics and socialists of his own time, Marx believed in the essential goodness of human nature; it is the world that plants the seed of corruption in the heart. All human conflict is at its root a conflict over things—gold, lands, animal herds, estates, inheritances, cities, tax revenues, harbors, mines, and trade routes. Clashing ideas and values are real, but secondary, and in fact are usually little more than rationalizations for the conflict over wealth. Marx calls this process **historical materialism**. Economic matters, in simplest terms, are the fuel that drives history forward. In all ages, he argues, change has come about through the conflict between those who produce the bulk of society's wealth with one technology and those who produce it under alternative technologies. In a nomadic, pastoral society, for example, ownership of the animal herds decides social status and hence political power. But when that society transitions into agrarian life, a new technology of wealth production is created, namely crop farming; control of land now determines economic value and therefore social status. The conflict between these modes of existence drives the change from a tribal society governed by unwritten customs to a bureaucratic state governed by written laws and contracts (such as land deeds). The rise of manufacturing and commerce propels the development of urban life and yet another stage of historical growth, especially as the urban economy eclipses the rural economy as the main producer of aggregate wealth. Hence the development of parliaments, with power in the hands of representatives from the urban economic elite. In each case, material life shapes social existence. Liberalism's emphasis on limiting society's claims on individual wealth and property therefore creates a society of free individuals.

But liberalism, in Marx's view, makes a fundamental and grievous error: it privileges the very things that we need to do away with, namely individual happiness and private property. Liberal notions of justice aim to protect us from one another, to restrict one person's ability to take or interfere with another person's property. And this means, Marx insists, that liberalism is essentially a philosophy of separation, whereas true human happiness consists of community, fellowship, and shared prosperity. Once we see liberalism as it really is, we will seek to move past it and to create a harmonious future without selfishness.

> Simply put, we must show the world what it is actually fighting over— for this, in the end, is what people need to recognize, whether they want to or not. In order to reform society's way of thinking, we must first help it to realize the way it is actually thinking already; we must awaken the world from its dreamy image of itself and show its actions for what they truly are. . . . Once we have accomplished this, the world will see that it can actually possess what it has hitherto only dreamed of [a truly happy and stable society].

So he wrote in a letter to a friend in September 1843.

Marx saw that the motivating forces in history are economic and technological. That insight surprises few readers today, but in its time it was strikingly original. What remains controversial is Marx's conclusion: the production and distribution of wealth determines culture. Marx argues that the struggle to control the means of production determines everything about a society from its political values to its laws, religious life, moral values, and intellectual outlook. The process is not even conscious—it does not need to be. Since the class that controls the dominant means of production also controls the state, it can perpetuate its position, just as it promotes its religious and moral values. The leading role in the British economy played by industrial capitalists, for example, finds its political expression in the House of Commons, which represents its interest. It also finds

Historical Materialism on Vivid Display   Scottish artist and poet William Bell Scott (1811–1890) painted this mural at Wallington Hall, in the English county of Northumberland. A viewer can almost hear the idealized steelworkers singing a Disneyesque tune as they swing their hammers in unison. No smoke, no dirt, no misery. A little girl even sits contently by while her father nobly toils. The coke-fueled heat coming out the furnace by which she sits could reach 2000 degrees Fahrenheit (1200 degrees Celsius).

its ideological expression in the cultural values of hard work, entrepreneurial drive, and free markets. As for religion, Marx holds that Christianity seems almost tailor-made to create a mass of docile workers: "Blessed are the poor"; suffering ennobles the soul; the affairs of this world do not really matter; reward comes in the next life; "turn the other cheek" to one's oppressors; and love one's enemies. He calls these teachings "slave morality."

But Marx insists that the painful cycle can be broken. Interrupting the march of capitalism will allow human altruism to emerge from its suppressed state. Indeed, the cycle is destined to be broken. The key is the transfer of economic and political power to the great mass of the proletariat, the modern industrial working class. That transfer culminates and concludes the historical process begun ages ago when the first nomad cut furrows in the earth and planted seeds. Marx does not, as some suggest, argue that its outcome is inevitable, but it is predictable. The interplay of economic, technological, and social forces produces the opportunities for social change; but human will and action are required to inaugurate each new development. To Marx, European capitalism in the middle of the 19th century had reached another decisive historical moment.

Since industrial capitalism, he argues, is incapable of self-reform, its death is imminent, but that death will not occur on its own. The struggle to wrest power and pass it to the workers may take a long, concerted effort—and may require force. As he writes in *The German Ideology*:

> A revolution is required because the ruling class cannot be overthrown in any other way, but also because the working class that dislodges it needs a revolution itself—a revolution that will purge the proletariat of the accumulated [cultural] trash of its past. Only thus can the workers rebuild society.

The act of revolution, in other words, creates the revolutionaries it needs to complete its own process. Marx abhors violence and never advocates it; he calls only for labor strikes, mass demonstrations, relentless political pressure, and the like. His rhetoric is always dramatic, but a call to confrontation is not the same thing as a call to arms.

THE COLLAPSE OF THE CONCERT OF EUROPE

Did the uprisings of 1848 significantly alter the political or economic trajectories of Europe? After all, they were quickly put down. Some writers insist that the year nevertheless marks a turning point: the severe economic and social problems catalyzed by industrialization had become impossible to ignore. One could no longer assume that the free market, left to itself, would set society along the path to a natural balance of prosperity, opportunity, and order. Henceforth, both conservatives and liberals would have to compromise their convictions with a practical commitment to economic regulation and government-sponsored social welfare. In this view, the second half of the 19th century represents a series of efforts to strike the right form of compromise.

Such writers also point to 1848 as the point of collapse of the Concert of Europe created by the Congress of Vienna in 1815. When King Frederick William IV of Prussia was confronted with armed insurrection in Berlin, he agreed to create a national assembly for Prussia and dissolve his absolute authorities. He thus catalyzed similar settlements for all of the German territories. Moreover, debates over whether to include the ethnic Germans residing in the

Austrian–Hungarian Empire brought Austria and Prussia to the brink of war. The possibility of the Habsburg Empire's ethnic Germans seceding from the megastate encouraged the nationalist hopes of the Magyars (ethnic Hungarians), Croats, Slovenians, and Czechs, which the Habsburgs quelled only with extreme force. Russia quickly became involved in the dispute, which in turn ignited Turkish concerns. A regional conflict threatened to expand into an international war. The failure of the 1815 settlement was all but officially recognized by the resignation of Klemens von Metternich as the Habsburg minister of foreign affairs in April 1848—even before most of the year's dramas had occurred.

Other writers regard 1848 not as a pivot point for European history but simply as a road sign confirming the path that Europe was already on. The rebellions and violent responses may have accelerated developments, but they did not fundamentally change the direction of history. To Marxists, the vast movement of history, like the current of a broad and powerful river, was toward the revolution of the proletariat, the destruction of capitalism, and the evolution of a new, classless society of freedom. Events like 1848 encouraged them to believe in the inevitability of Communism. As *The Communist Manifesto* proclaims (in the English edition prepared by Engels himself):

> Hitherto, every form of society has been based, as we have already seen, on the antagonism of oppressing and oppressed classes. But in order to oppress a class, certain conditions must be assured to it under which it can, at least, continue its slavish existence. The serf, in the period of serfdom, raised himself to membership in the commune, just as the petty bourgeois, under the yoke of feudal absolutism, managed to develop into a bourgeois. The modern laborer, on the contrary, instead of rising with the progress of industry, sinks deeper and deeper below the conditions of existence of his own class. He becomes a pauper, and pauperism develops more rapidly than population and wealth. And here it becomes evident, that the bourgeoisie is unfit any longer to be the ruling class in society, and to impose its conditions of existence upon society as an over-riding law. It is unfit to rule because it is incompetent to assure an existence to its slave within his slavery, because it cannot help letting him sink into such a state, that it has to feed him, instead of being fed by him. Society can no longer live under this bourgeoisie, in other words, its existence is no longer compatible with society.
>
> The essential condition for the existence, and for the sway of the bourgeois class, is the formulation and augmentation of capital; the condition for capital is wage-labor. Wage-labor rests exclusively on competition between laborers. The advance of industry, whose involuntary

THE CHARTIST MEETING ON KENNINGTON COMMON, 1848. *(From a Contemporary Print.)*

A Chartist Rally   Shown is a meeting of Chartist enthusiasts at Kennington Common on April 10, 1848. Located in south London, Kennington Common had previously been a site for public executions.

promoter is the bourgeoisie, replaces the isolation of the laborers, due to competition, by their revolutionary combination, due to association. The development of Modern Industry, therefore, cuts from under its feet the very foundation on which the bourgeoisie produces and appropriates products. What the bourgeoisie, therefore, produces, above all, is its own grave-diggers. Its fall and the victory of the proletariat are equally inevitable.

The revolutions of 1848 therefore accelerated historical change. Constitutions may have been jettisoned and franchises rescinded; nationalist aims thwarted, workers brought to heel, and the poor forced to submit, but the very success of the powerful and propertied ensured the ultimate success of the revolution. Common workers could now believe in the ultimate inevitability of victory, whether or not that victory appeared in a Marxist form, and that belief was the real revolution of 1848. The movement was only in embryonic form by midcentury, with Marx and Engels busily analyzing the workings of politics and economy in print, while organizing and rallying workers into labor unions and political factions in meeting halls. But the Communist model they created eventually became one of the leading political and social visions of the modern era.

WOMEN IN A CONSERVATIVE AGE

It was not only Marxist writers who felt that the dramas of 1848 had changed nothing or little. Most Western women remained legally controlled by their fathers until they married, at which point they came under the legal control of their husbands. Customs varied from country to country in regard to dowries, inheritance rights, and property ownership. Little formal education was available, except for those capable of hiring private tutors. Marriage and childbirth were the central events in most women's lives. Peasant and working-class girls usually married in their early twenties, but were considered marriageable by age sixteen; they were usually given to husbands anywhere from five to fifteen years older. Once she reached her mid-thirties an unmarried woman was considered a spinster, according to English law. By 1900, the British government sent annual shipments of spinsters to its overseas colonies, especially to India, where they might find work as governesses or teachers.

Women formed a large segment of the industrial workforce and indeed came to dominate certain manufactures. On average, however, they earned only about 40 percent of what male wage earners received, and efforts to unionize labor hardly helped. In fact, these unionizing campaigns as often as not began as efforts to drive women from the workplace altogether so that more men could find employment. Industrialism brought another change to family life as well—the physical separation of work space and domestic space. Throughout most of human history, the home was also where one worked—either a farm or a small shop, above which the shopkeepers lived. But the factory economy now meant that one went away to the job, whereas home was a refuge after a long day's labor. The effort to push women out of the job market and "back into the home" thus defined the home as a woman's terrain.

It was also part of a new **cult of domesticity** (also known as the "cult of true womanhood"), a prevailing value system among the middle and upper classes of the West during the 19th century. Proper society emphasized the impor- *Cult of Domesticity* tance of the home as a place of refuge, comfort, and nurture for hard-working husbands and fathers, overseen by "true women," wives and mothers who possessed the cardinal virtues of piety, purity, domesticity, and submissiveness. During this period, novels became the most popular genre of popular literature, overtaking poetry, and the overwhelming majority of them dealt with domestic themes: the discovery of love and its culmination in happy marriage and a cozily elegant domestic life.

Among the most popular new publications of the age were magazines for middle-class women like *La Belle Assemblée, Bell's Court and Fashionable Maga-* *Popular* *zine Addressed Particularly to the Ladies*, and *Wives' and Widows' Gazette of Fash-* *Magazines* *ions*, which began to appear in large numbers in every country. These offered

Domesticity Critiqued   *The Bellelli Family* (ca. 1858–1867), known also as *Family Portrait,* is an early masterwork of the French artist Edgar Degas (1834–1917). It depicts Degas's aunt Laura, her husband the Italian baron Gennaro Bellelli, and their two daughters, Giula and Giovanna. Laura is shown in black, mourning her recently deceased father, who appears in the framed picture behind her. Her countenance is dignified and austere, her gesture connected with her daughters but her gaze directed into space. Her husband, by contrast, seems separated from his family, his association with worldly affairs implied by his position at his busy desk. The different postures of the daughters suggest their divided loyalties in a scene of family alienation.

advice on fashions, décor, family relationships, home economics, sheet music, and dress patterns, along with serialized fiction and sentimental poetry. Also popular were guidebooks to maintaining happy, efficient, economical, and comfortable homes. The leading example, *Mrs Beeton's Book of Household Management* (1861), became one of the best-selling books of the century.[4] Isabella Beeton was only twenty-five when she published the first edition of this massive book of more than 1,100 pages. (She died only four years later of a uterine infection after the birth of her fourth child; her first two had already died.) She made her purpose plain at the start:

> What moved me . . . to attempt a work like this, was the discomfort and suffering which I had seen brought upon men and women by household

---

[4]   More than 2 million copies of *Mrs Beeton's Book of Household Management* sold in the United Kingdom in ten years—more than all the novels of Charles Dickens in his lifetime, combined.

mismanagement. I have always thought that there is no more fruitful source of family discontent than a housewife's badly-cooked dinners and untidy ways. Men are now so well served out of doors—at their clubs, well-ordered taverns, and dining houses—that in order to compete with the attractions of these places, a mistress must be thoroughly acquainted with the theory and practice of cookery, as well as be perfectly conversant with all the other arts of making and keeping a comfortable home.

Even more blunt is the first page of the opening chapter:

As with the Commander of an Army . . . so it is with the mistress of a house. Her spirit will be seen through the whole establishment; and just in proportion as she performs her duties intelligently and thoroughly, so will her domestics follow in her path. Of all those acquirements, which more particularly belong to the feminine character, there are none which take a higher rank, in our estimation, than such as enter into a knowledge of household duties; for on these are perpetually dependent the happiness, comfort, and well-being of a family.

Although the bulk of its pages consist of cooking recipes, Mrs. Beeton also offers detailed advice on cleaning, first aid, and the supervision of domestic servants. What surprises many modern readers is the attention she gives to legal matters, as in chapter 44:

In civil cases, a wife may now give evidence on behalf of her husband; in criminal cases she can neither be a witness for or against her husband. The case of assault by him upon her forms an exception to this rule. The law does not at this day admit the ancient principle of allowing moderate correction by a husband upon the person of his wife. Although this is said to have been anciently limited to the use of "a stick not bigger than a thumb," this barbarity is now altogether exploded. He may, notwithstanding, . . . keep her under restraint, to prevent her leaving him, provided this be effected without cruelty.

Despite their inferior legal status vis-à-vis their husbands, the millions of middle-class women who read Mrs. Beeton, and other authors like her, prided themselves on their domestic efficiency and propriety.

Women and the Novel

Middle- and upper-class women turned to novels as well as magazines. Not only did novels become the most popular literary genre of the 19th century, but also the majority of both their readers and their authors were women. This marked

Guidebook to Happiness *Mrs. Beeton's Book of Household Management*, published in 1861 when the author was only twenty-five years old, offers a striking contrast to Degas's critique of domesticity. Over 1,100 pages, it guides readers through everything necessary to create a happy, orderly, comfortable bourgeois home. Isabella Beeton died in 1865, from complications during the birth of her fourth child.

a sharp shift of opinion from the 18th century, when the new genre was blamed for spreading lax morals. Novels dangerously misled young women, it was said, filling their hearts and minds with fantasies of idle romance. As late as 1801, the father–daughter team of Robert and Maria Edgeworth wrote in their popular guide *Practical Education*:

> With respect to sentimental stories, and books of mere entertainment, we must remark, that they should be sparingly used, especially in the education of girls. This species of reading cultivates what is called "the heart" prematurely, lowers the tone of the mind, and induces indifference for those common pleasures and occupations, which, however trivial in themselves, constitute by the far the greatest portion of our daily happiness.

Popular novelists like the Englishwomen Jane Austen (1775–1817) and the Brontë sisters Charlotte (1816–1855), Emily (1818–1848), and Anne (1820–1849) published their books under male pseudonyms. Jane Austen even took to hiding her manuscripts under piles of knitting and sewing, lest any household visitors discover her life as an author. In 1856 another great English writer, Mary Anne Evans (1819–1880), published under the pseudonym George Eliot a delightfully vindictive article, "Silly Novels by Lady Novelists," in the *Westminster Review*. In it, Eliot castigates writers who:

> have evidently never talked to a tradesman except from a carriage window; they have no notion of the working-classes except as "dependents;" they think five hundred a-year a miserable pittance; Belgravia and "baronial halls" are their primary truths; and they have no idea of feeling interest in any man who is not at least a great landed proprietor, if not a prime minister. It is clear that they write in elegant boudoirs, with violet-coloured ink and a ruby pen; that they must be entirely indifferent to publishers' accounts, and inexperienced in every form of poverty except poverty of brains.

But not all the novels were silly. George Eliot's own novels—especially her masterpiece, *Middlemarch* (1871–1872)—depict England's rural and village settings with uncommon delicacy and intelligence. In France, the novels of George Sand (Amantine Dupin, Baroness Dudevant, 1804–1876) provide sympathetic portraits of agrarian and working-class men and women who struggle against poverty and social prejudice. Italy's Matilde Serao (1856–1927) published a series of novels in the 1880s whose melodramatic plots were laced with a powerful social conscience driven by her work as a journalist and newspaper editor. Rosalía de Castro (1837–1885), from northwestern Spain, was primarily a poet, but her novels detail with dignity and precision the lives of the rural poor. Austrian novelist Bertha von Suttner was the first woman ever to win the Nobel Peace Prize, for her passionate antiwar novel *A Farewell to Arms* (*Die Waffen nieder*; 1889). Annette von Droste-Hulshoff (1797–1848), from an old aristocratic family from the region of Westphalia, is best known in Germany for her religious poetry, but she also wrote a disturbing novel called *The Jew's Beech Tree* (*Die Judenbuche*; 1842), which may be the first murder mystery in modern fiction.

Caroline Norton's Campaign to Change Britain's Marriage Laws

If women found acceptance, however grudging, on the shelves of booksellers, they still faced determined opposition when it came to legal rights. Even privileged women faced great obstacles. An Englishwoman named Caroline Norton (1808–1877) came from a respectable family with military and colonial connections; her two sisters each married into the nobility, and she wed a prominent barrister and member of Parliament. Her husband, however, turned out to be a violent drunkard whose jealousy prompted him to suspect the lovely Caroline, unfairly, of constant infidelity and to hold her to a tight domestic budget. To make extra money, Caroline began to publish poetry and novels, which were well received and led to friendships with many prominent writers and statesmen. In 1836, re-solved to face no more verbal and physical abuse, she left her husband, who in turn abducted their three children (all sons), refused to let her see them, and sued to gain possession of all her book royalties—arguing successfully in court that ev-erything belonging to a wife is the rightful possession of the husband. For six years she was forbidden to see her boys and received none of her book earnings. In 1842 their eldest son died in a horse-riding accident, after which her husband re-lented and allowed her occasional visits to the remaining two boys. She had no legal grounds for divorcing her husband—wife beating not being against the law then—and did not become free of him until his death in 1875.

Caroline Norton devoted many years to the struggle for changes in the laws regarding marriage and divorce. The culmination of her efforts came with the Matrimonial Causes Act of 1857, which gave women the legal ability to initiate divorce; they could also retain possession of a share of the couple's wealth. The act reaffirmed their right—originally granted in 1839, also thanks in part to Caroline Norton—to shared custody of their minor children. Norton wrote a pamphlet-length letter, addressed to Queen Victoria (r. 1837–1901) herself:

> The one woman in England who *cannot* suffer wrong; and whose royal assent will be formally necessary to any Marriage Reform Bill which the Lord Chancellor, assembled Peers, and assembled Com-mons, may think fit to pass, in the Parliament of this free nation; where, with a Queen on the throne, all other married women are legally *NON-EXISTENT.*

She concluded:

> Nevertheless, so long as human nature is what it is, some marriages must be unhappy marriages, instead of following that theory of intimate and sacred union which they ought to fulfill: and the question is, there-fore, what is to be the relation of persons living in a state of alienation, instead of a state of union,—all the existing rules for their social position being based on the first alternative,—namely, that they are in a state of union,—and on the supposition that marriage is indissoluble, though Parliament has now decided that it is a civil contract? Divorced or undi-vorced, it is absolutely necessary that the law should step in, to arrange that which is disarranged by this most unnatural condition. It becomes perfectly absurd that the law which appoints the husband legal protector

of the woman, should not (failing him who has ceased to be a protector, and has become a very powerful foe) itself undertake her protection. She stands towards the law, by an illustration which I have repeatedly made use of,—in the light of an ill-used inferior; and she is the *only* inferior in England who cannot claim to be so protected. ("A Letter to the Queen on Lord Chancellor Cranworth's Marriage and Divorce Bill," 1855)

Britain stood ahead of the curve, compared with the Continent, in recognizing the legal rights of women.

◆

By the end of 1848 Europe was tiring of revolutions, and with good reason. The overthrow of absolutism and the forced march of industrialism had been wrenching experiences. The people had demanded the restructuring of the state and the reconsideration of long-standing social traditions. Conservatism and liberalism offered new paths out of the chaos; but although significantly distinct from earlier notions of political order, they were not revolutionary. Indeed, conservatism presented itself as the upholder of tradition, whereas liberalism offered itself as the intelligent way to control and channel the forces of change. By contrast, Marxism represented a true revolutionary development. It was a call to change hearts and minds as much as to transform the state and workplace.

WHO, WHAT, WHERE

Chartist movement	conservatism	Klemens von
Communism	cult of domesticity	Metternich
The Communist	historical materialism	liberalism
Manifesto	ideologies	proletariat
Concert of Europe	Karl Marx	socialism
Congress of Vienna		

SUGGESTED READINGS

Primary Sources

Beeton, Isabella. *Mrs. Beeton's Book of House-hold Management.*

Burke, Edmund. *Reflections on the Revolution in France.*

Engels, Friedrich. *Socialism: Utopian and Scientific.*

Maistre, Joseph-Marie de. *Considerations on France.*

Maistre, Joseph-Marie de. *Essay on the Generative Principle of Political Constitutions.*

Marx, Karl. *Capital.*

Marx, Karl. *The 18th Brumaire of Louis Napoleon.*

Marx, Karl. *The German Ideology.*

Marx, Karl, and Friedrich Engels, *The Communist Manifesto.*

Metternich, Klemens von. *Memoirs.*

Mill, John Stuart. *On Liberty.*

Mill, John Stuart. *The Principles of Political Economy.*

Norton, Caroline. *English Laws for Women in the 19th Century.*

Tocqueville, Alexis de. *Recollections.*

Anthologies

Leroux, Robert, and David Hart, eds. *French Liberalism in the 19th Century: An Anthology* (2012).

Marx, Karl. *Selected Writings* (2000). Edited by David McLellan.

Tucker, Robert C., ed. *The Marx–Engels Reader* (1978).

Studies

Alexander, Robert. *Re-writing the French Revolutionary Tradition: Liberal Opposition and the Fall of the Bourbon Monarchy* (2007).

Berend, Ivan T. *History Derailed: Central and Eastern Europe in the Long Nineteenth Century* (2005).

Boime, Albert. *Art in an Age of Counterrevolution, 1815–1848* (2004).

Boime, Albert. *Art in an Age of Civil Struggle, 1848–1871* (2008).

Cohen, G. A. *Karl Marx's Theory of History: A Defence* (2001).

Dénes, Iván Zoltán. *Conservative Ideology in the Making* (2010).

Devigne, Robert. *Reforming Liberalism: J. S. Mill's Use of Ancient, Religious, Liberal, and Romantic Moralities* (2006).

Fawcett, Edmund. *Liberalism: The Life of an Idea* (2014).

Fortescue, William. *France and 1848: The End of Monarchy* (2005).

Gross, Michael B. *The War against Catholicism: Liberalism and the Anti-Catholic Imagination in Nineteenth-Century Germany* (2005).

Hahn, Hans Joachim. *The 1848 Revolutions in German-Speaking Europe* (2001).

Jarrett, Mark. *The Congress of Vienna and Its Legacy: War and Great Power Diplomacy after Napoleon* (2013).

Kahan, Alan S. *Liberalism in Nineteenth-Century Europe: The Political Culture of Limited Suffrage* (2003).

Kertzer, David I., and Marzio Barbagli, eds. *Family Life in the Long Nineteenth Century, 1789–1913* (2002).

Langewiesche, Dieter. *Liberalism in Germany* (2000).

Leopold, David. *The Young Karl Marx: German Philosophy, Modern Politics, and Human Flourishing* (2007).

Liang, Hsi-Huey. *The Rise of Modern Police and the European State System from Metternich to the Second World War* (2002).

Pitts, Jennifer. *A Turn to Empire: The Rise of Imperial Liberalism in Britain and France* (2006).

Popkin, Jeremy D. *Press, Revolution, and Social Identities in France, 1830–1835* (2001).

Rapport, Michael. *1848: Year of Revolution* (2009).

Sack, James J. *From Jacobite to Conservative: Reaction and Orthodoxy in Britain, c. 1760–1832* (2004).

Siedentop, Larry. *Inventing the Individual: The Origins of Western Liberalism* (2014).

Sked, Alan. *Metternich and Austria: An Evaluation* (2008).

Sperber, Jonathan. *The European Revolutions, 1848–1851* (2005).

Sperber, Jonathan. *Revolutionary Europe, 1780–1850* (2000).

Vick, Brian E. *Defining Germany: The 1848 Frankfurt Parliamentarians and National Identity* (2002).

Wolff, Jonathan. *Why Read Marx Today?* (2002).

Zamoyski, Adam. *Rites of Peace: The Fall of Napoleon and the Congress of Vienna* (2008).

For additional resources, including maps, primary sources, visuals, web links, and quizzes, please go to **www.oup.com/us/backman**.

CHAPTER 20

Nationalism and Identity

1800–1900

O ne of the most dramatic and widespread cultural developments of the 19th century was the phenomenon of passionate,
urgent concern for national identity. What does it mean to be a
member of a particular ethnic or cultural group? What makes one
English, German, Hungarian, Polish, or Serbian? Can a foreign immigrant ever be truly assimilated into a new culture? Into a political
state, yes—but that is another matter entirely, a question of formal
citizenship. Can an ethnic
Russian truly become Irish? Is
it possible, or even desirable, for a Dutch man or
woman to become French—and if so, is not
some element of his or her "Dutchness" lost in
the process? Can the claims of civic membership ever trump the claims of blood? Attempts
to answer questions like these altered the map
of Europe. In turn, those changes led to renewed questions among and about, and to divisions within, Europe's Jewish population. They
also accelerated the forces tearing apart the
social fabric of the Ottoman Empire.

It might seem odd that questions of
identity still haunted peoples who had lived
together for more than a thousand years. Why
such a fuss over what makes a Frenchman

THE GREATER WEST, 1871

"A Hero of Two Worlds"
The great populist hero of Italian
unification was Giuseppe
Garibaldi (1807–1882). A born
adventurer, he served in the
merchant marine as a young man,
fought with republican rebels
against the then-imperial
government in Brazil, and
commanded a fleet of volunteer
soldiers in the Uruguayan Civil
War (1839–1851). Returning to
Italy in 1848, he defended Rome
against a French attack, after
which he avoided arrest (both the
French and the Austrian armies
were looking for him) by sailing
to New York. He returned to Italy
in 1860 and fought in the decisive
campaign to achieve Italy's
independence and unification.

French or an Austrian an Austrian? The explanation lay in the innumerable configurations of their joint existences. Political borders delineating kingdoms and states through past centuries had been drawn variously along dynastic lines, religious lines, geographic lines, lines of military conquest, lines demarcating zones of economic interest, linguistic lines, and negotiated lines of convenience: not on shared cultural identity. The willful drawing and redrawing of political boundaries at international congresses like Westphalia and Vienna, or at scores of local meetings over the centuries to settle regional disputes, had the effect for many of making states seem artificial at best and irrelevant at worst. If the state to which one owes political obedience and personal loyalty can be altered by something as small as a signature on a treaty, then how can one honestly feel any sense of deep identification with it? Given such persistent arbitrariness, the absence of any sure sense of communal identity becomes less of a surprise.

The upheavals of the late 18th and early 19th centuries only added to the confusion. As late as 1815 just under 10 percent of Europe's population lived in cities with populations above fifty thousand; only fifty years earlier than that, however, the figure had been closer to 2–3 percent. The threefold increase in urban population meant more than a quantitative growth in absolute numbers because urban populations tend to greater ethnic complexity than rural ones, which are more typically homogeneous in their ethnic makeup. Napoleon's Continental System had erased, for a while, at least, the legal barriers to peoples' free movement from

CHAPTER TIMELINE

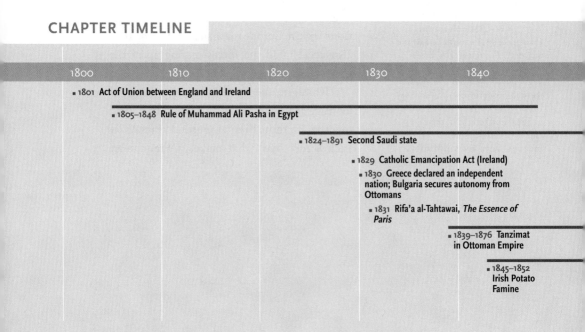

| 1800 | 1810 | 1820 | 1830 | 1840 |

- 1801 Act of Union between England and Ireland

- 1805–1848 Rule of Muhammad Ali Pasha in Egypt

- 1824–1891 Second Saudi state

- 1829 Catholic Emancipation Act (Ireland)

- 1830 Greece declared an independent nation; Bulgaria secures autonomy from Ottomans

- 1831 Rifa'a al-Tahtawi, *The Essence of Paris*

- 1839–1876 Tanzimat in Ottoman Empire

- 1845–1852 Irish Potato Famine

one territory to another, as they sought opportunities to learn new skills and access new markets. And industrialization encouraged even more movement and concentration of labor. The result was the presence of sizable communities of resident foreigners in cities across Europe: ethnic Poles living in Berlin or Paris, ethnic Sicilians residing in Milan or Hamburg, ethnic Greeks taking up new lives in Madrid or Genoa, ethnic Portuguese residing in Rotterdam or Marseilles. When the Continent began to industrialize at speed, post-1815, the pluriethnic character of urban life became even more pronounced. Under these conditions, when a city like Munich became home to a multiplex of cultural groups, what did "being German" or "being Bavarian" mean?

NATIONALISM IN THEORY

Edward Augustus Freeman (1823–1892), one of England's greatest 19th-century historians, confronted the question in an essay entitled "Race and Language" (1879):

> [What of] those parts of the world where people who are confessedly of different races and languages inhabit a continuous territory and live under the same government? How do we define nationality in such cases as these? The answer will be very different in different cases. . . . They may

1850	1860	1870	1880	1900

- 1848 **Europe rocked by revolutions**
- 1852–1870 **Second Empire in France**
- 1852–1856 **Crimean War**
- 1859–1870 **Unification of Italy**
- 1861 **Abolition of serfdom in Russia**
- 1862–1871 **Unification of Germany**
- 1870 **Franco-Prussia War**
- 1878 **Romania secures autonomy from Ottomans**
- 1881 **First appearance of the term "anti-Semitic" in English**
- 1896 **Theodore Herzl, *The Jewish State***
- 1903 **Publication of *The Protocols of the Elders of Zion***

form what I have already called an *artificial nation,* united by an act of its own free will. Or it may be simply a case where distinct nations, distinct in everything which can be looked on as forming a nation, except the possession of an independent government, are brought together, by whatever causes, under a common ruler. The former case is very distinctly an exception which proves the rule, [such a] nation is something different from those nations which are defined by a universal or at least a predominant language. We mark it as an exception, as something different from other cases. And when we see how nearly this artificial nation comes, in every point but that of language, to the likeness of those nations which are defined by language, we see that it is a nation defined by language which sets the standard, and after the model of which the artificial nation forms itself.

Freeman mentions Switzerland as an example of an artificial nation—one composed of several groups, each of which maintains its own language. He sees other examples in the Ottoman and Austrian–Hungarian empires of his time:

While in each Western country some one of the various races which have settled in it has, speaking roughly, assimilated the others, in the lands which are left under the rule of the Turk, or which have been lately delivered from his rule, all the races that have ever settled in the country still abide side by side. So when we pass into the lands which form the Austr[ian]–Hungar[ian] national government, another fragment is ruled by civilized strangers, a third is trampled down by barbarians. The existing states of Greece, Romania, and Serbia are far from taking in the whole of the Greek, Romanian, and Serbian nations. In all these lands . . . there is no difficulty in marking off the several nations; only in no case do the[se] nations [correspond] to any existing political power.

To Freeman, language defines national identity. But other possibilities exist. To some writers, one's nationality comprised race, loyalty to a unique political vision, religious practice, or even native cuisine. Rudyard Kipling (1865–1936), tireless champion of British imperialism and at one point the most popular writer in the English-speaking world, identified nationality with birthplace; one's nation is simply the homeland to which one remains loyal in one's heart.

Our hearts where they rocked our cradle
Our love where we spent our toil,
And our faith, and our hope, and our honor,
We pledge to our native soil.

God gave all men all earth to love
But since our hearts are small
Ordained for each one spot should prove
Beloved over all.

The search for national identity was intrinsically Romantic—self-fascinated, intuitive, multifaceted (and, inevitably, contradictory), and awe inspiring—and informed numerous aspects of Romantic thought and expression, from historical writing like E. A. Freeman's to the political essays of Frenchman Ernest Renan (1823–1892) and the poetical–philosophical works of the German composer Richard Wagner (1813–1883). In an influential speech entitled "What Is a Nation?" (1882), Renan argues that national identity is a voluntary rather than ethnic phenomenon—that is, it consists of the active desire of people to live together, to see themselves as collective historical actors who wish to preserve that togetherness. In his words, a nation is any large group of people "who have done great things in the past and desire to do great things in the future." Wagner, on the other hand, posits a mythical–spiritual element as the binding force in a nation, a Romantic awareness of shared culture that both consists of and transcends ethnicity. Like Romanticism, the influence of nationalism spread throughout the 19th century. Unlike Romanticism, nationalist passions continued to be felt throughout the 20th century, indeed to the present day, all too often in odious and destructive ways.

In all its forms, **nationalism** was and remains a potent force. It may in fact be the most vital element in modern political history. The word implies more than mere patriotism, although it includes that notion. Nationalism in the modern sense suggests a collective consciousness, an awareness that the members of an individual nation-state share a depth of feelings, values, and attitudes toward the world. Together, these sentiments give meaning to their aggregate existence and may in fact be the only way to realize a fully meaningful life. In the United States this conviction took the form in the 19th century of a belief in America's "manifest destiny" to move westward across the Great Plains and extend the national borders to the Pacific coast.[1] In Europe it took the form of popular desire to erase the artificial political lines drawn in 1815 and replace them with organic nation-states composed of the political and geographical union of all members of specific ethnic groups: a Germany made up of the aggregate of all ethnic Germans; an Italy that unites all ethnic Italians into a single state; an independent Hungary that gathers all Magyars under an autonomous government of their own (see Map 20.1).

---

[1] The phrase *manifest destiny* was coined in 1845, in an article by the American journalist John L. O'Sullivan (1813–1895), which called for the annexation of Texas (then an independent republic) into the United States: "our manifest destiny to overspread the continent allotted by Providence for the free development of our yearly multiplying millions."

MAP 20.1 The Peoples of Europe, ca. 1850 Ethnic diversity was on the rise across Europe from the start of the 19th century, especially in the cities. Wide expanses of countryside, however, still remained ethnically homogeneous by midcentury.

But the word *nation* did not always have this populist meaning. In the 16th and 17th centuries it was widely used to designate the aristocracy in most countries—that is, the people born into privilege, the people who mattered. That is why the Tennis Court declaration made in 1789 by the revolutionaries locked out of the meeting of the Estates General in Paris—that "we are the nation"—was so radically decisive. Rousseau had argued that a nation composed of all of its people in equal membership would create not only a more just society but a decidedly more powerful, dynamic, and harmonious one. Here the "General Will" of its constituents would find the freest and most perfect expression. This idea carried through into the Industrial Age, although differing political camps put it to different uses. To most conservatives, nation meant culture, language, and tradition—the political and social norms that bound people together under the paternal care of ancient hierarchies. To liberals, the word described the egalitarian gathering of people under a constitution that recognized rights, guaranteed the claims of property, and promoted individual freedom. To socialists, a nation was a fiction, an imagined grouping used by capitalists to control industrial production and promote the interests of the bourgeoisie. It is part of the complexity of nationalism that all of these views were, and are, to some extent correct.

The political narrative of 19th-century nationalism is episodic: it took decades either for discrete territories to unite into a single nation or for a subjugated land to break away from foreign domination and establish its independence. The most prominent political successes were the unifications of Germany and of Italy, whereas the most significant political failures were those of Hungary and of Ireland.

NATIONALISM IN PRACTICE: FRANCE, ITALY, AND GERMANY

Ironically, the borders of France—which had inflicted brutal war throughout Europe under Napoleon—were little altered by the Congress of Vienna, and so the French entered the industrial age with an already-realized nationalism. Without the need to pursue unification, France's nationalist passions aimed instead at influencing affairs across Europe by providing a model for adapting to industrial change and by seeking to preserve France's involvement in international geopolitics. As a result, France played a significant role in the unifications of both Italy and Germany in the years following the upheavals of 1848. *France*

Napoleon III (r. 1852–1870), who as Louis-Napoleon Bonaparte had served as president of the Second Republic (r. 1848–1852), dreaded an uprising of the urban laborers like the one that had toppled his predecessor Louis-Philippe (discussed in chapter 19). Now, as emperor, he pushed hard for France's industrial and commercial development while doing all he could to centralize political authority into something as close to absolutism as he could manage. His goal was to encourage a carefully controlled type of nationalism, one in which popular loyalty was not only to the country but also to the imperial state itself. By mobilizing the government behind industrial expansion, he hoped, people would associate national prosperity not with individual entrepreneurship outside of state regulation but with the government itself—and especially with the ruler at its head.

The emperor controlled state finances, commanded the military, determined foreign policy, and dictated domestic affairs to an impotent national assembly whose existence preserved the fiction of popular democracy. Two policies dear to Napoleon III's heart—industrial development and urban renewal—advanced because of innovations he made in public finance, the most notable being his establishment of the Crédit Mobilier, a publicly held investment bank whose capital financed, among other imperial adventures, the quintupling of France's miles of rail lines and the wholesale redesign of the city of Paris. The redevelopment of the city center involved demolition of well over thirty thousand buildings, wiping out entire neighborhoods, and laying more than 120 miles of new roads. A dozen broad boulevards now radiated out from the *Arc de Triomphe* (the Arch of Triumph commissioned by Napoleon in 1806 to commemorate his victories) in the heart of Paris. These not only provided a proud focal point to the city; their

PARIS   PLACE DE L'ÉTOILE. L'ARC DE TRIOMPHE   AERO-PHOTO 128

Urban Renewal on a Grand Scale   This aerial view shows the Place de L'Etoile and the Arc de Triomphe in Paris, the signature piece of Napoleon III's renovation of the city. Hundreds of buildings were destroyed to make room for this array of broad avenues. This intersection of twelve boulevards forms the symbolic center of the city. The remodeling had a practical benefit: it made it easier, should the need arise, for troops and police to control the crowds.

breadth also made it easier for the emperor's troops and police units to fan out into the neighborhoods, if necessary, to quell uprisings like those of 1848.

Eager for military glory, Napoleon III rushed into a conflict that had pervasive consequences for Italian and German unification. Late in 1853 the Russian tsar Nicholas I (r. 1825–1855) ordered his army into the Ottoman-controlled regions of Moldavia and Wallachia—roughly the territory of the eastern and southern part of today's nation of Romania, along the plain where the Danube River meets the Black Sea—arguing that the need to liberate the regions' Catholic and Orthodox populations from Islamic oppression justified the action. But since the quick Russian victory threatened the balance of power in southeastern Europe, France joined Britain in declaring a retaliatory war against Russia. This was the **Crimean War** (1853–1856), an ineptly managed and spectacularly bloody conflict that left approximately a million men dead, more than two-thirds from disease or starvation (see Map 20.2).

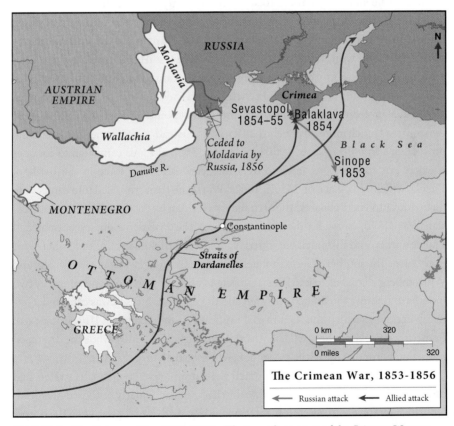

MAP 20.2   The Crimean War, 1853–1856   The immediate cause of the Crimean War was concern for the worsening treatment of the Christians who lived under Ottoman rule in the Holy Land. The more substantive cause was French and British determination not to let Russia gain any of the lands lost by the crumbling Turkish empire.

In the midst of this unfolding catastrophe, Alexander II (r. 1855–1881) ascended the Russian throne after the death of Nicholas I, his father. With casualties mounting, the new tsar asked for peace. In the 1856 Peace of Paris, Russia lost the right to base its navy in the Straits of Dardanelles and the Black Sea, which were declared neutral waters. Moldavia and Wallachia (which soon merged to form Romania) became autonomous Turkish provinces under the victors' protection, drastically reducing Russian influence in that region, too. More generally, the war severed the alliance between Austria and Russia, the two conservative powers on which the Congress of Vienna peace settlement had rested since 1815. It thus ended Austria's and Russia's grip on European affairs and undermined their ability to contain the forces of nationalism.

France's strong efforts in the Crimea emboldened Napoleon III to attempt to influence political matters closer to home, and so he plunged into Italy's unification struggle in 1859. His interests were divided: as a devout Catholic he wanted to preserve the autonomy of the Vatican (which ruled the Papal States), but as a nationalist he sincerely wanted to see a unified Italy. And the hard-nosed politician in him sought to wrest some territorial concessions from Italian nationalist leaders in return for military assistance against Austria. In the end, the hard-nosed politician won. French troops helped drive the Austrians from the region around Venice, and for their trouble France was granted in 1860 the city of Nice and its surrounding area (today's French Riviera), along with the region of Savoy.

Had Napoleon III ceased his adventures at that point, his reign would have been remembered much more positively than it now is. Instead, eager to wield international power like a true Bonaparte, he first undertook a vainglorious campaign to conquer Mexico. His troops were defeated by a Mexican nationalist force in the Battle of Puebla, which took place on May 5, 1862.[2] Worse, he then stumbled into direct conflict with Otto von Bismarck, the architect of German unification. The Franco-Prussian War (1870) proved a disaster for France. The Prussian military outmatched France's army, and Bismarck outwitted Napoleon III diplomatically and militarily at every turn. The southern German states of Baden, Bavaria, Hesse, the Palatinate, and Würtemberg all rushed to join Prussia in defending the Fatherland, and after only two months of fighting the French army fell and the emperor himself was captured. Germany declared victory and its imperial unification, and Napoleon III was deposed. France then declared the start of its Third Republic (1870–1940), while the disgraced former emperor fled into exile in London, where he died in early 1873.

Italy   Italy's unification involved as much high drama as Napoleon III's reign had provided France. Political decentralization had not particularly bothered most Italians through the centuries; fragmentation and localism had so long been the norms of Italian life that they were seldom questioned. This sort of regional particularism,

---

[2]   Although French troops remained in Mexico until 1867, Cinco de Mayo lives on as a national holiday.

in fact, had preserved much of what was best loved in Italian life—local customs, local cuisines, local dialects, and a strong sense of local identities. Until well into the 19th century, few people on the peninsula thought of themselves as Italians. Instead, they were Beneventans, Florentines, Lucchesans, Neapolitans, Perugians, or Venetians—or, for those with a more regional sense of identity, Ligurians, Sicilians, or Tuscans. The strongest impulse toward national identity came from resentment of foreign domination. "Italian patriotism is like the patriotism of the ancient Greeks," wrote a prominent Neapolitan official in 1850. "It consists of love for a single town, not for a whole country. Conquest by foreigners is the only thing that ever unites Italians. Left to themselves, they will always split into smaller groups."

At least since the 13th century, the Italian peninsula had been dominated by a shifting matrix of European powers, from Austrians and the French to Germans and Spaniards. In the 16th century Machiavelli had penned *The Prince* to urge a native uprising against the foreigners (at that point primarily the French) tearing apart the countryside. The chief villains in the 19th century were the Habsburg Austrians in the north and the Bourbon French in the south, both of whom had been either placed or ratified in power by the despised Congress of Vienna in 1815. In 1827 the Romantic poet Alessandro Manzoni (1785–1873) published his only novel, often considered Italy's greatest, *The Betrothed* (*I promessi sposi*), which dramatized, among much else, the suffering inflicted on northern Italy by foreign usurpers. The novel is set in the 17th century, when the region around Manzoni's birthplace of Milan was controlled by Spanish forces, but it alludes directly to the dominance of the Austrians in the 19th—a theme of his stage dramas as well.

Popular rebellion broke out in hundreds of small riots and demonstrations. Giuseppe La Farina (1815–1863), a government official and strong proponent of unification, wrote that:

Neapolitans Two youths enjoy a meal of the Neapolitan specialty, pasta. Naples is the Italian peninsula's largest port city. Commonly thought of as a place of squalor and crime, it was (and still is) the fourth largest urban economy in Italy, and the first Italian city to have a railway line. When Naples joined the Kingdom of Italy in 1861, national unification was nearly complete.

Italy's independence should be the aim of every spirited and intelligent man, for neither our schools, commerce, nor industry will ever flourish or develop so long as Austria's boot remains on our necks. . . . To gain freedom politically we must drive out the Austrians who dominate us. To gain freedom intellectually we must drive out the Austrians who keep us the slaves of the Holy See. And to create a national literature, too, we must drive out the Austrians who keep most of our people illiterate. . . . Everything tends toward political unification. Our science, industry, commerce, and arts require it. No great advancements are possible unless we first bring together the skills, minds, capital, and labor of our great nation. . . . Woe to anyone who dares to get in our way!

The Congress of Vienna had reshuffled the Italian peninsula into roughly a dozen autonomous small principalities and the German territories into a confederation of thirty-eight states. The middle classes in both places were the prime movers for unification because they stood to benefit the most: only by pooling the peoples' resources, they recognized, could the Italians or Germans catch up to industrialized England. National banks were needed to provide financing for start-up manufacturers, for example, and extensive systems of transport and communication had to be established. Moreover, they needed to be established quickly. To those of the working class, a unified state seemed the most feasible way to rein in the abuses and inequities of industrial capitalism. Both groups thus came to see national union as the most promising path to both economic growth and social reform. Italian and German conservatives balked at both developments and fought to protect their provincialism. The strong Romantic pulse of the young generation, however, inclined them to explore and exalt the collective genius of their cultures at large. It thus complemented the ledger-book mentality of the entrepreneurial class in its press for national union.

By 1860 the only open question, in most Italians' minds, was whether the unified country would be a monarchy (favored by many in the north) or a democracy (the general preference of those in the south). Diplomatic leadership came from the north in the persons of Vittorio Emmanuel II, the king of Piedmont–Sardinia (r. 1849–1861)—which was one of the arbitrary states created in 1815—and his wily chief minister, **Camillo di Cavour** (1810–1861). Military and populist leadership, however, came from the south in the person of **Giuseppe Garibaldi** (1807–1882), a charismatic adventurer who pursued the cause of liberating enslaved peoples everywhere from Tunisia and Brazil to Italy, the United States, and France.[3]

Garibaldi and his army of red-shirted volunteers had defeated the Bourbon-controlled south by the end of 1860, and Cavour (with some help from the French) had neutralized Habsburg power in the north by roughly the same time

---

[3]   Garibaldi offered his services in the American Civil War on two conditions: President Lincoln would abolish slavery immediately and make him commander in chief of the Union army. Lincoln politely declined.

Red Shirt Seamstresses Painted in 1863 by Edward Borrani (1834–1905), this image shows women sewing the red shirts that were the uniform of Garibaldi and his soldiers.

(see Map 20.3). In 1861 Vittorio Emmanuel journeyed to Rome and assumed the title of king of Italy (r. 1861–1878). By 1866, when Austria ceded Venetia, Cavour's vision of Italian unification had won the day.

The only remaining problem was the Holy See. The pope was not only the spiritual leader of the Catholic Church but also the political ruler of part of central Italy since the Middle Ages. His domain had long since been reduced, geographically, but Pope Pius IX (r. 1846–1878) refused to relinquish any aspect of his secular authority and to recognize the Kingdom of Italy. Thus, he and his successors

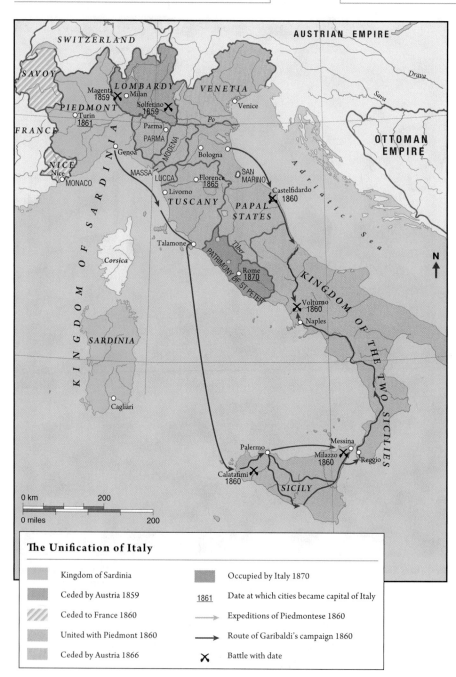

The Unification of Italy

░ Kingdom of Sardinia	▓	Occupied by Italy 1870
░ Ceded by Austria 1859	<u>1861</u>	Date at which cities became capital of Italy
▨ Ceded to France 1860	→	Expeditions of Piedmontese 1860
░ United with Piedmont 1860	→	Route of Garibaldi's campaign 1860
░ Ceded by Austria 1866	✕	Battle with date

MAP 20.3   The Unification of Italy The strongest opposition to unification came from within the peninsula, as the Papal State—which had been established in the 8th century—feared the loss of its autonomy as a political entity, much as the Church feared losing its spiritual authority to the rise of secular culture.

became "the prisoner of the Vatican," refusing to leave their enclave to avoid any appearance of accepting the authority of the Italian government. The dispute continued until 1929, when a concordat signed by the Holy See and the Italian government created the modern state of Vatican City and finally ended the matter.

But the Kingdom of Italy was united only in name. The north remained the center of economic might, with its banks, industry, and commercial links; the south, by contrast, was overwhelmingly rural and poorly educated. Since Italy's political leadership invariably came from the north, the economic disparity between north and south, and the unequal leverage of political power between them, would hamper Italian development for decades.

The Prussians had taken the early lead in the German Confederation created by the Congress of Vienna by reforming their military along meritocratic lines. *Germany* Reorganizing the officer corps signaled the end of the dominance in Prussian society of the old landed aristocracy, called Junkers (from the noble title "Junker"), and paved the way for other reforms: cities won the right to control their own finances, and German universities were opened to competitive admission. By 1848, tired of conservative foot-dragging and impatient of initial liberal efforts at reform, workers and bourgeois alike proposed schemes for German nationhood at a meeting of the Frankfurt Assembly.

Most of the delegates came from professional circles and confronted a pressing question: Did unification mean the union of all ethnic Germans everywhere or simply of those Germans residing in German-governed principalities? German populations living in Czech-dominated Bohemia, for example, or in Habsburg-controlled Austria, wanted to be included in a "Greater Germany" but could not do so without risking active resistance from their rulers. The Prussian king Frederick William IV (r. 1840–1861) was offered, but declined, the crown of a "Lesser Germany" that omitted those extraterritorial nationals. Not that his refusal had anything to do with the extraterritorial nationals; he refused the crown simply because it had been offered by the people, among them the rebels of 1848. A true conservative, he declared that the only crown he could ever wear was one that he placed upon his own head, lest he appear to condone liberal attitudes:

> This crown [that you offer] is no real crown. . . . [It] humiliates whoever wears it. . . . It smells of the gunpowder of the revolution of 1848—the most ridiculous, stupid, and vile (although not, thank God, the most evil) uprising of this century. . . . Let me state it outright: If the [true] crown of the united German nation, a crown with a one-thousand-year-old heritage . . . should ever be bestowed again, it will be I and my peers—alone—who bestow it. Woe to those who assume authorities to which they have no right. ("Proclamation of 1849")

Instead of an early union of the Lesser Germany, what came out of the Frankfurt Assembly was an even weaker version of the former German Confederation.

One thing remained clear: the debate over German unification boiled down to a political rivalry between Prussia and Austria, since either one of these seemed likely to take the lead in a single Greater Germany. As one of the Frankfurt delegates, the historian Johann Gustav Droysen (1808–1884), put it:

> There is no avoiding the fact that the whole issue of a united Germany comes down to a simple choice between Prussia and Austria. German life in these two states certainly has its positive and negative characteristics—in the first, the focus is on national union and reform, while in the second the focus is upon mere, and ultimately destructive, dynastic power. In this way, the whole issue of "Germany" is not about a constitution but about power, pure and simple. The monarchy in Prussia thinks about the whole of the German people, while that in Austria never will. ("Speech to the Frankfurt Assembly," 1848)

Historians still debate the consequences of the failure at Frankfurt. At the very least, unification, with the support of a broad cross-section of the people, happened only later. Yet it was also caused by a new political alliance between the Prussian monarchy and the military. This direct military element, some argue, forced German nationalism onto a unique path that led unavoidably to Nazism and Hitler. (Historians call this debate the *Sonderweg* controversy, after the German for "unique path.")

Unavoidably or not, the Prussian military did in fact take over the cause of unification. Under the leadership of Prime Minister **Otto von Bismarck** (1815–1898), a deeply conservative, complex, and brilliant figure, Prussian arms bullied and beat their neighbors into submission. Bismarck, it should be noted, neither enjoyed nor glorified war; he was simply willing to resort to it when there seemed no other way to achieve what he wanted. He started a war with Denmark (1866) to seize the disputed principalities of Schleswig and Holstein, then provoked a "Seven Weeks' War" against Austria (also 1866), which gained another half-dozen territories, while securing Venetia (previously under Habsburg control) as his Italian ally. He then engineered the Franco-Prussian War (1870), which returned, among other areas, the Alsace–Lorraine region to German control (see Map 20.4).

Bismarck, who regularly wore a military uniform but never served in the army himself, is most frequently remembered for his statement that "the great issues of our time will not be resolved by speeches and parliamentary votes (that was the mistake of the revolutionaries of 1848) but by blood and iron." Yet he also declared that "anyone who has ever looked straight into the glazed eyes of a soldier dying on a battlefield will think twice before starting a war." Above all, Bismarck was a master

The Unification of Germany

▨ Habsburg Empire	—	Border of German Customs Union (Zollverein) 1842
▨ Prussia 1815	—	Southern border of North German Confederation 1867
▨ Territory added to Prussia 1815–66	—	Border of German Empire 1871
▨ Territory added to Prussia/German Empire 1871		

MAP 20.4   The Unification of Germany The unification of Germany was the achievement, above all, of Otto von Bismarck (1815–1898), the Prime Minister of Prussia.

practitioner of **Realpolitik**, a practical, tough-minded politics born of the failed revolutions of 1848 that aimed at strengthening the state and tightening social order.

He was no nationalist, however; born into the Junker class, Bismarck regarded himself first and foremost as a Prussian. But since German unification seemed inevitable, he chose to bring it about in his own way, with Prussia very much the dominant player. Bismarck gambled that the German people would support his militarism in return for his championing of liberal social programs that he personally found odious: health insurance, unemployment insurance, and retirement pensions, in short, anything that avoided actual regulation of the marketplace. He was

Proclamation of the German Empire Kaiser Wilhelm stands before the crowd of dignitaries in the Hall of Mirrors at the palace of Versailles, where he became the first ruler of a united Germany (r. 1871–1888). His chief minister, Otto von Bismarck (1815–1898), stands at the base of the stairs, in white.

right. Germany became not only a single nation—the Second Reich (the first being the medieval empire established in the 10th century)—under Bismarck, but also both an unfettered industrial-capitalist economy and a social-welfare state. On January 18, 1871, at the end of the Franco-Prussian War, which destroyed the power of the French emperor Napoleon III, the Prussian king William I became the emperor of Germany (r. 1871–1888) with the following proclamation:

> I, . . . do hereby declare that I have concluded that it is my solemn duty to our common Fatherland to answer the call of the united German princes and free cities and to assume the German imperial title . . . while fully conscious of my responsibility to protect the rights not only of the empire of its loyal German subjects, to maintain peace, and to assure the independence of the German nation (which depends, in its turn, on the united strength of its people). I assume this title in the hope that the German people will be freely able to reap in lasting peace the rewards of its strenuous and selfless wars, within national boundaries that will grant the Fatherland safety from renewed French aggression—a safety that has been lacking for centuries. May God grant that I and my successors on this imperial throne will ever add to the wealth of our empire not by military conquest but through the blessings and gifts of peace, in the realm of national prosperity, freedom, and morality.

It is as concise a summary of nationalist sentiments as one could hope to find.

Once united, Germany accelerated its industrial development and efforts to "Germanize" the population. The first development is self-explanatory: the construction of new factories (especially in steel manufacture, railroads, and arms) and the building of both commercial and military fleets that could challenge England's dominance on the high seas. "Germanization" of the countryside involved the forced assimilation of ethnic minorities and the resettlement of ethnic Germans on farmland confiscated from groups such as the Danes, French, Lithuanians, and Poles. The languages spoken by these groups were forbidden in the

Nationalism and Power Founded in 1810 as a foundry for producing railway equipment, the Krupp Steel Works factory in Essen, Germany, turned to manufacturing cannons and other armaments in midcentury. Weaponry quickly became its primary manufacture after 1870. By 1900 Krupp was the largest company in Europe, with over 75,000 employees across the Germany, roughly one-third of whom worked in the original plant at Essen.

military, schools, books, newspapers, theaters, concert halls, museums, court-rooms, and most other public sites.

Bismarck, a devout Lutheran, also targeted Catholicism as an intrinsically non-German religion. This anti-Catholic campaign was known as the **Kulturkampf** ("culture struggle") and lasted from 1871 to 1878. Among the measures the government took were the banning of the Jesuit Order and the breaking of diplomatic relations with the Vatican. Internally, the Reich forbade Catholic priests from mentioning any political issue in the pulpit; clergy found guilty of "political preaching" faced two years' imprisonment.[4] The government also closed roughly one-third of all monasteries. It is difficult to know the extent to which the Kulturkampf targeted Catholics in general and how much it aimed to undermine specifically the Polish communities living under the authority of the Reich; Bismarck certainly had little sympathy for either group. In either case, however, it backfired. Voters sympathetic to the Catholics' plight turned out in high numbers, and Catholic representation in the Reichstag doubled over the seven years of government oppression.

---

[4]   By 1878 nearly two thousand Catholic clergy had been either jailed or exiled, including fully one-half of all Catholic bishops.

FRUSTRATED NATIONALISM: HUNGARY AND IRELAND

Nationalist passions may have been ubiquitous in the 19th century, but victories were not. Two of the most notable failed efforts of the century—although they succeeded in the 20th—occurred in Hungary and Ireland.

Hungary

Hungary had not been independent since 1526, when the Ottomans crushed the Magyar army and killed the Magyar king at the Battle of Mohács. The remaining independent Hungarian nobles had split over what to do next. Some elected a new Hungarian monarch and formed a rump mini-kingdom that lasted only a brief time before being absorbed into the Ottoman Empire, whereas the others threw their support to Ferdinand I (r. 1526–1564) of Habsburg Austria. Hungary remained divided between Habsburgs and Ottomans until 1687, when a vast military alliance organized by Pope Innocent XI (r. 1676–1689) and known as the Holy League (Austria, the Holy Roman Empire, the Venetian Republic, Poland–Lithuania, and Russia, plus others) routed the Turkish army at a second Battle of Mohács. Soon virtually the entire Hungarian homeland lay under Habsburg control. The century and a half of Austrian–Ottoman fighting had left much of Hungary in ruins, with many of its cities depleted or flattened and much of its urban population lost to emigration.

Austrian rule, autocratic, self-absorbed, and frequently brutal, weighed heavily on the Hungarians. Hardly a decade passed without a nativist rebellion somewhere in the Magyar lands. The Habsburgs responded in true absolutist style by destroying strongholds, choking off supplies to cities, forbidding the Magyar language, and keeping the peasantry (fully 90 percent of the population) dirt-poor.[5]

The temporary dismantling of absolutism under Bonaparte gave fresh hope to the people not only by ridding them of a detested monarchy but also by presenting an opportunity for economic development. Hungary's traditionally diversified subsistence farms gave way to large-scale monoculture that could provide food and materiel to Napoleon's eastward-heading army; the French also developed local roads, bridges, and transport vehicles. The enthusiasm created by the resulting economic boom, combined with the subsequent crushing of political hopes at the Congress of Vienna in 1815, catalyzed Magyar pride and resentment and sparked new demands for the creation of an autonomous Hungarian state. Led by charismatic leaders like István Széchenyi (1791–1860) and Lajos Kossuth (1802–1894), the Hungarians pushed continually to break free of the reinstated Habsburgs. Although they succeeded briefly during the raucous uprisings of 1848–1849 (during which Kossuth dramatically issued the Hungarian Declaration of Independence), Habsburg power was restored by force, with

---

[5]   Hungarians refused to use German in government councils or for public records. Denied the use of their native tongue, the Hungarians thus have the honor of being the European people with the longest tradition of spoken Latin anywhere.

Hungarian Patriot   Lajos Kossuth (1802–1894), the great national champion of Hungarian independence, called for his country's freedom from Austria in a stirring speech to the Hungarian Diet in 1848. "Gentlemen!" he cried, "The fate of our nation is now in our hands . . . God has placed each one of you in the position of arbiter of the life or death of Hungary!" This drawing shows Lossuth after his speech, in one of his many appearances around Hungary calling for recruits to the nation's militia.

the assistance of tsarist Russia. Kossuth was driven into exile and died abroad. Magyar nationalist hopes lived on, but would not fully revive until the ultimate collapse of the Habsburg Empire in World War I.

By contrast, many of the Irish actually wanted to remain under foreign control. After centuries of British rule and misrule, enough Anglo-Irish Protestants *Ireland* had lived in Ireland long enough to regard it as their native country. They were a minority of the total population, however, and the development of parliamentary government meant that, if Ireland were to gain political autonomy, they would always remain a minority—and thus, the Protestants feared, never receive fair representation in government or full equality before the law. To many British loyalists the solution was to continue to deny representation and equality to the Catholic majority and to reject Irish home rule. Irish nationalism, as it entered the 19th century, thus progressed in two stages—first the struggle for Catholic emancipation and then the fight for home rule. Protestants in Ireland opposed both campaigns.

Since the 16th century, royal writ had effectively restricted political rights in Britain to those willing to take the Oath of Supremacy—that is, to recognize the monarch as the supreme head of the church within the realm. This law barred Catholics from holding public office; moreover, anyone who refused to take the oath could be arrested for treason. With few exceptions, the law had effectively forbidden Irish Catholics to play any part in their own government. Rebellions against England had broken out regularly in the 17th century but were crushed by England's superior armed forces. Legal assaults usually followed on the heels of the military ones. By 1700, for example, Irish Catholics were forbidden to purchase new land or to inherit it from a Protestant, and the law required Catholic landholdings to be subdivided among all surviving sons on a landholder's death. Over generations these maneuvers undermined Catholic land tenure, turning the Irish majority from free owners to tenants-at-will who could be turned out by their Protestant landlords on a whim. Catholics could not vote, sit on juries, serve in the military, or work as schoolteachers or police. The Anglo-Irish Protestant minority therefore had a monopoly on economic and political power over the entire island.

A brief relaxation of the legal persecution in 1778 produced such a powerful anti-Catholic backlash within England that riots engulfed London, leaving more than four hundred people dead and hundreds more injured. These are known as the "Gordon Riots" (1780), named after Lord George Gordon (1751–1793), who in his position as head of the Protestant Association had led the effort to overturn the easing of legal oppression of the Catholics. Leading a mob of fifty thousand, Gordon tried to present a petition against the legal reforms to Parliament. Blocked from entry into Parliament, the mob then went out of control, destroying Catholic chapels, pillaging the homes of London Catholics, and setting fire to Newgate Prison. It took several days for the English army to quell the riots.[6] Hatred and mistrust across religious lines remained deeply ingrained as Ireland entered the 19th century.

England recognized that Catholic emancipation would have to be granted eventually or else the island would never cease to rebel. As a means of retaining control, however, the English now proposed an **Act of Union**, whereby the nominally independent Irish Parliament (composed solely of Protestant Anglo-Irish since the 17th century) was subsumed into the British Parliament. The Irish were slow to warm to the idea, but eventually they agreed, and in 1801 the union took place. Catholic emancipation followed a generation later. The Catholic Emancipation Act of 1829 gave Irish Catholic men (and only men) the right to vote and to serve in government. Their smaller numbers, in both the House of Lords and the House of Commons, however, meant that they were unable to form a sufficiently large bloc to affect policy.

Disputes about the nature of Irish nationalism continued to rage. To the majority Catholics, more than half of whom still spoke Gaelic rather than English,

---

[6]   The Gordon Riots provide the backdrop to Charles Dickens's novel *Barnaby Rudge* (1841).

the Protestant Anglo-Irish were not Irish at all. By blood, language, law, religion, and custom they were English and therefore foreigners on Ireland's soil. To the Protestants, national identity meant more than shared ethnicity or religious commitment. A nation could be as legitimately defined by dedication to a set of ideals and values—as the example of the United States showed.

Industrialization only worsened the bloody rivalry. Because of its ties to England, Ireland experienced a wave of industrialization earlier than the European continent, although it never advanced far enough to challenge English manufacturing might. (The English saw to that.) Textile factories predominated for the production of fine Irish linens, along with breweries and distilleries. These factories were scattered across the country but were found most frequently in counties where the Anglo-Irish Protestants predominated.[7] Most Irish still worked the land and never shared in the prosperity of the factory-owning class. Moreover, farm prices fell dramatically after 1815, when the barriers to trade with the Continent fell, so most farmers fell into ever worse poverty, widening the economic gap between the Catholic majority and the Protestant minority. Manufacturing wealth and agrarian poverty were a volatile mix; the rural poor grew angrier and more violent and even began to organize themselves into networks of underground movements. For the Anglo-Irish, their industrial prosperity meant that they had even more to lose in the event of a successful nationalist rebellion.

The 1820s and 1830s saw repeated attempts at reform. Some of these efforts, like the Catholic Emancipation Act of 1829, had salutary effects. Others, like the temperance movement, seemed a mixed blessing. By 1842, 5 million people in Ireland had publicly sworn themselves to total abstinence from alcohol, a figure large enough to worry the owners of the heavily capitalized breweries and distilleries. By 1844 distillery revenues across Ireland had fallen by 50 percent from what they had been only twenty years earlier. Ireland's population in 1844 was roughly 8.5 million, so the number of pledge takers represented more than half the country. Landlords began to fear sober tenants, who might thereby organize into a movement, more than drunken rowdies.

Given the slow emergence of something like an organized Irish majority and the willingness of the British to institute at least some reforms, a successful campaign for Irish independence might have come about by midcentury. But then catastrophe struck—the Great Potato Famine (1845–1852). The funguslike potato blight (*Phytophthora infestans*) is believed to have come to Ireland in 1844 from South America aboard ships transporting guano, a natural fertilizer widely used in western Europe at the time. The blight in fact infected much of western Europe, not

---

[7]   One landlord described his Catholic tenants and factory workers as "ignorant, prejudiced, vulgar, brutal [people] unacquainted with . . . an efficient police, kind or indulgent landlords, or a respectable clergy."

Conspirators   This Irish cartoon shows a group of rebels swearing-in (and toasting) a new recruit to the cause of "Captain Rock"—a euphemism for the cause of Irish nationalism.

just Ireland. Conditions in Ireland, however, allowed the disease to reach its maximum and most deadly effect. By 1845 fully one-third of the entire Irish population lived on potatoes, combined at best with bacon, buttermilk, and cabbage, since potatoes grew so abundantly as to allow even the poorest farmers with the tiniest landholdings a subsistence diet.[8] The blight—for which no cure is known even today—not only wiped out entire crops but also infected the soil itself and guaranteed the loss of subsequent plantings as well, even if one brought in fresh seed potatoes. Perhaps half of the 1845 harvest was lost, and the blight destroyed three-quarters of the 1846 harvest. Only in 1852 did the blight run its course, leaving Ireland permanently changed and Irish–English relations permanently scarred.

Somewhere between 1 and 1.5 million Irish died of starvation during the famine, and a slightly larger number, perhaps as many as 2 million, were forced to emigrate—mostly to America and Canada, in addition to other areas of Britain itself. Nearly one-third of the westward-sailing emigrants died before reaching their new homes, however, making the total mortality figures all the more horrific. The blight itself was a natural disaster, but one made considerably worse by British mismanagement of the crisis. The British blocked international relief efforts and refused to commit to long-term public works projects that would have enabled Irish workers to purchase foodstuffs from abroad. To Irish eyes, however, the two most odious of Britain's actions throughout the crisis were to continue shipping into England large quantities of the unblighted potatoes to make up for

---

[8]   Farm families, especially in western Ireland, ate as many as twenty potatoes per person daily.

The Face of Horror   The suffering of the Potato Famine in Ireland is starkly portrayed in this painting from 1850 by the English artist George Frederick Watts (1817–1904). Associated with the Symbolist movement, an offshoot of Romanticism, Watts wrote, "I paint ideas, not things."

England's own native losses and to refuse to redirect Irish grain crops (which provided the raw material for the distilleries and breweries owned by the Anglo-Irish) so that they could feed the people instead. As John Mitchel (1815–1875), a young Irish nationalist, bitterly wrote, "The Almighty, indeed, sent the potato blight, but the English created the Famine."

In the midst of this horror, the Revolutions of 1848 rocked Europe. Ireland's version of it lasted only a single day before being put down, but the implications of possible revolt loomed large in British minds afterward. Like the leading voices at Westphalia in 1648 or at Vienna in 1815, the leading political figures in Britain resolved to contain the revolutionary impulse and sought any means to forestall Irish independence. The issue of home rule did not emerge again as a live political issue until the 1880s.

Within Ireland, two essential demographic facts shaped matters. First, many of the most desperate, angry, and radical of the Irish had either died or emigrated. This may explain the political quiescence of Ireland after midcentury, since the presumed leaders of any populist movement were absent. Second, the enormity of the disaster, coupled with some easing of British restrictions on land tenure for Catholics, meant that those Irish who did remain on the land were able to increase their holdings: individual farms grew from as few as five acres to fifteen, or a hundred, or even more, which meant that something beyond mere survival was possible. Industrialization declined overall throughout the island but focused more intensely on the northern counties, such as Ulster, where a large shipbuilding industry took root. In other words, postfamine Ireland was less populous overall, more secure in its resources, and more ethnically and religiously demarcated. For the time being, peaceful order and relative calm and prosperity trumped the urgent demands of the frustrated Irish version of nationalism.

JEWISH IDENTITIES

The Psalmist's oath in exile has been a mainstay of Jewish prayers and aspirations for centuries: "If I forget you, O Jerusalem, let my right hand wither; let my tongue stick to my palette if I cease to think of you, if I do not keep Jerusalem in memory even at my happiest hour" (Psalms 137.5–6).

The Jews' dream of returning to Palestine had remained constant since the Diaspora ("exile" or "scattering") of the 6th century BCE, even if it seldom expressed itself in a mass movement. Some individual and small-group immigration trickled into the region, and on occasion it swelled—at it did, for example, after the establishment of the Crusader states in the 12th century and with the consolidation of the Ottoman Empire in the 16th and 17th centuries. For the most part, however, the bulk of Europe's Jews through the centuries chose either to coexist with mainstream Greater Western society or to assimilate while awaiting the messiah.

During the Enlightenment many Jews, especially the more well-to-do, em-

Assimilation braced the rationalism of the age in the hope that in a Europe without organized religion there would be no religious hatred. Some of these Jews abandoned Orthodoxy, accepted Western gentile forms of dress, diet, and thought, and joined the world of the salons. The great philosopher Moses Mendelssohn (1729–1786), whom we met in chapter 16, is perhaps the best example of an assimilated, Enlightened Jew. Still others went so far as to accept baptism as a means of gaining entry to mainstream society—like the parents of the German revolutionary Karl Marx (1818–1883) and of the British statesman Benjamin Disraeli (1804–1881).

Most European countries had given Jews—officially, at least—something like full civic and political equality by 1880: they struck down guild restrictions that had prohibited Jewish involvement in certain industries and crafts, they opened Europe's universities to Jews, and they permitted Jews to participate in newly emerging professions like journalism. Under the Old Regime Jews had not

Wie sich der Chanukaleuchler des Ziegenfellhändlers **Cohn** in Pinne zum Christbaum des Kommerzienrats **Conrad** in der Tiergartenstraße (Berlin W.) entwickelte.

Assimilation: An Evolutionary Perspective In this anti-assimilationist cartoon, the menorah used in celebration of Hanukkah metamorphoses into a Christmas tree. The message is clear: Jews cannot become assimilated into the German nation without losing their Jewish identity.

been permitted to reside in Paris; by 1880 more than forty thousand Jews lived there, nearly two-thirds of all the Jews in France. Throughout Germany, Jewish populations in cities of at least twenty thousand inhabitants quadrupled between 1815 and 1880. In Berlin alone the Jewish population increased from three thousand to thirty-six thousand over that period.

Most Jews in western Europe prospered in these years. Tax rolls tell the tale. England, for example, had admitted roughly ten thousand Jewish immigrants between 1750 and 1815, most of them simple peddlers; yet by 1850 virtually all of their families had achieved middle-class status. In Germany, 80 percent of all Jews reported incomes that made them solidly middle-class.

Given their urbanization, Jews figured large as business leaders, journalists, physicians, and lawyers.[9] Many Jews launched political careers as well. Adolphe Crémieux (1796–1880) served in France's Chamber of Deputies and twice held the position of minister of justice; Gabriel Riesser (1806–1863) became Germany's first Jewish judge. Benjamin Disraeli, mentioned before, was England's first (and still the only) Jewish prime minister, serving twice in that office (1868, 1874–1880).

Romantic nationalism, however, quickly ended the Enlightenment dream of a unified, rationalized human community, and Jews were once again seen as alien. *The New Anti-Semitism* Resistance to Jewish advancement occurred at the popular level, and it rose as rapidly as the Jews themselves did within society. But racial discrimination, not religious opposition, defined the new **anti-Semitism**. Marx may have been one of the first Westerners to write publicly about "the Jewish Question," but he was hardly the first to raise it. In 1844 a Frenchman named Alphonse Toussenel (1803–1885) published a vile attack titled *The Jews—Kings of Our Time: A History of Financial Feudalism*, which was quickly followed by another French work, Arthur de Gobineau's (1816–1882) *Essay on the Inequality of the Human Races*

---

9   Jews made up 10 percent of all lawyers in the city of Würtemberg. In Vienna in 1870 fully 40 percent of all medical students were Jewish.

(1855), one of the first books to argue for the inherent superiority of the "Aryan race."

These books represent the start of a century-long parade of anti-Semitic literature in Europe that culminated in an infamous forgery entitled *The Protocols of the Elders of Zion* (1903). This Russian work, soon translated into every major European language, purports to represent the blueprint for an international Jewish conspiracy to take over the world. In English the terms *anti-Semitic* and *anti-Semitism* first appeared in print in 1881, in the London journal *The Athenaeum*, with the laconic observation that "anti-Semitic literature is very prosperous in Germany."[10] Being disproportionately visible in industrial, urban Europe, the Jews were disproportionately blamed for its miseries. That meant everything from low wages and miserable housing for workers to overcrowding and disease.

The Jews' very success was seen as proof of their insidious intent. Surely it cannot be a coincidence that Jews own businesses, publish newspapers, fill the ranks of the medical and legal professions, manage theaters, and help write the laws? Either the Jews are engaged in an international conspiracy or they are simply mean and grasping. In either case, the bigots concluded, we tolerate the Jews at our peril.

But not all criticism of assimilation came from outside. Many Orthodox Jews viewed warily the rise of secularism. Jewish schools now taught secular subjects—geography, mathematics, and European languages—that pushed aside the traditional focus on the study of scripture and the Talmud. The Jewish High Rabbinical Court in Paris in 1808 had asserted the authority of civil law over religious law; in effect, Jews should be French citizens first and observant Jews second. In 1818 authorities in Hamburg issued a new prayer book written in German, not Hebrew, and printed from left to right, unlike Hebrew. It also introduced practices like choirs, organ playing, sermons in the local language, and integration of the sexes, and it dropped from the weekly prayers all references to a Jewish return to Zion (Jerusalem).

Zionism These tensions resulted in new efforts to establish at long last a Jewish state. Two fundamental convictions form the basis of those efforts, known as **Zionism**. One is the belief in the Jews' unique claim to possession of the Holy Land—a claim as old as the Abrahamic Covenant, whereby God appointed the Hebrews as His "Chosen People." The other is recognition of the historical fact that the Jews, despite two thousand years of effort, will never be wholly accepted into Western society. The Viennese journalist Theodor Herzl (1860–1904), who organized the First International Zionist Congress, summed up this view in a powerful pamphlet titled *The Jewish State* (1896):

---

[10] A German journalist named Wilhelm Marr appears to have invented the word anti-Semitism in 1879.

The anti-Semitism of today should not be confused with the persecutions that Jews have faced in the past, for while it does have a religious
tinge to it in some countries, the principle focus of this new aggression is
different. In most places where anti-Semitism thrives, in other words, it
does so because of the [civil] emancipation of the Jews. . . . Maybe, if we
would be left in peace for a generation or two, we could possibly assimilate completely into the peoples who surround us, but the simple fact is
that they will not leave us in peace. Instead, they manage to tolerate us
for a short time, but then their hostility returns—again and again. For
some reason our prosperity irritates the world, probably because for so
many centuries it had grown accustomed to regard us as the most con-
temptible of the poor. Society's stupidity and mean-heartedness have
made it blind to the fact that prosperity has actually weakened our Jewish
identity by eradicating those customs that used to distinguish us. . . . We
are a single people—our enemies have united us even without our consent. This has happened before. Suffering has brought us together, and in
that union we recognize our strength. Surely we are strong enough to
found a state of our own, one that will be a model for all states.

The Zionist movement found most of its support among the Jews of eastern
Europe. These Jews, in the 19th century, made up roughly two-thirds of the entire
world's Jewish population, so success here was essential to the ultimate spread of
Zionism.

Anti-Semitism in eastern Europe—including the area known as the **Pale of
Settlement**—was particularly vicious (see Map 20.5).[11] The Russian tsar and king
of Poland, Alexander II (r. 1855–1881), despite his liberalizing tendencies, was
widely unpopular and the subject of numerous assassination attempts. In fact, in
1881 members of the revolutionary *Narodnaya Volya* ("Will of the People") Party
did kill him. Although no Jewish individuals or groups had been involved, popular
sentiment blamed the murder on the supposed international Jewish conspiracy.

Wave after wave of organized persecutions known as **pogroms** now rolled
through the region, cutting down Jews, destroying synagogues, and setting
Jewish books aflame. As a result, more than 3 million Jews migrated farther westward into eastern and central Europe, desperate and hungry, carrying only the
possessions they had on their backs. To these exiles and the eastern European
Jews who welcomed them, Zionism was the only solution to the hatred and bigotry that had permeated Jewish history.

---

[11] The word *pale*, in this regard, means a "boundary" or "border." It derives from the Latin *palus*, meaning a
"stake" or "post" set in the ground as a border marker.

SWEDEN

St. Petersburg
(21,000)

Lake
Pskov

Novgorod
(4,700)
Lake
Ilmen

(80,000)

BALTIC PROVINCES

Baltic Sea

KOVNO

VITEBSK

Moscow
(9,000)

GERMANY

SUWALKI

VILNA

Smolensk
(10,500)

Tula
(2,700)

PLOCK

LOMZA

MINSK   MOGILEV

KALISZ   WARSAW   GRODNO   Pripet
Marshes

PIOTRKOW   SIEDLCE

R U S S I A

RADOM

CHERNIGOV

Kursk
(4,000)

Voroneth
(2,700)

KIELCE   LUBLIN

VOLHYNIA

AUSTRIA—
HUNGARY

Kiev   POLTAVA

KIEV

Kharkov
(14,000)

N

PODOLIA

0 km   200

RUMANIA

BESSARABIA

EKATERINOSLAV

KHERSON

0 miles   200

Nikolaev

TAURIDA

The Pale of Settlement, 1835–1917

Sea of
Azov

Kuban
(5,000)

———   The Pale of Settlement. Russian Jews were confined to this
area by laws of 1795 and 1835.

Sebastopol

Yalta

○   Towns within the Pale which were themselves barred to
Jews without special residence permits.

Black Sea

■   Towns outside the Pale with Jewish inhabitants (figures for 1897).

MAP 20.5   The Pale of Settlement, 1835–1917   The Pale of Settlement was the territory
within imperial Russia in which residency by Jews was allowed and beyond which Jewish residency was generally prohibited. It corresponds roughly to present-day Ukraine and Belarus.

Slowly, groups of Jewish settlers also began to return to the Holy Land. Between 1881 and 1914 nearly 100,000 Jews had taken up residence there, either living with distant relations and friends or purchasing land from Turkish landlords or Palestinian freeholders. Zionist organizations in Europe created their own financial networks that made capital available to would-be settlers. Many of the Turks who sold their lands were absentee landlords, and some were public

Aftermath of a Pogrom   Survivors of an anti-Jewish pogrom in Russia in 1881 pick through the remnants of a Torah scroll, prayer books, and other items in a pillaged synagogue.

officials determined to withdraw from a decaying Ottoman state with their purses full. These were fully legal purchases of property, but that fact did not appease many of the roughly 700,000 Palestinians who lived in the area and dreamed of a free homeland of their own.

ISLAMIC NATIONALISMS

Nationalism roiled throughout the Islamic world just as in Europe. The Ottoman state had expanded far into Europe, with a diverse religious and ethnic makeup, and through the centuries it had likewise struggled to guarantee a degree of religious toleration while preserving Islamic religious law, guarding the holy cities, and maintaining the pilgrimage routes that led to them. Moreover, the flexible structure of Ottoman administration had allowed non-Turks to serve in government and even to rise to positions of political and social prominence. But in the 18th century the empire went on the defensive against expansionist powers in Russia, Austria, and revolutionary France. And with the rise of industrial Europe, the empire as a unifying force for Muslims weakened dramatically, to be replaced by ethnically based nationalist sentiments. The Ottoman gift for accommodation proved no match for the newfound commercial and military might of European states, and the 19th-century reform efforts crumbled in the face of the increasingly urgent demands for local control over local fates.

As we saw in the previous chapter, Greece wrested its independence from the Ottomans in the 1820s. In the following decade France invaded Algeria and carved it away from Ottoman rule. At the same time, Tunisia and Egypt instituted political and economic reforms in an effort to secure their independence. The region of Bulgaria had gained autonomy by 1830, with Romania following in 1878. Off to the east, the Caucasus territories of Abkhazia, Georgia, Batumi, and Kars were wrenched away by Russia. By 1878 the Ottomans remained in control of only Anatolia, Iraq, Palestine, and the Hijaz—the coastal strip of Arabia that lay alongside the Red Sea, including the holy cities of Mecca and Medina. Persia had long since established itself as an independent—indeed a rival—state under the Safavids and then the Qajars. What had once been a universal Islamic empire stretching from the Atlantic Ocean to India was thereby reduced to a single Middle East state, kept alive by a shaky alliance among its Turkish, Persian, and Arab leaders.

Nationalistic passions were both fed and challenged by several new strains in Islamic thought. In the 19th century Russian intellectual life was divided between liberals and Slavophiles—that is, between those who promoted Western-style reforms on the one hand and those who urged a return to Russian cultural and religious tradition on the other; 19th-century Islamic thought was divided as well. Whereas many believed that new Muslim countries could be aligned with Europe without abandoning their Islamic character, others advocated instead a thorough turning away from the Greater West and delving deeper into Islamic tradition.

Muhammad Ali Pasha, Founder of Modern Egypt

An example of the first was the pro-Western reform promoted in Egypt under the dynasty established by **Muhammad Ali Pasha** (r. 1805–1848), often called the founder of modern Egypt. Born in the Ottoman Balkans (present-day Albania), Muhammad Ali worked his way up the military ranks and arrived in Egypt at the head of an army as part of the Ottomans' campaign to regain control of the region after Napoleon's forces had withdrawn. He assassinated most of his Mamluk rivals for power, which made him popular with the Egyptian masses, and subsequently drove the remaining Mamluk soldiers into the desert. By 1805 he had taken the title of *wali* ("governor") of the country and ruled independently, although he publicly proclaimed obedience to the sultan in Istanbul. His most important innovation was a popular army. Muhammad Ali understood the growing weakness of the regime in Istanbul and believed that Egypt was the right site for a renewal of Islamic power: its economic might, coupled with its proximity to the holy cities of the Arabian Peninsula, made it the natural successor as leader of the Islamic world. But for Egypt to assume that leadership, he believed, the Egyptians themselves had to form the basis of the state, and hence he remodeled the army.

By 1820 he had conscripted 30,000 Egyptians and turned them into a disciplined force, and by the end of his life in 1848 the army numbered 150,000 or more. This was the first truly Egyptian military force—with ethnic Egyptians making up the rank and file and gradually staffing the officers' ranks as well—since the days of the pharaohs. Muhammad Ali wanted a modern army too, with modern weaponry, and so he established close ties with industrialized England, from whom he acquired not only modern rifles and artillery but also military trainers to instruct his soldiers. He also put together a new navy with ships purchased from England, France, Italy, and Greece. By 1830 he had constructed his own new shipyard at Alexandria, which began to produce a steady stream of frigates and men-of-war. Once his navy was fully developed, Muhammad Ali launched a combined land and sea attack against the Ottomans, taking Jerusalem, Acre, Damascus, Beirut, and Aleppo in quick succession until, by peace treaty in 1833, he ruled all of Palestine and Syria in addition to Egypt. He also sent a force into Arabia itself and briefly controlled both Mecca and Medina.

Muhammad Ali ruled as an autocrat, but he reorganized and professionalized the government along Western lines, with a central cabinet composed of ministries of war, finance, foreign relations, education, and commerce. In trade, he directed Egypt's exports away from the Ottomans and toward Europe. He supported the introduction of cotton cultivation along the Nile, and soon Egyptian

Negotiating with the Europeans   This lithograph by the Scottish artist David Roberts (1796–1864) shows the great social and political reformer Muhammad Ali Pasha (r. 1805–1848) receiving European dignitaries in his palace at Alexandria, Egypt. Roberts spent several years in Egypt and the Middle East drawing sketches from which he later produced color prints, which he published in nine hugely popular volumes.

cotton began to be shipped to the factories of England. As soon as the engineering skill was available, Muhammad Ali also constructed his own textile plants and sugar refineries, too. He appointed European administrators and civil engineers to improve the sanitation of cities, and he hired Europeans to head new military academies and polytechnic (vocational) schools.[12] Newspapers were introduced, appearing in both Arabic and French. New centers for translating European technical manuals into Arabic were set up, along with publishing houses to produce the works.

REFORMING ISLAM

Al-Nahda

The opening up to Europe helped to inspire an intellectual and cultural revival in Egypt known as **al-Nahda** ("awakening" or "renaissance"), which some writers describe as an Islamic Enlightenment. Most of the thinkers associated with *al-Nahda* believed that Muslim society faced being surpassed by Europe's economic, military, and technological might and thus needed to open its arms and minds to ideas from the outside world. As in their great medieval empire, Muslims could actually strengthen and deepen their culture, they believed, because customs from abroad could be harmonized with Islamic values.

The first great figure in the movement was Rifa'a al-Tahtawi (1801–1873). He had been sent to Paris, along with a corps of younger students, by Muhammad Ali Pasha in 1826 to learn French, study Western ideas, and develop a closer understanding between Europe and the Islamic world. After a stay of five years, Tahtawi wrote a celebrated memoir, *The Essence of Paris,* in which he recounts his group's excitement at learning Western law, philosophy, mathematics, and science. He read Voltaire, Rousseau, and Montesquieu. He wrote volumes on social theory, political rights, and moral philosophy. After returning to Cairo, he established the School of Languages (1835), which not only instructed students in languages but also served as a central clearinghouse for ideas about secular government, national identity, and cultural pluralism. Tahtawi believed passionately in the integration of Islam and European culture. This was possible, he argues, because Europe had separated its religion from its political and civic traditions. Key to this integration, he contends, is the notion of citizenship—a form of group identity that is not determined by race, creed, or ethnicity. Rather, one chooses to join a community and acts as a member in good standing of it. A nation, in the modern sense, Tahtawi urges, consists of people who share an allegiance not just to a vision of the past but also to a vision for the future.

---

[12]   In the 19th century, roughly one-tenth of the urban populations in Egypt died each year from infectious disease.

The other major school of Islamic thought, however, thoroughly rejected, condemned, and demonized modernization and Western values. The clerics and *The* writers known ultimately as **Wahhabis** were conservatives and traditionalists, *Wahhabi* but nationalists too in their way. Named for a cleric from the Islamic heartland of *Movement* central Arabia, Muhammad ibn Abd al-Wahhab (1703–1792), the Wahhabi movement declared that the overwhelming majority of Muslims throughout the entire world—Sunni, Shi'a, and Sufi—had fallen into a state of spiritual ignorance and moral barbarism. What had caused this religious desolation? Ignorance of the meaning of the Qur'anic concept of *tawhid*—the "unity" of God. Interpreting this concept in the strictest possible fashion, Wahhabis emphasized that God is the One, the Only, the Creator, the Divine. Any act of religious observance that diverted attention from him was an abomination. As al-Wahhab once wrote:

> It is well-known that the Messenger of God (Peace be upon him!) obliged the faithful to observe *tawhid* many years before obliging them to the Pillars of Islam. . . . *Tawhid* is supreme among religious duties, more important than prayer, alms, fasting, and pilgrimage [with the testimony of faith, the Pillars of Islam].

Anything and everything that distracts the soul from recognizing the Supreme One is a transgression against Islam. Wahhabism accepts as historical facts the miracles performed by Islamic saints, but it forbids veneration of the saints who performed them or the shrines where they are entombed. That would be idolatry. To give alms to the poor is a religious requirement, but it is idolatrous to do so out of love for the poor rather than love of God. Only by returning to a pure and martial faith—ideally to practices in existence during the lifetime of the Prophet himself—could the moral horror of the modern world be erased and an authentic Muslim society established.

Abd al-Wahhab never articulated a full body of teachings on government. Drawing his inspiration from the 14th-century jurist Ibn Taymiyya, he stressed the moral responsibility of the ruler to destroy all forms of idolatry—if necessary, by force. Any ruler who adhered to Wahhabi ideals and enforced its strict moral code would be acceptable. Al-Wahhab taught that every true Muslim (meaning his followers) must refuse to obey political and clerical authorities who do not maintain the proper attitude toward *tawhid*. It was not until well after his death in 1792 that his clerical successors began to formulate a coherent set of ideas regarding governance; most drew their main ideas directly from Ibn Taymiyya, who had identified "innovation in religion" as a second abomination, equal to that of idolatry, and called for relentless state action to stamp it out in all its forms.

The Arab prince **Muhammad ibn Saud** (r. 1744–1765) enthusiastically embraced the teachings of the Taymiyya–Wahhabi sect in the mid-18th century. Ibn Saud was an ambitious figure, determined to free Arabia from foreign control and create a new Arab-led society that would restore Islam's greatness and purge it of the vile "innovations" that had crept into its practice through the centuries. Two enemies, as he saw it, stood out among many—the Ottomans and the Sufis. By 1765, when Ibn Saud died, he had conquered much of central Arabia and parts of the east. His succeeding son, grandson, and great-grandson extended the conquests, until by 1818 nearly the entire peninsula, including the holy cities, was under Saudi control (see Map 20.6). At this point, the Egyptian reformer Muhammad Ali, acting with the blessing of the Ottoman ruler in Istanbul, launched his own attack on Arabia to wrest the holy sites from Saudi control and liberate them from Wahhabi doctrine and practice. He succeeded for a time, but Saudi determination and the fast-growing sense of Arab nationalism won control back for them in 1824. This second Saudi state lasted from 1824 to 1891. Saudi-based Arab nationalism completed a historical cycle that restored leadership to the people who had been privileged to wield it first.

Tanzimat
Reforms

Istanbul, for its part, tried to counter the Wahhabi nationalism of the Saudis. The empire's **Tanzimat** ("reorganization") reform movement, which flourished from 1839 to 1876, represented a last-ditch effort to hold onto power. It emerged from the efforts of Sultan Mahmud II (r. 1808–1839) to modernize the empire in the face of French expansionism. By the end of his reign, Mahmud had abolished the entire corps of Janissaries, who had dominated the Ottoman army since the 13th century but had long since been surpassed in organization, training, and

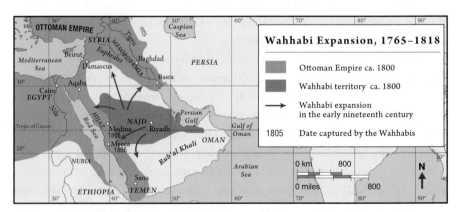

MAP 20.6   Wahhabi Expansion, 1765–1818   The Wahhabi movement gained power with its embrace by Muhammad ibn Saud and his successors, who set themselves up as the purifiers of Islamic culture and faith.

overall might by the Western national armies. Legal, administrative, and economic reforms followed, and even court-directed modernization of architectural and clothing styles.

The essence of the Tanzimat reform movement was to promote civic secularism while protecting religious pluralism. Especially within its shrunken political borders, the Ottoman realm was too diverse, both ethnically and religiously, to conflate religion and civic life. So the Ottomans proposed a different kind of nationalism—one based not on race or creed but on secular government and religious freedom. They built more schools, reorganized curricula, and encouraged newspapers and magazines. They enacted laws promising equality for all subjects regardless of faith. They even appointed Christians and Jews to reform councils to advise the government, as well as to the Supreme Judicial Council, which acted as an appellate court. Their efforts, however, faced determined resistance by Arab groups interested instead in establishing their own ethnically based nationalism. These Islamic conservatives became the most dependable support of Sultan Abdul Hamid II (r. 1876–1909), who abandoned the model of European liberalism in his long and repressive reign.

Uniformed Secularism   Portrayed are three leaders of the increasingly secular and professional Turkish army. The religiously trained and motivated Janissaries had been disbanded in 1826, after they had attempted a coup against Mahmud II (r. 1808–1839). The great reform era known as Tanzimat lasted from 1839 to 1876, during which the empire attempted to integrate its non-Muslim subjects more fully into society, while modernizing its institutions and legal processes. In the end, the empire fell victim to the intense nationalist passions of the 19th century.

◆

The nationalist movements that so stirred 19th-century hearts and minds apparently included no women, for none of them championed, or even mentioned, the role of women as fully participating citizens. Campaigns to extend voting rights explicitly spoke of enfranchising men—and men only. Many reforms across Europe helped to secure women more legal rights, but the fundamental right to participate in the shaping of public life was denied. To change this, women from all classes came together to insist on giving women the vote. As we shall see, they came for different reasons and followed different tactics, but in the process they formed a new identity for themselves—the New Woman.

WHO, WHAT, WHERE

Act of Union	Kulturkampf	pogroms
al-Nahda	Muhammad Ali Pasha	Realpolitik
anti-Semitism	Muhammad ibn Saud	Tanzimat
Camillo di Cavour	nationalism	Wahhabis
Crimean War	Otto von Bismarck	Zionism
Giuseppe Garibaldi	Pale of Settlement	

SUGGESTED READINGS

Primary Sources

Bismarck, Otto von. *Memoirs.*

Fichte, Johann Gottlieb. *Address to the German Nation.*

Herzl, Theodor. *The Jewish State.*

Herzl, Theodor. *Old New Land.*

Mazzini, Giuseppe. *The Duties of Man.*

Renan, Ernest. *What Is a Nation?*

al-Tahtawi, Rifa'a. *The Emancipation of Muslim Women.*

al-Tahtawi, Rifa'a. *The Essence of Paris.*

Anthologies

Gellner, Ernest. *Nations and Nationalism,* 2nd ed. (2009; org. 1983).

Kurzman, Charles, ed. *Modernist Islam, 1840–1940: A Sourcebook* (2002).

Melancon, Michael S., and John C. Swanson. *Nineteenth-Century Europe: Sources and Perspectives from History* (2006).

Spencer, Philip, and Howard Wollman, eds. *Nations and Nationalism: A Reader* (2009).

Studies

Aksan, Virginia H. *Ottoman Wars, 1700–1870: An Empire Besieged* (2007).

Akşin, Sina. *Turkey from Empire to Revolutionary Republic: The Emergence of the Turkish Nation from 1789 to the Present* (2007).

Anderson, Benedict. *Imagined Communities: Reflections on the Origin and Spread of Nationalism* (2006).

Baron, Beth. *Egypt as a Woman: Nationalism, Gender, and Politics* (2007).

Bayly, C. A. *The Birth of the Modern World, 1780–1914* (2003).

Bennette, Rebecca Ayako. *Fighting for the Soul of Germany: The Catholic Struggle for Inclusion after Unification* (2012).

Ceylan, Ebubekir. *The Ottoman Origins of Modern Iraq: Political Reform, Modernization, and Development in the Nineteenth-Century Middle East* (2011).

Choueiri, Youssef M. *Arab Nationalism: A History* (2000).

Çiçek, Nazan. *The Young Ottomans: Turkish Critics of the Eastern Question in the Late Nineteenth Century* (2010).

Clark, Christopher. *Iron Kingdom: The Rise and Downfall of Prussia, 1600–1947* (2009).

Eichner, Carolyn J. *Surmounting the Barricades: Women in the Paris Commune* (2004).

Eley, Geoff. *Forging Democracy: The History of the Left in Europe, 1850–2000* (2002).

Elon, Amos. *The Pity of It All: A Portrait of the German-Jewish Epoch, 1743–1933* (2003).

Fahmy, Khaled. *All the Pasha's Men: Mehmed Ali, His Army, and the Making of Modern Egypt* (2002).

Frankel, Richard E. *Bismarck's Shadow: The Cult of Leadership and the Transformation of the German Right, 1898–1945* (2005).

Gellner, Ernest. *Nations and Nationalism* (2009).

Gerwarth, Robert. *The Bismarck Myth: Weimar Germany and the Legacy of the Iron Chancellor* (2005).

Ghazal, Amal N. *Islamic Reform and Arab Nationalism: Expanding the Crescent from the Mediterranean to the Indian Ocean, 1880s–1930s* (2014).

Gross, Michael B. *The War against Catholicism: Liberalism and the Anti-Catholic Imagination in Nineteenth-Century Germany* (2005).

Hall, Catherine, Keith McClelland, and Jane Rendall. *Defining the Victorian Nation: Class, Race, Gender, and the British Reform Act of 1867* (2000).

Harris, Erika. *Nationalism: Theories and Causes* (2009).

Harvey, David. *Paris: Capital of Modernity* (2005).

Hewitson, Mark. *Nationalism in Germany, 1848–1866: Revolutionary Nation* (2010).

Hibbert, Christopher. *Garibaldi: Hero of Italian Unification* (2008).

Khuri-Makdisi, Ilham. *The Eastern Mediterranean and the Making of Global Radicalism, 1860–1914* (2010).

Langewiesche, Dieter. *Liberalism in Germany* (2000).

Lerman, Katharine Anne. *Bismarck* (2004).

Offen, Karen. *European Feminisms, 1700–1950: A Political History* (2000).

Pollard, Lisa. *Nurturing the Nation: The Family Politics of Modernizing, Colonizing, and Liberating Egypt, 1805–1923* (2005).

Porter, Brian. *When Nationalism Began to Hate: Imagining Modern Politics in Nineteenth-Century Poland* (2002).

Roshwald, Aviel. *The Endurance of Nationalism: Ancient Roots and Modern Dilemmas* (2006).

Salmi, Hannu. *Nineteenth-Century Europe: A Cultural History* (2008).

Smith, Anthony D. *The Ethnic Origins of Nations* (2009).

Smith, Anthony D. *Nationalism: Theory, Ideology, History* (2002).

Steinberg, Jonathan. *Bismarck: A Life* (2013).

Wawro, Geoffrey. *The Franco-Prussian War: The German Conquest of France in 1870–1871* (2005).

Wetzel, David. *A Duel of Giants: Bismarck, Napoleon III, and the Origins of the Franco-Prussian War* (2003).

For additional resources, including maps, primary sources, visuals, web links, and quizzes, please go to **www.oup.com/us/backman**.

CHAPTER 21

The Modern Woman

1860–1914

Throughout the second half of the 19th century, ever-increasing numbers of women across the Greater West began to agitate for equal rights, most particularly the right to vote. Calls for fairer treatment of women date back to the 14th century at least, but usually from solitary voices. Now the issue of women's rights was the subject of more widespread expectation and demand.

WOMEN AND THE RIGHT TO VOTE

Women first enfranchised:
pre-1914   1921–45   1971–
1914–20   1946–70   no suffrage

The first major step forward occurred in the labor protests of the early 1800s, when European women formed the majority of the workforce in industries such as textile manufacture. These women expected an improvement in their lot as part of the rise of workers' rights, but their hopes were beaten down for the most part and had to wait for another generation or two. The uprisings of 1848 brought new attention to women's demands, although little changed in their status right away. The first bill before the British Parliament to extend suffrage (the right to vote) to women was presented in 1867 and defeated by an overwhelming vote of 194 to 74. But the very industrial system that had kept women down before 1860 gave them the means to press forward in the latter decades of the century. These changes in the workplace, combined with the development of political liberalism, enabled the call for women's suffrage and

The New Woman This promotional poster for the original London production of *The New Woman* (1894), a play by English dramatist Sydney Grundy (1848–1914), suggests the ridicule that male-dominated society heaped on educated, independent-minded women in search of equality in the late 19th century. Grundy's subtitle was "A Comedy in Four Acts," and the play was a hit.

ultimately the rise of broader demands for women's social, economic, and political equality known as the **feminist movement**.

THE APPETITE FOR REFORM

The hunger for reform was acute. Popular attitudes regarding women's place in society ranged widely, but the majority emphasized their fundamental duty to maintain the family and household and insisted on the unnaturalness of their interest in civil society, politics, and intellectual life. As the popular London weekly newspaper *The Saturday Review* put it in 1871,

> The power of reasoning is so small in women that they need adventitious [additional] help, and if they have not the guidance and check of a religious conscience, it is useless to expect from them self-control on abstract principles. They do not calculate consequences, and they are reckless when they once give way, hence they are to be kept straight only through their affections, the religious sentiment, and a well-educated moral sense.[1]

---

[1]   Another example: "No woman can or ought to know very much of the mass of meanness and wickedness and misery that is loose in the wide world. She could not learn it without losing the bloom and freshness which it is her mission in life to preserve." *The Saturday Review.*

CHAPTER TIMELINE

1865	1870	1875	1880	1885

- 1867 National Society for Women's Suffrage formed in Britain; first bill presented to British parliament to extend suffrage; Russia and Finland open their universities to women
- 1869 John Stuart Mill, *The Subjection of Women*
- 1870 First commercially produced typewriter
- 1874 Women's labor and trade unions legalized in France
- 1878 First international congress for women's rights meets in Paris
- 1880 Naphey, *The Physical Life of Woman;* France allows girls to attend secondary school
- 1882 Aletta Jacobs establishes Europe's first birth control clinic in Amsterdam

The sanctity of the family as the fundamental unit of society, in this view, trumped any demand by women for civic equality. Hence opposition to female suffrage was primarily moral—which set it apart from the economic and class-based arguments levied against the demands of male workers and commoners. Thousands, if not tens of thousands or more pamphlets, sermons, domestic guidebooks, novels, stage-plays, popular songs, paintings, and family-oriented magazines pressed the point continually.

Industrialization had separated the work space from the domestic space, and among the middle class this led to a heightened popular vision of the home as *Early* a place of refuge (the "cult of domesticity" that we considered in chapter 19). *Feminists* A wife, as overseer of the domestic safe haven, both supplied and tended to *and Their* the essential emotional cohesion of family life; but until divorce laws were *Sympathizers* reformed she did so from a position of legal powerlessness. To those pressing for reform, both female and male, the liberal capitalist ideology that distinguished between the male-identified public sphere and the female-identified home front was the fundamental problem. The solution, therefore, was not merely to remove the barriers that excluded women from the man's world of commerce and government. It was to end the very notion of separate female and male spheres of belonging and action. As one Englishwoman recalled, in a biography of her suffragist mother published in the 1930s:

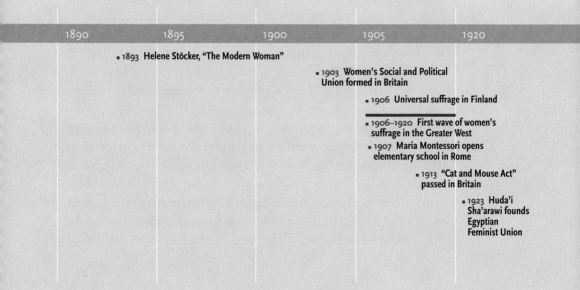

1890   1895   1900   1905   1920

- 1893 Helene Stöcker, "The Modern Woman"

- 1903 Women's Social and Political Union formed in Britain

- 1906 Universal suffrage in Finland

- 1906–1920 First wave of women's suffrage in the Greater West
- 1907 Maria Montessori opens elementary school in Rome

- 1913 "Cat and Mouse Act" passed in Britain

- 1923 Huda'i Sha'arawi founds Egyptian Feminist Union

To remain single was thought a disgrace and at thirty an unmarried woman was called an old maid. After their parents died, what could they do, where could they go? If they had a brother, as unwanted and permanent guests, they might live in his house. Some had to maintain themselves and then, indeed, difficulty arose. The only paid occupation open to a gentlewoman was to become a governess under despised conditions and a miserable salary. None of the professions were open to women; there were no women in Government offices; no secretarial work was done by them. Even nursing was disorganized and disreputable until Florence Nightingale recreated it as a profession by founding the Nightingale School of Nursing in 1860.

This was Louisa Garrett Anderson (1873–1943), an early feminist whose mother, Elizabeth Garrett Anderson (1836–1917), had been Britain's first-ever female licensed physician.

The same point was made at greater length by the British political philosopher John Stuart Mill (1806–1873) in his book *The Subjection of Women* (1869):

What we are now discussing is not the need which society has of the services of women in public business, but the dull and hopeless life to which it so often condemns them, by forbidding them to exercise the practical abilities which many of them are conscious of, in any wider field than one which to some of them never was, and to others is no longer, open. If there is anything vitally important to the happiness of human beings, it is that they should relish their habitual pursuit. . . . The injudiciousness of parents, a youth's own inexperience, or the absence of external opportunities for the congenial vocation, and their presence for an uncongenial, condemn numbers of men to pass their lives in doing one thing reluctantly and ill, when there are other things which they could have done well and happily. But on women this sentence is imposed by actual law, and by customs equivalent to law. What, in unenlightened societies, colour, race, religion, or in the case of a conquered country, nationality, are to some men, sex is to all women; a peremptory exclusion from almost all honourable occupations, but either such as cannot be fulfilled by others, or such as those others do not think worthy of their acceptance. Sufferings arising from causes of this nature usually meet with so little sympathy, that few persons are aware of the great amount of unhappiness even now produced by the feeling of a wasted life.

Mill (as you may recall from chapter 19) never used eight words to say something when he could think of eighty; but his perception was sharp and his character essentially sympathetic. His argument throughout *The Subjection of Women* is primarily utilitarian: women have proven themselves talented and resourceful despite the appalling constraints placed on them by centuries of cultural tradition, and therefore it can only benefit society to put these proven skills to full use by allowing women to participate in civic life. Mill was enough a man of his era to maintain that women ought not to enter the workplace, since that would remove them from their domestic responsibilities, yet he advocated full political rights for them and equality before the law. Early British feminists like Anderson and feminist sympathizers like Mill moved against the tide of their times.

Things were no better for women on the Continent. French law declared as a bedrock legal principle the notion that "a wife owes obedience to her husband." German law granted every husband the sole right to decide when the breastfeeding of his infant son by his wife should end. (The nursing of daughters, on the other hand, presumably was not sufficiently important to merit regulation by the state.) As late as 1900, German law denied all parental rights over her children to

Edward Degas, *Interior* (1869)   This painting—also known as *The Rape*, though Degas exhibited it under the less inflammatory title—presents a disturbing vision of male-female relations. The narrow bed, simple furnishings, and the prominent display of a sewing box suggest this is a scene of a prostitute and a customer in a hotel room. (In Paris at that time prostitutes often carried sewing boxes, both as an indicator of their profession but also, and more practically, so they could repair their clothing after a customer's rough assault.) The partially undressed woman has turned her back on the man, who stands, dark and menacing, against the door.

any woman who remarried after her husband's death; her new husband, the children's stepfather, assumed sole legal authority over them. Social pressures limited the movements that proper middle-class women could make in the world, while allowing men to roam freely, with predictable results. By 1900 nearly 17 percent of all the children born in France annually were illegitimate, and nearly one-quarter of all adult female deaths either resulted directly from or were complicated by sexually transmitted diseases.[2] In nearly every major statistical category—life expectancy, education, employment, and income, above all—women on the Continent lagged behind men, especially in the working class. To protect women's health and secure their rights under the law, feminist reformers quickly realized, two goals stood out as strategic necessities—suffrage and education.

WHOSE RIGHTS COME FIRST?

Opposition came in many forms and from many directions, some of them surprising. That most men in Europe opposed women's suffrage comes as no surprise. Neither does the opposition mounted by most of the mainstream churches, which dismissed ideas of the "modern woman" as a repudiation of the traditional roles of wife and mother. But large numbers of intelligent, talented, and ambitious women also refused to go along with the call to equal rights—such as the British nurse and organizer Florence Nightingale (1820–1910) and novelist Mary Ward (1851–1920). And often their reason was not so much lack of sympathy for women as passion for reform on behalf of others.

Women against Feminism

Nightingale, whose opposition to the women's movement was particularly fierce, shared many of the attitudes of contemporary males about female abilities and weaknesses. She had served heroically in the Crimean War of 1853–1856 (discussed in chapter 20), overseeing the care of thousands of wounded British soldiers. After the war she established a school in London that launched modern nursing as a profession; she also helped raise funds for the grand Royal Buckinghamshire Hospital outside the city. A deeply pious and determined woman, she maintained throughout her life that the cause of women's rights paled in comparison with the world's other sufferings. In fact, as she wrote to a friend in December 1861, it seemed to her nothing more than middle-class self-absorption:

> Now just look at the degree in which women have sympathy—as far as my experience is concerned. And my experience of women is almost as large as Europe. And it is so intimate too. I have lived and slept in the same bed as English countesses and Prussian *Bauerinnen* [peasant girls].

---

[2]   French law forbade unwed mothers to bring paternity suits against the fathers of their children.

No Roman Catholic *Supérieure* [mother superior] has ever had charge of women of the different creeds that I have had. No woman has excited "passions" among women more than I have. Yet I have no school behind me. My doctrines have not taken hold among women.... No woman that I know has ever *appris à apprendre* [attempted to understand]. And I attribute this to want of sympathy.... It makes me so mad, the Women's Rights talk.... Women crave for being loved, not for loving. They scream out at you for sympathy all day long, [but] they are incapable of giving any in return, for they cannot remember your affairs long enough to do so.... I am sick with indignation at what wives and mothers will do [out] of the most egregious selfishness.

To Mary Ward—who published two dozen novels under her married name, Mrs. Humphrey Ward—suffrage represented a perversion of female character. As she wrote in a magazine editorial in 1889, suffrage reform was an effort to fit women into roles to which they were not suited by nature or by Christian faith:

As voters for or members of School Boards, Boards of Guardians, and other important public bodies, women now have opportunities for public usefulness which must promote the growth of character, and at the same time strengthen among them the social sense and belief. But we believe that the emancipation process has now reached the limits fixed by the physical constitution of women, and by the fundamental difference which must always exist between their main occupations and those of men.... Nothing can be further from our minds than to seek to depreciate the position or the importance of women. It is because we are keenly alive to the enormous value of their special contributions to the community, that we oppose what seems to us likely to endanger that contribution. We are convinced that the pursuit of a mere outward equality with men is for women not only vain but demoralizing. It leads to personal struggle and rivalry, where the only effort of both the great divisions of the human family should be to contribute the characteristic labour and the best gifts of each to the common stock.

The first significant gains in women's rights were rights separate from suffrage itself. Tsarist Russia opened its universities to women in 1867, for example, as did Finland. The United States formally allowed women to enroll in its universities the following year, and Sweden did so the year after that.[3] In 1872 Sweden

First Advances in Women's Rights

---

3   By 1880 fully one-third of all university students in the United States were women.

Female Physician   Emily Shanks (1857–1936), a British-Russian painter who lived in Moscow until 1914, painted this scene of a female physician conducting an ear exam. Women were allowed to study medicine informally in Russia as early as the 1850s, but the first medical degree was not granted until 1867 when Nadezhda Suslova (1843–1918) became the country's first licensed female physician.

outlawed arranged marriages that did not have the expressed consent and agreement of the bride. The first women's labor and trade unions in France were legalized in 1874, and by 1900 French women had gained the right to practice law. In Russia, roughly one of every ten licensed physicians was female by 1914.

The question arises: Why were the dominant European states—the states with the most developed economies, highest literacy rates, most established democratic systems, and most elaborate and sophisticated networks of communication—so resistant to extend suffrage to women? The women's rights movement, after all, had actually arisen originally in those leading nations. Calls for women's full legal and political equality date back to the Enlightenment of the 1700s in England and France and became urgent after the post-1848 compromises left women out of the picture. The answer lies in the fact that many women of the 19th century shared Florence Nightingale's opinion that the developed world had far more pressing issues to deal with than the political rights of European women.

Englishwoman Harriet Martineau (1802–1876), for example, one of the founders of modern sociology, thought the feminist leaders of her time to be *Advocating* downright dangerous; her political passions focused on abolishing the slave *for Others* trade, extending suffrage to working-class men, and improving educational opportunities for women. Public health issues and poor relief, not political rights for middle-class women, were what mattered. Martineau's first two books, *Illustrations of Political Economy* (1832) and *Poor Laws and Paupers Illustrated* (1834), focused on the economic injustice of industrial capitalism and became bestsellers, ironically leaving her financially secure for life. Her three-volume study *Society in America* (1837) is one of the classic works of early sociology. The result of two years of travel in the United States, it offers a sharp critique of American values and practices. The chapter titled "The Political Non-Existence of Women" describes how American women are given "indulgence rather than justice" and have few prospects in life other than marriage. Toward the end of her life, Martineau signed petitions calling for female suffrage but refused to call herself a suffragist.

For many passionate reformers, the problems of the working poor were simply more dire than the plight of middle-class women. To the English activist Beatrice Webb (1858–1943)—coauthor with her husband, Sidney, of *The History of Trade Unionism* (1894) and *Industrial Democracy* (1897) and a founder of the socialist Fabian Society—the prospect of two oppressed individuals, one denied the vote and the other dying of starvation, created an obvious moral choice for action. Another noted socialist of the era, German activist Anna Maier (b. 1870), in her 1912 autobiography described the plight of her early life in distinctly economic rather than sexual terms. To Maier, economic oppression trumped sexual prejudice and had to be dealt with first:

> My father was a weaver and my mother a spooler, although whenever necessary they did any work they could find. I was the youngest of twelve children and learned at an early age what it is to work. . . . [From the age of six] I had to get up at five o'clock every morning to do some spooling before running off to school. My clothes were rags. After a morning at school I hurried home to do some more spooling before having lunch, and then I returned to school for the afternoon lessons, after which I went back to more spooling. . . . When I was thirteen my mother took me by the hand and we went to the manager of a nearby tobacco factory, to see if he would give me a job. He refused, but my mother begged him to take me on since my father had recently died and we were desperate, and so he hired me. . . . The way workers were treated at the factory was hellish. The older women berated the young girls and sometimes even

beat them. . . . Years went by, and eventually a new newspaper, the *Arbe-iterinnen Zeitung* ["Women Workers' Daily"], started to be published; one of the older women smuggled a few copies into the factory. . . . When a friend loaned me a copy I had to hide it at work and could not even let my mother see it at home. I learned many new things and met many new people. . . . When some men founded a workers' organization they said women could not join, but when a party agent came . . . I asked him if I wasn't enough of an adult worker to be a member. I remember that he was embarrassed at first, but he finally spoke up: "When do you want to start?" I joined, and remain a member to this very day.

The gradual success of antipoverty programs and the legalization of labor unions indirectly helped the cause of women's suffrage, however, because as they alleviated the sufferings of the working poor, they freed up energies to pursue other goals.

SUFFRAGISTS AND SUFFRAGETTES

National Society for Women's Suffrage

Suffragists and suffragettes were not the same thing. They pursued the same end—women's right to vote—but their methods differed. In simplest terms, **suffragists** worked peaceably and within the legal system for women's rights, whereas **suffragettes** favored confrontation, aggressive action, and, whenever they thought it necessary, even violence to change society. Britain's **National Society for Women's Suffrage** formed in 1867 and provided a model for similar groups that sprang up quickly on the Continent—like the VVV (*Vereeniging voor Vrouwenkiesrecht*, or "Society for Women's Legal Rights") in Holland. In 1878 a loose network of these associations convened the first international congress for women's rights in Paris, where they embraced the terms *feminist* and *suffragist* and charted out strategies for their cause. These drew heavily on their observations of (male) electoral politics of the age, which included fostering political alliances and courting sympathetic members of the press. Earlier campaigns by women to promote the abolition of slavery and alcohol had given them vital experience at shaping public opinion. But in the end these early feminist organizations proved more successful in enrolling members than in bringing about significant reform. Constitutional change is a slow-moving business, especially when it faces entrenched resistance.

The denial of female suffrage lingered into the 20th century, which resulted in a dramatic change in some reformers' tactics. Led by the redoubtable **Emmeline Pankhurst** (1858–1928) and her three daughters, Christabel

(1880–1958), Sylvia (1882–1960), and Adela (1885–1961), the new group *Women's* called themselves suffragettes. These activists broke away from the main suf- *Social and* fragist association in Britain in 1903 and established the **Women's Social and** *Political* **Political Union** (WSPU). The WSPU was a distinctly more militant organiza- *Union* tion than the National Society for Women's Suffrage; its motto was "Deeds, not words." The suffragettes provoked anger and outrage everywhere they went. Unaffiliated with any political party, they nevertheless attended and intention- ally disrupted political meetings by the score. They protested outside Parlia- ment and sometimes chained themselves to its doors; some vandalized shop windows and churches. One suffragette committed suicide by running into the path of a racehorse owned by the royal family to draw attention to the plight of women.

Pankhurst herself engaged in little overt violence other than trying to force her way into Parliamentary meetings (for which she was imprisoned for six weeks)—and once slapping a policeman to be arrested. But she declared that "the condition of our sex is so deplorable that it is our duty to break the law in order to

MRS PANKHURST ARRESTED IN VICTORIA STREET. FEB. 13. 1908.

Fighting for Women's Suffrage   Born in Manchester, in northern England, Emmeline Pankhurst (1858-1928) was one of the most prominent suffragettes. Repeatedly arrested (as here, in 1905), she regularly staged hunger strikes and was subjected to force-feeding— experiences that inspired her to more radical tactics in society, such as arson. Her daughter Christabel (1880-1958) followed in her mother's footsteps as a leader of the Women's Social and Political Union, but her other daughter Adela (1885-1961) repudiated Emmeline's embrace of violent methods. Emmeline responded by giving Adela £20 and a one-way ticket to Australia.

draw attention to the reasons why we do so." In a speech in the United States in 1913, she described her experience and the WSPU's tactics:

> I do not come here as an advocate, because whatever position the suffrage movement may occupy in the United States of America, in England it has passed beyond the realm of advocacy and it has entered into the sphere of practical politics. It has become the subject of revolution and civil war, and so tonight I am not here to advocate woman suffrage. American suffragists can do that very well for themselves. I am here as a soldier who has temporarily left the field of battle in order to explain—it seems strange it should have to be explained—what civil war is like when civil war is waged by women. . . . I am here [also] as a person who, according to the law courts of my country, . . . is of no value to the community at all; and I am adjudged because of my life to be a dangerous person, under sentence of penal servitude in a convict prison. So you see there is some special interest in hearing so unusual a person address you. I dare say, in the minds of many of you—you will perhaps forgive me this personal touch—that I do not look either very like a soldier or very like a convict, and yet I am both. . . . We have brought the government of England to this position, that it has to face this alternative: either women are to be killed, or women are to have the vote. I ask American men in this meeting, what would you say if in your State you were faced with that alternative, that you must either kill them or give them their citizenship,—women, many of whom you respect, women whom you know have lived useful lives, women whom you know, even if you do not know them personally, are animated with the highest motives, women who are in pursuit of liberty and the power to do useful public service? Well, there is only one answer to that alternative; there is only one way out of it, unless you are prepared to put back civilization two or three generations; you must give those women the vote. Now that is the outcome of our civil war.

Ultimately, she was arrested several dozen times before Parliament finally granted unrestricted women's suffrage in 1928.

Suffragettes on the Continent followed similar measures. In France, Hubertine Auclert (1848–1914) triggered a wave of copycat protests when she smashed a ballot box in a municipal election in Paris to express her disgust at being unable to vote. Madeleine Pelletier (1874–1939), a physician and France's first female licensed psychiatrist, made her mark by agitating not only for suffrage but also for women's rights to contraception and abortion (then a taboo subject) and by protesting the normative ideas of femininity by dressing as a man, complete with cane and bowler hat.[4] Moreover, she continued to provide abortion services despite their illegality. A German socialist, Clara Zetkin (1857–1933), edited a radical newspaper (*Die Gleichheit*, "Equality") and invited arrest by taking a public position against World War I.

Many imprisoned suffragettes protested their arrests by going on hunger strikes, hoping to win sympathy for their cause by sacrificing themselves even to the point of death. Governments quickly responded by ordering forced feedings, a brutal process in which the woman was bound to a chair, had rubber tubing pushed down her throat or through her nostrils and into her stomach, and then had a loose porridge poured into her. Worse still, the British government passed the "Cat and Mouse" Act (officially, the Temporary Discharge of Prisoners for Ill Health Act) in 1913. This ordered police to release from prison any hunger-striking suffragette, only to rearrest her after she had regained her health on the outside. The forced feedings and repeated arrests swung public sympathy toward the women prisoners—especially when their sufferings were made public. In her memoir, Lady Constance Bulwer-Lytton (1869–1923) wrote of disguising herself as a poor seamstress to avoid receiving preferential treatment because of her noble status. The harsh treatment she received in prison resulted in a stroke that left her right arm paralyzed. She taught herself to write with her left hand and produced *Prisons and Prisoners: Some Personal Experiences* (1914) in a year.

But extreme actions, including terrorist ones, cost the movement public sympathy too. To chain oneself to the houses of Parliament was one thing; to set fire to the homes of Parliamentarians was another. In February 1913 a group of WSPU members burned down the home of David Lloyd George, then the Chancellor of the Exchequer. Lloyd George privately supported women's suffrage but officially opposed it in 1913, for fear that it might

Rallying for Women's Suffrage Soon after its appearance, the German government banned this poster calling for a rally on behalf of women's suffrage in support of International Women's Day (March 8, 1914). Most copies have been destroyed.

---

4 Asked once why she dressed as a man, Pelletier responded, "I'll show my breasts when men start wearing pants that show their pricks."

MAP 21.1 Winning the Vote: Women's Suffrage in the Greater West, 1906–1971 In some ways, women's right to vote was held hostage to the conflicts that culminated in the world wars that dominated the 20th century.

disrupt preparations for the coming World War. The following year another suffragette took an axe to a painting of Venus by the great 17th-century Spanish artist Diego Velázquez in the National Gallery in London. She claimed that she was merely doing to one beautiful woman what society was doing to all.

As dedicated as the suffragists were, and as brave and selfless as many of the suffragettes were, winning the vote ultimately resulted more from the economic conditions in Europe after World War I. Before that, only Finland (1906) and Norway (1913) had universal suffrage; Denmark passed it in 1915. After the war, women were enfranchised in half of Europe—the reward, men in government claimed, for women's tremendous war efforts (see Map 21.1).

LOVE AND SEX

Helene Stöcker (1869–1943) was a leading German feminist who advocated suffrage but devoted most of her prodigious energy to women's sexual health. That issue turned out to be an increasing part of redefining a woman's role. It also went hand in hand with the growing availability of information about sex throughout society—and growing controversies over birth control.

Stöcker founded the Society for the Protection of Mothers in 1905 (later renamed the German Society for the Protection of Mothers and for Sexual Reform) and edited two journals—*Mutterschutz* ("Care for Mothers") and *Die neue Generation* ("The New Generation"). Through these she campaigned for publicly available sex education, including contraception and abortion, and advocated for the legal rights of children born out of marriage. In 1906 she published *Women and Love: A Manifesto for Emancipating Women and Men in Germany,* which described her plan to reinvent male–female relationships, preferably within marriage but not necessarily so. Her goal, she insisted, was not just to pursue equality for its own sake; it was to help relationships between men and women to become more true, more intimate, and more rich. The greatest harm of the gender inequity of the age was not the legal injustice of it, she argued, but the emotional aridity of the relationships it fostered and even encouraged.

Stöcker envisioned a world in which any woman who wanted to do so could rise above the traditional path of being a dutiful daughter, then a quiet, uncomplaining wife, and then a loving, selfless mother. If a woman wanted, she could pursue an independent life filled with emotional, intellectual, and sexual richness. Stöcker's essay "The Modern Woman" (1893) put the case with her typical candor:

> I am describing a unique species, . . . the modern woman, . . . who sets out from the shelter of her father's household . . . in order to gain financial independence, the prerequisite of every freedom. . . . The modern woman does not wish to become man-like but only to become a happier, because a more free, person, one who continues to grow in her unique womanly way. She long ago gave up the childish complaint that she was not born male; rather, she has learned to appreciate her unique feminine strength as a rare gift, a thing set apart, something beyond traditional categories. . . . [The modern woman] is born for love. With the fires of her nature—with all her heart, soul, and sensuality—she craves intimacy, and she needs it more than a man does. . . . She yearns to give and receive love as a woman, not simply to sit quietly by while clever men talk to one another. . . . She craves freedom too, and just as intensely. Only these two things, love and freedom, combined, can grant her the kind of inner peacefulness found among truly liberated people. She therefore maintains a critical distance, a composure, in order to avoid being overwhelmed by her intense youthful sensuality, lest, after a brief thrill, she end up making herself and another truly miserable. But she knows one

thing all too well: The greatest happiness that life can offer develops only in a relationship between two fully free people, a free man and a free woman. Of this there is no doubt.

Stöcker's concern was for a kind of freedom that included but was larger than mere political rights. She wanted, as did many people of her generation, to redefine sexual identity so as to free it from the constraints of Victorian morality. Surely there must be alternatives to brutish labor for working-class women and dreary if respectable marriage for the middle class. The 19th century witnessed a constantly growing call for just such alternatives.

Debating the "Woman Question"   Not everyone joined in the chorus. The "Woman Problem" or "Woman Question" was analogous to nationalism: just as the air was filled with passionate discussions of the "Englishness" of the English, the "Germanness" of the Germans, or the "Spanishness" of the Spaniards, so too were many people intent to define the essential qualities of womanhood. Advances in science were of little help here, since Darwinian evolution (discussed in the next chapter) appeared to reduce human life to a set of predetermined biological functions. And related sciences did not seem any more enlightened.

A popular American medical guide of the 1880s, *The Physical Life of Woman: Advice to the Maiden, Wife, and Mother,* by the doctor George Napheys, asserted that "the vast majority of women" possess only "moderate" sexual appetites, and "only in very rare instances do women experience one tithe of the sexual feeling which is familiar to most men. Many of them are entirely frigid, and not even in marriage do they ever perceive any real desire." A German gynecologist, Otto Adler, estimated in 1904 that "as many as forty percent" of all women experience no sexual desire in their lifetimes. Anatomists who studied the brain announced confidently that men are by nature between 12 and 20 percent more intelligent than women. Intellectual work, they proclaimed, when performed by women, diverts bodily energies away from their natural reproductive mission. An Englishwoman studying medicine at Cambridge's Girton College in 1888 summarized the attitude of physicians around her, in an anonymous article in the *Westminster Review,* as a sarcastic warning:

Women, beware! Beware! You are on the brink of destruction! You have hitherto been engaged only in crushing your waists [by wearing corsets], now you are attempting to cultivate your minds! You have been merely dancing all night in the foul air of ballrooms; now you are beginning to spend your mornings in study. You have been incessantly stimulating your emotions with concerts and operas, with French plays and French novels; now you are exerting your understanding to learn Greek and solve propositions in Euclid. Beware! Oh, beware!! Science pronounces that the woman who studies—is lost!

Knowledge of sex, and confusion about it, abounded. Condoms, which had been used in Europe at least since the early 18th century, were readily available at taverns, pharmacists, and outdoor markets.[5] Other methods of contraception included cervical caps and diaphragms (made of vulcanized rubber after 1850) and herbal abortifacients like Queen Anne's lace, which consisted of the crushed seeds of flowering wild carrots. The most commonly used methods were presumably *coitus interruptus* and what is known today as the "rhythm method." Abortion was illegal everywhere in Europe but was generally available— at a high price and at great risk to health. Christian churches had always condemned abortion, but doctrines on contraception were another matter. Until such measures became widely available, starting in midcentury, the churches had felt no need to take a definitive position except to condemn *coitus interruptus* as the "sin of Onan"—a reference to the tale in Genesis 38. (Onan was the brother of Judah, and according to the custom of the times Onan had a responsibility, after Judah's early death, to wed and provide offspring for Judah's childless widow. When Onan instead "spilled his seed on the ground" by interrupting the sexual union with his sister-in-law, God condemned him to death for disobedience to the Law.) Whatever the cause, birth rates among the middle class declined significantly between 1850 and 1914. In Britain, for example, one-quarter of all middle-class families had eight or more children in 1825. By 1925 fully one-half of all families had only one or two children each, and one family of every six was childless.

Arguing over "Family Management"

The distribution of information about birth control—"family management" or "family limitation," as it was known at the time—was highly contentious. Western countries struggled with the tension between traditional morals and the free exchange of scientific knowledge. In the United States, the distribution of material about contraception and sexually transmitted diseases was legal until 1870, when the federal government enacted the Comstock Law—which included such medical material in its definition of "obscene literature and articles of immoral use." President Theodore Roosevelt (1901–1909) spoke for many when he called family limitation "one of the most unpleasant and unwholesome features of modern life."

But women's demand for reliable contraception continued to grow. In 1877 a pamphlet on contraception by an American physician was published in England and sold 125,000 copies in one year. Aletta Jacobs (1854–1929), Holland's first female physician, established Europe's first birth control clinic in Amsterdam in

---

[5] Condoms occasionally were sold at concession stands in theaters. The German army after 1870 regularly handed them out to soldiers when they were about to go off duty.

1882, dispensing information about contraception and the materials for it. She next opened a similar clinic for poor women, to whom she gave care and medical advice for free. (In later years, she dedicated herself to the antiwar movement and helped to found the Women's International League for Peace and Freedom.) A German physician in Breslau (today's city of Wrocław, Poland), Richard Richter, published the first treatise on the use of intrauterine devices in 1909. Alarmed by this proliferation of materials, social critics in Germany began to express concern that the ensuing labor shortage would invite immigration by "alien people—especially Slavs and perhaps the eastern European Jews too."

Ignorance of sexual matters was widespread and, to an extent, deliberately imposed. If the moral code of "proper society" forbade the discussion of sex and tried to control the distribution of scientific knowledge about it, then it is not surprising that many men and women began their sexual lives without any accurate understanding of what they were starting. Experts still warned that masturbation was medically harmful to both men and women, since it depleted the body of "vital fluids and energies." That depletion supposedly left the body, according to a medical guide of the time, more vulnerable to "seminal weakness, impotence, dysury [painful urination], *tabes dorsalis* [a manifestation of syphilis], pulmonary consumption, dyspepsia, dimness of sight, vertigo, epilepsy, hypochondriasis, loss of memory, manalgia [catatonia], fatuity [dementia], and death." Male physicians treating their middle-class patients for "female hysteria"—a catch-all term for a supposed ailment characterized by emotional excess, anxiety, insomnia, and irritability—eased their symptoms by massaging the sexual organs until the women achieved a "nervous paroxysm" that the physicians steadfastly refused to recognize as a sexual orgasm.[6]

Male Antimasturbation Device
Masturbation had long been criticized in European culture as a sin or a personal failing, but it only became regarded as clinically unhealthy in the early 18th century, when a series of pseudo-scientific works warned of its supposedly harmful effects. In Victorian times, concerns about the dangers of masturbation grew so extensive that many parents began to employ physical methods to prevent their sons from indulging in the fearful practice. This piece dates to 1880. Made of copper, it was worn on a belt to protect boys both from masturbation and from unintentional nocturnal emissions.

Much of Western society held two contradictory beliefs at once—in the sexual rapaciousness of women and in their natural sexlessness. The explan-

---

[6]   Complaints by the doctors about the time needed for this treatment led directly to the invention of the vibrator—originally marketed as a medical device.

ation lay in the widespread view that there are two types of women.[7] Assuming that most women—proper women, in society's eyes—had no interest in sex, many felt there was no need to educate them about it, and the consequence was entrenched ignorance.

THE FEMALE IDENTITY

Many of the era's greatest works of literature are dedicated to exploring female identity in both its generalized essentials and its individual quirks. These are great works of art—and their authors are all male (see Table 21.1). Women writers also explored female character in depth, but generally with less of a singular focus on a specific woman, as in the works written by men, and generally with less artistic success. George Eliot's *Middlemarch* (1872), discussed in chapter 19, was undeniably the greatest novel written by a European woman in the late 19th century; the first in the 20th century by a woman to have truly changed the very shape of the novel was Virginia Woolf's *Mrs. Dalloway* (1925), which we will pick up in chapter 22. In the intervening fifty-plus years, women in every Western country continued to produce excellent fiction (Willa Cather and Edith Wharton in the United States, for example), but were their aims any less revolutionary than that of their male counterparts, and if so, why? It is an important question. Why, at the very time when the status of women in Western society was being most passionately and universally debated, were women novelists, poets, and playwrights stimulating any less of a debate? No doubt the deep involvement of so many women in suffragist and suffragette work partially explains the lack; the times called for action, not novels or poems. Moreover, political themes seldom make for enduring literature.

Women in Literature

TABLE 21.1   Literature of Female Identity: A Sampler

Madame Bovary (1857), by Gustave Flaubert

Anna Karenina (1878), by Leo Tolstoy

The Portrait of a Lady (1881), by Henry James

Fortunata and Jacinta (1887), by Benito Pérez Galdós

Hedda Gabler (1890), by Henrik Ibsen

Tess of the d'Urbervilles (1891), by Thomas Hardy

The New Woman (1893), by Bolesław Prus

Effi Briest (1894), by Theodor Fontane.

---

[7] As one physician in Oxford put it in 1914, "Speaking as a doctor, I can tell you that nine out of ten women are indifferent to or actively dislike [sex]; the tenth, who enjoys it, will always be a harlot."

Edith Wharton   One of the leading novelists of her time, Edith Wharton (1862–1937) came from New York's wealthy and privileged society, a world that she examines in works like *The House of Mirth* (1905), *The Custom of the Country* (1913), and *The Age of Innocence* (1920). Living in France when World War I broke out, she worked tirelessly to help the injured, the unemployed, and the displaced.

Sex itself may provide another explanation—not gender, but actual sex. European fiction and drama from 1850 to 1914 were dominated by the realist and naturalist schools, which aimed for a fuller and more detailed depiction of daily life. It lingered on its characters' gritty surroundings, the sounds and smells of the cities they inhabited, and the sense of despair and misery created by wretched food, hard labor, and oppressive social mores. A goal of these writers was to depict the whole array of pressures, demands, irritations, and longings that shape human lives. One of the greatest naturalist writers in France, Émile Zola (1840–1902), wrote a series of twenty novels with interlocking characters, families, settings, and events in an effort to portray the entire panorama of French life during the Second Empire. His descriptions of social snobbery, grueling manual labor, inadequate housing, the ruin of alcoholism, prostitution, marital bliss, and marital despair are often unnervingly vivid.

Many realist and naturalist writers depicted sexual relations with a candor that set the Victorians' teeth on edge. Although tame by 21st-century standards, the frank sexuality in European literature from 1850 to 1914 may have been off-putting to women writers—something they did not wish to attempt or felt that they could not do. Even Virginia Woolf, as late as her death in 1944, allowed no sex to enter any of her books.[8] Women writers already worked in the face of enough social prejudices. Did they feel that writing frankly about sexual feelings might be too much? No one can say for sure.

Women in Art   Overlooked for centuries, women artists came into their own at this time. The 18th century saw a handful of successful women artists, but not many, and most of them fitted into rather than challenged the prevailing attitudes and style. One such forerunner was the Austrian painter Angelica Kauffman (1741–1807); she spent many years in Italy and Britain, painted in the Neo-Classical style, and was famous for her portraits of scenes from history and her popular depictions of

---

8   Woolf's most subversive novel, the time-shifting, gender-bending fantasy *Orlando*, published in 1928, was inspired by her lesbian affair with Vita Sackville-West. But it contains no trace of eroticism.

scenes from the plays of William Shakespeare.

The women artists who emerged in the 19th century were more daring in their choices of topic and style. Eager to endorse the advancement of women, they highlighted the beauty and dignity of everyday women (not just the aristocrats) and their toil. An especially common motif in their works were scenes of women reading—an image that suggests the emergence of independent minds. Louise Abbéma (1853–1927), a French sculptor and painter, became famous while still in her twenties with her portraits of two of the great actresses of the time, Sarah Bernhardt (1844–1923) and Jeanne Samary (1857–1890)— each of whom may have been her lover. Exhibiting regularly at the Paris Salon, Abbéma also became a noted printmaker for various journals. Emma Lampert Cooper (1855–1920), an American, studied painting in Holland and specialized in landscapes, several of which won prizes at various World Expositions. The best-known, and arguably the best, woman painter of the century was another American, Mary Cassatt (1844–1926), who figured large in the artistic movement of Impressionism. Her works explored every facet of women's lives, from birth to death, and she experimented with style more so than any other artists associated with the Modern Woman.

Mary Cassatt, *Woman Reading*   Mary Cassatt (1844–1926) was born into a well-to-do American family but spent her adult life based in France. Her independent spirit, coupled with innate talent and hard work, turned her into one of the leading painters of the second half of the 19th century. Most of her best work captures the inner lives of women and children, which she portrays with affectionate intimacy but never sentimentality.

EDUCATION AND WORK

As the European industrial economy expanded, the late 19th century saw explosive growth in public education across the West. Even factory workers at the low end of the pay scale needed to be functionally literate and numerate, if only so that they could read the regulations governing the shop floor. Prior to the revolutions of 1848, most Western states had established only public secondary schools. Elementary education was thought to be needed only by the relatively well-to-do, who hired private tutors for their young children, which left poor working-class

Expansion of Public Education

youths free to be exploited in the factories. When the 19th century began, only Germany had a system of state-run primary schools; France created its system in 1833, and the schooling was not made compulsory until a few years later.

For most working-class girls, formal education ended there. France did not open its secondary schools to girls until 1880, and by the end of the century there were only three dozen such schools for girls in the entire country. Germany's first secondary school for girls appeared in 1872. In Britain, primary schooling became compulsory in 1880 but was not run by the state until 1902. In the Netherlands compulsory state-run schools did not exist for either boys or girls before 1901, but private primary and secondary education had long been among the best in Europe. Usually the creation of public primary education systems followed within a decade of the outlawing of child labor.

Secondary education expanded rapidly, as the economy created a demand for better-educated workers. New careers as railway employees, postal workers, shipping clerks, civil servants, accountants, public works employees, secretaries, teachers, journalists, and legal aides all appeared in the late 19th century—and all needed preparation. Public schools provided new opportunities for women, since the education of children seemed to many to be a natural extension of women's traditional role as caregivers. The United States led the way, with fully two-thirds of all primary and secondary school teachers being female by 1890. Europe's figures did not measure up, but the majority of primary school teachers in each country were women.

College for Women

So great was the demand, in fact, that entire colleges for training teachers were created; along with special colleges for medical training, they were the first cracks in the walls that kept women out of the university system. Aside from professional colleges, the first colleges for women were established in the 1870s and 1880s—such as Newnham and Girton Colleges in Cambridge and Lady Margaret Hall in Oxford—but were not formally accepted into their university systems until well into the 20th century. Overall, the numbers of women in all areas of education continued to grow until, on the eve of World War I in 1914, perhaps as many as 12–15 percent of European undergraduate students were female. In non-industrialized parts of Europe, such as partitioned Poland and Austrian-controlled Hungary, upper-class women created underground networks of elementary and secondary education with the dual aims of improving the status of women and promoting Polish and Magyar nationalism.

Montessori's Educational Methods

A different and special chapter in the development of education opened with the career of **Maria Montessori** (1870–1952), the first female licensed physician in Italy. Her training in psychology led to an interest in the education of mentally handicapped children. In 1896, with the support of the Italian minister for education, she worked with a group of special-needs children whom the state schools had dismissed as uneducable. Using her own experimental methods, she produced an impressive result: within three years, her eight-year-old students outscored public school students in reading and writing. This led to her opening a new elementary school in a rough neighborhood in Rome in 1907, where she wanted to see what effect her methods would have on mainstream students.

Montessori's methods were controversial among educators and remain so today, but produced consistently superior performance in every category, including social behavior, up to the age of twelve. Her method was based on the notion of self-directed education, or "spontaneous self-development." She believed that children, being naturally inquisitive, learn better by being allowed to explore at their own rate than by being drilled with data according to a state plan. As she wrote in *Education for a New World* (1947), the teachers in her schools thus acted more as facilitators or guides than as deliverers of knowledge:

> Scientific observation has established that education is not what the teacher gives; education is a natural process spontaneously carried out by the human individual, and is acquired not by listening to words but by experiences upon the environment. The task of the teacher becomes that of preparing a series of motives of cultural activity, spread over a specially prepared environment, and then refraining from obtrusive interference. Human teachers can only help the great work that is being done, as servants help the master. Doing so, they will be witnesses to the unfolding of the human soul and to the rising of a New Man who will not be a victim of events, but will have the clarity of vision to direct and shape the future of human society.

Schools using her methods, whether officially affiliated with the International Montessori Association or not, began to spring up across Europe and especially in the United States.

Meanwhile, the numbers of women in the workplace also increased. The development of the telegraph and telephone systems created a need for well-trained operators, whereas machines like the typewriter (invented in 1829, with the first commercially produced typewriter appearing in 1870) virtually created the modern business office, with its attendant pools of secretaries, clerks, and administrative managers. Women thus became essential elements of the modern commercial economy, all the while treated as inferior to men. Newspapers and magazines dedicated to them multiplied exponentially. Hundreds of popular

Women in the Workplace

songs, plays, and paintings focused on the **New Woman** of the start of the century, whether to celebrate, lampoon, or pillory her. Some were gently playful, as in the popular stage play *The New Woman* by Sydney Grundy (see the poster that opens this chapter), or in this anonymous poem of 1898:

> Rock-a-bye baby, for father is near.
> Mother is "biking"—she never is here!
> Out in the park she's scorching all day
> Or at some meeting is talking away!
> She's the king-pin at the women's rights show,
> Teaching poor husbands the way they should go!
> Close then your eyes; there's dishes to do.
> Rock-a-bye baby, 'tis Pa sings to you!

The Montessori Method   Beginning her career as a physician, Maria Montessori (1870–1952) was soon drawn to the field of education and child development. She herself never taught in the schools she opened. Regarding education as a science, she conducted research on educational methods, equipment, and personnel, as well as on interactions between teachers and children—all while she also planned the curriculum, trained new teachers in her methods, and oversaw administration of the schools. By the time she died, over four thousand "Montessori schools" were in existence around the world.

The reference to "biking" alludes to a popular new invention: the chain-driven bicycle. Earlier bicycles had employed direct drive—that is, the pedals were attached directly to the hub of the large front wheel. Although capable of significant speed, these early bicycles were notoriously unstable and required a man's strength to pedal. Chain-driven bicycles, however, suited women and were quickly adopted as a new means of locomotion that was doubly important. They enabled, in those pre-automobile days, a wider degree of maneuverability, and they symbolized, in their very propulsion, the spirit of independence shown by the New Woman.[9]

Free to move her own person, to control her own sexual life, to attend school, to pursue a career, and to seek a new kind of fulfillment in life, the New Woman entered the 20th century full of hope.

---

[9]   Bicycles also helped to get rid of the Victorian corsets and stays that had for so long restricted women's movements.

The finest achievement of the new woman has been personal liberty. This is the foundation of civilization; and as long as any one class is watched suspiciously, even fondly guarded, and protected, so long will that class not only be weak, and treacherous, individually, but parasitic, and a collective danger to the community. Who has not heard wives commended for wheedling their husbands out of money, or joked because they are hopelessly extravagant? As long as caprice and scheming are considered feminine virtues, as long as man is the only wage-earner, doling out sums of money, or scattering lavishly, so long will women be degraded,

Spirit of Independence This advertisement for the Grand Manège Central, a popular bicycling track and park in Paris, dates from about 1890. The American suffragist Susan B. Anthony (1820–1906) once declared: "I think [the bicycle] has done more to emancipate women than anything else in the world. It gives women a feeling of freedom and self-reliance. I stand and rejoice every time I see a woman ride by on a wheel... the picture of free, untrammeled womanhood."

The New Woman

even if they are perfectly contented, and men are willing to labor to keep them in idleness! Although individual women from pre-historic times have accomplished much, as a class they have been set aside to minister to men's comfort. But when once the higher has been tried, civilization repudiates the lower. Men have come to see that no advance can be made with one half-humanity set apart merely for the functions of sex; that children are quite liable to inherit from the mother, and should have opportunities to inherit the accumulated ability and culture and character that is produced only by intellectual and civil activity. The world has tried to move with men for dynamos, and "clinging" women impeding every step of progress, in arts, science, industry, professions, they have been a thousand years behind men because forced into seclusion. They have been oversexed. They have naturally not been impressed with their duties to society, in its myriad needs, or with their own value as individuals. The new woman, in the sense of the best woman, the flower of all the womanhood of past ages, has come to stay—if civilization is to endure.

So declared *The New Womanhood*, a best-selling manifesto of 1904 by Winnifred Harper Cooley. This hymn of victory to come is likewise expressed in fictional form in *The Doll* (1890) and *The New Woman* (1893) by one of Poland's greatest novelists, Bolesław Prus (1847–1912).

THE "WOMAN QUESTION" FOR MUSLIMS

Qasim Amin's Call for Women's Rights

Yet another book championed the rights of women and called for an end to their social seclusion, free access to education, and a guarantee of full political equality. In fact, it was also entitled *The New Woman* and appeared between Prus's novel and Harper Cooley's manifesto. It was *Al-Mar'a al-jadida*, published in Cairo in 1901, by **Qasim Amin** (1863–1908). His call was not alone, but it quickly ran into struggles over Arab nationalism and Ottoman decline.

Amin's father was a high Ottoman official of Kurdish descent and his mother an upper-class Egyptian. Apart from four years in France in the 1880s, he spent the whole of his brief life in Egypt. While in Paris, Amin had made contact with the great Islamic reformer Muhammad Ali Pasha (introduced in chapter 20), who inspired his conviction that Islam needed to remake itself to adapt to the modern world. Otherwise, it risked losing out to the conservative Wahhabi movement, which regarded every social innovation as an affront to sacred tradition.

To Amin (more so even than to Muhammad Ali himself), the most urgently needed reform was to improve the social status of women in Muslim society. He called for four essential changes: (1) women's access to education, (2) a constitutional guarantee of political equality, (3) abolition of the customary wearing of the veil, and (4) reform of marriage laws to deny husbands their rights to take multiple wives and to repudiate any wife at will. To make his full argument required two books, and *The New Woman* had been preceded in 1899 by the legal treatise *The Emancipation of Women* (*Tahrir al-mar'a*). These were bold positions to take even in the Islamic Enlightenment atmosphere of turn-of-the-century Egypt, and Amin stirred up considerable opposition. For several years he engaged in a public debate with conservative jurists on these issues, but when his proposals made little headway, he shifted tactics and devoted the bulk of his time to the establishment of Cairo University (1908), which Amin and his cofounders intended to be a Western-style university emphasizing liberal thought. It could therefore serve as a complement, even a counterbalance, to the religiously based al-Azhar University, which dated back to the year 972.

As in Europe, the question of women's status in the Islamic world was related to the issue of nationalism. Tanzimat efforts (1839–1876) to modernize the

Ottoman state proved, as we saw in chapter 20, to be impossible. For conservative *Opponents* Muslims, especially those of Arab ethnicity, modernization violated both the *of the* spirit of the faith and the dictates of nature; authentic Islamic identity and West- *"Modern* ern notions of human rights, democracy, and social progress, they insisted, were *Woman"* fundamentally incompatible. For many others, especially those who welcomed the socially liberalizing aspect of Tanzimat but rejected its insistence on the continuation of Ottomanism, the future lay in local autonomy, independence from both the universalizing claims of Ottoman political overlordship and ethnically Arab religious supervision. They wanted to break away from both constraints and establish instead new provincial societies that were free to define their own Islamic and national identities. Abu al-Qasim al-Shabbi (1909–1934), a Berber-Tunisian poet and social critic of the era, put it bluntly: "Everything the Arabs have produced throughout all the long centuries of their history is colorless and utterly devoid of inspiration."

Writers experimented with new literary forms, especially the novel, be- cause of its ability to express criticism of social ills and depict the struggles *Struggle* of individuals against various forms of oppression. As in Europe, the travails *against* of women were a theme for many novelists and playwrights, including *Oppression* Egypt's Taha Husayn (1889–1973), Mahmud Taymur (1894–1973), and *in Literature* Tawfiq al-Hakim (1898–1987). In al-Hakim's 1934 play based on *A Thou-* *and Life* *sand and One Nights*, Scheherazade's storytelling helps her survive her murderous husband, and at the play's end she achieves a mystical union with the ancient goddess Isis.

The reformers pressed especially for girls' rights to education and the reform of marriage practices to prohibit forcing girls into arranged marriages against their wills. Namik Kemal (1840–1888), an Ottoman court official turned playwright and journalist, championed girls' education in countless articles and essays. Midhat Pasha (1822–1884) edited a daily newspaper in Istanbul, *Tercüman-ı Hakikat* ("The Interpreter of Truth"), that promoted social reform and distributed a weekly supplement designed especially for schoolchildren. Midhat also wrote more than one hundred books of history, popular science, and social reform, reaching an enormous audience.

But the best-known feminist of her time was the Egyptian reformer **Huda'i Sha'arawi** (1878–1947), who organized a women's self-help society and the Union of Egyptian Women-Intellectuals. She also founded the Egyptian Feminist Union, in 1923, and served as its president until her death. Sha'arawi focused her prodigious energies on political involvement, speaking at conferences across Europe and organizing feminist demonstrations throughout Egypt. In addition to her book *Harem Years: The Memoirs of an Egyptian Feminist*, she published two

Huda'i Sha'arawi   The leading pioneer in feminism in the Islamic world, Huda'i Sha'arawi (1879–1947) was also prominent in the protest movement against Britain's colonization of Egypt. In the mass protests against the regime of Egyptian president Hosni Mubarak in 2011, many people carried signs and banners bearing her image.

feminist journals called *The Egyptian Woman*—one in French (*L'Égyptienne*) and one in Arabic (*al-Misriyya*).[10]

A few schools for girls opened in the 1880s and 1890s and received public funds, but more girls were probably enrolled in private or missionary schools than in the state-run system. Illiteracy remained a problem for both boys and girls, however; as late as 1914 perhaps only 10 percent of the Ottoman population could read and write. In general, reforms were most successful in those countries that had both close commercial and diplomatic relations with Europe and a higher percentage of non-Muslims among their populations: Egypt, Lebanon, Palestine, and what would eventually become the nation of Turkey. The countries of the Arabian Peninsula, Iraq, and Iran, however, saw little change. As late as 1908, in fact, the slave trade remained legal throughout much of Ottoman society, so long as the slaves in question were non-Muslim females. The American ambassador to Constantinople during World War I famously noted that Armenian girls could be purchased in Turkish cities for as little as eighty cents apiece.

---

[10]   Sha'arawi's memoir was left unfinished when she died in 1947. The original Arabic version—entitled *Mudhakkirati* ("My Memoirs")—was published in 1981 in Cairo. An English translation appeared first in 1986.

As nationalist aspirations among peoples long ruled by the Ottomans rose, certain ethnic and cultural practices not formally part of Islamic teaching began to revive. Two of these are especially significant in regard to women: honor killing and genital cutting. Neither is formally accepted by mainstream Islamic tradition today, whether Sunni or Shi'ite. Both, however, were widely practiced in the Islamic world and experienced a resurgence during the Ottoman breakup.

Honor Killing and Genital Cutting

Honor killing has a long history in many parts of the Islamic world, dating back to well before the arrival in the 7th century of the Prophet Muhammad, but it is hardly a custom unique to Arab culture. The ancient Romans practiced it: the paternal authority (*patria potestas*) of the head of a family entitled him, and in fact demanded of him, that he preserve the good honor and repute of his household by eliminating those whose licentiousness brought dishonor to the clan. Many of the pre-Christian Germanic tribes demanded that families protect the moral uprightness (*mundium*) of their clans by killing those unmarried females who lost their virginity.[11] To the Muslims who followed the practice, two distinct concepts of honor predominated. Male honor (*hasab*) was both hereditary and personal,

Modern but Pure   The contrast between the veiled Muslim women seated on a beach near Istanbul and the lightly clad male rower is striking in this photograph from around 1900. The modernizing Tanzimat reforms of the mid-19th century paid little attention to promoting the rights of women in the Ottoman state.

---

[11]   The Salian Franks allowed any member of the family to kill a wayward female. Early Burgundians ruled that a woman who had sex outside of marriage was to be drowned in a swamp.

the reputation held by virtue of one's birth and family status as well as one's personal integrity; like a bank balance, it could increase or decrease according to one's behavior and the actions of his family. Female honor (*'ird*), by contrast, was solely personal. More akin to the English-language concept of "purity" than "honor," *'ird* was a quality that a woman either possessed or did not: once lost, it was lost forever. But the moral stain of the loss of *'ird* spread to the members of the woman's family, which justified the action needed to restore the family's *hasab*: the killing of the sinner.

The heightened attention paid to the place of women in society worldwide by the rise of feminism brought these practices in closer scrutiny throughout the Greater West. Honor killings in the last decades of Ottoman rule nonetheless remained hidden from view and difficult to quantify. Most cases seem to have involved honor "lost" by a daughter's refusal to accept an arranged marriage agreed to by her parents. Those who perpetrated or witnessed such killings did not consider them a crime, and hence they saw no need to report them to authorities. The Ottoman Turks themselves, to whom honor killing was more culturally foreign, did not wish to stir up the anger of their non-Turkish subjects by investigating such deaths too intently.

Female circumcision was most widely and openly practiced in the northeastern quadrant of Africa—Egypt, Ethiopia, Somalia, and Sudan—and in many parts of the Middle East. The custom was publicly condemned but long remained a secret practice in northern Arabia, southern Jordan, and the Kurdish regions of Iran, Iraq, Syria, and Turkey—secret, but not rare. As many as 80–90 percent of females in some of these regions either submitted or were forced to submit to some form of circumcision. Men who frequently went off on lengthy trading journeys relied on circumcision as a way of guaranteeing their wives' fidelity. In the most extreme cases nearly the entire vaginal opening was sewn shut, in addition to the more customary removal of the clitoris.

The practice predates Islam and probably originated from a mixture of motives—hygienic, aesthetic, and moral. The hygienic argument held that circumcision allowed for easier and fuller cleansing of the body after menstruation or childbirth; the aesthetic argument maintained that the procedure enhanced the beauty of the female form. The moral argument was the most nefarious, as it remains today. The moral motive insisted that circumcision promoted chastity before marriage and fidelity within marriage. Because it denied women the ability to experience pleasure by removing the clitoris, it thus removed temptation. The Islamic position on genital cutting is open to interpretation. A verse in one collection of the hadith of the Prophet Muhammad relates that when Muhammad encountered a woman in Medina who worked as a ritual circumciser, he said to her. "But do not mutilate—it is better for the woman and more desirable for her husband [to cut less rather than more]." This would seem at least to permit the practice, but legal scholars have long debated the authenticity of the verse.

◆

The call for the emancipation of women in the Islamic world, then, required bravery and countercultural determination unlike anything faced by women in western Europe. But in both cases the call was met with considerably more indifference and hostility than sympathy. To alter the position of women in society meant to change the definition of the nation itself at a critical moment.

Within Europe, the women's movement was hampered by a persistent, although not always accurate, association of feminism and secularism. Many of the women mentioned in this chapter were indeed religious skeptics, a fact that should not surprise us, since many of the West's patriarchal values and customs had their origin (or at least found affirmation) in the Judeo-Christian tradition. To challenge society was indirectly to challenge the religion that had helped to shape it. And as we shall see in the next chapter, that religion was under attack on any number of fronts.

WHO, WHAT, WHERE

Emmeline Pankhurst	National Society for	suffragists
feminist movement	Women's Suffrage	Women's Social and
Helene Stöcker	New Woman	Political Union
Huda'i Sha'arawi	Qasim Amin	
Maria Montessori	suffragettes	

SUGGESTED READINGS

Primary Sources

Bulwer-Lytton, Constance. *Prisons and Prisoners.*

Martineau, Harriet. "The Political Non-Existence of Women," in *Society in America.*

Mill, John Stuart. *The Subjection of Women.*

Reid, Marion Kirkland. *A Plea for Woman.*

Sha'arawi, Huda'i. *Harem Years: The Memoirs of an Egyptian Feminist.*

Stöcker, Helene. *Women and Love: A Manifesto for Emancipating Women and Men in Germany.*

Verbitskaya, Anastasia. *The Keys to Happiness.*

Source Anthologies

Badran, Margot, and Miriam Cooke, eds. *Opening the Gates: A Century of Arab Feminist Writing* (2004).

Nelson, Carolyn Christensen, ed. *A New Woman Reader: Fiction, Articles, and Drama of the 1890s* (2000).

Patterson, Martha H., ed. *The American New Woman Revisited: A Reader, 1894–1930* (2008).

Studies

Ali, Kecia. *Sexual Ethics and Islam: Feminist Reflections on Qur'an, Hadith, and Jurisprudence* (2006).

Bartley, Paula. *Emmeline Pankhurst* (2003).

Brown, Kathryn. *Women Readers in French Painting, 1870–1890: A Space for the Imagination* (2012).

Bush, Julia. *Women against the Vote: Female Anti-Suffragism in Britain* (2007).

Capaldi, Nicholas. *John Stuart Mill: A Biography* (2004).

Clark, Linda L. *Women and Achievement in 19th-Century Europe* (2008).

Friedmann, Yohanan. *Tolerance and Coercion in Islam: Interfaith Relations in the Muslim Tradition* (2003).

Fuchs, Rachel G. *Gender and Poverty in 19th-Century Europe* (2005).

Haeri, Shahla. *Law of Desire: Temporary Marriage in Shi'i Iran* (2002).

Hatem, Mervat F. *Literature, Gender, and Nation-Building in Nineteenth-Century Egypt: The Life and Works of 'A'isha Taymur* (2011).

Keddie, Nikki R. *Women in the Middle East: Past and Present* (2006).

Kertzer, David I., and Marzio Barbagli, eds. *Family Life in the Long Nineteenth Century, 1789–1913* (2002).

Logan, Deborah Anna. *Harriet Martineau, Victorian Imperialism, and the Civilizing Mission* (2010).

Logan, Deborah Anna. *The Woman and the Hour: Harriet Martineau's "Somewhat Remarkable" Life* (2002).

Malone, Carolyn. *Women's Bodies and Dangerous Trades in England, 1880–1914* (2003).

Marchand, Suzanne, and David Lindenfeld, eds. *Germany at the Fin de Siècle: Culture, Politics, and Ideas* (2004).

Offen, Karen M. *European Feminisms, 1700–1950: A Political History* (2000).

Phillips, Melanie. *The Ascent of Woman: A History of the Suffragette Movement and the Ideas behind It* (2003).

Prieto, Laura R. *At Home in the Studio: The Professionalization of Women Artists in America* (2001).

Pugh, Martin. *The Pankhursts: The History of One Radical Family* (2008).

Roberts, Mary Louise. *Disruptive Acts: The New Woman in Fin-de-Siècle France* (2002).

Rosenthal, Angela. *Angelica Kauffman: Art and Sensibility* (2006).

Sharawi Lanfranchi, Sania. *Casting Off the Veil: The Life of Huda Shaarawi, Egypt's First Feminist* (2015).

Stansell, Christine. *The Feminist Promise: 1792 to the Present* (2010).

Tosh, John. *A Man's Place: Masculinity and the Middle-Class Home in Victorian England* (2007).

For additional resources, including maps, primary sources, visuals, web links, and quizzes, please go to **www.oup.com/us/backman**.

CHAPTER 22

The Challenge of Secularism

1800–1914

"God is dead." Many people know this quotation from the German philosopher Friedrich Nietzsche (1844–1900) without understanding it. Nietzsche's statement was not, as readers often assume, a bold declaration of intellectual freedom after centuries of superstition and thought control. For him, the death of God was tragic, perhaps the worst calamity ever to befall mankind, because human life without God

VOYAGE OF THE HMS *BEAGLE*, 1831–1836

ENGLAND

is tragically meaningless. Every individual's experience is nothing but a brief crack of light between two eternities of darkness, and nothing that happens during that brief crack matters in any absolute sense. The death of God is also the death of the soul: rather than an "interior self," what we think of as a soul is really just a temporarily lit-up neural network. We are simply random gatherings of molecules that cohere and experience "consciousness" (whatever we may mean by that word) for a short time before dissolving again

Pablo Picasso, *Les Demoiselles d'Avignon*
Picasso could paint exquisite representational art, but representational painting did not allow him to express what he wanted. His breakthrough, *Les Demoiselles d'Avignon* ("The Young Ladies of Avignon," 1907), portrays naked prostitutes along the Carrer d'Avinyó, a street in Barcelona then notorious for its sordid nightlife. Two of the women wear African masks with savage expressions while the remaining three scowl. All five stare blankly and disdainfully at the viewer—presumably their next customer—as though challenging his right to be there. Their bodies are shown from at least two separate perspectives, which breaks their forms into geometric shapes and flat fields of color. The painting makes viewers feel as though they are under attack.

into nothingness. Not a sunny view. "Hope in [a supposed] reality is the greatest evil that can befall anyone," he writes, "for all it does is prolong one's agony."

But Nietzsche's point is to rouse us to action, not to drive us to collapse in despair. This is where he parts company with the extreme form of skepticism known as *nihilism*, which holds that all values are baseless and that nothing can be known or communicated. For Nietzsche, we should not simply accept the world's randomness but actually do something about it. Let us not make the agony of our lives even worse by being stupid while we are here—so let us not tell ourselves comforting lies or live by values we do not genuinely hold. Instead, we should have the courage to face awful reality as it is and live authentically during our short time on earth.

His insights highlight the dilemmas of one of the 19th century's most striking changes: secularization, or the declining power of religious beliefs, values, and institutions and the subsequent decline in religious practice. The rise of **secularism** resulted from many factors, the most significant of which was the sheer volume of human dislocation brought on by industrialization and its accompanying urban blight. But it also derived in large part from two of the century's greatest scientific achievements: a new theory of earth's history put forth by geologists and the English naturalist Charles Darwin's theory of evolution by natural selection.

These two achievements alone, as they gained supporters, threatened religious tradition by offering for the first time an alternative model for the world's original and continuing creation—moreover, a *testable* model that became more convincingly true with every subsequent breakthrough. But then, at the start of the 20th century, a wave of new discoveries in fields like physics and psychology

CHAPTER TIMELINE

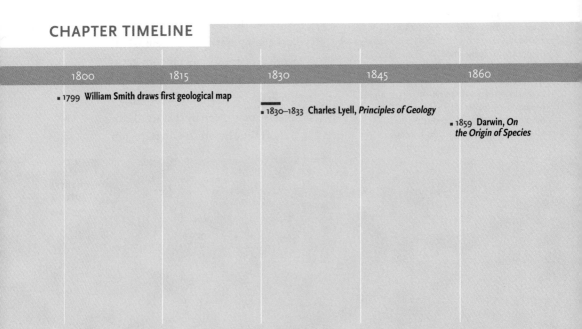

1800	1815	1830	1845	1860

- 1799 **William Smith draws first geological map**

- 1830–1833 **Charles Lyell, *Principles of Geology***

- 1859 **Darwin, *On the Origin of Species***

strengthened the challenge to tradition by probing deep into the mysteries of matter and mind—and likewise finding God nowhere present.

If science was secularism's handmaiden for the majority Christian world of the Greater West, it was less so for the West's Jewish and Muslim societies. As we shall see, the major factor in Jewish secularism was assimilation, not science. And for the Islamic world, secularism did not advance much at all. But this continuation of religious tradition came at a cost—the rejection of science.

WHO KILLED GOD?

The 19th century marks a watershed in European history, the period when Western culture began to turn decidedly secular. Since the dawn of Western history around 3000 BCE, religion had formed an essential part of the bedrock of its culture. Religious doubters, heretics, and critics existed in every faith and every age, but genuine nonbelief was rare. How else could one explain the existence of the world than by a god? From ancient Greece forward, virtually all leading scientists—from Aristotle to Newton—were people of religious conviction. Philosophers from Plato to Hegel all retained passionate, if sometimes quirky, convictions about God. Even the most irreligious of the Enlightened, Voltaire, acknowledged the existence of a divine creator. **Atheism** existed, and indeed the word dates back to the 16th century, but its usage was limited to "godlessness" in the moral sense—of "godless" behavior.[1]

---

[1]   The words *secularism, agnosticism,* and *atheism* (in the sense of disbelief) were all coined in the second half of the 19th century.

1875	1890	1905	1920	1935

- 1881 Ibsen, *Ghosts*
- 1886 Nietzsche, *Beyond Good and Evil*
- 1891 Oscar Wilde, *The Picture of Dorian Gray*; Leo XIII's *Rerum Novarum (Of New Things)*
- 1899 Freud, *Interpretation of Dreams*; van Gogh, *Starry Night*
- 1900 Max Planck formulates quantum theory
- 1905 Einstein publishes special theory of relativity
- 1907 Pius X issues decrees that reject modernism; Picasso, *Les Demoiselles d'Avignon*
- 1910 Kandinsky, *On the Spiritual Element in Art*
- 1915 Einstein publishes general theory of relativity
- 1920 Freud, *Beyond the Pleasure Principle*

Except for Baruch Spinoza (the 17th-century philosopher) and Nietzsche, almost everyone yet mentioned in this book accepted the existence of one or more deities—and based his or her ethical behavior at least partly on that belief.

What, then, had happened? Why did the rejection, or mere absence, of religious belief suddenly become so prominent an element in European society? In 1811 the Romantic poet Percy Bysshe Shelley (1792–1822) was expelled from Oxford University when he was discovered to be the author of a pamphlet called *The Necessity of Atheism*. Only two generations later, however, the Russian writer Leo Tolstoy (1828–1910) could have one character describe another, in his novel *Anna Karenina* (1877), as:

> an odd, uneducated fellow, one of those wild "modern" people one meets so often these days, a "freethinker" raised from birth with notions of non-belief, negation, and materialism. . . . It used to be the case that a "freethinker" was someone who had been brought up with the ideas of religion, law, and morality, and had reached the state of freethinking after long years of personal pain and struggle. But now there is this new kind of ready-made freethinker—the ones who grow up without ever even hearing that there once were such things as moral laws and religious convictions, and that these were the authorities in life. These new folks, now, simply grow up in a world where all this is rejected out of hand— which is to say, they grow up as savages.

Industrial Capitalism   The decline of Christianity in 19th-century Europe resulted from a host of factors. Industrial capitalism figures large. It wrenched millions of Europeans from their rural parishes and deposited them in dense urban settings, where there was little or no organized religious life. Forced to work twelve to fourteen hours a day in factories, six days a week, with few churches or clergy members available, many of the working poor simply lost the habit of attending church. And given widespread illiteracy, there was insufficient Bible reading or private devotions to compensate. In cities from Manchester to Milan, thousands of gleaming new churches were built or revamped, yet these lay overwhelmingly in tidy middle-class precincts that few working-class people could reach—and where they would have felt distinctly out of place and unwelcome even if they could have reached them.

Established Churches   Another cause of unease was the institution of the "established church," meaning the legal proclamation of a specific Christian tradition as the official faith of a nation. United Italy designated Roman Catholicism as its state religion; England had its Anglican Church and Scotland its Presbyterian Church. Each of the provinces of united Germany had its own state church, and the alliances between governments and the Orthodox Churches in eastern Europe and Russia date back to the Middle Ages. Popular discontent with a government's policies frequently resulted in popular dissatisfaction with the church. Meanwhile, the bourgeois classes that benefited most from the industrial economy came to represent the centers of power within each government.

Less directly involved, although still a factor, was prosperity itself. Nineteenth-century Europe witnessed a proliferation of new department stores, exhibition halls, museums, sports venues, theaters, music halls, and restaurants.[2] All these challenged the traditional role of churches as centers of community. As church became a once-a-week, Sunday-mornings-only affair, religious enthusiasm waned. And for those millions who did not share in the prosperity of the age, taverns and bodegas provided some relief from their miseries. Meanwhile, many of the most enthusiastic believers, both Protestant and Catholic, lay or clerical, left Europe to pursue missionary work overseas, often in Africa or eastern Asia. *New Centers of Community*

Another contributing factor to secularism may have been modern medicine. Physicians became able to treat and cure a broader array of ailments; vaccines mitigated the horrors of cholera and smallpox; and improvements in food production and distribution lessened famine. Child mortality decreased, life expectancy increased, and more and more people lived longer and healthier lives. These were undeniably positive developments, but they contributed to secularization *Modern Medicine*

by lessening the presence of death in peoples' lives. This is not a trivial point. Among the middle classes who had access to modern medical care, it was not uncommon to attend only a handful of funerals in a lifetime—usually later in life when older relatives died. By contrast, just over a century earlier England's Queen Anne (r. 1702–1707) – who presumably had the best care available at the time - had had eighteen pregnancies, thirteen of which ended in miscarriages; four children were born but died before the age of two. Her sole surviving child died just days after his eleventh birthday. The untimely death of deeply loved relations, friends, or romantic partners has proved through the centuries to be a powerful impulse to religious meditations. Without the painful presence of death, once a constant in life even with the best available medical care, it became easier to avoid thinking about it.

Temple of Consumerism   Many more women than men appear in this illustration of the grand staircase at Le Bon Marché ("The Good Market" or "The Good Deal") department store in Paris. The founder of the store was Aristide Boucicaut (1810–1877), who credited much his success to his promotion of the store as a place where proper bourgeois women could meet without chaperones.

---

[2]   The first two department stores were Bainbridge's in Newcastle-upon-Tyne, England, and Le Bon Marché in Paris; both opened in 1838.

Until the late 19th century, too, religious houses had been the main providers of social services throughout Europe: they had run hospitals and orphanages, provided education, organized soup kitchens and almshouses, and offered care for the elderly and destitute. The liberal nation-states, however, gradually took over most of these roles as the century progressed, which effectively marginalized the active presence of religious life in society. From the point of view of the disaffected, churches—especially established churches—were institutions that enjoyed their tax exemptions and government subsidies while apparently catering to the well-to-do middle and upper classes. But they played a constantly declining role in most people's lives.

Advance of Liberalism   The advance of liberalism, especially after 1848, also had an indirect philosophical effect. By promoting toleration of differing traditions and dissenting views as a civic virtue, it implicitly allowed and perhaps even encouraged the circulation of ideas that directly challenged religion's traditional position of cultural authority. By making a virtue of welcoming dissent, liberal society unintentionally added to the growing sense of distance from their religious roots felt by millions. And the religious and social debates of the age reached ever increasing numbers of people thanks to the proliferation of newspapers and magazines in the second half of the century. Finally, by inviting religious plurality, liberal Europe created a marketplace of ideas that provided encouragement to many but also fostered confusion when it came to people's religious convictions. The midcentury Oxford movement in England, for example, aimed to confront the problem of Anglicans who no longer adhered to the traditions of Anglican Christianity because they no longer really understood them. A parallel development in Protestant Germany was the so-called Neo-Lutheran movement. Sunday schools were established across Europe to combat religious ignorance or indifference.

Toleration contributed to the rise of secularism by redefining civic virtues. The earliest secularists did not present themselves publicly as enemies of Christianity but rather as champions of nonpartisanship. George Jacob Holyoake (1817–1906), the most prominent early campaigner for civic secularism in England, described his position in this way:

> Secularism is not an argument against Christianity; it is one independent of it. It does not question the pretensions of Christianity; it advances others. Secularism does not say there is no light or guidance elsewhere, but maintains that there is light and guidance in secular truth, whose conditions and sanctions exist independently, and act forever. Secular knowledge is manifestly that kind of knowledge which is founded in this life, which relates to the conduct of this life, conduces to the

welfare of this life, and is capable of being tested by the experience of this life. (*Origin and Nature of Secularism*, 1896)

Holyoake was briefly imprisoned for blasphemy in 1842. The secularist cause was given formal order by the creation of groups like England's National Secular Society, founded in 1866, and Germany's Freethinkers' League (*Freidenkerbund*), established in 1881.

THE THEORY OF CREATION

Secularism found a target in one of the most notorious false beliefs of its time— the date of Creation. It found new weapons, too—in science's attempts to trace history in the earth and in evolution by natural selection.

The Reverend James Ussher (1581–1656) was a brilliant Anglo-Irish Protestant scholar, the archbishop of Armagh and primate of all Ireland who helped calm the Irish religious and political scene during the panicked violence of the English Civil War; unfortunately, he is remembered today chiefly for a single ridiculous idea. In 1648, the same year when the Peace of Westphalia put an end to the Wars of Religion and inaugurated the age of absolutist governments, Ussher published a lengthy study of biblical history entitled *The Annals of the Old Testament*, which attempted to work backward through the detailed chronologies given in the Hebrew Bible and thereby calculate the likely dates of the most important events it describes. After years of painstaking research, Bishop Ussher opened his *Annals* with the solemn announcement that God began his six-day labor of Creation, as related in the initial chapter of *Genesis*, at sunset on the evening preceding Sunday, October 23, in the year 4004 BCE—making the world around him exactly 5,652 years old.

His conclusion was remarkable more for its precision than for its originality; attempts to determine the date of Creation by means of the Bible's many genealogies and royal lists were as old as the Bible itself. The Jewish calendar's Year 1—the year *before* God began his work of Creation—corresponds to the year 3760 BCE; the astronomer Johannes Kepler calculated Creation to have occurred in 3992 BCE. Isaac Newton himself, a half century after Ussher, concluded that the Creation took place in the year 4000 BCE. The belief that the world in the 19th century was approaching six thousand years old was surprisingly widespread, and Ussher's chronology was commonly printed inside editions of the Authorized (King James) Version of the Bible until the early 19th century. In the United States an edition known as the Scofield Reference Bible—from Cyrus Scofield (1843–1921), the American Bible student who updated and annotated Ussher's chronology—appeared in the early 20th century. It sold more than

2 million copies by 1950 and became the foundation of the Christian-fundamentalist challenge to the theory of evolution.

The Challenge of Geology

The theory of the 4004 BCE Creation never had official recognition from any of the mainstream Christian churches in the West, and it came under direct attack from the work of three British scientists: two geologists, William Smith and Sir Charles Lyell, and the biologist Charles Darwin. William Smith (1769–1839) was the self-educated son of a village blacksmith; apprenticed to a surveyor working to map out canals for the great industrial boom then underway, he developed a passionate interest in geological formations and fossils. He taught himself map drawing and in 1799 produced a geological map of the area around the city of Bath in Somerset. It showed consistent relationships between the various strata of stone and their fossil remains, illustrating the development over time of the entire region. The land formations he analyzed gave every sign of being layered; the deeper one dug into the earth, the further back into time one traveled.

The success of this map, and the enthusiasm it raised among other geologists, inspired Smith to his greatest project—a map of the entire geological structure of the island of Britain, which he published in 1815 in a volume called *A Delineation of the Strata of England and Wales*. Taking advantage of Britain's extensive railways, he traveled more than ten thousand miles a year in the process of gathering his data; especially useful were the rock walls created by construction crews building the nation's railroad tunnels and canal networks. Smith's maps, and the detailed data he published along with them, pointed to rock strata composed of like materials and containing similar fossils. These could be connected to create a picture of the formation of the land. In other words, he provided clear evidence that the British Isles emerged from sequential development over long periods of time rather than all-at-once creation.

Sir Charles Lyell (1797–1875) was in many ways the antithesis of Smith. Born to a prominent Scottish family of lawyers and civil servants, Lyell went to Oxford University, traveled extensively, moved easily in society, married a famous beauty who was also a scientist, and held a professorship at King's College London. A gregarious and generous man, he made his career less by conducting field research (his eyesight was poor) than by synthesizing the investigations of others. His most important work was also a bestseller: the three-volume *Principles of Geology* (1830–1833).

Lyell's main contribution was the popularization of the theory called **uniformitarianism**, originally proposed by another Scottish geologist, James Hutton (1726–1797). The theory stated that geological change consists of the slow accumulation of smaller changes—and these changes continue to happen in the present. The idea seems self-evident today, but it was a radical challenge to a world that believed that the earth's entire history covered less than six thousand years.

A Map that Changed the World   William Smith published his geological map of Britain in 1815, which made clear that the island emerged gradually over time, rather than appeared whole from a single act of creation. Unfortunately, others plagiarized his map and subsequent books, and he fell into debt. He spent two years in debtors' prison, and afterward worked as a surveyor. Shown here is a detail of the map showing southwest England and part of Wales.

Lyell's theory demanded hundreds of millions of years for the physical record to make sense. The fact that Lyell himself was known to be a deeply committed Christian gave his theory additional force; it was well known that he accepted his own theory only because the evidence for it was so overwhelming. And he continued to expand and revise this theory through twelve editions of *Principles* and through six editions of a subsequent study called *Elements of Geology.*

DARWIN AND EVOLUTION BY NATURAL SELECTION

The young English naturalist Charles Darwin (1809–1882) read Lyell's *Principles of Geology* while on a five-year voyage (1831–1836) aboard the HMS *Beagle*, exploring the coasts of South America and its outlying islands. Several papers that he delivered after his return to England, along with the publication of his travelogue *The Voyage of the Beagle* (1839), established his reputation as a scientist and writer of rare gifts. He and Lyell became lifelong friends, and their relationship grew ever closer despite Lyell's resistance to Darwin's great contribution—his **theory of evolution by natural selection**. Some of the fundamental ideas behind it had been around for several years, yet no one had pieced them together with as much geological support and analysis as Darwin. Moreover, although other scholars had suggested that species change over time, none had come up with an explanation for why they did so. Darwin supplied a powerful one, and it remains the central idea behind the science of biology today.

Darwin's theory dealt wholly with the plant and animal world, but it clearly implied that human beings evolved in a similar manner. Darwin posited natural selection as the means by which evolution occurs. First, nature produces a super-abundance of offspring in each generation. A single grain of wheat, for example, produces a wheat shaft that contains dozens of new grains, or a single female salmon lays hundreds of eggs that are then fertilized by the millions of sperm cells produced by the male salmon. Second, this superabundance results in a contest among those offspring for the resources necessary for life. This contest will favor individuals who have a unique ability that gives them an advantage over their rivals. And third, this preferred characteristic, whatever it might be, is then passed on to its offspring. Eventually, this will allow the species to develop into a new form.

Darwin spent fifteen years working out the details of his theory—which he finally published as **On the Origin of Species by Means of Natural Selection** in 1859. The following comes from the opening chapter:

Darwin's On the Origin of Species

> As many more individuals of each species are born than can possibly survive; and as, consequently, there is a frequently recurring struggle for existence, it follows that any being, if it vary however slightly in any manner profitable to itself, under the complex and sometimes varying conditions of life, will have a better chance of surviving, and thus be *naturally selected*. From the strong principle of inheritance, any selected variety will tend to propagate its new and modified form.

Darwin ended the book with a plea that it be seen as a celebration of life rather than as an attack on cherished assumptions:

> Authors of the highest eminence seem to be fully satisfied with the view that each species has been independently created. To my mind it accords better with what we know of the laws impressed on matter by the Creator, that the production and extinction of the past and present inhabitants of the world should have been due to secondary causes, like those determining the birth and death of the individual. When I view all

beings not as special creations, but as the lineal descendants of some few beings which lived long before the first bed of the Silurian[3] system was deposited, they seem to me to become ennobled. . . . As all the living forms of life are the lineal descendants of those which lived long before the Silurian epoch, we may feel certain that the ordinary succession by generation has never once been broken, and that no cataclysm has desolated the whole world. Hence we may look with some confidence to a secure future of equally inappreciable length. And as natural selection works solely by and for the good of each being, all corporeal and mental endowments will tend to progress towards perfection.

Within the scientific community, Darwin's theory of evolution carried the day. Even Lyell eventually endorsed it. Like many Christian believers, Lyell's problem was not with evolution itself but with the idea of natural selection, which seemed to undermine the notion of a heavenly plan; it could even dismiss the need for a Creator altogether. Others, however, saw no reason why Darwin's work had to be regarded as an attack on religion. A popular novelist and historian of the day, Charles Kingsley (1819–1875), who was also an Anglican priest, sent Darwin a letter immediately after reading *On the Origin of Species*:

> [It] is just as noble a conception of Deity to believe that He created primal forms capable of self development into all forms needful . . . as to believe that He required a fresh act of intervention to supply the lacunas [missing elements] which He Himself had made. I question whether the former be not the loftier thought.

Not only could the Anglican priest accept so "non-Christian a theory as evolution"; he also could admire it.[4]

A famous debate took place at the Oxford Association for the Advancement of Science in 1860 between Darwin's most vocal champion, Thomas Huxley *Early* (1825–1895), and Samuel Wilberforce (1805–1873), then the bishop of Oxford. *Opposition* (Darwin did not attend. His work on *The Origin of Species* had been so all- *to Evolution* consuming that his health broke down while he was completing it, and he needed months to recover from the strain. He remained in ill health, in fact, through the rest of his life.) Angry words flew across the stage at the debate, and the crowd roared and jeered; in the end, both sides declared victory. Although inconclusive, this debate set the tone for the war of words that ensued in lecture halls, pulpits,

---

3   *Silurian* is the name of an early geological period, roughly from 440 to 420 million years ago.

4   "What can be more delightful to me," Kingsley is said to have replied at an aristocratic dinner, "than to know that Your Ladyship and I sprang from the same toadstool?"

newspapers and magazines, common rooms, and at dinner tables across England and the Continent. Wilberforce led the charge against Darwin's book, and he saw immediately the repercussions of evolutionary theory for religious faith:

> Mr. Darwin writes as a Christian, and we doubt not that he is one. We do not for a moment believe him to be one of those who retain in some corner of their hearts a secret unbelief which they dare not vent; and we therefore pray him to consider well the grounds on which we brand his speculations with the charge of such a tendency. . . . Man's derived supremacy over the earth; man's power of articulate speech; man's gift of reason; man's free will and responsibility; man's fall and man's redemption; the incarnation of the Eternal Son; the indwelling of the Eternal Spirit—all are equally and utterly irreconcilable with the degrading notion of the brute origin of him who was created in the image of God, and redeemed by the Eternal Son assuming to himself His nature.

For many people, opposition to evolution was visceral. By validating the notion of natural selection, they felt, it removed God from the creation of life. It seemed not only to contradict biblical tradition but also to be holding it up to ridicule. The six-thousand-year-old world was being unceremoniously ushered out the door. But worse was yet to come. Darwin's later book *The Descent of Man* (1871) stated explicitly what *The Origin of Species* had only implied and what Wilberforce had pointed out: human beings themselves were the product of evolution and had emerged from more primitive species.[5] Cartoonists rushed to depict Darwin derisively as an ape-man. His bald head, strong facial features, and flowing white beard—which he had grown to cover some of the effects of his long illness—were well suited to caricature.

The notion of all earthly life as a struggle for existence seemed coldly harsh. That the fittest survive at the expense of the rest seemed irreconcilable with a loving Creator. The Bible's apparent evidence that the world was created in 4004 BCE could be set aside easily enough by interpreting its dates as merely symbolic. Abraham did not literally live to be 175 years old (Genesis 25.7), it might be said; the high number of years attributed to him simply symbolized great age and wisdom. However, Scripture repeatedly asserts that the loving God made the cosmos as a thing of supreme beauty and order, all set in motion according to his divine plan. This was tough to square with the arbitrary ruthlessness of Darwin's

---

[5]   Darwin never claimed that humans are descended from apes. Instead, humans and apes are descended from a remote common ancestor. "Some ancient member of the anthropomorphous subgroup gave birth to man," he writes in chapter 6 of *The Descent of Man*. This subgroup includes a variety of apelike creatures, such as the gorilla, chimpanzee, and orangutan (and their forebears).

world-as-battlefield. If the Bible's most fundamental traditions and moral teachings can be set aside as mistaken, then what is left?

A SECULAR UNIVERSE

The answer to that question came from a surprising place—physics—and it was, if anything, even more unnerving to traditional values. Europeans in the 19th century commonly regarded physics—the study of matter and energy and their interactions—as the least interesting of all sciences. It seemed a professional dead end; after Sir Isaac Newton (discussed in chapter 13), all that remained to do was to clear up a few minor things or add a few points to the general picture. Newton's three laws of motion had established classical mechanics (the movement of matter); his law of universal gravitation explained nature's fundamental force. The cosmos operated according to fixed laws and mathematical formulas. Alfred North Whitehead (1861–1947), the great British mathematician and philosopher, described the start of his career as "an age of successful scientific orthodoxy, undisturbed by much thought beyond the conventions . . . [and] one of the dullest stages of thought since the time of the First Crusade." The discovery of a new energy, electricity, stirred things up for a while, but James Maxwell (1831–1879), a Scottish physicist, soon calmed things down again. Maxwell showed how electricity, magnetism, and light are all manifestations of the same force— electromagnetism. The rest of physics, it seemed, was merely a matter of adjusting a few details.

Ape-man   Darwin suffered from ill health most of his adult life (he ultimately died of heart disease), and the intense exertion of writing his *Origin of Species* nearly killed him. During a long convalescence he grew out his beard, which together with his advancing baldness gave him a distinctive look that was easily and sometimes cruelly caricatured. Here he is shown as half man and half monkey, trying to teach another monkey about its identity.

But then a spate of new discoveries popped up, discoveries that could not be fitted into the Newtonian framework. In fact, they seemed to attack it. On *The New* November 8, 1895, Wilhelm Röntgen (1845–1923) discovered X-rays while ex- *Physics* perimenting with electrical current passing through a vacuum tube.[6] These rays

---

6   The "X" in X-rays derived from the mathematical sign for an unknown. Röntgen received the first Nobel Prize in Physics, in 1901.

Marie Curie   The brilliance of her work in science resulted in two Nobel Prizes for Marie Curie (1867–1934)—one in physics and one in chemistry. Polish by birth, she lived in France from 1891 on but kept close ties to her family and homeland. When she isolated and identified a new element in 1898 she named it after her homeland: polonium.

were yet another elemental force, but they could not be explained by the standard model. Then came the electron, discovered by 1897 by J. J. Thomson (1856–1940) at Cambridge University in England. Before Thomson, atoms were believed to be the smallest particles in nature—the fundamental building blocks. As Thomson deflected cathode rays through electromagnetic fields, he found subatomic particles less than 0.0005 times the mass of the smallest atom, hydrogen. The next year the Polish-French physicist and chemist Marie Curie (1867–1934) discovered a new element, radium, that somehow emitted radiation—and with it another new form of energy, radioactivity. Suddenly the universe, at the smallest of levels, looked stranger than it had since the time of the Scientific Revolution.

These discoveries showed the universe to be immensely more complex than anyone understood. But they were nothing compared to what came next. All of classical physics, and even the newer discoveries, had relied on the idea of the *ether*. This presumed medium had neither mass, nor weight, nor color; it was uniform, odorless, and tasteless; it was imperceptible to touch or measurement; it offered no physical resistance. Yet it had to exist, because all of those atoms and energies had to move *through something*. Otherwise atoms and energies could not interact, just as swimmers rely on water to move through the sea or a pool. The ether ensured that all movement, all changes in momentum and direction, and all interactions of force and counterforce would proceed smoothly and perfectly. But then came Max Planck (1858–1947) and Albert Einstein (1879–1955), and our understanding of the universe would never be the same.

Planck's Quantum Theory   Planck and Einstein seldom performed experiments; they both preferred to work out on paper the theories behind other people's data. Planck's first breakthrough came in 1900, after a group of physicists who were trying to coax the maximum brightness out of light bulbs with the least possible electricity sent the accumulated data of their experiments to him. He came up with an astonishing conclusion: the data could be explained only by introducing into the calculations a fixed unit of energy—a kind of packet of light energy, which Planck called a *quantum* (plural *quanta*). One could have x amount of light energy, or $2x$, or $3x$, and so on, but nothing in between. Light, therefore, was not a continuous wave of energy but instead a torrent of finite bits.

Further, these quanta of light behaved like physical particles possessing mass, even as they also had the characteristics of waves. Planck turned to this conclusion, he later wrote, "as an act of despair." It was the only way to make mathematical sense out of the data, although it upset the foundations of all of physics. In this he was remarkably like Copernicus four hundred years earlier, who had to wreck the system he had inherited to make his numbers crunch better. Planck had invented a new physics based on quanta, the **quantum theory**. Most physicists rejected his claims at first, although they could find no fault in his reasoning. It took Einstein's affirmation of Planck's theory for most to fall into line.[7]

Not even Einstein, however, was prepared for the next step. Matter, too, appeared to behave as both wave and particle. This idea of duality formed the basis of how quantum theory developed over half a century or more, to reveal the inner workings of atoms and molecules. Yet scientists found that they could make predictions about only the *probability* that any one particle would be anywhere at any particular moment in time. That "wave-particle duality" is also the basis of the *uncertainty principle*, which sets limits on what one can know about a particle at a given moment. No wonder Einstein initially rebelled against quantum theory. Besides, he had made some sweeping and precise predictions of his own.

Einstein finished the task of reinventing physics in 1905 when he published what came to be known as his special theory of relativity. His general theory of relativity followed in 1915. They are sophisticated, but it is important to understand the basics—and not solely to appreciate the science. Relativity could in fact stand for the entire cultural and intellectual ferment of the early 20th century. It could stand for the relativity of aesthetic values, of philosophical terms, and of literary judgments. Artists and poets did not derive their ideas from Planck and Einstein, although many were keenly aware of them, but there are parallels all the same. European culture had earlier periods of uncertainty about how to know what was true, but now the very idea of fixed truth seemed to be false.

Einstein's Theory of Relativity

The **special theory of relativity** maintains that all measurements of space and time are relative. This is not just a matter of perspective, like looking at a draftsman's ruler or waiting in line. A ruler may be 12 inches in length, but if one looks at it from a distance or at an angle, it appears considerably shorter. An hour spent waiting at the Registry of Motor Vehicles seems infinitely longer than an hour spent listening to Mozart. Einstein's results are something else again.

---

7   Speaking of one holdout against quanta, Plank recalled, "He's a perfect example of the type of theorist we do not need . . . the kind who says 'The facts don't fit my theory; too bad for the facts.'"

Consider a man bouncing a basketball. Suppose the ball moves with perfect regularity and in a perfectly vertical line—3 feet down, 3 feet up, over and over, exactly one bounce per second. The ball therefore travels a total of 6 feet per second. But now imagine that the man is standing on a flatcar on a train that is moving down the track as he bounces the basketball. To an observer watching from a platform some distance away, the ball moves not in a vertical line but at an angle to the vertical because of the horizontal movement of the train. Moreover, the ball turns out to travel at a different speed—say, 5 feet diagonally down and 5 feet diagonally up, for a total of 10 feet per second.

The special theory shows that this is not simply a difference of perspective. The ball does not just "seem" to be traveling at one speed and not the other; the special theory holds that the ball actually is traveling 6 feet per second *and* 10 feet per second, depending on the observer, *at the same time.* Time and space are elastic and should be conceived as different facets of a single dimension that Einstein called *space-time.*[8]

The **general theory of relativity** describes gravity's relationship to space-time. Newton had posited gravity as an attraction between all particles with mass, but he offered no insight into what gravity actually is. After all, why would two bodies hundreds of billions of miles apart feel attracted toward each other? Newton admitted defeat on this question and happily returned to his calculations on how great the force would nevertheless be. To Einstein, gravity is not a force at all. It is simply the name we give to an experience we have of space-time. A person in a stationary elevator can "feel gravity." It is the sensation of the floor of the elevator, preventing him from falling into the earth's core (or at least into the basement). But if now the elevator began to accelerate upward, even if there were no earth below pulling the person down, he would feel the exact same sensation of the floor pushing upward. In fact, he could not tell whether

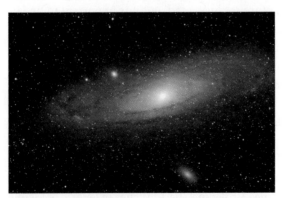

Space-time A photo of the Andromeda galaxy (also known as M31) taken through a Celestron 80ED telescope with a one-hour exposure. Andromeda is a spiral galaxy roughly 2.5 million light-years from Earth and contains over a trillion stars. Andromeda and our own Milky Way galaxy are drawing nearer to one another and will collide in about 4.5 billion years. You have been warned.

---

8   Einstein's special theory of relativity is the basis of the idea that nothing can go faster than the speed of light.

the elevator was moving. Einstein called this relationship of motion to gravity the *equivalence principle*.

In general relativity, every vantage point in the universe, whether moving or stationary, is as valid as every other vantage point. The laws of physics will look the same in each. There is no fixed and absolute center to anything: to space, to motion, to time. Everything is relative. From the point of view of a spectator, a football thrown by a quarterback appears to arc smoothly upward, reach a zenith, and then arc smoothly downward into the receiver's arms. That is true, says Einstein—but it is also true that the ball travels in a straight line through a space-time that is curved. It is the curvature of space-time that gives the impression of the ball's rising and falling. Adding to the wonder and complexity of it all, it is also true, from a different vantage point, that the ball is not moving at all. The curved space-time of the universe rushing past it gives the impression of the ball in flight. Each observation is equally valid.

Planck received the Nobel Prize in Physics in 1918 and Einstein in 1923. Their ideas have been confirmed by thousands of experiments and with unimaginable degrees of precision. They were sufficient to upend the entire scientific understanding of the cosmos, but taken together they add yet another level of confusion: quantum theory and general relativity, as we currently understand them, cannot both be true, or at least they have so far resisted the unity of a single theory. (The clash between the two models relates to the conflict between the fixed quantum nature of matter and the geometric description of space-time.) Much of the research done in the hundred years since Planck and Einstein has been devoted to reconciling them. Einstein himself spent the last twenty years of his life trying to determine a "unified field theory" that would harmonize his and Planck's ideas. Efforts continue in ways more open to the paradoxes of quantum theory than Einstein himself ever was, with variations on string theory today.

Although immensely sophisticated and mathematically complex, these ideas quickly entered 20th-century culture. Beliefs held by scientists for three thousand years had been shown to be false, and the two new truths that proved so actually conflict with each other. A story like that is hard to keep secret. What people took away from the new physics was the broader idea of relativity—no fixed points, no absolute time, no absolute space. And the more we learned about the universe, the more immense, confusing, unexpected, and, for some, more frightening it seemed to be.

NIETZSCHE AND THE WILL TO POWER

Like physics, philosophy since the turn of the 20th century has been insightful and brilliant. It has also been depressing—and that is not an unfortunate side effect. It is the work's very point. Coming down from the heights of idealism, its thrust has been the randomness, contingency, and disorder of life. Modern philosophy has argued for the inability of our minds to comprehend reality—and the slipperiness of language in trying to discuss it.

The key figure in the new bleakness was Friedrich Nietzsche (1844–1900), the prophet of God's death whom we met at the start of this chapter. Although little known in his lifetime, Nietzsche's work advanced the nihilistic philosophy of the age, although, as we saw, he himself rejected nihilism's extreme skepticism. Rather, Nietzsche insists that we must overcome the inevitable despair of life and at least live authentically while we are here.

False Values

But how do we know what is authentic? As usual, it is easier to identify what is false than what is true. One thing that is clearly false, Nietzsche argues, is the Western belief in democracy and the equality of mankind. In our heart of hearts, he insists, we know that we do not believe in this idea. One has only to look around—at one's neighbors, at passengers on a bus, at crowds gathered at a ball game. If we are honest, we will acknowledge that many people are ignorant. In contrast, democracy makes sense only if people are all equally capable of making intelligent decisions about how to govern society. We should therefore throw democratic values and institutions on the trash heap. Go ahead and admit it, Nietzsche urges. Life is already brief, purposeless, and meaningless. Why spend the little time we have living in a political system that gives fools an equal share of influence? Why should we refuse to acknowledge what we all actually think? Just to be nice? That sounds pleasant, he says, but niceness is no basis for a philosophy, except to idiots:

> What bizarre distortions and lies people put up with! It never ceases to amaze anyone who has eyes to see. "Oh, look! Isn't everything around us so cheery and free, so easy and simple! Isn't it wonderful how we have given ourselves a free pass to experience everything that is superficial! . . . And oh! how we figured out from the dawn of time how to keep ourselves ignorant so that we might enjoy a degree of freedom and escape from care, feel ourselves to be brave and cheerful, and to actually enjoy existence!" (*Beyond Good and Evil*, 1886)

What is another idea to reject? Christianity. All religions to Nietzsche (the son, grandson, and great-grandson of Lutheran ministers) are just emotional security blankets. And Christianity—at least as he saw it, in its late 19th-century form—is particular guilty because of its very niceness. The Christianity of his time, he finds, preaches what he terms a "slave-morality" of meekness and passivity, of self-denial and contempt for strength. As he put it in a late book:

I say that Christianity is the greatest single curse on mankind, [its] most gargantuan and deep-seated depravity, . . . the most enduring blemish on the human race, . . . for it favors everything that is weak, base, and malformed. . . . Some call it the "religion of compassion," but I say that compassion negates all the fundamental instincts that contribute to the vitality and meaning of life! (*The Twilight of the Idols*, 1888)

Reading Nietzsche is a visceral experience. He shouts, curses, and ridicules. He aims to shock. His books offer no calm, rational arguments; instead they consist of series of independent passages, each written at a white heat and usually in a single burst of inspiration. He writes in a confrontational and emotional style, like a firefighter trying to hurry people out of a burning building that is on the brink of collapse. Life is a state of continual emergency, and Nietzsche understands that we are our truest selves during emergencies. We may not be our best or most likeable selves, but we are truest to what we value most.

Nietzsche insists that we stop pretending that everything is fine. We must stop telling ourselves that everything is in God's hands, that history is progress, that democracy and capitalism will make the world better, that all people are

Friedrich Nietzsche   "What does man actually know about himself?" Friedrich Nietzsche (1844–1900), perhaps the most influential philosopher of the 20th century, is certainly the most bracing to read.

created equal, and that Christian platitudes can relieve human suffering. The only things he recognizes as absolutely good are the desire for life and the urge to create.

Thus he champions the **will to power**—the passionate striving to make meaning and leave a mark on the world. The phrase sounds ominously like a prelude to 20th-century fascism—and it has often been interpreted that way. Yet Nietzsche, despite his love of violent vocabulary and strident prose, was neither a fascist nor a sadist. (As a medical orderly during the Franco-Prussian War, he regularly fainted at the sight of blood.) By the will to power, he meant the *creative drive* or *creativity*. In one of his notebooks, he discusses his philosophical ideas in relation to recent discoveries in physics:

The Creative Drive

> The triumphant idea of force—namely, the thing by means of which our physicists have invented God and God's invention of the world—needs elaboration. It needs an interior element, one I call "the will to power." An insatiable desire to enact power, to wield it and use it, to spur creation.

Nietzsche envisions a world in which those with the will to power would emerge as natural leaders, whether in politics, intellectual life, or art. These **supermen** (*Übermenschen*) would do a better job of it than the general masses. They would also provide inspiration and models for people everywhere to tap into their own creative drives. Such a scheme might make for a messy, conflict-prone world—but, Nietzsche asks, isn't that the world we live in now? In the world of supermen, the conflicts would at least be noble ones.

The creative drive championed by Nietzsche, knowingly or not, was the foundation of a new trajectory in artistic life—**aestheticism**, the belief in art for art's sake. Its most famous proponent was one of the few people who read Nietzsche's works in his lifetime, a brilliant Oxford undergraduate from Ireland named Oscar Wilde.

ART FOR ART'S SAKE

Playwright and novelist Oscar Wilde (1854–1900) dismissed the average bourgeois capitalist as someone "who knows the price of everything, and the value of nothing." Mass production meant crass production—especially regarding the arts. It was fine to devote a nation's talent and treasure to spreading literacy and scientific knowledge among the masses. What good was it, however, if those skills went only to produce kitschy art and shallow pulp fiction?

Rise of "Low Culture"

Books became the dominant form of popular entertainment, with novels surpassing poetry as the favorite genre. Max Pemberton (1863–1950) was a popular British novelist who wrote many adventure stories aimed at working-class audiences. His most successful was *The Iron Pirate* (1896), about a steam-driven frigate that terrorizes the Atlantic. H. Rider Haggard (1856–1925) was even more successful, with novels like *King Solomon's Mines* (1885) and *She* (1887).[9] The latter tells of an English scholar of antiquities who travels to an uncharted kingdom "in darkest Africa," ruled by a mythical immortal beauty. "God help English literature," wrote one critic of the time, "when English people lay aside . . . the works of Defoe, Swift, Thackeray, Charlotte Brontë, [and] George Eliot . . . for the penny-dreadfuls of Mr. Haggard." (Cheap adventure novels were called "penny dreadfuls" because they appeared in installments in magazines costing only a penny.)

Oscar Wilde The endlessly quotable Anglo-Irish writer Oscar Wilde (1854–1900) lived brilliantly and died tragically. After earning fame and wealth as a playwright, poet, and social critic, he was convicted and imprisoned for homosexuality, at hard labor for two years (1895–1897). The experience broke him, and he spent his final years in obscurity and poverty in Paris.

The pressure of the marketplace drove down standards in popular music as well. The invention of the phonograph and radio, although good things in themselves, meant that people no longer had to learn to play instruments to have music in their lives. They could simply turn on the machine to hear whatever they wished. Light, popular songs crowded out more serious and challenging music. Culture, it seemed, was being split into high and low—and low culture was winning out.

Many writers, critics, and artists at the end of the 19th century therefore reacted by championing the high. "Art for art's sake" became their rallying cry. Art had to be dedicated to nothing but itself; it had to pursue beauty, truth, and deep feeling on their own terms, without any concern for the masses. "Nothing is truly beautiful unless it is useless," wrote the French critic Théophile Gautier (1811–1872). "Everything that is useful is actually ugly since its usefulness derives from its answering to a human need—and human needs are ignoble and disgusting. . . . The most useful thing in a house [after all] is the toilet."

Turn to Aestheticism

The preface to Oscar Wilde's novel *The Picture of Dorian Gray* (1891) served as a manifesto for this passionate aestheticism:

> The artist is the creator of beautiful things. To reveal art and conceal the artist is art's aim. . . .
>
> Those who find ugly meanings in beautiful things are corrupt without being charming. . . . Those who find beautiful meanings in beautiful things are the cultivated. For these there is hope. . . .

---

9 H. (for Henry) Rider Haggard's novels later became the models for the *Indiana Jones* movies.

> There is no such thing as a moral or an immoral book. Books are well written, or badly written. That is all.
>
> . . . It is the spectator, and not life, that art really mirrors. Diversity of opinion about a work of art shows that the work is new, complex, and vital. . . . We can forgive a man for making a useful thing as long as he does not admire it. The only excuse for making a useless thing is that one admires it intensely.
>
> All art is quite useless.

Wilde's career reached its zenith in his brilliant stage comedy *The Importance of Being Earnest* (1895); but his fall, after a conviction for "gross indecency" with his homosexual lover, inspired a keen self-investigation. Written in 1897 while in his prison cell, his *De Profundis* ("Out of the Depths") recognizes the need for moral seriousness and the pursuit of goodness in life. Without this sense of spiritual purpose, he writes, life is cast adrift. And this aimlessness permits the greed, power wielding, and self-serving hypocrisy of late Victorian society. In the words of the Danish philosopher Søren Kierkegaard (1813–1855), it was "the sickness unto death" and the principal curse of modern European life.

THE ILLNESS OF WESTERN SOCIETY

European society was "disintegrating, corroding, as a result of the decay of civilized life," proclaimed the first edition of *Le Décadent*, published in Paris in 1886. The "decadence" referred to was more than merely the decline of traditional moral and artistic standards; it was the positive assertion that such values did not hold because they did not exist. They were simply relative norms that the truly free individual could and should refuse to live by.

Imagery of Illness

Many critics of turn-of-the-century culture used the imagery and language of illness to describe what they saw around them. The Norwegian playwright Henrik Ibsen's drama *Ghosts* (1881) suggested a moral rot in European culture analogous to advanced syphilis, prompting one critic to describe the play as an open sewer. The Austrian writer Arthur Schnitzler used the same metaphor in his 1900 play *La Ronde* ("A Circle Dance"), in which pairs of lovers meet in various locales around Vienna, before or after their sexual encounters. Schnitzler's lovers come from every social class, from the Austrian aristocracy to street prostitutes, and they portray the moral decadence that so many thought endemic to the time. The novel *Against the Grain* (or *Against Nature*, *À rebours*, 1884) by French writer Joris-Karl Huysmans and Oscar Wilde's *The Picture of Dorian Gray* (1890) chronicle, in lushly lurid language, the physical and spiritual decay of their protagonists. The popular Welsh writer Arthur Machen (1863–1947) exploited themes of degeneration and sickness in horror stories like "The Great God Pan" (1894) and fantasy novels like *The Hill of Dreams* (1907). Tuberculosis—generally known as "consumption" at the time—appeared time and again in novels, plays, and operas whose heroes, antiheroes, and love interests waste away in settings of physical and emotional rot. *La Bohème* ("The Bohemian Girl," 1896), an opera by Italian composer Giacomo Puccini, traces the doomed love of a consumptive artist in a Parisian garret in sumptuous music. The novel *Buddenbrooks* (1901), by German writer Thomas Mann, chronicles the decline of German society through several generations of a physically and spiritually sickly mercantile family. Mann's *Tristan* (1903) and *The Magic Mountain* (1924) are set in a tuberculosis sanatorium.

With so many voices bearing witness to the illness of Western society, it is not surprising that other voices answered—with some unexpected diagnoses and treatments all their own. Political and social critics denounced the imperialist policies that had given the West control of much of the world (as we will see in the next chapter), but had cost it its soul. Chemistry had to reinvent itself after the discovery of new particles and new forms of energy. Physics replaced the Newtonian order with two new systems, quantum theory and relativity, that contradicted each other. Philosophy almost gave up on the external world to focus on our modes of perception, and literature described a culture suffering from terminal illness. And a new science of the mind emerged: psychology.

FREUD AND PSYCHOANALYSIS

Where there is illness, there will be physicians, or those acting as such, to treat the afflicted. Psychology emerged in the late 19th century and grew rapidly both in sophistication and in popularity. The existence of an unconscious or subconscious mind dates at least to 1889, with the work of the French psychologist Pierre Janet (1859–1947), and allusions to a mind within the mind can be traced back to the Enlightenment. But the idea gained new power with the work of Sigmund Freud (1856–1939).

After completing his medical studies, Freud specialized as a neurologist and general psychologist. In 1886 he married and set up a private practice in his hometown of Vienna. Freud first used hypnosis as a means to access the inner thoughts of his patients, but he noticed that its effects were temporary; besides, most of his patients spoke quite freely without it. He developed instead **psychoanalysis**, the technique of encouraging free association, and he saw meaningful patterns not only in what his patients said but also in what they avoided saying. From this he developed the concept of *repression*: certain thoughts were being held back not only from open expression but also from the patients' conscious thinking. And many of these repressed thoughts turned out to be sexual in nature. Freud hypothesized that neuroses resulted from patients' inability to address basic erotic instincts.

Freud's Theory of Consciousness

By the late 1890s, Freud had begun to elaborate a new theory of consciousness. For Freud, our waking minds are in continual dialogue with our unspoken urges and with equally powerful social and cultural norms that regulate those instinctive drives. In Freud's terminology, one's conscious mind, the *ego*, is a product of and a counterbalance to two additional processes. One is our biological instinct for sexual pleasure, the *id*. The other is the ethical conscience, the *superego*—consisting of social norms, religious teachings, and cultural values. Freud realized that he could test his theory by studying not only his patients' free-associative ramblings but also their unconscious ones—in their dreams. What is a dream, after all, but our minds still thinking and talking while our bodies rest?

In 1899 he published what he considered his greatest work, *The Interpretation of Dreams*, which argues that dreams originate as wish fulfillment. Common moral standards dictate that one ought not to act on every sexual impulse. In response, our superegos repress these feelings without our conscious effort. To Freud, however, these impulses are never annihilated; they simply find expression in indirect ways—chiefly through our dreams. But even in the dream state, our

Freud's Couch This is the original couch used in Sigmund Freud's psychoanalytic practice in Vienna, where much of the clinical work was done that led to the formulation of his theories of the human mind.

superegos remain active, which explains why erotic desires are often expressed in our dreams through disjointed images, dialogues, or sensations. Our ids also find delight and release in racy jokes (when in safe company) and "Freudian slips" of the tongue or pen. (The formal term is *parapraxis*—plural *parapraxes*.)

Freud's *Three Essays in the Theory of Sexuality* (1905) insisted on sex as the primal and primary human instinct, and it provoked a storm of protest. Victorian society was never as prudish as people often think it was; polite society did not relish open discussions of sexual matters, but it permitted them within the limits of propriety. *Three Essays* rankled not simply because it dealt with sexuality but also because of what it said about sex.

Freud describes sexuality as starting in infancy and progressing through stages. The first stage is the baby's intense focus on the delight derived from bodily contact with one's parents, in nursing or cuddling. The second, the "anal stage," lasting from about eighteen months to three years, finds relief in control of the lower digestive tract. In the third stage, spanning from three to six years, the child becomes fascinated with the genitals. This "Oedipal stage" was the most shocking of all. In Freud's theory, when a child becomes aware of genital pleasure, a complex chain reaction sets in—culminating in a son's desire to supplant his father as the object of his mother's attention. In the parallel "Electra" stage, a daughter desires to supplant her mother in her father's affection.[10] It is not that all children desire to have sexual intercourse with their parents. Rather, at some basic level, one's parents are the source of physical pleasure from the moment of one's birth, and hence we associate bodily pleasure with our parents. At the Oedipal stage, however, our bodies begin to feel an entirely new type of pleasure stimulus, one that our species is hardwired to dissociate from our parents. (This is what he meant as a taboo.) Learning to accept this new bodily pleasure as something wholly distinct from the body pleasure we associate in our minds with our parents is part of the inner conflict of adolescence.

Freud labored for years to earn acceptance of his theories. Despite his growing clinical practice and dedicated disciples, the psychological world resisted his focus on the role of sex in shaping human nature. Most people are still uncomfortable with his model. Freud is saying, after all, that everyone is driven by instinct; everyone's conscience represses true nature; everyone's consciousness has the same fundamental structure. To a class-obsessed world like Freud's, the notion that a duke experiences the same mental processes as a ditchdigger was unpardonable. The turning point came in 1909, when Freud accepted an invitation to

---

[10]   Freud had a lifelong fascination with ancient Greek mythology and drew freely from it for illustrations of his ideas. Oedipus is the mythical king of Thebes who fulfills the tragic destiny assigned to him by Fate when he unknowingly kills the man who was his father and marries the woman who was his mother. Electra is the daughter of Agamemnon, king of Mycenae, and his queen Clytemnestra, whose love for her father leads her, in some versions of the story, to kill the person who murdered him—Clytemnestra. In other versions, she does not participate in Clytemnestra's death but rejoices in it.

deliver a series of public lectures in the United States, later published as *Five Lectures on Psychoanalysis*. They helped correct the popular image of him as a sex-obsessed madman. His *Introductory Lectures on Psychoanalysis* (1917) also added to his reputation. His polite manner and the straightforward, accessible rigor of his thinking won people over and made them willing at least to consider his approach.

Many people wrote to Freud, from this time on, with questions or entreaties. One of his most famous letters (1935) was this response, in English, to an American woman's inquiry about her son:

Dear Mrs. [X].

I gather from your letter that your son is a homosexual. I am most impressed by the fact, that you do not mention this term yourself in your information about him. May I question you why you avoid it? Homosexuality is assuredly no advantage, but it is nothing to be ashamed of, no vice, no degradation, it cannot be classified as an illness; we consider it to be a variation of the sexual function produced by a certain arrest of sexual development. Many highly respectable individuals of ancient and modern times have been homosexuals, several of the greatest men among them (Plato, Michelangelo, Leonardo da Vinci, etc.). It is a great injustice to persecute homosexuality as a crime and cruelty too. If you do not believe me, read the books of Havelock Ellis [an English contemporary of Freud who wrote the first objective study of homosexuality].

By asking me if I can help, you mean, I suppose, if I can abolish [your son's] homosexuality and make normal heterosexuality take its place. The answer is, in a general way, we cannot promise to achieve it. In a certain number of cases we succeed in developing the blighted germs of heterosexual tendencies, which are present in every homosexual; in the majority of cases it is no longer possible. It is a question of the quality and the age of the individual. The result of treatment cannot be predicted. What analysis can do for your son runs in a different line. If he is unhappy, neurotic, torn by conflicts, inhibited in his social life, analysis may bring him harmony, peace of mind, full efficiency, whether he remains a homosexual or gets changed. If you make up your mind he should have analysis with me—I don't expect you will—he has to come over to Vienna. I have no intention of leaving here. However, don't neglect to give me your answer.

Sincerely yours with kind wishes,

Freud

P.S. I did not find it difficult to read your handwriting. Hope you will not find my writing and my English a harder task.

As his fame grew, Freud continued to revise his conclusions. Most significantly, he argued that an instinct toward aggression challenges sex for primacy. *Freud's* Aggression originates as the instinct for self-preservation. In a life-or-death situation, people will resort to violence. Aggression also represents an expression of *the* the sexual instinct: to secure access to a mate, human behavior ranges from competitive mating rituals to actual violence. Every act of creation is also an act of destruction. To grow a crop, one must first rip out existing plant life.

Freud's Beyond the Pleasure Principle

In 1920 he published *Beyond the Pleasure Principle*, a treatise on what he called the "death drive." This drive (Thanatos, named after the Greek god of death) represents the counterweight to the life-generating sexual impulse (Eros, the Greek god of love), but is also in some ways just another expression of it. Sexual enjoyment involves stimulation of our physical senses and mental energies—and yet there is a countervailing pleasure in the calming of the senses after great excitement. We experience the pleasure of relaxation not only after heated sex but also after a hectic day's work or a battle with heavy traffic. The desire for death is the purest and most complete craving for calm after the strain and clamor of life. It is a longing to return to the inanimate state from which we all originate.

Freud came slowly to the theory of aggression. In fact, it took World War I to convince him of humanity's innate barbarism. He began by analyzing and treating individual cases, but the horrors of the new century led him to psychoanalyze the culture itself. His late book-length essay titled *Civilization and Its Discontents* (1929) could with justice be called "Civilization and Everyone in It." It argues that to be civilized *is* to be unhappy. Civilized behavior begins in not giving expression to our most fundamental instincts. It means not having sex with every attractive person we encounter, not striking every person who raises our anger, and not always saying what we feel. Civilization is the superego given social form. But no degree of civilized conduct can extinguish our creative and destructive instincts:

> Civilization exacts a heavy toll on man's sexuality and his instinct for aggression.... [Our natural instincts] are not to love our neighbor but to indulge our aggressive impulses upon him—whether, that is, to hurt him for labor, to use him to satisfy our sexual desires, to seize his possessions, to humiliate him, hit him, torture him, kill him.

And then the cage door snaps shut:

> Who has the audacity to deny this, in the face of all the facts of history?

For Freud, civilization cannot bring happiness. Rather it is an example of the comforting lie that Nietzsche warns against.[11] Freud hardly wants to see a return to barbarism—although he lived to see it with the rise of the Nazis and his subsequent escape to London. He wants only to relieve as much of the pain of civilized life as possible. And the only way to do so was to alleviate the crushing control of the superego. To Freud, the end of the 19th century saw the West trapped in a hypocritical sexual morality, an outworn religious culture, a decayed social structure, brutal imperialist governments, and callous capitalism. Society itself suffered from a neurosis that was to develop in the mid-20th century into a full-blown case of mass psychosis.

Psychologists today have moved far beyond Freud's original model and have rejected much of it. Few psychology departments in Western universities even teach him or mention him. However, the effect of his ideas is still felt throughout Western culture. He stands with Darwin, Marx, Nietzsche, and Einstein as one of the most influential thinkers of the past two hundred years. Imagine *that* conversation.

MODERNISM: THE FIRST WAVE

Modernism was a movement that began around 1860 with the visual arts in Europe and spread to literature, architecture, and finally to music. Like the Romanticism that characterized the start of the century (discussed in chapter 18), modernism resists easy definition since it reached into so many different spheres. The sheer number of figures who made up the movement sets it apart from the past. Unlike other cultural eras and movements—aestheticism, classicism, decadence, Enlightenment, impressionism, Romanticism, symbolism—the term *modernism* offers no hint of its core ideas or values. After all, it means nothing more than "the new." That, already, however, was a distinctive cry. The American poet and critic Ezra Pound (1885–1972) coined a slogan for a generation of artists and poets when he called on them to "make it new."

The closest thing to a manifesto of modernism appeared in 1863, in "The Painter of Modern Life," an essay by the French poet Charles Baudelaire (1821–1867) that defended the Dutch painter (and one-time war correspondent in the Crimea) Constantin Guys (1802–1892). Guys, as Baudelaire sees it, is determined to cast off old ways of expression and demands radically new responses from viewers as well. Shock is part of the point, Baudelaire is honest enough to admit, but

---

[11] Freud and Nietzsche never met. By the time Freud reached adulthood, Nietzsche had collapsed into mental illness. Freud knew Nietzsche's ideas quite well (having heard lectures on them by his philosophy professor in college), but he steadfastly refused to read him and claimed throughout his life that Nietzsche's thinking had no influence whatsoever on the development of his psychoanalytic theories.

Constantin Guys   The subject of Charles Baudelaire's 1863 essay, "The Painter of Modern Life," Constantin Guys (1802–1892) was a Dutch painter who came to fame as a war correspondent in the Crimean War (1853–1856). He documented the war's savagery in drawings and watercolors for various newspapers. After the war, he charted the developments of French culture during the Second Empire (1852–1870).

only a part. New techniques, expertly employed, will also produce new perspectives on truth and beauty: "He is in search of something indefinable—something we may perhaps term *modernity*." Many artists of the time painted even contemporary scenes with figures cloaked in medieval dress or Asian finery (then a popular fashion). "This is, on the face of it, utter laziness—pure and simple!"

Modernism demands the new, but it also rejects modernity. It rejects the inherited attitudes about how artists should work—in structure, technique, and presentation. And yet it also rejects the impersonality of conformist, mass-produced, and mass-consumed culture. The same ambivalence applies to the public at large. Although nearly every leading modernist desired a wider following, most of them also railed at popular taste. (Recall the elitist disdain for "the penny-dreadfuls of Mr. Haggard.") They wanted an art and literature that could be understood and appreciated not just by the wealthy or the aristocracy, but they often dismissed the very audiences who viewed, read, or listened to their art.

Disdain for mainstream culture was felt passionately. To Baudelaire, respectable European society was "utterly worn out, brutalized, and greedy" and incapable of genuine feeling. The German playwright Bertolt Brecht (1898–1956), too, complained:

> Whenever anyone goes to conventional stage drama, he says of it, "Oh yes, I've felt that way too; that just how I experience things; that's

> real life. . . . That's what great art is. Everything is so clear and self-
> evident. I cry when everyone else cries and laugh when everyone else
> laughs."

He wanted to create a new type of drama that solicits a different reaction:

> "Who ever would think that way? You can't do that! It's too strange;
> it's beyond belief; and it has to stop!"

Search for the "Truth Within" There was more to modernism than contrariness. In the visual arts, painters and sculptures aimed to reproduce the "truth within" rather than just external appearance. They sought personal visions of the realities beneath the surface. Art became less representational and more intuitive, symbolic, and impressionistic—more expressive of the artist's response to the world than of the world itself. It parallels the philosophical currents of the age, sometimes consciously so. The Austrian composer Arnold Schoenberg (1874–1951) pronounced that the purpose of art was "to express oneself *directly*—not one's taste or upbringing, or one's intelligence, knowledge, or skill. Not all the *acquired* characteristics, but that which is *inborn* [and] *instinctive*."

The primitive self, driven by passion and instinct, is the only self that matters to art—because it is the source of art. Most of the modernists felt naturally drawn to the irrational, intuitive, and primitive. Paul Gauguin (1848–1903) abandoned his native France (not to mention his wife and five children) to live in Tahiti and to create a new art. Spanish-born Pablo Picasso (1881–1973), arguably the greatest painter of the 20th century, was fascinated with tribal African masks. Such writers as the Greek poet Constantine Cavafy (1863–1933) and the Bohemian-Austrian poet and novelist Rainer Maria Rilke (1875–1926) shared a passion for ancient Greek mythology. Thomas Mann's four-volume novel *Joseph and His Brothers* (1930–1943) reimagined the very roots of mythology in the Biblical tale. Schoenberg, along with Russian composers Igor Stravinsky (1882–1971) and Sergei Prokofiev (1891–1953), drew on ancient folktales and songs for their music.

Modernism broke with established forms in the quest to express subjective experience. Painters and sculptors abandoned the representational art they had inherited in favor of highly personal expression. Vincent van Gogh's (1853–1890) *Starry Night* (1889) draws its power from the artist's refusal to portray the sky as it appeared outside his asylum window so that he could convey instead the state of his troubled mind. Picasso could paint exquisite representational art, but representational painting did not allow him to express what he wanted. His breakthrough, *Les Demoiselles d'Avignon* ("The Young Ladies of Avignon," 1907), portrays naked prostitutes along the Carrer d'Avinyó, a street in Barcelona then notorious for its sordid nightlife. Two of the women wear African masks with

Picasso, *Les Demoiselles d'Avignon*   1907

savage expressions, whereas the remaining three scowl. All five stare blankly and disdainfully at the viewer—presumably their next customer—as though challenging his right to be there. Their bodies are shown from at least two separate perspectives, which breaks their forms into geometric shapes and flat fields of color. The painting makes viewers feel as though they are under attack. No wonder so many people hated it, starting when it was first exhibited, in 1916.[12] Picasso knew he had produced a masterpiece and so kept it in his private collection.

The Russian-born émigré Wassily Kandinsky (1866–1944), who spent most of his adult life in Germany and France, was the most direct and eloquent theorist *Art as* of modernism after Baudelaire. His 1910 book *On the Spiritual Element in Art* has *Faith* never been equaled as a meditation on art by a practicing artist. In it he asks why

---

[12] Picasso's great rival, French painter Henri Matisse (1869–1954), reportedly flew into a rage at *Les Demoiselles d'Avignon*, feeling that Picasso was mocking Modernism.

art matters, why it is worth material sacrifice, and why it can elevate the soul even in a time of deepening confusion and despair. Art, to him, is as much faith as aesthetics, in a world that no longer has a place for organized religion:

> The spirit strengthens itself and develops itself just as the body does; and just as a body can weaken and become worn out, so too can the spirit. The essential, life-generating force within every artist is precisely like the "talent of gold" described in the Gospel story—it is the priceless thing that must not be buried away, and any artist who lets his talents decay without putting them to use is like the "lazy servant" of the story. . . . Art is a force that has a goal: it must be made to serve the development and refinement of the human soul.

Art, in other words, supplants religion (as Nietzsche had already insisted); it is the only remaining means of achieving anything like spiritual salvation:

> An artist must train his soul as much as he trains his eye. . . . And above all he must have something to say; to master a technique, to gain control over physical form is not the goal of art. Art's only real goal is to adapt form to spiritual meaning.

This is precisely why abstraction is not only acceptable but also necessary. The only eternal realities that the spirit can attain and understand, the only transcendent truths available to us, are those experienced through aesthetic bliss. And art follows no rules but its own:

> Abstract forms, or representational forms that have been partially abstracted, can take the place of determinedly physical objects in almost any painting. . . . For "beauty" in art is nothing more nor less than the expression of the soul's desire. Whatever seems beautiful to our souls is beautiful in art.

Modernists like Kandinsky thought of art as the only substitute for religious faith, the only spiritual lifeline available in a world otherwise devoid of hope or meaning beyond our meager selves.

THE CATHOLIC COUNTERATTACK

The 19th century's social and intellectual challenge to faith affected Catholic Christianity less than it did the Protestant variety. At the urban street level, Catholics made up a high percentage of industrial workers across Europe and generally brought with them ingrained habits of communal identity. Irish immigrants, for example, filled many of northern England's largest factories, just as Polish, Czech, and Hungarian workers flocked into German manufacturing cities. And as immigrants, their minority status heightened their sense of solidarity. Catholic migrant workers also tended to live in congregated clusters, which led easily to the development of full parish life. Moreover, the Catholic Church was relatively quick to condemn the excesses of industrial capitalism and the wealth disparities between the bourgeoisie and the working poor. That meant that fewer Catholics fell away from their faith because of their church's supposed association with the capitalist elite.

The supreme expression of the church's warnings about unchecked capitalism appeared in 1891 when Pope Leo XIII (r. 1878–1903) issued the encyclical *Social* (papal decree) *Rerum novarum* (*Of New Things*). The Church recognized the *Catholicism* intrinsic rights of private property but insisted on the equal right of workers to form labor unions. Without a system of collective bargaining, Leo argues, the industrial capitalist economy gives a morally unacceptable permanent advantage to the wealthy:

> Let workers and employers therefore make free agreements, and in particular let them agree freely as to wages; nevertheless, there remains a fundamental requirement of natural justice older and more authoritative than any arrangement between man and man—namely, that wages

Noble Workers   Giuseppe Pellizza da Volpedo (1868–1907) was an Italian artist who dedicated most of his short life to promoting the rights of the working class and advocating for socialism. This famous work, *The Fourth Estate* (1901), commemorates striking workers (the "fourth estate") in Milan. The prominent role given to a woman in the picture was radical even among Italian progressives of the era, and the composition as a whole celebrates the power of mass movement.

ought not be so low that a frugal and well-behaved worker cannot support himself or his family. When a worker is forced, by need or by fear of something even worse, to accept wages lower than this threshold by an employer who refuses to pay more, the worker is nothing more than a victim of violent injustice.

At the same time he insists, in a swipe at Marxism, that the relationship between workers and owners must not be and need not be one of conflict:

The great error [of Marxists] is to insist on the idea that each class is inevitably hostile to the other, and that capitalists and workers are fixed by a law of nature in a state of perpetual conflict. This view is so wrong-headed and contrary to reason that in fact its exact opposite is true—for just as the harmony of the human body derives from the proper arrangement of its various parts, so too does nature ordain that in human society the various classes should dwell in harmonious accord. This is what produces the balance in a body politic. Each class needs the other, for capital cannot survive without labor, and labor cannot survive without capital.

The Catholic social movement, of which *Rerum novarum* was merely one part, had begun in the 1820s as soon as industrialization took root on the Continent, which insulated the faith from the slow pull of secularism. **Social Catholicism** was founded on the idea that the challenge to Christian society under industrialism was structural rather than personal. The question, in other words, was not "How do we help the poor?" but "How do we combat poverty?" Liberal economics in the industrialized state did not merely fail to eradicate poverty but actually caused it—and hence the response had to be principled and ideological as well as activist.

Clergy in Belgium, France, and Germany preached steadily against the systemic flaw of unregulated capitalism. In 1825 the first full-length moral indictment of industrial society appeared: *Regarding the Faith and Its Relations with the Civil and Political Order*, by a French priest named Hugues de Lamennais (1782–1854). A German priest and later bishop of Mainz, Wilhelm Emmanuel (Baron von Ketteler, 1811–1877), entered the fray immediately after his ordination, preaching on workers' rights and the need for state regulation of the marketplace. He called for the legalization of labor unions throughout Europe. In 1869, at a bishops' conference in the ancient German city of Fulda, he argued passionately that the problem of industrial capitalism was vastly more significant than any of the intellectual conflicts then confronting Christian society. Poverty, he insisted, not Charles Darwin, was the real scourge of the age. In England, Henry Edward

Manning (1808–1892), a convert from Anglicanism, regularly preached sermons on the rights of laborers; in 1889 he helped negotiate a settlement to the dock-workers' strike that paralyzed commerce in London. After he was made a cardinal in the church, Manning became a close adviser to Pope Leo XIII and indeed helped him to write *Rerum novarum*.

The Catholic Church had less success confronting the intellectual challenges of geology, evolution, and physics. The fundamental issue remained that pre- *The* sented by the original Scientific Revolution: how can the claims of Revealed *Challenge* Truth (as in the Bible) be reconciled with the claims of secular science, and who *of Modern* has the authority to render such judgments? Pope Pius IX (r. 1846–1878) staked *Science* out his own position by summoning the First Vatican Council (1869–1870), the convocation best known for pronouncing the dogma of papal infallibility.

The infallibility of the pope had been a traditional assumption among Catholics since the Middle Ages, but it had never been formalized as an official teaching. The Vatican Council determined that the dogma of infallibility, already established by tradition, needed formal definition to provide a guarantee of the Church's authority against the intrusion of new ideas upon Catholic faith. The pope, as head of the Church, must have recourse to the exercise of absolute authority over it in the definition of its central beliefs in certain circumstances. Pius IX's political travails in Italy made him increasingly conservative, and although he remained revered for his piety and gentle nature, his last years in office were marked by a deepening isolation from the world outside the palace walls. Pius's successor, Leo XIII (r. 1878–1903), resolved to bring the Church back into direct engagement with the world. Although no less conservative than Pius, Leo revitalized the Church's campaign to secure the rights of workers and the poor. He introduced the idea of *subsidiarity*, by which he meant that problems ought generally to be resolved locally. This principle, which governed Catholic social teaching throughout the 20th century, had two aims. First, it sought to preserve the dignity of persons and to help them recognize their own moral responsibilities. And second, it sought to safeguard against an overreaching centralized government.

Leo responded slowly to the scientific discoveries of the century. A natural diplomat, he set out not to respond to the intellectual assaults on Catholic tradition but to prepare the groundwork for such a response. His most important effort in this regard was the encyclical *Providentissimus deus* (*The God of All Providence*, 1893), which effectively established two guiding principles. First, the truths of science and Scripture can never contradict each other once they are fully known and understood. Since both are gifts from God, they must ultimately exist in harmony; apparent contradictions between them merely indicate where our understanding is imperfect. Second, the study of the Scriptures should be welcomed at all times. It merely requires an honest spirit that seeks a better understanding of

God's word, rather than a malicious spirit that desires only to point out textual inconsistencies for their own sake. In essence, Leo asserted that the relationship between science and faith is like the relationship between quantum theory and relativity theory: for the moment, they appear to contradict each other, but let us be patient. The ultimate truth will emerge to harmonize what appears irreconcilable.

Pius X's War on Modernity   Leo's successor would have none of it. Pius X (r. 1903–1914) railed against all forms of intellectual novelty—which he grouped under the heading "modernism." He was kindly, pious, and generous, but he regarded any new idea as a direct threat to the faith and stubbornly refused to consider it. Soon enough, he would not allow new ideas to be considered. In two encyclicals issued in 1907, *Lamentabili sane exitu (With Lamentable Consequence)* and *Pascendi dominici gregis (Feeding the Lord's Flock)* he formally condemned sixty-five teachings that he deemed irredeemably anti-Catholic. Calling them a **Syllabus of Errors**, he ordered all clerics to swear a loyalty oath that explicitly rejected every tenet of modernism. The oath, which was required of all clergy until 1967, ran in part as follows:

> I proclaim that God, Who is the origin and the end of all things, can be known with certainty by the natural light of reason; . . . that the teachings of the Faith have been handed down to us from the Apostles, through the orthodox Fathers, and always with exactly the same meaning and the same intent; . . . I declare my complete opposition to the errors of the modernists, who claim that there is nothing divine in sacred tradition [of the church]. . . . I firmly maintain and shall maintain to my last breath the belief of the Church Fathers in the sacred gift of Truth— Truth which most certainly exists, has existed, and always shall exist in the apostolic succession of bishops. . . . And I vow that I will keep these promises faithfully, wholly, and sincerely, keeping them inviolate, and in no way ever deviating from them in teaching or any other way. . . . All these things I do promise and swear, so help me God.

He followed up by instituting a clerical purge. He recommended the establishment of oversight committees (called *sodalitia*, or "fellowships") in every diocese in the church worldwide. These he charged with the detection of modernism and empowered to censor all clerical publications, and he entitled them to work in complete secrecy.[13] Accordingly, scores of books were banned and dozens of

---

13   Some censors went so far as to intercept private mail and to review a suspect's book purchases at local shops. Many kept notes in secret codes.

priestly careers ended—some by expulsion from clerical orders and some even by excommunication.

The effect of these measures was easy to imagine: much of Catholic intellectual life stagnated. It did not recover until after World War II, with the establishment of the Second Vatican Council (1962–1965). To many in the broader Western society, the church's war on modernism seemed a painful embarrassment, not merely a flat-out inability to understand modern scientific thinking but a petulant refusal by pious ideologues to think or to allow others to do so. Victims of the purges under Pius X—like the French priest and scholar Alfred Loisy (1857–1940) and the English Jesuit George Tyrell (1861–1909)—became martyrs to intellectual freedom for their supporters. Loisy was defrocked and excommunicated, whereas Tyrell was expelled from the Jesuit order and excommunicated. Both men were denied a Catholic burial. And the Roman Catholic Church entered the 20th century with a growing popular reputation as the enemy of thinking.

MODERNISM, SECULARISM, AND THE JEWS

The secularist trend did not trouble the Jewish worlds nearly as much as it did the Christian one, for the simple reason that skeptical questioning, doubting, and reevaluating have been the mainstay in Jewish thinking through the centuries. For many, Judaism has always been more about how one lives and what one does than it has been about what one believes. Reading the Scriptures with a critical eye was nothing new to them.

What was new, and increasingly troubling, was the trend toward assimilation into the broader cultures. This development had been accelerating since the 18th century, when reform-minded Jews embraced the ideals of toleration and secularism advanced by the Enlightenment. Casting off traditional clothing *The Challenge of Assimilation* and seizing the opportunities offered by the rise of liberal democracy and capitalism, the numbers of Jews who either formally, if emptily, converted to Christianity to escape anti-Jewish restrictions on their public lives, or who took non-Jewish spouses, steadily increased. Assimilation did not necessarily result in loss of Jewish identity—the bigots in society made sure of that—but over the generations it had a corrosive effect.

As we saw in chapter 16, the movement away from Orthodoxy had begun at least a century earlier, in the early 18th century. Yet Orthodox leaders failed to respond to developments effectively. It may be that they regarded the rise of anti-Semitism or the suffering of the industrialized poor as the more pressing problems; certainly nationalistic passions from one end of Europe to the other gave them reason to pause. But the fact remains that Jewish Orthodoxy by and large dug in its heels. Like Catholic conservatism, it fought against the new scientific understandings of religious tradition by simply saying no.

Surprisingly few Orthodox rabbis took on the Darwinian challenge, however. Instead, they just ignored it. Judaism had never accepted the notion of original sin and the Fall of Man—the idea that human life is a devolution from an earlier state of spiritual perfection. Thus, few Jews felt that humanity's rise from primitive beginnings threatened their tradition. Moreover, Orthodoxy had never insisted on a literal interpretation of the Six Days of Creation, which left the door open to accepting geological time.

Once again, social and economic changes led to the spread of nonobservance, but here the role of industrialization was less important than it was for Christian Europe. Over the course of the 19th century, Europe experienced two major waves of immigration—of Jews fleeing the troubled Ottoman Empire and of Jews escaping the pogroms in Tsarist Russia (discussed in chapter 20). The overall European population doubled to more than 400 million, and the number of Jews went from roughly 3 million to 8 million. Close to 5 million, however, lived specifically in eastern Europe, and most of them were poor—victims of the weak economic development of the area, of their own refugee status, or of legal barriers to advancement.[14] Given their dire condition, many emigrated yet again, farther west into cities like Warsaw (30,000 in 1800 and 300,000 in 1900), Berlin (12,000 in 1800 and 140,000 in 1900), and Vienna (2,000 in 1800 and 150,000 in 1900). There they followed the classic immigrant pattern of hard work, education, and advancement through subsequent generations to reach professional status—doctors, lawyers, journalists (see Map 22.1). Secularization, as a consequence, resulted from the drive to succeed and gain acceptance.

The family of Karl Marx fit this pattern, as did those of Theodor Herzl (the Zionist leader introduced in chapter 20) and Sigmund Freud. What was unusual in their cases was simply the degree of secularism and assimilation that they had achieved. Describing the same phenomenon among Jewish immigrants to the United States, Hungarian-born Moses Weinberger (1854–1940), a popular Orthodox writer, lamented in 1887:

> How awesome is the strength of America! In a single year it transforms "Rachel, wife of Reb Jaakov" into "Mrs. Jacobs" and "Reb Baruch, cobbler and shoemaker" into "Mr. Bennett, Shoe Manufacturer." The Enlightenments of Berlin and Europe put together did not accomplish as much in half a century.

---

[14] Most secondary schools at the time restricted Jewish enrollment to no more than 5 percent of the student body.

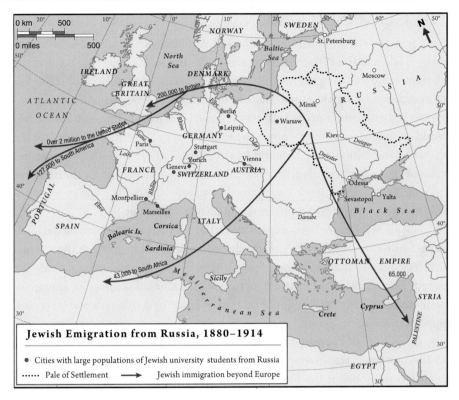

MAP 22.1   Jewish Emigration from Russia, 1880–1914   Bitter persecution of the Jews who lived in the Pale of Settlement—the expanse of steppe-land that bridged eastern Europe and western Russia—by the Romanov tsars led to either voluntary migration or forced expulsion of millions of Jews into eastern and central Europe.

A separate movement among 19th-century Jews is known variously as Secular Judaism, Secular Zionism, Humanistic Judaism, or Cultural Zionism. This *Secular Judaism* was not, as it might sound, a vision of Jewish identity shorn of religious convictions. Rather, it emphasized a fundamental unity of identity across the religious lines that divided the multiple Jewish traditions—Orthodox, Reform, and Conservative Judaism, plus the many subgroups and outcroppings belonging to each. Among the early leaders of this mission was Asher Ginsberg (1856–1927), a Russian Jew better known by his pen name, Ahad Ha'am. Ahad Ha'am clashed with Theodor Herzl over the issue of establishing a Zionist state in Palestine, thinking it was impractical. But he did want to help organize and maintain a Jewish presence in Palestine, one that would symbolize for all Jews everywhere their ancestral linkage. It would establish, in his words, "a Jewish state and not merely a state made up of Jews." Seeing the growing divisions among Jews as a greater problem, for the moment at least, than the vulnerable position of Jews in Western society, Ahad Ha'am devoted his life to calling all Jews to recognize their fundamental and eternal connectedness.

THE ISLAMIC EXCEPTION

Distance from Modern Science

The rapid growth—imposition, really—of Wahhabism was the major development in Islam in the 19th century, as we saw in chapter 20. Scientific study in the Muslim world had long since turned inward to focus on already-codified bodies of knowledge rather than new areas of investigation. Few of the European advances and discoveries of the 19th century made much of an impact in the Islamic world or, indeed, were even known there, and so they presented nothing like the threat to traditional faith they did in the West. Darwin's *Origin of Species* remained virtually unheard of; it appeared in an Arabic translation for the first time only in 2009.[15] The scientific vacuum this represented made it easier for Wahhabism's form of aggressive anti-intellectualism to take root.

Not all Muslim societies experienced the same distancing from modern science. Some embraced it wholeheartedly, at least in theory, although their actual involvement was somewhat marginal. Others, however, remained staunchly opposed. They saw the systematic structure of scientific thinking as an attempt to confound the complete freedom of action retained by Allah. In a few instances, opposition to science lasted until well into the 20th century. In Iran, for example, dissection of corpses remained forbidden in medical schools until the 1920s; moreover, traditional medicine (*yunani-tibb*, in Arabic) based on the ancient Greek model of the four humors is still taught, licensed, and practiced.

Al-Azhar University, Cairo, ca. 1910   Founded in the 10th century, Al-Azhar is one of the oldest universities in the world. For nearly a thousand years its curriculum—Islamic law and jurisprudence, Arabic, grammar, logic, and philosophy—barely changed.

---

[15]   A 2009 poll in Egypt found that only 9 percent of the adult population both knew of evolution and believed in it.

And at the leading Islamic university in Egypt, Al-Azhar University in Cairo, the Copernican heliocentric model was not officially accepted until 1961.

To many in the Islamic world strongly opposed to the new science, their position was not merely a knee-jerk rejection of innovative thinking. Rather, it was a rejection of European political imperialism—which was beginning to take place precisely at the end of the 19th century. Armed with technologies made possible by the new science—machine guns and artillery, especially—European powers encroached on the Islamic, African, and Asian worlds with a force that seemed demonic. Resistance was determined but futile. Relations across the Greater West were about to enter a dramatic new phase, one filled with hostility and dread. To many in the Islamic world, the brutality of the imperialist Europeans resulted not from their being Christian, but from their being God-less.

WHO, WHAT, WHERE

aestheticism
atheism
general theory
    of relativity
modernism
On the Origin of
    Species by Means of
    Natural Selection

psychoanalysis
quantum theory
secularism
Social Catholicism
special theory of
    relativity
supermen
Syllabus of Errors

theory of evolution
    by natural selection
uncertainty principle
uniformitarianism
will to power

SUGGESTED READINGS

Primary Sources

Darwin, Charles. *The Descent of Man.*
Darwin, Charles. *On the Origin of Species.*
Feuerbach, Ludwig. *The Essence of Christianity.*
Freud, Sigmund. *Civilization and Its Discontents.*
Freud, Sigmund. *The Interpretation of Dreams.*
Geiger, Abraham. *The Biblical Text and Its Transmission.*
Goldziher, Ignaz. *Muslim Studies.*
Kandinsky, Wassily. *On the Spiritual Element in Art.*
Leo XIII, Pope. *Rerum Novarum.*
Lyell, Charles. *Principles of Geology.*

Nietzsche, Friedrich. *The Gay Science.*
Renan, Ernst. *The Life of Jesus.*
Strauss, David Friedrich. *The Christ of Belief and the Jesus of History.*
Strauss, David Friedrich. *The Life of Jesus Critically Examined.*
Wellhausen, Julius. *Prolegomena to the Historical Origins of Islam.*
Wellhausen, Julius. *Prolegomena to the History of Ancient Israel.*
Wilde, Oscar. *De Profundis.*
Wilde, Oscar. *The Importance of Being Earnest.*

Anthologies

Albright, Daniel. *Modernism and Music: An Anthology of Sources* (2004).

Fritzsche, Peter, trans. and ed. *Nietzsche and the Death of God: Selected Writings* (2011).

Guy, Josephine, ed. *The Victorian Age: An Anthology of Sources and Documents* (2001).

Herbert, Sandra. *Charles Darwin and the Question of Evolution: A Brief History with Documents* (2011).

Otis, Laura. *Literature and Science in the 19th Century* (2009).

Otis, Laura, ed. *Literature and Science in the Nineteenth Century: An Anthology* (2009).

Perelberg, Rosine Jozef, ed. *Freud: A Modern Reader* (2005).

Rainey, Lawrence, ed. *Modernism: An Anthology* (2005).

Studies

Armstrong, Tim. *Modernism: A Cultural History* (2005).

Artigas, Mariano, Thomas F. Glick, and Rafael A. Martínez. *Negotiating Darwin: The Vatican Confronts Evolution, 1877–1902* (2007).

Bernardi, Peter J. *Maurice Blondel, Social Catholicism, and Action Française: The Clash over the Church's Role in Society during the Modernist Era* (2008).

Brown, Callum G. *The Death of Christian Britain: Understanding Secularisation, 1800–2000* (2009).

Browne, Janet. *Charles Darwin: A Biography* (2003).

Burrow, J. W. *The Crisis of Reason: European Thought, 1848–1914* (2002).

Chiron, Yves. *Saint Pius X: Restorer of the Church* (2002).

Crews, Robert D. *For Prophet and Tsar: Islam and Empire in Russia and Central Asia* (2009).

Fawaz, Leila Tarazi, and C. A. Bayly, eds. *Modernity and Culture: From the Mediterranean to the Indian Ocean* (2001).

Ford, Alan. *James Ussher: Theology, History, and Politics in Early-Modern Ireland and England* (2007).

Gay, Peter. *Modernism: The Lure of Heresy from Baudelaire to Beckett and Beyond* (2010).

Gay, Peter. *Schnitzler's Century: The Making of Middle-Class Culture, 1815–1914* (2002).

Gregory, Brad S. *The Unintended Reformation: How a Religious Revolution Secularized Society* (2012).

Hill, Harvey. *The Politics of Modernism: Alfred Loisy and the Scientific Study of Religion* (2002).

Jodock, Darrell. *Catholicism Contending with Modernity: Roman Catholic Modernism and Anti-Modernism in Historical Context* (2010).

Knight, Mark. *Nineteenth-Century Religion and Literature* (2006).

Koltun-Fromm, Ken. *Abraham Geiger's Liberal Judaism: Personal Meaning and Religious Authority* (2006).

Kragh, Helge. *Higher Speculations: Grand Theories and Failed Revolutions in Physics and Cosmology* (2011).

Kragh, Helge. *Quantum Generations: A History of Physics in the Twentieth Century* (2002).

Larsen, Timothy. *Crisis of Doubt: Honest Faith in Nineteenth-Century England* (2009).

Larsen, Timothy. *A People of One Book: The Bible and the Victorians* (2011).

McLeod, Hugh. *Secularisation in Western Europe, 1848–1914* (2000).

O'Connor, James, trans. *The Gift of Infallibility: The Official Relatio on Infallibility by Bishop Vincent Ferrer Gasser at Vatican Council* (2008).

Prusak, Bernard P. *The Church Unfinished: Ecclesiology through the Centuries* (2004).

Schultenover, David G., ed. *The Reception of Pragmatism in France and the Rise of Roman Catholic Pragmatism, 1890–1914* (2009).

Weller, Shane. *Modernism and Nihilism* (2011).

Winchester, Simon. *The Map That Changed the World: William Smith and the Birth of Modern Geology* (2001).

Young, Julian. *The Death of God and the Meaning of Life* (2003).

Young, Julian. *Friedrich Nietzsche: A Philosophical Biography* (2010).

For additional resources, including maps, primary sources, visuals, web links, and quizzes, please go to **www.oup.com/us/backman**.

CHAPTER 23

The Great Land Grab

1870–1914

There is, it seems, no end to empires. To individual megastates, yes—but to empires themselves, no. We have already had a parade of them: the Akkadians, the Hittites, the Assyrians, the Babylonians, the neo-Babylonians, and the Persians—empires all, and all only by the end of our first two chapters. Subsequent chapters presented the Athenian, the Alexandrian, the Roman, the Parthian, the Byzantine, the Umayyad, the Carolingian, the Abbasid, the Seljuk, the Mamluk, the Mongol, and the Ottoman empires. Then came the empires of Tamerlane and Charles V. The Venetian Empire in the Mediterranean. The Aztec and Incan empires of the Americas before European "discovery." The Spanish Empire in the Americas. The Safavid Empire in Iran. The Mughal Empire in India. The Polish–Lithuanian Empire. Napoleon's Empire. The Austrian–Hungarian Empire. France's Second Empire. Russia's Romanov Empire. Until one begins to list them, one hardly realizes the extent to which Greater Western history appears to be dominated by them.

EUROPEAN COLONIES AND PROTECTORATES, 1914

Is it possible that this is not accidental? Might empires, in fact, be the norm of human political life—the default position, so to speak? Many have thought so. Especially in the late 19th and early 20th centuries, this thought

African Missionary School
This postcard shows a young woman instructing African children in the basic tenets of Christianity. The Church Missionary Society for Africa and the East was formed in 1815 to train idealistic evangelists for work overseas. About 15% of the missionaries sent out by the Society were women, most of them married to other missionaries.

- "The White Man's Burden"
- The Second Industrial Revolution
- Looking Overseas
- Missionary Europe

- Industrial Warfare and Command Economies
- Western Ways: Emulation and Resistance

CHAPTER OUTLINE

seemed to drive the European nations, and others, into headlong competition to covet and to cover the earth. Belgium, Britain, France, Germany, and Italy all took part, as did, on a smaller scale, Japan and the United States. So striking was the expansion of European power that contemporaries spoke of the "**new imperialism**," which, unlike the old, was a process that took several forms. Sometimes one state controlled another through direct rule, by which the colonizing nation annexed territories outright and subjugated the peoples who lived there. At other times, imperialism worked through indirect rule, by which conquering nations reached agreements with local leaders and governed through them. Finally, imperialism could take the shape of **informal imperialism**, where stronger states allowed weaker ones to maintain their independence while reducing their sovereignty.

Ever since their global land grab, it has been commonplace to condemn Western nations for the crushing of cultures considered "Other"—subjugation made possible by the West's technological advantages over their victims. Racism and exploitation, a greed that flat out ignored the peoples and interests of the rest of the world, is what lay behind the Western feeding frenzy, critics charge. There is much to say for this view. Critics of European imperialism can literally point to the graves of millions who died in the mad dash to make rich Europe even richer. But the period from 1870 to 1914 was also a time of resistance to empire, as reformers, activists, politicians, journalists, writers, critics, and commoners of all stripes cried out in horror at what their society was becoming or had already become.

CHAPTER TIMELINE

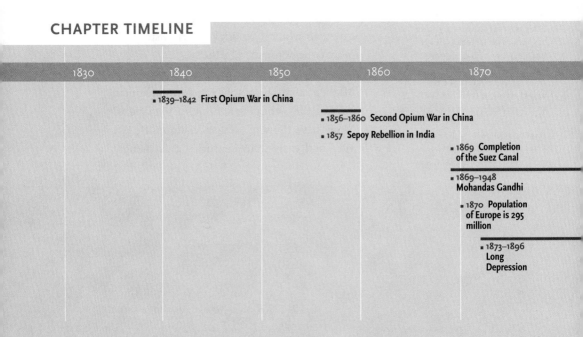

| 1830 | 1840 | 1850 | 1860 | 1870 |

▪ 1839–1842 **First Opium War in China**

▪ 1856–1860 **Second Opium War in China**

▪ 1857 **Sepoy Rebellion in India**

▪ 1869 **Completion of the Suez Canal**

▪ 1869–1948 **Mohandas Gandhi**

▪ 1870 **Population of Europe is 295 million**

▪ 1873–1896 **Long Depression**

"THE WHITE MAN'S BURDEN"

Karl Pearson (1857–1936), a prominent British mathematician and ardent champion of the British Empire, saw the new imperialism as simply the best use of the earth's resources. In an essay called "National Life from the Standpoint of Science" (1900), he wrote:

Justifying Subjugation

> History shows me one way, and one way only, in which a high state of civilization can be produced—namely, the struggle of race with race, and the survival of the physically and morally fitter race. If you want to know whether the lower races of man can evolve a higher type, I fear the only course is to leave them to fight it out among themselves. . . . Let us suppose that we could prevent the white man, if we liked, from going to lands of which the agricultural and mineral resources are not worked to the full; then I should say, "A thousand times better for him that he should not go, than that he should settle down and live alongside the inferior race."

Aside from its obvious racism, Pearson's argument was essentially amoral, and supporters of any of the empires mentioned above would likely have agreed. It runs something like this. The earth offers only finite amounts of natural resources, but the constantly increasing human population has constantly

1880	1890	1900	1910	1940

- 1880–1914 **Mass European emigration**
  - 1884 **First gasoline-powered automobile patented**

- 1884–1885 **Conference of Berlin**

  - 1898 **Battle of Omdurman in Sudan; Spanish–American War**
  - 1898–1901 **Boxer Rebellion in China**

  - 1899 **Rudyard Kipling, "The White Man's Burden"**
  - 1899–1902 **Boer War in South Africa; Philippine–American War**
    - 1901 **Naoroji, *Poverty and Un-British Rule in India***
    - 1903 **Ford Motor Company founded**
      - 1904–1905 **Russo-Japanese War**
        - 1911 **Taylor, *Principles of Scientific Management***
          - 1914 **Population of Europe is 450 million; more than 90 percent of Africa partitioned among European states**

increasing needs. Given those needs, the right to access and exploit resources belongs to whoever is in the best position to get the most value from them. A society that has failed, for whatever reason, to put its resources to proper use has effectively renounced its right to control them. And any foreign group who exploits those materials for productive gain not only is right to do so but also benefits the society shunted aside. Imperialism is therefore best understood as a vital instrument in the evolution of human civilization, and its benefits far exceed any harm it causes. From Pearson again:

> The struggle for existence between the white man and the red man in America, painful and even terrible as it was in its details, has given us a good far out-balancing its immediate evil. In place of the red man, who contributed practically nothing to the work and thought of the world, we have a great nation, mistress of many arts, and able, with its youthful imagination and fresh, untrammeled impulses, to contribute much to the common stock of civilized man.
>
> The great function of science in national life is to show us what national life means, and how the nation is a vast organism subject to the great forces of evolution. . . . Is it not a fact that the daily bread of our millions of workers depends on their having somebody to work for? That if we give up the contest for trade routes, free markets, and waste lands, we indirectly give up our food supply? Is it not a fact that our strength depends on these and upon our colonies, and that our colonies have been won by the ejection of inferior races, and are maintained against equal races by respect for the present power of our empire? . . . The path to progress is strewn with the wreck of nations; traces are everywhere to be seen of the slaughtered remains of inferior races, and of victims who found not the narrow way to perfection. Yet these dead people are, in very truth, the stepping-stones on which mankind has arisen to the higher intellectual and deeper emotional life of today.

The thought is odious, even vile. But does that mean it is incorrect?

To believe in the innate superiority of one's race or culture is nothing new. The ancient Persians had no doubt about the inferiority of every culture they overran. To the ancient Greeks the word for "barbarian" (*barbaroi*) applied to any non-Greek ethnic group; neither Charlemagne nor Tamerlane considered any of his conquered peoples his equal. And Napoleon was confident in France's divine mission to lead the world. The nations that set out after 1880 to dominate the globe shared the same confidence in their rights to rule others. But a new element crept into their thinking. The imperialism of the late 19th and early 20th centuries differed from earlier imperial adventures in this one important regard: the European champions of the new imperialism thought of their actions in Darwinian terms—as a necessary step in the evolutionary development of the entire human species. This was **social Darwinism**, the misuse of Darwin's theory of evolution by natural selection to justify competition among societies. It was all the more self-confident because of what many Europeans regarded as its scientific certitude. Belief in the "survival of the fittest" justified their actions as morally necessary—the best, or even perhaps the only, means by which human civilization itself could advance.

For English writer Rudyard Kipling (1865–1936), imperialism was "The White Man's Burden," the title of his most famous poem (1899), whose last stanzas ran:

> Take up the White Man's burden—no tawdry rule of kings,
> But toil of serf and sweeper—the tale of many things.
> The ports ye shall not enter, the roads ye shall not tread,
> Go mark them with your living, and mark them with your dead.
>
> Take up the White Man's burden—and reap his old reward:
> The blame of those ye better, the hate of those ye guard-
> The cry of hosts ye humour (ah, slowly!) toward the light:-
> "Why brought ye us from bondage, our loved Egyptian night?"
>
> Take up the White Man's burden—ye dare not stoop to less-
> Nor call too loud on Freedom to cloak your weariness;
> By all ye cry or whisper, by all ye leave to do,
> The silent, sullen peoples shall weigh your gods and you.
>
> Take up the White Man's burden, have done with childish days-
> The lightly proferred laurel, the easy, ungrudged praise.
> Comes now to search your manhood, through all the thankless years,
> Cold, edged with dear-bought wisdom, the judgment of your peers!

Kipling's call to bravado was written to persuade the United States to colonize the Philippine Islands (which the United States did in 1902, after a three-year war) as a moral duty, but it carries a trace of irony. Having been born in India, Kipling knew first-hand the emotional and moral costs that imperialism can have on the colonizers as well as the colonized. Deeply entrenched resentment and anger, not gratitude, were the wages of imperial sin.

THE SECOND INDUSTRIAL REVOLUTION

An empire is a machine—an ordered system of tools, institutions, and communications to govern people and administer goods. And that is a much more difficult thing to accomplish than the military conquests that lead up to it. Military conquest, after all, is nothing more than a bloodstain on a map, however great or small the area. An empire is so much more. True empires require engineers, jurists, civil officials, industrialists, financiers, teachers, missionaries, skilled laborers, and the infrastructures that can connect them efficiently and reliably. From 1870 to 1914 western Europe developed an abundance of all these, in what is known as the **Second Industrial Revolution**. And the natural resources needed to fuel and feed that revolution lay increasingly overseas—as did the new shape of empire.

As we saw in chapter 18, the first wave of industrialization had focused on the production of consumer goods—textiles and food, especially, with housewares and furniture running second. All were fueled by the new energy technologies of coal and by high-grade refined iron. The Second Industrial Revolution was essentially a continuation of the earlier process but with a focus instead on producing capital goods—goods used to produce other goods, such as steel, heavy machinery, chemicals, electrical power, and refined petroleum. Many of these are the "capital" of industrial capitalism, or resources in the hands of factory owners. Many are also public goods, like automobiles and radios, open to everyone and bringing people together. Other key developments of this period were the telegraph and telephone, lighter and stronger steamships and railroads, subways, the internal combustion engine, the airplane, and modern weaponry—like repeating rifles, artillery, and machine guns. The chemical industry produced soaps, detergents, dyes, photographic plates and films, medicines, gasoline and other petroleum products, synthetic textiles, paints, fertilizers, and explosives.

Advances in Chemistry   In the second half of the 19th century, chemistry, along with medicine, was the liveliest science, the site of the most exciting advances. The creation of the periodic table of elements in 1869—a table that showed regular patterns in the properties of elements arranged according to atomic weight—was the breakthrough work of Russian chemist Dmitri Mendeleev (1834–1907). With this foundation established, the discovery of new elements and chemical processes followed quickly.

When the French chemist Louis Pasteur (1822–1895) discovered germs—the microorganisms that cause many diseases—he established an entire new science, microbiology (the study of microscopic organisms), which in turn led to two critical innovations. One was *pasteurization,* in which foodstuffs are heated to destroy the bacteria that cause spoilage. The other was *immunology,* the study of vaccines and other means to protect people from disease. Pasteur perfected a vaccine against rabies by 1885, and by the end of the century other scientists had developed vaccines against cholera, diphtheria, and typhus. Joseph Lister (1827–1912), an English chemist, developed the first successful antiseptic and the process of disinfection.[1] Their work helped launch modern medicine, as did that of Madame Marie Curie (1867–1934), introduced in chapter 22. Curie, who won the Nobel Prize in Physics (1903) and then again in Chemistry (1911), established radiology, the study of radioactivity, and her work led to the development of X-rays.

Apart from their inherent intellectual values, discoveries like these made possible a large number of new manufactures and manufacturing processes, the pursuit of which allowed imperialist conquest.

Although railroads had been in use for decades, they did not overtake rivers and canals as the dominant means of transporting cargo in Europe until the 1880s. Once advances in steel production dramatically reduced the cost of laying and maintaining rail lines, the cost of shipping cargo along those lines decreased as well, which spurred further production of goods. The development of electrical grids, telegraph and telephone networks, and radio systems enabled communication at speeds never before known. It felt like a whole new era in human development. "The economic changes that have occurred during the last quarter of a century—or during the present generation of living men—have unquestionably been more important and more varied than during any period of the world's history," crowed an enthusiastic American economist, David Ames Wells (1828–1898).

Advances in Manufacture

German engineer Karl Friedrich Benz (1844–1929) patented the first gasoline-powered automobile in 1884, but it was the American industrialist Henry Ford (1863–1947) who revolutionized personal transportation. He founded the Ford Motor Company in 1903, with its innovative assembly-line model. Mass production became the norm, or at least the desired one. With plentiful cheap oil, high-grade steel machinery, and endless quantities of electrical power, goods could be produced literally around the clock. By 1900, the half dozen leading European nations produced two-thirds of all the manufactured goods on the planet. Modern transportation and communication allowed these goods to reach markets around the world, and they brought back to Europe the resources to produce more goods, which in turn stimulated new cycles of production and consumption (Map 23.1).

New technologies appeared with stunning rapidity. In the United States alone nearly a million patents were issued for inventions between the end of the

---

[1]   Listerine, the antiseptic mouthwash named for Joseph Lister, was originally marketed as a floor cleaner and a treatment for gonorrhea.

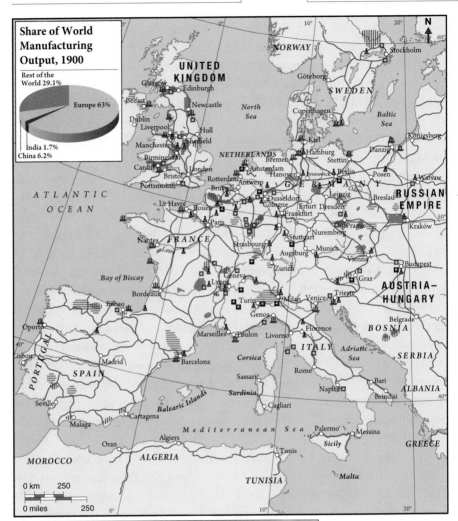

Share of World Manufacturing Output, 1900

Rest of the World 29.1%

Europe 63%

India 1.7%
China 6.2%

Industrialization and Manufacturing in Europe, 1870–1914

Industry in 1870

- Coal mining
- Iron working
- Textile production
- Major railway lines, 1914

Industry in 1914

- Steel
- Shipbuilding
- Chemicals
- Electrical industry

MAP 23.1   Industrialization and Manufacturing, 1870–1914   Industrialization required enormous investments of capital as well as technological innovation. The European nations that were able to do so—Britain, France, Belgium, Germany, and Italy—quickly dominated the global economy.

Civil War in1865 and the start of World War I in 1914—everything from pneumatic braking systems (1872) and the phonograph (1877) to the telephone (1879), light bulb (1880), jackhammer (1890), radio (1893), semiautomatic rifle (1898), safety razor and electric vacuum cleaner (1901), airplane (1903), helicopter (1907), and dental braces (1910). So quickly were new industries created that in a single five-year period, 1896–1901, the volume of stocks sold on the New York Stock Exchange increased by a factor of six. Not only did new technologies appear constantly, but also the amount of time taken to bring those technologies to market and general use shortened dramatically. The telephone, invented in 1879, had become a standard business necessity across Europe and the United States by 1900. The automobile was a novelty item at first, but with the development of the petroleum industry it was soon transforming entire cities. Petroleum also supplied the asphalt on which automobiles ran.

Modern management techniques must be counted among the innovations of the era. Called **scientific management** by its founders, this set of ideas aimed at a single goal: to improve the efficiency of the manufacturing workplace by increasing the productivity of labor. Machines, after all, could be set to function at a constant rate for as long as they were fueled and maintained, but workers were less predictable. Some were more intelligent and skillful than others, some more energetic and diligent, and some more highly motivated and determined; still others were lazy, inconsistent, awkward, and slow. To even out

Scientific Management and Its Consequences

Charting a New Course   The first automobile maps appeared in 1900 in both France and Germany. In both countries, bicycle tire manufacturers, all of whom quickly started manufacturing tires for cars, sponsored or created automobile maps to encourage people to buy their new products. In 1910, the French tire company Michelin published its first road map of France, which included information on local attractions and restaurants. Shown above is the cover of this early Michelin Guide, bearing an advertisement for Renault automobiles.

these differences, scientific management sought to break down manufacturing into small, distinct steps, along an assembly line. Rather than have a hundred furniture makers each build an entire dining table, for example, one worker could plane lumber for the tabletop, the next join the pieces, the third trim the edges, the fourth shape the table legs on a lathe, and so on, step by step, over and over, again and again. Finally, the finished dining tables emerged from the assembly line—identical, at a steady pace, and with maximum efficiency. In *The Principles of Scientific Management* (1911), American mechanical engineer Frederick Winslow Taylor (1856–1915) called for the minute study of workers' physical movements to design steps with perfect efficiency. The point was to get workers to adapt themselves to the machines they operated.

This was time management: the efficiency of the machines set the pace of manufacture. It still sometimes called for intelligent, highly skilled workers, but Taylor also saw that many tasks could be performed by any worker regardless of skill, intelligence, or motivation. At times, in fact, industry could exploit workers' lack of education or intellectual sharpness. The booming steel industry, he noted, had a particular need for dullards, since the handling of pig iron (iron ore at the intermediate stage of the smelting process) called for more brawn than brains:

> Now one of the very first requirements for a man who is fit to handle pig iron as a regular occupation is that he shall be so stupid and so phlegmatic that he more nearly resembles in his mental make-up the ox than any other type. The man who is mentally alert and intelligent is for this very reason unsuited to what would, for him, be the grinding monotony of work of this character. Therefore the workman who is best suited to handling pig iron is unable to understand the real science of doing this class of work. He is so stupid that the word *percentage* has no meaning to him, and he must consequently be trained by a man more intelligent than himself into the habit of working in accordance with the laws of this science before he can be successful. The writer trusts that it is now clear that even in the case of the most elementary form of labor that is known, there is a science, and that when the man best suited to this class of work has been carefully selected, when the science of doing the work has been developed, and when the carefully selected man has been trained to work in accordance with this science, the results obtained must of necessity be overwhelmingly greater than those which are possible under the [traditional] plan of "initiative and incentive."

The condescending tone and debt to social Darwinism are on display throughout the book. Even Taylor balked at calling workers mere appendages to machinery,

Unscientific Management   This still shot from English filmmaker Charlie Chaplin's comic masterpiece *Modern Times* (1936) illustrates how human labor was made to accommodate the workings of machines in industrial manufacture. The machine itself became the workers' boss, and occasionally (as here, with Chaplin trying to rescue a fellow worker trapped in the gears) it not only directed the workers' lives, but it consumed them.

but that is the essence of his management science and the key to his vision of efficiency.[2]

One of the chief problems with improved industrial capacity was overproduction. When manufactures outpaced consumption, prices tumbled and profits slumped or even disappeared. The problem was noted as early as the 1820s, when the word "depression" was used for the first time in its economic sense. Every advance in technology, it seemed, only made the problem worse by making it easier to produce and deliver more goods. Modern railroads and steamships could cross continents, oceans, and soon even the most daunting natural barriers. The Transcontinental Railroad crossed America in 1869, the same year that the Suez Canal was completed, cutting in half the time needed for ships to sail from Europe to India. The 12-mile-long Simplon Tunnel through the Alps, along the Swiss–Italian border, sped people and goods

---

[2]   At Harvard Business School, founded in 1908, *The Principles of Scientific Management* was the core textbook used until the start of the Great Depression in 1929.

The Suez Canal   Crowds watch the first ships to sail through the Suez Canal on November 17, 1869, in this print from a German magazine. The canal was designed by a French engineer, Ferdinand de Lesseps (1805–1894), the same man who later formally presented (though he did not design or build) the Statue of Liberty, to President Grover Cleveland of the United States.

between northern and southern Europe. Never before in Western history were so few people able to feed so many, with less than 10 percent of the population engaged in farming. This freed more workers to seek employment in cities, which pushed wages down, but production levels remained so high that food prices fell even faster.

A growing population lessened the risks of a complete collapse in prices, or deflation. The birthrate in most of western Europe declined sharply between 1870 and 1914, especially among the bourgeois and skilled-labor classes. This decline was in part a result of the availability of contraception but probably even more because of the (slowly) growing alternatives to motherhood available to women. However, advances in medicine brought about an even sharper decline in mortality, with the net result that a European population of 295 million in 1870 ballooned to more than 450 million by the start of World War I—a gain of 60 percent in two generations. Such impressive growth ensured steadily expanding markets for goods of all sorts. Even this was not enough, however. Markets, like the homes they supplied, filled to bursting with a seemingly never-ending stream of household goods, foodstuffs, appliances, tools, and decorative objects. As production grew in pace, the only solution to declining profit margins was to find ever more markets to flood with commodities. That meant looking overseas.

LOOKING OVERSEAS

Overseas resources were definitely within reach. Commercial contacts with Africa, India, eastern Asia, and the South Pacific islands had continued since the late 16th century, so the routes, harbors, and geography were mostly familiar. Now the telegraph, radio, and telephone enabled regular contact with far-flung territories, and modern weaponry gave Europeans a decisive battlefield advantage. The industrialized West seized roughly one-quarter of planet earth (and roughly one-third of its human population) in an astonishingly short span of time.

The unification of Germany in 1870 (discussed in chapter 20) played an important role. German industrial capacity had grown rapidly under Bismarck's *Economic* leadership—so quickly that even the expense of a vastly enlarged military and *Triggers for* extensive social programs did not slow economic expansion. Moreover, since *the New* Germany had been a comparative latecomer to industrialization, its factories *Imperialism* benefited from newer technologies. Germany was also one of the few countries in Europe to have a rising birthrate in the late 19th century, which meant that its population was younger than that in Britain, France, or Italy. The rush of youthful energy and optimism seemed to be on Germany's side. All it lacked were overseas opportunities—which soon came with the global weakening of the Spanish and Portuguese empires as a result of their failure to industrialize.

Another trigger was Reconstruction, the remaking of the American South after the Civil War. The South had long been among the principal suppliers of raw cotton for European textile factories, but the catastrophic Civil War (1861–1865) had essentially cut off those supplies. In the postwar decades American policy aimed primarily at developing domestic industry, and this inward turn not only decreased the export of raw materials, but also increased competition on world markets by introducing American finished goods. Like Germany, America was a young nation filled with energy and ambition, and it soon became a major producer of everything from textiles and food-stuffs to steel, machinery, weapons, automobiles, and electrical appliances.

America also invested heavily in public education. The Morrill Act of 1862 (renewed and expanded in 1890) granted states the right to sell or develop federal lands for the creation of colleges

News from around the World   The White House became wired for telegraph and telephone in the 1880s. (Computers were introduced during President Jimmy Carter's term, 1977–1981.) Here a trio of engineers monitor the telegraph system bringing news of the Spanish-American War in 1898.

and universities. These land-grant colleges meant continued innovation in arts, engineering, and sciences.[3] America's growing military might was also a factor. Although still recovering from the Civil War, American fighting forces, once fully modernized, had the potential to rival the great European powers, especially on the sea-lanes. In response, industrialized Europe had to seize the moment.

The British led the way by transforming their long commercial domination of India into full-scale exploitation, led by the privately held British East India Company. India produced cotton on a massive scale, which compensated for the loss of American cotton, and its enormous population was an irresistible potential market. An uprising against British control by Indian soldiers, or *sepoys*, in 1857— known in India as the Great Mutiny of 1857 and in Britain as the Sepoy Rebellion—led to a sharp military crackdown, after which the entire subcontinent was formally declared a colony (1858) of Her Majesty Queen Victoria (r. 1837–1901). So great a prize was India that for nearly a dozen years the British scarcely looked elsewhere for further colonial adventures.

With Germany's and Italy's unifications, however, that had to change. The Continent was now awash with goods, and prices plummeted. The Long Depression (1873–1896), known in its time as the Great Depression until a still greater one struck in 1929, was marked by severe deflation and loss of profits. In the United States the price of cotton fell by 50 percent; grain fell to only a third of its previous value. Declines in Europe were at times even worse because of panics on the Vienna, Paris, and London stock exchanges. Since decreasing production was unthinkable, the answer was two pronged. First, increase access to markets abroad by seizing them; and second, seek protection by discouraging competition within an industry and by government subsidies. Firms joined or cooperated, forming cartels, to thwart the natural workings of the market.

Until the 1870s few governments, whether liberal or conservative, favored outright colonialism. In 1852 the British Prime Minister Benjamin Disraeli (1804–1881), a conservative, had dismissed England's handful of colonies as "a millstone around our necks" that cost far more to protect and maintain than they produced. William Gladstone (1809–1896), a liberal politician who also served as prime minister (four times, more than any other person), declared that "the lust-love of territory has been among the greatest curses of mankind." But by the mid-1880s newspapers were describing the race to extend Western industrial might throughout the entire world. "When I left the Foreign Service in 1880," wrote one British diplomat, "nobody thought about Africa. When I returned to it in 1885, the nations of Europe were almost quarreling with each other as to the various portions of Africa which they should obtain." A contemporary French

---

[3]   The first land-grant university created from scratch was Kansas State University in 1863.

official expressed his amazement, saying, "We are witnessing something never before seen in history—the actual partition of a foreign continent [Africa] by a handful of European countries." He quickly added, however, that "France, of course, is entitled to the largest share in these spoils."

Egypt, a convenient and profitable stop on the way to Asia, was an early target. Beginning with Muhammad Ali Pasha (introduced in chapter 20, r. 1805–1848), *Europeans* Egypt's modernizing rulers transformed Cairo into a bustling city with lively *Scramble* commercial and manufacturing enterprises. Production of raw materials, such *for Africa* as cotton for textile mills, was booming. Europeans invested heavily in the region, first in ventures such as building the Suez Canal in the 1860s, then in laying thousands of miles of railroad track, improving harbors, creating telegraph systems, and finally and most important, loaning money at exorbitant rates of interest.

In 1879, the British and the French took over the Egyptian treasure, allegedly to secure their investments and guarantee the repayment of loans. In 1882, after striking a deal with the French, the British invaded and essentially took control of the government, an act they claimed was necessary to put down those Egyptian nationalists who protested the seizure of the treasury. The English, in alliance with local entrepreneurs, shifted the Egyptian economy from a system based on multiple crops—a system that maintained the country's self-sufficiency—to one that emphasized the production of a few highly marketable crops, notably cotton and wheat, which were especially useful to the English. As the colonial powers and Egyptian elites grew rich, the bulk of the rural population barely eked out an existence.

An international congress met in Berlin in 1884–1885 to lay out the legal framework for further European expansion into Africa. Organized by Otto von Bismarck, the **Conference of Berlin** included Austria–Hungary, Belgium, Denmark, France, Germany, Italy, the Netherlands, the Ottoman Empire, Portugal, Russia, Spain, and Sweden (in union with Norway at the time). The United States was invited but did not attend.[4] Of course, no African countries were invited; in fact, none was even informed of the congress's intentions. The Conference did not actually divide Africa among the European powers; it merely established the standards by which any European country could claim an African territory against another European rival. Yet its effect was immediate. In the ensuing "scramble for Africa," France extended its traditional hold over central North Africa by seizing the territory of French West Africa (today's Benin, Burkina

---

[4] The United States had little interest in Africa apart from the nation of Liberia, which was founded in 1847 by African Americans freed from slavery and returned to Africa with the help of the American Colonization Society, a private antislavery organization established in 1816. The capital of Liberia, Monrovia, is named after U.S. president James Monroe (1817–1825), an early supporter of the Society.

Faso, Ivory Coast, Guinea, Mali, Mauritania, Niger, and Senegal) in 1895. Italy invaded Ethiopia in the same year, but was beaten off; a few years later, however, the Italians captured Somalia and eventually Libya (see Map 23.2).

With government backing, a British businessman and diamond merchant, **Cecil Rhodes** (1853–1902), used his position as prime minister of the British Cape Town Colony in southern Africa to instigate the **Boer War** (1899–1902), a conflict between Britain and the Dutch settlers—known as Afrikaners or

MAP 23.2   The Scramble for Africa, ca. 1880–1914   In less than thirty years, the imperial powers of Europe took control of roughly 10 million of Africa's 11 million square miles.

Boers—in the Orange Free State and the Transvaal Republic, where a large deposit of diamonds had recently been discovered. Rhodes, an ardent imperialist, once declared, "If I could, I would annex other planets." His brand of imperialism was more economic and informal than political. Rhodes wanted a world under the political umbrella of London but locally governed, either directly or through influence, by the industrial elite. In the first will he wrote (1877), he outlined his desire to establish a "secret society" for global domination and bequeathed money to the creation of one:

> The true aim and object whereof shall be for the extension of British rule throughout the world, the perfecting of a system of emigration from the United Kingdom, and of colonisation by British subjects of all lands where the means of livelihood are attainable by energy, labour and enterprise, and especially the occupation by British settlers of the entire Continent of Africa, the Holy Land, the Valley of the Euphrates, the Islands of Cyprus and Candia, the whole of South America, the Islands of the Pacific not heretofore possessed by Great Britain, the whole of the Malay Archipelago, the seaboard of China and Japan, the ultimate recovery of the United States of America as an integral part of the British Empire, the inauguration of a system of Colonial representation in the Imperial Parliament which may tend to weld together the disjointed members of the Empire and, finally, the foundation of so great a Power as to render wars impossible, and promote the best interests of humanity.

Did Rhodes really think that other states would embrace British rule? In any event, unprepared for the ferocity of Boer resistance, the British fought a costly guerilla war that would last for three years. The British tactics became more brutal as the campaign went on, with the setting up of concentration camps—the first use of the term—where Boer civilians were forced to live under appalling conditions so that they could not help the guerillas.

In the end, the Boers ceded control of their republics to a new British Union of South Africa that gave them a share of political power. A further result was the extension of British sovereignty northward into what came to be called Rhodesia (today's Zambia and Zimbabwe). Portugal seized Angola and Mozambique. Germany secured Cameroon, Namibia, and Tanzania. By 1914, more than 90 percent of Africa had been partitioned among the dominant European states; only Ethiopia and Liberia remained independent (see Map 23.2).

The rush to carve away parts of Asia was no less feverish or violent, but not as all-encompassing. Direct commercial relations, circumventing the Ottoman middleman, had gone on since the 16th century with permanent trading posts *Imperialism in Asia*

Driving Back the Europeans   Italy was a latecomer to European imperialism. The Italians invaded Ethiopia (one of the few parts of Africa not yet taken) in 1896. In a decisive battle at Adowa, at the northernmost point of the country, an Ethiopian army, armed with the latest Western military technology, crushed the ill-placed and ill-trained Italian forces. This painting by an unknown Ethiopian artist depicts the victory over the Italian soldiers—shown in formation on the right.

established from India to the Malay Peninsula and from southern China to Japan. The British East India Company had held sway over most of India, by grant of Parliament, since the second half of the 18th century. In the early 19th century Britain then expanded further east and seized control of Burma before turning south and taking Malaya.

The Dutch were the first European nation to take full political control of an Asian country. The government-chartered Dutch East India Company had been established in 1602 with an awarded monopoly on the movement of goods into and out of Indonesia. When the Dutch government took over Indonesia in 1816, it instituted a "Cultivation System" (*Cultuurstelsel*) that forced a bound peasantry to replace their rice fields with plantings of money crops like indigo and sugar. The Dutch also minted a debased coinage for use in Indonesia that cut in half the real value of what they paid for those money crops while weakening the peasants' purchasing power for foodstuffs. In a resulting rebellion known as the Java War (1825–1830), more than 200,000 people were killed.

The Europeans sometimes turned to even nastier measures, as when the British forced the Chinese to accept India-grown opium in lieu of money to pay for Chinese silks and tea. By 1840 opium addiction was so widespread in China that the emperor attempted to deny the British entrance to Chinese harbors, which prompted so-called gunboat diplomacy to force the opening of the ports. The First Opium War (1839–1842) ended with China forced to cede to

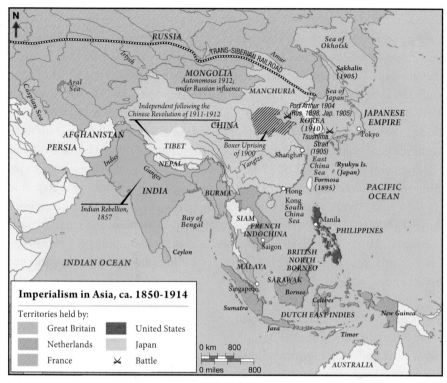

MAP 23.3   Imperialism in Asia, 1850–1914   The same countries that divided Africa between themselves fought to control southern and eastern Asia as well. The United States joined the Europeans in colonizing Asia; after helping the Filipinos win their independence from Spain, the Americans decided to keep the islands for themselves.

Britain permanent control of the harbor at Hong Kong.[5] A Second Opium War (1856–1860) soon followed, in which American and French troops assisted the British in their campaign to force open more Chinese ports to the trade in opium and other commodities and to make it easier for Western ships to export indentured Chinese laborers (coolies). France moved aggressively into Southeast Asia in the 1850s and 1860s, using the murder of a Spanish missionary by a group of resentful Vietnamese as an excuse to colonize much of southern Vietnam. By 1883 France was in control of the northern regions of Vietnam, along with much of Cambodia. Ten years later it added Laos to French Indochina (see Map 23.3).

All that remained up for grabs by 1890 were the outlying islands of the South Pacific. Britain snatched up Fiji and a few surrounding sites, whereas Germany seized the Marshall and Samoan Islands. France moved into Tahiti and into New

---

[5]   Hong Kong remained the last outpost of the British Empire in Asia; it was not restored to Chinese control until 1997.

Caledonia, an archipelago off the eastern coast of Australia. The biggest prize in the Pacific, however, was the widespread group of Philippine Islands. These had long previously belonged to Spain, but a successful revolution in 1898 brought about a short-lived period of independence. In that same year the United States ended its brief but bloody conflict with Spain—the **Spanish–American War** of 1898, fought over the issue of control of Cuba and Puerto Rico. Among other things, the peace treaty gave the Philippines to America. Not all Americans were enthusiastic about taking up colonial responsibilities so far from home. Rudyard Kipling composed "The White Man's Burden" at this time precisely to rouse Americans to imperialist action. The United States and the Philippine Republic signed a peace treaty after the three years of fighting known as the **Philippine–American War** (1899–1902); warfare continued in some of the outer islands, however, as late as 1913. In 1934, Congress guaranteed Philippine self-rule in ten years. World War II intervened, however, and Philippine independence did not become a reality until 1946.

Japanese Imperialism   Only Japan managed to retain full independence among Asian nations, which it did by becoming an imperialist power itself. Rapid industrialization had begun in 1868 after the Meiji Restoration overthrew a backward-looking network of feudal regimes and restored the imperial dynasty, but the new government was intensely aware of Japan's weakness: it had no modern navy. Moreover, Japan had ample agricultural land but virtually no metal ore for mining. That meant that the nation could industrialize only by importing raw materials and exporting finished products, and it had to unload its ships in reliable markets. With so many of the Pacific and East Asian markets snapped up by Europe and the United States, Japan had to carve out its own colonial zones, which brought it into conflict with Russia.

The **Russo-Japanese War** (1904–1905) was fought for control of Manchuria, Korea, and the island of Sakhalin (see Map 23.3). The first two were prized as rich in resources and heavily populated; the latter was the sole major source of petroleum in East Asia. This was primarily a naval war, with a handful of battles for control of ports. Small Japan's victory over its giant neighbor surprised most observers, but the treaty that ended the war awarded Japan no territory and released Russia from having to pay for the costs of the conflict.[6] Riots erupted across Japan in response to the news and fostered a powerful sense of betrayal. Doubting that it would ever receive a fair hearing on the international scene, the imperial government, with popular backing, decided to turn aggressive. Five years after the war, Japan annexed the Korean peninsula; Russia agreed to withdraw from

---

[6]   U.S. President Theodore Roosevelt won the 1906 Nobel Peace Prize for helping to negotiate a peace treaty between Japan and Russia.

Japanese Victory   This Japanese screen shows the 1905 naval Battle of Tsushima, a crucial episode in the Russo-Japanese War (1904–1905). Japan's forces annihilated two-thirds of the Russian imperial fleet.

Manchuria, opening the way for further Japanese expansion. Japan continued to develop its military might, and when World War I ended in 1918 the Japanese quickly seized Germany's Asian colonies.

MISSIONARY EUROPE

The global land grab was without precedent in history. The political and economic factors behind it, importantly, were buttressed by religious and humanitarian motives. Armies of missionaries, women as well as men, traveled before, with, and after the troops, spreading Christianity and attempting to quell the long-standing tribal hatreds and class and ethnic rivalries that they encountered wherever they went. With their various Christian moralities in tow, missionaries confronted a parade of cultural values and practices they found not only foreign but also authentically horrifying. In much of east Africa, for example, the tradition of female genital cutting aroused shock and disgust. The stoning of women for alleged adultery or the enslavement of children elicited a special sympathy. The Hindu folk practice of *sati* also demanded some sort of response: in parts of old India, a widow was thrown alive onto the burning funeral pyre of her deceased husband so that she could accompany him into the life beyond. If imperialist subjugation was the price of putting an end to such brutalities, missionaries preached, then it was a price well worth paying.

Humanitarian Motives for Imperial Conquest

The British banned sati in 1829 but the practice continued (even as it does in parts of rural India today). A famous anecdote relates a confrontation between the British commander Sir Charles James Napier (1782–1853) and an embassy of

Hindu leaders who came to him in 1860 to complain about the British ban on a Hindu tradition. Napier replied:

> Be it so. This burning of widows is your custom; prepare the funeral pyre. But my nation has also a custom. When men burn women alive we hang them, and confiscate all their property. My carpenters shall therefore erect gibbets on which to hang all concerned when the widow is consumed. Let us all act according to national customs.

Napier's response was gratuitously snide, but the episode usefully illustrates the clash of values for which imperialism was, in European eyes, a justifiable venture if not an outright moral duty.

Writing a quarter century later about Britain's seizure of Egypt in 1882, Sir Evelyn Baring (1st Earl of Cromer, 1841–1917), Britain's first colonial governor of that country, offered a classic defense of imperialism. It needed to be done as much for Egypt's benefit as for Britain's, he insisted, since the Egyptians had proven themselves to be incapable of running their own affairs. And if it needed doing, then better the British than anyone else:

> Egypt may now almost be said to form part of Europe. It is on the high road to the Far East. It can never cease to be an object of interest to

Doing God's Work   Missionaries conduct a baptism ceremony in the French Congo. In 1900 there were approximately 9 million Christians in Africa; by the year 2000 that number had grown to nearly 400 million, an increase of about 150 percent. The continent's traditional religions have declined dramatically. Africa north of the Sahara Desert is now overwhelmingly Islamic, but south of the desert it is chiefly Christian.

all the powers of Europe, and especially to England. A numerous and intelligent body of Europeans and of non-Egyptian orientals have made Egypt their home. European capital to a large extent has been sunk in the country.... In addition to these peculiarities, which are of a normal character, it has to be borne in mind that in 1882 the [Egyptian] army was in a state of mutiny; the treasury was bankrupt; every branch of the administration had been dislocated.... [The people of Egypt] have, for centuries past, been a subject race. Persians, Greeks, Romans, Arabs from Arabia and Baghdad, Circassians, and finally, Ottoman Turks, have successively ruled over Egypt, but we have to go back to the doubtful and obscure precedents of Pharaonic times to find an epoch when, possibly, Egypt was ruled by Egyptians. Neither, for the present, do they appear to possess the qualities which would render it desirable, either in their own interests, or in those of the civilized world in general, to raise them at a bound to the category of autonomous rulers with full rights of internal sovereignty. If, however, a foreign occupation was inevitable or nearly inevitable, it remains to be considered whether a British occupation was preferable to any other. From the purely Egyptian point of view, the

Slaves in Chains   Slavery was officially abolished in Zanzibar in 1873. Until then it had been the busiest slave market in eastern Africa, with as many as fifty thousand slaves a year passing through its ports; most of these were sent to the Persian Gulf region, to work as laborers or domestic servants.

answer to this question cannot be doubtful. The intervention of any
European power was preferable to that of Turkey. The intervention of
one European power was preferable to international intervention. The
special aptitude shown by Englishmen in the government of Oriental
races pointed to England as the most effective and beneficent instrument
for the gradual introduction of European civilization into Egypt. (Lord
Cromer, *Modern Egypt*, 1908)

Nothing can justify the orgies of violence and theft that attended empire building, yet European control did put an end to the international slave trade. It also
attempted to halt practices like female circumcision in Africa and *sati* in India. At
the same time, one can argue that imperialism simply replaced one form of servitude with another.

INDUSTRIAL WARFARE AND COMMAND ECONOMIES

The Europeans' technological superiority gave them the most lopsided military
victories in human history. Some of them had nearly a carnival atmosphere,
resembling nothing so much as the digital mayhem in some of our modern video
games. And once in power around the globe, the Europeans instituted many of
the practices of **command economies**—economies that aim to provide the highest possible yield for whoever held the raw materials and captive markets.

Industrial Warfare in Action

Shooters simply mowed down the resistance with seemingly endless numbers of clicks—except that Europe's remote controls consisted of real weapons.
Remington and Winchester breechloading rifles, elephant guns, Jarmann
M1884 repeating rifles, Kropatschek 11-millimeter carbines, Maxim and Gatling
machine guns, and seven-pound field artillery—all these squared off against warriors armed with little more than spears and arrows. The results were horrifying
and became horrifyingly familiar.

In 1897, a French force of only 32 Europeans and 507 African mercenaries
massacred a native army near Sokoto, in today's Nigeria, that numbered more
than 30,000. Two years later only 320 Senegalese fighters, under French
command, wiped out more than 12,000 Sudanese troops. And in 1908, a company of 389 French soldiers annihilated a 10,000-man army from the kingdom
of Ouaddai, near today's province of Darfur along the Chad–Sudan border in
east-central Africa.

The British scored their one-sided victories as well, including the campaign
to conquer Sudan in 1898. Sudan itself was of relatively little value to the British
in terms of natural resources. The country, directly south of Egypt, mattered principally for strategic purposes: those who controlled Sudan could impede traffic

along the Nile (see Map 23.2). An army of Sudanese Mahdist fighters, numbering more than fifty thousand, met the British at Omdurman, now a suburb of the Sudanese capital of Khartoum. The well-armed British were aided by a flotilla of gunboats that had steamed up the river. Winston Churchill (1874–1965), the future prime minister, served there as a second lieutenant and described the battle in an 1899 memoir:

> [The infantry] fired steadily and stolidly, without hurry or excitement, for the enemy were far away and the officers careful. Besides, the soldiers were interested in the work and took great pains. But presently the mere physical act [of repeated firing] became tedious. . . . But at the critical moment the gunboat arrived on the scene and began suddenly to blaze and flame from Maxim guns, quick-firing guns, and rifles. The range was short; the effect tremendous. The terrible machine, floating gracefully on the waters—a beautiful white devil—wreathed itself in smoke. The river slopes of the Kerreri Hills, crowded with the advancing thousands, sprang up into clouds of dust and splinters of rock. The charging Dervishes [Mahdists] sank down in tangled heaps. The masses in the rear paused, irresolute. It was too hot even for them. . . . And all the time out on the plain on the other side bullets were shearing through flesh, smashing and splintering bone; blood spouted from terrible wounds; valiant men were struggling on through a hell of whistling metal, exploding shells, and spurting dust—suffering, despairing, dying.

The carnage lasted for five hours and left ten thousand Mahdists dead, fifteen thousand wounded, and another five thousand captured; the British lost fewer than fifty men. As described in Churchill's vivid memoir, the British gunmen, apart from a few losses, suffered nothing worse than the effects of carpal tunnel syndrome from pulling the triggers of their weapons so many times.

Lopsided advantages like this did more than ensure battlefield success; they altered the perceptions of warfare itself and of the participants as well. The Europeans appeared not simply as the victors. Rather, a society that could engineer such stunning conquests must in some sense be superior. As for its victims, a nation that clings to spears and arrows in an age of steel and gunpowder may not deserve massacre and foreign oppression, but it can hardly be surprised when they result. Such, at any rate, was the attitude of many in the West. An officers' manual for British forces fighting in Sierra Leone described "the weird and treacherous surroundings and the nerve-wracking effects of the climate" in the region. It contrasted the "cunning savages . . . like the wild animals of [their] own forests" with "the stern discipline and enthusiastic *esprit de corps* of the British army"

BATTLE OF OMDURMAN. SEPTEMBER 2, 1898.

Industrial Warfare   Field Marshall Horatio Herbert Kitchener (1850–1916), major-general of Britain's imperial troops in Africa, defeated the Mahdist forces in battle at Omdurman, in Sudan, in 1898. The British killed over 10,000 Mahdists and wounded another 15,000, while suffering only 47 losses themselves. According to an eyewitness: " . . . It was not a battle but an execution . . . The bodies were not in heaps—bodies hardly ever are; but they spread evenly over acres and acres. Some lay very composedly with their slippers placed under their heads for a last pillow; some knelt, cut short in the middle of a last prayer. Others were torn to pieces."

under the command of "that indispensible factor in the machine of West African warfare—the British officer." European readers more often felt wonder and pride than revulsion.

Leopold II of Belgium   Even the most ardently imperialistic Europeans, however, were disgusted by the excesses of King Leopold II of Belgium (r. 1865–1909). Leopold, who had long been keen to develop colonial holdings in Africa, cast his eye on the vast natural wealth of the Congo: "To open to civilization the only part of the globe where it has not yet penetrated, to pierce the darkness which envelops whole populations, is a crusade, if I may say so, a crusade worthy of this century of progress." Unable to stir the Belgian parliament into action, he hit on the idea of establishing instead a private company, the International African Association, to help the Congolese "develop." He hired the ruthless British explorer Henry Morton Stanley (1841–1904) to represent the association and get local tribal rulers to sign friendship pacts with it, but the pacts turned out to be sales contracts—giving ownership of the entire region to Leopold. He thus found himself in personal possession of 30 million people and an area of 900,000 square miles (an area the size of Alaska and Texas, combined). The enslaved Congolese were brutally whipped and beaten and forced to harvest rubber, palm oil, and ivory (the three most profitable products of the region). Workers who failed to meet their quotas were punished by having their hands chopped off.

Leopold's thugs were organized into the *Force Publique*, whose savagery was so methodical that they kept accounts of the number of hands they had severed. They were expected to produce a hand for every bullet they fired, lest they be charged with wasting military resources. At the height of the butchery, nearly a metric ton of severed hands was delivered to Leopold's officials per day. As one historian wrote,

> The baskets of severed hands, set down at the feet of the European post commanders, became the symbol of the Congo Free State. . . . The collection of hands became an end in itself. *Force Publique* soldiers brought them to the stations in place of rubber; they even went out to harvest them instead of rubber. . . . They became a sort of currency. They came to be used to make up for shortfalls in rubber quotas, to replace . . . the people who were demanded for the forced labour gangs; and the *Force Publique* soldiers were paid their bonuses on the basis of how many hands they collected.[7]

An estimated 5 to 8 million Congolese were murdered during Léopold's reign, with an equal number dying of starvation and disease.

In 1908, after proof of the Belgians' sadistic cruelties was published (1904) by a British diplomat, the Belgian Parliament forced Leopold to relinquish personal control of the Congo and placed it under the authority of the Belgian state. Yet Leopold was among the richest people in the Western world, and among Belgians today he is remembered for the large number of public buildings he constructed with his wealth, including the Musée de Congo in Tervuren. Now known as the Royal Museum for Central Africa, it contains thousands of artifacts of Congolese life. It makes no mention,

The Horror   This photograph shows Congolese with their hands chopped off, the common punishment for failure to meet work quotas.

---

[7]   Peter Forbath, The River Congo: The Discovery, Exploration, and Exploitation of the World's Most Dramatic Rivers (1974), p. 374.

however, of the savagery that brought them to Belgium and reduced the Congolese population by one-half.[8]

On the last day of December in the year 1900, Mark Twain (Samuel Clemens;
1835–1910) penned a brief "Salutation-Speech from the 19th Century to the 20th,"
which appeared the next day in the *New York Herald*. Like most of the American
writer's late work, this piece is marked with a sharp, bitter humor. In it, he regrets
the era he has lived through and holds little hope for the century to come:

> I bring you the stately matron named *Christendom*, returning be-
> draggled, besmirched, and dishonored from pirate-raids in Kiaw-Chow
> [Guangzhou], Manchuria, South Africa, and the Philippines, with her
> soul full of meanness, her pocket full of boodle, and her mouth full of
> pious hypocrisies. Give her soap and a towel, but hide the looking-glass.

Western values needed a thorough cleansing, and a younger Mark Twain might
have hoped one was possible. But the imperial, rapacious world he lived in offered
no reason for optimism.

Workings of the Command Economy

Around the colonized world European governments and chartered companies "expropriated"—that is, stole—lands, crop fields, mines, flocks, and businesses at will. They forced locals to work at reduced wages (when they paid them
at all), and they seized mineral rights and monopolized control of imports and
exports. They dismantled centuries-old commercial routes, since neighboring
territories were likely to be subjects of a rival European power. They also built
tariff barriers that kept competitors' goods out of domestic markets. They ensured that their colonies sold only the goods produced by their imperialist masters, at whatever prices those masters set.

Their goal was clear: to maximize profit for the European power in control
of each region, its government, its officials, and its merchants. The imperial age
thus strongly resembled the absolutist era—but with a difference. Compared to
mercantilism, the command economy worked better, because it covered a
broader area and its tools of oppression were more deadly. The larger the empires grew, too, the greater grew the need to protect their business interests.
Mining and manufacturing, and the banks used to back them, were seen as too
big to allow to fail.

---

[8] Similarly, the official website of the Belgian monarchy makes no reference to the brutality of Leopold's
criminal regime. Instead, it credits him with establishing the antislavery campaign in central Africa and
blames the "excesses" on others: "Following the excesses committed by the Europeans in Africa, Leopold's reputation and his overseas venture were questioned. The King set up an International Commission
of Inquiry, which recognised the merits of the royal action in Congo, while pointing out abuses and
shortcomings."

MAP 23.4 European Emigration, 1880–1914   The nations that were unable to industrialize enough to compete with the great powers were effectively locked out of the international economy. Faced with unemployment and poverty, millions of people from nations like Ireland, Italy, Greece, Poland, and Sweden emigrated abroad—chiefly to the United States.

Britain's industries found it difficult to compete with Continental rivals, but no matter: they simply consolidated into larger and larger corporations in the hopes of improving profits. Many banks and investment houses consolidated as well and worked out special relations with the government-led Bank of England. In this way, Britain gradually exposed itself to crushing debts, and the shakiness of the entire structure increased the need for government manipulation. In fact, it was partly to write off debt from the construction of the Suez Canal that the British decided in 1882 to annex it.

The command economies of imperialism and its repeating cycles of boom and bust effectively locked out underdeveloped nations within Europe from international markets. Unable to compete or to secure funding for their own industrialization, many of these countries—Greece, Ireland, Italy, Norway, Poland, and Sweden, most notably—lost tens of millions of their people to emigration between 1880 and 1914. Approximately one-half of these emigrants made their way to the United States, with the other half divided among Australia, Canada, and Latin America (see Map 23.4).

Mass European Emigration

WESTERN WAYS: EMULATION AND RESISTANCE

Once in control of their colonies, the Europeans encountered consistent but relatively minor unrest. Their technological edge made resistance seem futile to most of their subjects, many of whom were long accustomed to rule by small numbers of tribal elites. Although they smarted under European oppression, they none-theless benefited from the disappearance or at least the neutralization of long-standing tribal and clan conflicts.

Argument for Westernization   Some colonial subjects emulated Western ways as a means to modernize their societies. They prized Western education, technology, and civil gov-ernment, and they sought to promote improved understanding between rulers and ruled, although the treatment they received from their European gov-ernors was shoddy. "However well-educated and clever a native might be," wrote a British military officer in India, "and however brave he may prove himself, I believe that no rank we can bestow on him would cause him to be considered an equal of the British." Contrast that with an 1871 speech by Dadabhai Naoroji (1825–1917), an Indian statesman who served in the British Parliament from 1892 to 1895:

> The introduction of English education, with its great, noble, elevat-ing, and civilizing literature and advanced science, will for ever remain a monument of good work done in India and a claim to gratitude upon the Indian people. . . . Britain may well claim credit for law and order, which, however, is as much necessary for the existence of British rule in India as for the good of the Indian people; for freedom of speech and press, and for other benefits flowing therefrom. . . . [But] the benefits are more than counterbalanced by evils inseparable from the system of a remote foreign dominion. . . . Commonsense will suggest this to any thoughtful mind. These evils have ever since gone on increasing, and more and more coun-terbalancing the increased produce of the country, making now the evil of the bleeding and impoverishing drain by the foreign dominion nearly or above £30,000,000 a year. (*Poverty and Un-British Rule in India*, 1901)

His book *Poverty and Un-British Rule in India* (1901) brought to popular attention within Britain the devastating effect of colonialism on the Indian people, while still expressing hope for a shared prosperity.

Mohandas Gandhi   But it was **Mohandas Gandhi** (1869–1948) who emerged as the charismatic leader for Indian independence. Born to a prominent provincial Hindu family near Bombay (today's city of Mumbai), Gandhi—also known as Mahatma, a Hindu honorary title meaning "Great Soul"—traveled to London in 1888 and studied law at University College London for three years. He spoke fluent Eng-lish, adopted Western dress and manners (although he hated British cooking), and hoped to make a living as a barrister back in British India. His career faltered, however, and he took a position in British South Africa, where his encounters with racism and discrimination turned him gradually against the empire.

For a time, Gandhi exhibited a measure of Western-style race prejudice, too: "Kaffirs [a derogatory term for black South Africans] are as a rule uncivilized. . . . They are troublesome, very dirty, and live almost like animals," he wrote in the newspaper he founded while in South Africa, the *Indian Opinion*. On another occasion he asserted, "We believe as much in the purity of race [as white South Africans do]. . . . We believe also that [whites] should be the predominating race." He finally returned to India in 1915, renounced Western dress, embraced strict Hindu asceticism (for example, taking a vow of lifelong celibacy), and began the nonviolent protest campaign against British rule in India for which he became famous.

The largest sustained rebellion against the Europeans, the **Boxer Rebellion** (1898–1901), occurred in China. It began when a millennial Buddhist sect from northern China opened a campaign of violence against European missionaries and native Chinese who had converted to Christianity. The rebels came largely from the peasantry and called themselves the society of the *Yihequan*, meaning "Righteous and Harmonious Fists." They believed themselves the sanctified saviors of China from foreign imperialism, fighters whose religious rituals made them invulnerable to Western guns and cannon. The *Yihequan* believed they would be reincarnated as "spirit warriors"—an entire ghost army that would rout the Western corrupters of China's world. They opposed Western culture as much as Western colonial rule and hence had much in common with other nationalist movements around the globe.

The Young Gandhi   This photograph was taken when Mohandas Gandhi (1869–1948) worked as a barrister in South Africa. Remembered best as the champion of India's independence from Britain and as the apostle of non-violence, Gandhi also campaigned tirelessly for the rights of women. He wrote in *Young India* (1930), a newsweekly he published from 1919 to 1932: "to call woman the weaker sex is a libel; it is man's injustice to woman. If by strength is meant brute strength, then, indeed, is woman less brute than man. If by strength is meant moral power, then woman is immeasurably man's superior. Has she not greater intuition, is she not more self-sacrificing, has she not greater powers of endurance, has she not greater courage? Without her, man could not be. If nonviolence is the law of our being, the future is with woman. Who can make a more effective appeal to the heart than woman?"

Later Chinese nationalists were ambivalent about the Boxers and remain so today. They admired the patriotism the *Boxer* rebels evinced but wanted to distance themselves from both the Boxers' low *Rebellion* origins and their unorthodox religious convictions. After uprisings in the

Boxer Rebellion Between 1899 and 1901 a large group of anti-imperialist fighters tried to rid China of the Europeans who had colonized much of the land. Called "Boxers" for their martial arts training, they numbered perhaps a quarter of a million. In this recruitment poster, several Boxers have not only killed some Europeans (pictured with beast heads) but are taking aim at the symbol of Christianity itself. The legend reads, "Jesus, the Pig, is put to death."

countryside, the Boxer forces, perhaps a quarter million strong, moved into Beijing and other cities to target missionaries, merchants, and diplomats. They killed several hundred Westerners, along with several thousand Chinese Christian converts. The empress dowager of the weak Qing dynasty was personally sympathetic to the Boxers but was compelled by her treaties with the Europeans to help put them down. In the end, the Boxers were routed by an alliance of soldiers from the five leading European states (Austria–Hungary, Britain, France, Germany, and Italy) plus forces from Japan, Russia, and the United States. To avenge the murdered missionaries and converts, the Eight Army Alliance committed widespread atrocities, including murder, rape, and arson, against civilians.

Mark Twain, soon after his toss-away "Salutation to the 20th Century," wrote a parody of the "Battle Hymn of the Republic," the stirring Civil War song of 1861 beloved to this day. In it he curses the imperialist greed that, he believed, had overtaken Western society. The aftermath of the Boxer Rebellion—which he had publicly supported—was particularly galling to him.

> Mine eyes have seen the orgy of the launching of the Sword;
> He is searching out the hoardings where the stranger's wealth is stored.
> He hath loosed his fateful lightnings, and with woe and death has scored;
> His lust is marching on.
> I have seen him in the watch-fires of a hundred circling camps,
> They have builded him an altar in the Eastern dews and damps;
> I have read his doomful mission by the dim and flaring lamps—
> His night is marching on.
> I have read his bandit gospel writ in burnished rows of steel:
> "As ye deal with my pretensions, so with you my wrath shall deal;
> Let the faithless son of Freedom crush the patriot with his heel;
> Lo, Greed is marching on!"
> We have legalized the strumpet and are guarding her retreat;
> Greed is seeking out commercial souls before his judgment seat;
> O, be swift, ye clods, to answer him! Be jubilant my feet!
> Our god is marching on!
> In a sordid slime harmonious, Greed was born in yonder ditch,
> With a longing in his bosom—and for others' goods an itch—
> As Christ died to make men holy, let men die to make us rich—
> Our god is marching on.

His daughter advised him that this scornful rendition of a revered song was too bitter and was certain to offend his readers. He never published it.

◆

Imperialism may or may not be the "default position" of history, but it certainly has been a mainstay of it. But nothing like the imperialism of the late 19th century had ever happened before. This was conquest and subjugation on a uniquely colossal scale. So too would be the industrial-scale war that followed it.

WHO, WHAT, WHERE

Boer War	Mohandas Gandhi	Second Industrial
Boxer Rebellion	new imperialism	Revolution
Cecil Rhodes	Philippine–American	social Darwinism
command economies	War	Spanish–American War
Conference of Berlin	Russo-Japanese War	
informal imperialism	scientific management	

SUGGESTED READINGS

Primary Sources

Baring, Evelyn. *Modern Egypt.*

Churchill, Winston S. *The River War: An Historical Account of the Reconquest of the Soudan.*

Gandhi, Mohandas. *An Autobiography: The Story of My Experiments with Truth.*

Hobson, J. A. *Imperialism: A Study.*

Taylor, Frederick Winslow. *The Principles of Scientific Management.*

Anthologies

Bowman, William D., Frank M. Chiteji, and J. Megan Greene, eds. *Imperialism in the Modern World: Sources and Interpretations* (2006).

Brown, Judith M., ed. *Mahatma Gandhi: The Essential Writings* (2008).

Fischer, Louis, ed. *The Essential Gandhi: An Anthology of His Writings on His Life, Work, and Ideas* (2002, orig. 1983).

Martin, Susan K., Caroline Daley, Elizabeth Dimock, Cheryl Cassidy, and Cecily Devereaux, eds. *Women and Empire, 1750–1939: Primary Sources on Gender and Anglo-Imperialism* (2009).

Naoroji, Dadabhai. *Poverty and Un-British Rule in India* (2010, orig. 1923).

Smith, Bonnie G., ed. *Imperialism: A History in Documents* (2000).

Studies

Appleby, Joyce Oldham. *The Relentless Revolution: A History of Capitalism* (2010).

Bickers, Robert A. *The Scramble for China: Foreign Devils in the Qing Empire, 1800–1914* (2011).

Bickers, Robert A., and R. G. Tiedemann, eds. *The Boxers, China, and the World* (2007).

Broadberry, Stephen, and Kevin H. O'Rourke, eds. *The Cambridge Economic History of Modern Europe* (2010).

Brody, David. *Visualizing American Empire: Orientalism and Imperialism in the Philippines* (2010).

Cannadine, David. *Ornamentalism: How the British Saw Their Empire* (2002).

Curtin, Philip D. *The World and the West: The European Challenge and the Overseas Response in the Age of Empire* (2002).

Delmendo, Sharon. *The Star-Entangled Banner: One Hundred Years of America in the Philippines* (2004).

Deringil, Selim. *The Well-Protected Domains: Ideology and the Legitimation of Power in the Ottoman Empire, 1876–1909* (2011).

Drayton, Richard. *Nature's Government: Science, Imperial Britain, and the "Improvement" of the World* (2000).

Ferguson, Niall. *Colossus: The Rise and Fall of the American Empire* (2004).

Ferguson, Niall. *Empire: The Rise and Demise of the British World Order and the Lessons for Global Power* (2003).

Gelber, Harry G. *Opium, Soldiers, and Evangelicals: Britain's 1840–42 War with China and Its Aftermath* (2004).

Hanioğlu, M. Şükrü. *Preparation for a Revolution: The Young Turks, 1902–1908* (2001).

Harrington, Peter. *Peking, 1900: The Boxer Rebellion* (2001).

Hochschild, Adam. *King Leopold's Ghost: A Story of Greed, Terror, and Heroism in Colonial Africa* (2000).

Jasanoff, Maya. *Edge of Empire: Lives, Culture, and Conquest in the East, 1750–1850* (2006).

Karabell, Zachary. *Parting the Desert: The Creation of the Suez Canal* (2004).

Kern, Stephen. *The Culture of Time and Space, 1880–1918* (2003).

Lelyveld, Joseph. *Great Soul: Mahatma Gandhi and His Struggle with India* (2012).

Linn, Brian McAllister. *The Philippine War, 1899–1902* (2000).

McCoy, Alfred W., and Francisco A. Scarano. *Colonial Crucible: Empire in the Making of the Modern American State* (2009).

Meyer, Karl E., and Shareen Blair Brysac. *Tournament of Shadows: The Great Game and the Race for Empire in Central Asia* (2006).

Pomeranz, Kenneth. *The Great Divergence: China, Europe, and the Making of the Modern World Economy* (2001).

Ringmar, Erik. *Liberal Barbarism: The European Destruction of the Palace of the Emperor of China* (2013).

Silbey, David J. *A War of Frontier and Empire: The Philippine–American War, 1899–1902* (2007).

Watts, Sheldon. *Epidemics and History: Disease, Power, and Imperialism* (2000).

Wesseling, H. L. *The European Colonial Empires, 1815–1919* (2004).

Wong, J. Y. *Deadly Dreams: Opium and the Arrow War (1856–1860) in China* (2002).

Xiang, Lanxin. *The Origins of the Boxer War: A Multinational Study* (2002).

Ziegler, Philip. *Legacy: Cecil Rhodes, The Rhodes Trust, and Rhodes Scholarships* (2008).

For additional resources, including maps, primary sources, visuals, web links, and quizzes, please go to **www.oup.com/us/backman.**

L.532a

CHAPTER 24

The World at War (Part I)

1914–1918

The day after the signing of the armistice that ended World War I, the British novelist D. H. Lawrence (1885–1930) wrote to a friend with a gloomy warning:

THE WORLD AT WAR, 1914–1918

• Major clashes, 1914-1918

> I suppose you think the war is over and that we shall go back to the kind of world you lived in before it. But the war isn't over. The hate and evil is greater now than ever. Very soon war will break out again and overwhelm you. . . . The crowd outside thinks that Germany is crushed forever. But the Germans will soon rise again. Europe is done for. . . . The war isn't over. Even if the fighting should stop, the evil will be worse because the hate will be dammed up in men's hearts and will show itself in all sorts of ways.

Armed to the Teeth At the beginning of the 20th century, the European powers engaged in a massive arms race that was part of industrial innovation. Even as sophisticated weaponry was one key to advancing global conquest, it also became part of national rivalries including economic, military, and imperial ones. Shown here is the Krupp armaments factory in Essen, Germany, 1912.

He had good reason to be pessimistic. The war that ended in November 1918 had been the cause of more bloodshed and horror than any conflict in Western history. Three empires—the Austrian–Hungarian, the German, and the Ottoman—lay in ruins.

Three others—the British, the French, and the American—had been knocked staggering.

Along the war's 400-mile-long western front, in northern and eastern France, entire towns and villages had been obliterated, crop fields and mines devastated, and roads and bridges ruined. Millions of corpses lay buried or rotting in the sun. Some 65 million soldiers had taken part. By the time the war ended, 10 million of them lay dead, another 21 million of them had been wounded, and still another million remained missing. The deaths were shared by all: 1.8 million Germans, 1.2 million Austrian–Hungarians, 1.7 million Russians, 1.4 million French, and nearly a million British. The late-coming Italians lost 460,000 soldiers, and the even later-coming Americans lost 115,000. The rest of the dead consisted primarily of Serbs (850,000), Turks (750,000), Romanians (600,000), Poles (one-fourth of whose 1.9 million soldiers died), Czechs, Slovaks, and Arabs (for all of whom precise numbers are difficult to tabulate). Small wonder that contemporaries named World War I the "Great War" for its staggering human toll.

By the war's end, the political map of the Greater West had already changed, with America's entry into a European war, a revolution in Russia, and the birth of what would become the Soviet Union. It was to change still more after the war, with a harsh peace treaty, the bitter resentment of the losers, and the end of the Ottoman Empire.

CHAPTER TIMELINE

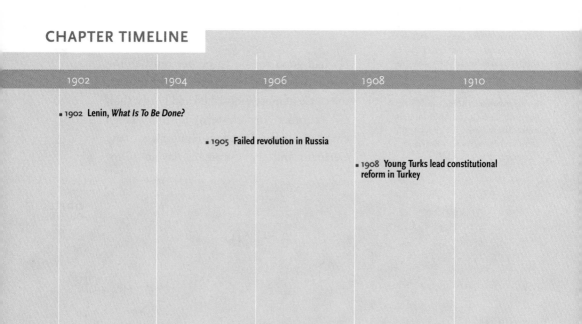

| 1902 | 1904 | 1906 | 1908 | 1910 |

■ 1902 Lenin, *What Is To Be Done?*

■ 1905 Failed revolution in Russia

■ 1908 Young Turks lead constitutional reform in Turkey

THE RUN-UP TO WAR

With hindsight, one can see the war coming as early as 1905, but not as the result of any presumed inevitable march of political events or economic developments. The popular demand for war simply rose continually. World War I was *willed* into being by a Europe drunk with nationalistic pride, with each nation eager to claim its victor's cup in the social Darwinian battle of life. Militarism had been on the rise across Europe ever since German unification in 1870, and it had to be. The "balance of power" codified by the Congress of Vienna in 1815 had presupposed a permanently fragmented German people, but unification had tipped the scale heavily in Germany's favor. Some sort of direct action was necessary, and that action found expression in the rapid development of military might—put to use in the colonization of Africa and much of Asia. And once the imperialist land grab was completed, the massive militaries remained.

Europe around 1900 was armed to the teeth, much as in the age of absolutism by 1715. As armies swelled and stockpiles of weapons ballooned, popular pres- *War Fever* sure built up to put them to use. In capitalist terms, unexercised muscle was a wasted resource. In Germany the Colonial Society, a nationwide group that championed imperialism, issued vague but insistent calls for war. "Peace is rotten," declared the Berlin-based poet Georg Heym (1887–1912) in a private notebook. He hoped for a war, "any war, even an unjust one," and in that same year (1912) he published a disturbing paean to it. Opening "War" with the line

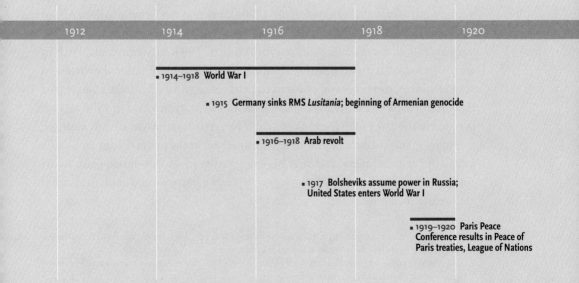

1912   1914   1916   1918   1920

• 1914–1918 **World War I**

• 1915 **Germany sinks RMS *Lusitania*; beginning of Armenian genocide**

• 1916–1918 **Arab revolt**

• 1917 **Bolsheviks assume power in Russia; United States enters World War I**

• 1919–1920 **Paris Peace Conference results in Peace of Paris treaties, League of Nations**

"He is risen that was long asleep," Heym describes the awesome, mythic power of War as it sweeps across the countryside, smashing towers, obliterating cities, devouring woods and fields. The nightmarish effect of the poem, however, derives not from Heym's powerful portrayal of War's terrible strength, but from his admiration of it.[1]

The popular journalist-lawyer Heinrich Class (1868–1953) was a member of another patriotic group, the Pan-German League. He wrote in the same year:

> If any nation has just cause to seek to expand its sphere of influence, it is the German one, whose population is rapidly growing, whose industry needs new markets, and whose overall economy needs new land from which to derive new resources. . . . We need these things and we need them now, and we need to acquire them by any means whatsoever. . . . We must engage in a proactive politics abroad—in fact, let us state it bluntly: we must be aggressive. . . . To begin with, any expansion within Europe can only come from direct conquest since neither France nor Russia will be so obliging as to give away part of their territories to us. . . . Another consideration is whether or not southeastern Europe might do for us, specifically the parts of the Austrian Empire and of the Balkans generally where the Slavic peoples (a "sub-German people," if I may put it thus) currently reside.

The Germans were not alone in their ardor for conflict. French politicians, writers, university students, and workers everywhere smarted from their country's defeat in the Franco-Prussian War of 1870. They were further demoralized by a public controversy that erupted in the 1890s known as the Dreyfus Affair. Alfred Dreyfus (1859–1935) was a French army captain unjustly accused of passing military secrets to the German embassy in Paris in 1894. His two trials, both of which ended with his conviction, were the cause of intense national debate and scandal since Dreyfus was a Jew and the charges against him were at least partially motivated by anti-Semitic hatred. He was fully exonerated in 1906 and reinstated in the army with the rank of major. Nevertheless, he had already endured five years of imprisonment in solitary confinement at the penal colony on Devil's Island in French Guiana, and after his exoneration he was wounded in an assassination attempt.[2] For many French people, only victory on the battlefield could restore national honor.

---

[1] "He is risen that was long asleep. / Risen now from caverns deep, / He stands in the twilight, unknown, and grand, / And crushes the moon in His black hand."

[2] Dreyfus retired from the army in 1907 but reenlisted when World War I broke out, eventually earning promotion to the rank of lieutenant colonel.

In Britain, too, many people looked eagerly forward to a contest that would settle, once and for all, the intense competitions begun with the founding of the German Empire. British confidence ran high. After all, the country had not had a serious military setback since the American Revolution, and British forces in the past twenty years had put more than 300 million people around the world under their control.

Not everyone had war fever, of course. Trade unionists and socialist reformers in all countries were among the loudest voices condemning the march to conflict. Members of the clergy also spoke up frequently against the militarist wave. One of the best known opponents of war was Norman Angell (1872–1967), the Paris-based editor of the British newspaper *The Daily Mail*, who in 1909 published a pamphlet called *Europe's Optical Illusion*. (It appeared in expanded form the following year as *The Great Illusion*.) In it Angell strategically speaks the language of business. He argues that, aside from purely moral issues, a European war would be disastrous simply because the economies of the countries involved had become too interdependent. Unlike manufacturing, the finance industry crossed too many international borders to survive a conflict. Credit was extended in such an extended web that any prolonged disruption to a single commercial sector would be felt everywhere. Angell sees an appeal to economic interests as the only argument that might succeed in a society that so romanticizes bloody conflict:

Voices against War

> War has no longer the justification that it makes for the survival of the fittest; it involves the survival of the less fit. The idea that the struggle between nations is a part of the evolutionary law of man's advance involves a profound misreading of the biological analogy. . . .
>
> Are we, in blind obedience to primitive instincts and old prejudices, enslaved by the old catchwords and that curious indolence which makes the revision of old ideas unpleasant, to duplicate indefinitely on the political and economic side a condition from which we have liberated ourselves on the religious side? Are we to continue to struggle, as so many good men struggled in the first dozen centuries of Christendom— spilling oceans of blood, wasting mountains of treasure—to achieve what is at bottom a logical absurdity, to accomplish something which, when accomplished, can avail us nothing, and which, if it could avail us anything, would condemn the nations of the world to never-ending bloodshed and the constant defeat of all those aims which men, in their sober hours, know to be alone worthy of sustained endeavor?

Back in England, Angell campaigned incessantly against the slaughter. He later served briefly as a Member of Parliament, was knighted in 1931, and in 1933 received the Nobel Peace Prize.

These arguments could not hold out against the passions of the age, however. What argument could prevail against the sentiments expressed and shared by millions of people across Europe? As a prominent German general declared once hostilities in fact had begun, "Even if it all ends in ruin, it has been beautiful to see."

THE BALANCE OF POWER

The assassination of Archduke Franz Ferdinand of Austria–Hungary triggered the catastrophe. It happened in the Bosnian capital of Sarajevo, on June 28, 1914, at the hand of a bitter nineteen-year-old Serb nationalist (and member of a Serbian terrorist group known as the "Black Hand") named Gavrilo Princip. But if it had not been this event that started the war, it would have been another. The entire Habsburg state by this time floated like a loosely joined raft on a sea of nationalist passions that wanted to break away from it and watch it sink: Poles, Czechs, Slovaks, Magyars, Serbs, Slovenians, Bosnians, Croatians, and others, tired of seeing themselves fall further behind industrialized Europe, roiled with anger and frustration. The assassination of Franz Ferdinand did not cause the war; it was simply the spark that set off a chain reaction of measures and countermeasures, alliances and counteralliances, resulting in a war that included nearly every nation in Europe. Tensions had been running so high for so long that anything could have set the calamity in motion.

Economic Tensions The main elements in these tensions were economic. Industrial overproduction continued throughout the carving up of Africa and Asia, and it had not lessened once the European empires had achieved full size. The result was a cycle of economic booms and busts between 1885 and 1914 that was made even worse by the growing availability of cheap transportation. Petroleum and electricity, for example, allowed massive imports of American, Argentinian, and Canadian foodstuffs to Europe. Against this threat, Europeans could either erect punitive tariff barriers or prop up their native industries with subsidies. To varying degrees, they did both. Manufacturers formed cartels to regulate output and fix prices. Banks organized themselves into consortia to set interest rates and control the movement of capital.

State interventions and cartel manipulations not only distorted markets but also solidified the divide that separated Europe's rich, developed nations from its poorer, undeveloped ones. Ireland, Greece, Portugal, Poland, and the Scandinavian and Balkan countries could not compete internationally, and their sharp economic declines drove more and more of their populations abroad. As we saw in chapter 23, between 1815 and 1900 more than 40 million people had already emigrated from Europe—primarily to the United States, Canada, Argentina, Brazil, and Australia. Almost 15 million more did so between 1900 and 1914.

Only Belgium and the Netherlands experienced a net gain in population through migration. Artificial controls in the markets also hardened the distinction between the wealthy and the poor within each industrialized country. With little capital available for smaller businesses, labor wages stagnated from 1900 to 1914, whereas prices for most consumer goods rose.

The leading states formed alliances that they hoped would preserve economic and military balance. These alliances often changed, however, as each boom-and-bust cycle altered the relative strengths of each partner. One year's ally might be next year's diplomatic and commercial rival (see Map 24.1). But the alliances generally tried to counterbalance the economic and military weight of the German Empire. Britain aimed above all to secure its naval superiority. It wanted to maintain sufficient strength to battle any two European nations combined—usually Germany and any country with which it could be allied. In the Anglo-French Entente of 1904, also known as the Entente Cordiale, for example, France recognized British interests in Egypt and Suez in return for British recognition of

Shifting Diplomatic Alliances

European Alliances, 1878-1918

◇ Austro-German alliance 1879–1918
◆ Three Emperors' alliance 1881–87
◆ Austro-Serbian alliance 1881–95
◆ Triple alliance 1882–1915
◇ Anglo-Russian Entente 1907
◆ Anglo-French Entente 1904
◆ Franco-Russian alliance 1894–1917

Alliance on the eve of the war
Allied Powers 1914
Central Powers 1914
Neutral states 1914

MAP 24.1 European Alliances, 1878–1914 As individual nations' economies coursed through boom-and-bust cycles, their governments tried to counterbalance matters by making and breaking alliances with other countries. One effect of the constant shifting of connections was to make no country completely trust another.

French interests in Morocco. The Anglo-Russian Entente of 1907 (sometimes erroneously called the Triple Entente) settled border disputes between British and Russian zones of influence in Afghanistan and Persia. These agreements, and others like them, did not create actual military alliances, yet they did pave the way to them by preemptively removing points of contention. Germany, for its part, responded to these ententes by forming pacts of its own with Austria–Hungary and the Ottoman Empire. Surging nationalism among many of the Slavic and Arab peoples living under Habsburg and Ottoman rule, respectively, weakened those empires dramatically. And the cost of putting down their rebellions helped to keep the two states near bankruptcy as the century began.

Relations between Britain and Germany had grown especially strained during the Boer War of 1899–1902 (discussed in chapter 23), which pitted the British against the Dutch-descended Afrikaners in South Africa. The British, who had already colonized parts of South Africa under Cecil Rhodes's leadership, wanted to extend their jurisdiction over the Afrikaner Orange Free State after the discovery of vast gold mines there. The Germans had predictably taken the side of the Afrikaners against the British. Britain won a modest victory in the war, but one that came at a heavy price in men, material, and prestige. Germany enjoyed the Britons' embarrassment and the apparent vulnerability of British forces.

Relations worsened several years later, thanks to the blundering of Kaiser William II, who had a long track record of putting his foot in his mouth. In an interview with England's *Daily Telegraph* on October 28, 1908, he described the British people as "mad as March hares." He claimed to have personally drawn up the battle plan that helped the British win a campaign against the Afrikaners and to have forwarded it to his "revered grandmother" Queen Victoria. He further, and bizarrely, laid down a public challenge to England for naval supremacy. Public opinion in Britain was outraged, and the German parliament (Reichstag) took action to limit the emperor's authority on the international scene. Subsequent crises in North Africa and the Balkans, in the context of the fast-decaying Habsburg and Ottoman Empires, brought matters to a fever pitch.

War Declared

In 1905 the German chief of general staff, Alfred Graf von Schlieffen (1833–1913), had developed a detailed battle plan in the event of a two-front war with France and Russia. Kept secret for nine years, the **von Schlieffen Plan** called for a rapid strike at France via Belgium and Luxembourg to circumvent French defenses. It would attack Paris from the north and score a quick victory before Russian forces could marshal in the east. When the Austrian archduke was assassinated in June 1914, the Habsburg state declared war on Serbia, which called in its ally, Russia, which in turn prompted Austria to summon its ally, Germany.

Dreading its two-front vulnerability, Germany took preemptive measures by declaring war on France and putting the Schlieffen Plan into effect. Belgium, however, was a neutral country without any alliances at all.[3] To aid this innocent victim and to uphold international law, Britain, on August 4, 1914, declared war on Germany. Within six weeks, a provincial crisis in the Balkans had swelled into a global conflict.

World War I pitted Germany, Austria–Hungary, the Ottoman Empire, and Bulgaria—the Central Powers—against the British Empire, France, Russia, Serbia, and Belgium—the Allied Powers. Eventually Japan (1914), Italy (1915), Romania and Portugal (1916), and Greece and the United States (1917) joined the fray, on the side of the Allies. The empires drew on all their dominions for soldiers and material support, leading to further conflict around the globe. Casualties mounted quickly. By 1916 both alliances resorted to forced conscription. And resistance to the draft, combined with events in the colonies, shook up societies far from the war's center in Europe.

A NEW MAP OF HELL

The narrative of the war is dismal to recount. Most Western accounts of the war emphasize the importance of the western front—the long, entrenched line along the French–German border, from Belgium to Switzerland—but other fronts proved equally as significant and deadly (see Table 24.1). World War I was fought in seven separate arenas: on the western front, on the eastern front with Russia, in northern Italy, in the Balkans, along the periphery of the Ottoman Empire, in the European colonies, and at sea. Each had its own unique horrors. And each forced the nations involved to mobilize "the home front" to share those horrors (see Map 24.2).

On the western front, the initial German advance through the Low Countries was halted a few miles short of Paris at the First Battle of the Marne (1914). *Battlefronts* More than 2 million soldiers took part in all, roughly one-quarter of whom died or were wounded. After this defeat, the Germans withdrew to a line that ran in a rough arc from Ypres in Belgium, through Soissons in northern France, and down to Verdun in northeastern France. This line moved little over the years and became a site of trench warfare that claimed more than 300,000 French and German lives before the war's end. More than 500,000 more were wounded. Both sides tried to break the deadlock by mounting major offensives—most notably at Verdun (1916), at the Somme (1916), and at Passchendale in Belgium (1917).

---

[3]   In fact, the 1831 treaty that established Belgium as an independent nation had explicitly forbidden it to form alliances.

TABLE 24.1   **Major Events of World War I**

June 28, 1914	Archduke Ferdinand of Austria–Hungary assassinated in Sarajevo
August 4	Germany invades Belgium
August 26–30	Russia invades Germany and is defeated at Battle of Tannenberg
September 4–10	German advance on Paris halted at Battle of the Marne
February 19, 1915	Allied campaign against Gallipoli begins (lasts until January 1916)
April 24	Start of Armenian genocide
May 7	Germany sinks the *Lusitania*
May 23	Italy enters war, joining the Allies; German counteroffensive drives Russians from most of Poland
February 21, 1916	Battle of Verdun begins; lasts until 15 December
June 6	Arab Revolt begins
June	Russian forces against Austria suffer 1 million casualties
July 1	Battle of the Somme (lasts until 18 November); Allies lose 600,000 soldiers
August 27	Romania enters the war
November 28	First German air-raid on London
February 1, 1917	German U-boats begin unrestricted attacks
March 11	British forces capture Baghdad
March 15	Russian tsar is overthrown, forced to abdicate
April 6	United States enters the war on the Allied side
November 16	Vladimir Lenin and his Bolsheviks come to power in Moscow
December 9	British capture Jerusalem
March 3	Treaty of Brest-Litovsk: Russia withdraws from the war
June	German army advances to within 60 miles of Paris
August	British victory at Amiens
August–September	Second Battle of the Somme
October 30	Ottoman Empire and Austrian–Hungarian Empire surrender
November 11	Austria and Germany sign armistice agreements with Allies, ending the war
January 12, 1919	Paris Peace Conference begins (lasts until January 21, 1920)
June 28	Treaty of Versailles is signed

These gained little territory but left hundreds of thousands of corpses lying on the muddy fields. A final effort to break the standoff came in 1918, with the Second Battle of the Marne, when German forces made a last-ditch effort to get through Allied lines and seize Paris. This too resulted only in more slaughter—a quarter million dead, all told.

The eastern front saw a handful of initial victories for the Russians, who dashed forward while German forces were mired in the west. Before long, however, Germany repelled the Russians' advance, and by the end of 1915 a German and Austrian counteroffensive drove the Russians out of Poland. Fighting in 1916 pummeled Russia's forces with extremely heavy losses, and 1917 brought another shock—the Bolshevik Revolution (discussed later in this chapter) and the fall from power of the tsar. This led to Russia's formal withdrawal from the war. The Treaty of Brest-Litovsk, formalized on March 3, 1918, freed Vladimir Lenin's Bolshevik forces to concentrate on securing their control over Russia.

The war in northern Italy was fought primarily between the Italians and Austrians. This third front, along Italy's northeastern border with Austria, did not open until Italy joined the war in 1915, and Allied hopes that it might break the deadlock elsewhere were soon dashed. No fewer than a dozen fierce campaigns were fought near the Isonzo River in the Italian Alps. Fighting ended with an Austrian surrender in October 1918.

The Central Powers armies marched into the Balkans early in the war, and by October 1915 they routed the Serbian forces and seized the Serb capital of Belgrade. They then joined with Ottoman and Bulgarian forces and took Romania. An effort to conquer Greece failed, and the last years of the war were spent in trying to quell rebellions among the Serbians and Bosnians.

For decades, the Ottoman Empire had been dismissed as "the sick man of Europe." However, despite predictions of its speedy collapse, Ottoman forces surprised the Allies with their resilience. The Turks held off a major Allied invasion (composed largely of soldiers from Australia, New Zealand, Canada, and South Africa) at Gallipoli, on the Dardenelles straits, for eight months in 1915. In the plain between the Tigris and Euphrates rivers, the British hoped to launch a sudden strike straight into Baghdad; the Turks stopped the Allies at Kut al-Amara. More than twenty thousand British soldiers died in the siege of Kut (December 1915) and another ten thousand were marched off across the desert as prisoners of war, two-thirds of them dying along the way.

The Turkish economy, however, could not keep Ottoman forces supplied, which left the empire severely weakened. The Allies capitalized on this by organizing the **Arab Revolt**, a 1916–1918 uprising of Middle Eastern Arab tribes against Turkish rule. Lieutenant Colonel T. E. Lawrence (1888–1935), the British

MAP 24.2 World War I, 1914–1918 There were seven principal battle fronts in the war: the western and eastern fronts, northern Italy's border with Austria, the Balkans, the periphery of the Ottoman Empire, the North Sea and Atlantic Ocean, and the sprawl of overseas colonies.

officer popularly known as Lawrence of Arabia, played a pivotal role. The revolt aimed to replace Ottoman imperial rule with autonomous Arab countries. Unknown to Lawrence, however, the British and French governments had

World War I, 1914–1918

	Central Powers
1915	Neutral state that joined Central Powers, with date
	Allied Powers (including colonies)
1914	Neutral state that joined Allied Powers, with date
	Country that remained neutral
	Furthest advance by Central Powers on date marked
	Furthest advance by Allied Powers on date marked
	Allied convoy route
- - -	Naval blockade of Central Powers
—	Borders in 1914
⚔	Major battle

already agreed secretly to divide up the Middle Eastern dominions between themselves, once the war was over. This pact, known as the **Sykes–Picot Agreement** (1916), after the two diplomats who were instrumental in forming it, arranged for Britain to receive what is today southern Iraq, Jordan, and most of

Colonial Troops   Many of the combatants in World War I came from the European colonies. Here, for example, is a photo of a Ugandan color guard on march (led by a British officer, of course).

what is now Israel. France received northern Iraq, today's Syria and Lebanon, and the southeastern corner of today's Turkey. Imperial Russia, a junior partner in the arrangement, was to receive the city of Istanbul and the Bosporus—but Russian claims were nullified by the Bolshevik Revolution of 1917.

Compared with the bloody land battles, there were few pitched naval battles. At the Battle of Jutland in June 1916, British and German naval forces fought to a draw, leaving the British in control of the North Sea. More significant were the attacks of German submarines, or U-boats, on international shipping. German strategy was to cut off the resupply of Britain: it imposed an embargo on all ships, of whatever origin, carrying any civilian or military goods to the United Kingdom. In practice, this meant attacking British and American ships. The U-boats proved highly effective, but at the cost of slowly drawing America into the general conflict.

U.S. Entry into War   The United States entered World War I on April 6, 1917, "to make the world safe for democracy," in the words of President Woodrow Wilson (r. 1913–1921). Wilson had recently won election to a second term, largely on the platform of having kept America out of the conflict, although in a state of "armed neutrality." In reality, the country had never been altogether neutral. Between 1914 and 1916, American trade with the Allies had increased fourfold, and most of the goods sold had been war material—weapons and ammunition, military rations, and supplies like tents, boots, and uniforms. U.S. banks had extended the Allies more than $2 billion in loans and credits, which meant that only an Allied victory would ensure repayment. Britain and France's debt alone equaled $45 billion in today's dollars. When the British imposed a naval blockade on Germany's Baltic coast, American ships never even attempted to challenge it.

Germany launched its U-boats into the Atlantic primarily to interdict American supplies to the Allies, an action that provoked American anger but failed to rouse the country to join the fight. Even when a German U-boat, in May 1915, sank the RMS *Lusitania*—a British transatlantic passenger liner that had 128 Americans on board—and Germany refused to apologize, the U.S. position did not change.[4] An intercepted telegram from Berlin to the German ambassador in Mexico City, in January 1917, added fuel to American outrage. The Zimmermann Telegram (named for the diplomat who had sent it) showed that Germany had offered military aid if Mexico was willing to declare war on the United States, to regain the territories lost in 1845 when the United States annexed Texas. One month later, when the Russians overthrew the tsar and pulled out of the conflict, Germany was able to gather its forces for a single massive campaign against the western front. America finally stirred to action.

America's entry—although not immediately decisive—gave a quick, colossal boost to British and French morale, while severely undermining Germany's. When it became clear that the American entry would only prolong the slaughter, all sides agreed to an armistice, signed on November 11, 1918. The Treaty of Versailles formally ended the war on June 28, 1919—five years, to the very day, after the assassination of the Austrian archduke in Sarajevo.

THE WAR IN THE TRENCHES

The narrative of the war and its strategies is important. So are the political wrangling and diplomatic schemes surrounding them. Indeed, one can view the entire twentieth century as a long, drawn-out consequence of the Great War. But two elements of the war deserve special notice—the experience of common soldiers and the customs of the military officers who commanded them.

Along most of the western, eastern, and Italian fronts, the war quickly devolved into a brutal war of attrition. Battlefronts moved little, which meant that *War of* the physical desolation of these areas was severe. The western front especially was *Attrition* dominated by trench warfare—parallel lines of muddy ditches, separated by a "no man's land" of landmines and barbed wire. From these ditches, soldiers fired rifles and machine guns, threw grenades and canisters of poison gas, tended mortar batteries, and occasionally charged one another with bayonet-fitted rifles. Most trenches were between 7 and 8 feet deep and perhaps 4 feet wide. Proper drainage was not possible under such conditions, so soldiers lived daily in water- and urine-soaked mud up to a foot deep. Worse still, trenches ran in zigzag patterns rather than straight lines to minimize the damage from grenades and artillery shells. The patterns also limited a sniper's ability to fire down a long line of crowded men. Yet they meant that most soldiers lived day in and day out seeing only walls of mud on all sides. The mounds of filth and piles of corpses encouraged a large rat population, which spread disease. Well behind the trenches were various supply

---

[4]   Germany claimed that the RMS *Lusitania* was carrying war supplies to Britain—and, as it later turned out, it was. The total number of passengers aboard the ship was 1962, of whom 1191 perished.

Trench Warfare "The Price of Victory" reads the original caption to this candid news photo of French soldiers in a trench near Argonne, in northern France, in June 1915. The pipe-smoking central figure steps casually over a wounded comrade as he helps to carry out a corpse.

camps; even further behind was the heavy artillery. Most higher-ranking officers took up stations somewhere behind the artillery, often separated from the fighting by several miles.

It was too much heavy firepower in too concentrated an area. Opposing trenches were sometimes so close that enemy soldiers could converse with one another. Artillery barrages intended to weaken the enemy's position fell all too often on the gunners' own comrades, and clouds of poison gas needed only the mildest of breezes to bring the fumes onto the very soldiers who had released them. By 1916 cheaply made gas-masks were standard issue for all soldiers, but they never provided any real protection. Chlorine gas left countless soldiers blinded, with permanently blistered faces and scarred lungs.

Siegfried Sassoon (1886–1967), an English soldier who became one of the greatest World War I poets, described the horrors of trench warfare in his poem "Attack":

> At dawn the ridge emerges massed and dun
> In the wild purple of the glow'ring sun,
> Smouldering through spouts of drifting smoke that shroud
> The menacing scarred slope; and, one by one,
> Tanks creep and topple forward to the wire.
> The barrage roars and lifts. Then, clumsily bowed
> With bombs and guns and shovels and battle-gear,
> Men jostle and climb to, meet the bristling fire.
> Lines of grey, muttering faces, masked with fear,
> They leave their trenches, going over the top,
> While time ticks blank and busy on their wrists,
> And hope, with furtive eyes and grappling fists,
> Flounders in mud. O Jesus, make it stop!

The heavy weaponry—giant howitzers and concrete machine-gun pillboxes, especially—was designed for defensive rather than offensive purposes. That left both sides unable to move forward even if they did score an occasional victory. Small wonder that photographs of battlefields often look like blasted moonscapes.

Small wonder too that officers' reports on both sides, trying to show evidence of progress for their home offices, rarely spoke of strategic gains. Instead of territory, they used a grim tally of corpses as indices of achievement. At Verdun, in 1916, 1.5 million Allied soldiers died to advance the battlefront a mere 3 miles—thirteen deaths for every inch of ground gained. On the eastern front, woefully ill-equipped Russian soldiers faced unending volleys of Central Power artillery shells and machine-gun fire. The tsar's officers could respond only by ordering wave after wave of soldiers into the barrage, in the hope that, eventually, the Germans and Austrians would run out of ammunition. Russian losses mounted so quickly that when rebels rose up against the tsar, in 1917, the army joined with them. At the time of the Treaty of Brest-Litovsk, the truce between Russia and the Central Powers, more than 3 million Russian soldiers had died and 4 million more were held as prisoners of war by Germany and Austria.

In the face of these grim realities, it became more and more difficult to sustain popular support for the war effort. Both sides had touted that the war would

Ghostly Battlefield   Soldiers of the 10th Field Artillery Brigade, Australian 4th Division, march in the battlefield near Ypres, Belgium, in October 1917. The bloodiest battles of all—those that epitomize World War I—came in 1916–1917, when first the Germans and later the British and French launched major offensives in attempts to end the stalemate.

be over by Christmas 1914, a mere six months after it began. In reality, as November's freezing rains gave way to a gray and bitter December, all that had happened was more than a million senseless deaths. At the same time, the Irish playwright George Bernard Shaw published a pamphlet, "Common Sense about the War," in which he argued that it was every patriotic British soldier's duty to rise from the trenches, turn about-face, and shoot his own officers for their incompetence and moral idiocy.

Shaw's outrage stemmed in part from how officers were placed in command. At the start of the war, only 250 of the more than 12,000 officers in the British regular army had earned their positions by promotion from within the ranks. The rest had acquired their posts thanks to aristocratic status, family connections, or British public school ties. They had little military experience or knowledge of military affairs, but the social elite was supposedly better suited to command. No wonder their blunders brought on so many deaths.

Prisoners of War

Soldiers captured in battle became prisoners of war, held according to standards set by the Hague Conventions of 1899 and 1907. These international agreements called for prisoners to receive the same standards of housing, diet, medical attention, and general treatment as soldiers serving the host country. Not all prisoners were so lucky. When the war ended, Germany held roughly 2.5 million prisoners, and Britain and France each held approximately three-quarters of a million. The United States had about fifty thousand in its possession. Most of these received adequate to fair treatment. But prisoners in the non-European theaters of the war fared far worse. At least one-third of the Allied soldiers captured by the Ottomans died during their imprisonment. Disease, malnutrition, thirst, and forced labor were the main causes. The Turks generally established their prisoner-of-war camps far from the battlefronts—in the Balkans, the Middle East, or in Mesopotamia—which seems, on the one hand, a sensible precaution. On the other hand, they regularly forced their prisoners to march the hundreds of miles to the camps—ostensibly to reserve transport vehicles and fuel for the war effort. These forced marches of prisoners across mountains and through deserts, without enough food or water, produced predictable results.

Armenian Genocide

The worst single chapter of this grim history was the death of as many as 1.5 million Armenians—victims of massacre, deportation, forced march, and starvation. This Armenian genocide began with the arrest in Istanbul of 250 leaders of the Armenian community in April 1915, right after the Allied raid at Gallipoli. These leaders were suspected of complicity in a plot to bring down the Ottoman state. From that point on, Armenian populations across eastern Anatolia were subject to torture, beatings, burnings, drownings, and even injections with morphine and typhoid fever.

An Armenian Genocide?   Starvation, dehydration, exposure, and forced marches killed most of the victims of the Armenian tragedy, 1915–1916. The government of Turkey does not deny the deaths of 1.5 million Armenians; it insists rather that they were the result of wartime happenstance instead of an intentional policy.

No official record has ever been found in the Ottoman archives directing a conscious, intentional campaign of annihilation (although access to those archives is heavily restricted even today). To this day, the Republic of Turkey passionately denies the accusation of genocide, although Turks do not dispute the deaths of the Armenian people. But the evidence seems overwhelming. On July 16, 1915, the American ambassador to the Ottoman state, Henry Morgenthau Sr. (1856–1946), sent a telegram to Washington, DC, which read:

> Deportations of and excesses against peaceful Armenians is increasing and from harrowing reports of eye witnesses it appears that a campaign of race extermination is in progress under a pretext of reprisal against rebellion.
>
> Protests as well as threats are unavailing and probably incite the Ottoman government to more drastic measures as they are determined to disclaim responsibility for their absolute disregard of capitulations and I believe nothing short of actual force which obviously United States is not in a position to exert would adequately meet the situation. Suggest you inform belligerent nations and mission boards of this.

As early as August 1915 the *New York Times* reported that Turkish actions amounted to "a plan to exterminate the whole Armenian people." The Ottomans never altered their policy of forced marches, not even when the certainty of massive numbers of Armenian deaths became obvious. By the end of 1916 hundreds of thousands of corpses lay strewn along the roads and tracks from the Armenian highlands to the Syrian desert.

THE HOME FRONT

Mobilizing Industry

Mobilizing the home front was every bit as vital as mobilizing the military, especially since none of the countries had prepared for a long war. France had entered the conflict with only a one-month supply of ammunition. The Germans, confident of a quick victory, never bothered to requisition winter boots and coats for their infantrymen until winter had set in.[5] Retooling the industrial economies for war thus became a top priority. The transition involved nationalizing industries, rationing most consumer goods, forbidding labor strikes, and raising capital by selling war bonds. To keep society in line, most states instituted some form of censorship and mounted extensive propaganda campaigns. Britain's Defense of the Realm Act (1914), for example, empowered the government to censor newspapers, read private mail, search homes without a warrant, and imprison or deport anyone guilty of unpatriotic utterances.

Mobilizing Civilians

In every country the compulsory military draft left a severe shortage of laborers in fields and factories. The German Reichstag not only forbade labor strikes but also made it illegal for any able-bodied man to be unemployed. Women had to step in to keep domestic production going. Food shortages became common; in Germany alone more than 750,000 civilians perished from starvation or complications from malnutrition. State investment in manufacturing, however, tended to go to the same large industrial and agricultural firms as before the war began. At least, it was thought, they could operate on a large enough scale to meet wartime needs. But the close relationships between them and the government raised alarms about war profiteering at the expense of small businesses and common workers.

A steady barrage of war propaganda kept the public in support of the war for quite some time, even in the face of mounting fatalities. In fact, the longer the war dragged on, the greater the effort was to rally support. Only the nature of the propaganda changed—from early enthusiastic posters ("The Great Game Has Begun!" crowed one early British poster) to cartoon depictions of the enemy as bloodthirsty savages.

---

5   The winter of 1914–1915 was a bad one on the western and eastern fronts. Soldiers complained that grenades froze together in their supply crates.

Women's Work   Workers take inventory in a British munitions factory during World War I. The extraordinary amount of munitions used in the war necessitated continuous production. As millions of men went into active service, women in all the involved countries stepped up to fill the factory positions.

However, thousands on all sides took public stances against the conflict. Their reasons differed. Some argued along class lines, others along economic or racial lines; still others staked out a moral position against all forms of militarism. In Britain, more than fifteen thousand individuals officially registered for "conscientious objector" status, as permitted by the Hague Conventions, risking social ostracism and even imprisonment.

Growing Opposition

In November 1914 a group of 101 British suffragists signed their names to an "Open Christmas Letter" addressed to "the Women of Germany and Austria":

> Sisters,
> Some of us wish to send you a word at this sad Christmastide, though we can but speak through the Press. The Christmas message sounds like mockery to a world at war, but those of us who wished and still wish for peace may surely offer a solemn greeting to such of you who feel as we do. Do not let us forget that our very anguish unites us, that we are passing together through the same experiences of pain and grief.

Dehumanizing the Enemy   This poster was one of many propaganda pieces made to persuade the United States to join World War I. A fierce gorilla, representing militarism and carrying a club marked "Kultur," stomps ashore in America. Russia's withdrawal from the war in 1917 freed Germany from fighting on two fronts and triggered widespread fear that the Central Powers would defeat France and Britain.

Caught in the grip of terrible circumstance, what can we do? Tossed on this turbulent sea of human conflict, we can but move ourselves to those calm shores whereon stand, like rocks, the eternal verities—Love, Peace, Brotherhood.

We pray you to believe that come what may we hold to our faith in Peace and Goodwill between nations; while technically at enmity in obedience to our rulers, we owe allegiance to that higher law which bids us live in peace with all men....

Do you not feel with us that the vast slaughter in our opposing armies is a stain on civilization and Christianity, and that still deeper horror is aroused at the thought of those innocent victims, the countless women, children, babes, old and sick, pursued by famine, disease, and death in the devastated areas, both East and West?

As we saw in South Africa and the Balkan States, the brunt of modern war falls upon non-combatants, and the conscience of the world cannot bear the sight....

Relief, however colossal, can reach but few. Can we sit still and let the helpless die in their thousands, as die they must—unless we rouse ourselves in the name of Humanity to save them? There is but one way to do this. We must all urge that peace be made with appeal to Wisdom and Reason. Since in the last resort it is these which must decide the issues, can they begin too soon, if it is to save the womanhood and childhood as well as the manhood of Europe?

Even through the clash of arms we treasure our poet's [Percy Bysshe Shelley] vision, and already seem to hear:

A hundred nations swear that there shall be
Pity and Peace and Love among the good and free.

May Christmas hasten that day. Peace on Earth is gone, but by renewal of our faith that it still reigns at the heart of things, Christmas should strengthen both you and us and all womanhood to strive for its return.

> We are yours in this sisterhood of sorrow.

The author of the letter was Emily Hobhouse (1860–1926), a longtime social activist. Hobhouse got her start in public life when she campaigned against the brutal conditions that she had witnessed in British concentration camps in South Africa during the Boer War. The Christmas Letter created a rift among suffragists, since many of them supported the war. Despite their differences, however, most suffragists agreed to set aside the issue of women's rights until the war was over and to dedicate themselves to humanitarian work in the meantime.

A group of 150 German suffragists responded in March 1915 with an open letter (in English) of their own:

> To our English sisters, sisters of the same race, we express in the name of many German women our warm and heartfelt thanks for their Christmas greetings, which we only heard of lately.
>
> [Your] message was a confirmation of what we foresaw—that women of the belligerent countries, with all faithfulness, devotion, and love to their country, can go beyond it and maintain true solidarity with the women of other belligerent nations, and that really civilised women never lose their humanity.

OFFICERS AND GENTLEMEN

Every war introduces new weapons and new technologies of communication and transport and confronts new and usually unforeseen challenges. However, it takes time to understand these innovations and translate them into military tactics. As the saying goes, commanders are always fighting the last war. When World War I began, none of the top officers on either side of the conflict was familiar with trench warfare, submarine warfare, or aerial warfare. None had experienced poison gas or the gargantuan howitzers of modern artillery. Joseph Joffre (1852–1931), the French commander in chief at the outbreak of hostilities, had never even commanded an army before. His entire career up to that point had consisted of working as a military engineer. King George V (r. 1910–1936) read repeated concerned reports from his general staff about the incompetence of the chief commander of the British Expeditionary Force, General John French (1852–1925) ("An ignorant little fool," in the words of a rival general; "a vain, ignorant and vindictive old man with an unsavoury society backing," in the words of another). The leading commanders on both sides had inherited a tradition that still mimicked the military strategy and tactics used by Napoleon Bonaparte—a fast-moving infantry, pressing ever forward, complemented by portable artillery. This had worked brilliantly at Austerlitz in 1805—but not in 1915, when the German field commander, Erich von Falkenhayn (1861–1922), earned the nickname "the Blood Miller of Verdun."

Mistakes and Miscommunications   Mistakes in command, even elementary ones, marked the war effort on all sides. Miscommunication between the German and Austrian–Hungarian leaders, for example, left their realms exposed to Russian advance in 1914. Each had expected the other to protect the Russian front while they pressed ahead in Belgium and Serbia, respectively. The confusion allowed Russia's forces to advance through all of Poland before they were stopped. At the eight-month siege of Gallipoli (1915–1916), civilian crews were assigned to the ships designed to clear the waterways of explosive mines ("minesweepers") in preparation for the Allied attack—crews who, unsurprisingly, fled once they came under heavy Ottoman artillery fire. As a result, one-third of the Allied battleships used in the campaign were sunk. On the Italian front officers launched twelve direct assaults against dug-in Austrian alpine units that held a clearly superior uphill position—protected by minefields, barbed wire, machine-gun nests, and artillery units. Fully one-half of all of Italy's 600,000 casualties in the war were suffered right here.

Just as sobering were the losses in the air and at sea. Both the airplane and the submarine made their military debut in the war and proved vital to its outcome. France put sixty-eight thousand airplanes into service; fifty-two thousand of them were destroyed in battle. The design of the planes had to be kept simple, since many pilots went into battle after as little as a single week's instruction in how to fly. Airplanes and airships were used initially for surveillance, but commanders quickly got the idea of dropping explosives. However, early airplanes did not fly at high altitudes, which left them vulnerable to enemy ground fire. Airplanes had their most dramatic effect in the Arab Revolt against the Turks, since the Ottomans had little heavy artillery and had dedicated it to other theaters. T. E. Lawrence described a battle at Megiddo in Palestine toward the end of the war, when British and Australian forces trapped a division of Turkish soldiers in a narrow defile and then strafed them from the air:

> When the smoke had cleared it was seen that the organization of the enemy had melted away. They were a dispersed horde of trembling individuals, hiding for their lives in every fold of the vast hills. Nor did their commanders ever rally them again. When our cavalry entered the silent

Flying above the Pyramids   Airplanes were used almost entirely for reconnaissance in the first year of the war, since their engines could not carry the additional weight of bombs. Pilots were not even issued parachutes, at first, since those too proved too heavy for most engines. Guns were of little use until they could be synchronized with the propellers, lest they shoot off their own blades.

valley the next day they could count ninety guns, fifty lorries, and nearly a thousand carts abandoned with all their belongings. The RAF [Royal Air Force] lost four killed. The Turks lost a corps [unit].

Despite Allied victories, lives were increasingly seen as wasted, the tragic collateral damage of incompetent military and political leaders. More than that, complaints ran, members of the labor and rural classes were regularly ordered into the worst of the fighting; so were recruits from colonial territories. In Australia today, commemoration of the slaughter at Gallipoli is a more emotionally powerful holiday than Armistice Day itself.

Siegfried Sassoon, the soldier-poet, protested the war with a letter read aloud in Parliament on July 30, 1917, and published subsequently in the *Times* of London:

> I am making this statement as an act of willful defiance of military authority because I believe that the war is being deliberately prolonged by those who have the power to end it. I am a soldier, convinced that I am acting on behalf of soldiers. I believe that the war upon which I entered

as a war of defense and liberation has now become a war of aggression and conquest. I believe that the purposes for which I and my fellow soldiers entered upon this war should have been so clearly stated as to have made it impossible to change them and that had this been done the objects which actuated us would now be attainable by negotiation.

I have seen and endured the sufferings of the troops and I can no longer be a party to prolonging these sufferings for ends which I believe to be evil and unjust. I am not protesting against the conduct of the war, but against the political errors and insincerities for which the fighting men are being sacrificed.

On behalf of those who are suffering now, I make this protest against the deception which is being practiced upon them; also I believe it may help to destroy the callous complacency with which the majority of those at home regard the continuance of agonies which they do not share and which they have not enough imagination to realize.

Despite government censorship, news about the war and its horrors circulated widely. After the initial elation in 1914, a popular attitude of grim resignation and determination set in. The war was no longer popular, but few saw any alternative, once it had begun, except victory. When Russia pulled out of the conflict and American entered it, in late 1917, fear arose that the war would drag on interminably. After the Allied victory at the Second Battle of the Somme (August–September 1918), the exhausted Germans were not long to submit.

Spanish Flu Epidemic

Even so, the suffering was not over, for another tragedy struck in the immediate postwar period—the influenza epidemic of 1918–1920. The so-called Spanish flu epidemic that spread across the entire world between January 1918 and December 1920 was the worst natural disaster since the Black Death in the mid-fourteenth century and the smallpox pandemic in the New World in the sixteenth century. The origin of the flu virus is uncertain; theories have placed it in France, Austria, China, Sierra Leone, and even a military installation in north-central Kansas. Wherever it originated, its effects were vast and rapid. People worn out by years of war and deprivation, among whom large numbers of close-quartered soldiers were in constant movement, were uniquely vulnerable. By the time the virus ran its course, the disease had spread globally, even to remote Pacific islands and into the Arctic, infecting some 500 million people and killing as many as 100 million of them—approximately 5 percent of the global population. (Despite its name, there was nothing Spanish about the flu. The virus was so called because Spain's noninvolvement in World War I meant that it was the only European country not to be under news censorship, and so the first detailed reports of flu appeared in that country.) Curiously, this flu was deadliest among the segment of the population that is usually least affected by flu viruses—adults between the ages of eighteen and forty.

The Spanish flu disappeared almost as quickly as it had arisen, presumably the result of a fast mutation of the virus into a less deadly form. In retrospect, it supplied a suitably horrific end to a horrifying war.

RUSSIA'S REVOLUTION

Reaching from Germany and Poland in the west to China and Japan in the east, Russia comprises one-sixth of the world's land mass. It is an enormous territory, made up largely of flat grassland with an icy northern fringe and no natural internal boundaries in its western reaches, and of forests, steppes, and fertile valleys interspersed with mountainous stretches in its eastern expanses. It is also vast, open, and, despite its large population, chiefly an empty space. It is a land of extensive ethnic and cultural diversity, marked by long distances, poor communication, an adverse climate, and above all defensiveness and an ingrained sense of vulnerability. Through much of its history it lacked both an effective government and any natural borders to keep enemies out.

For long centuries the people of Russia suffered waves of invasion from all sides. According to tradition, Russia's history begins with an invasion of Swedish Vikings who established the first Kingdom of Kievan Rus' in the ninth century. Subsequent invaders included the Khazars, Slavs, Byzantines, Poles, Lithuanians, Germans, and French. Still other attackers included the Huns, Chinese, Mongols, and Turkish peoples of the east. Without adequate means to defend themselves, Russia's rulers traditionally relied on two tactics. One was to relinquish territory by retreating; this forced invaders to maintain long supply lines while exposing them to brutal winters. The other tactic was to hurl wave after wave of common soldiers at their attackers to use up the invaders' stores of ammunition.

With a few exceptions, the Romanov rulers held tight to autocracy and resisted efforts to reform. The development of democratic traditions, capitalist economies, industrialization, and liberal societies in the West frustrated and frightened Russia's rulers more than they inspired them. If Bonaparte had not been enough to convince Russia of Europe's dangerousness and untrustworthiness, the Crimean War in the 1850s was. Through the second half of the nineteenth century, nevertheless, pressure for reform did increase. The question was how to reform. Many Russians supported Western values and championed Enlightened reforms like human rights, democracy, and economic development; others hoped for a uniquely Russian version of change, something homegrown and rooted in tradition. The tension between these competing notions of change underlay much of Russia's social and cultural development of the era. It also

The Last Tsars

provides the backdrop for the parade of great literary artists Russia produced: Nikolai Gogol (1809–1852), Ivan Turgenev (1818–1883), Fyodor Dostoevsky (1821–1881), Leo Tolstoy (1828–1910), and Anton Chekhov (1860–1904), to name but a few.

Calls for reform gained momentum in the 1860s and 1870s. Serfdom was abolished in 1861, and independent judiciaries with trials by jury were established. But in 1881 a terrorist assassinated Tsar Alexander II, which led his successor, Alexander III (r. 1881–1894), to strengthen the police state. He reached out for popular support by promoting a Pan-Slavism that masked an obsessive personal hatred of Jews, with the result that anti-Jewish pogroms became common and vicious. Alexander also tried to force rapid industrialization; his signature project was the Trans-Siberian Railroad, begun in 1891. Russia's loss in the war with Japan in 1905, combined with a failed attempt that year at revolution in Moscow and Saint Petersburg, led the next tsar, Nicholas II (r. 1894–1917), to dismiss the Russian parliament.

The deaths of millions of poorly trained and ill-equipped soldiers, several years of horrendous crop failures, and the collapse of the currency led to a wave of food riots and labor strikes in early 1917. Unlike in 1905, the army supported the

Bloody Sunday   Tsarist soldiers fire on demonstrators at the Winter Palace in Saint Petersburg, Russia, on "Bloody Sunday," January 9, 1905.

rebels this time in their "February Revolution." Nicholas realized the situation was hopeless and abdicated, bringing the three-hundred-year-old Romanov dynasty to a sudden end.

But as with revolutions elsewhere, most notably in France in 1789, the people could not agree on what government would replace the old administration. They were united only in their opposition to the tsar and to Russia's further involvement in World War I. A dizzying array of rival parties quickly formed, and each party was just as quick to raise an army of its own. Soon a civil war raged across Russia. By 1920 Vladimir Lenin and his Bolshevik party had crushed all rivals and established a Communist rule that would govern Russia until 1991 (see Map 24.3).

Bolshevik Takeover

MAP 24.3   The Russian Civil War, 1917–1922   The Russian Civil War was fought by more than a half-dozen rival groups, among them the pro-tsarist Whites and the communist Menshevik and Bolshevik factions. The Western powers and Japan sent in troops to put down the threatening revolution, but the Bolsheviks ultimately triumphed by the end of 1920. Fighting continued, however, into 1922.

The **Bolshevik Revolution** (also known as the "October Revolution" for the month in 1917 when the Bolsheviks seized control of the provisional government established after Nicholas's abdication) succeeded in part because the Bolsheviks understood the depth of the popular desire for radical agrarian reform—how desperately the peasants wanted Russia's farmland redistributed. It succeeded, too, because the Bolsheviks believed unapologetically in the use of violence and terrorism to achieve their ends.

The civil war and Bolshevik takeover shaped Russian Communism. Leon Trotsky (1879–1940), Bolshevik commissar of war, built the highly disciplined "Red Army" by ending democratic procedures, such as the election of officers, that had originally attracted soldiers to Bolshevism. Lenin and Trotsky introduced the policy of war Communism—seizing grain from the peasantry to feed the civil war army and workforce. Marx had promised that revolution would bring a "withering away" of the state. Instead, the result was authoritarian government.

BOLSHEVISM AND THE LAWS OF HISTORY

Lenin and Leninism

Vladimir Lenin (1870–1924) possessed the unwavering drive and personal discipline of a true zealot. Lenin's real name was Vladimir Ilyich Ulyanov, and his father had worked for the imperial bureaucracy as a provincial school inspector. He converted to radicalism as a youth, after Tsar Alexander III ordered Lenin's older brother executed in 1887 for his involvement in an assassination plot, and spent much of his young adulthood in Europe, where he made contacts with a network of dedicated reformers. (He became a Marxist in 1890 or 1891, during his study of the law at the University of Saint Petersburg, and changed his name to confuse the police.) Lenin sympathized with poor workers and farmers but never identified with them. He saw himself instead as a Romantic leader of the masses, a passionate intellectual superior to those whom he led.

His elitism carried over into his political thinking as well. Lenin's party positioned itself as a vanguard party: it held all authority and ruled the masses directly, rather than, as some Marxist groups had called for, through public referendum. He championed a separate group of professional revolutionaries whose ideological purity would ensure the success of the revolution. It would also conveniently legitimize whatever tactics the party elite chose to employ. The incorruptibility of the Bolshevik leaders, he was convinced, would prevent them from being seduced by the trappings of the power they so ruthlessly reserved for themselves.

Intellectually, Lenin had to alter Marxist theory to make it fit the Russian situation, and the changes he made helped set the tone for much of the twentieth century's international politics. Marx had argued that the inevitable transfer of wealth and power to the working class would and could happen only in an industrialized society. Industrial capitalism as he saw it, for all its evil, was a necessary stage en route to Communist freedom. The proletarian class who would inherit the earth consisted first and foremost of urban laborers. Russia by 1920, however, had not become an industrialized society by any stretch of the imagination. Dirt-poor farmers and unskilled laborers still made up easily 80 percent of the population. Lenin needed to tweak the Marxist formula so that historical development could leapfrog over the industrial-capitalist stage straight to socialism.

Russian Peasants   Russian villagers pose for a photographer in this picture from the 1890s. Their wooden huts with thatch roofs can be seen, as well as the simple dirt roads that were the norm. In spring these became nearly impassable as the melting snow turned them into rivers of mud.

Lenin wrote his most interesting books during his two-decade European exile before coming to power, when he was trying to establish himself among the revolutionary elite. His first significant publication was *The Development of Capitalism in Russia* (1899). It is here that he reworks Marxist theory by arguing that Russia's agricultural production already had all the labor specialization, class structure, and market competition called for by Marx. Lenin also extends his argument against *populism*, the liberal political philosophy supporting the rights and power of the people in their struggle against the privileged elite. Populism, as he sees it, is moral compromise dressed up as common sense: True reform means centralizing all authority among professional revolutionaries because the servitude of the masses allows them to be co-opted by capitalist landowners.

In the 1890s there were widespread calls within Russia for land reform—all within a structure of social democracy that would preserve the rights and citizenship of the elite. Lenin would have none of that. He insisted that only the revolutionary caste can lead the masses to freedom, and it can do so only by ignoring the opinions of those they lead. As he put it in *What Is To Be Done?* (1902): "The history of the world shows that workers by themselves can achieve nothing more than a trade-union level of consciousness." The leaders of the revolution, in other words, are of not the same stock as the workers they control, and they should not apologize for it.

Lenin's next major publication was *Materialism and Empirio-criticism: Critical Comments on a Reactionary Philosophy* (1909). It represents Lenin's only attempt at genuine philosophical writing, and no other book of his betrays more of Lenin's thin, hard, and brittle personality. He argues that there are only two real possibilities in a philosophical view of the world—materialism and idealism. There is the world of objects, things, bodies, atoms, molecules, and natural forces on the one hand, and there is the world of theories, abstract ideas, and impersonal notions on the other. Any philosophy that attempts a middle position or claims somehow to transcend the poles is either short-sighted or just plain verbal tomfoolery. His point is reminiscent of Thomas Hobbes in *Leviathan* (discussed in chapter 15): a society can consist only of absolute chaos or absolute order, and any position in between is simply the sweep of the pendulum on its way from one extreme to the other. Materialism, Lenin concludes, must be the truth, since it alone is supported by modern science. Physical reality exists outside of human thought for the simple reason that the universe existed before human beings did—millions of years before, in fact. Moreover, human thought emerges from the human brain, which is itself a physical object. No brain, no thought; materialism alone has verifiable existence.

Lenin's argument is neither elegant nor original, but he presents it with evangelical intensity. The theory of **dialectical materialism**, or of the pendulum swings of history in a firmly materialist world, is actually a fairly minor aspect of Marx's own thought. But in Leninism it appears front and center as the force driving history forward—to the confrontation of the peasants and the bourgeoisie. There is no way for human beings to avoid this force, any more than they can avoid Newton's universal laws. Just as all molecules are subject to gravity, all humanity is driven by dialectical materialism. Most of Lenin's contemporaries lambasted the book as cold, crude, and shallow—which it is. The book quickly sank from view, but it was revived in the 1930s by a new leader of the Bolshevik regime, Joseph Stalin (g. 1922–1952)—whose ability to regard people as mere objects was even more pronounced than Lenin's.

Exporting Revolution Lenin's most interesting book was inspired by the experience of World War I, which he watched unfold in all its tragedy from a safe distance in Zurich, in neutral Switzerland. *Imperialism, the Highest Stage of Capitalism* was published in Petrograd ("Peter's City"), the former Saint Petersburg, in 1917. (The imperial government renamed the city in 1914, after the outbreak of World War I, to remove the German words "Sank" and "Burg.") Lenin here confronts a significant problem: Karl Marx had not foreseen imperialism. According to Marx, industrial capitalism would result in a consolidation of economic power among the most prominent members of the bourgeoisie. Once this institutional lock on further economic development was in place, the proletarian revolution would take place.

Lenin had to address why a revolution had not occurred to stop imperialism before it began. His adroit answer also buttresses his earlier contention—that agrarian Russia could bypass the industrial stage and still effect a Marxist revolution. In late capitalism, he argues, finance and industry form a union of their own that shuts out all competition. Once it has taken over an entire national economy, its profits become stagnant, which drives the cartel overseas in search of new markets and larger profits. By investing its capital abroad, the cartel divides the world between the imperialist industrial nations and the colonized countries that are locked out of industrial development. Because the undeveloped nations depend on monopolistic capital, they assume the role of the proletariat as the actors in the revolution. Lenin asserts that imperialism is neither an aberration nor an accidental consequence of capitalism; it is actually the *goal* of capitalist societies, and the Great War is the initial stage of the revolution yet to come. And the agents of the revolution will be the agrarian workers of the undeveloped periphery—meaning Russia.

Once the Bolsheviks took control of the government, Lenin and his comrades indeed led the country as a vanguard. He introduced two final major revisions of Marx's thought. First, he insisted on violent action to bring the revolution to fruition. And second, he insisted on the need to export the revolution to the colonized nations living under capitalist rule. Just as Bonaparte had believed that absolutism had to be crushed everywhere to preserve the revolution in France, Lenin concluded that revolutionary Russia needed to promote the rising up of oppressed rural workers everywhere.

For the time being, however, that was not possible, Lenin declared. The Bolsheviks had to get Russia in order first. In 1920 they instituted a complete state takeover of the land and whatever manufacturing base the country possessed. They conscripted labor, confiscated all foodstuffs and goods, and began an emergency redistribution of provisions. Peasant bands called Green Armies revolted against the confiscation of their crops. Industrial production stood at only 13 percent of prewar levels, and millions of refugees clogged the cities and roamed the countryside. In the spring of 1921, workers in Petrograd and sailors at the naval base at Kronstadt revolted, protesting the privileged standard of living that Bolshevik supervisors enjoyed. They called for "soviets without Communists"— that is, a worker state without elite leaders. (The word *soviet* entered the English language in 1917; derived from the Russian noun *sovèt* ["council"], it designated, in general, any sort of council dedicated to socialist principles. Later, of course, it came to identify uniquely the conglomerate state of the Soviet Union.)

The revolts pushed Lenin to institute reform. Under his **New Economic Policy,** the government retained control of finance, transportation, and industrial output but returned the rest of the economy to a modest degree of private

The Leninist Regime

enterprise. Peasants contributed a certain percentage of their crops to the state, but they were free to sell the rest on an open market. Traders were allowed to buy and sell as they pleased. In essence, Lenin throughout the 1920s introduced a "mixed" system—socialism in the large-scale economy and capitalism in the small, local economies.

Politically, Communist Russia was a dictatorship led by a Bolshevik party of some the party—by which he meant keeping the party subservient to his authority—by instituting regular purges. Spying and terrorism began on a massive scale, along with a network of forced labor camps. "Let us cleanse the Russian land of every type of harmful insect . . . by which I mean the rich, the miscreants, the lazy—all those not dedicated entirely to the revolutionary cause."

The Bolsheviks wiped out, by imprisonment, extermination, or both, the entire professional class of financiers half million members, and Lenin himself reigned supreme. He maintained the "ideological purity" of entrepreneurs, civic officials, engineers, and administrators, seeing them as unreliable. They abolished the Russian Orthodox Church, confiscated its possessions, and forbade all religious ceremonies and religious education. An internal security bureau, the forerunner of the KGB, strictly censored all publications, broadcasts, and public

Lenin in the Vanguard   Lenin addresses a Moscow crowd in 1918 at the first anniversary of the Bolshevik Revolution. He mobilized the masses with his oratory, but he also used traditional weapons of the Russian Empire such as secret police, torture, and executions to secure the Revolution.

addresses. Mandatory public education introduced the new generation to socialist ideals and the unquestioned correctness of the Leninist model of communal existence. Lenin himself remained in complete control until his death in 1924, but he seemed diminished as a personality. His strength was as a firebrand, attacking old systems, rather than as the administrator of a bureaucracy, even if a ruthless one. Writings from his final four years are filled with complaints: "Russians are lousy workers compared to those in the West. . . . One out of every ten lazy workers should be shot on the spot." "Treat the Jews in the Ukraine with an iron rod. . . . Transfer them to the front, and never let them into government offices." "Tell every member of the Security Bureau to kill anyone who does not show up to work because he wants a stupid Christmas celebration."

Emancipated Women   This Soviet propaganda poster honors the heroines of socialist labor. It proclaims, "What the October [Bolshevik] Revolution brought to the female worker and the peasant woman."

Still, despite the horrors of the civil war and of Lenin's brutal governance, daily life for most Russians was probably better in the 1920s than it had been under the tsars. Food and shelter become more available, as did some forms of education and medical care. Visitors from the West brought back to Europe breathless reports about Marxism as a viable new path of development. The West could and should consider that path, they said, as it rebuilt from the ruins of World War I.

HOW NOT TO END A WAR

After armistice was declared on November 11, 1918, the difficult work of ironing out a permanent peace settlement began. The actual settlement punished the losers, angered both sides, and practically ensured anything but permanent peace. The collapse of the Ottoman Empire was just one more sign that although the old order was gone for good, the grounds for resentment still simmered.

The Allied leaders—U.S. President Woodrow Wilson, British prime minister David Lloyd George, French prime minister Georges Clemenceau, and Italian prime minister Vittorio Orlando—gathered in Paris in January 1919 along with teams of diplomats, historians, lawyers, and economists amid high hopes.

Signing the Peace Treaty This painting by Sir William Orpen (1878–1931) shows the scene in the Hall of Mirrors, at Versailles, on June 28, 1919, when the Peace Accord was formalized. The body language between U.S. president Woodrow Wilson and French prime minister Georges Clemenceau, with their backs to each other, is telling.

Negotiations deadlocked almost instantly. Wilson, head of the growing world power that had contributed to the Allied victory, had his own agenda. His **Fourteen Points** were steeped in the language of freedom and called for open diplomacy, an "open-minded" settlement of colonial issues, and the self-determination of peoples— meaning the right of national groups to have autonomy if they wanted it. Wilson pressed especially hard for a political redivision of central and eastern Europe to respect ethnic nationalities. The French, however, considered themselves the victims of German aggression. The overwhelming bulk of the fighting on the western front, after all, had taken place on French soil. The only acceptable option to France was to punish Germany so that it could never again threaten France. The British took a position somewhere between the two. After months of talks and no progress at all, the governments finally agreed out of exhaustion and frustration to France's demands.

Peace of Paris

The **Peace of Paris** (1919–1920), often called the Treaty of Versailles, actually consists of five separate treaties, one with each of the Central Powers (Germany, Austria, Hungary, Bulgaria, and Turkey), and each one created as many problems as it resolved. The treaty with Germany—the **Treaty of Versailles** (1919) proper—proved the most controversial. France insisted on, and won, vast concessions. Germany was stripped of all overseas colonies and internationally held funds, which were duly reapportioned among Belgium, Britain, France, and Italy. The regions of Alsace and Lorraine were ceded to France, and the rest of Germany west of the Rhine River was given over to a new international body dedicated to world peace and cooperation, the **League of Nations**. Germany's borders were in essence pushed back to what they had been in 1871. The German military was limited to 100,000 soldiers and was denied aircraft, heavy artillery, and warships.

The League of Nations also organized the administration of the former colonies and territories of the defeated empires through systems of political control called **mandates**. Although the victorious powers exercised their mandates, local leaders retained limited authority. The league justified the mandate system as providing governance by "advanced nations" over territories "not yet able to stand by themselves under the strenuous conditions of the modern world." As we will see in the next chapter, the mandate system would not only keep imperialism alive at a time when the powers were bankrupt and weak but also, like the Treaty of Versailles, arouse anger and resistance.

Most galling of all to the Germans were articles 231 and 232 of the treaty, which to their minds forced Germany to accept sole blame for the entire war:

> Article 231: The Allied and Associated Governments affirm and Germany accepts the responsibility of Germany and her allies for causing all the loss and damage to which the Allied and Associated Governments and their nationals have been subjected as a consequence of the war imposed upon them by the aggression of Germany and her allies.
>
> Article 232: The Allied and Associated Governments recognize that the resources of Germany are not adequate, after taking into account permanent diminutions of such resources which will result from other provisions of the present Treaty, to make complete reparation for all such loss and damage. The Allied and Associated Governments, however, require, and Germany undertakes, that she will make compensation for all damage done to the civilian population of the Allied and Associated Powers and to their property during the period of the belligerency of each as an Allied or Associated Power against Germany.

These articles obliged Germany to make reparations for all civilian losses to the Allied powers, which a separate commission reckoned at a sum of 226 billion reichsmarks (roughly $680 billion in today's currency). This was an impossible sum, since so much of Germany's accumulated wealth had been confiscated. The treaty, after all, had taken away territories that supported most of the nation's industrial capacity—75 percent of its iron ore deposits, 30 percent of its steel production, and nearly 30 percent of its available coal. Further, outraged Germans especially viewed Article 231 as a "war guild clause." It is uncertain, however, whether these clauses were indeed assignations of guilt. Nearly identical clauses were included in the separate treaties that ended the war against Germany's allies—and none of them regarded the clauses in that way.

As stringent as it was, the treaty represented far less than France had originally wanted. Criticism of the pact emerged almost instantly. The British Parliament and the U.S. Congress refused to ratify it, which left France feeling exposed, with unreliable allies. A leading British economist who had in fact been a delegate to the peace conference, John Maynard Keynes (1883–1946), repudiated the treaty. In his *Economic Consequences of the Peace* (1919), Keynes had a gloomy prediction not only for Germany but also for the entire Continent:

> The essential facts of the situation, as I see them, are expressed simply. Europe consists of the densest aggregation of population in the history of the world. This population is accustomed to a relatively high standard of life, in which, even now, some sections of it anticipate improvement rather than deterioration. In relation to other continents Europe is not self-sufficient; in particular it cannot feed itself. Internally the population is not evenly distributed, but much of it is crowded into a relatively small number of dense industrial centers. This population secured for itself a livelihood before the war, without much margin of surplus, by means of a delicate and immensely complicated organization, of which the foundations were supported by coal, iron, transport, and an unbroken supply of imported food and raw materials from other continents. By the destruction of this organization and the interruption of the stream of supplies, a part of this population is deprived of its means of livelihood. Emigration is not open to the redundant surplus. For it would take years to transport them overseas, even, which is not the case, if countries could be found which were ready to receive them. The danger confronting us, therefore, is the rapid depression of the standard of life of the European populations to a point which will mean actual starvation for some (a point already reached in Russia and approximately reached in Austria). Men will not always die quietly. For starvation, which brings to some lethargy and a helpless despair, drives other temperaments to the nervous instability of hysteria and to a mad despair. And these in their distress may overturn the remnants of organization, and submerge civilization itself in their attempts to satisfy desperately the overwhelming needs of the individual.

Europe after the war did indeed have difficulty feeding itself, and not just Germany and Austria. For a time the Allied countries could draw on the resources of their colonies. Now, however, the collapse of the Ottoman and Habsburg Empires gave fresh hope to colonized peoples throughout the world. They might finally achieve freedom from all European control. Germany, meanwhile, was forced to swallow a humiliating treaty that left a legacy of resentment and betrayal.

The settlement with Austria was not as punitive as that with Germany, although the Austrians felt that it was. Austria and Hungary became separate countries, much to the rejoicing of the Hungarians, and an autonomous Czechoslovakia was established. A short-lived kingdom of Serbia, Croatia, and Slovenia soon evolved into the federated state of Yugoslavia; smaller territorial concessions were made to Italy and Romania. Austria itself was thus reduced to a landlocked republic and was forbidden to unite with Germany into a larger German state. The Hungarians celebrated independence from Vienna and were left with an ethnically cohesive state. However, they resented losing control of the Slovak, Slovenian, and Balkan peoples—who had at one time made up 60 percent of their subjects (see Map 24.4).

YOUNG TURKS

The demise of the Ottoman Empire both was and was not a consequence of the war. The revolt in 1908 of a faction called the **Young Turks** had already led to a constitutional reform that reinstated the Turkish Parliament and severely limited the power of the imperial government. A number of peripheral territories, primarily in the Balkans and much of today's country of Libya, took advantage of the political disorder to win independence from Istanbul. Although the rebellion contributed to a shrinking of the empire, it nonetheless produced a more stable and reform-minded government.

The Young Turks were not democrats, although they posed as such when negotiating with the Western powers. Interested above all in promoting pan-ethnic Islamic nationalism, they overthrew the sultan Abdul Hamid II in 1909 and replaced him with his half brother Mehmed V (r. 1909–1918). The Young Turks had modernizing ambitions, and some of them, at least, hoped to govern a united Islamic world under a partially secularized regime, seeing this as the best hope of resolving the religious sectarianism among Muslims. The position of non-Muslims under Young Turk rule was uncertain. Indeed, the policies of the Young Turks were contradictory—what they proposed was not a truly secular government but a special kind of Muslim monopoly of power—which prompted groups like the Armenians and Jews to seek to break away from Turkish rule altogether. The Young Turk administration, not the sultan, entered the war on the Central Powers side.

The Arab Revolt of 1916–1918 had weakened Turkish power further by causing most of the Middle East to rise up against Istanbul. Defeat in the war meant the effective end of the empire, and the ensuing political confusion meant that it took until 1920 to formalize a peace treaty with the Allies. The treaty cut away even further at the Turkish dominion. Greece was awarded sites in Thrace, whereas Italy received control of Rhodes and the Dodecanese Islands. Independent republics of Armenia and Kurdistan were carved out of the eastern reaches of the former empire (although all three were short lived), and all the Arab

Emergence of Modern Turkey

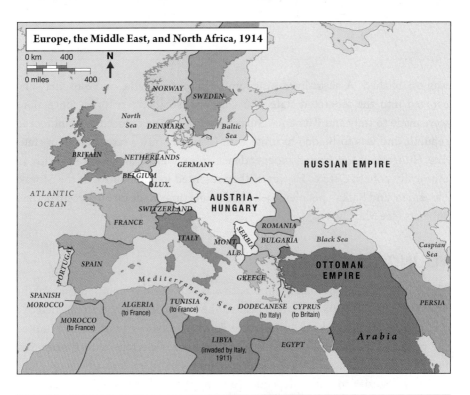

Europe, the Middle East, and North Africa, 1914

Europe, the Middle East, and North Africa, 1923

MAP 24.4 Europe and the Middle East in 1914 and 1923 In 1916, only halfway through the First World War, Britain and France (with Russia assenting) had already concluded the Sykes-Picot Agreement, a secret pact that would divide the Middle East between them in the event of the Ottoman Empire's fall. When Russia pulled out of the war in 1917, Leon Trotsky, one of the leaders of the Bolshevik Party, exposed the Agreement to the international public.

Prince Faisal at the Paris Peace Conference in 1919.   The British colonel T.E. Lawrence (Lawrence of Arabia) is in the group behind—second from the right.

territories were given over to the Allies. Syria became a French mandate, whereas Iraq, Palestine, and Transjordan became British mandates.

Turkey was left, in essence, with only those territories that were primarily Turkish in population. The settlement hurt Turkish pride, which was further harmed by international accusations of guilt for the Armenian genocide. A charismatic new leader, Mustafa Kemal (1881–1938), who later adopted the name Atatürk ("first among Turks"), took advantage of wounded Turkish nationalism to declare in 1923 a new Republic of Turkey. He was committed to secularism and republican government, but rigidly determined to defend Turkey against any criticism from outside.

◆

Thus, the Great War ended, at last, with bristling resentment, constrained economies, and damaged national pride on all sides. The coming years did not look hopeful. In every country, old and new, the civic fabrics were torn: some factions were filled with the desire to restore past glories and certainties; others wanted to simply return to their jobs and families, keep quiet about politics, and get on with daily living; still others felt the time was ripe to slough off the political ideas and practices of the nineteenth century, like a snake shedding its dead skin, and to move boldly into the approaching Communist paradise. But the possibility of this last group succeeding set off alarmed reactions, and soon Europe was awash in political groups dedicated to confronting the threat of Marxism. It is time for heroic action, these groups proclaimed, a radical realignment of priorities and values that would confront the Communist danger while repudiating the dead past of democracy.

WHO, WHAT, WHERE

Arab Revolt	mandates	Treaty of Versailles
Bolshevik Revolution	New Economic Policy	Vladimir Lenin
dialectical materialism	Peace of Paris	Von Schlieffen Plan
Fourteen Points	Sykes–Picot	Young Turks
League of Nations	Agreement	

SUGGESTED READINGS

Primary Sources

Angell, Norman. *The Great Illusion: A Study of the Relation of Military Power to National Advantage.*

Antonius, George. *The Arab Awakening.*

Graves, Robert. *Goodbye to All That.*

Jünger, Ernst. *Storm of Steel: From the Diary of a German Shock-Troop Officer on the Western Front.*

Keynes, John Maynard. *The Economic Consequences of the Peace.*

Lawrence, T. E. *Seven Pillars of Wisdom.*

Lenin, Vladimir. *Imperialism, the Highest Stage of Capitalism.*

Lenin, Vladimir. *The State and Revolution.*

Lenin, Vladimir. *What Is To Be Done?*

Shaw, George Bernard. *Common Sense about the War.*

Anthologies

Little, Jean. *If I Die Before I Wake: The Flu Epidemic Diary of Fiona Macgregor—Toronto, Ontario, 1918* (2007).

Neiberg, Michael S., ed. *The World War I Reader: Primary and Secondary Sources* (2006).

Shevin-Coetzee, Marilyn, and Frans Coetzee. *World War I: A History in Documents* (2010).

Weinberg, Robert, and Laurie Bernstein. *Revolutionary Russia: A History in Documents* (2010).

Studies

Akçam, Taner. *A Shameful Act: The Armenian Genocide and the Question of Turkish Responsibility* (2007).

Azak, Umut. *Islam and Secularism in Turkey: Kemalism, Religion, and the Nation State* (2010).

Barry, John M. *The Great Influenza: The Epic Story of the Deadliest Plague in History* (2004).

Bass, Gary Jonathan. *Stay the Hand of Vengeance: The Politics of War Crimes Tribunals* (2002).

Beckett, Ian F. W. *The Great War, 1914–1918* (2007).

Bein, Amit. *Ottoman Ulema, Turkish Republic: Agents of Change and Guardians of Tradition* (2011).

Bloxham, Donald. *The Great Game of Genocide: Imperialism, Nationalism, and the Destruction of the Ottoman Armenians* (2007).

Buttar, Prit. *Collision of Empires: The War on the Eastern Front in 1914* (2014).

Campos, Michelle. *Ottoman Brothers: Muslims, Christians, and Jews in Early Twentieth-Century Palestine* (2010).

Ceadel, Martin. *Living the Great Illusion: Sir Norman Angell, 1872–1967* (2009).

Englund, Peter. *The Beauty and the Sorrow: An Intimate History of the First World War* (2011).

Fitzpatrick, Sheila. *The Russian Revolution* (2008).

Gregory, Adrian. *The Last Great War: British Society and the First World War* (2008).

Hanioğlu, M. Şükrü. *Atatürk: An Intellectual Biography* (2011).

Herwig, Holger H. *The First World War: Germany and Austria–Hungary, 1914–1918* (2014).

Herwig, Holger H. *The Marne, 1914: The Opening of World War I and the Battle That Changed the World* (2011).

Kévorkian, Raymond. *The Armenian Genocide: A Complete History* (2011).

Kramer, Alan. *Dynamic of Destruction: Culture and Mass Killing in the First World War* (2009).

Martel, Gordon. *The Month That Changed the World: July 1914* (2014).

Martel, Gordon. *Origins of the First World War* (2008).

McMeekin, Sean. *The Berlin–Baghdad Express: The Ottoman Empire and Germany's Bid for World Power* (2010).

McMeekin, Sean. *The Russian Origins of the First World War* (2011).

Paice, Edward. *World War I: The African Front* (2010).

Philpott, William. *Three Armies on the Somme: The First Battle of the Twentieth Century* (2011).

Samson, Anne. *World War I in Africa: The Forgotten Conflict among the European Powers* (2012).

Sanborn, Joshua A. *Imperial Apocalypse: The Great War and the Destruction of the Russian Empire* (2014).

Sharp, Alan. *The Versailles Settlement: Peacemaking after the First World War, 1919–1923* (2008).

Sondhaus, Lawrence. *The Great War at Sea: A Naval History of the First World War* (2014).

Strachan, Hew. *The First World War.* Vol. 1, *To Arms* (2003).

Suny, Ronald Grigor, Fatma Müge Göçek, and Norman M. Naimark, eds. *A Question of Genocide: Armenians and Turks at the End of the Ottoman Empire* (2011).

Thompson, Mark. *The White War: Life and Death on the Italian Front, 1915–1919* (2010).

Wawro, Geoffrey. *A Mad Catastrophe: The Outbreak of World War I and the Collapse of the Habsburg Empire* (2014).

Zürcher, Erik J. *The Young Turk Legacy and Nation Building: From the Ottoman Empire to Atatürk's Turkey* (2010).

For additional resources, including maps, primary sources, visuals, web links, and quizzes, please go to **www.oup.com/us/backman.**

CHAPTER 25

Radical Realignments

1919–1939

The Greater West entered the postwar era with little confidence and many worries. Europe remained politically unstable and economically vulnerable, and the Middle East churned with new turmoil and resentment toward Europe. America largely wanted to wash its hands of foreign entanglements, and a new government in Moscow declared its goal of liberating the world from capitalist oppression. Desolation and confusion reigned. The immediate crisis, however, was economic. Most of Europe emerged from the war either bankrupt or perilously close to it. "The military crisis may be over," wrote the French poet Paul Valéry (1871–1945) in 1919, "but the economic crisis is still here with us in all its ferocity."

THE GREAT DEPRESSION IN EUROPE

Decline in industrial production of over 30%
Decline in industrial production of up to 30%

Force of Will   Never a great orator, Benito Mussolini (1883–1945), the Italian architect of fascism, compensated by being a passionate one. His expressive nature came across to many as buffoonish and insincere. An egoist who despised democracy and Christianity as refuges for the weak, he likened himself to a Nietzschean "superman" but lacked the positive qualities Nietzsche had expected in such a figure.

The European countries had lost their dominance in many international markets to relative newcomers—Australia, Canada, Japan, and the United States. Even worse, most of Europe's governments were deeply in debt. They had financed the war by selling billions of dollars in bonds and by borrowing both public and private funds from the United States. England and France responded to their debt problem, initially, by simply printing more money; but when bondholders, including the United States, objected to receiving repayment in devalued currency, they stopped. The United States emerged from the war in better economic and political shape than any other participant. Even so, America found it difficult to convert back to a peacetime economy and struggled with inflation that reached as high as 18 percent in 1919–1920.

Everything seemed in flux even before the beginning, in 1929, of the great economic crash called the Great Depression. Educators were revisiting the entire history of Western civilization. Attempts to create a strong international League of Nations foundered; national aspirations were emerging on the peripheries of Europe and in the Middle East; and runaway inflation set the stage for economic unrest. The tyrannies of fascism and totalitarianism further threatened peace. Amid all this, modern literature entered a new stage with its own experiments and trauma. "What caused this disorder in the European mind?" asked Valéry; "[Nothing but] the mere co-existence, in all of Europe's cultivated minds, of the most conflicting ideas and the most incongruous values in life and learning. And this is now the fundamental characteristic of the modern age."

HISTORY FOR BEGINNERS

How on earth had the Western world got itself into such a mess? Europe, after all, was the cradle of democracy, philosophy, modern science, and Western Christian

CHAPTER TIMELINE

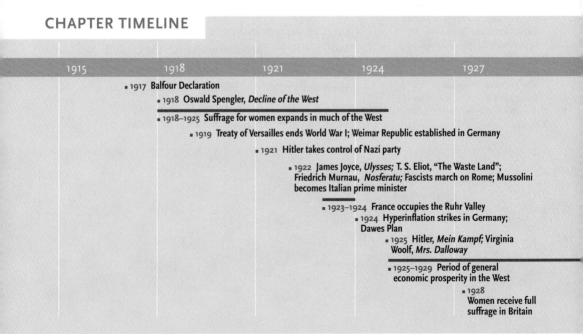

| 1915 | 1918 | 1921 | 1924 | 1927 |

- 1917 Balfour Declaration
- 1918 Oswald Spengler, *Decline of the West*
- 1918–1925 Suffrage for women expands in much of the West
- 1919 Treaty of Versailles ends World War I; Weimar Republic established in Germany
- 1921 Hitler takes control of Nazi party
- 1922 James Joyce, *Ulysses*; T. S. Eliot, "The Waste Land"; Friedrich Murnau, *Nosferatu;* Fascists march on Rome; Mussolini becomes Italian prime minister
- 1923–1924 France occupies the Ruhr Valley
- 1924 Hyperinflation strikes in Germany; Dawes Plan
- 1925 Hitler, *Mein Kampf;* Virginia Woolf, *Mrs. Dalloway*
- 1925–1929 Period of general economic prosperity in the West
- 1928 Women receive full suffrage in Britain

values. Its contributions to the arts were incalculable. It had produced both industrial genius and the most trenchant criticism of industrialization. Europe had the world's highest literacy rates and standards of living. Its technological development was unmatched. Although still hampered by legal and social prejudices, women played a larger public role than in any other society on the globe. A vigorous and determined press enabled citizens to stay informed. Yet this civilization had sunk to an extraordinary depth of savagery. All across Europe large numbers of the postwar generation lost faith in the very values that had led, in their minds, directly to the catastrophe, and therefore they turned to the apparent success story unfolding in Communist Russia as an alternative path of development. Interest in Marxism, which had never caught on in the nineteenth century, grew exponentially in Europe—and also, although in a much smaller way, in the United States—in the postwar period.

People across both Europe and America cried out for an explanation, which resulted in a dramatically increased popular interest in history. American colleges and universities responded with what came to be called "Western civilization" courses that followed the story from the West's origins in ancient Mesopotamia to the Treaty of Versailles. Although these survey courses did not shy away from the horrors of war, they emphasized positive achievements such as democracy, liberalism, education, and prosperity. At the same time, literature and philosophy departments crafted "great books" and "great ideas"

Study of "Western Civilization"

| 1930 | 1933 | 1937 | 1940 | 1943 |

- 1929 Start of the Great Depression; Stalin's first Five-Year Plan; Lateran Agreement
- 1932 Unemployment in Germany more than 43 percent
- 1933 United States abandons the gold standard; Hitler appointed German chancellor
- 1936 Great Purge under Stalin in Soviet Union; Keynes, *The General Theory of Employment, Interest, and Money*
- 1936–1939 Spanish Civil War
- 1938 Munich Conference gives Sudetenland to Germany
- 1939 World War II in Europe begins

surveys of Western culture—to which publishers responded by producing new series of the "Western classics" in translation. Such courses presumed, and preached, that the Western way of life still offered the best chance for a bright human future. Before long, the courses created at the University of Chicago and at New York City's Columbia University established models that were quickly adopted by other schools around the country. The fundamental problem, they urged, was not with Western values themselves but with radical misrepresentations of them. Capitalism was not at fault; only the most unchecked and rapacious form of it. Democracy was not the culprit either; if anything, it was the too-limited and constrained versions of it that led to the trouble. The answer, therefore, was to pursue more and better capitalism, more and better democracy.

European curricula changed as well, moving sharply away from the nation-based focus of their history departments and placing new emphasis on the histories of other countries and cultures. A two-volume history by a sickly German loner became almost overnight the most talked-about book in Europe. In universities, coffeehouses, public libraries, and private studies everywhere, everyone read it and debated it. The book was *The Decline of the West*, by Oswald Spengler (1880–1936); the first volume appeared in 1918 and the second four years later. In it, Spengler argues that Western civilization has evolved through three major phases of development—the Magian, the Apollonian, and the Faustian. Spengler describes these, respectively, as the belief in magic (including the major religions), the striving for order (classical Greece and Rome), and the pursuit of power and knowledge (the modern West). For him, Europe in the early twentieth century had reached the end of its Faustian period, after which life ceases to be creative and vital and becomes bureaucratic and superficial.

Spengler's book proved popular not for the strength of its arguments but for the resonance of its dark outlook with the prevailing mood of postwar Europe. Indeed, once Europe recovered some stability in the 1920s, interest in Spengler evaporated until the gloom of yet another postwar era (in the late 1940s this time) made him once again a figure of interest.

Rival visions of history were quick to appear. For H. G. Wells (1866–1946), a popular English novelist and science-fiction writer, hope for the future remains—so long as we remain dedicated to educating all people. Catastrophes like the Great War occur only when ignorance and prejudice reign supreme, he assures readers. "Human history becomes more and more a race between education and catastrophe." Wells published *The Outline of History* in 1920. In its 1,300 pages he argues for an evolutionary view of history. Mankind, he says, is in a continual state of adaptation. Although periods of crisis and ruin may occur, human history progresses upward—or it will if we let it:

The need for a common knowledge of the general facts of human history throughout the world has become very evident during the tragic happenings of the last few years. Swifter means of communication have brought all men closer to one another for good or for evil. War becomes a universal disaster, blind and monstrously destructive; it bombs the baby in its cradle and sinks the food-ships that cater for the non-combatant and the neutral. There can be no peace now, we realize, but a common peace in all the world; no prosperity but a general prosperity. But there can be no common peace and prosperity without common historical ideas. Without such ideas to hold them together in harmonious co-operation, with nothing but narrow, selfish, and conflicting nationalist traditions, races and peoples are bound to drift towards conflict and destruction. . . . A sense of history as the common adventure of all mankind is as necessary for peace within as it is for peace between the nations.

Even more massive works appeared, too. *A Study of History* (twelve volumes, starting in 1934) by the English historian and philosopher Arnold Toynbee (1889–1975) and *The Story of Civilization* (eleven volumes, starting in 1935) by the American historian Will Durant (1885–1981) and his Russian-born wife Ariel Durant (1898–1981) made bookshelves groan across the world.

The war was only one reason for the sudden fascination with history. The other was fear of Marxism. To many oppressed laborers and struggling émigrés, the Bolshevik success in Russia gave a jolt of encouragement, just as the American Revolution had inspired reformers in eighteenth-century France. Radical change seemed within grasp and worth pursuing. Across Europe workers' rights had been rolled back during the war, including the right to unionize, and that convinced many workers that the labor struggles of the previous century had to be fought anew. Capitalism, it seemed to them, was as likely to regress as to reform. Labor strikes across Europe and America prompted a broad array of legal and extralegal crackdowns by Western governments.

Concern about the "Red Menace" was especially strong in the United States, where fears of Bolshevism reached near-panic levels. In 1919 alone came the Seattle General Strike, the Boston Police Strike, the Pennsylvania Steelworkers' Strike, and the United Mineworkers' Strike. It is easy to see why Western civilization courses placed such emphasis on the rise of modern democracy and the strength of economic liberalism. They displayed a special fascination with the American and French Revolutions, as twin birthplaces of freedom, and they focused on capitalism's self-correcting powers, as guarantors of prosperity and justice. The pure "Western tradition," they argued, still represented humankind's

"*Look, you boob . . . !*"

What
BERNARD SHAW
told the Americans
about **RUSSIA !** *HIS FAMOUS BROADCAST*

PRICE **5** CENTS (Threepence)

Worker's Paradise   Irish playwright George Bernard Shaw's faith in human nature was bitterly shaken by World War I, and in the mid-1920s he lost faith in democracy and drifted into admiration for strong leaders. An early enthusiast for Mussolini, he visited Russia in 1931 and returned full of enthusiasm for Joseph Stalin. On October 11 of that year he broadcast a lecture on American national radio in which he told his audience that "any skilled workman . . . of suitable age and good character" would be welcomed and given work in the Soviet Union.

best hope as long as it was allowed to work. An interesting contrast appears between two major publishing efforts that literally book-ended the two world wars: the 51-volume "Harvard Classics" series published in 1909, only two volumes of which are dedicated to the French 18th century, and the 54-volume "Great Books of the Western World" series published by the Encyclopedia Britannica in 1952—no fewer than ten volumes of which are dedicated to the Enlightenment and French Revolution. (The second edition of the "Great Books" series added extra volumes on Voltaire, Diderot, and de Tocqueville, for good measure.) The message seems clear: when catastrophe threatens to undermine the central values of Western life, the response is to redouble efforts to champion and proclaim those values.

A renewed passion for history also characterized Arab society. Although Arab chroniclers and memoirists had always been numerous and some had earned a wide readership, no Arab historian of any note had emerged since Ibn Khaldun in the fourteenth century. The breakup of

New Arab Histories   the Ottoman world, however, coupled with the surging nationalism of the ethnic Arabs seeking independence, inspired an energetic new wave of historical writing. Most of these works view earlier ages through the prism of nineteenth-century imperialism and colonialism. The medieval Crusades, for example, had been regarded for centuries in the Muslim world as a series of bitter but local frontier wars of relatively minor importance. No full-length Arab-language history of the Crusades, in fact, had ever even been written. Instead, the wars for the Holy Land had taken a backseat to the conflicts that really mattered—those between the Arabs and the Turks, between the Arabs and the Persians, and between the Arabs, Persians, and Turks combined against the Mongols. In the aftermath of nineteenth-century imperialism and global conflict, however, Arab writers reinterpreted the Crusades dramatically. The best example of this new intensely nationalistic and bitterly anti-European history is the *History of Jabal 'Amil* by Muhammad Jaber al-Safa (1875–1945), in which he depicts the history of his Lebanese home district as emblematic of the entire course of Arab oppression by the West, from the Crusades to the partitioning of the Holy Land by the Sykes–Picot Agreement. Suddenly these frontier skirmishes stood out as the first

chapter of Western Christianity's incessant war on Islam, the start of a determined crime spree to strangle Islam in its crib and seize control of the Arab lands.

PARCELING OUT NATIONS

President Woodrow Wilson had arrived at the Paris Peace Conference with an
outline of how to structure the peace settlement and lay the foundations for postwar rebuilding. But as we saw in chapter 24, the plan, known as the Fourteen
Points, quickly proved unworkable. So, it soon proved, did Europe's economy.

Wilson's main ideas—apart from preserving free movement on the seas and
free trade between countries—were to redraw Europe's political boundaries. *Postwar*
After the collapse of the Habsburg, Ottoman, and Romanov empires, he sought *Political*
to recognize the ethnic and nationalist aspirations of the peoples in central and *Boundaries*
eastern Europe. But creating new borders faced two difficulties. First, the move- *in Europe*
ment of peoples in the preceding hundred years made it impossible to establish
countries without ethnic minorities. Europe's populace was now intermixed (see
Map 25.1). Second, political rivalries between the dominant nations frustrated
efforts to build stable new countries. The contours of Poland, for example, resulted from a desire to establish a buffer zone between Russia and Germany. Bye-
lorussian, German, Jewish, and Ukrainian minorities made up at least a third of
the new country's population, and no fewer than twenty-five political parties
formed, each with a different constituency and a different vision of Poland's
future. Similar problems confronted the newly created Bulgaria, Czechoslovakia,
Hungary, Romania, and Yugoslavia. Compounding their problems, the new
states of eastern Europe were industrially undeveloped. Anywhere between 60
and 80 percent of their populations was still engaged in primitive farming.

Many of the same problems existed outside of Europe. The League of Nations
had parceled out the former Ottoman Empire to Britain and France, since it *Middle*
judged the Middle East to be unready to stand on its own. Britain took control of *East*
Iraq, Palestine, and Transjordan, and France was given Lebanon and Syria. Brit- *Mandates*
ain also oversaw Arabia, Egypt, and Iran. The creation of these not-quite-inde-
pendent states, or mandates, outraged their inhabitants. Not only did they violate
promises made by the Allies during the war, but also they seemed simply to substitute one form of foreign imperialism for another. Moreover, the Western
powers took little notice of local conditions, including culture and religion. The
Turks had at least understood the difference between Shi'a and Sunnis; among
ethnic Arabs, Armenians, Kurds, Palestinians, Syrians, and Turkmen; and among
the various tribes. In establishing a unified British Iraq, for example, the League
of Nations fused distinct territories that the Ottomans had governed as independent provinces.

MAP 25.1   Ethnic Minorities in East-Central Europe, 1930   The movement of peoples in the 19th and early 20th centuries resulted in the presence of ethnic minorities in all European countries, but the populations of east-central Europe were especially mixed.

Global politics and dynastic rivalries within the Arab world complicated matters. Britain, for example, had established close ties with the Hashemite clan, a prominent Arab family said to be the last direct descendants of the Prophet Muhammad, and planned to install its leader, Faisal ibn Ali, as ruler of a unified Palestine and Transjordan. The **Balfour Declaration** in 1917, however, bound Britain to support a national Jewish homeland in Palestine. Caught between opposing allegiances, Britain divided Palestine and Transjordan as autonomous units, installed Faisal as king of Iraq (r. 1921–1933), and placed Faisal's brother, Abdullah ibn Hussein, on the throne as ruler of Transjordan (r. 1921–1951). Meanwhile a descendant of the nineteenth-century tribal emir Muhammad ibn Saud (discussed in chapter 20) emerged as the leader in Arabia itself. This was Abd al-Aziz ibn Saud, the first king of the modern state of Saudi Arabia (r. 1926–1953).

The Palestinian Mandate roiled with tensions between the native population (mostly Palestinian Arabs, but with sizable Jewish and Christian communities) and Zionist immigrants from Europe. Thousands of Jews migrated to Palestine in

White City   Ben-Yehuda Street in Tel Aviv was famous for its Bauhaus- or International-style architecture, which was used during a construction boom in the 1930s when thousands of Jewish refugees from Nazi Germany poured into the British mandate of Palestine. The neighborhood takes its nickname from the local practice of covering the exteriors of buildings with heat-reflecting white plaster.

the postwar years, most of them settling on lands that they had purchased from departing Turks or from Palestinian landowners pursuing a better life under one of the Hashemite rulers or the Saudi dynasts; others wanted simply to get away from the British. Although these transfers were legal, it did not take long for concern to arise about Jewish "displacement" of the Palestinians. By 1922, Britain decided to slow the migration of Jews into the region to appease its millions of Muslim subjects. The Arabs opposed Jewish settlement (at this stage, at least) less out of resistance to the idea of Zionism than as a cudgel with which to beat the British. These developments pleased no one and set the stage for decades of turmoil.

NEW RIGHTS AND NEW ECONOMIES

Most European countries after the war received new constitutions or significantly revised existing ones, and the most significant revision was the extension of the vote to women. As we saw in chapter 21, before the war only Finland (1906) and Norway (1913) had universal suffrage; Denmark passed it in 1915. Campaigns for female suffrage had taken a backseat to the war, but calls for the vote rose anew before the ink on the peace treaty was dry. Women received the right to vote in the new Czechoslovakia in 1918, in Germany in 1919, in Austria and the United

Suffrage for Women

States in 1920, and in Poland in 1921. Limited rights of suffrage were introduced in Britain and Hungary in 1918 and 1925, respectively; British women finally received full rights in 1928. Women in France and Italy were denied the vote until 1945, however, and Switzerland rejected female suffrage until 1971. Delays were largely the fault of the Liberal parties, who warned that women would vote overwhelmingly for Conservatives.

Economic Strains   Economic concerns dominated the postwar years. Except for the regions around the old western front, the war had left most of Europe's factories intact. These factories needed to be retooled for commercial manufacture from their wartime activities, but they did not need to be rebuilt from the ground up. Industrial production could therefore begin again as soon as capital and raw materials became available. France, for the moment, was almost entirely dependent on German reparations and American credit for capital. Britain and Belgium also relied heavily on German payments but were better prepared to relaunch their manufacturing base. A problem blocked their path, however. Republican president Warren G. Harding (1921–1923) placed high tariffs on imports to protect American businesses. This meant that Europeans could not sell their products and thereby earn the money they needed to pay off their American creditors. For Britain and Belgium, it also meant a greater reliance on their colonies and Middle Eastern mandates, whereas Germany turned instead to trade with eastern Europe and Communist Russia.

Inflation set in as governments let their currencies depreciate to make their goods cheaper and more competitive. The tactic worked to an extent, but the falling currencies made it harder for Europeans to purchase American goods—which in turn triggered concerns for U.S. growth. Instability in the markets threatened to impede economic recovery. When Germany failed to make a reparation payment to France in 1923, the French took drastic action and sent an army into the Ruhr Valley. There it seized German factories and effectively held the German workers and their families for ransom, while demanding payment in full of Germany's entire reparations debt.

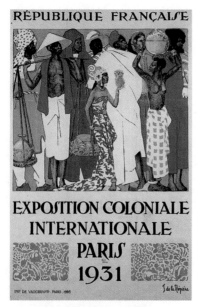

RÉPUBLIQUE FRANÇAISE

EXPOSITION COLONIALE
INTERNATIONALE
PARIS
1931

IMP. DE VAUGIRARD - PARIS - 1931   J de la Nézière

Selling the Empire   Paris hosted the International Colonial Exposition in 1931, one of the last large-scale celebrations of imperialism. This poster invites visitors to delight in the colorful costumes and quaint handcrafts of France's happy underlings.

Germans everywhere were outraged, and the government of the new Weimar Republic urged Ruhr citizens to stay at home and refuse to work for the French. When talks failed to resolve the dispute, Berlin responded by wildly printing trillions of marks—and declared the reparations bill "paid" with worthless currency. Feverish hyperinflation followed.

A single U.S. dollar in January 1924 purchased four German marks; by September a dollar equaled nearly 4.5 *trillion* marks. Personal savings, life-insurance policies, bond holdings, and pensions were wiped out instantaneously. Germans who received their pay in cash found that it lost half its value by the time they reached a shop in which to spend it. In October 1923, Betty Scholem, a woman living in Berlin, wrote to her son, the famous Jewish scholar Gershom Scholem, then living in Switzerland, describing conditions:

German Hyperinflation

> Streetcar fare is twenty million marks, and tomorrow it will probably be fifty. You can't even imagine what it is like. My God, it's like witnessing a witches' Sabbath, only a million times more wicked. As you know, we sell women's magazines to [a certain friend]. A few days ago her husband sent us a cashier's check for five million marks—but when we went to the local branch of their bank, here in Berlin, to pick it up, they charged us forty million marks in transfer fees! . . . [Some other friends of ours] went out to lunch and had rabbit. It cost 1.75 *billion*.

One needed a wheelbarrow full of marks to purchase a single loaf of bread.

The United States responded to the crisis with the Dawes Plan, named for its chief architect, the director of the federal Bureau of the Budget, Charles G. Dawes—who won the Nobel Peace Prize in 1925 and became vice president under President Calvin Coolidge. This massive bailout restructured reparations so that Germany had a chance to meet its obligation without crippling its own economic development. The currency was stabilized within a year, but the issue of reparations and the moral stain of responsibility for the war continued to rankle Germans. Even as the economy improved, many Germans, nostalgic for imperial glory, associated defeat with the new Weimar government. Voters responded to candidates who

Germany's Hyperflation   The decision in 1924 to print endless amounts of marks, supposedly to satisfy French demands for reparations' payments, was catastrophic for the German economy. The worthless currency had value only as fuel for kitchen fires, or as building blocks for people to play with. In this photo it is being used as wallpaper.

announced their determination to do something about the "guilt payments" and restore Germany's honor. International pressure forced the French to relinquish their occupation of the Ruhr valley in August 1925, after two years of holding it hostage, but the scandal created considerable sympathy for Germany across the West, even as it accelerated the development of right-wing political parties within Germany.

Economic Recovery   Several years of impressive growth across Europe began in 1925. With order restored to markets and the threat of new French–German hostilities removed, relief and hope filled the air. Within four years, in fact, western Europe reached its prewar levels of industrial production. Radios, telephone systems, automobiles, phonographs, tractors, motion pictures, televisions, and gas lighting were manufactured. A new era was dawning, with an infinite number of new technologies and products on the horizon. Or so it seemed to governments and private banks, which lent money for new businesses at previously unimagined rates. Entrepreneurs drew investment from all quarters.

But two underlying economic problems festered. First, machines like gasoline-powered tractors and combine harvesters, together with new chemical fertilizers, made agriculture more productive than ever. But that meant that prices could easily collapse just when farmers were taking on debt to purchase the machinery. Second, the rush of investment in new technologies and manufactures left less capital for established industries. For the time being, these were potential problems only. All they needed, however, was the right jolt, or series of jolts, to become a full-blown catastrophe.

THE GREAT DEPRESSION

Not everyone shared in the economic growth of the mid-1920s. In the United States, which was by then the largest and most influential economy in the world, the top 5 percent of the population received nearly 35 percent of all income, whereas 70 percent of the nation lived in or near poverty—mostly those who were still engaged in small-scale family farming and sharecropping. Disparities in total wealth were even more lopsided. In Europe, matters varied from country to country. France, for example, had traditionally championed small and medium-size companies over large publicly-held firms, and so it was less at risk from stock-market fluctuations. Britain, too, had a less inequitable concentration of wealth than the United States, because it had had an indexed income tax since 1798. Germany did not yet have one, since the Kaiser had preferred to fund the Great War on debt, fearing that a tax on wealth would anger the wealthy.

The web of debt nevertheless ensnared every Western country: governments owed other governments, banks owed other banks, and companies owed other companies. And the web grew more dangerous as people became more hopeful for the future. With so many exciting new products, people felt that the potential for riches was almost limitless. Urged on by zealous stockbrokers, they were therefore willing to invest their entire savings—and to borrow more to invest. For a while, all that cash did prompt growth; but rising stock prices quickly turned into a bubble, and when the bubble burst, stocks and bonds lost value, and credit dried up.

On Black Tuesday, October 29, 1929, on the New York Stock Exchange, prices tumbled. It was the beginning of the **Great Depression**. Banks and com- *U.S. Stock* panies failed by the tens of thousands, throwing millions of people out of work. *Market* Farmers who had invested in new machinery only to see the agricultural prices *Crash* fall could not make their loan payments and lost their farms. To staunch the flow of red ink, American banks all but stopped lending to Europe. This meant that credit-dependent countries like France and Germany could not purchase U.S. goods, which in turn added to America's woes. Popular culture demonized bankers and portrayed them as incompetent, self-serving, soulless, or corrupt tricksters—or a combination of all four.[1]

The largest commercial bank in Austria came close to liquidation, which triggered a panic among European banks. Assets were frozen, which meant that depositors could not access their own savings, and lines of credit were cut off. Fearing a repeat of the miseries of the early 1920s, governments made the mistake of trying to stabilize currency rates rather than stimulate consumption and production by injecting new money into the system. Pressure placed on currencies by the Depression led most Western countries to abandon the **gold standard**. This monetary system, introduced in the West by Britain in 1821 (and adopted by the United States in 1873), pegged a currency to the price of gold, so that a British sovereign, a German mark, or an American dollar always bought the same amount of the precious metal. Since worldwide supplies of gold, and the demand for it, were relatively constant through the nineteenth century, currency values and exchange rates remained stable. The problem with the gold standard, however, was that gold prices alone did not reflect any given currency's actual value at any particular time: inflation and interest rates also played a part. In the run-up to World War I most Western governments needed to print money rapidly to cover their military costs—and this forced up both interest rates and the inflation rate. The United States abandoned the gold standard in 1933.

The statistics are grim. Banks failed; by 1933, in the United States alone more *Economic* than five thousand banks failed. Many of these failed banks were purchased, at *Collapse*

---

[1] Bank robbers like Pretty Boy Floyd (Charles Arthur Floyd [1904–1934]) and Bonnie and Clyde (Bonnie Parker [1910–1934] and Clyde Barrow [1909–1934]) became popular-culture heroes.

bargain prices, by larger banks—which recouped their expenses by confiscating the homes, farms, and businesses of the failed banks' borrowers. Millions of Americans lost their homes, their farms, and their jobs. Unemployment reached as high as 25 percent, three years into the crisis. In Europe, the numbers were even worse (see Table 25.1). More than 40 percent of the German workforce was unemployed. In France, where three-fourths of all farms were less than 25 acres in size, farmers had no way to produce enough to meet their debt payments and often were lucky to be able to feed their families. In Poland roughly three-quarters of a million farmers lost their farms to debt.

TABLE 25.1 **Unemployment Rates during the Great Depression (in percentages), 1929–1936**

	BRITAIN	GERMANY	SWEDEN	UNITED STATES	NETHERLANDS
1929	10.4	13.1	10.7	3.2	5.9
1930	16.1	22.2	12.2	8.7	7.8
1931	21.3	33.7	17.2	15.8	14.8
1932	22.1	43.7	22.8	23.6	25.3
1933	19.9	26.3	23.7	24.9	26.9
1934	16.7	14.9	18.9	26.7	28.0
1935	15.5	11.6	16.1	20.1	31.7
1936	13.1	8.3	13.6	16.9	32.7

The decline in international trade hit the shipping industry especially hard. The Dutch shipping industry fell by two-thirds in three years, whereas parts of coastal northern England and Scotland had unemployment rates of 90 percent or more. With tax revenues plummeting and the need for social services rising, Western governments relied on deficit spending and cut salaries and wages for government employees, including the military. Cuts to soldiers' pay made by the governments of Britain and of the Netherlands, for example, resulted in the first mutinies in their modern histories. The British mutiny (1931) consisted of one thousand soldiers on four warships; the conflict was brief and was resolved peacefully. The Dutch mutiny (1933) was another matter. When the crew of a warship likewise refused to obey orders, the government responded by bombing the ship and killing twenty-two sailors. Cuts in civil service pay also sparked protests around the continent.

Manufacturing output declined by nearly 40 percent worldwide between 1929 and 1933. The effects were widespread, but as always they were felt most

Hunger Marchers   A series of protests against food shortages occurred throughout Britain during the Depression of the 1930s. The largest single demonstration took place in 1932. A group of 3000 protestors set out from Glasgow in Scotland, and by the time the march reached London there were as many as 100,000 involved. The metropolitan government summoned a police force of 75,000 to break up the crowd before it could reach Parliament.

stingingly among the urban and rural poor. Unemployment was particularly high among young people, those aged sixteen to twenty-six, who had little to do except sit idly in cafes and parks and nurse their resentment. Many of these made easy targets for recruiters from radical and reactionary political groups. Both Communist and Fascist parties relied on these feelings to gain followers.

THE SEARCH FOR SOMEONE TO BLAME

Ideology and its appeal are a recurring theme in fiction of the 1920s and 1930s. The German writer Thomas Mann (1875–1955) powerfully depicted this sort of seduction in two novellas; both "Disorder and Early Sorrow" (1925) and "Mario and the Magician" (1929) illustrate the bitterness and hopelessness of the time. Less well known in the English-speaking world is the novelist Hans Fallada (1893–1947), whose *What Now, Little Man?* (1932), *A Wolf among Wolves* (1937), and *Iron Gustav* (1938) portray the miseries of life in Depression-era Germany with unforgettable power. Fallada's books gave such a powerful description of life in the Weimar Republic that later the Nazi propaganda minister, Joseph Goebbels (1897–1945), used them as a way of justifying the Nazi regime. Goebbels also tried to blackmail Fallada into writing an anti-Semitic and pro-Nazi novel, but Fallada, who detested the Nazis and their anti-Semitism, avoided filling the request for a few years. In 1944, however, Goebbels had Fallada arrested and placed in an insane asylum until he produced. *The Drinker*, published ultimately in 1950, was instead an autobiographical work criticizing Fallada's own difficulties with drug and alcohol addiction. He died in 1947, leaving behind the manuscript of his greatest novel, *Every Man Dies Alone*, his indictment of the entire Nazi era. It was published shortly after his death.

A journey through the Congo turned the French writer André Gide (1869–1951) against Western imperialism and led him to become, briefly but passionately, a Communist. "Communism," he wrote, "is the only promise for the salvation of mankind; I would lay down [my life] for it in an instant, to make it succeed." Membership in Britain's Communist Party increased dramatically after the 1929 crash, especially in the heavily hit industrial towns and coalfields of the north and west, where local newspapers began to refer to certain neighborhoods as "Little Moscows" because of their active Communist groups. Another site popularly regarded as a haven of Communism was the Jewish neighborhood in the East End, in London.

Europe's Jews

Popular and official attitudes toward Europe's Jews worsened. Jews were singled out either as presumed leaders of socialist cells or as corrupt merchants and financiers. In Poland, employers were ordered to test their workers and apprentices for their knowledge of Polish—and thus to root out Yiddish-speaking Jews. The government of Austria forced all Jewish-owned banks to close, whereas the government in Romania ordered Jewish companies of any sort to take on Christian partners or else forfeit their ability to obtain credit. The Greek state rescinded its contracts with Jewish businesses. In Britain, formal actions regarding Jews were confined to policy debates over Zionism and Palestine, but the tone of those debates was often ugly. According to the *Times* of London Zionist Jews were "pushing, grasping, and domineering," and the *Morning Post* bemoaned the fact that British citizens were being "compelled to pay for establishing a national home" for Jews. As late as 1938 the *Weekly Review* declared that the goal of Zionism, "though not definitely avowed, is to secure world domination for the members of its race."

Among the charges leveled against Jews everywhere was the rumor that they were benefiting from a demographic crisis: birthrates across Europe fell sharply after 1929 because married couples feared they could not feed many mouths. But fewer children—who previously had worked on family farms, in factories, or in odd jobs—meant lower incomes for poor families. Some political circles saw the decline as part of the decline of the nation, and they singled out the Jews as a factor in both developments. Regarded as a race of financiers and merchants, they were blamed for economic woes everywhere, and as one of the few groups with population growth, they were seen as "taking over" society by biological means. Not everyone felt this way, of course, but complaints remained widespread throughout the Depression.

American industrialist Henry Ford (1863–1947), founder of the Ford Motor Company, spoke for many when he wrote about the supposed dangers of "the International Jew" (1920) in the Michigan newspaper he owned, *The Dearborn Independent*:

> In Russia [the Jew] is charged with being the source of Bolshevism, an accusation which is serious or not, according to the circle in which it is made; we in America, hearing the fervid eloquence and perceiving the prophetic ardor of young Jewish apostles of social and industrial reform, can calmly estimate how it may be. In Germany he is charged with being the cause of the Empire's collapse and a very considerable literature has sprung up, bearing with it a mass of circumstantial evidence that gives the thinker pause. In England he is charged with being the real world ruler, who rules as a super-nation over the nations, rules by the power of gold, and who plays nation against nation for his own purposes, remaining himself discreetly in the background. In America it is pointed out to what extent the elder Jews of wealth and the younger Jews of ambition swarmed through the war organizations—principally those departments which dealt with the commercial and industrial business of war, and also the extent to which they have clung to the advantage which their experience as agents of the government gave them.
>
> In simple words, the question of the Jews has come to the fore, but like other questions which lend themselves to prejudice, efforts will be made to hush it up as impolitic for open discussion. If, however, experience has taught us anything it is that questions thus suppressed will sooner or later break out in undesirable and unprofitable forms.

Ford's warning seems unnervingly prescient, although not in the sense he meant it:

> The Jew is the world's enigma. Poor in his masses, he yet controls the world's finances. Scattered abroad without country or government, he yet presents a unity of race continuity which no other people has

> achieved. Living under legal disabilities in almost every land, he has
> become the power behind many a throne. There are ancient prophecies
> to the effect that the Jew will return to his own land and from that center
> rule the world, though not until he has undergone an assault by the
> united nations of mankind.

The agonies of the Depression, in sum, added to concerns for Western decline left over from the war. A new generation, raised to believe in the unique injustice of their suffering, came of age determined to rescue their honor as well as their livelihoods. And they were willing to take desperate action.

MODERNISM: THE SECOND WAVE

The war, the divisive Peace of Paris, the Bolshevik Revolution, the Red Menace, the Ruhr Valley disaster, hyperinflation, the Depression—all these traumas strengthened modernism in the arts, which now seemed prophetic (see chapter 22). The Irish poet William Butler Yeats (1865–1939) summed up the atmosphere in "The Second Coming" (1920):

> Things fall apart; the centre cannot hold;
>   Mere anarchy is loosed upon the world,
> The blood-dimmed tide is loosed, and everywhere
>   The ceremony of innocence is drowned;
> The best lack all conviction, while the worst
>   Are full of passionate intensity.

The proud confidence of the imperial age had given way to anxious doubt. Without a fixed center, Yeats suggests, life's only point of reference becomes the personal. Still, if our consciousness is all we have, we would be wise to investigate it. Interwar modernism did precisely that, in complex, enduring art characterized by innovations and experiment.

This second generation of modernists was born after 1880 and therefore reached intellectual and artistic maturity during or after the war. For them, Freud's theories about human nature being driven by forces we imperfectly control resonated loudly. These impulses for creation (Eros) and destruction (Thanatos) helped shape the literary and artistic culture of the 1920s and 1930s.

Joyce,
Ulysses

A high point in modernism occurred in 1922, when three artistic masterpieces appeared: the novel *Ulysses*, by the Irish writer James Joyce (1882–1941), the poem "The Waste Land," by the transplanted-from-America Englishman

T. S. Eliot (1888–1965), and the film *Nosferatu*, by the German writer and director Friedrich W. Murnau (1888–1931). *Ulysses* depicts the events of a single crucial day in the life of Leopold Bloom, an assimilated Irish Jew living in Dublin. He visits the post office, attends the funeral of a friend, stops in the National Library, performs a business errand, eats lunch, walks along the beach, and visits a friend who is giving birth in a hospital. Along the way Bloom encounters a young aspiring writer named Stephen Dedalus, with whom he forms an unexpectedly close bond. They drink together in a pub; Bloom then follows a drunken Stephen into a brothel to watch over him and helps him after Stephen gets into a scuffle with a policeman. After he and Stephen part, Bloom returns home to his wife, Molly, who has spent the afternoon with her lover, and collapses into bed. A magnificent long stream-of-consciousness monologue by Molly closes the novel.

Joyce narrates this day with a riot of narrative innovations. Patterned on Homer's epic *The Odyssey*, the novel presents Bloom as a modern-day Odysseus (Ulysses, in Latin), with Stephen as his son, Telemachus, and Molly as his wife, Penelope. Each chapter employs a different style and a new set of motifs and imagery. One chapter—the visit to the brothel—is written as a play, complete with stage directions. It dramatizes not only the two men's activities but also their thoughts and fears. Another section appears in the dry question-and-answer format of a Catholic catechism. A third episode shatters the narrative into nineteen vignettes of minor characters, who function as a chorus commenting on the main action. Yet *Ulysses* tells a traditional, or indeed mythical, tale of middle-aged loss, sadness, and longing. Stephen, Bloom's symbolic spiritual son, is a frustrated artist who rails against the political and religious bonds that shackle Irish society. At one point Stephen states, "History is a nightmare from which I am trying to awake." Molly, meanwhile, reawakened to sexuality after her afternoon tryst, meditates on the role that love and loneliness have played in her life. She confides in her soliloquy that she and Leopold have not had intercourse in a decade, but she resolves to tell Bloom in the morning about her infidelity and to renew their marriage.

Ulysses is a virtuoso performance and, for many, the supreme modernist novel. Its technical experimentations are not merely vehicles for displaying Joyce's talent; they are part of the point. The realist novel is dead, *Ulysses* proclaims. It is dead not only because nothing new can be done in that genre but because there is no reality to portray outside the perspectives of each individual character. Even those perspectives, however, cannot be fully trusted. Stephen and Leopold's states of mind are continually interrupted by impulses, hallucinations, visions, and suppressed memories; Molly's musings may just as likely be self-delusion as self-confession, a way of justifying to herself her infidelity. One cannot be sure. And that is one of the book's many hidden revelations.

T. S. Eliot, "The Waste Land"

Following hard on *Ulysses*'s footsteps was T. S. Eliot's "The Waste Land." Like many of Eliot's poems, it was composed in fragments over the course of many months and possibly several years. Shifting between different voices, multiple situations, and abrupt jumps in time, it is filled with literary, historical, and mythical allusions. As its opening reveals, the poem's overall effect is of collage:

> April is the cruelest month, breeding
> Lilacs out of the dead land, mixing
> Memory and desire, stirring
> Dull roots with spring rain.
> Winter kept us warm, covering
> Earth in forgetful snow, feeding
> A little life with dried tubers.
> Summer surprised us, coming over the Starnbergersee [a lake near
>   Munich]
> With a shower of rain; we stopped in the colonnade,
> And went on in sunlight, into the Hofgarten [a park in Munich],
> And drank coffee, and talked for an hour.
> Bin gar keine Russin, stamm' aus Litauen, echt deutsch ["I am not
>   Russian at all, I am a German from Lithuania"].
> And when we were children, staying at the archduke's,
> My cousin's, he took me out on a sled,
> And I was frightened. He said, Marie,
> Marie, hold on tight. And down we went.
> In the mountains, there you feel free.
> I read, much of the night, and go south in the winter.

Imagine a vast museum filled with all the treasures of Western art, literature, and music. "The Waste Land" is what you might have if you picked through the ruins of such a museum after a catastrophic explosion—shards of memories, bits of mangled newsprint, fragments of sculptures, scraps of painted canvas, torn pages from volumes of verse. After the wreck of civilization, the poem suggests, individual artists must piece together their own set of references and touchstones to create their own ordering of the world. The reader does not "understand" the poem in the traditional way, since no one can recognize without help the origins of all the bits of charred ruin. But one knows that a catastrophe has occurred—and that the museum will never again exist as it once did.

Murnau, Nosferatu

Nosferatu, also released in 1922, revises the legend of the vampire Dracula as it had been popularized in the 1897 novel by Bram Stoker. The film relocates the story from Stoker's contemporary England to a fictional Baltic port city in northern Germany in the 1830s. A representative of a German manufacturing firm is sent to Transylvania to meet with a new client, one Count Orlok, who turns out to be a vampire. He attacks the businessman in his sleep but does not kill him, as he usually does with his victims. Why? The businessman had shown Orlok a portrait of his wife back in Germany, and the vampire is smitten. He follows the businessman back to Germany and purchases the house directly across the street from the happy couple—all the while planning his attack and satisfying his bloodlust by killing dozens of other innocents. The wife, suspicious of her new neighbor, realizes what Orlok is when she reads a book on vampires. It informs her that the only way to kill a vampire is for a virtuous woman to offer herself to him as a sacrifice. One

Count Orlok   The role of Count Orlok, the vampire in *Nosferatu* (1922), was played by Max Schreck (1879–1936). A favorite of playwright Berthold Brecht's, Schreck spent most of his career in theater, but he also appeared in a silent film version of Shakespeare's *Merchant of Venice* (1923).

night she does so, for the sake of humanity, and Orlok, in his orgiastic enjoyment of her blood, fails to notice the rising of the sun. It vaporizes him.

Visually stunning, the film can still enthrall. Its distorted physical sets, unnatural lighting (white trees against a black sky, for instance), and oblique camera angles mirror and heighten the psychological discomfort felt by the film's protagonists—but also by its viewers. As with *Ulysses* and "The Waste Land," the formal technique not only propels the story but also is an intrinsic element of it. Orlok represents the unfulfilled human soul, condemned to an existence it did not choose and in pursuit only of its own desire. What it desires most is what will kill it. The Freudian echoes may or may not be intentional on the filmmakers' part. Either way, the film shows how much the interwar modernist movement had absorbed Freud's theories and made them its own.

The fact that the film relocates the novel's setting to northern Germany in the 1830s is significant. Germany in the 1830s had recently established the Customs' Union (*Zollverein*, discussed in chapter 18), which presaged the German Empire under Bismarck. The seed of industrial capitalism and nationalism, in other words, had been planted. *Nosferatu* is in large part an allegory of the rise of modern capitalist Germany, a society expanding its borders and pursuing its dream of wealth. It is the Germany that marched headlong into the Great War.

These masterpieces aside, the second wave of Modernism proved to be more varied, inclusive, and popular than the first. The most visible change in this second generation was the prominence of women writers and artists among the avant-garde. Freed at last from the struggle for the right to vote, women emerged as important figures in modernist cultural life (see Table 25.2). Among all women modernists, however, pride of place belongs to Virginia Woolf (1882–1941), one of the twentieth century's greatest writers.

TABLE 25.2 **Women in Modernist Cultural Life**

Editors, Publishers, Critics	Painters and Sculptors
Sylvia Beach (1887–1962)	Camille Claudel (1864–1943)
Adrienne Monnier (1892–1955)	Natalia Goncharova (1881–1962)
Rebecca West (1892–1983)	Georgia O'Keefe (1887–1986)
Poets	**Short-story Writers**
H. D. (Hilda Doolittle, 1886–1961)	Katherine Mansfield (1888–1923)
Marianne Moore (1887–1972)	
Novelists	**Composers**
Djuna Barnes (1892–1982)	Alma Mahler (1879–1964)
Ivy Compton-Burnett (1884–1969)	Nadia Boulanger (1887–1979)
Edith Södergran (1892–1923)	Germaine Tailleferre (1892–1983)
Virginia Woolf (1882–1941)	Lili Boulanger (1893–1918)

Virginia Woolf

Woolf was born into a prominent and famously complicated English family; privately educated, she grew up in an atmosphere of extraordinary intellectual stimulation.[2] The death of her mother in 1895, when Virginia was thirteen, was the first great emotional shock in her life and triggered an inward turn in her consciousness and behavior. The death of her father in 1904 resulted in a full-blown nervous breakdown; she recovered gradually but spent the rest of her life on the edge of mental instability. She killed herself in 1941, when World War II and a resurgence of manic depression made her fear losing her mind once and for all.

Woolf's greatness as a novelist lies in her unique combination of technical virtuosity and intense emotion. Starting with her third novel, *Jacob's Room* (1922), and through to her masterworks *Mrs. Dalloway* (1925) and *To the Lighthouse* (1927), she employs stream-of-consciousness monologues, unpredictable shifts in time and perspective, unreliable narrators, and at times a complete absence of plot. In this way, she focuses instead on the inner lives and intricate,

---

[2]   Woolf's father, Sir Leslie Stephen (1832–1904), a well-regarded author and journalist, was the chief editor of the *Dictionary of National Biography*.

unspoken bonds between her characters. Little ever "happens" in a Woolf novel. The plot of *Mrs. Dalloway* consists simply of the preparations over a single day, in an upper-middle-class London family, for a dinner party that evening. Yet Woolf captures an astonishing range of emotions, impressions, memories, and longings among the novel's characters. And these inchoate threads of feeling intertwine in intricate patterns. Few novels depict such emotional richness so quietly and yet so successfully.

Yet Woolf's novels can leave the reader with a feeling of incompleteness. Emotional life ends only when life itself ends, and the close of each Woolf novel does not feel like an ending at all. The same characters will awaken the next morning, and their inner maelstroms of sensation, regret, delight, and doubt will begin all over

Virginia Woolf Photographed here in 1932, Virginia Woolf (1882-1941) was one of the greatest modernist writers. Her major works include the novels *Mrs. Dalloway* (1925), *To the Lighthouse* (1927), and *The Waves* (1931).

again. That, of course, is part of the modernist point: we are *beyond* ideas, values, beliefs, and convictions. Life is by definition aimless, since no one can be certain of the target at which we should aim. Woolf skillfully depicts the emotionally corrosive effects of prejudice against women, but nowhere does she propose a specific idea of how to combat it. Woolf occasionally allowed her name to be added to petitions and helped her husband, Leonard Woolf, with some of his correspondence in his own political career. Otherwise, her political activities extended no further than conversation among her writer friends. Despite her professed admiration for the suffragists and the urgency of the political issues of the 1920s and 1930s, there is no evidence that she ever bothered to cast a vote in any election.

But then neither did Joyce nor Eliot. Second-generation modernism emphasized the unfixed, shifting nature of reality. They viewed most systems of belief and intellectual constructs with ironic detachment. Before the Great War and the Great Depression, modernism found few avid supporters and was at best an interesting marginal culture phenomenon. The generation that came of age during those horrendous times, however, felt modernism's creative aimlessness and self-exploration to resonate profoundly with their own aching uncertainty.

THE RISE OF FASCISM: ITALY AND SPAIN

At its root Fascism is the cult of power—the belief that force, directly applied to achieve a specific end, is the best form of government. Of course, all governments are in the business of reining in the actions of the people they govern; governments place limits on our daily activities, our business dealings, the ways in which we pass estates on to our heirs, the people we are allowed to marry. We agree to controls on our personal freedom in return for the stability and order of communal life. But *control* implies *force*, and no government can long survive without possessing the ability to make the populace feel its sting. Good government therefore consists of knowing the right kind and amount of force to apply, and when, and toward what end.

For an astonishing number of Europeans in the 1930s the best form of government, and perhaps the only form of government possible, considering the enormity of Europe's troubles, was one in which the state abandoned any pretence of moderation, shared authority, or the consent of the governed and simply assumed the direct, open, and unchallenged exercise of its own will. This was **Fascism**—a word that derives from the name of one of the ancient symbols of Roman power, the *fasces,* a long, tightly bound bundle of birch rods, from which the blade of a battle-ax emerges at the upper end. It was not a weapon but the symbol of one.[3]

As an ideology, Fascism differed in a fundamental way from the earlier form of authoritarian government, royal absolutism. Absolutism had been founded on the simple conviction that *someone* had to exert absolute external control on society; the absolute control mattered more than the identity of the person wielding it. In Fascism, however, the identity of the dictator was everything because Fascism embraced the Romantic notion of the collective soul of a national group— the mystical shared spirit (or *genius*, in the nineteenth-century sense of the term) of a people that expressed their deepest needs and longings. As the living embodiment of that spirit the Fascist leader knew—in his blood and sinews as much as in his mind—what his people desired, needed, hoped for, and feared, and for that reason his actions *were* the nation's actions. He did not impose his will on the people, as in absolutism, but rather expressed their will—and the more forcibly, the better. Fascist leaders emphasized their mystical connection with the nation and presented their rule as the organic expression of the general will.

Mussolini's Rise to Power

Fascism originated in Italy as a product of World War I. When Italy entered the war on the side of the Allies in 1915, many Italians, including the socialist journalist **Benito Mussolini** (1883–1945), welcomed the war as a cleansing force, a powerful disinfectant that would purify Italian society. Because the Socialist Party opposed Italy's entry into the war, Mussolini broke with the socialists, joined the army, and fought until he was wounded in 1917. When the war ended,

---

3   Carried by the bodyguards of Roman magistrates, the *fasces* represented the Republic's authority over its citizens and the idea of strength through unity.

he sought to create a new politics that would build on the camaraderie and exhilaration of combat.

In March 1919, Mussolini and about one hundred followers—mostly men but also some women—gathered in Milan and declared themselves the Fascist movement. Like Mussolini, many of these "Fascists of the first hour" were war veterans, a number of whom had served in the *arditi*, elite commando units that fought behind enemy lines. The arditi uniform, a black shirt, became the Fascist badge of identity.

Just three and a half years after the first Fascist meeting in Milan, Mussolini became prime minister of Italy. His rise to power occurred against a backdrop of social turmoil. In 1919 and 1920, more than 1 million workers were on strike and a wave of socialist-inspired land seizures spread across the countryside. Fearing that Communist revolution would engulf Italy just as it had destroyed tsarist Russia, landowners and industrialists looked to Mussolini's Fascists for help. Fascist squads disrupted Socialist Party meetings, broke up strikes, beat up trade unionists, and protected aristocratic estates from attack. By 1922, the Fascists were a powerful political force with thirty-five parliamentary seats. In October of that year, thousands of Fascists from all over Italy converged in the "March on Rome," a powerful demonstration of the disciplined might of Mussolini's followers. An intimidated King Victor Emmanuel III (r. 1900–1946) quickly invited Mussolini to become prime minister.

Mussolini ran Italy with a combination of terror and traditionalism. Victor Emmanuel remained on the throne, the official head of state, but power lay in the *Fascism in* hands of Mussolini, "the Leader" (*il Duce*). Using his special corps of thuggish *Italy* loyalists, the Blackshirts, he crushed all political dissent, broke the labor unions, suppressed the free press, and brutalized anyone who stood in his way. He ingratiated himself with Italy's economic and aristocratic elites and made it clear that he would gladly leave them in control of their property and privileges in return for their political support. Most of them agreed, including the papacy. The **Lateran Agreement** of 1929 officially recognized the Vatican City as a sovereign nation within Italy—indeed within the confines of Rome—and in return for this recognition Pope Pius XI (r. 1922–1939) urged all good Catholics in Italy to support his government.

The Fascist brand of nationalism appealed to many Italians, but more people accepted Mussolini's regime out of fear of retaliation, or out of a greater fear of the political alternatives like Communism, than out of true enthusiasm. Although workers' rights were severely curtailed by the disbanding of labor unions and the close relations between the government and industrial leadership, the Fascists' enormous expenditures on public works kept unemployment relatively low. Mussolini thought of himself as the modern exemplar of a Renaissance man—scholar, statesman, soldier, lover, athlete—and the embodiment of all manly virtues. In *The Doctrine of Fascism* (1932), which like most of his "scholarly" publications was ghost-written for him, he argues that the Fascist state should be directly connected to the people without intermediaries like unions: "Fascism provides the only freedom that can be taken seriously—the freedom of the state, and the freedom of the individual within the state. To the Fascist, the state is everything; nothing human or spiritual exists or has any meaning outside of the state. Thus Fascism is totalitarian; and the Fascist State brings together and harmonizes every value, and it alone interprets, develops, and strengthens the life of the entire people."

Mussolini's determination to expand Italy's authority in the Mediterranean also proved popular. He sent his forces into Libya in 1923 and by 1935 had annexed the entire country; in 1935 he invaded Ethiopia and took it over the next year; and in 1939 he seized Albania (see Map 25.2). Despite international protests, these moves improved Mussolini's standing at home and with the army, which was central to maintaining his hold on power.

Rise of Fascism in Spain

Military support was also the key element in the rise of General **Francisco Franco** (1892–1975), the leader of Fascist Spain. A career military man, Franco had worked his way through the ranks and in 1920 became Spain's youngest-ever general. Nationalist sentiments ran as strong in Spain as anywhere else in Europe in the nineteenth century; however, those sentiments were regional and divisive rather than uniting. Groups like the Basques and Catalans regarded themselves as autonomous nations instead of parts of a greater Spain. They sought independence from Madrid, not union with it. Passionate in his conviction that Communism represented the greatest evil of the modern era, Franco believed in monarchy, the Catholic Church, and Spanish cultural tradition (by which he meant Castilian, his own heritage)—and he was determined to eliminate everything that threatened them.

In the nineteenth century Spain had endured two bloody civil wars (1833–1840 and 1872–1876) that left it with a weak constitutional monarchy and a deeply divided parliament. Industrialization and the loss of Spain's last colonies (Cuba, Guam, the Philippines, and Puerto Rico) to the United States in the Spanish–American War of 1898 had added new strains to the situation, causing Spain to enter the twentieth century with even stronger centrifugal momentum than in the nineteenth. Officially neutral in World War I, the parliamentary government in Madrid had made an ill-fated attempt to conquer Morocco as a salve to wounded pride. In 1923 the army, under the command of a liberal general named Miguel Primo de Rivera (1870–1930) and with the support of King Alfonso XIII (r. 1886–1981), had staged a coup and tried to institute republican reform. This new regime recognized the rights of workers to form unions and admitted

MAP 25.2 **Expansion of the Italian Empire, 1922–1939** Promising his followers Roman glory, Mussolini quickly expanded Italian holdings in the Mediterranean and north Africa.

moderate socialist parties to the political process. But these concessions had triggered a conservative backlash by Spain's landowning elite and industrial leaders, and in 1930 Primo de Rivera was forced to resign as prime minister, which opened the door to yet another civil war—and the rise to power of the Fascists.

In 1931 a republican form of government replaced the Spanish monarchy; in 1936 a so-called Popular Front government, a coalition of Communists, socialists, and radicals, took office in the name of the Republic of Spain. Army officers, *Spanish Civil War* led by Franco, rebelled, and the **Spanish Civil War** of 1936–1939 began. The struggle between the left-wing Republican forces and the right-wing Nationalist rebels quickly became an international issue. Fascist Italy and Nazi Germany supported the rebellion. The Republic of Spain appealed to the democracies for aid, but the only state that came to its assistance was the Soviet Union. Unnerved by Soviet involvement, the French, British, and American governments remained neutral, although tens of thousands of volunteers from Britain, France, the United States, and elsewhere joined the Republicans. The small but highly influential contingent of officers and airmen from Stalinist Russia helped to radicalize many of the Republican fighters—a trend that only added urgency to the Nationalist cause. The bitterness of the struggle polarized the political divisions: the liberals became increasingly revolutionary, whereas the conservatives grew increasingly reactionary.

Witness the description of Barcelona, a Republican stronghold, in George Orwell's *Homage to Catalonia* (1938), the English writer's firsthand account of the Spanish Civil War:

> Practically every building of any size had been seized by the workers and was draped with red [Communist] flags or with the red and black flag of the Anarchists [a party that sought the abolishment of state government]; every wall was scrawled with the [Soviet] hammer and sickle and with the initials of the revolutionary parties; almost every church had been gutted and its images burnt. Churches here and there were being systematically demolished by gangs of workmen. Every shop and cafe had an inscription saying that it had been collectivized [taken over by the state]; even the bootblacks had been collectivized and their boxes painted red and black. Waiters and shop-walkers looked you in the face and treated you as an equal. Servile and even ceremonial forms of speech had temporarily disappeared. Nobody said *Señor* or *Don* or even *Usted*; everyone called everyone else "Comrade" or "Thou," and said *Salud!* instead of *Buenos dias*. Tipping had been forbidden by law since the time of Primo de Rivera; almost my first experience was receiving a lecture from a hotel manager for trying to tip a lift-boy. There were no private motorcars, they had all been commandeered, and the trams and taxis and much of the other transport were painted red and black. The revolutionary posters were everywhere, flaming from the walls in clean reds and blues that made the few remaining advertisements look like daubs of mud. Down the Ramblas, the wide central artery of the town where crowds of people streamed constantly to and fro, the loud-speakers were bellowing revolutionary songs all day and far into the night.

The Horror of War   The bombing of a small Basque town in 1937 (by Nazi German and Fascist Italian airplanes, acting on behalf of the Nationalist forces led by Francisco Franco) inspired Pablo Picasso to paint his great mural *Guernica*, which he exhibited at the World's Fair in Paris of that year. Using a stark black, gray, and white palette, he layered images of horror on top of each other in the center of the scene (note the human skull and the attacking bull located inside the image of the shrieking horse), which he counter-balanced with images of dismemberment along the base and figures of women in pain and despair at either side.

The war raged until March 1939, when the last remnants of the Republican forces surrendered to Franco. More than half a million people had perished in the fighting, and Franco executed hundreds of thousands more after he took power and established an authoritarian state that increasingly became a Fascist dictatorship. The new regime outlawed all competing political parties and imposed strict censorship of the media and school curricula. It mandated the use of Castilian Spanish, promoted conservative Catholicism, and built a network of concentration camps where criminals and political enemies were imprisoned, tortured, and killed.

NAZISM IN GERMANY

The Weimar government was all but powerless in the face of Fascism's rise in Germany. Many Germans could not separate the birth of the Weimar Republic from the national humiliation imposed by the Versailles Treaty. The Nazi Party was in fact only one of many extremist factions that had formed throughout Europe almost immediately after the signing of the treaty. It would take a charismatic leader to bring the Nazis to power.

Adolf Hitler (1889–1945), a German nationalist, was not a citizen of Germany for much of his life. Born in the Austrian half of the Austrian-Hungarian Empire, Hitler came of age in Vienna, where he made a meager living as a painter while absorbing the anti-Semitic German nationalism that permeated this capital

Hitler's Rise to Power

city. By the start of World War I, however, Hitler had settled in Germany. De-lighted by the chance to fight the war in German rather than Austrian uniform, Hitler served as a German soldier until he was temporarily blinded by poison gas in 1918. He then returned to Munich, home to large bands of unemployed war veterans and a breeding ground for nationalist and racist groups.

The Nazi Party began as one of those groups, with Hitler quickly emerging by 1921 as its leader. *Nazi* is shorthand for Nationalist Socialist German Workers' Party, but this title is a misnomer. Nazism opposed socialism, Communism, and trade unionism. Like Italian Fascism, **Nazism** was a nationalistic, antidemo-cratic, and militaristic ideology.

In Nazism, however, racism, particularly anti-Semitism, played the central role. To Hitler, all history was the history of racial struggle; in that racial struggle, the Jews were always the principal enemy. Hitler regarded Jewishness as a biologi-cal rather than a religious identity, a toxic infection that threatened "Aryans," a linguistic term that Hitler misused to identify the "racially pure"—white north-ern Europeans. In Hitler's distorted vision, Jewishness and Communism formed two parts of the same evil whole. He saw the Bolshevik victory in Russia as part of a wider struggle for Jewish world domination, and he promised his followers that the Aryan race would defeat the forces of "Judeo-Bolshevism" and establish a mighty empire encompassing all of eastern Europe, including the Soviet Union.

The early Nazi movement appealed to men like Hitler, individuals without power or, apparently, much chance of getting it—unemployed ex-soldiers, small shopkeepers wiped out by postwar hyperinflation, the myriad workers who had lost their jobs. By November 1923, party membership stood at about fifty-five thousand—a small, insignificant fringe party.

That month, however, Hitler and his supporters achieved national renown by attempting to overthrow the Weimar government. Although this "Beer Hall Putsch" (so-called because it originated in a beer hall) failed miserably—in con-trast to Mussolini's "March on Rome," which Hitler intended to emulate—it won Hitler a wide audience. In the ensuing trial for treason, a sympathetic judge sen-tenced Hitler to a mere nine months in prison. He emerged from his cell with a bulky manuscript that he soon published: *Mein Kampf* ("My Struggle"), pub-lished in two volumes (1925–1926). Whatever personal demons haunted Hitler's mind, his book resonated with the bruised and embittered egos of many Germans.

Mein Kampf devotes most of its pages to a theory of the superiority of the German race, on the basis of which it promotes two strategic goals. The first goal was *Lebensraum*—"living space," literally. By this term Hitler meant not just the return of ethnically German territories carved away from the nation by the Ver-sailles Treaty; he also meant the right of Germany to expand into eastern Europe and the Balkans at the expense of the inferior Slavic peoples who resided there. His second goal was to promote an organic, classless, national community of the Germanic people. It would unite them in spirit and blood and would express its spiritual unity in Nazism and its leader. It insisted that the spiritual purity of the German "folk" (*Volk*) could be achieved only by removing from its midst the polluting presence of Communists, homosexuals, the physically and mentally handicapped, and, above all, the Jews. Like a true paranoid, he sees himself (and the entire German nation) surrounded by enemies, whom he ultimately conflates into one:

> Marxism, a Jewish philosophy, rejects Nature's aristocratic ways and substitutes the mass of sheer numbers of people and all their dead weight for the eternal right of power and strength—and in so doing it denies the values of human personality, the importance of nationality and race, and thereby denies the human race the very foundation of its existence and culture. . . . The application of such a philosophy can only lead to chaos on earth and the destruction of the human population. If the Jew, aided by his Marxist creed, emerges victorious over the other races of the earth, his crown will be the funeral wreath of humanity.

Hitler in Landsberg Prison   During his 1924 imprisonment, Adolf Hitler wrote the ghoulish manifesto *Mein Kampf* ("My Struggle"), which describes his racial theories, political ideas, and vision of Germany's future.

Amid the desperate conditions of postwar Germany, Hitler appealed to ever-growing numbers of disaffected and resentful Germans. His skill as a speaker and the brilliance of his propaganda director, Joseph Goebbels, made Hitler's political rise seem unstoppable. The impact of the Great Depression provided the last boost needed to bring the Nazis to power. In the national elections of 1928, the Nazis were still a minor, although growing, power; in the next election cycle of 1930 (one year after the onset of the Depression), they became the second largest party in Germany.

From this point, the Nazis quickly turned to the use of violence, blackmail, and intimidation to

Nazi Anti-Semitism   "Behind our Enemy-Powers—the Jew," reads this typical piece of anti-Semitic propaganda.

strengthen their hand. Hitler purged the party of any possible rivals to his personal rule. The personality cult of "the Leader" (*der Führer*) promoted by Goebbels grew in intensity, and the desire to cleanse Germany of moral guilt for World War I intensified too. Finally, in January 1933, after a new round of elections, the Nazis emerged as victors, and Hitler won appointment as chancellor of the nation. In September he delivered a speech that summarizes the Nazi view of politics and German history:

> In 1919 when the Nazi Party came into existence in order to replace the Marxist-democratic republic with a new nation, the very idea seemed hopeless and foolish—especially to those pseudo-intellectuals who, with their shallow understanding of history, looked upon us with a simpering and pitying smile. Most of them knew that our nation was about to fall upon evil times, because they recognized that the men in charge of the November Republic were both too evil and too inept to lead our great nation. What they did *not* know, however, was that our party would *never* fall victim to the ideas and sentiments that caused *them* to run from the attacks of Marxism for the last fifty years. . . . We were ready from the start for the long and difficult struggle to build up a party that would destroy Marxism. . . . The former leaders, the bourgeois leaders, of society talked endlessly about making "quiet progress" . . . while we held hundreds and thousands of demonstrations. . . . They blathered about democracy, but kept away from the people. National Socialism, on the other hand, talked about authority, but engaged with the people, wrestled with the people, as no movement in German history had ever done. . . .
>
> As the sole legitimate possessor of state power, our party understands that it is responsible for the entire course of German history. . . . We may reject the principles of democracy and parliamentary government, but we passionately believe in the peoples' right to govern themselves. Parliaments, we insist, do not express the will of the masses, but actually pervert and violate that will. The will of the people finds its only true and effective expression in its most gifted leaders. . . . Power and its ruthless application can accomplish much.

The appeal of such a message was deep because it offered a chance to rewrite history as well as to chart a new future. And the people of Germany desperately desired to do both.

Growth of Fascist Parties   Fascism's appeal was wide reaching. Austria had at least two Fascist parties of note—the "Fatherland Front" and the "Home Defense Force." Belgium's "Rexist

Party" grew large enough to hold one-tenth of the seats in the national parliament. Britain had fifty thousand members in its "Fascist Union," Croatia had the "Fascist Insurrection Party," and in Finland the "Lapua Party" (named after the town in which it was founded) nearly seized power in a coup in 1932. Greece had its "Fascist Party of Free Believers"; Hungary had its "Arrow Cross Party." The "National Union Party" came briefly to power in Norway, as did the "New State" in Portugal. Poland's "Fascist Falanga Party" (deriving its name from the ancient Greek mass military formation, the phalanx) was led by Bolesław Piasecki (1915–1979), who spouted torrents of anti-Semitic bile that rivaled anything uttered by Hitler. Corneliu Codreanu (1899–1938) was the charismatic, anti-Semitic head of Romania's leading Fascist party, known primarily as the "Iron Guard" but occasionally using the names "Everything for the Fatherland," the "League of Christian Defense," and the "Legion of the Archangel Michael."

France felt the tug toward Fascism too, producing as it did an abundance of extremist parties: the "Cross of Fire," which may have had as many as a million members; "French Action," the "French Popular Party," "French Solidarity," and the "Young Patriots." It may be the case, in fact, that France avoided becoming a Fascist country only because it had so many Fascist parties, which kept splitting the votes among themselves. In all of these countries, Fascism appealed to two distinct groups: the poor, who wanted retribution against real and perceived enemies, and the industrial and financial elites, who craved social and economic stability.

OPPRESSION AND TERROR IN RUSSIA

Fascism and Communism stood as opposite ends of the political spectrum in the 1920s and 1930s, and each presented itself as the only defense against the other. Yet they resembled each other closely in methods of social control—so closely that observers as early as 1926 coined the word **totalitarianism** to describe their shared form of political oppression. Like the Fascist groups across Europe, Russia's Communist regime under **Joseph Stalin** (1879–1953) was an intensely centralized society. The Bolshevik Party held all authority and openly used systematic police terror to dominate and manipulate the general population.

Stalin had come to Lenin's attention early in the century and by 1912 was appointed to the Bolshevik Central Committee. An enthusiast from the start for *Stalinism* Lenin's insistence on the use of violence against political enemies, Stalin indulged his taste for cruelty, and for the rest of his life he relied on assassinations, purges, enslavement, and intimidation to achieve his ends. After Lenin's death in 1924, Stalin resolved to increase Russia's industrial and agricultural output by any means necessary, and that meant dismantling the economic structures created by

Lenin's New Economic Policy, which, as we saw in chapter 24, combined elements of Marxism and capitalism.

In 1929 Stalin replaced the New Economic Policy with the first of several **Five-Year Plans** intended to mobilize Soviet citizens to industrialize the nation. Stalin's program called for massive increases in the output of coal, iron ore, steel, and industrial goods over successive five-year periods. Without an end to economic backwardness, Stalin warned, "the advanced countries . . . will crush us." He thus established central economic planning, a policy of government direction of the economy, as used during World War I and increasingly favored by economists and industrialists around the world. Between 1929 and 1940, the number of Soviet workers in industry, construction, and transport nearly tripled, and production soared. Stalin's first Five-Year Plan helped make the Soviet Union a leading industrial nation.

The Soviet government also drastically changed conditions on the land. Faced with peasants' refusal simply to turn over their grain to the government, Stalin called for the "liquidation of the kulaks." The word *kulak,* which literally means "fist," was first an insulting Soviet term for a prosperous peasant, but it came to apply to any independent farmer. State officials massacred hundreds of thousands of farmers and their families, confiscated their lands to form new collective farms under the direct control of the government, and forced the rest into exile and starvation. Many millions more perished of famine and exposure.

Stalin relentlessly blamed all food shortages and failures to meet the goals of his vaunted Five-Year Plans on conspiracies led by corrupt officials, lazy workers, inept engineers, political rivals, and, of course, their Jewish financial cronies. The degree and ferocity of his paranoia can hardly be overstated. Starting in 1936 in the **Great Purge** he orchestrated a series of show trials in which phony evidence was used to prove false charges against these "enemies of socialism"—and then to justify their execution. By the next year he did away with even the show trials. He simply ordered mass arrests and confinements in a vast network of brutal concentration camps that stretched across Russia from Moscow to Siberia—the *gulag* (an acronym for the Russian phrase meaning "Central Administration of Corrective Labor Camps"). From 1938 to Stalin's death in 1953, roughly 1 million prisoners died in these camps. Some were starved and worked to death; others were simply beaten to death or shot. And perhaps another million or more died after being sentenced to internal exile. By the time World War II began, Stalin had already murdered 90 percent of his generals and 80 percent of his colonels—a purge that left the Russian army at a distinct disadvantage when Hitler invaded.

The Bolshevik regime had initially improved the social and political status of Russian women by establishing a high-level Women's Department within

Building Socialism   Women and children were also sent to the gulag during Stalin's murderous reign. Here a group of prisoners work at digging a canal out of the frozen Russian ground.

its ranks, granting women the right to seek divorce, and securing access to abortion services. Stalin rolled back many of these gains, but less out of opposition to women's rights in theory than from a need to stem a demographic hemorrhage. He killed so many millions that the nation had difficulty maintaining a national workforce. He therefore ordered improved health care available to women (although access to birth control was tightly restricted) and education focused on improving literacy rates. The number of female engineers, physicians, and civil officials rose significantly; the lower ranks of the party itself became in time filled with female members. At the same time, Stalin redefined the family. What Marx had dismissed as an outdated bourgeois institution was officially rehabilitated as a "school for socialism." To encourage large families, Stalin bestowed a new award—that of the "Heroic Mother" (*Mat'eri Geroi*)—on women who produced ten children. Propaganda posters of the 1930s vividly depict all these changes in the significance of women to the socialist dream.

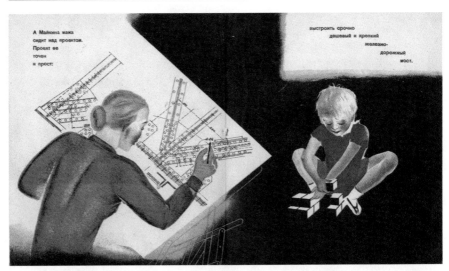

Working Mother   This illustration comes from a children's book called *Mommy's Bridge* (1933). The book aims to show that women working to create a socialist state could do so without fear of failing as mothers. Stalin emphasized a cult of motherhood in order to encourage women to produce more little socialists.

A NEW DEAL?

When Hitler became chancellor on January 3, 1933, his aims could hardly have been clearer. *Mein Kampf* had spelled them out in rambling detail, and the thuggish tactics used by his uniformed and civilian supporters gave overwhelming evidence of the Nazis' willingness to beat, murder, rob, and swindle to accomplish those aims. Whatever else might be said about Hitler, he seldom shied away from speaking his mind. Why, then, did the nations of the West give him more or less free rein for six years to do whatever he wanted? Before looking for answers, it is important to emphasize the continuing economic crisis.

The steps needed to confront the Depression seemed clear enough: the only way to spark economic recovery was to put people back to work by spending on public projects like highways, dams and levees, electrical grids, schools, and parks. The creation of welfare-state programs could offer nonworking sectors of the population, such as children and the elderly, essential services like housing and health care. This was, in fact, how Hitler enabled Germany's recovery. Massive investment in rebuilding the military and constructing large-scale projects like the Autobahn system (the highways) all but eradicated Germany's sky-high unemployment rate by 1937. In the United States, President Franklin Delano Roosevelt's torrent of new programs known as the **New Deal** followed the same basic path. It put millions of men and women back to work, provided price supports for cash-strapped farmers, offered unemployment insurance and retirement benefits to those no longer working, and made welfare payments to dependent mothers and their children.

Opposition to such expensive schemes was widespread, however, and in many countries the opposition undercut recovery. Some of the opposition was simply personal: those with capital and incomes did not relish paying higher taxes—often dramatically higher—to benefit others. Much, however, was a matter of principle, since government intervention on such a scale smacked of socialism. Two brilliant economists squared off in the debate and set the terms for much of the philosophical divide between liberalism and conservatism for the rest of the twentieth century—John Maynard Keynes (1883–1946) and Friedrich Hayek (1899–1992).

Keynes was the author of *The Economic Consequences of the Peace* (1919). After his bitter experience at the Paris Peace Conference (described in chapter 24), he *Keynesian* moved between Cambridge, where he was a fellow at King's College, and London, *Economics* where he advised the Treasury on economic matters. He was also associated with the group of writers, artists, and philosophers (including Virginia Woolf) who became known as the "Bloomsbury Group," after the London neighborhood in or near which many of them lived.

In 1936 he published his greatest work, *The General Theory of Employment, Interest, and Money*, which some have called the most important work of economics of the twentieth century. Believing that unemployment was the single most severe problem posed by the Depression, Keynes argues in *The General Theory* that market forces alone cannot solve the problem. As profits decline, wages will fall indefinitely to restore profits, given enough time, and in unacceptably unpredictable ways. The rehiring of displaced workers and the taking on of new laborers will always be the last step taken by businesses on the mend. Moreover, Keynes adds, many failed or failing businesses will simply never return; some might reinvent themselves and produce new manufactures and services that rely less on labor—but this will only extend the problem. The solution to endemic unemployment, he maintains, is direct government action. The wages earned by labor will allow them to spend more, and the return to normal demand levels for products and service will mean a return to normal prices and profits to businesses.

Friedrich Hayek was born in Vienna, then the still-vibrant capital of the Austrian–Hungarian Empire. His family was wealthy and academic, and he served *Hayek's* bravely in World War I in an artillery unit on the Italian front. His personal sense *Conservative* of the loss of the comfort, stability, and refinement of the prewar era never left *Alternative* him. After the war he studied law and economics at the University of Vienna, earned a doctorate, and published his first book, *Monetary Theory and the Trade Cycle*, in 1929—the year of the crash. On its strength Hayek was appointed a professor at the London School of Economics, where he taught until 1950. He later taught at the University of Chicago (1950–1962) and the University of Freiburg (1962–1968), and in 1974 he received the Nobel Prize in Economics. Hayek challenged Keynes both theoretically and empirically, book for book, article for article, lecture for lecture, throughout the 1930s and 1940s. Their rivalry was a friendly one, but the differences between the two men were profound.

Hayek endorsed the pre-1848 vision of classical economic liberalism, one that asserted the supreme importance of individual liberty, personal responsibility, and the sacrosanct rights of property. A free market, he insisted, was the best and ultimately the only reliable guarantor of all three. Government intervention is a violent interruption of a natural process and leads only to demands for further interruptions. Think of how erecting a levee or a dam on a river protects a flood-plain: it may protect that particular plain, but it only passes the problem of river-flow further downstream, where more calls for action will result in still more levees and dams, built at ever greater expense. Eventually, the river becomes un-manageable and a disaster vastly greater than that posed to the initial floodplain will occur. Better to recognize that rivers sometimes flood, and one should not build homes below the high-water level. In his two most famous attacks on Keynesian economics, *The Pure Theory of Capital* (1941) and *The Road to Serfdom* (1944), his conclusion is stark: government intervention in a free economy, no matter how well intentioned, is the first step toward totalitarianism, whether of the liberal/Communist or conservative/Fascist variety.

APPEASEMENT AND PACIFISM

How evil does a regime have to be before other countries will take preemptive action against it? Who may take such action—only the regime's immediate neighbors? Why did the Western world respond to Hitler's Fascism by tolerating it? This is the essential, urgent question posed by the 1930s, and it still rankles millions of people.

There is no single answer. The guiding policy of the West toward Hitler in the 1930s was called **appeasement**—the granting of political and territorial concessions to preserve peace—and each Western country appeased Hitler in different ways and for different reasons. And because of the continued economic crisis, the stakes were high. Each nation debated how to confront the Nazi danger without risking its plans for much-needed economic recovery.

Causes of Appeasement

France had perhaps the easiest choice to make, since it had really no choice at all. After World War I and the Depression, France could not even feign a direct challenge to Hitler's aggression. It took instead a purely defensive posture by building a barricade along the French–German border—the "Maginot Line," named after the minister of war, André Maginot (1877–1932). An interlocking chain of artillery casements, machine-gun pillboxes, tank formations, barbed wire, minefields, and concrete bunkers, it was a variation on the trench networks of World War I—and proved in the end to be just as ineffective. The point, however, is that France could do little else.

The causes of American appeasement were rather more complicated. First, a strong popular sentiment in favor of isolationism dominated the 1930s. The Paris Peace Conference had spoiled the hopes of many regarding their country's ability to influence Europe for the better, and the crushing urgency of the Depression—which had left nearly one-half the U.S. population in dire poverty—demanded immediate, unwavering attention. Senate Republicans led the case for nonintervention by establishing a special commission to examine America's involvement in World War I. Its 1936 report concluded that munitions manufacturers had influenced the U.S. decision to enter the war, out of a simple but coldhearted desire for profits. Outrage at these "war profiteers" fueled noninterventionist passions across America.

But another factor mattered just as much, namely the concern over aggressive Communism. Although the full extent of Stalin's humanitarian crimes remained unclear, enough was known to make Washington wary. Hitler clearly sought to force his will over central Europe, but Stalin wanted the entire world under his boot-heel. Given a choice between evils—which many in Washington thought was all they had, in the 1930s—it might make strategic and even moral sense to prefer a strong Nazi Germany as a barricade against a Stalinist Europe.

The causes of British appeasement were perhaps the most complicated of all. Most people in Britain agreed that the Versailles Treaty had been a disaster and that the refusal of the Parliament to ratify it had been correct. But if the West had been wrong in 1919 to strip Germany of its peripheral territories, how could it oppose Germany's desire to have those territories restored? So long as Hitler's demands called only for rolling back an unfair treaty, many British concluded, they were not worth foiling at the cost of another war. For example, Hitler repeatedly demanded the return to Germany of the Saar Valley. Britain, loath to quarrel yet again with France, at first hesitated and denied the claim, citing the Versailles Treaty as justification. But when German demands became shriller and Hitler declared his willingness for war, if necessary, Britain relented. In 1936 it agreed to allow the Nazi regime to take control of and remilitarize the district.

For the moment, tensions calmed, but then Hitler began the gamble again the following year by calling for Germany's right to unite with Austria (the *Anschluss*). Similar demands, similar arguments, similar threats—and once again, British compliance in Germany's annexation of Austria. Then in 1938 Hitler insisted on the return of the Sudetenland—the region of northern Czechoslovakis where the majority of the population was ethnically German. Once again the

British prime minister, Neville Chamberlain, had to explain his position on the floor of the Parliament in March 1938:

> The position that we had to face in July was that a deadlock had arisen in the negotiations which had been going on between the Czechoslovak Government and the Sudeten Germans and that fears were already entertained that if it were not readily broken the German Government might presently intervene in the dispute. For His Majesty's Government there were three alternative courses that we might have adopted. Either (1) we could have threatened to go to war with Germany if she attacked Czechoslovakia, or (2) we could have stood aside and allowed matters to take their course, or, finally, (3) we could attempt to find a peaceful settlement by way of mediation. The first of those courses we rejected. We had no treaty liabilities with Czechoslovakia. We always refused to accept any such obligation. Indeed, this country, which does not readily resort to war, would not have followed us if we had tried to lead it into war to prevent a minority from obtaining autonomy, or even from choosing to pass under some other Government.
>
> The second alternative was also repugnant to us. However remote this territory may be, we knew, of course, that a spark once lighted there might give rise to a general conflagration, and we felt it our duty to do anything in our power to help the contending parties to find agreement.
>
> We addressed ourselves to the third course, the task of mediation. We knew that the task would be difficult, perhaps even perilous, but we felt that the object was good enough to justify the risk.

Chamberlain substitutes the word "mediation" here for "appeasement," which actually had a positive connotation at the time—a sense of reasonableness and diplomatic maturity. Only after World War II did it acquire its current taint.

The Call for Pacifism

Another English word entered common use in the West in the 1930s, carried over from French—**pacifism**. It appeared first in 1902 to describe French social reformers who opposed the military buildup that culminated in World War I. From 1919 on, however, it denoted any principled and total rejection of violence as a means of resolving disputes. In an early treatise dedicated to the subject, the British social critic Philip S. Mumford wrote in his *Introduction to Pacifism* (1937), that "the Pacifist believes: 1. That war, i.e. mass murder, as a political policy is morally wrong, and consequently will never produce good results. . . . 2. That security for nations, ideals, or personal freedom can be obtained only by non-violent resistance." Pacifism therefore meant not merely the preference for peace but also the belief that any form of violence is intrinsically evil.

Munich Conference   This carefully staged photograph from September 28, 1938 shows negotiations between Neville Chamberlain and Adolf Hitler, with attendants, to resolve the issue of
Nazi claims to control the Sudetenland region in Czechoslovakia. After returning home from
the Munich Conference, Chamberlain spoke to a crowd outside 10 Downing Street: "My good
friends, this is the second time in our history that [there has come back from Germany to
Downing Street peace with honour.] I believe it is peace for our time. We thank you from the
bottom of our hearts. And now I recommend you to go home and sleep quietly in your beds."
World War II broke out almost exactly one year later.

The most famous name among British pacifists of the time was the novelist
and critic Aldous Huxley (1894–1963), best remembered today for his novel
Brave New World (1932), in which he warned of the harmful effects of society's
growing dependence on technology. Urged on by figures like him, the Student
Union of Oxford University in 1935 swore a public oath that they "would not take
up arms in defense of King and country . . . under any conditions whatsoever,"
should conflicts with Nazi Germany, Fascist Italy, or Communist Russia come to
war. This "Oxford Oath" circulated through Cambridge University as well before
coming to the United States. By the end of 1936 no fewer than sixty thousand
American undergraduates had also taken the pledge.

Britain found itself in a bind—caught between loathing and distrust of
Hitler on the one hand and a grudging willingness to consider his demands on
the other. Despite urgent warnings in Parliament, the ruling Conservative Party
hoped to the last that nations could deal with even a tyrant like Hitler with cau-
tion and reasonableness. Many in the country, and in Britain's closest ally, the

United States, feared Stalin even more and hoped against hope that Hitler could be used as a foil against him. And leading groups of the generation that would do the actual fighting, if it came to that, had already announced their refusal to fight at all.

Churchill's Argument against Appeasement

In the face of all this, Winston Churchill (1874–1965), then First Lord of the Admiralty and future prime minister of Great Britain, rose in Parliament on October 5, 1938. His stirring speech against any further appeasement or pacification ended with a quote from the Bible (Daniel 5.27):

> The Prime Minister desires to see cordial relations between this country and Germany. There is no difficulty at all in having cordial relations with the German people. Our hearts go out to them. But they have no power. You must have diplomatic and correct relations, but there can never be friendship between the British democracy and the Nazi Power, that power which spurns Christian ethics, which cheers its onward course by a barbarous paganism, which vaunts the spirit of aggression and conquest, which derives strength and perverted pleasure from persecution, and uses, as we have seen, with pitiless brutality the threat of murderous force. That power cannot ever be the trusted friend of the British democracy.
>
> What I find unendurable is the sense of our country falling into the power, into the orbit and influence of Nazi Germany, and of our existence becoming dependent upon their good will or pleasure. It is to prevent that, that I have tried my best to urge the maintenance of every bulwark of defense—first, the timely creation of an Air Force superior to anything within striking distance of our shores; secondly, the gathering together of the collective strength of many nations; and thirdly, the making of alliances and military conventions. . . . It has all been in vain. Every position has been successively undermined and abandoned on specious and plausible excuses. We do not want to be led upon the high road to becoming a satellite of the German Nazi system of European domination. In a very few years, perhaps in a very few months, we shall be confronted with demands with which we shall no doubt be invited to comply. Those demands may affect the surrender of territory or the surrender of liberty. I foresee and foretell that the policy of submission will carry with it restrictions upon the freedom of speech and debate in Parliament, on public platform, and discussions in the Press. . . .
>
> But [the British public] should know the truth. They should know that there has been gross neglect and deficiency in our defenses; they

should know that we have sustained a defeat without a war, the consequences of which will travel far with us along our road; they should know that we have passed an awful milestone in our history, when the whole equilibrium of Europe has been deranged, and that the terrible words have for the time being been pronounced against the Western democracies: "Thou art weighed in the balance and found wanting."

The Nazi regime bet its survival on the belief that the nations of the West would acquiesce so long as Nazi demands were couched in terms of the Versailles Treaty. The six years of breathing space accorded Hitler by the policies of appeasement and the popular call for pacifism were all he needed to rebuild Germany's military system and to turn it into the most awesome fighting force in Europe. On September 1, 1939, Hitler took his decisive step by sending his army into Poland—the first territory outside any conceivable German claim to legitimate dominion. At that point it was at last undeniable that Nazi aims were pan-European. Within three days, World War II had begun.

WHO, WHAT, WHERE

Adolf Hitler	Francisco Franco	Nazism
appeasement	gold standard	New Deal
Balfour Declaration	Great Depression	pacifism
Benito Mussolini	Great Purge	Spanish Civil War
Fascism	Joseph Stalin	totalitarianism
Five-Year Plans	Lateran Agreement	

SUGGESTED READINGS

Primary Sources

Hayek, Friedrich A. *The Road to Serfdom.*

Hitler, Adolf. *Mein Kampf.*

Keynes, John Maynard. *The General Theory of Employment, Interest, and Money.*

Orwell, George. *Homage to Catalonia.*

Spengler, Oswald. *The Decline of the West.*

Toynbee, Arnold J. *A Study of History.*

Valéry, Paul. "A Crisis of the Mind."

Wells, H. G. *The Outline of History.*

Anthologies

Aster, Sidney, ed. *Appeasement and All Souls: A Portrait with Documents, 1937–1939* (2005).

Crew, David F. *Hitler and the Nazis: A History in Documents* (2006).

Studies

Berend, Ivan T. *Decades of Crisis: Central and Eastern Europe before World War II* (2001).

Bosworth, R. J. B. *Mussolini's Italy: Life under the Fascist Dictatorship, 1915–1945* (2007).

Brendon, Piers. *The Dark Valley: A Panorama of the 1930s* (2009).

Caldwell, Bruce J. *Hayek's Challenge: An Intellectual Biography of F. A. Hayek* (2003).

Diepeveen, Leonard. *The Difficulties of Modernism* (2002).

Evans, Richard J. *The Coming of the Third Reich* (2004).

Evans, Richard J. *The Third Reich in Power, 1933–1939* (2005).

Fitzpatrick, Sheila. *Everyday Stalinism: Ordinary Life in Extraordinary Times—Soviet Russia in the 1930s* (2000).

Geifman, Anna. *Death Orders: The Vanguard of Modern Terrorism in Revolutionary Russia* (2010).

Gregor, A. James. *Marxism, Fascism, and Totalitarianism: Chapters in the Intellectual History of Radicalism* (2008).

Griffin, Roger. *Modernism and Fascism: The Sense of a Beginning under Mussolini and Hitler* (2011).

Hagedorn, Ann. *Savage Peace: Hope and Fear in America, 1919* (2007).

Hodgson, Keith. *Fighting Fascism: The British Left and the Rise of Fascism, 1919–39* (2010).

Hoffmann, David L. *Stalinist Values: The Cultural Norms of Soviet Modernity, 1917–1941* (2003).

Kennedy, David M. *Over Here: The First World War and America Society* (2004).

Kitchen, Martin. *Europe between the Wars: A Political History* (2006).

Lampe, John R. *Balkans into Southeastern Europe: A Century of War and Transition* (2006).

Lampe, John R., and Mark Mazower, eds. *Ideologies and National Identities: The Case of Twentieth-Century Southeastern Europe* (2004).

North, Michael. *Reading 1922: A Return to the Scene of the Modern* (2001).

Overy, Richard. *The Twilight Years: The Paradox of Britain between the Wars* (2009).

Paxton, Richard O. *The Anatomy of Fascism* (2005).

Pfannestiel, Todd J. *Rethinking the Red Scare: The Lusk Committee and New York's Crusade against Radicalism, 1919–1923* (2003).

Pine, Lisa. *Education in Nazi Germany* (2011).

Romero Salvadó, Francisco J. *The Spanish Civil War: Origins, Course, and Outcomes* (2005).

Steiner, Zara. *The Lights That Failed: European International History, 1919–1933* (2007).

Steiner, Zara. *The Triumph of the Dark: European International History, 1933–1939* (2011).

Thomas, Hugh. *The Spanish Civil War* (2001).

Tooze, Adam. *The Deluge: The Great War, America, and the Remaking of the Global Order, 1916–1931* (2014).

Tooze, Adam. *The Wages of Destruction: The Making and Breaking of the Nazi Economy* (2008).

Tubach, Frederic C. *German Voices: Life during Hitler's Third Reich* (2011).

Wapshott, Nicholas. *Keynes Hayek: The Clash That Defined Modern Economics* (2011).

Weitz, Eric D. *Weimar Germany: Promise and Tragedy* (2009).

Widdig, Bernd. *Culture and Inflation in Weimar Germany* (2001).

Worley, Matthew. *Oswald Mosley and the New Party* (2010).

For additional resources, including maps, primary sources, visuals, web links, and quizzes, please go to **www.oup.com/us/backman**.

"THIS WORLD CANNOT EXIST HALF SLAVE AND HALF FREE"

SACRIFICE FOR FREEDOM!

CHAPTER 26

The World at War (Part II)

1937–1945

Fifty to sixty million deaths. Adolf Hitler's invasion of Poland on September 1, 1939 inaugurated the war in Europe, and Japan's attack on the U.S. naval base at Pearl Harbor, Hawaii, on December 7, 1941, triggered war in the Pacific. World War II ended with the unconditional surrenders of Germany in May and Japan in August of 1945. More than 110 million soldiers participated; 27 million of them perished. Six million Jews, almost all of them civilians, were murdered in the Nazi concentration camps; another 20 to 25 million civilians from among all the other combatant nations died of starvation or exposure, in air raids, or by artillery shelling, or were deported to the death camps. In one way or another the war involved most of the nations on earth, and the great powers formed into two camps—the Allies (led by Britain, France, the Soviet Union, and the United States) and the Axis (Germany, Italy, and Japan, principally).

THE WORLD AT WAR, 1937–1945

Major clashes

Fight for Freedom A patriotic call to duty in wartime Britain (note the Anglican collar on the clergyman at left—already wholly in shadow), this poster was produced by the U.S. government. The threatening figure brandishing the whip is artfully drawn: he could be interpreted as either a Nazi German or a Stalinist Russian.

World War II nearly wiped out entire populations and entire cities. Its unparalleled atrocities sparked a determination to seek justice, however. Along with the atomic bomb, the postwar years saw trials that prosecuted the atrocities as war crimes and the recognition of international law in the United Nations. A replacement for the ineffective

League of Nations, the United Nations was created "to prevent succeeding generations from the scourge of war."

The largest, bloodiest, most destructive, and most expensive conflict in human history, World War II holds a special place in memory. To the people of Russia, where by far the greatest number of victims fell, it is called the "Great Patriotic War" to honor their extraordinary suffering. To them, the eastern front marked the center of the conflict, and the Battle for Stalingrad was the turning point of the entire war. Western Europe recalls instead the Nazi seizure of Holland, Belgium, and France; the Battle of Britain; the Normandy Invasion; the North African and Italian campaigns; and the final march on Berlin. In China, which remained apart from the broader conflict, it is the "War of Resistance" against Japan, whereas in Japan it is either the "Japan–China Incident" or simply the "China Incident." (Neither country ever issued a formal declaration of war.) Japanese historians long described the war against America and its allies as simply one facet of the "Greater East Asian War"—a broad independence movement that aimed to free East Asia of Western meddling. Americans speak of "World War II," but the phrase "the Good War" has also taken hold. That goodness lay, at least in nostalgic memories, in the moral clarity of America's involvement—as a conflict between obvious Good and obvious Evil. By whatever name the war is known, it left scars on the hearts and minds of all who participated in it (see Figure 26.1).

CHAPTER TIMELINE

1937	1938	1939	1940	1941

- 1937–1945 Second Sino-Japanese War
- 1938 Germany annexes Austria; Munich Conference
- 1939 Germany occupies Czech lands; German–Soviet Nonaggression Pact; Germany invades Poland; Britain and France declare war on Germany
- 1940 German army captures Paris; Japan signs formal alliance with Germany and Italy
- 1940–1941 Battle of Britain
- 1941 Germany invades Soviet Union; Japan attacks Pearl Harbor; United States enters war
- 1941–1945 Six million Jews killed in Nazi concentration camps

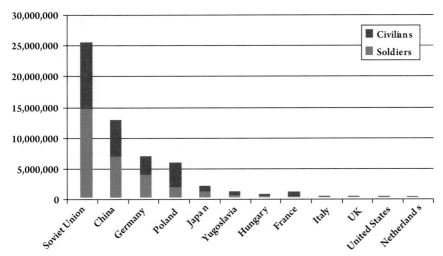

FIGURE 26.1   Deaths in World War II

THE WAR IN EUROPE

Unlike the start of World War I, no jubilant crowds greeted this conflict. Popular
sentiments were decidedly grim. After the West acquiesced at the Munich *Failure of*
Conference of 1938 (discussed in chapter 25) to Hitler's annexation of the *Appeasement*

1942   1943   1944   1945   1948

- 1942 Battle of Midway Island

- 1942–1943 Battle of Stalingrad

- 1944 D-Day (June 6): Allied forces land at Normandy

- 1945 Battle of Iwo Jima; fall of Berlin;
United States drops atomic bombs on
Hiroshima and Nagasaki; World War II ends;
United Nations established; Nuremberg and
Tokyo War Crimes Trials begin

- 1948 Universal
Declaration of
Human Rights;
creation of state of
Israel

Sudetenland from Czechoslovakia, few people shared British Prime Minister Neville Chamberlain's stated confidence in the policy of appeasement. Most believed that another international conflict was imminent, and the last six months before the war were filled with desperate strategic maneuvers. Britain and France, fearing the worst, promised to defend Greece, Poland, Romania, and Turkey in case of Nazi aggression. Hitler countered by forging the "Pact of Steel" with Fascist Italy in May 1939. In Moscow, meanwhile, Stalin was exasperated at the West's delay in protecting eastern Europe and so began private negotiations with Hitler. In a surprise nonaggression pact signed in August 1939, each side vowed not to attack the other and to remain neutral in the event of war elsewhere. And Stalin counted on that pact. He needed every last month and week of delay to replenish the officer corps that he had decimated with his brutal purges.

The news of the German–Russian pact stunned Europe and the United States, since the ideology of each nation was so opposed to the other. What the West did not know was that a secret clause in the agreement arranged for the two countries to divide the lands of Poland, Estonia, Latvia, and Lithuania. At some future date, their conquest was to be undertaken by either Germany or Russia—and that future arrived more quickly than even Hitler and Stalin may have guessed.

Blitzkrieg

The broad narrative of the war divides easily into three stages—early Nazi success after success, then decisive battles in Russia and against Italy, and finally Allied success in France and Germany. From 1939 to 1942 Germany quickly overran, in order, Poland, Denmark, Norway, Holland, Belgium, and France (see Map 26.1). The Nazis made the fullest possible use of Germany's advantages in technology and numbers to break through defensive barriers at speed. Their **Blitzkrieg** ("lightning war") strategies concentrated heavy but mobile firepower (tanks and aircraft especially) and rapid troop movement in small areas. Having split their opponents' forces, the Germans then rapidly advanced straight ahead, which forced the shattered defense forces to attempt to regroup against a fast-moving enemy.

Time and again, in the first three years of the war, Nazi strategies forced their opponents to capitulate before they ever had a chance to mount a countercampaign. In less than two months in 1940, before the French army could even muster, the Nazis raced through the Low Countries, circumvented the Maginot Line altogether, and, on June 14, marched into Paris. The French assembly voted to disband and to hand over power to the World War I war hero Marshal Philippe Pétain (1856–1951), who established an authoritarian government. On June 22 this new **Vichy regime** (named after the southern city Pétain chose for his capital) signed an armistice with Germany and pledged collaboration with the Nazi regime. Theoretically, Pétain's authority extended over all of France, but in reality the Vichy regime was confined to the south. As of June 1940, Germany not only

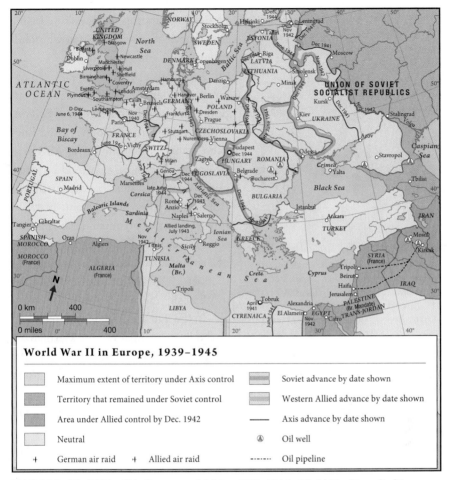

MAP 26.1 **World War II in Europe and Africa, 1939–1945**   World War II resulted in massive loss of life and destruction of property. Ultimately the Allies crushed the Axis powers by moving from east, west, and south to inflict a total defeat.

occupied western and northern France, but also—with its allies and satellites—held most of the continent. A jubilant Hitler, who arrived in Paris shortly after the armistice was signed, celebrated the crushing of an era established by the hated Versailles Treaty.

After the fall of France, Hitler hoped that Britain would accept Germany's domination of the continent and agree to a negotiated peace, but his hopes went unrealized. The failure of appeasement and the subsequent military disasters had thoroughly discredited Chamberlain, who left office in disgrace. The British parliament suspended party politics for the duration of the war, and power passed to an all-party coalition headed by Winston Churchill, the long-time leading critic

Hitler in Paris After the collapse of French defenses, the Nazi army seized control of France in a matter of a few weeks. Here a triumphant Hitler poses with Albert Speer (1905–1981), his Minister of Armaments and War Production, and Arno Breker (1900–1991), his favorite sculptor, before the Eiffel Tower.

of Britain's appeasement policy. In his first speech as prime minister, Churchill promised, "Victory—victory at all costs."

Faced with the British refusal to negotiate, Hitler ordered his General Staff to prepare for a land invasion of Britain. But placing German troops in the English Channel while the Royal Air Force still controlled the skies would be a certain military disaster. The destruction of Britain's air power had to come first. On July 10, German bomber raids on English southern coastal cities opened the **Battle of Britain**, a battle waged in the air and in the factories and that ended in Germany's first significant setback.

In the Battle of Britain—or the Blitz, as the British called it—the German air force (*Luftwaffe*) bombed monuments, public buildings, and industry. In response, Britain poured resources into its

Battle of Britain highly successful code-breaking group called Ultra, the further development of radar and air weaponry, and in outproducing Germany by 50 percent. By the fall of 1940, when the Germans finally gave up the effort to take Britain, the Royal Air Force had shrunk from approximately two thousand aircraft to five hundred, but Nazi losses had been even heavier.

War against Britain had never been one of Hitler's central goals, however.

Invasion of the Soviet Union His dreams of the Third Reich, a German empire that was to last a thousand years, centered on capture of the agricultural and industrial resources of the Soviet Union. But Hitler sought far more than resources. He envisioned war with the Soviet Union as an apocalyptic clash of Good versus Evil: the superior German Aryan race against the twin evils of the inferior Slavic race and "Judeo-Bolshevism." Thus his fateful decision to break the Nazi–Soviet Pact and attack the Soviet Union.

As early as July 1940, as the Battle of Britain began, Hitler ordered his military to plan a Soviet invasion. By December the plan was set: German troops were to attack the Soviet Union in April 1941. But they did not. Hitler postponed the invasion for two crucial months because the ambitions of an incompetent ally—Mussolini—threatened to undermine the economic base of the Nazi war machine.

Hoping to expand his Mediterranean empire, Mussolini ordered Italian troops into British imperial territories in North Africa in July 1940, followed by an invasion of Greece in October. But with a military budget one-tenth the size of

Germany's, outdated tanks and aircraft, and a limited industrial base, Italy was ill-equipped to fight. By the spring of 1941, the British army had pushed the Italians back into Libya while the Greeks mounted a strong resistance.

Thus, Hitler delayed the invasion of the Soviet Union while the German army took over for Mussolini in the Balkans and North Africa. In April 1941 German forces punched through Yugoslavian defenses. Greece came next. Meanwhile, in North Africa German troops recaptured all the territory taken by the British the previous year. By the summer of 1941, Hitler stood at the apogee of his power. But these victories came at a high price: the postponement of the German invasion of the Soviet Union from April to June.

At first, that postponement did not seem to matter. On June 22, 1941, the largest invading force the world had yet seen began to cross the Soviet borders. The campaign into Russia, called **Operation Barbarossa** (for the great twelfth-century Holy Roman emperor and German king Frederick Barbarossa), caught Stalin by surprise and progressed rapidly. Barbarossa was the largest single military action in Western history, involving 3 million German soldiers (75 percent of the entire Nazi army and 66 percent of its total air power), who went east against the nearly 5 million soldiers of the Red Army. Stalin's forces were already established in the half of Poland ceded to him by Hitler in 1939, and so the initial Blitzkrieg strikes occurred there. After breaking through the Russian ranks, the Germans pressed a three-pronged attack: to the northeast, against Leningrad (Saint Petersburg); due east, toward Moscow; and to the southeast, to Stalingrad (Volgograd). Each of the three campaigns ended in Nazi defeats. The Nazis reached Leningrad in September of 1941 but were unable to storm the city. Instead, a miserably protracted siege lasted more than two years, until January 1944, during which more than a million city dwellers died of starvation, cold, and disease. German forces dropped more than 100,000 bombs and 200,000 artillery shells on the city, to no avail. The Nazis themselves incurred extraordinarily high casualties because they were exposed to brutal winters for which they were unprepared and poorly resupplied. The Battle for Moscow, from October 1941 to January 1942, ended with a decisive Russian victory, however, as did the Battle for Stalingrad, from August 1942 to February 1943 (see Map 26.1).

Matters worsened for the Germans quickly thereafter. The Allies in the west moved steadily through North Africa and turned north, invading Sicily and the Italian mainland in the late summer of 1943. Stalin had wanted the Allies to relieve the pressure on Russia by opening a second front in the west, but Churchill persuaded President Roosevelt that attacking "the soft underbelly of Europe" first made better sense strategically, by removing Italian armies from the conflict and gradually encircling German forces. When the Allies seized control of Sicily, the Fascist government in Rome toppled Mussolini and imprisoned him, although he quickly escaped, with German help, and became leader of the small "Italian Social Republic," a German client regime in northern Italy. In late April 1945, with total defeat looming, Mussolini and his mistress, Clara Petacci, tried to flee to neutral Switzerland, only to be captured and executed near Lake Como by Italian partisans. Their bodies were then taken to Milan and proudly put on public display.

After the government in Rome overthrew Mussolini, it broke with the Axis and joined the Allied side, which set the stage for the third and final act of the war in Europe. It began with the Allied invasion of Normandy on D-Day, June 6, 1944.

Invasion of Normandy The Nazis had long anticipated an Allied invasion but were surprised at the precise location and date when it did finally come. Nevertheless, their defenses were strong. An Allied force of 130,000 men, made up primarily of U.S. and British soldiers, landed on the beaches, whereas another 20,000 parachuted far behind the Nazi defenses to cut off reinforcements. Although enormously costly in lives, the D-Day landing proved a huge success, and that year Allied forces liberated most of Holland (the densely populated northern part remained under German occupation until May 1945), Belgium, and France, while their troops in Italy pressed continually northward.

Gradually, as 1945 began, Allied armies from the west and the south and Russian forces moving in rapidly from the east closed in on Germany and then on Berlin itself. As the Allied vice tightened, Hitler refused to spare the German people by surrendering. Instead, he committed suicide with his wife, Eva Braun, in their Berlin bomb shelter. The Soviet army took Berlin in April. On May 7, 1945, Germany surrendered unconditionally.

D-Day   Allied troops land on the beach at Normandy on D-Day, June 6, 1944. The invasion proved a turning point in the war.

WAR IN THE PACIFIC

The war in the Pacific began on December 7, 1941, when Japan attacked the U.S. naval base at Pearl Harbor in Hawaii. Within a few hours, the U.S. Pacific fleet lay gutted. Roosevelt immediately summoned the U.S. Congress to declare war on Japan.

Tensions between the two countries had been rising for at least twenty years before the Pearl Harbor attack, however. Japan had long feared domination from *The Road* the mainland, from China or Korea, and the coal-powered American maritime *to War* rivals added a new threat. Only by rapid industrialization, and the means to deliver its manufactures to world markets, could Japan feel protected. But the islands of Japan have little in the way of mineral ores—which forced them to look for outside sources of raw materials, fuel to process and ship them, and secure markets in which to sell them.

Japan's imperialist adventures began, as we saw in chapter 23, in 1904–1905 with the Russo-Japanese War. This war had been fought principally for control of the island of Sakhalin off the coast of Russia, where sizeable deposits of oil were known to exist. In 1910 Japan forcibly annexed Korea too, which had much-needed natural resources and a large population that could serve as a captive market. When World War I broke out, Japan formed an alliance with Britain and laid claim to Germany's East Asian and Pacific Island colonies—which it duly received. Japanese sailors also fought briefly in the Great War in the Mediterranean, against the Ottomans. By this point Japan was fully in the grip of militarism, every bit equal to that of Europe prior to 1914. When the Great Depression hit in 1929, it combined with population growth—from about 45 million in 1900 to 65 million in 1930—to highlight the fundamental fact that Japan alone among developed nations could not feed itself. (Japan today remains the only industrialized country that depends on imported food for survival.)

Thus, the military took an even more active role in government, touting itself as the only real solution to the economic problem. Its solutions in the 1930s focused on stirring up trouble in China to justify direct military action (see Map 26.2). For the generation who fought in World War II, imperial might and the martial spirit that sustained it were the best guarantors of prosperity and proof of the people's superior nature.

Two "incidents" provided all the justification Japan needed. In September 1931 the Japanese staged a supposed Chinese terrorist attack on the South Manchurian Railway, which was then under lease to Japan. They placed a small bomb a short distance from a little-used piece of track and detonated it. The explosion caused only minor damage, but it attracted the attention of nearby Chinese soldiers, who hurried to investigate. The sudden "onslaught" of Chinese forces provided a pretext for Japanese action—and the seizure of all of Manchuria within five months

MAP 26.2   The Japanese in China, 1931–1941   Japanese expansion in the 1930s was intended to cap the earlier annexation of Taiwan and Korea and lead to the conquest of China, bringing the island nation enormous new territory and resources.

of the faked terrorist attack.[1] The United States condemned Japan's action—known variously as the Mukden Incident or the Manchurian Incident—and vowed never to recognize any government established in Manchuria by Tokyo.

The second incident—the Marco Polo Bridge Incident—triggered the start of the Second Sino-Japanese War (1937–1945) and was a murkier affair. It occurred in July 1937 at the Marco Polo Bridge (the Lugou Bridge in Chinese, or Roku in Japanese), a long stone bridge over a tributary of the Hai River located a dozen miles southwest of Beijing. The bridge formed part of the rail line that linked Beijing with the rest of the province and was thus of great strategic importance. The Chinese government, as a courtesy, had long allowed any nation that had trade legations in Beijing to place armed guards along this rail line. These guards had the right to perform occasional maneuvers—but Japan was the only country actually to do so. Either by plan or by accident, a squad of Japanese

---

[1]   An exhibit in the Yushukan Military and War Museum in Tokyo still blames the 1931 Manchurian Railway bombing on Chinese militias.

soldiers performed night maneuvers without informing local Chinese officials as they were supposed to do. One of the Japanese soldiers disappeared, and when Chinese officials began to search for him and to investigate the matter, Japan claimed that a cover-up conspiracy was under way and used this as a pretext for a full-scale invasion of Beijing and the entire province. When the United States condemned the aggression, announced economic sanctions, and ultimately cut off oil and steel to Japan, the Japanese military began the preparations that led ultimately to the attack on Pearl Harbor.

As with the war in Europe, the war in the Pacific falls neatly into three stages. The years from 1937 to 1941 mark the first stage, when Japan imposed its will throughout *The* eastern and southeastern Asia, snatching up territories like Singapore and the Dutch *Course* East Indies and campaigning aggressively in China. The second stage consists of the *of the War* start of the war with the United States in 1941 to the **Battle of Midway** in 1942. Midway Island lay roughly 1,500 miles west of Hawaii; although small, it had great strategic value because of its location midway between Hawaii and Japan. When Japan attempted a joint naval land and air assault on it, a smaller American force successfully fended off the attackers—and turned the tide of the war (see Map 26.3).

The final stage ran from 1942 to the Japanese surrender in 1945, as the Allies pressed in on the Japanese Empire from all sides. A ferocious battle to take the garrison island of Iwo Jima in February–March 1945 was the bloodiest single episode in a campaign that featured many. Iwo Jima lay 750 miles due south of Tokyo and was the site of strategic airfields that the Japanese used to resist American air attacks on Japan itself. Of the roughly eighteen thousand soldiers stationed there, only two hundred survived and were captured; the rest perished in the assault. The United States attacked with a force of seventy thousand, nearly seven thousand of whom perished; another twenty thousand were wounded. Overall, it was a heavier U.S. toll than in the invasion of Normandy on D-Day.

Devastation continued with the American decision to drop atomic bombs on Hiroshima and Nagasaki on August 6 and 9, killing 140,000 people instantly, with tens of thousands later dying from wounds, burns, and other bomb-related afflictions. Military hardliners wanted to continue the war, but on August 15, 1945, the Japanese government surrendered.

ATOMIC FISSURES

Harry S. Truman, U.S. president from 1945 to 1952, gave the orders to drop the atomic bomb on Hiroshima and Nagasaki. As Franklin Roosevelt's vice presi- *The U.S.* dent, he had succeeded to the presidency on April 12, the day Roosevelt died after *Decision* months of declining health. Four months later, Truman faced making a decision *to Bomb* about a program unknown to him before he took the oath of office. *Japan*

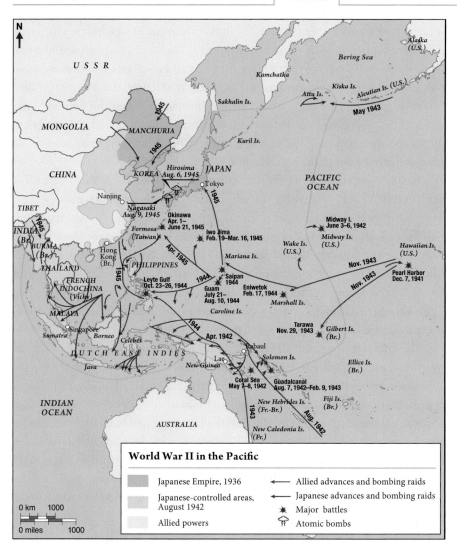

MAP 26.3   **World War II in the Pacific**   The "Europe first" strategy of the Allies permitted Japan a comparatively free hand in the Pacific. Japan's victories were short-lived, however, despite the determined efforts of its civilians and military to sacrifice everything for victory. The Japanese strategy of fighting to the last person instead of surrendering when a loss was in sight was one factor in President Truman's decision to drop the atomic bomb in August 1945.

Without unconditional surrender, Truman warned, Japan would face "the inevitable and complete destruction of [its] armed forces and just as inevitably the utter devastation of the Japanese homeland." The Americans had long been at work on a weapon of unparalleled destructiveness. The **Manhattan Project**, as the secret program to develop an atomic bomb was known, had begun in 1939 at the Los Alamos National Laboratory in New Mexico under the scientific direction of J. Robert Oppenheimer (1904–1967). It was generally and correctly assumed that

Nazi Germany was trying to develop atomic weapons as well. Although Hitler would hardly have kept the Japanese emperor Hirohito (r. 1926–1989) informed of the Nazis' progress, Japan six years later must have suspected that the United States might be attempting something of dramatic scale. After all, there were nuclear physicists in Japan who had undertaken their graduate studies in the United States with some of the very scientists involved in the Manhattan Project.

Hiroshima and Nagasaki were important but not vital hubs of industry, shipping, and military communications, and neither had been the site of any fighting or bombing prior to that August. The Americans wanted "untouched" targets, the better to assess the effectiveness of their new weapons. According to the *U.S. Strategic Bombing Survey*, a report on the bombs' effectiveness:

> The morning of 6 August 1945 began bright and clear. At about 0700 [7:00 A.M.]
>
> there was an air-raid alarm and a few planes appeared over the city. Many people within the city went to prepared air-raid shelters, but since alarms were heard almost every day the general population did not seem to have been greatly concerned....
>
> After the all-clear sounded, persons began emerging from air-raid shelters and within the next few minutes the city began to resume its usual mode of life for that time of day. It is related by some survivors that they had watched planes fly over the city. At about 0815 there was a blinding flash. Some described it as brighter than the sun, others likened it to a magnesium flash. Following the flash there was a blast of heat and wind. The large majority of people within 3,000 feet of Ground Zero were killed immediately. Within a radius of about 7,000 feet almost every Japanese house collapsed. Beyond this range and up to 15,000–20,000 feet many of them collapsed and others received serious structural damage. Persons in the open were burned on exposed surfaces, and within 3,000–5,000 feet many were burned to death while other received severe burns through their clothes. In many instances clothing burst into spontaneous flame and had to be beaten out. Thousands of people were pinned beneath collapsed buildings or injured by flying debris. . . . The people appeared stunned by the catastrophe and rushed about as jungle animals suddenly released from a cage. . . . Pandemonium reigned as the uninjured and the slightly injured fled the city in fearful panic.

Hiroshima's population then stood at around 350,000 and Nagasaki's around 250,000. The bombs killed about 20 percent of each city's population instantly and turned their cityscapes instantly into moonscapes. Most of the dead were

Mushroom Cloud over Nagasaki Mushroom-shaped clouds have become associated with nuclear explosions, even though they are commonly produced by gunpowder-based explosions as well. This photo shows the frightening cloud produced by the atomic bomb dropped on Nagasaki, Japan, on August 9, 1945. The original target was the city of Kokura (now absorbed into the city of Kitakyushu), but heavy cloud cover there forced the crew to opt for Nagasaki instead. Within one second of the bomb's detonation, tens of thousands of people were dead.

killed either by the force of the explosion or from "flash burns" caused by the tremendous heat it generated, reaching 7,000°F (3,900°C). Within five years of the bombings, an equal number of people died from the effects of radiation as had died in the explosions themselves—a total of perhaps 250,000—and many tens of thousands more suffered from radiation wounds and diseases for decades to come.

Why not give Japan an explicit warning, or even a preview by detonating the bomb on a deserted Pacific island? Was it truly necessary to incinerate seventy thousand people in Hiroshima and another forty thousand in Nagasaki, most of them civilians? As recalled by Henry Stimson (1867–1950), Truman's Secretary of War:

> We carefully considered such alternatives as a detailed advance warning, or a demonstration, in some uninhabited area. But both of these suggestions were discarded as impractical. They were not regarded as likely to be effective in compelling a surrender of Japan, and both of them would involve risks. Even the New Mexico test did not give final proof that any given bomb was certain to explode when dropped from an airplane. Quite apart from the generally unfamiliar nature of atomic explosives, there was the whole problem of exploding a bomb at a predetermined height in the air by a complicated mechanism which could not be tested in New Mexico. Nothing would have been more damaging to our effort to obtain Japan's surrender than a warning or a demonstration followed by a dud. . . . Furthermore, we had no bombs to waste. ("The Decision to Use the Atomic Bomb," *Harper's Magazine*, February 1947)

Stimson's matter-of-fact tone masks the complexities of the issue. Japan had expressed a possible willingness to surrender in the spring of that year and passed word to Joseph Stalin, who had offered to serve as intermediary with the Americans. But Stalin never forwarded the Japanese offer to Washington, in the hope that by prolonging the struggle in the Pacific, he might strengthen his own hand in East

Asia. In fact, he was already hurriedly sending his troops, recently relieved of battle in Europe after the Nazi surrender, across the massive Russian countrywide into Japanese-controlled Manchuria. On August 8, only two days after the bombing of Hiroshima, 1.5 million Soviet troops invaded Manchuria and presumably would have continued into Japan itself. The prospect of Stalin replacing imperial Japan as the supreme lord of eastern Asia was untenable to the United States, which proceeded to drop their second atomic bomb on Nagasaki the very next day—as much a warning shot across Stalin's bow as a final blow against Emperor Hirohito.

Arguments that the bombings were necessary to spare the millions of lives that would have been lost in a conventional attack cannot be wholly dismissed, but neither can they be taken at face value. There is no way of knowing for certain what would have happened had America simply continued its conventional advance. The question therefore changes. America could certainly have defeated Japan without the atomic bombs—but could it have reached Tokyo before Stalin's troops did? By August 1945, it was clear that the Russians had no intention of withdrawing from eastern Europe. Were the Allies ready to accept a Stalin also in control of East Asia?

Except for the iconic images of the mushroom clouds over the two cities, photos and film of the devastation were strictly controlled or suppressed altogether. America may have wished to avoid comparison with images then circulating of the Nazi death camps. Photos of mangled, bloodied, and charred bodies, the government feared, might raise doubts about the legitimacy of American actions precisely when the country faced the possibility of continuing the war against the Communist regime.

Some scientists in Russia, in fact, had been engaged in nuclear research since the early 1930s, but Stalin's government was intensely focused on practical industrial development, so little of this "pure research" was therefore given sufficient funding or encouragement. What changed Stalin's mind was a letter in 1942 from a Russian physicist that pointed out a singular fact: no American, British, or German physicist had published any research on nuclear fission in scientific journals since 1939. Clearly something was up. Why else the sudden and total silence from the most brilliant scientists in the West? Stalin began to give priority to nuclear research in Russia, although progress was slow until 1945, when Russian troops reached Berlin and started transporting truckloads of captured German physicists back to Moscow.[2]

The Spread of Nuclear Power

---

2   A German-born British physicist named Klaus Fuchs (1911–1988), whose hatred of Nazism inspired him to join the British Communist Party in 1933, began passing sensitive scientific material to Russia as early as August 1941. An early member of the British team investigating the building of an atomic bomb, he eventually was welcomed into the Manhattan Project in 1943. Transferring to Los Alamos itself in 1944, Fuchs kept Stalin's scientists informed of the general developments in atomic research. His espionage continued until 1949. He was tried by the British in 1950 and sentenced to fourteen years in prison. Released in 1959, Fuchs emigrated to Communist East Germany and continued his nuclear research until his death.

With the help of these new recruits, the Soviet Union developed its first atomic bomb in 1949. Britain became an atomic power in 1952 and France in 1960. As the postwar tensions between the West and the USSR rose higher and higher, they did so in a frightening new context of potential mass annihilation.

WOMEN IN, AND AGAINST, FASCISM

By the 1930s, Western women had secured political equality and the right to vote. They found the challenge of *social* equality more stubborn, however, despite the appearance, as we saw in chapter 25, of major female scientific, literary, and artistic talents. The Depression and the totalitarian threat further pressed most women back into the home. Yet when war came, women were in the thick of it.

Women in Totalitarian Regimes   Nazi ideology, based on a somewhat mythical traditionalism, had made women's place in society clear: it emphasized women's duty to produce more Aryan children to offset the growth of Jewish and Slavic peoples. As Hitler put it in a speech to the Nazi Women's League in September 1934:

> The catchphrase "Emancipation for Women!" was coined by Jewish intellectuals, who also shaped the whole of the so-called women's movement. But surely no German woman needs emancipation in an era as full of promise as our own.

Fighting Fascism on the Farm   This Russian poster from 1942, with the words "A Tractor in the Field Is Worth a Tank in Battle," proclaims the importance of farm work and of women workers. The poster's calm, reassuring image ignores the wartime devastation that Hitler's armies were then wreaking in Russia.

Remilitarization and the revival of heavy industry under the Nazis put men back to work. As in Fascist Spain, however, women were essentially driven from the workplace. (Women did, however, supply much of the clerical and lower administrative staff of the regime.) Italy differed from its totalitarian allies. There, women not only had owned and run businesses and estates, but also many worked in factories and served in the civil service. Expectations about their domestic roles did not alter much, but a public life was widely considered acceptable as well.

Communist Russia experienced the most dramatic change in women's roles, since Marxist ideology insisted on a radical equality of gender roles. Women worked in factories, toiled on the land, ran offices, and served as bureaucrats, at least on the lower levels. In fact, they served on something like an equal level with men—although also equal to men in their lack of freedom. To accelerate industrial production, Stalin outlawed abortion in 1936 and increased state aid to families with young children, so that women could afford to remain in the workplace. When war finally broke out, women in Russia saw active combat. By 1940 women made up almost half of the workforce in Russia. Just over 100,000 women were decorated for valor after service in artillery and tank units or in the signal corps by the end of the war.

In Western Europe a more complex picture emerged. The economic misery *Women* of the 1930s undermined many of the political gains made by women after 1918, *in Western* since government revenue had declined so precipitously. In Britain, for example, *Europe* unemployment benefits were withheld from all women who lost their positions as domestic staff—as cooks, maids, and housecleaners—and from women who worked out of their own homes as seamstresses, launderers, or typists. Consider a woman who had lost a clerical or manufacturing job and was compelled to take a position in domestic service at dramatically reduced pay. If she accepted the job, she became ineligible for unemployment insurance if she later lost the domestic position; but if she declined the job, she was ineligible for state help since she was considered to be not actively seeking work. As conditions worsened, married women who lost their jobs were denied unemployment payments as well, whether their husbands were working or not. In Austria, government statistics on unemployment regularly consisted only of men who were out of work, since women were regarded as workers but not as employees. And that, too, ate into welfare payments and other social benefits.

Although Mussolini boasted that Fascism had created a utopia, Italian women in the 1930s experienced unending want, oppression, and despair. Most trade unions were broken, and labor strikes were outlawed—which made it difficult for any workers, much less women, to show discontent. Government funding for education, health programs, and unemployment faced regular cuts to make room for military expenditures. The Italian military made up more than 30 percent of government costs in the 1930s and approached 40 percent when war finally came. As conditions worsened, birthrates fell. Women either put off marriage or did what they could to avoid pregnancy (contraception was forbidden). The Italian birthrate fell 30 percent between 1911 and 1941, and this came amid a decline in overall population thanks to heavy emigration.

Women had featured prominently in the pacifist campaigns of the 1930s. Taking up where the antiwar groups of World War I had left off, many women's *Women* groups that had formed to pursue suffrage turned to the cause of avoiding war. *against* The Women's International League for Peace and Freedom convened for the first *War* time in the Netherlands, in The Hague, in the spring of 1915; it later moved its headquarters to Geneva, Switzerland, where it still resides. Its founders were an American, Jane Addams (1860–1935); two Germans, Anita Augsburg (1857–1943) and Lida Heymann (1868–1943); and the Dutch physician and reformer, Dr. Aletta Jacobs (1854–1929).[3] The Women's International League for Peace and Freedom campaigned for equal rights for all citizens, economic justice, and greater understanding and empathy between peoples.

Members were divided, sometimes passionately, on whether socialism had to be a part of the movement for peace and freedom—but the real crisis confronting it was Fascism. To work tirelessly for peace and fairness in the long term is one thing. What should one do, however, when aggressive, violent evil has burst on the scene? Some activists and writers formed a new group, the Women's Congress against War and Fascism. Founded in Paris in 1934, it advocated the use of force as a last resort against international Fascism. Given the general popularity of appeasement, however, anti-Fascist groups like the Women's Congress against War and Fascism came under suspicion of possible connections with Communism.

The decade's most famous statement in favor of pacifism was *Three Guineas* (1938) by Virginia Woolf. Woolf was then at the height of her fame as a novelist and had long been active in, and publicly associated with, women's issues. The book offers three essays, each written in the form of a letter responding to a solicitation for a financial contribution to a social cause. The first cause is a drive to enlarge and refurbish a women's college at Cambridge University; the second, to help professional women advance in their careers; and the third, "to prevent war by protecting culture and intellectual liberty." The third essay, which is as long as the first two combined, is not only Woolf's statement of radical pacifism but also an attempt to decode the root cause of all war. She sees war as the extreme expression of a uniquely male desire for aggression. To offer direct resistance to Fascism is simply to extend the male need to dominate, to beat down, to control, and to rule.

Changing Roles for Women

World War I had been chiefly a soldier's war. At least along the western front, only a small number of British, French, German, and Italian women witnessed any fighting or were direct casualties of it, although millions of them suffered the loss of loved ones. But World War II was different. The battlefronts were too numerous and too mobile, and air assaults like the London Blitz or the Allies' firebombing of Dresden respected neither gender nor age. No matter which side they were on and whether they supported the war or not, women were involved from start to finish.

Britain called its women to active service almost immediately after fighting began in 1939, requiring every woman aged eighteen to fifty to register either for

---

[3]   Jane Addams became the first American to win the Nobel Peace Prize in 1931. Another American leader of the Women's International League for Peace and Freedom, Emily Greene Balch (1867–1961), received the prize in 1946.

military or for civil service. By 1941, as soon as the Blitz was over, unmarried British women aged twenty to thirty were drafted directly into one of the noncombat units. In the countryside, women were called into the "Land Army" to maintain food production; in the cities somewhere between 80 and 90 percent of all adult females worked either in industry or directly in the war effort. They served as clerks, radio operators, drivers, warehouse and shipping personnel, instructors, nurses, or searchlight handlers. In Italy, women served as nurses and physicians, teachers, and military staff. France, however, whether Occupied or Vichy, kept women in traditional household roles as much as possible.

American women probably made the greatest social and economic gains during the war years. Women filled factories, offices, the professions, and schools in record numbers in the 1940s. One area of particular significance was journalism. Women had long worked in the U.S. news industry, whether print or radio, but usually in behind-the-scenes positions like clerks, production assistants, and general staff; the Women's National Press Club had

Rosie the Riveter   More than eighteen million women worked fulltime in the United States during World War II in farming, manufacturing, shipping, and communications. The popular figure of "Rosie the Riveter" came to symbolize these women and to honor their efforts. (The name first appeared in a popular song in 1942.) It has been argued that the experience of so many millions of women working together regardless of differences of race helped to lay the foundation for the postwar civil rights movement.

formed as early as 1919. When female correspondents began losing their jobs during the Great Depression, Eleanor Roosevelt organized weekly press conferences to which only women journalists were invited. The practice sent out a symbolic message and preserved at least a few dozen jobs for women in Washington. When the war came, nearly 150 women journalists became accredited war correspondents and photographers. They reported from foreign battlefields, military bases and ships, hospitals and concentration camps across Europe and East Asia.

Dorothy Thompson   Dorothy Thompson (1893–1961) was a leading journalist in the 1930s and 1940s, prominent both in print and on radio. *Time* magazine in 1939 described her as the second most influential woman in the country, following Eleanor Roosevelt. After reporting on the suffragist and Zionist movements in the 1920s, she became the Berlin bureau chief for the *New York Post* in 1927, where she covered the rise of Nazism. In 1934, she was the first U.S. journalist to be expelled from Germany by the new Nazi government.

Women received only 50–75 percent of the pay men earned for the same work. It did not matter whether they worked in offices, schools, factories, the military, journalism, hospitals, or scientific labs. It did not matter whether they worked alongside men or in place of men who had entered the military. They were also largely expected, and even forced, to give up employment after 1945, as men returned from war. Many of women's gains disappeared after the war ended, setting the stage for the domestic era of the 1950s. Yet women in every country contributed mightily to the war effort—and just as much to the effort to promote peace.

ATROCITIES AND HOLOCAUST

All wars have their atrocities, but technology has made modern warfare particularly savage. From the introduction of gunpowder weapons and the creation of mass armies, the frequency and scale of massacres in wartime have increased dramatically. The mere pulling of a trigger can produce carnage to equal that at defining battles like Thermopylae, Hastings, and Lepanto. For one generation, World War I seemed the summit of human horror; but airplanes and armored vehicles came into wide use only toward the end of that conflict, and World War II began with even more destructive weapons. Ironically, interwar recovery efforts made those weapons possible, thanks to the heavy investment in industry. The roll call of massacre sites is a long one: Auschwitz, Babi Yar, Dresden, Hiroshima, Katyn, Manila, Nagasaki, Nanking, Novi Sad, Port Arthur, and Treuenbrietzen are simply the best-known episodes. We know as much as we do about the atrocities in part because the Nazis, confident of their ultimate victory and certain of the morality of their actions against "inferior peoples," kept meticulous film and documentary archives of their own activities and in part, too, because the Allies insisted on international tribunals for investigating and prosecuting war crimes.

T-4 Project Massacres were only part of the heartless savagery of the war. Another was the Nazis' program to cleanse the gene pool of the Aryan race by euthanasia. From the start of Hitler's rule in 1933, the Nazis had forcibly sterilized thousands of "undesirables"—meaning individuals with severe physical or mental handicaps. But from 1939 on, the cost of the surgical procedures was considered too great, and so the regime decided to switch to quick "mercy-killings." Known as the *T-4 Project*—from the address of its administrative center in Berlin, No. 4 Tiergartenstrasse—this campaign performed at least 200,000 chemical executions. Officially closed in 1941, the T-4 Project operated unofficially almost to the end of the war. Hitler recruited physicians, engineers, chemists, and administrative personnel with great care to ensure that their ideological zeal matched their technical expertise. His chancellors Philipp Bouhler (1899–1945) and Viktor Brack (1904–1948) served as administrative heads of the project, and his personal physician, Karl

Brandt (1904–1948), oversaw the review, selection, and disposal of the victims. In the end, the Nazis' official T-4 records report that some 70,000 men, women, and children were put to death in a half-dozen sites built especially for the program; in the Nuremberg trials that followed the war, evidence of an additional 150,000 victims emerged. Initially, the victims were killed by lethal injections—but the process took too long and the poisons became too costly once the war began, so Brandt recommended custom-designed gas chambers instead. Bouhler was arrested at the war's end but committed suicide before he could be tried; Brandt and Brack were tried, convicted, and executed for crimes against humanity.

T-4 was prologue to a still greater tragedy—the systematic murder of 6 million Jews, the **Holocaust**, or *Shoah* (Hebrew for "catastrophe"). Nazi hatred of the Jews was fanatical, but unlike other anti-Semitic episodes in Western history, the war on the Jews had primarily a racial rather than a religious basis. The Jews, it was feared, polluted the Aryan race. First, their mere presence in Europe fouled the atmosphere and corrupted the culture; second, by intermarriage they weakened the racial purity of the Germanic people; and third, their supposed championing of both the hated ideologies of Communism and untrammeled capitalism gave them a dangerous degree of control over the material lives of the people. Hitler had made it clear in *Mein Kampf* what he intended to do about the Jewish problem, if he ever had the chance. "We must free ourselves from the forces that now control our public life.... Our first objective must be to wipe out Jewish society as it currently exists."

The Holocaust

The Jewish population of prewar Germany had been roughly 500,000; another 200,000 were added when Hitler annexed Austria. Just over half of these had fled the Nazis before the start of the war. When Hitler swept into Poland, however, some 2 million more Jews came under his control, and the increased numbers added to the frenzy of Nazi hatred. The solution to the Jewish problem, he concluded, was to ship Jews to concentration camps where they could be forced to labor on behalf of the Germans. At the infamous Wannsee Conference (named for the Berlin suburb in which it was held) in January 1942, a committee of senior Nazi officials endorsed a protocol that called explicitly for the extermination of the Jews in Europe—the so-called Final Solution. The conference lasted only ninety minutes.

A report written by two escapees from the Auschwitz–Birkenau extermination camp complex, Alfred Wetzler (1918–1988) and Rudolf Vrba (1924–2006), describes the scene that met them when they arrived at Birkenau in early 1942:

> By the middle of May a total of four Jewish male transports had reached Birkenau from Slovakia. All received the same treatment as ourselves. From the first and second transports, 120 of us were sent to Auschwitz on orders of the Auschwitz camp command, which had asked for doctors, dentists, university students, and professional administrators

Warsaw Ghetto Uprising   In 1943, after five months of Jewish resistance, Nazi soldiers brutally put down the rebellion in Warsaw's ghetto. This photograph, one of the most famous of World War II era images, appeared in the official report on the uprising submitted to Heinrich Himmler (head of the Nazi *Schutzstaffel*, or SS). The identity and fate of the small boy in front have never been confirmed.

and clerks. After one week at Auschwitz 18 doctors and nurses, as well as three clerks, were selected from the 120 professionals. The doctors were assigned to the Auschwitz hospital and the three clerks, including myself, were sent back to Birkenau. Two of my companions, . . . both of whom have since died, went to the Slovak block. I went to the French block, where we were given administrative work. The remaining 99 persons were sent to work in the Auschwitz quarry, where they perished within a short time.

Shortly afterwards a so-called hospital was established in one of the buildings. This was the notorious Block No. 7. I was assigned there as head-nurse at first; later I became the manager. . . . This hospital was nothing other than an assembly point for those awaiting death. All prisoners unable to work were sent here. Naturally, there could be no question of medical treatment or nursing. Every day about 150 people died and their corpses were sent to the Auschwitz crematorium.

At the same time the so-called "selection" was started. The number of prisoners who were to be gassed and their bodies burned was determined twice weekly, on Monday and Thursday, by the camp doctor. Selectees were loaded on a truck and taken to the birchwood. Those who reached there alive were gassed in the big barrack built for the purpose and located next to the hole for burning bodies, and then were cremated in that hole. Approximately 2,000 from Block No. 7 died each week, of which about 1,200 deaths resulted from "natural causes" and about 800 from "selection." Death reports on those dying from natural causes were made out and sent to camp HQ at Orianenburg. Selectees were marked up in a book labeled "Special Treatment." I was manager of Block No. 7 until 15 January 1943, during which time I could observe what was going on. About 50,000 prisoners were destroyed during that period, either from "natural causes" or through "selections."

This report, quoted here in its official English translation for the courts, was among the most valuable pieces of evidence presented at the Nuremberg Trials.

The Nazis killed Jews everywhere they found them, but six camps, all located in Poland, formed the main sites of industrialized murder: Auschwitz–Birkenau, Belzec, Chelmno, Majdanek, Sobibor, and Treblinka (see Map 26.4). Those Jews deemed fit

MAP 26.4   Nazi Concentration Camps, 1941–1945   This map shows the major concentration camps in Europe, but the entire continent was dotted with thousands of lesser camps to which the victims of Nazism were transported. Many of these camps served as way stations on the route to ultimate extermination.

Auschwitz-Birkenau   Jewish children gather in this haunting image of the death camp.

for labor received temporary reprieves and were set to work. The rest faced quick annihilation in gas chambers, followed by cremation in special ovens built for the purpose.

For a time, the English language failed before the scale of the evil; a new word was needed for a crime of this magnitude. Fittingly, a Polish Jew, Raphael Lemkin, coined the term **genocide** in 1944. Lemkin (1900–1959) had been a public prosecutor in prewar Poland, and in 1939 he joined the army to fight against the Nazis. Wounded in battle, he escaped to Sweden and eventually to America, where he subsequently taught law at Duke, Yale, and Rutgers universities. He served as an adviser to Robert H. Jackson, the U.S. Supreme Court judge who later served as chief counsel at the Nuremberg Trials.

Six million Jews died in the Holocaust—the great majority in a single eighteen-month spasm of psychotic violence from late 1942 to mid-1944. By the time it ended, when advancing Russian and Allied troops closed in on Germany, the Jewish societies of Austria, Germany, Lithuania, the Netherlands, Poland, Romania, and the Ukraine had been all but annihilated.

Jews were not the only victims of the Nazi's industrialized murder scheme. Somewhere between 2 million and 3 million Russian prisoners of war died in the camps, as did 3 million Polish Gentiles who had resisted Nazi power or impeded the Germans' roundup of Jews. Other victims included homosexuals, the physically disabled, the Roma (Gypsies), Freemasons, and Jehovah's Witnesses; this last group was persecuted less for their religious beliefs than for their refusal to serve in the German army (see Table 26.1).

The Nazis and Japanese were not the only participants to commit atrocities. In May 1941 Croatian members of a Fascist militia group massacred 260 Serbs in the village of Glina by driving them into a local church, which they then set ablaze. British guards at the "London Cage" (a prisoner-of-war camp established in the Kensington Palace Gardens by British Intelligence) repeatedly beat, waterboarded, and otherwise tortured the inmates held there in 1943. French Resistance fighters stormed the prisoner-of-war camp at St.-Julien-de-Crempse in September 1944 and executed the seventeen German soldiers held there. The Russian troops who entered the city of Vienna in early 1945, for example, raped as many as 87,000 women in only three weeks. US navy personnel, acting under orders, tortured eight surviving crewmen of a sunken German U-boat in April 1945.

TABLE 26.1   **Victims of the Nazi Death Camps (figures are approximate)**

Jews	6,000,000
Soviet POWs	2,000,000–3,000,000
Poles	2,000,000
Roma (Gypsies)	350,000
The disabled	250,000
Freemasons	120,000
Homosexuals	15,000
Jehovah's Witnesses	4,000

Four million is the rough tally of Chinese troops killed while fighting Japan during the 1937–1945 war, although the figure rises as high as 20–22 million *Rape* when one factors in civilian casualties. The most notorious atrocity in this Second *of Nanjing* Sino-Japanese War was the **Rape of Nanjing**. (The First Sino-Japanese War had occurred 1894–1895.) In the weeks following the Marco Polo Bridge Incident (July 1937), a large force of 150,000 Japanese soldiers advanced on Nanjing, then the capital of China. Accounts of what happened differ—and the Japanese either destroyed or removed their records on the affair—as American forces drew closer to Tokyo in 1945. Enough evidence, however, survives to make it clear that

The Rape of Nanjing   In just six weeks, after taking the then-capital of Nanjing in December 1937, Japanese soldiers beat, raped, tortured, and killed as many as three hundred thousand Chinese men, women, and children. To many ardent nationalists in Japan, even today, none of this ever happened. Most Japanese today acknowledge that a gruesome battle took place, but they place the number of the dead at only one-tenth of the real casualties and attribute even those deflated numbers to regular battlefield occurrences.

somewhere around 250,000 Chinese civilians were slaughtered by the Japanese army, all in a period of only five to six weeks. (That averages to more than 6,000 deaths per day.) Another 20,000–50,000 Chinese women and girls were raped, most of them repeatedly. Civilians were shot, stabbed to death, or beheaded. Others were doused with gasoline and set aflame. Hundreds were plowed, alive, into ditches and covered with tons of dirt. In the end even the Japanese commanding officer, General Iwane Matsui (1878–1948), expressed confusion and regret over how it had all happened; his soldiers, he claimed, had simply gone briefly mad.

Japan's "Comfort Women"   Another crime was the Japanese abduction and sexual enslavement of 200,000 women and girls to serve as so-called **comfort women** for their soldiers. These women were taken overwhelmingly from the occupied territories, although there is evidence that some Japanese women—primarily the relatives of critics of the government—were also forced to work as prostitutes throughout the empire. The official purpose of the "comfort stations" was, first, to control the spread of sexually transmitted diseases among the soldiers by giving them access to a regulated sex trade. Second, it was said to protect against espionage by foreign agents posing as prostitutes. It seems likely that the basic aim was more elemental—to curry favor with the soldiers by giving them what they would have simply taken anyway. Numerous women who survived their enslavement testified that even the Japanese doctors who came regularly to examine the women for sexually transmitted diseases raped them.

The program began as early as 1932, when the first comfort station was introduced in Shanghai. The government actively recruited women to work in the brothels, even to the point of placing advertisements in newspapers; but as the empire and the army grew, volunteers no longer sufficed. By 1937, at the start of the Second Sino-Japanese War, civilian agents hired by the government to manage and provide for the military brothels resorted to fraud and kidnapping. Ultimately, many tens of thousands of Chinese, Indonesian, Korean, Malay, Philippine, Thai, and Vietnamese women were abducted, raped, humiliated, and enslaved. Although several Japanese prime ministers have apologized for the abuse of women during the war, the government still denies any legal liability for the military brothels. Many Japanese political leaders still hold that the total number of comfort women was no larger than twenty thousand—none of whom, they insist, were forced into the work.

MAKING AMENDS

How does a nation make amends for horrors? Can crimes of the magnitude of those committed in World War II be atoned for or forgiven? Who has the right to judge? One result of the war was the creation of a setting where such questions could be debated and decided on the basis of international law.

The **Nuremberg Trials** of German leaders and **Tokyo Trials** in Japan did more than set the stage.

The idea of international law dates to the Treaty of Westphalia in 1648 but started to assume its modern character in the nineteenth century, with the growth of multinational businesses and modern empires. The Allies, however, had planned at least since early 1942 to bring the Nazis to justice for war crimes, and they had worked out the mechanisms for doing so long before Germany actually surrendered. The Tokyo Trials were another matter. Although the Allies agreed in principle to bring charges against the leaders of Imperial Japan, the joint process was preempted by General Douglas MacArthur (1880–1964), who used his position as supreme commander of the Allied Powers in the Pacific to order the arrests of nearly forty Japanese leaders and to begin their prosecution. The tribunal worked out the details as it conducted its work.

Nazi Germany and Imperial Japan were not the first nations to commit war crimes; nor were they the only ones to commit appalling acts in World War II. *The* Germany and Japan were unique in that their crimes were conceived, imple- *Nuremberg* mented, and administered by the state as conscious elements of national policy. *Trials*

Göring on Trial   Hermann Göring (1893–1946) was the commander-in-chief of the Nazi air force (*Luftwaffe*) and Hitler's presumed successor. Convicted of crimes against humanity at the Nuremberg Trials, he committed suicide the night before he was to be hanged. In a late conversation with an interviewer he boasted that "people can always be talked into doing what their rulers want. It's easy—all one has to do is tell them that they are being attacked, and then blame it on unpatriotic pacifists who are exposing everyone to harm. It will work in any country."

At Nuremberg, the Allies placed 24 top Nazi officials on trial, 21 of whom were convicted; subsequent trials of lower-tier officers convicted 142 of 185 defendants. Still more trials took place in several of the concentration camps, adding hundreds more to the list of criminals brought to justice before the trials closed in 1956: camp guards, doctors, special operations paramilitaries (*Einsatzgruppen*), and others. Most of the guilty were either hanged or imprisoned for life, although several of the most prominent defendants, like Herman Göring (1893–1946, the head of the German Air Force, *Luftwaffe*), committed suicide before their executions could be carried out.

These courts marked a crucial point in the establishment of fundamental standards of international justice. As one of the leading judges at the trials, the U.S. Supreme Court Justice Robert H. Jackson (1892–1954), declared in his opening statement for the prosecution on November 21, 1945:

> Never before in legal history has an effort been made to bring within the scope of a single litigation the developments of a decade, covering a whole continent, and involving a score of nations, countless individuals, and innumerable events. Despite the magnitude of the task, the world has demanded immediate action. This demand has had to be met, though perhaps at the cost of finished craftsmanship. In my country, established courts, following familiar procedures, applying well-thumbed precedents, and dealing with the legal consequences of local and limited events, seldom commence a trial within a year of the event in litigation. Yet less than eight months ago today the courtroom in which you sit was an enemy fortress in the hands of German S.S. troops. Less than eight months ago nearly all our witnesses and documents were in enemy hands. . . .
>
> I should be the last to deny that the case may well suffer from incomplete researches, and quite likely will not be the example of professional work which any of the prosecuting nations would normally wish to sponsor. It is, however, a completely adequate case to the judgment we shall ask you to render, and its full development we shall be obliged to leave to historians. . . . At the very outset, let us dispose of the contention that to put these men to trial is to do them an injustice, entitling them to some special consideration. These defendants may be hard pressed but they are not ill used. . . . If these men are the first war leaders of a defeated nation to be prosecuted in the name of the law, they are also the first to be given the chance to plead for their lives in the name of the law.

Although few people complain about the trials' outcomes, the manner in which they took place raises questions about the quality of their justice. As pointed out at the time—for instance, by U.S. Supreme Court Justice William O. Douglas (1898–1980)—the laws defining war crimes were written after the atrocities had been committed. The trials were therefore *ex post facto* ("after the fact"), appearing more like revenge than fair judgment.[4] Both Winston Churchill and the American Secretary of the Treasury, Henry Morgenthau Jr. (1891–1967), were adamantly opposed to the trials. Churchill advocated summary executions without any kind of trial whatsoever. Morgenthau's position had more nuance. He pointed out that Stalin in his show trials of the 1930s had written the laws under which the defendants were charged, appointed the judges and prosecutors, and determined the place for the proceedings. For the Allied Powers to do so could give the impression of a similar sort of rough justice. It did not help matters that Stalin made a point of repeatedly endorsing the Nuremberg trials in public. In the end, however, most observers, along with the German nation as a whole, recognized that some form of atonement, even an imperfect one, was necessary for the atrocities committed.

The Tokyo Trials were a different matter. At least since the Battle at Midway Island in 1942, the Imperial Japanese government had carefully searched out and *The Tokyo* destroyed documents regarding their crimes, and in the weeks before their sur- *Trials* render in 1945, they undertook a mass purging of their records. Above all, they wanted to protect the emperor Hirohito and his family from any possible legal charge. Second, they wanted political and military leaders to claim plausible deniability about their role in criminal action. The tribunals therefore operated with distinctly inferior standards of evidence: documents could be submitted to the courts, for example, without their authenticity or provenance clearly established. "The tribunal shall not be bound by technical rules of evidence," declared the foundation charter of the Tokyo Trials, "and it shall admit any evidence which it deems to have probative value."

The tribunals forbade the cross-examination of some witnesses for the prosecution. They disallowed hearsay evidence from the defense that contradicted the hearsay evidence presented by prosecutors, and they adopted a new standard for "negative criminality." They condemned Japanese officials for not preventing actions that were legal when they were performed. In the end, the Allies and nearly every nation formerly under Japanese rule staged trials of more than ten thousand Japanese officials, more than half of whom were convicted and roughly one thousand of whom were executed.

---

4   Göring, presented with a copy of the indictment against him, penned the comment, "The victor is always the judge, the defeated is always the accused"—with his signature.

Creating a New World Order   Delegations from the United States, Great Britain, the Soviet Union, France, and China met in Washington, D.C., at the Dumbarton Oaks Conference in August 1944 to draft the charter of a new international institution—what would become the United Nations. The five chartering countries became the permanent members of the Security Council.

THE UNITED NATIONS AND HUMAN RIGHTS

The **United Nations** set in formal order the standards and procedures for maintaining peace and international law. Established in 1945, this organization of member nations established a special tribunal for hearing specific cases as well as the permanently standing International Court of Justice and International Criminal Court. War crimes and crimes against humanity came under the jurisdiction of the International Criminal Court.

Universal Declaration of Human Rights   To prevent further war crimes and to establish a sounder basis for trials when they should occur, the United Nations on December 10, 1948, approved the **Universal Declaration of Human Rights**, whose drafting and promotion were chiefly the work of Eleanor Roosevelt (1884–1962), the wife of president Franklin Delano Roosevelt. It was the first, and is still the most important, statement of global rights in history—the standard of civic values for the world. In 1990, forty-five Muslim nations withdrew from the Universal Declaration and provided a substitute for it, known as the Cairo Declaration of Human Rights in Islam, that is in essence a declaration of a separate set of values that are unique to the Muslim world. (We return to the Cairo Declaration on Human Rights in Islam in chapter 27.)

The key articles of the Universal Declaration assert:

Article 1: All human beings are born free and equal in dignity and rights. They are endowed with reason and conscience and should act towards one another in a spirit of brotherhood.

Article 2: Everyone is entitled to all the rights and freedoms set forth in this Declaration, without distinction of any kind, such as race, color, sex, language, religion, political or other opinion, national or social origin, property, birth or other status. . . .

Article 3: Everyone has the right to life, liberty and security of person.

Article 4: No one shall be held in slavery or servitude; slavery and the slave trade shall be prohibited in all their forms.

Article 5: No one shall be subjected to torture or to cruel, inhuman or degrading treatment or punishment. . . .

Article 7: All are equal before the law and are entitled without any discrimination to equal protection of the law. . . .

Article 9: No one shall be subjected to arbitrary arrest, detention or exile. . . .

Article 13: (1) Everyone has the right to freedom of movement and residence within the borders of each state.

Article 14: (1) Everyone has the right to seek and to enjoy in other countries asylum from persecution. . . .

Article 16: (2) Marriage shall be entered into only with the free and full consent of the intending spouses. . . .

Article 18: Everyone has the right to freedom of thought, conscience and religion; this right includes freedom to change his religion or belief, and freedom, either alone or in community with others and in public or private, to manifest his religion or belief in teaching, practice, worship and observance.

Article 19: Everyone has the right to freedom of opinion and expression; this right includes freedom to hold opinions without interference and to seek, receive and impart information and ideas through any media and regardless of frontiers.

Article 20: (1) Everyone has the right to freedom of peaceful assembly and association. . . .

Article 21: (1) Everyone has the right to take part in the government of his country, directly or through freely chosen representatives. (2) Everyone has the right of equal access to public service in his country. (3) The will of the people shall be the basis of the authority of government; this will shall be expressed in periodic and genuine elections which shall be by universal and equal suffrage and shall be held by secret vote or by equivalent free voting procedures.

Article 23: . . . Everyone, without any discrimination, has the right to equal pay for equal work. . . .

Article 26: (1) Everyone has the right to education.

The UN General Assembly adopted the declaration by a nearly unanimous vote. Saudi Arabia, South Africa, the Soviet Union, Czechoslovakia, and Yugoslavia abstained. Their various domestic policies of female subjection, apartheid, and rejection of private property and free speech contradicted its central tenets.

Although supported by all the nations that signed it, the Declaration bears the marks of its Western and Enlightenment origins. It could have been written by Rousseau himself—personal safety, political participation, due process, equality before the law, and social egalitarianism. The Enlightenment had championed education but never asserted an individual right to it; Voltaire, for one, would have been alternately amused and horrified at the prospect of teaching the masses to read. That difference sets the Declaration ahead of its eighteenth-century forebears.

The looming Cold War between Communist and Western nations (discussed in the next chapter) made it impossible for the Declaration to be a binding treaty. Eleanor Roosevelt and her colleagues had to settle for its acceptance as a set of universal guidelines or standards of behavior. Subsequent regional treaties such as the European Convention for the Protection of Human Rights and Fundamental Freedoms (1953) and the African Charter of Human and Peoples' Rights (1981), however, based their articles on the Declaration and made its principles binding.

WORLD WAR II AND THE MIDDLE EAST

Although not directly active in the conflict, the peoples of the Middle East were profoundly affected by World War II, and their aspirations affected both Allied and Axis strategies. The war also led to growing tensions among European mandates, Arab nationalism, and a Jewish homeland.

Independent Nations The Muslim lands that already existed as autonomous nations—Egypt, Iran, and Turkey most notably—declared neutrality in the conflict but were drawn in nonetheless. The Fertile Crescent regions that existed as European mandates (Lebanon and Syria under France; Palestine, Jordan, and Iraq under Britain) were important factors in Allied strategies from the start. Egypt, technically independent since 1922, had endured a British military occupation that aimed above all to keep the Suez Canal open—and popular sentiment against the British presence rose throughout the 1930s. When the war began in 1939, Egyptian hopes of freedom from British influence led the nominal ruler, King Farouk I (r. 1936–1952), to start secret negotiations with Berlin, offering to join the Axis if Britain should be driven from the region. German forces under Field Marshal Erwin Rommel (1891–1944) advanced almost to Cairo before being turned back at the battle of El Alamein in late 1942, which dashed the prospect of a British withdrawal.

Iran, too, was a neutral power. Under Reza Shah Pahlavi (r. 1925–1941) it was engaged in an array of ambitious modernization projects. Public schools, modern hospitals, a national system of trains and buses, a comprehensive radio and telephone grid, the University of Tehran—all were paid for with revenues from oil. But oil in wartime becomes a weapon, and neither the Allies nor the Axis wanted Iran's oil to fall to the other side. Roughly a thousand German nationals resided in Iran in the early years of the war; most were engi-

Muhammad Reza Pahlavi Shah of Iran from 1941 to 1979, Muhammad Reza Pahlavi (1919–1980) began as a pro-modernizing, pro-Western, secularist who shared power with a series of democratically elected prime ministers, but over time he transformed into a autocrat who employed a brutal secret police force to suppress all opposition to his increasingly remote and corrupt rule. He was finally overthrown by the Iranian Revolution led by Ayatollah Ruhollah Khomeini.

neers and businessmen developing a local steel industry in return for oil. When the shah rejected Allied demands that he deport the Germans, both British and Soviet forces invaded the country and forced him to abdicate in favor of his son, Muhammad Reza Shah Pahlavi (r. 1944–1979), who immediately aligned himself with the Western Allies. Reza Pahlavi remained in power until the Iranian Revolution of 1979 toppled him and instituted the Islamic Republic.

Turkey likewise faced pressure from both Allied and Axis governments but remained neutral until the last year of the war, when it seemed clear that Nazi Germany would fall. Like Egypt, the country joined the Allies simply to earn the right to participate in the UN end-of-war negotiations for a permanent settlement. By holding to a neutral position for so long, Turkey was able to advance its internal development as a secular democracy and so to serve as a bridge between the West and the Middle East.

The Fertile Crescent itself was under French and British rule. Nations did not exist here—only an administrative grid of Western mandates and regional gover- *Mandates* nors who tried to manage an interlocking yet fluid array of tribes, clans, and sects. The Ottomans had known better and had not tried to force the Arabs into larger units. France and Britain governed their mandates by allying themselves with self-selected conservative elites—landowners, clerical leaders, leading merchants, tribal chieftains, and military officers—all of whom expressed, and in some cases genuinely felt, a willingness to work with their European masters. In return, Europe tacitly recognized their positions as leaders, ready and fit to take over whenever the Europeans left.

Syria, technically, was enemy territory to the Allies after 1940, since the Nazi seizure of Paris had left control of Syria to the compromised regime of Vichy. Hitler used Damascus at a staging and refueling site for planes bringing Iraqi oil to Germany, and this in turn led to the British decision to invade. Aided by "Free France" forces in exile, Britain took control of Syria in July 1941 and held it until the end of the war. When the war ended, however, Syria declared itself an independent republic, wrote a constitution, and elected a prime minister. Newly liberated France responded by bombing Damascus (in May 1945) and reasserting its rights under the UN mandate.

Britain opposed the French claim and wanted to secure an advantageous position with the new Syrian Republic. First, it pressured France to withdraw its troops (reluctantly done by April 1946). Second, it recognized the republic's claim to a "Greater Syria" that extended its borders to the Mediterranean. Finally, Britain promised to do all it could to prevent further Jewish immigration into Palestine; at the same time, Britain was formally committed to a Jewish homeland there.

ARAB NATIONALISM AND GROWING ZIONISM

As we have seen, Arab nationalism differed from European models in that it emphasized shared language and culture over shared territory. Autonomy from the West meant more than an independent form of government. Secularism was a means to an end, rather than a genuine value. Most Arabs, whether Sunni or Shi'i, were devout Muslims and desired to recreate an Islamic caliphate—although only in the sense of a symbolic spiritual realm. But most declared allegiance to secularism to placate Western concerns for the many Jews and Arab Christians who lived in the region. As one writer expressed it:

> The nationalism we are talking about is nothing more than Love—the feeling that binds a man to his family. For our country is simply a large household, our nation a large family. Nationalism thus makes the heart glad and the soul joyful, just as any form of love does, and whoever feels this joy shares it with everyone who feels the same. It raises one beyond oneself and brings one closer to spiritual perfection. (*The Battle for Our Destiny*, 1958)

Ba'athism   The writer was Michel Aflaq (1910–1989), an Arab Christian from Damascus who founded the **Ba'ath Party**—which he envisioned as the representation of secular pan-Arabism, combined with socialist ideals of state-sponsored care for the masses. (The Arabic word *ba'ath* means "rebirth.") To Ba'ath supporters, and many other "nationalist" groups of the 1930s and 1940s, the "nation" of the Arabs implied something larger than any political arrangement and should not be thought of in Western political terms; the Arab nation, to them, was a spiritual state, an elevated sense of communal and cultural identity, a renewal of the original, founding community of the united Arab *peoples*.

Britain had established a pro-Western monarchy in Iraq with the elevation of King Faisal I (r. 1921–1933), who maintained good relations with Britain. After a brief coup that was caused in part by the effects of the Depression, Faisal's grandson took over and ruled as Faisal II (r. 1939–1958). Like his grandfather, Faisal hoped to foster a sense of political unity among the peoples living in Iraq. Ethnic, sectarian, and even geological divisions, unfortunately, stood in the way. As it had been determined by the UN mandate, Iraq consisted of two oil-rich zones, one in the north and one in the south, with an arid desert zone in between and centered on the ancient capital of Baghdad. The Kurds lived in the north, the Iranian-allied Shi'a in the south, and the Ba'athist, pan-Arab, Sunnis in the arid middle. Without the resources of the north or south, the Sunni middle could hold Iraq together and impose its will only by force.

Palestine was both the most and the least significant of the mandate territories. In earlier centuries its religious importance had matched its commercial sig- *Palestine* nificance: it bridged the Mediterranean-based economy of the West and the *and Israel* caravan route–based economy of Asia. Trade routes, however, had long since moved, with the development of modern shipping, rail, and air-cargo traffic. The Suez Canal, opened in 1869, and the Trans-Siberian Railroad, completed in 1916, opened still more routes for goods. When Mark Twain visited Palestine in the latter half of the nineteenth century, he described it as a barren expanse of dust, rocks, and weeds that was almost devoid of habitation. As he put it in his best-selling travel book, *The Innocents Abroad* (1869):

> The further we went the hotter the sun got, and the more rocky and bare, repulsive and dreary the landscape became. There could not have been more fragments of stone strewn broadcast over this part of the world, if every ten square feet of the land had been occupied by a separate and distinct stonecutter's establishment for an age. There was hardly a tree or a shrub anywhere. Even the olive and the cactus, those fast friends of a worthless soil, had almost deserted the country. No landscape exists that is more tiresome to the eye than that which bounds the approaches to Jerusalem. The only difference between the roads and the surrounding country, perhaps, is that there are rather more rocks in the roads than in the surrounding country.

Conditions had changed by the mid-twentieth century, of course, and the most dramatic change was the growing Jewish presence. Between 1869 and 1923 roughly 50,000 Russian and European Jews had migrated to the Holy Land, where they

Exodus to Nowhere   The *SS Exodus 1947* carried 4,500 German Jews, most of them Holocaust survivors, from France to the Holy Land in July 1947. Britain was then still in possession of the Palestinian Mandate and had a determined policy not to worsen its relations with the Arabs by allowing increased Jewish immigration: when the *Exodus 1947* reached port in Haifa, British authorities refused to let the passengers disembark. The fate of the Jews became international news for months. With the formal creation of the nation of Israel in 1948, all bars to the group's repatriation were removed, but by then half of the original 4,500 had either died or fled.

purchased farmlands, pastures, homes, and businesses from departing Turks and emigrating Arabs. Another 60,000 arrived by 1932; and during the early years of Hitler's rule, while the West pursued appeasement, perhaps 150,000 more Jews came. The British did all they could to restrict immigration during the war to avoid upsetting their Arab subjects. The British also saw it as a first step toward resolving the tensions between Arab claims and the founding of a Jewish state.

The Jews were still a minority in the Holy Land in 1945, although they constituted a majority in Jerusalem and several other cities. The Jews who moved into Palestine included poor farmers and laborers but also large numbers of professionals—physicians, lawyers, business managers, engineers, teachers, labor organizers, and scholars—whose skills transformed the landscape. New industries, schools, and trades appeared on the scene, health care improved, malarial swamps were drained, and transportation and communication networks were established. New political and legal institutions were introduced as well. Unlike their Arab neighbors, the Jews formed modern political parties based on ideology—pro-labor, pro-business, pro-socialist, secular, or religious. These organizations unified the populace across the region. Palestinian Arabs remained wedded to a more traditional tribal and clan-based social organization.

The Jews, in other words, developed a Western variety of political nationalism that proved more effective than the cultural and spiritual variety of nationalism familiar to the Arab world. This powerful sense of nationhood, and the legal and institutional practices that operated within it, combined with the immense emotions produced by the Holocaust, which demanded a safe homeland for the Jews. In 1947, an exhausted Britain ceded Palestine to the newly created United Nations, which voted to partition Palestine into an Arab region and a Jewish one (see Map 26.5). Hostility turned into open war, which Jewish forces won. On May 14, 1948, the state of Israel came into being.

◆

The suffering and destruction of World War II challenges any ability to describe. A recent bestselling history—*Postwar*, by Tony Judt—begins with a powerful thirty-page catalog of the physical desolation of the continent. The human

MAP 26.5   The Partition of Palestine and the Creation of Israel, 1947–1948   The creation of the Jewish state of Israel in 1948 against a backdrop of ongoing conflict between Jews and indigenous Arab peoples turned the Middle East into a powder keg, a situation that has lasted to the present day.

geography was equally desolate and traumatized. Making things even worse, two of the Allies who had won the war now looked upon one another with suspicion, namely the United States and the Soviet Union. As Winston Churchill declared in a famous speech delivered at Westminster College, in Missouri, in 1946, soon after the war's end:

> It is my duty, however, to place before you certain facts about the present position in Europe. From Stettin in the Baltic to Trieste in the Adriatic an iron curtain has descended across the Continent. Behind

that line lie all the capitals of the ancient states of Central and Eastern Europe. Warsaw, Berlin, Prague, Vienna, Budapest, Belgrade, Bucharest and Sofia; all these famous cities and the populations around them lie in what I must call the Soviet sphere, and all are subject, in one form or another, not only to Soviet influence but to a very high and in some cases increasing measure of control from Moscow. The safety of the world, ladies and gentlemen, requires a unity in Europe, from which no nation should be permanently outcast.

The Iron Curtain that descended on Europe divided not only the continent but the entire world, as the strategic tensions between West and East played out around the globe.

WHO, WHAT, WHERE

Ba'ath Party	Holocaust	United Nations
Battle of Britain	Manhattan Project	Universal Declaration
Battle of Midway	Nuremberg Trials	of Human Rights
Blitzkrieg	Operation Barbarossa	Vichy regime
comfort women	Rape of Nanjing	
genocide	Tokyo Trials	

SUGGESTED READINGS

Primary Sources

Gilbert, G. M. *Nuremberg Diary.*

Levi, Primo. *Survival in Auschwitz.*

Stimson, Henry L., and McGeorge Bundy. *On Active Service in Peace and War.*

Swanwick, Helena. *The Roots of Peace* (1938).

Woolf, Virginia. *Three Guineas* (1938).

Zweig, Stefan. *The World of Yesterday.*

Anthologies

Coetzee, Frans, and Marilyn Shevin-Coetzee, eds. *The World in Flames: A World War II Sourcebook* (2010).

Goldensohn, Leon. *The Nuremberg Interviews* (2005).

Laqueur, Walter, and Barry Rubin, eds. *The Israel–Arab Reader: A Documentary History of the Middle East Conflict* (2008).

Madison, James H. *World War II: A History in Documents* (2009).

Marrus, Michael R., comp. *The Nuremberg War Crimes Trial, 1945–46: A Documentary History* (1997).

Martel, Gordon, ed. *The World War Two Reader* (2004).

Simmons, Cynthia, and Nina Perlina. *Writing the Siege of Leningrad: Women's Diaries, Memories, and Documentary Prose* (2005).

Studies

Bass, Gary Jonathan. *Stay the Hand of Vengeance: The Politics of War Crimes Tribunals* (2001).

Bellamy, Chris. *Absolute War: Soviet Russia in the Second World War; A Modern History* (2008).

Bix, Herbert. *Hirohito and the Making of Modern Japan* (2000).

Browning, Christopher R. *The Origins of the Final Solution: The Evolution of Nazi Jewish Policy, September 1939–March 1942* (2007).

Carpenter, Stephanie. *On the Farm Front: The Women's Land Army in World War II* (2003).

Evans, Richard J. *The Coming of the Third Reich* (2003).

Evans, Richard J. *The Third Reich at War, 1939–1945* (2008).

Evans, Richard J. *The Third Reich in Power, 1933–1939* (2005).

Friedländer, Saul. *Nazi Germany and the Jews.* Vol. 1, *The Years of Persecution, 1933–1939* (1998).

Friedländer, Saul. *Nazi Germany and the Jews.* Vol. 2, *The Years of Extermination, 1939–1945* (2008).

Gelvin, James L. *The Modern Middle East: A History* (2011).

Glendon, Mary Ann. *A World Made New: Eleanor Roosevelt and the Universal Declaration of Human Rights* (2002).

Gregor, Neil. *Haunted City: Nuremberg and the Nazi Past* (2008).

Hasegawa, Tsuyoshi. *Racing the Enemy: Stalin, Truman, and the Surrender of Japan* (2006).

Hitchcock, William I. *The Struggle for Europe: The Turbulent History of a Divided Continent, 1945 to the Present* (2004).

Knox, Macgregor. *Common Destiny: Dictatorship, Foreign Policy, and War in Fascist Italy and Nazi Germany* (2009).

Laucht, Christoph. *Elemental Germans: Klaus Fuchs, Rudolf Peierls and the Making of British Nuclear Culture, 1939–59* (2012).

Mawdsley, Evan. *Thunder in the East: The Nazi–Soviet War, 1941–1945* (2007).

Megargee, Geoffrey P. *War of Annihilation: Combat and Genocide on the Eastern Front, 1941* (2007).

Merridale, Catherine. *Ivan's War: Life and Death in the Red Army, 1939–1945* (2007).

O'Shea, Paul. *A Cross Too Heavy: Pope Pius XII and the Jews of Europe* (2011).

Pike, Francis. *Empires at War: A Short History of Modern Asia since World War II* (2011).

Power, Samantha. *A Problem from Hell: America and the Age of Genocide* (2013).

Rees, Laurence. *World War II behind Closed Doors: Stalin, the Nazis, and the West* (2008).

Snyder, Timothy. *Bloodlands: Europe between Hitler and Stalin* (2012).

Steiner, Zara. *The Lights That Failed: European International History, 1919–1933* (2007).

Steiner, Zara. *The Triumph of the Dark: European International History, 1933–1939* (2011).

Thorpe, Julie. *Pan-Germanism and the Austrofascist State, 1933–38* (2012).

Totani, Yuma. *The Tokyo War Crimes Trial: The Pursuit of Justice in the Wake of World War II* (2009).

Vaizey, Hester. *Surviving Hitler's War: Family Life in Germany, 1939–48* (2010).

Weikart, Richard. *Hitler's Ethic: The Nazi Pursuit of Evolutionary Progress* (2011).

Wendehorst, Stephan E. C. *British Jewry, Zionism, and the Jewish State, 1936–1956* (2011).

Wette, Wolfram. *The Wehrmacht: History, Myth, Reality* (2007).

Wintle, Michael, and Menno Spiering, eds. *European Identity and the Second World War* (2011).

For additional resources, including maps, primary sources, visuals, web links, and quizzes, please go to **www.oup.com/us/backman**.

CHAPTER 27

Theater of the Absurd: The Postwar World

1945–1968

It was no easy thing to survive the first half of the twentieth century and still believe in the essential goodness of humanity, the inevitability of progress, or the existence of a loving God. And, in fact, millions of people ceased to believe in all three. An immense task of rebuilding once again confronted the Greater West. Hundreds of thousands of corpses needed burial, and millions of wounded and displaced people needed care. Billions of tons of rubble had to be cleared. Rivers and fields had to be reopened. Whole cities had to be fixed up or entirely reconstructed. The agricultural sector, too, needed to be reestablished. The destruction was immense, even awe inspiring.

THE GREATER WEST, ca. 1950

— "Iron Curtain"

Dresden after the Fire-Bombing Nearly four thousand tons of explosive and incendiary bombs were dropped on Dresden in forty-eight hours in February 1945, resulting in over twenty thousand deaths and this desolate scene. This photograph was taken from atop the tower of the city hall. The sculpture in the foreground, ironically, is a personification of Goodness (*Bonitas*).

The Italian novelist Elsa Morante (1912–1985), who was half Jewish, spent part of the war hiding from the Nazis in the Apennine Mountains. She described the physical and emotional desolation of the time in her novel *History* (*La storia*, 1974). It depicts the brutality of everyday life in war-torn Rome—searching for food and cast-off clothing, trying to find a safe place to sleep amid ruins, running from looters and rapists. Morante evokes the horror of the war not by narrating large-scale scenes of battle but by describing intimate events. When her main character Ida encounters a train filled with Jews on their way to the death camps, she singles out of the noise within the closed car the sound of several children singing a song—and rushes to the door to join in singing with the doomed children.

The effect is all the more powerful because of the smallness of its scale. Ida's quest is both material and ethereal: to survive, keep her children safe, and restore some kind of normal life, but also to make sense of horrors. Suffering that does not *mean something* is unbearable. "Man in his fundamental nature needs to explain the world into which he was born," Morante writes. "This is what separates him from other animals. Every last person, even the least intelligent and the lowest of the world's castaways, explains the world to himself from childhood on, and this is what enables him to keep living. Without it, all would be madness."

Many in Europe never found safety or meaning, and an aura of persistent gloom lasted long after the war. It influenced literature with the idea of "the absurd." Millions of others, however, rolled up their sleeves and set to work. They rebuilt nations and economies. They faced down the tensions and violence of the Cold War—a rivalry between the United States and the Soviet Union born out of postwar tensions that would dominate world affairs for decades—by moving away from imperialism as well as into a "second wave" of feminism. Some of the same tensions stirred conflict and change in Islamic states as well.

CHAPTER TIMELINE

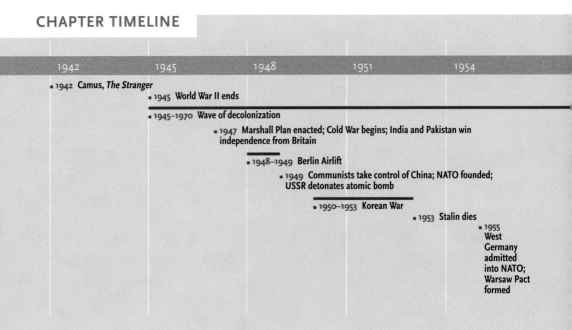

| 1942 | 1945 | 1948 | 1951 | 1954 |

- 1942 Camus, *The Stranger*
- 1945 World War II ends
- 1945–1970 Wave of decolonization
- 1947 Marshall Plan enacted; Cold War begins; India and Pakistan win independence from Britain
- 1948–1949 Berlin Airlift
- 1949 Communists take control of China; NATO founded; USSR detonates atomic bomb
- 1950–1953 Korean War
- 1953 Stalin dies
- 1955 West Germany admitted into NATO; Warsaw Pact formed

As the peoples of the Greater West redefined themselves, the U.S. and Soviet superpowers took the world to the brink of nuclear disaster. From the dropping of the atomic bomb on Japan in 1945 to the Cuban Missile Crisis of 1962, fear and anguish gripped much of the world, even in the midst of the West's economic recovery.

SETTING TO WORK

The refugee crisis called for attention first. Roughly 50 million refugees and several million prisoners of war had to be repatriated—that is, sent home—or, failing that, resettled into their host countries. The difficult process was made even more confusing by the new postwar national boundaries and by Stalin's unwillingness to withdraw his troops from eastern Europe. Germany was divided into zones of Allied control. Brutal forms of ethnic cleansing became commonplace in the east, as ethnic minorities were shuffled from one location to another. In Poland, for example, the non-Polish population constituted one-third of the nation before the war; by 1945 it was reduced to a mere 5 percent. Wartime criminals, collaborators, and postwar looters were sought out for punishment. Judicial punishments and mob justice reached many who had collaborated with the Nazis. In Belgium alone, more than 600,000 people (roughly 8 percent of the population) were prosecuted.

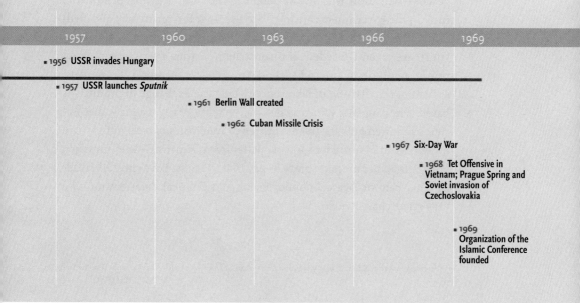

1957   1960   1963   1966   1969

- 1956 **USSR invades Hungary**

- 1957 **USSR launches** *Sputnik*

- 1961 **Berlin Wall created**

- 1962 **Cuban Missile Crisis**

- 1967 **Six-Day War**

- 1968 **Tet Offensive in Vietnam; Prague Spring and Soviet invasion of Czechoslovakia**

- 1969 **Organization of the Islamic Conference founded**

The Marshall Plan

Europe could not feed itself. Agricultural production in 1945 was less than half its prewar level, and strict rationing was put in place everywhere. Lacking markets in which to sell and having no fuel with which to operate their machinery, farmers refrained from growing crops and turned instead to raising livestock. Shipments of food from the United States helped to keep people alive, but rationing continued in many countries well into the 1950s. The **Marshall Plan**, named after U.S. Secretary of State George Marshall (1880–1959), began in 1947. It provided cash, credit, raw materials, and technical assistance to jump-start industrial production.[1]

Marshall described the agricultural crisis in a public lecture he delivered at Harvard University in June of 1947:

> The farmer has always produced the foodstuffs to exchange with the city dweller for the other necessities of life. This division of labor is the basis of modern civilization. At the present time it is threatened with breakdown. The town and city industries are not producing adequate goods to exchange with the food-producing farmer. Raw materials and fuel are in short supply. Machinery is lacking or worn out. The farmer or the peasant cannot find the goods for sale which he desires to purchase. So the sale of his farm-produce for money which he cannot use seems to him an unprofitable transaction. He, therefore, has withdrawn many fields from crop cultivation and is using them for grazing. He feeds more grain to stock and finds for himself and his family an ample supply of food, however short he may be on clothing and the other ordinary gadgets of civilization. Meanwhile people in the cities are short of food and fuel. So the governments are forced to use their foreign money and credits to procure these necessities abroad. This process exhausts funds which are urgently needed for reconstruction. Thus a very serious situation is rapidly developing which bodes no good for the world. The modern system of the division of labor upon which the exchange of products is based is in danger of breaking down. The truth of the matter is that Europe's requirements for the next three or four years of foreign food and other essential products—principally from America—are so much greater than her present ability to pay that she must have substantial additional help or face economic, social, and political deterioration of a very grave character.

---

[1]   Within five years the Marshall plan provided more than $17 billion in aid—worth more than $150 billion today.

The Marshall Plan ran until 1952. By the end of the program, every one of the sixteen countries that had benefited from the program had surpassed its economic output before the start of the war. By the mid-1950s western Europe was exporting manufactured goods around the globe. The Plan did more than pump capital into its clients' economies: it modernized their technology, introduced American-style business practices, and helped reduce tariff barriers between countries. In this way, the Marshall Plan paved the way for the integration of Europe as well as its recovery. The long period of widespread and steady growth enabled most nations to undertake a great social experiment—the modern welfare state.

Full Speed Ahead   "The Open Road of the Marshall Plan" proclaims this German poster produced to promote the rebuilding effort.

On Stalin's orders the nations of eastern Europe, now under Communist control, declined U.S. assistance and denounced it as poorly disguised imperialism. Moreover, the creation and rapid growth of the **North Atlantic Treaty Organization** (NATO) in 1949, despite the emphasis on the alliance as a defensive one, looked to Soviet eyes like the laying of the groundwork for an attack on the Communist world. By 1952, the year the Marshall Plan formally ended, NATO consisted of fourteen nations (the United States, Belgium, Canada, Denmark, France, Greece, Iceland, Italy, Luxembourg, the Netherlands, Norway, Portugal, Turkey, and the United Kingdom). West Germany joined in 1955. Stalin responded, in part, by forming the **Warsaw Pact**, an alliance of the eight Communist nations (Albania, Bulgaria, Czechoslovakia, East Germany, Hungary, Poland, Romania, and the Soviet Union itself), while ordering East Germany, Hungary, and Romania to pay reparations for World War II damages to Russia—and using the money received to pay for further industrialization of Russia (see Map 27.1).

Eastern and Western Blocs

Within a decade of the end of the war, the Greater West was already polarized between two hostile international networks.

ALIENATION AND THE ABSURD

The determination and hard work of so many people did not translate, however, into optimism. Gloom predominated, even among the war's victors. In fact, much of European culture (and at least some pockets of it in America) hardly believed

Sartre and Existentialism

Military Blocs in Europe, 1948-1955

Neutral country

Warsaw Pact

Communist country, not member of Warsaw Pact

North Atlantic Treaty Organization *plus Canada and United States. France withdrew from Integrated Military Command in 1966.*

—— "Iron Curtain"

MAP 27.1   Military Blocs in Europe, 1948–1955   The "Iron Curtain" was the ideological conflict and physical boundary dividing Europe into two separate areas from the end of World War II in 1945 until the end, nearly fifty years later, of the Cold War. The term, coined by Winston Churchill, symbolized efforts by the Soviet Union to block itself and its satellite states from open contact with the West and non-Soviet-controlled areas.

what it saw—a vast ruin of shattered hopes and beliefs. The notion of absurdity summed up, for many, the meaninglessness of existence and the inscrutability of fate, and the philosophy of **existentialism** became the rage among cultural elites. This philosophy explored the meaning of human existence in a world where evil flourished. In the formula made famous by the French existentialist thinker Jean-Paul Sartre (1905–1980), "existence precedes essence": my nature is the product of my choices in life, not vice versa. It is easy to trace these ideas back to Nietzsche, the great champion of freedom of the will.

Camus and the Absurd

The French-Algerian writer Albert Camus (1913–1960), Sartre's contemporary and the first great writer of postwar Europe, made the existential quest for meaning in an absurd world the emblematic quest of his generation. As Camus sees it, we can bear the unhappiness of today because we have some hope for tomorrow; but the absence of real hope leaves only fearful doubt for the future. That uncertainty, or ambiguity, is endurable. It leaves a tension, however, that can be resolved only by a lie: we believe that our lives matter, but if we are honest we must acknowledge that they do not. To Camus that is the drama of life and its tragedy. A world that can continue to exist after 60 million deaths is a world in which no individual life has real meaning. We do not choose to come into this world, but we are powerless to leave it, short of suicide. Life is thus reduced to mere existence—and the absurdity of it all.

Camus enjoyed enormous success with his first novel, *The Stranger* (1942), one of the most widely read books of the twentieth century. In *The Stranger*, the protagonist, Meursault, at one point argues with a priest who is trying to redeem his soul after Meursault has committed a murder:

> Something inside me snapped. I do not know why. I began to scream at him, as loudly as I could, berating him, telling him his prayers were wasted on me. I seized him by the collar of his cassock and let fly with all the anger and passion in my heart: *You're so confident about everything, aren't you? But there's not a belief in your head that is weightier than a hair, a single hair on a woman's head!* The poor fellow couldn't even be sure he was alive, since he was living like one already dead. And he thought *I* was the one with an empty existence! But I knew the truth—about me, about everything—better than he ever did; I knew my life and the death that was coming for me. Yes, that was all, is all. But I had as strong a grip on it as it had on me. . . . I had done this, but not that; a third thing, but not a fourth— and so what? It was like I had been waiting just for this moment, this crack of light at dawn, to win my vindication. Nothing mattered, nothing, and I knew why. . . . What did it matter that some people died, or that a mother loved her child? What could his God, or the lives that people choose for themselves, or the fates they think they control, possibly mean to me?

Camus summarizes the problem of absurdity in a famous essay also published in 1942, *The Myth of Sisyphus*:

> I do not know if the world has any transcendent meaning, but I do know that if such meaning exists I cannot know it; it is impossible for me to know it. What can a meaning outside of my own existence possibly mean to me? I can understand things only in human ways—the things that I touch, the things that press back against me. These things I under- stand. But I also know that I cannot reconcile my desire for absolute truth and unity with the impossibility of reducing the world to a rational, understandable principle. What truth about these things can I state without lying? Without invoking a sense of hope that I do not possess—a hope that means nothing outside my own existence?

Albert Camus   This picture shows the philosopher of the "absurd" and Nobel Prize-winning novelist, Albert Camus (1913–1960), soon after the publication of his novel *The Plague* (*La peste*, 1947). "People, on the whole, are more good than bad; but this isn't the point that really matters, for people are also more or less ignorant. . . . And the most incurable vice is the type of ignorance that thinks it knows everything for certain and therefore claims for itself the right to kill."

Camus rejected nihilism, the denial of all meaning to life, in the 1950s, however. Deciding that "courage is the only moral virtue," he championed the rights of the poor and oppressed around the world, campaigned against admitting Fascist Spain into the United Nations, protested the brutality of the Soviet regime, and advocated an end to capital punishment. He never renounced his ideas about the absurdity of life. He simply decided that he could still try to create a better existence for himself and others.

Much of postwar literature and philosophy took up the themes of absurdity and alienation. The view of life that they portrayed was grim—from the existentialist writings of Sartre to the plays and novels of the Irish writer Samuel Beckett (1906–1989), the French Romanian playwright Eugène Ionesco (1909–1994), and the Czech dramatist and statesman Václav Havel (1936–2011). Among the less well known but still significant "absurdists" is the Swiss playwright Friedrich Dürrenmatt (1921–1990), whose dramas *The Distinguished Lady's Visit* (1956) and *The Physicists* (1962) explore people's willingness to compromise their deepest and most humane values for the sake of money and power. Many of the plays and novels of the postwar decades were comic, but the laughter they produced was nervous and never far from despair.

THE COLD WAR

To some politicians and military commanders, the fall of Berlin in 1945 should not have been the end of the war. Worries about Stalin's Russia and the role it would play in global politics had emerged as early as 1943 and were an important factor in the closing military strategies of the Allies. Communism under Lenin and then Stalin had always been feared, but Communist Russia had looked inward during the run-up to the war. Now that the war had left Stalin in possession of half of Europe, his long-stated goal of exporting revolution to other nations could be put into effect. An American general, George Patton, proclaimed his readiness in 1945 to keep his tank divisions rolling eastward until they brought Moscow to its knees, and he had his share of supporters.

Winston Churchill, too, wanted to continue on to Russia after Hitler's defeat—which helps to explain why the British voted him out of office in the first postwar election. They were grateful for his role in saving the country from the Nazis, but they wanted no part in a new war with their former ally in the east. To many observers, President Truman's decision to drop the atomic bombs on Hiroshima and Nagasaki was motivated at least in part by Russia. It was, they felt, a warning to Russia not to expand its role in the east as it had done in Europe.

The **Cold War** between the Soviet bloc and western European nations allied with the United States received its name from Bernard Baruch (1870–1965), a wealthy American financier and presidential advisor who was appointed in 1946 to the UN Atomic Energy Commission. He advocated a World Atomic Authority that would have complete control over atomic weapons. By this point, however, Stalin's scientists had begun work on their own atomic program. Baruch borrowed the term from George Orwell; the British writer had used it to describe the "peace that is no peace" that would exist if two atomically armed countries opposed one another. Neither nation would dare to use its weapons, and yet neither would dare to disarm. Orwell coined the term in 1945, before Stalin had begun the Soviet nuclear program. Baruch applied it to the high-tech rivalry that became real when Russia tested its first atomic bomb in 1949.

The Cold War unfolded in three main stages. The years from 1947 to 1962 marked the first and most hostile stage. The United States and western Europe were determined to prevent any revival of Fascism by promoting democracy and capitalism. They naturally viewed Soviet expansion with suspicion. Most Russians, however, had no doubts that the West was the real aggressor. How many times had a European power invaded Russia? Hitler had been only the most recent would-be conqueror, in a line that ran all the way back to the age of the Vikings. Yet when had Russia ever invaded Europe? After 1945, Russia at last possessed a buffer zone of European states that allowed it to export its Communist ideals while remaining somewhat safe from attack.

One of those buffer states nearly broke away from Soviet control in 1956. The attempt failed, but was a crucial turning point for many in the West who had been inclined to favor Marxism as an alternative model for development. The Hungarian People's Republic, under its brutal leader Mátyás Rákosi (1892–1971), had governed Hungary since the end of World War II. Gleefully referring to himself as "Stalin's best pupil," Rákosi killed, arrested, or exiled more than 300,000 Hungarians—military and civil officials, writers, artists, and scholars—and by 1956 had so alienated the populace that a mass rebellion against his government broke out, first in the capital Budapest but soon engulfing the whole nation. Rákosi fled to Russia, where he died fifteen years later. A more moderate faction of the Communist government took over, one that was committed to Marxism

Soviet Invasion of Hungary

but desired to break away from Moscow's control and govern independently. The Soviet Union responded by invading Hungary, violently suppressing the rebels, and executing the leader of the faction that succeeded Rákosi, Imre Nagy, for the crime of treason.

The invasion of Hungary took the mask off the Soviet Union's international image as a misunderstood country wanting only to help its people in the face of a hostile West. This event changed the whole tenor of the Cold War.

Sputnik

In October 1957 the Soviet Union successfully launched *Sputnik 1*, the first rocket-cum-satellite, into orbit around the Earth, which stirred fears of a nuclear attack. Prior to this, the only way either the United States or the USSR could launch an attack would have been to place a nuclear bomb on an airplane and fly it across the Atlantic Ocean—a trip that took ten to fourteen hours. Radar systems gave ample warning of such an approaching aircraft, allowing for some sort of defensive maneuver. But with *Sputnik*, which could orbit the entire globe in only ninety minutes, the "delivery time" for a nuclear weapon was reduced to a mere twelve minutes.

The Berlin Airlift Berlin—controlled by the United States, Great Britain, France, and the Soviet Union—was deep in the Soviet zone of occupation and became a major point of contention among the former allies. When the Soviet Union blockaded the Allied-controlled western half of the city in June 1948, the United States responded with a massive airlift. By the time the blockade ended in May 1949, over 200,000 flights had delivered roughly 5,000 tons of supplies a day. Twelve years later, in 1961, the USSR built the Berlin Wall to stop movement between the Soviet and Western zones of the city.

Throughout the initial phase of the Cold War, each side aggravated tensions. The United States and Russia supported separate sides in the Greek Civil War of 1946–1948. Stalin blockaded West Berlin (1948–1949) in an effort to starve the city until it accepted Soviet rule; the Allies responded with the **Berlin airlift**, dropping more than 200,000 planeloads of food over the city. The Soviet Union saw NATO as a marshalling of forces to attack Russia, and with every country added to the alliance, the battlefront moved closer and closer to the Soviet border (see Map 27.1). Even such peaceable institutions as the International Monetary Fund and the World Bank (both started in 1946) struck Moscow as aggressive, since they aimed to promote capitalism—which, since the days of Lenin, was assumed always to culminate in imperialism.

As tensions rose in Europe, the Cold War spread to Asia. In 1945 as the defeated Japanese surrendered, Korea, like Germany, was divided into Soviet and American zones of occupation, which became in 1948 a Communist North Korea and an anti-Communist South Korea. In late 1949 the Communists under Mao Zedong *Escalating* (1893–1976) triumphed in China, frightening and angering many Americans, *Tensions* who saw new evidence of a powerful worldwide Communist conspiracy. When the Russian-backed Communist forces of North Korea invaded South Korea in the spring of 1950, President Truman acted swiftly. American-led UN forces under U.S. general Douglas MacArthur intervened.

The **Korean War** was bitterly fought. Initially, the well-equipped North Koreans almost conquered the entire peninsula, but the South Koreans and the Americans rallied and drove their foes north to the Chinese border. At that point China intervened, and its armies pushed the South Koreans and Americans back south. The war then seesawed back and forth near where it had begun. President Truman rejected MacArthur's call to attack China and fired him. In 1953 a fragile truce was finally negotiated, and the fighting stopped.

THE KOREAN WAR, 1950-1953

Stalin's death in 1953 led to a temporary calming of hostilities, but these roared back to life with the **Cuban Missile Crisis** of 1962, when the USSR's new *Cuban* leader, Nikita Khrushchev (1894–1971), ordered missiles with nuclear warheads *Missile* installed in Fidel Castro's Communist Cuba. With only 90 miles separating Cuba *Crisis* and the U.S. mainland, reaction times to a sudden launch were negligible. U.S. president John F. Kennedy (1917–1963) countered with a naval blockade of the island. After two weeks of intense negotiations and threats, Khrushchev withdrew the missiles. The world had come within minutes of a full-scale nuclear war. After this close escape, both sides agreed to ease hostilities and, if possible, to limit the spread of nuclear weapons.

The second stage of the Cold War stretched from 1962 to 1979. This was the era of **détente**, when the USSR and the West tried to ease the tensions between *The Era of* them by diplomacy, cultural exchange, and treaties to limit arms. The first break- *Détente* throughs were the Partial Test Ban Treaty (1963), the Outer Space Treaty (1967), and the Nuclear Non-Proliferation Treaty (1968), under President Lyndon Johnson (1918–1973) and Soviet Premier Leonid Brezhnev (1906–1982), whereby both sides agreed to restrict the testing of new nuclear weapons, to maintain the demilitarization of outer space, and to work together to prevent new nations from acquiring nuclear capability. But the problem remained that both the United States and the Soviet Union were armed to the teeth with nuclear weaponry of constantly increasing deadliness.

The first round of Strategic Arms Limitation Talks (SALT) produced a treaty (1972) that froze the number of nuclear missile launch systems held by each side; President Richard Nixon (1913–1994) and Brezhnev signed it in May of that year. West Germany played an important role here by pursuing closer relations with Communist East Germany. A younger generation increasingly warned of the dangers of the weapons buildup. A second round of SALT negotiations began almost immediately, with the aim of actually reducing the number of nuclear warheads held by each side. After seven years of negotiations, a SALT II treaty was signed by President Jimmy Carter (b. 1924) and (once again) Brezhnev in June 1979.

We pick up the final phase of the Cold War in chapter 28. It began with the Soviet invasion of Afghanistan in 1979, the effort to suppress the Solidarity reform movement in Poland, and the rise to power in Moscow of Mikhail Gorbachev (b. 1931) in 1985. Gorbachev's willingness to tear down the Berlin Wall in 1989 began the end of the Cold War—a process that both sides declared complete in 1991.

DECOLONIZATION IN A COLD WAR WORLD

This was also the era of **decolonization**, when Europe gave up, willingly or unwillingly, the bulk of its overseas territories. Independence movements had

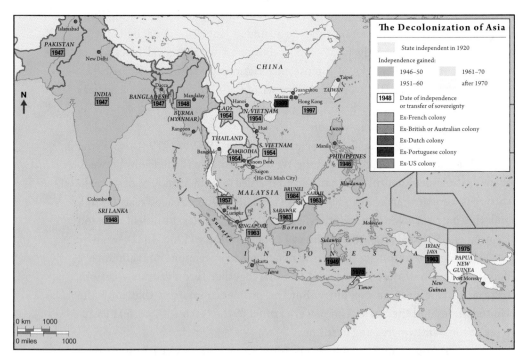

MAP 27.2   The Decolonization of Asia   Divided primarily along religious lines into two states, British India was the first and largest of the European colonies to win self-government after World War II.

already picked up their pace when the Depression made it harder for the imperial nations to afford their overseas involvements. First, the former colonies of the Ottomans gained freedom—although often, as we have seen, only a partial freedom, under a government named by the Europeans. Next came those of the Japanese Empire. (Japan had held Burma, Cambodia, parts of China, Laos, and Vietnam for only a decade, after seizing them from the Europeans, who had held them much longer.)

The European-held colonies followed. First came those in south Asia. India, Pakistan, Indonesia, and Sri Lanka all gained freedom in the late 1940s (see Map 27.2). In the 1950s the decolonizing wave passed to Southeast Asia, and in the 1960s it came at last to Africa (see Map 27.3). By 1970 the process was nearly complete.

MAP 27.3   The Decolonization of Africa   The liberation of Africa from European rule was an uneven process, sometimes occurring peacefully and at other times demanding armed conflict. Most African territories achieved statehood by the mid-1960s, as European empires passed away, unlamented.

Cleaning House   The Dutch East India Company, chartered by the government of The Netherlands, had controlled Indonesia from the late-16th century to 1800, when the government took over direct rule of the archipelago. Seized by imperial Japan in 1942, Indonesia demanded independence after the war but the Dutch fought to re-establish their colony. After two years of fighting, Indonesia won independence in December 1949. In this photograph, Indonesian workers remove the portraits of the three hundred Dutch governors who had ruled the country since 1595.

A host of problems confronted each of the newly independent countries, often before the ink had dried on their new charters. One problem was particularly prevalent in Africa: the political borders of the new nations did not correspond to ethnic, religious, or cultural boundaries. The borders of Somalia, for example, consisted only of the extent of Italian military conquest. The new "nation" after the Italian withdrawal did not exist in any meaningful way for the native peoples, who found themselves grouped together in a state not of their own choosing.

From Colony to Nation

Nigeria was formed from no fewer than 420 distinct ethnic and tribal groups. Although Kenya, for instance, had a more traditional structure to it, the problem of borders accounted for much of the political instability in African nations.

Independence from Europe also did not translate directly into economic self-sufficiency. Too many natural resources had been stripped away in cases such as Cambodia, the Congo, and India. Elsewhere resources remained monopolized by foreign corporations or the descendants of the colonizers, who often remained in what was for them their homeland. Even as the twentieth century drew to a close, Africans and Asians of European descent and their associates held much of the productive land, mineral resources, and commercial properties in the former European colonies. They also dominated political life. In Zimbabwe, for instance, white citizens made up a mere 1.5 percent of the total population but as late as 1987 they were guaranteed 20 percent of the seats in parliament. The Dutch East Indies, colonized in 1602, had been seized by Japan in World War II, and after the war the independent nation of Indonesia began to draft a constitution. The Dutch, however, waged a two-year war (1947–1949) to reestablish control; they were willing to compromise on sovereignty but fought bitterly to retain possession of the profitable trades in coal, coffee, oil, rubber, and spices. In the end, as many as eighty thousand Indonesians were killed and several million were displaced from their homes, especially on the islands of Java and Sumatra.

Superpower Rivalry

Decolonization also added to the rivalry between the West and the Soviet Union. In nearly every former colony hundreds, if not thousands, of diplomatic, economic, and military agents worked to encourage the new country to join their paths of development. Communism appealed strongly among the poorest and most powerless of the freed peoples and to many left-leaning intellectuals. Its message of economic equality resonated with desires to settle old scores with the West. Khrushchev supported independence movements across Africa and Asia but lacked capital for direct investment. Hence he offered trade credits in return for the raw materials that could supply Russia's factories. America's sales pitch to the new countries was more complex. It offered substantial investment—especially through the newly chartered International Monetary Fund and the World Bank—in return for guarantees to keep markets open to American goods and to resist Communism.

To keep an eye on Soviet attempts to spread their influence, the United States developed the Central Intelligence Agency. Its mission was officially limited to the gathering of intelligence, but in practice it often engaged in direct political intervention. In Iran, for example, the Central Intelligence Agency orchestrated the overthrow of a democratically elected new prime minister, Muhammad Mosaddegh, in 1953, after he nationalized the oil industry and its petroleum reserves. For good measure, they also had Mossaddegh arrested by the new government of the pro-Western Muhammad Reza Pahlavi, who ruled as shah until his own overthrow in the Iranian Revolution of 1979. In Korea (1950–1953) and, as we will see, in Vietnam (1955–1975), the confrontation of Communist and Western interests reached the point of military action. Neither war ended satisfactorily for either side.

RISE OF THE WELFARE STATE

While trying to contain Communist expansion, western Europe also devised programs to put economic development back on track and to prevent a reemergence of Fascism. These programs aimed at the creation of **welfare states**—societies in which the central government, funded by heavy taxation, provided all essential social services. They did this out of two central convictions: that education, health care, and a secure retirement are fundamental human rights and that people who have their basic needs met will not be tempted by radicalism.

Purposes and Principles

The welfare state differed in each country. In France, for example, the government focused on protecting children through education, family allowances, and childcare assistance. The British placed special emphasis on security for adults through health care, unemployment insurance, and pensions. The fundamental goal of maintaining stable life for all citizens remained the same, however. The United States did not travel as far down this road as western Europe did, but it went further than many people today remember. By the 1960s the United States offered a broad range of social benefits—Social Security for retirees, unemployment insurance, health care for the elderly and the indigent (Medicare and Medicaid), assistance with securing mortgages through the Federal Housing Administration, and access to college education (the GI Bill, Pell Grants, and loan guarantees)—even while undertaking massive infrastructure projects like the interstate freeway system.

Sir William Beveridge (1879–1963), a prominent economist, stated the British case for social welfare in 1942 in a report to Parliament called *Social Insurance and Allied Services* but known commonly as the *Beveridge Report*. He called on three essential principles:

> The first principle is that any proposals for the future, while they should use to the full the experience gathered in the past, should not be restricted by consideration of sectional interests established in the obtaining of that experience. Now, when the war is abolishing landmarks of every kind, is the opportunity for using experience in a clear field. A revolutionary moment in the world's history is a time for revolutions, not for patching. . . .
>
> The second principle is that organisation of social insurance should be treated as one part only of a comprehensive policy of social progress. Social insurance fully developed may provide income security; it is an attack upon Want. But Want is one only of five giants on the road of reconstruction and in some ways the easiest to attack. The others are Disease, Ignorance, Squalor and Idleness. . . .
>
> The third principle is that social security must be achieved by cooperation between the State and the individual. The State should offer security for service and contribution. The State in organising security should not stifle incentive, opportunity, responsibility; in establishing a national minimum, it should leave room and encouragement for voluntary action by each individual to provide more than that minimum for himself and his family.

Beveridge was arguing that the purpose of the state is to remove want, disease, ignorance, squalor, and idleness—as opposed simply to guaranteeing an individual's freedom to do so on his or her own.

This marks a significant change from nineteenth-century liberalism, although (as we saw in chapter 19) liberalism had insisted as early as 1848 on the state's responsibility to intervene. Free-market capitalism, for all its positive elements, gives profound advantages to some parts of society and disadvantages others. Intervention should thus be seen as reestablishing the freedom of the majority (the workers) rather than curtailing the freedom of the minority (the entrepreneurs). In protecting workers, for example, the state is simply correcting the imbalance

Subsidized Housing   Architects and urban planners review plans for creating more high-rise housing in a poor district in postwar Glasgow (1953). Postcolonial immigration increased demand for housing in western Europe's bigger cities, and the development of the welfare state gave high priority to providing housing.

that the marketplace gives to company owners. Workers must have the right to form unions and negotiate collectively for wages and work conditions, because company owners otherwise control labor. Another example is progressive taxation—requiring those with higher incomes to pay higher percentages of that income in tax. In this way, the state breaks up self-perpetuating concentrations of wealth so that a larger number of people gain the freedom to achieve success themselves.

The postwar welfare state extended such thinking. No one is free who is born into want, disease, ignorance, and squalor—and no such person can achieve freedom. Even idleness, Beveridge thought, is not simply a vice. It is imposed by unemployment, lack of education, and lack of opportunity. Removing these bars to freedom, liberalism argued, is the responsibility of the state. The purpose of government is to care for its citizens rather than to preserve owners' rights to control their property. Higher taxes on the wealthy are needed to pay for basic services.

Not everyone was pleased. Friedrich Hayek in the 1930s and 1940s warned of the "road to serfdom" (see chapter 25). Economic freedom, to Hayek, was the engine of all other freedoms, and any interference in capital, goods, services, and labor invited totalitarianism. (After reading a subsequent report by Beveridge in 1944 called *Full Employment in a Free Society*, Hayek declared that Beveridge "knows no economics whatever.") A leading American theorist who dissented

Arguments against the Welfare State

from welfare-state orthodoxy was Russell Kirk (1918–1994), the author of *The Conservative Mind: From Burke to Santayana* (1953).[2] Kirk's brand of conservatism emphasizes morality, tradition, and right living: "All culture arises out of religion." No amount of wealth or poverty can stand in the way of living by, and for, shared values. Nevertheless, Kirk insisted that the rights of private property were essential to freedom, since without the means to support oneself one cannot be truly free; attacks on property, as represented by the taxation required for the welfare state, undermined freedom.

British voters reelected the Conservative Party in 1951, then under the renewed leadership of Churchill, largely out of fear of the costs of a welfare state. Although welcome in the abstract, the welfare society was proving expensive to sustain. As the Party's manifesto put it:

> The attempt to impose a doctrinaire Socialism upon an Island which has grown great and famous by free enterprise has inflicted serious injury upon our strength and prosperity. Nationalisation has proved itself a failure which has resulted in heavy losses to the taxpayer or the consumer, or both. . . . Our finances have been brought into grave disorder. No British Government in peace time has ever had the power or spent the money in the vast extent and reckless manner of our present rulers. Apart from the two thousand millions they have borrowed or obtained from the United States and the Dominions, they have spent more than 10 million pounds a day, or 22 thousand millions in their six years. No community living in a world of competing nations can possibly afford such frantic extravagances.

Although successful in the short run, this line of thinking was too negative. There had to be more to the Conservative program than an argument that the nation could not afford the Liberal program. After four brief years, the British returned the more liberal Labour Party to power in 1955 and gave the welfare state a renewed endorsement. It was not until Margaret Thatcher (1925–2013) took the leadership in 1979 that Conservatism reemerged as a powerful force in British life.

SOCIAL CONSERVATISM AND ECONOMIC LIBERALISM

Germany lay divided into the democratic Federal Republic of Germany, or West Germany, and the Soviet-dominated Democratic Republic of Germany, or East Germany. West Germany, aided by the Marshall Plan and various UN

---

[2]   "When religious faith decays, culture must decline, though often seeming to flourish for a space after the religion which has nourished it has sunk into disbelief."—Russell Kirk

programs, achieved a stunning economic and political recovery under Konrad Adenauer (1876–1967), its chancellor from 1949 to 1963. Adenauer led the Christian Democratic Union, the party that has dominated German politics for the past sixty years. He was polite but reserved, and he could be coldly autocratic, especially in his later years, yet his vision for Germany was generous, welcoming, and humble regarding the sins of the Nazi past.

Adenauer was determined to create a prosperous and decent society that would integrate with the rest of western Europe. He set German–French relations on a better course, and he started the effort to reconcile Germany with the new State of Israel. He acknowledged the horror of the Holocaust, offered unconditional and repeated apologies, and extended reparations and aid to the fledgling Jewish state. By 1955 he had restored West Germany's reputation so much that NATO welcomed it into the alliance. At home Adenauer set in motion the

Konrad Adenauer   The tag-line on this photograph reads: "Together with the Chancellor, all Germans eye with worry their capital city." Adenauer was one of the founders of the Christian Democratic party in postwar West Germany and served as Chancellor of the Federal Republic from 1949 to 1963. He oversaw the reconstruction of the nation and its economy, restored diplomatic relations with Britain, France, and the United States, advocated restitution to all Jews, and was a resolute champion of the new state of Israel. Participants in a television poll in 2003 named him "the greatest German of all time."

welfare state. Education, health care, pensions, and unemployment insurance all became hallmarks of the Christian Democrats. Austria, Belgium, Italy, the Netherlands, and Norway for many years were (and in some instances, still are) dominated by Christian Democratic parties. Other nations with prominent Christian Democrat parties include Czechoslovakia, Denmark, France, Hungary, Ireland, Luxembourg, Portugal, Poland, Romania, and Sweden.

Christian Democrats have figured large in most western European nations— and in fact in most developed non-Communist countries worldwide since World War II. As an ideology, **Christian democracy** is a hybrid of social conservatism and economic liberalism. It blends forward-looking economic growth with a regard for traditionally Christian moral values. The movement started in the nineteenth century with a Catholic twist. Pope Leo XIII's encyclical *On New Things* (*De Rerum Novarum*), discussed in chapter 22, had focused on the impact of industrial capitalism on society. Yet the central thrust of most Christian Democrat parties has been moral, not theological—the importance of family, help for the poor and oppressed, communal identity, and social justice. After World War I

Christian Democracy

many Protestant groups joined forces with the early Christian Democrat parties out of concern for the growth of secularism in European society. They affirmed the Christian heritage of their societies, not to exclude other religious communities but to challenge secular ethics and Communism.

On the economic front, Christian democracy staked out a position midway between free-market capitalism and socialism. Commercial competition is generally good, it holds, but it must be used for the benefit of society as a whole, and that requires regulation. Unchecked capitalism creates wealth, but the problems of the twentieth century resulted not from lack of wealth-production but from its unequal distribution. Hence the welfare state. Substantial and indexed taxation, with tax rates increasing with income levels, exists both to fund essential services and to engineer a society that has less income imbalance. To a significant degree, however, western Europe could afford its welfare structure because the United States provided the cost of military defense through direct aid and subsidization of NATO.

THE POSTWAR BOOM

With the state providing for their basic needs, western Europeans could spend more of their incomes on the new consumer goods that rolled off factory lines: televisions, automobiles, refrigerators, laundry machines, record players, mass-produced cigarettes and alcohol, motorcycles, electric coffee makers, vacuum cleaners, hair dryers, power tools, and gas and electric ovens. High taxes naturally reduced "disposable income," the money left over to buy such items, but a new tool kept the purchases coming—consumer credit. Credit has been the fuel for capitalism since the thirteenth century, but it had always been limited to governments, banks, investment houses, companies, merchants, and entrepreneurs. Now that consumers too could purchase items on credit, consumption could keep pace, and more so, with production, assuring manufacturers a steady demand for their products.[3] Demand spurred continuous production and continual innovation, which in turn generated profits that could be taxed to fund the welfare state.

Consumerism   The economic uplift of the 1950s led to the manufacture of a new item—the word *consumerism*. It had existed before, but only in the sense of "advocacy for the rights of consumers"—the right to a fair price or to a product that is safe to use. Starting around 1960, however, it acquired a new meaning, one that has since become one of its main, if not its principal, uses: "excessive preoccupation with acquiring consumer goods." Consumption for consumption's sake, whether conspicuous or not. The ability to produce unprecedented quantities of consumer

---

3   The first true credit card, the Diners Club Card, appeared in 1950, and American Express brought out its card in 1958. Sweden introduced the *Eurocard* in 1960. France's *Carte Bleue* appeared in 1967.

Conspicuous Consumption in the Postwar Years   The recovery of the Western economy was based on construction and the manufacture of consumer goods: cars, electrical appliances, stoves, stereos, and televisions. Here one of the first color televisions is proudly displayed in a Frankfurt store in 1967.

goods, coupled with the decline in captive markets as a result of decolonization, led to a culture of acquisitiveness unlike anything Europe or America had experienced before. As late as 1900, perhaps 80 percent of the people in the industrialized West still exhausted their incomes on housing, food, and necessary services; with little or no "disposable income" (a phrase that made its first appearance in 1948) available, the purchase of non-necessary items remained beyond the reach of most people. The massive production levels of the postwar economy, however, especially in the context of the welfare state, meant that more people could purchase more goods. Consider televisions. In 1946 only seven thousand televisions existed in the entire United States, yet by 1949 more than twenty thousand televisions were purchased every day, and by 1960 more than 50 million televisions were in use.

It worked well, until the late 1960s. As long as the Western economies kept growing, so did tax revenues, and governments remained solvent. But Western economic growth depended on the growing postwar population, the so-called baby boom, which demanded more and more goods—more food and toys, more athletic equipment, more clothing, more schools and school supplies, more stereo systems, and more ways to care for all of them. But when the population increase leveled off, so too did demand for goods. Economic confidence crumbled and profits fell. To continue funding the welfare state, taxes rose; and as profits declined, credit became tighter. The miraculous recovery of the postwar West suddenly appeared vulnerable.

TURNING POINT: 1967–1968

Cold War tensions had eased somewhat after the near catastrophe of the Cuban Missile Crisis, but they reignited in 1967 and 1968. They were fueled by three events—the Six-Day War in the Middle East, the Soviet invasion of Czechoslovakia, and the Tet Offensive against American forces in Vietnam.

Six-Day War

Relations between Israel and its Arab neighbors had remained difficult, since the Arab states refused to recognize Israel. Border clashes occurred regularly, and members of the Palestinian Liberation Organization, an organization founded in 1964 with the purpose of the "liberation of Palestine," regularly carried out terrorist attacks on Israeli citizens and property. Rivalries and disagreements among the Arab states, however, impeded any sort of collective action against Israel until 1967, when alliances between Egypt, Jordan, and Syria left Israel surrounded by declared enemies. Preempting the coming invasion from all sides, Israel launched the **Six-Day War**. Air strikes and rapid troop movements paralyzed the Arabs' military capabilities, and in only six days Israel seized the Gaza Strip, the Golan Heights along the Israeli border with Syria, the Sinai Peninsula, and the entire West Bank. It also took possession of the eastern part of the then-divided city of Jerusalem (see Map 27.4).

The speed and completeness of the Israeli victory deeply embarrassed the Arab nations, including the eight countries that had provided armed assistance to Egypt, Jordan and Syria but did not participate in the actual fighting: Algeria, Iraq, Kuwait, Libya, Morocco, Saudi Arabia, Sudan, and Tunisia. Apart from what it meant to the combatants and local populations, the war had important implications for the Cold War. Arab popular opinion quickly decided that their stunning defeat was possible only through secret U.S. intervention on Israel's behalf. Nothing less than a massive international conspiracy could have brought about so complete and humiliating a reversal. Although America had indeed staunchly supported the state of Israel prior to the war, most Arabs prior to 1967 had regarded the British and French as the biggest meddling outsiders. After the war, most Arab popular resentment turned toward the United States.

Soviet Invasion of Czechoslovakia

The following year, on the night of August 20, 1968, Soviet tanks rolled into Czechoslovakia and put an end to the liberalizing reforms of its Communist government. Czechoslovakia had been Communist since 1948, but a new leader, Alexander Dubček (1921–1992), had hoped to create a less repressive form of government, a "socialism with a human face." Reforms instituted

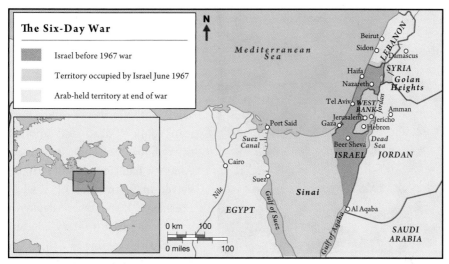

MAP 27.4 The Six-Day War In 1967, Israeli forces, responding to Palestinian guerrilla attacks, quickly seized Gaza and the Sinai peninsula from Egypt, the Golan Heights from Syria, and the West Bank from Jordan. Israel's stunning victory in this action deeply embarrassed the Arab nations and turned public opinion against the United States as well as Israel.

early in 1968, known as the **Prague Spring**, permitted independent political parties; this development appalled the Soviet ruler, Leonid Brezhnev (1906–1982), who ordered the military intervention. Overnight, 20–21 August, two hundred thousand Soviet soldiers and two thousand tanks poured into Czechoslovakia.[4] The action was more threatening than violent, but it sent a chill throughout Europe. The USSR, after all, had killed more than twenty thousand civilians in its 1956 invasion of Hungary under Stalin's successor, Khrushchev. Now under Khrushchev's successor, Brezhnev, the leadership in Moscow had shown yet again its willingness to secure and expand its dictatorial authority. The attack on Czechoslovakia was the first direct experience of Soviet brutality for the generation that came of age in the late 1960s, and it made clearer than ever the perilous state of the world. To Moscow's surprise, protests against the invasion came from multiple corners: America and western Europe, of course, but also the Communist governments of Albania, Finland, and Romania, as well as the Communist parties in places like Italy and Portugal. Chastened, the Soviets quickly worked out a compromise settlement with the government in Prague and withdrew.

Also in 1968, a surprise wave of attacks by the troops of Communist North *Tet* Vietnam against the U.S.-supported government in South Vietnam nearly *Offensive*

---

[4]   Many of the invaders got lost, since dozens of villages and towns took down their local road signs and quickly put up new ones, each renaming itself "Dubček". The Russians' maps were thus rendered useless.

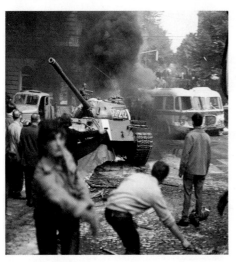

Prague Spring The term "Prague Spring" refers to the liberalizing reforms instituted by the Communist government in Czechoslovakia under Prime Minister Alexander Dubček. (Its echo can be heard in the "Arab Spring" rebellions of 2011.) Dubček promoted freedom of speech, freedom of the press, and the option for a multiparty government. Here people are shown resisting the Soviet tanks that rolled into the city to put an end to the Prague Spring. Dubček was removed from power and his reforms undone.

toppled the American-backed regime in Saigon. Called the Tet Offensive, these attacks targeted roughly 120 separate towns and cities in the south and left ten thousand South Vietnamese and American soldiers dead and another thirty-five thousand wounded. America had become directly involved in Vietnam in 1955, when President Eisenhower deployed several hundred military advisers to assist the regime in Saigon. By 1963 U.S. troops were still as few as sixteen thousand, but under President Lyndon Johnson the military presence escalated dramatically, passing the half million mark by 1968. The sharp impact of the Tet Offensive made it abundantly clear that, even with increased numbers and superior technology, the United States could look forward to no quick and easy victory in Vietnam. Chinese and Soviet support for the Communist North Vietnamese further assured a long and drawn-out war (see Map 27.5).

The 1967–1968 turning point drove home some harsh realities. The economic bonanza of the postwar years was coming to a halt, threatening to unravel the safety net provided by the welfare state. The Cold War turned out not to be merely a strategic game between bureaucrats and armchair generals; the threat was real and deadly.

THE FEMALE FACTOR

The postwar decades saw dramatic shifts in the legal and social rights of women. Despite women's wartime work in farming, in manufacturing, and in clerical and administrative positions, cultural pressures pushed them back into the home after 1945. At the same time, the millions of men who were released from military service sought reentry in the postwar economy.

Many Americans like to remember the 1950s as a period of particularly happy and stable home life. In Europe, privation and rationing gave the lie to that

MAP 27.5   The Vietnam War   The Cold War drew the United States to Vietnam, where they tried to stem what they saw as the tide of Communist influence behind the Vietnamese liberation movement. The ensuing war in Vietnam in the 1960s and 1970s spread into neighboring countries, making the region the scene of vast destruction.

view. Europe had lost tens of millions of young men in the war, resulting in the labor shortage that had led to guest workers and immigration. Women in Europe consequently were not driven from their jobs to the same degree as in the United States; the primary injustice they experienced was unequal pay. In Britain, Italy, the Netherlands, and West Germany, women received only two-thirds the pay that men did in the 1950s and 1960s for the same work; in France women often received only half. With low wages and salaries, companies earned greater profits and so paid more in taxes—which in turn kept social programs running.

Rise of Second-Wave Feminism

Another factor also came into play to affect deeply Western women and society—the availability of reliable contraception. The birth-control pill, the result of decades of scientific research, reached the U.S. and European markets in the early 1960s. Women began to have fewer children, and the postwar baby boom came to a close: from its peak in 1955, the birthrate in western Europe fell 40 percent by 1975. With fewer children to care for at home and with demand for labor in the workplace, women—especially middle-class women—began to think of employment outside the home. Work could be a lifelong career, rather than a way to support oneself until marriage.

By 1970 fully one-half of European mothers had stopped having children by the age of twenty-seven or twenty-eight, which meant that forty years of productive work still lay ahead of them, if they were interested. And they *were* interested. They wanted careers, not merely jobs, and they demanded equal pay for equal work. Feminism at this time thus focused on economic and social justice. Men still predominated in heavy industry and manufacturing, but new careers opened up in schools and universities, in health care, in management, in journalism, and in law. Women were drawn to these "white collar" careers in large numbers.

The movement for equality for women in the 1960s and 1970s came to be known as **second-wave feminism**. Feminism's first wave, starting in the nineteenth century, had a single goal—the right of women to vote. Crusaders for contraception were then relatively few, and they were widely regarded as radicals. The second wave focused on personal life, sexual health, access to abortion and contraception, equal rights in the workplace, the availability of childcare services, gender roles in society, and the portrayals of women in popular culture. Since then, a third wave of feminism, from the 1990s to the present, has had two main streams. One was a broadening of the movement to include the poor and ethnic minorities. The other was an examination of the very concepts of gender, race, and sexuality.

The second wave scored signal achievements. In the United States, new institutions dedicated to improving women's lives were established—from the Presidential Commission on the Status of Women (1961) to the National Organization for Women (1966), the National Abortion Rights Action League (1968), and the Coalition of Labor Union Women (1974). The Supreme Court in 1965 struck down states' bans on the sale of contraception, and in 1973 it upheld women's right to abortion. The first shelters for battered women opened their doors. Universities across the nation created programs in women's studies. Military academies admitted women applicants, and female undergraduates in colleges outnumbered males by 1978.

Feminism in western Europe did not have the vibrancy of America's reform movement, largely because the extensive welfare-state structures had already achieved—at least on paper—many of its goals. The new French constitution of 1946, for example, had already mandated equal legal rights for men and women, and women were already vital to the workforce. Although discrimination persisted, especially in pay, political instability seemed the more immediate problem. Between 1946 and 1958 the French government went through no fewer than twenty-seven cabinet reshufflings, which made it difficult to mount any extended campaigns for reform. Only in 1968 was the first national organization for women's rights formed—the Mouvement de Libération des Femmes. Even then, the Mouve-

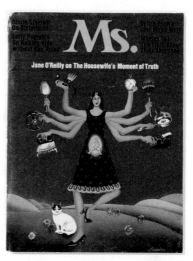

Second-Wave Feminism   This photograph reproduces the cover of the first issue of *Ms.* Magazine, which appeared in January 1972 and was for the next decade the leading periodical in second-wave feminism. The magazine was founded by Gloria Steinem (b. 1934) and Dorothy Pitman Hughes (b. 1938), and currently has a circulation over 100,000.

ment saw itself as a network of psychologists, psychoanalysts, philosophers, and legal scholars rather than a group of activists. Practical, hands-on reform had to wait until the 1971 formation of Choisir ("Choice"), a group that advocated for contraception and abortion rights.

Feminism and the Welfare State

In West Germany too, the welfare state had already addressed many women's issues. That assumption helps explain why no government between 1945 and 1961 had a single woman in a cabinet-level post. As Franz Josef Würmeling, the West German minister for the family and social affairs, put it in 1961:

> The [German] family has responded to the economic constraints of our time in two main ways: with housewives and mothers taking jobs outside the home, and then limiting the number of children they have.... But for housewives and mothers to work outside the home is not a solution; it is in fact a compulsive evil.

In Britain feminist concerns were the program of the Labour Party, along with social welfare and reform. Labour was in power from 1945 to 1951 under Clement Atlee (1883–1967) and then again from 1964 to 1970 and 1974 to 1976 under Harold Wilson (1916–1995). The laws regarding abortion, contraception, divorce, education, and sexual preference were all liberalized, but a vital feminist movement comparable to the American one failed to appear.

WOMEN, ISLAM, AND THE STATE

The status of women in postcolonial Islamic society played out between the opposing forces of modernization and traditionalism. The ideologies of the Cold War did not affect Muslim states directly, since atheistic Communism held no appeal, but the political conflict mattered to them very much. Three broad issues had a particular impact on women: national identity, the role of Islamic law in civic life, and the nature of state government.

Forces of Modernization

First, national identity. The states created out of European decolonization sometimes crossed, and sometimes divided, traditional ethnic borders. Creating a sense of national identity thus represented a challenge to traditional social structures and values. Some factions believed that Western-style pluralism could be harnessed to produce a modern democratic society based on individual rights and capitalism even while retaining the core values of Islam. This reformed tradition, they believed, would allow Islamic states to remain open to the West and rid Muslim life of centuries-old norms regarding women, while still retaining an authentic religious identity.

One example of this reform-minded strain emerged in Turkey. There the secular constitution ensured equal treatment of women before the law, moderated customs regarding marriage and divorce, and allowed women economic freedom, access to education, and freedom of dress. In Algeria after liberation in 1962, men and women came to possess full and equal civil rights. Lebanon also experimented with democracy, civil rights, religious pluralism, and greater participation and freedom for women in public life. Conflicts with Israel and Syria kept Lebanon a fragile society, but the capital city of Beirut became known in the 1960s and 1970s as the "Paris of the eastern Mediterranean." In Iran, too, under the autocratic regime of Shah Muhammad Reza Pahlavi, westernizing policies opened the state to economic development, the growth of a vivid cosmopolitan culture, and an easing of restrictions on female participation in society.

Learning New Ways   An Iranian teacher assists one of her students during class in this photograph from the late 1960s.

No political freedom existed, of course, and the rewards of economic development were hoarded by the shah and his cadre. But Iranian society seemed set on a
liberalizing trajectory, prior to the Islamic Revolution of 1979.

Other factions in response raised the second issue of importance to women—
the role of Islamic law, or shari'a. They argued that Islam cannot be harmonized *Forces of*
with Western ways, and the only correct path was a complete rejection of Western *Religious*
values and the embrace of ancient Islamic practices. In the words of one conserva- *Conservatism*
tive reformer, Mona Fayyad Kawtharani, ancient practices like the veiling of
women represent resistance to the West. Ethnic and tribal traditions also contributed, but civic rights and social freedoms for women became ideological statements. After the 1979 overthrow of the shah and the declaration of Iran as an
Islamic Republic, the fundamentalist new regime ordered women to relinquish
Western styles of dress, forbade them from venturing out in public without an
accompanying male family member, and pressed them back into domestic life.

The role of conservative Islam in national life thus became crucial to determining women's fates. The Organization of the Islamic Conference (OIC) formed
in 1969 to present a united Islamic face to the world. With fifty-seven member
states, it is the largest international organization in the world after the United Nations itself, and it came to reject the 1948 UN Declaration on Human Rights (discussed in chapter 26) because of its basis in secular values. The OIC's **Cairo
Declaration on Human Rights**, adopted in 1990, states in its preamble that the
only valid foundation for human rights is in faith:

> Convinced that mankind which has reached an advanced stage in
> materialistic science is still, and shall remain, in dire need of faith to sup-
> port its civilization as well as a self-motivating force to guard its rights;
>
> [and] believing that fundamental rights and freedoms according to
> Islam are an integral part of the Islamic religion and that no one shall
> have the right as a matter of principle to abolish them either in whole or
> in part or to violate or ignore them inasmuch as they are binding divine
> commands, which are contained in the Revealed Books of Allah and
> which were sent through the last of His Prophets to complete the preced-
> ing divine messages;
>
> and [believing] that safeguarding those fundamental rights and
> freedoms is an act of worship whereas the neglect or violation thereof is
> an abominable sin, and that the safeguarding of those fundamental
> rights and freedom is an individual responsibility of every person and a
> collective responsibility of the entire *Ummah*;
>
> [We do] hereby and on the basis of the above-mentioned principles
> declare as follows.

Among the Declaration's highlights were the following:

> Article 1: (a) All human beings form one family whose members are united by submission to God and descent from Adam. All men are equal in terms of basic human dignity and basic obligations and responsibilities, without any discrimination on the grounds of race, colour, language, sex, religious belief, political affiliation, social status or other considerations. . . .
>
> Article 2: Life is a God-given gift and the right to life is guaranteed to every human being. It is the duty of individuals, societies and states to protect this right from any violation, and it is prohibited to take away life except for a Shari'ah-prescribed reason. . . .
>
> Article 6: (a) Woman is equal to man in human dignity, and has rights to enjoy as well as duties to perform; she has her own civil entity and financial independence, and the right to retain her name and lineage. (b) The husband is responsible for the support and welfare of the family. . . .
>
> Article 9: (a) The quest for knowledge is an obligation, and the provision of education is a duty for society and the State. . . . (b) Every human being has the right to receive both religious and worldly education from the various institutions of education and guidance, including the family, the school, the university, the media, etc. . . .
>
> Article 19: (a) All individuals are equal before the law, without distinction between the ruler and the ruled. (b) The right to resort to justice is guaranteed to everyone. . . .
>
> Article 22: (a) Everyone shall have the right to express his opinion freely in such manner as would not be contrary to the principles of the Shari'ah. (b) Everyone shall have the right to advocate what is right, and propagate what is good, and warn against what is wrong and evil according to the norms of Islamic Shari'ah. . . . (d) It is not permitted to arouse nationalistic or doctrinal hatred or to do anything that may be an incitement to any form of racial discrimination.
>
> Article 25: The Islamic Shari'ah is the only source of reference for the explanation or clarification to any of the articles of this Declaration.

The Cairo Declaration recognizes the innate dignity of all people. It asserts their rights to live in peace, to own property, and to receive public services like education and health care. Because "the Islamic Shari'ah is the only source of reference for the explanation or clarification to any of the articles of this Declaration" (article 25), however, exceptions exist to almost every one of its guarantees.

As far as women are concerned, the OIC's declaration recognizes that "woman is equal to man in human dignity, and has rights to enjoy as well as duties to perform" (article 6), but that is not the same thing as saying that a woman has equal rights to men—as the UN declaration explicitly declares.

The third issue affecting women's status was the debate regarding the role of the state itself. To hold together their ethnically plural nations, with diverging interpretations of the role of religion in national life, postcolonial governments have relied on centralized authority. "Strongmen" with authoritarian regimes have included the shah Muhammad Reza Pahlavi in Iran (r. 1941–1979), Hafez al-Assad in Syria (r. 1971–2000), General Muhammad Zia ul-Haq in Pakistan (r. 1978–1988), and Muammar al-Qaddafi in Libya (r. 1969–2011). In each case, wealth has been hoarded by elites rather than distributed throughout society, and countries without oil have been mired in poverty. In the poorer states—Afghanistan, Bangladesh, Jordan, Libya, Pakistan, Syria—lack of economic opportunity drove women further into isolation within the home.

◆

To many Muslims, the legacy of imperialism and the advance of secularism in Europe and America were proofs of entrenched Western hostility toward the Islamic world and of a general moral decrepitude that made any aspect of Western culture, however seemingly benign, something suspicious and dangerous. The only sure path to stability and happiness was the return to religious truth. According to Abu'l-Hasan Ali Nadwi (1914–1999), a prominent religious scholar from northern India, Islam's conservative turn, in the face of Western secularism, was a sign of the eventual global supremacy of the Muslims. "The only cure for the world's current evils is for world-leadership to pass from those who worship materialism to those who worship Allah." With such sentiments, the phenomenon of modern Islamist belief begins.

For Europe and America, though, it was still necessary to have something to believe in—even if that something was not divine. A parade of candidates existed: democracy and human rights, free markets, the authority of science, the sanctity of cultural tradition, the essential centrality of the nuclear family, the primacy of the individual. The sight of so many alternatives was confusing but also exciting.

WHO, WHAT, WHERE

Berlin airlift

Cairo Declaration
    on Human Rights

Christian democracy

Cold War

Cuban Missile Crisis

decolonization

détente

existentialism

Korean War

Marshall Plan

North Atlantic Treaty
    Organization

Prague Spring

second-wave
    feminism

Six-Day War

Warsaw Pact

welfare states

SUGGESTED READINGS

Primary Sources

Barthes, Roland. *Mythologies.*

Camus, Albert. *The Myth of Sisyphus.*

Camus, Albert. *The Stranger.*

Kirk, Russell. *The Conservative Mind.*

Lévi-Strauss, Claude. *The Savage Mind.*

Nkrumah, Kwame. *Neo-Colonialism: The Last Stage of Imperialism.*

Powell, Enoch. *Freedom and Reality.*

Anthologies

Bekes, Csaba, Malcolm Byrne, and Janos Rainer. *The 1956 Hungarian Revolution: A History in Documents* (2003).

Hanhimäki, Jussi, and Odd Arne Westad, eds. *The Cold War: A History in Documents and Eyewitness Accounts* (2003).

Pierson, Christopher, and Francis G. Castles, eds. *The Welfare State Reader* (2007).

Prince, Althea, and Susan Silva-Wayne, eds. *Feminisms and Womanisms: A Women's Studies Reader* (2004).

Winkler, Allan M. *The Cold War: A History in Documents* (2011).

Studies

Azoulay, Ariella. *From Palestine to Israel: A Photographic Record of Destruction and State Formation, 1947–1950* (2011).

Barrett, Roby C. *The Greater Middle East and the Cold War: US Foreign Policy under Eisenhower and Kennedy* (2010).

Fowkes, Ben. *Eastern Europe, 1945–1969: From Stalinism to Stagnation* (2000).

Fraser, Derek. *The Evolution of the British Welfare State: A History of Social Policy since the Industrial Revolution* (2009).

Gaddis, John Lewis. *The Cold War: A New History* (2005).

Gati, Charles. *Failed Illusions: Moscow, Washington, Budapest and the 1956 Hungarian Revolt* (2006).

Geller, Jay Howard. *Jews in Post-Holocaust Germany, 1945–1953* (2005).

Grossmann, Atina. *Jews, Germans, and Allies: Close Encounters in Occupied Germany* (2009).

Harrison, Brian. *Seeking a Role: The United Kingdom, 1951–1970* (2011).

Hilton, Matthew. *Consumerism in Twentieth-Century Britain: The Search for a Historical Movement* (2003).

Judt, Tony. *Postwar: A History of Europe since 1945* (2005).

Kusin, Vladimir. *The Intellectual Origins of the Prague Spring: The Development of Reformist Ideas in Czechoslovakia, 1956-1967* (2002).

Lukes, Igor. *On the Edge of the Cold War: American Diplomats and Spies in Postwar Prague* (2012).

Lüthi, Lorenz. *The Sino-Soviet Split: Cold War in the Communist World* (2008).

Palier, Bruno, ed. *A Long Goodbye to Bismarck?: The Politics of Welfare Reforms in Continental Europe* (2010).

Patten, Howard A. *Israel and the Cold War: Diplomacy, Strategy, and the Policy of the Periphery at the UN* (2012).

Pugh, Martin. *Women and the Women's Movement in Britain, 1914–1959* (2000).

Roth, Benita. *Separate Roads to Feminism: Black, Chicana, and White Feminist Movements in America's Second Wave* (2004).

Wendehorst, Stephan E. C. *British Jewry, Zionism, and the Jewish State, 1936–1956* (2011).

Westad, Odd Arne. *The Global Cold War: Third World Interventions and the Making of Our Times* (2007).

Zubok, Vladislav M. *A Failed Empire: The Soviet Union in the Cold War from Stalin to Gorbachev* (2008).

For additional resources, including maps, primary sources, visuals, web links, and quizzes, please go to **www.oup.com/us/backman.**

CHAPTER 28

Something to Believe In

1960–1988

Europe's movement away from traditional religious ob-servance accelerated in the second half of the twentieth century. The revolt was intuitive rather than intellectual. Many who had survived World War II simply concluded either that no God would allow such suffering or that any God who would allow it did not deserve worship. Others re-tained their belief but not their former practice; with entire cities in ruins, there were not enough churches left standing. Still others felt that Europe could not afford the time for churchgoing. The task of rebuilding was too important—and once the econo-mies did begin to hum along, there were too many opportunities to "get ahead." Millions of Europeans felt trapped by the tension between the United States and the Soviet Union. Regardless of what happened with missiles, few doubted that Europe itself would once again become a battlefield and responded to the knowledge with despair.

Yet amid secularism and spiritual anxiety, there was also revival. As atten-dance in churches declined, both Catholic and Protestant thinking became more diverse. Pope John XXIII (r. 1958–1963) in-stituted the most sweeping Catholic reform in centuries, with concern for the plight of Jews after the Holocaust and for Catholics in the Soviet bloc. Protestantism saw a "new or-thodoxy" in Europe, but also new modes of worship and new spiritual energy in the

PREDOMINANT RELIGIONS OF THE GREATER WEST, ca. 1988

Predominant/state-supported religion:
Roman Catholicism — Sunni Islam
Orthodox and other Eastern Churches — Shiite Islam
Protestantism — Judaism

Believing in Prosperity The 60s generation, Italian-style. Postwar youths, full of energy and brio, secure in their comfort and care, but already showing signs of rebellion against conformity.

United States and the Third World. Postwar realities also brought on important changes in Jewish and Islamic observance across the Greater West. Jews fractured into new denominations and contested histories of Israel, and the tensions between traditional Islamic cultures and modernity sparked another revolution.

A GENERATION OF REBELLION

Strains in the Welfare State

Welfare-state spending grew steadily through the 1960s until, as early as 1964, it strained budgets across western Europe and the United States. In Britain, annual costs for social services rose 50 percent between 1964 and 1970. With the U.S. military shield protecting Europe from the Soviet Union, European states were still able to sustain their generous welfare programs with ease. In the United States, however, the combination of social spending and military costs threatened ruin. For millions of baby boomers coming of age in the 1960s, the economy and society appeared to be unraveling, along with the political system that oversaw it. As America entered the war in Vietnam, it seemed to many to have lost its moral authority as well. A generation of rebellion began to question received values and to protest against unjust norms and failed policies.

In western Europe, however, the rebellious 1960s had a different focus. Heavy public investment in higher education continued. Britain created dozens of public universities in the 1950s and 1960s, which British students attended for

CHAPTER TIMELINE

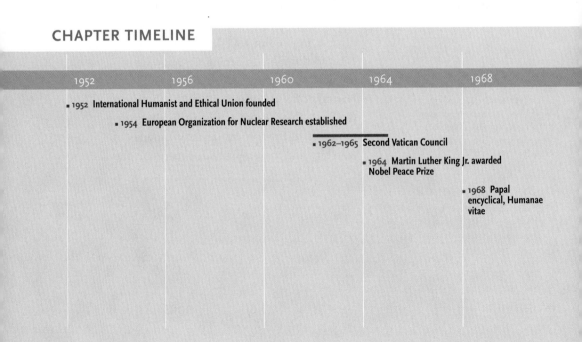

| 1952 | 1956 | 1960 | 1964 | 1968 |

- 1952 International Humanist and Ethical Union founded
- 1954 European Organization for Nuclear Research established
- 1962–1965 Second Vatican Council
- 1964 Martin Luther King Jr. awarded Nobel Peace Prize
- 1968 Papal encyclical, Humanae vitae

free. Discontent arose not from limited access to education but from social preju-dices that preserved old privileges. One could be brilliantly educated at a new "red brick" university—yet one could get the best jobs or most promising careers, many believed, only if one had attended the elite private universities of Oxford and Cambridge.

France, too, expanded access to its university system, but at a much slower rate—and with preferred treatment for the middle class. As late as 1968 only 4 per-cent of university students nationwide came from the working class. Italy invested in fewer new universities but admitted students in large numbers and also helped pay for their tuition; the average student-to-faculty ratio rose higher than 200 to 1. The quality of their education, or at least the perception of its quality, declined pro-portionally. By 1968 only half of university graduates were able to find work in the fields of their study. The liberalization of higher education across western Europe, in other words, had failed to alter ingrained social privilege and class stratification.

Similar complaints arose about economic strata. In 1967 in West Germany, despite twenty years of reform, the top 2 percent of the population still owned more than one-third of the nation's wealth—a pattern that echoed the inequity of the era before World War I. France and Britain had comparable concentrations of wealth. Western society, overall, was better off than ever before, but the ideal of social justice, many complained, had been sold out. People had ceased to be think-ing and feeling actors on the world stage and had become mere consumers.

1972	1976	1980	1984	1988

■ 1973 Yom Kippur War

■ 1975 European Space Agency founded; UN Resolution 3379

■ 1979 Peace treaty between Egypt and Israel; Iranian revolution

■ 1987 Morris, *The Birth of the Palestinian Refugee Problem, 1947–1949*

■ 1988 Founding of Hamas

A Generation in Rebellion   University students in Paris, in 1968, seized the buildings of the Sorbonne in protest against the Cold War and the failures of the welfare state. The photos visible here are portraits of Karl Marx, Friedrich Engels, Joseph Stalin, and Mao Zedong. Workers across the nation joined in a general strike, which nearly brought down the government of Charles de Gaulle. The motives of the rebels are still debated. Many were Communists or Socialists, but others seem to have joined in a spirit of unfocused anarchy. One of the graffiti left behind by the students on the walls of the Sorbonne read: "We do not want a world in which the price for a guarantee of not starving to death is to die of boredom."

The 1960s were also the age of **civil rights** struggles in the United States—the struggles for equal access for African Americans to the voting booth, transportation, lunch counters, jobs, schools, and every other part of society. The Reverend Martin Luther King Jr. (1929–1968) was a powerful moral force who advocated the use of civil disobedience to obtain these goals. His shocking assassination in 1968, four years after he won the Nobel Peace Prize, did not deter other groups, including Hispanic Americans, American Indians, and gays and lesbians, from also advocating for their own rights in the face of sometimes enormous hostility. Major civil rights laws were passed by the U.S. Congress starting in 1964.

The decade also saw immigration conflicts in western Europe. Millions of Africans, South Asians, and Muslim Arabs, Turks, and Pakistanis migrated into Europe during decolonization. They came for many different reasons. Some feared the instability of the postcolonial societies and their underdeveloped economies. Others felt a sense of cultural identity with the withdrawing Europeans.

U.S. Civil Rights Struggles   Still others were openly recruited by Western powers that, after 80 million war deaths, faced the hard work of rebuilding. Jobs were plentiful in western Europe, and economic futures in Africa, Asia, and the Middle East seemed uncertain, so why not migrate?

Immigration Conflicts   West Germany had the greatest need for workers, given the scale of postwar reconstruction. Chancellor Konrad Adenauer (1876–1967) invited "guest workers" (*Gastarbeiter*) from Turkey to work in construction and in factories. In 1964 the West German labor minister, Theodor Blank (1905–1972), commemorated the arrival of the one-millionth Turkish guest worker:

> These million workers contribute vitally to the steady growth of German industry, the maintaining of stable prices, and upholding Germany's reputation on the world marketplace. . . . To judge from available statistics, our native labor pool will continue to shrink for the foreseeable future. . . . We are in fact wholly dependent on the guest workers

to keep our economy moving forward. . . . In fact we can no longer even imagine economic life without them, a situation that entitles them to share in the benefits of our [welfare] society.

Tensions between the guest workers and their German hosts were growing, he acknowledged, but "the coming together of people from different backgrounds and cultures has worked—and for that we owe our guest workers our gratitude."

But popular resistance to immigration kept growing. In 1982 a group of professors at the University of Heidelberg went so far as to publish an open letter that warned of:

> the infiltration of our German people by millions of foreign immigrants and their families—the infiltration of our language, our culture, our national traditions. . . . In many workplaces and neighborhoods, in fact, our German people are made to feel like strangers in their own land.

In Britain, immigrants included Indians, Pakistanis, Arabs, Africans, Chinese, and Southeast Asians. Throughout the 1960s a Conservative British politician, Enoch Powell (1912–1998), warned of the growing expense of the welfare state. He is best remembered, however, for a speech in the spring of 1968 on the threat of immigration:

> In 15 or 20 years, on present trends, there will be in this country three and a half million Commonwealth immigrants and their descendants. That is not my figure. That is the official figure given to parliament by the spokesman of the Registrar General's Office.
>
> There is no comparable official figure for the year 2000, but it must be in the region of five to seven million, approximately one-tenth of the whole population, and approaching that of Greater London. Of course, it will not be evenly distributed from Margate to Aberystwyth and from Penzance to Aberdeen. Whole areas, towns and parts of towns across England will be occupied by sections of the immigrant and immigrant-descended population.
>
> As time goes on, the proportion of this total who are immigrant descendants, those born in England, who arrived here by exactly the same route as the rest of us, will rapidly increase. Already by 1985 the native-born would constitute the majority. It is this fact which creates the extreme urgency of action now, of just that kind of action which is hardest for politicians to take, action where the difficulties lie in the present but the evils to be prevented or minimized lie several parliaments ahead. . . .

But while, to the immigrant, entry to this country was admission to privileges and opportunities eagerly sought, the impact upon the existing population was very different. For reasons which they could not comprehend, and in pursuance of a decision by default, on which they were never consulted, they found themselves made strangers in their own country. They found their wives unable to obtain hospital beds in childbirth, their children unable to obtain school places, their homes and neighbourhoods changed beyond recognition, their plans and prospects for the future defeated; at work they found that employers hesitated to apply to the immigrant worker the standards of discipline and competence required of the native-born worker; they began to hear, as time went by, more and more voices which told them that they were now the unwanted. . . .

As I look ahead, I am filled with foreboding. Like the Roman, I seem to see "the River Tiber foaming with much blood" [quote from Virgil's *The Aeneid*]. That tragic and intractable phenomenon which we watch with horror on the other side of the Atlantic [U.S. civil rights struggles] but which there is interwoven with the history and existence of the States itself, is coming upon us here by our own volition and our own neglect. Indeed, it has all but come. In numerical terms, it will be of American proportions long before the end of the century. Only resolute and urgent action will avert it even now. Whether there will be the public will to demand and obtain that action, I do not know. All I know is that to see, and not to speak, would be the great betrayal.

Powell's "Rivers of Blood" speech set off a stormy debate. Although many Britons denounced his comments as racist, most rallied to his cause. The argument against immigration was the same one used by societies dating back to Roman efforts to block Germanic tribesmen from overwhelming the empire in the third century CE: too many, too fast. Mass assimilations can be difficult for the host society, as they are for the immigrants themselves. Popular support for Powell's comments swelled, because immigration was seen as a threat to the welfare state.[1] Powell argued that welfare programs could continue at steady levels even while reducing Britain's basic tax rate—but only if the country avoided military entanglements abroad and reduced the immigrant population. Those were two big ifs.

---

[1]   In polls between 1969 and 1974, Enoch Powell was repeatedly identified as the single most admired politician in Britain.

Migrant Labor   An immigrant from Portugal arrives in Britain, in search of a better life. He was lucky to get out. A repressive quasi-Fascist regime, led by António de Oliveira Salazar, ran Portugal from 1932 to 1974.

BIG SCIENCE AND EXPANDING SECULARISM

The Cold War marked the beginning of the era of **Big Science**, involving everything from the space race to subatomic particle colliders, from cancer research *Scientific* to genetic engineering, and from biochemical processes to digital micropro- *Achievements* cessing. Total spending on scientific research in Europe and the United States *and Funding* quintupled between 1945 and 1980 (even after adjusting for inflation); so did the number of scientists and engineers engaged in research. In Europe, according to the Organization for Economic Cooperation and Development, roughly 65 percent of scientific research is either conducted or funded by industry; another 20 percent is supported by European universities, and another 10 percent is funded by the various governments. In the United States, by contrast, the federal government funded roughly 30 percent of research through the 1960s and 1970s—a share three times larger than that of its European counterparts. As Table 28.1 indicates, spending on so vast a scale produced numerous scientific breakthroughs.

Given the high costs of scientific research, these achievements could not have occurred without the support of governments and other institutions. In nuclear physics, for example, leadership belonged to the European Organization for Nuclear Research (known as CERN, an acronym of its original French

TABLE 28.1   **Major Advances in Science and Technology, ca. 1950–2000**

1946	ENIAC, first digital computer
1952	Polio vaccine developed by Jonas Salk
1953	Francis Crick and James Watson model DNA molecule
1962	Thomas Kuhn publishes *The Structure of Scientific Revolutions*
1963	Tectonic plate theory confirmed
1964	Louis Leaky identifies *Homo habilis*
1965	Cosmic microwave background radiation (echo of Big Bang) detected; Noam Chomsky posits theory of generative grammar
1968	ARPANET (precursor of Internet) established
1969	First microprocessor; Neil Armstrong lands on the moon
1970	Stephen Hawking and Robert Penrose prove the universe must have had a beginning in time
1971	Biologists identify the gene that controls an organism's sense of time
1972	Astronomers identify the first-ever confirmed black hole; Stephen J. Gould presents theory of evolution by punctuated equilibria
1973	First successful experiment of recombinant DNA; development of TCP/IP, allowing diverse computer networks to communicate with each other
1976	Confirmation of theory of a genetic component in development of cancer
1977	First transmission of television signals on optical fibers
1978	Mary Leaky discovers fossilized human footprints 3.5 million years old
1981	Programmers at Microsoft Corporation develop MS-DOS operating system
1982	Experimental proof of Einstein's predicted "spooky action at a distance" theorem
1984	Discovery of *Homo erectus* skeleton, 1.6 million years old
1987	Genealogical model shows how all human mitochondrial DNA can be traced back to a common African maternal ancestor
1988	Etienne Baulieu develops the RU-486 abortion pill
1990	Tim Berners-Lee invents the World Wide Web
1993	First evidence published of a possible genetic role in homosexuality in humans
1995	Discovery of first extrasolar planet; first complete sequencing of a genome of a living organism (*Hemophilus influenzae*); first preventative treatment for sickle-cell anemia
1996	First lander/rover on Mars; Java programming language released
1997	First cloning of an adult mammal: Dolly, the sheep; Fermilab reports discovery of the Top Quark
1998	The expansion of the universe is discovered to be accelerating; construction begins, in orbit, on the International Space Station; vaccines discovered for Lyme disease and for rotavirus

First Landing on the Moon   On July 20, 1969 *Apollo 11* astronauts Neil Armstrong (1930–2012) and Buzz Aldrin (b. 1930) landed on the moon. (A third member of the mission, Michael Collins, b. 1930, remained in orbit and never set foot on the moon; he retired in 1970.) American astronauts made five more moon landings before NASA (the National Aeronautics and Space Administration) retired the *Apollo* program in December 1972.

name—Conseil Européen pour la Recherche Nucléaire), established in Geneva in 1954. Funded by twelve governments, CERN had an operating budget in 2010 of approximately $1.2 billion, but it rests on a much larger endowment that enables CERN to construct projects like the Large Hadron Particle Collider, which cost between $5 and $10 billion. The European Molecular Biology Laboratory, established in 1974, conducts research at five principal sites, with a 2010 operating budget of $170 million. The European Space Agency, created in 1975, is headquartered in Paris and had a 2010 budget of $5 billion. Supervising a dozen other groups is the Joint Research Council of the European Union, with expenditures in 2010 of roughly $500 million, up from $275 million just five years earlier.

The proportional distribution of public support for science research relative to the arts, humanities, and social sciences says much about the values of *Big Science as Cultural Value* the modern era. In the United States, in 2010, for example, the operating budget for the National Science Foundation was $7 billion and that for the National Institutes of Health was $31 billion. The amounts dedicated to the National Endowment for the Arts and the National Endowment for the Humanities, in contrast, were $158 million and $167 million, respectively. In other words, nonscientific research comprised roughly 8 percent of the government's commitment, whereas scientific research garnered 92 percent of it. Whatever one may think about these relative emphases, the fact of them is historically significant. It would not have occurred to any Renaissance prince or absolutist monarch to favor science so overwhelmingly. Big science is more than an area of active and exciting research. It is itself a cultural value, one that separates the West from the undeveloped world (as a matter of financial capability) and from much of the Islamic world (as a matter of cultural choice).

Is the relation of science and secularism one of cause and effect, and if so, which is which? Has science driven religious faith from the European scene or has the modern West championed science because it presumes a secular view of the cosmos? And does any of this matter? Few believers abandoned their faith because they learned about evolution, DNA, or stem cells. Rather, most secular Westerners since the 1960s have been simply indifferent to organized religion, making it difficult to keep tradition going.

Rise of Secularization
Groups dedicated to a secularized society proliferated after World War II. The International Humanist and Ethical Union, formed in Amsterdam in 1952, brought together more than a hundred smaller groups across Europe. The union, which today claims a membership of 5 million people around the world, promotes a secular basis for society but recognizes the right to freedom of belief:

> Humanism is a democratic and ethical life stance, which affirms that human beings have the right and responsibility to give meaning and shape to their own lives. It stands for the building of a more humane society through an ethic based on human and other natural values in the spirit of reason and free inquiry through human capabilities. It is not theistic, and it does not accept supernatural views of reality.

In 1956 several thousand secularists met in Oslo and formed the Norwegian Humanist Association to campaign against the established Lutheran Church. The British Humanist Association came together in 1967 (although its origins lay in the 19th century); among its chief aims is to maintain the strict separation of church and state. Activists in Stockholm created the Swedish Humanist Association in 1979. The European Humanist Federation brought together several smaller institutions when it formally organized in Berlin in 1993. Now based in Brussels, it participates actively in the work of the European Union. Membership in such groups has grown steadily, and their chief goals have been to remove religion from civic life and to encourage reasoned interpretations of science, government, ethics, and society.

The great bulk of Europe's secularization, however, has resulted from waning participation in organized faith. It was not an intellectual rebellion or a conscious rejection, but a fading away. Even in staunchly secular France (with church attendance only 12 percent), the majority of the population self-identifies as Christian.

Three factors head the list of probable causes: the nature of capitalist society, religious pluralism, and antagonism toward institutional churches. First, life in the West

No Time for Church   The United Kingdom hosted the 1966 World Cup, which pitted England against West Germany in the final (England won, 4-2). Shown here is the contest between Spain (in red) and Argentina (in blue and white). The World Cup is, by a long lead, the most popular sporting event in the world; held every four years, it draws a television-viewing audience of roughly one-tenth of the earth's population.

offered unending opportunities for work, leisure, and entertainment—cinemas, television, sports events, restaurants, cafes, radio, museums, theaters, concerts, parks. These took over part of the social function of churchgoing, just as the welfare state assumed the caring role of churches. Second, the many religious choices eroded a strong sense of religious identity, especially among Protestants. So did intermarriage. Since at least the 1960s, fewer and fewer people say that they can differentiate between the teachings of various denominations. The third factor was consciousness of the established churches' real and perceived failings. For many who came of age in the late 1960s, the institutional churches had much to answer for.

ANOTHER CATHOLIC REFORMATION

A series of problems confronted the Roman Catholic Church throughout the twentieth century and contributed to the loss of lay members. Especially painful for many Catholics was the Church's response to Fascism and the Holocaust—or

Crisis in Moral Authority

rather its lack of one. Pope Pius XII (r. 1939–1958), although personally opposed to Fascism, charted a moderate course in opposing Mussolini and Hitler; officially, the Vatican remained neutral throughout the war. Pius feared a military assault on Catholic communities across Europe or even on the Vatican itself if it took public positions on political matters. Many Jews looked to Rome to take a strong moral position, and Pius secretly protected many thousands of Jews throughout the war, in churches and monasteries as well as inside the Vatican itself. In the end, roughly 80 percent of Rome's Jewish population received direct aid from the Church in avoiding capture by the Nazis via their Fascist allies.

Still, Pius never unmistakably condemned the ongoing Holocaust. The closest he came was in a radio speech on Christmas Day in 1942. Near the end of his talk, he called for the restored promise of honesty, fairness, generosity, and mercy toward all of God's people:

> Humanity owes such a vow to the innumerable dead who lie buried on battlefields: the sacrifice of their lives in their fulfillment ought to be a holocaust for a new and better social order. Humanity owes such a vow to the unending cries of mothers, widows, and orphans who have had the light, comfort, and sustenance of their lives torn from them. Humanity owes such a vow to the innumerable exiles whom the hurricane of war has blown from their homes and left stranded in foreign lands: they can lament with the Prophet [Jeremiah], "Our inheritance has been handed over to strangers, our homes to foreigners" [Lamentations 5.2]. Humanity owes such a vow to the hundreds of thousands of people who, without any just cause and only on account of their nationality or race, have been sent either to their deaths or to a gradual decline. Humanity owes such a vow to the many millions of noncombatants—women, children, the sick, the elderly—to whom the aerial bombardments (whose horrors we have repeatedly condemned from the start) have destroyed lives, goods, possessions, houses, hospitals, and places of worship without discernment or sufficient care. Humanity owes such a vow to the rivers of tears and bitterness, to the clouds of sorrow and torment, which have proceeded from the deadly ruin of the present conflict, darkening the heavens and calling out for the descent of the Holy Spirit—that It might free the world from the spread of violence and terror.

Even this moving invocation does not specify the suffering of the Jews. His description of persecution and his quotation from Jeremiah might be veiled references to the Jews, but many Catholics wanted something more from their leader. Pius was no anti-Semite, but to his critics he is the pope who failed to speak out. To them the Church—or at least the papacy—lost moral authority.

After the war, Pius encouraged the rebuilding of Europe and the creation of the European Union of 1957 (see chapter 29). He also focused on the plight of Catholics in the Soviet bloc. His positions on the State of Israel mixed altruism and stubbornness. Pius showed concern for everyone suffering from persecution and war, but he refused to recognize Israel. (The Vatican finally recognized Israel late in 1993.) The crux of the conflict was Jerusalem, which the Vatican maintained should be an internationally controlled city. Pius's legacy regarding Judaism is complex, and it will become clear only when the archives of his pontificate are fully available to researchers.[2]

Pius XII's successor was Pope John XXIII (r. 1958–1963), who dedicated his pontificate to *aggiornamento*, "a bringing up to date" of the Church. John believed *Second* that the Church needed to confront head-on the rift between the practices of the *Vatican* church and the lived realities of everyday Catholics. He convened the **Second** *Council* **Vatican Council**, also known as Vatican II, which met from 1962 to 1965. John did not live to see the conclusion of the Council, but his spirit dominated its proceedings. The Council's work was wide ranging. It refined the relations between the papacy and bishops. It reformed the liturgy to allow greater lay participation. It expressed regret for the centuries-long hostilities between the Catholic and Orthodox Churches. It renewed a spirit of missionary work around the globe. And it rededicated the Church to seeking union, whenever possible, with the Protestant and other churches.

Most controversially, the Council rejected the tradition of blaming the Jews for the killing of Christ:

> True, the Jewish authorities and those who followed their lead pressed for the death of Christ; still, what happened in His passion cannot be charged against all the Jews, without distinction, then alive, nor against the Jews of today. Although the Church is the new people of God, the Jews should not be presented as rejected or accursed by God, as if this followed from the Holy Scriptures. All should see to it, then, that in catechetical work or in the preaching of the word of God they do not teach anything that does not conform to the truth of the Gospel and the spirit of Christ. Furthermore, in her rejection of every persecution against any man, the Church, mindful of the patrimony she shares with the Jews and moved not by political reasons but by the Gospel's spiritual love, decries hatred, persecutions, displays of anti-Semitism, directed against Jews at any time and by anyone. (*Nostra Aetate*, "In Our Time")

---

[2]   There has never been an effort to block research into the Church's activities in World War II. The Vatican Archives is one of the most professional archives in the world, but its holdings are massive. Since opening their doors to researchers in the eighteenth century, the archivists have gathered, authenticated, preserved, cataloged, and indexed the billions of individual records it holds, one pontificate at a time; once complete, the records of the entire pontificate are released. Pius XII's pontificate is the current object of this activity.

Many bishops had opposed the change. Except for a few individuals, they were motivated not by anti-Semitism but by a desire to uphold another tradition—the Church's "infallibility," or freedom from error. How could the central ritual of the Church, the Mass, have been wrong when for centuries it had blamed the "perfidious Jews" for the Crucifixion? The reformers won the day, however.

The end of Vatican II did not stop further reforms. Pope Paul VI (r. 1963–1978), John XXIII's successor, instituted the Mass in languages other than Latin, by simple decree. For liberal-minded Catholics, the work of the Council and then the reforms of Paul offered hope for a faith newly adapted to the needs of contemporary society.

Continuing Decline in Church Attendance   In sheer numbers, however, they were proved wrong. Attendance at Mass continued its steep decline, and vocations to the priesthood fell off at a startling rate. Conservative Catholics attributed the decline to the reforms themselves. They argued that, in the attempt to make the Church relevant to the modern world, it had cut itself off from its roots. Liberal Catholics pointed to two other issues—the church's ban on contraception and its refusal to allow women to be priests.

Adapting to the Needs of Contemporary Society   Roman Catholicism, though still the single largest branch of Christianity, has struggled to keep abreast with the social and cultural changes since World War II—and has in fact debated whether or not it should do so. The reforms of the Second Vatican Council (1962–1965) displeased many Catholics, many of whom thought the Council had compromised too much with modernity, and many others who felt that it had not reformed nearly enough. Shown here is a Mass on behalf of the then gravely ill Pope John Paul II (r. 1978–2005), at Our Lady of Angels Cathedral in Los Angeles.

The debate over artificial contraception had been around for a long time, at least since the twelfth century, but it became urgent with the commercial availability of the birth - control pill in 1961. Paul VI spent several years investigating the science behind the new method. He also reviewed Church doctrine on the nature of sexuality and the purpose of marriage, and set up advisory committees that included laymen and laywomen, both married and unmarried. He reviewed the documents of Vatican II and consulted with both physicians and theologians. Finally, in 1968, he issued *Humanae Vitae* ("Of Human Life"), perhaps the most famous papal encyclical in history.

The encyclical recognizes (in an innovation) that sexual intercourse between a man and a woman has a twofold purpose. Besides producing offspring, it ex- Humanae presses love. All the more reason, then, that marriage is the only licit venue for Vitae sex, because without a lifelong commitment, sex is reduced to mere coupling. Marriage does more than unite a man and woman into "one flesh." It unites the married couple with the loving God who brought them together:

> Marriage, then, is far from being the effect of chance or the result of the blind evolution of natural forces. It is in reality the wise and provident institution of God the Creator, whose purpose was to effect in man His loving design. As a consequence, husband and wife, through that mutual gift of themselves, which is specific and exclusive to them alone, develop that union of two persons in which they perfect one another, cooperating with God in the generation and rearing of new lives.
>
> The marriage of those who have been baptized is, in addition, invested with the dignity of a sacramental sign of grace, for it represents the union of Christ and His Church.

Married love, then, is a human analogue to the Holy Trinity itself. *Humanae vitae* consequently rejects all forms of artificial contraception and insists that "each and every" act of sexual union must be left open to the possibility of new life.

The crowds stayed away in droves. Studies of European Catholics from 1970 on showed that a major factor in their falling away from Church attendance was the Church's stance on contraception. A clash was perhaps inevitable—even more so with the rise of second-wave feminism. To many women, *Humanae vitae* resentenced them to lives of endless reproduction just when they were winning their freedom to pursue other goals.

Of secondary significance was the issue of women's ordination as priests— *Continuing Ban* secondary because fewer women were interested in pursuing the priesthood than *on Female* in avoiding pregnancy. The Church's traditional position was that Jesus, in select- *Ordination* ing his twelve apostles, had chosen only men, and so only men were called to priesthood. The Church therefore did not have the authority to ordain women, even if it wanted to do so. At Vatican II many bishops and their theological advisors argued against this strict interpretation of the Gospel. The apostles, they pointed out, were also all married men and all Jewish. Did it not then follow that the Church does not have the authority to ordain anyone other than Jewish husbands to the Catholic priesthood? Moreover, the New Testament clearly distinguishes between the apostles and bishops. The Church would have none of this, however. Paul VI and his successor, John Paul II (r. 1978–2005), insisted that the priesthood is a uniquely male calling, and the question is closed.

Vatican II was the most thoroughgoing reform of the church since the sixteenth-century Catholic Reformation. But the legacy of the Council is still debated. To conservatives, the Council is to blame for the church's European decline; it substituted modern fashions for a two-thousand-year tradition. To liberals, the Council failed to enact enough reform; it left the same old patriarchy, perhaps with a friendlier face. In either case, the results are still to be seen Sunday after Sunday, in row after row of empty seats in the pews.

POSTWAR PROTESTANTISM

The story of postwar European Protestantism is also one of loss, and yet Protestant Christianity grew as fast in the postcolonial Third World as it faded in Europe. Moreover, when it came to spiritual energy, the United States became a leader in the Protestant world.

Protestantism in Europe   Attendance at and active membership in church life declined at roughly the same pace and to the same extent as with Catholic Europeans. Protestantism in Europe, however, experienced a fragmentation that the Catholic Church did not. The decline started in the nineteenth century, gained pace with the disillusionment of World War I, and turned severe after World War II. By 1989, when the Soviet Union began to disintegrate (discussed in chapter 29), it became apparent that Protestant Christianity had survived four decades of Communist persecution in eastern Europe better than it had survived in the postwar west. This tenacity of faith in the east perhaps resulted from the persecution itself, as Protestants resisted the official state atheism. In the west, Protestantism faced many of the same factors that affected Catholic Christians—modern capitalism, religious pluralism, and frustration with the institutional churches.

The Protestant churches, as institutions, had been organized along national lines since the sixteenth century. The blow that the World Wars dealt to nations, and to nationalism, thus affected the churches as well. In Nazi Germany, a National Socialist brand of Lutheranism, the "German Christian" movement, had received official support. The German Evangelical Church (EKD, for

Evangelische Kirche in Deutschland), formed in 1933, had roots in the World War
I era. Some 600,000 members strong, the EDK had supported Hitler and defrocked all Lutheran ministers of Jewish descent. It also established a "research
institute" charged with preparing a new translation of the New Testament—one
that would eliminate all references to the Jewishness of Jesus and his apostles and
turn them all into Aryans.

Although the EKD survived until the end of the war, there was heroic resistance to it. A group of Lutheran, Calvinist, and Moravian theologians and pastors
met in Barmen (the birthplace of Friedrich Engels, ironically enough) and formed
the Confessing Church. As a religious group, they did not denounce Nazism itself
but only the Nazification of their faith in the EKD. Nevertheless, several leading
figures in the Confessing Church became prominent activists against the Nazi
regime, most notably the Lutheran pastors Hermann Maas (1877–1970) and Dietrich Bonhoeffer (1906–1945). Maas, an ardent Zionist from his youth, risked
his life many times to shield Jews from arrest and helped many to flee Germany.[3]
Bonhoeffer campaigned actively against the Nazi regime and in 1943 even joined
the conspiracy of some German intelligence officers to assassinate Hitler. Bonhoeffer was arrested and died in the Flossenbürg concentration camp on April 9,
1945, only three weeks before the end of the war.

Uneasy over their churches' collusion with the Nazis during the war and left
without a clear leadership after it, German Protestantism lost momentum. The
faithful had enough to do clearing rubble, finding food and shelter, and reviving
the economy. Churchgoing, to many of them, was hardly a priority. In October
1945 ecumenical figures from outside Germany persuaded the Protestant leaders
to issue a somewhat tepid and vague acknowledgment of their failures during the
Nazi years; known as the "Stuttgart Confession of Guilt," it acknowledged that
"enormous wrong befell many peoples and countries on account of us," but insisted, "We fought for many years, in the name of Jesus Christ, against the mindset
that exemplified the Nazis' violent regime." The leaders' shortcomings, the "Confession" said, consisted of "not standing up for our beliefs more courageously, not
praying more faithfully, not believing more joyfully, and not loving more ardently."
The murders, pogroms, book burnings, arrests, deportations, and concentration
camps of the previous twenty-five years are never mentioned.

This is no time, the leaders seemed to say, for looking back. Besides, the main
Protestant denominations were undergoing some painful rifts. Theologians and
church leaders across the Continent reinterpreted their traditions, seeking to ex-
punge ideas that, in their eyes, had contributed to the two world wars—national

---

[3]   Israel placed Hermann Maas on the list of "Righteous among the Nations" at the official Yad Vashem
Holocaust Memorial in Jerusalem.

pride, belief in progress, support for liberal capitalism, confidence in "justification by faith" and the guidance of the elect. In Britain, the decline of religious life also became apparent after the war. Economic straits meant less money for the support and maintenance of church buildings, and the sunny tone of much Anglican preaching seemed out of place. The loss of empire also meant the decay of prestige for the Church of England and its head, the archbishop of Canterbury. Just as Britain ceased to be a political superpower, so too did mainstream Anglicanism, and the state religion lost ground.

In Africa, Asia, and South America, Protestant communities ceased to look to Europe for leadership. Missionary work in the developing nations increased steadily starting in the 1950s, bringing many new faithful into the fold. It also affected the substance of the faiths themselves. As described by an Anglican missionary to India, William Robertson (1894–1955):

Protestantism in Developing Nations

> Christianity is not a product of the West. Its divine Founder lived in an Eastern land. The great churches of its glorious youth with that roll of doctors and martyrs belonged chiefly not to Europe but to Africa and the East. We must therefore desire to go to a land like India as little as possible as Westerners. We must give every encouragement to the clothing of the catholic faith and the worship that enshrines it in Indian garments. Our vision must be that of a real Indian Church.
>
> Our ideal is to live in simplicity as far as possible in the Indian way. Our hope is that if we are faithful God will enable us to make some contribution to the Church in India by helping forward the naturalizing of her theology and worship. . . .
>
> Our hope is that our Ashram will be so Indian in character that many Hindus will feel at home in it, and will readily stay with us. Hospitality will always be part of our programme, and we hope to have accommodation for a number of guests. We hope also to undertake works of social service, and some of us may teach in schools. It has been suggested that we should visit the prison, the leper asylum, and the hospitals. In this way rather than in preaching we believe that we can show forth the spirit of Jesus, our Lord.

By the end of the Cold War, the number of practicing Christians outside of Europe vastly exceeded the number within Europe. And they stamped the faith with elements of their native cultures. [4]

---

[4]   The nation with the highest proportion of active Christians today is Nigeria, where 85 percent of the Christian population attends church regularly. Christians make up one half of the total population.

Despite upheaval in the 1960s and 1970s, the United States never experienced the severe popular decline in Christian practice seen in Europe. America was also the site of three important developments—Pentecostalism, fundamentalism, and evangelicalism. All three are styles of worship rather than separate denominations, and all three took root in the mainstream Protestant churches.

Pentecostalism takes its name from the descent of the Holy Spirit on the original twelve apostles, as told in the New Testament. Taking the appearance of tongues of flame, the Spirit filled the twelve with heavenly grace; and the sign of this gift was that they could suddenly speak in foreign tongues. Pentecostalism first appeared in the last years of the nineteenth century, in a revival movement among poor rural groups in the American South. It is at root a mystical union with God. The believer is seized by a spiritual ecstasy, speaks aloud in unrecog-

Mystical Union with God Worshippers at a Pentecostal revival in Brazil. The explosive growth of Pentecostalism has been in a statistical sense, one of the major success stories in recent Christian history. Its appeal has been particularly strong in South America. Estimates of the worldwide Pentecostal population are difficult to make, since Pentecostalism is more a style of worship than a discrete denomination; figures range from 200 to 500 million.

nizable speech, and often receives or performs miraculous healings. It preaches of a second baptism "in the Holy Spirit," and it celebrates a surrender of the believer's heart to the resurrected Christ. As such, Pentecostalism is openly, even proudly, anti-intellectual in its approach—based on a conviction that traditional Protestantism has tied itself into knots by a dependence on rational inquiry. By the 1960s and 1970s it entered mainstream Protestantism as a charismatic reform. Moreover, Pentecostal missionaries in the 1980s and 1990s found many welcoming audiences in South America and parts of Asia, especially China, where it now forms the fastest-growing Christian movement. But it has failed to take root in Europe.

Protestantism in the United States

The key element of **fundamentalism** is "scriptural inerrancy." It too is a mode of worship rather than a distinct denomination, and scholars trace its origins to nineteenth-century debates in the United States over Darwinian theory and the biblical record.[5] It can mean the strictest and simplest type of literalism when reading the Bible, but more commonly it insists merely on the presence of a fundamental truth in every scriptural passage. For example, when the Bible states

---

[5]   The publication in 1910–1915 of a twelve-volume anthology of pamphlets called *The Fundamentals: A Testimony to the Truth* is often taken as the symbolic start of the movement.

that Abraham lived 175 years (Genesis 25.7), it is not talking about calendar years; it is simply proclaiming that obedience to God guarantees a heavenly blessing—in this case, long life. Morally earnest, fundamentalism has an element that urges personal and societal reform before the approach of Armageddon—Jesus's return and the final battle between good and evil, which certain fundamentalist groups describe as the "Rapture."

Evangelicalism, too, emphasizes the work of the Holy Spirit in the world and the centrality of biblical truth. However, it retains more of the traditional elements of Protestant denominations than Pentecostalism does—and less millennial urgency than does fundamentalism. Evangelicals also focus more on *ecumenicalism*, or bringing Protestant churches together. They seek simply to enliven what they regard as staid forms of Protestant worship. Evangelicalism is the only trend of the three that has gained any footing within Europe, where it tries to bring energetic Christian worship back into Anglican, Calvinist, and Lutheran life.

In sum, European Protestantism in the later twentieth century struggled to disassociate itself from the elements that, for many people, had made it complicit in two world wars. The attempt did not succeed, and the vital centers of Protestant Christianity thus passed beyond Europe's borders. In the United States, South America, Africa, and Asia, the faith has adapted itself to local worship traditions, giving it new life in new forms.

JEWISH REVIVAL AND CONFLICT

Jews throughout the world experienced both elation and sorrow in the years after Israel's success in the Six-Day War (see chapter 27). Although still surrounded by hostile neighbors, Israel had proven its might and extended its borders to more easily defensible positions. Jews from throughout the Diaspora migrated in a large new wave, especially from Muslim countries, now that the fledging state seemed likely to survive (see Map 28.1). More than 90 percent of the quarter million Jews living in Morocco, for example, returned to the Holy Land within a decade of the 1967 war, whereas virtually the entire Jewish population in Libya (roughly thirty-five thousand) did the same.

Not all Arab Jews showed such confidence in Israel. The quarter million or so Jews in Algeria, for example, migrated instead to France, with some continuing on to the United States. Their Sephardic traditions and greater degree of religious observance changed the tone of French Jewish life. Yet tens of thousands poured into Israel from Iraq and Iran, and the small number of Jews remaining in Egypt were essentially forced out by the government of Gamal Abdul Nasser. For the first time, many Jews arrived from the United States and western Europe as well.

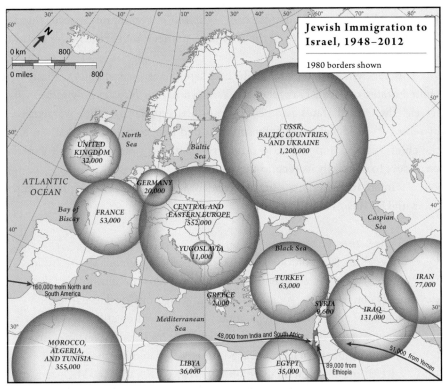

Jewish Immigration to Israel, 1948–2012

1980 borders shown

0 km   800
0 miles   800

USSR, BALTIC COUNTRIES, AND UKRAINE
1,200,000

North Sea

UNITED KINGDOM
32,000

ATLANTIC OCEAN

Baltic Sea

GERMANY
20,000

Bay of Biscay

FRANCE
53,000

CENTRAL AND EASTERN EUROPE
552,000

Caspian Sea

YUGOSLAVIA
11,000

Black Sea

160,000 from North and South America

GREECE
2,000

TURKEY
63,000

IRAN
77,000

SYRIA
9,600

IRAQ
131,000

Mediterranean Sea

48,000 from India and South Africa

51,000 from Yemen

MOROCCO, ALGERIA, AND TUNISIA
355,000

LIBYA
36,000

EGYPT
35,000

89,000 from Ethiopia

MAP 28.1   Jewish Immigration to Israel since 1948   Since its establishment as a state in 1948, waves of Jews from throughout the Diaspora have migrated to Israel.

The new wave of immigrants profoundly altered Israeli society. The nation had been founded largely by refugees and immigrants from central and eastern Europe. Many brought with them a passionate Zionism and a commitment to socialism. The new arrivals of the 1950s, 1960s, and 1970s were different. The North African Jews were Sephardic, spoke Ladino and Arabic rather than Yiddish and Hebrew, were highly observant, and were generally blue-collar laborers eager for an opportunity to prosper. Meanwhile, the Jewish immigrants from the Arabian peninsula, Iraq, and Iran, as well as those from the United States and western Europe, were educated professionals and entrepreneurs. A new money-driven consumer culture developed in challenge to the older, idealistic communal identity.

Tensions between Old and New Settlers

Israel's compulsory military service was an engine of social integration. Yet strong prejudices among many of these groups polarized society. Survivors of the Holocaust and their descendants often regarded the Sephardim and the Jews from the prosperous West with disdain. They viewed them as opportunists who wanted to connect with their Jewish roots only now that the suffering was over. Sephardic religious traditions seemed alien and out of place to many established

Israelis, and so did the Sephardic habit of living in communities according to their national origin. Moreover, the commercial orientation of the newer arrivals seemed crass and shallow.

This reorientation of Israeli life had significant consequences. First, the United States replaced France as the Western nation most closely allied with Israel.[6] The United States also became the chief supplier of military assistance, by selling its most technologically sophisticated weaponry to Israel. (It was also the chief weapons supplier to several Arab states in the 1970s, but it usually made sure to offer only its second-tier technology.)

UN Resolution   International opinion turned decidedly against Israel—most notoriously
3379   with **UN Resolution 3379**, in 1975:

> The General Assembly,
>
> Recalling its resolution 1904 (XVIII) of 20 November 1963 . . . that "any doctrine of racial differentiation or superiority is scientifically false, morally condemnable, socially unjust and dangerous" and its expression of alarm at "the manifestations of racial discrimination still in evidence in some areas in the world, some of which are imposed by certain Governments by means of legislative, administrative or other measures,"
>
> Recalling also that, in its resolution 3151 G (XXVIII) of 14 December 1973, the General Assembly condemned, inter alia, the unholy alliance between South African racism and Zionism,
>
> Taking note of . . . the principle that "international co-operation and peace require the achievement of national liberation and independence, the elimination of colonialism and neo-colonialism, foreign occupation, Zionism, apartheid and racial discrimination in all its forms, as well as the recognition of the dignity of peoples and their right to self-determination,"
>
> Taking note also of Resolution 77 (XII) adopted by the Assembly of Heads of State and Government of the Organization of African, . . . which considered "that the racist regime in occupied Palestine and the racist regimes in Zimbabwe and South Africa have a common imperialist origin, forming a whole and having the same racist structure and being organically linked in their policy aimed at repression of the dignity and integrity of the human being,"
>
> Taking note also of the Political Declaration and Strategy to Strengthen International Peace and Security and to Intensify Solidarity

---

6   America was home to 6 million Jews, more than lived in the Holy Land itself, and American public and private economic aid to Israel grew rapidly.

and Mutual Assistance among Non-Aligned Countries, . . . which most severely condemned Zionism as a threat to world peace and security and called upon all countries to oppose this racism and imperialist ideology,

Determines that Zionism is a form of racism and racial discrimination.

This diplomatic shift had many causes, including anti-Americanism as a consequence of the Cold War and the war in Vietnam. Moreover, yet another war *Yom* had been fought in the Middle East on October 6, 1973. On Yom Kippur, the *Kippur* holiest day in the Jewish calendar, united Egyptian and Syrian forces had *War* launched a surprise assault on Israel. Caught unawares, the Israeli forces nearly fell, but after two weeks they managed to drive off their attackers and advanced far toward Cairo and Damascus before agreeing to a cease-fire. The **Yom Kippur War** did not change territorial borders much, but it destroyed Israel's aura of invincibility, assuaged hurt Arab pride, and emboldened anti-Israel forces to push for the UN resolution. Under pressure from the United States, the United Nations ultimately revoked Resolution 3379 in 1991. It is the only revoked declaration in UN history.

Within Israel, by the mid-1970s the majority of the population consisted of *Rise of the* the non-European immigrants of the previous decades or their offspring. That *Likud* change placed the earlier settlers in the minority for the first time. One conse- *Party* quence was a sharp shift to the political right, since Jews of Middle Eastern heritage generally took a more hard-line stance toward the Arabs. The conservative Likud Party, founded by Menachem Begin (1913–1992), now rivaled the Labor Party for dominance, with Begin in office from 1977 to 1983. In an effort for peace, Egypt's President Anwar Sadat (1918–1981) boldly traveled in 1977 to Jerusalem to deal directly with the government. Begin and Sadat had a surprisingly good personal rapport and, aided by U.S. president Jimmy Carter (b. 1924), signed a peace treaty in 1979.

U.S. and Israeli Assault This Egyptian political cartoon from September 1973, published in the run-up to the Yom Kippur War, shows a joint U.S.-Israeli bomb falling on the home of an Egyptian boy. In reality, the war began when Egypt and Syria launched a surprise two-front assault on Israel.

The political shift reflected a second major development in Israel, religious conflict. Israel had had a diverse population from the start. In 1948, at the nation's founding, about 10 percent of Israel's citizenry was Arab; by 2010 Arabs comprised nearly 20 percent of the population,

The Camp David Accord   In March 1979, the first peace treaty between the state of Israel and a Muslim nation was signed. Shown here are U.S. president Jimmy Carter, Egyptian president Anwar Sadat, and Israeli prime minister Menachem Begin. Sadat was reviled by Muslim leaders around the world for this act, and he paid for it with his life: Islamist military officials in his own army assassinated him two years later. Despite occasional tensions, the peace treaty has remained in effect.

not counting Palestinians residing in the occupied West Bank and Gaza Strip. The Jews themselves were divided among wholly secular Jews (roughly 20 percent), those who identified as nonobservant but believing Jews (50–55 percent), observant Orthodox Jews (15–20 percent), and *Haredim* (or Ultra-Orthodox) Jews (5–10 percent). Differences that exist in the United States between Reform, Conservative, and Reconstructionist Judaism have little significance for Israeli Jews, who identify themselves more by the degree of their religious observance than by their denominational type. Between 1 and 2 percent of Israel's citizens are Christian; another 1–2 percent of the citizens are Druze (a monotheistic religion that evolved out of Shi'a Islam). But Israel's constitutional system of proportional representation has meant that small and even fringe parties have figured in every governing coalition.

Together with the virtual deadlock between Labor and Likud since the 1970s, the divisions make it difficult to unify the government behind any plan to resolve the conflict with the Palestinians. Moreover, the Ultra-Orthodox have demanded, as the price of their joining any coalition, control of the ministry that determines and enforces religious law regarding marriage. (Israel has no civil marriage.) That has largely meant strict Orthodoxy on marriage law. Many Reform immigrants, converts, and children of a Jewish father and non-Jewish mother have found, to their surprise, that the government does not legally recognize them as Jews at all—although it grants them citizenship.

INTERNATIONAL JUDAISM AND THE STATE OF ISRAEL

International Judaism has undergone a wide range of changes and evolutions since the hard-fought establishment in 1948 of the state of Israel. Nearly one-third of all Jewish marriages in the United States and in western Europe *Multiple* since the 1970s have been mixed, and the majority of families resulting *Denominations* from those mixed marriages have become culturally or religiously Christian by the third, and sometimes by the second, generation.[7] Reform Jews, whether observant or not, have proved the most willing to enter mixed marriages, and Orthodox and conservative Jews have proved the least willing. Reform Jews in the West have also been quickest to accept homosexuality as a normal aspect of human life, regardless of biblical and *halakhic* (rabbinical legal) condemnations of it. They have been the first to allow women to enter the rabbinate as well.[8]

Conservative Judaism, in contrast, although permitting men and women to sit together during worship, accepted female rabbis only starting in the late 1980s. Conservative Judaism also initiated the formal ritual of a *bat mitzvah* for girls, to correspond to the centuries-old *bar mitzvah* for boys. Both rituals take place at the traditional coming of age at thirteen years. The *bat mitzvah*, begun only in 1922 in the United States, proved popular and was gradually accepted by all *Continuing* major Jewish traditions, although the Orthodox held out against it the longest. *Persecution* Orthodox Judaism rejects women rabbis as contrary to *halakha* and tradition, but several rabbinical schools since 2000 allow women to participate in rabbinical study and to qualify as educators. In recent decades several new versions of Judaism have emerged in the West: Humanistic, Liberal, Reconstructionist, Renewal, and Tradition Jews have all emerged since the 1970s.

Jews of every denomination have also endured continued persecution, and Jews living in the Soviet bloc faced some of the worst of it. Under Stalin and Khrushchev, thousands of synagogues, schools, Jewish newspapers, theaters, and youth clubs were all closed. By the middle of the 1960s there were fewer than a hundred synagogues in the entire USSR. More than a million Jews left eastern Europe and Russia in the 1990s, heading chiefly to Israel and the United States. As late as 2002, in Russia proper, Jews made up less than one-fifth of 1 percent of the total population.

Rabbi Naamah Kelman Born in New York City in 1955, Kelman moved to Jerusalem in 1976 and in 1992 became the first woman ever to be ordained a rabbi in Israel. She currently serves as the dean of the Institute of Religion at Hebrew Union College.

---

[7] In the United Kingdom, fully half of all Jewish marriages were mixed by the year 2000.

[8] The first woman rabbi, Regina Jonas (1902–1944), was killed at Auschwitz after two years caring for fellow concentration-camp prisoners and delivering lectures on Jewish history and law.

Lower birth rates combined with emigration to reduce what had once been the center of Jewish population to the tiniest fraction of what it had been.

Hundreds of thousands asked to emigrate to Israel but were denied exit visas on the excuse that they had access to information vital to state security. And, in fact, Jews were prominent in many professions. In the 1960s a mere four thousand were allowed to repatriate to the Holy Land. In Poland and Czechoslovakia, where Soviet officials often appointed Jewish members of the Communist Party to administrative positions, anti-Communist rebellions took on an ugly anti-Semitism. The Soviets could always blame, and did blame, government failures on Jews in positions of power. Romania's brutal dictator Nicolae Ceauşescu (1918–1989), in power from 1965 until his death, held his Jewish subjects for ransom; he granted them exit visas only in return for large cash payments to support his lavish lifestyle.

The New Historians

An unexpected challenge to Jews everywhere came from within Israel itself, starting in the 1980s, with the young scholars and journalists known as the **New Historians**. Mostly born in Israel, they came of age just when the thirty-year hold (a common practice internationally) expired on government records pertaining to the establishment of the state of Israel. With access to these declassified documents, historians like Benny Morris (b. 1948), Tom Segev (b. 1945), and Avi Shlaim (b. 1945) offered fresh—and to many older Israelis, treacherous—views of Zionism.

The standard history up until then had described the early Zionists as peaceful idealists. These stout pioneers longed to settle in the Holy Land side by side with their Arab neighbors. When Hitler came to power, they spared no effort to save their doomed European compatriots, but could do nothing in the face of such evil. And when the nation of Israel was formally proclaimed in 1948, these Zionist heroes watched in surprise as their good Palestinian neighbors suddenly abandoned the land. Surrounding Arab states had ordered it, promising a glorious return once Arab armies trounced the inexperienced Jewish forces. But when that plan failed, the Zionist victors had no alternative but to claim the abandoned land as Jewish territory. "We did not have real history in this country," argues Segev. "We had mythology."

The debate began in earnest in 1987, with the publication of Benny Morris's study *The Birth of the Palestinian Refugee Problem, 1947–1949*. Here Morris argues that the 700,000 Palestinians who fled the Holy Land at the time of Israel's war of independence did so for a variety of reasons—but the chief cause was the Israeli army, which forced village after village to flee. Morris sees no evidence of a central policy of ethnic cleansing. Rather, he insists that Palestinians were expelled in location after location, on orders of commanders on the ground, depending on their strategic needs in the war.

Another New Historian, Ilan Pappé (b. 1954), entered the fray in 1988. His *Britain and the Arab–Israeli Conflict, 1948–1951* maintains that the British colonial government had favored the establishment of a Palestinian Arab, not a Jewish, state. Most disturbing of all was Segev's *The Seventh Million: The Israelis and the Holocaust* (1993), which criticizes the Zionist leaders of the 1930s for caring more about the establishment of Israel than about helping the Jews facing mass murder under the Nazis. To older Israelis, this was inexcusable slander.

The debate was intense, and it remains so today. Morris and his peers insist that they want only to discover the truth about their nation. A permanent peace settlement between Israelis and Palestinians, they say, can come about only if both sides confront honestly the strengths and weaknesses of their claims to the land. But to their critics, the New Historians are mounting an assault on Zionist belief itself—the belief in a unique Jewish identity and a unique Jewish fate, both tied to the Holy Land. The impact of the New Historians probably would not have been so great had not Jewish identity already been so endangered by secularization, assimilation, mixed marriages, and divisions among denominations. To attack the "myth of Israel" was, to many, to attack Judaism itself. Without that, what does it mean to be a Jew? As more records become declassified, the historical picture changes and takes on more detail. But this remains only half the story. Modern Arab archives remain largely closed to researchers—and absolutely closed to Jews. Until full access is available to all, the truth of what happened to those 700,000 Palestinians, how, and why will be unknown. And a just and permanent settlement of the Israeli–Palestinian dispute will be impossible.

ISLAMIC REVOLUTIONS

The idea of revolution holds an uneasy place in classical Islamic teaching. Unlike the English word *revolution*, which is morally neutral (as in "digital revolution"), the most frequent Arabic terms are decidedly negative. *Al-fitnah* ("rebellion"), *al-ma'siyah* ("disobedience"), and *al-riddah* ("apostasy") all imply efforts to overturn a divinely established order. Misrule is no justification for revolution; only impiety is. A ruler may be autocratic, corrupt, and venal, but unless he has violated religious law and damaged the spiritual well-being of the community, he must be obeyed. To oppose a ruler who is guilty of impiety is not "revolution" but jihad. But even a righteous jihad poses dangers, since the anarchy it produces if it fails might lead believers astray. It is best to accept any government that does not flout the basic tenets of the faith, no matter how inept or despotic it may be. Thus the great Kurdish scholar Ibn Taymiyyah (d. 1328), an inspiration for the modern Wahhabi movement, justified rebellion against the Mongols (who had described Genghis Khan as the Son of Allah) but insisted on obedience to the despised Mamluks.

In the eighteenth century, in response both to the Enlightenment and to European incursions into the Islamic world, a new word entered the popular vocabulary. *Al-thawrah* ("uprising") implied secular insurrection against a foreign regime and thus had an element of nationalist sentiment. Wahhabi groups across North Africa and throughout the Middle East used this term when calling for Arab rebellion against the Ottoman Turks and their European enablers (see chapter 20). Both the Arab struggle under Muhammad ibn Saud (d. 1765) against the Turks and the Egyptian insurrection against the British in 1919 were described by contemporaries as *al-thawrah*.

The Islamic world of the late twentieth century was filled with political upheaval and refusal to settle for an unacceptable status quo. The 1950s saw military *coups d'état* in Egypt, Iran, Iraq, and Pakistan. Uprisings in the 1960s occurred in Libya, Syria (four times), and Yemen. Still more revolts came in the 1970s in Iran, Iraq, Lebanon, Pakistan, Syria, and Yemen. The 1980s were relatively quiet, with civil insurrection only in Lebanon and Yemen, but the 1990s saw rebellion in Lebanon, Pakistan, and Yemen. And these were only the successful uprisings; scores more failed revolts took place in every country. It is an impressive record of determined opposition.

Still, what was the status quo against which they rebelled? And why was it unacceptable? There are two obvious explanations and another two that are less obvious. All four are colored by profound religious concerns.

Role of Nationalism

First was the issue of nationalism and the emotional residue of European imperialism and the Cold War. Many Muslim states were the creation of Europe. The imperialist countries left behind them, after their withdrawal, not only nations with artificial international borders but also as often as not new nativist regimes and new constitutions to prop them up. European motives were seldom altruistic. If a government was willing to oppose the spread of Communism, open its country's markets to Western commerce, and keep oil production going, then the West cared little how corrupt and oppressive that government might be. The result was a series of pro-Western autocracies that were widely viewed by their Arab subjects as puppets. They were also constant targets for ambitious new leaders who wanted to show their eagerness to confound the West and to stoke Arab pride.

Time magazine, for example, in 1973 described Muammar al-Qaddafi, who had seized power in Libya in 1969, this way:

> The leadership of the 100 million Arabs is, in the famous words of Egypt's Gamal Abdel Nasser, "a role wandering aimlessly about in search of an actor to play it." Now that Nasser is dead, now that his successors are gray and conventional, it is the implausible figure of Muammar Gaddafi that has acquired the role of an Arab Parsifal [a legendary knight]. He is a mere 31 years old, handsome, devout, ardent, even fanatical. "The Arabs need to be told the facts," he is fond of saying. "The Arabs need

someone to make them weep, not someone to make them laugh." Nasser once told the young Gaddafi: "You remind me of myself when I was your age." Gaddafi was profoundly moved. To be the new Nasser is his obsession—to succeed where Nasser failed.

The new Arab leaders, although anti-Western in their public stances, were often eager to retain good relations with Europe and the United States privately to preserve the flow of Western dollars. By Islamic standards, their false piety was cause for legitimate revolt.

Second was the issue of Israel. With the possible exception of Jordan, few of the Arab countries genuinely cared about the plight of the Palestinians, whom *The Israeli* popular prejudice among the broader Arab populace regarded as poor, backward *Issue* rustics. But other countries cared very much about using them as a cudgel with which to beat the Israelis. Repeated defeats at the hands of the Israeli Defense Force wounded Arab pride. It also threatened to undermine the legitimacy of the national governments. As Islamist groups repeatedly pointed out, the Qur'an itself (3.110–112) had proclaimed of the Arabs:

> You are the best nation formed out of mankind, commanding what is good, forbidding what is evil, and believing in Allah. If only the People of the Book [Jews and Christians] had had faith, it would have been well for them. Some of them do have faith, but most of them are perverted transgressors. They will never be able to do you any serious harm, only minor annoyance. When they come out to fight you, they will turn their backs [to flee], and will not be succored. Shame is their lot, pitched over them [like a tent] wherever they might go. . . . They have incurred Allah's wrath, and humiliation covers them [like a blanket]—all because they rejected Allah's signs, impiously killed His prophets, and have continually rebelled and transgressed.

That was a hard pill to swallow after seven straight military defeats. The need to take the lead in opposing Israel, and to be seen to take the lead, became a central plank of Middle Eastern politics. Any regime that faltered or failed in this regard paid a price in popular discontent.

A third explanation is less obvious: decolonization let loose long-simmering ethnic and tribal rivalries. These contests frequently played themselves out *Impact of* as power struggles within nations, but from the 1970s on, they took the *Decolonization* form of angling for leadership of the broader Islamic world. Ethnic Arabs had not been in such a role since the late eighth century, when power passed to the Persians. In the fourteenth and fifteenth centuries, leadership in the Muslim world

Demonstrating for Pan-Arabism   Gamal Abdel Nasser was the president of Egypt from 1956 to 1970 and one of the leading statesmen for the pan-Arab movement. Among his achievements was a brief formal union of Egypt and Syria into a single United Arab Republic. Formed in 1958, the union ended when Syria withdrew in 1961. Here, an Egyptian crowd, carrying Nasser's portrait, protest the Syrian secession.

passed to the Ottoman Turks, who held it until World War I. Wahhabism originated in the eighteenth century as an intellectual movement to restore Arab primacy, and the Arab states began to adopt it after World War II. The rebel leaders who managed to hold onto power through the twentieth century consistently presented themselves as leaders of a pan-Arab movement to guide Islam into the new age. The state-run media in ethnically Arab countries referred to the 1979 uprising in Iran as *al-thawrah al-Iraniyyah* ("Iranian secular rebellion"). They wished to deny both the ethnic Persians and the dominant Shi'a of that country the honor of leading an "Islamic revolution."

       This brings up the final, fourth major issue—Islam's relationship with modern

The Challenge of Modernization

culture. Islamic modernism had emerged in the nineteenth century, when progressive religious scholars were eager to adapt Islamic life to technological and secular society. These modernizers included, as we have seen, the Young Turks at the Ottoman court, the Islamic Enlightenment in Egypt, and writers as broadly based as Beirut, Damascus, and Baghdad. The ideas associated with Islamic modernism fell into disrepute, however, in the twentieth century. Religious and nationalist conservatives rejected modernism out of hand because of its pro-Western taint. The enduring problems in the Islamic world, to the conservatives, did not need a Western solution but rather a traditional Islamic one, rooted in ancient values and customs.

The theocratic government established in Iran after the overthrow of the shah in 1979 offered one variation on this theme. As the Ayatollah ("Supreme Leader") Ruhollah Khomeini (1902–1989) put it in his best-known book, *Islamic Government* (1970):

> Islamic government is a government of law. In this form of government, sovereignty belongs to God alone and law is His decree and command. The law of Islam, divine command, has absolute authority over all individuals and the Islamic government. Everyone, including the Most Noble Messenger(s) and his successors, is subject to law and will remain so for all eternity—the law that has been revealed by God, Almighty and Exalted, and expounded by the tongue of the Qur'an and the Most Noble Messenger(s). If the Prophet(s) assumed the task of divine vice-regency upon earth, it was in accordance with divine command.

Free-market capitalism, with its emphasis on individual freedom and the rights of property, did not fit well with a conservative Islamic view that championed community and egalitarianism. Better suited to Muslim values, and specifically to Arab ones, was the political ideology known as *Ba'athism*.

BA'ATHISM AND BROTHERHOOD

As we saw in chapter 26, Ba'athism is at root a form of Islamic socialism. It calls for a state-run capitalism in which the government, or the Ba'athist Party, provides essential services to all citizens. Ba'athism originated in Syria in the 1940s and gained popularity in the postwar decades. Although a secular political ideology, it complemented the conservative religious movement of the Wahhabis. Like them, the Ba'athists emphasized the unique role of the Arabs in securing a new future for international Islam. Their mission was to turn back the course of history to the social and cultural ideal of the first Arab caliphate. This vision may or may not have been a genuine political goal; what mattered was Arab unity as an expression of religious culture.

The desire to restore an Islamic culture of the past meant first the rejection of Western ideas, values, and civic norms. Democracy, equal rights for women, freedom of speech, and the separation of religion and government appear not as universal ideals but as Western customs incompatible with Islamic culture. Hence the decision to replace the UN Declaration of Human Rights with the Cairo Declaration, which, as we saw in the last chapter, subordinates all claims of human rights to shari'a. Hence, too, the 1988 charter of **Hamas**, a conservative religious–political Palestinian group that devoted itself equally to charitable campaigns and social work among the Palestinians and to a terrorist war on Israel.

Hamas

Hamas originated as an offshoot of the Egyptian **Muslim Brotherhood**, founded in Egypt in 1928. The Brotherhood called for a return to Islam along with a rejection of the secular, "modern" mindset. "Islam is the solution," was the Brotherhood's catch phrase as it sought to end British influence in the country. Hamas took as its own slogan the declaration, "Allah is our goal, the Prophet [Muhammad] our model, the Qur'an our constitution, jihad our method, and death for Allah's sake our most sublime conviction." With financial backing from the Brotherhood, a poor religious scholar named Shaikh Ahmed Yassin (1937–2004) cofounded the group with Abdel Aziz al-Rantissi (1947–2004) in 1988. Hamas's determination to liberate Palestine from Israeli occupation is expressed clearly in its founding charter:

> In the name of Allah the Merciful and Compassionate . . .
> "You are the best nation" [*Qur'an 3.110*].
>
> [Hamas] is a free-standing Palestinian movement; ever loyal to Allah, it embraces Islam as its way of life and aims to raise Allah's flag over the entirety of Palestine. Those who follow other religions [of the Book] may continue to live in the secure enjoyment of their lives, property, and personal rights, even though without Islam disagreements arise, injustice spreads, and corruption thrives, leading to never-ending strife and war. . . .
>
> Ours is a global movement, worthy to fulfill our role because of the clarity of our ideals, the loftiness of our purpose, the exalted nature of our goals. . . .
>
> We are one element in the jihad-struggle to confront the Zionist invasion. . . . The Prophet (may Allah's prayer and peace be ever upon him!) himself said: "The hour of judgment will not come until the Muslims fight the Jews and kill them all—such that every tree and stone will say "Oh Muslim, servant of Allah! There is a Jew hiding behind me. Come kill him!'" . . . There is no solution to the Palestinian problem except by *jihad*.

Less well known is its position regarding modernism:

> Our movement began at a time when true Islam had all but disappeared from Arab life: its laws had been broken, its teachings ignored, its values altered. Wicked people had seized power, and under them there was nothing but oppression and darkness. . . . Homelands were usurped,

people sent into exile and made to wander aimlessly through the world; justice disappeared and lies took its place. Nothing was as it should have been—which is the case whenever true Islam is driven out. . . .

In order to bring up the generations in an authentic Islamic way, it is necessary to teach the duties of religion, to study the Qur'an and the Prophet's traditions in their completeness, and to learn Islam's history and ways from authentic sources. . . .

We respect [nationalist] movements, understanding the conditions and circumstances that gave birth to them, and so long as they reject both the Communist East and the Crusading West we encourage them in their work. . . . We detest opportunism and seek only the good of all people. We reject material wealth and celebrity, seeking no return from any human being.

Such groups commanded significant popular support, but less for their anti-modern stance than for their anti-Zionism. A unified pan-Arab movement, they

Marching to Annihilate the Zionist Enemy   Hamas members and sympathizers rally in Gaza City on the first anniversary of the death of Abdel Aziz al-Rantissi (1947–2004), the group's co-founder. Rantissi helped to popularize the false notion that the Holocaust was the result of a secret Jewish conspiracy with the Nazi leaders; the conspiracy, he claimed, aimed to drive more Jews to emigrate to Palestine while making the rest of the world feel sorry for them and thereby allow the creation of Israel.

confidently believed, emboldened by a pure and disciplined application of traditional Islamic morality, could not fail to achieve the annihilation of the Zionist enemy. And success would be the crowning achievement of the Arab campaign to regain its rightful place at the head of international Islam. This is why Israel's repeated military victories in the 1960s and 1970s stung: while the Zionist state continued to thrive at the physical center of the Arab lands, Arab dreams to regain their status remained frustrated.

Groups like the Muslim Brotherhood and Hamas shared that frustration with political parties like the Ba'athists. They wished to revitalize a past vision of Islamic–Arab greatness rather than pursue a new one. They sought not a revolution but a restoration.

◆

Looking forward by looking back has long been a hallmark of the Greater West. As the Islamic world closed out the twentieth century, many of its most prominent voices were calling for a return to traditional values and practices, while resisting, or attempting to resist, the tug of the modern. In Europe and the United States the contest was rather between competing visions of capitalism and individualism. Is it the best course of action to free the economy from constraints and allow market forces to operate, or to regulate the economy in order to provide stability for all? Should the governments of Europe pursue their individual interests, or accede to the continent-wide interests of the European Union? And, above all, does the idea of the Greater West still have meaning in a world when the essential values held by the various peoples in it follow such separate arcs?

WHO, WHAT, WHERE

Big Science	Hamas	Second Vatican Council
civil rights	Muslim Brotherhood	UN Resolution 3379
evangelicalism	New Historians	Yom Kippur War
fundamentalism	Pentecostalism	

SUGGESTED READINGS

Primary Sources

John XXIII. *Pacem in terris.*

Paul VI. *Humanae vitae.*

Tillich, Paul. *The Courage to Be.*

Tillich, Paul. *Theology of Culture.*

Anthologies

Bonhoeffer, Dietrich. *Conspiracy and Imprisonment, 1940–1945* (2006).

Hahnenberg, Edward P. *A Concise Guide to the Documents of Vatican II* (2007).

Studies

An-Na'im, Abdullahi Ahmed. *Islam and the Secular State: Negotiating the Future of Shari'a* (2010).

Asad, Talal. *Formations of the Secular: Christianity, Islam, Modernity* (2003).

Bauman, Zygmunt. *Modernity and the Holocaust* (2001).

Bethge, Eberhard. *Dietrich Bonhoeffer: A Biography* (2000).

Bowler, Peter J., and Iwan Rhys Morus. *Making Modern Science: A Historical Survey* (2005).

Calvert, John. *Sayyid Qutb and the Origins of Radical Islamism* (2010).

Campos, Michelle U. *Ottoman Brothers: Muslims, Christians, and Jews in Early Twentieth-Century Palestine* (2011).

Fernando, Mayanthi L. *The Republic Unsettled: Muslim French and the Contradictions of Secularism* (2014).

Gerlach, Wolfgang. *And the Witnesses Were Silent: The Confessing Church and the Persecution of the Jews* (2000).

Heschel, Susannah. *The Aryan Jesus: Christian Theologians and the Bible in Nazi Germany* (2010).

Hockenos, Matthew D. *A Church Divided: German Protestants Confront the Nazi Past* (2004).

Jenkins, Philip. *God's Continent: Christianity, Islam, and Europe's Religious Crisis* (2009).

Karsh, Efraim. *Fabricating Israeli History: The "New Historians"* (2000).

Lamb, Matthew L., and Matthew Levering, eds. *Vatican II: Renewal within Tradition* (2008).

Mahmood, Saba. *Politics of Piety: The Islamic Revival and the Feminist Subject* (2011).

Mahmood, Saba. *Politics of Religious Freedom: Contested Genealogies* (2014).

Morris, Benny. *Righteous Victims: A History of the Zionist–Arab Conflict, 1881–2001* (2001).

Morris, Benny. *The Birth of the Palestinian Refugee Problem Revisited* (2004).

O'Malley, John W. *What Happened at Vatican II* (2010).

Roy, Olivier. *Holy Ignorance: When Religion and Culture Part Ways* (2009).

Sánchez, José. *Pius XII and the Holocaust: Understanding the Controversy* (2002).

Segev, Tom. *One Palestine, Complete: Jews and Arabs under the British Mandate* (2001).

Segev, Tom. *1967: Israel, the War, and the Year That Transformed the Middle East* (2008).

Segev, Tom. *The Seventh Million: The Israelis and the Holocaust* (2000).

Taylor, Charles. *A Secular Age* (2007).

Warner, Michael, Jonathan VanAntwerpen, and Craig Calhoun, eds. *Varieties of Secularism in a Secular Age* (2010).

Young, Julian. *The Death of God and the Meaning of Life* (2003).

For additional resources, including maps, primary sources, visuals, web links, and quizzes, please go to **www.oup.com/us/backman**.

CHAPTER 29

Global Warmings

SINCE 1989

In late 1989 Mikhail Gorbachev, then general secretary of the Soviet Union, opened the Berlin Wall. The collapse of the Soviet Union followed quickly thereafter. As winter came and 1990 began, another Soviet-bloc country emerged into freedom almost every month: East Germany, Bulgaria, Czechoslovakia, Romania, Lithuania, Latvia, Estonia, Poland, Hungary. Soon even nations within the Russian Confederation declared their independence, most notably Ukraine and Georgia (see Map 29.1). Every emergent state, and eventually Russia itself, announced its intent to write a new constitution, to dismantle its state-run economy, and to adopt democracy and free-market capitalism. The transitions were rocky, but people everywhere spoke optimistically of a "postideological era." The ideological battle between East and West belonged, it seemed, to the past. Western values and ideas had triumphed over Soviet ideology.

A surprise international bestseller, *The End of History and the Last Man* (1992) by

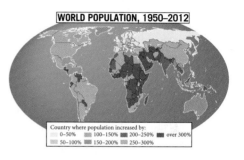

WORLD POPULATION, 1950–2012

Country where population increased by:
0–50%   100–150%   200–250%   over 300%
50–100%   150–200%   250–300%

The End of History? German youths celebrate the opening of the Berlin Wall on November 9, 1989. That date is also the anniversary of other crucial events in German history: the end of the Revolution of 1848, the declaration of the Weimar Republic (1918), Adolf Hitler's failed "Beer Hall Putsch" (1923), and the *Kristallnacht* ("Crystal Night") attacks by the Nazis upon Germany's Jews (1938).

Francis Fukuyama, argued that with Communism's failure the battle for human hearts and minds was ended. Conflicts still lay ahead, but they would be mere economic or territorial disputes, not philosophical ones:

> What we may be witnessing is not just the end of the Cold War, or the passing of a particular period of postwar history, but the end of history as such: that is, the end point of mankind's ideological evolution and the universalization of Western liberal democracy as the final form of human government.

The debate between differing visions was settled—or so it seemed.

However, triumph soon gave way to profound tensions. Open markets and democratic government, it turns out, are difficult to institute overnight. Outgoing government figures in many ex-Soviet nations made private deals to share power, sell off national industries and public resources, and arrange guarantees of immunity from prosecution for crimes committed while in power. With price controls lifted on consumer goods, inflation skyrocketed. The opening of secret-service archives triggered disputes over the settling of old scores with informants. The need to secure nuclear weapons and fissile-material laboratories raised concerns for safety. Many earnest, and many overearnest, emissaries from Western churches rushed in to win godless former-Communist souls for Christ, numb to local desires to revive their Orthodox traditions.

CHAPTER TIMELINE

1989	1992	1995	1998	2001

- 1989 Fall of Berlin Wall; Rushdie, *The Satanic Verses*; *Exxon Valdez* environomental disaster; revolt in Tiananmen Square
- 1990–1991 First Gulf War
- 1991–1992 Algerian civil war
- 1991–2001 War in the Balkans
- 1992 Soviet Union formally dissolved; Fukuyama, *The End of History and the Last Man*
- 1993 Treaty of Maastricht creates European Union
- 1994–1996 First war in Chechnya
- 1995 UN Women's Conference in Beijing; World Trade Organization founded
- 1999 EU introduces the euro; Good Friday Accord signed; "Battle of Seattle" against World Trade Organization
- 1999–2009 Second war in Chechnya
- 2000 Vladimir Putin becomes president of Russia; world population 6.1 billion
- 2001 9/11 terrorist attacks; United States invades Afghanistan

The end of the Cold War and the independent demands of peoples and nations thus introduced a host of new challenges. Globalized capitalism and the enormous influence of the United States as the only remaining superpower raised both hopes and fears that the values of the West would become universalized. Among the most immediate concerns were the debates over how to promote economic development while protecting the environment and how to protect the rights of women and the poor without imposing, or appearing to impose, Western cultural values that were at odds with those of non-Western states. These concerns dramatically and suddenly complicated relations within the Greater West as the Muslim states struggled to determine their own relations with modernity. Trouble emerged right from the start in 1989.

1989: ONE YEAR, THREE CRISES

In the wake of the Soviet Communism's fall, what remained to do, it seemed at first, was to set to work bringing the world into the golden dawn of prosperity, freedom, and progress. Freed of the need for Cold War nuclear deterrence, people spoke of a "peace dividend." Now governments could balance their books, lower taxes, promote economic growth, and even expand social services. It was heady optimism unlike anything the West had seen since before the two World Wars. Hundreds of thousands of people rushed into western Europe, fleeing poverty and oppression, and were received as heroic survivors of

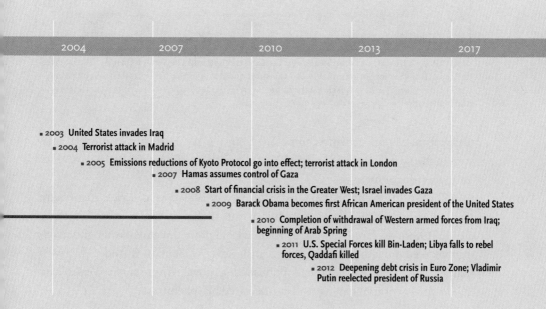

2004   2007   2010   2013   2017

- 2003 United States invades Iraq
- 2004 Terrorist attack in Madrid
- 2005 Emissions reductions of Kyoto Protocol go into effect; terrorist attack in London
- 2007 Hamas assumes control of Gaza
- 2008 Start of financial crisis in the Greater West; Israel invades Gaza
- 2009 Barack Obama becomes first African American president of the United States
- 2010 Completion of withdrawal of Western armed forces from Iraq; beginning of Arab Spring
- 2011 U.S. Special Forces kill Bin-Laden; Libya falls to rebel forces, Qaddafi killed
- 2012 Deepening debt crisis in Euro Zone; Vladimir Putin reelected president of Russia

The Fall of Communism in Eastern Europe and the Soviet Union

Former republic of the Soviet Union gaining independence in 1991	Independence from Soviet Union declared 1991; at war with Russia, 1994–2000	▬ Boundary of the former Soviet Union to 1991
Boundary of Russian Federation after December 1991	Former Warsaw Pact country holding free elections, 1990–1992	✥ Violent ethnic conflicts

MAP 29.1   The Fall of Communism in Eastern Europe and the Soviet Union   The sudden collapse of the Soviet Union in 1989 and the subsequent end of the USSR itself brought an end to the Cold War. The new Russian nation, however, remained influential as it began drawing on and marketing its natural resources more effectively.

despotism. Manufacturing companies from the West saw huge potential markets in the East. Churches looked hopefully to the millions who had been denied religious life for forty years.

Rushdie's The Satanic Verses   Three other events in that remarkable year of 1989 presaged a less rosy future. First, the leader of the Islamic Republic of Iran, the Ayatollah Ruhollah Khomeini (1902–1989), declared a *fatwa*, or Islamic legal pronouncement, that ghoulishly pronounced a death sentence on a British novelist, Salman Rushdie (b. 1947). Earlier that year Rushdie had published a novel, *The Satanic Verses*, that Khomeini—without having read it—declared blasphemous:

I would like to inform all courageous Muslims throughout the world that the author of the novel *The Satanic Verses* . . . as well as those publishers who were aware of its contents, are hereby sentenced to death. I call upon all pious Muslims to execute them all, quickly, wherever they might find them, so that afterwards no one will dare to insult the holiness of Islam. Anyone who is killed in carrying out this sentence will be regarded as a martyr and will go directly to heaven.

The novel takes its title from a dream sequence in which the fever-stricken main character imagines that the Prophet Muhammad has made a deal with three ancient pagan deities to insert some of their pseudo-revelations into the text of the Qur'an. Even more repugnant to some Muslims was a later episode set in India, in which the prostitutes in a brothel have all taken the names of the Prophet's wives as pseudonyms.

Khomeini died four months after pronouncing the death sentence, but his call spurred fanatics into action. The novel's Japanese translator, a recent convert to Islam, was stabbed to death; its Italian translator, knifed in Milan, survived; its Norwegian publisher was shot in the back four times, but also survived. A mob set fire to a hotel where the novel's Turkish translator was participating in a literary conference; thirty-five people burned to death. The Turkish translator himself escaped the fire, but several of the firefighters, recognizing him, beat him senseless. Rushdie stayed in protective custody with the British government for nine years, and the death sentence remains, although Iran has agreed not to pursue it.

Of course, a handful of would-be assassins do not represent an entire religion or culture, but the reaction of the Muslim world alarmed the West. The Union of Muslim Organisations, Britain's largest Islamic group, petitioned Parliament to ban the distribution of the novel.[1] Bookshops were vandalized and firebombed, and hundreds more received bomb threats. The Organisation of the Islamic Cooperation, a group for coordinating policy between Muslim states at the United Nations, requested all its member states to ban the book. The Islamic Union of Students' Associations in Europe also endorsed the demand for Rushdie's murder. Numerous other Islamic groups opposed the killing, but on legal rather than moral grounds. They argued that Khomeini's *fatwa*, or Islamic legal pronouncement, had not followed the proper guidelines, and anyway a *fatwa* could not be enforced in a non-Islamic country such as Britain.

---

[1] Within a year of publication, *The Satanic Verses* was banned in nineteen countries, including Bangladesh, Egypt, Indonesia, Malaysia, Pakistan, Qatar, Saudi Arabia, Somalia, South Africa, and Sudan.

Demonstrating Against *The Satanic Verses*
Ayatollah Khomeini's call for the assassination
of novelist Salman Rushdie prompted dozens of
demonstrations worldwide, both for and against
the *fatwa*. In this photo, Khomeini supporters
in Tehran declare their support for the *fatwa*
with the assertion that freedom of speech does
not extend to religious insult.

The Rushdie affair brought home the anger
of many Muslims worldwide at Western values.
The Khomeini regime had instituted public
whippings, stonings, beheadings, and firing
squads for its enemies. "Those who attempt to
undermine or ruin our Republic in the name of
democracy," Khomeini warned, "will be suppressed; they are worse than the Jews of Banu
Qurayza, and must be hanged." (The reference is
to a group of seventh-century Jews from Medina,
some eight hundred of them, who had opposed
Muhammad's rise and were consequently captured and beheaded.) The Iranian Revolution
pursued not only a separate path of development
for Islamic nations but also active opposition to
the West's "oppressive, un-Islamic" ways of life.

Arab states feared the Iranian Revolution
as a sign of both Shi'a and Persian ascendance
and therefore a threat to Arab and Sunni dominance. But rejection of the West's politics, econ-
omy, popular culture, and moral values proved popular throughout the Islamic
world, and militant organizations had at least the tacit support of the broader
population—and even several governments. Soon news and debates in the West
regularly referred to groups with names like *Islamic Jihad*, *Party of God*, *Party of
Islam*, and *Party of Liberation*. Like the nations in which they were founded, most
of these institutions are of recent origin. All promote a restoration of conservative
Islamic values, but not all advocate for anti-Western violence. Many of these
groups are quite small, with only a few hundred members. But some claim membership in the hundreds of thousands.

Until the Rushdie affair, the West had generally regarded developments in
the Islamic world as regional concerns, of interest to the West only as they affected Israel or the price of oil. Muslim immigration into Europe and the United
States still worried relatively few. But the sudden sight of tens of thousands of
European Muslims on the streets of Berlin, Copenhagen, The Hague, London,
Paris, Rome, and dozens of smaller cities provided a wake-up call. This might not
be the "end of history" after all.

**Exxon
Valdez Oil
Spill**
The second alarming incident of 1989 was the grounding of the *Exxon Valdez*,
an oil tanker, in Prince William Sound, Alaska. The tanker was plump with
55 million gallons of heavy, thick crude oil from Alaska's far-northern Prudhoe
Bay when its hull was crushed against a reef. It created an environmental disaster

Environmental Disaster   The work to clean up the oil spilled by the *Exxon Valdez* took decades. Here workers use high-power sprays on coastal rocks and the beach. Even twenty years later, marine and coastal wildlife were dramatically reduced in numbers. While the sound itself now looks clean, as much as 20,000 gallons of oil still lie beneath the surface. Many local plant species and the animal populations that feed on them have declined over 90 percent and show little likelihood of recovering.

greater than anything the United States had ever experienced. The responsibility lay with the Exxon Corporation; an Alaskan court ordered it to pay more than $25 billion in compensation and another $5 billion in punitive damages. To finance its payments, Exxon received a multi-billion-dollar line of credit from the J. P. Morgan investment bank, which invented a new kind of financial instrument to provide the capital. They called it a "credit default swap," and it was to play a role, as we shall see, in another disaster—the financial crisis of 2008.

The spill awakened millions in the West to the threat that industrial development posed the environment, and debates about Western dependency on oil, its effects on the environment, and the dangers of what seemed the only real alternative—nuclear energy—escalated. After a drought in 1988, government officials spoke for the first time of **global warming**, a sweeping change in the earth's climate (see Map 29.2). Britain's prime minister, Margaret Thatcher, in 1988 called for political action to combat climate change, but promoted nuclear energy as the solution. The *Valdez* oil spill accelerated calls for international action.

The first significant step was the UN Conference on Environment and Development, or Earth Summit, held in Rio de Janeiro in 1992. Its Rio Declaration

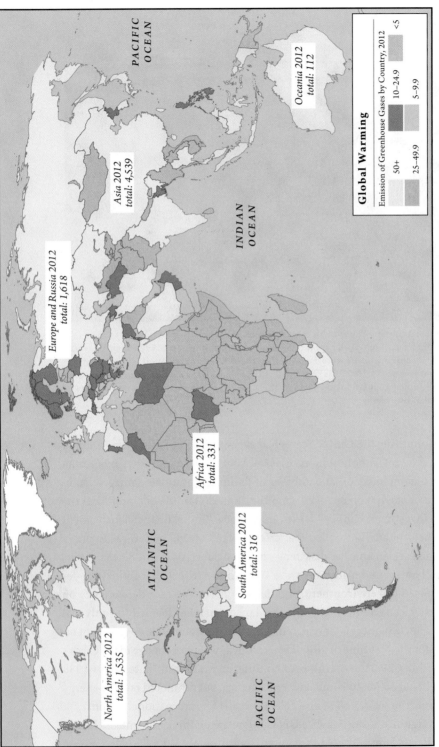

MAP 29.2 Global Warming As industry advanced and population grew, the earth itself came under assault. By the late 1980s, scientists determined that the use of chlorofluorocarbons (CFCs), chemicals found in aerosol and refrigeration products, had blown a hole in the earth's ozone layer, the part of the blanket of atmospheric gases that prevents harmful ultraviolet rays from reaching the planet. Simultaneously, industrial emissions, especially of carbon dioxide produced by the burning of fossil fuels, were adding to the thermal blanket. The buildup of pollutants produced a "greenhouse effect" that resulted in global warming—an increase in the temperature of the earth's lower atmosphere. By the 1990s the Arctic ice pack was breaking up, and scientists predicted dire consequences: if unchecked, the rate of global ice melting would eventually flood coastal areas, disturb fragile ecosystems, and harm the fresh water supply.

called environmental protection an "integral part of the development process," one that "cannot be considered in isolation from it." It also committed nations to "the essential task of eradicating poverty as an indispensable requirement for sustainable development." Critics complained that the two goals were contradictory, at least in the short term, since only economic development could overcome poverty in developing nations. The demand to reduce carbon emissions from fossil fuels while also resisting the spread of nuclear energy, critics said, was simply unrealistic. Transportation of goods and people alone accounted for 40 percent of carbon emissions. For all its ecological drawbacks, oil is effective, relatively inexpensive, and easy to move. One can have economic health or environmental health, critics insisted, but not both.

The conflict between economic development and environmental preservation came to a head with the document known as the **Kyoto Protocol**, an international response to global warming in 1997. The English cleric and scholar Thomas Malthus (1766–1834) had raised a related issue as long ago as 1826, in his *Essay on the Principle of Population*. To Malthus, human history has always been the contest of a growing population for the finite material goods of the earth. "The power of population is indefinitely greater than the power in the earth to produce subsistence for man." When the tension between the two powers becomes too great, nature alleviates it by famine and disease. Knowingly or not, those who argued most for environmental protections were Malthusians. They believed that human and economic catastrophe could be averted only by protecting the environment.

Others took the opposite view, insisting that economic growth was the answer to the ecological problem. In two books, *The Ultimate Resource* (1981) and *The Resourceful Earth* (1984), the American economist Julian Simon (1932–1998) laid the intellectual foundation for many conservative leaders at the end of the century. For Simon, the competition for scarce resources in a free market promotes innovations, as he wrote in *The Ultimate Resource*:

> The basic idea is that growth in population creates a demand that provokes an increase in prices. The increase in prices creates opportunities that attract businesses and scientists to be able to satisfy the demand and thus increase their income. Most of them fail and they personally absorb the costs. But after a while, some are successful and find solutions. At the end you have a situation better than if there had not been a problem of scarcity.

If environmental doomsayers were too negative, the "free-market environmentalists" may have been naive idealists. But once again the "end of history"—either as the birth of a capitalist utopia or as the death of planet Earth—had not yet arrived.

A third crucial event of 1989 occurred in China. In April, students at Beijing *Tiananmen* University used the funeral of a popular dissenting politician as an occasion to *Square* demonstrate for reform in Tiananmen Square. More than 100,000 people joined the demonstration, which soon became a direct challenge to the Communist government. The demonstrators in the square were peaceful and stopped short of calling for party leaders to leave office; rather, they demanded democracy, freedom of speech, freedom of association, an end to political cronyism, and increased funding for education. Urban workers, who generally supported the government's economic liberalization but had begun to experience inflation, voiced support for the students.

Violent rioting broke out in several cities, although not in Beijing itself. The government portrayed the demonstrators as plotting to overthrow the state, which only strengthened student resolve. On June 4, the army took action, both within Beijing and across the nation. Estimates of the number of protestors, onlookers, and soldiers killed nationwide ranges from 241 (the official government reckoning) to as many as 5,000 (as estimated by the local branch of the Red Cross). Thousands more, and possibly tens of thousands, were wounded.

The government tried to control how these events appeared to the world, but too late. Satellite phones and radio and television broadcasts had leaked too many

Tank Man The identity of this lone figure, staring down a column of tanks en route to Tiananmen Square, is still unknown—and he may well be grateful for that fact, given the continuing crackdown on dissidents by China's ruling elite.

reports and videos. The benign image that the regime had presented was stripped away, to reveal a brutal autocracy with the power of tanks and fact-twisting propaganda:

> A group of ruffians banded together about 1,000 people to push down the wall of a construction site near Xidan [a major commercial area in Beijing] and seized large quantities of tools, reinforcing bars and bricks, ready for street fighting. They planned to incite people to take to the streets the next day, a Sunday, to stage a violent rebellion in an attempt to overthrow the government and seize power at one stroke.
>
> At this critical juncture, the martial law troops were ordered to move in by force to quell the anti-government rebellion. . . . Over 1,280 vehicles were burned or damaged in the rebellion, including over 1,000 military trucks, more than 60 armoured cars, over 30 police cars, over 120 public buses and trolley buses and over 70 motor vehicles of other kinds. More than 6,000 martial law officers and soldiers were injured and scores of them killed.
>
> Such heavy losses are eloquent testimony to the restraint and tolerance shown by the martial law enforcement troops. For fear of injuring civilians by accident, they would rather endure humiliation and meet their death unflinchingly, although they had weapons in their hands. It can be said that there is no other army in the world that can exercise restraint to such an extent. (*Official Report of the Editorial Board of the Truth about the Beijing Turmoil*, Beijing Publishing House, 1990)

In response to the crackdown, the European Union and the United States embargoed the sale of weaponry to China, and the World Bank suspended all developmental loans to Beijing. Billions of dollars in foreign investments were canceled, and international tourism to China fell by 25 percent.

Communist and Maoist ideology no longer convinced most Chinese, but the party could still command obedience by appeals to nationalism. The party presented itself as the only sure guarantor of stable economic reform and the protector of national pride. The Communist government in effect played a double game. It showed a friendly face to the outside world and courted international investment, yet internally it portrayed the Chinese people as the victims of misunderstanding and imperialist aggression. China's political leader at the time, Deng Xiaoping, remained in power for three more years after the Tiananmen Square rebellion, and retired in 1992. His extensive reforms opened China to a market economy, which began China's extraordinary climb as a global leader in manufacturing and commerce. Between 1985 and 2000, China's gross domestic product increased by a factor of ten, and it doubled again in the first six years after the turn of the millennium. Like the ancient rulers of Rome, the Chinese Communists had learned that people will relinquish political freedom if given an opportunity to prosper economically.

The Former Soviet Bloc The rise of radical Islamism and the flourishing of Arab and Chinese nationalism have shaped Western life ever since. The Cold War may have ended in 1989, but a profoundly unsettled world took its place. The post-1989 changes in fact echoed many of the experiences of the post-1815 era, when an economic and social time-lock opened, and an accelerating wave of aggressive capitalism rushed in. Scores of huge fortunes were amassed almost instantly, as people with access to capital snatched up privatized state monopolies, whereas the bulk of the populations, unaccustomed to and suspicious of Western-defined "market forces," found themselves with no means to support themselves. Unemployment in Poland, for example, reached 20 percent. The gross national product of Ukraine collapsed 50 percent within ten years of the Soviet breakup, whereas hyperinflation threatened to make the national currency useless; even after another decade, by 2009, more than one-third of the adult population was unemployed. Hungary lost three-fourths of its export markets when protectionist measures closed access to its former trading partners; the national trade deficit soon grew to nearly triple the amount of total exports.

Soon enough, the predictable backlash occurred, and currents of political ultraconservatism emerged across eastern Europe that advocated a return to centralized control. Intense nationalistic sentiments rose, which prompted many nonmajority populations—especially large numbers of Jews—to emigrate. Right-wing coups were attempted in Georgia, as people denounced the corruption and cronyism of democratically chosen administrations. Assassinations and attempted assassinations poisoned the political atmospheres.

The West responded by injecting capital through the International Monetary Fund, increasing private investment, bringing at least some of the nations (Bulgaria, Estonia, Hungary, Latvia, Lithuania, Poland, Romania) into the European Union and most of the same into NATO. The economic malaise improved through the 1990s as a result, but this improvement came at the cost of leaving the not-included nations feeling exposed and vulnerable, especially in the face of renewed political swagger from Russia's leader, Vladimir Putin. Putin had led Russia, either as President or Prime Minister, since 1999, during which time he benefited from the sharply rising oil and gas prices of the early 2000s (Russia being a major producer of both) to restabilize the economy after its post-Communist transition to a market orientation. Flush with cash, Putin pursued aggressive foreign policy initiatives in central Asia and the Caucasus region. He carried on a brutal war to suppress rebels against Moscow's authority in Chechnya (1999–2003), interfered in

Georgia's attempt to restore control of its breakaway province of South Ossetia (2008), gave military support to the regime of Bashar al-Assad in Syria against rebels (2010), and railed against Ukraine's campaign to join NATO—finally going so far as to annex the Crimea and to give military support to Russian-speaking rebels within Ukraine who wished to win autonomy from Kiev (2014).

THE UNITED STATES OF EUROPE?

The idea of uniting Europe in a single superstate can be traced back at least to Charlemagne in the early ninth century. Several medieval popes had imagined it. Most of the Habsburgs had probably fantasized about it. Napoleon almost achieved it. Hitler almost destroyed the place in his fanatic attempt make it happen. But the idea existed outside the minds of would-be dictators too.

Unification's appeal lay in the hope that it might be the one force powerful enough to contain nationalist passions, and it expressed the idea that European *Values of* civilization stood for more than material progress—that the values by which the *European* various people live transcend ethnic and political lines. At the Continent's center, *Unification* German thinkers have traditionally been at the forefront of the call to unification. Nietzsche had devoted a long section of *Beyond Good and Evil* (1886) to the question of national and civilizational identity:

> No matter what you wish to call the thing by which Europe is made distinctive—its "civilization," "humanization," or "progress"—or if you simply call it (without praise or blame) Europe's political "democratization," there is an overarching physiological process occurring, indeed accelerating, behind all the moral and political theorizing around it: namely, Europeans are becoming more and more alike, more and more detached from those elements of climate and class that lead to the creation of separate races. . . . An essentially super-national, free-wandering European man is emerging, one who physiologically possesses as his defining trait a superfluity of the ability to adapt. (*chapter 242*)
>
> Because of the pathological soul-estrangement created by the utter insanity of nationalism . . . and because of the short-sighted sleight-of-hand performed by today's politicians (who got to where they are precisely by playing off this madness), . . . people are overlooking or perhaps (willfully?) misunderstanding the most obvious thing in the world: namely, that *Europe wants to unite*. (*chapter 256*)

The aspiration to unite was cultural, moral, and even spiritual. At stake were shared values and beliefs, a commitment to human rights, civic-mindedness, reason, and personal freedom. Politics and the economy played their roles, but what mattered most was the idea of Europe as a civilization, not just a commercial entity.

Creation of the European Union

The leaders of western Europe, after years of wrangling, had agreed in March 1957 to the first step toward union—the Treaty of Rome, which established the European Economic Community (EEC), an organization comprising the six nations of Belgium, France, West Germany, Italy, Luxembourg, and the Netherlands. More of a corporate merger than a cultural confluence, the EEC created a competitive commercial bloc that could hold its own on the world market. Its goals were to help postwar recovery and to counterbalance American economic power. Two other groups, the European Coal and Steel Community and the European Atomic Energy Community, were merged with the EEC in 1967, creating the European Community. Already it sounded less like a chamber of commerce and more like an association of cultures.

The next step to full integration came late in 1993, when a treaty signed a year earlier at Maastricht, in the Netherlands, took effect. This treaty established the **European Union** (EU), as not a single institution but a united group of independent European nations. This flexible web of institutions would provide a process for coordinating policies formed at the level of member states:

> The European Union (EU) is not a federation like the United States. Nor is it simply an organisation for co-operation between governments, like the United Nations. It is, in fact, unique. The countries that make up the EU (its "member states") remain independent sovereign nations but they pool their sovereignty in order to gain a strength and world influence none of them could have on their own. Pooling sovereignty means, in practice, that the member states delegate some of their decision-making powers to shared institutions they have created, so that decisions on specific matters of joint interest can be made democratically at the European level.

From the six members of the original EEC, the EU grew steadily (see Map 29.3). It now numbers twenty-seven member states, with another five official candidates for membership. Each nation must meet three criteria before joining:

- It must have a democratic government that recognizes human rights and the rule of law.
- It must have a free-market economy.
- It must meet administrative standards to participate seamlessly with other member states.

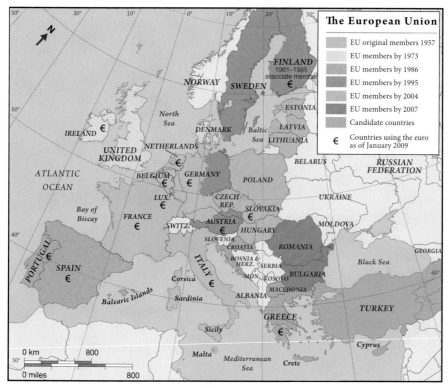

MAP 29.3 **The European Union** The European Union helped end the traditional competition between its members and facilitated trade and worker migration by providing common currency, passports, and business laws and open borders. But many critics feared a loss of cultural distinctiveness among peoples in an age of globalization.

Of those standards, the most crucial is the ability to limit governmental debt to an acceptable percentage of the gross national product. Once a member, each country may choose to join in a common currency—the *euro*—which was introduced in 1999. By eliminating or reducing bureaucratic barriers, the EU promoted the free movement of workers, goods, services, and capital. All these, combined with the low price of oil caused by Middle East overproduction, made the 1990s an economic boom time. Still-developing economies in countries like Greece, Ireland, and Portugal benefited from substantial investment in new manufacturing and financial ventures.

Unified Europe was not without its problems. More people flowed from poor nations into wealthy ones than euros flowed from wealthy nations into poor ones. This meant rising unemployment in countries like Britain, France, and Germany; it also meant uncertain growth in countries like Greece, Portugal, and Spain. Labor surpluses put downward pressure on wages in the developed countries, since by far the most migration took place among the *Challenges to European Unification*

MAP 29.4   Immigration in the European Union   The rising tide of globalization ushered in as many challenges as opportunities. With its policy of open borders, the European Union witnessed a dramatic increase in immigration.

working class. Meanwhile, the developing nations took on excessive debt in proportion to their growth. For the time being, however, the availability of cheap capital, which included substantial investments from the United States and China, made the decade feel more prosperous, as we will see, than it was.

A more immediate problem was the social assimilation of so many new foreign workers. Concern about immigration had become an issue as early as the late 1960s, but the creation of the union put increased numbers on the move (see Map 29.4). It was chiefly the migration of individuals rather than entire families.

Libyan Immigrants   The Arab Spring of 2011 led to civil wars across North Africa and in Syria, creating hundreds of thousands, and eventually million, of refugees, many of whom attempted, and still attempt, to emigrate to Europe. Here refugees from the fighting in Libya arrive at the Italian island of Lampedusa. Overcrowding on these ships make for a dangerous passage, and many refugee ships sink. On the ship shown here, a 65-foot trawler, 760 people were crammed aboard.

Since many such workers sent parts of their pay back to their families, they often could afford only crowded and squalid housing. They remained socially isolated in their host countries and struggled for acceptance. They were also the first workers to be laid off during bad times. The need for their wages back home, however, often kept them in their host countries where they looked for new work. The emotional strain on these workers, not to mention on their distant families, was great.

When a recession hit, the unemployed in Britain alone grew from 1.6 million workers to 3.0 million between 1990 and 1993. The downturn contributed to the rise of reactionary popular movements in Europe. Neo-Nazi skinheads led race riots and railed against "foreigners," both European and non-European. "France for the French!" became the cry of the far-right National Front Party, which by the middle of the 1990s was earning 15 percent of the vote. The French government, eager to capitalize on anti-immigrant passions, in 1996 chartered aircraft to fly undocumented workers back to their native countries. In Austria and the Netherlands as well, immigration was the crucial issue in determining the outcome of elections.

ECONOMIC GLOBALIZATION

"Battle of Seattle"

Protesters gathered in Seattle in 1999, in advance of the scheduled ministerial conference of the **World Trade Organization** (WTO), an intergovernmental organization founded in 1995 to promote international trade. They blocked intersections and organized large street demonstrations. Speeches and worker protest songs rang out from street corners. Some protestors set fire to dumpsters. Others broke shop windows and halted almost the entire city's commerce. Police reacted with pepper spray, tear gas, and rubber bullets to clear the streets. In the end, police arrested more than six hundred people. The disruption of business and the task of cleaning up cost the city more than $20 million.

The "Battle of Seattle" drew attention to the intense emotions surrounding economic globalization—the development of a single, interconnected global market. A global market is much like the digital Internet, a network of networks, crossing all borders of nationality, language, culture, and class. Globalization itself was nothing new. One can think of it as an extension of long-standing regional or continental trade. The arc dates back at least to the wave of European imperialism in the 1880s and 1890s. Some historians of antiquity, fancifully enough, date the movement all the way back to the Sumerian era, when the grain-rich Mesopotamian south was linked with northernmost reaches of the Fertile Crescent, rich in iron ore. What is new today are modern systems of communication and transportation. Strawberries harvested one day in California can appear the next day in markets in Tokyo.

The WTO promotes international trade by resolving disputes between nations (see Map 29.5). It also implements trade agreements between nations and, most controversially, oversees the national trade policies of individual countries. The protestors in Seattle represented labor unions, environmental groups, women's organizations, immigration activists, and others. Their opposition to the WTO—indeed to globalization itself—sprang from many issues, but all ones related to the differing standards and legal protections between countries. Workers in countries like China and India do not have the same rights as American workers in regard to wages, work conditions, and employment benefits. It is therefore to any manufacturer's advantage to shift its production overseas. The savings in labor costs vastly outweigh the expense of transporting their finished goods. Some countries offer tax benefits to companies that other countries cannot afford. Still others do not require industry to observe the same environmental protection. The uneven international playing field represented a danger to the standards of living that Westerners had come to expect. Hence the trouble in Seattle.

Globalization had been opposed before, but never in such a dramatic way. More demonstrations followed, all across the United States, in opposition to the World Bank and the International Monetary Fund, two institutions viewed as the

N

0 km   3000

0 miles   3000

The World Trade Organization

Countries that joined WTO 1995-2000   Countries that joined WTO 2001-2012   Observer governments

MAP 29.5   The World Trade Organization   Formed in 1995 to promote international trade, the WTO works to resolve disputes between nations, implement international trade agreements, and, most controversially, oversee the national trade policies of individual countries.

financiers of globalization. Opposition to globalization occurred in Europe too, although generally in quieter forms.

The world population rose steadily throughout the 1990s and will continue to do so until 2050 (see Figure 29.1). And that means a steady rise in the demand for everything from food and textiles to pharmaceuticals and computer components. Yet the populations of Europe and the United States are stagnating. Between 2010 and 2050 the U.S. population is projected to grow from 300 million to 400 million (a 33 percent growth, compared to the global increase of 100 percent), and the population of Europe will actually decline from 700 million to 690 million.[2] For Western corporations that want to expand their businesses, the choices are clear—either import workers (which means immigration, whether legal or illegal) or export jobs. Or both. And in their varying ways, global institutions like the WTO and the International Monetary Fund help them do just that. Both responses to the demographic gap between the West and the world—exporting jobs and immigrating workers—present political and social challenges. European unification, globalization, and immigration came together in the 1990s and helped trigger a sudden series of unnervingly bitter wars.

Impact of Population Growth

---

[2]   In 2010, the United States and Europe held 15 percent of the world's population; by 2050, they may hold as little as 8.5 percent.

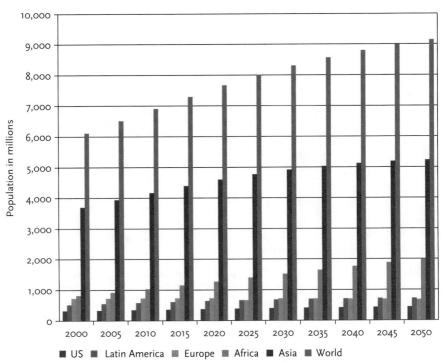

FIGURE 29.1   World Population, 2000–2050 (in millions)

WAR AND PEACE, FROM THE BALKANS TO PAKISTAN

The Balkans

Nationalist passions in the Balkans had been kept in check by the heavy hand of totalitarian rulers. After the collapse of Communism, they sprang back to poisonous life. Serbs, Croats, Bosnians, and Slovenians after 1991 all wanted to secede from the political union that the Communists had forced on them, but a demographic mixing had taken place during Yugoslavia's forty years of existence. It was impossible to draw satisfying political borders when every configuration left remnants of some group as a minority among others. Of all the peoples involved, the Serbs proved the most willing, even eager, to resort to war. Under their leader, Slobodan Milosevic (1941–2006), who commanded what was left of the old Yugoslav army (the fourth largest military machine on the Continent), the Serbs began a series of wars against their neighbors (see Map 29.6). They hoped to establish a Greater Serbia that would unite all ethnic Serbs, to reclaim Balkan land claimed as their patrimony, and to purge those lands of non-Serbs. In 1994, after Serbian soldiers had massacred tens of thousands of Bosnians and driven hundreds of thousands more into exile, NATO forces finally took action with bombing raids against Serb artillery. Eventually, the United Nations brought in peacekeeping forces. These wars lasted until 1995 and witnessed many scenes of

MAP 29.6   Wars and Conflicts in the Greater West, 1990–2012   The end of the Cold War ushered in a series of regional conflicts, often inspired by nationalist passions kept in check by decades of superpower control.

Mourning the Dead   In July 1995, soldiers of the Serbian army executed eight thousand Muslim men and boys in the Bosnian city of Srebrenica. The massacre was preceded by several days of horrendous torture of civilians, including the systematic rape of Bosnian women, even as a Dutch-staffed UN peacekeeping force looked on. Here a Srebrenica survivor, Hajra Èatiae, who lost her husband and son in the attack, helps to maintain a photo archive of the victims.

horror and near genocide. A peace deal was finally negotiated with the help of the United States, but the Serbs soon opened a new front in Kosovo and Albania, extending the violence until 2001. Milosevic himself was arrested in that year and brought to The Hague to face trial for crimes against humanity. He died in prison before the trial had run its course.

Apart from bookending the twentieth century with Balkan violence, the wars there added fuel to Muslim anger toward the West. The Bosnians, who were the chief victims of Serb massacre, are a predominantly Muslim people.[3] Would the European and American powers have waited two years to come to the rescue if the Bosnians had been Christians and the Serbs had been Muslims? To countless Muslims around the world, the wholesale slaughter of the Bosnians took place with the silent complicity of the West. The mass murder of eight thousand Bosnian men and boys at Srebrenica in July 1995 would never have occurred, they insisted, had the religions of attackers and victims been reversed.

Chechnya   Many critics perceived a similar anti-Muslim bias in the West's reaction to the warfare between Russia and Chechnya. Chechnya is a Muslim territory in the North Caucasus (see again Map 29.1). As the USSR eroded in the 1980s, a

---

[3]   Bosnians are the largest Islamic population in Europe after the Turks.

Chechen independence movement arose. The Chechen National Congress achieved independence in 1991, but only three years later, Russia sent in a large army to end it. The war lasted from 1994 to 1996, when a truce was declared. War broke out again shortly thereafter, lasting from 1999 to 2009. The conflicts were marked by atrocities on both sides. Russia proved unable to bring the province to heel despite enormously superior numbers and weaponry. The Chechens could not drive the Russians from the region, but they proved ruthless and adept at terrorist bombings in Moscow and elsewhere. Muslims felt a lack of interest in the West in their suffering. Europe barely responded to Russia's heavy-handedness, but it condemned the terrorism that many Chechens felt was their only option. As if to prove their point, the Chechen War drew little media attention in the West, and even when it has been covered, Western news outlets seldom mention the issue of religion.

Two wars in the Persian Gulf, however, claimed the attention of the entire world. The first war (1990–1991) was a tense but brief affair. Iraq's ruler, Saddam *Persian* Hussein (1937–2006), deeply in debt after a disastrous war with neighboring Iran *Gulf* (1980–1988), needed new oil revenues and invaded the tiny but wealthy Gulf nation of Kuwait. Kuwait was in fact one of Iraq's two principal creditors, the other being Saudi Arabia. International condemnation of Iraq came swiftly, and in seven months a U.S.-led coalition drove the Iraqis from Kuwait and established a "no-fly zone" over southern Iraq. Its goal was to protect Kuwait from fresh attack and to protect Shi'i Iraqis from retribution by Saddam Hussein's Sunni army. The coalition's forces were mostly American soldiers, with the next largest contingents from the United Kingdom and the Arab League, composed of Morocco, Oman, Qatar, Saudi Araba, Syria, and the United Emirates. Saudi Arabia was the staging post of the coalition's armies, and it paid the bulk of the war's cost. Both facts had dramatic consequences, since they drew the ire of Osama bin Laden, head of the militant Islamic organization al-Qaeda. As we will see, the sheer presence of a Western army on the sacred soil of Arabia became bin Laden's justification for ordering the 9/11 and 7/7 attacks on the United States and the United Kingdom.

The United States launched air assaults against the Taliban regime in Afghanistan in October 2001, since the Taliban had granted refuge to al-Qaeda for years. Within a matter of weeks the Taliban were crushed, although Osama bin Laden escaped into Pakistan. Rather than focusing on building up the shaky new government in Afghanistan, however, the United States under President George W. Bush (b. 1946) turned its attention back to Saddam Hussein in Iraq. He had been behind the 9/11 attacks, Bush argued, and was stockpiling advanced chemical, biological, and perhaps even nuclear weapons. In March 2003, after months of diplomatic pressure and posturing, the United States invaded Iraq—but no link between Iraq and al-Qaeda was ever found. Indeed, Hussein had long been an active hunter of groups like al-Qaeda, since their religious ideology was directly at odds with his secular Ba'athism. Nor were any of the advanced weapons systems ever found, which left the United States and its British allies open to charges of willful war-making. Most Iraqis cheered the capture, trial, and execution of Hussein, but few felt that his downfall was worth the price of the invasion.

Charges of imperialism were quickly levied against the West throughout the Arab world, charges supported by critics within the West. Accusations of oil theft, war crimes, corruption, and high-handedness swirled around the Western forces, and scandals only added to the West's public relations difficulties with the Muslim world. American forces mistreated Iraqi prisoners at the Abu Ghraib prison complex, at a military facility in Guantanamo Bay in Cuba, and at secret prisons operated by the Central Intelligence Agency. Such episodes undercut the positive image the West tried to create for its involvements in the region, which it presented as efforts to bring democracy to nations that have known only tribalism and corrupt dictatorship.

In 2007 Great Britain got a new prime minister, Gordon Brown (2007–2010), and one year later Barack Obama (b. 1961) was elected as the first African

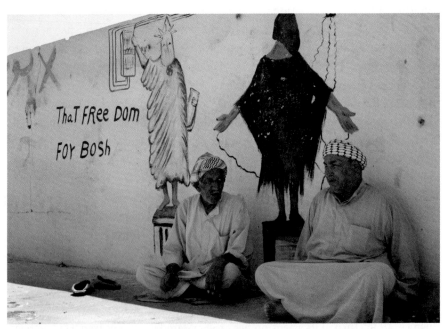

Public Relations Difficulties   U.S. efforts to restore order in Iraq after the overthrow of Saddam Hussein confronted one challenge after another. One of the most infamous episodes was the public release of photos showing the torture of Iraqis held in the U.S.-controlled prison at Abu Ghraib in 2004. This photos shows two Iraqi men resting in the shade provided by a wall—a wall bearing graffiti criticizing the U.S. behavior. "That freedom for Bosh" castigates U.S. President George W. Bush's policy.

American president of the United States. Under these two leaders the West withdrew its troops from Iraq, bringing to a gradual end (in October 2010) a struggle that had lasted for seven years. A shaky democratic government under a new constitution now runs Iraq, but it remains to be seen whether it can withstand the separatist leanings of parts of the country and the continued attacks of Islamist splinter groups.

Meanwhile, al-Qaeda's relocation to Pakistan opened a new front in the West's war against terrorism. Pakistan's diplomatic position had always been delicate, since its chief diplomatic and military concern centered on its troubled *Pakistan* relations with India, to the east. The issue of Afghanistan was important to the Pakistani government mainly as a way to coax military and economic aid out of the United States. That led the government in Islamabad to play a double game of claiming to oppose al-Qaeda and the Taliban, even while privately giving them aid and refuge. On May 2, 2011, U.S. Special Forces launched a secret raid on a secure compound in Abbottabad in Pakistan, where it found and killed Osama bin Laden, who was still directing the activities of al-Qaeda after ten years on the run. His discovery at a safe house only a short distance from a Pakistani military academy prompted questions about Pakistan's role in harboring him.

ISLAM AND ITS DISCONTENTS

Militant Islamism continued to spread throughout the 1990s and 2000s and caused sharp political ruptures in North Africa and the Middle East. With the exception of Iran, most of the foment came from nongovernmental organizations. Indeed, most militants opposed their own governments as much as they resented what they regarded as Western neocolonialism. These groups turned to terrorist tactics as their main form of political action, fearing that no other tactic could bring reform. The danger lay not only in the attacks themselves but also in the repressive response of Arab governments.

In Algeria, for example, the Islamic Salvation Front won local and national elections with its calls for government by Islamic law, or shari'a. The Algerian *Government* government voided the elections and declared martial law, triggering a civil *Suppression* war (1991–1992) that killed 100,000. Fearing comparable scenes in their own *of Islamic* countries, the governments of Egypt and Tunisia also suppressed Islamist *Groups* groups. In Egypt, President Hosni Mubarak (b. 1928) placed every mosque in the country under direct government control in an effort to root out radical clerics. In Turkey, the Rifah (or Welfare) Party rose quickly, scoring local electoral victories in 1994 and two years later electing Necmettin Erbakan (1926–2011) as prime minister. Erbakan had the demeanor of an academic, which he was (he was a professor of mechanical engineering), but his political convictions were those of an

Islamist radical. He rejected the idea of Turkey joining the European Common Market, which he disparaged as a joint Catholic and Zionist conspiracy to engulf and assimilate the Islamic world. His policies antagonized the overwhelmingly secular Turkish army, however, which pressed him to resign after only twelve months in office.

WHY TERRORISM?

Terrorism erupted in the 1990s and early 2000s. The most frequently used techniques were car bombings and shootings, although by 2000 suicide bombings became increasingly common as well. And the victims were global. Colombia suffered the greatest number of terrorist attacks, all connected to the trade in illegal drugs. Other hot spots included India, Indonesia, Pakistan, and Sri Lanka.

The greatest number of attacks came from domestic rather than foreign enemies. Algerians fought against their own government, separatists in Northern Ireland against the United Kingdom, Kurdish rebels against the Turkish state, and Basque separatists in the Spanish capital of Madrid. In only a handful of cases was terrorism directed outward against foreign nations. Those cases, however, included Israel's struggle with the Palestinians and the horrific attack on the United States on September 11, 2001.

Fringe-group terrorism seldom works. In the short term it terrifies, even paralyzes, whole populations; but it also steels their resolve not to give in to the terrorists' aims. The conflict in Northern Ireland, for example, was resolved only after terrorist groups on both the Catholic and the Protestant sides, tiring of the decades of conflict, renounced violence, surrendered their arms, and agreed to negotiate. The process proved to be long and difficult, but it finally succeeded. The **Good Friday Accord** (or Belfast Agreement), signed in May 1998, went into effect in December 1999, ending eighty years of strife. Similarly, the constitutional struggle in Spain ended only when the Basque group ETA realized that their brutality only made their goal of more freedom from Madrid less likely. When they declared a halt to terrorism in 2006, negotiations for greater autonomy began at once; by 2011 a permanent settlement had been made. If terrorism worked, Israel would have been brought to its knees decades ago.[4]

Economic Interpretation   Why then did terrorism spread so viciously at the end of the twentieth century? Two schools of thought predominate, one pointing to economic and the other to political factors. The economic theorists argue that the poor are attracted to terrorism out of desperation. They are recruited to become

---

[4]   State-run terrorism is another matter. Testimonials could be given by any number of people—the ancient Assyrians, Attila the Hun, Genghis Khan, Tamerlane, and Stalin come to mind.

suicide bombers by organizations that use terrorism against a declared enemy as a tool to gain power and influence among their own people. These groups also build strength by courting popular support through social work and by appealing for aid outside of their country. Sustained terrorist campaigns, after all, require money—lots of money.

For example, Hamas, the Palestinian group founded in Gaza in 1987 by Shaikh Ahmed Yassin (introduced in chapter 28), acquired financial backing from the Muslim Brotherhood. Yassin quickly brought physicians into the leadership and set to work providing free health services to the Gazan poor, which helped establish a popular base. Tens of millions of dollars annually (an estimated 50 percent of its money) comes from Saudi Arabia; perhaps another 10 percent comes from the government in Iran. Ironically, Hamas in its first years also received financial backing from the Israeli government, which had sought to draw support away from

Day of Infamy   September 11, 2001. Terrorists from Osama bin Laden's organization al-Qaeda hijacked four U.S. airliners and flew them into chosen targets. One plane crashed into the Pentagon in Washington, D.C. Two others took down the Twin Towers of the World Trade Center in lower Manhattan, shown here. The fourth crashed in rural Pennsylvania when the passengers stormed the cockpit. In this photograph, the south tower has already collapsed, and the north tower has just been hit by the airplane targeting it. More than 2,700 people died and 2,200 more were injured in the 9/11 attacks.

the Palestinian Liberation Organization under Yasser Arafat. As it gained financial heft, however, Hamas supplemented its charitable work with armed terrorism. Most recent Western estimates of Hamas's funding place it in the range of $400 to $500 million dollars a year.

The case of **al-Qaeda** ("the Foundation" or "Base")—the group behind the 9/11 terrorist attacks—is similar. Its leader and co-founder, **Osama bin Laden** (1957–2011), was born to wealth, a member of the Saudi royal family. He expanded his fortune through owning and managing several large construction companies. A longtime religious conservative, bin Laden fought against the Soviet Union in Afghanistan with the *mujahideen*, and his politics became radicalized during the first Gulf War (1990–1991), when he objected to "infidel armies" in the land of the Prophet. From this point on, he called the United States the greatest of the four "enemies of Islam," against which he dedicated his life. The other three were Jews, Shi'i Muslims, and unspecified "heretics."

The second leading theory sees political and social conditions as terrorism's richest source. Repressive governments and discriminatory societies, this line of thinking goes, create their own terrorists as individuals come to feel the *Political Interpretation* need for dramatic action. The Irish Republican Army in Northern Ireland is the best example. Created in the 1910s, the group had as its goal a single objective—to overthrow what it regarded as 750 years of English tyranny over the Irish people. Irish Republican Army fighters saw themselves as champions of Irish freedom and of Catholic vengeance on Protestant persecutors. Consider, too, the Kurdish PKK (Partiya Karkerên Kurdistan, or Kurdistan Workers' Party), which Abdullah Öcalan (b. 1948) founded in 1978. Nursing an intense resentment of the Republic of Turkey, the PKK fought to gain independence for the Turkish Kurds. It also had the long-term aim of a united Kurdistan, made up of the Kurds in northern Iran and Iraq too. Financial support poured in from Syria, which hoped to profit from Turkey's trouble. Later the bulk of its funding came from extortion, racketeering, and the drug trade.

However, a political explanation of terrorism must be subtler than a simple formula like "terrorism as revenge." If a strong-armed regime can persuade its subjects that the real cause of their misery is foreign meddling, then the repressed people will lash out against that enemy. In this scenario the tyrannical authority casts itself as the true champion of the people, their only alternative to corruption and humiliation from abroad.

In the case of Syria, for example, which is perhaps the most repressive Arab regime of the past forty years, the Assad family has held control, although it represents the small, and largely detested, Alawite minority. In fact, it has turned its minority status into its strength by building up a national myth, thanks to a steady diet of anti-Semitic and anti-American propaganda. Only the Assads, they repeat, can hold at bay the strife between Arab tribes and sects within Syria. Only they can stand up to Zionists and Western imperialists.

In an editorial published in September 2003 *Tishreen*, Syria's largest and state-run newspaper, Ghazi Hussein declared that the Holocaust was an invention of the Jews—a plan they had hatched with the Nazis. Why arrange to have 6 million fellow Jews killed? So that the world will feel sorry for the survivors and allow them to create the Zionist state:

> Zionism lurks in the darkest chapter of [Israel's] history, and invents fictions about Jewish suffering in the "Nazi Holocaust" which it then inflates astronomically. . . . The fundamental problem is not the fact that the Zionists attempt to re-write history but that Zionist groups use this false history to deceive international opinion, win the world's sympathy, and then engage in blackmail. . . . Two goals are paramount to Israel and the Zionist organizations that support it: to get more money out of Germany and the other European entities, and to use the myth of the Holocaust as a sword held over the necks of anyone who opposes

Zionism and to accuse them of anti-Semitism. . . . The truth though is that Israel herself—the supposed heir of Holocaust victims everywhere— has committed in the past and still commits today crimes much worse than anything supposedly done to them by the Nazis.

Hussein was not a random commentator. At the time he wrote the article he was both a legal advisor to the Assad government and the head of the political section of the Palestinian Liberation Organization's office in Damascus.

Similar stories run in other newspapers, like *Balsam*, published in the West Bank by the Palestinian Red Crescent, and appear regularly on Syria's state-operated radio. The thuggish rule of Saddam Hussein in Iraq used the same technique, blaming the country's woes on American imperialists and Muslim-hating Zionists.

Both the economic and the political interpretations of terrorism have had their followers. Europeans have often favored the first and the United States the second. Some, however, have raised a third possibility—that Islam itself promotes violence as a way to attain martyrdom. This sentiment is found more frequently in the United States than in Europe—or at least it is given freer expression in America. Predictably, it also feeds the belief of many Muslims that the West is biased against Islam. Whatever the causes, bitter discontent and terrorism show no signs of abating.

"WHY DO THEY HATE US?"

On September 11, 2001, the long-simmering tensions between the West and the Muslim Middle East came to a full boil. And well after the 9/11 terrorist attacks on the United States, the violence kept coming. Hardly a week passed in 2002 without a suicide bomber maiming innocents in Israel; in 2003 the pace slowed to perhaps one massacre every other week. In March 2004 a coordinated sequence of bombs on train lines in Madrid killed 191 and wounded more than two thousand innocents. On July 7, 2005, or "7/7" in British common parlance, a team of bombers struck London's public transport system, killing fifty-two and injuring more than seven hundred. Only a few months later, in September 2005, a Danish newspaper published a dozen cartoons that depicted the Prophet Muhammad in ways that Muslims around the world found offensive and blasphemous. One Danish cartoon depicted the Prophet with a black turban that was actually a lit bomb. Scores of angry demonstrations took place, and arsonists set the Danish embassies in Beirut, Damascus, and Tehran aflame. A wealthy regional politician in India offered a $10 million reward to any Muslim who beheaded the cartoonist who had drawn the most offensive of the cartoons.

"Americans are asking," said U.S. President George W. Bush, "'Why do they hate us?'" Terrorism, however, was not by any means the whole story—perhaps not even the most important one when it comes to understanding Islam or the future of the West. The challenges include independence movements and recovery from dissolution of the USSR, hopes for strengthening of the EU, a second Iraq war, and the status of Muslim women. The turmoil includes the hope and struggles of an "Arab Spring," a deep economic downturn, and conflict over the purpose and limits of government.

As the killings continued, non-Muslim majorities in Europe and the United States reacted in horror. That was sensible enough, but many of them also reacted less sensibly, by seeing all Muslims as terrorists, potential terrorists, or supporters of terrorism. Racism lies behind such attitudes, but so does a willful ignorance—and, in Europe, a greater indifference to religion. Few non-Muslim Westerners knew much about Islam prior to 9/11 and 7/7, and surprisingly few are better informed today.

Western Hypocrisy   In fact, the Muslim world in general does not hate democracy, human rights, or free speech; it hates only what it perceives as Western hypocrisy about them.

Demonstrating for Religious Freedom   Muslim women and girls demonstrate, in 2004, for the right to wear Islamic headscarves in publicly funded schools. French law requires that public schools be entirely secular, which means, among other things, a ban on religious clothing and religious symbols (Jewish skullcaps and Christian crucifixes are likewise forbidden). The protestors carry a banner that calls for "Equality" and "Fraternity"—echoes of the call-to-arms of the French Revolution of 1789. Critics of the Muslim protests point out that demonstrators have left out the first word in the call-to-arms, "Liberty."

How committed was the United States to democracy, Muslims have asked, when it overthrew the democratically elected prime minister of Iran (Muhammad Mossadegh, r. 1951–1953) and installed an autocrat like the shah, Muhammad Reza Pahlavi? How committed was it when it lavished military aid on a dictatorial regime like Hosni Mubarak's in Egypt? How dedicated to religious freedom is a country like France when it forbids Muslim schoolgirls to wear the traditional head-covering, the hijab? How committed to freedom of speech is Germany when it forbids, on penalty of imprisonment, the expression of doubt about the extent of the Holocaust? In the minds of many Muslims, we have been weighed in our own balance and found wanting.

ISRAEL, PALESTINE, AND THE ARAB SPRING

Meanwhile, the conflict between Israel and the Palestinians shows no sign of nearing resolution. In 2007 Palestinian leadership split between two rival factions—the Fatah party under Mahmoud Abbas (b. 1935), which administers the West Bank, and Hamas, which took control of the Gaza Strip. This split introduced an unexpected difficulty into the peace process because Hamas, despite its genuine social and charitable work, is widely recognized as a terrorist organization; thus, Israel steadfastly refuses to negotiate with it. Yet Hamas rose to power through open election by the Gazan Palestinians. To Israel, the way in which Hamas won power is irrelevant. Above all, what matters is what the group has done in the past with the power it had: it murdered and maimed thousands of innocent Israelis. *Israeli–Palestinian Conflict*

But there is more. Since 2007 Hamas has actively encouraged the radicalization of the populace. It instituted an official "Virtue Committee" whose members patrol the streets in search of anyone not observing strict rules of sexual segregation, dress, and comportment. Verbal harassment and physical coercion are common tactics. Critics have likened their actions to the excesses of the Taliban in Afghanistan.

For three weeks at the end of 2008 and the start of 2009, Israel conducted a surprise bombing campaign against Hamas called Operation Cast Lead. Inevitably, interpretations of it vary widely. Hamas and Fatah claim that the Israeli action was a callous act of aggression that killed well over a thousand Palestinian civilians and virtually destroyed Gaza's infrastructure. Israel maintains that it launched a precisely limited series of strikes against known sites of Hamas's terrorist activity and provided warnings in advance to local residents to clear each target area. A flawed UN investigation into the campaign was widely criticized, leaving the dispute alive.

Finally, a chain of spontaneous popular rebellions against corruption, oppression, and ineptitude spread through the Arab world starting in December 2010. The first eruption occurred in Tunisia, where a local street vendor, *The Arab Spring*

Muhammad Bouazizi, who was in despair after years of mistreatment by local officials, set himself ablaze in a busy intersection and killed himself. Crowds took to the street by the hundreds of thousands to protest the actions of the government. They saw Bouazizi as a martyr to civic freedom, and they chanted over and over their demand for vengeance. After attempting to calm the protests, the Tunisian president, who had held dictatorial authority for twenty-three years, fled to France, and a new government came to power. Only a week later the government in neighboring Algeria surrendered the emergency powers it had held for nearly twenty years.

Lebanon and Jordan came next, with crowds demanding, and receiving, new parliamentary regimes. Demonstrations in Sudan prompted its controversial president, Omar al-Bashir (b. 1944), to announce that he would step down from office at the end of his current term. Apart from his oppression of the people in Darfur, he is believed to have embezzled as much as $8 billion of the nation's funds. The atrocities in Darfur have killed as many as 400,000 people and left 2.5 million homeless: Bashir is charged with crimes against humanity, including genocide, by the International Criminal Court. In Oman and Saudi Arabia, protestors won economic concessions and the right to hold elections to fill local government offices and to initiate legislation at that level.

The most spectacular revolt yet occurred in Egypt, where massive demonstrations in Cairo's Tahrir Square in 2011 brought down the forty-year dictatorship of Hosni Mubarak (in June 2012 he was sentenced to life in prison). The military took temporary control of the government, dissolved the parliament, and suspended the constitution. Subsequent mass movements arose in Morocco, Yemen, Iraq, Bahrain, and Kuwait and won at least a partial lifting of heavy-handed governments, the shifting of cabinets, release of political prisoners, and certain economic concessions. The reforms are ongoing although the prospect for the future is unclear.

The only Arab regimes to have mounted prolonged resistance to uprisings have been Libya and Syria, both nations where the government's military forces remained reliably on the regime's side. In each case, civilians withstood months of repressive measures—beatings and arrests, artillery bombardments, systematic rape, and the cutting off of food, water, and electricity. Rebels against Libya's Muammar Qaddafi finally defeated the regime after NATO airstrikes paralyzed the dictator's defenses, which allowed the rebels to stage a decisive land campaign into the capital of Tripoli. Qaddafi himself was captured and killed by a rebel mob when he fled to his hometown of Sirte in October 2011.

Government intransigence has been even stronger in Syria, where the Assad regime has not only held out but also violated UN-brokered cease-fires and intensified its resistance. The political and military situation in Syria, however, is

The Arab Spring   Tawakkol Karman, the leader of the organization "Women Journalists without Chains," protests against the government of Yemen in 2011. Yemen's president, Ali Abdullah Saleh, had been in power since 1978; he was forced to resign his office in early 2012.

considerably more complicated than it was in Libya. Syria's historical role as the original center of the Islamic empire and its proximity to Israel (with which it has had officially hostile yet surprisingly stable relations since the 1990s), together with international concerns to have an Arab counterweight to the regional ambitions of Iran, have disinclined groups like the United Nations, NATO, or the Arab League to provide direct support to the rebels.

These rebellions are known collectively as the **Arab Spring**. They are taking place in the ethnically Arab lands and represent part of the broad awakening of Arab national identity and pride (see Map 29.7). A revitalized and democratic belt of Arab nations across North Africa and throughout the Middle East could do much to help the people of the region prosper. As things have stood, the immense oil wealth of the area has been monopolized by either royal or dictatorial families and their cronies. Freer societies could mean not only a broader sharing of that wealth but also more varied and diverse economies that would help strong democratic traditions to take root. At the same time, the rebellions have been secular. Islamist groups have inevitably been involved at the margins, but the Arab Spring has been overwhelmingly a civic movement, a demand of the masses for control over their own lives. If they can succeed, and in their success remove one of the chief factors behind the desperate appeal of radical Islamism, the possibility of a real, lasting, and just peace in the region could be within reach.

MAP 29.7   The Arab Spring   At the end of 2012, protests erupted in Tunisia over the corruption of its longtime dictator Zine El Abidine Ben Ali and his family. The overthrow of Ben Ali inspired others across the Arab world to demand change.

Confounding such hopes has been the striking success of the extremist group known variously as the Islamic State, ISIL (the Islamic State in Iraq and the Levant), and ISIS (the Islamic State in Iraq and Syria). ISIS is a Sunni group dedicated to a strict Islamist vision of conservative theocracy. It formed as an offshoot of al-Qaeda in response to the US-led invasion of Iraq in 2003. During the regime of Saddam Hussein, the Sunni majority in Iraq treated the Shi'a (who predominate in the southern part of the country) with disdain and considerable oppression, and the U.S. forces disbanded the Sunni government and military forces, being doubtful of their reliability, which opened the way for the Shi'a to end up leading the post-invasion new government. Fearing a Shi'ite backlash against the Sunnis, ISIS quickly formed, found widespread support from the disbanded Sunni military, and in a surprisingly quick wave of conquests carved out a wide zone in both Syria and Iraq that it declared as a new caliphate, under the group's leader Abu Bakr al-Baghdadi. ISIS is also an apocalyptic group that expects the imminent approach of the Day of Judgment, which, in their eyes, justifies the brutality of their efforts to "cleanse" the Middle East those it deems blasphemers, idolators, and "enemies of Allah". Mass executions, usually by beheading, are a signature act of the group.

WOMEN AND THE GLOBAL WORLD

Feminism as practical action did not cease in the 1990s. In fact, it went global. Under the leadership of institutions like the UN Women's Conference, the call to recognize women's rights as human rights grew louder. Meetings in Mexico City *Women's* (1975), Copenhagen (1980), and Nairobi (1985) recognized the different priori- *Rights as* ties of Western and non-Western women. Western speakers, in general, had ad- *Human* dressed economic, legal, and political rights, whereas representatives from the *Rights* non-Western countries emphasized disease, hunger, poverty, and violence. The difference did not show a lack of caring or understanding. It showed instead how much Western women had achieved—on fundamental issues still faced every day by women in Africa, Asia, and Latin America.

A rousing call to action came in the 1995 conference held in Beijing. Hillary Rodham Clinton (b. 1947), then the First Lady of the United States, enumerated the horrors confronting women around the globe:

> It is a violation of human rights when babies are denied food, or drowned, or suffocated, or their spines broken, simply because they are born girls.
>
> It is a violation of human rights when women and girls are sold into the slavery of prostitution for human greed—and the kinds of reasons that are used to justify this practice should no longer be tolerated.
>
> It is a violation of human rights when women are doused with gasoline, set on fire, and burned to death because their marriage dowries are deemed too small.
>
> It is a violation of human rights when individual women are raped in their own communities and when thousands of women are subjected to rape as a tactic or prize of war.
>
> It is a violation of human rights when a leading cause of death worldwide among women ages 14 to 44 is the violence they are subjected to in their own homes by their own relatives.
>
> It is a violation of human rights when young girls are brutalized by the painful and degrading practice of genital mutilation.
>
> It is a violation of human rights when women are denied the right to plan their own families, and that includes being forced to have abortions or being sterilized against their will.
>
> If there is one message that echoes forth from this conference, let it be that human rights are women's rights and women's rights are human rights once and for all. Let us not forget that among those rights are the right to speak freely—and the right to be heard.

The rising ethnic pluralism in Europe probably did more than the Internet to increase awareness of women's global plight. Poverty and violence are harder to ignore when they happen here rather than thousands of miles away.

The "United States of Europe" began to resemble the United States itself, not only as an institution but also in its cultural pluralism. And not everyone was pleased.

Veiled Threats

The future of its women may yet determine the fate of Greater Western society in the twenty-first century. Despite discouraging trends in places like India and China, where gender-selective abortion thrives despite its official illegality, women still outnumber men and comprise the bulk of global society. Within the Greater West, however, a sharp divide exists in how women are treated in society.

The World Economic Forum publishes an annual "Report on the Global Gender Gap," using statistics provided by the member countries themselves, that examines the status of women worldwide. The reports examine five criteria in each country: the level of economic opportunity available to women; educational opportunity and attainment; the availability of health care, whether publicly or privately funded; levels of gender-specific crimes like rape; and the degree of political empowerment, which includes female participation in government, the right to vote, and equal treatment under the law. The 2010 report highlights and quantifies the divide within the Greater West. Sixteen of the highest-scoring twenty nations—that is, those countries that provide the greatest equality and respect to women—are Western. Fifteen of the lowest-scoring twenty nations are Muslim. Subsequent studies have focused on discrete countries and regions, and have confirmed that little has changed.

The World Economic Forum's criteria can be, and often are, argued to have a pro-Western bias. They represent the values of the UN Declaration of Human Rights rather than those of the Cairo Declaration. They assume that individually based gender values matter as much as family cohesion, for example, and that personal independence is superior to communal stability and cultural tradition.

The Muslim West treats women and girls profoundly differently than men and boys. In the most conservative lands women may not vote, drive a car, give testimony in court, or hold a job. Education for girls, when available at all, is often limited to the elementary level and is focused on religious schooling. In many Islamic countries the law allows women greater choice in deciding whom to marry, and it has liberalized the criteria that allow women to seek divorce. Yet domestic violence remains commonplace. It may be technically illegal, as in the case of honor killings—the deaths of women who are thought to have tarnished the family's reputation. Even then, however, the violence is seldom prosecuted and frequently goes unpunished. In 2003 the government of Pakistan alone documented more than 1,200 such killings. Thanks to the Internet, the practice has become far harder to overlook. Gruesome videos of women being beaten, whipped, and stoned to death are readily available to anyone with the stomach to watch them. One of the most attacks was the attempted assassination in 2012 of a then fifteen year old Pakistani girl named Malala Yousafzai who had gained renown by writing a blog on the importance of girls' education. On October 9 in that year a member of the local Taliban faction boarded the school bus that carried Malala and her friends to school, and shot her in the head. Remarkably, Malala survived, after extensive surgery in a British hospital, and has dedicated herself since to continue the campaign for girls' education around the world—work for which she received the Nobel Peace Prize in 2014.

The phenomenon has spread to the West with the rise in Muslim immigration to Europe. Recent reports estimate that two hundred Muslim girls and women have been killed by their families in Spain in the past twenty years. Roughly a dozen honor killings occur each year in the United Kingdom. In a recent BBC poll, in fact, 10 percent of British Muslim men—which would calculate to some fifty thousand of them, nationwide—said that they would unhesitatingly kill a daughter or sister who had dishonored the family.

But 90 percent of them said they would not. Worldwide, Muslims who reject the idea of honor killing are clearly in the majority, but proponents of the practice remain a sufficiently large minority that concern for the persecution of women cannot abate. Recent studies have shown that the predominant motive behind honor killings, when they occur in Islamic countries, is some sort of real or perceived sexual impropriety. But when they occur among Muslims within Europe, the main cause—by more than a two-to-one margin—is that the women or girls were considered to have "become too Western." Even more disturbing, the honor killings committed for the supposed crime of becoming Westernized usually involve some sort of torture before the victims are actually killed. Given the virulence of such crimes, it is no wonder that Europe's Muslims have not assimilated into their surrounding cultures at a rate fast enough to please their non-Muslim neighbors. Yet the Western media pay little attention to the slow but steady advances made by Muslim women both in Europe and in the Middle East.[5] Girls' schools in Egypt and Jordan are growing, albeit slowly, in number and in sophistication. Prominent women teach at some of the premier universities in Egypt, Iraq, and Turkey.

Aside from traditional cultural conservatism, economic factors also play a role in shaping Arab attitudes toward women. Since 85 to 90 percent of Arab wealth comes from a single industry, petroleum, their nations do not have the varied economies that would allow women to advance as they have done in Europe and in the non-Arab Muslim countries. Proven oil reserves in the Middle East, at current rates of production and consumption, will run dry by the year

---

[5]   Women in Iran hold 10 percent of the nation's political offices, including three of its twelve vice presidencies.

Leaders of the Revolution   A group of Iranian schoolgirls listen to their president, Mahmoud Ahmadinejad, addressing the parliament in February 2011. Women have the right to vote in Iran, and currently about 8 percent of parliamentary seats are held by women.

2050, leaving the region economically crippled unless other sources of revenue can be found. As of 2010 plastics and petrochemicals are the two largest nonoil industries—but together they produce only enough money to cover the cost of food imports into the region.

Muslim women's growing involvement in the post-oil economy should lighten some of the social strictures under which they lived throughout the twentieth century. But given the experience of women in Europe, this may take some time.

Feminism in Europe and the United States has entered its third wave. To the chagrin of some, however, **third-wave feminism** has been largely, although not entirely, an intellectual endeavor. The collapse of Communism introduced eastern European women to the ideas of modern feminism. And the expansion of the EU to include countries like the Czech Republic, Hungary, and Poland provided opportunities for women to migrate westward in search of work and a new life. However, that only heightened awareness of the differences between national cultures when it came to women's rights and roles.

Feminism's Third Wave

For every move toward liberalization in the 1990s, there was an equal trend toward conservatism. In both Ireland and Italy, efforts to liberalize laws pertaining to divorce met powerful resistance from traditional-minded women's groups. Although homosexuality to most people was no longer a pathology or a crime, the "gender wars" brought thuggish attacks on homosexuals. Other disadvantaged groups in society—from ethnic minorities to the physically disabled, from under-represented religious groups to the urban poor—demanded more attention to their own agendas.

The active center of third-wave feminism was firmly fixed in the United States, but much of its intellectual leadership came from Europe, and it has focused not on social change but on the intellectual assumptions about gender that shape it. The two leading figures were French speaking. Luce Irigaray (b. 1932), a Belgian psychoanalyst, became especially influential as her books appeared in English translation. Both *An Ethics of Sexual Difference* (1984, in English in 1993) and *Speculum of the Other Woman* (1974, in English in 1985) display her eclectic ideas and methods. Her central theme is the struggle to create an authentic understanding of femaleness. For her, ideas of gender are socially constructed around a system of binary relations. Every aspect of Western culture, Irigaray writes, right down to the use of gendered nouns and adjectives in Western languages, presents the male as the norm. Everything that is "He," meaning "not She," fails to comprehend fully the Otherness of the female. Business practice, too, tends to use male experience as the default. Would men ever have thought of maternity leaves had women not fought for them? Even the physical sciences cannot escape the trappings of gender. "Is $E = mc^2$ a gendered equation?" Irigaray once asked. "It may be." She explained her reasoning: "The equation [for Einstein's special theory of relativity] is sexist because, like male-ness, it is hierarchical. In privileging the speed of light over all other speeds, it enacts a form of domination that is expressive of gendered relations."

Is Irigaray excessive in seeing a "gendered nature" in everything? In one essay she criticizes the sexual tyranny of men:

> It is important to rediscover the uniqueness of female sexual delight. . . . Are not these women being de-personalized, abandoned without vitality, sensations, perceptions, gestures or images of their own, things expressive of their own true identity? For women, at least two types of orgasms exist—one that is attuned to the male sexual economy . . . ; but there is another more in harmony with women's true identity, their true sexual nature. There are many women who feel nothing but guilt and unhappiness, who are paralyzed and dismissed as frigid, simply because they cannot enjoy their true sensations, their true sexuality . . . , within the norms established by the phallocratic sexual economy. Such women could embrace sexuality if they were allowed to pursue a norm of sexual delight more attuned to their bodies and their sex.

To Irigaray's critics, the relentless focus on language defeats any practical social change. In the past decade, however, she has been involved in several studies for the EU investigating the conditions of women's lives. She has also played a role in developing possible legislation for the European Parliament.

If Irigaray made her name by drawing attention to language, Julia Kristeva (b. 1941) made hers by rejecting "essentialism." To this Bulgarian French sociologist and literary critic, there is no such thing as *femaleness* in the first place. Rather than a fixed essence, Kristeva writes, femaleness is an ongoing process. All that one can do is to take a snapshot of it at any particular moment in time. But process, to Kristeva, is also crisis. She posits an instinct called the *semiotic* that underlies self-consciousness. Resembling Freud's concept of the id, the semiotic consists of the unspoken—the thing that we are trying to say when we use language but can never get quite right. Our lived experiences, she argues, can never be completely described in language, since language is fixed in time. Reality is always more complex, more immediate and dynamic, than language can convey.

Kristeva calls the gap between language and reality the *space of abjection*. For her, this space is the domain of women, ethnic minorities, gays, lesbians, and the poor, since the language and value systems that create our "snapshot" of experience are inevitably male, white, heterosexual, and prosperous. To be outside the dominant structure is therefore to live in continuous crisis.

To her critics, Kristeva distances herself from the everyday problems of women in the world—discrimination, violence, unequal pay, and control over their bodies' sexual expression. Unless it is dedicated to programs for social change, they argue, feminism risks becoming only an interesting academic specialty. To discuss the space of abjection does little to improve the lives of Portuguese girls trapped in French textile sweatshops. It cannot help Turkish daughters who fear "honor killing" at the hands of their own fathers or brothers in Germany. Admirers of the third wave, however, have a reply: this is exactly what we are talking about. Why should women *have* to justify feminism through its results? No one, after all, discounts intellectual fields like literary criticism, art history, mathematics, or astronomy for not addressing social problems. Criticism of the irrelevance of third-wave writers, they say, is simply another form of sexism.

DEBT, TAXES, AND LIBERTY

Financial Crisis of 2008

With increased interconnectedness came a series of shocks to the global economy as the twenty-first century began. In 2008 a real estate bubble burst in the United States, setting in motion a financial crisis of enormous proportions. The economic crash highlighted painfully the problem of Western debt. Since capitalism runs on credit, debt and even long-term indebtedness are inescapable—and are not in itself harmful. People commonly purchase homes that leave them in debt to their banks or mortgage servers for thirty years. They may even refinance their loans at any point, lowering their payments but extending the indebtedness further into the future. They also pay for college with loans that may extend into their middle age or even beyond. Cities and states issue bonds to provide revenues to improve infrastructure or to pay for school construction. National governments borrow domestically and internationally to fund special projects or to spur economic growth. Small companies rely on loans to expand their business, invest in new products, and modernize their equipment. Large corporations take on debt to acquire smaller companies—and sometimes even larger debt to purchase companies larger than themselves.

Problems arise, however, when too much red ink appears on the ledger. How much is too much? It depends on one's assets and their current and projected values, but also on other factors. These include the viability of the project for which the debt is assumed, the interest rate charged, and the security of the revenue stream that will repay the loan. This is all elementary finance—but the West still got itself into a mess in 2008. Public and private debt threatens to collapse the Euro Zone and has brought the United States close to default. Looking at public debt as a percentage of gross domestic product (GDP)—the value of all goods and services produced in a year and the best way to judge the problem—is a sobering exercise.

The problem with Greece, for example, is obvious. The nation's debt is almost one hundred times its annual GDP, and its 2010 budget added another GDP's worth of debt to the pile. At the same time, its national revenues are declining by more than 12 percent a year. Caught in so severe a bind, the nation has no way to pay its creditors and return to fiscal health without help. Portugal, in comparison, owes sixty-four times its GDP and slashed its 2010 budget by almost 3 percent of GDP. Its growth rate is only enough to hold steady, and it can avoid drowning only by forcing its creditors underwater. The euro, the single currency of the EU, was supposed to lessen problems like this. The easy availability of credit, however, enticed too many people, in all countries, to take on more debt. For a time it seemed that economic growth and the increase in value of what they owned would compensate.

Something similar happened in the United States. Government debt had been on the rise since the 1960s but had remained manageable, as a percentage of GDP, until the 1990s. At that point, a series of tax increases and cuts in social programs, combined with a decade-long rise in the stock market, created a significant budget surplus. The federal budget entered the twenty-first century well under control, but three events reversed the trend. First, a surge of interest in high-tech companies had driven the stock market upward in the 1990s, but now the collapse of this "dot-com bubble" put many Americans out of work. Second, President George W. Bush pressed for substantial tax cuts that radically reduced federal revenues just as demand for social services began to rise dramatically. Third, the country went to war in Afghanistan and Iraq without raising taxes to pay for either conflict—essentially funding two wars on a credit card.

These factors combined to produce the largest budget deficits in the country's history. Soon millions of Americans took on enormous personal debt, in part because of artificially high housing values. Unscrupulous and even fraudulent loan agencies and mortgage brokers walked right in, earning specious profits by extending loans to people who could not afford them and then selling the mortgages. The sale went to the financial markets, repackaged as the hazily understood "collateralized debt obligations," which, together with the credit default swaps made popular twenty years earlier by the *Exxon Valdez* settlement, helped trigger the financial crisis of 2008.

How to Solve the Crisis? The combination of widespread debt and economic recession presents a problem—how to spur economic growth and get unemployed people back to work. To do both, governments have traditionally invested heavily in infrastructure and other projects, and they have done so by taking on debt. As more people become wage earners, their taxes pay off the public loan. But opposition to tax increases remained fervid in 2010 in the United States, especially among conservatives who prefer to balance budgets by cutting expenditures. In Europe, calls for debt financing to help out countries in critical condition (Greece, Ireland, Italy, Portugal, Spain) and to fuel job growth have been resisted by those nations (Germany especially) that would have to provide the credit.

More is involved in these debates than reconciling figures in a ledger. The Greater West has entered the twenty-first century engaged in full-throttle disputes over the purpose and limits of government and the responsibilities of individuals in society. The disputes are not new, but they are being addressed with a fervor not witnessed since the mid-nineteenth century (see chapter 19).

Debate over Role of Government Two related issues are at stake. The first is taxation as economic stimulus: do higher taxes help the economy or not? Remember that the story of capitalism is capital—wealth that can be used to produce more wealth. No one disputes that injecting new capital into an economy spurs investment, production, and consumption. But should that capital come from the public (that is, the government) or from private sources?

The conservative argument holds that the best way to trigger growth is to reduce taxes and spending on social programs to "free" capital. We should allow business owners to keep more of their wealth to invest in production, and we should let consumers retain more of their own wealth to spur the purchase of goods. That way, activity will be stimulated throughout the economy. This is the free-market view described in the twentieth century by economists like the Austrian-born Friedrich Hayek (introduced in chapter 25) and the American Milton Friedman (1912–2006). An unregulated market, these economists wrote, will produce the greatest efficiency. A small but thriving portion of the economy will always produce more than a larger, intrusive portion of a halting, staggering economy. Moreover, it respects individuals' rights to control their own property.

The second issue is taxation as wealth redistribution: Taxes take from those with money and give it to those without it, in the form of social services. But should that be the goal of society? The libertarian argument holds that any taxation at all is evil because it is theft. By claiming its right to a portion of someone's income, a government is in essence claiming its right to a portion of that person's labor—the labor that produces the income. But to claim someone else's capital as one's own is theft. Even worse, the ownership of someone else's labor is slavery. Once, before the American Revolution, colonists protested British taxes. No taxation, they cried, without representation. Now, the argument goes, any form of taxation at all is an attack on individual liberty. Obviously, certain services are essential ones that people need not

Greek Prime Minister Alexis Tsipras Of all the countries in the European Union, Greece struggles the most under the burden of crushing debt, and the EU has demanded strict austerity measures be implemented. After several years of belt-tightening, popular resentment resulted in the election in 2015 of Alexis Tsipras (b. 1974) as prime minister. His appeal lay in his insistence that austerity has failed, and the only solution to the crisis is for Greece's creditors to forgive its debts. For good measure, Tsipras' government has also called for Germany to make reparations payments to Greece for the harm done to the country in World War II.

provide for themselves. National defense, most obviously, cannot be provided for without public funding. And it is unreasonable, for another example, to expect each of us to build our own roads when we wish to travel somewhere. So some compromise on principle is necessary. But libertarians hold that government ought to be as small and inexpensive as possible: it should provide only those services that citizens cannot be expected to provide for themselves.

What might those services be? Infrastructure, certainly (meaning roads, electrical grids, sewer systems, and so on), and national defense. But anything beyond that is debatable. Retirement pensions? Health care? Many conservatives would respond by asking why people shouldn't be expected to save for their own retirement. A publicly funded pension, after all, might be a disincentive to save. And if someone *has* saved but finds, on retirement, that his or her savings still fall short of what is needed, why shouldn't the individual's family help first? Why is it *everyone's* responsibility to care for individuals who chose to spend all of their money as they were making it? For government to step in is not only contrary to an efficient economy; it actually weakens society by lessening the role of the family.

As for health care, shouldn't people be responsible for themselves? If you choose to smoke forty cigarettes a day, avoid exercise, and drink to excess, that is absolutely your right. But why is it then society's responsibility to pay for your cancer treatment, liver transplants, and physical therapy? Or consider school lunches, a fine idea for those who wish to purchase them. Why should they be publicly subsidized? Is it wrong to expect parents to feed their own children? Why is it right to subsidize a lunch provided by the school, but not the lunch a parent prepares for a child to carry to school?

The conservative argument against taxation rests on the principle that people are responsible for themselves and for their own families. Taxation to provide services that ought not to be the government's business in the first place is therefore unjustifiable. In the end, it does more harm than good. For the state to intrude on such matters is unprincipled, inefficient, costly, harmful to the economy, and damaging to the moral values of society.

FREE MARKET? WHAT FREE MARKET?

The Liberal Argument

All this is willful blindness and moral idiocy, counter liberals. The blindness consists of a refusal to see that no such thing as a free market exists. People are not autonomous, self-owned, rational actors in a marketplace of open and equal competition. Capitalism is at root a numbers game, especially as the libertarians claim to practice it. Real human actions are not governed by and cannot be understood by numbers and formulas alone. A skilled electrician who cannot get hired because he is a member of a racial or religious minority is not subject merely to market forces. No matter how good his work or how low his rates, his struggle against prejudices—even if successful—is not played out on the same economic playing field as his white competitor. Or take a midlevel manager working for a software firm who earns only 80 percent of what her male colleagues in the same position receive. Equal pay for equal work is a matter of fundamental justice, not of artificial manipulation of a free market. The problem with the call for small government and unregulated economies, liberals argue, is that free-market economists do not believe in sin. Or at least they talk that way, whenever the subject is the economy.

Not only are injustices like racism, sexism, cronyism, and class discrimination built into the system, but so are inequalities of opportunity. Large, well-stocked supermarkets provide full selections of fresh produce, artisanal breads, and shelves packed with dietary supplements. They are almost always located in suburbs, with ample parking, not in inner cities and in poorer neighborhoods. Why then is it solely the responsibility of the urban poor to maintain their own healthy diets? Even when suburban supermarkets are located near bus lines, it may take a city dweller an hour and a half to get there. A simple grocery trip can turn into an all-day affair that may get in the way of work and other responsibilities.

Moreover, even in a perfect world, capitalism has a built-in bias toward the concentration of capital. For one thing, property is inheritable but labor is not: the owner of a manufacturing plant can hand over that ownership to a son or daughter, but the factory workers cannot pass on their jobs to their heirs. Even allowing for business failures, real assets generally grow in value over time, whereas the long-term value of labor diminishes as workers age or as technology replaces them. Thus thriving capitalist societies do experience a degree of enrichment overall, but within that general trend lives another pattern entirely—the consolidation of wealth at the top.[6] So much for total assets, but what about annual income? In the United States more than twenty cents out of every dollar in new income is paid to the top 1 percent of wage and salary earners. In the United Kingdom from 1997 to 2007, the overwhelming bulk of the new jobs created were added at the very top and the very bottom of the pay scale: the executives, in other words, and their minimum-wage workers.

Economists measure wealth and income distributions using a standard called the *Gini coefficient*, named after the Italian statistician (and former Fascist bureaucrat) Corrado Gini (1884–1965).[7] The Gini scale ranges from a score of 0, meaning that a country has perfect equality of wealth among all citizens, to a score of 100, meaning that 100 percent of the wealth is owned by a single individual. According to the Gini scale, the West maintained the lowest concentrations of wealth during the decades of the welfare state. Since free-market economic policies came into effect beginning with U.S. President Ronald Reagan and British Prime Minister Margaret Thatcher in the 1980s, however, the trend has been toward ever-greater concentrations of wealth in their two countries. From 1980 to the present, these pro-market economies have improved overall wealth, but the concentration of that wealth among the richest citizens (a 50 percent increase in Britain between 1980 and 2000 and a 33 percent increase in the United States) is clear.

These trends lead to another idea: **redistributive taxation**, taxes intended not only to pay for essential services but also to force a broader distribution of

---

[6]   In the United States in 2010, the four hundred richest individuals (0.000125 percent of the population) owned as much wealth (capital and assets) as the least wealthy 150 million Americans combined. In 2014 the richest 400 Americans had a combined wealth of 2.29 trillion dollars – an amount equal to the gross national product of Brazil in that year.

[7]   When he was not busy calculating his coefficients and indexing the birth rates of inferior peoples, Gini wrote a pamphlet called *The Scientific Basis of Fascism* (1927).

wealth. Liberal economists argue that these taxes *must* exist, as a matter of justice. Besides, taxes also assure continued economic growth, as a matter of practical policy. Take redistribution as justice first. A just society gives priority to treating its people, not its material wealth, with fairness and respect, goes the argument. If there are human rights, then all people possess them, and society should see that every citizen has his or her rights recognized and protected. Does that mean that all wealth should be handed out in equal parcel to everyone? Socialists might say yes, but most liberals say no. Rather, society serves justice by seeing to it that everyone has an equal opportunity to prosper. The children of a billionaire investor and the children of a coal miner do not begin life with the same opportunities and the same chances to succeed, and hence the state has a responsibility and a right to extract, in taxes, more of the billionaire's wealth so that it can be directed to the coal miner.

No one lives independently, in this view, and all our fates are connected. You can wear a seatbelt while driving a car, for example, or not—but you had better wear one. The choice is not simply a matter of personal freedom versus a paternalist state, and it is selfishness to think that it is. If you are without a seatbelt in an accident, your medical costs will be vastly greater than if you had worn one. Even if private insurance pays that bill, the rest of society remains affected because the demand on medical services raises the prices of medical care and insurance for all.

Justice Is Fairness   The distribution of wealth has become increasingly a focus of political attention. Here a well-dressed figure in London's financial district walks past a homeless beggar outside the Royal Exchange (formerly a financial center, now a luxury shopping mall).

Two other major issues stand out, among many, as pressing challenges to economic growth. First is the aging of the West. The population of Europe, es- *Challenges* pecially the western half of it, is getting older, since birth rates are in decline *to Economic* and the advantages of skilled medicine allow people to live longer lives. This *Growth* problem also exists to some extent, although a lesser one, in the United States, where immigration, both legal and illegal, makes up for some of the stagnation in net population. As Britain discovered at the end of the nineteenth century, its aging population factored heavily in its economic and political competition with Germany, whose larger and younger population was a catalyst for its imperial growth. In parts of eastern Europe, and especially throughout the Islamic part of the Greater West, populations are growing rapidly and average ages are declining (see Map 29.8). In Iran alone, nearly two-thirds of the entire population is under the age of thirty-five; moreover, overall growth, in absolute numbers, has been dramatic: the population has nearly doubled in size since the Islamic Revolution in 1979.

An aging population means increased health costs—which forms the other major challenge to the West. The European countries provide cradle-to-grave medical care to their people, but this generosity depends on two factors to keep it going: continuing military subsidies from the United States, which frees up capital for the EU nations to dedicate to social programs, and a sizable labor force whose taxes can support the cost of medical care. Both factors are currently in doubt for the foreseeable future. In the United States, the cost of entitlement programs (Medicare for the elderly, Medicaid for the poor, and Social Security pensions for the retired) has been straining or breaking budgets for decades. The need both to address these ballooning costs and to balance that effort against the need to stimulate a sluggish recessionary economy will dominate national politics for at least another generation.

WHAT IS THE GREATER WEST NOW?

The names of historical periods and movements matter. It matters that the educated of the eighteenth century called themselves *the Enlightened*—even if only to expose their self-regard. In the third century CE, when Germanic tribes swept into the western Roman Empire, the Romans called it an *invasion*, but the Germans later described it as a *migration* (*Völkerwanderung*). And they were both right, each from their own point of view.

The Greater West may be experiencing a similar two-side moment now. Migration within and immigration from without is changing the entire European continent. New faiths are filling the spaces left by a declining Christianity. The languages heard on the streets are often unfamiliar; so are the smells and tastes emanating from shops and restaurants. Nationalist passions contend with a vision

MAP 29.8   Population Growth in the Greater West, 2012   Rising life expectancy caused the entire world's population to surge in the early 21st century. In the Greater West, populations especially increased in the Islamic regions.

of European unity that, like new clothing, seems to fit but still feels uncomfortable. Political and economic rivalries come and go, but most Europeans are cheered that no wars have broken out between any members of the EU, the EC before it, or the EEC before that. This most warlike of continents may finally have stumbled onto the path to peace.

Other parts of the Greater West are undergoing almost precisely the opposite pressures and trends. The ethnic makeup of the Arab countries is becoming more, not less, homogenous. Christian populations are small and declining; the Jewish populations are even more so. Israel is the most pluralistic of the Middle East nations and the most democratic, although optimists see in the Arab Spring the start of a democratic swing. If it can overcome its current crisis with ISIS, Iraq may yet prove to be the first viable Arab democracy. Religious conviction runs deep, but the rifts between Sunni and Shi'i Muslims and the rivalries between clans are a continuous challenge. The likely major struggle to come within the Islamic world will be the rivalry among Arabs, Persians, and Turks; and in the working out of that contest the fate of Islam's women will be both cause and consequence. Iran's nuclear ambitions are perhaps the most pressing issue at present, but the contest will continue to heat up, especially as Arab oil wealth declines. For now, the two halves of the Greater West are confronting the challenge of understanding their own identity—as nations? Religions? Economic actors?

The question has already run into roadblocks. Speaking to the Council of Europe in 2005, Pope Benedict XVI (r. 2005–2013) urged the EU not to deny its own history. Christianity, for good or ill, has been a central element in the

Malala Yousafzai   Malala Yousafzai (b. 1997), who as a Pakistani schoolgirl survived a shooting by the Taliban to become an activist for children's education rights around the world, is the youngest recipient of a Nobel Prize. She shared the 2014 Peace Prize with Kailash Satyarthi (b. 1954), a Hindu child-rights advocate in India.

development of European culture. He insisted that the faith still has a crucial role to play in the future:

> Only a Europe with peaceful social coexistence and the exchange of cultural riches, both material and non-material, will be able to be featured as the common house of all Europeans, in which each and every one is accepted and feels at home, no one is subject to discrimination but all are required to live as responsible members of one great family of peoples. . . . Christianity has been an essential factor of unity among peoples and cultures. For two millennia, it has never ceased to promote an integral vision of the human being and human rights, and the history of the nations of the Continent as a whole attests to its extraordinary cultural fruitfulness.

There is an obvious difficulty here. To deny the significance of the Christian faith in shaping the Greater Western tradition is historical nonsense, but the Greater Western world is increasingly and actively Islamic. To center Western

The Face of the Greater West   A group of Berlin youths gather at the annual Holocaust Remembrance Day for an activity known as "Cleaning the Cobblestones [Stolpersteine]." Christian, Muslim, Jewish, and Bahai youths walk through the streets to clean and care for the roughly 3,500 commemoration-stones planted along sidewalks. Each stone bears the name of local Jewish citizens of Berlin who became victims of the Holocaust. The idea has grown in popularity, and hundreds of cities all across Europe now have Stolpersteine. By the end of 2011 more than thirty thousand stones had been created.

identity on Christianity is just bad politics; hence the EU's refusal to acknowledge a Christian core to European culture. But the Islamic world, too, will have to adapt to non-Muslim society. It has done so in the past, with notable success. The challenge to Islam today is the small but violent minority of Muslims who oppose any adaptation and demand an immediate and uncompromising return to the strictest shari'a. The only reform they desire is a return to a mythical pure past, a golden age—a common trope of Greater Western culture, but not necessarily the most admirable or helpful one.

Efforts are underway to speed adaptation along, to improve understanding across religious lines. A controversial figure, the Swiss Egyptian academic Tariq Ramadan (b. 1962), has emerged with a distinctive European version of Islam. Born and raised in Geneva, Ramadan is the grandson of the founder of the Muslim Brotherhood in Egypt (Hassan al Banna, whom we met in chapter 28), a family connection that makes many of his critics suspicious of his claims that he is not a fundamentalist. Ramadan argues that the Qur'an is the essential authority in Islamic life, but it must be interpreted in light of the time and place in which one lives. Muslims within Europe, he insists, have an obligation to observe the laws of the secular state. They should devise a code of Islamic life that harmonizes Qur'anic teaching and social expectation. As he expressed it in his book entitled *To Be a European Muslim* (1999):

> The European environment is a space of responsibility for Muslims. This is exactly the meaning of the notion of "space of testimony" (*dar al-shahada*) that we propose here, a notion that totally reverses perspectives: whereas Muslims have, for years, been wondering whether and how they would be accepted, the in-depth study and evaluation of the Western environment entrusts them, in light of their Islamic frame of reference, with a most important mission. . . . Muslims now attain, in the space of testimony, the meaning of an essential duty and of an exacting responsibility: to contribute, wherever they are, to promoting good and equity within and through human brotherhood. Muslims' outlook must now change from the reality of "protection" alone to that of an authentic "contribution."

Ramadan's outlook is not altogether new. We have often forgotten that Islam has been a Western religion from the start. The events of the Arab Spring are still recent, but the slow integration of the European and Muslim worlds now underway in the Greater West has a chance to succeed. As it happens, one of its first test cases will occur where our civilization began—in Iraq.

WHO, WHAT, WHERE

al-Qaeda	Good Friday Accord	third-wave feminism
Arab Spring	Kyoto Protocol	World Trade
European Union	Osama bin Laden	Organization
global warming	redistributive taxation	

SUGGESTED READINGS

Primary Sources

Fukuyama, Francis. *The End of History and the Last Man.*

Irigaray, Luce. *The Ethics of Sexual Difference.*

Khomeini, Ruhollah. *Islamic Government.*

National Commission on Terrorist Attacks upon the United States. *The 9/11 Commission Report* (2004).

Ramadan, Tariq. *Islam, the West, and the Challenges of Modernity.*

Ramadan, Tariq. *The Quest for Meaning: Developing a Philosophy of Pluralism.*

Ramadan, Tariq. *Western Muslims and the Future of Islam.*

Rushdie, Salman. *The Satanic Verses.*

Anthologies

Euben, Roxanne L. and Muhammad Qasim Zamin. *Princeton Readings in Islamist Thought: Texts and Contexts from al-Banna to Bin Laden* (2009).

Freedman, Estelle B., ed. *The Essential Feminist Reader* (2007).

Kamrava, Mehran, ed. *The New Voices of Islam: Rethinking Politics and Modernity—A Reader* (2007).

Laqueur, Walter, and Barry Rubin, eds. *The Israel–Arab Reader: A Documentary History of the Middle East Conflict* (2008).

Oliver, Kelly, ed. *The Portable Kristeva* (2002).

Roded, Ruth, ed. *Women in Islam and the Middle East: A Reader* (2008).

Sandel, Michael J., ed. *Justice: A Reader* (2007).

Vallentyne, Peter, and Hillel Steiner, eds. *The Origins of Left-Libertarianism: An Anthology of Historical Writings* (2007).

Volpi, Frédéric, ed. *Political Islam: A Critical Reader* (2010).

Studies

Berman, Eli. *Radical, Religious, and Violent: The New Economics of Terrorism* (2009).

Browers, Michaelle. *Political Ideology in the Arab World: Accommodation and Transformation* (2009).

Budgeon, Shelley. *Third Wave Feminism and the Politics of Gender in Late Modernity* (2011).

Calhoun, Craig, and Georgi Derluguian, eds. *Business as Usual: The Roots of the Global Financial Meltdown* (2011).

Council on Foreign Relations. *The New Arab Revolt: What Happened, What It Means, and What Comes Next* (2011).

Frieden, Jeffry A. *Global Capitalism: Its Fall and Rise in the Twentieth Century* (2007).

Garcelon, Marc. *Revolutionary Passage: From Soviet to Post-Soviet Russia, 1985–2000* (2005).

Gillis, Stacy, Gillian Howie, and Rebecca Munford, ed. *Third Wave Feminism: A Critical Exploration* (2007).

Holton, Robert J. *Globalization and the Nation State* (2011).

Hoogvelt, Ankie. *Globalization and the Postcolonial World: The New Political Economy of Development* (2001).

Huntington, Samuel P. *The Clash of Civilizations and the Remaking of World Order* (2011).

İnce, Başak. *Citizenship and Identity in Turkey: From Atatürk's Republic to the Present Day* (2012).

Judt, Tony. *Postwar: A History of Europe since 1945* (2005).

Keddie, Nikki R. *Modern Iran: Roots and Results of Revolution* (2006).

Kenney, Padraic. *The Burdens of Freedom: Eastern Europe since 1989* (2006).

Krueger, Alan B. *What Makes a Terrorist: Economics and the Roots of Terrorism* (2008).

Malik, Kenan. *From Fatwa to Jihad: The Rushdie Affair and Its Aftermath* (2010).

Marquand, David. *The End of the West: The Once and Future Europe* (2011).

Mearsheimer, John J. *The Tragedy of Great Power Politics* (2003).

Mittelman, James H. *The Globalization Syndrome: Transformation and Resistance* (2000).

Mockaitis, Thomas R. *The "New" Terrorism: Myths and Reality* (2008).

Mottahedeh, Roy. *The Mantle of the Prophet: Religion and Politics in Iran* (2008).

Nussbaum, Martha C. *The New Religious Intolerance: Overcoming the Politics of Fear in an Anxious Age* (2012).

Ohana, David. *Israel and Its Mediterranean Identity* (2011).

Pope, Nicole. *Honor Killings in the Twenty-First Century* (2011).

Post, Jerrold M. *The Mind of the Terrorist: The Psychology of Terrorism from the IRA to al-Qaeda* (2008).

Rashid, Ahmed. *Jihad: The Rise of Militant Islam in Central Asia* (2002).

Reid, T. R. *The United States of Europe: The New Superpower and the End of American Supremacy* (2005).

Roy, Sara. *Failing Peace: Gaza and the Palestinian–Israeli Conflict* (2006).

Roy, Sara. *Hamas and Civil Society in Gaza: Engaging the Islamist Social Sector* (2011).

Ruiz, Teofilo F. *The Terror of History: On the Uncertainties of Life in Western Civilization* (2011).

Sandel, Michael J. *What Money Can't Buy: The Moral Limits of Markets* (2012).

Sarotte, Mary Elise: *1989: The Struggle to Create Post–Cold War Europe* (2009).

Sen, Amartya. *The Idea of Justice* (2011).

Sen, Amartya. *Identity and Violence: The Illusion of Destiny* (2008).

Shapiro, Daniel. *Is the Welfare State Justified?* (2007).

Sinno, Abdulkader, ed. *Muslims in Western Politics* (2008).

Stiglitz, Joseph E. *Globalization and Its Discontents* (2003).

Suri, Jeremi. *Power and Protest: Global Revolution and the Rise of Détente* (2005).

Tavassoli, Sasan. *Christian Encounters with Iran: Engaging Muslim Thinkers after the Revolution* (2011).

Van Dam, Nikolaos. *The Struggle for Power in Syria: Politics and Society under Asad and the Ba'th Party* (2011).

Westad, Odd Arne. *The Global Cold War: Third World Interventions and the Making of Our Times* (2007).

Wikan, Unni. *Generous Betrayal: Politics of Culture in the New Europe* (2002).

Young, Elise G. *Gender and Nation Building in the Middle East: The Political Economy of Health from Mandate Palestine to Refugee Camps in Jordan* (2012).

Zürcher, Christoph. *The Post-Soviet Wars: Rebellions, Ethnic Conflict, and Nationhood in the Caucusus* (2009).

For additional resources, including maps, primary sources, visuals, web links, and quizzes, please go to **www.oup.com/us/backman**.

Reference Maps

The Greater West: Physical Features

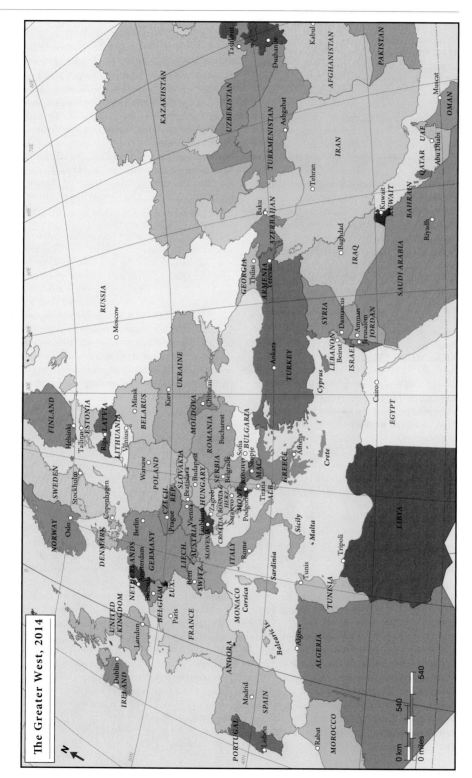

The Greater West, 2014

Glossary

A

Abbasids Dynasty of Islamic caliphs who came to power in 750 and remained formal heads of the Islamic Empire until 1258, when they were unseated by the Mongols. Moved Islamic capital from Damascus to Baghdad.

absolutism Political theory granting limitless authority to a sovereign ruler, holding that a sovereign entrusted with absolute power will best protect the sovereign's subjects from disorder and chaos.

Academy The school founded by the philosopher Plato in Athens in 385 BCE.

Act of Union (1800) Parliamentary legislation that united Great Britain and Ireland.

Acts of Toleration Throughout the 17th and 18th centuries, laws promulgated to offer full or partial constitutional rights to Jews.

aestheticism The belief, popular in the late 19th century, that art and artists have no obligation other than to strive for beauty.

Afrikaners The descendants of the first Dutch settlers of South Africa; formerly known as the Boers; the language they speak is called Afrikaans.

Ahura Mazda The One Lord or eternal God, worshipped by Zoroastrians, who believe he is the creator of all living things.

Akhenaten (r. 1352–1336 BCE) Pharaoh whose attempt to promote the worship of the sun god, Aten, ultimately weakened his dynasty's position in Egypt.

Alexander the Great (356–323 BCE) The Macedonian king whose conquest of the Persian Empire led to the greatly increased cultural interactions of Greece and the Middle East in the Hellenistic Age.

Anabaptists Apocalyptic sect of Swiss exiles who rejected infant baptism, called for a second baptism in adulthood, and embraced a literal reading of scripture and the imminent approach of Christ's Second Coming.

Ancien Régime **(Old Regime)** The French aristocracy from 1648 to 1789, seen as a golden age (for those privileged enough to enjoy it) before the French Revolution.

anti-Semitism Term coined in 1881 to describe the vicious hatred toward and persecution of Jews, both officially and unofficially, that emerged across Europe in the 19th century.

apartheid Official policy of racial segregation instituted in South Africa by the Afrikaner-dominated National Party in 1948.

appeasement In the 1930s, the granting of political and territorial concessions to Hitler's Germany by many Western countries to preserve peace.

Arab Revolt Uprising (1916) of Middle Eastern Arab tribes against Turkish rule, which aimed to replace Ottoman imperial rule with autonomous Arab countries but instead furthered the European imperialist project by dividing the Middle East between England and France. See also **Sykes–Picot Agreement**.

Arab Spring Wave of rebellions in ethnically Arab countries, beginning in Tunisia in December 2010 and rippling across Morocco, Yemen, Iraq, Bahrain, Egypt, and Kuwait. The rebellions turned violent in Libya, resulting in the eventual overthrow and death of the dictator Muammar Qaddafi, and in Syria, which plunged into civil war.

Ark of the Covenant A chest containing the stone tables on which the Ten Commandments were inscribed, which Moses received from God on Mount Sinai. Captured by the Philistines around 1050 BCE, the ark was recovered by King David (r. ca. 1005–965 BCE), whose son Solomon (r. ca. 965–928 BCE) built a temple in Jerusalem to house it. The ark vanished after the Babylonians conquered Jerusalem in 586 BCE.

Ashkenazim Northern European Jewish cultural tradition uniquely focused on the preservation of Talmudic tradition.

atheism The rejection, or absence, of religious belief.

Augustus Original title of the Roman emperors; given first to Octavius.

Avesta The holy book of the Zoroastrians.

ayatollah Arabic, "sign from God"; the supreme clerical authority in Iran.

B

Ba'ath Party Founded in 1947 by Arab Christian writer Michel Aflaq as the political representation of secular **pan-Arabism**, applying socialist ideals of state-sponsored care for the masses (from the Arab word for "renaissance").

baby boom Demographic bubble in the United States (1946–1964) when postwar prosperity and the return of soldiers from combat resulted in an elevated birth rate.

Babylonian Captivity After the Chaldaeans destroyed Jerusalem and the Temple in 587 BCE, they took many of the surviving Jews back east as slaves, where they remained until they were released in 538 BCE by the Persian emperor Cyrus the Great (r. 576–530 BCE).

Bacon, Francis (1561–1626) British philosopher and scientist who—by arguing that thinkers should amass many observations and then draw general conclusions based on these data—pioneered the scientific method and inductive reasoning.

Baghdad   The capital and largest city of modern Iraq, in the center of the country on the Tigris River. Founded in the 8th century, it became a large and powerful city whose greatness is reflected in the *Arabian Nights*.

Balfour Declaration   Agreement (1917) that announced Britain's support for a national Jewish homeland in Palestine.

Baroque Age   Concurrent with the **Ancien Régime**, an era in Europe of extraordinary artistic accomplishment in the service of the tremendously wealthy and privileged aristocratic class.

Bastille   A royal fortress and prison in Paris. In June 1789, a Revolutionary crowd attacked the Bastille to show support for the newly created National Assembly. The fall of the Bastille was the first instance of the people's role in Revolutionary change in France.

Battle of Britain   The World War II air campaign waged by the German Air Force (Luftwaffe) against the United Kingdom during the summer and autumn of 1940. The failure of Nazi Germany to achieve its objective of destroying Britain's air defenses is considered by historians its first major defeat and a crucial turning point in the war.

Battle of Midway   A crucial naval battle in the Pacific theater of World War II; between June 4 and 7, 1942, six months after Japan's attack on Pearl Harbor, the U.S. Navy decisively defeated an attacking fleet of the Imperial Japanese Navy.

Battle of Waterloo   The last battle lost by Napoleon; it took place near Brussels on June 18, 1815, and led to the deposed emperor's final exile.

Bayle, Pierre   (1647–1706) French **philosophe** best known for his seminal work, the *Historical and Critical Dictionary*, published beginning in 1697.

Berlin airlift   The 1948 transport of vital supplies to West Berlin by air, primarily under U.S. auspices, in response to a blockade of the city that had been instituted by the Soviet Union to force the Allies to abandon West Berlin.

Big Science   A term used by scientists and historians to describe a series of changes in science that occurred in industrial nations during and after World War II as scientific progress increasingly came to rely on large-scale projects usually funded by national governments or groups of governments.

bin Laden, Osama   (1957–2011) Leader of the militant Islamic group al-Qaeda, which executed terrorist plots, including the September 11, 2001, attacks on the United States, to end the presence of U.S. forces in his home country, Saudi Arabia.

bishop   A high-ranking Christian cleric, in modern churches usually in charge of a diocese and in some churches regarded as having received the highest ordination in unbroken succession from the **twelve apostles**.

von Bismarck, Otto   (1815–1898) Leading Prussian politician and German prime minister who waged war to create a united German Empire, which was established in 1871.

Black Death   Successive outbreaks of bubonic plague, beginning in 1347, that killed up to a third of European and Muslim populations over the course of the 14th century.

Blitzkrieg   Nazi strategy of "lightning war" that used rapid motorized firepower to overwhelm an enemy before it could mount a defense.

Boer War   Conflict (1899–1902) between British and **Afrikaners** (formerly known as "Boers") in South Africa, with terrible casualties on both sides.

Bolsheviks   Political party led by Vladimir Lenin in the Russian (Bolshevik) Revolution that overthrew the Russian government in 1917, establishing a form of Communism that maintained power in the Soviet Union until 1991. A variation on classical Marxism, requiring the systematic use of violence, the establishment of a supposedly temporary dictatorship by party members to effect the overthrow of pre-revolutionary practices, and the violent exportation of revolution to other countries.

Boniface VIII   (r. 1294–1303) The pope whose clash with King Philip IV of France left the papacy considerably weakened.

Book of the Dead   An anthology of prayers, poems, and similar texts collected during the Egyptian Middle Kingdom (2035–1640 BCE). Placed in the coffin, the Book of the Dead was believed to allow the deceased to enter paradise.

bourgeoisie   The prosperous and primarily urban middle class of Enlightenment Europe.

Boxer Rebellion   Violent attempt (1898–1901) by Chinese peasants, motivated by millennial Buddhist beliefs, to purge Westerners and Western influence from China.

Bronze Age   The period between 4000 and 1500 BCE characterized by the ability of ancient Near East inhabitants to smelt copper (and its alloy, bronze, which combines copper with tin) for weapons, farm implements, and tools.

C

Caesar, Julius (100–44 BCE) The Roman general who conquered the Gauls, invaded Britain, and expanded Rome's territory in Anatolia. He became the dictator of Rome in 46 BCE. His assassination led to the rise of his grandnephew and adopted son, Gaius Octavius Caesar, who ruled the empire as Caesar Augustus.

Cairo Declaration on Human Rights Adopted in 1990 by the Organization of the Islamic Conference to replace the earlier (and secular) **Universal Declaration of Human Rights** with a specifically Islamic conceptualization.

caliph Successor to the Prophet Muhammad as political and religious leader of the Islamic world. Meaning "deputy" in the literal sense, in common usage it was roughly comparable to the English word "emperor."

Calvin, John (1509–1564) French-born theologian and reformer whose radical form of Protestantism, known as Calvinism, was adopted in many Swiss cities, notably Geneva.

capitalism The modern economic system characterized by an entrepreneurial class of property owners who employ others and produce something (or provide services) for a market to make a profit.

capitulations Trade agreements between the Ottoman Empire and European nations that by the 19th century overwhelmingly favored European interests.

Carolingian Renaissance A cultural and intellectual flowering that took place around the court of **Charlemagne** in the late 8th and early 9th centuries.

Carolingians Ambitious Frankish dynasty that overthrew the **Merovingians**, defended western Christendom against Muslim invaders, and united France.

Catholic Reformation General reform of Catholic life initiated by the **Council of Trent** (1546–1563). Also known as the "Counter-Reformation."

di Cavour, Camillo (1810–1861) Prime minister of Piedmont-Sardinia and founder of the Italian Liberal Party; he played a key role in the movement for Italian unification under the Piedmontese king, Victor Emmanuel II.

censor A powerful office in the Roman Republic, whose duties were to maintain the census, to administer the state's finances for public works, and to preserve public morals.

Charlemagne (r. 767–814) The Carolingian king whose conquests vastly expanded the Frankish kingdom. In 800, he was crowned emperor by the pope in Rome, establishing a precedent that would have wide-ranging consequences for western Europe's relationship with the eastern Roman Empire in Byzantium and for the relationship between the papacy and secular rulers.

Charles Martel (r. 718–741) The Frankish ruler who began the series of military campaigns that established the Franks as the undisputed masters of all Gaul; grandfather of Charlemagne, Charles Martel ("the Hammer") laid the groundwork for the rise of the Carolingian dynasty.

Chartist movement Labor movement begun by the London Working Men's Association in 1838.

chivalry In 12th-century Europe, an ethic that embraced ideal knightly behavior: comportment, noble demeanor, learning, and piety.

Christian democracy Western European ideological hybrid of social conservatism and economic liberalism.

Christian humanism Anticlerical movement of the northern Renaissance that emphasized the simple reading of scripture (especially the New Testament), the singing of hymns, and communal prayer.

Church of England Protestant church founded by King Henry VIII of England when he broke with the Catholic Church in 1533. Also known as the Anglican Church; the monarchy is its supreme head.

Ciompi Rebellion Popular uprising in Italy in 1378.

city-state A form of political organization that incorporates a single city with its surrounding countryside and villages.

civilization A way of life based in cities with dense populations organized as political states, large buildings constructed for communal activities, the production of food, diverse economies, a sense of local identity, and some knowledge of writing.

classicism Artistic movement that replaced the flourishes of the Baroque with a more controlled and formal sensibility.

Cleisthenes (ca. 570–508 BCE) Statesman regarded as the founder of Athenian democracy, serving as chief archon (highest magistrate) of Athens (ca. 525–524 BCE). He successfully allied himself with the popular Assembly against the nobles and imposed democratic reform. Perhaps his most important innovation was the basing of individual political responsibility on citizenship of a place rather than on membership in a clan.

Cold War Term coined by American financier and presidential advisor Bernard Baruch to describe the relationship (1947–1991) between the Soviet bloc and Western nations allied with the United States; each side possessed nuclear weapons, yet neither side dared to either use those weapons or disarm.

College of Cardinals   Created by Pope Nicholas II (r. 1059–1061) and given sole power to elect the next pope.

Columbian Exchange   The widespread exchange of peoples, plants, animals, diseases, goods, and culture between the African and Eurasian landmass and the region that encompasses the Americas, Australia, and the Pacific islands, precipitated by the 1492 voyage of **Christopher Columbus**.

Columbus, Christopher (1451–1506) A Genoese sailor who persuaded King Ferdinand and Queen Isabella of Spain to fund his expedition across the Atlantic, with the purpose of discovering a new trade route to Asia. His miscalculations landed him and his crew in the Bahamas and the island of Hispaniola in 1492.

comfort women   Euphemism used in imperial Japan for the quarter-million Chinese, Filipino, and other women captured and forced into sexual slavery in World War II.

command economies   Economies that aim to provide the highest possible yield for whoever holds the raw materials and captive markets.

Communism   Socialist movement that advocates the destruction of capitalism and the development of a new, classless society of freedom.

The Communist Manifesto   Book by Karl Marx and Friedrich Engels (1848) that presents a Marxist view of history as class struggle.

Concert of Europe   The body of diplomatic agreements designed primarily by Austrian minister Klemens von Metternich between 1814 and 1848 and supported by other European powers until the start of World War I in 1914. Its goal is to maintain a balance of power on the Continent and to prevent destabilizing social and political change in Europe.

Concordat of Worms   The agreement between pope and emperor in 1122 that ended the investiture conflict and established the independence of the papacy.

Conference of Berlin   International conference (1884–1885) of European nations that set the standards by which any European country could claim an African territory over another European rival, touching off the "Scramble for Africa."

Congress of Vienna   Conference of European diplomats convened from 1814 to 1815 to redraw boundaries and work toward peace after decades of conflict.

conquistadores   The 16th-century Spanish forces who subdued South and Central America.

conservatism   Political approach that values tradition and stability above the individual.

Constantine the Great   (r. 312–337) The first emperor of Rome to convert to Christianity, Constantine founded a new imperial capital, **Constantinople**, in 324.

Constantinople   Founded by the emperor Constantine on the site of a maritime settlement known as Byzantium, Constantinople became the new capital of the Roman Empire in 324 and continued to be the seat of imperial power after its capture by the Ottoman Turks in 1453. It is now known as Istanbul.

constitutionalism   A system of government in which rulers share power with parliaments made up of elected representatives.

consul   In the Roman Republic, the executive office in charge of the government.

Continental System   Economic system, implemented by Napoleon, with two key aims: to create an integrated Continental economy and to bring about the collapse of Britain through the imposition of a strict trade embargo.

Copernicus, Nicolaus   (1473–1543) Polish astronomer who advanced the theory that the Earth moved around the sun.

cottage industry   The transfer of textile production from urban industry, where it was controlled by guilds, to rural producers, particularly women. Also known as the "putting-out system."

Council of Trent   Ecumenical council convened from 1546 to 1563 to address the challenges of Protestantism by clarifying the teachings and practices of the Catholic Church.

Counter-Reformation   See **Catholic Reformation**.

covenant   The special promise God made to the Jews, symbolized by Moses's leading of the Hebrews out of bondage in Egypt and into the Promised Land; in return, the Jews agreed to live by the Torah.

Crimean War   Rooted in the longstanding desire of Russia to increase its influence over the Ottoman Empire, the immediate cause of the war (1853–1856) had to do with Russian claims to protective oversight over Orthodox Christians in the Ottoman Empire, but more strategic goals were at stake. The war pitted France and Britain, who were allied with the Ottomans, against Russia. Although Russia accepted unfavorable terms at a conference in Paris in 1856 that ended the conflict, both sides performed ineptly, a fact that became widely known because the war was the first conflict to be covered by journalists and photographers.

Cuban Missile Crisis   Standoff between the Soviet Union and the United States in 1962, when Soviet leader Nikita Khrushchev built military bases in Cuba equipped with nuclear missiles. After two weeks of intense negotiations, Khrushchev withdrew the missiles.

cult of domesticity   Cultural view in the 19th century that idealized women's role in the home, discouraging them from seeking work or other opportunities outside of their domestic duties.

cuneiform   Technique of writing developed in Mesopotamia whereby wedge-shaped marks were impressed in clay tablets.

curiales   The class of urban elites in ancient Rome who, although they were unsalaried, were responsible for municipal government and tax collection; obliged to make up any shortfalls in civic finance from their own personal wealth, they were entitled to retain a portion of the tax revenues they collected for personal use.

Customs Union   The free-trade zone established by Prussia in the early 19th century; an important early step in German unification. Also known as *Zollverein* (German for "Customs Union").

Cynicism   In philosophy, the school of thought that originated in ancient Greece and believes virtue to be the only good and self-control to be the only means of achieving virtue.

Cyrus the Great   (ca. 585–529 BCE). Founder of the Persian Empire.

D

Dark Ages   The period in western Europe from the 4th to the 8th centuries, so named because of the chaos that reigned after the fall of the western Roman Empire and the endless depredations of various barbarian invasions. See also **Late Antiquity**.

David (r. ca. 1005–965 BCE)   Hebrew king who pushed the borders of the Israelite kingdom to their greatest extent and established Jerusalem as the capital city.

Declaration of the Rights of Man and Citizen   The preamble to the French constitution drafted in August 1789; it established the sovereignty of the nation and equal rights for citizens.

decolonization   European withdrawal during the 20th century from its former colonies.

deism   Enlightenment-era belief in a single and possibly benevolent God who created the cosmos—but who plays no active role in it. As a result, a dual policy of religious freedom and of freedom from religious intolerance is essential to human progress.

Delian League   A military alliance formed in 478 BCE (Athens assumed control a year later) among all the Greek poleis, dedicated to maintaining a strong defense—particularly against Persia.

democracy   In its original incarnation in ancient Greece, this form of government allowed a class of propertied male citizens to participate in the governance of their polis (city-state) but excluded women, slaves, and citizens without property from the political process.

Descartes, René   (1596–1650) French philosopher and mathematician who emphasized the use of deductive reasoning.

détente   A "loosening" of tensions between two nations. Used especially to describe efforts to improve diplomatic ties between the United States and the Soviet Union in the 1970s and 1980s. Ironically, *détente* is also a colloquial French term for the trigger of a gun.

dhimmi   Legal status of Jewish and Christian populations living under Muslim rule; officially granted freedom of religion, Jews and Christians had to accept certain restrictions on their communal practice and pay a poll tax (*jizya*) in return for Islamic protection. Restrictions included bans on any public expression of faith and curtailment of the ability to build or repair synagogues and churches.

dialectical materialism   In Marxist theory, the idea that history is driven forward by materialist concerns; to Lenin, this led inevitably to confrontation between the proletariat and the bourgeoisie.

Diaspora   The "exile" or "scattering" of the Hebrews after the Assyrians brutally conquered the Kingdom of Israel in 721 BCE and the Chaldaeans (or Neo-Babylonians) conquered Judah in 587 BCE.

Diderot, Denis   (1713–1784) French **philosophe** who was the guiding force behind the publication of the first encyclopedia. The *Encyclopedia* showed how reason could be applied to nearly all realms of thought and aimed to be a compendium of all human knowledge.

Diet   The medieval German parliament.

Diocletian   (r. 284–305) Roman emperor who established the **tetrarchy** (rule by four) and initiated the **Great Persecution**, a time when many Christians became martyrs for their faith.

Documentary Hypothesis   The belief of many modern biblical scholars that the Torah was compiled from four original sources: "J," by the Yahwist (ca. 950 BCE); "E," by the Elohist (ca. 750 BCE); "D," by the Deuteronomist (ca. 650 BCE); and "P," by the Priestly Author (ca. 550 BCE).

Dominicans Mendicant order focused on education that established schools across Europe.

E

Edict of Milan Issued by the Roman emperor Constantine in 313 CE, it legalized Christianity and guaranteed religious freedom for all faiths within the empire.

Edict of Nantes Decree by Henri IV in 1598 that guaranteed religious freedom, with certain restrictions, throughout France.

Elizabeth I (r. 1558–1603) English queen who oversaw the return of the Protestant Church of England and, in 1588, the successful defense of the realm against the Spanish Armada.

empire A centralized political entity consolidated through the conquest and colonization of other regions and peoples to benefit the ruler and his homeland.

enclosure movement Trend of aristocratic landowners toward evicting small farmers (by enclosing formerly open fields with stone walls or hedges) and instead using those fields for the more profitable grazing of livestock, especially sheep.

English Peasants' Revolt Popular uprising in England in 1381.

En-Heduanna (ca. 2285–2250 BCE) Daughter of King Sargon of Akkad and the poet who is the world's first author known by name.

Enlightenment Term coined in the second half of the 18th century to describe an array of intellectual and cultural activities of the 1700s distinguished by a worldview informed by rational values and scientific inquiry.

Epic of Gilgamesh One of the earliest known works of literature, originating in Sumer but first recorded by Babylonian scribes; relates the adventures of the semimythical Sumerian king Gilgamesh as he battles gods and monsters in pursuit of enlightenment.

Epicureanism Philosophy based on the work of the Greek philosopher Epicurus (341—270 BCE) that promotes a life free of pain and fear as the way to happiness.

epistemology The philosophical inquiry into the nature of knowledge (and, by extension, learning).

equestrians In ancient Rome, an upper class ranking immediately below senators.

Erasmus, Desiderius (ca. 1469–1536) Dutch-born scholar, social commentator, and Christian humanist whose new translation of the Bible influenced the theology of Martin Luther.

Essenes An ascetic and eschatological sect within Second Temple Judaism.

Estates General French parliament, established by the Capetian kings. Reestablished in 1789 (after having last met in 1614) at the behest of the French aristocracy. The three estates were the nobles, the clergy, and the common people.

Etruscans A literate and prosperous people who associated with the **Latins** and profoundly influenced the emerging religious and moral culture of Rome.

European Union United group of independent European nations established in 1993 to provide a process for coordinating policies formed at the level of member states.

evangelicalism Protestant style of worship developed in the Protestant Church that emphasizes the work of the Holy Spirit in the world and the centrality of biblical truth while retaining more of the traditional elements of Protestant denominations.

existentialism Rationalist philosophy associated with Jean-Paul Sartre whose key tenet, "existence precedes essence," demands that we take action and make something of the world, or at least of our lives in it.

F

Fascism The belief that force, directly applied to achieve a specific end, is the best form of government, exemplified by the dictatorships of Adolf Hitler (r. 1934–1945) and Benito Mussolini (r. 1922–1945).

fatwa An Islamic legal pronouncement.

feminist movement A series of movements from the 19th century through the present day that aim to reform policies and practices that oppress the rights and well-being of women.

Fertile Crescent The region of the Middle East roughly framed by the Mediterranean to the west, the Arabian peninsula to the south, and the Tarsus and Zagros mountains to the north and east. The Tigris and Euphrates rivers flow through the center of this region, whose rich soils and abundant water gave rise to early agriculture. The Fertile Crescent connected central Asian and eastern Mediterranean economies.

feudal bonds The relationship between lord and vassal, whereby the lord granted dominion over property to the vassal in exchange for the vassal's pledge of service to the lord.

Final Solution Nazi program of systematic deportation and murder of Jews throughout Germany and all German-occupied territories during World War II.

Five-Year Plans Soviet effort launched under Joseph Stalin in 1928 to replace the market with a state-owned and state-managed economy to promote rapid economic development over a five-year period and thereby catch and overtake the leading capitalist countries.

flying shuttle Invented by Englishman John Kay in 1733, this device sped up the process of weaving.

Fourteen Points Woodrow Wilson's proposal, presented to the Paris Peace Conference (1919), for rebuilding Europe in the aftermath of World War I; ultimately rejected because of French and British concerns.

Franciscans Mendicant order established by Saint Francis of Assisi (1181–1226) dedicated to preaching and service to the urban poor.

Franco, Francisco (1892–1975) Right-wing general who in 1936 successfully overthrew the democratic republic in Spain and instituted a repressive dictatorship.

freemasonry Secret society that claimed its origins lay in medieval trade guilds; its members, wealthy bourgeoisie and noblemen alike, met in private clubs (or "lodges") to conduct business.

Fronde Rebellion (1648–1653) of French aristocrats against the tax policies of Cardinal Mazarin during the regency for the underage King Louis XIV.

fundamentalism American Protestant style of worship that insists on the presence of a fundamental Truth in every scriptural passage and urges personal and societal reform before the approach of Armageddon; from the 1980s, fundamentalism has had considerable influence on American politics, particularly the Republican Party.

G

Galilei, Galileo (1564–1642) Italian physicist and inventor; the implications of his ideas raised the ire of the Catholic Church, and he was forced to retract most of his findings.

da Gama, Vasco (ca. 1460s–1524) A Portuguese explorer and the first European to reach India by sea (1497–1499), linking Europe and Asia for the first time by ocean route.

Gandhi, Mohandas (Mahatma) (1869–1948) Indian leader who advocated nonviolent noncooperation to protest colonial rule and helped win home rule for India in 1947.

Garibaldi, Giuseppe (1807–1882) Italian revolutionary leader who led the fight to free Sicily and Naples from the Habsburg Empire; the lands were then peacefully annexed by Sardinia to produce a unified Italy.

general theory of relativity Einstein's theory (1915) describing gravity's relationship to **space-time**.

German Peasants' Revolt A widespread popular rebellion in the German-speaking areas of central Europe from 1524 to 1525.

ghettos In early modern and modern Europe, segregated communities of Jews in cities.

Girondists One of several factions during the French Revolution; a relatively moderate group, they championed a constitutional monarchy until they were driven from power by the more radical **Jacobins**.

glasnost "Openness," literally, in Russian. Specifically, the policy in the Soviet Union under Premier Mikhail Gorbachev to relax the traditional censorship of Soviet television, radio, and print media and to permit greater freedom of speech.

Glorious Revolution Coup in 1688 that deposed the Catholic king James II of England and replaced him with the popular Protestant ruler of Holland, William of Orange (who was married to James II's daughter, Mary).

gold standard Monetary system, initially introduced in the West by Britain in 1821 and abandoned by most countries in the aftermath of the Great Depression, that pegs a currency to the price of gold.

Good Friday Accord Treaty signed in 1998 that ended eighty years of terrorist conflict in Northern Ireland.

Great Depression (1929–1936) Global economic depression that began with the crash of the New York Stock Exchange on October 29, 1929, resulting in massive unemployment and economic crises worldwide.

Great Fear The term used by historians to describe the French rural panic of 1789, which led to peasant attacks on aristocrats or on seigneurial records of peasants' dues.

Great Persecution The violent program initiated by the Roman emperor Diocletian in 303 to make Christians convert to traditional religion or risk confiscation of their property and even death.

Great Purge Brutal efforts, beginning with show trials in 1936, by Josef Stalin (r. 1931–1953) to eliminate anyone he considered an enemy of the Soviet Union.

Great Pyramids The ancient Egyptian pyramids located at Giza, on the outskirts of modern Cairo.

Great Schism The papal dispute of 1378–1417 when the church had competing popes. Also known as the "Great Western Schism," to distinguish it from the longstanding rupture between the Greek East and Latin West.

Gregorian Reform The papal movement for church reform associated with Gregory VII (r. 1073–1085). Its ideals included ending three practices: the purchase of church offices, clerical marriage, and **lay investiture**.

guilds Artisanal and commercial trade associations that set prices, quality standards, methods and volume of production, and wages paid to workers. Guilds also assigned market shares to individual artisans or merchants.

gulag Network of Soviet Russian prison camps used to incarcerate political dissidents and enemies. Begun under Vladimir Lenin and greatly expanded under Joseph Stalin, the gulag accounted for the deaths of roughly a million prisoners annually from the 1930s to the 1980s.

H

hadith The written record of the actions and non-Qur'anic teachings of the Prophet Muhammad. The two most significant collections are those by al-Bukhari (d. 870) and al-Muslim (d. 875).

hajj The pilgrimage of Muslims to Mecca, held annually. All able-bodied Muslims are expected to undertake the hajj at least once in their lives.

Hamas Conservative religious–political Palestinian group (and offshoot of the **Muslim Brotherhood**) equally devoted to charitable campaigns and social work among the Palestinians and to a terrorist war on Israel.

Hammurabi (r. ca. 1792–1750 BCE) Ruler of Babylon who issued a collection of laws that constitutes the world's oldest surviving law code.

Hasidim Adherents to a revivalist movement in Judaism, started in the mid-18th century in the Polish–Lithuanian Commonwealth by the Ba'al Shem Tov (d. 1760). Using highly emotive language and physical expression, Hasidic Judaism challenged the rather staid formalism of synagogue worship.

Haskalah Hebrew term for "enlightenment."

Hatshepsut (r. ca. 1479–1458 BCE) New Kingdom Egyptian pharaoh who launched several successful military campaigns and extended trade and diplomacy. She was an ambitious builder who probably constructed the first tomb in the Valley of the Kings. Although she never pretended to be a man, she was routinely portrayed with a masculine figure and a ceremonial beard.

heliocentrism First articulated by Copernicus, the observation that the Earth is one of several planets that orbit around a stationary sun.

helot Slave owned by the city-state of ancient Sparta. Comprising roughly 75 percent of the Spartan population, helots performed virtually all the labor, leaving the Spartans themselves free to perform military and civic service.

hieroglyphs System of writing used in ancient Egypt, especially in official records.

hijab The "covering" of women required in Islamic society. Varies widely from country to country, depending on ethnicity, denomination, and, to some extent, class. Least extensive covering is a simple headscarf; most extensive is the full-length burqa.

Hijrah The migration, or exodus, of Prophet Muhammad and his company of the faithful from Mecca to Medina in 622 CE. Marks Year 1 in the Islamic calendar (1 AH).

Hippocratic oath An oath historically taken by physicians, it is one of the most widely known of Greek medical texts. Scholars widely believe that Hippocrates (ca. 460–378 BCE), often called the father of Western medicine, wrote the oath.

historical materialism In Marxist theory, the process by which economic concerns propel historical change.

Hitler, Adolf (1889–1945) The author of *Mein Kampf* ("My Struggle") and leader of the Nazis who became chancellor of Germany in 1933. Hitler and his Nazi regime started World War II and orchestrated the **Holocaust**.

Holocaust The systematic murder of some 6 million Jews by the Nazis during World War II in an attempt to exterminate European Jewry.

Homer (8th century BCE) Greece's first and most famous author, who composed *The Iliad* and *The Odyssey*.

honestiores The Roman senatorial and equestrian classes, municipal officials, and army veterans, and their status entitling them to immunity from torture, lesser criminal fines, and, in capital crimes, exemption from crucifixion.

hoplites Ancient Greek infantrymen serving in a phalanx; name derives from Greek word (*hoplos*) for the smallish, circular shields they carried.

hubris Arrogant self-pride, the deadliest of moral sins to the ancient Greeks; specifically, the delusional belief that one is in control of one's own fate. Frequently used as a plot device to trigger the dire events in Greek tragedy.

Huguenots The Calvinists in 16th-century France, led by Henri de Navarre.

humanism A literary and linguistic movement cultivated particularly during the Renaissance (ca. 1350–1600) and founded on reviving classical Latin and Greek texts, styles, and values.

humiliores Everyone in the Roman Empire apart from the honestiores and the slaves (the latter, in terms of the law, were counted as property rather than people). The humiliores were expected to obey the law, pay their taxes, participate in public religious rites, and hold to the ethical duties of family care and public service.

Hundred Years' War From 1337 to 1453 CE, the war fought between England and France, beginning when England's king Edward III (r. 1327–1377) laid claim to the French throne; France (led, at one point, by the young girl Joan of Arc) eventually won.

Hyksos ascendancy The Second Intermediate Period (1640–1570 BCE) of the Middle Kingdom, so named because of the revolt of foreign laborers against the Egyptian government.

I

Ideal Forms In Plato's philosophy, the concept of a perfect and ultimate reality, of which our own perceived reality is but a flawed and flimsy reflection. Because we have a dualistic nature composed of an eternal soul temporarily housed in a flawed and mortal body, we can apprehend and aspire to that perfection.

ideologies Coherent sets of beliefs about the way the social and political order should be organized.

illuminationism Twelfth-century Persian philosophical program that attempts to harmonize Sufism, Shi'ism, and rational philosophy.

imam In Sunni Islam, a community leader who recites Qur'anic verses during prayer services. In Shi'i Islam, a charismatic spiritual leader, a successor and descendant of the Prophet Muhammad through the line of Fatima and Ali.

imperator Title assumed by Augustus and all subsequent rulers of Rome; often translated as "emperor," but in the Republic referred to a triumphant military general.

imperialism European (and, later, American) dominance of non-Western cultures for the exploitation of natural resources as well as political gain. See also **informal imperialism** and **new imperialism**.

Indo-European A horde of nomadic and herding nations, loosely related by their dialects of the language family, who began to migrate from their homeland near the Black Sea toward western Europe, the Aegean, and Anatolia from about 2000 BCE. Other groups migrated eastward.

indulgences Donations to the Catholic Church as a means of satisfying the requirements for the forgiveness of sin.

Industrial Revolution The burgeoning 19th-century economy driven by mechanization, factories, an investment in infrastructure, and a growing workforce.

informal imperialism The use of indirect means to control an area. Indirect means can be a military presence but is usually centered on economic control. Trading and loans are two essential parts of economic-centered informal imperialism.

inquisition Campaign by the Catholic Church to identify and correct heresy; heretics who would not admit their errors were punished, in some instances brutally.

Intifada "Uprising." Organized mass protests of Palestinians against Israeli occupation of the West Bank and Gaza (1987–1993). The Second Intifada lasted from 2000 to 2005.

Ionian League An alliance (ca. 750 BCE) of several Greek coastal cities in Anatolia organized by the vibrant and prosperous city of Miletus.

Iron Curtain Military and ideological barrier dividing the Soviet bloc from western Europe between the end of World War II and the dissolution of the Soviet Union.

Israel In antiquity, one of two Hebrew kingdoms (937–721 BCE), this one in the north of Palestine with Shechem as its capital. See also **Judah**.

J

Jacobins Radical party that seized power from the **Girondists** during the French Revolution. Resolutely antimonarchist, the Jacobins executed King Louis XVI and his family in 1793, outlawed Christianity, and sought to create a classless society based on radical principles.

Jacquerie Popular uprising in France (1358).

al-Jahiliyya Term (literally "Age of Ignorance" or "Age of Barbarism") used by Arab historians to describe the era between the death of Jesus and the birth of Muhammad.

Janissaries Elite military caste in the Ottoman Empire, 14th–19th centuries. The ranks of Janissaries were filled with Christian children, either orphaned or kidnapped from their parents, who were then converted and given a special, highly disciplined military upbringing.

Jesuits Ecclesiastical order, founded by Saint Ignacio de Loyola in 1540, particularly devoted to education and missionary work.

Jesus of Nazareth (ca. 4 BCE–30 CE) A Jewish preacher and teacher who was arrested for seditious political activity, tried, and crucified by the Romans. After his execution, his followers claimed that he had been resurrected from the dead and taken up into heaven. They began to teach that Jesus had been the divine representative of God, the messiah foretold by ancient Hebrew prophets, and that he had suffered for the sins of humanity and would return to judge all the world's inhabitants at the end of time.

jihad "Struggle," literally. Refers to any conscious, intentional, and persistent effort to advance the cause of Islam in the world. The term has a broad range of meanings, from something as innocuous as a personal vow to live a more committed Islamic life to a determination to wage religious war against the perceived enemies of God.

Joan of Arc (1412–1431) A French peasant girl whose conviction that God had sent her to save France in fact helped France win the **Hundred Years' War**.

John the Baptist (late 1st century BCE–ca. 35 CE) An itinerant preacher and a major religious figure in Christianity, he is described in the Bible as following the unique practice of baptism for the forgiveness of sins. Most scholars agree that John baptized Jesus.

Judah One of two Hebrew kingdoms (937—721 BCE), this one in the south of Palestine and centered on Jerusalem. See also **Israel**.

judges As described in the Bible, the leaders of each of the twelve tribes of Hebrews who moved into Palestine around 1200 BCE, after being delivered from Egypt.

Junkers Landed aristocracy in Brandenburg–Prussia in the 17th–18th centuries. In popular usage the term came in the 19th century to designate all types of conservative, wealthy elites.

justification by faith alone Luther's understanding that one attains salvation not through the purchasing of **indulgences** or other outward acts but simply by having faith in Christ.

Justinian I Sixth-century emperor of the eastern Roman (Byzantine) Empire, famous for waging costly wars to reunite the empire.

K

Ka'ba The holiest shrine of Islam. Temple in Mecca housing the stone believed to mark the site of Abraham's altar to Allah. Originally a pagan shrine dedicated to all the deities of the pre-Islamic Arab tribes. Site of the **hajj**.

Kabbala A mystical interpretation of scripture developed by rabbis that became newly popular in the 17th century in part via the influence of Sabbatai Zvi (1626–1676).

kalam "Theology." Unsystematic effort to provide rational explanation of basic religious mysteries in early Islam on the nature of the Qur'an and the attributes of Allah.

khan The hereditary leader of a given tribe of Mongols.

Khan, Genghis (Chinggis) (r. 1206–1227) Founder and Great Khan (emperor) of the Mongol Empire, which became the largest contiguous empire in history under his successors.

Korean War A war (1950–1953) between North and South Korea, in which a UN force led by the United States fought for the south and China fought for the north, which was also assisted by the Soviet Union. The war, which ended in stalemate, arose from the division of Korea at the end of World War II and from the global tensions of the Cold War that developed immediately afterward.

Kristallnacht "Crystal Night," literally; the "Night of Broken Glass," poetically. The organized Nazi attacks on Jewish businesses, synagogues, and homes throughout Germany on November 9, 1938. Widely regarded as the turning point from Nazi anti-Semitic discrimination to blatant pursuit of genocide.

kulak "Fist," literally. Term popularized by Lenin and Stalin to designate relatively wealthy peasant freeholders who opposed the Communist regime in early-20th-century Russia.

Kulturkampf Otto von Bismarck's "cultural war" against Catholicism in Germany.

Kyoto Protocol International agreement, adopted in 1997, to combat global warming by reducing greenhouse gas emissions. The United States is not among the almost two hundred nations that have since signed and ratified the protocol.

L

laissez-faire "Leave it alone" (French), literally. Term used to identify the economic doctrine of allowing markets to self-regulate, without government interference. First articulated by Adam Smith in *The Wealth of Nations* (1776).

Late Antiquity Term ancient historians use for the **Dark Ages**.

Lateran Agreement Agreement (1929) between Mussolini and Pope Pius XI that recognized the Vatican as a sovereign state in exchange for the Catholic Church's support of Mussolini's Fascist regime.

latifundia Slave-worked plantations in ancient Rome, especially during the Republic.

Latins   Name of the original settlers of the region of Latium.

lay investiture   The installation of clerics into their offices by lay rulers.

League of Augsburg   Alliance forged by Holy Roman Emperor Leopold I in 1686 for defense against French expansionism; members included England, the Low Countries, Sweden, and several German principalities as well as the Holy Roman Empire.

League of Nations   Woodrow Wilson's proposed international body that would arbitrate disputes, oversee demilitarization, and provide for collective security.

Lebensraum   "Living space," literally. The conviction that the territorial losses forced on Germany by the Treaty of Versailles (1919) had denied the German people sufficient space in which to live and thrive. Under the Nazis, it evolved into the policy of demanding the unification of all German-inhabited lands.

legate   Commander of a legion selected by the Roman emperor from members of the Senate. In smaller provinces, the legate also served as the provincial governor.

Lenin, Vladimir   (1870–1924) Leader of the Bolshevik Revolution in Russia (1917) and the first leader of the Soviet Union.

liberalism   Political view calling for civil liberties, equality under the law, the right to vote, and a free-market economy.

libertarian   Political stance that supports small and highly limited government and opposes almost all forms of taxation.

Linear A   Script used by Minoan culture on ancient Crete. Its underlying language has not been identified, and hence the script has not been deciphered.

Linear B   Syllabic script used by ancient Mycenaeans in Crete. Its underlying language is an early dialect of Greek, and the script was deciphered by 1953.

Locke, John   (1632–1704) English philosopher and political theorist known for his contributions to **liberalism**. Locke had great faith in human reason and believed that just societies were those that infringed least on the natural rights and freedoms of individuals.

Logos   "Word," literally. Neoplatonic term for the spirit of wisdom that lies at the center of creation, from which emanate the **Ideal Forms** and all the elements of the cosmos. Term adopted by early Christians (see Gospel of John) to refer to Christ as the "Word of God" made flesh.

lord   In the feudal system, the figure who could grant vassals dominion over manors.

Louis XIV   (r. 1643–1715) Called the "Sun King," he is famous for his success at strengthening the institutions of the French absolutist state.

Louis XVI   (r. 1774–1792) French king who was tried for treason during the French Revolution; he was executed on January 21, 1793.

lugal   Old Sumerian title of city-state kings in Mesopotamia.

Luther, Martin   (1483–1546) A German monk who started the Protestant Reformation in 1517 by challenging the practices and doctrines of the Catholic Church and advocating salvation through faith alone.

Lyceum   School founded by the philosopher Aristotle in Athens in 335 BCE.

M

ma'at   Concept of cosmic order in ancient Egypt in which everything is in perfect balance; includes the notions of meaning, justice, and truth, although in a passive sense, asking people not to upset divine harmony by attempting to alter the political and religious order.

madrasa   Islamic religious school attached, administratively and often physically, to a mosque. Study focuses on memorization of the Qur'an, with subsequent forays into Islamic law and literature.

magi   Zoroastrian priests.

Maginot Line   Barricade of artillery casements, machine-gun pillboxes, tank formations, barbed wire, minefields, and concrete bunkers built by France along its border with Germany.

Magna Carta   Agreement in 1215 between the king of England and English lords establishing certain constraints on royal power.

Mahdi   Messianic figure expected by Shi'i Muslims; believed to be the return of the "Hidden Imam" who has gone into seclusion until the end of time.

mamluk   A slave-soldier in the medieval Islamic world.

mandates   Semi-independent states created in the Middle East by the League of Nations after World War I, dividing territories of the former Ottoman Empire between Britain and France.

Manhattan Project   Secret American program to develop an atomic bomb, begun in 1939 under the scientific direction of J. Robert Oppenheimer.

manors   In a feudal system, collective farms under the authority of lords.

market   Term coined by economist Adam Smith (1776) to describe commerce as a rational pattern of human behavior.

Marshall Plan   American plan to rebuild western Europe after World War II by providing cash, credit, raw materials, and technical assistance to jump-start industrial production.

martyr   Greek for "witness," the term for someone who dies for his or her religious beliefs.

Marx, Karl   (1818–1883) German philosopher and economist who believed that a revolution of the working classes would overthrow the capitalist order and create a classless society. Author of *Das Kapital* and, with Friedrich Engels, *The Communist Manifesto*.

mawali   Non-Arab Muslim converts in the Islamic Empire.

Mehmed II   (r. 1444–1446) The sultan under whom the Ottoman Turks conquered Constantinople in 1453.

Mehmet Ali Pasha   (r. 1805–1848) Pro-Western dynastic leader of Egypt who built a powerful Egyptian military force, professionalized the government along Western lines, and developed both industry and education.

mendicant orders   Groups (such as the Dominicans and the Franciscans) dedicated to assisting the clergy in the performance of their evangelical mission.

Menes   (r. ca. 31st century BCE) Ancient Egyptian ruler credited with the unification of Egypt. Also known as "Narmer."

Mensheviks   Faction of the Russian Revolution that was generally more moderate than Lenin's Bolshevik faction and was ultimately defeated by the **Bolsheviks** in 1917.

mercantilism   The economic policy of **absolutism**, defining economic wealth as tangible assets and promoting protectionism with the aim of concentrating wealth among as few individuals as possible.

Merovingians   Warrior dynasty who ruled as kings of the Franks from ca. 500 to the ascent of the **Carolingians**   (ca. 754).

messiah   In the Jewish tradition, an earthly savior who would bring justice and create a safe, unified state for the Jews.

von Metternich, Klemens (1773–1859)   Austrian prince who took the lead in devising the post-Napoleonic settlement arranged by the Congress of Vienna (1814–1815).

modernism   1. To the Catholic Church in the early 20th century, a deplorable trend toward intellectual novelty that trivialized scriptural truth and claimed "that there is nothing divine in sacred tradition [of the church]." 2. Highly diverse cultural movement (roughly 1860–1950) that simultaneously rejects previous attitudes about how artists should work and resists the contemporary impersonality of mass-produced culture.

monasticism   In the rapidly Christianizing world, the movement to reject normal family and social life, along with the concern for wealth, status, and power, in favor of a harsh life of solitude and spiritual discipline in communities of other monks.

Mongols   Diverse group of nomadic Asian tribes that, through a series of brutal conquests in China, Russia, and the Muslim world, covered at its height in 1279 nearly one-quarter of the Earth's land surface.

monotheism   The belief in a single, supreme deity.

Montesquieu   (1689–1755) An Enlightenment thinker and writer whose most influential work was *The Spirit of Laws*, in which he analyzed the structures that shape law and characterized governments according to three types: republics, monarchies, and despotisms.

Montessori, Maria   (1870–1952) An Italian physician and educator best known for the philosophy of education that bears her name. Montessori education emphasizes independence, freedom within limits, and respect for a child's natural psychological, physical, and social development.

Muhammad   (ca. 570–632) The prophet of Islam. He united a community of believers around his religious tenets, above all that there that was one God whose words had been revealed to him. Later, written down, these revelations became the Qur'an.

Muhammad Ali Pasha   (r. 1805–1848) An Ottoman Albanian commander in the Ottoman army who became leader of Egypt with the Ottomans' initial approval. Although not a modern nationalist, he is often cited as the founder of modern Egypt because of the dramatic reforms in the military, economic, and cultural spheres that he instituted.

Muhammad ibn Saud   (r. 1744–1765) Founder of the first Saudi state and the Saud dynasty.

mullah   A Persian word used primarily in non-Arabic speaking Shi'i Muslim countries (e.g., Iran, Afghanistan, Pakistan) to designate a low-level cleric. It is a term of respect rather than a designation of office. With a literal meaning of "guardian" or "caretaker," it carries a colloquial sense analogous to the English word *reverend*, stripped of any ecclesial meaning. Used primarily by Shi'i Muslims and throughout Pakistan and India by both Sunnis and Shi'a.

Mulla Sadra   The greatest Muslim philosopher of the modern era; his most important book is *The Four Journeys of the Intellect* (1638).

Muslim Brotherhood   Religious–political group founded in Egypt in 1928 that, after years of repression by Egypt's military and secular regime, assumed power following elections in 2011.

Mussolini, Benito   (r. 1922–1945) The Italian founder of the Fascist Party who, after the March on Rome in 1922, became dictator of Italy; allied himself with Hitler and the Nazis during World War II.

mystery religions   Religious worship that provided initiation into secret knowledge and divine protection, including hope for a better afterlife.

N

al-Nahda   Arabic, "awakening" or "renaissance"; 19th-century Islamic intellectual and cultural movement centered in Egypt that advocated the integration of Islamic and European culture.

Napoleon Bonaparte   (1769–1821) The French general who became First Consul in 1799 and emperor (Napoleon I) in 1804; he dominated European affairs for nearly two decades while leading France against a series of coalitions in the so-called Napoleonic Wars. One of the greatest commanders in history, his campaigns are studied at military schools worldwide; his lasting legal achievement, the **Napoleonic Code**, has been adapted by dozens of nations. After losing the battle of Waterloo in 1815, he was exiled to the island of St. Helena.

Napoleonic Code   Systematic law code established by Napoleon that (among other principals) emphasized individuals' rights to property and standardized the legal structures for contracts, leases, and establishing stock corporations.

Narmer   See **Menes**.

National Assembly   In France, the governing body that succeeded the Estates General in 1789 during the French Revolution. It was composed of, and defined by, the delegates of the Third Estate.

nationalism   A collective consciousness or awareness that the members of an individual nation-group share a depth of feelings, values, and attitudes toward the world.

National Society of Women's Suffrage   The first national group in the United Kingdom to campaign for women's right to vote. Formed in 1867, the organization helped lay the foundations of the women's suffrage movement.

Nazism   The political movement in Germany led by Adolf Hitler, which advocated a violent anti-Semitic, anti-Marxist, pan-German ideology.

Neoplatonism   Spiritual philosophy derived from Plato that influenced both late Roman paganism and early Christian theologians.

New Deal   American economic initiatives launched by President Franklin Delano Roosevelt to help the nation recover from the Great Depression by increasing government spending to employ men and women, provide price supports for farmers, offer unemployment insurance and retirement benefits, and create welfare programs.

New Economic Policy   The policy adopted in 1921 by the **Bolsheviks** after they abandoned War Communism. Under the NEP, the state still controlled all major industries and financial concerns, although individuals could own private property, trade freely within limits, and farm their own land for their own benefit. Fixed taxes replaced grain requisition. The policy successfully helped Soviet agriculture recover from civil war.

New Historians   Young Jewish scholars and journalists, mostly born in Israel, whose archival research and writing has led to a more complex and less idealistic understanding of Zionism and the founding of Israel.

new imperialism   A period of colonial expansion—and its accompanying ideologies—by the European powers, the United States, and the empire of Japan during the late 19th and early 20th centuries.

New Testament   Canon of twenty-seven works written after the death of Christ by or about various apostles.

Newton, Isaac   (1642–1727) One of the foremost scientists of all time, Newton was an English mathematician and physicist; he is especially noted for his development of calculus, work on the properties of light, and theory of gravitation.

New Woman   The subject of innumerable journalistic and literary works in Europe, America, and parts of the Islamic world; a woman who, from the 1880s on, thanks to tremendous economic, cultural, and political shifts, was free to travel, get an education, and have a career.

Nicene Creed   Statement of fundamental Christian beliefs issued by an ecumenical council convened by the Roman emperor Constantine in 323–325.

nihilism   Philosophical position of extreme skepticism that holds existence to be random, even meaningless.

Ninety-Five Theses A list, published by **Martin Luther** in 1517, of assertions condemning the theology of **indulgences**.

North Atlantic Treaty Organization (NATO) Defensive alliance created by the United States in 1949 to protect western Europe.

Nuremberg Trials Trials of Nazi leaders for war crimes before an international tribunal of judges and prosecutors from the Allied countries, held in 1945–1946 in Nuremberg, Germany.

O

Olympian deities The numerous gods, worshipped by the ancient Greeks, whose passions and exploits are recounted in Greek mythology.

Operation Barbarossa The codename for Hitler's invasion of the Soviet Union in 1941.

Organization of Petroleum Exporting Countries (OPEC) Group of twelve oil-exporting countries that strongly influences both the production and the pricing of oil. A 1973 boycott by OPEC drove gas prices to record levels, disrupting the American economy.

Ottoman Turks Dynasty founded by Osman (r. 1281–1324) that established a powerful state from the Balkans to Mesopotamia to North Africa.

P

pacifism In the aftermath of World War I, a term used to describe any principled and total rejection of violence as a means of resolving disputes.

Pale of Settlement Region of Russian Empire where Jews were allowed to live (they were generally not allowed to live anywhere else in Russia), and the site of devastating pogroms in the late 19th century.

Palestinian Liberation Organization (PLO) Political organization of Palestinian Arabs created in 1964 in opposition to the existence of the Jewish state of Israel.

pan-Arabism Ideology promoting the unification of all Arabs, particularly in opposition to Western imperialism. See also **Ba'ath Party**.

Panhellenism The "all-Greek" culture that allowed ancient Greek colonies to maintain a connection to their homeland and to each other through their shared language and heritage.

Pankhurst, Emmeline (1858–1928) Organizer of a militant branch of the British suffrage movement, working actively for women's right to vote.

pan-Slavism Populist approach of Tsar Alexander III (r. 1881–1894) that resulted in vicious persecution of Russian Jews, who were portrayed as exploiters of the common Russian people.

Pantheon A temple built by the emperor Hadrian (r. 117–138 CE) in Rome and dedicated to the whole roster of major deities within the empire.

parlements Ancient French aristocratic-led system of legal courts reestablished during the regency of Louis XV as a way to extend aristocratic privileges; Louis XV tried to overturn the parlements when he came of age.

parliament A representative body having supreme legislative powers within a state or multinational organization.

pater familias In the Roman Republic, the head (always male) of a household. The pater familias had complete authority over the familia and was the sole possessor of its property.

patrician In ancient Rome, a member of a noble family or class.

patrilinear Describes a social system in Mesopotamia and elsewhere, in which only men can inherit property.

Pax Romana The "Roman Peace," a period of general peace and prosperity in the Roman Empire from Augustus (d. 14 CE) to Marcus Aurelius (d. 180 CE).

Peace of Augsburg Compromise settlement (1555) between Charles V and Lutheran princes that granted Lutheranism legal recognition. With this policy, the religion of the local ruler determined the state religion of the principality, with certain guarantees offered for the rights of the religious minority.

Peace of Paris The series of peace treaties (1919–1920) that provided the settlement of World War I. The Treaty of Versailles with Germany was the centerpiece of the Peace of Paris.

Peace of Westphalia A collection of treaties (1648) negotiated by the first general diplomatic congress in Western history. Involving more than one hundred delegations, it brought a century of European conflict to a close.

Peloponnesian War (431–404 BCE) Prolonged war between Athens, which sought to dominate all of Greece, and Sparta, one of the last holdouts against Athenian supremacy. An epidemic of typhus in 429 BCE weakened Athens, while the Spartans' alliance with Persia allowed them to challenge and defeat the Athenian navy.

Pentecostalism American Protestant style of worship that is charismatic, even anti-intellectual, in its emphasis on a mystical union with God manifested by the ability to speak in tongues and perform miraculous healings.

perestroika   Collective term for the economic policies of Mikhail Gorbachev in the Soviet Union that allowed for the limited introduction of free-market mechanisms. "Restructuring," literally.

Pericles   (ca. 495–429 BCE) Athens's political leader during Greece's Golden Age.

Peter I   (r. 1689–1725) Russian tsar who undertook the Westernization of Russia and built a new capital city named after himself, St. Petersburg.

phalanx   A fighting unit of Greek foot soldiers: eight horizontal lines of ten to twenty men each, who stood shoulder to shoulder and moved as a single unit.

pharaoh   A term (meaning "household") that became the title borne by the rulers of ancient Egypt. The pharaoh was regarded as the divine representative of the gods and the embodiment of Egypt itself.

Pharisees   One of three "philosophical sects" into which Judean society was divided. Unlike other Jews, they held a belief in the immortality of the soul and the resurrection of the dead; they also anticipated the arrival of a messiah.

Philippine–American War   Armed conflict (1899–1902) between the United States and Filipino revolutionaries that arose from the struggle of the First Philippine Republic to secure independence from the United States following the latter's acquisition of the Philippines from Spain after the **Spanish–American War**.

philosophes   French for "philosophers"; public intellectuals of the Enlightenment, applied to all regardless of their homeland.

plebeians   The class of free landowning Roman citizens, represented in the government of the Roman Republic by the Plebeian Council.

plutocracy   From the Greek terms for "wealth" (*ploutos*) and "power" (*kratos*), a society or system ruled and dominated by the small minority of the richest citizens.

pogroms   Beginning in 1881, vicious attacks from 1648 on against entire Jewish communities in the **Pale of Settlement**.

polis   The ancient Greek city-state (plural form *poleis*).

pope   Bishop of Rome and leader of the worldwide Catholic Church. The power of the Roman bishop is largely derived from his role as the traditional successor to St. Peter, to whom, according to the Bible, Jesus gave the keys of Heaven, naming him the "rock" on which the church would be built.

Prague Spring   Reforms initiated in 1968 Communist Czechoslovakia by moderate leader Alexander Dubček, who described it as "socialism with a human face"; the reforms were squashed by a Soviet military intervention in August 1968.

predestination   The doctrine of **John Calvin** that God preordained salvation or damnation for each person before Creation; those chosen for salvation were considered the "elect."

Princeps   Title taken by the emperor Octavian, meaning "first in honor" (because his name appeared first on the censor's list of Roman citizens).

proletariat   A term popularized by Marx to describe the working classes. A revolution of the proletariat, Marx believed, would bring about the end of capitalism and the birth of a classless society.

protectionism   The blocking of imports by tariff barriers or other legal means to promote the interests of a domestic mercantilist economy.

Protestant Reformation   Movement initiated by Martin Luther that sought to re-create what he believed to be Christian belief and practice as they had existed in the apostolic church.

psychoanalysis   Technique associated with Sigmund Freud (1856–1939) that seeks to understand the unconscious mind.

Punic Wars   Three wars Rome fought with Carthage between 264 and 146 BCE, resulting in Roman dominance of the entire western Mediterranean basin.

putting-out system   See **cottage industry**.

Pythagoreans   Group of philosophers named after Pythagoras (570–495 BCE), who had developed the famous theorem about right triangles. They sought to identify rational order and laws governing the natural world; hence their focus on mathematics.

Q

qadi   Islamic religious judge.

al-Qaeda   "The Base," literally. Islamic terrorist organization created in the late 1980s by former rebels against the Soviet Army in Afghanistan. Led by Osama bin Laden until his death in 2011.

quantum theory   New theory of physics proposed by Max Planck (1858–1947) suggesting that both light and matter exist as waves and as particles.

Qur'an   The holy book of Islam, revealed to the Prophet Muhammad.

R

rabbi   An honorific Hebrew word meaning "my master." Rabbis were originally teachers of Jewish Law. During the Babylonian Captivity, far from their ruined Temple, many Jews turned to their rabbis for religious guidance. Rabbis became leaders of the exiled Jews and during this time refined the laws governing Jewish life.

Ramses II   (r. ca. 1279–1213 BCE) Also known as Ramses the Great, he is often regarded as the most powerful and celebrated pharaoh of the Egyptian Empire. In addition to building cities, temples, and monuments, he led several military expeditions eastward, reasserting Egyptian control over Canaan, and also southward, into Nubia.

Rape of Nanjing   Atrocities perpetrated by invading Japanese soldiers in the Chinese capital of Nanjing in December 1937–January 1938. Hundreds of thousands of Chinese civilians were brutally murdered.

rationalism   The essential characteristic of Greek thought, from Mycenaean times to the earliest known philosophers of Miletus (Thales, Anaximander, and Anaximenes); attempts to explain the natural world through observation rather than through mythology.

Realpolitik   Politics based on strategic and tactical realities instead of idealism.

Reconquista   "Reconquest," in Spanish. Refers to the long struggle (985–1492) between Christian and Muslim warlord-princes for control of the Iberian Peninsula.

redistributive taxation   Taxation that is intended to spread incomes more fairly among people by taxing rich people more and poor people less.

Reichstag   Name of the lower parliamentary chamber in the German imperial government, 1871–1945.

Reign of Terror   Brutal period of the French Revolution (1792) during which, at the direction of Robespierre, tens of thousands of French citizens believed to be opposed in any way to the Revolution were executed.

relativity   In physics, the concept that every vantage point in the universe, whether moving or stationary, is as valid as every other vantage point; as a cultural metaphor, the new and possibly frightening idea that there are no fixed points, no absolute time, and no absolute space.

Renaissance   Literally "rebirth" (French); an era of tremendous cultural achievement as artists, scholars, and philosophers rediscovered the works of classical Greece and Rome and applied those ideas and aesthetics to contemporary arts, humanism, and modern statecraft.

res publica   Latin term for "republic" or "commonwealth"; a form of government based on a system of checks and balances that emerged in Rome in 509 BCE.

Rhodes, Cecil   (1853–1902) A British businessman, mining magnate, and politician in South Africa. An ardent believer in British colonialism, Rhodes was the founder of the southern African territory of Rhodesia (modern Zimbabwe), which was named after him in 1895.

Risorgimento   "Resurgence," literally; the name given to the 19th-century movement for Italian national reunification.

Robespierre, Maximilien   (1758–1794) A French lawyer and politician who, as leader of the Committee of Public Safety, laid out the principles of a "republic of virtue" and of the Terror, a period of French Revolutionary violence marked by mass executions of "enemies of the Revolution." His arrest and execution in July 1794 brought an end to the Terror.

Romanticism   Cultural and artistic movement in opposition to industrialization, preferring emotion and instinct over structural order and rational thought.

Rousseau, Jean-Jacques   (1712–1778) One of the most important **philosophes**, he argued that only a government based on a social contract among the citizens could make people truly moral and free.

Rule of Saint Benedict   A communal handbook written by Saint Benedict of Nursia (480–547) to guide the monastery he had established; its focus on the physical and intellectual as well as spiritual well-being of monks led to its being widely adopted by monastic communities across medieval Europe.

Rumi   (1207–1273) Sufi poet whose work championed Islam without disparaging other faiths.

Russo-Japanese War   In this armed conflict (1904–1905), Japanese and Russian expansion collided in Mongolia and Manchuria. Russia was humiliated after the Japanese navy sank its fleet, which helped provoke a revolt in Russia and led to an American-brokered peace treaty.

S

Sadducees   One of three "philosophical sects" into which Judean society was divided; a party of aristocrats who were reputedly strict upholders of Temple ritual, dedicated to the literal reading of scripture and the rejection of the oral Torah.

Saint Bartholomew's Day Massacre   Riot (August 23–29, 1572) between Catholics and Protestant Huguenots that began in Paris and spread across France, resulting in the deaths of thousands.

salons   In urban, Enlightenment-era society, regular gatherings, often hosted by wealthy or aristocratic women in their own homes, to which **philosophes**, artists, and other cultural figures were invited to discuss ideas.

sans-culottes   "Those without breeches," literally. Colloquial reference to political Revolutionary militants in Paris drawn from the lower orders.

Sappho   (ca. 620–550 BCE) The most famous woman lyric poet of Ancient Greece, Sappho was revered as the "Tenth Muse" and emulated by many male poets. "Lesbian" is derived from Lesbos, her native island.

Sargon I   (r. 2334–2279 BCE) The Akkadian ruler who consolidated power in Mesopotamia.

Schlieffen Plan   Military strategy created by German chief of general staff Alfred Graf von Schlieffen in 1905 that called for German forces to circumvent French defenses by striking swiftly through Belgium and Luxembourg; this was exactly how Germany proceeded at the start of World War I nine years later.

scholasticism   Method of research and teaching in medieval universities, characterized by the application of Aristotelian logic and the attempt to harmonize all knowledge.

scientific management   Management theory that increases the productivity of labor by breaking down manufacturing into small, distinct steps.

scientific method   The combination of experimental observation and mathematical deduction used to determine the laws of nature; first developed in the 17th century, it became the secular standard of truth.

Scientific Revolution   From 1500 to 1700, a cultural, philosophical, and intellectual shift from a view of the universe as divinely created to a concept of the natural world as a system that could be understood through study and observation.

Second Industrial Revolution   Continuation of the earlier Industrial Revolution, but with a focus instead on producing capital goods (goods, such as steel and chemicals, used to produce other goods).

Second Vatican Council   Convened by Pope John XXIII (r. 1958–1963) as part of the effort to modernize the church's teachings and governance.

second-wave feminism   Women's movement in the 1960s and 1970s that focused on sexual health, access to abortion and contraception, equal rights in the workplace, childcare services, gender roles in society, and portrayals of women in popular culture. (The "first wave" of feminism had focused almost exclusively on women's suffrage.)

secularism   The declining power of religious beliefs and institutions and the subsequent decline in religious practice.

Sephardim   Jewish people centered around the Mediterranean, where they remained in constant contact with Arab, Greek, and Latin cultural developments.

Septuagint   A Greek translation of the Hebrew Bible created by a group of seventy-two scholars who convened in Alexandria around 260 BCE (the name is derived from the Greek word for "seventy"). It includes several books later excluded from the Jewish canon.

serfs   Dependent farmers who performed labor on manors in exchange for the security and primitive justice provided by the landlord.

Seven Years' War   A worldwide series of battles (1756–1763) between Austria, France, Russia, and Sweden on the one side and Prussia and Great Britain on the other.

Sha'arawi, Huda'i   (1879–1947) Pioneering Egyptian feminist leader, nationalist, and founder of the Egyptian Feminist Union.

shah   Persian term for "emperor."

shari'a   Islamic religious law.

Shi'a   Muslims who believe that political and religious legitimacy can pass only to members of the Prophet Muhammad's hereditary line.

simony   Paying money or presenting gifts in return for ecclesiastical office, a widespread abuse in the Roman Catholic Church in the post-Carolingian era that inspired the Gregorian Reform.

Six-Day War   Military action (June 5–10, 1967) initiated by Israel against Egypt, Jordan, and Syria; Israel seized the Gaza Strip, the Golan Heights along the Israeli border with Syria, the Sinai Peninsula, and the entire West Bank, including the eastern part of the then-divided city of Jerusalem. After the stunning defeat of Arab allies, much of Arab popular resentment turned toward the United States.

Skepticism   In ancient Greece, the philosophical school based on the fundamental idea that nothing can be known for certain: our senses are easily fooled, and reason follows too easily our desires.

Smith, Adam   (1723–1790) Scottish economist and liberal philosopher who proposed that competition between self-interested individuals led naturally to a healthy economy. He became famous for his influential book *The Wealth of Nations* (1776).

Social Catholicism Nineteenth-century European Catholic movement founded on the idea that the challenge to Christian society under industrialism was structural rather than personal.

social contract Articulated in Thomas Hobbes's *Leviathan* (1651), the theory that when people decide to live in community they enter a covenant with each other, compromising their individual free wills in return for the benefits of society. Government, which bears responsibility for preserving social stability, may therefore legitimately assert its will on the community whenever it deems it necessary to do so.

social Darwinism Misuse of Darwin's theory of evolution by natural selection to morally justify imperialism as a healthy competition among societies.

socialism A social and political ideology, originating in the early 19th century, that advocated the reorganization of society to overcome the new tensions created by industrialization and restore social harmony through communities based on cooperation.

Socratic method The Athenian philosopher Socrates's method of teaching through conversation, in which he asked probing questions to make his listeners examine their assumptions.

Solomon (according to tradition, r. ca. 970–931 BCE) A king of Israel and son of **David**; the Hebrew Bible credits Solomon as the builder of the First Temple in Jerusalem.

Solon (d. 559 BCE) Athenian political reformer whose changes promoted early democracy.

Song of Songs Biblical book, also known as the Song of Solomon, consisting of a poetic dialogue between a bride and bridegroom. Centuries of scholars have interpreted the Song of Songs as an allegory of the covenant between God and his people.

Sophists In Greece in the 5th century BCE, a group of thinkers who traveled from city to city teaching rhetoric and philosophy.

South Sea Bubble Economic crash (1720) sparked when the South Sea Company, an English company formed to trade with Spanish colonies in the New World, encouraged investors to speculate wildly on its supposed ventures but then could not make good on its unrealistic promises.

space-time Einstein's concept of time and space as elastic and therefore understood as different facets of a single dimension.

Spanish–American War War (1898) between the United States and Spain in Cuba, Puerto Rico, and the Philippines. It ended with a treaty in which the United States took over the Philippines, Guam, and Puerto Rico; Cuba won partial independence.

Spanish Civil War Internal conflict (1936–1939) between conservative and liberal forces in Spain that drew anti-Fascist support from around the world. The conservatives, under the Fascist dictator Francisco Franco (r. 1936–1975), won.

special theory of relativity Einstein's theory (1905) that maintains that all measurements of space and time are relative; the basis of the idea that nothing can go faster than the speed of light.

spinning jenny Invention of Englishman James Hargreaves (ca. 1720–1774) that revolutionized the British textile industry by allowing a worker to spin much more thread than was possible on a hand spinner.

Stalin, Joseph (1879–1953) Soviet leader who, with considerable backing, formed a brutal dictatorship in the 1930s and forcefully converted the country into an industrial power.

Stöcker, Helene (1869–1943) German feminist, pacifist, and sexual reformer. In 1905 she helped found the League for the Protection of Mothers.

Stoicism Philosophy most famously described and taught by Seneca (4 BCE–65 CE) and Epictetus (55–135 CE) that conformed to Roman morals through an emphasis on duty, forbearance, self-discipline, and concern for others.

suffrage The right to vote.

suffragettes European activists for women's rights who, in contrast with **suffragists**, favored confrontation, aggressive action, and, whenever they thought it necessary, even violence to change society.

suffragists Activists for women's rights who, in contrast with **suffragettes**, worked peaceably and within the legal system for women's rights.

Sufism A mystical, esoteric approach to Islam that flourished in the Ottoman Empire.

sultan "Commander," literally. Term for chief military officer in the Turkish Empire. Under the Ottomans, the word came to represent the head of state.

Sultanate of Women Period (1640s and 1650s) of the Ottoman Empire when leading members of the imperial harem effectively controlled the state, directed foreign policy, and oversaw the fiscal system.

summa A "summary," or an encyclopedic effort to organize all thought on a given topic; a popular genre among the scholastic writers of the 13th and 14th centuries, representing the conviction that a rational order underlies all of human life.

sunnah The collected sayings and actions of the Prophet Muhammad, used to establish Islamic legal precedents.

Sunni Muslims who regard selection by the community as the sole legitimate means to leadership of the Islamic world.

supermen Term used by Friedrich Nietzsche (1844–1900) to describe cultural, political, and intellectual figures with a will to power.

Sykes–Picot Agreement Pact between England and France (1916) that took advantage of the **Arab Revolt** to divide the dominions of the Middle East between the two nations.

Syllabus of Errors Sixty-five teachings Pope Pius X decreed irredeemably anti-Catholic in two 1907 encyclicals.

symposia All-male drinking parties in ancient Greece where philosophical ideas were discussed.

syncretism The merging of religious doctrines.

T

Talmud Codification of rabbinical law and commentary that became central to Jewish life starting in the Middle Ages. Two dominant forms exist: the Babylonian Talmud, compiled around 500 CE, and the Palestinian Talmud (also known as the Jerusalem Talmud), compiled around 400 CE. Reference to the "Talmud" usually means the Babylonian Talmud.

Tamerlane (r. ca. 1370–1405) A Turkish-Mongol conqueror and the founder of the Timurid dynasty in Central Asia, Tamerlane is considered the last of the great nomadic conquerors of the Eurasian steppe; his empire set the stage for the rise of the more structured and lasting gunpowder empires in the 16th and 17th centuries. Also known as "Timur."

Tanakh A common name for the canonical Hebrew Bible—an acronym based on the letters T (for Torah, meaning "Instructions"), N (for Nevi'im, or "Prophets"), and K (for Ketuvim, or "Writings"). Traditionally believed to have been assembled by the "Men of the Great Assembly" around 450 BCE, modern scholars believe the compilation occurred later, between 200 BCE and 200 CE.

Tanzimat (Turkish, "reorganization"); a 19th-century movement by the Ottoman government to promote economic development and the integration of the empire's non-Muslims and non-Turks into civil society.

telos According to Aristotle, the intrinsic purpose or necessary role in the cosmic drama of every existing thing.

Tennis Court Oath Oath taken by representatives of the Third Estate in June 1789, in which they pledged to form a **National Assembly** and write a constitution limiting the powers of the king.

tetrarchy Under Diocletian, a new system whereby the Roman Empire was formally divided into two halves, with a separate emperor (*augustus*, in Latin) for each. Each half was further divided in half again, and each augustus therefore had a subordinate vice emperor, or *caesar*.

themes New system of organizing the army under Byzantine emperor Heraclius in the 7th century that redistributed land to military officers and soldiers.

theory of evolution by natural selection As explained by Charles Darwin in his 1859 book *On the Origin of Species by Means of Natural Selection*, the process by which the superabundance of offspring produced by all living beings results in their competition for resources; over time, that competition favors traits in offspring that provide an advantage over their rivals.

Thermidorian Reaction The violent backlash against the rule of **Robespierre** that dismantled the Terror.

Third Estate The branch of the French legislative body made up of elected representatives of the common people, including the bourgeoisie and wage earners. See also **Estates General**.

third-wave feminism A movement beginning in the early 1990s and continuing to the present, it arose partially as a response to the perceived failures of and backlash against **second-wave feminism**. Unlike the determined positions of second-wave feminists, third-wave feminists emphasize the diversity of female experience and multiple avenues to female empowerment.

Thirty Years' War Conflict that began in 1618 between Protestants and Catholics in Germany and gradually enveloped most of Europe, ending in 1648 after massive losses of life and property.

Tokyo Trials Trials (1946–1948) of Japanese officials for war crimes before an international tribunal of judges and prosecutors from the Allied countries.

Torah The first five books of the **Tanakh**, attributed to Moses.

totalitarianism A system of government that controls all aspects of society, using fear and intimidation to maintain power.

Treaty of Rome Treaty agreed to by western European leaders in 1957 that established the European Economic Community to help postwar recovery and counterbalance American economic power.

Treaty of Verdun   The treaty that, in 843, split the Carolingian Empire into three parts; its borders roughly outline modern western European states.

Treaty of Versailles   Controversial agreements that formally ended World War I on June 28, 1919; ruinous concessions demanded from a defeated Germany were a contributing factor in the run-up to World War II.

trireme   Ancient Greek warship with three tiers of oarsmen and a bronze-tipped battering ram on the prow.

twelve apostles   According to the Bible, the primary disciples of **Jesus**, who became the primary teachers of his gospel message.

Twelve Tables   The first written law code of the Roman Republic, ca. 450 BCE.

tyrant   A person in a Greek polis who took power temporarily to bring about dramatic reform in a politically deadlocked state. In terms of social class, the tyrants were aristocrats but were allied with the masses.

U

'ulama   Arab for "brotherhood" or "community," a central focus of Sunni life.

Umayyads   Name of the ruling dynasty in the Islamic Empire, 661–750. Governing the empire from their new capital at Damascus, the Umayyads were overthrown in 750 by the **Abbasids**, who transferred the capital to the newly built Baghdad.

ummah   The community of Muslim believers.

uniformitarianism   Scottish geologist James Hutton's theory that geological change consists of the slow accumulation of smaller changes—and these changes continue to happen in the present.

United Nations (UN)   Organization of member nations established in 1945, including a permanently standing International Court of Justice and International Criminal Court.

Universal Declaration of Human Rights   The first statement of global rights in history, drafted and promoted by American First Lady Eleanor Roosevelt and approved on December 10, 1948, by most members of the United Nations (Saudi Arabia, South Africa, and the Soviet Union abstained).

urbanism   The growth of towns and cities resulting from the movement of people from rural to urban areas; this trend was encouraged by the development of factories and railroads.

V

vassal   In a feudal system, a free man who pledges to serve a lord in exchange for dominion over a manor or manors bestowed by the lord.

vizier   Regional administrator under the Abbasid dynasty and later under the Ottomans. From the word meaning "burden sharer."

Voltaire   (1694–1778) The pen name of François-Marie Arouet, leading **philosophe** and one of the most influential writers of the Enlightenment.

W

Wahhabism   Conservative reform movement within Sunni Islam, taking its name from the 18th-century figure Muhammad ibn Abd al-Wahhab. The movement stresses returning to strict reliance on the Qur'an and hadith, purging Islam of non-Arabic traditions, and restoring ethnic Arabs to leadership in international Islam. The official sect in Saudi Arabia in the 20th and 21st centuries.

War of the Roses   English civil war for the throne (1455–1485) fought between the noble houses of York and Lancaster.

welfare states   In post–World War II Western Europe, societies in which the central government, funded by heavy taxation, provided all essential social services.

Wergild   Old Germanic term—"man money," literally—for the compensation owed by an offender to his victim, according to custom.

will to power   Term used by German philosopher Friedrich Nietzsche (1844–1900) to describe the passionate striving to make meaning and leave a mark on the world.

Women's International League for Peace and Freedom   Pacifist group founded in 1915 that campaigned for equal rights for all citizens, economic justice, and greater understanding and empathy between peoples.

Women's Social and Political Union   Militant organization founded in 1903 that campaigned for women's suffrage in Great Britain. It was led by **Emmeline Pankhurst** and is best known for hunger strikes, for breaking windows in prominent buildings, and for arson of unoccupied houses and churches.

World Trade Organization   Intergovernmental organization seeking to liberalize trade between nations.

Y

YHWH   The term for "God" used by the Yahwist author of the Torah (see **Documentary Hypothesis**), represented in English-language Bibles by the all-capitals word LORD.

Young Turks   Modernizing faction in Turkey that promoted pan-ethnic Islamic nationalism, overthrowing the sultan Abdul Hamid II in 1909 and replacing him with his half-brother Mehmed V (r. 1909–1918).

Z

ziggurats Step-pyramid temples of ancient Mesopotamia, believed to be the dwelling places of the gods.

Zionism From Hebrew *Tsiyon*, the name for the central portion of Jerusalem, but by extension referring to all of Israel/Palestine. Movement by Jews (especially from eastern Europe) to establish a Jewish state in the Holy Land as a refuge from European persecution beginning in the 19th century.

Zollverein See **Customs Union**.

Zoroastrianism Monotheistic religion founded by Zoroaster in Persia ca. 1300 BCE. In its emphasis on moral behavior, personal salvation, and the eventual victory of Good in a cosmic battle with Evil, Zoroastrianism is considered by many a precursor of Judaism (and, by extension, Christianity).

Credits

Scala/Art Resource, NY; pg. 298: Iman Zahdah Chah Zaid Mosque, Isfahan, Iran/Index/Bridgeman Images; pg. 302: BN, Arabe 5847, fol 5v

CHAPTER 10: pg. 308: Bridgeman-Giraudon/Art Resource, NY; pg. 317: Bibliotheque Nationale, Paris, France/Bridgeman Images; pg. 319: Alfredo Dagli Orti/The Art Archive at Art Resource, NY; pg. 327: Textile/Universal History Archive/UIG/Bridgeman Images; pg. 330: Photononstop/SuperStock; pg. 334: bpk, Berlin/Dietmar Katz/Art Resource, NY; pg. 339: Erich Lessing/Art Resource, NY; pg. 342: Art Resource, NY; pg. 347: Erich Lessing/Art Resource, NY

CHAPTER 11: pg. 352: © DeA Picture Library/Art Resource, NY; pg. 359: Erich Lessing/Art Resource, NY; pg. 362: Erich Lessing/Art Resource, NY; pg. 363: Archive Timothy McCarthy/Art Resource, NY; pg. 368: © JTB MEDIA CREATION, Inc./Alamy; pg. 370: Album/Art Resource, NY; pg. 374: © RMN-Grand Palais/Art Resource, NY; pg. 377: Snark/Art Resource, NY; pg. 380: Scala/White Images/Art Resource, NY; pg. 384: Image copyright © The Metropolitan Museum of Art. Image source: Art Resource, NY; pg. 384: National Palace Museum, Beijing; pg. 387: The John Work Garrett Library, The Sheridan Libraries, The Johns Hopkins University; pg. 390: Werner Forman Archive/Museum of Islamic Art, Cairo. HIP/Art Resource, NY; pg. 395: Erich Lessing/Art Resource, NY

CHAPTER 12: pg. 398: Erich Lessing/Art Resource, NY; pg. 403: Santa Maria Novella, Florence, Italy/Bridgeman Images; pg. 405: © National Gallery, London/Art Resource, NY; pg. 408: Scala/Art Resource, NY; pg. 410: The Granger Collection, NYC—All rights reserved.; pg. 414: public domain; pg. 416: Scala/Art Resource, NY; pg. 419: Scala/Art Resource, NY; pg. 420: Deutsches Historisches Museum, Berlin, Germany/© DHM/Bridgeman Images; pg. 421: © amphotos/Alamy; pg. 425: Photo: Albertina, Vienna, from Geisberg, Der deutsche Holzschnitt in der ersten Halfte des 16. Jahrhundert, Munchen 1923-1930; 30. Lieferung, Nr. 1243."; pg. 427: The Pierpont Morgan Library/Art Resource, NY; pg. 432: © Sergej Borzov -Fotolia.com; pg. 434: National Portrait Gallery, London; pg. 438: Courtesy of the Library of Congress; pg. 442: Scala/Ministero per i Beni e le Attività culturali/Art Resource, NY; pg. 442: © RMN-Grand Palais/Art Resource, NY; pg. 443: Courtesy José Luís Fernández-Castañeda, S.J., parish priest of the Church of San Pedro, Lima, and Administrator of the Jesuit Order in Peru.

CHAPTER 13: pg. 448: Private Collection/© Look and Learn/Bridgeman Images; pg. 457: Snark/Art Resource, NY; pg. 459: Library of Congress, Rare Book and Special Collections Division; pg. 460: Peter Newark American Pictures; pg. 463: public domain; pg. 465: Erich Lessing/Art Resource, NY; pg. 465: Courtesy of the Library of Congress; pg. 467: Erich Lessing/Art Resource, NY; pg. 470: Caja de Ahorros de Valencia, Valencia, Spain/Index/Bridgeman Images; pg. 472: Erich Lessing/Art Resource, NY; pg. 475: Erich Lessing/Art Resource, NY; pg. 477: Scala/Art Resource, NY; pg. 477: Bridgeman-Giraudon/Art Resource, NY; pg. 483: bpk, Berlin/National Portrait Gallery/Jochen Remmer/Art Resource, NY; pg. 488: Private Collection/Bridgeman Images

CHAPTER 14: pg. 492: Scala/Art Resource, NY; pg. 498: Scala/White Images/Art Resource, NY; pg. 501: Palazzo Barberini, Rome, Italy/Bridgeman Images; pg. 502: Woburn Abbey, Bedfordshire, UK/Bridgeman Images; pg. 505: Deutsches Historisches Museum, Berlin, Germany/© DHM/Bridgeman Images; pg. 509: The Granger Collection, NYC—All rights reserved.; pg. 512: public domain ; pg. 515: Gianni Dagli Orti/The Art Archive at Art Resource, NY; pg. 518: Erich Lessing/Art Resource, NY

CHAPTER 15: pg. 526: National Trust Photo Library/Art Resource, NY; pg. 533: © RMN-Grand Palais/Art Resource, NY; pg. 536: © British Library Board/Robana/Art Resource, NY; pg. 538: Gianni Dagli Orti/The Art Archive at Art Resource, NY; pg. 541: akg-images; pg. 543: © Chad Ehlers/Alamy; pg. 544: Erich Lessing/Art Resource, NY; pg. 547: © Bristol Museum and Art Gallery, UK/Bridgeman Images; pg. 548: © liszt collection/Alamy; pg. 550: Nimatallah/Art Resource, NY; pg. 551: Norton Simon Collection, Pasadena, CA, USA/Bridgeman Images; pg. 553: © Photo: Bayerisches Nationalmuseum München, Bastian Krack. Fork: Inv. No. 36/37; Knife: Inv. No. 36/38; pg. 555: © Danita Delimont/Alamy; pg. 559: The Pierpont Morgan Library/Art Resource, NY; pg. 566: © Roger Wood/CORBIS; pg. 572: Eileen Tweedy/The Art Archive at Art Resource, NY

CHAPTER 16: pg. 578: Gift of Vernon Stroud, Eva Linker, Gerda Mathan, Ilse Feiger and Irwin Straus in memory of Frederick and Edith Straus, The Magnes Collection of Jewish Art and Life, UC Berkeley; pg. 584: Gianni Dagli Orti/The Art Archive at Art Resource, NY; pg. 586: Library of Congress, Rare Book and Special Collections, Washington, D.C.; pg. 592: Erich Lessing/Art

Resource, NY; pg. 594: SSPL/Science Museum/ Art Resource, NY; pg. 594: Alfredo Dagli Orti/ The Art Archive at Art Resource, NY; pg. 595: © BnF, Dist. RMN-Grand Palais/Art Resource, NY; pg. 597: Bridgeman-Giraudon/Art Resource, NY; pg. 598: Chateau de Coppet, Paris, France/ Bridgeman Images; pg. 599: Eileen Tweedy/The Art Archive at Art Resource, NY; pg. 601: Erich Lessing/Art Resource, NY; pg. 603: Tate, London/Art Resource, NY; pg. 606: Private Collection/Photo © Bonhams, London, UK/Bridgeman Images; pg. 610: Kimbell Art Museum, Fort Worth, Texas/Art Resource, NY; pg. 616: Alfredo Dagli Orti/The Art Archive at Art Resource, NY

CHAPTER 17: pg. 620: Musee de la Ville de Paris, Musee Carnavalet, Paris, France/Archives Charmet/Bridgeman Images; pg. 626: Musee de la Ville de Paris, Musee Carnavalet, Paris, France/ Archives Charmet/Bridgeman Images; pg. 628: © Corbis; pg. 630: © RMN-Grand Palais/Art Resource, NY; pg. 633: Gianni Dagli Orti/The Art Archive at Art Resource, NY; pg. 637: Bridgeman-Giraudon/Art Resource, NY; pg. 640: Courtesy of the Library of Congress; pg. 645: Erich Lessing/ Art Resource, NY; pg. 650: Bibliotheque Nationale, Paris, France/Archives Charmet/Bridgeman Images; pg. 652: Courtesy of the Library of Congress; pg. 654–655: From SEED Project

CHAPTER 18: pg. 658: The Granger Collection, New York – All rights reserved.; pg. 662: Universal History Archive/UIG/Bridgeman Images; pg. 666: Science Museum, London, UK/Bridgeman Images; pg. 668: National Trust Photo Library/Art Resource, NY; pg. 671: DEA PICTURE LIBRARY/De Agostini/Getty Images; pg. 676: Courtesy of Charles Cavaliere; pg. 683: ©Roger-Viollet/The Image Works; pg. 688: HIP/Art Resource, NY; pg. 688: HIP/Art Resource, NY; pg. 690: Eileen Tweedy/The Art Archive at Art Resource, NY; pg. 692: Musee de la Ville de Paris, Musee Carnavalet, Paris, France/ Archives Charmet/Bridgeman Images; pg. 693: Mary Evans Picture Library; pg. 698: © National Gallery, London/Art Resource, NY

CHAPTER 19: pg. 702: Courtesy of the Library of Congress; pg. 707: The Granger Collection, NYC—All rights reserved.; pg. 711: Bibliotheque des Arts Decoratifs, Paris, France/Archives Charmet/Bridgeman Images; pg. 715: © Peter Wheeler/Alamy; pg. 720: Eileen Tweedy/The Art Archive at Art Resource, NY; pg. 724: The Granger Collection, New York – All rights reserved.; pg. 729: © AISA/Everett Collection; pg. 731: National Trust Photographic Library/Derrick E.

Witty/Bridgeman Images; pg. 734: Private Collection/© Look and Learn/Bridgeman Images; pg. 736: Erich Lessing/Art Resource, NY; pg. 738: John Meek/The Art Archive at Art Resource, NY

CHAPTER 20: pg. 744: Gianni Dagli Orti/The Art Archive at Art Resource, NY; pg. 752: Lebrecht Music and Arts Photo Library/Alamy; pg. 755: Neopolitan Boys Eating Maccheroni, from Francesco de Bourcard, Usi e costume de Napoli (1858); pg. 757: Scala/White Images/Art Resource, NY; pg. 762: Schloss Friedrichsruhe, Germany/Bridgeman Images; pg. 763: bpk, Berlin/Art Resource, NY; pg. 765: bpk, Berlin/ Art Resource, NY; pg. 768: Nicholas K. Robinson Collection of Caricature, held within the Early Printed Books Department of Trinity College Library, Dublin; pg. 769: © Trustees of Watts Gallery/Bridgeman Images; pg. 771: bpk, Berlin/Art Resource, NY; pg. 775: HIP/Art Resource, NY; pg. 777: Adoc-photos/Art Resource, NY; pg. 781: Bibliotheque des Arts Decoratifs, Paris, France/ Archives Charmet/Bridgeman Images

CHAPTER 21: pg. 784: CCI/The Art Archive at Art Resource, NY; pg. 789: Philadelphia Museum of Art, Pennsylvania, PA, USA/The Henry P. McIlhenny Collection in Memory of Frances/P. McIlhenny, 1986/Bridgeman Images; pg. 792: © Chelmsford Museums, Essex, UK/Bridgeman Images; pg. 795: Mary Evans Picture Library/Alamy; pg. 797: bpk, Berlin/Dietmar Katz/Art Resource, NY; pg. 802: Science & Society Picture Library; pg. 804: Everett Collection Inc/Alamy; pg. 805: Private Collection/ Bridgeman Images; pg. 808: ullstein bild/The Granger Collection, NYC—All rights reserved.; pg. 809: Gianni Dagli Orti/The Art Archive at Art Resource, NY; pg. 812: AP Photo/Ahmed Abd el Fattah; pg. 813: from the Collection of Wolf-Dieter Lemke

CHAPTER 22: pg. 818: Digital Image © The Museum of Modern Art/Licensed by SCALA/Art Resource, NY; pg. 823: Private Collection/Bridgeman Images; pg. 827: Courtesy of the Library of Congress; pg. 831: HIP/Art Resource, NY; pg. 832: © Corbis; pg. 834: © SakvaUA; pg. 837: bpk, Berlin/Nationalgalerie, Staatliche Museen, Berlin, Germany/Photo by Klaus Goeken/Art Resource, NY; pg. 839: Private Collection/Ken Welsh/Bridgeman Images; pg. 842: Freud Museum, London, UK/Bridgeman Images; pg. 847: Musee de la Ville de Paris, Musee Carnavalet, Paris, France/Bridgeman Images; pg. 849: Digital Image © The Museum of Modern Art/Licensed by SCALA/Art Resource, NY; pg. 851: De Agostini

Index

Page numbers in *italics* indicate a map, table, or figure on the designated page.